The Classical Hollywood Cinema

The Author

David Bordwell is Professor of Film at the University of Wisconsin at Madison. He is the author of *The Films of Carl-Theodor Dreyer* (University of California Press, 1981); of *Narration in the Fiction Film* (Methuen, 1987), and, with Kristin Thompson, *Film Art: An Introduction* (Knopf, 1985).

Janet Staiger is Associate Professor of Film at the University of Texas-Austin. She has published articles in *Cinema Journal, Screen, Wide Angle, Film Reader 4, The Velvet Light Trap* and other journals.

Kristin Thompson is Honorary Fellow at the University of Wisconsin at Madison. She has taught Film studies there and at the University of Iowa. She is the author of *Eisenstein's Ivan the Terrible* (Princeton University Press, 1981), *Export Entertainment* (British Film Institute, 1985) and numerous articles on film.

THE CLASSICAL HOLLYWOOD CINEMA

Film Style & Mode of Production to 1960

David Bordwell, Janet Staiger and Kristin Thompson

Routledge

London

Dedicated to
Ralph Bellamy, Margaret Booth, Anita Loos,
Arthur C. Miller, and their many co-workers
in the Hollywood cinema

First published in 1985
First published as a paperback 1988
by Routledge

11 New Fetter Lane,
London EC4P 4EE

Reprinted in 1991, 1994, 1996

Set in Century 9 on 11 pt
by Columns, Reading
and printed in England
by Clays Ltd, St Ives plc

British Library Cataloguing in Publication Data

Bordwell, David

The classical Hollywood cinema.
1.Moving-pictures—United States—History
I. Title   II. Staiger, Janet
III. Thompson, Kristin
791.43'0973   PN1993.5.U6

ISBN 0-415-00383-0

Contents

Figures

Acknowledgments

We thank the University of Wisconsin-Madison Graduate School, the University of Wisconsin-Madison Communication Arts Department, and the University of Delaware Department of English for financial support of this research. Several libraries, archives, and film distributors helped immeasurably: the Museum of Modern Art, the New York Public Library at Lincoln Center, the George S. Amberg Film Study Center at New York University, the Library of Congress, the Wisconsin Center for Film and Theater Research, the Wisconsin State Historical Society, the Cleveland Public Library, the National Film Archive, the Danish Film Archive, the UCLA Theatre Arts collection, the UCLA Film Archive, the Margaret Herrick Library at the Academy of Motion Picture Arts and Sciences, the American Film Institute Library, the American Society of Cinematographers, the Eastman Kodak Research Library, Macmillan Audio-Brandon, and Films, Inc.

We also thank the many friends and colleagues who aided us in our work; these include Jeanne Allen, J. Dudley Andrew, David Armitage, Tino Balio, Dana Benelli, Jane and Berney Berninghausen, Edward Branigan, Mike Budd, Elaine Burrows, Keith Cohen, Mary Corliss, Michael Drozewski, Thomas Elsaesser, Maxine Fleckner, Douglas Gomery, Ron Gottesman, Rob and Kit Hume, Robert C. Hummel, Roberta Kimmel, Barbara Klinger, Jay Leyda, William Luhr, Russell Merritt, Judith Milhaus, Charles Musser, Al P. Nelson, Geoffrey Nowell-Smith, Rodney Recor, David Rodowick, Bob Rosen, Phil Rosen, Paul Sandro, Peter Schofer, Robert Self, Emily Sieger, Charles Silver, Three Tyler, Marc Wanamaker, and Alan Williams.

We are particularly grateful for the kindness of Charles G. Clarke, Stanley Cortez, Linwood Dunn, William K. Everson, William Hornbeck, Sidney P. Solow, and Karl and Ethel Struss, and for the patience of Peter Staiger.

Preface

Hollywood as the dream factory: 'How can you tell if people would want drugs so much today, if we still gave them this dream-world on film?' (Ruth Waterbury). Hollywood as an arm of the culture industry: 'The tone adopted by every film is that of the witch handing food to the child she wants to enchant or devour, while mumbling horribly: "Lovely, lovely soup. How you're going to enjoy it!" ' (T.W. Adorno). Hollywood as celluloid imperialism: 'Hollywood may be physically situated in this country, but it is an international enterprise.' (Will H. Hays). Hollywood as escape: 'All the adventure, all the romance, all the excitement you lack in your daily life are in – Pictures.' (Advertisement for a film). Hollywood as nostalgia: 'Take a good look, because we'll never see its like again.' (*That's Entertainment!*). Hollywood as imaginary landscape: 'Hollywood is a place you can't geographically define. We don't really know where it is.' (John Ford).[1]

The number of books promulgating all these versions of Hollywood (and more) would fill the library of a small town in America. Hollywood has been celebrated by cultists and camp followers, castigated by reformers and social theorists, and boosted by an army of publicists. Anthropologists have treated it as a tribal village, economists as a company town. The films of Hollywood have been lumped together as indistinguishable vulgarity, and they have been splintered into a hundred categories: the films of Garbo, of Goldwyn, of Griffith; the Paramount pretties, automobiles in the cinema, the gangster film, the serial, music for the movies; direction by Alfred Hitchcock, costumes by Edith Head, cinematography by Gregg Toland, sets by Van Nest Polglase; silent films, sound films, color films, films noirs.

Yet another treatment of the subject requires some justification. This book is an examination of Hollywood cinema as a distinct artistic and economic phenomenon. We will look at American studio filmmaking much as an art historian would trace the stylistic traits and business transactions of Parisian academic painting in the nineteenth century, or as a historian of music would examine the aesthetic and economic forces involved in the development of Viennese classicism. We take Hollywood seriously, treating it as a distinct mode of film practice with its own cinematic style and industrial conditions of existence.

A mode of film practice is not reducible to an *oeuvre* (the films of Frank Capra), a genre (the Western), or an economic category (RKO films). It is an altogether different category, cutting across careers, genres, and studios. It is, most simply, a context. And we cannot arrive at this context simply by adding up all the histories of directors, genres, studios, producers, etc.; this would be, as George Kubler suggests, like trying to determine a country's network of railroads by studying the itinerary of every traveler.[2] Just as the railroad system is of another logical order than your or my trip on it, so the Hollywood mode of film practice constitutes an integral system, including persons and groups but also rules, films, machinery, documents, institutions, work processes, and theoretical concepts. It is this totality that we shall study. And while we could justify this book as filling in the background for this or that individual's achievement, our aims go further. We hope to show that understanding this mode of film practice is indispensable to a full grasp of the art and industry of cinema as it has existed in history.

Recent academic film criticism has focused more and more exclusively upon the text. Sophisticated methodologies drawn from anthropology, semiotics, psychoanalysis, and literary criticism have dramatically broadened our sense of how a film works. But too often critical analysis has been unable to specify the historical conditions that have controlled and shaped textual processes.[3] On the other hand, the new generation of film historians, while an exciting development, has generally avoiding confronting the films themselves.[4] Detailed accounts of Hollywood financing, labor, distribution, exhibition, and technology have not usually sought to link economic factors to stylistic ones. In this book, we show how the concept of a mode of film practice can historicize textual analysis and connect the history of film style to the history of the motion picture industry.

The concept of a mode of film practice situates textual processes in their most pertinent and proximate collective context. This context includes both a historically defined group of films and the material practices that create and sustain that group. Raymond Williams has posed the problem:[5]

> We have to break from the common procedure of isolating an object and then discovering its components. On the contrary we have to discover the nature of a practice and then its conditions. . . . The recognition of the relation of a collective mode and an individual product — and these are the only categories we can initially presume — is a recognition of related practices. That is to say, the irreducibly individual projects that particular works are, may come in experience and analysis to show resemblances which allow us to group them into collective modes. These are by no means always genres. They may exist as resemblances within and across genres. They may be the practice of a group in a period, rather than the practice of a phase in a genre. But as we discover the nature of a particular practice, and the nature of the relation between an individual product and a collective mode, we find that we are analyzing, as two forms of the same process, both its active composition and its conditions of composition, and in either direction this is a complex of extending active relationships.

For the Hollywood cinema, the practices of film production constitute a major component of that process of which Williams speaks. Film production must be understood not simply as a background to individual achievement but as a crucial

'condition of composition' of resemblances among texts. The ways that films are conceived, planned, and produced leave their marks upon the films — not only directly, in telltale details, but structurally as well.[6] At the same time, stylistic aims have shaped the development of the mode of production. The relations between film style and mode of production are, we argue, reciprocal and mutually influencing.

A mode of film practice, then, consists of a set of widely held stylistic norms sustained by and sustaining an integral mode of film production. Those norms constitute a determinate set of assumptions about how a movie should behave, about what stories it properly tells and how it should tell them, about the range and functions of film technique, and about the activities of the spectator. These formal and stylistic norms will be created, shaped, and supported within a mode of film production — a characteristic ensemble of economic aims, a specific division of labor, and particular ways of conceiving and executing the work of filmmaking. Through time, both the norms and the mode of production will change, as will the technology they employ, but certain fundamental aspects will remain constant. Thus to see Hollywood filmmaking from 1917-60 as a unified mode of film practice is to argue for a coherent system whereby aesthetic norms and the mode of film production reinforced one another. This argument is the basis of this book.

If we have taken the realms of style and production as primary, it is not because we consider the concrete conditions of reception unimportant. Certainly conditions of consumption form a part of any mode of film practice. An adequate history of the reception of the classical Hollywood film would have to examine the changing theater situation, the history of publicity, and the role of social class, aesthetic tradition, and ideology in constituting the audience. This history, as yet unwritten, would require another book, probably one as long as this. While we have not treated reception fully, the present book does introduce certain issues — e.g., the activities which the Hollywood film solicits from the spectator, or the importance of early advertising in establishing classical canons — which we believe to be necessary to any future study of how the classical film has been consumed under specific circumstances.

As a historical account, our argument makes use of a great deal of empirical data about filmmaking, including much information not previously brought to light. But we should stress that the concept of a mode of film practice is not one that can be retrieved by 'simply looking' at films, documents, and machines. For rhetorical purposes, our argument is cast chronologically, but the idea of a 'classical Hollywood cinema' is ultimately a theoretical construct, and as such it must be judged by criteria of logical rigor and instrumental value. This book thus stands out not only as a history of the Hollywood cinema but also as an attempt to articulate a theoretical approach to film history.

There are many ways to organize a study such as this one. It would be possible to trace the history of the Hollywood cinema three times – once recounting changes in the mode of production, then treating changes in film style, then tracing technological developments. This we rejected, since the length of the three sections would be likely to break apart the parallels and causal connections we wished to bring out among the three realms. And placing one realm, such as the mode of production, first might imply that it had a monolithic determining status. But another alternative, that of simply limning a chronological account of American cinema and raising each argument *seriatim*, was clearly too atomistic. It would not allow us to treat broad institutional and stylistic patterns in a systematic way. We finally settled upon a format which permits us to delineate theoretically distinct realms while still weaving our arguments into a fundamentally chronological pattern. Our seven-part structure is a compromise between the need to analyze several 'levels' of historical change (style, economics, technology) and the need to cut 'vertically' across those levels at moments in which significant changes occurred. In this way, we balance localized accounts and generalized explanation. The book should then be seen as outlining the fundamental principles of historical stability and change at work in the Hollywood cinema and as displaying those principles in detail in particular instances.

The result can be sketched out in broad strokes. Part One establishes the stylistic norms fundamental to Hollywood filmmaking from 1917 to 1960. It is here that the concepts of norm, function, and style are defined and the ordinary Hollywood film is analyzed.

In Parts Two, Three, and Four, we consider three aspects of pre-1930 Hollywood filmmaking: the economic, the stylistic, and the technological. Part Two examines the economic aims and principles of the Hollywood mode of production and traces how that mode created a series of hierarchical, divided work systems. Part Three shows that while the Hollywood mode of production found its definitive form, the stylistic norms were also becoming consolidated. Part Four shows how the norms and the mode of production impel and respond to technological change.

Parts Five and Six deal with developments in the classical Hollywood cinema in the sound era. Part Five examines the effects of organized labor and large-scale financing upon the mode of production and traces further changes in production processes during the period. Part Six relates developments in technology to changes in film style during the same years.

Part Seven suggests the historical influences and the current state of this mode of film practice and concludes with some consideration of alternative modes.

This book has had its own stylistic norms and its own mode of production. Although parts and chapters are the work of single authors, we have conceived and executed the book as a unified argument, sharing common assumptions and terminology. We have not, however, striven for complete homogeneity. Differences of emphasis, value, argument, and style thus remain to remind the reader that the forms of the medium and the division of labor leave their marks, for better or worse, upon any cultural artifact.

Part One The classical Hollywood style, 1917-60

DAVID BORDWELL

Neither normative criticisms nor morphological description alone will ever give us a theory of style. I do not know if such a theory is necessary; but if we want one we might do worse than approach artistic solutions in terms of those specifications which are taken for granted in a given period, and to list systematically, and even, if need be, pedantically, the priorities in the reconciliation of conflicting demands. Such a procedure will give us a new respect for the classical but will also open our minds to an appreciation of non-classical solutions representing entirely fresh discoveries.[1]

E.H. Gombrich

1

An excessively obvious cinema

We all have a notion of the typical Hollywood film. The very label carries a set of expectations, often apparently obvious, about cinematic form and style. We can define that idea, test and ground those expectations, by using the concept of *group* style.

Historians routinely speak of group style in other arts: classicism or the Baroque in music, Impressionism or Cubism in painting, Symbolism or Imagism in poetry.[1] Cinema has its own group styles; German Expressionism, Soviet montage cinema, and the French New Wave afford time-honored instances. But to suggest that Hollywood cinema constitutes a group style seems more risky. In other national schools, a handful of filmmakers worked within sharply contained historical circumstances for only a few years. But Hollywood, as an extensive commercial enterprise, included hundreds of filmmakers and thousands of films, and it has existed for over six decades. If it is a daunting challenge to define a German Expressionist cinema or a Neorealist one, it might seem impossible to circumscribe a distinctive Hollywood 'group style.'

The historical arguments for the existence of such style are examined later in this book. At this point, a *prima facie* case for a 'classical Hollywood style' depends upon critically examining a body of films. Suppose that between 1917 and 1960 a distinct and homogeneous style has dominated American studio filmmaking – a style whose principles remain quite constant across decades, genres, studios, and personnel. My goal here is to identify, at several levels of generality, to what extent Hollywood filmmaking adheres to integral and limited stylistic conventions.

We could start with a description of the Hollywood style derived from Hollywood's own discourse, that enormous body of statements and assumptions to be found in trade journals, technical manuals, memoirs, and publicity handouts. We would find that the Hollywood cinema sees itself as bound by rules that set stringent limits on individual innovation; that telling a story is the basic formal concern, which makes the film studio resemble the monastery's *scriptorium*, the site of the transcription and transmission of countless narratives; that unity is a basic attribute of film form; that the Hollywood film purports to be 'realistic' in both an Aristotelian sense (truth to the probable) and a naturalistic one (truth to historical fact); that the Hollywood film strives to conceal its artifice through techniques of continuity and 'invisible' storytelling; that the film should be comprehensible and unambiguous; and that it possesses a fundamental emotional appeal that transcends class and nation. Reiterated tirelessly for at least seventy years, such precepts suggest that Hollywood practitioners recognized themselves as creating a distinct approach to film form and technique that we can justly label 'classical.'

We are not used to calling products of American mass culture 'classical' in any sense; the word apparently comes easier to the French speaker. As early as 1925, a French reviewer described Chaplin's *Pay Day* (1922) as a representative of 'cinematic classicism,' and a year later Jean Renoir spoke of Chaplin, Lubitsch, and Clarence Brown as contributors to a 'classical cinema' of the future, one 'which owes nothing to tricks, where nothing is left to chance, where the smallest detail takes its place of importance in the overall psychological scheme of the film.'[2] It was probably André Bazin who gave the adjective the most currency; by 1939, Bazin declared, Hollywood filmmaking had acquired 'all the characteristics of a classical art.'[3] It seems proper to retain the term in English, since the principles which Hollywood claims as its own rely on notions of decorum, proportion, formal harmony, respect for tradition, mimesis, self-effacing craftsmanship, and cool control of the perceiver's response – canons which critics in any medium usually call 'classical.'

To stress this collective and conserving aspect of Hollywood filmmaking also affords a useful counterweight to the individualist emphases of auteur criticism. Bazin criticized his protégés at *Cahiers du cinéma* by reminding them that the American cinema could not be reduced to an assembly of variegated creators, each armed with a personal vision:[4]

What makes Hollywood so much better than anything else in the world is not only the quality of certain directors, but also the vitality and, in a certain sense, the excellence of a tradition. . . . The American cinema is a classical art, but why not then admire in it what is most admirable, i.e., not only the talent of this or that filmmaker, but the genius of the system, the richness of its ever-vigorous tradition, and its fertility when it comes into contact with new elements.

Bazin's point struck the *Cahiers* writers most forcefully only after his death, partly because the decline of the studio system faced them with mediocre works by such venerated filmmakers as Mann, Ray, and Cukor. 'We said,' remarked Truffaut bitterly, 'that the American cinema pleases us, and its filmmakers are slaves; what if they were freed? And from the moment that they were freed, they made shitty films.'[5] Pierre Kast agreed: 'Better a good *cinéma de salarie* than a bad *cinéma d'auteur*.'[6] It is the *cinéma de salarie*, at least in its enduring aspects, that represents Hollywood's classicism.

All of which is not to say that Hollywood's classicism does not have disparate, even 'non-classical' sources. Certainly the Hollywood style seeks effects that owe a good deal to, say, romantic music or nineteenth-century melodrama. Nor do Hollywood's own assumptions exhaustively account for its practice; the institution's discourse should not set our agenda for analysis. The point is simply that Hollywood films constitute a fairly coherent aesthetic tradition which sustains individual creation. For the purposes of this book, the label 'classicism'

serves well because it swiftly conveys distinct aesthetic qualities (elegance, unity, rule-governed craftsmanship) and historical functions (Hollywood's role as the world's mainstream film style). Before there are auteurs, there are constraints; before there are deviations, there are norms.

Norms, paradigms, and standards

In the final analysis, we loved the American cinema because the films all resembled each other.

François Truffaut[7]

The first, and crucial, step is to assume that classical filmmaking constitutes an aesthetic system that can characterize salient features of the individual work. The system cannot determine every minute detail of the work, but it isolates preferred practices and sets limits upon invention. The problem is, in other words, that of defining what Jan Mukařovský has called aesthetic *norms*.

When we think of a norm, especially in a legal sense, we tend to think of a codified and inflexible rule. While Mukařovský recognized that the aesthetic norms of a period are often felt by artists as constraints upon their freedom, he stressed the norms' comparative flexibility. He argued that the aesthetic norm is characterized by its non-practical nature; the only goal of the aesthetic norm is to permit art works to come into existence. This has important consequences: disobeying the aesthetic norm is not necessarily a negative act (may, indeed, be quite productive); and aesthetic norms can change rapidly and considerably. Mukařovský goes on to inventory several different kinds of norms, all of which intertwine within the art work. There are norms deriving from the *materials* of the art work. Poetry, for instance, takes language as its material, but language does not come raw to the task; it brings along norms of everyday usage. Secondly, there are *technical* norms, basic craft practices such as metrical schemes and genre conventions. Thirdly, there are *practical*, or sociopolitical norms; e.g., a character's ethical values represented in the work. Finally, Mukařovský speaks of *aesthetic* norms as such, which seem to be the basic principles of artistic construction that form the work. These would include concepts of unity, decorum, novelty, and the like.[8]

Mukařovský's work helps us move toward defining the Hollywood cinema as an aesthetic system. Plainly, the Hollywood style has functioned historically as a set of norms. It might seem rash to claim that Hollywood's norms have not drastically changed since around 1920, but Mukařovský points out that periods of 'classicism' tend toward harmony and stability. Moreover, the idea of multiple norms impinging upon the same work helps us see that it is unlikely that any Hollywood film will perfectly embody all norms: 'The interrelations among all these norms, which function as instruments for artistic devices, are too complex, too differentiated, and too unstable for the positive value of the work to be able to appear as virtually identical with the perfect fulfillment of all norms obtaining within it.'[9] No Hollywood film *is* the classical system; each is an 'unstable equilibrium' of classical norms.

Mukařovský's work also enables us to anticipate the particular norms which we will encounter. Evidently, classical cinema draws upon practical or ethico-socio-political norms; I shall mention these only when the particular ways of appropriating such norms are characteristic of the classical style. For example, heterosexual romance is one value in American society, but that value takes on an aesthetic function in the classical cinema (as, say, the typical motivation for the principal line of action). Material norms are also present in the cinema; when we speak of the 'theatrical' space of early films or of the Renaissance representation of the body as important for classical cinema, we are assuming that cinema has absorbed certain material norms from other media. Similarly, I will spend considerable time examining the technical norms of classical filmmaking, since to a large extent these pervasive and persistent conventions of form, technique, and genre constitute the Hollywood tradition. But in order to understand the underlying logic of the classical mode, we must also study how that mode deploys fundamental aesthetic norms. How, specifically, does Hollywood use such principles as unity and aesthetic function? As all these points indicate, the chief virtue of Mukařovský's work is to enable us to think of a group film style not as a monolith but as a complex system of specific forces in dynamic interaction.

My emphasis on norms should not be taken to imply an iron-clad technical formula imposed upon filmmakers. Any group style offers a *range* of alternatives. Classical filmmaking is not, strictly speaking, formulaic; there is always another way to do something. You can light a scene high- or low-key, you can pan or track, you can cut rapidly or seldom. A group style thus establishes what semiologists call a paradigm, a set of elements which can, according to rules, substitute for one another. Thinking of the classical style as a paradigm helps us retain a sense of the choices open to filmmakers within the tradition. At the same time, the style remains a unified system because the paradigm offers *bounded* alternatives. If you are a classical filmmaker, you cannot light a scene in such a way as to obscure the locale entirely (cf. Godard in *Le gai savoir*); you cannot pan or track without some narrative or generic motivation; you cannot make every shot one second long (cf. avant-garde works). Both the alternatives and the limitations of the style remain clear if we think of the paradigm as creating *functional equivalents*: a cut-in may replace a track-in, or color may replace lighting as a way to demarcate volumes, because each device fulfills the same role. Basic principles govern not only the elements in the paradigm but also the ways in which the elements may function.

Our account of this paradigm must also recognize how redundant it is. Not only are individual devices equivalent, but they often appear together. For instance, there are several cues for a flashback in a classical Hollywood film: pensive character attitude, close-up of face, slow dissolve, voice-over narration, sonic 'flashback,' music. In any given case, several of these will be used together. In another mode of film practice, such as that of the European 'art cinema' of the 1960s, the same general paradigm governs a movement into flashback, but the conventional cues are not so redundant (e.g., pensive close-up but with no music or dissolve). The classical paradigm thus often lets the filmmaker choose how to be redundant, but seldom how redundant to be.

One more conception of Hollywood cinema as a unified system plays a part in understanding the classical style. This book will also refer to a 'standardized' film style. In general, this suggests only adherence to norms. But the term also implies that Hollywood cinema has been made stringently uniform by its dependence upon a specific economic mode of film production and consumption. Calling the Hollywood style 'standardized' often implies that norms have become recipes, routinely repeating a stereotyped product.

Yet the avant-garde has no monopoly on quality, and violating a norm is not the only way to achieve aesthetic value. I assume that in any art, even those operating within a mass-production system, the art work can achieve value by modifying or skillfully obeying the premises of a dominant style.

Levels of generality

If the classical style is a set of norms, we need a way to distinguish greater and lesser degrees of abstraction in that set. A match-on-action cut is a classical convention; so is the principle of spatial continuity. But the first convention is a particular application of the second. Broadly speaking, we can analyze the classical Hollywood style at three levels.

1 Devices. Many isolated technical elements are characteristic of classical Hollywood cinema: three-point lighting, continuity editing, 'movie music,' centered framings, dissolves, etc. Such devices are often what we think of as the 'Hollywood style' itself. Yet we cannot stop with simply inventorying these devices.
2 Systems. As members of a paradigm, technical devices achieve significance only when we understand their functions. A dissolve between scenes can convey the passage of time; but so can a cut. To say that the classical Hollywood style ceased to exist when most scenes were linked by cuts is to presume that a style is only the sum of its devices. A style consists not only of recurrent elements but of a set of functions and relations defined for them. These functions and relations are established by a system. For example, one cinematic system involves the construction of represented space. In classical filmmaking, lighting, sound, image composition, and editing all take as one task the

articulation of space according to specific principles. It is this systematic quality that makes it possible for one device to do duty for another, or to repeat information conveyed by another. Thus employing a cut to link scenes conforms to one function defined by classical premises; within this paradigm, there must be some cue for a time lapse between scenes, and a cut may do duty for a dissolve (or a swish-pan, or a shot of a clock's moving hands). The systematic quality of film style also sets limits upon the paradigm; in representing space, for instance, ambiguous camera positions and discontinuous cutting are unlikely to occur because they violate certain principles of the system.

In this book, we shall assume that any fictional narrative film possesses three systems:

A system of narrative logic, which depends upon story events and causal relations and parallelisms among them;

A system of cinematic time; and

A system of cinematic space.

A given device may work within any or all of these systems, depending on the functions that the system assigns to the device.[10]

3 Relations of systems. If systems are relations among elements, the total style can be defined as the relation of those systems to each other. Narrative logic, time, and space interact with one another. Does one of them subordinate the others? Do all three operate independently? How are the principles of one justified or challenged by another? In the Hollywood style, the systems do not play equal roles: space and time are almost invariably made vehicles for narrative causality. Moreover, specific principles govern that process. At this level, even irregularities in the various systems can be seen as purposeful. For instance, if we do find a passage of discontinuous cutting, we can ask whether it is still serving a narrative function (e.g., to convey a sudden, shocking event). In such a case, the relation among systems would remain consistent even if the individual device or system varied from normal usage.

We can, then, characterize the classical Hollywood style by its stylistic elements, by its stylistic systems, and, most abstractly, by the relations it sets up among those systems. No single level of description will work. It is too narrow to define classical norms by devices, and it is unwarrantably broad to define them solely by relations among systems. (The domination of narrative logic over cinematic time and space is common to many styles.) Hence the importance of the second level, the stylistic systems. The categories of causality, time, and space enable us both to place individual devices within functional contexts and to see the classical style as a dynamic interplay of several principles. Finally, no categorical explanation of one level can wholly swallow up another. The systematic principle of depicting space unambiguously does not logically entail the use of three-point lighting. Those specific devices are the products of diverse historical processes; other elements might do as well. The specificity of the classical style depends upon all three levels of generality.

My account here will construct the classical stylistic paradigm across several decades, emphasizing the continuity at the second and third levels. But by stressing continuity of function I do not imply that the systems' paradigmatic range did not change somewhat. For example, before the mid-1920s, the use of high and low angles was severely codified: for long-shots (especially of landscapes), for optical point-of-view, or for shot/reverse-shot patterns when one person is higher than other. (In shot/reverse-shot editing, an image of one element in the scene, typically a person talking, is followed by a shot of another element which is spatially opposite the first, typically, a person listening. Chapter 5 furnishes a more systematic explanation. See the examples in figs 16.65 and 16.66 in Chapter 16.) A medium-shot of an object or a human figure would seldom be framed from a sharp high- or low-angle. Yet in the late 1920s, Hollywood's spatial paradigm widened a bit, probably as a result of the influence of certain German films. Examples can be found in *Bulldog Drummond* (1929) and *The Show* (1927), which dramatically use high and low angles (see figs 1.1 and 1.2). With the coming of sound, an occasional odd angle could compensate for what was felt to be an excessively 'theatrical' scene (see fig 1.3). Throughout the 1930s and 1940s, steep angles took their place as common functional equivalents for normal framings in many situations. Across

history, the paradigm develops chiefly through changes in the first level of analysis – that of devices. This process will be examined in detail in Parts Three, Four, and Six.

Viewers, schemata, and mental sets

Considering the classical cinema as a system of norms operating at different levels of generality can seem to create a reified object, a colossal block of attributes that says little about how film viewers see films. The language of objectivism is hard to avoid, especially when we apply spatial metaphors like 'levels.' How, then, are we to characterize the viewer's work, or what E.H. Gombrich calls 'the beholder's share'?

An intricate and comprehensive theory of film viewing has yet to be constructed, and it is not within the scope of this book to do it. Yet if we want to consider how the Hollywood film solicits a specific way of being understood, we need to recognize at least how passive an 'illusionist' theory makes the spectator. Illusionist theorists usually insist that only avant-garde texts make the viewer perform an 'active' reading, or force the viewer to 'work to produce meaning.'[11] The Hollywood spectator, it is claimed, is little more than a receptacle; few skills of attention, memory, discrimination, inference-drawing, or hypothesis-testing are required. Now this is clearly too simple. Classical films call forth activities on the part of the spectator. These activities may be highly standardized and comparatively easy to learn, but we cannot assume that they are simple.

Consider, as one problem, the spectator as perceiver. Illusionist theory emphasizes the deceptive quality of projected movement or of shot space: the spectator is duped into taking image for reality. As Noël Burch puts it, 'spectators experience the diegetic world as environment.'[12] But recent explorations in aesthetic perception and cognition have shown that 'illusion' is not simply a matter of fooling the eye. The spectator *participates* in creating the illusion. R.L. Gregory, for instance, speaks of perception as inferential, which makes 'illusion' dependent upon errors of inference: either biological 'mechanism' errors (e.g., the *phi* phenomenon as creating the illusion of movement) or cognitive 'strategy' errors (e.g., assuming that the whole is consistent with displayed parts). Gombrich has also shown that visual illusion demands that the spectator propose, test, and discard perceptual hypotheses based on expectation and probability.[13] For illusion to work, the spectator must meet the art work at least half way.

If perceptual illusion requires some spectatorial activity, even more is required for that imaginative involvement solicited by narrative. No story tells all. Meir Sternberg characterizes following a tale as 'gap-filling,' and just as we project motion on to a succession of frames, so we form hypotheses, make inferences, erect expectations, and draw conclusions about the film's characters and actions.[14] Again, the spectator must cooperate in fulfilling the film's form. It is clear that the protocols which control this activity derive from the system of norms operating in the classical style. For example, an insistence upon the primacy of narrative causality is a general feature of the classical system; the viewer translates this norm into a tacit strategy for spotting the work's unifying features, distinguishing significant information from 'noise,' sorting the film's stimuli into the most comprehensive pattern.

Gombrich describes this process in terms of 'schemata' and 'mental sets.' Schemata are traditional formal patterns for rendering subject matter. Gombrich points out that the artist cannot simply copy reality; the artist can only render the model in terms of one schema or another. Thus even new shapes will be assimilated to categories which the artist has learned to handle. As Gombrich puts it, 'making precedes matching' – the creation of a schema precedes copying the model.[15] After the making, the schema can be modified in each particular case by the artist's purpose (usually, the sort of information the artist wants to convey). So far, much of this is congruent with Mukařovský's argument: we might think of the artist's schemata as technical norms and the artist's purpose as involving specific aesthetic norms. But Gombrich goes on to show that the schemata and the purpose function for the viewer as well. The artist's training is paralleled by the spectator's prior experience of the visual world and, especially, of other art works. The painter's traditional schemata constitute the basis of the viewer's expectations or *mental set*: 'A style, like a culture or climate of opinion, sets up a horizon of expectation, a mental set, which registers deviations and modifications with exaggerated sensitivity.'[16] For Gombrich, this mental set is defined in terms of probabilities: certain schemata are more likely to fit the data than others.

By pairing concepts like schemata and mental set, we can spell out the ways in which the classical film solicits the spectator. For instance, one well-known schema of Hollywood film editing is the shot/reverse-shot pattern. The filmmaker has this ready to hand for representing any two figures, groups, or objects within the same place. This schema can be fitted to many situations, whatever the differences of figure placement, camera height, lighting, or focus; whether the image is in widescreen ratio or not; whether the figures are facing one another or not; etc. Because of the tradition behind the schema, the viewer in turn expects to see the shot/reverse-shot figure, especially if the first shot of the combination appears. If the next shot does not obey the schema, the spectator then applies another, less probable, schema to the second shot. The spectator of the classical film thus riffles through the alternatives normalized by the style, from most to least likely. Through schemata, the style's norms not only impose their logic upon the material but also elicit particular activities from the viewer. The result is that in describing the classical system we are describing a set of operations that the viewer is expected to perform.

To stress the tasks which the film allots to the spectator allows us to abandon certain illusions of our own. We no longer need subscribe to copy-theories of cinema, whereby a certain style simply replicates the real world or normal acts of perception; schemata, tied to historically defined purposes, always intervene to guide us in grasping the film. Nor need we imagine a Svengali cinema holding its audience in thrall. The classical schemata have created a mental set that still must be activated by and tested against any given film. Of course, the classical style defines certain spectatorial activities as salient, and the historical dominance of that style has so accustomed us to those activities that audiences may find other schemata more burdensome. Yet this dynamic concept of the viewer's role allows us to explain the very processes that seem so excessively obvious; as we shall see, even the spectator's rapt absorption results from a hypothesis-checking that requires the viewer to meet the film halfway. We can also envision alternative viewing practices, other activities that the spectator might be asked to perform. The chapters that follow, then, suggest at several points how the norms of the classical Hollywood style encourage specific activities on the part of the spectator.

Style in history

If you're not working for Brezhnev Studio-Mosfilm, you are working for Nixon-Paramount. . . . You forget that this same master has been ordering the same film for fifty years.

Wind from the East

To construct the classical Hollywood style as a coherent system, we also need to account for the style's historical dimension. In one sense, this entire book tries to do that, by examining the Hollywood mode of production, the consolidation of the style in a specific period, and the changes that the style undergoes in subsequent years. At this point, I must indicate that my overall description of the classical style applies to a set of films across an extensive period. What historical assumptions underlie such a broadly based analysis?

The three levels of generality indicate some of those assumptions. My enterprise assumes a historical continuity at the two most abstract levels of style (systems and relations among systems); it assumes that the most distinct changes take place at the level of stylistic devices. For example, through its history Hollywood cinema seeks to represent events in a temporally continuous fashion; moreover, narrative logic has generally worked to motivate this temporal continuity. What changes through history are the various devices for representing temporal continuity such as inter-titles, cuts, irises, dissolves, whip-pans, and wipes.

By stressing the enduring principles of the classical style, we lose some specific detail. In this part, I shall not reconstruct the choices available to filmmakers at any given moment. If I say that a scene can begin by drawing back from a significant figure or object, that suggests that an iris, a cut, and a camera movement are all paradigmatic alternatives. But in 1917, the most probable choice would have been the iris; in 1925, the cut; in 1935, the camera movement. In discussing the general principles of classical style, I shall often project the historically variable devices on to the same plane to show their functional equivalence. This bird's-eye view enables us to map the basic and persistent features of the style in history. The more minute history of the devices themselves forms the bulk of Parts Three, Four, and Six.

Historical analysis demands a concept of periodization. Since we are concerned here with a stylistic history, we cannot presuppose that the periods used to write political or social history will demarcate the history of an art. That is, there is no immediate compulsion to define a 'cinema of the 1930s' as drastically different from that of 'the 1940s,' or to distinguish pre-World War II Hollywood style from postwar Hollywood style. What, then, will constitute our grounds for periodization? Norms, yes; but also the film industry, the most proximate and pertinent institution for creating, regulating, and maintaining those norms. This is not to say that film style and mode of production march across decades in perfect synchronization. Parts Two and Five will provide a periodization for the Hollywood mode of production that while congruent in some respects, cannot be simply superimposed upon stylistic history. Nevertheless, we have chosen to frame our study within the years 1917-60.

The earlier date is easier to justify. Stylistically, from 1917 on, the classical model became dominant, in the sense that most American fiction films since that moment employed fundamentally similar narrative, temporal, and spatial systems. At the same time, the studio mode of production had become organized: detailed division of labor, the continuity script, and a hierarchical managerial system became the principal filmmaking procedures. Parts Two and Three detail how style and industry came to be so closely synchronized by 1917. But why halt an analysis of the classical Hollywood cinema in 1960?

The date triggers suspicion. Stylistically, there is no question that 'classical' films are still being made, as Part Seven will show. Variants of the Hollywood mode of production continue as well.

There are thus compelling reasons to claim that 1960 is a premature cutoff point. On the other hand, some critics may assert that this 'classical' period is far too roomy; one can see any period after 1929 as the 'breakdown' of the Hollywood cinema (the tensions of the Depression, the anguish of war and Cold War, and the competitive challenge of television).

The year 1960 was chosen for reasons of history and of convenience. In the film industry, it was widely believed that at the end of the decade Hollywood had reached the end of its mature existence. *This Was Hollywood*, the title of a 1960 book by publicist Beth Day, summarizes many reasons for considering the year as a turning point. Most production firms had converted their energies to television, the dominant mass-entertainment form since the mid-1950s; many had reduced their holdings in studio real estate; stars had become free agents; most producers had become independent; the B-film was virtually dead.[17] To Day's account we can add other signs of change. By 1960, a certain technological state of the art had been reached: high-definition color films, wide formats, and high-fidelity magnetic sound had set the standard of quality that continues today. Moreover, other styles began to challenge the dominance of classicism. The international art cinema, spearheaded by Ingmar Bergman, Akira Kurosawa, certain Italian directors, and the French New Wave, offered a more influential and widely disseminated alternative to Hollywood than had ever existed before. Not that Hollywood was significantly shaken (Part Seven tries to show why), but the force of the classical norm was reduced somewhat. Despite these reasons, it remains somewhat arbitrary to see 1960 as closing the classical period. We have chosen it partly because it makes our research somewhat manageable while still conveying the powerful spread of the classical cinema's authority.

The ordinary film

Film historians have not generally acknowledged the place of the *typical* work. In most film histories, masterworks and innovations rise monumentally out of a hazy terrain whose contours remain unknown. In other arts, however, the ordinary work is granted considerable importance. Academicism, mainstream works, the canon, tradition – the history of music, painting, and literature could not do without such conceptions. 'I believe,' remarks Roman Jakobson, 'that a very important thing in analyzing trends in the cinema or the structure of a film, is the necessity of considering the base, the *background* of the spectator's habits. What films is the spectator used to seeing? To what forms is he accustomed?'[18] My analysis of the norms of the classical style thus gives privileged place not to the aberrant film that breaks or tests the rules but to the quietly conformist film that tries simply to follow them.

Between 1915 and 1960, at least fifteen thousand feature films were produced in America. It is impossible to analyze such a corpus. To construct a model of the ordinary film, we have selected in an unbiased fashion, 100 films from this period. (Appendix A explains the sampling procedures and lists the films.) We studied each film on a horizontal viewing machine, recording stylistic details of each shot and summarizing the film's action scene by scene. This body of data constitutes our unbiased sample (abbreviated UnS), and when we cite such a film, an asterisk signals it.

In the stylistic analysis of the cinema, the practice of unbiased sampling is unprecedented, but we believe it to be a sound way to determine historical norms. When the sample turned up what might be regarded as auteur films, we accepted this as inevitable in an unbiased sample and treated these films exactly as we did others. At least four-fifths of the sample, however, constitute a body of fairly obscure productions ranging across decades, studios, and genres. Furthermore, we have sought to test the conclusions about the UnS films by closely analyzing almost two hundred other Hollywood films of the 1915-60 period. We chose many of these films for their quality or historical influence, but many were as undistinguished as our UnS items. We shall refer to this second set of films as the Extended Sample (ES). My analysis of the classical style takes the UnS films as the central source of evidence and examples, drawing upon ES films occasionally. This means that many of the films mentioned will be unfamiliar to readers, but since I argue for their typicality, the reader will recognize qualities present in many other films.

In one sense, the concept of group style simply makes manifest what we and Hollywood itself 'already know.' Concepts like norm, paradigm, stylistic alternatives, levels of systemic function, periodization, and schemata are, from this perspective, simply tools in making our habitual intuitions explicit. But these concepts also enable us to reveal the patterned and stable quality of our assumptions. The concepts can show that the classical cinema has an underlying logic which is not apparent from our common-sense reflection upon the films or from Hollywood's own discourse about them. The theoretical concepts introduced in this chapter are indispensible to grasping the classical style's systematic quality. Armed with them, we can go on to examine how that style characteristically organizes causality, time, and space. The next five chapters, then, should trigger a certain *déja vu*; the reader will recognize some familiar filmmaking practices. But these chapters also seek to explain in a systematic way how these practices work together to create a distinct film style which, like Poe's purloined letter, 'escapes observation by dint of being excessively obvious.'[19]

2

Story causality and motivation

There are several ways of analyzing fictional narrative cinema; the approach taken here can be broadly called formalist. As Chapter 1 proposed, a narrative film consists of three systems: narrative logic (definition of events, causal relations and parallelisms between events), the representation of time (order, duration, repetition), and the representation of space (composition, orientation, etc.). Any given technical parameter (e.g., sound, editing) can function within any or all of these systems. Lighting or camera movements can emphasize a causally significant object while endowing the represented space with depth and volume. Offscreen sound can operate as a narrative cause, can work to specify duration, or can define an unseen space. In short, while this account stresses what Mukařovský calls technical norms, the techniques are not simply isolated devices but rather functional components in the three basic formal systems.

A narrative film seldom treats its systems as equals. The Russian Formalist critics suggested that in any text or tradition, a certain component – the *dominant* – subordinates others. 'The dominant,' writes Jakobson, 'may be defined as the focussing component of a work of art: it rules, determines, and transforms the remaining components. It is the dominant which guarantees the integrity of the structure.'[1] This integrity deserves to be seen as a dynamic one, with the subordinated factors constantly pulling against the sway of the dominant. In Hollywood cinema, a specific sort of narrative causality operates as the dominant, making temporal and spatial systems vehicles for it. These systems do not always rest quietly under the sway of narrative logic, but in general the causal dominant creates a marked hierarchy of systems in the classical film.

Another distinction cuts across these three systems. Most film theorists recognize a difference between the narrative material of a film (the events or actions, the basic story) and the manner in which that material is represented in the film. The Russian Formalist literary critics distinguished between *fabula* ('story') and *syuzhet* ('plot'), and throughout this book, we will use the story/plot distinction in a sense akin to that of the Formalists.[2] 'Story' will refer to the events of the narrative in their presumed spatial, temporal, and causal relations. 'Plot' will refer to the totality of formal and stylistic materials in the film. The plot thus includes all the systems of time, space, and causality actually manifested in the film; everything from a flashback structure and subjective point-of-view to minutiae of lighting, cutting, and camera movement. The plot is, in effect, the film before us. The story is thus our mental construct, a structure of inferences we make on the basis of selected aspects of the plot. For example, the plot might present certain events out of chronological order; to understand the film, we must be able to reconstruct that chronological, or story, order. One virtue of this scheme is its acknowledgment of the viewer's activity; if the viewer knows how a certain tradition of filmmaking habitually presents a story, the viewer approaches the film with what Gombrich calls a mental set. In the next chapter, we shall be able to specify certain tasks which the classical film assigns to the spectator. The work at hand is to bring to light basic principles of story causality in the classical Hollywood film. Once we have done this, we will be in a position to understand how the classical story creates its particular unity.

Causes and effects

This extra is called an actor. This actor is called

a character. The adventures of these characters are called a film.

Wind from the East

'Plot,' writes Francis Patterson in a 1920 manual for aspiring screenwriters, 'is a careful and logical working out of the laws of cause and effect. The mere sequence of events will not make a plot. Emphasis must be laid upon causality and the action and reaction of the human will.'[3] Here in brief is the premise of Hollywood story construction: causality, consequence, psychological motivations, the drive toward overcoming obstacles and achieving goals. Character-centered – i.e., personal or psychological – causality is the armature of the classical story.

This sounds so obvious that we need to remember that narrative causality could be impersonal as well. Natural causes (floods, genetic inheritance) could form the basis for story action, and in cinema we might think of the work of Yasujiro Ozu, which installs a 'natural' rhythm or cycle of life at the center of the action. Causality could also be conceived as social – a causality of institutions and group processes. Soviet films of the 1920s remain the central model of cinematic attempts to represent just such supraindividual historical causality. Or one could conceive of narrative causality as a kind of impersonal determinism, in which coincidence and chance leave the individual little freedom of personal action. The postwar European art cinema often relies upon this sort of narrative causality, as Bazin indicates in relation to Bresson's *Diary of a Country Priest* (1950): 'Events do indeed follow one another according to a necessary order, yet within a framework of accidental happenings.'[4]

Hollywood films of course include causes of these impersonal types, but they are almost invariably subordinated to psychological causality. This is most evident in the classical film's use of historical causality. Pierre Sorlin points out that classical films typically present historical events as uncaused; a war simply breaks out, disrupting characters' lives very much as a natural disaster might.[5] When history is seen as caused, that cause is traceable to a psychologically defined individual. (A chief instance here is *The Birth of a Nation* [1915], which links Reconstruction abuses to the ambitions of Austin Stoneman.) Thus the classical film makes history

unknowable apart from its effects upon individual characters. As an old Russian émigré says at the end of *Balalaika* (1939): 'And to think that it took the Revolution to bring us together.'

Impersonal causes may initiate or abruptly alter a line of story action which then proceeds by personal causes. A storm may maroon a group of characters, but then psychological causality takes over. A war may separate lovers, but then they must react to that condition. Coincidence is especially dangerous in this context, and Hollywood rule-books insist upon confining coincidence to the initial situation. Boy and girl may meet by accident, but they cannot rely upon chance to keep their acquaintance alive. The later in the film a coincidence occurs, the weaker it is; and it is very unlikely that the story will be resolved by coincidence. We see here the influence of the well-made play (e.g., the mischance that triggers the intrigue in Scribe or Sardou) and the appeal to Aristotelian notions of plausibility and probability. Unmotivated coincidences do occasionally crop up in Hollywood films. *The Courage of Commonplace* (1917) deals with a miners' strike, and the film's protagonist, the mine supervisor, will not yield to the strikers. He declares: 'Something's got to happen.' The next day, a mine collapses by natural causes. (A more careful scenarist would have made a disgruntled foreman sabotage the mine.) Or, in *Parachute Jumper* (1933), it is not unmotivated to have the romantic couple first meet by accident, but in the last scene they meet again by sheer chance. Most often, though, coincidence is motivated by genre (chance encounters are conventions of comedy and melodrama). And 'coincidental' encounters may be prepared causally. In *Parole Fixer* (1940), the crooked Craydon must encounter the government agents at a cafe, so the script motivates the encounter as probable. His secretary asks why Craydon eats at the cafe so often, and he answers: 'Our friends of the FBI eat here.'

If the character must act as the prime causal agent, he or she must be defined as a bundle of qualities, or traits. Screenplay manuals demand that a character's traits be clearly identified and consistent with one another. Sources for this practice, of course, go back very far, but the most pertinent ones are the models for characterization present in literature and theater. From the nineteenth-century melodrama's stock characterizations, Hollywood has borrowed the need for sharply delineated and unambiguous traits.[6] (Some of melodrama's types, such as certain ethnic types, the old maid, and the villainous lawyer, get reincarnated in the Hollywood cinema.) From the novel comes what Ian Watt calls a 'formal realism': characters are individualized with particular traits, tics, or tags.[7] Watt highlights, for instance, the importance of the unique proper name (Micawber, Moll Flanders) which creates a greater singularity of personality than the stereotyped names of the melodrama (Paddy the Irishman, Jonathan the Yankee). The popular short story acted as a model for narrowing such individualized characterization to fixed limits. The novel can explore many character traits and trace extensive character change, but the dominant aesthetic of the short story in the years 1900-1920 required that the writer create characters with few traits and then focus those upon a few key actions. The short story in a sense struck an average between the fixed character types of the melodrama and the dense complexity of the realist novel, and this average appealed to the classical Hollywood cinema during its formative years. (Chapter 14 will trace how the popular short story became a model for Hollywood dramaturgy.) It was thus possible for Frank Borzage to claim in 1922 that 'Today in the pictures we have the old melodramatic situations fitted out decently with true characterizations.'[8]

The classical film's presentation of character traits likewise follows conventions established in earlier theoretical and literary forms. Characters will be typed by occupation (cops are burly), age, gender, and ethnic identity. To these types, individualized traits are added. Most important, a character is made a consistent bundle of a few salient traits, which usually depend upon the character's narrative function. It is the business of the film's exposition to acquaint us with these traits and to establish their consistency. At the beginning of *Saratoga* (1937), a garrulous grandfather tells another character (and us) how his daughter has become 'high and mighty' since she went to Europe. We see her almost immediately, and her snooty behavior is consistent with his description. At the start of *Casbah* (1948), police officers discuss Pepe's susceptibility to women; the next scene introduces Pepe, singing

about women and fate to an audience of admiring women. Sometimes, as in *Lorna Doone* (1923) and *Wuthering Heights* (1939), the film borrows the novelistic device of introducing us to the characters in childhood; the already-formed principal traits we observe will carry over into the adult lives. More commonly, the character's salient traits are indicated — by an expository title, by other characters' description — and the initial appearance of the character confirms these traits as salient. In such ways, the spectator forms clear first impressions about the characters as homogeneous identities.

The importance of character consistency can be seen in the star system, which was a crucial factor in Hollywood film production. Although in the United States, the theatrical star system goes back to the early 1800s, it was not until the period 1912-1917 that film companies began consistently to differentiate their products by means of stars.[9] On the whole, the star reinforced the tendency toward strongly profiled and unified characterization. Max Ophuls praised Hollywood's ability to give the actor an already-existing personality with which to work in the film.[10] The star, like the fictional character, already had a set of salient traits which could be matched to the demands of the story. In describing the filming of *I Was a Male War Bride* (1949), Hawks suggested that one scene did not coalesce until he discovered the scene's 'attitude': 'A man like Cary Grant would be amused' — that is, the star's traits and the character's traits became isomorphic.[11]

In his book *Stars*, Richard Dyer has shown how the 'roundness' of the novelistic character is lacking in Hollywood film characterization and traces this lack to the need for 'perfect fit' between star and role.[12] It is also the case that the classical film both trades upon the prior connotations of the star and masks these connotations, presenting the star as character as if 'for the first time.'[13] For example, the star may portray a character who grows into the star's persona. In *Meet John Doe* (1941) the selfish pitcher John Willoughby becomes the rustic idealist John Doe because Willoughby was, in latent form, Gary Cooper to begin with. We discover the Gary Cooper persona afresh, even while knowing that it was there before the start. This is perhaps the most common way to represent character change in the classical cinema, since it affirms a basic consistency of character traits.

'Guys like you end up in the stockade sooner or later.' A single line in *From Here to Eternity (1953) shows how strongly classical character traits are tied to action. Fatso's remark follows his fight with Maggio, and so sums up Maggio's act of defiance. But the 'guys like you' assumes Maggio to be a fixed identity, a permanent type (the hotheaded bucker of authority). Moreover, that type is defined not only by traits but by deeds. Maggio will continue to act according to type. That he does indeed wind up in the stockade does not make Fatso a prophet; his remark simply acknowledges the close causal relation between a character's traits and actions; traits are only latent causes, actions the effects of traits. We reason, as screenwriting manuals remind us, from cause to effect and vice-versa; the writer's procedure of 'foreshadowing' is nothing more than preparing a cause for an eventual effect.

If characters are to become agents of causality, their traits must be affirmed in speech and physical behavior, the observable projections of personality. While films can entirely do without people, Hollywood cinema relies upon a distinction between movement and action. Movement, writes Frederick Palmer,[14]

> is merely motion. Action is usually the outward expression of inner feelings. . . . For instance, one might write: 'The whirring blades of the electric fan caused the window curtains to flutter. The man seated at the massive desk finished his momentous letter, sealed it, and hastened out to post it.' The whirring fan and the fluttering curtain give motion only − the man's writing the letter and taking it out to post provides action.
> It is of action that photoplays are wrought.

Palmer's scene provides a precise hypothetical alternative to the classical style (one that Ozu will actualize in his shots of objects interrupting passages of character 'action'). Hollywood cinema, however, emphasizes action, 'the outward expression of inner feeling,' the litmus test of character consistency. Even a simple physical reaction − a gesture, an expression, a widening of the eyes − constructs character psychology in accordance with other information. Most actions

in the classical film proceed, as Bazin put it, 'from the commonsense supposition that a necessary and unambiguous causal relationship exists between feelings and their outward manifestations.'[15]

Hollywood cinema reinforces the individuality and consistency of each character by means of recurrent motifs. A character will be tagged with a detail of speech or behavior that defines a major trait. For example, the *nouveau riche* Upshaw in *Going Highbrow (1935) is associated with his craving for tomato juice and eggs, a sign of his ordinary tastes. The 'fallen woman' in *Woman of the World (1925) is defined by her exotic tattoo, executed at a lover's request. In *Mr. Skeffington (1944), Fanny's flightiness is conveyed by her habit of mentioning a luncheon engagement with another woman but then always standing her up. The motif may associate the character with an object or locale. The heroine of *The Tiger's Coat (1920) is associated with a painting that compares her to a 'tawny tiger skin.' In *His Double Life (1933), Farrell meets a woman who talks of her garden while the soundtrack plays 'Country Gardens'; once he has married her, they are seen sitting in her garden. Consistency of character is conveyed by repeating the motif through the film. With a minor character, the motif may be a running gag that aids easy identification, as when one soldier in *The Hasty Heart (1949) has been curious about what a Scotsman wears under his kilts and at the end peers under the kilts to find out.

For major characters, the motif serves to mark significant stages of story action. In *A Lost Lady (1934), the older man tells Marion that she must face life 'with banners flying,' and the motif defines his pride and sets a goal for her. Once they are married, the phrase becomes a bond between them. At the film's close, after having decided not to leave him, Marion says: 'Nothing to be afraid of, no more ghosts − banners flying!' A similar use of another line, 'I can take it on the chin,' runs through *Show People (1928) tracing the heroine's career as a movie actress. In *Prince of Players (1954), Junius Booth drunkenly orders an audience to wait ten minutes and he'll give them 'the damnedest King Lear you ever saw. The name is Booth!' After his son Ned becomes an actor, he calms an unruly crowd by promising 'the damnedest Richard you ever saw. The name is

Booth!' When, at the film's end, Ned decides to perform despite his wife's death, he explains, 'The name is still Booth!' The tiny word 'still' confirms that the father's defiant attitude persists in the son, and Ned has not changed a bit.

Once defined as an individual through traits and motifs, the character assumes a causal role because of his or her desires. Hollywood characters, especially protagonists, are goal-oriented. The hero desires something new to his/her situation, or the hero seeks to restore an original state of affairs. This owes something to late nineteenth-century theatre, as seen in Ferdinand Brunetière's dictum that the central law of the drama is that of conflict arising from obstacles to the character's desire: 'That is what may be called *will*, to set up a goal, and to direct everything toward it.'[16] Plainly the star system also supported this tendency by insisting upon a strongly characterized protagonist. The goal-oriented hero, incarnated in Douglas Fairbanks, Mary Pickford, and William S. Hart, was quickly identified as a distinguishing trait of the American cinema. In 1924, a German critic wrote of the Hollywood character as 'the man of deeds. In the first act his goal is set; in the last act he reaches it. Everything that intervenes between these two acts is a test of strength.'[17] Through thirty years, the claim generally held good. In *The Michigan Kid* (1928), the hero resolves in his childhood to flee to Alaska, make a fortune, and come back to marry his sweetheart. One of the policemen in *Sh! The Octopus* (1937) vows: 'We're gonna catch that Octopus and get that fifty thousand dollar reward.' The immigrant protagonist of *An American Romance* (1944) has a burning desire to manufacture steel. In *My Favorite Brunette* (1947), the hero declares: 'All my life I wanted to be a hard-boiled detective.' The teenage heroine of *Gidget* (1959) states her aim of attracting a handsome boy on the beach. It is easy to see in the goal-oriented protagonist a reflection of an ideology of American individualism and enterprise, but it is the peculiar accomplishment of the classical cinema to translate this ideology into a rigorous chain of cause and effect.

Other characters get defined by goals. Melodrama's formula of hero versus villain, never too hoary for Hollywood, depends upon the clash of opposed purposes. Even when the oppositions are not absolute, characters' goals produce causal chains. Characters may have complementary or independent goals. In *Sweepstakes Winner* (1939), when Jenny comes into a betting parlor and announces her goal (to buy a race horse), two touts see how that can serve their own aims (to fix races and make money). In *Indianapolis Speedway* (1939), a racedriver's girlfriend wants only a home and family; he tells her that she'll get both after he has put his brother through college. Goals become latent effects in the causal series: they shape our expectations by narrowing the range of alternative outcomes of the action.

Making personal character traits and goals the causes of actions has led to a dramatic form fairly specific to Hollywood. The classical film has at least two lines of action, both causally linking the same group of characters. Almost invariably, one of these lines of action involves heterosexual romantic love. This is, of course, not startling news. Of the one hundred films in the UnS, ninety-five involved romance in at least one line of action, while eighty-five made that the principal line of action. Screenplay manuals stress love as the theme with greatest human appeal. Character traits are often assigned along gender lines, giving male and female characters those qualities deemed 'appropriate' to their roles in romance. To win the love of a man or woman becomes the goal of many characters in classical films. In this emphasis upon heterosexual love, Hollywood continues traditions stemming from the chivalric romance, the bourgeois novel, and the American melodrama.

We sometimes think of a play's second line of action as an independent subplot, such as a comic love affair between servants. Classical Hollywood cinema, however, makes the second line of action causally related to the romantic action. Instead of putting many characters through parallel lines of action, the Hollywood film involves few characters in several interdependent actions. For example, in *Penthouse* (1933), the protagonist tries to solve a murder while wooing one of the suspects. Sometimes, as in the love-triangle story, the second line of action also involves romance. More commonly, the second line of action involves another sort of activity — business, spying, sports, politics, crime, show business — any activity, in short, which can provide a goal for the character. In *Saratoga* (1937), the protagonist Duke must win Carol from her fiancé Hartley and he must help her grandfather to obtain a successful racehorse. In *Steamboat Bill Jr.* (1928), the son falls in love with the daughter of the town entrepreneur while trying to show his father that he can save their steamboat line. *High Time* (1960) presents a middle-aged businessman setting out to prove that he can graduate from college and falling in love in the process: in his valedictory speech, he looks out at the woman and says: 'If there's anything a man can't achieve by himself he shouldn't hesitate to join with someone else.' The tight binding of the second line of action to the love interest is one of the most unusual qualities of the classical cinema, giving the film a variety of actions and a sense of comprehensive social 'realism' that earlier drama achieved through the use of parallel, loosely related subplots. This specific form of unity is well described by Allan Dwan: 'If I constructed a story and I had four characters in it, I'd put them down as dots and if they didn't hook up into triangles, if any of them were left dangling out there without a significant relationship to any of the rest, I knew I had to discard them because they're a distraction.'[18]

Psychological causality, presented through defined characters acting to achieve announced goals, gives the classical film its characteristic progression. The two lines of action advance as chains of cause and effect. The tradition of the well-made play, as reformulated at the end of the nineteenth century, survives in Hollywood scenarists' academic insistence upon formulas for Exposition, Conflict, Complication, Crisis, and Denouement. The more pedantic rulebooks cite Ibsen, William Archer, Brander Matthews, and Gustav Freytag. The more homely advice is to create problems that the characters must solve, show them trying to solve them, and end with a definite resolution. The conventions of the well-made play — strong opening exposition, battles of wits, thrusts and counter-thrusts, extreme reversals of fortunes, and rapid denouement — all reappear in Hollywood dramaturgy, and all are defined in relation to cause and effect. The film progresses like a staircase: 'Each scene should make a definite impression, accomplish one thing, and advance the narrative a step nearer the climax.'[19] Action triggers reaction: each step has an effect which in turn becomes a new cause.[20*]

Chapter 6 will show how the construction of each scene advances each line of action, but for now a single film will stand as an instance of the overall dynamics of cause and effect.

The Black Hand (1949) begins in New York's Little Italy in 1900. The Mafia murder a lawyer, and his young son Gio vows to find the murderers. This becomes the overarching goal of the film. Eight years later, Gio returns from Italy and begins to investigate. He goes to the hotel where his father was killed and is told that he can find the night clerk with the help of the banker Serpi. When Gio visits Serpi's bank, he meets Isabella, and in a prolonged scene several goals get articulated: Gio declares that he wants to be a lawyer, she suggests forming a Citizen's League to fight the Black Hand, and a romantic attachment is defined between the couple. Gio continues to investigate the night clerk, but he finds that the Mafia have killed him. The romance is here a subsidiary line of action; the two principal causal lines are Gio's drive for revenge and the civic aim of driving out the Mafia. Both lines are advanced when Gio and Isabella form a Citizen's League. As Gio puts it: 'If I haven't got any leads, I'll make some.' This initiative sparks an immediate reaction: the Mafia capture and beat Gio, and the League dissolves. The next Mafia outrage, the bombing of a shop, plunges Gio into an alliance with the policeman Borelli. They bring the bomber to trial and Gio's legal training turns up evidence that leads to the bomber's being deported. Since he is also one of the men who killed Gio's father, Gio is brought a step closer to his initial goal.

The bomber's trial causes Gio to hit upon a new, legal way to achieve his goal. He suggests that Borelli go to Italy to check on illegal immigration; the information will enable the city to deport many Mafiosi. In Italy, Borelli finds that the banker Serpi has a criminal record. In another counterthrust, the Mafia kill Borelli — but not before he mails Gio the incriminating evidence. From now on, cause and effect, action and reaction, alternate swiftly. The New York gang kidnaps Isabella's brother Rudy in order to silence Gio; recovering Rudy thus becomes a new short-range goal. Gio discovers where Rudy is imprisoned, but he is himself captured. He now realizes that Serpi arranged the murder of his father. Serpi's gang acquire Borelli's documents, but before they can destroy them, Gio manages to touch off a bomb in their hideout. In the melee, Gio fights with Serpi and recovers the evidence. At the film's end, Gio has achieved both his personal goal and the community's goal. This was accomplished through a series of causally linked short-term goals (law studies, Citizen's League, immigration investigation, kidnapping) that grew out of several mutually dependent lines of action. This process is at work in virtually every classical narrative film.

The Black Hand exemplifies how the classical story constitutes a segment of a larger cause-effect chain. The beginning, as Chapter 3 will show, introduces us to an already-moving action which has a first cause, a distant but specified source. (Gio's father is killed because he wants to divulge his knowledge of the Mafia to the police.) What of the end? The ending is, most simply, the last effect. It too should be justified causally. One screenplay manual asks about the characters: 'What is their mental attitude in the beginning of the story? Just what traits are responsible for their struggle and conflict? How do these traits of character lead to the solving of the plot problem?'[21] Just as the *scene à faire* of the well-made play shows the hero triumphing over obstacles, the classical Hollywood film has a 'big scene where matters are settled definitely once and for all.'[22] In *The Black Hand*, the romance line of action is hardly in doubt; the last moments simply celebrate the couple's union. The same thing happens in the last two shots of *At Sword's Point* (1952): (1) The musketeers, having restored the monarchy, shout, 'Long live the King!'; (2) Clare and D'Artagnan embrace. In other films, such as *His Girl Friday* (1939), the romance line of action is unresolved until the film's last moments. In either case, the ending need not be 'happy'; it need only be a definite conclusion to the chain of cause and effect.

This movement from cause to effect, in the service of overarching goals, partly explains why Hollywood so prizes continuity. Coincidence and haphazardly linked events are believed to flaw the film's unity and disturb the spectator. Tight causality yields not only consequence but continuity, making the film progress 'smoothly, easily, with no jars, no waits, no delays.'[23] A growing absorption also issues from the steadily intensifying character causality, as the spectator recalls salient causes and anticipates more or less likely effects. The ending becomes the culmination of the spectator's absorption, as all the causal gaps get filled. The fundamental plenitude and linearity of Hollywood narrative culminate in metaphors of knitting, linking, and filling. Lewis Herman eloquently sums up this aesthetic:[24]

Care must be taken that every hole is plugged; that every loose string is tied together; that every entrance and exit is fully motivated, and that they are not made for some obviously contrived reason; that every coincidence is sufficiently motivated to make it credible; that there is no conflict between what has gone on before, what is going on currently, and what will happen in the future; that there is complete consistency between present dialogue and past action – that no baffling question marks are left over at the end of the picture to detract from the audience's appreciation of it.

What would narrative cinema without personalized causation be like? We have some examples (in Miklós Jancsó, Ozu, Robert Bresson, Soviet films of the 1920s), but we can find others. Erich Von Stroheim's *Greed* (1924) shows that a Naturalist causal scheme is incompatible with the classical model: the characters cannot achieve their goals, and causality is in the hands of nature and not people. From another angle, Brecht's ruminations upon Aristotelian dramaturgy suggest that causality could be taken out of the power of the individual character. 'The attention and interest that the spectator brings to causality must be directed toward the law governing the movements of the masses.'[25] It is also possible to view Brecht's theories as leading toward a narrative which interrupts the action to represent actions that might have happened, thus revealing the determinism that underlies psychologically motivated causality in the classical narrative.[26] Even when personal causation remains central to a film, however, there is still the possibility of making it more ambiguous and less linear; characters may lack clear-cut traits and definite goals, and the film's events may be loosely linked or left open-ended. Chapter 30 will examine how these qualities become significant in the postwar European 'art cinema.'

Motivation

Understanding classical story causality takes us toward grasping how a classical film unifies itself. Generally speaking, this unity is a matter of *motivation*. Motivation is the process by which a narrative justifies its story material and the plot's presentation of that story material. If the film depicts a flashback, the jump back in time can be attributed to a character's memory; the act of remembering thus motivates the flashback.

Motivation may be of several sorts.[27] One is *compositional*: certain elements must be present if the story is to proceed. A story involving a theft requires a cause for the theft and an object to be stolen. The classical causal factors we have reviewed constitute compositional motivation. A second sort of motivation is *realistic* motivation. Many narrative elements are justified on grounds of verisimilitude. In a film set in nineteenth-century London, the sets, props, costumes, etc. will typically be motivated realistically. Realistic motivation extends to what we will consider plausible about the narrative action: in *The Black Hand*, Gio's quest for revenge is presented as 'realistic,' given his personality and circumstances. Thirdly, we can identify *intertextual* motivation. Here the story (or the plot's representation of it) is justified on the grounds of the conventions of certain classes of art works. For example, we often assume that a Hollywood film will end happily simply because it *is* a Hollywood film. The star can also supply intertextual motivation: if Marlene Dietrich is in the film, we can expect that at some point she will sing a cabaret song. The most common sort of intertextual motivation is *generic*. Spontaneous singing in a film musical may have little compositional or realistic motivation, but it is justified by the conventions of the genre.[28] There is, finally, a rather special sort of motivation, *artistic motivation*, which I shall discuss later.

It should be evident that several types of motivation may cooperate to justify any given item in the narrative. The flashback could be motivated compositionally (giving us essential story information), realistically (proceeding from a character's memory), and intertextually (occurring in a certain kind of film, say a 1940s 'woman's melodrama'). Gio's search for revenge is

likewise justified as compositionally necessary, psychologically plausible, and generically conventional. Multiple motivation is one of the most characteristic ways that the classical film unifies itself.

The Hollywood film uses compositional motivation to secure a basic coherence. Compositional motivation is furnished by all the principles of causality I have already mentioned – psychological traits, goal orientation, romance, and so on. Realistic motivation typically cooperates with the compositional sort. When Fatso alludes to Maggio as 'Guys like you,' the film appeals to the audience's sense of a culturally codified type. At certain moments, realistic motivation can override causal motivation. In *T-Men* (1948), a Treasury agent passing counterfeit money is trapped because one counterfeiter recognizes the bill as the work of a man in jail. This is coincidental, but the film's semidocumentary prologue motivates this as realistic: it 'really happened' in the case upon which the film was modeled.

More commonly, compositional motivation outweighs realistic motivation. Gérard Genette has explained that in poetics the classical theory of the *vraisemblable* depends upon a distinction between things as they are and things as they should ideally be; only the latter are fit for artistic imitation.[29] In Hollywood cinema, verisimilitude usually supports compositional motivation by making the chain of causality seem plausible. Realism, writes one scenarists' manual, 'exists in the photoplay merely as an auxiliary to significance – not as an object in itself.'[30] Frances Marion claims that the strongest illusion of reality comes from tight causal motivation: 'In order that the motion picture may convey the illusion of reality that audiences demand, the scenario writer stresses motivation – that is, he makes clear a character's reason for doing whatever he does that is important.'[31] Classical Hollywood narrative thus often uses realism as an alibi, a supplementary justification for material already motivated causally. When the photographer-hero of *Rear Window* (1954) is attacked, he uses flashbulbs to dazzle the intruder: the realistic motivation (a photographer would 'naturally' think of flashbulbs) reinforces the causal one (he must delay the attacker somehow). Or, as Hitchcock put it: 'It's really a matter of utilizing your material to the fullest dramatic extent.'[32]

Intertextual, particularly generic, motivation can also occasionally run afoul of compositional motivation. If Marlene Dietrich is expected to sing, her song can be more or less causally motivated. In Busby Berkeley's musicals, the story action grinds to a halt when a lavish musical number takes over. The melodrama genre often flouts causal logic and relies shamelessly upon coincidence. In *Mr. Skeffington* (1944), for instance, Fanny and George watch a war newsreel and just happen to see her lost brother in it. Comedy justifies even a non-diegetic commentary, such as the drawing of an egg used to symbolize the failed show in The Band Wagon (1953). Yet obviously such operations do not radically disunify the films, since each genre creates its own rules, and the spectator judges any given element in the light of its appropriateness to generic conventions.

On the whole, generic motivation cooperates with causal, or compositional, unity. Genres are in one respect certain kinds of stories, endowed with their own particular logic that does not contest psychological causality or goal-orientation. (The Westerner seeks revenge, the gangster hero seeks power and success, the chorus girl works for the big break.) Multiple motivation – causal logic reinforced by generic convention – is again normal operating procedure.

A simple example from the history of Hollywood lighting shows how complicated the interplay of various kinds of motivation can be. Lighting was of course strongly motivated compositionally: salient causal factors – the characters – had to be clearly visible, while minor elements (e.g., the rear walls of a set) had to be less prominent. As usual, this compositional need overrode 'realism,' so that light sources were often not justified realistically. (Examples of such unrealistic lighting would be the edge lighting of figures or day-for-night shooting.) But after the mid-1920s, lighting was coded generically as well. Comedy was lit 'high-key' (that is, with a high ratio of key plus fill light to fill light alone), while horror and crime films were lit 'low-key.'[33] The latter practice was considered more 'realistic,' since one could justify harsh low-key lighting as coming from visible sources in the scene (e.g., a lamp or candle). By means of this generic

association with 'realism,' filmmakers began to apply low-key lighting to other genres. Sirk's melodramas of the 1950s are sometimes lit in a sombre low key, while Billy Wilder's Love in the Afternoon (1957) elicited comment for using low-key lighting for a comedy.[34] Thus the appeal to 'realism' changed some generic conventions.

Specifying these three types of motivation can clarify some murky narrative issues in the classical cinema. For example, overtly psychotherapeutic films of the 1940s might seem 'unclassical' in that they present inconsistent character action. The neurotic and psychotic characters of Shadow of a Doubt (1943), The Lodger (1944), Spellbound (1945), The Locket (1946), et al., would seem evidence for a less linear, more complex relation between mind and behavior than that operating in earlier classical films. In his analysis of 'Freudian' films of the period, the French critic Marc Vernet has shown that such films none the less respected classical dramaturgy.[35] We can subsume his explanations to the types of motivation we have already considered. First, psychoanalytic explanations of character behavior were motivated as a new 'realism,' a scientifically justified psychology. (That such a 'realism' was itself a vulgarization of Freudian concepts does not affect its status as verisimilitude for the period.) Secondly, certain aspects of psychoanalysis fitted generic models. Hollywood films stressed the cathartic method of psychoanalysis (not important for Freud after 1890) because of its analogy to conventions of the mystery film. The doctor's questioning recalls police interrogations (the patient as witness or crook who won't talk). Like the detective, the doctor must reveal the secret (the trauma) and extract the confession. One could add to Vernet's account that the subjective points of view and expressionistic distortions in many of these films also hark back to generically codified treatments of madness in the cinema of the 1920s. Most important, the vulgarized psychoanalytic concepts in the films of the 1940s respected the causal unity required by compositional motivation. In The Locket, Shadow of a Doubt, Guest in the House (1944), Spellbound, Citizen Kane (1941), and others, the childhood trauma functions as the first cause in what Vernet calls 'a linear determinism of childhood history.'[36] This is not to say that such films do not pose important narrative problems, but we need to recognize that Hollywood's use of Freudian psychology was highly selective and distorting, trimming and thinning psychoanalytic concepts to fit an existing model of clear characterization and causality. This can be seen in *Kings Row* (1942), which overtly thematizes psychoanalysis as a science (the protagonist goes to Vienna to study this new discipline) and yet ends with a chorus singing, 'I am the master of my fate, I am the captain of my soul.'

I have already suggested that compositional, generic, and realistic motivation do not always work in perfect unison, and I shall examine some typical dissonances in Chapter 7. But these are exceptional. Normally, any element of a classical film is justified in one or more of these ways. When it is not, it may be subsumable to yet another sort of motivation, one usually (if awkwardly) called 'artistic' motivation. By this term, Russian Formalist critics meant to point out that a component may be justified by its power to call attention to the system within which it operates. This in turn presupposes that calling attention to a work's own artfulness is one aim of many artistic traditions – a presupposition that challenges the notion that Hollywood creates an 'invisible' or 'transparent' representational regime. Within specific limits, Hollywood films do indeed employ artistic motivation in order, as the Formalists would put it, to make palpable the conventionality of art.[37]

Hollywood has eagerly employed spectacle and technical virtuosity as means of artistic motivation. 'Showmanship' consists to a considerable extent of making the audience appreciate the artificiality of what is seen. Early talkies were especially prone to slip in a song for the slightest reasons. A distant historical period often serves as a pretext for pageantry, crowd scenes, and lascivious dancing. Hollywood producers allotted time and money to create responses such as that triggered by the costumes in *The Great Ziegfeld* (1936): 'The designer and the producer of the picture felt that the expenditure was more than justified when the first appearance of the costumes brought exclamations of delight from the audience.'[38]

Flagrant technical virtuosity can also contribute to spectacle. What Parker Tyler called Hollywood's 'narcissism of energy' applies as much to cameramen as to Fred Astaire, Buster Keaton, or Sonja Henje.[39] In the silent cinema, complex and daring lighting effects; in the sound cinema, depth of field and byzantine camera movements; in all periods, exploitation of special effects – all testify to a pursuit of virtuosity for its own sake, even if only a discerning minority of viewers might take notice. During the 1940s, for example, there was something of a competition to see how complicated and lengthy the cinematographer could make his tracking shots.[40] This impulse can be seen not only in famous films like *Rope* (1948) but also in very minor films with one striking shot, such as *Casbah* (1948), at the climax of which the camera smoothly follows the hero, moves down an airport crowd, picks up the heroine (fig 2.1), follows her into the plane (figs 2.2 to 2.4), and settles down beside her seat, while the hero gets arrested outside (fig 2.5). It is probable that such casual splendors offered by the Hollywood film owe a great deal to its mixed parentage in vaudeville, melodrama, and other spectacle-centered entertainments. Nevertheless, digressions and flashes of virtuosity remain for the most part motivated by narrative causality (the *Casbah* example) or genre (pageantry in the historical film, costume in the musical). If spectacle is not so motivated, its function as artistic motivation will be isolated and intermittent.

Artistic motivation can emphasize the artificiality of other art works; this is usually accomplished through the venerable practice of parody. Hollywood has, of course, never shrunk from parody. In *Animal Crackers* (1930), Groucho Marx shows up the soliloquys in *Strange Interlude*, while in *Hellzapoppin* (1941), Olson and Johnson mock *Kane*'s Rosebud sled. In *My Favorite Brunette* (1947), Ronnie Johnson tells Sam McCloud he wants to be a tough detective like Alan Ladd; McCloud is played by Alan Ladd. Parody need not always be so clearly comic. At the climax of *The Studio Murder Mystery* (1929), the Hollywood montage sequence is parodied when the director explains at gunpoint what will happen after he kills Tony: 'Quick fade out. Next, headlines in the morning papers.' The following exchange from *The Locket* (1946) parodies the already mannered conventions of the psychoanalytic film of the 1940s. The doctor's wife has just returned from a movie.

Nancy: I had a wonderful time. I'm all goose pimples.

Dr Blair: A melodrama?

Nancy: Yes, it was ghastly. You ought to see it, Henry. It's about a schizophrenic who kills his wife and doesn't know it.

Dr Blair (laughing): I'm afraid that wouldn't be much of a treat for me.

Nancy: That's where you're wrong. You'd never guess how it turns out. Now it may not be sound psychologically, but the wife's father is one of the . . .

Dr Blair: Darling, do you mind? You can tell me later.

When an art work uses artistic motivation to call attention to its own particular principles of construction, the process is called 'laying bare the device.'[41]* Hollywood films often flaunt aspects of their own working in this way.[42] In *Angels Over Broadway* (1940), a drunken playwright agrees to help a suicidally inclined man get money and thus to 'rewrite' the man's 'last act.' The playwright then looks out at the audience and says musingly: 'Our present plot problem is money.' In von Stroheim's *Foolish Wives* (1922), the susceptible Mrs Hughes reads a book, *Foolish Wives*, by one Erich von Stroheim. In *His Girl Friday* (1939), as Walter starts fast-talking Hildy into staying with the newspaper, she begins to mimic an auctioneer's patter; this not only mocks Walter but foregrounds speech rhythm as a central device in the film. The show-business milieux of the musical film make it especially likely to bare its devices. The 'You were meant for me' number in *Singin' in the Rain* (1952) shows Don Lockwood staging his own spontaneous song; the way he sets up romantic lighting, mist, and backdrops calls attention to the conventional staging of such songs. An even more flagrant baring of this device occurs in 'Somewhere there's a someone' in *A Star Is Born* (1954).

Classical films are especially likely to bare the central principle of causal linearity. In *One Touch of Nature* (1917), when the hero succeeds as a baseball player, an expository title dryly remarks: 'In the course of human events, we come logically to the deciding game of a World's Series.' In *The Miracle Woman* (1931), a despairing writer is about to commit suicide because, having received a rejection slip from Ziegler Company, he

exclaims: 'I've tried them all from A to Z. What comes after Z?' He hears an evangelist's radio broadcast and resolves to try again: 'What comes after Z? A!' *A Woman of the World* (1925), contains an amusing image of the story's own unwinding. Near the beginning of the film, two old women sit on porch rockers gossiping and knitting, with their balls of yarn smaller each time we see them. At the film's end, the camera shows the chairs rocking, now empty, and the yarn all gone.

Hollywood's use of artistic motivation imputes a considerable alertness to the viewer: in order to appreciate certain moments, one must know and remember another film's story, or a star's habitual role, or a standard technique. To some extent, artistic motivation develops a connoisseurship in the classical spectator. Yet most artistic traditions show off their formal specificity in some way. We must ask what limits classical cinema imposes on artistic motivation. Generally, moments of pure artistic motivation are rare and brief in classical films. Compositional motivation leaves little room for it, while generic motivation tends to account for many flagrant instances. Indeed, baring the device has become almost conventional in certain genres. Comedies are more likely to contain such *outré* scenes as that in *The Road to Utopia* (1945), in which Bing Crosby and Bob Hope, mushing across the Alaskan wilds, see the Paramount logo in the distance. Likewise, the melodrama is likely to contain a shot like that in *The Fountainhead* (1949), in which two characters stand at opposite edges of the frame (fig 2.6) while the woman asserts: 'This is not a tie but a gulf between us.' In *His Girl Friday*, Walter can describe Bruce (Ralph Bellamy) as looking like Ralph Bellamy, but in *Sunrise at Campobello* (1960), no one notices FDR's resemblance to the same actor.

Preston Sturges's *Sin of Harold Diddlebock* (1947) permits us to watch compositional motivation take artistic motivation firmly in hand. The opening scene of the film is silent and is announced to be from Harold Lloyd's *The Freshman*. But this fairly overt reminder of the work's conventionality is undermined by the covert insertion of shots not from the original film. These interposed shots, filmed by Sturges, show a businessman watching the football game. The businessman is compositionally necessary, since he will offer Harold a job in the next scene, but remotivating *The Freshman*'s opening to create a smooth causal link between the two films tones down the silent segment's distinct, palpably conventional qualities.

The classical cinema, then, does not use artistic motivation constantly through the film, as Ozu does in *An Autumn Afternoon* (1962) or as Sergei Eisenstein does in *Ivan the Terrible* (1945). It does not bare its devices repeatedly and systematically, as Michael Snow does in *La région centrale* (1967) or Jean-Luc Godard does in *Sauve qui peut (la vie)* (1980). Compositional motivation for the sake of story causality remains dominant.

3 Classical narration

A film's story does not simply shine forth; as viewers, we construct it on the basis of the plot, the material actually before us. The classical guidelines for this construction are those principles of causality and motivation already sketched out in Chapter 2. A film's plot usually makes those guidelines applicable by transmitting story information. This aspect of plot I shall call *narration*.

Hollywood's own discourse has sought to limit narration to the manipulation of the camera, as in John Cromwell's remark that, 'The most effective way of telling a story on the screen is to use the camera as the story-teller.'[1] And the classical film's narration itself encourages us to see it as presenting an apparently solid fictional world which has simply been filmed for our benefit. André Bazin describes the classical film as being like a photographed play; the story events seem to exist objectively, while the camera seems to do no more than give us the best view and emphasize the right things.[2] But narration can in fact draw upon any film technique as long as the technique can transmit story information. Conversations, figure position, facial expressions, and well-timed encounters between characters all function just as narrationally as do camera movements, cuts, or bursts of music.

From this standpoint, classical narration falls under the jurisdiction of all the types of motivation already surveyed. In a classical film, narration is motivated compositionally; it works to construct the story in specific ways. Narration may also be motivated generically, as when performers in a musical sing directly to the spectator or when a mystery film withholds some crucial story information. Narration is less often motivated 'realistically,' although the voice-over commentary in semidocumentary fiction films might insist that the story action is based on fact.

Artistically motivated narration is very rare in classical films and never occurs in a pure state. A non-classical director like Jean-Luc Godard can 'lay bare' a film's narrational principles, as does the beginning of *Tout va bien* (1972), in which anonymous voices play with alternative ways of opening the film, hiring cast and crew, and financing the film. But when a classical film wants to call attention to the 'palpability' of its narration, it must create a context that motivates baring the device by other means as well. For instance, in scene after scene of *The Man Who Laughs* (1928), the narration conceals Gwynplaine's deformed mouth from us (by veils, strategically placed furniture, etc.). But in one scene, the narration lays bare this very pattern. During his stage act, Gwynplaine looks out at us and deliberately reveals his deformity; then a clown in his act slowly covers it again. The shot thus stages the act of revelation and concealment that has been central to the narration throughout. However, this baring of the device is partly motivated by realism (Gwynplaine is on stage, revealing his deformity to an audience in the fiction) and by causal necessity (for the story to proceed, a woman in the audience must see his mouth and take pity upon him). We encounter again the familiar multiple motivation of the classical text.

We could follow Hollywood's lead and simply label such carefully motivated narration 'invisible.' Hollywood's pride in concealed artistry implies that narration is imperceptible and unobtrusive. Editing must be seamless, camerawork 'subordinated to the fluid thought of the dramatic action.'[3] Some theorists have called the classical style transparent and illusionist, what Noël Burch has called 'the zero-degree style of filming.'[4] This is to say that classical technique is usually motivated compositionally. The chain of cause and effect demands that we see a close-up of an important object or that we follow a character into a room.

'Invisible' may suffice as a rough description of how little most viewers notice technique, but it does not get us very far if we want to analyze how classical films work. Such concepts play down the constructed nature of the style; a transparent effect does not encourage us to probe beneath its smooth surface. The term is also imprecise. 'Invisibility' can refer to how much the narration tells us, upon what authority it knows or tells, or in what way it tells. A tangle of different problems of narration is packed into this 'invisibility.'

How then to characterize classical narration? Meir Sternberg has put forth a clear theory that will prove useful.[5] Sternberg suggests that narration (or the narrator) can be characterized along three spectra.[6] A narration is more or less *self-conscious*: that is, to a greater or lesser degree it displays its recognition that it is presenting information to an audience. 'Call me Ishmael' marks the narrator as quite self-conscious, as does a character's aside to the audience in an Elizabethan play. A novel which employs a diarist as narrator is far less self-conscious. Secondly, a narration is more or less *knowledgeable*. The omniscient speaker of *Vanity Fair* revels in his immense knowledge, while the correspondents in an epistolary novel know much less. As these examples suggest, the most common way of limiting a narrator's knowledge is by making a particular character the narrator. Thus the issue of knowledge involves point-of-view. Thirdly, a narration is more or less *communicative*. This term refers to how willing the narration is to share its knowledge. A diarist might know little but tell all, while an omniscient narrator like Henry Fielding's in *Tom Jones* may suppress a great deal of information. Some of Brecht's plays use projected titles which predict the outcome of a scene's action: this is less suppressive than a normal play's narration, which tends to minimize its own omniscience.[7]

Sternberg's three scales can be summarized in a series of questions. How aware is the narration of addressing the audience? How much does the narration know? How willing is the narration to tell us what it knows?

Sternberg's categories help us analyze classical narration quite precisely. In the classical film, the narration is omniscient, but it lets that omniscience come forward more at some points than at others. These fluctuations are systematic. In the opening passages of the film, the narration is moderately self-conscious and overtly suppressive. As the film proceeds, the narration becomes less self-conscious and more communicative. The exceptions to these tendencies are also strictly codified. The end of the film may quickly reassert the narration's omniscience and self-consciousness.

The modest narration

Classical narration usually begins before the action does. True, the credits sequence can be seen as a realm of graphic play, an opening which is relatively 'open' to non-narrational elements. (Certainly it is in credits sequences that abstract cinema has had its most significant influence upon the classical style.) Yet the classical Hollywood film typically uses the credits sequence to initiate the film's narration. Even these forty to ninety seconds cannot be wasted. Furthermore, in these moments the narration is self-conscious to a high degree. Musical accompaniment already signals the presence of this narration, and often musical motifs in this overture will recur in the film proper. The title will most probably name or describe the main character (*Mickey* [1918], *Gidget* [1959], *King of the Rodeo* [1928]) or indicate the nature of the action (*Going Highbrow* [1935], *Impact* [1949]). If not, the title can suggest the locale of the action (*Adventure Island* [1947], *Wuthering Heights* [1939]), a motif in the film (*Applause* [1929], *Balalaika* [1939]), or the time of the action (*The Night Holds Terror* [1955]). The credits that list the cast may reinforce the title (e.g., *The King and the Chorus Girl* [1937], starring Fernand Gravet and Joan Blondell), but they will certainly introduce the film's narrative hierarchy. Protagonist, secondary protagonist, opponents, and other major characters will be denoted by the order, size, and time onscreen of various actors' names. Some films strengthen this linkage by adding shots of the characters to the credits, in which the amount of the screen surface a character is allotted indicates the character's importance (fig 3.1).

(Compare the flattening effect of credits which make no distinction among major actors and walk-on parts, such as the 'democratic' credits of Jean-Marie Straub and Danièle Huillet's *Not Reconciled* [1964].) Even the studio logo, the MGM lion or the Paramount mountain, has been analyzed as a narrational transition.[8] The credits are thus highly self-conscious, explicitly addressed to the audience.

In the silent period, many films went no further than these cues, laying the credit sequence against black backgrounds or a standardized design (e.g., curtains, pillars, or picture frames). Some credits sequences, however, used 'art titles' whose designs depicted significant narrative elements. William S. Hart's *The Narrow Trail* (1917), for instance, displays its credits against a painting of a stagecoach holdup. By the 1920s, such art titles were commonly used for exposition (see fig 3.2). Lettering could also indicate the period or setting of the story, a practice probably influenced by playbills and illustrated books: narration rendered as typography. In the 1920s, a credits sequence might appear over moving images (e.g., *Merry-Go-Round* [1923]) or might be animated (e.g., *The Speed Spook* [1924]). The sound cinema canonized this stylized 'narrativization' of the credits sequence, assigning it a range of functions.

The credits can anticipate a motif to appear in the story proper. In *Woman of the World* (1925), the protagonist's scandalous tattoo is presented as an abstract design under the credits; in *The Black Hand* (1950), a stiletto forms the background for the titles. Credits' imagery can also establish the space of the upcoming action, as do the snowy fir trees in *The Michigan Kid* (1928) or the city view in *Casbah* (1948). Credits often flaunt the narration's omniscience and tantalize us with glimpses of action to come. As early as *The Royal Pauper* (1917), we find the credits summarizing the rags-to-riches story action by dissolving from a shot of the star, dressed as a poor girl, to a shot of her wearing expensive clothes. Thierry Kuntzel has shown how the opening credit sequence of *The Most Dangerous Game* (1932), a shot of a hand knocking at a door, stages an important gesture of the ensuing film and anticipates several motifs in the setting and action. The credits sequence of *Bringing Up Baby* (1938) presents stick-figure man, woman, and leopard engaged in actions that will reappear in the film; *Sweepstakes Winner* (1939) employs the same strategy (see fig 3.3). As Kuntzel points out, such sequences are explicitly narrational: the unknown hand knocking at the door can only be the viewer's, giving an idealized representation of the viewer's entry into the film.[9] Such overt address to the spectator can also be seen in those still-life compositions of book pages or album leaves turned by unknown hands (e.g., *Penthouse* [1933], *Easy to Look At* [1945], *Play Girl* [1941]). In the postwar period, direct address in credits sequences could also be accomplished through a voice-over narrator. In such ways, the credits sequence flaunts both the narration's omniscience and its ability to suppress whatever it likes.

Like credits, the early scenes of the action can reveal the narration quite boldly. Before 1925, the film might open with a symbolic prologue, mocked by Loos and Emerson as 'visionary scenes of Heaven or Hell, of the Fates weaving human lives in their web.'[10] (See, for example, fig 3.4, from *The Devil's Bait* [1917].) More often, silent films simply used expository titles to announce the salient features of the narration. In the sound era, other film techniques take on this role of foregrounding the narration. After the credits, *Partners in Crime* (1928) reveals a city landscape and an inter-title, 'Gangsters and Gun War – A City Steeped in Crime' (see fig 3.5). Suddenly the title shatters as hands holding guns break through to fire directly at the audience (see figs 3.6 and 3.7). At the start of *Housewife* (1934), the camera tracks with a milkman up to the front door and lingers on the front door as he leaves. There is a cut to the welcome mat, and the camera tracks in and tilts up to the doorbell and name card. The shots have treated the camera as if it were a guest strolling up to the house. *Easy to Look At* (1945) opens with a voice-over narrator describing the heroine's arrival in the city: 'And thus New York's population is increased by one – and quite a number . . .' as a man on the street gawks at her. Such passages reveal the narration to be widely knowledgeable and highly aware of addressing an audience.

The narration can also exploit the opening moments to stress its ability to be more or less communicative. *The Case of the Lucky Legs* (1935) opens with a flurry of women's legs striding up a flight of steps (see fig 3.8) and then dissolves to a sign (see fig 3.9). Several pairs of legs are revealed (see fig 3.10). At the end of the scene, as a former contest winner tries to claim her prize, the swindler pushes her away (see fig 3.11) and the camera pans to an advertisement for the Lucky Legs contest (see fig 3.12). The image dissolves to a pair of legs stretched out (see fig 3.13) and pans to their owner, the latest bilked woman, sobbing. The gratuitous camera movement to the sign and the opening of the next scene provide overtly ironic commentary on the contest.

The explicit presence of the narration in these heavily expository beginnings is confirmed by the eventual emergence of the 'pre-credits sequence.' Here the film opens truly *in medias res*, with the credits presented only after an initial scene or two of story action. This practice began in the 1950s, possibly as a borrowing from television's technique of the 'teaser.' The effect of pre-credits action was to eliminate the credits as a distinct unit, sprinkling them through a short action sequence that conveyed minimal story information (e.g., the establishment of a locale or the connecting of two scenes by a trip). The postponement of the credits tacitly grants the narrational significance of whatever scenes open the film.

Yet once present in these opening passages, the narration quickly fades to the background. In the course of the opening scenes, the narration becomes less self-conscious, less omniscient, and more communicative. Very flagrant examples allow us to trace this fading process at work.

*The Caddy (1953) has a highly stylized credits sequence that signals the genre (comedy), repeats the principal motif (golf clubs, tees, tartan), and anticipates story events (the cartoon figures). (See fig 3.14.) The film's first shot reveals a theatre marquee which carries caricatures similar to those in the credits (see fig 3.15). The bandstand's design repeats the caricatures, linking the figures to the live protagonists we finally see (fig 3.16). In a sliding movement, the narration's cartoon images of Dean Martin and Jerry Lewis have become gradually replaced by the story's images of the characters themselves. A more complex example occurs in *The Canterville Ghost (1944). While a voice-over commentator tells of the Ghost's history, the image shows the relevant passage in a book, *Famous Ghosts of England*. There follows a flashback to 1634, which shows how the cowardly Simon was bricked up in a wall of the mansion. The camera tracks into a close-up of a birthmark on Simon's neck (see fig 3.17), which freezes into an illustration in the book as the voice-over commentary resumes (see fig 3.18). The page is turned as the narrator describes the castle today; the illustration of the castle (see fig 3.19) dissolves to the same image on film, into which the heroine Jessica rides (see fig 3.20). Action has replaced the non-diegetic voice, and we never see or hear the narration so evidently again.

The phasing out of the narrator is also visible in historical changes in the silent cinema's expository tactics. Before 1917, films commonly introduced characters in ways that called attention to the act of narration. An expository title would name and describe the character and attach the actor's name; then a shot might show the character striking a pose in a non-diegetic setting (e.g., a theater stage). After several characters were introduced this way, the fictional action would begin. After 1917, such signs of narration diminished. Characters would be introduced upon their first appearance in the action. Overt commentary in the titles ('Max, a Bully') would be replaced by images of the character enacting typical behavior (e.g., Max kicking a dog).[11]

The role of expository inter-titles changed as well. Silent scenarists were aware that the expository title foregrounded narration. One writer compared the expository title to a Greek chorus, 'someone who is behind the scenes. They are in the secret of the play.'[12] Another critic was even more aware of the intrusion: 'The title may say no more than "Dawn" or "Night" or "Home"; but it clearly is the injected comment of an outsider who is assumed, by the author's own terms, to be absent.'[13] (This, he claimed, 'breaks the spell of complete absorption.') The presence of an unseen fictional narrator was also marked in expository titles by the use of the past tense, which became standard after 1916. After 1917, Hollywood film became less and less reliant upon expository inter-titles and more dependent upon dialogue titles. Between 1917 and 1921, one-fifth to one-third of a film's inter-titles would be expository; after 1921, expository titles constituted less than a fifth of the total. In the later silent years, we find films with no expository titles at all. Placement and length changed too: after 1921, the early scenes of the film contain more and longer expository titles than do later scenes. The cultivation of the art title, the expository title enhanced by a pictorial design, further substituted image for language. Expositional tasks were shifted to character dialogue and action, not only across the period but within the individual film.

The judicious combination of expository titles, dialogue titles, and exemplary character action created a fairly knowledgeable and communicative narrator. Consider the opening scene of *Miss Lulu Bett* (1921). The family assembles for dinner, and an expository title introduces each family member. The title is then followed by a character performing a typical action which confirms the title's description. After the narration identifies the youngest daughter, the images show her swiping food playfully. After the father is identified, he goes to the clock to check his watch. Once most of the family are introduced, another expository title introduces the elder daughter but adds the information that she wants to leave the family. This title is followed by a shot of her at the front gate, holding a boy's hand. Because the narration has already accurately characterized the other family members, we trust its information about the daughter's purely private desires − information which is in turn immediately confirmed by her action. The narration is omniscient and reliable. The smoothness of such narration was recognized in Europe in the silent era; a Parisian critic noted that the Hollywood film always begins with a long expository title explaining the film's theme, followed by the rapid introduction to and delineation of characters by means of titles and actions. The critic emphasized that Hollywood films avoided the gradual psychological revelation characteristic of Swedish and German films of the period.[14]

What enables the narration to fade itself out so quickly? Any narrative film must inform the viewer of events that occured before the action which we see. The classical film confines itself almost completely to a sort of exposition described by Sternberg as *concentrated* and *preliminary*.[15] This means that the exposition is confined principally to the opening of the plot. In explaining how to write a screenplay, Emerson and Loos claim that the opening should 'explain briefly but clearly the essential facts which the audience must know in order to understand the story,' preferably in one scene.[16] Such advice may seem commonplace, but we need to remember that this choice commits the Hollywood film to a slim range of narrational options. Scattered or delayed exposition has the power to alter the viewer's understanding of events; making the spectator wait to fill gaps of causality, character relations, and temporal events can increase curiosity and even create artistic motivation, baring the device of narration itself. But concentrated and preliminary narration helps the classical film to make the narration seem less omniscient and self-conscious.

Classical narration also steps to the background by starting *in medias res*. The exposition plunges us into an already-moving flow of cause and effect. As Loos and Emerson put it, the action must begin 'with the story itself and not with the history of the case which leads up to the story.'[17] When the characters thus assume the burden of exposition, the narration can seem to vanish.

The Mad Martindales (1942) offers a simple case. After an expository title ('San Francisco 1900'), the film opens with a close-up of a cake, inscribed 'Happy Birthday Father.' The camera tracks back, and while a maid and butler decorate the cake they discuss household affairs. The camera follows the butler to the piano, where Evelyn, the elder daughter, sits. Evelyn and the butler converse. We then follow the butler to the study, past the younger daughter Cathy, who is sitting at the desk writing. The camera holds on her while the butler leaves. Bob, Cathy's friend, thrusts his head in the window, which gives her a chance to explain what she's writing (a feminist tract, surprisingly enough). The phone rings and Evelyn answers it. The caller is her boyfriend Peter, who proposes marriage to her. At this juncture, the girls' father arrives, having just bought a Poussin painting. While workmen uncrate the painting, the family discuss Cathy's graduation, Martindale's birthday, the news about Peter, etc. When the butler brings birthday champagne, Cathy raises the issue of unpaid bills; at this point, the lights go out, cut off by the utility company. As the scene ends, the family discovers that it is penniless and Cathy sorrowfully reveals her gift to her father – a wallet. You are right to think that this scene is overstuffed with information, but it is typical of Hollywood cinema's almost Scribean loading of exposition into a film's first scenes. By plunging *in medias res* with the first shot of 'Happy Birthday Father,' the film lets the characters tell each other what we need to know.

Classical narration may reemerge more overtly in later portions of the film, but such reappearance will be intermittent and codified. In the silent cinema, the expository art title may include imagery that comments overtly on the action. Occasionally, the narration will reassert its omniscience by camera movement: the cliché example is the pan from the long shot of the stagecoach to the watching Indians on the ridge. In the sound film, an overlapping line of dialogue can link scenes in ways that call attention to the narration. Many of the examples of artistic motivation and 'baring the device' that I considered in the last chapter can now be seen as examples of self-conscious and flagrantly suppressive narration. Narrational intrusions may also be generically motivated: in a mystery film, framing only a portion of the criminal's body as the crime is committed, or in a historical film, making the narrator 'the voice of history.'[18] Whatever the genre, however, there is yet another moment that narration comes strongly forward in the classical film – during montage sequences.

Typically, the montage sequence compresses a considerable length of time or space, traces a large-scale event, or selects representative moments from a process.[19] Cliché instances are fluttering calendar leaves, brief images of a detective's search for witnesses, the rise of a singer given as bits of different performances, the accumulation of travel stickers on a trunk, or a flurry of newspaper headlines. Rudimentary montage sequences can be found in Hollywood films of the teens and early twenties. By 1927, montage sequences were very common, and they continue to be used in a variant form today.

From a historical perspective, the montage sequence is part of Hollywood's gradual reduction of overt narrational presence. Instead of a title saying 'They lowered the lifeboats,' or 'While the jury was out, McGee waited in a cold sweat,' the film can reveal glimpses of pertinent action. The montage sequence thus transposes conventions of prose narration into the cinema; Sartre cites *Citizen Kane*'s montages as examples of the 'frequentative' tense (equivalent to writing 'He made his wife sing in every theater in America').[20] Moreover, the montage sequence aims at continuity, linking the shots through non-diegetic music and smooth optical transitions (dissolves, wipes, superimpositions, occasionally cuts). Yet the montage sequence still makes narration come forward to a great degree. Extreme close-ups, canted angles, silhouettes, whip pans, and other obtrusive techniques differentiate this sort of segment from the orthodox scene. When newspapers swirl out of nowhere to flatten themselves obligingly for our inspection, or when hourglasses and calendar leaves whisk across the screen, we are addressed by a power that is free of normal narrative space and time. What keeps the montage sequence under control is its strict codification: it is, simply, the sequence which advances the story action in just this overt way. Flagrant as the montage sequence is, its rarity, its narrative function, and its narrowly conventional format assure its status as classical narration's most acceptable rhetorical flourish.

Causality, character, and point-of-view

After the concentrated, preliminary exposition and except for intrusions like montage sequences, the classical film reduces narration's prominence. Chapters 4 and 5 will show how this process shapes cinematic space and time. For now, I want only to indicate the general ways that classical Hollywood narration reveals self-consciousness, omniscience, and communicativeness.

After the opening portions of the classical film, the narration's self-consciousness is generally kept low, chiefly because character action and reaction convey the ongoing causal chain to us. It is here that the effect of an enclosed story world, Bazin's objectively existing play simply transmitted by the camera, is at its strongest. Many devices of nineteenth-century realist theater – exposition by character conversation, speeches and actions which motivate psychological developments, well-timed entrances and exits – all assure the homogeneity of the fictional world. This homogeneity has induced many theorists and most viewers to see the classical film as composed of a solid and integral diegetic world occasionally inflected by a narrational touch from the outside, as if our companion at a play were to tug our sleeve and point out a detail. We must, however, make the effort to see the film's diegetic world as itself constructed and, hence, ultimately just as narrational as the most obtrusive cut or voice-over commentary. Yet we need to recognize how important this apparently natural, actually *covert* narration is to the classical cinema. In what follows, I shall assume that this narration-through-character-interaction constitutes the most normal and least noticeable ploy of Hollywood narration.

The narration reinforces the homogeneity of the fictional world by means of a non-theatrical device: the use of public and impersonal sources of information that can be realistically or generically motivated within the film. The most common instrument is the newspaper. ROSEN FOUND GUILTY: the headline or article becomes an unquestioned surrogate for the narrator's presence. In many films of the 1930s, newspaper reporters become an expository chorus, initiating us into the action. Other public transmitters of information include radio, television, bulletin boards, posters, ticker tape, tour guides, and reference books (e.g., the *Ghosts of England* volume in *The Canterville Ghost*). These impersonal sources of story information also prove invaluable in toning down the self-consciousness of montage sequences.

Classical narration is potentially omniscient, as credits and openings show and as Hollywood's own discourse generally acknowledges. A. Lindsley Lane, for example, refers to 'omniscient perception' as the basic law of film. In the bulk of the Hollywood film, this omniscience becomes overt occasionally but briefly, as when a camera angle or movement links characters who are unaware of each other.[21] The same omniscience becomes overt in the *anticipatory* qualities of narration – the character who enters a scene just before she or he is needed, the camera movement that accommodates a character's gesture just before it occurs, the unexpected cut to a doorbell just before a thumb presses it, the music that leads us to expect a prowler to jump out of the shrubbery. 'There is only one way to shoot a scene,' Raoul Walsh claimed, 'and that's the way

which shows the audience what's happening next.'[22]

The most evident trace of the narration's omniscience is its *omnipresence*. The narration is unwilling to tell all, but it is willing to go anywhere. This is surely the basis of the tendency to collapse narration into camerawork: the camera can roam freely, crosscutting between locales or changing its position within a single room. 'The camera,' writes Lane, 'stimulates, through correct choice of subject matter and setup, the sense within the percipient of "being at the most vital part of the experience – at the most advantageous point of perception" throughout the picture.'[23] Sometimes this ubiquity becomes only artistically motivated, as in those 'impossible' camera angles that view the action from within a fireplace or refrigerator.[24] Spatial omnipresence is, of course, justified by what story action occurs in any given place, and it is limited still further by specific schemata, as we shall see in Chapter 5. To avoid treating the camera as narrator, however, we should remember that what the camera does *not* show implies omnipresence negatively – the site of an action we will learn of only later, the whole figure of the mysterious intruder. The narration could show us all, but it refuses.

Classical narration admits itself to be spatially omnipresent, but it claims no comparable fluency in time. The narration will not move on its own into the past or the future. Once the action starts and marks a definite present, movements into the past are motivated through characters' memory. The flashback is not presented as an overt explanation on the narration's part; the narration simply presents what the character is recalling. Even more restrictive is classical narration's suppression of future events. No narration in any text can spill all the beans at once, but after the credits sequence, classical narration seldom overtly divulges anything about what will ensue. It is up to the characters to foreshadow events through dialogue and physical action. If this is the last job the crooks will pull, they must tell us, for the narration will not become more self-conscious in order to do so. If the love affair is to fail, the characters must intuit it: 'These things never happen twice' (*Interlude* [1957]). At most, the narration can drop self-conscious hints, such as pointing out a significant detail that the characters have overlooked; e.g., the camera movement up to the 'Forgotten Anything?' sign on the hotel-room door in *Touch of Evil* (1957). More commonly, anticipatory motifs can be included if the shot is already motivated for another purpose. Near the end of *From Here to Eternity* (1953), the attack on Pearl Harbor is anticipated when the camera pans to follow a character and reveals a calendar giving the date as December 6.

Classical narration thus delegates to character causality and genre conventions the bulk of the film's flow of information. When information must be suppressed, it is done through the characters. Characters can keep secrets from one another (and us). Confinement to a single point-of-view can also suppress story information. Genre conventions can cooperate, as the editors of *Cahiers du cinéma* point out in their analysis of *Young Mr. Lincoln* (1939). Here the narration must juggle three points of view so as to keep certain information from the spectator. Two brothers accused of murder each believe the other is guilty, while their mother also believes that one is guilty. When all three meet, it would be plausible for them to talk to one another and thus reveal each one's beliefs. But if this happened, the plot twist – that neither is guilty – would be given away prematurely. So the family's reunion is staged as a silent vigil the night before the trial's last day. This convention of courtroom dramas motivates withholding information from the audience.[25]

Any narrative text must repeat important story information, and in the cinema, repetition takes on a special necessity; since the conditions of presentation mean that one cannot stop and go back, most films reiterate information again and again. The nature of that reiteration can, however, vary from film to film.[26] In a film by Godard or Eisenstein, the narration overtly repeats information that may not be repeated within the story. Sequences late in *October* (1928) and *Weekend* (1967) replay events that we have seen earlier in the film, and this repetition is not motivated by character memory. But a classical film assigns repetition to the characters. That is, the story action itself contains repetitions which the narration simply passes along. For example, after the credits for the film *Housewife* (1934) have concluded, the opening scene shows the heroine harassed by her domestic duties. At the

scene's close, a polltaker calls on her and asks her job; 'Oh . . .,' she says, '. . . just a housewife.' 'Housewife,' the polltaker repeats at the fade-out. In one scene of *The Whole Town's Talking* (1935), we learn a man's profession the moment he enters the room; a group of police officials greet him in a chorus:

'Warden!'
'Warden, Chief!'
'Hello, Warden.'
'Hiya, Warden.'

Such repetition is not extensive – that would be as transgressive as no repetition at all. Optimally, a significant motif or informational bit should be shown or mentioned at three or four distinct moments, as in the warden chorus. Three is in fact a mystical number for Hollywood dramaturgy; an event becomes important if it is mentioned three times. The Hollywood slogan is to state every fact three times, once for the smart viewer, once for the average viewer, and once for slow Joe in the back row.[27] Leo McCarey recalls: 'Most gags were based on "the rule of three." It became almost an unwritten rule.'[28] Irving Thalberg is reported to have said, 'I don't mean tell 'em three times in the same way. Maybe you tell 'em once in comedy, maybe you tell 'em once directly, maybe you tell 'em next time with a twist.'[29] For a rare instance of audacious repetition in the narration rather than the story, see fig 3.21.

Since classical narration communicates what it 'knows' by making characters haul the causal chain through the film, it might seem logical to assume that the classical film commonly restricts its knowledge to a single character's point-of-view. Logical, but wrong. If we take point-of-view to be an *optical* subjectivity, no classical film, not even the vaunted but misdescribed *Lady in the Lake* (1947), completely confines itself to what a character sees. If we regard a character's point-of-view as comprising what the character knows, we still find very few classical films that restrict themselves to this degree. The overwhelmingly common practice is to use the omnipresence of classical narration to move fluidly from one character to another.

The classical film typically contains a few subjective point-of-view shots (usually of printed matter read by a character), but these are firmly anchored in an 'objective' frame of reference. Moreover, Hollywood's optical point-of-view cutting is seldom rigorously consistent. While in one shot a camera position will be marked as subjective, a few shots later the same viewpoint may be objective – often resulting in anomalies such as a character walking into his or her own field of vision (see figs 3.22 through 3.25). In a similar fashion, classical narration will confine itself to one character's limited knowledge, but this will then be played off against what other characters know. Clever narrational twists often depend upon restricting us to one character's point-of-view before revealing the total situation. Even flashbacks, which are initially motivated as limited, subjective point-of-view, seldom restrict themselves solely to what the character could have known. For such reasons, it is accurate to describe classical narration as fundamentally omniscient, even when particular spatial or temporal shifts are motivated by character subjectivity.

The Hollywood cinema quickly mastered shifts in point-of-view. As early as *Love and the Law* (1919), one can find extensive sequences of optical point-of-view cutting (see figs 16.44 and 16.45). *The Michigan Kid* (1928) begins with a montage of gold prospecting in Alaska and then moves our attention to a gambling hall. At one table sits Jim Rowen, identified by an inter-title as the owner of the hall. In talking to two customers, Jim reveals that he is selling out to go back to the States and rejoin the girl he left behind. As Jim packs to leave, he stares at his tattered picture of Rose. This triggers a flashback introducing Jim as a boy, playing with Rose and fighting off the delinquent Frank. The flashback ends and dissolves into Jim's optical viewpoint of Rose's picture. At this point, however, the film widens its narrational view. There is a cut to a customer in the gambling den. He looks at his watch before offering it as a stake. Thanks to another point-of-view shot, we see Rose's picture in his watch. Thus we know before Jim does that Frank has reentered his life. A bartender takes the watch to Jim, who appraises it; we are in suspense as to whether he will notice the picture. At first he does not, which increases the tension, but then he does. As he looks at the picture, the shot superimposes his memory image of Rose as a girl, then his

newspaper picture of her. He asks the barkeep to bring Frank in. Using only two expository titles, the narration has presented the essential background of the story action and has fluently moved among various degrees of subjectivity. Beginning *in medias res* and letting the characters reveal exposition, the classical Hollywood film thus moves to subjectivity only occasionally – something possible for a narration endowed with omniscience.

The example from *The Michigan Kid* shows that classical narration can exploit omnipresence to conceal information that individual characters possess. Occasionally the classical film flaunts such suppressive operations, opening up a gap between the narration's omniscient range of knowledge and its moderate communicativeness. Consider the opening of *Manhandled* (1949), which shows a man sitting in a study. The framing carefully conceals his face. His wife and her lover return, but we see only their feet. After the lover leaves, the husband follows her upstairs, his face still offscreen. He approaches his wife and starts to strangle her. The sequence seems transgressive because the narration has overtly suppressed the faces of the killer and the lover. Yet at the end of the sequence, there is a dissolve and a voice says: 'At that point the dream always ends, doctor.' The overtness of the narration is justified retroactively as subjective. The greater emphasis placed upon 'psychoanalytic' explanations of causality in the 1940s created a trend toward such occasionally explicit narration. Similarly, play with point-of-view is a minor convention of the mystery film. *Through Different Eyes* (1929) and *The Grand Central Mystery* (1942) both use flashbacks to recount the same events from inconsistent points of view. The subjective film and the mystery film can thus make narration self-conscious and overtly suppressive, but only thanks to compositional and generic motivation. Consistently suppressive narration, such as that of Jean-Marie Straub and Danièle Huillet's *Not Reconciled* (1964) or Alain Resnais's *Providence* (1977), is unknown in the Hollywood paradigm.

Classical narration, then, plunges us *in medias res* and proceeds to reduce signs of its self-consciousness and omniscience. The narration accomplishes this reduction by means of spatial omnipresence, repetition of story information, minimal changes in temporal order, and plays between restricted and relatively unrestricted points of view. It is in the light of these aims that we must assess the power of that celebrated Hollywood 'continuity.' Because we see no gaps, we never question the narration, hence never question its source. When, in *Penthouse (1933), the scene shifts from a nightclub to a luxury yacht and the voice of the club's bandleader continues uninterrupted, now broadcast from a radio on board the yacht, we can recognize the narration's omnipresence but we are assured that no significant story action has been suppressed. At the end of a scene, a 'dialogue hook' anticipates the beginning of the next (e.g., 'Shall we go to lunch?'/long-shot of a cafe); such a tactic implies that the narration perfectly transmits the action. Crosscutting signals omnipresence and un-restricted point-of-view, while editing within the scene delegates to the characters the job of forwarding the story action. Chapters 4 and 5 will assess how narrational concerns have shaped classical patterns of space and time. At this point, it is worth looking briefly at one technique that is seldom considered a part of narration at all.

Music as destiny

From the start, musical accompaniment has provided the cinema's most overt continuity factor. In the silent cinema, piano or orchestral music ran along with the images, pointing them up and marking out how the audience should respond. Non-diegetic music was less pervasive in the early 1930s, but the rise of symphonic scoring in the work of Max Steiner, Erich Wolfgang Korngold, Ernest Newman, *et al.* reasserted classical cinema's interest in using music to flow continuously along with the action. Stravinsky's comparison of film music to wallpaper is apt, not only because it is so strongly decorative but because it fills in cracks and smoothes down rough textures.[30] Filmmakers have long recognized these functions. As early as 1911, a theater musician advised players not to stop a number abruptly when the scene changed.[31] Hollywood composers claimed that sudden stops and starts were avoidable by the process of imperceptibly fading the music up and down, the practice known in the trade as 'sneaking in and out.'[32]

This continuous musical accompaniment functions as narration. It would be easy to show that film music strives to become as 'transparent' as any other technique − viz., not only the sneak-in but the neutrality of the compositional styles and the standardized uses to which they are put ('La Marseillaise' for shots of France, throbbing rhythms for chase scenes). Theodor Adorno and Hanns Eisler have heaped scorn upon Hollywood music as pleonastic and self-effacing; Brecht compared film music's 'invisibility' to the hypnotist's need to control the conditions of the trance.[33] Yet calling the music 'transparent' is as true but uninformative as calling the entire Hollywood style invisible. If music functions narrationally, how does it accomplish those tasks characteristic of classical narration?

The sources of Hollywood film music show its narrational bent very clearly. In eighteenth-century melodrama, background music was played to underscore dramatic points, sometimes even in alternation with lines of dialogue. American melodrama of the 1800s used sporadic vamping, but spectacle plays and pantomimes relied upon continuous musical accompaniment.[34] The most important influence upon Hollywood film scoring, however, was that of late nineteenth-century operatic and symphonic music, and Wagner was the crest of that influence. Wagner was a perfect model, since he exploited the narrational possibilities of music. Harmony, rhythm, and 'continuous melody' could correspond to the play's dramatic action, and leitmotifs could convey a character's thoughts, point up parallels between situations, even anticipate action or create irony. Adorno's monograph on Wagner even argues that the dream of the *Gesamtkunstwerk* anticipated the thoroughly rationalized artifact of the culture industry, as exemplified in the Hollywood film.[35]

In the early teens, film trade journals solemnly supplied theater pianists with oversimplified accounts of Wagner's practice. One pianist explained: 'I attach a certain theme to each person in the picture and work them out, in whatever form the occasion may call for, not forgetting to use popular strains if necessary.'[36] When Carl Joseph Breil proudly claimed to be the first composer to write a score for a film, he said he used leitmotifs for the characters.[37] Silent film scores, usually pasted together out of standardized snatches of operas, orchestral music, and popular tunes, adhered to the crude leitmotif idea (see fig 12.16). Early synchronized-sound films with musical tracks continued the practice: when we see the Danube, we hear 'The Blue Danube' (*The Wedding March* [1928]). With the post-1935 resurgence in film scoring, Wagner remained the model. Most of the major studio composers were trained in Europe and influenced by the sumptuous orchestration and long melodic lines characteristic of Viennese opera.[38] Max Steiner and Miklós Rózsa explicitly acknowledged Wagner's influence, as did Erich Wolfgang Korngold, who called a film 'a textless opera.'[39] Characters, places, situations – all were relentlessly assigned motifs, either original or borrowed. When motifs were not employed, certain passages functioned as a recitative to cue specific attitudes to the scene (e.g., comic music, suspense music).[40] Brecht complained that with such constantly present music, 'our actors are transformed into silent opera singers.'[41] But Sam Goldwyn gave the most terse advice: 'Write music like Wagner, only louder.'[42]

Like the opera score, the classical film score enters into a system of narration, endowed with some degree of self-consciousness, a range of knowledge, and a degree of communicativeness. The use of non-diegetic music itself signals the narration's awareness of facing an audience, for the music exists solely for the spectator's benefit. The scale of the orchestral forces employed and the symphonic tradition itself create an impersonal wash of sound befitting the unspecific narrator of the classical film.[43] The score can also be said to be omniscient, what Parker Tyler has called 'a vocal apparatus of destiny.'[44] In the credits sequence, the music can lay out motifs to come, even tagging them to actors' names. During the film, music adheres to classical narration's rule of only allowing glimpses of its omniscience, as when the score anticipates the action by a few moments. In *Deep Valley* (1947), for instance, just before the convict approaches the lovers, the music swiftly turns from pleasant to sinister. As George Antheil puts it, 'The characters in a film drama never know what is going to happen to them, but the music always knows.'[45]

Most important, musical accompaniment is communicative only within the boundaries laid down by classical narration. Like the camera, music can be anywhere, and it can intuit the dramatic essence of the action. It remains, however, motivated by the story. When dialogue is present, the music must drop out or confine itself to a subdued coloristic background. 'If a scene is interspersed with silent spots, the orchestration is timed so closely that it is thicker during the silent shots. It must then be thinned down in a split second when dialogue comes in.'[46] Just as classical camerawork or editing becomes more overt when there is little dialogue, so the music comes into its own as an accompaniment for physical action. Here music becomes expressive according to certain conventions (static harmony for suspense or the macabre, chromaticism for tension, marked rhythm for chase scenes).[47] A 'sting' in the music can underline a significant line of dialogue very much in the manner of eighteenth-century melodrama.

Music can also reinforce point-of-view. It establishes time and place as easily as does an inter-title or a sign: 'Rule Britannia' over shots of London, eighteenth-century pastiche for the credits of *Monsieur Beaucaire* (1946). In scoring *Lust for Life* (1956), Rózsa modeled his score upon Debussy in order to suggest Van Gogh's period.[48] To this 'unrestrictive' use of musical narration, Hollywood counterposes the possibility of subjective musical point-of-view. The music often expresses characters' mental states – agitated music for inner turmoil, ominous chords for tension, and the like. In *The Jazz Singer* (1927), we know Jakie is thinking of his mother when, as he sees her picture, we hear the 'Mammy' tune in the score. During the spate of subjective films of the 1940s, musical experiments increased (the theremin in *Spellbound* [1945], a playback reverberation in *Murder, My Sweet* [1944]). As one critic noted at the time, weird coloristic effects became more common because of 'the vogue for films dealing with amnesia, shock, suspense, neurosis, and kindred psychological and psychiatric themes. The music counterpart of the troubled mental states depicted in these films is a musical style which emphasizes vagueness and strangeness, especially in the realms of harmony and orchestration.'[49] By the mid-1930s, music could shift easily from unrestrictive to restrictive viewpoints, as when a character hums a tune to himself and then, as he steps outdoors, the orchestra takes it up.[50] Hollywood music could even create misleading narration, as in *Uncertain Glory* (1944): when the prisoner Jean tells Bonet he wants to go to church to confess, the music is sentimental, but once Bonet lets him go, Jean flees and the music becomes flippant. The first musical passage is now revealed as having presented only Bonet's misconception about Jean's sincerity. Such practices, even such deceptions, are the logical consequence of making music-as-narration dependent upon character causality.

Since classical narration turns nearly all anticipations and recollections of story action over to the characters, music must not operate as a completely free-roaming narration. Here is one difference from Wagner's method, which did allow the music to flaunt its omniscience by ironic or prophetic uses of motifs. The Hollywood score, like the classical visual style, seldom includes overt recollections or far-flung anticipations of the action. The music confines itself to a moment-by-moment heightening of the story. Slight anticipations are permitted, but recollections of previous musical material must be motivated by a repetition of situation or by character memory. At the close of *Sunday Dinner for a Soldier* (1944), Tessa's wave to Eric is accompanied by the ballroom music to which they had danced in an earlier scene. The classical text thus relies upon our forming strong associations upon a motif's first entry.

The narrational limits which the classical film puts upon music are dramatically illustrated in *Hangover Square* (1945). During the credits, a romantic piano concerto plays non-diegetically but does not conclude. Early in the film, when the composer George Bone goes to his apartment, his friend Barbara is playing the opening of his concerto, the same music we had heard over the credits. But Bone's version is also unfinished, and Barbara's father advises him to complete it. In the course of the action, Bone is plagued by murderous amnesiac spells triggered by discordant noises, which are rendered as subjective by means of chromatic and dissonant harmonies. Completing the concerto drives these from Bone's head, but in the film's climactic scene, when he plays the concerto at a soiree, he suffers another breakdown. Yet the performance continues, and the action of the last scene is accompanied throughout by Bone's concerto. Bone's romantic score wins out over the psychotic

discordances, but only by becoming identical with the score of the film, the score that had been 'rehearsed' under the credits. The narration's power lies in the fact that Bone is allowed to score the last scene only by writing the score that the narration 'had in mind' all along. The narration's limits are revealed by its *almost* complete anticipation of Bone's concerto: the film cannot complete the piece before he does. Only the conclusion of the action – Bone finishing the performance alone in a burning building – brings the concerto and the film itself to a close. As 'The End' appears on the screen, the (non-diegetic) orchestra swallows the solo piano; now the narration can have the last word, and chord.

The reappearing narration

The finale of *Hangover Square* also illustrates the way in which the narration can reappear overtly but briefly at the film's very close. This close would minimally consist of a 'The End' title, usually against a background identical to that of the opening credits, and a non-diegetic musical flourish. Such devices buckle the film shut, making the 'narrator' simply a discreet curtailer, like the curtain that closes a play or 'The End' that concludes a novel. This narrational movement toward finality is laid bare in the credits of *King Kong* (1933). The opening credits are set against a triangular shape which steadily narrows as they proceed (see figs 3.26 and 3.27). Not until the end credit does the triangle diagram a complete closure (see fig 3.28).[51] After about 1970, it seems, films seldom exploited these narrational possibilities and instead dropped the 'The End' credit, shifted most of the opening credits to the final spot (as a signal of the end), and expanded the credits sequence to a Talmudic intricacy.

The narration can afford to be so modest at this point because the film has already informed the audience when it will end. Chapter 4 shows how deadlines work in this fashion. Characters also constantly look forward to closure. In *The Arkansas Traveler* (1938), Traveler tells John: 'When this is all over, I want you to remember just one thing.' In the final moment of *Play Girl* (1941), the heroine calls her maid to fetch the perfume she has worn for every flirtation: 'The last time, Josie, the last time.' *Uncertain Glory* (1944) ends with Jean about to sacrifice his life. Bonet: 'It's been a long road.' Jean: 'But it's come to the right ending.' The conditions for closure have also been non-diegetically anticipated by the narration. *The Shock Punch* (1925) begins with expository titles that describe Dan Savage as a man who believes that life is a battle and the winner is one who 'can command the last reserve of physical power.' The next title continues: 'And as he wanted his son Ranny to be like that − to carry a final, deciding punch into every conflict −.' Needless to say, the film's action is resolved when Ranny flattens the man he is fighting. At the start of *The Black Hand* (1950), a crawl title tells of Italian immigrants living in New York at the turn of the century. Most were good citizens, the narration explains, who fought the Black Hand and eventually purged their community of its influence. The title thus anticipates Gio's success in overthrowing the Mafia. At the film's close, a fireman mutters, 'Ah, these dagoes!' and the captain turns. 'I wonder where you think Americans come from.' His retort confirms the narration's initial estimate of the immigrants' civic virtues. In contrast, it is no trivial description of an avant-garde or modernist film to say that such films often do not let us know when they will stop. Films in these traditions deliberately exploit a sense of uncertainty about their boundaries, as when, in *Last Year at Marienbad* (1961), the narrator announces that 'The whole story has come to its end,' but neglects to add that the film is only half over.

The work of classical narration may also peep out from the film's epilogue − a part of the final scene, or even a complete final scene, that shows the return of a stable narrative state. The screenwriter Frances Marion suggests ending the film as soon as possible after the action is resolved, but 'not before the expected rewards and penalties are meted out. ... The final sequence should show the reaction of the protagonist when he has achieved his desires. Let the audience be satisfied that the future of the principals is settled.'[52] Emerson and Loos call this a short 'human interest' scene, an equivalent of 'And so they lived happily ever after.'[53] All the films in the UnS did include an epilogue, however brief; in two-thirds of them, the epilogue was a distinctly demarcated scene. A 1919 film

Love and the Law (1919), signalled its epilogue by a very self-conscious title: 'Patience, gentle audience, just one thing more.' Soon, however, no such cues were necessary and an epilogue could be included as a matter of course.

Epilogues will often tacitly refer back to the opening scene, proving the aptness of Raymond Bellour's remark that in the classical film the conclusion acknowledges itself as a result of the beginning.[54] *You for Me* (1952) begins with Tony being peppered in the buttocks by a shotgun blast; a freeze frame catches him in a comic posture. The film ends with him sitting down on a knitting needle, accompanied by a freeze frame. *Sunday Dinner for a Soldier* (1944) frames its story by the habitual action of the family waving to planes overhead; at the start, the planes are anonymous, but by the close, Tessa is in love with one pilot. The familiar here-we-go-again, or cyclical, epilogue is a variant of the same principle. The epilogue can even be quite self-conscious about its symmetry, as is the framing narration of *Impact* (1944). The opening of the film corresponds to the opening of a dictionary by an anonymous hand, and the word 'impact' is enlarged. A voice-over commentary reads the somewhat improbable definition: 'Impact: The force with which two lives come together, sometimes for good, sometimes for evil.' At the end, the epilogue returns to the dictionary, but the definition has changed: 'Impact: The force with which two lives come together, sometimes for evil, sometimes for good.' The restoration of 'good' as the stable state creates an explicit balancing effect, as does shutting the book to announce the close of the film.

Most classical films use the story action to confirm our expectations of closure without further nudgings from the narration. But *Impact* does show that during the last few seconds of the film, the narration can risk some self-consciousness. The familiar running gag, a motif repeated throughout the film to be capped in the final moments, reminds the audience to some degree of the arbitrariness of closure. Another self-conscious marking of the narration's perspective upon the story world is the camera that cranes back to a high angle upon a final tableau. Most overt is a finale like that of *Appointment for Love* (1941), in which an elevator man turns from the couple and winks at the audience. As we would expect, such direct address is usually motivated by genre (e.g., comedy) or realism (as in a frame story stressing the factual basis of the fiction).

The winding corridor

The belief that classical narration is invisible often accompanies an assumption that the spectator is passive. If the Hollywood film is a clear pane of glass, the audience can be visualized as a rapt onlooker. Again, Hollywood's own discourse has encouraged this. Concealment of artifice, technicians claim, makes watching the film like viewing reality. The camera becomes not only the storyteller but the viewer as well; the absent narrator is replaced by the 'ideal observer.'[55] Few theorists today would agree with Hollywood's equation of its style with natural perception, but contemporary accounts have still considered the spectator to be quite inactive. Most commonly, film theorists have employed concepts taken from perspective painting to explain the spectator's role. Yet terms like 'spectator placement,' 'subject position,' and other spatial metaphors break the film into a series of views targeted toward an inert perceiver.[56] In Chapter 5, I will consider 'perspective' as an account of the representation of classical space. For now, a metaphor involving both space and time will be useful. The spectator passes through the classical film as if moving through an architectural volume, remembering what she or he has already encountered, hazarding guesses about upcoming events, assembling images and sounds into a total shape. What, then, is the spectator's itinerary? Is it string-straight, or is it more like the baffling, 'crooked corridors' that Henry James prided himself upon designing?[57]

The film begins. Concentrated, preliminary exposition that plunges us *in medias res* triggers strong first impressions, and these become the basis for our expectations across the entire film. Meir Sternberg calls this the 'primacy effect.'[58] He points out that in any narrative, the information provided first about a character or situation creates a fixed baseline against which later information is judged. As our earlier examples indicate, the classical cinema trades upon the primacy effect. Once the exposition has outlined a character's traits, the character should remain consistent. This means that actions must

be unequivocal and significant.[59] The star system also encourages the creation of first impressions. 'The people who act in pictures are selected for their roles because of the precise character impressions that they convey to audiences. For instance, the moment you see Walter Pidgeon in a film you know immediately that he could not do a mean or petty thing.'[60] All of these factors cooperate to reinforce the primacy effect.

Many films open with dialogue that builds up an impression of the yet-to-be-introduced protagonist; when the character appears (played by an appropriate star, caught in a typical action), the impression is confirmed. In the first scene of *Speedy* (1928), the young woman says that Speedy (Harold Lloyd) has a new job; her father comments that Speedy cannot keep any job because he is obsessed by baseball. Scene two begins with an expository title identifying the crucial game being played in Yankee Stadium, and shots of the game follow. Another expository title informs us that Speedy now works where he can phone the stadium. We then see a soda fountain, with Speedy as the soda jerk, going to the phone to learn the game's score. The rest of the scene confirms Pop's judgment of Speedy's character through gags showing Speedy carrying his baseball mania into his work. Dialogue title, expository title, character action, and star persona (Harold called himself 'Speedy' in *The Freshman* [1925]) all reinforce a single first impression.

The primacy effect is not confined to characterization, although first impressions are probably most firm in that realm. In some silent films, an unusually emphatic narration previews the essential theme and establishes the most coherent reading of what will follow. By extension, all the devices of 'planting' and foreshadowing motifs — objects, conditions, deadlines — gain their saliency from the primacy effect.

Once first impressions get erected, they are hard to knock down. Sternberg shows that we tend to take the first appearance of a motif as the 'true' one, which can withstand severe testing by contrary information. When, for instance, a character first presented as amiable later behaves grumpily, we are inclined to justify the grumpiness as a temporary deviation.[61] This tactic (again, reinforced by the star system) is a common way in which the classical film presents character change or development. In the opening of *The Miracle Woman* (1931), Florence Fallon is so distraught by her father's death that she denounces his congregation as hypocrites and launches into a sermon on the need for kindness. An opportunistic promoter takes advantage of her fervor and talks her into getting revenge on people by becoming a phony faith healer. When we next see her, she behaves cynically. Because of first impressions, we see her cynical selfishness as a momentary aberration, caused by exceptional circumstances, and so we are not surprised when love recalls her to her father's ideals. The primacy effect helps explain why character change in the Hollywood film is not a drastic shift but a return to the path from which one has strayed.

First impressions in place, the spectator proceeds through the film. How does this process work? The narration creates gaps, holding back information and compelling the spectator to form hypotheses. Most minimally and generally, these hypotheses will pertain to what can happen next, but many other hypotheses might be elicited. The spectator may infer how much a character knows, or why a character acts this way, or what in the past the protagonist is trying to conceal. The viewer may also hypothesize about the narration itself: why am I being told this now? why is the key information being withheld? Sternberg sees every viewing hypothesis as having three properties. A hypothesis can be more or less *probable*. Some hypotheses are virtual certainties (e.g., that Bill will survive the flood in *Steamboat Bill Jr.* [1928]). Other hypotheses are highly improbable (e.g., that Bill will not get the girl he loves). Most hypotheses fall somewhere in between. Hypotheses can also be more or less *simultaneous*; that is, sometimes we hold two or more hypotheses in balance at once, while at other moments one hypothesis simply gets replaced by another. If a man announces that he will get married, we hold simultaneous hypotheses (he will go through with it or he won't). But if a sworn bachelor suddenly shows up with a bride on his arm, the bachelor-hypothesis is simply replaced; the bachelor-hypothesis never competed with another possibility. Evidently, simultaneous hypotheses promote suspense and curiosity, while successive hypotheses promote surprise. Finally, a set of hypotheses can be more or less *exclusive*. Narration may force us to frame a few sharply distinguished hypotheses (in a chess game, there can only be win, lose, or draw), or the film may supply a range of overlapping and indistinct possibilities (setting out on a trip, one may undergo a wide variety of experiences).[62]

The three scales of probability, simultaneity, and exclusivity take us a considerable way toward characterizing the activities of the classical spectator. Broadly speaking, Hollywood narration asks us to form hypotheses that are highly probable and sharply exclusive. Consider, as a naive example, *Roaring Timber* (1937). In the first scene, a lumber-mill owner comes into a saloon looking for a new foreman. He tells the bartender he needs a tough guy for the job. Since we have already seen our protagonist, Jim, enter the bar, we form the hypothesis that the owner will ask him. The expectation is fairly probable, and there is no information to the contrary (no other man in the room is identified as a candidate). There is also a narrow range of alternatives (either the owner will ask Jim or he will not). Few hypotheses are as probable as this, but one of the indices of classical narration's reliability is that it seldom equivocates about the likeliest few hypotheses at any given moment. Similarly, the classical film sharply delimits the range of our expectations. The character's question is not 'What will I do with my life?' but 'Will I choose marriage or a career?' Even subtle cases operate by the same principles. *Beggars of Life* (1928) begins with a wandering young man coming up to a farmhouse and finding a dead man inside. He then encounters a young woman who tells, in flashback, how the farmer tried to rape her and how she killed him. The alternative explanations (suicide, accident, homicide, etc.) narrow to a single one (self-defense), and this becomes steadily more probable as the woman's tale accounts for the details the young man had noticed. True, farcical forms of comedy permit almost anything to happen next, but there the improbability and open-endedness of permissable hypotheses are motivated as generic conventions, and we adjust our expectations accordingly. On the whole, classical narration creates probable and distinct hypotheses. Characters' goal orientation often reinforces and guides the direction these hypotheses will take. Incidentally, in *Roaring Timber*, Jim accepts the foreman's job.

By threading together several probable and quite exclusive hypotheses, we participate in a game of controlled expectation and likely confirmation. There is, however, more to the spectator's activity. Any fictional narration can call our attention to a gap or it can distract us from it. In a mystery film, for instance, the crucial clue may be indicated quite casually; the detective may notice it but we do not. If the narration thus distracts us, we do not form an appropriate hypothesis and the narration can then introduce new information. These successive hypotheses, as Sternberg calls them, create surprise.[63] Now it is characteristic of classical narration to use surprise very sparingly. Too many jolts would lead us to doubt the reliability of the narration, and the advantages of concentrated, preliminary, *in medias res* exposition would be lost. In our itinerary through the classical film, the banister cannot constantly collapse under our touch.

For this reason, classical narration usually calls our attention to gaps and allows us to set up simultaneous, competing hypotheses. The scenes from *Roaring Timber* and *Beggars of Life* afford clear instances, as does a sequence in *Interlude* (1957). The heroine calls on the conductor Tonio Fischer; our knowledge of him has been identical with hers. While she waits for him, the narration takes us to another room, where Tonio is playing the piano for another woman. The scene raises questions about the woman's identity and Tonio's character traits, and these gaps encourage us to construct simultaneous alternatives to be tested in subsequent scenes.

Our hypothesis-forming activity can be thought of as a series of questions which the text impells us to ask. The questions can be posed literally, from one character to another, as in the beginning of *Monsieur Beaucaire* (1946): 'Will there be war?' Or the questions can be more implicit. Roland Barthes speaks of this question-posing process as the 'hermeneutic code' and he shows how narratives have ways of delaying or recasting the question or equivocating about the answer.[64] The classical cinema always delays and may recast, but it seldom equivocates. At the start of *Play Girl* (1941), we are uncertain whether Grace is a gold-digger or whether the title is ironic. But when the father of her current beau denounces her, not only does she not deny her scandalous past but she accepts a bribe to let the son go. The answer to our question, somewhat delayed, is unequivocal.

All of the foregoing instances illustrate another feature of the gaps that classical narration creates: they are filled. Sternberg distinguishes between *permanent* gaps, which the text never authoritatively lets us fill (e.g., Iago's motives), and *temporary* gaps, which sooner or later we are able to fill.[65] It is a basic feature of classical narration to avoid permanent gaps. 'The perfect photoplay leaves no doubts, offers no explanations, starts nothing it cannot finish.'[66] The questions about Tonio in *Interlude* are eventually answered. Concentrated preliminary exposition, causal motivation, the use of denouement and epilogue – all seek to assure that no holes remain in the film. This process of gap-filling helps create the continuity of impression upon which Hollywood prides itself. Each sequence, every line of dialogue, becomes a way of creating or developing or confirming a hypothesis; shot by shot, questions are posed and answered. Our progress through the film, as our first impressions are confirmed and our hypotheses focus toward certainty, resembles the graphic design in the titles of *King Kong* (figs 3.26-3.28): a pyramid narrowing to a point of intelligibility. One screenplay manual puts it well: 'In the beginning of the motion picture we don't know anything. During the course of the story, information is accumulated, until at the end we know everything.'[67]

Again, one should not conclude that classical narration is naive or shallow, for subtle effects can be achieved within the admittedly constrained bounds of such narration. *Wine of Youth* (1924) begins with three expository titles:

When our grandmothers were young, nice girls pretended to know nothing at all.
When our mothers were young, they admitted they knew a thing or two.
The girls of today pretend to know all there is to know.

There follow two parallel scenes. At a ball in 1870, a suitor proposes to a woman, and she accepts: 'There has never been a love as great as ours!' At another dance in 1897, a suitor proposes to the couple's daughter, and she too accepts, repeating the line her mother had uttered years before. The symmetry is quite exact: similar situations, same setting (a sofa in an alcove), even the identical number of shots in each scene. At this point, the narration has established itself as highly reliable: the scenes have confirmed the titles' knowledge of women, and we have already formed strong first impressions about what the 'girls of today' will be like. (The word 'pretends' strongly suggests omniscience.) When the scene moves to the present, our impressions are confirmed. Jazz babies and lounge lizards are engaged in a wild party. Mary, the granddaughter and daughter of the other two women, refuses to marry her suitor. We form a hypothesis that this will not in the long run violate the pattern established in the first two scenes. Over the whole film we wait for Mary to reconcile herself to the decent young man who loves her. A harrowing family crisis demonstrates both the strains and the possibilities of marriage. Mary and her suitor are sitting on the sofa (the site of both previous courtships) and he proposes. She accepts: 'There has never been a love as great as ours!' It has been a long wait, but the narrational gap has finally been closed, and by an ironic repetition at that. The narration can even afford a twist — embracing, the couple tumble off the sofa — that lends a small surprise to the finale. Our hypotheses about the conclusion, established as very narrow and highly probable, are tested but finally validated, and in a way that also illustrates the recurrence of the Rule of Three.

There is one genre that may seem to run counter to all these claims about spectator activity in classical narration. The mystery film sometimes makes its narration quite overt: a shot of a shadowy figure or an anonymous hand makes the viewer quite aware of a self-conscious, omniscient, and suppressive narration. Similarly, the mystery film encourages the spectator to erect erroneous first impressions, confounds the viewer's most probable hypotheses, and stresses curiosity as much as suspense. (The mystery tale always depends upon highly retarded exposition, the true account coming to light only at the end.) The narration may even be revealed as retrospectively unreliable. Thus *The Maltese Falcon* (1941) offers an interesting contrast with *Wine of Youth*. Not only does the narration abandon its initial adherence to Sam Spade's point-of-view by showing the killing of his partner Archer, but the narration also declines to show the killer (we see only a gloved hand). More important, the narration misleads us in an expository title at the very outset. Over a still-life of the Maltese falcon, the title recounts the statuette's origin and ends by remarking that its whereabouts remain a mystery 'to this day' (fig 3.29). When the characters find only a lead replica of the falcon, the opening title stands revealed as doubly misleading. The falcon in the still-life may be the phony, and the phrase 'to this day' which we might take as meaning 'until this story started,' actually means 'even after the story concluded.' The opening title's equivocation is apparent only in retrospect. The same kind of misleading narration is at work in the beginning of *Manhandled*, as I've already suggested (p. 32). A more drastic example, probably a limit-case, is Hitchcock's duplicitous flashback in the beginning of *Stage Fright* (1950).

The unreliable and overt narration of the mystery film remains, however, finally bound by classical precepts. First, the narration still depends chiefly upon suspense and forward momentum: the story is primarily that of an investigation, even if the goal happens to be the elucidation of a past event. Secondly, the mystery film relies completely upon cause and effect, since the mystery always revolves around missing links in the causal chain. Third, those links are always found, so even the gaps of the mystery film are temporary, not permanent. Most important, the mystery film's overt play of narration and hypothesis-forming is generically motivated. Since Poe and Doyle, the classical detective story has stressed the game of wits that the narrator proposes to the reader. In this genre, we want uncertainty, we expect both characters and narration to try to deceive us, and we therefore erect specific sorts of first impressions, cautious, provisional ones, based as much upon generic conventions as upon what we actually learn. We do not feel betrayed by the *Falcon*'s opening title, since it is equivalent to the deceptive but 'fair' narrational manipulations in certain novels by Agatha Christie, John Dickson Carr, or Ellery Queen. The classical film thus can generically motivate an unreliable and overt narration.

The spectator moves through, or with, classical Hollywood narration by casting expectations in the form of hypotheses which the text shapes. Narration is fundamentally reliable, allowing hypotheses to be ranked in order of probability and narrowed to a few distinct alternatives. Surprise and disorientation are secondary to suspense as to which alternatives will be confirmed. Curiosity about the past takes a minor role in relation to anticipation of future events. Gaps are continually and systematically opened and filled in, and no gap is permanent. Lest this process seem obvious or natural, recall such a film as *Last Year at Marienbad* (1961), which creates a fundamentally unreliable narration, a lack of redundancy, an open and relatively improbable set of hypotheses, a dependence upon surprise rather than suspense, a pervasive ambiguity about the past that makes the future impossible to anticipate, and many gaps left yawning at the film's close. This is of course an extreme example, but other narrative films contain non-classical narrative strategies. A film's narration could make the initial exposition less clear-cut, as does Godard's *Sauve qui peut (la vie)* (1980), or the narration could establish a firm primacy effect but then qualify or demolish it, as do films as different as Carl Theodor Dreyer's *Day of Wrath* (1943) and Resnais's *Providence* (1977). The Hollywood film does not lead us to invalid conclusions, as these films can; in the classical narrative, the corridor may be winding, but it is never crooked.

4 Time in the classical film

Our examination of exposition has shown that the narrational aspect of plot manipulates story time in specific ways. More generally, classical narration employs characteristic strategies for manipulating story *order* and story *duration*. These strategies activate the spectator in ways congruent with the overall aims of the classical cinema. We shall also have to pay some attention to how narration uses one device that is commonly associated with the Hollywood style's handling of time: crosscutting.

Temporal order: the search for meaning

After dramas supposedly without endings, here is a drama which would be without exposition or opening, and which would end clearly. Events would not follow one another and especially would not correspond exactly. The fragments of many pasts come to bury themselves in a single now. The future mixed among memories. This chronology is that of the human mind.[1]

Jean Epstein, writing in 1927, thus describes his film *La Glace à trois faces*. Hollywood cinema, however, refuses the radical play with chronology that Epstein proposes; the classical film normally shows story events in a 1-2-3 order. Unlike Epstein, the classical filmmaker needs an opening, a threshold – that concentrated, preliminary exposition that plunges us *in medias res*. Events unfold successively from that. Advance notice of the future is especially forbidden, since a flash*forward* would make the narration's omniscience and suppressiveness overt (see Chapter 30 on alternative cinemas' use of the flashforward). The only permissible manipulation of story order is the flashback.

Flashbacks are rarer in the classical Hollywood film than we normally think. Throughout the period 1917-60, screenwriters' manuals usually recommended not using them; as one manual put it, 'Protracted or frequent flashbacks tend to slow the dramatic progression' – a remark that reflects Hollywood's general reluctance to exploit curiosity about past story events.[2] Of the one hundred UnS films, only twenty use any flashbacks at all, and fifteen of those occur in silent films. Most of these are brief, expository flashbacks filling in information about a character's background; this device was obviously replaced by expository dialogue in the sound cinema. In the early years of sound, when plays about trials were common film sources, flashbacks offered a way to 'open up' stagy trial scenes (e.g., *The Bellamy Trial*, *Through Different Eyes*, *The Trial of Mary Dugan*, *Madame X*, all 1929). Another vogue for flashbacks ran from the late 1930s into the 1950s. Between 1939 and 1953, four UnS films begin with a frame story and flash back to recount the bulk of the main action before returning to the frame. Yet those four flashback films still comprise less than 10 per cent of the UnS films of the period. What probably makes the period seem dominated by flashbacks is not the numerical frequency of the device but the intricate ways it was used: contradictory flashbacks in *Crossfire* (1947), parallel flashbacks in *Letter to Three Wives* (1948), open-ended flashbacks in *How Green Was My Valley* (1941) and *I Walked With a Zombie* (1943), flashbacks within flashbacks within flashbacks in *Passage to Marseille* (1944) and *The Locket* (1946), and a flashback narrated by a dead man in *Sunset Boulevard* (1950).

It is possible, of course, to present a shift in story order simply as such, with the film's narration overtly intervening to reveal the past.

In *The Ghost of Rosie Taylor* (1918), an expository inter-title announces that it will explain how the situation became what it is; the title motivates the flashback. *The Killing* (1956) uses voice-over, documentary-style narration to motivate 'realistically' its jumps back in time. The rarity of these overt intrusions shows that classical narration almost always motivates flashbacks by means of character memory. Several cues cooperate here: images of the character thinking, the character's voice heard 'over' the images, optical effects (dissolve, blurring focus), music, and specific references to the time period we are about to enter. If we see flashbacks as motivated by subjectivity, then the extraordinary fashion for temporal manipulations in the 1940s can be explained by the changing conception of psychological causality in the period. Flashbacks, especially convoluted or contradictory ones, can be justified by that increasing interest in vulgarized Freudian psychology which Chapter 2 has already discussed.

Classical flashbacks are motivated by character memory, but they do not function primarily to reveal character traits. Nor were Hollywood practitioners particularly interested in using the flashback to restrict point-of-view; one screenwriters' manual suggests that 'unmotivated jumping of time is likely to rattle the audience, thereby breaking their illusion that they participate in the lives of the characters.'[3] Even the contradictory flashbacks in *Through Different Eyes* or *Crossfire* serve not to reveal the teller's personality so much as they operate, within the conventions of the mystery film, as visual representations of lies. Jean Epstein's aim in *La Glace à trois faces* − to reflect the mixed temporality of consciousness, fragments of the past in a single now − is far removed from Hollywood's use of flashbacks as rhetorical 'dispositions' of the narrative for the sake of suspense or surprise. Nor need the classical flashback respect the literary conventions of first-person narration. Extended flashback sequences usually include material that the remembering character could not have witnessed or known. Character memory is simply a convenient immediate motivation for a shift in chronology; once the shift is accomplished, there are no constant cues to remind us that we are supposedly in someone's mind. In flashbacks, then, the narrating character executes the same fading movement that the narrator of the entire film does: overt and self-conscious at first, then covert and intermittently apparent. Beginning with one narrator and ending with another (e.g., *I Walked With a Zombie*), or compelling a character to 'remember' things she never knew or will know (e.g., *Ten North Frederick* [1958]), or creating a deceased narrator (e.g., *Sunset Boulevard*) − all these tactics show that subjectivity is an arbitrary pretext for flashbacks.

Classical manipulations of story order imply specific activities for the spectator. These involve what psychologists call 'temporal integration,' the process of fusing the perception of the present, the memory of the past, and expectations about the future. E.H. Gombrich points out that temporal integration depends upon the search for meaning, the drive to make coherent sense of the material represented.[4] The film which challenges this coherence, a film like *Not Reconciled* (1964), *Last Year at Marienbad* (1961), or *India Song* (1975), must make temporal integration difficult to achieve. In the classical film, however, character causality provides the basis for temporal coherence. The manipulations of story order in *Not Reconciled* or *Marienbad* are puzzling partly because we cannot determine any relevant character identities, traits, or actions which could motivate the breaks in chronology. On the other hand, one reason that classical flashbacks do not adhere to a character's viewpoint is that they must never distract from the ongoing causal chain. The causes and effects may be presented out of story order, but our search for their connections must be rewarded.

Psychological causality thus permits the classical viewer to integrate the present with the past and to form clear-cut hypotheses about future story events. To participate in the process of casting ever more narrow and exclusive hypotheses, we must have solid ground under our feet. Therefore, through repetition within the story action and a covertly narrated, 'objective' diegetic world, the film gives us clear memories of causal material; on this basis we can form expectations. At the same time, the search for meaning of which Gombrich speaks guides us toward the motifs and actions already marked as potentially meaningful. For example, motifs revealed in the credits sequence or in the early scenes accumulate significance as our memory is amplified by the ongoing story. Kuntzel suggests that these reinscribed motifs create a vague *déjà-vu* that becomes gradually more meaningful: 'The entire itinerary of *The Most Dangerous Game* is to make its initial figure *readable*, to progressively reassure the subject plunged *ex abrupto* into the uncertainty of the figure.'[5] The classical aesthetic of 'planting' and foreshadowing, of tagging traits and objects for future use, can be seen as laying out elements to be recalled later in the cause-effect logic of the film. If temporality and causality did not cooperate in this way, the spectator could not construct a coherent story out of the narration.

Our survey of narration has shown that the viewer's successive hypotheses can be thought of as a series of questions. Hollywood cinema's reliance upon chronology triggers the fundamental query: What will happen next in the story? Each shot, wrote Loos and Emerson, 'is planned to lead the audience on to the next. At any point, the spectator is wondering how things will come out in the next scene.'[6] The forward flow of these hypotheses may be related to the irreversibility of the film-viewing experience; Thomas Elsaesser has speculated that the channeling of chronology into causality helps the viewer 'manage' the potentially disturbing nature of the film-viewing situation.[7] The relatively close correspondence between story order and narrational order in the classical film helps the spectator create an organized succession of hypotheses and a secure rhythm of question and answer.

Duration, deadlines, and dissolves

Like order, classical Hollywood duration respects very old conventions. The narration shows the important events and skips the intervals between them. The omitted intervals become codified as a set of punctuation marks: expository inter-titles ('The Next Day') and optical effects. From 1917 to 1921, fade-ins and -outs and iris-ins and -outs were the most common optical transitions between scenes. Between 1921 and 1928, the iris fell into disuse, replaced by the fade as the most common transition. In the sound era, fades and dissolves were the most common signs of temporal

ellipsis. Wipes enjoyed a vogue between 1932 and 1941 and appeared occasionally thereafter. Such optical punctuation marks were often compared with theatrical or literary conventions (curtain, end of chapter). Within a scene, of course, some of the same ellipses could be used. After the late 1920s and until the early 1950s, scenes often began with a shot of a building or a sign and then dissolved to the action proper. In the same period, a wipe, either hard- or soft-edged, might follow a character moving from one sub-scene to another. (Not until the late 1950s did a few films begin to eliminate such internal punctuation and simply use the straight cut to link scenes and sub-scenes.[8]) Such a clear set of cues creates an orderly flow of action; compare the disruptive effect, in the films of Eisenstein and Godard, of beginning a scene's action and then, part of the way through, interrupting the action with a title that tells us when the action is occurring.

Punctuation marks enable the narration to skip unimportant intervals by simple omission. The montage sequence lets the narration represent, however briefly, those intervals. The montage sequence does not omit time but compresses it. A war, a prison sentence, or a career can be summed up in a few shots. Films which cover a great length of time may make heavy weather of montage sequences, as does *High Time* (1960), which employs montages of seasons and semesters to cover four years on a college campus. The montage sequence was especially important in literary adaptations, since the plots of novels tended to cover extensive periods.[9] So critical were montages to temporal construction that they were also called 'time-lapse' sequences.

The classical film creates a patterned duration not only by what it leaves out but by a specific, powerful device. The story action sets a limit to how long it must last. Sometimes this means simply a strictly confined duration, as in the familiar convention of one-night-in-a-mysterious-house films (*The Cat and the Canary* [1927], *Seven Footprints to Satan* [1929], *One Frightened Night* [1935], *Sh! The Octopus* [1937]). More commonly, the story action sets stipulated *deadlines* for the characters.

The mildest and most frequent form of the deadline is the appointment. This is most evident in the romance line of action, wherein a suitor will invite a woman out for dinner, to a dance, etc.

If the film makes romance primary, the acceptance, rejection, or deferral of such invitations forms a significant part of the drama (e.g., *Interlude* [1957], *The King and the Chorus Girl* [1937]). The very title of *Appointment for Love* (1941) conveys the same idea. Even if the film does not rely completely upon the romance line of action, many scenes include the making of appointments for later encounters. Just as motifs anticipate future actions, so appointments gear our expectations toward later scenes.

The deadline proper is the strongest way in which story duration cooperates with narrative causality. In effect, the characters set a limit to the time span necessary to the chain of cause and effect. Over three-quarters of the UnS films contained one or more clearly articulated deadlines. The deadline may be stipulated in a line of dialogue, a shot (e.g., a clock), or cross-cutting; whatever device is used, it must specify the durational limit within which cause and effect can operate. Most frequently, the deadline is localized, binding together a few scenes or patterning only a single one. Scenes in *Miss Lulu Bett* (1921) are structured around the repeated deadline of the family's dinner hour. A series of short episodes in *High Time* (1960) are governed by the fact that the freshmen must build a bonfire by seven o'clock. The localized deadline is of course most common at the film's climax. In *Fire Down Below* (1957), one of the protagonists is trapped in the hold of a ship; it is on fire and sinking, and the suspense is predicated upon the slow drainage of time until the situation becomes hopeless. *The Canterville Ghost* (1944) presents the climactic scene of the ghost and young William proving their courage by towing a ticking bomb across the landscape. When William says, 'If it'll hold for twenty seconds more!' the Ghost starts to count the seconds off. The conventional last-minute rescue is the most evident instance of how the classical film's climax often turns upon a deadline.

A deadline may also determine the entire structure of a classical film. The protagonist's goal can be straightforwardly dependent upon a deadline, as when in *Roaring Timber* (1937), Jim agrees to deliver eighty million feet of lumber in sixty days. *The Shock Punch* (1925) gives the protagonist the task of finishing construction of a building by a certain date; the film's last scene

occurs on the deadline day. In 1940s films, the use of the flashback can also limit the duration of the story action. For example, *No Leave, No Love* (1946) begins with the protagonist rushing to a maternity ward; while he waits for news of his child's birth, he tells another husband the story of how he met his wife. By halting the action at a point of crisis and flashing back to early events, the film makes those events seem to operate under the pressure of a deadline. (See also *The Big Clock* [1948] and *Raw Deal* [1948].)

Uncertain Glory (1944) offers a clear example of how appointments mix with deadlines to unify the duration of the classical Hollywood film. The film's action takes place in France under the Nazi Occupation. The first six scenes present the escape of the convict Jean and his capture by the police detective Bonet; in these portions, alternating point-of-view creates suspense. When Bonet has captured Jean, we learn that the Gestapo will shoot one hundred hostages if a partisan saboteur does not surrender in five days. This long-term deadline structures the bulk of the film, as Bonet tries to convince Jean to pose as the saboteur, help the Resistance, and save the hostages. While the deadline hovers over the action, the two men quarrel, villagers conspire against them, Jean falls in love with a village woman (entailing small-scale appointments), and Jean tries several times to escape from Bonet. Finally, in the penultimate scene, at five o'clock Jean decides to surrender himself: 'Deadline's six o'clock, isn't it?' He turns himself in.

It should be evident that deadlines function narrationally. Issuing from the diegetic world, they motivate the film's durational limits: the story action, not the narrator, seems to decide how long the action will take. Planning appointments makes it 'natural' for the narration to show the meeting itself; setting up deadlines makes it 'natural' for the narration to devote screen time to showing whether or not the deadline is met. Moreover, appointments and deadlines stress the forward flow of story action: the arrows of the spectator's expectations are turned toward the encounter to come, the race to the goal. When, in *Applause* (1929), the sailor from Wisconsin asks April for a date, we expect to see the date; when he says he has only four days of leave, we are not surprised that he should ask her to marry him before his leave is up. Deadlines and appointments thus perfectly suit classical narration's emphasis upon eliciting hypotheses about the future.

As a formal principle, the deadline is one of the most characteristic marks of Hollywood dramaturgy. Alternative styles of filmmaking can often be recognized by their refusal to set such explicit limits on the duration of story action. The alternatives vary. Ozu structures his films by repeated routines and cycles of family behavior. Jacques Tati uses a fixed duration (a week, a day or two) simply as a block of time without a deadline. Eisenstein often composes a film of separate, durationally distinct episodes (e.g., *Ivan the Terrible* [1945]). The 'art cinema' of Federico Fellini, Ingmar Bergman, or Michelangelo Antonioni is characterized partly by its refusal of deadlines, its replacement of appointments by chance encounters, and its 'open' endings that do not allow the audience to anticipate when the chain of cause and effect will be completed. A Hollywood version of *L'avventura* (1960) would be sure to include a scene in which someone says: 'If we don't find Sandra in three days, her supply of food will run out.'

Within the classical scene, the viewer assumes durational continuity unless signals say otherwise. The individual shot is assumed to convey a continuous time span which only editing can disrupt. Yet the classical cinema is a cinema of cutting; the single-shot sequence is very rare. Thus classical editing strategies have to signal temporal continuity. *Match-on-action* cutting is the most explicit cue for moment-to-moment continuity. If a character starts to stand up in one shot and continues the movement in the next shot, the classical presumption is that no time has been omitted (see figs 4.1 and 4.2). Editors are warned that if they mismatch action, audiences will be confused about temporal progression.[10] But the match-on-action cut, expensive and time-consuming, is relatively rare; of all the shot-changes in a classical film, no more than 12 per cent are likely to be matches on action. In the absence of information to the contrary, spatial editing cues, such as eyeline-match cutting, imply durational continuity.

The adoption of synchronized sound-on-film had a very powerful effect on how the classical cinema represented story time, as Chapter 23 will show in detail. Diegetic sound created a concrete perceptual duration that could aid editing in creating a seamless temporal continuity. If two characters are talking, the sound editor could make the continuous sound conceal the cut. A British editor summarized American practice:[11]

> This flowing of sound over a cut is one of the most important features of the editing of sound films — in particular, of dialogue films. The completely parallel cut of sound and action should be the exception rather than the rule. . . . Most editors today make a practice of lapping the last one or two frames of modulation on the soundtrack of the shot they are leaving over onto the oncoming shot.

That is, the shot change precedes the dialogue change by a syllable or a word. This 'dialogue cutting point' (Barry Salt's term) became standard by 1930.[12] On other occasions, of course, the sound can lead the image; very commonly a classical film will motivate a cut by an offscreen sound. The noise of a door opening, a character starting to speak, the music of a radio from another room — these can all help sound flow over a cut.

Another way of using sound to secure durational continuity is to employ diegetic music. Of course non-diegetic music, as accompaniment, had been present in the silent cinema, but there its quality as narration made it temporally abstract. In the sound film, diegetic music could cover certain gaps at the level of the image while still projecting a sense of continuous time. For example, in *Flying Fortress* (1942), a couple sit down to dinner in a restaurant while a band is playing. The meal is abbreviated by means of dissolves, creating ellipses on the visual track; but the band's music continues uninterrupted. The bleeding of music over large ellipses suggests how easily the temporal vagueness of music can make sound fulfill narrative functions.

The dissolve, the most common indication of duration, affords us an instructive example of how classical narration does its temporal work. Visually, the dissolve is simply a variant of the fade — a fade-out overlapped with a fade-in — but it is a fade during which the screen is never blank. 'To the layman or the average theatregoer, a lap dissolve passes unobtrusively by on the screen without his being aware that it had happened. A lap dissolve serves the purpose of smoothly advancing the story.'[13] The dissolve was quickly restricted to indicating a short, often indefinite interval, if only a few seconds (e.g., a dissolve from a detail to a full shot). This makes the dissolve a superb way to soften spatial, graphic, and even temporal discontinuities. The dissolve could blend newsreel footage with studio shots, cover mismatched figure positions or screen direction, or blend an extreme-long shot with a close-up (see figs 4.3 through 4.5). Filmmakers of the 1920s in Europe and Russia showed that the dissolve opens up a realm of sheerly graphic possibilities, but Hollywood severely curtailed these: apart from a few exceptions (such as Josef Von Sternberg's work), the Hollywood dissolve became, as Tamar Lane puts it, 'a link. . . . It bridges over from one situation to another without a jarring break of action and without need for explanatory matter.'[14]

After 1928, the dissolve on the image track was accompanied by a sound transition as well. At first, the procedures of sound editing and the uncertainties of sound perspective made technicians puzzled. 'Imagine switching abruptly from the blast of a jazz orchestra to a flash of a whispered conversation, then to the rush of a train and back to the silken vampire sleeping peacefully in her boudoir. Such a rush of conflicting sound ought to leave an audience as nervous as a doe at a waterhole.'[15] Sound dissolves were declared distracting; while a close-up of a face could dissolve to a long shot of a crowd, to mix even briefly the character's speech with the crowd's babble would result in cacophony. Instead, the character would complete the dialogue and pause; the crowd noise would then be sneaked in over the dissolve. Like the offscreen sound that motivates the cut to a new space, the sound bridge here may sometimes very slightly anticipate the next image. Both image and sound dissolving procedures show how, once a transition became codified, it could provide a continuous and unself-conscious narration.

Like our experience of story order, the viewer's experience of story duration depends upon a search for meaning. Gombrich writes: 'We cannot judge the distance of an object in space before we have identified it and estimated its size. We cannot estimate the passage of time in a picture without interpreting the event represented.'[16] In the classical cinema, the narration's emphasis upon the future gears our expectations toward the resolution of suspense. It is this that determines what periods the narration will eliminate or compress. When this does not happen, when the narration dwells upon 'dramatically meaningless intervals,' duration comes forward as a system in the film and vies with causality for prominence. (See the various critiques[17] of Hitchcock's use of the long take in *Rope* [1948].) Time in the classical film is a vehicle for causality, not a process to be investigated on its own. Hence the stricture that a walk without dialogue is 'dead' or wasted time. (Compare the durational importance of the silent walk in Dreyer, in Antonioni, and, from a different culture, in the Navajo films described by Sol Worth and John Adair.[18])

More generally, classical narration's insistence upon closure rewards the search for meaning and makes the time span we experience seem a complete unit. Even from shot to shot, our expectation of causally significant completion controls how we respond. 'We hardly realize that we look at two different shots if the first one shows the beginning of an action and the next one its continuation.'[19] The match-on-action cut, the bleeding of sound over a cut, the use of dissolves and diegetic music all confirm our expectation of completion. The viewer's ability to test hypotheses against a film's unfolding cause and effect means that duration again becomes secondary to a search for narrative meaning.

Hollywood has also exploited our search for temporal meaning by shaping the felt duration of our experience. Narrative 'rhythm' can be thought of as a way in which narration focuses and controls successive hypotheses. Camera movement, especially if it is independent of the figures and closely timed to music, can create a moment-by-moment arc of expectation.[20] Editing was the earliest rhythmic realm which the classical cinema systematically exploited; by 1920, scenarists were recommending using short shots to increase excitement.[21] Rhythmic editing is still far from clearly understood theoretically, but certainly the time needed to grasp a new shot depends partly upon expectation. It appears that if the viewer is prepared and if the shot is graphically comprehensible, the viewer requires between half a second and three seconds to adjust to the cut.[22] Slowly paced editing leaves a comfortable margin, so that the new shot is on the screen quite long enough for the viewer to assimilate it. But in Hollywood's use of accelerated editing, the viewer is primed to expect a very narrow range of alternative outcomes and the shots then flash on the screen so quickly that the viewer can 'read' them only in gross terms: do they confirm or disconfirm the immediate hypothesis? This process is evident in the last-minute rescue, when all the viewer wants to know is whether the rescuers will arrive in time, so the accelerating editing builds excitement by confining each shot to posing, retarding, and eventually answering this question. The ability of rapid editing to funnel the spectator's hypotheses into very narrow channels is confirmed by Robert Parrish's claim that fast pace can cover story problems. Asserting that *The Roaring Twenties* (1939) works like 'one big ninety-minute montage,' Parrish notes: 'The audience never gets a chance to relax and think about the story holes. They're into the next scene before they have time to think about the last one.'[23]

Crosscutting

Strictly speaking, crosscutting can be considered a category of alternating editing, the intercalation of two or more different series of images. If temporal simultaneity is not pertinent to the series, the cutting may be called *parallel* editing; if the series are to be taken as temporally simultaneous, then we have *crosscutting*. For example, if the film alternates images of wealth and poverty with no temporal relation to one another, we have parallel editing; but if the rich man is sitting down to dinner while the beggar stands outside, we have crosscutting. Griffith's *Intolerance* (1916) uses both types: parallel editing makes abstract analogies among the four epochs, while crosscutting within each epoch depicts simultaneous actions. In the classical Hollywood cinema, parallel editing is a distinctly unlikely alternative, since it emphasizes logical relations rather than causality and chronology.

Crosscutting is a narrational process: two or more lines of action in different locales are woven together. Our hero gets up in the morning; cut to the boss looking at the clock; cut to our hero eating breakfast; cut to the boss pacing. Christian

Metz has pointed out that such a sequence manipulates both order and duration.[24] Within each line of action, the events are consecutive; but between the lines of action taken as wholes, the temporal relations are simultaneous. The hero gets up somewhat *before* the boss looks at the clock, but across the whole sequence, we understand that *while* the hero gets up and comes to work the boss waits for him. There is yet another factor involved, which Metz does not mention: usually, crosscutting creates ellipses. If we cut from hero waking up to boss to hero leaving, the shot of the boss covers all the time it takes our hero to dress, wash, etc. Crosscutting almost always skips over intervals in exactly this way. Crosscutting, then, creates a unique set of temporal relations – order, ellipsis, simultaneity – which function for specific narrational ends.

Alternation of narrational point-of-view has a long history in literature and other arts, but crosscutting is often linked to specifically nineteenth-century theatrical and literary sources. Nicholas Vardac found 'cross-cut' scenes in nineteenth-century drama, which used dual box sets and area lighting to switch between lines of action.[25] Eisenstein traced Griffith's parallel montage through theatrical melodrama back to Dickens's novels.[26] The analogies with other arts emphasize the brevity of the scenes alternated and the simultaneity of the actions represented. Chapter 16 will show that both these aspects of crosscutting were common in American film-making long before 1917. But such analogies with other arts do not specify all the features of classical crosscutting.

Classical crosscutting traces out personal cause and effect, creates deadlines, and frees narration from restricting itself to a single character's point-of-view. We most commonly think of crosscutting as supporting a deadline – supremely, the last-minute rescue situation. But a silent film might employ crosscutting in a great many scenes – as exposition, as a reminder of characters' where-abouts, and especially as a way in which narration could control the viewer's hypothesis-framing. Crosscutting thus reveals narration to be omniscient (the narration knows that something important is happening in another line of action), but this omniscience, true to classical precept, is rendered as omnipresence.

In 1920, Loos and Emerson advised the screenwriter that two crosscut lines of action would help keep the audience interested.[27] Of the UnS silent films, 84 per cent use extensive passages of crosscutting. With the coming of sound, however, crosscutting became far less frequent. Of the UnS sound films, only 49 per cent use any crosscutting at all, and only 16 per cent use it as extensively as did silent films. The reasons are evident. Dialogue would not be cut as quickly as silent action, and crosscutting lines of dialogue (done in Europe by René Clair and Fritz Lang) probably seemed too narrationally intrusive for Hollywood film-making.[28] The abandonment of crosscutting thus became consonant with a greater reticence on the part of sound-film narration.

None the less, the principle behind crosscutting remained important for the sound film. As Chapter 23 will show, the rhythm of silent film editing found a functional equivalent in the sound film's rapid shifts from scene to scene. In *The Whole Town's Talking* (1935), our hero's boss notices that he is late and begins to interrogate other employees. The scene switches to Jones at home, asleep; he wakes up, notices the time, and rushes off. We then see Jones arrive at work. Such shifts in locale could be motivated by sound links as well (music, radio or television broadcasts, phone conversations, etc.). In such ways, a rapid alternation of distinct scenes could stimulate crosscutting's characteristic play with time – consecutive order, ellipsis, and an overall sense of simultaneity. A discreet narration oversees time, making it subordinate to causality, while the spectator follows the causal thread.

5 Space in the classical film

The motion picture industry for many years has been trying to remove the one dimension of the screen. By lighting, with lenses of inexplicable complexity, through movement, camera angles, and a variety of other techniques, the flatness of the screen has largely been overcome.[1]

Ranald MacDougall, 1945

In making narrative causality the dominant system in the film's total form, the classical Hollywood cinema chooses to subordinate space. Most obviously, the classical style makes the sheerly graphic space of the film image a vehicle for narrative. We can see this principle at work negatively in the prohibitions against 'bad' cuts. 'The important subjects should be in the same general area of the frame for each of the two shots which are to be cut together,' but 'as long as the important subject is not shifted from one side of the screen to the other, no real harm is done.'[2] In describing the classical cinema's use of space we are most inclined to use the term 'transparent,' so much does that cinema strive to efface the picture plane. 'The screen might be likened to a plate-glass window through which the observer looks with one eye at the actual scene.'[3] We need, however, a fuller account of how classical narration uses image composition and editing to create a powerful representation of three-dimensional space.

The image: composition

While recognizing that Hollywood cinema subordinates space to narrative causality, we ought also to acknowledge that the classical spatial system is, in a strictly logical sense, arbitrary. We could imagine other systems that privileged different devices (e.g., decentered framings, discontinuity editing) but which were equally coherent and equally supportive of causality. Historically, however, the classical construction of space appears far from arbitrary, since it synthesizes many traditions which have dominated various Western arts.

Post-Renaissance painting provided one powerful model. Cinematographers and directors constantly invoked famous paintings as sources. Cecil B. De Mille claimed to have borrowed from Doré, Van Dyck, Corot and one 'Reubens.'[4] Robert Surtees cited the Impressionists, Leon Shamroy imitated Van Gogh. Discussions of lighting invariably invoke Rembrandt.[5] To a point, such assertions are simply hyperbole. Allan Dwan remarked: 'Once in a while we would undertake the imitation or reproduction of something artistic – a famous painting, let's say.'[6] (Staged replicas of famous pictures were also a convention of theatrical melodrama.) But in a more significant sense, Hollywood did perpetuate many precepts of post-Renaissance painting. The very name 'film studio' derives from the term for the workroom of the painter or sculptor. While no major cinematographers were professional painters, many (Charles Rosher, Karl Struss, Stanley Cortez, James Wong Howe) had been portrait photographers, a field in which academic rules of composition and lighting prevailed. And occasionally a cinematographer would articulate principles of filmmaking that directly echo those of academic painting.[7] We ought not to be surprised, then, that Hollywood's practices of composition continue some very old traditions in the visual arts.

An outstanding example is the Hollywood cinema's interest in centered compositions. In post-Renaissance painting, the erect human body provides one major standard of framing, with the face usually occupying the upper portion of the picture format. The same impulse can be seen in the principle of horizon-line isocephaly, which guarantees that figures' heads run along a more or less horizontal line.[8] Classical cinema employs these precepts. While extreme long shots tend to weight the lower half of the image (this derives from landscape painting traditions), most shots work with a privileged zone of screen space resembling a T: the upper one-third and the central vertical third of the screen constitute the 'center' of the shot. This center determines the composition of long shots, medium shots, and close-ups, as well as the grouping of figures (see figs 5.1 through 5.8). In widescreen films, the center area is proportionately stretched, so even slightly off-center compositions are not transgressive (especially in a balanced shot/reverse-shot cutting pattern). Classical filmmaking thus considers edge-framing taboo; frontally positioned figures or objects, however unimportant, are seldom sliced off by either vertical edge. And, as the illustrations indicate, horizon-line isocephaly is common in classical filmmaking. Thus the human body is made the center of narrative and graphic interest: the closer the shot, the greater the demand for centering.

But how to center moving figures? The classical style quickly discovered the virtues of panning and tilting the camera. The subtlest refinement of this practice was the custom of *reframing*. A reframing is a slight pan or tilt to accommodate figure movement. Every film in the UnS contained some reframings; after 1929, one out of every six shots used at least one reframing. The chief alternative to reframing is what Edward Branigan has called the *frame cut*.[9] Within a defined locale, a figure leaves the shot, and, *as the body crosses the frame line*, the cut reveals the figure entering a new shot, with the body still crossing the (opposite) frame line (see figs 5.9 through 5.14). Frame-cutting is extraordinarily common in classical cinema, partly because it is the least troublesome match-on-action cut to make but also because it confirms the importance of the center zone of the screen. In a frame cut, the image's edge becomes only a bridge over which figures or objects pass on their way to center stage.

With centering comes balance, but the complex and dynamic equilibrium of great Western painting is usually lacking in Hollywood compositions. Overall balance and an avoidance of distractingly perfect symmetry generally suffice. Once centered, the human body provides enough slight asymmetries to yield a generally stable image, and camera viewfinders, engraved with cross-hatchings, enabled cameramen to balance the shot. When balance is lost, the results leap to the eye. In figures 5.15 and 5.16, from *The Bedroom Window* (1924), William C. deMille's practice of multiple-camera shooting has pushed the shots off-center and off-balance. Of course, such imbalance can be causally motivated, as in *Harvey* (1950), for which cinematographer William Daniels had to frame the shots asymmetrically to include the invisible rabbit.[10] The value of balance in the classical cinema can be seen in the way that a vacancy in the frame space will be reserved for the entry of a character; that figure will complete the balanced composition (see figs 5.17 through 5.19).

Both centering and balancing function as narration in that these film techniques shape the story action for the spectator. The narrational qualities of shot composition are also evident in the classical use of frontality. Renaissance painting derived many principles of scenography from Greek and Roman theater, so that the idea of a narrative action addressed to the spectator became explicit in Western painting. The classical film image relies upon such a conception of frontality. The face is positioned in full, three-quarter, or profile view; the body typically in full or three-quarter view. The result is an odd rubbernecking characteristic of Hollywood character position; people's heads may face one another in profile but their bodies do not (see figs 5.20 and 5.21). Standing groups are arranged along horizontal or diagonal lines or in half-circles; people seldom close ranks as they would in real life (see figs 5.22 and 5.23). The dyspeptic Welford Beaton was one of the few critics who noticed this practice:[11]

> In most of our pictures the directors make their characters face the camera by the simple expedient of turning them around until they face it, no matter how unnatural the scene is made thereby. In *Gentlemen Prefer Blondes* [1928], there is an exhibition of flagrant disregard of common sense in grouping characters. Ruth Taylor, Alice White, and Ford Sterling are shown seated at a round table in a

restaurant. Instead of forming a triangle, they are squeezed together so closely that Sterling, in the center, scarcely can move.

Yet complete frontality – e.g., direct address to the camera – is rare; a modified frontality requires that a wedge be driven into the space, opening up the best sightlines.

Frontality constitutes a very important cue for the viewer. When characters have their backs to us, it is usually an index of their relative unimportance at the moment. George Cukor points out a scene from *Adam's Rib* (1949) in which Katharine Hepburn was turned from the camera: 'That had a meaning: she indicated to the audience that they should look at Judy Holliday.'[12] Groupings around tables often sacrifice a good view of the least significant character in the scene. One UnS film, *Saratoga* (1937) vividly illustrates how troubled the film's space becomes when frontality is disrupted. Jean Harlow died in the course of the film's production, before several scenes were shot. In those scenes, Harlow was replaced by a double who never faces the camera, resulting in the odd phenomenon of having no portrayal of the heroine's expressions during climactic moments of the action.

Most important, frontality can be lost if it is then regained. Over-the-shoulder shot/reverse-shot cutting decenters a figure and puts his or her back to us, but the reverse shot reinstates that character front and center. Once the figures are arranged for us in the image, editing can introduce new angles, but then closer shots will typically be centered, balanced, and frontal in their turn. Even if one minimizes editing, as Orson Welles and William Wyler are often thought to do, the deep-focus composition cannot forfeit frontality – indeed, in films like *The Magnificent Ambersons* (1942) and *The Little Foxes* (1941), classical frontality is in fact exaggerated (see figs 5.24 and 5.25).

The most obvious way that the classical cinema works to treat the screen as a plate-glass window is in the representation of depth. Probably the most important depth cue in cinema is movement. When a figure moves and creates a continuous stream of overlapping planes and receding shapes, when the camera glides through or across a space – under these circumstances it becomes very difficult to see the screen as a flat surface. This is

perhaps one of the reasons that modernist and avant-garde films have often suppressed the kinetic depth effect by such devices as flicker, still images, and graininess.

Classical Hollywood space is created in planes through various depth cues. To the usual cues of visual overlap (the object that overlaps must be closer) and familiar size, the classical image adds pattern, color, texture, lighting, and focus to specify depth. Geometrical patterns and colors, especially of costumes, stand out from plainer backgrounds (see figs 5.26 and 5.27). Even in black-and-white filming, set designers painted sets in different colors to create planes in depth.[13] More dense and concentrated textures were reserved for the figures in the foreground, and cinematographers would diffuse the light on backgrounds to make them more granular. Lighting is particularly important in establishing depth. Cinematographers were careful to alternate planes in contrasting keys and half-tones (a silhouetted foreground, a bright middle ground, a darker background).[14] Hollywood's standardized three-point lighting system (key, fill, and backlighting), supplemented by background lighting, eye lights, and other techniques, had as its effect the careful articulation of each narratively relevant plane. The importance of backlighting cannot be overestimated here. Commonly thought of as a Griffith cliché or a sudden lyrical effect, back-lighting is in fact one of the most common ways the Hollywood filmmaker distinguishes figure from background: A pencil-line of light around the body's contour pulls the figure forward (see figs 5.28 and 5.29).[15] Edge lighting of figures remained common even after fast film stocks and color films enhanced figure separation (see fig 5.30). Low-key lighting could be very effective in picking out planes if edge-lighting supplemented it (see fig 5.31). Finally, the planes of the classical image also usually get defined by selective focus, an equivalent of aerial perspective in painting. In framings closer than medium shot, the characters are in focus while other planes are not.[16] Variations are possible – in deep-space compositions, a figure in the foreground might be out of focus while another in the background is in focus – but the principle generally holds good. No classical films throw figures out of focus to favor insignificant objects (kegs, stoves) in the manner of Ozu's films or of certain avant-garde works.[17]

Stacked planes are not enough; the classical style stresses volumes as well. Cinematographers valued 'roundness' as much as depth, using highlights to accentuate curves of face and body or to pick out folds in drapery.[18] As early as 1926, the cinematographer was compared to the sculptor:[19]

> It is chiefly by the use of such lighting equipment that the sculptor-director seeks his worshipped 'plasticity.' Failing a true stereoscopic effect in film, he models his figures to a roundness with lights behind and above and on either side, softening here and sharpening up for accent elsewhere with a patience and skill inevitably lost on the layman.

Make-up was designed to enhance the roundness of faces. Likewise, a set had to be represented as a volume, a container for action, not a row of sliced planes. Designers often built three-dimensional models of sets in order to try out various camera positions. Even the ceiling, which usually could not be shown, had to be implied through shadow.[20] Camera movement could endow the set with a sculptural quality too, as Dwan observed: 'In dollying as a rule we find it's a good idea to *pass* things in order to get the effect of movement. We always noticed that if we dollied past a tree, it became solid and round, instead of flat.'[21]

The importance of planes and volumes in defining classical scenographic depth makes academic perspective rather rare. Developed during the Renaissance as a revision of ancient Greek perspective, central linear perspective organizes planes around the presumed vantage point of a stationary monocular observer. The impression of depth results from the assumption that parallel lines receding from the picture surface seem to meet at a single point on the horizon, the vanishing point.[22] Now it is indisputable that certain aspects of Hollywood film production, such as set design and special-effects work, frequently draw upon principles of linear perspective.[23] But images in the Hollywood cinema seldom exhibit the central vanishing point, raked and checkered floorplans, and regular recession of planes characteristic of what Pierre Francastel calls the 'Quattrocento cube.'[24] (Such conventions are far more common in pre-classical

films; see fig 5.32.) The classical shot is more usually built out of a few planes placed against a distant background plane – in a long shot, the horizon; in a closer view, the rear wall of a room (see figs 5.33 and 5.34). A limited linear perspective view can be supplied by the corner of a room or ceiling or the view out of a window. Sometimes, especially in 1940s films, a more explicit sense of perspective emerges; an occasional establishing shot exhibits a deep recessional interior (see fig 5.35) or a skewed vanishing point (see fig 5.36). But in medium-long and medium shots (the majority of the shots in a film), linear perspective remains of little importance, and pronounced depth is achieved by interposing figures and objects on various planes.

Such art-historical traditions would not seem easily applicable to the scenographic space constructed by the soundtrack. But the classical cinema modeled its use of sound upon its use of images. (Chapter 23 examines how this occurred historically.) As one technician wrote:[25]

> With the two-dimensional camera, which bears the same psychological relation to the eye as monaural sound does to the ear, the illusion of depth can be achieved by the proper use of lighting and contrast, just as by the manipulations of loudness and reverberation with the microphone. And just as the eye can be drawn to particular persons or objects by the adjustment of focal length, so can the ear be arrested by the intensification of important sounds and the rejection of unimportant ones.

What Hollywood technicians called 'sound perspective' was the belief that the acoustic qualities of dialogue and noise had to match the scale of the image. Engineers debated how to convey 'natural' sound while granting that strictly realistic sound recording was unsuitable. Microphones had to be rotated in the course of conversations; musical numbers had to be prerecorded; some dialogue had to be post-synchronized; and, most importantly, sounds had to be segregated onto separate tracks for later mixing. In the theater, the speakers were placed behind the screen, as centered as were the figures in the frame. The same conceptions of balance, centrality, and spatial definition were applied to stereophonic sound in the early 1950s.[26]

Thus in the Hollywood cinema the space constructed by the soundtrack is no less artificial than that of the image. Alan Williams points out that like visual perspective, sonic perspective is narrational, yielding not 'the full, material context of everyday vision or hearing, but *the signs of* such a physical situation.'[27] He shows how selective the sonic space of a Hollywood locale is in comparison with that of the racket-filled café in Godard's *Two or Three Things I Know About Her* (1966). Similar effects occur in the dense, layered montage of offscreen sound in Rainer Werner Fassbinder's *Third Generation* (1980) and *In a Year of Thirteen Moons* (1980), during which radios, television sets, and several conversations compete for our attention. In this sense, classical sound technique articulates foreground (principal voice) and background (silence, 'background' noise, music 'under' the action) with the same precision that camera and staging distinguish visual planes.

Centering, balancing, frontality, and depth – all these narrational strategies – encourage us to read filmic space as story space. Since the classical narrative depends upon psychological causality, we can think of these strategies as aiming to *personalize* space. Surroundings become significant partly for their ability to dramatize individuality. Hence the importance of doors: the doorway becomes a privileged zone of human action, promising movement, encounters, confrontations, and conclusions. The classical film also charges objects with personal meanings. Props (guns, rings, etc.), and especially representational props (photographs, dolls, portrait paintings) all bear an ineluctable psychological import. (How many classical films convey a lover's disgust by violence against the picture of the beloved.) Shot scale is also geared to expressivity, with the *plan américain* (the knees-up shot) and the medium shot the most common ones because they 'retain facial expressions and physical gestures – partially lost in the long shot – and relate these, dramatically, to the action involved.'[28] A close-up, which can theoretically show anything, becomes virtually synonymous with the facial close-up, the portrait that reveals character. It is significant, however, that *extreme* facial close-ups – framings closer than full facial shots - are almost absent from the classical cinema, as if cutting the face completely free of

the background made the close-up too fragmentary. (Compare the frequency of enlarged portions of faces in the Soviet cinema of the 1920s.) Lighting brings out the personality of the character, while diffusion distinguishes women by spiritualizing them.[29] In the sound cinema, the voice parallels the face as a vehicle of personalization. In all these ways, the classical cinema declares its anthropocentric commitment: Space will signify chiefly in relation to psychological causality.

Classical narration of space thus aims at orientation: The scenography is addressed to the viewer. Can we then say that a larger principle of 'perspective' operates here – not the adherence to a particular spatial composition but a general 'placing' of the spectator in an ideal position of intelligibility?[30] Certainly Hollywood's own description of its work emphasizes the camera as an invisible witness, just as the soundtrack constitutes an ideal hearing of the scene. This aesthetic of effaced present is anthropocentric (camera and sound as eye and ear) and idealist (the witness is immaterial, an omniscient subject), hence also ideological. Yet the viewer is not wholly a passive subject tyrannized by a rigid address. Analogies with perspective, being spatial, tend to neglect the spectator's activities. Just as the viewer must meet causal and temporal systems halfway, the viewer must contribute something in order to make classical space work. That contribution includes the sort of hypothesis-forming and -testing that I have emphasized in earlier chapters. That we tend to anticipate data, that we frame our hunches as more or less likely alternatives (or paradigmatic choices), that we retroactively check our hypotheses – all these activities operate in our construction of classical space.

So, for instance, centering procedures quickly lead the viewer to perform certain operations. Confining significant narrative action to any constant zone of screen space effectively insures that attention paid to other areas will not be rewarded. Moreover, psychologists have long known that it is hard to read a configuration as three-dimensional if we are markedly aware of the edges of the image: our eye tests for consistency, and the depth of the represented space conflicts with the boundary of the picture.[31] Centered film compositions, either static or moving, draw our attention away from the frame edge. Even the viewing situation encourages this, since black masking on the theater screen conceals the aperture line. Cinematographers often darkened the edges of the image to avoid a glaring contrast between the picture and the theater masking.[32] Distracting our attention from the edge thus discourages us from testing the image as a flat space. Compare, however, the flattening effect of edge-framed compositions in non-Hollywood traditions (see fig 5.37).

Similarly, frontality functions as a strong cue for the spectator. Since the classical Hollywood cinema is predominantly anthropocentric, the representation of the expressive body arouses in us an interest nourished not only by art but by everyday life. Our principal information about people's mental states is derived in large part from posture, gesture, facial expression, and eye movement (as well as voice), so that if classical cinema is to represent psychological causation in its characters, narrational space must privilege these behavioral cues. Moreover, as Gombrich points out, some objects give a more exact feeling of frontality than do others. We are remarkably sensitive to anglings of body, face, and especially eyes, and we tend to orient ourselves to postures and gazes with a precision that we do not apply to walls or trees.[33] In addition, of course, 'normal' camera height, standardized at between 5 and 6 feet, corresponds to a gaze from an erect human body, a position canonized not only in art but also in culture generally.[34] Imagine a classical film with only one difference: it is entirely shot from straight above the characters. The consistent bird's-eye view would destroy the expressive basis of the narrative because the classical filmmaker lacks schemata for rendering such an orientation and the film viewer has no appropriate repertoire of expectations.

And what of the spectator's construction of depth? The various depth cues, most prominently movement, require an act of spatial integration on the viewer's part. If classical space does not pose the visual paradoxes of images in some German Expressionistic cinema or in abstract film, that is partly because we scale our expectations to a limited set of possibilities. But consider the baffling space of figure 5.38, from Griffith's *Trying to Get Arrested* (1909). A tiny man runs in at the lower left corner. The cue of familiar size

dictates that he looks small because he is far away, but the receding planes of the shot seem to deny this. Is the man then a leprechaun? No, he is indeed in the distance, as a later frame (fig 5.39) makes clear. The peculiarity of this primitive shot arises from the way the image foils those expectations about planes and volumes that the classical cinema would have confirmed by composition and framing. Certainly seeing an image as deep is 'easier' in cinema than in other arts, but even film depth must be *achieved* to some degree, relying upon what Gombrich has called 'the beholder's share.'[35]

Continuity editing

Theorists are still a long way from fully understanding how the viewer contributes to the creation of classical space, but some consideration of the process of editing may help. Certainly editing can work against the orientation achieved within the image, as it does in the films of Eisenstein, Ozu, Nagisa Oshima, Godard, and other filmmakers.[36] Classical continuity editing, however, reinforces spatial orientation. Continuity of graphic qualities can invite us to look through the 'plate-glass window' of the screen. From shot to shot, tonality, movement, and the center of compositional interest shift enough to be distinguishable but not enough to be disturbing. Editors seldom discussed graphic continuity, but the procedure was explained as early as 1928 by two visitors to the Hollywood studios, who claimed that either the point of interest in shot B should be on the screen 'almost' where the point of interest of shot A ended, or B should continue A's movement:[37]

This has no reference to the story itself, but merely to the making of the pictures considered only as spots of colour and centres of pictorial interest. The eye should be led a gentle dance, swaying easily and comfortably from side to side of the picture, now fast, now slow, as the emotional needs of the story demand.

Compare the graphically gentle cut of the typical shot/reverse-shot series, which only slightly shifts the center of interest (see figs 5.40 through 5.43) with the graphically jarring cut which alters that center of interest quite drastically (see figs 5.44 and 5.45).

Once graphic continuity is achieved, the editing can concentrate upon orienting us to scenographic space. Crosscutting creates a fictive space built out of several locales. As Chapter 4 points out, classical crosscutting presupposes that shifts in the locale are motivated by the story action. More often, editing fulfills the narrational function of orienting us to a single locale (a room, a stretch of sidewalk, the cab of a truck) or to physically adjacent locales (a room and a hallway, the rear of the truck). Thus the principles and devices of continuity editing function to represent space for the sake of the story.

André Bazin has summarized the basic premises of classical continuity editing:[38]

1 The verisimilitude of the space in which the position of the actor is always determined, even when a close-up eliminates the decor.
2 The purpose and the effects of the cut are exclusively dramatic or psychological.
In other words, if the scene were played on a stage and seen from a seat in the orchestra, it would have the same meaning, the episode would continue to exist objectively. The changes of point of view provided by the camera would add nothing. They would present the reality a little more forcefully, first by allowing a better view and then by putting the emphasis where it belongs.

Besides spelling out the classical assumptions about consistent spatial relations and the determining role of character psychology, Bazin reveals the extent to which classical editing continues and elaborates the scenography of nineteenth-century bourgeois theater. Bazin's mobile-yet-stationary spectator in the orchestra personifies the viewpoint created by the classical '180°' or 'axis-of-action' system of spatial editing. The assumption is that shots will be filmed and cut together so as to position the spectator always on the same side of the story action. Bazin suggests that the 'objective' reality of the action independent of the act of filming is analogous to that stable space of proscenium theatrical representation, in which the spectator is always positioned beyond the fourth wall. The axis of action (or center line) becomes the imaginary

vector of movements, character positions, and glances in the scene, and ideally the camera should not stray over the axis. In any scene, explains Robert Aldrich, 'You have to draw the center line. . . . You must never cross the line.'[39] If we assume that two conversing characters are angled somewhat frontally (as is usual), the classic 180° system will be as laid out in diagram 5.1. Camera positions A, B, C, and D (and indeed any position within the lower half-circle) will cut together so as to orient the viewer, while camera position X (or any position on the other side of the center line) is thought to disorient the spectator.

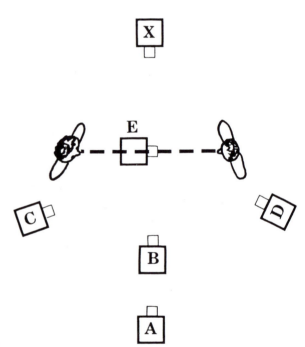

The 180° principle governs all the more specific devices of continuity editing. *Analytical* editing moves the spectator into or back from a part of a total space. A cut from position A to position B (or vice versa) would be an analytical cut, respecting the axis of action. *Shot/reverse-shot* cutting assumes that the series of shots alternates a view of one end-point of the line with a view of the other. Thus cutting from camera position C to that of D would be a shot/reverse-shot pattern. Typically, shot/reverse-shot editing joins shots of characters facing one another, but it need not.

The same principle applies to vehicles, buildings, or any entities posited as being at opposite ends of the axis of action. *Eyeline-match* cutting uses character glance as a cue to link shots. The assumption is that the eyeline runs parallel to the axis, so the camera positions will remain on one side of the line. Shots C and D when cut together will yield correct eyeline matches in a way that, say, shots X and D would not. A comparatively uncommon case of eyeline-match cutting, *point-of-view* cutting, reveals the limits of permissibility in the 180° system. The first shot shows the character looking at something offscreen; the second shot shows what the character is seeing, but more or less from the character's optical vantage point. Remarkably, critics continue to reduce shot/reverse-shot cutting to point-of-view cutting. A recent monograph defines shot/reverse shot in a conversation scene as taking the second shot 'from the first character's point-of-view.'[40] Hollywood shot/reverse-shot cutting is more properly what Jean Mitry calls *semi*-subjective: we are often literally looking over a character's shoulder.[41] (Edward Branigan has shown that camera angle is the critical variable here: camera distance is often inexact in classical point-of-view cutting.[42]) But even the point-of-view shot remains within the 180° convention because it represents a camera position *on the axis itself* (e.g., position E on the diagram). The power of the 180° system may also be seen in what we may call the 'earline-match' cut, in which a character listens from outside the space of the scene. The assumption is that the sound travels in a straight line, which constitutes the axis of action. If a listener at a door cocks his ear to screen left, a cut to someone inside the room walking to that door must show the character moving screen right.

Obviously, across a series of shots all these editing devices work smoothly to reinforce each other, so that an establishing shot will be linked by an analytical cut to a closer view, and then a series of shot/reverse shots will follow. But the system, being part of a stylistic paradigm, has a certain latitude as well, so that one can use the shot/reverse-shot schema if one character has turned his back to the other, if there are five or six characters present, and so on.

One more device of the 180° system deserves mention, not least because it dramatizes the extent to which the system defines a coherent but limited field for the spectator. Editing for *directional* continuity translates the imaginary line into a vector of movement. If a character or vehicle is moving left to right in shot 1, it should continue to do so in shot 2. Directional continuity cutting is like eyeline cutting: just as two shots of figures looking in opposite directions imply that the figures are looking at each other, so two shots of figures moving in opposite directions lead us to expect the figures to meet. Directional continuity also resembles point-of-view cutting in that one can show the movement from a position *on* the axis of action – i.e., either a heads-on or a tails-on shot of the action. (A shot from this position can function as a transition if one wants to cross the line.) Directional continuity is often used within a circumscribed space, as when a character goes from the window (exit frame left) and comes to the desk (enter frame right). In these cases, Hollywood directional continuity depends upon the frame cut. What is more revealing, though, is that directional continuity can be maintained across separate spaces, for in that case the 180° system presupposes that the ideal spectator is situated on one side of an axis perhaps miles long! The closed chamber-space of the theater has been left behind, but Bazin's spectator-in-the-orchestra and his or her relation to proscenium space remain intact.

The devices of continuity editing are best seen as traditional schemata which the classical filmmaker can impose upon any subject. As King Vidor wrote: 'The filmmaker should be consciously aware of this 180° rule throughout the whole field of film action. It is not only beneficial in sports, but in chase sequences, with cowboys, Indians and cavalry, animal pursuits, moon landings, dinner-table conversations, and a thousand other movie subjects.'[43] Most film critics are aware of these schemata but consider them simply a neutral vehicle for the filmmaker's idiosyncratic themes or 'personal vision.' What makes the continuity devices so powerful is exactly their apparent neutrality; compositional motivation has codified them to a degree of rigidity that is still hard to realize. In each UnS film, less than 2 per cent of the shot-changes violated spatial continuity, and one-fifth of the films contained not a single violation. No wonder that, of all Hollywood stylistic practices, continuity editing has been considered a set of firm rules.

As with other classical techniques, continuity editing cues form a redundant paradigm. Conventional 180° editing assumes that the establishing shot *and* the eyeline match cut *and* directional continuity of movement *and* the shot/reverse-shot schema will all be present to 'overdetermine' the scenographic space. The redundancy of the paradigm becomes evident when we watch a non-classical filmmaker simply remove one or two cues. In Dreyer's *Day of Wrath* (1943), the characters' eyelines in medium shot often violate the 180° axis, but there are frequent establishing shots to orient us. Conversely, in Bresson's *Procès de Jeanne d'Arc* (1961), the eyelines respect the axis of action, but scenes frequently lack establishing shots.[44] In neither film do we lose our bearings (although, since each filmmaker exploits his devices systematically, the result is significantly different from the space of the classical scene).

What are the narrational consequences of spatial continuity editing? One answer might be based on a broad conception of perspective. In perpetuating the playing space of post-Renaissance bourgeois theater, classical editing makes the spectator an ideally placed onlooker. To paraphrase Bazin, the action and the viewer are separate ('the episode would continue to exist objectively'), yet the narration acknowledges the onlooker by implicitly addressing her or him ('by allowing a better view'). In sum, the intelligible orientation created within the single shot is kept consistent across shots by positing a spectator that can be moved only within the limits of a theatrical space of vision.

This account is certainly correct as far as it goes. Its drawbacks are the passivity it imputes to the spectator and its neglect of certain significant irregularities in the continuity system. For one thing, the space constructed by continuity editing is rarely a total one, even on the favored side of the axis of action. Not only do we seldom see the fourth wall of the typical interior, but areas immediately in front of the camera remain relatively undefined. Films of the late teens and the 1920s sometimes have holes in their scenographic space; the establishing shot may not show all adjacent areas from which characters may emerge. And Hollywood practitioners have long employed the aptly named 'cheat cut,' in which the shift of camera distance and angle during a cut covers a distinct change in character position (see figs 5.46 through 5.49). The cheat cut works to enhance balance, centering, or frontality:[45]

> 'Cheating' is the great game between the camera operator and the Continuity girl. To compose a foreground or a background the operator will sometimes move or substitute objects, or have the artiste raised or lowered in relation to his surroundings. Actually, after a long while in pictures, I realised that such 'cheating' is seldom noticeable to an audience, but in the studio it often seems fantastic.

The viewer's willingness to ignore unshown areas of space and to overlook cheat cuts suggests that the viewer actively forms and tests specific hypotheses about the space revealed by the narration. The always-present pockets of non-established space are, in the absence of cues to the contrary, assumed to be consistent with what we see. (We assume that there is more wall, a door, etc.) If a technician or a lighting unit peeped into the shot, that would provoke us to revise such assumptions. The cheat cut suggests that a process of hierarchical selection is at work. Since we are to attend to story causality, the fact that a character is first three feet and then suddenly two feet from another character becomes unimportant if our expectations about the action are confirmed from shot to shot. Of course, there are limits to how much the cut can cheat before the operation distracts us from story causality, and these warrant psychophysical study.[46]

Our hierarchical selection of what to watch is evident from the very schemata of classical cutting. For example, the repetition of camera position becomes very important. Typically, any classical series of shots will include several identical camera set-ups. The reestablishing shot will usually be from the same angle and distance as the establishing shot; shot and reverse-shot framings may be repeated several times. Such repetitions encourage us to ignore the cutting itself and notice only those narrative factors that change from shot to shot. In a similar way, the first occurrence of a set-up often 'primes' us for a later action. In *The Caddy* (1953), Harvey hides from dogs in a locker room. A *plan américain* reveals him leaning on the door; on the right of the frame are clothes lying on a coat rack. Cut: the dogs outside the door wander off. The next shot repeats the *plan américain* of Harvey, but now Harvey notices the clothes. The first set-up unobtrusively asked us to hypothesize that Harvey would disguise himself, and the guess is confirmed by keeping set-ups constant. A similar process occurs in figures 5.50 through 5.53. This priming of later actions does not occur in films by Eisenstein and Godard, for instance, who seldom exactly repeat set-ups and who thus demand that we reorient ourselves after every cut.

The phenomenon of priming illustrates Gombrich's point that schemata set the horizon of the viewer's expectations. Classical editing is organized paradigmatically, since any shot leads the viewer to infer a limited set of more or less probable successors. For example, an establishing shot can cut away to another space or cut in to a closer shot; the latter alternative is more likely. An angled medium shot of a character or object is usually followed by a corresponding reverse shot. Cutting around within a locale is most likely to be based upon eyeline matches and upon shot/reverse-shot patterns, less likely to be based upon figure movement, and least likely to be based upon optical point-of-view. (In this respect, Hitchcock relies upon point-of-view cutting to an almost unique degree.) The classical construction of space thus participates in the process of hypothesis-forming that we saw at work in narration generally. Julian Hochberg compares the viewer's construction of edited space to 'cognitive mapping': 'The task of the filmmaker therefore is to make the viewer pose a visual question, and then answer it for him.'[47]

The process of viewer expectation is particularly apparent in the flow of onscreen and offscreen space. Consider again the shot/reverse-shot schema. The first image, say a medium shot of Marilyn, implies an offscreen field, foreshadowing (by its angle, scale, and character glance) what could most probably succeed it. The next shot in the series, a reverse-angled view of Douglas, reveals the narratively significant material which occupies that offscreen zone. Shot two makes sense as an answer to its predecessor. This backing-and-filling movement, opening a spatial gap and then plugging it, accords well with the aims of classical narration. Furthermore, shot/reverse-shot editing helps make narration covert by creating the sense that no important scenographic space remains unaccounted for. If shot two shows the important material outside shot one, there is no spatial point we can assign to the narration; the narration is always elsewhere, outside this shot but never visible in the next. This process, which evidently is at work in camera movement and analytical cutting as well, is consistent with that unself-conscious but omnipresent narration described in Chapter 3.[48]*

Classical offscreen space thus functions as what Gombrich calls a 'screen,' a blank area which invites the spectator to project hypothetical elements on to it.[49] Given classical viewing priorities, we are more concerned with the distinct persons and things visible within space than with the spaces between and around them. If a shot shows a person or object that was implicit in the previous shot, we check the new material against our projection rather than measuring the amount of space left out. Since Hollywood scenography seldom represents a locale in its entirety, we must construct a spatial whole out of bits. And if those bits not only overlap in what they show but agree with the fields we have inferred to be lying offscreen, we will not notice the fuzzy areas that have never been strictly accounted for. Classical editing supports orientation according to Gombrich's negative principle of perspective: A convincing image need not show everything in the space as long as nothing we see actually contradicts what we expect.[50] If classical cinema makes the screen a plate-glass window, it is partly because it turns a remarkably coherent spatial system into the vehicle of narrative causality; but it is also because the viewer, having learned distinct perceptual and cognitive activities, meets the film halfway and completes the illusion of seeing an integral fictional space.

Shot and scene

From montage to découpage

> O Minotaur, here is your Ariadne's thread: decoupage.[1]
>
> André Bazin

Part by part, brick by brick: the Hollywood cinema often evokes metaphors from architecture and masonry. What Soviet filmmakers of the 1920s called *montage* – shot-assembling as the basic constructional activity – Hollywood filmmakers called cutting or editing, terms associated with trimming off unwanted material. The best term for the Hollywood practice is another French one, *découpage*: the parceling out of images in accordance with the script, the mapping of the narrative action onto the cinematic material. This decoupage became standardized in sheerly quantitative terms. In production, scriptwriters were expected to be able to estimate scenes in advance, and one specific production role – the timer – existed to provide exact calculations of a script's total running time. As T.W. Adorno proposes: 'It is a justification of quantitative methods that the products of the culture industry, secondhand popular culture, are themselves planned from a virtually statistical point of view. Quantitative analysis measures them by their own standard.'[2]

For Hollywood, the shot is the basic unit of material. But this unit of material is already a unit of meaning. Before 1950, technicians usually called a shot a 'scene,' defining the strip of images as a narrative action. The shot was also Hollywood's basic unit of production. Chapter 11 will show how, after 1913, the development of the classical mode of film production depended upon the continuity script, which made the shot the minimal unit of planning. Once the story was divided into shots, the planning of the shooting could begin. The filmmakers could tick off the shots one by one as they were completed. Rehearsals of entire scenes were uncommon, since the actors' performances were constructed wholly in the editing. Using long takes was discouraged, since a paucity of shots took crucial decisions about timing and emphasis out of producers' and editors' hands. The routine procedure of making shots also tended to standardize and limit the ways each shot was handled. The Soviet cinematographer Vladimir Nilsen criticized the American method for fetishizing the shot as an end in itself rather than as part of a total editing unit.[3]

The shot became the brick which built the film long before 1915, but with the help of our Unbiased Sample we can distinguish some significant quantitative developments. It would be possible to compute some general statistical norms, as Barry Salt has done in his discussion of average shot lengths, but such abstractions mean little without a concept of the range of paradigmatic choice dominant at a given period.[4] For instance, in the years 1915–16, a feature film (itself often only seventy-five minutes long) might contain as few as 240 shots or as many as 1000. The most common range was between 250 and 450 shots per film, or (at 16 frames per second) about 275-325 shots per hour. (In all figures for the silent cinema, inter-titles are counted as shots. Throughout the years 1915-1928, inter-titles comprised around 15 per cent of the total number of shots per film.) To say, then, that the average shot length of films of the years 1915-16 was about twelve to thirteen seconds is true but misleading. The crucial point is that a director or cutter had a specific range of choices and constraints: no feature film would contain fewer than two hundred shots and only a very few, such as Walsh's *Regeneration* (1915), might have over five hundred.

After 1916, however, the paradigmatic choices and constraints shifted drastically. A film would be composed of many more shots, and the shots would be significantly shorter. The typical Hollywood feature film of the years 1917-28 contained between 500 and 1000 shots, with never fewer than 400 and seldom more than 1300. While the average shot length (ASL) can thus be considered to be between five and seven seconds, what is more significant is the sharp widening of paradigmatic choice. A filmmaker might employ anything between 360 and 900 shots per hour, the most common range being 500-800 shots per hour. The increase in cutting rhythm has causes which will be discussed in Chapter 16, but one effect was to broaden the filmmakers' options. A Douglas Fairbanks or Erich von Stroheim film might have an ASL of around three seconds, while Maurice Tourneur might rely on much longer takes (an average of ten seconds in *Victory [1919]).

Our intuitive assumption is that the cutting rate slowed with the introduction of sound, and to some extent the belief is correct. The ASL of the period 1929-60 is ten to eleven seconds, twice that of the classical silent decade. But this alone cannot reveal the ways in which the paradigmatic range changed with the coming of sound. The typical film of the sound era contained between 300 and 700 shots, or between 200 and 500 shots per hour. This afforded only slightly less choice than the range of the classical silent period. Normal practice between 1917 and 1928 gave the filmmaker a leeway of 'plus or minus' 300 shots per hour, while sound-period practice yielded a leeway of 250 more or less. Furthermore, the breadth of the paradigm increased after 1928; if no sound film could be cut as fast as, say, von Stroheim's *Wedding March* (1928; ASL, 3.7 seconds), the range of permissible shot lengths was none the less greater. A sound film could have an ASL of five seconds (*Indianapolis Speedway* [1939]) or an ASL of thirty-seven seconds (*Caravan* [1934]). Films of comparable length might employ 600 shots (*The Locket* [1946]) or 177 shots (*Fallen Angel* [1945]).

Similarly, we tend to assume that the typical shot got longer during the sound era. The history of average shot lengths bears this out, but only at the expense of ignoring the wide range of alternatives that were always available. During the years 1929 to 1934, the mean ASL in the Unbiased Sample was eleven seconds, which corresponds to common intuitions about lugubrious cutting pace in the early sound period. But this average is derived from a set of films with ASLs ranging from 6.3 seconds (*Housewife [1934]) to 14 seconds (*Applause [1929], *Penthouse [1933]). The Extended Sample is even more revealing, indicating that between 1929 and 1934 filmmakers could choose to use anything between 170 and 600 shots per hour. Some contemporary sources confirm these figures. Several writers claim 200-500 shots as normal for an early 1930s film. A 1937 source cites ten seconds as appropriate for a typical shot.[5] The average cutting rate speeds up a little in the years 1935-46 (ASL 9 seconds) and slows down between 1947 and 1960 (ASL 11-12 seconds), but the range of choice remains constant: many films favor short shots (7-8 seconds), many favor medium-length shots (9-11 seconds), and others favor longer takes (12-14 seconds). (The UnS average in the years 1947-60 is skewed by a few films with very long takes; it is in the post-1946 period that the UnS registers the first feature films since 1917 to contain fewer than 300 shots. So the general belief that long-take filming became more common in the postwar period is warranted, but both the UnS and the ES suggest that it was by no means the dominant practice.) Even in 1957, during the presumed heyday of widescreen long takes, one CinemaScope film might have 200 shots per hour (*Young and Dangerous*), another 267 (*Interlude), another 450 (*Fire Down Below). A 1959 widescreen film, *Journey to the Center of the Earth*, could have an ASL of around six seconds, the same as that of a 1931 Warners' film, *Dangerous Female*. If the paradigm's center of gravity shifted somewhat in the course of the sound era, the overall breadth of choice was hardly affected.

Like the shot, the Hollywood sequence is more a narrative entity than a material one. The consensus among contemporary theorists is that the classical sequence possesses the Aristotelian unities of duration, locale, and 'action,' and that it is marked at each end by some standardized punctuation (dissolve, fade, wipe).[6] This rough description serves us well if we remember that each film establishes its own scale of segmentation. In *One Frightened Night* (1935), the action sets up a very limited duration within a single setting (a mansion), so slight lapses of time (usually signaled by wipes) and shifts of locale (from room to room) constitute significant breaks between sequences. But in *An American Romance* (1944), which spans several decades and jumps across the country, the same shifts in time and space do not mark new sequences. For instance, after Anton explains to Steve where the coal goes, the shot dissolves to the two men walking out of the mine; the lapse of time is as brief as that between scenes in *One Frightened Night*, but in this context only longer intervals demarcate separate scenes. Most classical films are overwhelmingly clear about the appropriate time scale for distinguishing among sequences.

Shortly I shall examine the classical sequence's internal structure. At this point, I am concerned only with external aspects of decoupage. How many sequences make up a classical film? How many shots does a sequence typically contain?

Again, comparing the silent era with the sound period reveals differences in the range of paradigmatic choices. Between 1917 and 1928, the ordinary Hollywood film contained between nine and eighteen sequences (not including the credits sequence), with a tendency for a film to have somewhat more sequences before 1921 than after. In the same period, the typical segment contained between forty and ninety shots and ran from four to eight minutes. In the period 1928-60, however, the available alternatives shifted. A sound film would most commonly contain between fourteen and thirty-five sequences. The typical sound sequence was composed of between twelve and thirty shots and ran from two to five minutes. Thus while shot lengths increased with the introduction of sound, the number of sequences in a Hollywood film almost doubled and the duration of those sequences roughly halved. (It can be argued that the dynamic rhythm of editing in the silent film was, after 1933, regained to some degree by a swift succession of short scenes.) There is also some historical variation: post-1946 films tend to have more sequences than their predecessors, and post-1952 films average somewhat fewer shots per sequence. What is more important, though, is that the sound decoupage paradigm was very flexible; a sound film might have six sequences or sixty, a scene might run one minute or ten, and a sequence might contain a great many shots.

Claude Chabrol once remarked that where an MGM editor would use four shot/reverse shots, a Universal editor would use eight.[7] The UnS, taken with the ES, suggests that in fact decoupage varied only a little from studio to studio. In the silent period, films from Douglas Fairbanks's and Harold Lloyd's units have unusually short shots. Undoubtedly, the average Warner Bros film of the 1930s is cut faster than its mate elsewhere. There was also a tendency for MGM and Paramount films to have slightly longer ASLs. On the whole, however, studio differences are minimal. Nor is genre a differentiating factor; there is no clear tendency for, say, musicals to have a longer ASL or for comedies to have a shorter one.

Generally, ASL varies somewhat more consistently among directors. Certain directors habitually used comparatively long takes throughout a film: Maurice Tourneur, John Stahl, Josef Von Sternberg, Buster Keaton, W.S. Van Dyke, Vincente Minnelli, William Wyler, William Dieterle, and Otto Preminger. Directors with an unusually rapid editing rhythm include D.W. Griffith, Erich von Stroheim, Mervyn LeRoy, Lloyd Bacon, and (despite the tours de force of *Rope* [1948] and *Under Capricorn* [1949]) Alfred Hitchcock. A few films inevitably stand out. *Caravan* (1934), directed by Erik Charrell, has only 160 shots; the ASL of thirty-seven seconds is due to spectacular camera movement. Contrariwise, George Stevens's *Shane* (1953) is remarkable for averaging 720 shots per hour (even if this rapid cutting rate seems due chiefly to an inability to stage movement within a sustained shot).

In a broader perspective, all the historical, institutional, and individual variations are relatively minor. Whatever the options within the classical paradigm, certain constraints remained fixed. No Hollywood films have exploited either that radical use of short shots to be seen in Soviet films or that radical use of the long take to be seen in films by Jancsó, Dreyer, Marguerite Duras, Roberto Rossellini, and Kenji Mizoguchi. The very existence of the shot as a material unit has been questioned in films by Dziga Vertov, Michael Snow, Hollis Frampton, and other avantgarde filmmakers; in these works, superimpositions, single-frame sequences, and other strategies refuse to articulate shots as discrete units. In a similar way, work upon narrative or upon the soundtrack can break down our expectations about distinct sequences; Vertov's *Enthusiasm* (1930) and Godard's *Le gai savoir* (1969) pose problems of segmentation that the stable narrative relations of Hollywood film-making never raise.

Anatomy of the scene

Montage sequences, chase scenes, and extended passages of crosscutting are part of the classical paradigm, but the straightforward scene – one or more persons acting in a limited locale over a continuous duration; what Christian Metz calls the 'ordinary sequence' – remains the building block of classical dramaturgy.[8] A scene, one rule book says, is a series of shots 'naturally collected together, usually in the same or adjacent locales or sets'; here, durational continuity is assumed.[9] Yet, as Thierry Kuntzel has pointed out, the autonomy of the classical scene is a mixed one; the scene is both a detachable segment and a link in a chain.[10] As such, the scene can be taken as having two roughly distinct phases, the exposition and the development. These phases organize all the narrative systems at work – causality, time, and space.

In the scene's expository phase, narration specifies the time, place, and relevant characters. The time is assumed to be after the previous scene, unless otherwise indicated, and usually the preceding scene has stipulated when this scene must be occurring (a few minutes later, the next day). If not, an expository title, a montage sequence, or some indication at the start of the scene's action (e.g., calendar, clock, dialogue) will announce this scene's place in the film's time scheme.

The scene's locale will usually be indicated generally (e.g., an exterior shot of a building, or a sign), then specifically (the immediate site of the action). Multiple cues set to work: the locale will have been anticipated in an earlier scene, a long shot or medium-long shot will establish the totality of the relevant space, and sound and visual action will all cooperate in defining the locale. Signs ('Inspector Miller's Office') or telephone-answering (*Morning Post*) will also help. (Signs can be thought of as realistically motivated equivalents of the silent film's expository inter-title.) In a silent film, sometimes an expository 'art' title will establish the space, not only by naming it but by including a drawing of the locale. Typically, the space is a room, and the expositional phase of the scene will emphasize the room's furniture and its windows and doors. (In this respect, classical film reveals its debt to nineteenth-century theater.[11]) Ernst Lubitsch is reported to have said that the main character in his films was the door, but the claim has some broader validity, too.[12] Classical cinema is indeed 'door-knob cinema,' strongly reliant upon signaling character entrances and exits from an interior.

At the scene's start, the classical paradigm offers two ways of establishing the space: immediate or gradual. The narration may begin with a long shot that establishes the total space; this is by far the most common method. Most scenes in the UnS films start on an establishing long shot. Or the narration may begin the scene by showing only a portion of the space – a character, an object, a detail of decor, a door-way.[13] In this alternative, the scene will begin by framing a detail and then by means of various devices (dissolve, cut, iris, or tracking shot) will soon reveal the totality of the space. The establishing shot is simply delayed, seldom eliminated (as it often is in the films of Bresson, for instance). In locales that we know from previous scenes the narration may omit the establishing shot, though even in such instances establishing shots are more common than not.

The expository phase does not simply signal the locale, it places characters within it. The Hollywood screenplay format is revelatory here, in that it first indicates the place, then the time, and then the character action. (For specimens, see figs 12.9-12.12.) Space becomes chiefly a container for character action; the story has appropriated it. That a locale is of little interest in its own right is shown by the fact that typically the exposition of space takes up the least time of any phase of the scene (often less than twenty seconds and seldom more than thirty). By this point, the characters have taken over the narration.

The classical scene must immediately reveal two things about the characters: their relative spatial positions and their states of mind. The establishing shots should, while exposing the surroundings, also indicate where everyone is. Previous scenes and current demeanor and dialogue should reveal to us, if not to other characters, each participant's psychological state. Our hypothesis-building activity must be constantly fed and usually confirmed; if a character is furious with his opponent at the close of scene A but is meek and amiable at the beginning of scene B, we had better be quickly shown why the behavior has changed. The centrality of characters' interaction may incline the narration to begin with close shots of them. In *Love and the Law* (1919), after an art title establishes the overall locale (see fig 6.1), the scene begins with tight shots of the various characters – governor, McIlvaine, and Mina (see figs 6.2 through 6.5). Only after nine of these detail shots does the establishing shot appear (fig 6.6). The delay in revealing the total space is determined by the scene's role as a crisis in the plot. More commonly, however, the narration will establish the scene's space quickly and then plunge into the characters' relations. For example, following walking characters provides a common way to reveal space and to initiate character interaction. After the 1930s, a common strategy was to begin in a corridor or on a street, pan to follow a passing supernumerary, then pick up the main character, and follow that character until he or she encounters another character (e.g., figs 6.7 to 6.9).[14]

Hollywood practitioners recognized the scene's exposition to be as formulaic as I have indicated. Taking a hypothetical scene, two editors described the scene's opening as 'setting the stage – the introduction of the characters – their purpose in the scene – and their relation to each other.'[15] Or, as Howard Hawks put it offhandedly: 'You know which way the men are going to come in, and then you experiment and see where you're going to have Wayne sitting at a table, and then you see where the girl sits, and then in a few minutes you've got it all worked out, and it's perfectly simple, as far as I am concerned.'[16]

Once the central characters are picked out and their psychological states established, the developmental phase of the scene begins. Characters act toward their goals, enter into conflict, make choices, set deadlines, make appointments, and plan future actions. In general,

causal development shapes how time and space are represented.

Dramaturgically, the classical scene participates in two processes. First, it continues, develops, or closes off lines of cause and effect previously left open. If Paul has been trying to borrow money in the previous scene, this scene may show him still trying. Or the previous causal line may be completed; Paul gets his money. The classical scene's other duty is to open and perhaps develop at least one *new* causal chain. Against the backdrop of old lines of action, the scene initiates new conflicts, new goals, new questions. Once Paul has asked everyone he knows for money, he may decide to try stealing some; in the classical film, this decision will not be allocated a separate scene but will be introduced after an earlier line of action has been developed in the scene. It is important that at least one new line of action be suspended in the scene; it will become an old line for later scenes to develop or close off. Typically, only the film's last scene closes off all the lines of action.

What is noteworthy about the scene's continuation of old plot lines and the revelation of new ones is their rigorously formulaic quality. In *S/Z*, Barthes points out that the narrative text (*textus*, 'woven thing') is a fabric, in which the sequential codes are threaded together, suspended, then taken up again.[17] The Hollywood film reveals some such weaving, but of a simpler sort. Most scenes continue or close off the old line of action before starting the new one. Other scenes may reintroduce the old line, toy with it, suspend it again, introduce a new causal line, then close out the old and introduce yet another before the scene ends. Changes in lines of action are often punctuated by the entry or exit of characters or by slight shifts in locale (e.g., from room to room). Usually the new line will get final say in the scene (even if a motif or a brief reaction is the last thing actually presented). The new causal line thus motivates the shift to the next scene. The famous 'linearity' of classical Hollywood cinema thus consists of a linkage which resembles a game of dominoes, each dangling cause matched by its effect in the following scene. Diagrammed, the pattern looks like this:

$$\text{scene 1} \quad \text{scene 2} \quad \text{scene 3}$$
$$C_1 \longrightarrow \overbrace{E_1 C_2} \longrightarrow \overbrace{E_2 C_3} \longrightarrow \overbrace{E_3 C_4} \longrightarrow E_4 \qquad \text{etc.}$$

A simple example will illustrate how conventional such phases can be. In scene 6 of *The King and the Chorus Girl* (1937), Dorothy Ellis is brought to meet King Alfred, but he is in a drunken stupor, and she leaves, furious. When Alfred awakes and learns that an American chorus girl has spurned him, he indignantly orders 'eggs and ham – American style.' This bit of speech provides a dialogue hook to scene 7. The Count is speaking: 'Eggs and ham, that's what he said.' The camera tracks back to reveal the Count and the Duchess in Dorothy's room, telling her what happened after she left. The characters are thus established in space and time while the dangling cause is tied up; the whole process takes only seventeen seconds. After Dorothy asks why they insist that she go to Alfred, the scene returns to an old causal line. The Count and the Duchess explain that they need a girl of 'independent spirit' to keep Alfred from drinking. They explain that they've tried other women, but only Dorothy seems to have had the desired effect. This phase of the scene consumes thirty-eight seconds. Now the scene opens a new causal line. The Duchess begs Dorothy to have supper with Alfred tonight (appointment proposed). Dorothy agrees, but only if Alfred comes to fetch her. 'The independent spirit. That's what you want, isn't it?' This new line of action takes thirty-one seconds to open and develop. The Count opines that Alfred cannot call for a commoner: 'A Bruger call for an Ellis? Never!' This becomes the (negative) dialogue hook to the next scene, which begins with Alfred's car driving up to Dorothy's apartment building.

If these principles of linearity seem self-evident or 'natural,' recall that other filmmakers have used quite different principles to structure and connect scenes. Antonioni will commonly protract the establishment phase of a scene, lingering upon environmental features for some time before a causal line is broached. Bresson will often abruptly start a scene on a new line of action without any evident connection to the previous scene; our uncertainty is exacerbated by ambiguous temporal relations and an absence of establishing shots. Other filmmakers exploit unexpected narrational intrusions during the scene. In Eisenstein's *October* (1928), the 'July days' sequence begins suddenly, with several shots of crowds, and only then does an expository inter-title 'christen' the sequence. The sequence

on the Paris-Nanterre train in Godard's *La Chinoise* (1967) begins with a medium shot of two pairs of hands at a compartment window. Voices chat offscreen. Eventually Véronique and François Jeanson lean forward into the frame. Now an inter-title ('Encounter with François Jeanson') intercedes to give us our bearings. Whereas the classical film strives to link scenes smoothly and to reserve narrational intrusions for the transitional moments, Eisenstein and Godard disorient us by shifting the narration's interjection to an unconventional point within the scene.

Within the classical scene, characters act and react according to principles of individualized character psychology. They struggle, collide, and make decisions. Because such patterns resemble those of orthodox drama, we are already inclined to see them as following the crisis/climax/resolution trajectory beloved of late nineteenth-century dramatic theory. But the classical scene is not structured like an act in a well-made play. The classical scene climbs toward a climax, certainly, but the peculiar domino-linearity of the scene's construction makes limited kinds of resolution occur *early* in the scene, as old lines of action get closed off. And the dangling cause often leaves the scene unresolved, open, and leading to the next. The classical scene progresses steadily toward a climax and then switches the resolution of that line of action to *another*, later scene.

From the standpoint of reception, this pattern enhances the spectator's confidence in understanding the story action. Closing off certain causal lines early in the scene gives the viewer a sense of cumulatively following the action, retroactively clinching his or her reading of earlier scenes. Such short-term resolutions also promise a final resolution as well. Compare this process with the operations of scenes in *Persona* (1967) or *L'eclisse* (1963) or *Pierrot le fou* (1965). In these films, the scene will not necessarily answer earlier questions; constantly posed and suddenly dropped enigmas lead to a moment-by-moment frustration that makes the viewer suspect that closure may never come.

Both time and space fit themselves snugly to the contours of the classical scene's action. As in the *King and the Chorus Girl* segment, the expositional phase of the scene occupies little screen duration; most is given over to the developmental phase. Order is assumed to be chronological, unless a flashback or some crosscutting takes place. There can be a brief ellipsis within the scene, but it will be either signalled by dissolves or wipes or covered by cutaways (e.g., while the boss chases his secretary, her suitor waits outside). Durational continuity from shot to shot is secured through all the devices examined in Chapter 4 (matches on action, sound overlaps, etc.). Certainly, the use of deadlines and appointments, not only between scenes but also within them, helps the viewer to create stable and narrow hypotheses about what turns the various lines of action can take.

Space is also rigidly codified by the scene's flow of cause and effect. The characters' activity is the fulcrum of the construction of 180° space. The initial establishing shots are followed most probably by two-shots (*plan américain* or medium-long-shot framings). Then come shot/reverse shots or eyeline-matched medium shots which can alternate for some time. Ticking and tocking against one another, these images will usually keep the figures in the same scale in shot and countershot. Then, least commonly, may come subjective point-of-view shots. This accentuation of the space follows the flow of cause and effect, the opening, development, and closing of lines of action. When a character changes position, a broader view must resituate us; when a new character enters, the almost inevitable eyeline matches must be reinforced by an eventual establishing shot. These re-establishing shots can in turn anticipate the next cause in the chain, as we saw in the way that one camera set-up

'primed' us for the next in *The Caddy* (1953). All of these factors are illustrated in the sample scene analyzed on pages 66-9.

The classical scene ends, as I have suggested, with a dangling cause − a new line of action, a step toward a goal, a character's reaction to a new piece of information. This pattern is echoed in the scenographic space. While a classical film begins most scenes on an establishing shot, it does not necessarily *end* most scenes on a re-establishing shot. The classical scene typically ends on only a part of the total space − usually a character. Just as narrative causality impels us to look forward to the next scene, so the decoupage carries us to the heart of the space, the site of character interaction, and leaves us there to anticipate how the dangling cause will be taken up later.

As always, the individual devices that construct the scene are historically variable. Before 1927, for instance, dissolves might be used to link a detail to a long shot during the scene's exposi-tional phase. After 1927, that link would probably be made by a camera movement. Similarly, the 1930s insisted more strongly upon intermediary stages between establishing shots and closer views than did the 1940s, which allowed cutting from establishing shots to close, over-the-shoulder reverse angles. But these minor fluctuations simply eliminate one of several redundant cues and do not affect the basic principles of the classical paradigm. Those principles can be seen at work in a typical classical scene such as that analyzed below.

PLAY GIRL (1941)
Specimen Scene

1   (ls) Sofa: Grace and Ellen are seated and drinking coffee (fig 6.10).

    Grace: 'How are things going with you and Tom?'

    Ellen: 'We're having fun.' She sets down her coffee cup.

    Grace: 'What've you been doing about it?'

    Ellen: 'Why, nothing. What makes you think I ought to do anything about it?'

    Grace: 'No reason at all. I just thought I'd ask.'

Commentary

Shots

1   The opening of the scene immediately establishes the two characters in space and reveals their different states of mind. (They talk about their feelings.) Grace's questions pick up the suspended romance-line of action from the previous scene. Non-diegetic music plays softly. Ellen's last line motivates the next shot, Grace's reaction.

Ellen rises and walks around the edge of the sofa (fig 6.11).

    Ellen: 'Tom's a nice boy and we have a lot of good times together, but I'd never marry him.'

2   (ms, high angle) Grace: 'Well, you certainly had me fooled. I could've sworn you were in love with him.' (fig 6.12)

3   (mls) Ellen, walking to sofa toward Grace: 'I am in love with him.' (fig 6.13) She leans on the sofa back. 'I think I have been ever since that first day out on the road.' (fig 6.14)

4   (ms, high angle as 2) Grace (fig 6.15).

    Ellen, offscreen: 'I've never stopped thinking about him.'

5   (ms) Ellen: 'Every night – all night long – I dream about him.' (fig 6.16)

6   (ms, as 2) Grace sets down coffee; she rises and walks around sofa (figs 6.17-6.18).

    Grace: 'My advice to you is to marry him.' Grace comes to Ellen in the right foreground (fig 6.19). 'Marry him the very first moment he proposes.'

    Ellen: 'He won't propose.'

7   (ms as 5) Ellen, Grace on the left edge of the frame.

    Ellen: 'He almost did today, but I stopped him.' She stands up angrily (fig 6.20). 'Don't be alarmed. I'll see to it that nothing like this happens and this little corporation of ours will continue to do business just as it is.'

8   (ms, as end of 6) Grace: 'Oh, I know how you feel, darling, but don't take it so much to heart.' (fig 6.21)

    Ellen, backing away: '*You* wouldn't, would you?'

9   (ms, as 7) Ellen snorts (fig 6.22). 'There are other men, lots of them. Your Bill Vincents and your Van Pacens. But there aren't any of them like Tom. He's the only one that's shown me any genuine respect since the very first day . . .'

10   (ms, as 8) Grace, seen past Ellen's shoulder (fig 6.23).

    Ellen: '. . . I met you.'

    Grace: 'I wish you hadn't said that, Ellen.'

2-5 Analytical cuts (1/2, 3/4) and eyeline matches (2/3, 4/5) break the space into its components to emphasize the dialogue. Edge lighting separates the characters from the backgrounds. Reframing is used to follow Ellen as she rises. The previous line of action is developed to a climax: Ellen admits she loves Tom. Music continues, aiding shot continuity.

6   Grace rises and walks to Ellen, marking the new line of action. She advises Ellen to marry Tom. The camera follows Grace and picks up Ellen in the right foreground, reorienting us. This composition prepares for a characteristic shot/reverse-shot pattern. Music continues.

7-10 Shot/reverse-shot cutting traces the rising tension between the two women. The repeated set-ups let us ignore minutiae of space and concentrate upon changes in character behavior, as when Ellen pulls away in shot 8. Sound bleeds over one cut (9/10) in order to anticipate character reaction. Music continues.

She smiles and walks left (figs 6.24 and 6.25). 'As a matter of fact I was rather wishing you would marry . . .'

11   (1s, as 1) The two women at either end of the sofa (fig 6.26).

Grace: '. . . Tom.'

Ellen: 'Of course. Nothing would give you greater pleasure than to get your hands on eleven million dollars.'

Grace: 'I was thinking first of all of your happiness.'

Ellen, voice rising: 'And your future! But I won't do a thing like to Tom!'

Grace: 'Ellen!'

Door buzzer rings.

Grace: 'You'd better fix your face.'

Ellen goes out right (fig 6.27). Buzzer sounds again. Grace goes out right (fig 6.28).

12   (1s) Foyer. Grace comes in left (fig 6.29); pan with her to door. She opens it (fig 6.30).

Grace: 'Good evening, Tom.'

Tom: 'Hello, Grace.' He enters.

Grace: 'Ellen will be here in just a moment.'

Tom: 'Say, that's an awfully nice dress you've got on.'

Grace, as she and Tom walk to the sofa: 'Oh, this isn't a dress, it's a negligee. I'm staying in tonight.' (fig 6.31)

Tom: 'You are?'

Grace, sitting down on the second sofa: 'Sit down, Tom. I want to talk to you.' (fig 6.32)

13   (mls) The second sofa, Tom sitting by Grace (fig 6.33).

Grace: 'You're very fond of Ellen, aren't you?'

Tom: 'Well, I've heard tell.'

Grace: 'Going to marry her?'

Tom: 'I would if I could.'

Grace: 'Give me one good reason why you can't.'

Tom: 'I don't think she'd have me.'

Grace: 'Ever try asking?'

Tom: 'No, not exactly.'

Grace: 'I want to tell you a secret. If you were to ask her tonight, I wouldn't be a bit surprised if she said yes.'

Tom, eagerly: 'Sh! Here she comes.'

Grace looks off left and Tom turns (fig 6.34).

11   Grace's walk left motivates a re-establishing shot. The conflict between the women reaches its climax, with Ellen accusing Grace of wanting her to marry Tom for his money. Instead of resolution, there is simply an interruption: the door buzzer. This sound cuts off the non-diegetic music for the rest of the scene, thus increasing the sense of irresolution. Grace starts out of the frame after Ellen has gone.

12   A frame cut and a panning movement follow Grace to the door. As Tom enters, the framing re-establishes the characters in space. The camera reframes and tracks to follow them to the second sofa. Grace's 'I want to talk to you' announces that they will take up a suspended line of action.

13   After ascertaining Tom's state of mind (he loves Ellen), Grace opens a new causal line for Tom, one parallel to that she opened for Ellen in shot 6. Grace also suggests a deadline for Tom's proposal. Again, the action is left unresolved; Ellen's entry, like Tom's arrival earlier, breaks off the conversation.

14 (1s, as end of 12) Tom, rising as Ellen enters:
        'Hello, Ellen.' (figs 6.35-6.36)
    Ellen: 'Hello, Tom.'
    Tom: 'You look mighty grand.'
Josie the maid enters with Ellen's gloves.
    Ellen: 'Thank you.'
    Tom: 'Well, here we go.'
He leads Ellen out, winking back at Grace
(fig 6.37).
    Josie, coming to Grace: 'What's he winking
        about?'
    Grace: 'I think he's going to propose
        tonight.'
    Josie: 'Well, that's fine. For Ellen.' Josie
        sits down (fig 6.38).

14 The cut matches on Tom's action of turning.
    Reframing creates a new establishing shot as
    Ellen and then Josie enter. After Tom leads
    Ellen out in the background, Josie and Grace
    summarize what Grace has accomplished.
    Josie's 'For Ellen' reintroduces Ellen's point
    (shot 11) about Grace's future.

15 (mls, as 13) Josie and Grace on the second
    sofa (fig 6.39).
    Josie, turning Grace's chin toward her:
        'But what happens to you?'
    Grace: 'Oh, I always get along.'
Her smile fades as she picks up a magazine;
Josie looks skeptical (fig 6.40).
                    Dissolve

15 As Josie sits, another match-on-action cut
    keeps temporal continuity. Two causes are
    left dangling: one immediate (will Ellen
    accept Tom's proposal tonight?), the other
    long-term (what will happen to Grace if she
    does?). The scene ends by lingering upon only
    a portion of the space, that charged with
    expressivity by Josie's concern and Grace's
    feigned nonchalance.

The scene is an object of fascination, for viewer and for analyst, partly because it offers in microcosm the possibility of charting the classical spectator's activity. Chapter 3 has already shown that classical narration emerges quite overtly in the film's opening moments, during the credits and the early scenes, and then becomes more covert, letting character causality caught in *medias res* carry the narrational burden. Later chapters have shown how systems of time and space permit this narration to become relatively less self-conscious, to render omniscience as omnipresence, and to justify narration's suppression of information by character action and shifting point-of-view. At the film's end, the action resolves itself 'on its own terms,' according to an internal causal or generic logic, but a final narrational intrusion (e.g., the wink to the audience in *Appointment for Love* [1941]) is permissible. Now we can see that this pattern of fluctuating presence is at work in the scene as well. In the establishing phase, the narration is most self-conscious and omniscient, with signs, ostentatious camera movements, and telling details leaving the traces of a relatively overt narration. Once the action gets going, the narration slips into the background. The peculiar domino-linkage of cause and effect takes over the scene, but the narration may become overt again by an anticipatory cut or a stressed sound-image juxtaposition. And perhaps, at the scene's end, the narration re-emerges more boldly: It might call our attention to a detail which will prove important later or which will aid the transition to the next scene, or non-diegetic music might sneak in to link this scene with the next. This is not to say that the classical film is only the scene writ large, since, for one thing, the film comes to rest and resolution in a way the typical scene does not. Scene and film do, however, rely upon the same viewing activities – creating and checking first impressions; linking actions by their anticipated consequences; weighing and testing alternative hypotheses about causality, time, and space. Brick by brick, scene by scene, and inference by inference, the classical film impells the spectator to undertake a particular but not naive work.

7 The bounds of difference

So far, I have emphasized the unity and uniformity of the classical stylistic paradigm. But any complete account of Hollywood filmmaking must recognize deviations from the norm. Hollywood itself has stressed differentiation as a correlative to standardization. Novelty and originality were taken to be valuable qualities, and scriptwriters evolved an entire vocabulary for describing variation (gimmick, twist, boff, yak, weenie, old switcheroo). Cameramen likewise claimed to see each story as requiring a unique visual style. The question, though, is what principles governed this search for differentiation. What limits were set upon variety? In what permissible ways could films differ from one another? And at what points can the overall unity of the classical style be said to break down altogether? We must not expect gaps and breakdowns everywhere. The principle of motivation gives the classical paradigm a great range of non-disruptive differentiation.

Benson's cubist picture

In *Suspicion* (1941), police detectives are calling upon Lina Aysgarth to inquire about her husband Johnnie. Before and after their questions, one detective pauses to glance at a cubist painting on the wall. Stephen Heath has found in this gesture a significant rupture of narrative unity: 'problem of point of view, different framing, disturbance of the law and its inspecting eye, interruption of homogeneity of the narrative economy, it is somewhere else again, another scene, another story, another space.'[1] Yet although officer Benson's painting lacks compositional motivation – it is causally irrelevant – the picture can be justified by other means. The cubist painting is generically motivated; Diane Waldman has shown that the woman's Gothic film of the 1940s conventionally casts suspicion upon the husband's sanity by associating him with the distorted style of modern art.[2] Benson's interest is itself generically motivated (the detective scans the room for clues to Johnnie's personality) and 'realistically' motivated as well: the philistine policeman is baffled by the artifacts of upper-class life, and the narration here comically reiterates the motif of class difference that runs through the film. (The piano phrase on the soundtrack further marks this as a narrational joke.) Finally, it is possible to see the cubist picture as an instance of artistic motivation, calling attention to the significance of imagery (paintings, photographs) and vision (point-of-view, correct judgment of appearances) in *Suspicion* as a whole. In sum, Benson's picture breaks unity only if we limit our notion of unity to straightforward causal motivation.

Most instances of apparent transgression in the classical film are like Benson's picture – intrusions which momentarily contest causality but which are motivated in other ways. We have already seen (in Chapter 2) how artistic motivation in Hollywood cinema can justify spectacle, parody, and baring of the device. Motivation can also explain some apparent disruptions in the role of the star. For Parker Tyler, the star is more important than the story, Hollywood acting is but a charade, and the star's voice functions disjunctively, as something detachable from the star's personality. For Richard Dyer, the star more often than not poses problems for creating character.[3] But we must remember that genre shapes how the star is understood. Tyler claims that since the star does not 'act' in the theatrical sense, he dominates the story; he cites as an example the way that a Fred Astaire film exists only to reveal Fred's talents.[4]

But this is only a way of saying that the star has found his genre; the musical motivates its narrative to allow occasions for ingratiating dance. The same point holds when a star crosses genres. In *The Black Hand* (1949) Gene Kelly plays an Italian who fights the Mafia; this crime film does not lead us to expect that he will burst into an angular dance, nor is there what Dyer calls a 'problematic fit' between the brash, streetwise protagonists of *Cover Girl* (1944) and *Anchors Aweigh* (1945) and the impetuous, idealistic Gio. Disruptions arise only when the star's presence or actions cannot be motivated by any means, and this seems to be rare.

Benson's cubist picture suggests that it is an error to overlook realistic motivation, but it is also an error to make too much of it. A conception of the classical film as a 'realist text' tends to see the stylization of certain films as outrageous and jolting. Yet stylization, of various sorts, is a convention of many Hollywood genres, most notably the comedy, the musical, and the melodrama. Historically, all three descend from episodic and composite forms in the American popular theater (e.g., vaudeville, melodrama). The nineteenth-century popular play was commonly interrupted by orchestral interludes, songs, dances, animal acts, magicians, acrobats, and other novelties.[5] To some degree, musicals, melodramas, and comedies have followed the episodic bent of their forebears. This seldom disturbs us, however, because in such instances the typical multiple motivation of the classical text simply gives way to a more linear series: a scene motivated compositionally, then a song or gag motivated generically, then another scene, and so forth.

We should not, however, make too much of the episodic quality of these genres, since the classical cinema tended to unify each genre's disparate appeals and to limit the genre's stylization. Compositional motivation provided each genre with a coherent baseline against which the genre's conventions could react. For example, in the films of the Ritz Brothers, Abbott and Costello, and the Marx Brothers, the vaudeville skit or comic dialogue rests within a relatively unified narrative. The backstage musical encouraged interpolated songs and dances while still maintaining an ongoing causal chain. The 'big scenes' favored by stage melodrama became

more compositionally motivated in film melodrama. For the most part, space and time remained classically coherent. The bursts of stylization (a Busby Berkeley number, a Mamoulian rhythmic passage, or a Harpo Marx sight gag) remain tied to the classical norm in that the norm defines the duration and range of permissible stylization. What Alan Williams remarks of the musical applies to all these genres: their conventions seem stylized not in relation to 'life' but in relation to the aesthetic norm of the classical film.[6] Compositional unity and generic conventions are as important as 'realism' in locating the specific dynamics of these genres.

All of which suggests that the most wrenching aspects of these films, their most 'radical' moments, are in fact codified through generic conventions. Recently critics have put forward the melodrama as a subversive genre — most crudely because its lack of verisimilitude yields unpleasure, more subtly because it reveals contradictions in bourgeois ideology (family, business, sexual relations).[7] Yet critics have yet to construct the melodrama as an empirically or conceptually coherent genre. If we did construct such a model, we would probably find that the genre's 'subversiveness' is itself conventionalized. For example, Thomas Elsaesser's generally excellent essay on melodrama cites a scene in *Margie* (1946) in which a girl rushes downstairs to see her teacher, only to find that he is going to the dance with someone else. Elsaesser writes: 'The strategy of building up to a climax so as to throttle it the more abruptly is a technique of dramatic reversal by which Hollywood has consistently criticized the streak of incurably naive moral and emotional idealism in the American psyche.'[8] But as early as 1926, the Russian Formalist critic Sergei Balukhatyi had pointed out that stage melodrama relied upon exactly this convention of sudden ups and downs. Daniel Gerould summarizes Balukhatyi's point:[9]

Melodrama always finds ways to introduce the *unexpected* into the action. The dynamic effect of this device lies in the fact that it violates the 'course of events' as it has been outlined and already grasped by the spectator, turning it in new, unknown directions through the introduction of a new fact or deed, not stipulated by the previous action.

This is not to deny the powerful effect of such twists, nor is it to assert that they should not be studied from a political standpoint. The point is only that the contradictory emotional wrenchings of melodrama are generically motivated, no more socially or textually disruptive than interpolated numbers in a musical.[10] In such ways, conventions of the more stylized genres operate as limited plays with the classical compositional dominant.

The assimilation of the European avant-garde

You cut to the back of the Big Fellow, then three lap dissolves of the presses − give 'em that Ufa stuff, then to the street − a newsboy, insert of the front page, the L roaring by − Kerist, it's the gutsiest thing in pictures! Call you back, chief![11]

S.J. Perelman, 'Scenario'

Like Benson's cubist picture in *Suspicion*, the European avant-garde might be thought to have had a disruptive effect when it entered Hollywood in the period 1925-50. Yet on the whole, Hollywood absorbed and modified alternative artistic practices which had been developed in Europe and Russia. It is not too much to say that Hollywood has perpetually renewed itself by assimilating techniques from experimental movements. Hollywood has done this by correlating new devices with functions already defined by the classical style. Three examples − avant-garde music, German Expressionist cinema, and Soviet montage cinema − illustrate how this has happened.

Contrary to what we might expect, the celebrated philistinism of Hollywood producers did not bar avant-garde composers from studio work. George Antheil recalled with astonishment that he was hired to write discordantly: 'We engaged you to do "modernistic" music − so go ahead and do it!'[12] Stravinsky and Schönberg were both approached to score films. Yet however modern the musical technique might be, it got motivated in conventional ways.

It should go without saying that experimental music since Debussy need not express anguished or tormented feeling, although some pieces certainly do. In this respect, Schönberg's

'Accompaniment for a Film Scene' (1930), subtitled, 'Danger Threatens, Panic, Catastrophe,' was prophetic, for Hollywood quickly identified dissonant music with just such qualities. Disturbing music could convey disturbed states of mind: David Raksin's 'piano track' for the dreamlike scenes of *Laura* (1944), Miklós Rózsa's theremin for expressing psychosis in *Spellbound* (1946), or Bernard Herrmann's dissonances which trigger the homicidal drives of the composer-protagonist of *Hangover Square* (1945). Atonality was similarly domesticated. In *East of Eden* (1955), Leonard Rosenmann assigned tonal music to the teenagers and reserved atonality for 'adult conflicts'; for *The Cobweb* (1955) Rosenmann used serial music because 'I wanted more neurosis.'[13] Quite often in these films, the 'modern' music becomes identified with the narrative conflict itself, so that the resolution of the action calls for a reassertion of 'normal' music. At the close of *Hangover Square*, the composer's romantic concerto constantly shifts between diegetic and non-diegetic status, thus overriding the dissonances in his psyche. Of the last ten minutes of *East of Eden*, Rosenmann writes: 'The final cue returns to a more tonal, classical setting, reflecting the resolution of the struggle, in Carl's repentance and reconciliation.'[14] There is also generic motivation. Just as single-source lighting could signal the thriller genre, so 'modern' music was reserved for horror films, psychiatric subjects, and science fiction. The latter genre also motivated the use of electronic music. After scoring experimental shorts for Ian Hugo and others, Louis and Bebe Barron went on to compose electronic music for *Forbidden Planet* (1956).[15] Even in recent years, horror and science fiction have remained the principal Hollywood genres that permit 'avant-garde' scores (*2001* [1968], *Planet of the Apes* [1968], *The Exorcist* [1973], *Halloween* [1978], *Alien* [1979]). In short, the expressive range and formal innovations of experimental music of this century have been stringently confined by Hollywood's narrative conventions.

What of experimental movements within cinema itself? Of all national cinemas, the 1920s German film had the greatest influence on Hollywood. This itself is significant, for in many respects that cinema most resembled the classical American practice. Ufa, the major German production company, had shown how films could be made in the completely controlled environment of a studio, a lesson that was not to be lost on Hollywood when sound came. Moreover, certain Expressionist techniques of lighting, camerawork, and special effects were quickly imitated by Americans. The set designs of such films as *The Cabinet of Dr. Caligari* (1920), one commentator remarked in the 1920s, made Hollywood 'no longer terrified by shadows.'[16] From 1926 to 1928, films like *Variety* (1925) and *The Last Laugh* (1924) created a vogue for unusual angles and the so-called 'free' camera. Charles Clarke recalls that at Fox, German films would be screened for directors and cinematographers and discussions would be held afterward: 'Well, that's a great shot; why can't we do that?'[17] At the end of 1928, one writer pointed out the technological demand created by the new fashion:[18]

> With the advent of the so-called 'German influence' several years ago, the first camera to be called into service in the production of creative angles was the Akeley. Because of its light weight, facile leveling device, and gyroscopic control, directors found chimerical ideas efficiently screened by this remarkable camera. The Akeley specialists were called upon to lash their instruments high on the masts of ships, on the arms of derricks, or to be still different, in deep holes looking up.

When Charles Rosher was at Ufa as a consultant on *Faust* (1926), he learned how to suspend a camera from the ceiling for overhead moving shots, a technique employed later in *Sunrise* (1927). The false perspectives of *The Last Laugh* and the miniatures in *Metropolis* (1926) introduced Hollywood to more sophisticated special effects, a practice that was also to expand considerably in the studio-bound era.

The assimilation of Germanic technique, however eager, was selective. Some devices were inserted into generic contexts: low-key lighting for mystery, distorted perspectives for horror, odd angles for shock effects. With a few exceptions, camera movement was used to establish locales or follow principal characters. Most important, German Expressionist techniques for indicating character subjectivity were seized upon for momentary, intensified inserts. The drunken camera in *The Last Laugh* and the somersaulting point-of-view in *Variety* became quickly copied, since they were easily motivated by characters' psychological states. In the late 1920s, Hollywood films began to include prismatic or distorted imagery, multiple superimpositions, skewed perspective in set design, and camera gyrations to indicate a character's intoxication, delirium, dream, or emotional anxiety. Such devices, more rare in the 1930s, were revived in the subjective point-of-view films of the 1940s. Other formal traits of Expressionist cinema – the more episodic and open-ended narrative, the entirely subjective film, or the slower tempo of story events – were not imitated by Hollywood; the classical style took only what could extend and elaborate its principles without challenging them.

Most significant of all is the manner in which the classical Hollywood paradigm blunted the stylistic challenge of the experimental Soviet cinema. At the level of story, the works of Eisenstein, Pudovkin, Dovzhenko, and others frequently refused to create individualized, psychologically defined protagonists. Point-of-view was manipulated by a narration that constantly flaunted its presence. Stylistically, montage editing tended to break down the unified diegetic world. Montage forced the viewer to recognize a reworking of the raw event through constant editing gaps and mismatches: overlapping cutting distended time, disjunctive cuts created spatial and temporal ambiguities. Even the shot itself offered uncertain cues, since extreme close-ups, canted angles, and abstract compositional patterns against sky or neutral backgrounds tended to disorient the viewer. In sum, Soviet montage cinema constituted a challenge to classical narrative and decoupage on almost every front: narrative unity, narrational voice and point-of-view, spatial and temporal continuity.

Hollywood was able to assimilate certain traits of Soviet films because its earliest awareness of 'montage' was based on German films. Except for *Potemkin*, which was seen in the United States in 1926, Soviet montage films were not generally imported until after 1928. But 'montage sequences' begin to appear in the Hollywood cinema before this; a good example is the scene of the artists' ball in *So This Is Paris* (1926). At this period, complicated dissolves with superimposed effects were often called 'Ufa shots.' Recognized as specifically Germanic, these shots were motivated as dreams, visions, or hallucinations. Such early montage sequences established two crucial qualities of later American ones: the linkage of several short shots by dissolves rather than cuts, and the motivation of montage by character psychology or other story factors. Later, acquaintance with Soviet films induced Hollywood to add an abstraction accomplished through framing: extreme close-ups, low angles, and canted framings. The combination of Soviet and German techniques thus became highly functional. The stylized framings signaled that these shots did not belong to the same narrational level as the 'normally' shot scenes, while the dissolves and wipes — already codified as indicating a time lapse — implied the compression of a considerable interval. Locked within an 'ordinary' context, the montage passages became codified as a symbolic shorthand, not a new way of seeing.

Early talkies soon began using the montage sequence to summarize a lengthy process. In *The Dance of Life* (1929), a performer's decline from success is rendered through canted angles of theater marquees, prismatic shots of his hectic dissipation, and rotating shots of his binges, all linked by slow dissolves. *Say It With Songs* (1929) includes a montage of the hero in prison, with his face singing in the center and superimpositions of canted angles of prison routines; a later sequence shows a ticking clock with calendar pages superimposed. In the montage sequence, the sound cinema had found its equivalent for the expository title, 'Time passes and brings many changes . . .'

Furthermore, decoration could make the montage a source of spectacle in its own right, enhancing emotional and rhythmic effect. Good examples may be found in *Flying Down to Rio* (1933) and in *Melody Cruise* (1933), in which montage runs wild. Montage became a rhetorical device used 'to get over a dramatic point in a minimum of footage and with maximum force.'[19] Hollywood's leading specialist, Slavko Vorkapich, filled his montages with visual rodomontade, employing portentous symbolism (e.g., the Furies in *Crime Without Passion* [1934]) and a frantic editing pace (e.g., the opening of *Meet John Doe* [1941]). Vorkapich's ostentatious sequence in *Maytime* (1937), tracing the rise of an opera singer, seems to be parodied in Susan Alexander's

decline in the opera montage of *Citizen Kane* (1941). No matter how elaborate, montage introduced some discontinuity, but because it was confined to short bursts for narrow purposes, the disjunctiveness was not a drawback; indeed, it was ideally suited to express momentary disruption, as in the montage of the earthquake in *San Francisco* (1936). Moreover, since any discontinuities were overridden by a unified musical passage, the montage sequence gave the film composer a chance to write a short but integral piece. The French term itself connoted virtuosity and sophistication; when the Academy of Motion Picture Arts and Sciences started an official magazine in 1939, the publication was called *Montage*.

By the mid-1930s, when the Soviet films were better known, Hollywood began to articulate what it had done with montage. Articles explaining Soviet film theory began to appear in professional journals. Karl Freund pointed out that the very fast cutting of Soviet films was 'adapted' by American studios through the technique of optical printing.[20] Most self-consciously continental was Vorkapich, who justified his work by appeal to the commonplaces of silent film theories of 'pure cinema' and who called the motion picture a 'symphony' in space and time. Echoing Eisenstein, Vorkapich claimed a behaviorist basis for montage: 'It is possible to stimulate a spectator into various psychological and physical reactions by means of certain visual imitations coming from the screen.'[21] But whereas Eisenstein celebrated the possibility of doing this throughout the film and without use of narrative, Vorkapich insisted on the need to let the story determine the film's shape and to use montage chiefly in 'transitional passages.'[22] A feedback loop was closed: the early Hollywood cinema's use of rapid cutting for suspense initially influenced the Russian formulation of montage, which was in turn revised and corrected for decades of use in Hollywood.[23] To this day, the classically constructed film has included orthodox montage sequences (albeit without dissolves); see, for example, the arrival of the vacationers in *Jaws* (1974) or the packing of the ransom money in *The Taking of Pelham 123* (1973).

The case of film noir

Issues of transgression and subversion, stylization

and realism, foreign influence and domestic genre intersect in that body of work known as film noir. It is an extraordinarily amorphous body; critics have defined it as a genre, a style, a movement, a cycle, even a tone or mood. Two respected critics find only twenty-two films noirs; a recent book on the subject lists over two hundred and fifty. Another critic's list includes *High Noon* (1952) and *2001* (1968).[24] The concept of motivation as we have been using it can help clarify what is often regarded as the most deeply problematic group of films produced in Hollywood.

What is film noir? Not a genre. Producers and consumers both recognize a genre as a distinct entity; nobody set out to make or see a film noir in the sense that people deliberately chose to make a Western, a comedy, or a musical. Is film noir then a style? Critics have not succeeded in defining specifically noir visual techniques (one that would include, say, *Laura* [1944] and *Touch of Evil* [1957]) or narrative structure (one that would include *policiers*, melodramas, and historical films like *Reign of Terror* [1949]). The problem resembles one in art history, that of defining 'non-classical' styles. Gombrich reminds us that most style terms – Gothic, mannerist, Baroque – originally characterized a new style solely by its repudiation of a norm. Such terms of exclusion cannot be simply translated into a set of traits for the style in question because the original epithet intended no more than negative characterization. ('Gothic' simply meant 'barbarous.') Historically, however, critics tend to take the term as a positive definition and to try to find the essential traits of the style. As Gombrich points out:[25]

The cook may divide fungi into edible mushrooms and poisonous toadstools; these are the categories that matter to him. He forgets, even if he ever cared, that there may be fungi which are neither edible nor poisonous. But a botanist who based his taxonomy of fungi on these distinctions and then married them to some other method of classification would surely fail to produce anything useful.

A look at the history of 'film noir' shows substantially the same process at work. Initially, the term served less to define than to differentiate. In the summer and fall of 1946, the French public saw a new sort of American film. Years of

occupation had withheld *The Maltese Falcon* (1941), *Laura* (1944), *Double Indemnity* (1944), *Murder, My Sweet* (1944), *The Woman in the Window* (1944), and *The Lost Weekend* (1945). In November of 1946, *La Revue du cinéma* published Jean-Pierre Chartier's article, 'Les américains aussi font des films "noirs"' ('Americans Also Make Films "Noirs"'). Chartier found these films to resemble the brooding *Quai des brumes* (1938) and *Pépé le moko* (1937), works which the French called *films noirs*.[26] From the start, then, the American *films noirs* were defined chiefly by their difference from the mainstream Hollywood product. But later critics, such as Raymond Borde and Etienne Chaumeton, began to search for traits that would constitute film noir as a unified grouping, or *série*.[27] Since then, film critics have continued to use 'film noir' as a constitutive category, forgetting that it emerged as what Gombrich calls a term of exclusion. The consequence was the still-current dispute about what film noir really 'is.' We might as easily, and as fruitlessly, ask what 'the Baroque' essentially is. The term accretes meaning, or rather meanings, only from the history of criticism. This is not to say that the term is thereby phantasmic or trivial, since once a critical tradition has introduced the term, filmmakers can take their cue from the critics' very struggle to define it positively. Borde and Chaumeton speak of French films noirs influenced by the American sources, and recent years have seen the release of such films as *Chinatown* (1974) and *The Big Fix* (1978), which clearly are responses to the critical canonization of film noir.

Thus we inherit a category constructed *ex post facto* out of a perceived resemblance between continental crime melodramas and a few Hollywood productions. As a result, 'film noir' has functioned not to define a coherent genre or style but to locate in several American films a challenge to dominant values. It is not a trivial description of film noir to say that it simply indicates particular patterns of nonconformity within Hollywood. This is why films of many different sorts can be considered to belong to 'film noir.'

What are these patterns of nonconformity? In general, film noir has been considered to challenge the classical Hollywood cinema in four ways.

1 An assault on psychological causality. The film
noir protagonist often suffers internal conflict,
'with an existential awareness of his or her
situation.'[28] As Borde and Chaumeton put it,
the classical conventions of logical action,
defined characters, and a psychologically stable
hero are subverted by film noir's attractive
killers, repellent cops, confused actions,
gratuitous violence, and weary or disoriented
heroes.

2 A challenge to the prominence of heterosexual
romance. The film noir heroine is sexually
alluring but potentially treacherous. The
psychological uncertainty of the protagonist
finds its counterpart in this enigmatic
characterization of the female. Christine
Gledhill points out that the narration often
compels the hero to decide whether the woman
fits the type or not. Instead of winning her as a
romantic partner, the hero finds her barring
access to his goal or holding him in her power;
at the limit, he may have to kill her or die
himself to break free.[29]

3 An attack on the motivated happy ending. The
resolution of the plot often expresses the
working of the fate that has overseen the entire
action; in this event, the film ends unhappily.
Or, if that is too shocking, the enforced happy
ending comes to seem lame and tacked-on.
How, ask Borde and Chaumeton, can we be
satisfied by the resoration of justice when the
film has shown representatives of justice as
monstrously corrupt? 'Is the disturbing effect of
the film completely wiped out by the last five
minutes?'[30]

4 A criticism of classical technique. According to
Paul Schrader, film noir uses night-lighting,
location shooting, a 'restless and unstable'
space, and tense compositions; such a style can
even undercut conventional middle-class
themes.[31] According to other critics, film noir's
visual style unsettles the viewer in order to
express the hero's disorientation.[32] For the
same ends, film noir traces the protagonist's
mental states by means of voice-over narration,
flashbacks, and subjective point-of-view. All of
these devices are said to challenge the
neutrality and 'invisibility' of classical style.

Such aspects of film noir have attracted critical
attention because they attack certain American
values prominent in mainstream Hollywood
cinema. But formally and stylistically, all four of
film noir's challenges none the less adhere to
specific and non-subversive conventions derived
from crime literature and from canons of realistic
and generic motivation.

Chartier's term film noir came from the phrase
roman noir, used in the early 1940s to refer to
hard-boiled detective novels on the American
model.[33] This etymology is significant because
every characteristic narrative device of film noir
was already conventional in American crime
fiction and drama of the 1930s and 1940s. Borde
and Chaumeton correctly emphasize the crucial
influence of hard-boiled detective fiction, which
had in the 1930s become more respectable with
the commercial success of books by Dashiell
Hammett, James M. Cain, Raymond Chandler,
and especially James Hadley Chase. One can even
claim that Hammett's first four novels (1929-31)
defined most of the conventions of noir detective
films, including first-person narration and
expressionist subjectivity (e.g., the protagonist's
dream in Red Harvest [1929]). By 1944, the hard-
boiled detective story had become conventional
enough for Raymond Chandler to sum it up in his
celebrated essay, 'The simple art of murder.'[34]
The evidence is clear: using the Alain Silver–
Elizabeth Ward list (disputable but no more
arbitrary than any), we find that adaptations of
hard-boiled novels constitute almost 20 per cent of
the films noirs made between 1941 and 1948.
Another sub-genre of crime literature, the
'psychological thriller,' underwent rejuvenation
during the 1930s, in novels and plays by Frances
Iles, Emlyn Williams, and Patrick Hamilton.[35]
The result was a series of films stressing
abnormal psychology and murder in a middle-
class setting: Gaslight (1944, adapted from
Hamilton's successful play Angel Street), Sleep My
Love (1948), Laura (1944), The Big Clock (1946),
and Secret Beyond the Door (1948). The espionage
thriller, made respectable during the late 1930s
by Graham Greene and Eric Ambler, was also
quickly transposed into film, in such works as The
Mask of Dimitrios (1944), Journey into Fear
(1942), The Confidential Agent (1945), and The
Ministry of Fear (1944).[36] And the postwar vogue
for semi-documentary films owes something to the
police-procedural novel in crime fiction, usually
considered to have emerged with Lawrence

Treat's *V as in Victim* (1945).

Clearly, the narrative 'problems' posed by films noirs are in fact conventions taken over by Hollywood cinema from popular literature. The relativity of right and wrong, the city as a jungle of corruption and terror, the solitary investigator walking down 'mean streets' – such devices of the hard-boiled novels and espionage tales were easily assimilated by the cinema. Similarly, film noir's atmosphere of fear and peril, psychological ambiguity, and abnormal mental states had already been conventionalized in psychological thrillers.

The stylistic features of film noir are just as strongly motivated. Subjective effects (flashbacks, voice-over commentary) were part of a general trend toward the representation of extreme psychological states. Location shooting, encouraged by wartime limits on set construction and the 'realism' of combat documentaries, became common after *Kiss of Death* (1947) and *Naked City* (1948).[37] Cinematographers began to employ 'mood lighting' – typically, low-key lighting. In normal filming, the ratio of key to fill light was 4:1 (key plus fill to fill alone). To light low-key, say 5:1, cinematographers usually shot with normal key and less fill, then adjusted the negative during processing or printing to bring out shadow detail.[38] In extreme cases, cinematographers used no fill light at all. Such 'weird lighting' was often considered realistic in contrast to three-point studio glamour lighting, and the effect could be plausibly motivated as coming from a single, harsh source – say, a street light or a feeble lamp (see fig 7.1). But here again, realistic motivation operated as an alibi. Low-key lighting was already a staple of certain genres (horror films, *policiers*), especially in scenes treating crime or morbid psychology (see fig 7.2). It is possible that crime literature also contributed to noir lighting effects. John Baxter cites this passage from Cornell Woolrich's *Black Path of Fear* (1944):[39]

> We went down a new alley . . . ribbons of light spoked across this one, glimmering through the interstices of an unfurled bamboo blind stretched across an entryway. . . . The bars of light made cicatrices across us. . . . For a second I stood alone, livid weals striping me from head to foot.

One can even find film noir visual conventions in 1940s comic strips like *Dick Tracy* and *The Spirit*. The Germanic influence upon Hollywood lighting during the 1920s and 1930s re-emerged in films noirs because current conceptions of realism came to reinforce existing generic norms.

The case of film noir can be solved by investigating realistic and generic motivation. Mystery writers had already turned away from the orthodox detective story toward a new 'realism'; this new realism in turn revivified certain film genres. Moreover, the new forms were better suited to classical cinema than the cerebral detective puzzle had been; they promised action and atmosphere. The crucial point, however, is that formally and technically these noir films remained codified: a minority practice, but a unified one. These films blend causal unity with a new realistic and generic motivation, and the result no more subverts the classical film than crime fiction undercuts the orthodox novel.

The reappearing author

The most influential argument for differentiation within Hollywood cinema has been advanced by auteur critics. To choose a body of work attached to a director's signature and to claim it as individual, personal, even subversive is the most common way to show that the Hollywood cinema is not monolithic. And auteur critics are right; like 'film noir,' the category of 'authorship' does locate important differences within the classical style. But we need to recognize several different senses in which any film can be said to have an 'author.'

The author can be thought of as a person, the actual agent (or agents) creating the text. Traditionally, this has raised problems of attribution, authentication, the relevance of biographical data and statements of intention, etc. In mass-production cinema, which has traditionally involved collaborative labor, scholars have found it difficult to assign authorship to any individual. Hollywood's own discourse has tended to recognize the innovative worker (as Chapter 9 will show in detail), and that worker can sometimes be granted the status of 'author' (e.g., Griffith, von Stroheim, possibly Welles). But identifying an innovative worker is seldom a relevant textual factor; however Vernon Walker's special effects for *Citizen Kane* (1941) might be praised within the trade, his work has acquired no authorial status in the realm of reception or criticism.

The author can also be thought of as a social code. Here the name of the person is invested with ideological, even mythological status. 'Picasso' is more than a man; the name connotes a complex set of artistic techniques, historical epochs, and social attitudes.'[40] In this sense, the author is constructed in and through the social institution of the specific art. Hollywood cinema has seldom constructed 'authors' as part of its institution. With rare exceptions (Disney, Hitchcock, and directors who are also stars, such as Chaplin and Jerry Lewis), the Hollywood cinema does not give directors, or even producers, authorial status. Consider by contrast the European art cinema, which has created a complicated set of processes (criticism, film festivals, retrospectives) to fix 'Bergman' or 'Fellini' as trademarks no less vivid than 'Picasso.'

Both the author as empirical agent and as institutional trademark stand outside the texts themselves. We can also think of the author as a name we give to certain operations of the art work. When we ask about the director's 'attitude' toward the action or speak of authorial manipulation or deception, we are identifying the author to some degree with the narrational process. Thus in a film one could sometimes equate the 'narrator' with the author.

The *politique des auteurs* went further, seeking narrational constants in many works possessing the same signature. This constitutes a fourth sense of 'authorship.' Insofar as the auteur critic is not simply talking intuitively about 'personality,' he or she is committed to the unearthing of common stylistic or thematic strategies within a body of work. 'Unearthing' is the right word because the 'invisibility' of Hollywood technique, the director who claims only to be a storyteller, and the aggrandizement of rules all tend to downplay the authorial process.

The following pages assume that identifying the 'author' with the narrational process, either within a film or across several films, is the approach most pertinent to the history of film style. If we think of authorship as characteristic processes of narration, we shall find that authorial presence in the Hollywood cinema is usually consonant with classical norms.

It would be possible to locate authorial differences by using two of the three levels of stylistic description I have already proposed. Authors are most readily characterized by the recurrence of particular technical devices – Wyler's deep focus, Von Sternberg's cluttered compositions. Since the classical style is a paradigm, a filmmaker may habitually and systematically choose one alternative over another. Whereas John Ford might customarily stage an action around a doorway, Sirk might stage it in front of mirrors. At the second level, that of formal systems, an author's work may also reveal distinctive manipulations of causality, time, and space. One common mark of the auteur film is ambiguity about character psychology. Welles's *Citizen Kane* is the *locus classicus* of this practice, but similar strategies are at work in the films of Hitchcock, Preminger, and Fritz Lang. It is equally possible to define authorial uniqueness by virtue of a distinctive treatment of time and space. Hawks's *His Girl Friday* (1939) accelerates plot duration by compressing story time, while Von Sternberg prolongs duration through static poses, slowed conversations, and lengthy dissolves which no longer convey simple ellipses but graphically superimpose two discrete story actions. Hollywood auteurs have also presented a rich variety of spatial systems, ranging from Preminger's sober, long-held two-shot to Lubitsch's fastidious breakdown of the space into revealing objects and expressions. Such variety will not surprise us if we recall Leonard Meyer's point: 'For any specific style there is a finite number of rules, but there is an indefinite number of possible strategies for realizing or instantiating such rules. And for every set of rules there are probably innumerable strategies that have never been instantiated.'[41]

There is, as Meyer's remark suggests, also a limit to authorial uniqueness in Hollywood. At the most abstract level of generality, narrative causality dominates the film's spatial and temporal systems. We have already seen how genre, spectacle, technical virtuosity, and other factors encourage narrative to slip a bit from prominence, only to allow the narration to compensate for this slip by adjusting its overall structure. In a similar fashion, authorial reshifting of the hierarchy of systems can only be intermittent. The modernist cinema and the avant-garde can make temporal and spatial systems vie for prominence with narrative causality and even override it; Bresson, Tati, Mizoguchi, Ozu, Snow, Frampton, et al. can in various ways problematize narrative, making overt narration a pervasive presence. But there is little chance in Hollywood of what Burch calls 'organic dialectics,' the possibility of using purely stylistic parameters to determine the shape of the film (including its narrative).[42] When George Melford directed *East of Borneo*, he could not have made Joseph Cornell's *Rose Hobart*, although the latter contains almost no shot that is not in the former; Cornell's film creates a play of spatial and temporal relations among elements discovered in but freed from a narrational matrix. In the classical film, such a play cannot permanently displace story causality from its privileged role.

This is to say that overt narration, the presence of a self-conscious 'author' not motivated by realism or genre or story causality, can only be intermittent and fluctuating in the classical film. We have already seen that the classical film contains certain codified moments when narration can be foregrounded: the beginning and ending of the film, beginnings and endings of scenes, montage sequences, and certain (usually generically motivated) moments within scenes. The self-conscious, omniscient, and suppressive narration of the film comes forward usually at such points. To some extent the auteur, either within the film or across films, can be identified with characteristic treatments of the intrusive narrational moments. For instance, expository inter-titles always acknowledge a certain omniscience on the narration's part; the film may play down this omniscience (as in a majority practice) or play it up to create a specific kind of narration (brooding and bardic in Griffith's films, cynical and worldly in Lubitsch's). Similarly, the opening is a particularly self-conscious moment in the film, so one may use it to erect false impressions (as Lubitsch does in *So This is Paris*) and thus emphasize the viewer's dependence upon the narration. The author may not intrude when we expect it: Hawks's or Cukor's narration almost never lapses into self-consciousness or overt suppressiveness. Or the author may intrude more often than is usual, as in the films of Lang, Hitchcock, and Welles.

The authorial possibilities within classical narration may be usefully illustrated by the work of two auteurs – Alfred Hitchcock and Otto Preminger. Hitchcock's narration capitalizes on every permissible chance to display self-consciousness, flaunt its superior knowledge, and mark its suppressive operations. This takes place in two ways. On the one hand, the narration confines us to a single character's point-of-view to a greater degree than is normal; this is reinforced by Hitchcock's unusual insistence upon optical subjectivity. On the other hand, blatant narrational intrusions freely comment on the action (symbolic inserts like the waltzing couples in *Shadow of a Doubt*, revelatory camera movements, unexpected angles and sound overlaps). There is thus a tension between what a character knows and what the narration tells. But the narration must never tell all; again and again, the narration points out its suppressive operations. When in *Shadow of a Doubt* Uncle Charlie sees the telltale newspaper story, the narration could show it to us; but the narration does not do so until little Charlie discovers the story in the library. When in *Psycho* Norman Bates climbs the stair to his mother's room, the camera tentatively follows him up and cranes back to a bird's-eye view just outside the doorsill, self-consciously displaying its deliberate withholding of information. By exploiting certain polar possibilities of the classical schemata of narration, Hitchcock's authorial persona oscillates between being modest and omnicommunicative within very narrow limits (i.e., presenting a single character's point-of-view) and flaunting its omniscience by suppressing crucial information.

It is exactly between these poles that Preminger's narration lives. Preminger planes classical narration down to a flat, almost inexpressive ground. In films like *Fallen Angel* (1944) or *Daisy Kenyon* (1947), a poker-faced author presents contradictory or enigmatic character behavior without supplying causal explanations. Preminger's reluctance to use even shot/reverse-shot cutting can be seen as a symptom of the narration's unwillingness to specify character psychology through reaction shots. To this end, the films forego both character subjectivity and narrational commentary, preferring instead to shift point-of-view between scenes, moving from one combination of characters to another. Two such different authorial styles are the results of narration and not of 'realism' or of 'round' versus 'flat' characters; as V.F. Perkins remarks, 'Hitchcock tells stories as if he knows how they end, Preminger gives the impression of witnessing them as they unfold'[43] Yet both auteurs remain within classical bounds: Hitchcock cannot always keep us aware of his narrational presence, whereas Preminger will often claim his *droit du seigneur* at the end of a film by an overt camera movement.

Historically, the degree of authorial intervention has fluctuated. Griffith is probably the first director systematically to foreground narration, a stratagem most clearly seen in his early features. In *The Birth of a Nation* (1915), Griffith synthesizes many contemporary but sporadic and partial forms into a coherent narrational process. The film becomes a mosaic of events to be interpreted by means of the historical argument and dramatic parallels urged by the omniscient narration. Moreover, the expository inter-titles register a specific voice issuing from the film — one which analyzes history, certifies verisimilitude (some titles have footnotes), anticipates action, and poetically meditates upon the images (one title refers to 'War's peace'). In a final beatific vision of peace, the omniscient narration carries us to a divine perspective outside history. Even this omniscient narration, however, is not always visible; most scenes rely upon covert, diegetically motivated narration.

Many of Griffith's devices became fashionable. At least one director, Erich von Stroheim, continued Griffith's search for a novelistic cinema that would make the narration quite overt, and in *Greed* (1924), a Naturalistic causal scheme attempted to eliminate individual psychological motivation. But, as released, the film remains an unresolved mixture of authorial intervention (in certain camera angles and in the symbolic inserts), expressionistic subjectivity (in the dreams and fantasies of the junk dealer), and compositionally motivated psychological narration. Most of the great Hollywood directors of the 1920s — F.W. Murnau, Lubitsch, Ford, Buster Keaton, Borzage — utilize authorial presence in various ways, but none displaced the sovereignty of story in the classical model. After the coming of sound, the bounds of difference were firmly set.

The intermittent presence of the author in classical films contributed to the very shape that auteur criticism has taken. Auteur criticism has relied almost completely upon thematic interpretation, consistently minimizing film form and technique. The typical thematic interpretation of an auteur film commences by summarizing the story action, moves to a psychological description of the characters and abstract thematic oppositions, and buttresses the reading with a rundown of privileged motifs that reinforce the themes. The very form of such essays confirms the fluctuation of classical narration. In each film, the auteur critic invariably turns up great swatches of the classical style — sequences, even whole films, whose visual and sonic organization cannot be thematized. Even auteurs, that is, spend a lot of time obeying the rules.

An auteur critic might argue in response that by looking at several films signed by the same director one could find traces of the author in aspects which an analysis of a single film might consider simply conventional. This is why auteur criticism implies, as Peter Wollen puts it, 'an operation of decipherment; it reveals authors where none had been seen before.'[44] Auteur criticism tries, in effect, to make aspects of the single film into narrational systems of a larger text, that of the *oeuvre*. But no auteur critic has in practice shown that, say, the shot/reverse-shot patterns or the usage of lighting across all of Sirk's films constitute a distinct handling of the classical paradigm; what stands out in an individual film is what stands out in the work as a whole (e.g., a tendency toward blatant symbolism for some purposes). Wollen does indicate that 'noise' from other codes (genres, studios, technical staff) blocks the critic from finding a consistent authorial presence in the Hollywood film: 'Any single coding has to compete, certainly in the cinema, with noise from signals coded differently.'[45] The most powerful of those signals, I am asserting, is the classical tradition itself.

The intermittence of authorial presence works to reaffirm classical norms. Because the classical paradigm encourages redundancy, the director can choose how to be redundant. By showing us how a particular range of choices can be organized systematically, the auteur revivifies the norm and makes us appreciate its depth and range. In *His Girl Friday*, Hawks pushes temporal continuity in a new direction, thus reaffirming it as a value. Every variant upon classical space testifies to the roominess of the original paradigm. When Hitchcock exploits optical point-of-view for surprise effect, we recognize new possibilities in such a simple classical device. Different handlings of genres – Sirk's and Preminger's of the melodrama, Berkeley's and Minnelli's of the musical, Keaton's and Lloyd's of the action comedy, Hawks's and Sam Fuller's of the war film – only confirm the genre's fertility. In such ways, conceptions of authorship enable us to appreciate the richness of the classical cinema.

The fluctuating quality of authorial presence in the Hollywood film suggests that radical disruptions crop up rarely. Genuine breakdowns in classical narration are abrupt and fleeting, surrounded by conventional passages. In Hollywood cinema, there are no subversive films, only subversive moments. For social and economic reasons, no Hollywood film can provide a distinct and coherent alternative to the classical model. Nothing in any Hollywood auteur film rivals the idiosyncratic systems of space or time operating in the work of Dreyer, Bresson, Mizoguchi, Straub/Huillet, Ozu, Resnais, or Godard. In such works, narration is pervasive, constantly foregrounded, because these modernist works create unique *internal* stylistic norms. Even the most deviant Hollywood films, however, must ground themselves in the external norms of group style. Hitchcock's *Psycho* (1960) is certainly one of the most deviant films ever made in Hollywood since it attacks several fundamental classical assumptions (e.g., the psychological identity of characters, the role accorded to narration). Yet *Psycho* remains closer to *His Girl Friday* than to *Diary of a Country Priest* (1951) or *Pierrot le fou* (1965). Really problematic Hollywood films become limit-texts, works which, while remaining traditionally legible, dramatize some limits of that legibility. They do not, however, posit thoroughgoing alternatives. So powerful is the classical paradigm that it regulates what may violate it.

It follows that authorial 'disruption' of classical norms can throw the spectator off-balance only momentarily. The classical paradigm supplies a set of hypotheses, ranked as alternatives and in order of likelihood, and the spectator uses those hypotheses in following the film. The narration can trigger one story hypothesis and deliver on it, or delay delivery, or confirm the hypothesis in a fresh way; all these are variants which do not drastically challenge the reliability of the narration. The classical spectator is somewhat more sorely tried if the narrator is proven to be fundamentally unreliable. Meir Sternberg points out that some narrations create a firm primacy effect only to demolish it or qualify it.[46] When this occurs in classical filmmaking, it is usually motivated generically, especially for mystery or comedy. Chapter 3 pointed out how the expository title in *The Maltese Falcon* undermines the primacy effect. A comic deflation of first impressions occurs in the opening of *Trouble in Paradise* (1932), when the sophisticated wealthy couple is slowly revealed to be a pair of hardened thieves. On those rare occasions when this rise and fall of first impressions is not motivated generically, it can have genuinely disruptive consequences. It is worth looking at one instance in detail.

Like *Psycho*, Fritz Lang's *You Only Live Once* (1937) is widely recognized as a deviant film. The film's disruptions arise from a play with our expectations about the limited and intermittent intrusions of classical narration. Specifically, we assume that narrational manipulations will be marked as such when they appear, as Hitchcock's camera movements are. In Lang's film, however, we do not notice authorial intrusions when they occur; only later, when our inferential steps have gone astray, do we retrace our path and realize how we jumped to conclusions. Lang thus foregrounds narration *ex post facto*. To make us run ahead of the evidence, *You Only Live Once* draws on basic assumptions of causal and generic motivation and encourages us to assume that, given classical narration's omnipresence, no crucial action taken by the protagonist will be withheld from us. The narration smoothes our inferential path still more by creating unusually strong continuity between scenes: a dissolve from parcels to the heroine's suitcase as she packs for her honeymoon; the heroine saying, 'Gas,' followed by a shot of the hero pulling into a gas station. Moreover, Lang's first scenes quietly signal the film's obedience to the convention of starting a scene by tracking back from an object.

All of these procedures force us to jump to conclusions during one central scene.

Eddie, an ex-convict, is jobless and frustrated. At the end of one scene, the camera shows us Eddie's hat, then Eddie eyeing a gun. In the next scene, we see Eddie's hat on the seat of a car, and the camera pans to show a man's face encased in a gas mask. The man robs an armored car and flees. In the rain, the truck crashes. Then Eddie, drenched by the rain, staggers into his home and tells his wife, Jo: 'The bottom's dropped out of everything.'

Cause and effect, point-of-view, continuity hooks from scene to scene, and details in scene openings all encourage us to infer that Eddie pulled the robbery. Just as important, no information has *contradicted* these inferences. But Eddie now explains that his hat was stolen and someone else robbed the car. Lang's narration has concealed the real criminal from us by trading upon the assumption that foregrounded narration will be immediately noticeable; as we have seen, classical narration usually does not distract us from gaps. In *You Only Live Once*, however, continuity devices link trivial items, concealing crucial events without any cue that something is being concealed. Indeed, so strong are first impressions in this case that even Eddie's explanation to Jo does not resolve all doubts about his guilt; the possibility that he may be lying creates a lingering simultaneous hypothesis that is not ruled out until the police discover the real robber's body many scenes later. (To make this even more complex, the film's generic identity is dubious; if it belongs to the 'they-made-me-a-criminal' sub-genre, Eddie is likely to be legally guilty, even if he is a victim of circumstances.)

The purpose of creating such an unreliable narration is evidently to compel the viewer to judge Eddie as unfairly as do all the respectable citizens who brand him incorrigible. More generally, Lang's American films frequently construct a 'paranoid' spectator through a narration that brutally and abruptly manipulates point-of-view in order to conceal gaps and force the viewer to false conclusions. An analysis of this process is indispensible to any account of Lang as an 'author.'

In Western music, the classical style creates dynamism by departing from and returning to a stable tonal center. Something like this dynamism appears in the Hollywood auteur film. The auteur film draws its sustenance from the classical base, which is visible in the film. The film mixes narrational modes – some systems operating according to classical probabilities, others intermittently foregrounded as less probable and more distinctive. Far from being a fault or flaw, this mixture can be a source of aesthetic value to those prepared to perceive it. Most often, an idiosyncratic exploration of causality, time, or space works to reaffirm the norm by revealing the suppleness and range of the paradigm. At rarer moments, a deviant narrational process can be glimpsed. We see the norm afresh, understand its functions better, recognize previously untapped possibilities in it, and – on a few occasions – reflect upon how our trust in the norm can mislead us. The Hollywood auteur film offers a particular pleasure and knowledge: the spectator comes to recognize norm and deviation oscillating, perhaps wrestling, within the same art work, that work being actively contained by the pressures of tradition.

Norms, subversion, conditions of production

Any account of the classical Hollywood film as an ideological product, a representational commodity, must recognize the specific formal operations through which classical principles reinforce dominant ideological positions. Hollywood has assimilated the challenge of avant-garde styles and of apparently deviant cycles such as film noir. Certainly the stress upon goal-oriented individuals, upon character psychology as desire, upon an 'objective' and inflexible story order, upon a space derived from theatrical scenography – all these factors cluster around assumptions about the nature of social existence. Narrative resolution can work to transcend the social conflict represented in the film, often by displacing it onto the individual (the hero torn between duty and personal urges), the couple (the romance-plot taking precedence over the pretext-action), the family, or the communal good.[47] Recent Marxist critiques of Hollywood cinema have demonstrated its persistent habit of reconciling social antagonisms by shifting the emphasis from history and institutions to individual causes and effects, where ethical and even religious moral terms can operate.[48] Spectacle can be used to elide or wish away uncomfortable contradictions. Classical temporal continuity between episodes can deny the audience time to reflect about alternatives to the events presented. Adorno even criticized the montage sequence for dissolving humanity into prefabricated segments, cheating the human out of lived duration.[49] Our examination of classical narration has shown that it accustoms spectators to a limited and highly probable range of expectations. Classical narration's reliability habituates the viewer to accepting regulated impersonality and sourceless authority.

At the same time, however, we cannot denounce the Hollywood style as uniformly suspect. Narration can, however momentarily, break down the ideological unity of the classical film. There can be no typology of such break-downs, although all of the analyses in the last six chapters will suggest where trouble might occur. If a model is needed, the arbitrary happy ending serves as well as any.

'A good director can contrive a happy ending that leaves you dissatisfied. You know that something is wrong − it just can't end that way.'[50] Fassbinder's remark indicates one extreme edge of 'subversion' within the classical text, whether it be film noir or *film d'auteur*. The classical ending, both as resolution and epilogue, tends to usher in the narration as self-conscious and omniscient presence. Yet even this overt narration should harmonize with the story action and generic demands. If the ending, especially the happy ending, is inadequately motivated, then the film creates a possibly productive split of story from narration. By including an ending that runs counter to what went before, deviant narration indicates certain extratextual, social, historical limits to its authority. Films like *Suspicion, Meet John Doe, Woman in the Window, The Wrong Man* (1957), and *How Green Was My Valley* (1941) tend to foreground the arbitrary conventionality of the ending and can even raise ideological questions. The cursory resolution or epilogue can put on display the requirements of social institutions (censorship agencies, studios) which claim to act as delegates of audience desires. The happy ending may be there, but to some extent the need for it is criticized.[51]

Conflicts of various conventions, operating at given historical moments, can create such problematic moments in Hollywood texts. We can understand those moments only by recognizing the norms operating in the Hollywood cinema and by being alert for glimpses, within the film, of another cinema, a cinema of multiplicity and formal tensions not finally resolved into a 'classical' unity.

It is not enough to locate principles of unity and alternatives to those principles. An adequate historical account of the classical Hollywood cinema must see the style as related to a specific mode of film production. Just as we must scrutinize form and style carefully, we must go beyond a general dismissal of Hollywood as an assembly-line operation. It is true that the American film industry does resemble certain modes of manufacture, but we must remember that art works have been produced by collective labor for centuries (e.g., Raphael's frescoes, academic painting in the nineteenth century). Marx and Engels point out that artistic creation was always linked to general and specific modes of production:[52]

Raphael as much as any artist was determined by the technical advances made in art before him, by the organization of society and division of labor in his locality, and, finally, by the division of labor in all the countries with which his locality had intercourse. . . .

In proclaiming the uniqueness of work in science and art, Stirner adopts a position far inferior to that of the bourgeoisie. At the present time [1845-7] it has already been found necessary to organize this 'unique' activity. Horace Vernet would not have had time to paint even a tenth of his pictures if he regarded them as works which 'only this Unique person is capable of producing.' In Paris, the great demand for vaudevilles and novels brought about the organization of work for their production, organization which at any rate yields something better than its 'unique' competitors in Germany.

While the culture industry has carried this tendency further, we shall see that Hollywood's division of labor, grounded in serial manufacture, still remains qualitatively different from assembly-line production.

The classical style can be linked to its conditions of production much more precisely than is generally acknowledged. Every cut testifies to narration, but every cut also implies some sort of work. The principles of a unified narrative both demanded and arose from a filmmaking process based upon the scenario; stylistic continuity has depended upon a 'continuity' script and a 'continuity girl.' The division of the film into shots and scenes bears the traces of divisions within the labor process. The repetition of camera set-ups so important for classical spatial orientation also mirrors a rapid, economical production procedure that depends upon shooting 'out of continuity.'[53] Soft-focus backgrounds in medium shots can save money in set construction.[54] Even authorial differences, those systematic choices within the stylistic paradigm, can be translated back into production procedures; alternative schemata correspond to concrete choices available to the filmmakers, and the limits upon those schemata parallel the work options open at any specific historical juncture.

For a specific example, consider once more the montage sequence. It not only fulfilled stylistic functions; it had the virtue of economy. Action too expensive to shoot as a scene could be conveyed by montage, thus saving 'both the budget and the continuity.'[55] Cheaper films relied upon the montage because they could draw on stock footage. We cannot say that the montage sequence was used simply because it was cheap, since it would have been even cheaper to use an expository title. Neither can we say, however, that the montage would not have been used if it had not been amenable to budgetary constraints. The film industry built the montage sequence into its production practices. Studios began to script such sequences carefully and to create production units specializing in them (e.g., Donald Siegel's unit at Warner Bros).[56] Once the stylistic device had proven its narrational virtues, it was rationalized economically.

In such ways, the classical norms became important causes of and guidelines for the organization of production. The remainder of this book is devoted to showing how the classical mode of filmic *representation* both sustained and was sustained by the development of a specific mode of film *production*.

Part Two The Hollywood mode of production to 1930

JANET STAIGER

8

The Hollywood mode of production: its conditions of existence

Introduction

The making of a product – particularly when it is a film – can sometimes fascinate us as much as the product itself. Rumors of offscreen affairs between the stars create auxiliary dramas and, when the film is seen, provide two plots for the price of one. Fascinating, too, are accounts of fabulous extravagance and ingenuity: 35,000 extras, real cream baths on the sets, multi-million-dollar location shooting ruined by hurricanes, dangerous stunt work actually performed by the hero or heroine. Part of the fascination must be that these are presented as true stories. In a wide-spread contagion they fascinate both those who worship Hollywood, its aura, its glamour, and those who condemn it. It infects film critics and historians as well, few of whom suspect themselves to be colleagues of Rona Barrett. Nor is this book immune. But we might ask questions about the implications of those stories, what they do tell us about Hollywood production practices, including, in fact, the reasons for generating such stories.

We want to know more about Hollywood production practices primarily because of the films that group of filmmakers created. Hollywood films and their stars have been a source of pleasure for us. Often we use that term, 'the Hollywood film,' as if we know exactly what it means. Analyzing the classical Hollywood cinema as a group style is the work of this entire book. Part One has indicated that this concept has a valid claim for a concrete historical existence as a group style. By systematically surveying typical films, we have been able to verify and refine that group style as a historical film practice. If the similarities among the Hollywood films cannot be attributed to accident, we must account for the uniformity.

The purpose of this part is to ground the film practices of Hollywood in the particular historical situation of their making. I assume that because production practices allowed the films to look and sound the way they did, we need to understand the production practices, how and why those practices were what they were. As noted in the Preface, Raymond Williams has outlined the question: 'We have to discover the nature of a practice and then its conditions.' We need to understand that the production of meaning is not separate from its economic mode of production nor from the instruments and techniques which individuals use to form materials so that meaning results. Furthermore, the production of meaning occurs in history; it is not without real changes in time. This suggests that we need to establish the conditions of the existence of this film practice, the relations among the conditions, and an explanation for their changes.

Some historians have already theorized what the conditions of existence of a film practice would include. Jean-Louis Comolli has pointed out the need to consider a socio-economic base, the ideological result of that base, and technology as an effect of both. He would include, as well, the influence of other signifying practices besides the medium of film. By using the term 'signifying practices,' Comolli stresses that film is a production of meaning, a work which, as an art, is not reducible to an ideology, but is a socio-historical practice with an ideological function. As a signifying practice, the material specificity of the medium has to be considered, that it can exceed any communicative meaning. Any film is a site of the interrelations, reinforcements, and contradictions of these terms at that time.[1]

In a somewhat different version, John Ellis has constructed four sorts of conditions of a film practice: the ideological (which includes various forms of visual representation as well as narrative developments, and so forth), the economic, the political, and the technological. Unlike Comolli, Ellis, and more recent theorists, do not privilege the socio-economic as a basis causing any 'superstructure' of ideology and technology. Rather, as Geoffrey Nowell-Smith has suggested, the history of cinema needs to be posed as 'immersed in a series of histories,' the histories of economy, technology, politics, ideology/representation, and the unconscious. For Nowell-Smith, histories do not accumulate but become the terrain of possibilities. Finally, Ellis stresses that production and stylistic practices cannot be seen as necessarily the result of these histories: 'The history of cinema cannot be read off from its conditions of existence.' By this, Ellis means that, for instance, 'the existence of a particular form of factory production did not "make" the studio develop its studio system, though it did provide one model for securing the reproduction of capital involved in mass cinema.'[2]

It is this latter course which most closely typifies my position. While economic practices are an important condition of existence for Hollywood's production practices, equally significant was the film industry's commitment to particular ideological/signifying practices such as those typified by the group style examined in Part One. Both practices were part of a socio-political formation which also often influenced their construction (e.g., instances of censorship, current social debates, state intervention in labor relations, patent and copyright formulations). These practices, as well, were influenced by other media both in terms of their economic practices (e.g., systems of production, distribution, and exhibition for theater, vaudeville, side shows) and their ideological/signifying practices (e.g., narrative structures, systems of constructing meaning). Yet as Ellis suggests, the conditions of existence must also be seen as internal to the industry. Once initiated, the industry generated its own economic and ideological/signifying practices that interacted with practices in adjacent industries.

Moreover, this commitment to particular practices was not due to some essentialist 'force' but rather to specifiable discourses discussing, describing, and validating these practices. These discourses appeared throughout the institutions within and connected to the film industry. This part will develop their historical construction and context.

This part will also show that these discourses and practices were the conditions of the existence of the particular mode of production. Thus, rather than considering Hollywood's mode only as the historical conditions allowing a group style to exist, we must also see production practices as an *effect* of the group style, as a function permitting those films to look and sound as they did while simultaneously adhering to a particular economic practice. The circularity needs concrete explanation.

No film historian has ever questioned that the American film industry was an instance of the economic system of capitalism. Films' manufacturers intended to produce films to make a profit. But capitalism has changed over the past eighty-five years. The implications of these changes have to be analyzed. In addition, many people have noted that the production practices were an instance of, as Ellis puts it, 'a particular form of factory production.' Now we need to specify what that form of factory production was, how it affected the dominant production practices, and why and how it changed during subsequent years. Among other things, to the present, the organization of the US film industry has utilized six kinds of management structures and after 1907, film production increasingly subdivided its work into more and more specialities to handle new technologies and increased output. Furthermore, many of Hollywood's production practices result from a tension in the economic practices: a movement toward standardizing the product for efficient, economical mass production and a simultaneous movement toward differentiating the product as the firms bid competitively for a consumer's disposable income. This tension helps explain why Hollywood film style remained so stable through the years and still manifested minor changes.

However, equally significant in the construction of production practices were ideological/signifying practices. The organization of this part may imply that the economic practices are the more potent explanation for the mode of production. While in the last instance economic practices may have been determinant, this part will stress that ideological/signifying practices continually influenced the necessity to divide labor and to divide it in its particular configuration. Here we have to understand the intertwining of determinants. A very particular group style became the film practice for Hollywood, and this did not exist *in toto* in 1896; in fact, it was a result of a process of movements among alternative practices, culminating around 1917 in the style that finally characterized Hollywood's films. (See Part Three.) What is most revealing is that *the mode of production constructed was by no means the cheapest filmmaking procedure*. Take, for instance, editing. By the 1920s, the post-shooting phase of production not only involved a film editor but also an assistant editor (to keep track of thousands of pieces of film), a writer (to construct additional bits of narrative information and dialogue for intertitles), and an elaborate system of paperwork (including a continuity script, notes taken during shooting by a script secretary, notes from a cameraman's assistant, and written directions from producers and directors.) In the balance between economical production and a presumed effect on the film, the latter won out. Thus, while economic practices helped produce a divided labor system of filmmaking, in many cases, ideological/signifying practices influenced how the firms divided that labor.

Technology enters here as a result of not only scientific developments (another history) but of both these economic and ideological/signifying practices. On the one hand, we shall find that technological changes in the industry increased production economies, differentiated products for competitive market positions, and 'improved' the product. On the other hand, technological change had to be accommodated within both production and film practices. That Hollywood was able to do so is attributable to the ways in which the industry developed its technologies and assimilated those changes. (See Parts Four and Six.)

Finally, what was occurring was not a result of a *Zeitgeist* or immaterial forces. The sites of the distribution of these practices were material: labor, professional, and trade associations, advertising materials, handbooks, film reviews. These institutions and their discourses were mechanisms to formalize and disperse descriptive and prescriptive analyses of the most efficient production practices, the newest technologies, and the best look and sound for the films. It is with these terms, then, that we can construct a history of the conditions of the existence of US film production practices.

A mode of production: initial definitions

Understanding the Hollywood mode of production requires analyzing what factors are involved in its organization and the relationship of those factors to each other. ('Mode of production' will refer specifically to production practices. The 'mode' is distinct from the 'industry' which is the economic structure and conduct of the particular companies which produced, distributed, and exhibited the films. For a brief history of the industry, see Appendices B and C.) A dynamic relationship – each element affects and influences each of the others. Generally, three elements will be referred to in this relationship: 1) the labor force, 2) the means of production, and 3) the financing of production.

This concept of a mode of production comes from Karl Marx. As Marx puts it: 'In the social production of their life, men enter into definite relations that are indispensable and independent of their will, relations of production which correspond to a definite stage of development of their material productive forces.' In his writings, Marx outlined various prior modes of production but concentrated his analyses on capitalism.[3]

The first term, labor force, includes all workers involved directly and indirectly in the production of the films or the production of physical means to make them. In cinema, these workers include cameramen, scriptwriters, stagehands, lensmakers, producers, breakaway-prop-makers, and so on.

The fact that these workers are not labeled by proper names indicates one aspect of this mode: it is organized by the work functions, not the identity of individuals. In addition, we all know that the breakaway-prop-maker, while a contributor to the final product, has a lot less to say about how a film will look and sound than will a scriptwriter or cameraman – who in turn will have different things to say about the film than will a producer. A hierarchical and structural arrangement of control over subordinate and separate work functions and hence, input into the product, is also a characteristic of the labor force. A system of management controls the execution of the work. The mode assigns work functions to each key management position, making the worker in that position responsible for supervising part of the total labor process.

The second term, the means of production, includes all physical capital related to the production of the commodity. Generally, the means of production consists of the physical aspects of a company such as its buildings, its sets and paints and glue, its costumes. A very particular part of the means of production for filmmaking is its technology, its tools and materials (cameras, film stock, lighting equipment). Technology also implies technique: the methods of use of those tools and materials. Thus, the cameraman's placement of an arc lamp is a concrete example of one of the relationships between the labor force and the means of production and, hence, part of the history of the mode.[4]

The third term is the financing of the production. In a capitalist firm, individual persons and other companies supply capital to a legal entity (the firm) which purchases labor power and physical capital. The purpose of providing capital is to make a profit, usually to maximize the profit. Some historians have argued that different forms of financing affected the films; we will examine that issue in Chapter 24. Ownership of a firm is a separate concept from the work function of managing a company. At times ownership and management will be congruent; at other times they will not. This theoretical and historical separation will become useful in understanding changing divisions of responsibility in the studios.

The historical context

Hollywood's mode of production has been characterized as a factory system akin to that used by a Ford plant, and Hollywood often praised its own work structure for its efficient mass production of entertaining films. The employment of a mass-production system fulfilled the owners' goals of profit maximization. Concurrent US business practices had set up a particular mode of production which seemed to insure the most efficient and economical work arrangement. It was within that context that the film industry began operating.[5]

Two major changes in the relationship between the workers and the work processes which led to the typical factory mode of production need to be described: 'mass production' and 'division of labor.' 'Mass production,' Henry Ford wrote, 'is the focussing upon a manufacturing product of the principles of power, accuracy, economy, system, continuity and speed . . . and the normal result is the productive organization that delivers in *quantities* a useful commodity of standard material, workmanship and design at a minimum cost.'[6] Ford's definition is debatable (are all mass-produced products 'useful'?), but it does include certain requisites for understanding mass production, and these can be summed up as interchangeability, standardization, and assembly.

Interchangeability is by no means a modern concept. As John Perry points out, interchangeability of parts goes back to ancient times. What Eli Whitney as a 'father of mass production . . . did was standardize production operations and narrow tolerances for the dimensions of parts.' But Perry also notes that genuine mass production implies standardization at a distance: parts made by a worker in one plant must fit with parts made by other workers in other plants.[7] Whitney managed this interchangeability primarily by designing machine-tools and precision gauges. A less skilled laborer could operate these tools with a precision and speed that the gunsmith craftsman could never have reached. Whitney's example was rapidly disseminated to others, and the 1820s and 1830s saw the quick expansion of machine-tool technology. One economist summarized the cost advantages in this degree of interchangeability: '(a) the percentage of spoiled work will probably be lower; (b) the parts are more likely to be interchangeable, which would decrease the assembly cost; and (c) the [tool] can probably be [used] by a less skilled workman, receiving a lower hourly rate.'[8] Necessary goods, such as tools, shoes, and clothes, and upper-class luxuries, such as harpsichords, clavichords, and spinet pianos, went into mass production by the 1840s. Lower costs and more goods available meant a better consumers' market, and mass production practices increased correspondingly.

Standardization, necessary for precision fit, had economic advantages within any firm which mass produced goods, but not so apparent to the firm were the advantages of inter-company uniformity. Companies traditionally varied their products for competing in the markets and used patent protection over these variations to effect a monopoly not only of the product but of replacement parts. For example, in the 1840s, railroad lines were operating under a variety of gauges which effectively prevented use of one road's lines by another company. The advantages of standardization − facilitation of economies of production, research and design; minimization of engineering problems; and reduction of costs of patterns, retooling, carrying large stocks, labor retraining, and accounting − eventually began to outweigh its disadvantages. The post-Civil-War shift toward company mergers and the move to eliminate ' "idiotic competition" '[9] (a phrase used to rationalize the collusion of firms), also enhanced the change. 'Industrial standardization,' as the full-blown movement was known, eventually included:[10]

1 *Nomenclature* and definitions of technical terms used in specifications and contracts; also technical abbreviations and symbols.
2 *Uniformity in dimensions* necessary to secure interchangeability of parts and supplies, and makes [sic] possible the interworking of apparatus. Dimensional standards.
3 *Quality specifications* for materials and equipment; composition, form, and structure.
4 *Methods of testing* to determine standards of quality and performance.
5 *Ratings* of machinery and apparatus under specific conditions.
6 *Safety provisions* and rules for the operation of apparatus and machinery in industrial establishments. Safety codes and standards of practice.
7 *Simplification* by the elimination of unnecessary variety in types, sizes, grades, this selection being usually based upon the relative commercial demand.

Prime movers in the trend were engineers and efficiency experts who created an institutional discourse about standardization in their technical journals, societies, textbooks, and handbooks. The creation in 1901 of the federal government's Bureau of Standards provided not only a new repository for physical objects defining standards of length, weight, volume, time, and temperature but now a testing facility for quality and performance of materials. One of the bureau's first activities was determining standards for electric lamps, which led to new testing equipment: needing a measure of brightness, it developed a rapid commercial photometer. The federal bureau gave the State's blessing to standardization and supplied national rather than state or industry guidelines.

Assembly, a third aspect of mass production, also involves 'division of labor.' Just as with all other elements of this changing work system, division of labor has very old sources. Societies have commonly parceled out work, often on the basis of gender: men and women may do different tasks. Within initial splits may be further ones − some laborers making pottery, others weaving, and others growing and harvesting crops. This is usually termed a *social division of labor*.[11] Within social division of labor, a worker will know and perform an integral series of tasks, from conceiving an object to be made and gathering the materials to working on those materials and completing the object. Even if the worker at times performs only parts of the whole task, knowledge of and skill in the entire craft belongs to the worker's repertoire.

This situation changed with mass production. Within a capitalist economy, a laborer must sell his or her labor power to a company. The company has the option of relying upon the social division of labor to define the worker's job. Analysts of capitalism have pointed out, however, that a company with a profit motive seeks to obtain as much labor power for its wages as it can. Although the social division of labor was adequate for certain tasks, mass production could be more efficient with a new type of work arrangement: *detailed division of labor*. Here the process of making a product is broken down into discrete segments, and each worker is assigned to repeat a constituent element of that process. Harry Braverman explains why the change to a new mode was made: 'The subcontracting and "putting out" systems [entailed by the social division of labor] were plagued by problems of irregularity of production, loss of materials in transit and through embezzlement, slowness of manufacture, lack of uniformity and uncertainty of the quality of the product.'[12] Capitalists saw possibilities in labor which were wasted in the social division mode. Furthermore, that mode could not insure the standardization of the product parts or rapid assembly necessary for mass production – which detailed division of labor could.

Braverman argues that the central difference between the modes is that in a detailed division of labor the conception and execution of the work is divided: management does all of the former and laborers do only the latter. As the work is complicated and the tasks are segmented further, the individual worker becomes more and more specialized and loses understanding of the entire process.[13]

Capitalism found detailed division of labor less costly: only the laborer doing the most skilled portion of the work had to be paid the highest rate. Marx makes several other distinctions which will become important in understanding Hollywood's mode of production. Within divided labor, he locates two phases – manufacturing and, later, machine-tool (or modern) industry. Manufacturing developed either when a capitalist assembled workers with multiple handicrafts into one workshop or when a capitalist gathered a group of craftsmen to make the same product and then divided their labor. Marx also defines manufacturing as either 'heterogeneous' or 'serial.' In 'heterogeneous' manufacture, all the parts of a product are made by separate workers; then the commodity is assembled by one individual. The case example is the manufacture of a watch. In 'serial' manufacture, the commodity goes through 'connected phases of development.' Thus, the workers are dependent on one another. In such a work process, the laborer must spend no more time than is necessary on his or her part, mass production requiring 'continuity, uniformity, regularity, order' for best profits. It is in serial manufacture that a hierarchy of skilled and unskilled workers forms.[14]

Machine-tool, or modern, industry is organized via the machines. Detailed division of labor meshed well with the introduction of machine-tool technology and the centralized work place. We have seen that the move to machine-tool technology had distinct economic advantages: less spoiled work, increased interchangeability, and less-skilled (hence cheaper) laborers. Machine-tool technology, in turn, required a centralized work place. More complicated technology necessitated the physical unification of the work, centralization reduced waste of time and cost in moving work from site to site, and centralization made it easier for management to control the workers' use of the machines. Once the company taught the laborer one process with one machine all training costs were over, and uniformity and standard quality in the product were assured. Thus, detailed division of labor and the new technology and work organization reinforced one another.

Both the changing industrial structure in contemporary United States and the mode of production supported one another. A steady supply of raw materials enhanced the assembly system – which in turn encouraged vertical integration of the corporate unit. Mass-production industries came to depend upon efficient distribution and marketing (which produced more vertical integration), the use of by-products (which resulted in diversification), and the elimination of competition (which induced horizontal integration).[15]* The shift to mass production and the growth of the corporate industrial structure went hand-in-hand.

For Marx, manufacturing had the potential of collective cooperation; in modern industry, any cooperation is only simple.[16] We shall see that although it is accurate to define the Hollywood mode of production as mass production and detailed division of labor, its organization most closely approximates serial manufacture, allowing some collective activity and cooperation between craft workers.

Detailed division of labor and commercial filmmaking

It is useful to classify the Hollywood mode of production as mass production, but that does not explain the disparity between D.W. Griffith at the Biograph Company in 1910 and Dore Schary at Metro-Goldwyn-Mayer in 1950. In one sense, both men were managing the mass production of films, but there is a significant difference between producing one one-reel Biograph after another and turning out reels of glossy MGM features. A description of all Hollywood production systems at one broad level of generality cannot account for more specific levels of description nor can it account for changes over time.

Theoretical models have the advantage of any generalization – they permit a simplification and unification of detail into a pattern. Likewise, they have the disadvantage of the loss of individual differences. Just as no single film is *the* classical Hollywood film, no actual production company is the site of the classical Hollywood production mode. Furthermore, just as the classical film can be subdivided into genres or styles with distinctive characteristics, so too can Hollywood's production mode. Because no one has attempted before to characterize or construct the mode in any extended analysis, no precedents form a basis for categorizing the available information.

I will be analyzing the mode of production by virtue of two descriptive and explanatory schemata related to the organization of the labor force: the division of the work and the management systems. Theoretically, these are separate concepts, and any historical explanation must consider different patterns of change in each.

In examining the division of the work, I will trace the increasing subdivision of the initial work functions and order. For instance, the cameraman's duties subdivided to laboratory technicians, to assistants, and to continuity clerks. This subdivision happened regardless of the management system; the causes lie not in the management structure per se, but in economic practices (increased production rate, increased technological complexities) and in ideological/signifying practices (demands for certain stylistic qualities in the films).

For the management systems, I will identify two modes. The distinction between the modes of social and detailed division of labor applies to the US film industry, which seems to have used both. The detailed division of labor mode, however, quickly became dominant when commercial filmmaking started emphasizing the production of narrative fiction films after 1906. Just as in the general sector, detailed divisions of labor in filmmaking allowed faster and more predictable product output. But as we shall see, in filmmaking mass production never reached the assembly-line degree of rigidity that it did in

other industries. Rather it remained a manufacturing division of labor with craftsmen collectively and serially producing a commodity. After describing the social division mode manifested in the 'cameraman' system, I will split the detailed division mode into five specific systems which appeared in a sequential order (I will use the term 'mode' for the broader description of the work structure as defined by Braverman and the term 'system' for a more specific description of one form of a mode):

1) the 'director' system, the dominant system from 1907 to 1909;
2) the 'director-unit' system which developed as the manufacturers increased output after 1909;
3) the 'central producer' system which became dominant around 1914;
4) the 'producer-unit' system which resulted from a major rearrangement in the early 1930s; and
5) the 'package-unit' system which started in the early 1940s and became dominant by the mid-1950s.

All five systems display a detailed division of labor.

In detailed division of labor systems, Braverman argues, work positions are divided between those who conceive the work and those who execute it. At the lowest echelons of the structural hierarchy, the split between conception and execution has caused the worker to lose the overall knowledge he or she had of a craft. Instead, the worker knows only the part that the company or schools train him or her to do. For Braverman, this helps explain the alienation of the worker from the work.

Although Braverman mentions a 'middle-layer' of employment, he generally avoids the problem of analyzing the managerial level of workers in the modern corporation. In the approach of Antony Cutler, Barry Hindess, Paul Hirst, and Athar Hussain, 'managers are economic agents employed to exercise the capacity of direction on behalf of a capital.' Four functions are involved in that management direction:[17]

1) *Direction of Investment:* the central function here is the calculation of financing (source and level of funds), the definition of the areas of operation of the capital – this will take the

form of an overall investment decision or plan. . . .

2) *Production Planning:* as a consequence of basic investment decisions this level involves decisions as to the products, type of production process, general level of production, etc. . . .

3) *Production Operation:* decisions as to the purchases of raw materials, labour-power, etc., are made on the basis of assessment of market conditions within the constraints imposed by the financial strategy. . . .

4) *Co-ordination and Supervision:* the integration of the phases of a process of production and the maintenance of production performance.

Functions 1 and 3 involve decisions which directly affect the nature and level of economic operation of the enterprises – they are functions which in some sense must be united in a single agency of calculation and decision. These functions define the *economic subject* – the agency of direction of a capital. Functions 2 and 4 are in general technical consequences of factors in economic and operational decisions, and are subordinate to them. . . .

. . . 'Managers' performing functions 1 and 3 are specialists hired to act as agents of an economic subjectivity, directors of capital. Specialists performing functions 2 and 4 exclusively are technical functionaries ancillary to the economic subject.

Alfred D. Chandler, Jr, has distinguished between management decisions along roughly the same lines, calling those decisions involving long-range capital direction (functions 1 and 3) *strategic* decisions, and those involving the day-to-day carrying out of the plans of a company (functions 2 and 4) *tactical* decisions. Both Cutler *et al.* and Chandler note that in actual operation in capitalist firms, strategic-decision managers top the pyramid in the hierarchy. In other words, they have the power to countermand any subordinate decision – a prerogative, we shall see, they will seldom employ in the larger companies because of the lack of familiarity with the lower-level work processes and technology. The tactical-decision makers (which Cutler *et al.* call technical functionaries) are the middle management.[18]

Thus, three levels of work exist: strategic management, tactical or technical management, and execution. At least at the technical level, the managers have retained craft knowledge and will probably be directly involved with varying amounts of its execution.

Besides focusing on the division of the individual work functions and the management structure and hierarchy, I will be emphasizing the importance of the script as a blueprint for the film. While a written plan of the film has always been useful, I will show how in the early teens a detailed script became necessary to insure efficient production and to insure that the film met a certain standard of quality defined by the industry's discourse. While pertinent before the early teens, the simultaneous diffusion of the multiple-reel film and certain stylistic options at that point placed such demands on the production crew that a precise pre-shooting plan became necessary. The script, furthermore, became more than just the mechanism to pre-check quality: it became the blueprint from which all other work was organized. These issues will be raised in the discussions of the first three systems of management in a detailed division of labor, culminating in the central producer system in which the continuity script became standard practice.

Throughout this chapter, I have suggested that various more specific formats of management organizations and the subdivision of work appeared in sequential order. I need to provide, then, causal explanations of these changes. Changes within the mode will be attributed to its conditions of existence: economic and ideological/signifying practices. Regarding the latter, I have already referred to standards of systems of representation which I said the filmmakers' institutions constructed – and in many cases, appropriated in mediated form from other signifying practices. As I suggested, a major part of my explanation as to why the mode of production developed as it did is the standards which the film industry discourse established. In particular, we will be looking at certain traits of the classical Hollywood group style: the primacy of the narrative, 'realism,' causal coherence, continuity, spectacle, stars, genres. These traits, among others, influenced the emphasis on certain job tasks and in some cases caused firms to create individual jobs. Two of the more obvious instances of this are the addition of research staffs in the mid-teens and the continuity clerk in the late teens.

Hollywood production practices related to the prevalent capitalist mode of production, justifying a broad claim of the mode being a mass-production, factory system. Furthermore, extensive analysis reveals subtleties in its organization which can be described and explained, and the practices can account for the uniformity and stability of the style of the films. This analysis also provides an explanation for the fascinating stories about making films in Hollywood. In the next chapter, we will see how in capitalism advertising the values of the films is an important selling technique. Thus, publicity releases, true or apocryphal, about thousands of extras, millions of dollars, and unique star personalities are all part of the Hollywood mode of production.

Standardization and differentiation: the reinforcement and dispersion of Hollywood's practices

Thus, when D.W. Griffith began to use his soft-focus lens to give added beauty or mystery to a shot and the idea was hailed as an advance in art, we had an era of fuzzy pictures which I am afraid did more to irritate the fans than to charm them. If a cameraman didn't have a real soft-focus lens, he merely threw his regular lens a bit out of focus and felt artistic for the rest of that day. And when the Germans began using 'unusual' angles, generally with a definite, psychological purpose, we kissed the idea on both cheeks and indulged in an orgy of 'unusual' angles, generally with no psychological or dramatic purpose whatsoever, but just to keep ahead of the procession. Love scenes were shot from the ceiling, giving an excellent view of the tops of both lovers' heads; mirror shots, always the directors' darlings, became so rampant that the audience frequently had trouble untangling the scene from its reflection; cameras were placed on the floor, whence the full depth and beauty of the heroine's nostrils could be viewed; cameras were placed behind bureaus, so that as the heroine pulled out the drawer we could peek up at her just as if we were actually in the drawer, a rare and most artistic viewpoint.[1]

William de Mille, 1939

Describing and explaining Hollywood's production practices and their changes over the years are the work of subsequent chapters. In this chapter I shall describe how the film companies established their production and stylistic practices throughout the industry. How could these practices have acquired such uniformity and stability? Standardization and differentiation are useful concepts in answering this question.

'Standard' means two slightly different things. One is regularity or uniformity. For example, 'the industry sought to standardize perforations' – or to make them uniform in size, number, and position relative to each photographed image. In the survey of the movement toward standardization in Chapter 8, I pointed out that industrial standardization included uniformity in nomenclature and dimensions, simplification in types, sizes, and grades, and safety provisions and rules of practice. Such standardization facilitated mass production. Standardization also included specifications, methods of testing quality, and ratings under specific conditions. The latter set of elements in standardization have another connotation: a criterion, norm, degree or level of excellence. Both the movement toward uniformity and attainment of excellence coexisted in the trend. The standardization process must be thought of not as an inevitable progression toward dull, mediocre products (although many may be that for reasons of aesthetic differences or economy in materials and workmanship) but instead, particularly in competitive cases, as an attempt to achieve a precision-tooled, quality object. Once established, the standard becomes a goal to be attained.

Just as the specifications for a machine involve degrees of tolerance in individual parts so too we might think of the standardized film. As we study the industry's discussion of its product and the grounds on which it competed, we find a repetition of characteristics considered desirable in the film. Primary ones are narrative dominance and clarity, verisimilitude, continuity, stars, and spectacle. We might think of these as product specifications which guide the boundaries of the film's construction but within those boundaries tolerance is permitted. As a system of elements, films operate within a cultural context that defines (and is defined by) the meaning of its systems. As the film industry and its institutions adapted representational and aesthetic systems from other media and constructed their own specifications of meaning for the US commercial film, they simultaneously set up hierarchies of quality work.

At a certain point in the history of the American film industry, specific industrial mechanisms appeared which facilitated standardization. Three of these mechanisms are of interest to us: advertising practices, industrial interest groups, and institutions adjacent to but not directly part of the industrial structure. These mechanisms dispersed a number of different types of standards ranging from stylistic practices (disseminated by advertising, writers' and cinematographers' groups, how-to books, trade papers, and critics), to technology (the professional engineers' society, cinematographers' clubs, projectionists' unions), to business, production, and exhibition practices (trade associations and trade papers). Although existing in part at the start of commercial filmmaking, these mechanisms coalesced into formal networks with the formation of distribution alliances in 1908-10. By the late teens, the industry had a full array of systematic techniques to spread industrial discourse and standards rapidly. This foundation provided the conditions for the existence of the uniformity in the industry's film practices.

The emphasis on uniformity does not mean that a standard will not change in small ways. New technology, new products, and new models are continually put forth as alternative standards for the field. One analyst of standardization wrote: 'An innovation is successful only when it has become a new standard.'[2] That process is dynamic, with multiple practices creating the change. In fact, for the film industry, changing its product was an economic necessity. In the entertainment field, innovations in standards are also prized qualities. The economic reason is that the promotion of the difference between products is a competitive method and encourages repeated consumption. The phrase *differentiation of the product* is used to describe the practice in which the firm stresses how its goods or services differ from other ones.

Economists explain that such product differentiation can create the appearance of a monopoly, and, as a result, the manufacturer attains more control over the price of the product.[3] Furthermore, this marketing advantage will affect the production sector which through styles and packaging may even engineer *product cycles*: as Braverman argues, in an 'attempt to gear consumer needs to the needs of production instead of the other way around.'[4]

In a particularly vulnerable consumption field, film has had to contend with rapidly shifting product cycles which it helped induce. The film industry, like other industries, faced innovations – a value it has itself standardized in its search for novelty and competitive advantage in differentiating its product. Innovations have sometimes replaced prior norms of excellence; sometimes they have not. Thus, I will also be stressing the implications of this economic practice for the production procedures and the group style.

'Absolutely the superior of any moving picture film ever made'

One of the major mechanisms which established the standards for quality filmmaking was advertising discourse. Advertising is important because it is the economic practice directing consumers to the product's possibilities for exchange-value. What advertising stressed became grounds for competition and a large part of the set of standards for film practice. That the major values we associate with later Hollywood ballyhoo were actively promoted by the early teens helps explain the formation of the classical style so early.

Advertising was not a recent invention, but a remarkable transformation in its strategies occurred during the 1800s in the United States. Goods which were originally sold generically began to acquire brand names. Techniques for advertising rapidly proliferated from ads in newspapers and magazines to posters on billboards and barnsides. Tie-ins were common by the mid-1800s, and slogans became popular at the end of the century. Businesses were not left on their own to advertise. As early as 1841 an advertising agent organized near Philadelphia and soon had branch offices in other cities. In 1899 Ayer's developed what would now be called a full-service campaign for the newly formed National Biscuit Co. It launched a national campaign through all media, did publicity work, advised on marketing, and created the trade names Uneeda and Nabisco. Overall, expenditures on advertising changed dramatically. They rose from only about $8 million in 1865 to $200 million in 1880 and exceeded $800 million in 1904. At that point, expenditures amounted to 3.4 per cent of the gross national product, the same percentage level current today.[5]

With these practices as their example, the first motion picture manufacturers used as their routine advertising method catalogues which listed the order number for the film, a brief, hopefully enticing, description, and the length of the film. The firms also organized the industrial structure in part to serve their marketing tactics. When distribution alliances formed in 1908-10 (see Appendices B and C), they contracted to supply the exhibitor not only a varied, quality product but a service of a predictable supply of films so that the exhibitor could change his program daily. As the Motion Picture Patents Company lawyers rationalized the motives for the organization of General Film Company, they stressed that prior exchange systems failed to provide the standard of service the exhibitors demanded. 'The market value of motion picture service,' they argued, 'depends entirely upon the age of the motion picture, counting from the release date.'[6] Although developed later, zoning (assuring exhibitors of a market area) and clearance (setting lengths of runs and intervals between runs) were economic practices which responded to and reinforced the ideology and profit advantage of new, quality product.

Advertising superlatives started with the catalogue ads. Excerpts from three Edison ads will exemplify what qualities were being promoted:[7]

Life of an American Fireman (1903)
In giving this description to the public, we unhesitatingly claim for it the strongest motion picture attraction ever attempted in this length of film. It will be difficult for the exhibitor to conceive the amount of work involved and the number of rehearsals necessary to turn out a film of this kind. We were compelled to enlist the services of the fire departments of four different cities, New York, Newark, Orange, and East Orange, N.J., and about 300 firemen appear in the various scenes of this film.

From the first conception of this wonderful series of pictures it has been our aim to portray *Life of an American Fireman* without exaggeration, at the same time embodying the dramatic situations and spectacular effects which so greatly enhance a motion picture performance. . . .

This film faithfully and accurately depicts his thrilling and dangerous life, emphasizing the perils he subjects himself to when human life is at stake.

Uncle Tom's Cabin (1903)
The photographic and dramatic qualities of our latest moving picture production, *Uncle Tom's Cabin*, are excellent. We offer this film as one of our best creations and one that will prove a great headline attraction. The popularity of the book and play of the same title is a positive guarantee of its success. The story has been faithfully studied and every scene posed in accordance with the famous author's version.

In this film we have made a departure from the old methods of dissolving one scene into another by inserting announcements with brief descriptions as they appear in succession.

The Great Train Robbery (1903)
This sensational and highly tragic subject will certainly make a decided 'hit' whenever shown. In every respect we consider it absolutely the superior of any moving picture film ever made. It has been posed and acted in faithful duplication of the genuine 'Holds Ups' made famous by various outlaw bands in the far West, and only recently the East has been shocked by several crimes of the frontier order, which fact will increase the popular interest in this great *Headline Attraction*.
. . . .

SCENE 14 – REALISM. A life size picture of Barnes, leader of the outlaw band, taking aim and firing point blank at each individual in the audience. . . . The resulting excitement is great.

These ads seem vaguely familiar because they exhibit many of the exchange-values the industry has consistently promoted as the qualities in their films: novelty, specific popular genres, brand names, 'realism,' authenticity, spectacle, stars, and certain creators of the product whose skills as artists were considered acknowledged. Emotional effects are emphasized. Once film exhibition flourished, advertising emphasis has also included the theater as an institution which supplied valuable entertainment that was more than just the moving pictures. In order to understand how advertising worked as a mechanism to disperse product standards and to implant principles which would help develop the classical film style, we can survey some of these values, noting their implications and in the case of the star system its emergence in the industry around 1910.

Examples of appeals to *novelty* manifest themselves continually in the catalogues and later newspaper advertising. The words 'novelty' and 'innovation' became so common as to be clichés: 'one of the most genuine motion picture novelties,' 'an innovation in picture making.'[8] When nothing new in the films themselves was worth promoting, the advertisers turned to related material. The ads (figs 9.1, 9.2) displayed the high costs of spectacles, stars, and acknowledged artist-creators as evidence of the films' value – which was one reason for the publicity about filmmaking and the stars' lives in fan articles and magazines.

These fan materials started around 1910 in conjunction with the promotion of particular personalities. Cited as the first major national exploitation of the movies in print format is the *Motion Picture Story Magazine*. Started by J. Stuart Blackton, owner and producer for Vitagraph, the *Motion Picture Story Magazine* announced its format:[9]

It is a symposium of film scenarios, as its name implies, but these have been amplified by competent writers into really interesting storiettes of the approved magazine style. The first number of over 100 pages, is sumptuously illustrated with engraved reproductions of scenes in the film. With such a source to draw upon the 'Motion Picture Story Magazine' can provide its readers with vivid and realistic

illustrations beyond the reach of any other periodical.

Exhibitors could order copies for sale in the theaters. Within a year, two other such publications were available: *Moving Picture Tales* (published by the trade paper *Motion Picture News*) and the Sunday edition of the Chicago *Tribune*. Such tie-ins quickly expanded. Film serials commonly were accompanied by story versions in the newspapers. By 1914, book publishers were promoting leather-bound, numbered, limited edition copies of the motion picture edition of a novel, with tipped-in stills from the films. This practice was exploited with greater and greater finesse in subsequent years.[10]

Publicity directly emphasizing the lives and loves of the stars was not far behind the first issue of *Motion Picture Story Magazine*. By early 1911, the *Cleveland Leader* was holding contests for the best amateur criticism of films, the Sunday metro section had articles about current films, and its latest 'innovation' was a copper-plate section with pictures of 'leading photoplayers.' *Photoplay* also began in 1911.[11] In 1919, statistics gathered for investment bankers Kuhn, Loeb and Company indicated the tremendous, nationwide extent of such publicity:[12]

Circulation *per issue* of Motion Picture Magazines, 1918-19

	1918	1919
Photoplay Magazine	204,434	no record
Motion Picture Magazine	248,845	400,000
Motion Picture Classic	140,000	275,000
Picture Play Magazine	127,721	200,000
Photoplay Journal	100,000	no record
Shadow Land	—	75,000
	821,000	950,000

Source: *American Newspaper Annual and Directory*

Brand name advertising and slogans were common US economic practices by 1900. For filmmakers, the purpose of brands was to spread the value of each film to all the films, hoping to entice repeated consumption of the manufacturer's offerings. If the manufacturer could succeed in this, the firm would gain the advantage of an apparent monopoly. As a trade paper article, 'The efficiency plan of film salesmanship,' cautioned, this worked a lot better if the films were all of good quality. It also required some element in which to specialize – often a genre – and an advertising campaign which promoted that element – perhaps through a trademark or a slogan (fig 9.3). Thus we have Biograph's 'AB' in a circle, Edison's 'Circle E,' Vitagraph's ' "V" surmounted by an eagle with spreading wings,' Selig's Diamond S, Bison's 'buffalo rampant' for its Westerns, Essanay's Indian head, Kalem's blazing sun, Pathé Frères' red rooster, Lubin's liberty bell. Other qualities besides genre and trademark could be used. One early film critic helped out by distinguishing among the 1911 licensed manufacturers. The consumer could tell the individual producers by the 'manner of acting, the style of the construction and the character of the story.'[13] In general, however, the use of brand names as a primary advertising tactic declined in subsequent years when multiple-reel films supplanted the less differentiated one-reelers.

'Realism' was an important advertising claim. An Edison ad of 1898-9 asserted:[14]

Edison's latest marvel, The Projectoscope. The giving of life to pictures so natural that life itself is no more real.

Life motion, realism, photographed from nature so true to life as to force the observer to believe that they [sic] are viewing the reality and not the reproduction.

If you have never seen animated pictures, don't fail to see this one. If you have seen them, see this one, the greatest of them all!

'Realism' in these ads shifts in meaning. While in this case, the ad promoted the photographic representation of physical reality, in *Life of an American Fireman*, 'realism' was re-enacted events. The story would be presented 'without exaggeration, at the same time embodying the dramatic situations and spectacular effects which so greatly enhance a motion picture performance.' Obviously, here values start to conflict with and contradict one another. The consumer was to receive the 'best' views as well as 'real life.' This tension among values was only partially resolved by conventions (often generic) of verisimilitude to which the quality film tried to adhere.

A third meaning of 'realism' was *authenticity*; as Chapter 1 has shown, this appeal persisted through American film history. The trade papers promoted this value in part by encouraging consumers to write in about 'mistakes' they caught in the films. Companies, in turn, advertised meticulous research. Behind *Custer's Last Fight* (1912) were 'months of preparation and careful study of the many historical accounts of the great battle. The photoplay . . . follows the historical facts with the utmost accuracy possible.' The argument for authenticity was that if a consumer noted some inauthentic occurrence, his or her 'illusion' of reality would be destroyed and with it the effect of the film.[15] (Legitimate theater had for over a century been promoting this value.[16]) This value eventually affected the division of labor by moving the research on historical topics into the work positions of technical experts and research departments.

Spectacle was a value imported from legitimate theater and other entertainments, and film advertisers sought new and better displays of extravagance. Advertisements for a 1912 multiple-reel film *Homer's Odyssey* compared it to an earlier success: 'Bigger in plot – more strikingly realistic – better in story – more scenically sensational than Dante's *Inferno*.' Or as Sam Goldwyn reputedly requested many years later: 'I want a film that begins with an earthquake and works up to a climax.' The enumeration of the number of players, the size and value of the sets, the costs in thousands and millions of dollars signaled areas of spectacle, and 'production value' and 'showmanship' became its euphemism (see figs 9.4, 9.5). Ensuring that the consumer knew these were installed within the film was part of the work of the publicity and exploitation segments of the sales departments, and the source of many of the stories we have of Hollywood's production practices.[17]

One particular warrant of quality was the appeal to an *established success* in entertainment. In Edison's 1903 ad for *Uncle Tom's Cabin*, the faithful reproduction of a famous work, the description argued, was a 'positive guarantee of its success.' At the time of this ad, the legitimate theater was in a cycle of adapting copyrighted fiction into plays, and the imitation of this practice by film companies responded to the same perceived economic advantages. Not only were famous works exploited but Edison's 'eminent authors' pre-dated Goldwyn's by a decade. The hiring of writers and dramatists to compose stories either in their own medium or in film scenario form began about 1909 in the United States. French Gaumont announced in the US trade papers it had signed contracts with French dramatists, and later Edison advertised the signing of 'exclusive' contracts for the writing services of Edward W. Townsend, Carolyn Wells, Richard Harding Davis, and Rex Beach.[18]

Finally, and, with the possible exception of the story, the most important value was the *stars*. The 'star system' already functioned in the other entertainment products of theater and vaudeville (dating back to at least the 1820s in the United States). In September 1909, Edison's publicity men claimed that while other press men tried to bring out 'some new press story' about their 'star's lives,' Edison knew it had secured 'some of the best talent the theatrical profession affords.' In its stock company it had 'under contract actors from the best companies in the business, companies such as Charles Frohman, David Belasco, E.S. Sothern, Ada Rehan, Otis Skinner, Julia Marlowe, Mrs Fiske, the late Richard Mansfield.' Subsequently, Edison introduced in its catalogues its stock players with individual lengthy descriptions of their prior experiences and successes. Kalem and Vitagraph innovated lobby display cards in early 1910 (see fig 9.6), and information about the 'real lives' of the players started to appear in the trade papers. Marion Leonard (see fig 9.7) was 'shanghaied' in January 1912 and King Baggott denied he was dead a week later (see figs 9.8, 9.9, 9.10).[19]

Whether the demand for stars came first from the consumers or was created by enterprising capitalists is immaterial in this case since the precedents in theater and vaudeville are so immediate. The argument that the licensed manufacturers did not exploit the stars because of fear of rising costs until they were forced into it by the independents' competition also does not hold up. Instead, the licensed manufacturers led the way although the independents may have outbid them for services of stars in later years. In addition, film manufacturers were competing directly with vaudeville and theater both of which were using the star system.

The emergence of the indigenous motion picture star occurred around 1910. Anthony Slide locates articles about Ben Turpin, Pearl White,

and Mary Pickford in April 1909 and December 1910.[20] It was but a step from being a personality to being a star. Florence Lawrence, the 'star that radiates and scintillates more than other luminaries in the film firmament,' appeared in the front pages of the *New York Dramatic Mirror*, a major trade paper for theater and vaudeville, in a 1912 story, 'Florence Lawrence, famous picture star.'[21]

The appearance of the theatrical and vaudeville star in movies was delayed somewhat because the producers could not afford established stars. In the middle of 1910 Edison promoted the appearance of Mlle Pilar Moran from the theater, and isolated campaigns increased thereafter. It was not until multiple-reel films became more common in 1911 and 1912, however, that film companies induced many stage stars to play roles.[22] The star system became the order of the day in 1912, and publicity promoted 'all star casts' from the Royal Theater of Copenhagen, Sarah Bernhardt, and the 'All Star' Film Company (see fig 9.11).[23]

None of this is meant to explain why this culture was and is fascinated by stars. Economically, the star may be thought of as a monopoly on a personality. The unique qualities of Mary Pickford or Lana Turner or Robert Redford permit a company to declare the merchandising of an exclusive product, and the competitive value of that justified paying the salaries those stars have been able to demand. The star became a means to differentiate product to achieve monopoly profits, and only lower-budget films would not have had stars.

All of these values of novelty and quality allowed the firms to differentiate their product so that exhibitors would seek their merchandise at the exchange and consumers would buy the opportunity to view the films in the theaters. Furthermore, advertising reinforced standard requirements for a film by stressing a certain set of characteristics in a certain way. In addition, in emphasizing these standards, advertising simultaneously outlined the boundaries for variation. For instance, in the case of spectacle, the standard was the bigger the better; the variant was the kind of spectacle. Or for famous writers, the variant was the latest literary or theatrical success. If one considers alternatives, it is easy to see the boundaries of the standard.

Imagine, for example, advertising a story as 'just like every other film you have ever seen' or 'written by an unknown who will remain that' or 'a drama completely unrealistic and unnatural.' (Of course, with just a twist, all of these could be turned around, exploiting favorite genres, the mystery of the writer's identity, or the uncanny.)

Advertising as a discourse created standards and exploited innovations. It established the grounds on which competition would occur and set up prescriptive values which became requirements for film practice in the United States. Stars, spectacle, 'realism,' popular genres, and so forth became necessary for a film. To the historian of production practices, advertising is a guide to the areas of exchange-value between the producer and consumer, and, as such, to the standards that those production practices would have to achieve in their films.

Coalescence of industrial interest groups

While advertising's effect was the standardization of product practices, industrial interest groups affected practices in film style, production, technology, business, and exhibition. Furthermore, in some instances, these groups deliberately attempted to standardize segments of the industry. The list of areas of industrial standardization (Chapter 8) includes, besides uniformity and quality specifications, standardization of nomenclature and codes of practice. In the case of trade associations, besides their informal exchange of information, they established codes of ethical conduct (self-regulation) and agreements regarding what subject matter would be available for competition (self-censorship). In later years, the professional engineers' society set up not only standards of technological design but lists of terms with approved definitions.[24]

By the late teens, the Hollywood film industry had a number of these organizations, originally formed for various purposes. There is no reason to assume that the primary reason for individuals forming such groups was to standardize the industry; in fact, most sought personal advantages from the combinations. Although there were a number of these organizations, three types seem most pertinent: trade associations, the professional engineers' association, and the labor associations. Each of these had different reasons for forming; each had a number of effects and functions within the industry; each, in addition, contributed to the standardization of practices.

Trade associations

The formation of trade associations was in response to various problems to which the individual firms responded by combining into protective associations. One problem was the threat of State censorship (when I use the capitalized term 'State,' I mean any one or more of the federal, state or local governmental branches, legislative, judicial or executive); another was, first, the fear, and then the advantage, of collusion between firms. These trade associations allowed intra-industrial exchange of information and eventually resulted in combined action against other segments of the industry. Such alliances promoted standardization.

Protective organizations were a common business practice by 1900, having started in some cases before the Civil War. Initially, some attempted to control prices and production, but when the government declared that illegal, major activities by the turn of the century focused on inter-company standardization and improvement of business conditions (indirect collusion). A valuable function was the establishment of credit bureaus to exchange information about risks in their clients. Trade groups also developed standard cost accounting systems, shared industry information, pooled and exchanged patents, fought unfavorable State legislation, lobbied for favorable laws, and formed codes of ethics to prevent unfair competition.[25] Although we shall not examine all of the film industry's trade association activities, the above list describes their range of projects as well.

Two early attempts at a trade association were in direct response to the 1908 formation of the Motion Picture Patents Company. In January 1909 the Independent Film Protective Association formed to ally non-licensed producers, distributors, and exhibitors against the Patents Company. In September 1909, it reorganized into the National Independent Moving Picture Alliance which had broader goals: fighting unfavorable legislation and unproductive business practices.[26]

These two trade associations for independents did not last. Around the early part of 1911 the trade papers reported the renewed interest in a national organization primarily for exhibitors. Membership was open, regardless of exhibitors' ties to competing distributors. Local and state exhibitor organizations went back at least to 1908, and the common cause for their appearance was local difficulties: taxes, regulations, and censorship. The call for a national group was made on the grounds of the size of the film exhibition business (which promoters estimated at 10,000 theaters, with daily attendance of 4 to 5 million, and a capital investment of at least $60,000,000). In addition, the promoters pointed out, the auxiliary businesses supplying furnishings and sundries greatly extended the reach of film exhibition's economic impact. At the first meeting in August 1911, over 200 exhibitors attended, formed the Motion Picture League of America, elected officers, and urged state associations to affiliate.[27]

Besides the exchange of personal information and tactics at the national and state meetings, trade shows accompanied such conventions. Auxiliary businesses (we shall call them support firms) found such gatherings a convenient, cheap means of reaching exhibitors with their latest products. At the July 1913 show, displays included the latest Bell & Howell perforators and printers, the Wurlitzer organ, lithograph supplies, ticket handling machines, slides, chairs, screens, fans, projectors, and lenses — a rapid dissemination of the latest wares with implicit claims as to the standards of quality expected from the most recent state-of-the-art equipment and exhibition practices.[28]

Like the exhibitors, the distributors organized regionally. Alliances of local exchanges went back to about 1912. These groupings became the Film Boards of Trade. Organized to exchange information on credit risks and illegal practices by exhibitors, the Film Boards spread. In May 1914 the New York City renters cooperatively hired a detective agency to eliminate bicycling of prints. If exhibitors were found guilty of that or of not paying bills or of unnecessarily damaging prints, the associates uniformly refused to rent to them. Thus, at local and state levels, licensed versus independent alliances were superceded by cooperative moves to improve the industry for all, and sharing information between distribution groups became possible.[29]

Film advertising men began to coalesce into a formal association in mid-1914. An industrial film company urged their banding together and 'the adoption of standards of practice.' In August 1916 the Associated Motion Picture Advertisers incorporated with representatives from all but two of the major companies.[30]

In September 1914 William Fox proposed another across-the-industry trade association for the independents. Under the New York Board of Trade act, Fox incorporated the National Independent Motion Picture Board of Trade, Inc., with a charter whose purposes included:[31]

> to diffuse accurate and reliable information as to the standing of manufacturers, distributors and exhibitors; to procure uniformity and certainty in the customs and usages of trade and commerce; to obtain a standardization of machines, films, appliances and apurtenances . . . to settle and arbitrate differences between and among its members.

When a permanent organization was effected a year later, it dropped the 'independent' segregation for a strong producers-distributors orientation. That alliance reorganized within a year into the National Association of the Motion Picture Industry which was the predecessor of the Motion Picture Producers and Distributors Association (MPPDA) which organized in 1922.[32]

One more early important trade association was the Los Angeles producers' organization, the Motion Picture Producers Association, formed in 1916. Main causes for it were local attacks on the morality of the industry, interference with granting permits for location shooting, and threats of censorship.[33]

Besides aligning to serve mutual business advantages, fear of State censorship was a primary motive for combination. These associations resulted in agreements of industry-wide standards of acceptable handling of certain subject matter. Random censorship occurred through the first years of film exhibition, but a major crisis was the New York City mayor's revocation of all film theater licenses on Christmas Eve, 1909. Other cities followed suit. Stating their willingness to be censored rather than lose all profits, the New York City exhibitors secured the cooperation of the People's Institute, a 'citizen bureau of social research,' which offered to set up committees to preview films before their release and to suggest elimination of offensive subject matter. Both the Patent and independent manufacturers agreed to submit their films to those committees. With the rejection of parts or all of some films and, consequently, an improved public sentiment, the Patents Company in June 1909 asked the Institute to organize a national preview system to aid other troubled exhibition areas. Accordingly, it set up the National Board of Censorship using committees proposed by civic agencies, and by late 1910 it censored virtually all of the US market. The industry exhibitors and producers paid part of the costs until 1914; thereafter, a set fee financed the Board. Although the Board could not prohibit a film showing, the industry cooperated out of fear that the voluntary system could be replaced by State-imposed censorship. On request, the Board also examined scenarios and offered pre-shooting advice on questionable material. It did taboo certain subjects: in 1911, 'brutal or wilful murder, highway robbery, suicide, kidnapping, theft, ... [and] scenes of an immoral or suggestive nature,' setting up precedents which the MPPDA followed in later years.[34]

Self-censorship was also profitable in that it encouraged a product acceptable to all cultural groups. As Charles R. Metzger was to point out many years later, the film industry responded to numerous pressure groups. Besides the vague notion of the general public, he listed public officials and religious, social, racial, ethnic, and trade groups. Such groups were already operating in the early teens. In 1911, Chinese in Los Angeles protested *The Chinese Trunk Mystery* for creating a poor 'reflection on the characters of members of their race,' and Northwest Indians were 'registering strenuous objections' about the industry's representation of their culture and life. Epes Winthrop Sargent in 1913 characterized the significance of the flourishing international market: 'Stick to the idea that will be as good a year from now [as] it is today and that will appeal equally to audiences in Bombay and Boston and you will have a story that is likely to sell.' As a result, the industry sought to mute any controversial material that might harm profits. The passage of various state and local laws requiring censorship also produced a national uniformity. A

film was made so that it would satisfy everyone.[35]

Thus, by the late teens, across-the-industry groups existed: a national trade association and organizations of exhibitors, distributors, advertisers, and producers. Although the primary purposes were protective, these trade associations reinforced and disseminated standardized business practices. Following the lead of other industries, these cross-company organizations also supplied a climate for informational exchange of company activities and techniques to improve efficiency and quality in production and stylistic practices. While providing a consistent public image for the industry, they also established formal and informal standards of practice.

Although the concern here is the pre-1917 period, it should be stressed that these activities certainly continued with the MPPDA (see Chapter 19). The MPPDA participated in the standardization of technology, continued the trend toward self-censorship including more and more uniform practices, and promoted an industrial harmony that affected labor activities, financing, and other economic practices.

A professional engineers' association

The one early interest group which purposely formed to promote the standardization movement was the Society of Motion Picture Engineers, which organized in 1916. The need to standardize film technology had been apparent earlier to its users. F.H. Richardson, who wrote a weekly column for projectionists in *Moving Picture World*, advocated standardization of machine-part terminology in 1912.[36]

When the National Motion Picture Board of Trade formed in 1915, it called for standardization. Organizing a bureau of standards chaired by C. Francis Jenkins, it proposed setting up standards for the trade's technology. When that trade association reorganized, rather than tie its existence to the new group, Jenkins proposed a permanent association for film standardization because 'every industry has its society of engineers, an association of men who are responsible for the form of the structure of the mechanisms used in their trade.' In July 1916, the Society of Motion Picture Engineers formed, with Jenkins as president and 'a dozen manufacturers and their technicians. ... its avowed purpose "advancement in the theory and practice of

motion picture engineering and the allied arts
and sciences, the standardization of the
mechanisms and practices employed therein and
the dissemination of scientific knowledge by
publication." ' The keynote speaker of the first
meeting which was held in Washington, DC, was
the Secretary of the US National Bureau of
Standards. The Society allied with the film trade
association, set up committees on cameras,
perforation, projection, optics, electrical devices,
and auditing, and published an engineering
journal, *Transactions* (later the *Journal*). In
summarizing its work, the Society wrote later:
'the Society through a permanent Standards
Committee, has made possible the interchangeability of apparatus parts throughout the
industry.' As a mechanism for standardizing the
technology, and its techniques of usage, the work
of the Society has been extremely influential.[37]

Labor associations

According to Alex Groner, the first US labor
groups were primarily 'more concerned with
regulating the conduct and improving the
industry of their members than in commencing
adversary representation against the employers.'
Craft guilds and benevolent societies for skilled
workers were old institutions. From the 1830s on,
unionism to improve wage and labor conditions
increased, as did strikes, which had some judicial
protection.[38]

Most of the early labor associations in the film
industry began as social or benevolent organizations. One of the earliest ones, however, did
not. Theater projectionists organized locally as
craft unions before 1910. As one advocate in 1907
argued, besides imparting craft knowledge, such
an 'operators' league' would be to the workers'
'mutual advantage.' Generally, the locals allied
with the AFL union, the International Alliance of
Theatrical Stage Employees (IATSE) which
provided a national network for the projectionists.
Fostered in part by Richardson in his trade paper
column, unionism also promoted standardization:
the Cleveland local, for instance, sent through
Richardson a new film cement for testing by
other locals. Based on its start in the projectionists' field, IATSE eventually became the
dominant union for many of the moving picture
crafts.[39]

Other crafts gathered as social clubs. Following

the Friars Club example, the Screen Club
organized in New York City in 1912, and a Los
Angeles version, the Reel Club (later the
Photoplayers) followed three months later. The
first long-term writers' clubs were basically
discussion and criticism groups. The writers,
however, were worried about prices and theft of
plots, and in March 1914, the Photoplay Authors'
League (PAL) incorporated with its head Frank
Woods, a former leading trade paper critic and
then head of scenario-writing for D.W. Griffith
(see fig 9.12).[40] Articles of incorporation included
the following objectives:[41]

to affiliate for the purpose of mutual protection
and for the general uplift and advancement of
the heretofore only partially recognized art of
motion picture play construction, and . . . to
publish as often as possible a bulletin
announcing new members, reporting new laws
that may be enacted for the benefit of its
members, and all photoplay authors, and
containing a complete forum for the exchange
and dissemination of the experiences and ideas
of its members.

In October PAL reported in its new journal, *The
Script*, three cases in which it had successfully
helped writers get proper credit and payment for
scripts.[42]

Cameramen organized about the same time as
the photoplaywrights. The Static Club received its
state charter in California in April 1913 and
adopted a constitution. The Cinema Camera Club
organized in New York City, in later April
1913.[43] An early member, Arthur Miller,
explained the clubs' functions:[44]

Because I hadn't met many cameramen in
California, I joined the Static Club. . . . These
clubs were partly social gathering-places, but
they also provided the chance for members to
discuss problems of lighting, standardization of
frame-line, and other matters concerned with
the art of cinematography.

The Static Club's motto in 1915 was 'efficiency'; it
had a clubhouse; and it published a journal, *Static
Flashes* (see fig 9.13). The editor, Jack Poland,
described the club:[45]

The objects of the club are to enjoy social and educational advantages through personal meetings of cinematographers with each other at the club, and to advance the cause of screen photography by a more intimate knowledge of the various details through lectures that will increase the practical efficiency of cameramen, the 'men who make the movies,' as their slogan mentions.

The New York Camera Club also proposed to keep members informed of technical developments through its journal *Cinema News*, to build professional prestige, and to secure screen credit. In 1918 the Static Club consolidated with a more 'aggressive organization,' the American Society of Cinematographers, which formally incorporated in 1919 and later published *American Cinematographer*.[46]

During the 1920s, these labor associations continued to form, reorganize, and voice in concert the desires of the workers. In 1920, the Screen Writers Guild organized. Headed for a time by Woods, it was so respected that it was admitted to the Los Angeles Chamber of Commerce. Film directors and assistant directors formed guilds. Concerted union activities by crafts were rare, however. In the early 1920s, the union for theatrical stage actors, Actors' Equity Association, claimed jurisdiction over two fledgling motion picture actor unions. Equity was not particularly successful in attracting film-worker memberships or in negotiating contracts. In 1928, the cinematographers unionized into International Photographers, which affiliated with the AFL. Because of labor unrest, in 1927, the producers and workers incorporated the Academy of Motion Picture Arts and Sciences, in large part to arrange for peaceful negotiation of minimal work conditions. For the next six years, the Academy was to play a large role in labor activities and standardization of the technology and work practices, and it became a central site for inter-craft communication (see chapter 19).[47]

These labor associations, and later unions, provided the exchange and reinforcement of many stylistic and production practices. Their journals widely disseminated and discussed standards and techniques, and the approval of a member's work became the state-of-the-art, the model for future work in the field.

Adjacent institutions

Other mechanisms for standardization included ones somewhat connected to the industry – trade publications and critics and 'how-to' books – and ones external to the industry – college courses, newspaper reviewing, theoretical writing, and museum exhibitions. Undoubtedly there are others, but these will suggest how standards were available to influence the company's and worker's conception of how the motion picture ought to look and sound. While these mechanisms presented themselves as educational and informative, they were also prescriptive. A how-to-write-a-movie-script book advised not only how it was done but how it ought to be done to insure a sale. In the case of reviewers or theorists, the references to established standards in other arts (theater, literature, painting, design, music, still photography) perpetuated ideological/signifying practices – although, of course, in mediated form.

Although society journals were important, so were the trade papers. Trade papers in the entertainment field (such as the *New York Dramatic Mirror*, *Show World*, the *New York Clipper*, and *Variety*) discussed stylistic and production practices, and three early ones were devoted exclusively to motion pictures (*Moving Picture World*, founded in 1907; *Motion Picture News*, 1908; and *The Nickelodeon*, 1909). Through their columns and articles many early standards were discussed, prescribed, and disseminated.

Two of the more important trade critics in the early teens were Frank Woods who used the pseudonym 'Spectator' in the *New York Dramatic Mirror* and Epes Winthrop Sargent in *Moving Picture World*. The trade consensus was that Woods was particularly important for his acting criticism. Sargent began as a critic for music, theater, and vaudeville in the 1890s and had been a scenario editor and press agent for Lubin before he arrived at the *Moving Picture World* in 1911. At that point he began a series of columns, the 'Technique of the photoplay,' which included formats of scenarios and film production information primarily aimed at the freelance writer and the manufacturers' scenario departments. Those columns appeared in book form in 1912 and in an extensively revised edition in 1913. Although other handbooks of film practice preceded his, Sargent's work became a classic in a field that from that point on rapidly expanded.[48]

In December 1909 an article, 'How moving picture plays are written,' informed freelance scenario writers of the format for their submissions to film companies. It is worth note as an early but typical example of the trade paper and handbook discourse. After discussing the differences between the film play and the 'drama of words,' the writer comments:[49]

The stories must have situations plainly visible, a clearly defined story, and, with it, an opportunity for artistic interpretation. Dramatically, a motion picture story must be more intense in its situations than the spoken drama. It is often dragged into inconsistency but this is pardonable if the story is sufficiently strong to warrant it. The point of situation cannot be too strongly emphasized.

. . . .

We are told by our masters in short story writing and in drama writing that we must have one theme and one theme only. Too many characters will spoil the spell that grips us when we have but two or three people to watch. We are told to avoid rambling into green hedges off the roadside and to grip the attention of the audience from the very start. The complications should start immediately and the developments come with the proper regard for sequence.

. . . .

The period of action in a motion picture play is not restricted although it is best to follow the arrangement as depicted in the vaudeville drama. A single episode or incident which might occur within the length of time it takes to run the film is better than dragging the tale through twenty or thirty years. Too many notes and subtitles interrupt the story and detract from the interest. . . .

. . . .

A motion picture play should be consistent and the nearer to real life we get the more is the picture appreciated. Complications which are too easily cleared up make the story unsatisfying, smacking of unreality, thus destroying the illusion that, as the producer faithfully endeavors to portray, the scene is not one of acting, but that we have an inside view of the comedy or tragedy of a real life. Let your stories, though they be strong in plot, be

convincing, the situations not merely possible but probable. The producer will then have no trouble in making his actors appear to be real.

The types of normative practices that Part One has described as characteristic of the Hollywood film from 1917 on were already being promoted in their nascent form. Furthermore, the sources for these standards were the discourse of existent signifying practices.

Allusions to standards in other arts suggest the range of sources that filmmakers called on in constructing their film practice. In 1910 Woods called Griffith 'the Belasco of motion pictures' and in 1911 the *Moving Picture World* argued that the best pictures came from scenarios from 'old masters.' One letter writer believed that '[In the photoplay there is] lack of true *technical construction* − not sufficient *introduction* and *preparation*; things just happen, regardless of *logic* and consistency − "logical sequence of events" and "verisimilitude." I contend that a photoplay should be as carefully constructed as a play for the speaking stage.'[50] A reviewer likened the opening compositions of *A Corner in Wheat* (1909) to 'an artistic farm scene after the style of Millet,' and Vitagraph advertised lighting effects *a la* Rembrandt in 1912. One photoplay advisor in 1912 justified the 'American foreground' in which figures were 'cut off at the knees or waist' as having precedents in the 'greatest sculptors and painters.' Another critic analyzing shots from several films compared their styles to Repin, Lorraine, Titian, and Veronese. Besides painting, still photography was a model. Publicity releases of 1914 claimed that Griffith had achieved effects 'hitherto attained only in "still" photography,' with a 'series of films d'art which rival the pseudo-impressionistic productions of the Fifth Avenue "still" ateliers.' While we have to be careful in using such references, what is of interest to us are the appeals to 'high art' and the suggestion of some standardization.[51]

Besides helping to standardize the Hollywood group style, the trade papers affected other practices. Richardson's column for projectionists started in early 1908, and Sargent began one on advertising techniques in September 1911. Clarence E. Sinn ran a column on 'Music for the picture,' (see fig 9.14) which in 1911 explained Wagner's technique of leitmotifs as an approach to film music accompaniment:[52]

> To each important character, to each important action, motive, or idea, and to each important object (Siegmund's sword, for example), was attached a suggestive musical theme. Whenever the action brought into prominence any of the characters, motives, or objects, its theme or *motif* was sung or played. . . .
>
> In addition to his *leit motif*, Wagner employed scenic, or descriptive music, and this idea, too, comes well within the lines of moving picture music.

In October of that year Clyde Martin started a column on sound effects. By 1913 handbooks such as the *Sam Fox Moving Picture Music* volume printed music under topical headings such as 'Indian,' 'Oriental,' 'Spanish,' or 'Mexican.' In 1915, Carl Louis Gregory began a column on photography. The trade papers supplied stories on varied aspects of the business from the results of a film in Bombay and Boston, from the latest indirect lighting fixtures and opera chairs to the newest cameras with turret-mounted lenses and gyroscopes.[53]

Not to be neglected, either, was the trade papers' impact in educating the various members of the industry about the entire film production process. As Harry Braverman points out, the increase in subdivision of skills results in the workers' decrease in understanding the work as a whole. These journals, particularly in later years, often included articles explaining to their readers other craft activities, functions, and processes within the industry.

Some mechanisms in this early period worked explicitly to standardize the industry. Others simply helped perpetuate standard practices already in widespread use; such standard practices undoubtedly gained part of their normative power through their distended usage. Raymond Williams speaks of such a cultural hegemony in his discussion of a model of dominant social ideology:[54]

> I would say that in any society, in any particular period, there is a central system of practices, meanings and values, which we can properly call dominant and effective. . . . In any case what I have in mind is the central,

effective and dominant system of meanings and values, which are not merely abstract but which are organized and lived. That is why hegemony is not to be understood at the level of mere opinion or mere manipulation. It is a whole body of practices and expectations; our assignments of energy, our ordinary understanding of the nature of man and of his world. It is a set of meanings and values which as they are experienced as practices appear as reciprocally confirming.

Although we are not dealing with a culture as a whole, certainly we have a group of film workers in a constant social relationship, working to provide films with meaning to such a culture. In detailing this set of institutions within the early industry, I have wanted to show the physical sites for the dispersion, coalescence, and reinforcement of a specific set of meanings, values, and practices. This institutional discourse explains why the production practices of Hollywood have been so uniform through the years and provides the background for a group style which we show as also stable through the same period. The standardization we find is a result of the hegemony of the discourse.

'The balance between formula and showmanship'

Although certainly dominant, standardization was not the only process at work. There do exist smaller internal shifts within the larger framework. As Part One pointed out regarding the group style, these changes were at the levels of devices and systems rather than relations between the systems. These more specific changes in the norm must also be accounted for in some way. To understand why the Hollywood film looked as it did throughout the years and also why production practices changed in minor ways, we must return to that tension in the economic practices between standardization and differentiation. Standardization was a dual process − both a move to uniformity to allow mass production and a move to attain a norm of excellence. Standardizing stylistic practices could make the production fast and simple, therefore profitable. However, differentiation was also an economic practice, and advertising sought to use the qualities in the films as a ground for competition and repeated consumption. Thus, difference and 'improvement' in film practice was also necessary. (For this reason filmmaking did not achieve the assembly-line uniformity prevalent in other industries.) This tension results in two additional effects on the Hollywood style and production practices: an encouragement of the innovative worker and the cyclical innovation of styles and genres.

The innovative worker

The mode's need for product differentiation encouraged the innovative worker, however much he or she may have seemed to challenge the standard. Characteristically, Hollywood's style effaced the techniques of making the film (or else recuperated them into the story line). It was a cinema of concealed artifice. Rather than a display of the apparatus and art of filmmaking, the standard was the story and what was lifelike, or verisimilar. The coherence of the story and its 'logic' controlled the systems of time (ellipses and condensations) and space (image compositions, matches-on-action, screen direction, establishing shots and cut-ins with re-establishing shots). Causality thus harnessed time and space to a coded continuity. In these systems, spectacle, stars, and novelties had their place, occasionally with problematic results (such as the bogus happy endings discussed in Chapter 7).

The classical stylistic standard was systematized by the late teens, as Part Three will show. Once in place, the standard controlled variations. The industry encouraged innovations, but they had to support or at least not interfere with the controlling standard. Thus, the standard set up boundaries for variation. Throughout the discourse of the industry, examples of this repeatedly appear, as though reinforcement would assure the manufacturers and their sales people that their stylistic practice was naturally the best.

For example, in line with William de Mille's playful description in this chapter's epigraph, after the critical attention paid to the imported German films of the mid-twenties, industrial personnel analyzed the 'correct' use of camera techniques. Sargent wrote in a screenwriters' journal about the new fancy camerawork called 'cinematics': 'If it tells an idea better than straight shooting, then it is good cinematics. If it overshadows the telling of the story, it is poor, no matter how novel the idea may be.'[55] Or the director Rouben Mamoulian in 1932:[56]

[Camera movement] focuses the attention of the audience on the mechanical rather than upon the story, and confuses instead of clarifies the issue. Unjustified movement is a sign of directorial weakness, rather than strength.

Likewise spectacle and settings serve the needs of the plot. *Photoplay* writer Harry C. Carr claimed in 1917: 'A spectacle is only permissible if it is subsidiary to character development.'[57] And Hugo Ballin, an important early set designer in 1921:[58]

Perfect sets have never made a drama. The audience follows the story. The story can be explained by the settings. Settings are dramatic rhetoric. They should be indications of breeding. When settings receive uncommon notice the drama is defective. When they are not noticed they are badly thought out.

The title of Ballin's article, 'The scenic background,' might well have served as the heading for Cedric Gibbons' comments on MGM art direction in 1938: 'The audience should be aware of only one thing – that the settings harmonise with the atmosphere of the story and the type of character in it. The background must accentuate that person's role, and show him off to the best advantage.'[59] These attitudes can be summarized by George Cukor:[60]

In my case, directorial style must be largely the absence of style. It is all very well for a director whose reputation is based on a certain hallmark which he imprints on all his work to subject every new story and scene to his own style and artistic personality. He may achieve wonderful results. He may take a poor story and poor performances, and by making them merely the groundwork of a brilliant exercise in cinema technique, evolve a distinguished picture. But such directors are very rare, so I shall stick to my own case of a director whose end is to extract the best that all his fellow-workers have to give, and who is best pleased when the finished picture shows to the layman in the audience no visible sign of 'direction,' but merely seems to be a smooth and convincing presentation by the players of the subject in hand.

This collage of quotations not only lets us read the same logic across spans of time and profession but also shows that practitioners justified changes as adding story improvements, authorial touches, or novelties. The industry required novelty for product differentiation and materially rewarded innovative workers. Take as another instance cameraman Lee Garmes in 1938: 'I would be in the end a bad photographer if I created photographic gems which shone so brightly that they dazzled the spectator and diverted his interest from the purpose of the scene as a whole.'[61] And a page later: 'There may come a time when the photographer is called upon to bring forth a photographic *tour de force* to strengthen a dramatically weak scene, or to introduce novelty in what would otherwise run the risk of being commonplace.'[62] The conflict between standardization and differentiation is explicit in a 1957 discussion of the industry's reaction to *Love in the Afternoon*:[63]

From the point of photography, *Love in the Afternoon*, has become one of the most controversial productions of the year. . . . cinematographers are divided into two camps regarding its lighting treatment: 1) those who hold that a comedy always should be lit in high key, and 2) those who believe that picture makers should dare to be different and break with tradition when something is to be gained by it.

MGM producer Hunt Stromberg in 1938 described 'formula' as giving the public what it wants and 'showmanship' as 'something novel, something truly "different"': 'Holding the balance between formula and showmanship is a problem in itself.'[64]

Hollywood's marketing practices meant that the workers had a goal of making a film so that it would both satisfy the received opinion of standard quality filmmaking and yet would introduce a departure from that standard. Instead of holding back the innovative worker, the

Hollywood mode of production cultivated him or her as long as the results provided profits. The man or woman whose work produced returns in the box office could demand and receive higher salaries and broader decision-making powers – which continued as long as earnings came back. 'You are only as good as your last film' – while perhaps an overstatement during the studio period – reflects this sort of power. As a result, some directors, writers, cameramen, designers, and so on, had no trouble overcoming the Hollywood system: they were part of one tendency within it. For instance, directors such as John Ford and Cecil B. De Mille commanded great sums of money or special units within studios otherwise run by strong producers. Or Gregg Toland could boast in an article how 'I broke the rules in *Citizen Kane*' and receive qualified praise by the industry for doing so.[65] The promotion of the innovative worker who might push the boundaries of the standard was part of Hollywood's practices. Normally, furthermore, the innovations were justified as 'improvements' on the standards of verisimilitude, spectacle, narrative coherence, and continuity. Hollywood's goal was a certain type of stylistic practice, *not* the display of the hand of a worker. For some workers, such as Cukor, the goal was playing by the rules of 'invisibility' – pursuing the standard of quality filmmaking; for others, such as Toland it was breaking the rules within the overall standards of stylistic practice. Those whom criticism has canonized as auteurs may thus be understood as strikingly innovative workers. Individuals who elaborated upon the norms were not necessarily subverting the group style but may very well have been furthering Hollywood's economic aims.

Cycles

We all steal from each other. We are all stimulated by each other. I think this is true of any art form. I think it's true in the field of writing, of painting, of music. I think we're all influenced by our contemporaries and also our past masters.[66]

Vincent Sherman

Innovation leads to a second effect of standardization versus differentiation: cyclical change within classical stylistic practice. Given a classical standard for quality filmmaking, an individual film still had great leeway in minor deviations in order to establish its differentiation within the consumption market. Indeed, we have seen that the marketing practice of publicity worked toward the appearance of novelty, and that, in fact, trade critics functioned to support that practice.

However no retrospective 'first' has any significance if it has not become a prized element in the system. To quote John Perry again, 'an innovation is successful only when it has become a new standard.' Hollywood has been described as running in cycles: one film that is successful spawns a host of others. The economic practice of profit maximization accounts in part for this. If a genre or style or technique produces positive results (usually measured in box office receipts), other companies try an imitation of that success. Witness de Mille's description of the effects of Griffith's use of a 'soft focus' style and the introduction of 'German-style' camerawork. Thus, within its circumscribed limits, Hollywood has attempted innovations and has standardized successes. As a result, similar films often appear closely together and constitute cycles.

The repetition of an innovation, then, leads to series. Part One has described the genesis of one such subgroup, film noir. In the teens, a vogue for Westerns was followed by fashions for military films and later 'vamp' pictures. Moderate sharpness, 'soft' style, and 'pan-focus' each constituted quality cinematography at one time or another. Stanley Cortez wrote about fads in color:[67]

We have so often had to follow the studios' specific styles. I remember that M-G-M and 20th used to fight; Louis B. Mayer saw one of [Darryl] Zanuck's pictures in the early days, and Mayer decided to change all his pictures from soft to hard colour as a result, and told Karl Freund and his other cameramen what to do. The other studios followed suit. So as a result we got 'Christmas package' colours in Hollywood films of the forties and after – a distorted sense of colour values in which everyone wanted to put more and more colour in.

In an analysis of the pan-focus style, a trade writer noted:[68]

The innovations which marked the late Gregg Toland's photography of *Citizen Kane* not only contributed to the very great success of the picture, but set a new standard in feature film photography. The immediate result was that other cinematographers adopted Toland's 'deep focus' technique and gave it new and interesting application.

Thus, the new trend becomes the new standard, a minor change within the group style of the classical film.

These innovations, in fact, often played off conceptions of the standards. For example, Warner Bros in the early 1930s wanted to make a film within the horror genre, but its head of studio production wanted it different from the then-standard films of Universal. The producers intentionally varied the design of the product by switching characteristic elements in the genre; the indefinite time and place settings in Universal films were transformed into present-day urban United States, and the peasants became the lower class.[69]

Bwana Devil combined two earlier technologies to bill itself 'the world's first three-dimensional feature in color.' Salesmen advertised a 1929 Ford film *The White Flame* as the 'first sound film without a heroine.'[70] Such methods of innovation also suggest techniques were periodically recovered and recombined within more particular genres and styles. In fact, director George Stevens described it in such terms:[71]

Something sort of cannibalistic is taking place. Producers, writers and directors have got into the habit of screening over and over again the pictures that have been proved in the past to possess something that made them box office successes. I don't mean that they simply make them over. They break them down into their component elements, study these carefully, and then use them again in different arrangement, as parts of a new story, depending on them to exert the same appeal they did the first time.

Thus the appearance of any 'progress' may be illusory. In addition, the order of such changes, while not chaotic, cannot be predicted.

By the end of the teens, then, a large number of

various types of mechanisms reinforced and disseminated standards. Advertising, trade associations, professional and labor associations, trade papers, and critics promoted uniformity and quality. A tension between standardization and differentiation in the economic system also helps explain similarities and variations among the individual films as well as the appearance of changes in subject matter, genres, and styles. With these practices in place, the production practices operated to achieve them; how they managed to do so is the focus of the rest of this part.

1.1 (above left) *Bulldog Drummond* (1929)
1.2 (above right) *The Show* (1927)
1.3 (left) A striking high angle for *The Garden of Eden* (1928)

2.1-2.5 Phases of a shot from *Casbah* (1948)
2.6 (below right) *The Fountainhead* (1949)

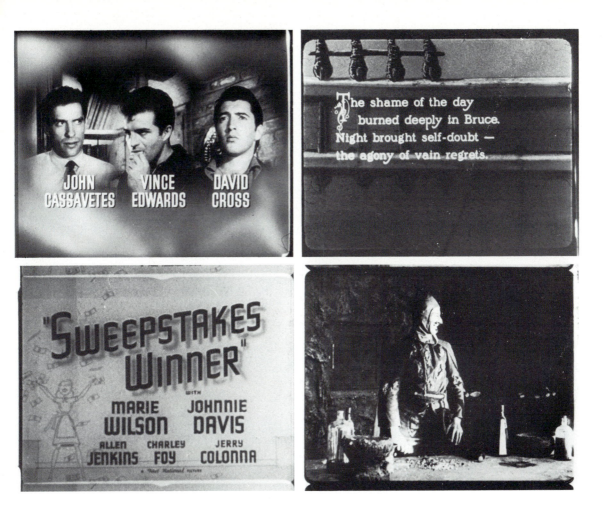

3.1 (above left) *The Night Holds Terror* (1955)
3.2 (above right) *Code of the Sea* (1924)
3.3 (below left) *Sweepstakes Winner* (1939)
3.4 (below right) Prologue in Hell: *The Devil's Bait* (1917)

 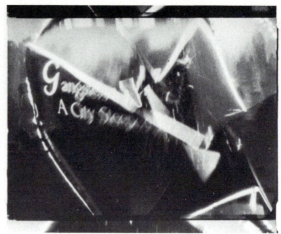

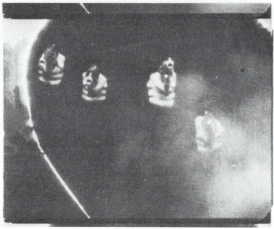

3.5-3.7 *Partners in Crime* (1928)

3.8-3.13 *The Case of the Lucky Legs* (1935)

3.14-3.16 *The Caddy* (1953)

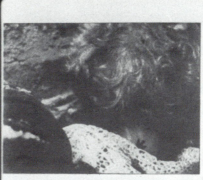

3.17-3.20 *The Canterville Ghost* (1944)

3.21 (below) *One Touch of Nature* (1917)

3.22-3.25 The protagonist walks into a shot initially defined as his field of vision: *The Whip Hand* (1951)

3.26-3.28 Narration in the credits of *King Kong* (1933)

4.1-4.2 (above) A match-on-action cut from *Mr. Skeffington* (1944)
4.3-4.5 (centre and below) A dissolve during a scene's exposition softens the transition to a closer view:
The King and the Chorus Girl (1937)

5.1-5.8 The T-composition at work in long shots (5.1, 5.2), closer views (5.3 through 5.6), and close-ups (5.7)

5.1 (above left) *The Caddy* (1953)
5.2 (above right) *The Clodhopper* (1917)
5.3 (centre left) *The Four Horsemen of the Apocalypse* (1921)

5.4 (centre right) *The Bedroom Window* (1924)
5.5 (below left) *Laura* (1944)
5.6 (below right) *The Best Years of Our Lives* (1946)

5.7 *A Farewell to Arms* (1932)

5.8 The T-principle is also common in the composition of widescreen shots: *Carmen Jones* (1954)

5.9-5.10 A partial frame cut. The figure crosses the frame line at the end of one shot (5.9) and this provides a transition to a full view (5.10): *Sweepstakes Winner* (1939)

5.11-5.14 (above and centre) A complete frame cut. The character leaves the shot (5.11), crossing the frameline (5.12). Cut to his body crossing the opposite frame line (5.13) as he moves to the center area (5.14): *The Whip Hand* (1951)
5.15-5.16 (below) *The Bedroom Window* (1924)

5.17 (right) Reserving frame space for a character's entrance: *The Royal Pauper* (1917)

5.18-5.19 (centre) Reserving space for an entering character: *Sweepstakes Winner* (1939). A reframing camera movement compensates for any loss of balance.

5.20 (below left) Modified frontality of body position in *Victory* (1919)
5.21 (below right) Modified frontality in Lady Windermere's Fan (1925)

5.22 (above left) Frontality in the dispersed group: *The Three Musketeers* (1921)

5.23 (above right) Frontality realistically motivated by the characters' environment: **Affair in Havana* (1957)

5.24 (centre left) *The Magnificent Ambersons* (1942)

5.25 (centre right) *The Little Foxes* (1941)

5.26 (below left) *The Four Horsemen of the Apocalypse* (1921)

5.27 (below right) **Manhandled* (1949)

5.28 (above left) *Wine of Youth* (1924)
5.29 (above right) *The Pride of the Yankees* (1942)
5.30 (centre left) *Dangerous Mission* (1954)

5.31 (centre right) *The Enchanted Cottage* (1945)
5.32 (below left) *The Unwritten Law* (c. 1907)
5.33 (below right) *The Four Horsemen of the Apocalypse* (1921)

5.34 (above left) *Are Parents People?* (1925)
5.35 (above right) **Manhandled* (1949)
5.36 (centre left) Perspective construction in *Anthony Adverse* (1936)
5.37 (centre right) Decentered framing in non-classical space: *La Passion de Jeanne d'Arc* (1928)
5.38-5.39 (below) Spatial manipulation in *Trying to Get Arrested* (1909)

5.40-5.41 (above) The 'gentle dance' of shot/reverse-shot, in which each composition's center of interest corresponds roughly to that of the next: *So This Is Paris* (1926)

5.42-5.43 (centre and below) Widescreen filmmaking generally obeyed the principle of keeping the viewer's eye close to the previous shot's center of interest: *Heaven Knows, Mr. Allison* (1957)

5.44-5.45 (above) Decentered shot/reverse-shot from a nonclassical tradition: *Not Reconciled* (1964)

5.46-5.47 (centre) A cheat cut from *Play Girl* (1941). In the second shot, the figures are closer together, and the young woman's hands are clasped

5.48-5.49 (below) *Each Dawn I Die* (1939). This spectacular cheat cut makes the James Cagney character vanish from the second shot. The viewer does not normally notice the lapse, probably because the cut crosses the axis of action

5.50-5.53 Four frames from *Mr. Skeffington* (1944). In 5.50, the armchair in the foreground is 'primed'
by the establishing shot. The camera tracks in (5.51) and a short scene ensues (5.52). When Mr
Skeffington sits, the chair is waiting for him (5.53)

6.1-6.6 Spatial fragments eventually get 'placed' by an establishing shot: *Love and the Law* (1919)

6.7-6.9 (above and left) A passing couple smoothly guides us to the significant action: *The Fountainhead* (1949)

6.10-6.40 (this page below and following pages) Frames from a scene of **Play Girl* (1941)

6.12-6.17 Frames from a scene of *Play Girl* (1941)

6.18-6.23 Frames from a scene of *Play Girl* (1941)

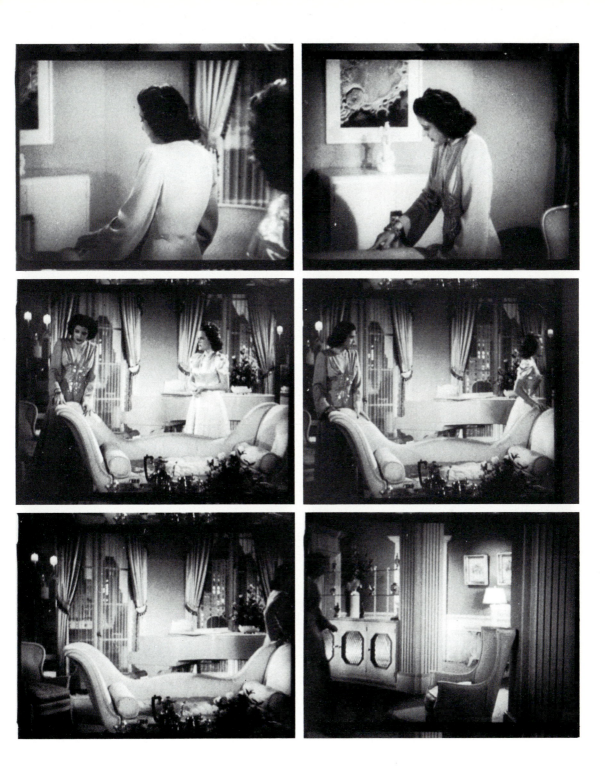

6.24-6.29 Frames from a scene of *Play Girl* (1941)

6.30-6.35 Frames from a scene of *Play Girl* (1941)

6.36-6.40 Frames from a scene of *Play Girl* (1941)

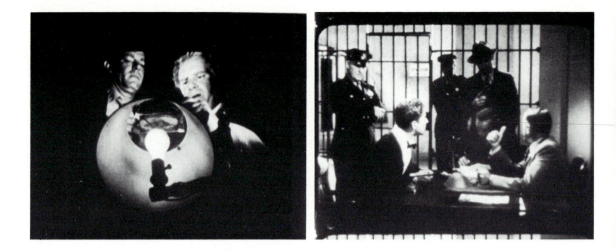

7.1 (left) *T-Men* (1948)
7.2 (right) **Penthouse* (1933)

Marion Leonard

A Message from the Stars to the Brightest One of Them

TWINKLE, TWINKLE, LITTLE STAR,
HOW WE WONDER WHERE YOU ARE!
UP ABOVE OUR SALARIES SO HIGH—
WILL YOU TELL US BY AND BY?
AND ECHO ANSWERS, "WHERE?"

9.1 (left) High salaries for some players were already drawing comment in November 1911
9.2 (right) A 1913 advertisement for the multiple-reeler *Atlantis*

9.3 In 1911, American Film used the 'Flying A' trademark and specialized in Westerns that were 'extremely original' and 'astoundingly realistic'

9.4 A 1913 advertisement for *The Battle of Waterloo*

9.5 (left) In 1911 New York Motion Picture Co. heralded its hiring of the Bison 101 Wild West Show

9.6 (right) By May 1911, companies were competing over the quality of the paper advertising available to exhibitors

9.7 A theater display in August 1911. Marion Leonard was one of the earliest players to receive headline credit. (Also see fig. 9.1)

Opposite page
9.8 (above left) A September 1911 advertisement using King Baggott as the primary exchange-value for the film
9.9 (above right) 'Little Mary' [Pickford] in a January 1911 advertisement
9.10 (below left) Owen Moore and Mary Pickford in October 1911
9.11 (below right) The distributing firm Film Supply Company of America transferred the star system to its cast of manufacturers (October 1912)

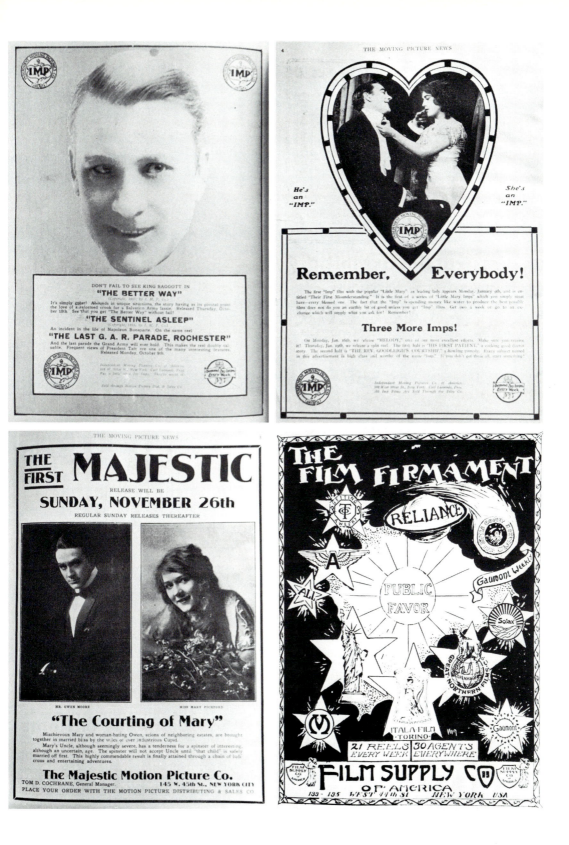

HETTIE GRAY BAKER.
SECRETARY

RUSSELL E. SMITH.
VICE PRESIDENT

FRANK E. WOODS.
PRESIDENT

RICHARD WILLIS.
TREASURER

DAVID W. GRIFFITH.
BOARD OF CONTROL

WM. E. WING.
BOARD OF CONTROL

MARY H. O'CONNOR.
BOARD OF CONTROL

WM. LORD WRIGHT.
VICE PRESIDENT

OFFICERS OF THE PHOTOPLAY AUTHOR'S LEAGUE.

picture to be filmed. It is to his interests and those of his employers to secure the highest class of photographic results at the least possible expense and to create the picture of quality.

One of the first ideas instilled into the minds of cameramen applying for membership in The Static Club of America is that of efficiency, which is the motto of the club. Advancement and progress through personal ability is the watchword, and operating the club along such lines of development the cameramen

events, dances, receptions at the clubhouse, an annual ball, and monthly banquets at leading cafes of Los Angeles, to which members of the motion picture industry, newspaper and publicity men and friends are invited. The prestige of The Static Club and the popularity of its members is attested by courtesies extended the organization by other clubs, a recent feature being a notable entertainment given The Static Club by The Press Club of Los Angeles, which was attended by many notables in film and press circles.

The Static Club.

Capt. Jack Poland, Editor Static Flashes.

W. J. Piltz, Vice-President.

E. G. Ullman, President.

W. C. Foster, Secretary.

S. S. Norton, Treasurer.

Officers of the Static Club.

9.12 (above) The officers of the
Photoplay Authors' League in 1915

9.13 (right) The Static Club in
1915

9.14 (opposite) Clarence E. Sinn's
column for 21 October 1911

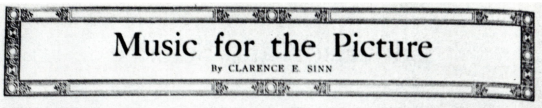

Music for the Picture

By CLARENCE E. SINN

A DRUMMER writes: "I am thinking of buying a complete outfit of effects and going on the road playing two or three night stands. I am experienced in putting on sound effects. It is a work that I like. Now I want your advice; do you think it would pay me to buy a complete outfit and work the way I mentioned, and what salary do you think I ought to ask for doing the above?" (I omit the name and address of the writer.)

Giving advice is an easy matter; giving sound, practical advice is another thing. It's almost as hard as following any kind of advice, which is the hardest proposition of all. There are many things which would have a bearing on the question in the above letter. In the first place, he evidently has no outfit of his own, though he says he is an experienced man. One would think he would like to have a complete outfit of his own just on general principles, even if he did not undertake the venture in question. But aside from that, I think if it was myself contemplating this thing, that I would address the people I expected to do business with—i.e., the managers. A neatly written form letter setting forth my proposition briefly and exactly would probably be an inexpensive starter. Have this printed on a good quality of paper (no cheap work) and mail it to managers of moving picture theaters. I should figure as nearly as possible my probable weekly expenses and add a fair wage to that in order to arrive at an idea of the remuneration to be asked. It might be considered good business to add interest on money invested, but that is a matter which would depend upon other circumstances. There are two proverbs, trite but true, which are applicable. First: "Nothing venture, nothing win." Second: "Begin nothing of which you have not well considered the end." I should suggest to the writer that he first post himself thoroughly; second, to be sure he can deliver the goods. Then get out and toot your horn—let folks know you have the goods. I might also call your attention to the fact that the Moving Picture World is the **one** medium through which to notify moving picture people that you have something in the moving picture line, whether buying or selling. This young man contemplates selling his services, talents and experience to managers of moving picture theaters. This paper is read by every one of them in North America and most of those in other English speaking countries.

The following suggestions are offered:

"Foul Play" (Edison), First Reel.

1. Neutral till change of scene.
2. Livelier (any intermezzo) till Robert exits.
3. Dramatic till "Robert's Father."
4. Same as No. 1 till "General Rolleston and His Daughter."
5. Bright waltz till check is shown.
6. Neutral (something like "Passion," by Helf & Hager) till two men enter.
7. Semi-pathetic ("Apple Blossoms") till "His Guilty Conscience," etc.
8. Pathetic till "Convicted for Another's Crime," then
9. Dramatic (softly) till jury stands up; increase in intensity till Robert's father goes to him.
10. Pathetic till close.

Second Reel.

1. Neutral ("Little Trifler," by George Bernard) till change.
2. Hurry, p and f, according to action, till shake hands.
3. At change of scene, soft agitato till Robert conceals pistol and exits.
4. Waltz till Bulletin Board.
5. Intermezzo till "Wylie, mate of the Prospering."
6. Short mysterious (heavy) till change.
7. Neutral till "Preparing to Sink the Ship."
8. Mysterious-gloomy, till "Land at Last."
9. "Autumn Breezes" (Leo Feist) till "Land at Last."
10. (Warning cue: "Where is Helen?") Wait till Arthur sinks in chair, then dramatic music till close.

Third Reel.

1. Intermezzo, "Martinique" (by Loraine) till "General Rollinson Leaves to Search the Seas."
2. Agitato (for vision) till change of scene.

3. "Reign of the Roses" (by Ellis Brook) till "Helen Tells Robert's Father of His Safety."
5. "Reconciliation" (by Theo. Bendix) till Robert climbs aboard ship.
6. At change to street scene, Wylie recognizes Robert, agitato till "Justice at Last."
7. Dramatic till shot.
8. Pathetic till close.

Through courtesy of Mr. Grover Kayhart, I am enabled to submit the following suggestions of appropriate music to be used in Kalem's pretentious release, "The Colleen Bawn":

"Colleen Bawn" (Kalem), First Reel.

1, Paddy Carey. 2, St. Patrick's Day. 3, Wearing of the Green. 4, College Hornpipe. 5, Irish Washerwoman. 6, Come Haste to the Wedding. 7, The Girl I left Behind Me. 8, My Lodgings on the Cold Ground. 9, Colleen Bawn. 10, The Brown Maid. 11, Aileen Aroon. 12, Gramachree.

Second Reel.

13, Lough Sheeling. 14, The Fairy Boy. 15, **The Song of Sorrow.** 16, Killarney. 17, The Dear Irish Boy. 18, Pretty Girl Milking Her Cow. 19, Crooghan a Vence. 20, Kathleen Mavourneen. 21, Molly Bawn. 22, Woods of Green Erin. 23, The Groves of Blarney. 24, Moll Roone.

Third Reel.

25, I'm Leaving Old Ireland. 26, Shamama Hulla. 27, I Once Had a True Love. 28, 'Tis the Last Rose of Summer. 29, The Angels Whisper. 30, Low Backed Car. 31, Cushla Machree. 32, Fagan. 33, Kitty Tyrell. 34, Kathleen Aroon. 35, Cean Dubh Delish. 36, Sly Patrick.

For the benefit of those who have not these numbers or are unable to get them, I will explain that Nos. 1, 2, 3, 4, 5, 6, 7, 22, 30, 33 and 36 are lively tunes. No. 8 is also known by the title, "Believe Me If All Those Endearing Young Charms." Nos 9, 11, 15, 16, 18, 20, 23, 25, 28, 29, 31 and 34 are sentimental and plaintive in character. No. 23 ("The Groves of Blarney") is said to be an ancient Irish tune from which Thomas Moore took the melody, "The Last Rose of Summer." The other numbers are characteristic Irish tunes, and are all very appropriate.

MORE HELP FOR PICTURE PIANISTS.

Elsewhere in this issue will be found the advertisement of Mr. Walter C. Simons, who has something of interest to say to pianists who are playing in picture, vaudeville and dramatic theaters. Mr. Simons is qualified to give instruction as to the proper method of playing picture and vaudeville accompaniments. He has filled the position of pianist in various theaters of the West and was pianist for Lyman Howe for one year; he also has a number of song successes to his credit, which places him in the composer class. Wherever Mr. Simons has appeared, either in pianologue or as accompanist, his work has been characterized as a feature of the entertainment by the critics. He is a young man of pleasing address and speaks with authority upon his chosen subject.

HANDSOME LOBBY DISPLAY FOR "HANDS ACROSS THE SEA."

Two special posters, one mammoth lobby hanger, a complete set of 8 x 10 actual photos and an interesting eight-page booklet, liberally illustrated, make up the line of advertising matter prepared for the new American Eclair Company's initial production in two reels, "Hands Across the Sea in '76." The posters and lobby hanger are superbly lithographed in six colors, the latter measuring 42 x 84 inches and is the first of its character ever made to order by a lithographer for a regular release. The photos are intended for display in frames in theater lobbies, while the booklets may be secured from the company in quantities for local distribution.

All exchanges will display an advance showing of samples, and bookings for the production should be made early to avoid disappointment.

11.1 The IMP stock company, February 1911, including Mary Pickford, Owen Moore, King Baggott, and Thomas Ince

Opposite page

11.2 (above left) In June 1912, Vitagraph's main studio in Brooklyn, New York, was a departmentalized factory able to plan, shoot, cut, and print four to five reels per week

11.3 (below) Plans for the Fox Studio, 1919

11.4 (above right) Dressing rooms that could double for a prison set (late 1910s)

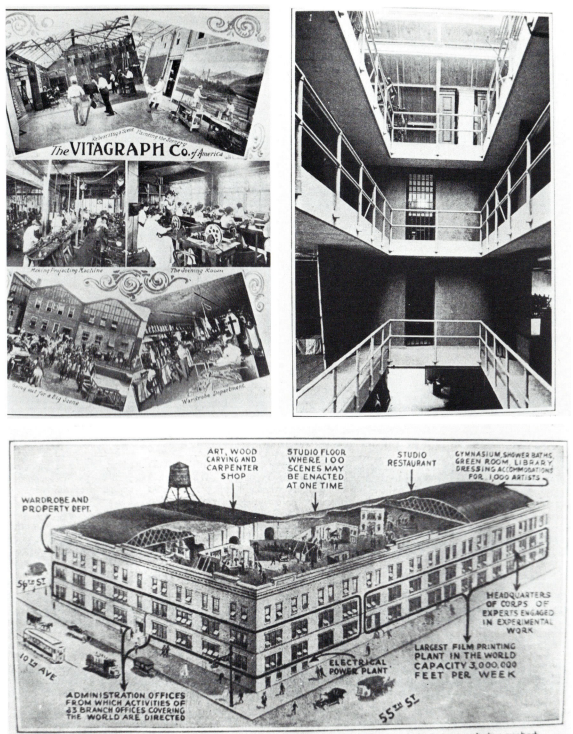

An entire motion-picture colony will be housed in this unusual building which is now being rushed to completion in New York City

Siegmund Lubin, his Executive Staff, Directors and Factory Employees.—Group Taken on Mr. Lubin's Birthday, April 20th, at the Plant.

11.5 The Lubin Firm, 1912

11.6 New York Motion Picture's Santa Ynez studio, 1915

feet in capacity, surrounded by a garage, a stable and a lemon orchard. Today there is a stage 185 by 60, of which an area 60 by 60 is under glass. The lot occupies practically a block in extent, and it is filled. Cecil B. De Mille has been the head of the studio from the beginning. Today he is aided in his producing staff by George Melford, James Neill and Frank Ricker. Wil-

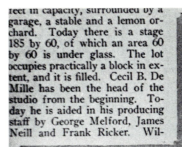

play. Also there was the castle used in "The Puppet Crown," W. C. De Mille's film version of Harold MacGrath's story. The players' dressing rooms are on each side of Lasky Lane, not a short thoroughfare by any means. There are many property rooms and scene docks. At the extreme rear of the lot quarters are being constructed for the scenario

THE MAIN STAGE, ADJOINING THE GLASS STUDIO.

PROPERTY ROOMS - LASKY STUDIO.

WILLIAM C. DE MILLE - SCENARIO EDITOR

CARMICHAEL CHIMMIE FADDEN

THE BIG GLASS STUDIO, LASKY CO.

fred Buckland, formerly technical director for Belasco, is art director. William C. De Mille is the chief of the scenario department. He is assisted by Miss Margaret Turnbull, who wrote "The Fighting Hope" for Belasco, and by Hector Turnbull, her brother, formerly on the New York Tribune.

One of the outstanding factors

department. Near the stage carpenters were putting the finishing touches on a special dressing room for Geraldine Farrar. Special it really is. There is a bathrooms, and there is a piano, too, and sufficient room for the accommodation of two maids and a secretary. Something was said also about a private runway to the stage! Overhead are being prepared permanent quarters for

11.7 The Lasky studio, 1915

Left, tower constructed full size only to the first window, upper part being miniature; center, another example of miniature work. Black line indicates portion of set actually constructed; right, street scene in Tokio. The buildings were photographed through a glass transparency.

11.8 (above) A London street set for the 1920 version of *Dr. Jekyll and Mr. Hyde*, under construction in the dark studio of the Famous Players-Lasky firm

11.9 (below) A December 1922 *Photodramatist* article explained how mattes and glass shots were accomplished

12.1 Photographed in 1911, the Star Theater (Boston, Massachusetts) was built in 1907

12.2 (below left) The Victoria Theater (Lawrence, Massachusetts) had a seating capacity of 900 in 1911
12.3 (below right) In Los Angeles, the Liberty Theatre in 1911 boasted of being 'one of the city's eight first-class moving picture theatres.' The gold leaf statue on the cornice was 10 feet in height and held an electric torch

Lectures on Notable Reels.

By W. Stephen Bush.

LECTURE ON "FAUST." (Two reels.)

Note.—It is suggested that the music and lecture of this reel be carefully rehearsed. The music, if not too loud, will not interfere with the lecture. Those who wish to alternate the lecture with the music will find useful suggestions in the body of the lecture.

Scene 1, Faust in his study.—"All the weary years have gone and brought me nothing, life's great secrets are dark as ever. Thus have I turned in my despair to magic's wonders to lure from this great book of Nostradamus the wisdom that explains the world. Alas, it's vain. How vain is too my life surrounded here by ancient books and by the wretched dust of centuries. There yonder vial is the most precious thing I have, it holds a drink, that will cure all—Hail you bitter drops, that beckon me to unknown shores, many a time you passed of yore from guest to guest around the merry throng—this is the last, the sweetest toast of all.

Scene 2.—A low and mocking laugh restrains the hand of Faust. Mephisto comes from his dark realm and laughs the doctor's misery to scorn: "Faust, wisdom's champion, ready to despair, this is the foolish mortal's way, there's time enough to die and I will show you that, which will make you want to live." Mephisto hurries Faust from the window and shows him

Scene 3.—Marguerite, taking leave of her brother Valentine, who is going away to war. Finish this scene with music.

Scene 4.—The sight of Marguerite has stirred the heart of Faust, his pulses beat faster, he is eager to see her again and with his servant he goes out to mingle with the people at the springtide festival, hoping to find Marguerite. Mephisto transformed into a dog follows Faust and the servant.

Scene 5.—The Faust waltz.

Scene 6.—The dog follows Faust on his return to his study and as he scolds the dog and bids him be still and stop his running and his growling, his jumping and his barking, Mephisto changes back into his own proper shape again, stirs the heart of Faust and brings before his ravished senses the lovely image of Marguerite. (Soft music.) (Short pause.) All scruples vanish. Mephisto urges Faust to sign the compact with a drop of blood. "I will serve you here, but yonder you must forever serve Mephisto." The compact is signed, Mephisto changed in garb to a cavalier urges Faust to come with him to shake off old age, lose the long beard and again feel all the joyous impulses of youth.

Scene 7.—Faust speaks: "Is it here, where I will drop the burden of the years, must I ask counsel of the withered hag?" Mephisto cries: "Yes, this is my monarchy, the drink given to you by her at my command will take off the weight of thirty years." Finish the scene with music and continue the music during the next scene, when Marguerite is seen coming out of church.

Scene 9.—Burning with love for Marguerite, Faust begs of Mephisto to deliver her into his possession. Mephisto protests he is powerless, as Marguerite has just come from confession and is free from sin; he promises, however, to exert all his power. Music.

Scene 10.—Marguerite is followed into her garden by Faust and Mephisto, the latter tells Faust he will tempt Marguerite with priceless jewels. Music.

Scene 11.—In her chamber Marguerite is thinking of the handsome knight, who spoke to her as she was leaving church, while innocently admiring herself in the mirror and singing an ancient German song, Mephisto, invisible to Marguerite, appears and places a casket with priceless jewels on her table. Finish scene with music.

SECOND REEL.

Scene 1.—The second reel begins with the famous garden scene. Marguerite shows the jewels to a neighbor Martha, and while Mephisto in his grotesque fashion woos Martha, Faust declares his love to Marguerite. Music and short pause in lecture. The plucking of the petals from the stem of the flower of love shows Marguerite that Faust loves her and she rejoices over cupid's oracle. (Music and short pause.) In the midst of the young lover's happiness Mephisto and Martha return, at the sight of Mephisto's leers and sneers Marguerite recoils and

Scene 2.—leaves Faust and returns the jewels. Music continues up to the title "Marguerite regrets her love, etc."

Scene 3.—Here resume the lecture as follows: Marguerite has been deserted by Faust and now tastes all the bitterness of man's betrayal. She comes to the shrine of the Virgin and prays: "Bend down your eyes to my distress, oh, Lady of Sorrows. Wherever I go, wherever I go, the grief in my bosom goes with me, my heart is poured out in tears, the flowers I bring thee are bedewed with drops of misery, even as the rays of the rising sun struggled into my room, I sat watching on my bed overburdened with fear; help and save me from shame and death, oh Lady of Sorrows bend down your eyes to me and my distress." Note: Where in the course of this scene Mephisto appears, suspend lecture and substitute music. The appearance of Mephisto is very brief, but the contrast between the prayer and the music will be found effective.

Scene 4.—Valentine returns from the war. (Strains of the Faust march.) He is eager to see his sister, but is disturbed by disquieting rumors he hears from Marguerite's old friend Seybel and from other neighbors. He meets Marguerite, assures her of his faith and love. Finish with music.

Scene 5.—Mephisto comes with Faust to Marguerite's window to lure her away. "We will sing a moral song to fool her all the better." Mephisto begins the song, which is a veiled insult to Marguerite and Valentine comes to avenge the insult. Mephisto changes into the shape of the dog and in the duel that ensues guides Faust's sword and parries every thrust of Valentine. After a few passages Faust kills Valentine and flees with Mephisto.

Scene 6.—Marguerite, attracted by the clash of arms and her brother's groans hastens to his side, but is cruelly repulsed. "Stop your tears," cries Valentine, "'Twas you who gave me the fatal stab. . . . I die bravely as a soldier should."

Scene 7.—Suspicion points to Marguerite, she is arrested and cast into prison. Music.

Scene 8.—Brooding over the past, Marguerite's mind has become clouded. She speaks: "To die so young . . . the wreath is broken . . . scattered are the flowers . . . they say I have sinned . . . but whatever led me on was good and sweet." Music.

Scene 9.—By means of phantom horses, the creation of Mephisto, the latter and Faust gain access to Marguerite's prison.

Scene 10.—Marguerite speaks again: "Pity me and let me live, let me live just through the night . . . wait, wait until the dawn." Music.

Scene 11.—Faust enters and seeks to rescue Marguerite, but she mistakes him for her executioner and though later she recognizes him, she cannot realize her danger and after renewing her vows of love, she dies. Faust is seized by Mephisto. Finish with music.

LECTURE ON "ENOCH ARDEN" (two reels, Biograph).

Tennyson's poem has been followed as far as the deviations of the film maker allowed.

Scene 1.—Here on this beach, a hundred years ago, three children of three houses, Annie Lee, the prettiest damsel in the port, and

Scene 2.—Philip Ray, the miller's only son, and

Scene 3.—Enoch Arden, a rough sailor's lad, made orphan by a winter shipwreck, had built their castles of dissolving sand, but

Scene 4.—when the dawn of rosy childhood past and the new warmth of life's ascending sun was felt by either.

Scene 5.—either fixed his heart on that one girl and Enoch spoke his love.

Scene 6.—the girl seemed kinder unto Philip than to him, but she loved Enoch and, when she saw them quarrel, she said, as in her days of childhood, she would be little wife to both.

Scene 7.—Then on a golden autumn eventide, fast by the rocky, surf-tossed shore Philip saw Enoch and Annie, sitting hand in hand. Philip looked and in their eyes and faces read his doom; then, as their faces grew together, groaned and slipped aside, crept down close to the surging billows, there

Scene 8.—while the rest were loud in merry-making

Scene 9.—had his dark hour unseen and rose and passed, bearing a life-long hunger in his heart.

Scene 10.—So these were wed and merrily rang the bells and Enoch had made a home, neat and nestlike, halfway up the narrow street that clambered toward the mill. Into the home he brought his pretty wife and all seemed bright and radiant and full of promise.

Scene 11.—Alas, there came a change, as all things human change. Fortune had been unkind to Enoch, though there had come to them a daughter first and then a boy, to be the rosy idol of her solitudes, and then another son, a sickly one. He seemed as in a nightmare to see his children poor,

---

12.7 (above) W. Stephen Bush's 1911 lectures for multiple-reelers *Faust* and *Enoch Arden*. ('Scene' is the period term for 'shot')

Opposite page

12.4 (above left) A 1915 Selig advertisement for its multiple-reel adaptation of *The Circular Staircase*

12.5 (above right) Lubin's five-reel film of Louis Reeves Harrison's *The Rights of Man* (1915)

12.6 (below) The Monopol Film Company advertisement for *Dante's Inferno* (1911)

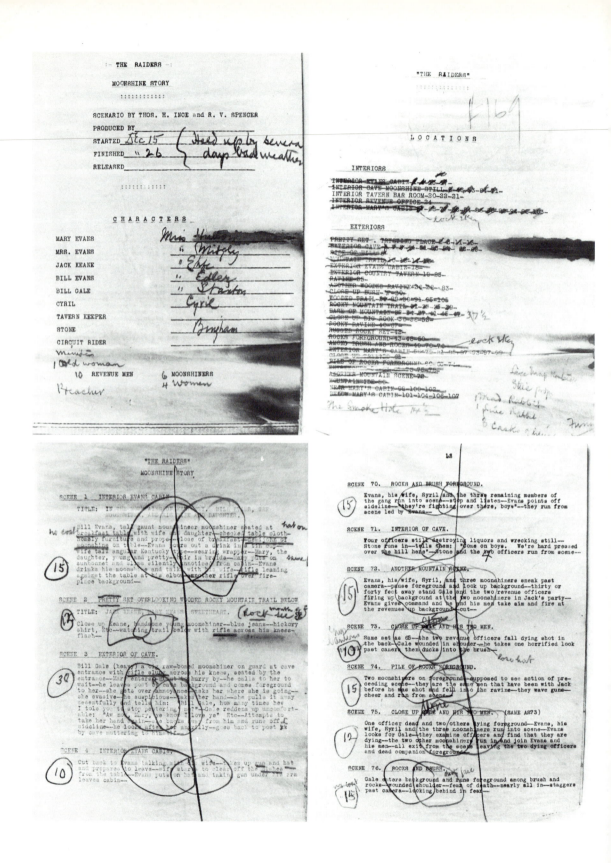

:- THE RAIDERS -:

MOONSHINE STORY

:::::::::::::

SCENARIO BY THOS. H. INCE and R. V. SPENCER

PRODUCED BY _____

STARTED *Dec 15* ⎫ (Held up by several
FINISHED " *26* ⎬ days bad weather)
RELEASED _____

::::::::::::

C H A R A C T E R S

MARY EVANS	*Miss Hart*
MRS. EVANS	" *Witzel*
JACK KEANE	" *Eke*
BILL EVANS	" *Edler*
BILL GALE	" *Stanton*
CYRIL	*Cyril*
TAVERN KEEPER	*Brigham*
STONE	
CIRCUIT RIDER	

Minster
1 Old woman

10 REVENUE MEN   6 MOONSHINERS

Preacher   *4 Women*

"THE RAIDERS"
:::::::::::::::

#169

L O C A T I O N S

INTERIORS

~~INTERIOR EVANS CABIN 1-4-8~~
~~INTERIOR CAVE MOONSHINE STILL~~ 5-10-23-31-71
INTERIOR TAVERN BAR ROOM-30-32-31-
~~INTERIOR REVENUE OFFICE 24~~
~~INTERIOR MARY'S CABIN~~ 97-98-91-92-94-95-96-103-
rock sky

EXTERIORS

~~PRETTY SET - TRYSTING PLACE 2-6-11-16~~
~~EXTERIOR CAVE 3-7-9-12-34-40-51-69~~
~~HARD ON TRAIL~~ 13
~~WOODED TRAIL 15-19-14-22~~
~~EXTERIOR EVANS CABIN 18~~
~~EXTERIOR COUNTRY TAVERN 19-25~~
~~RAVINE 65~~
~~ANOTHER WOODED RAVINE 26-28-83~~
~~CLOSE UP BUSH 7-30~~
~~WOODED TRAIL 50-85-90-91-65-105~~
~~ROCKY MOUNTAIN TRAIL 37-2~~ 35-36 *37½*
~~BARE OF MOUNTAIN 38-34-39-41-46-49~~
~~CLOSE UP BIG ROCK 38-36-53~~
~~ROCKY RAVINE 40-87~~
~~RUGGED ROCKY SET 42~~
ROCKY FOREGROUND-43-48-50- *rock sky*
~~RUGGED BRUSH AND ROCKS 49-70-73~~
~~EXTERIOR MARY'S CABIN 51-75-82-85-87-93-97-99~~
~~CLOSE UP TRAIL 52~~
~~PILE OF ROCKS FOREGROUND 60-74-77~~
~~ANOTHER MOUNTAIN SCENE-72~~
~~MOUNTAINSIDE 86~~
~~NEAR MARY'S CABIN 95-100-102~~
~~BELOW MARY'S CABIN 101-104-106-107~~
The Smoke Hole 14½

Large Mag Lantern
Stile props

Brad Rabbit
1 Jacke Rabbit
6 Chicks or hens
furn...

"THE RAIDERS"
MOONSHINE STORY

SCENE 1.   INTERIOR EVANS CABIN

TITLE: IN THE HEART OF KENTUCKY, BILL EVANS, THE
        MOONSHINER, AND HIS WIFE AND DAUGHTER.

(15)   Bill Evans, tall gaunt mountaineer moonshiner seated at
        breakfast table with wife and daughter—checked table cloth—
        homely furniture and props—close of leisure—meal. ONE OF
        THEM on title—Evans pours out a drink in tin cup—his
        wife angular Kentucky type—wearing wrapper—Mary, the
        daughter, young and pretty—hair in braids—lazy puts on
        sunbonnet and picks silently—notices from cabin—Evans
        drinks his moonshine and talks with his wife—rifle leaning
        against the table at his elbow—another rifle over fire-
        place background.

SCENE 2.   PRETTY SET OVERLOOKING WOODED ROCKY MOUNTAIN TRAIL BELOW

        TITLE: JACK KEANE, MARY'S SWEETHEART. *(Rock with sky)*

(12)   Close up Keane, handsome young moonshiner—blue jeans—hickory
        shirt, Etc.—watching trail below with rifle across his knees—
        flash.

SCENE 3.   EXTERIOR OF CAVE.

(30)   Bill Gale (heavy) a big raw-boned moonshiner on guard at cave
        entrance with rifle slung across his knees, seated by the
        entrance—Mary enters and starts hurry by—he calls to her to
        wait—he leaves post by cave background and comes foreground
        to her—she gets over annoyance—asks her where she is going—
        she evasive—the suspicious—takes her hand—she pulls it away
        resentfully and tells him: Bill Gale, how many times hev
        I tole you to stop pestering me?—Gale reddens up uncomfort-
        able: "Aw now, Mary, yer know I love ya" Etc—Attempts to
        take her hand—she breaks away from him and runs off—
        sideline—he looks after her and sadly—goes back to post by
        cave muttering to himself.

SCENE 4.   INTERIOR EVANS CABIN

(10)   Cut back to Evans talking with wife—takes up gun and hat
        and prepares to leave—wife starts to clear off the dishes
        from the table—Evans puts on hat and taking gun under his arm
        leaves cabin—

L3

SCENE 70.   ROCKS AND BRUSH FOREGROUND.

(15)   Evans, his wife, Cyril and the three remaining members of
        the gang run into scene—stop and listen—Evans points off
        sideline—"they're fighting over there, boys"—they run from
        scene led by Evans.

SCENE 71.   INTERIOR OF CAVE.

        Four officers still destroying liquors and wrecking still—
        Stone runs in—tells them: "Come on boys. We're hard pressed
        over the hill here"—Stone and the two officers run from scene—

SCENE 72.   ANOTHER MOUNTAIN SCENE.

(15)   Evans, his wife, Cyril, and three moonshiners sneak past
        camera—pause foreground and look up background—thirty or
        forty feet away stand Gale and the two revenue officers
        firing up background at the two moonshiners in Jack's party—
        Evans gives command and he and his men take aim and fire at
        the revenues up background—cut—

SCENE 73.   CLOSE UP GALE AND HIS TWO MEN.

(10)   Same set as 65—the two revenue officers fall dying shot in
        the back—Gale wounded in shoulder—he takes one horrified look
        past camera then ducks into the brush—

SCENE 74.   PILE OF ROCKS FOREGROUND.

(15)   Two moonshiners on foreground—supposed to see action of pre-
        ceeding scene—they are the same men that have been with Jack
        before he was shot and fell into the ravine—they wave guns—
        cheer and run from scene—

SCENE 75.   CLOSE UP GALE AND HIS TWO MEN. (SAME AS 73)

(12)   One officer dead and two others dying foreground—Evans, his
        wife, Cyril and the three moonshiners run into scene—Evans
        looks for Gale—they examine officers and find that they are
        dying—the two other moonshiners run in and join Evans and
        his men—all exit from the scene leaving the two dying officers
        and dead companion foreground—

SCENE 76.   ROCKS AND BRUSH.

(14)   Gale enters background and runs foreground among brush and
        rocks—wounded shoulder—fear of death—nearly all in—staggers
        past camera—looking behind in fear—

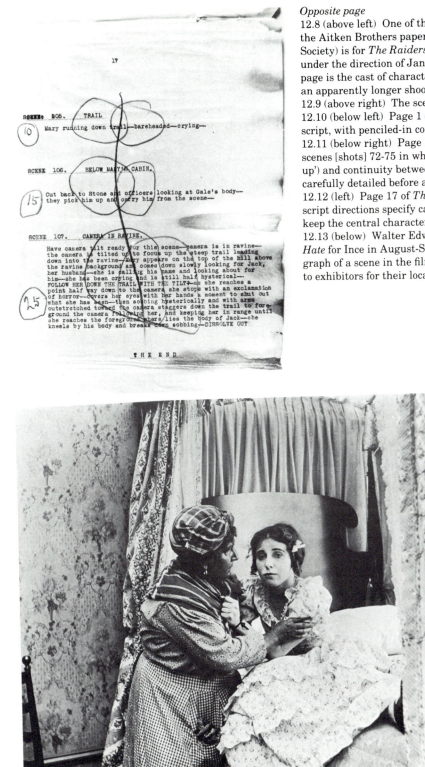

17

SCENE: 105.   TRAIL
Mary running down trail—bareheaded—crying—

SCENE 106.   BELOW MARY'S CABIN.
Cut back to Stone and officers looking at Gale's body—they pick him up and carry him from the scene—

SCENE 107.   CAMERA IN RAVINE.
Have camera tilt ready for this scene—camera is in ravine—the camera is tilted up to focus up the steep trail leading down into the ravine—Mary appears on the top of the hill above the ravine background and comes down slowly looking for Jack, her husband—she is calling his name and looking about for him—she has been crying and is still half hysterical—FOLLOW HER DOWN THE TRAIL WITH THE TILT—as she reaches a point half way down to the camera she stops with an exclamation of horror—covers her eyes with her hands a moment to shut out what she has seen—then sobbing hysterically and with arms outstretched toward the camera staggers down the trail to foreground the camera following her, and keeping her in range until she reaches the foreground where lies the body of Jack—she kneels by his body and breaks down sobbing—DISSOLVE OUT

THE END

Opposite page

12.8 (above left) One of the earliest scripts available in the Aitken Brothers papers (Wisconsin State Historical Society) is for *The Raiders*, shot in December 1913 under the direction of Jan Hunt for Thomas Ince. This page is the cast of characters. Note the explanation for an apparently longer shooting schedule than planned
12.9 (above right) The scene plot for *The Raiders*
12.10 (below left) Page 1 of *The Raiders'* continuity script, with penciled-in commentary and footage lengths
12.11 (below right) Page 13 of *The Raiders'* script. Note scenes [shots] 72-75 in which analytical editing ('close up') and continuity between shots ('lose hat') are carefully detailed before and during shooting
12.12 (left) Page 17 of *The Raiders'* script. Here the script directions specify camera movement that will keep the central character in the center of the frame
12.13 (below) Walter Edwards directed *The Bride of Hate* for Ince in August-September 1916. This photograph of a scene in the film would have been available to exhibitors for their local advertising

-:- Specially selected and compiled by M. Winkler.
The timing is based on a speed limit of 14 minutes per reel.
THEME: "DON'T YOU SIGH NO MORE" (Southern Love Song) Lake.

TO BE PLAYED UNTIL TITLE OR S(CENE)	LENGTH OF SCENE	NO. TITLE AND TEMPO OF MUSICAL COMPOSITION
At. Screening	1 min. 30 sec.	2. THEME
T. Doctor Dudley Dupres	3 min. 45 sec.	2. Love's Acclaim--Amino (False Melodique)
T. I have lost heavily at	2 min. 25 sec.	3. Mysterious Nights--Berg (False Dramatique)
T. His love for his dead son	1 min. 50 sec.	4. continue pp
T. Aboard the Mississippi	1 min. 10 sec.	5. The Coon's Patrol--Lotter (Char.)
T. Mercedes, a slave girl	1 min. 10 sec.	6. Dramatic Reproach--Berge
T. The gambling saloons of	1 min. 10 sec.	7. Virginia Reel or Old style Southern Lancers to action
T. While at Bayou	1 min. 30 sec.	8. THEME
T. Off with the old love	3 min. 10 sec.	9. Continue to seion
S. Black Mammy running up stairs	4 min. 10 sec.	10. Agor Motif--Kilenyi
T. Fate intervenes of judge	15 sec.	11. Continue pp
T. Home	3 min. 40 sec.	12. THEME
T. His Mama, the scoundrels	2 min. 55 sec.	13. Humours--Kilenyi (Dram.)
T. Grimly awaiting Gren-shaw's	4 min.	14. Dramatic Tension--Amino
S. Slave girl coming down stairs	1 min. 25 sec.	15. THEME
T. The quickly conceived	1 min. 30 sec.	16. Scramia Argonaise--Bare
T. The awaited day	2 min. 40 sec.	17. THEME
T. Stop	2 min. 20 sec.	18. Dramatic Conflict--Levy
T. Dawn, the following morning	1 min. 30 sec.	19. Weird Mysterioso--Kilenyi
S. Interior of hospital	5 min. 40 sec.	20. Last Lullaby--Baron (Dramatic)
S. Close up of girl in bed	2 min. 25 sec.	21. Majestic Mysterious Kilenyi
T. In answer to the Doctor's	3 min.	22. THEME ff.

THE END.

All numbers listed on this cue sheet are non-taxable and can be obtained through Belwin Inc. 701 Seventh Ave., New York City, or your local music dealer.

"The Bride of Hate"
-: HIS SLAVE :-

SCENARIO BY JOHN LYNCH
PICTURIZED BY J. G. HAWKS
PRODUCED BY Walter Edwards
STARTED
FINISHED
RELEASED

CHARACTERS

DR. DUDLEY DUPREZ,
PAUL CRENSHAW,
MERCEDES MENDOZA,
ROSE DUPREZ,
MARY LOU,
JUDGE SHORE,
DON RAMON ALVAREZ,
DON PATON'S DAUGHTER,
DOCTOR DUPREZ'S SON
NEGRO SERVANTS, GUARDS, NURSES
WEDDING GUESTS, MINISTER, STRETCHER BEARERS

It is earnestly requested by Mr. Sullivan that no changes of any nature be made in this scenario either by elimination of any scenes or the addition of any scenes or changes of any of the action as described, or titles, without first consulting him.

12.14 (left) *The Bride of Hate*'s cast list includes a standard admonition regarding changing the script without permission. C. Gardner Sullivan managed Ince's scenario department

12.15 (right) An early proposal for music for *The Bride of Hate*

Music Cues For "The Bride of Hate"

BY S. M. BERG

This "Musical Suggestion Cue Sheet" is intended as a partial solution of the problem—what to play for the picture. Together with the suggested music at the title or descriptive cues, the tempo or characteristic is given, so that the leader can select or substitute any or all of the numbers from his own library.

The timing of the picture is based on a speed of 15 minutes to a thousand feet. The time indications will help the leader to anticipate the various cues, which may consist of the printed sub-title (marked T) or a described action (marked D). For instance, 2¼ T "Bayou Petite plantation—" is a sub-title and is printed reading matter on the screen. But 19 D "When Rose ascends stairs" is a description of action.

The theme selected is Chopin's "Valse Lente," Op. 34 No. 2.

Time.		Sub-Titles or Descriptive Cues.	Music.
0	D	Opening	The Sunny South—Lampe (Selection of Southern Songs)
2¼	T	Bayou Petite plantation—	Valse Lente—Chopin Op. 32 No. 2 (THEME)
4	T	"I wanted to tell you"—	
5	T	"Then you must see him—"	Novellette—Marquis (Allegro grazioso)
9	T	"I can't stop now—"	
9¾	T	His love for his dead son—	Repeated: THEME
10¾	T	"While I'm in St. Louis—"	
11¾	T	On the "Father of Waters." (Wave effects)	Arkansas Traveller (Nigger break-down)
12¾	T	"Mighty pretty slave I'd say."	Southern Girl—Kremer (Caprice Gavotte)
13¾	T	"She acts like a lady—"	
14½	T	In the Gilded Saloon of—	Dance of the Marionettes—Gurney (Allegretto 6-8)
15¾	T	While at his Louisiana—	Dramatic Andante No. 32—Berge
19	D	When Rose descends stairs	Misterioso Dramatico No. 22—Sorch
21	D	When Mammy ascends stairs.	
22¼	T	"I have lost all my—"	"Andante Dramatic No. 15—Herbert
26¼	D	Duprez talks to Mercedes	Allegro Agitato No. 1—Kiefert
27	T	One of the sailors thought—	Enchanted Hour—Mouton (Andantino Barcarolle) (Boston)
28	T	Home.	
29	T	"Where is Miss Rose?"	Dramatic Tension No. 9—Andino
31	D	Duprez at Rose's bed	Dramatic Andante No. 24—Borch
32	T	"Tell me!"	Andante Pathetique No. 10—Berge
36	T	Waiting, knowing that the man	
37	T	"De Doctor is on de—"	Longing—Bendix (Andante pathetique)
40¼	T	"I am heavily in your debt—"	
42½	D	When Mercedes enters room	Meeting—Bendix (Andante con moto)
45	T	"I am going to marry you—"	
46¾	T	The day of his revenge (Wedding scene)	Piano or Organ Solo.
49	T	"Whom God hath joined—"	
50	T	"Stop!"	Ein Marchen—Bach Op. 40 (Dramatic Andante)
51¾	T	"—and husband of a nigger"	
53¼	T	The dawn of following—	Repeat: THEME
55	T	"I am going to report to Chief"	
55½	T	"I have a typical case—"	Recollections—Williams (Allegretto)
57½	T	"I am not Judge Shone—"	
58½	T	"The old Spaniard who—"	Lullaby—Williams (Andante con espressione)
60	T	"From now on you are—"	
61½	T	The struggle. Whether—"	Meditation—Williams (Andante affetuoso)
63	T	"That's the man who—"	
64	T	"This is the dead line—" (Shots)	Agitato No. 6—Kiefert
65	T	In answer to the doctor's—	Repeat: THEME
69	T	The End.	

12.16 Music cues released in the company's press sheet for exhibitors

"The Bride of Hate"

No. 494.

Director: Edwards	Cameraman: Jennings
Commenced Aug. 16th,	Completed Sept.30th,
Stock, Directors, Actors, etc.	8,552.69
Labor & Operation, Carpenters, etc.	1,842.82
Auto Expense, Driver's Salaries	60.00
Ranch R & M, Salaries	14.83
Laboratory, Operation, Salaries	1,057.01
Wardrobe, Salaries	233.69
Payroll, Undist.	7,483.66
Payroll, Total	19,244.70
Picture Expense, Direct	1,835.50
Props, Scenery, Wardrobe	230.24
Arsenal, Asset	15.50
Wardrobe, "	82.48
Scenery "	282.04
Props, Rented	3.60
Laboratory, Material	208.27
Auto Expense, Use of Machines	225.00
General Picture Expense, Undist	3,095.37
" " " Depreciation	2,894.44
Total Picture Expense	28,117.14
Negative Film Used	18,200 Ft.
Positive " "	22,140 "
Cost per Reel (5 Reels)	5,623.43
" " " Foot	5.62
Total Calif. Picture Expense	28,117.14
18,200 Ft. Negative Stock @.03125	568.75
22,140 " Positive " @. 02775	614.38
Grand Total Calif. Picture Expense	29,300.27
" " Cost per Reel	5,860.05
" " " " " Foot	5.86
Star— Frank Keenan 6 wks—3 days	4,925.00

12.17 The accounting page for *The Bride of Hate*. Over 68 per cent of the direct costs were for salaries

SCENE 13.   DRAWING ROOM WHITNEY HOME

   BEAUTIFUL SET -- everything the finest -- some of the
   guests are scattered about in this room -- others are
   entering from a sideline doorway -- Whitney is coming from
   the background doorway -- he nods pleasantly to the
   people about him, stops a moment to talk to them but all
   the time manoeuvering to get out -- he finally exits --
   contrast him with the others -- even they notice it and
   smile as they say "A wonderful character" --

SCENE 14.   SG GARDEN   NIGHT

   BEAUTIFUL SET -- some of the guests are strolling about--
   a group of young men are sauntering along, smoking --
   Whitney enters over the foreground -- he lights a cigar
   and puffing on it impatiently, starts into the background,
   steering his course so as to avoid the others as much
   as possible --

SCENE 15.   WHITNEY BALLROOM

   Flash back to the dance -- show Octavia and her escort
   in the foreground --

SCENE 16.   CLOSE UP ON FOUNTAIN: GARDEN   NIGHT

   Whitney is standing by the fountain watching the water --
   he is smoking moodily -- as he watches the rising smoke
   from his cigar mechanically, INSERT TITLE --

                    MEN OF THE YESTERDAYS

   BACK TO ACTION -- and as Whitney stares at and beyond the
   smoke, DISSOLVE OUT INTO THE FOLLOWING --

SCENE 17.   ALASKAN MINING STREET

   VERY CRUDE AND ROUGH -- a bunch of young miners with dogs
   and picks come on -- pick stalwart men for this -- they
   are of the red blooded rough and ready type who conquered
   the ice and cold -- good scene of fellowship among men --
   it is not necessary to show Whitney here --

12.19 Triangle produced *Framing Framers* in 1917. This script page indicates the beginning of a series of shots that represent the character Whitney remembering his youth. Three cues suggest this: the inter-title, Whitney's stare, and the dissolve. In subsequent action, this subjective sequence motivates Whitney's interference in his granddaughter Octavia's choice of a husband

10

The director system: management in the first years

The introduction of a new product

Initially, the exhibitors marketed the new medium of film on the basis of its technological novelty, but they had to find new rationales in order for consumers to repeat consumption of the product. This resulted in a need to supply a variety of product, and several firms entered the field to produce these films. Between Edison's first public exhibition in 1896 and 1908 when the Film Services Association formed, the manufacturers moved to an output which was predominantly fictional narratives. Robert Allen's research indicates that an important cause for this was the fact that narratives could be made in a central location and on a predictable basis – making possible a start of efficient and profitable mass production.

With this shift to narratives, the first detailed division of labor started to dominate a craft mode of making films. Modelled in part on the working practices of legitimate theater, the director system of filmmaking allowed rapid, predictable, and efficient production, and it quickly became the standard labor organization in the industry.

The first methods of marketing the product

The exhibition of projected Vitascope films on 23 April 1896, at Koster & Bial's Music Hall, may be considered a case of the introduction of a new product into a market. Many new products fail; this one did not. The reason can be traced to both economic and ideological/signifying practices.

Film entered the entertainment field, which meant that it would compete for consumers' disposable income. Consumers had to be willing to value the product enough to spend money on it rather than on a beer or a weekly illustrated magazine or a new phonograph record. The new product also faced an organized market which had already realized some of the advantages of national distribution and mass production. Legitimate theater had theater chains and national touring road companies presenting famous plays and stars. Set pieces for the stage were manufactured for mass distribution with these groups. Mark Klaw and Abraham Erlanger controlled a substantial string of theaters in major cities, which created an efficient national circuit and a syndicate by 1896. Opera houses and theaters had graduated-price seating, and penny arcades, Wild West, minstrel, and educational shows, circuses, and fairs were available to those with modest incomes. Popular magazines, such as the *Ladies Home Journal*, which was first to reach a circulation of $1\frac{1}{2}$ million in 1891, used the inexpensive mails for distribution and sold advertising to pay part of its production costs. Dime novels and children's fiction were widely available through inexpensive mass printing.[1]

Raff & Gammon exhibited the Vitascope and its films under Edison's name at a vaudeville house, vaudeville being another competitor in the entertainment field. The first Vitascope presentation consisted of a series of six vaudeville-like scenes: an umbrella dance by a variety act; a scenic of the seashore; a burlesque boxing match by Walton and May, 'the long and short comedians'; a section of a Hoyt farce, 'A Milk White Flag,' in which 'a couple of dozen people appeared'; a serpentine 'skirt dance by a tall blonde'; and a comic allegory called 'The Monroe Doctrine,' 'showing an argument between John Bull and Uncle Sam.' According to Robert Allen, Raff & Gammon's decision to exploit films through an acknowledged leader in retailing middle-class entertainment seems a conservative one. Advantages of vaudeville were apparent: typical acts could be filmed, and their length made them compatible with the short moving pictures. Working on the presentation of an interchangeable set of acts which were not linked together thematically, vaudeville intentionally varied its parts for widest audience appeal. It also regularly presented 'dumb acts' such as tinted stereopticon slide shows, acrobatics, and animal acts. Theater circuits had developed, legitimate stars were appearing on its stages, and middle-class money was arriving at the box offices of the well-appointed houses. Thus, moving pictures fitted into an already-existent market. To achieve profits, Raff & Gammon needed to supply projectors and films – a much smaller investment and distribution problem, than, for instance, moving into exhibition.[2]

Although Edison chose to concentrate on manufacturing and distributing projectors and films, other firms solved the marketing problem differently. Following another established pattern of selling entertainment to consumers, itinerant showmen armed with a camera, projector, and supply of film would tour the countryside and set up wherever audiences were available. These black-top, traveling tent shows were common in the United States through at least 1908. Combining the two methods, many firms contracted with vaudeville houses to supply projectionist, projector, and films as a set act. The advantage to this was that the house did not have to invest in a projector or worry about ordering films. The house only paid the act's salary. This distributing and merchandising method also meant rapid variation of the act with no loss of capital investment once audience interest declined.[3]

Luring the customer

At first films were marketed on the basis of the technological novelty of moving pictures. But novelty has a breaking point – Allen says, sometimes only a couple of months for the early films. The problem was to find new rationales for consumers repeatedly to purchase the product. The solution was to shift the publicity emphasis from films as a technological novelty to a variety of consumer appeals: stories, genres, spectacle, information, new novelties. Selling the product by differentiating it – even in slight ways – resulted in a need for a varied and increased supply of films.

The companies' films fell into several broad types, five of which are worth special attention. I have already mentioned the variety act and the fictional narrative. The earliest Vitascope films made by the Edison Company exemplified these two categories, as do films made by Vitagraph and Biograph. Typically, such films were produced in permanently located studios such as Edison's Black Maria. In 1897, *Scientific American* devoted a three-page article describing Biograph's technological apparatus, explaining that it was built 'for taking photographs of celebrated scenes from plays or of individual performances in which it is desired to reproduce the motions as well as the features of the subject.'[4] (The description indicates a revolving stage like the Black Maria and a camera which moved to and from the stage with its 'necessary scenery'.) These two types of films exploited the value of famous performers, sketches, and stories.

A third type was 'scenics,' a kind of family or tourist's collection of views of everyday life: the baby eating, workers leaving factories, vacation spots, exotic peoples and customs, far-away lands, and celebrities. A moving record of present-day life around the world, these documentaries were the medium's adaptation of written and oral accounts, paintings, and photographs. Hale's Tours (1905) even took the spectator/consumer on simulated trips by projecting films of scenic views while mechanically rocking the audience in specially constructed railroad cars. Scenics did not have to take spectators to picturesque locales; they might take them no farther than the home town. Cameramen would visit a town, take films, develop them, and then exhibit them on the spot. When Biograph visited Rochester, New York, in 1899, the firm photographed the town's fire department, police, employees from Eastman Kodak and Bausch & Lomb, and casual passers-by for exhibition at the local opera house.[5]

'Topicals' were a fourth major type. These differed from scenics in their exploitation of the timeliness of current events – a direct appeal to the freshness of the product. Early newsreels, these were filmings of coronations, funerals, fires, floods, and – with the advent of the Spanish American War – armed conflict. There were editorials: a crowd pleaser was a Vitagraph film showing the hoisting of an American flag after the pulling down of a Spanish one. Even re-enacted representations of the war's battles had consumer interest. Sport was also one of the earliest subjects for filming. Enoch Rector filmed the Corbett-Fitzsimmons bout in 1897, for an atypically long film of 11,000 feet, and the 1899 Biograph shooting of the Jeffries-Sharkey prize fight required an early use of artificial lighting. Unlike many other subjects, sports films held their value in repeated showings, particularly if controversial calls benefited from replays.[6]

Finally, 'trick' films provided an extension of the initial marketing appeal of the technology. Once moving pictures as such faded as a novelty, other aspects of the technology were exploited.

Economically and ideologically, moving pictures followed established, conservative business practices. In marketing, companies retailed the product as other entertainments had been retailed. Once the initial novelty of the product was gone, new visual, topical, and technological lures were the loci of advertising promotion to entice viewers to repeated consumption. The types of product — fictional narratives, variety entertainment, scenics, topicals, and tricks — had appealed to customers before film companies introduced moving pictures commercially; they still constitute the fare of television and other entertainment sources.

While it is not unusual for a company to introduce a new product, in a capitalist economy there remains the task of stimulating a demand so that production can increase. In early US film production the combination of a low cost and an accepted entertainment fare fostered a wide consumer demand. The low cost was a result of a series of developments in the industrial structure. Exchanges developed after 1903, which lowered the exhibitors' cost, which in turn permitted the establishment of the nickelodeon era about 1906. Moving pictures could then present entertainment — often vaudeville acts or short narratives — at a significantly lower price than vaudeville or theater. (The average admission prices in Boston in 1909 were: moving picture shows, $.10; vaudeville and moving pictures, $.15; vaudeville, $.50; regular theatre, $1.00; and the opera, $2.00.[7]) Even if the consumer had to give up live, three-dimensional spectacle, the ticket-price difference won out. As *Moving Picture World* said in 1908, 'A great portion of the public is satisfied with a reasonably good substitute for the real article [stage and vaudeville], providing it can be

obtained as a sufficiently reduced price.' Furthermore, scenics and topicals offered a moving recording — not possible in other entertainment media. In other words, some consumers with limited disposable income settled for the less expensive product, while consumers with even less income could now afford one form of commercial entertainment. This is not a case of the poor discovering cinema as their own, but the increased availability of films — both in exhibition outlets and in footage — to all income levels. The middle-class had had moving pictures in vaudeville; now the product's market expanded, and, with that expansion, it could move to a volume output and achieve economies of scale.[8]

The production shift to fictional narrative

With an increase in demand in the years 1906-7 (the nickelodeon boom), Allen claims commercial filmmakers weighted their output toward fictional narratives because of their suitability to mass production. This shift to narratives takes hold by 1907-8. (If spectators had not found these stories acceptable entertainment, the industrial concentration would not have been possible.) The change was remarked upon after the fact by several commentators, and their explanation makes good economic sense — for capitalist filmmakers. Discussing why the American manufacturers chose fictional narratives, Hugo Münsterberg wrote:[9]

It is claimed that the producers in America disliked . . . topical pictures because the accidental character of the events makes the production irregular and interferes too much with the steady production of the photoplays.

Or, in Harry C. Carr's picturesque language in a 1917 *Photoplay* article 'the demand for plays being greater than the supply of floods and fires, picture people began making pictures in the studios.'[10]

As Allen points out, fictional films could 'be made at a low, predictable cost per foot, produced in or near a centralized studio, and released on a regular schedule.' Irregularity hinders mass production. The producer needs both a constant, assured supply of raw materials and a routine assembly process. Topicals and scenics could not yield regular production, since a large number of cameramen spread throughout the United States sat idle for indefinite periods of time.[11] Moreover, the new (1908) distribution system, the Film Service Association, which sold exhibitors a *regular*, weekly supply of new films compounded the need for a steady production schedule.

Thus requirements of production and distribution which needed to ensure a supply of films explain the shift away from unpredictable options and toward fictional narratives. Changes in demand and supply affected all three branches of the film industry. Manufacturers began to consider efficient ways of ordering and expanding production; these techniques increased after the nickelodeon boom of 1906. Distributors helped that demand increase by regularizing the films' availability. Exhibitors expanded the number of outlets and, through lower prices, the overall market. The film had become generally accepted as a competitor for the consumer's dollar in the entertainment field, and filmmakers shifted to fictional narratives to provide efficient, steady mass production.

The 'cameraman' system of production (1896-1907)

In 1896, the manufacturers actually used two modes of production: a social division of labor and a detailed division of labor. The 'cameraman' system dominated until about 1907. As a type of social division of labor, the cameraman system represents a particularly unified craft situation. In general, cameramen such as W.K.L. Dickson, Albert Smith, Billy Bitzer, and Edwin S. Porter would select the subject matter and stage it as necessary by manipulating setting, lighting, and people; they would select options from available technological and photographic possibilities (type of camera, raw stock, and lens, framing and movement of camera, etc.), photograph the scene, develop and edit it. Dickson, in fact, not only was an inventor, but in 1899-1900 he spent ten months in South Africa photographing the Boer War for Biograph. Dickson recounted staging a typical film:[12]

February 26th [1900] – I am lost in admiration over the stoical manner in which our men suffer and joke over it all [the war]. To-

day I photographed the men as they were being carried from the Red Cross waggons to the trains at Colenso. Before they were lifted out I went from waggon to waggon telling them about the Biograph, and how their friends at home would see them, and that they must put the best foot forward. Although suffering severely they were cheery, and amused themselves chaffing with each other. The stretcher-bearers fell in with my idea and gave them every assistance, and soon a lot of them on stretchers, carried on each other's backs, &c., were ready to march past the machine, one fellow remarking as he tried to rise, 'Hello, old chap, are you winding us up for another go at old Krooger?'

Bitzer shot narratives, variety acts, and news footage, including covering the Spanish-American War and the Galveston hurricane. Porter concentrated on studio production for Edison. Workmanship precedents came from the examples of the still photographers during the second half of the 1800s.[13]

This description of the first work system seems comparable to the analysis of the social division of labor. Like the artisan/craftsman, the cameraman knew the entire work process, and conception and execution of the product were unified. In early film production, some individuals functioned as both owners/managers (with the work responsibilities of capital direction) and cameramen (with product responsibilities); in other cases the responsibilities were split among individuals. What is important is that those who actually made the films were craftsmen.

The cameraman system could supply films but not as predictably, rapidly, and inexpensively as was necessary once the nickelodeon boom started in 1906. To produce scenics and topicals, the firms needed many cameramen to cover the entire physical space where news might occur. Even when an event did occur, the success of the film might depend on uncontrollable factors such as the weather: if the film jammed or was inadequately exposed, news events did not repeat themselves for retakes. While cameramen continued making newsreels on their own, the entire growing industry could not rely on such a method to increase production at a time when demand warranted expansion.

In the production of narratives, variety acts, and trick films in a studio, a skilled artisan such as Porter who organized, directed, photographed, and edited most of his firm's product could only do so much. The number of cameramen so skilled in a variety of work processes was also limited. Furthermore, while the companies might have trained other workers in all aspects of the craft, that would counter the cost advantages of dividing labor. Only the most skilled workers had to be paid high salaries; if a few workers could specialize in the technical phases, the less-skilled workers could execute the work — for lower salaries. Training craftsmen was more expensive than dividing labor.

In both location shooting and studio production, the cameraman system — as of that period — was not able to supply films in mass production. That the firms should shift away from a social division of labor to a detailed division of labor follows the economic example set by many other profitable industries. The cameraman system did not die out as such (Hal Mohr describes working in it for a small firm in 1913 and it continues today), but by sheer weight of capital investment another mode and system began to dominate the film industry after about 1907.[14]

The 'director' system of production (1907-1909)

You will find that the kinetoscope world is much like the dramatic, that it has its actors and actresses, its playwrights and stage directors, its theatrical machinery, its wings, its properties, its lights, its tricks, its make-ups, its costumes, its entrances and exits.[15]

Moving Picture World, 1907

Even before 1907, some firms developed a different organization of work. Vitagraph, for instance, hired its first director in 1904. Although Bitzer had been in charge of all his product at Biograph, about 1907, a separate worker began to take over parts of the direction. In this system of production, one individual staged the action and another person photographed it. Moreover, the director managed a set of workers including the craftsman cameraman. The historical precedent for this system was the legitimate theater and its stage director.[16]

Historians of the theater generally date the emergence of the modern stage director from the 1870s. Although directorial work functions were part of the labor process before then, usually the director was also a member of the cast. The productions between 1874 and 1890 of Georg II, Duke of Saxe-Meiningen, are particularly significant:[17]

> The most important factors in the Duke's approach were his complete control over every aspect of a production, and his long and careful rehearsals. A painter and draftsman, he designed the scenery, costumes, and every movement of the actors. He did not utilize stars and each actor was subordinated to the over-all effect. . . . Furthermore, stage scenery and properties were carefully designed in terms of the action, and the total stage picture as it developed moment by moment was worked out with extreme care.

In the United States, Augustin Daly, an early non-acting manager, also countered the prevalent star system by stressing ensemble acting. Describing Daly's techniques from the 1870s on, a biographer writes that 'he treated his artists as puppets in his scheme of *mise en scène*.' By 1900 it was common both abroad and in the United States to consider each play as having its own needs in style, scenery, and staging which the director organized, controlled, and rehearsed in detail. Oscar Brockett comments that for directors like Max Reinhardt a script was 'the meager outline offered by the playwright which the director must complete.'[18]

Many of the early film directors came from stage acting experience: G.M. Anderson (with Selig from 1903), Hobart Bosworth (with David Belasco until hired by Selig in 1909), D.W. Griffith (with Biograph in 1907), Herbert Brenon (with IMP, 1909), Al Christie (with Nestor, 1909), and Sidney Olcott (with Kalem, 1907). When the 1907-8 shift to fictional narratives occurred, film production was able to take as a model the stage director who controlled the choices of scenery, costumes, and acting, and used a script as an 'outline' of the narrative.[19]

In the film studio, the director made most of the major and minor decisions involved in the filming of the product. As a producer, his employment with a company ensured that finances were available. (At this point in the industry, the terms 'producer' and 'director' were even used synonymously.) The director/producer like Griffith either furnished the idea for the film or rewrote one the firm had available. He selected his stage settings and gave directions to the carpenters, painters, and property men. If any research was needed, he would do it. He selected the people from the stock company; he found locations. One director in 1907 described his shooting procedures: 'I rehearsed the child and dog a good many times, so's to get just the right kind of curves to the performance and when they were letter perfect in their parts I had the machines planted and gave the word for the snapping to begin.' Once the cameraman or laboratory staff developed the film, the director edited it.[20]

The parallels between film director and the theatrical counterpart are evident. Edward W. Townsend made the comparison explicitly when he described production procedures in 1909:[21]

> Work preliminary to production runs parallel with that in a Broadway theater. Plays, some in scenario form, some fully developed, are received in every mail and examined by professional readers who select the possible for managerial consideration. Those finally accepted, if in scenario − the sketch of the play − are given to a playwright to be fully developed. In their final form plays are turned over to a stage manager, who first proceeds as does his brother of Broadway, to draw off scene plots for the painters and carpenters, and property and costume lists for those in charge of those departments. Then the people of the play are cast.

The firms copied other aspects of the stage work system by employing actors and actresses, stage managers, property men, and wardrobe mistresses. There were also 'assistants with signs, costumes and various properties.' In 1908 Selig hired carpenters and scene shifters who were members of the local theatrical Stage Hands Union.[22]

The director system differs significantly from the cameraman system. Most obviously, the director system split responsibility for the production between jobs, thus separating the conception and execution of the work among individual craftsmen. This was due in part to the technology.[23]* The cameraman, almost invariably, made several important decisions: the sufficiency of light, the photographic acceptability of a take, and the quality of the negatives he or an assistant developed and printed. He may also have been involved in other aspects of the camera's set-up. Generally, the knowledge of this technology was outside the province of the director, whose major photographic criterion at that time was visibility of action. After 1907, it became atypical in fictional narrative production for the work functions of director and cameraman to be combined. In later years, around 1913, Thanhouser publicized its employee Carl L. Gregory as 'one of the two moving picture directors who actually operate their own cameras.'[24]

A further separation of conception and execution began to isolate another specific function: writing the script outlines. (From the beginning, companies had supplied some stories for the workers to reconstruct for filming. Credited by the early industry as the 'first' person hired by a company to produce stories, Roy L. McCardell worked for Biograph from 1897.[25]) The cause for this split seems to be one of increasing the supply of raw product (stories) for the move to mass production. Epes Winthrop Sargent suggested that the nickelodeon boom and the shift to fictional narratives created an intense need for a constant and plentiful supply of plots. As Sargent wrote in 1913:[26]

> It was seen that the studio force could not produce each week a sufficiently strong story, and outside writers were invited to contribute suggestions, for which they were paid from five to fifteen dollars. These mere synopses were developed in the studio into scripts, since few of the writers possessed the knowledge of picture-making requisite to enable them to develop the script.

By subcontracting stories from freelance writers or hiring its own writers, the company organized script production into two phases: 1) selecting subject material and constructing a plot, and 2) breaking the plot into parts for filming. The director or another individual in the firm did the latter. These 'outlines' ranged from the causal scenario to the more formal play. Gene Gauntier recalls the scenarios which Kalem owner-writer Frank Marion was supplying to director Sidney Olcott in the summer of 1907: 'And he [Marion] would hand Sid a used business envelope on the back of which, in his minute handwriting, was sketched the outline of six scenes, supposed to run one hundred and fifty feet to the scene − as much as our little camera would hold. A half dozen words described each scene; I believe to this day Mr. Marion holds the championship for the shortest working scenario.' Gauntier's evaluation of Marion's scenarios indicates that his ran toward the more informal end of the continuum. The more detailed plays mentioned by Townsend in 1909 were 'picture-play manuscripts [which] consist largely of descriptions of character, explanations of emotions, instructions for entrances and exits and other stage directions, and contain but a few lines [of dialogue] (and those merely for guidance).'[27]

The director still had great leeway in the use of these scenario outlines. In an interview with the 'stage director' filming a civil war story on location in suburban Chicago in 1909, the director explained:[28]

I expect to call this piece 'Brother Against Brother,' but we don't always know until we see how they turn out. The idea is that the Union captain has taken his own brother prisoner as a spy, and then is compelled to have him shot. I don't know exactly what we'll do with it yet. We may have the Union captain commit suicide rather than shoot his own brother. We'll have to work this out later.

While the director may have been in charge of the film, planning was apparently not always very advanced.

The division between the story writer and the director had become so common by 1911 that trade paper writers were already saying that while the ideal would be a combined 'author-director,' few individuals could successfully be both.[29] Probably the separation of functions also owed a good deal to the mode of legitimate theater.

By 1907, then, the artisanal cameraman mode had been replaced by a system which separated conception and execution of the work among at least director, cameraman, and writer. There was an additional significant difference between the cameraman and director systems. As Marx predicted regarding serial manufacture, more craft positions created a hierarchy of management. As in the theatrical model, the director topped a pyramid of workers: the rest of the staff followed his decisions and directions.

The split of conception and execution and the creation of a management hierarchy signal a fundamental change in the mode of film production − a change from a social division of labor to a detailed one. Now several individuals were functioning both as managers (with technical decision-making power) and workers (with execution power). Part of this was due to the means of production, with its combination of crafts (writing, directing, photographing); part, to the advantages of detailed division of labor in improving the rate of output. After management and work processes had become clearly divided, subsequent production systems revised the director system, generally separating the various management decisions among more and more work positions, creating hierarchies of management and non-management workers, and further parceling out the labor. While the future systems would be different, they all worked out of the director system's distribution of management and craft knowledge among various jobs.

Finally, it is not unimportant that this system of production centralized its work processes in the studio/factory. This allowed an ease in controlling labor time, eliminating irregularity of production, and permitting detailed division of labor as well as reducing material and labor cost. The film studio/factory was the focal site of the manufacturing of fictional narrative films, and the shift away from the scenics and topicals has to be attributed in part to the advantages of studio production. Even when the firm sent out a group to shoot exteriors for a one-reel narrative, the locations at first were usually within one-day round-trip distance. Only later when the firms made work procedures more regularized did they take advantage of another characteristic of standardization: if parts were interchangeable, they could be made in different and distant locations and then assembled in yet another place.

The studio need not be a site for the complete construction of the film, but for efficient mass production, a centralized place of planning and assembly was perceived as a minimal condition.

The director system dominated US film production only a few years — most centrally, the period 1907-9. It remains a distinct and important system, however, because it did continue as a sporadic or minority practice. Taking its immediate precedents from theatrical work models, it did not immediately develop the rigid work organizations then current in a very few mass production industries such as the automotive one. As we shall see, subsequent systems in the detailed division of labor revised and reworked the basic features of this initial system. By 1909, demand for films had increased to the point that a new system took over.

11

The director-unit system: management of multiple-unit companies after 1909

The 'director-unit' system of production (1909-14)

> The Selig plant is an enormous art factory, where film plays are turned out with the same amount of organized efficiency, division of labor and manipulation of matter as if they were locomotives or sewing machines.[1]
>
> *Motography*, July 1911
>
> 'There's another sausage.'[2]
>
> Attributed to D.W. Griffith during his Biograph employment

In 1911 Selig Polyscope was releasing four one-reel films per week. This was typical of the manufacturers, who through their distribution alliances were selling a regular supply of varied goods to exhibitors. By then, the exhibitors required twenty to thirty new films per week, and the distribution alliances, to regularize the system and spread the product evenly across the week, assigned weekly release schedules. This required manufacturers to systematize their production output so that the reels of film would roll out the studio doors as regularly as those locomotives or sewing machines. Advertising practices also reinforced this need for system. In order to achieve maximum benefit from advertising any particular film, the exhibitor had to count on its appearance on the release date. We can attribute the dominance of a new production system after 1909 to economic practices – the need to increase production and maintain it year-round to meet exhibitor demand.[3]

Selig Polyscope and the other manufacturers could have stuck with their former one reel a week, but more profits could be made with four. A single director-producer could shoot one reel a week; he could not shoot four. The solution was logical: hire more directors. This expansion started in 1908, as the industrial structure began to coalesce into what became the Motion Picture Patents Company later that year. With the anticipated stabilization of the industry, manufacturers shifted capital and attention from patent litigation to investment in the manufacturing of more product. It was easy to increase production: the director system made for a fully integrated work force; all the components to produce a film resided within a predictable set of employees. By late 1909, Selig had four director-producers in three permanent locations: Francis Boggs in California, Louis J. Howard in New Orleans, and Otis Turner and Frank Beal in Chicago. In 1911, D.W. Griffith, Frank Powell, and Mack Sennett all directed units for Biograph.[4]*

Another cause of the move to the director-unit system was the necessity for year-round production to supply the distribution exchanges. The headquarters and studios of the manufacturers had, understandably, located themselves in the centers of the entertainment business: New York and Chicago. New York was the staging area for the national circuits in theater and vaudeville, which provided a trained supply of labor, and Chicago was a major midwest center. Neither city, however, was immune from the vagaries of winter snow and grey skies. Artificial lighting in the studios might overcome the latter, but bad weather eliminated exteriors on low-light days. As a result, some companies began sending units to better climates during the winter.

Furthermore, this type of expansion allowed the manufacturers to retain certain aspects of the popular scenics and topicals while making sure production schedules were met. Sending a director-unit on an extended trip to make a series of narratives, the manufacturers combined location shooting and its values of authenticity, realism, and spectacle with the fictional narrative and its production efficiency.

Selig, which had used a traveling unit from 1904, visited California in fall 1907. 'Nowhere,' it later claimed, 'but in the real West could the proper atmosphere and wide vistas have been found [for Selig films].'[5] The Independent Motion Picture Company (IMP) headed to Cuba in January 1911 because 'local color is the order of the day in moving picture making.' It continued:[6]

Of course there is nothing remarkable in this fact of manufacturers being located hundreds of thousands [sic] of miles from New York City. The apple that we ate this morning was probably from Oregon; there is no reason why the moving picture that we looked at last night should not also have been made in the same distant State. The telephone, the telegraph, the aeroplane, as well as the fast railroad are, in modern business economics, rapidly annihilating time and space. . . .

IMP then used this as a mark of quality production for its first Cuban film: 'If the excellency of this picture is any criterion by which to judge, the expense of sending two producing companies to a clime where exterior scenes can be filmed in the dead of winter has been justified.' Or in a publicity article on Nestor's location work and a 1912 release: ' "White Cloud's Secret" holds the interest of the onlooker not only in the working out of the plot but also in the splendid choice of scenes, the novelty of which thrills the Easterner, and all unaccustomed to the Western desert scenery.'[7]

Both the licensed and the independent manufacturers were avid travelers. Besides Selig's various trips and then permanent locations of units in 1909 in California and New Orleans, Kalem found its 1908-9 trip to Jacksonville, Florida, valuable since it had no permanent studio. It also sent a unit to Ireland where the workers produced films using Irish plays and novels as sources. In 1911 Kalem made films in the Holy Land including *From the Manger to the Cross*, a six-reeler using the authentic locales. G.M. Anderson directed a unit for Essanay

Westerns from 1908 on. Traveling throughout the southwest, his unit eventually established a permanent studio outside San Francisco. Lubin had two stock companies location shooting in 1912. One with thirty people journeyed from Florida to New Orleans and up the Mississippi River. The other, also with thirty people, roamed Arizona. Both units had a Pullman standard sleeping and day coach and a baggage car with scenery, props, and furniture. The variety of the exteriors must have compensated for the lack of variation in the interiors. Nor is the imitation of a touring stage company coincidental. The independents also used this production method of units, some of which were shooting on varied locations in 1911 and 1912. American Film traveled the Old Santa Fe Trail doing comedies and dramas; Thanhouser had its New Rochelle Studio units and a unit in Jacksonville; and Powers had three units in New Mexico.[8]

The location of permanent studios in Southern California developed out of these odysseys. That the studio sections of the firms should settle in California is not surprising. In 1911, the Los Angeles correspondent to the *Moving Picture World* described a series of reasons for spending part or all of the production season there: 1) good weather (the US Weather Bureau figured that on the average 320 days of the year were acceptable for filming); 2) a variety of exteriors (these included not only topology and climates but also residential areas, missions, and fine parks such as Griffith Park); 3) a good labor supply (Los Angeles had a population in 1910 of 319,198 people with up to 500,000 during the winter season); 4) advantages as a major west coast theatrical center (both the Belasco and Burbank stock companies were there, and 'with the growth of the city dramatically there came the booking agencies, the scene painting studios, theatrical costumers, and other supply companies' — including Max Factor); 5) good transportation to other parts of the country; and 6) a number of film firms already located there (this, as we noted, provided exchange of workers and amenable industrial ties). The interest in Hollywood and other suburbs was due to their lower costs in labor and real estate. Room for standing sets was also plentiful. Firms which had winter or permanent companies there in spring 1911 included the licensed firms of Selig, Pathe West Coast,

Biograph, Kalem, Essanay Western, and the independent Bison brand of New York Motion Picture Company. By 1915, one trade paper writer estimated 15,000 workers were employed in Hollywood's moving picture industry with over 60 per cent of the US films produced there. Despite competition from other locales, particularly Jacksonville, Los Angeles won out as the producing center for the United States film industry.[9]

While financing units for location filming, the manufacturers expanded their home studio staffs in the same manner — by units, often referred to as stock companies (see fig 11.1). Simultaneously, the firms expanded their stage area to allow several companies to film at the same time. The trade papers repeatedly report these expansions.[10]

The dominance of a director-unit system after 1909 resulted from two advantages: increased, efficient production eliminated troubles from winter weather; and a variety of locations yielded exchange-values of authenticity, realism, and spectacle. This type of increase in size in the firm justifies a distinct category. As the firms organized the work, the director of the unit remained in charge of the producing, rewriting, directing, and editing functions. Generally, he retained the same production staff with him from film to film, but now there was some combining, sharing, and dividing of work by the middle-level workers such as the cameramen, prop men, the stock company, and so on. What changes significantly is that the workers in each unit only participated in the work of their unit or only for sections of many films rather than in the production of all the firm's films. As before, knowledge of the conception and execution of the product was separated among several workers.

At the same time, the method of worker payment started to affect the work relations. The increase in the rate of product output encouraged the use of wage payment based on fast work and deadlines. With time as the calculator of wages, the fewer people involved for the shortest time, the less the cost. This proceeded to reduce the involvement in planning by workers in subordinate positions in the hierarchy. The firm used most of the workers in straight execution of work rather than in design contribution. (Had payment been by quality of output or perhaps a profit-sharing scheme, the tendency toward dis-

associating certain workers might have been reduced. For the effect when there is a change to profit-sharing, see the 'package-unit' system in Chapter 26.) Furthermore, with mass production, variation in design should be minimal (standardization being the dominant goal, with only occasional differentiation) so that production is faster; a few workers could supply variations while most of the others followed standard production design and practices. For instance, sets could be lit basically the same way for illumination of the action no matter what happened in the narrative or who was playing the lead. Even effects lighting (which became common after 1915) could be standardized.

Deadlines not only discouraged sharing of planning activities and encouraged standardizing the style, they forced the further subdivision of labor. As Fred Balshofer remarked about his situation in 1912: 'Nevertheless, directing, preparing the next story for shooting, plus the full responsibility for the company became more than any one individual could find time to handle properly.' As a *Moving Picture World* writer in 1911 urged: 'a proper system and division of labor' with specialists in scene design, photography, lighting, and locations were necessary because a 'stage director' could not know and do all those things.[11]

Although there had been some detailed division of labor and hierarchy in the director system, with the advent of the director-unit system and the overall expansion of the number of employees, subdivision and separation of knowledge began to proliferate, and work functions coalesced into departments. Technical specialists (middle-level, tactical managers) took charge of these departments. Upper-level managers made long-term decisions as to methods of financing, type of products, hiring of middle-level specialists and the rest of the workers, and assessing of market conditions and trends. These managers left short-term, day-to-day production to the middle-level management. In such a line-and-staff administration, information was generalized as it moved up the hierarchy, although the upper management might develop methods to keep somewhat in touch. For instance, H.M. Horkheimer, general manager and president of Balboa in 1915, said:[12]

I have a fixed time each day for meeting my

directors. We go over the work in hand. I have confidence in them, hence I never ask them why they are doing a thing while they are at work. I wait until the production is finished and then pass on it. In the same way, I have conferences with the various cameramen. I visit the laboratory and keep in touch with the wardrobe department.

The period 1909-14, then, marks the separation and subdivision of the work into *departmentalized* specialities with a structural hierarchy.

The director-unit system started the large-scale movement to specialization of work. I would point out, however, that the film industry has shown a flexibility in its use of individuals. Even though the industry separated the jobs, it was not uncommon for a person to hold several simultaneously or successively. Certain routines and combinations, because they were closely related in the work process, were more susceptible to movement between them. But it is clear that the categories of work were distinct with their specific duties and responsibilities within the overall process. In later years, this compartmentalization increased.

The efficient, departmentalized organization of the means of production

That departmentalization was rapidly developing is evidenced by publicity descriptions of the physical arrangements of the studios. The permanent studio was one option as a site of filmmaking, and its centralization of the labor process with a steady supply of narrative material helped to permit a regular output of product. Early descriptions of these studios use the term 'factory,' and their large brick buildings with glass-enclosed stage spaces have an evident kinship with turn-of-the-century industrial plants. Usually, the entire requirements for making a film stood within the factory area: laboratories for film developing and printing, outdoor lot space for exteriors, and by the early teens, restaurants for employees' lunches and hospital facilities in case of accidents (see fig 11.2). With the firms' expansion, the studios, like the labor force, grew larger to accommodate the needs of the multiple stock companies at work.[13]

By 1912, following the standard assembly system in mass production, Solax had reorganized the means of production at its studio. Its departments included executive, production, direction, art, wardrobe, small properties, electrical, mechanical, laboratory, sales, publicity, shipping, and accounting, and it positioned them physically so that 'harmonious co-operation [can] be maintained and thus the highest average of efficiency secured.' 'The laboratory,' Solax's publicity boasted, 'is so arranged that the whole process of film manufacture after the camera man turns in his negative proceeds logically from room to room in each succeeding process without needlessly making a single step that would tend toward delay or entail a waste of movement and consequently a waste of energy.'[14] Solax was typical. An exchange of 1913 boasted of using the 'exact business practices to-day.'[15]

> The departmental lines in our organization are carefully and rigidly drawn. . . . Every department has its distinct functions with a responsible department head in charge. While our departments are physically separated from each other, our work is so systematized that the co-operation of departments is perfect.

This organization intensified in later years. In 1916, 'efficiency engineers' rearranged the Triangle-Fine Arts studio 'to meet the needs of increased production and large numbers of companies.' The Bosworth Company used the new building material of re-inforced concrete for its stages. *Scientific American* described the building of Fox's new combined facility in 1919 (see fig 11.3): 'It has been laid out along scientific lines by authorities on factory and office construction, with a view to speed, economy, and concentration in every possible phase of efficient motion-picture production, from the filming to bookkeeping to stenography to starring.' Firms also constructed their studios for multiple purposes. At Universal City in 1916, 'the principal bridge across this stream is simply a foundation bridge and may be hastily transformed from a Roman bridge into a railroad-crossing.' Architects also designed dressing rooms with various fronts (see fig 11.4), and they planned landscaping so it could double as an exterior.[16]

Not only were the plants efficiently organized,

but following progressive business leaders, the film firms also participated in contemporary corporate welfare for their employees. As early as 1911 Sigmund Lubin established a restaurant at his Philadelphia plant (see fig 11.5): 'Mr. Lubin feels . . . that it is a good investment aside from any philanthropic aspect, because it adds to the health and comfort, and, therefore, to the capacity for accomplishment of the employees.'[17] The New York Motion Picture Company refurbished the Keystone scenario department in 1915:[18]

Soft carpets, easy chairs, subdued colors and every little detail of comfort and restfulness have been resorted to with the idea that the staff of writers will do better in the improved surroundings. A library of reference books, individual stenographers for each writer, dictating machines, and other conveniences are combined in the most up-to-date scenario department in the west.

By the mid-teens, the companies were adding equipment to insure continuous production. Vitagraph manufactured its own arc-lamps in 1912, and most firms had shops to make break-away and explosive props by 1915. Electrical lighting, even in sunny California, became standard equipment in case of inadequate natural light, and by 1916 some companies had moved from outdoor stages with muslin overhangs to glass studios with lights for all their interior settings (see figs 11.6, 11.7). Inceville's eight California stages were all 'equipped with the most up-to-date lighting devices, including the wonderful nitrogen light, so that on dark days during rainy seasons pictures may be made with every effect and value of sunlight.' In 1921, one cameraman wrote that interiors were almost always lit with artificial lighting and that the light for exterior sets was often boosted by electrical lights as well.[19]

This move was also due to the films having acquired specific realistic and compositional standards for quality work including, in particular, effects lighting. To achieve realistic lighting for night scenes and interiors, some companies built 'dark studios.' Vitagraph had one in 1912: 'Arc-lamps . . . are used for artificial lighting purposes, where concentrated light effects are needed in a scene at night or during

the day. These produce very strong Rembrandt effects, particularly in a picture which is produced in the Dark Studio in the day-time.' By the late teens, the firms had painted some of the glass studios black for the same reason (see fig 11.8).[20]

The firms began a steady exodus from location shooting into the studio and back lot after the mid-teens. One 1916 writer pointed out that producers used to go away to shoot foreign scenes; now they were done in the United States 'where the producers have better laboratory facilities, understand the light better, can secure experienced players — and save time.' With a particular standard for the quality film, location work even miles away became more difficult and expensive. Negative development, lighting control and cost, electrical current access, location set problems (low ceilings in houses which hampered quality lighting arrangements), and transportation of larger labor staffs and more equipment all decreased location shooting's desirability. Besides, better set construction, with the use of miniatures and glass shots (see fig 11.9) when necessary, adequately represented exterior locales and 'local color' sets.[21]

Changes in script writing practices: the scenario script

The director-unit system not only saw specialization and departmentalization, including the reorganization of studios into a predictable, efficient assembly system, but the studios' script writing practices changed. The causes for this are economic and ideological: efficient production and the standards of the quality product.

In the director system, the story outline sufficed as a production plan. But the manufacturers found two defects in the casual story outline. First, for efficient production, filmmakers quickly realized that they saved time and money if all the shots to be taken at one place or on one set were done at the same time, rather than in the order of the final film. The director could break the story into shots and could supervise the drawing up of a 'scene plot' which listed the shots to be taken in each setting. After the crew photographed all the shots, the director could put them into order during editing. To insure that this disjunctive shooting order would supply all the story parts, a prepared script was useful.

Moreover, to achieve a quality product, the director's primary duty in his assembly process was to structure a narrative in which an initial cause produced a chain of effects which ended in a satisfactory resolution. This, the filmmakers believed, achieved a clear, logical, and realistic story. This conception of quality product was no problem for filmmakers at first because if the film failed the manufacturer could either pay to shoot the necessary plot linkage or could send out the film as it was – even if a bit jumbled by standards of the best narrative.

This approach to production received a setback when around 1908 film distributors and exhibitors adopted the 1,000-foot length as the standard size of the purchased product. (As the exchange system developed and nickelodeon theaters proliferated, manufacturers turned out films which were priced by the foot and sold in a standard length for convenient pricing and handling.) With this new constraint on the film, the producers found themselves pressured to provide a narrative with the requisite beginning, middle, and end. A 1911 trade paper critic pointed out that stories often ended up with abrupt connections and sudden conclusions or seemed dragged out. Arguing that the length of the film should not be standardized so strictly, the critic wrote: 'There is too much evidence of "cutting up" and "cutting off" to the detriment of the continuity of the pictures, and this slaughtering of the subject only increases the ambiguity of the whole.'[22] The problem for the producers, then, was to insure complete narrative continuity and clarity despite the footage limitation.

The solution was to pay more rigorous attention to preparing a script which provided narrative continuity before shooting actually started. In that way the director could make an initial estimate of the footage per shot and add up all the shots to precheck that they would not exceed the footage limit. In the early teens, directions to freelance writers repeatedly cautioned them to choose stories which could be presented within one reel. Descriptions of shooting practices indicate that rehearsals served in part to check in advance the shots' lengths and that action would be compressed if necessary to meet the predetermined footages. One of the functions of the cameraman was to measure each take's footage which was matched to the length established by the script. If the shot ran over its limit, it might be retaken. Tricks to get more narrative within footage limits included quickening entrances and exits of characters or 'discovering' them in the scene; inter-titles and crosscutting were also used to eliminate or abbreviate action. Here is an instance in which economic practices (the one-reel limit) directly influenced film style.[23]

Thus both shooting out of final continuity and the standard of clear, continuous action militated for a script written prior to shooting. It is evident that the manufacturers transformed the theatrical and vaudeville script into their working blueprint for the film. A 1909 trade paper article set out the format for the standard script: the title, followed by its generic designation ('a drama,' 'a comedy'), the cast of characters, a 200-word-or-less 'synopsis' of the story, and then the 'scenario,' a shot-by-shot account of the action including inter-titles and inserts. This scenario script could insure that the standard of continuous action would be met within the footage requirement. It also listed all the story settings so that shooting out of order was faster, easier, and safer, and, hence, cheaper. With this method of production, the manufacturer achieved both efficient production and a quality product. As we noted in Chapter 10, playwright Edward Townsend who was writing picture plays for Edison in 1909 mentioned that all the stories at that firm were put into just such a shooting format for the firm's directors.[24]

Although descriptions of and advice about this working procedure were common in trade literature, shooting from a scenario script was not a requirement. Some directors still followed the outline approach. Griffith even composed the story as he went along. Since at this point, each narrative event was almost always equivalent to a shot, and since the one-reel film was a linkage of fifteen to thirty shots, it was possible for the director to carry the parts of the story in his head throughout the length of the three- to six-day production schedule. If the director was able to meet the footage requirements and to handle the nonsequential shooting order, connecting each of the story parts was no difficult matter.

Had the films produced by the US manufacturers remained in the style of the tableau, with general lighting, and only moderate attention to continuity and authenticity, it seems probable that work practices might have remained this way, with some planning in advance through simple scenario scripts. However, two major changes occurred: first, the practices of quality stylistic representation changed between 1909 and 1917; and second, the standard length of the film increased during the same period. Both of these changes caused the manufacturers to shift from the scenario to the continuity script, a script which carefully detailed every shot of the film.

12

The central producer system: centralized management after 1914

The next change in the mode of production can be traced to profit maximization goals and to the shifting and coalescing standards of quality filmmaking. This new system centralized the control of production under the management of a producer, a work position distinct from staff directors. The producer used a very detailed shooting script, the continuity script, to plan and budget the entire film shot-by-shot before any major set construction, crew selection, or shooting started. This system, while part of a major shift in US business practices to 'scientific management,' was also due to two specific changes in the film industry: first, the techniques for achieving continuity, verisimilitude, and narrative dominance and clarity coalesced to create what we call the classical Hollywood film; second, the films lengthened from an average of eighteen minutes to seventy-five minutes or more. Both of these factors required production planning. A continuity script insured the quality of the film, and it permitted budget control, becoming the design blueprint for the film and all of the work. Since the lengthening of the film is integral to this, we shall look at multiple-reel film's innovation and diffusion before examining the new production system and script practices.

The diffusion of longer films

The shift to the multiple-reel film was part of an intentional attempt to improve profits by making the film appear to be a quality product. The exhibitors created such an image by improving their theaters and service, and, consequently, they sought a film which could be effectively advertised as a 'feature.' One of the ways to insure that a film would succeed was to adapt a prior success – a play or novel. But because the

producers wanted to claim that they were true to the source (the standard of fidelity operated here), a problem developed: these adaptations, sometimes starring famous players from legitimate theater, could not easily be crammed into the constrictive one-reel length. As a result, the adaptation of famous works became a major cause in the lengthening of the film into the multiple-reeler.

Dirty little dumps and quality theaters

Producers and distributors sold films; exhibitors sold entertainment.[1] With a theater and a marketing area in a specific physical space, the exhibitor could vary and enhance the makeup of the entertainment package to achieve maximum profits; he, too, emphasized the novelty and quality of the product as its exchange-value.

Vaudeville was the first site of projected film exhibition and with it came a contemporary standard of quality theater. For Keith's Union Square Theater in 1895 that meant – besides the rotation of variety acts and continuous shows – ushers in uniform, leaf fans and ice water in the summer, and a cool, palmed grotto.[2]

The first all-film theaters (which started around 1905) have been described as dank, dark, dirty, and disreputable. These theaters were small (often with fewer than two hundred seats to avoid the need for an amusement license). Part of this seediness may be due to the conversion from stores and to the initially low capital with which the exhibitors started. Rather than seeing the growth of the nickelodeons as a chaotic mushrooming, however, the research of Russell Merritt, Douglas Gomery, and Robert Allen has found that the theaters' early locations functioned to promote the best chance of profits. Generally, the exhibitors established the nickelodeons along commercial thoroughfares, near mass transit routes, and by and in established shopping and entertainment areas. Such locations could take advantage of the passing consumer of any economic class who might stop in for a short period of relaxation before continuing on her or his way.[3]

The period of the impoverished theater must have been relatively short, just long enough to increase capital, because by 1907-8 some exhibitors were already emulating high-class vaudeville and theater techniques of service and style with the product. This tendency may also have been exacerbated by competition between film exhibitors. If there were three or four nickelodeons within a shopping area and the only product came from a small set of producers, how could the exhibitor compete? One method was advertising a quality product: brand names were an important asset since the exhibitor could announce he always had the latest Vitagraph drama or Essanay Western.

Another way of competing was to offer extras. Such an early technique was the recombination of live acts interspersed with the films. William Fox introduced small-time (lower-cost) vaudeville into his New York City theater in 1908 and by 1910 had a circuit of fourteen houses with long programs, seven or eight live acts, a policy of comfortable surroundings, and an admission price of 10 to 25 cents. In late 1907, a magazine writer claimed: 'the tendency is clear toward fewer, bigger, cleaner, five-cent theatres and more expensive shows.'[4] (See figs 12.1 through 12.3.) By early 1911, *Moving Picture World* wrote:[5]

> To-day things have changed, the dirty little dumps, with small seating capacity and poor ventilation are fast passing away to make room for large, palatial houses, and the moment that the exhibitor called the attention of the public to a much better class of houses, a new class of spectators appeared and are now eager for motion pictures.

Of course these theaters hardly approximated the extravagance of the edifices of the 1920s, but the underlying causes of those palaces were already in place.

As the *Moving Picture World* passage implies, the *representation* of the quality status of the product was important in the shift. One signifi-

cant way to create an image of a respectable theater was to raise the admission price. By mid-1911, the 5-cent theater was facing a potent rival: the theater whose prices ranged from 10 to 25 cents, a cost still below other entertainment offerings, but a theater which offered the aura of respectable middle-class entertainment. Many trade paper writers advised exhibitors to raise the price to at least 10 cents (which even the poor could afford) to avoid the appearance of a 'cheap and common' show. Justifying the raise did require, however, presenting an appearance of greater entertainment value.[6] (Many small theaters stayed with the nickel price even up to 1915, however.)

With an exhibition image at stake, the theater location, construction, and presentation had to be planned with care. Advice poured in; one writer in 1911 suggested: 'Study every point of difference which can be found between the theater in question and its competitor or competitors: The color of the front; the decorations of the front; the announcement signs for number, attractiveness, and general desirability; the poster service used for the films; the style of the ticket window' and on and on. Architects who had been building theater and vaudeville houses for years advertised they would plan the film exhibitor's newest one; examples in the trade paper columns of outstanding theaters provided models for future houses; and the exhibitors exchanged little techniques to improve the atmosphere or increase house control. Throughout all this, the exhibitors also looked for quality films to go with their quality theaters.[7]

The feature film

Promulgating the feature film depended upon creating the sense of a greater exchange value. Before 1908, advertising by posters, on billboards, and in newspapers was standard practice, but differentiating the individual films was difficult. Faced with several short varied subjects, a daily change, and unpredictable supply, the exhibitor could not advertise much more than good films and entertainment at low prices. Borrowing a technique from vaudeville, however, he might try promoting a 'headline' or 'feature' attraction in his program. That is what Kleine Optical Company proposed in 1904:[8]

The exhibitor who purchases a small quantity of films, say from 300 to 500 feet, is necessarily compelled to confine himself to short subjects. But if the purchase is 1000 feet, we advise one feature film of 400 to 500 feet, the balance from 50 to 100 feet each; if 2000 feet, there should be at least one long feature film, such as *The Great Train Robbery*, 740 feet, or *Christopher Columbus*, 850 feet. These long films admit of special advertising, that is to say, special emphasis on one subject, which is more effective than equal emphasis on a number of shorter films. The public has been educated to appreciate these long films which tell an interesting story, and need few words of explanation.

Applied to moving pictures, the term 'feature' implied a film which could merit special advertising and billing because it was different from the other films. As one trade writer emphasized in 1912:[9]

In the matter of scenarios, in the direction, in the selection of scenery, in the preparation of big spectacles, in the choice of artists, from the leading player down to the super, the feature film must bear distinct characteristics of its own which at once differentiate it from an ordinary release.

The feature film as it began depended not on length but on a conception of its anticipated exchange-value and its place in an exhibitor's entertainment package.

The shift in 1908 to a regularized production and exchange service helped the exhibitor with his advertising. Once systematic mass production set in, producers could disseminate information about upcoming releases, and with such preparation the exhibitor who did the local consumer advertising could plan an advertising campaign emphasizing the feature film. In effect, the feature film was part of the overall campaign to improve profits.[10]

Bigger pictures, bigger prices

The quality film (as Chapter 9 mentions) publicized its source in famous works and authors, including, for instance, the adaptation of *Uncle Tom's Cabin* in 1903. Producers sporadically used such adaptations in hopes of a carry-over of quality from drama and fiction to the filmed version. Drawing on *Ben-Hur*'s enormous literary and theatrical success, Kalem in 1907 filmed an unauthorized version of it and advertised: 'Sixteen magnificent scenes with illustrated titles, positively the most superb motion picture spectacle ever made.'[11] With little attention to copyright, directors and others in the companies 'borrowed' plots from the masters, but their massive exploitation occurred after one producer set an example. In 1906-7, Pathé released a three-reel version of the *Passion Play* in France and the United States. A success in both places, it stimulated several films and, in France, the formation of Film d'Art, a production company. Film d'Art purchased stories from famous French writers — Anatole France, Jules LeMaitre, Henri Lavedan, Jeanne Richepin, Victorien Sardou, and Edmund Rostand — and employed some of the famous players from the Comédie Française, scenic artists, and musicians. The firm's successes included a production of the *Assassinat du Duc de Guise*, directed by Le Bargy and Calmettes, play by Lavedan, music by Saint-Saëns, and acting by Le Bargy, Albert Lambert, Gabrielle Robinne, and Berthe Bovy. The appeal was to values of established literature, music, and theater. Following Film d'Art's lead, French Gaumont signed up some of Film d'Art's writers, and Edison followed the practice in the United States by 1909.[12]

About the same time, feature films started coming more often in longer-than-one-reel lengths. These multiple-reelers were almost all adaptations. In October 1909, Pathé released *The Drink*, a two-reel drama; Vitagraph released a four-reel version of *Les Miserables* over three months, September to November 1909, and then a three-reeler of *Uncle Tom's Cabin* in July 1910. In 1911, the number of these features increased: in June, the *Moving Picture World* listed the productions which were being filmed in two- and three-reel lengths: *The Fall of Troy, A Tale of Two Cities, Enoch Arden, The Battle of the Republic, The Maccabees,* and *Faust* — all adaptations. 'We cannot do justice,' the article commented, 'to the subjects especially worth while in a thousand feet of film. The play, even with the aid of the spoken word, takes from two to three hours to present, and cannot be condensed into a pantomime, which must be rushed through in generally less than thirty minutes.'[13] In August the trade papers noted than two-reelers had become more common and sometimes drew the audience back to see them again:[14]

> The filming of some great opera or a popular literary or dramatic or historical subject requires more than a reel. . . . The larger production likewise makes a deeper impression on the memory and to that extent advertises itself much better than the shorter one-reel affair. . . . [The best way to raise prices] in the general run of moving picture houses is the two and three and four-reel production. With better and bigger pictures the public will readily see the fairness of bigger prices.

In September in the regular column reviewing notable films all those selected for special attention were multiple-reel adaptations: *Foul Play* (Edison, novel by Charles Reade), *David Copperfield* (Thanhouser, Charles Dickens), and *The Colleen Bawn* (Kalem, play by Dion Boucicoult). The successful importation of *Dante's Inferno* (five reels), *The Crusaders* (four reels), and *Jerusalem Delivered* (four reels) in the same year encouraged a view that length was no inhibition to profits. At this point, too, companies started hiring stage stars to appear in films of their famous performances. In 1911 Cecil Spooner played his *The Prince and the Pauper* (Edison), Sidney Drew directed and acted in his *When Two Hearts are Won* (Kalem), and Mabel Taliaferro appeared in a three-reel version of her *Cinderella* (Selig). The independent Powers hired Mildred Holland who performed her play *The Power Behind the Throne*.[15]

While there may be exceptions to his generalization, one commentator gave a plausible summary in October 1911: 'No feature [multiple-reel] film, of which we have any knowledge, has been produced from an original scenario.'[16] The evidence overwhelmingly supports a connection between the famous play, novel, and story adapted into film and the increasing length of the product. The longer film enabled a more faithful reproduction of these classics well-known to a middle-class audience, a ploy in step with contemporary exhibition practices. Although the advertising and status advantage of the adapta-tion was probably dominant in the events which took place, another element must, however, be considered as part of the shift.

Copyrights and sources of fictional narratives

While the move to established literary works was an attempt to transfer their perceived value into the film product, the new legal status of the film story as subject to federal copyright laws reinforced the changeover to these narrative sources. Before 1911, crediting sources was an economic tactic to improve profits; afterward, crediting sources, at least by purchasing rights, was legally necessary.

Writers had been hired for some time to provide plots, and firms increasingly sought freelance contributions when production output increased after 1907. Up to this point, manufacturers had freely adapted anything, but then Kalem's *Ben-Hur* ran into legal trouble. Harper and Row, publishers of Lew Wallace's original novel, and Klaw and Erlanger, authorized producers of the stage version, sued Kalem for copyright infringement.[17]

Copyright laws, like patents, were meant to insure that the monopoly profits from invention returned to the original inventors, thus stimulating creativity. The history of US copyright law is in part a history of the expansion of the term 'published writing,' as technology and methods of mass producing works increased: maps and charts (1790); engravings, etchings, and prints (1802); performances of copyrighted drama (1856); paintings, drawings, chromolithographs, statues, models, designs, photographs, and negatives (1870).[18]

The Kalem suit became a test case for the status of filmed versions of copyrighted works, and, as such, the Motion Picture Patents Company helped underwrite Kalem's defense. In 1909 the lower court held: 1) that when films were projected, they became a dramatization, with drama being defined as a succession of events, and 2) that historically copyright laws had included in the term 'writings' things which were other than printed matter; thus, moving pictures were subject to copyright laws. The US Supreme Court upheld that decision in 1911. This also meant that an original film narrative could be protected from infringement.[19]

The decision affected filmmakers in at least two

ways. Anticipating such a decision, Edison's lawyers had already instituted for any freelance submissions an 'ironclad release form' in which the writer of the scenario asserted that he or she was the original creator. Such releases had become standard in the industry by 1911. The other major reaction was the turning to already published works because of the assurance of the source of the plot, and the gingerly handling of any freelance submission that displayed 'earmarks of being filched from the columns of some readily accessible magazine or book.'[20]

In summary, about 1911, two practices were in operation which contributed to a shift to film narrative sources coming from published literature and drama. First, advertising, which stressed the value of prior literary and dramatic successes, promoted the adaptation of famous works, sometimes played by the stars who had made them a success. Secondly, adjudication of copyright laws necessitated acquiring the rights to narratives to be filmed – and as long as those purchases had to be made, the companies might as well advertise any valuable ones. Negatively, manufacturers began declining freelance plots, and within a decade, freelancers either published their work in print first or worked through agents.

Common news in the trade papers thereafter was the announcement of the latest acquisition of copyrighted work. In March 1911, Selig signed a contract with magazine publishers Street & Smith for the 'exclusive scenario rights' to all stories in its publications which included *Popular*, *Ainslee's*, and *People's Smith's*; Reliance, Edison, Selig, Bison, Nestor, and Vitagraph were noted as turning to magazine material in mid-1912; and Eclair picked up the 'exclusive rights' to O. Henry's stories in early 1913. Besides short fiction, the adaptation of plays and novels proceeded at a rapid pace: in early 1913 Lubin bought the film rights to Charles Klein's successful muckraking plays for a series of multiple-reel films. Famous Players Film Company hired theater producer Daniel Frohman to stage manage the company's policy 'to immortalize the most noted characterizations of the famous players of the day'; a trade paper called Famous Players' president Adolph Zukor 'the Benefactor of Posterity.' And a *coup de maître* was the Jesse L. Lasky Company's securing of film rights in mid-1914 to David Belasco's productions.[21] (See figs 12.4, 12.5.)

By the mid-teens the interchange between copyright fields had become systematic. A trade paper writer commented in 1916 that five photoplay writers had had dramas purchased for stage presentation, and the dramatic rights to the screen success *The Cheat* had been sold. To handle this increase in possible auxiliary profits from sale of rights, publishing houses had from about 1912 tried to secure film rights when they purchased a story. By 1918 they had film rights departments and agents who sold the firm's novels as they came off the presses.[22]

To handle the competitive bid for rights, a film producer as early as 1915 offered to finance stage productions with the stipulation that he controlled the film rights. By 1920, one theater critic warned that Famous Players-Lasky with Wall Street backing had invaded Broadway and was 'actually controlling the production of spoken drama.' The critic's fears were that soon only plays thought suitable for subsequent filming would find room in Broadway's theaters.[23]

The standardization of the multiple-reel feature film

By 1916, the multiple-reel feature film had prevailed. While its increasing dominance in the output of the industry was in part due to the perceived exchange-value of the feature's narrative sources and its ability to be differentiated in advertising, another factor needs to be taken into account. The film industry's institutions played a role in standardizing the longer film as the dominant exhibition practice. Trade advice continually reminded the exhibitor that the longer film offered something 'extra and of more importance than the ordinary single reels' and that the distribution and exhibition of these films required some changes in present standards. The films needed to be presented in a unit to reap the rewards of the advertising. Although producers began distributing the films one reel at a time following the single-reel practice, that procedure had fairly well ceased by late 1911, early in the period of the changeover to multiple-reel films. And, again, to take advantage of advertising and to increase the length of runs, the trade papers reported the successes of exhibitors who tried runs of two or three days or a week.[24]

Multiple-reel films intensified the trade papers' disseminating of exhibition techniques. An example is the mid-1911 Monopol Film Company release of *Dante's Inferno*, advertised as 'the greatest spectacle in exhibition history' with 'one night stands transformed into week stands'; Gustave Doré's illustrations accompanied the ads (see fig 12.6). Road-showed in first-class theaters and with prices between $.25 and $.75, the film completely sold out its opening at the best theater in Baltimore. Stephen Bush enhanced it with a simultaneous lecture, and the music had 'careful and well rehearsed effects.'[25] The *Moving Picture World* commented:[26]

The presentation of this film marks truly an epoch in the history of moving pictures. It has added . . . prestige to the moving picture art. It will win most desirable friends for the photoplay everywhere. It has destroyed the absurd idea, that people will not pay high prices for a moving picture entertainment, regardless of its high character.

Repeatedly, the analysis of exhibition was: 'There are hundreds of persons who will gladly pay twenty-five cents to see a feature who would refuse to enter the smaller houses simply because the price is cheap.' For special films, the *Moving Picture World* printed lectures for oral presentation and music cues (see fig 12.7). When Selig released a three-reeler in 1912, General Film promised special advertising materials to 'boom the films' and appropriate music prepared by S.L. Rothapfel, 'the widely known manager of the Lyceum Theatre, Minneapolis.' Rothapfel's techniques had already become familiar to exhibitors. In 1911, an article on him entitled 'The Belasco of motion picture presentation' described his managing and unifying control of the entire show — like the director in legitimate theater.[27]

For the hesitant exhibitor who knew that the one-reelers were good for secure profits, the trade papers assured him that longer films had even better stories than his single-reelers. One reviewer wrote that Great Northern's early 1912 two- and three-reelers had no lags in the stories: 'Rather, the extended picture makes possible a more connected and logical narration of the story.' The Bison two-reel Westerns did not seem padded:

'They merely contain the many intermediate and connecting scenes that are so often omitted from the one-reel subjects for want of space, but are really valuable in properly carrying the story along. Furthermore, none of the scenes are [sic] dragged out.'[28] The main difference these analysts saw was in the narrational structure of the reels. A critic noted:[29]

The scenes are curtailed always at a point of keenest interest in just such a manner as are the different portions of a serial story — just when the suspense is greatest and the imaginative system is keyed up to the highest, the vision is cut off, leaving the onlooker at a tension of irresistible curiosity.

Such narration was, of course, an aid to the exhibitor who wanted a fascinated audience who would return for more such exciting features.

Part of the reason for this plot construction with minor climaxes may be exhibition practices. It could be a carry-over from the separate-day release system or the model of the acts of the theater play. Also important was that at least for theaters with small-time vaudeville the reels were separated by live acts, retaining the continuous, varied show from vaudeville exhibition. Some smaller theaters also used only one projector. It was worth special note in the trade papers when a theater exhibited in February 1913 a five-reel film without interruption between the reels.[30]

By 1914, the economic potentials of the multiple-reel film had influenced exhibition to the point where about one-fifth of New York City's theaters were running them and people were paying $1.00, 'Broadway prices.' In October of that year, *Photoplay* pondered the reason for the delay in total conversion to the longer films and located it in exhibition practices: people entered at any time; if they came in in the middle of a five-reeler, they had to sit through its end without knowing the beginning. With a one- or two-reeler, they did not miss much and could go on to the next film. Also business still came off the streets during lunch times and the consumer did not have time for more than one or two reels. This conservative trend slowed the changeover.[31]

In 1911 entertainment journalist Robert Grau had asked hopefully, 'Is the two-dollar-a-seat picture theater in sight?' Four years later, *The Birth of a Nation* opened on Broadway and ran at theater prices of $2.00, for forty-four consecutive weeks, which was represented to the exhibitors as more than any attraction 'in the history of the American stage.' *The Birth of a Nation* capped the rise of the longer film and encouraged the longer-run, higher-priced *special* feature — since multiple-reel features were common by then.[32]

Thus, the diffusion of the multiple-reel film had two economic causes: 1) the extensive adaptation of classic works, in part for advertising reasons (tie-ins to former successes and differentiation of the product) and in part for legal ones (copyright laws), required longer films for faithful reproduction of the stories; and 2) the multiple-reel film allowed the exhibitor to increase prices and runs, which bolstered profits. These were strong incentives. Assured that the film did not suffer but improved in quality with more logical development and greater suspense, the exhibitor exploited it with more and more showmanship. By 1916, the multiple-reel feature dominated the market and special features brought theater prices.

The 'central producer' system of production (1914-31)

'Efficiency experts' and 'production-line' practices appeared in the US film industry by 1912 and became the order of the day around 1914. With this came the 'central producer,' the modern manager of a well-organized mass production system which was now necessary to produce the quality multiple-reel film.

'Efficiency' was commonly valued by businessmen early in the century although wide-spread use of practices which became categorized as 'scientific management' started a decade later. Two aspects of these management practices are significant for what happened in film's mode of production: the application of scientific management to the worker in the production line and to the manager of the firm. Frederick Winslow Taylor was the chief developer of work practices leading to these new tactics.

Participating in a general trend to improve the output of the worker, Taylor responded to a production problem of wage payment. His

'experiments,' published in 1895 and 1903, led to his conclusion that a manager must plan and control all decisions and steps in the work process so that waste could be eliminated. For the production worker on the job, he urged the institution of time- and motion-studies so that companies could set standards of performance and efficient labor. For managers, he advocated a 'functional type of management,' a military style 'line and staff' hierarchy, and the initiation of a planning department which would determine *in writing* in advance of each job the instructions for each worker and the cost of materials and labor. (David F. Noble points out that Taylor's work can be seen as part of the concurrent standardization movement: just as business standardized its product and technology, so it standardized its labor force.)[33] One promoter of scientific management wrote:[34]

One of the greatest problems of adjustment to this mechanical age is the coordination of the efforts of large numbers of people under one plan. These people are sometimes widely separated in space, producing different parts of an ultimate product in different parts of the world. Different elements have to be assembled somewhere later on. . . . In order to coordinate the efforts even of two men who work at different times, there must be some durable substance to connect the two. . . . You may do it by memory, but then you are the physical substance. Yet individual memory cannot do all the uniting. There must be something or other, some physical substance — it may be nothing but a book or manuscript.

Planning departments and paper records would also improve economies in other areas. At the turn of the century, companies commonly had decentralized purchasing and storage which meant over- and under-stocking of raw materials. Accounting supplied double-entry profit-and-loss statements but few analyses of waste and inefficiency. In 1898 universities formed several business schools, after 1900 books on business management became much more common, and in 1908 the Harvard Graduate School of Business Administration was founded and accepted Taylor's ideas as its guiding management principles. It was not, however, until Taylor received national notoriety in a 1910-11 Inter-state Commerce Commission hearing that his techniques spread into general use. It was only a very little later than another change within the US film mode of production started.

A 1916 article, 'Putting the move in the movies,'[35] is worth summarizing in detail as an anecdotal description of the shift from a director-unit system to a 'central producer' system in which planning by a manager with a carefully prepared script controlled the design of the product. An anonymous director claimed that, although others said it could not be done: 'System and Efficiency have found their way into the manufacture of motion pictures.' To prove this he described the situation before and after the installation of a new management system at his company a couple of years earlier. Before, everything was up to the director. He hired his staff and found a scenario either from his own creation or from among those the company had available. Because each director had his own staff, he kept people on salary, even when they were not needed. Purchasing was erratic and so were set and costume accuracy. The property people took his oral suggestions and either borrowed props from other sets, sometimes surreptitiously (thus wreaking havoc on the other units) or rented supplies which no one remembered to return. He had at least three purchasing agents at once, and bills did not always make their way to accounting. No one seemed to care about cost.

Then, the author writes, the company hired a general manager − but one from business, not the entertainment field. The general manager estab-lished a production office in the center of the studio lot, which became a clearing house for all departments. These departments 'assumed definite duties and responsibilities.' The director left the production office alone, but he did notice that his assistant director began to use the office to get everything he needed. One day, the manager of production had a conference with this director. The company was going to plan and estimate the cost of the picture *before* it was shot. The company wanted to know if the film would make a profit before funds were expended. The supply now exceeded the demand, this manager told the director, and exhibitors could 'pick and choose' their films. How would the cost be figured in advance? On the basis of the scenario the

director had chosen to film, estimates had been made: the number of sets and their cost, the number of characters and extras, the number of days of wages, the approximate cost of 'rented props, negative stock, laboratory work, lunches on location,' etc., and overhead. One-third of the estimate was added on to cover costs of stage space, wardrobe, props, stage hands, carpenters, painters, artists, and administration. Overhead was calculated on the number of shooting days; if the director brought the film in faster, less overhead would be added. The director received his estimate sheet with authorized expenses. In addition, the production department helped him in a new way. Prepared by 'experts' hired by the firm, detailed sketches of all sets were ready for his approval. These sketches indicated the types of doors, floor paint, wall paper by pattern number, the baseboard and moulding types, and what scenes would be seen through open windows. All the director had to do was approve the plans, and he had no more worries. Crews worked at night; when he arrived to shoot, everything was prepared as he had approved. The result? The director said he cut the time of making that film from a normal twelve days to seven days and brought it in under budget. The director was pleased; things were much less tense on the set, and he was now responsible only for shooting the film. Others took care of the rest. The money expended for purchases by the single purchasing agent for the firm, he believed, was now visible in the product.

This account illustrates important changes. For one thing, planning the work and estimating production costs through a detailed script became a new, extensive, and early step in the labor process. This improved regularity and speed of production, use of materials, and uniformity and quality of the product. The script became a blueprint detailing the shot-by-shot breakdown of the film. Thus, it could function as a paper record to coordinate the assembly of the product shot out of order, prepared by a large number of people spread at various places through the world (location shooting, for instance, to be matched to an interior in Santa Monica), and still achieve a clear, verisimilar and continuous representation of causal logic, time and space.

The management organization also changed significantly. The functions of the producer and director were split. More typically, the work of the producer was split further. Now the producer took over the management of the pre- and post-shooting work for *all* the films in the studio while the new manager of the production department coordinated the studio facility's planning, budgeting and accounting, and the day-to-day record-keeping. This system introduced a new set of top managers – producers such as Thomas Ince and later Irving Thalberg who meticulously controlled the making of their firm's films.

As a result, the management responsibilities and status of the director changed. The director still had some managerial input into the entire product. The producer and staff solicited his ideas and approval on the script, casting, sets, wardrobe, and editing, but the producer's approval superceded his, and much actual creation was now done by departmental experts. Although the director had complete charge over the shooting activities, he lost the function of being a unit head. Instead, directors became, in a sense, a separate department of technical experts in directing the actors and crew during the shooting. The producer chose a director from that department just as he would select a writer or a designer or a cameraman to be combined with a story and cast. In shooting, the director topped the hierarchy of workers, but the producer took over coordinating production decisions. The producer became a top manager and economic agent for the firm. He was responsible for the output of a specific number of quality films produced within carefully prepared budgets; the producer selected and coordinated the technical experts.

The central producer system started in 1912 and became the dominant practice by 1914. For example, when the Universal Film Manufacturing Company merger occurred in June 1912, Universal announced a reorganization. Dropping a multiple-unit system, it centralized and specialized.[36]* Those firms with the best facilities took over the work for all the companies' films; Bison and Rex did the printing and developing; a single scenario department supplied all scripts; scenarios were distributed to the directors who excelled in particular types of subjects (another instance of increasing specialization); and a studio-wide pool of players was formed. By 1916, H.O. Davis, Universal's general manager, supervised a system which might well have been

that of the director in the anecdotal article. The production office estimated costs before the shooting of any scenes, and within the most recent two months for one hundred films, the cost was 'a variation of but 5 per cent.' After the firm selected a story, it gave it to writers to put into continuity format and on that basis the director, construction department, and art director discussed the sets. They chose props from a property department which had been organized and indexed. Shooting time had been cut in half.[37]

At the New York Motion Picture Company, Ince had established the central producer as distinct from the director by 1913. A writer described his efficient studio:[38]

> With preparations laid out in detail from finished photoplays to the last prop, superintended by Mr. Ince himself, far in advance of the action, each of the numerous directors on the job at Santa Ynez canyon is given his working script three weeks ahead of time. . . . Filled with the theme and action, he goes out and, with the cogs of the big Ince machine oiled to the smallest gear and the entire plant running as smoothly as an automobile in the hands of a salesman, the picture travels from the beginning to end without delays. To my mind this is the modern miracle.

Ince's studio provides a good example of the process of an actual changeover in one company. Directing a unit for the New York Motion Picture Company, Ince traveled to Edendale, California, in 1911 to take charge of the Bison-brand films. In June 1912, Ince split his work staff into two production units because it had become so large. This marked the move to a director-unit system with Francis Ford the second director. To control Ford's filmmaking, Ince used a detailed continuity script which carefully laid out the film shot-by-shot. Ince gradually relinquished the directorial duties of writing and rewriting, and he stopped directing and then editing. In 1913, he hired George B. Stout as a production manager. Stout was educated at Rutgers University as a public accountant. Stout reorganized the studio into a functional, departmentalized system which watched costs closely. With that accomplished and Ince acting as 'Director-General,' the studio had moved to a central producer system.[39]

In mid-1913, the Lubin Company instituted a management hierarchy over the directors. According to the firm's publicity, it followed Biograph, Edison, and Vitagraph in removing script selection from the directors' prerogatives. Planning a reorganization along 'modern lines,' the firm insisted that the director consult with the script department, which had now been divided into two parts. After a new split in writing functions, one section handled incoming submissions; as for the other:[40]

a new section has been established to handle those scripts accepted and put them in perfect technical shape before they are handed to the director for production, permitting the latter to give his full attention to production without requiring him to handle the editorial and revision work that he has hitherto performed, this work now being done by the trained staff writers whose literary qualifications and technical training in combination better fit them for the work.

After the technical experts prepared the script, the director selected the cast to fit the story. If the plans met the general manager's approval, the director could proceed to 'make the production without departing from the lines laid down.' Lublin explained a further aspect of its plan:[41]

In the business department careful cost data is kept, segregated for each picture, so that it is possible, at any time, to ascertain what the pictures are costing and, by comparison, to tell which methods are wasteful and which are profitable.

Efficiency techniques spread. Balboa announced that it received weather reports from the US Weather Bureau so that it could plan the next day's activities; it had a 'location book' with snapshots of locations; it had indexed all the items (over 100,000) in the prop room; and it owned a complete stock of furniture so it wasted no time or money in rentals. Another studio organized a manual with work regulations and responsibilities for every position; the company then assigned each worker a number by which she or he found her or his spot in the production

schedule. In 1918 World-Pictures had color-coded the work clothes of painters, carpenters, electricians, and stage hands.[42]

The separation of the former director-producer's functions had become so common by 1917 that when Jesse L. Lasky announced a return to a director-unit system it became noteworthy:[43]

Each director in our four studios will be absolutely independent to produce to the best of his efficiency and ability. With the discontinuance of a central scenario bureau each director will have his own writing staff and the author will continue active work on every production until its conclusion, staying by the side of the director even when the film is cut and assembled.

The descriptions of the mode of production are generalizations: no individual company can be considered a perfect instance of the pattern. At this point with the growth in size of the firms and the types of managerial organizations possible, some mixture of these systems occurred. Some large firms had combinations: a central producer who managed most of the product and a director-producer whose crew formed a fairly distinct unit but who used the planning and centralized departments available to the central producer. William S. Hart, for instance, maintained a separate unit in Ince's Triangle studio. Such differences depended on the size of the firm and the top management's analysis of marketing conditions and of strengths and weaknesses of its personnel. Another factor related to the employee's marketability of his or her own skills: those with greater marketability (e.g., Hart) could demand certain work conditions. None the less, the central producer system remained the dominant system of production until 1931.[44]

Another change in script writing: the continuity script

Two factors contributed to a new type of script: the standardization of the multiple-reel film between 1911 and 1915 and the development of the central producer system. Another factor, the simultaneous movement toward the classical style, also promoted the change.

As Part Three will show, between 1909 and 1917, the Hollywood film developed a specific set of stylistic techniques and a particular arrangement of the systems of narrative logic, time, and space. These changes now started complicating the method of production and assembly of the film. The representation of a continuous time and space started to permit direct cuts between scenes not spatially and temporally contiguous, as long as cues to the gaps were present. Cues included timing of the entrances and exits of characters and the insertion of inter-titles. Techniques of matching action and maintaining screen direction became conventions to signal continuing action and placement of adjacent spaces. Crosscutting increased, serving a variety of purposes.

With a standard of continuity and conventions of achieving that continuity, the mode of production faced greater demands on its system of memory. As the scientific management expert pointed out, a paper plan and record was a lot more reliable and predictable than an individual's memory, particularly in recalling plans for assembling a multiple-reel film now containing hundreds of shots. Staging entrances and exits, matching movements to adjacent spaces while maintaining conventions of screen direction, and correlating crosscutting were more certain if workers kept a record of what was done. But records made on the spot without consideration of potential difficulties in the next set-ups were hardly as efficient and reliable as a work practice that arranged shot relations in advance. A written script which included descriptions of each shot and its adjacent shots provided a long-term cost advantage. It was cheaper to pay a few workers to prepare scripts and solve continuity problems at that stage than it was to let a whole crew of laborers work it out on the set or by retakes later. Because the scripts provided the means to ensure the conventions of continuous action, they soon became known as 'continuities.' This work practice assured meeting the standard of a quality film.

Maintaining the group style might have been simple with a one-reel film; with a longer film problems multiplied. In fact, the continuity script made possible the increase in the films' lengths and the retention of the standards for a good film. The producer could use the script to check in advance the quality of the product. The producer

did not even have to be present at shooting or editing; the written instructions organized the assembly of the film throughout the various separate phases and places of its creation.

The detailed continuity script was normal practice by 1914. Trade papers and 'how-to' handbooks helped standardize its format. Since continuity scripts and associated paperwork varied little from studio to studio, those from Ince's productions can be taken as typical (see figs 12.8 through 12.19).[45] The firm assigned each of the scripts a number, which provided a method of tracing the film even though its title might shift. A cover page indicated who wrote the scenario, who directed the shooting, when shooting began and ended, when the film was shipped to the distributors, and when the film was released. The next part was the 'Complete Picture Report' which summarized production information in more detail. Following that was a list of titles and inter-titles and an indication as to where they were to be inserted in the final print. (Inter-titles were usually rewritten after editing and printed separately.) At the end of the set of associated paperwork was the entire cost of the film, broken into a standard accounting format. Following 'scientific management' practices, this history on paper recorded the entire production process for efficiency and control of waste.

The continuity script started with the location plot. This scene plot listed all exterior and interior sites along with their shot numbers, providing efficient cross-checking and saving time and labor. Then came the cast of characters. Typed portions listed the roles for the story and penciled in were the names of the people assigned to play each part. After a one-page synopsis, the script followed. Each shot (with multiple shots per narrative action) was numbered consecutively and its location was given. Temporary inter-titles were typed in, often in red ink, where they were to be inserted in the final version. The description of the *mise-en-scène* and action was very detailed. Since these scripts were used on the set, staff would mark with a pencil each completed shot and sometimes would note on the side the footage. The continuities included meticulous technical instructions such as special effects and tinting directions and notes to the cutters. Most importantly, these continuity scripts became the design blueprint for the workers in the central producer system of production.

Alternatives within the mode of production

Such efficient production practices were dominant in Hollywood filmmaking between 1914 and 1931, but there were also variations and alternatives. Three deserve special note. During the 1920s, some production companies permitted a looser script than the shot-by-shot continuity. A contemporary described it:[46]

> Frank Borzage is a champion for the continuity synopsis, a running account of the plot, undivided into scenes [shots]. Many other directors prefer this method dividing their pictures into the desired and natural number of scenes [shots] during actual work.

Since in many studios, changes after shooting could be extensive, the scene-by-scene synopsis preserved the advantages of a script in setting up the estimated budgets, scene plots, and so forth without detailing the individual type or number of cut-ins. Shooting scripts in the sound period generally followed this format (the master-scene) rather than the more rigorous shot-by-shot continuity.

A director might also adhere to the older method of a script outline. D.W. Griffith provides an outstanding example although Charles Chaplin and others also used it. Employing a more theatrical work procedure, Griffith used the general outline script even in the multiple-reel era. During the teens and early 1920s, through extensive rehearsals, he worked on and refined the action of the scenes. Griffith could follow such a method for a couple of reasons. His style of assembling the material often overrode subtleties of matching action and continuity. He used crosscutting extensively, and this produced fewer continuity difficulties. Griffith's cutter also recalled that Griffith shot the long shots, decided during rushes where he wanted close-ups, and then went to a neutral background and did those for insertion. Both of these techniques, cross-cutting and order of shooting, needed less planning of a 'continuity' than in the standard system.[47] Moreover, Griffith was atypical in another way:[48]

> Mr. Griffith's method of working has its advantages and, under certain circumstances, it would have its grave disadvantages. Mr. Griffith, being his own employer, can take all the time he wishes on the making of his productions. A director working on a schedule that makes some consideration of time would be quite at a loss in working without a 'script.

During this period, Griffith participated in the capitalization of the companies for which he directed films. He also had enough weight from established box office successes to control his working conditions until his move to Paramount in 1925. Paid by profits rather than time he had no necessity for efficient, quick production; his films were not scheduled into a regular distribution deadline either. He was, accordingly, not pressured to move to other systems of production. Descriptions of his companies, however, suggest that in most other ways he and his employees participated in the standard mode of detailed division of labor. While he often consulted his staff for ideas, for instance, they had little or no conception of the design of the entire project, that remaining within Griffith's control as he worked it over the course of the making of the film.[49]

Cecil B. De Mille's method provided a further alternative (which his brother William also used): multiple-camera shooting. De Mille chose during the 1920s to shoot a film in its dramatic order so that the actors would build up characterization and psychological intensity as they would in a stage play. To do this and still have efficient and economical production while maintaining the classical style, he varied the system very slightly. First he prepared a story in continuity form so that only three or four sets would be needed at a time, and subsequent sets would replace these as the staff progressed through the story. Then he used multiple cameras, some for long shots and others for close-ups. Descriptions of this vary but it appears that he set up one camera at a long shot, a second one right next to it with a longer focal length lens for a close-up, and several other cameras at angles for more close-ups and two-shots. Thus, the scene could be played through, the various shots could be edited together to provide the classical establishing shots and cut-ins, and the action would match. This system did, however, provide several problems for the classical style. It was difficult to light every part of the set equally well for the different cameras and to achieve any special lighting for the close-ups. In addition, the multiple-camera system required multiple cameramen and equipment, which could be costly. On the other hand, Bert Glennon who shot for De Mille said that with rehearsals in the morning and shooting in the afternoon, the team could do up to fifty shots per day – fast work. The reduction in shooting time probably compensated for the increased labor costs. Besides, De Mille, like Griffith, had great power at Paramount and in his own production firm.[50]

These alternatives were scarcely challenges to the dominant production practices, but the fact that some variance was tolerated as long as satisfactory results came in is important in understanding Hollywood. It allowed difference from the standard when that difference was minimal but brought in profits.

Legal control of the quality of the product

It was during this same period that the State intervened in production practices, assigning product quality control to the hierarchy of a firm's management rather than to any individual worker. This is of tremendous importance to issues of product design. Anyone who has read stories about Hollywood has probably run across instances of superiors changing the work of a subordinate. (For instance, Samuel Goldwyn appended a 'happy ending' to *Wuthering Heights* against William Wyler's wishes.[51]) In the next chapter, I will analyze the hierarchy in the mode of production and show what positions controlled various aspects of production. At this point, a more general question arises: what legal mechanism assured management's hierarchical control?

The case of *Charles Chaplin* vs *Essanay* (1916) became an industry precedent in this regard. After Chaplin moved to Mutual, he sued Essanay and distributor V-L-S-E to prevent release of *Charlie Chaplin's Burlesque on 'Carmen.'* When he worked on it, its length ran about 2,000 feet, but he charged that after he left, the company padded the film to 4,000 feet with material 'of such quality as seriously to injure his fame.'

Chaplin lost the case. The courts reasoned, among other points, that unless a contract stipulated otherwise, a firm, not a particular employee, controlled the product. The courts were clearly following legal and economic precedent that in an employer-employee relationship, the contract of employment must expressly indicate what rights the worker retains; otherwise, the company is entitled to the ownership and profits of whatever the employee produces.[52]

That the firm positioned the managers of capital and the technical experts at the top of the hierarchy as agents for the firm resulted in their legal control over all decisions in design. At least two factors, however, qualified this. First, managers of capital usually dissociated themselves from direct involvement in making the films, and technical managers (the studio heads and producers) took varying degrees of interest in varying parts of the design. Secondly, a 'talent,' a star or writer or director or cameraman, with prestige in the industry could parlay his or her exchange-value into securing agreeable contractual arrangements by inducing the studios to bid for his or her services. If final control of a cut, for instance, was exceptionally important to a valuable director, he could get it. When Ernst Lubitsch signed with Warner Bros in the 1920s, he demanded and received a contract entitling him to complete control over rushes and negatives, final cut, and all decisions regarding cast and subject.[53] The problem was that only a few individuals had such power within the industry, and setting precedents of giving up controls was not a move the company wanted to make. At any rate, the State indirectly reinforced the hierarchy of the mode of production, and management controlled the making of the films. Thus in future years, we hear stories such as that told by William Castle about Columbia producer Irving Briskin's re-editing of Castle's *The Chance of a Lifetime* (1943):[54]

Briskin took the end of the picture and put it at the beginning, then spliced a section of Reel Four into Reel Two, a section of Two into Four, and some of Five into Six. Reel Seven he took out entirely. Eight he trimmed, and Nine he left alone. After his glowing contribution, *Chance of a Lifetime* became even more muddled and screwed up than it had been originally, if that was possible.

Two transitions in the design of the product between 1909 and 1917 affected the mode of production: changes in the standards of quality filmmaking and in film length required a detailed script. In addition, by 1914, with 'scientific management,' the firms started to utilize extensive management precalculation of the films. Thus, the script served management both as an efficient blueprint, a paper record for the assembly of the product, and as an effective precheck for quality. 'Scientific management' also intensified production planning work so that the director's tasks subdivided: the producer planned and coordinated the work while the director specialized in managing the shooting activities. Finally, the State reinforced this by assigning control of the product to the hierarchy of the firm's economic agents rather than to specific work positions. Control over parts of the film work, however, could be negotiated in contracts between the firm and the individual worker (and later the labor organizations representing the collective rights of the workers). This central producer system remained dominant until 1931 when the industry tried a new management organization.

13

The division and order of production: the subdivision of the work from the first years through the 1920s

By the mid-teens, the feature had established its dominance over the one-reelers, and production, distribution, and exhibition practices standardized the product's design and marketing. The production system for which Hollywood would become famous was in full operation. The standard working procedure involved a producer, a large, fully-staffed studio, a set of departmentalized technical workers and specialists, all guided by a continuity script. This system is particularly manifest in the physical plant of a Hollywood studio. As a major producer of multiple-reel films, the Lasky studio in 1918 (see fig 13.1) was described by *Photoplay* as 'a veritable city within a city.' Following the numbers around the lot, we note whole buildings devoted to properties (1, 2, and 11), wardrobes (4 and 30), casting (5), management (6, 7, and 26), direction (8), story selection and screenwriting (9), art direction (13 [Wilfred Buckland's office]), scene docks and set construction (15, 20, 27, 29, 31-4). Besides open stages (12 and 19), there were glass-enclosed ones (17, 18, and 23) and even a 'dark stage' (22). A large back lot with standing sets (37) and a sailboat in a tank (21) provided massive, three-dimensional exteriors – close to the rest of the studio. Also included were hospital facilities (24) and a full service system with 'police, fire, street cleaning, water and electrical departments.' *Photoplay* reported that the studio used so much lumber that it had bought a tract of timberland in Oregon and a private sawmill and steamers to transport the wood to Southern California.[1] If there was a 'golden age' of the studio, it is in full operation by 1918. The last three chapters have focused on the management hierarchy; now we need to review how the work was executed and how it became systematized during the central producer period.

In the early years of filmmaking, the cameraman for all intents and purposes created the entire product on his own. In later years, the firms split the work into more and finer subdivisions and achieved a set regime. One might think of the subdivision of the execution of the work as a tree with its trunk in an earlier period and its branches at later points. The trunk contained all the work functions unified in one worker. At one historical juncture, a set of subdivisions, main branches, appears. Later, these branches subdivide again.

These subdivisions can be attributed to several causes, two of which are most pertinent. For economic reasons, subdividing the work into small segments allowed expertise and increased speed and efficiency. Moreover, the standards of the quality film caused certain work positions to appear. It is true that production practices, on occasion, caused certain stylistic techniques. But overall, Hollywood's production practices need to be seen as an *effect* of economic and ideological/signifying practices. In some instances, as we have seen, a production practice affected the film's style, but in general, we have to look elsewhere for explanations of why films looked and sounded as they did.

About 1907, with the increased production of narratives and the ascension of the director system of management, the first set of subdivisions appeared. The second set occurred in the mid-teens, simultaneous with the move to the central producer. At this point, the new standards for the quality film created greater attention to continuity, verisimilitude, narrative clarity, and spectacle. As design and quality standards become more complicated, film companies established jobs to handle the specialized parts of the work. In addition, the move by distribution alliances such as Paramount, World, Triangle, Warners, and V-L-S-E to a full schedule distribution of multiple-reel films produced profits and a competitive standard of hiring experts from outside the moving picture industry. These experts from legitimate theater, painting, music, architecture, and fashion design separated specialities still further. Technological innovation within the industry resulted in experts in special effects, make-up, and materials and tools of production.

This chronology and periodization are based on the changes in the management system, but the subdivision process, an effect of the detailed division of labor, might have occurred in the same order whatever the management system. Whether a studio used a director-unit or a central producer system, the research department or the continuity clerk would probably have developed. Standards of authenticity and continuity would still have created a need for this work. By the late teens the major subdivisions and work procedures had a set pattern. In Part Five, noteworthy additions to the structure will be mentioned, but, as will become apparent, the changes were minor modifications.

The conception of the production

Direction of capital

Generally, managers functioned either as directors of capital, guiding investment and purchasing raw materials and labor power, or as technical specialists, coordinating, supervising, and maintaining production. In the management hierarchy, technical managers were subordinate to the directors of capital. The ownership function was separate from these.

Most of the people who owned the first film production firms worked in both management capacities, although some owner/managers concentrated on one or the other. Some subcontracting also occurred, with technical specialist responsibilities given those workers (e.g., cameramen with a contract to provide films). Such subcontracting, of course, predated the commercial introduction of the moving pictures, the instance in point being the experimentation period at Edison. These cameramen/managers often chose what to film and almost always how to

film it; their own levels of quality were dependent only in a general way on the owner/managers' acceptance of the finished product. Thus, the initial separation between ownership and management occurred when owners hired separate technical managers. Not only was this a parting of ownership and management but it was a sectioning of management between the two types, capital direction remaining united with ownership. Significantly, owners did not hire non-owner capital-direction managers. Capital direction remained exclusively the owners' prerogatives until the firms went public and ownership spread.

Initial decisions about the product and production process

In the periods dominated by the cameraman, director, and director-unit systems (1896-1914), the director and cameraman made the major decisions in filmmaking. With the introduction of the central producer system about 1914, however, division of responsibility started in earnest. The producer (or studio head or supervisor) and the production department took over what had been the director's and cameraman's responsibilities for selecting the type of product, type of production processes, level and integration of production, and maintenance of production performance. The director and cameraman were given the latter two responsibilities for an individual film, but at a subordinate level to the producer. Such a splitting of responsibility also produced a collective activity by the workers. As cinematographer Lucien Ballard said many years later: 'Another thing you learn is that a cameraman cannot do a picture the way he wants to, because he's not the boss. It's a collaboration of the director, the art director, and the cameraman.'[2] As we noted in Chapter 8, in serial manufacture, craftspeople are gathered into a central workshop, labor is divided, and a hierarchy of management occurs. But as Marx points out, complex collective work is possible in this mode of production.

By the end of the teens, production planning was standardized. At the start of the production season, the producer (usually located in Los Angeles) would consult with the president and various board members (the directors of capital) in New York City. There, the group would calculate expected income for the year. With that figure as the overall budget, the group then determined how many of what types of films at what levels of financial investment the firm would make.

These decisions were based on experience in the business and a forecast of next season's market. Both considerations entailed marketing analyses. One source of information was the opinion of exhibitors as to what the public was buying, but the use of more rigorous marketing research seems to have started with the move to scientific management.[3] In 1915, Paramount instituted a film rating system to tabulate the opinions of its distributors and exhibitors, and Essanay in 1917 established an 'Investigation Department' 'to discover not only what the sales organizations and theater managers desired but to keep a record of critics' reviews and secure all available information from the public direct.' In subsequent years the industry tried other methods, but the general attitude seems to have been that film cycles moved too fast to allow decisions to be based on present buying trends, and directors of capital relied mostly on informal analyses.[4] (In the late 1920s, Universal tried a few other market analysis techniques including audience questionnaires and a psychologist to analyze public response.)

The calculation at the yearly budget meeting included not only the budget and some product determination but also the precise number of films at certain cost brackets of expenditures. The directors of capital and the producer made, in addition, some initial decisions as to casting and story. Generally, once feature fiction films were the principal product, the companies separated them into two and (after 1930) three cost levels with brackets within each group: the specials (those which would 'roadshow' before going into the regular exhibition circuit), the programs (those which filled out the company's contractual commitment to provide so many films at such and such costs to the exhibitors), and after 1930 the low-cost B films (films for the second spot in the double-feature). The firm would then choose whether to spread its costs across a wide number of films or to count on fewer films at higher prices or some variation of both. The company also planned various shorts, comedies, serials, and newsreels to fill out the exhibitor's program needs.[5]

With the budget and decisions from that meeting, the producer returned to the studio and with his staff set in motion the actual production operation. The producer oversaw all of the departments, and depending upon his proclivities, he gravitated toward various degrees of involvement in the routine work on individual films.

The production department

Assisting the producer in his planning was the production department which handled all the day-to-day management and economic coordination for the studio. This department estimated costs, organized studio physical facilities, and kept production records. It also relied on the continuity script as the source of its cost estimates: once the producer, director, and writers had a story in continuity format, the production department and the assistant director for that film broke the script apart into a scene plot, a costume plot, and the number of players and scenes in which they appeared. With this design 'breakdown,' the individual departments did initial plans and cost estimates, cutting expenditures if necessary to meet the story's assigned budget.

The assistant director's breakdown of the script is a logical historical development of his role. The position of assistant director had separated from the director's as production rates increased, and by the early teens he generally took care of routine, pre-shooting organizational work. This might include checking out locations, finding authentic properties, and reviewing the rushes of the previous day's work. As elaborate planning developed, the assistant director took over laying the work out, determining how many shots would be taken daily, deciding which shots would be grouped together on which exteriors and interiors, hiring extras, organizing location shooting, and prechecking sets, costumes, and lighting. His work relieved the director of details, and he acted as the director's liaison with the people on the set and those in the production office.[6]

Besides its planning function, the production department also had overall responsibility for an efficient, economical work process. Controlling costs demanded intensive use of labor-power and the means of production. Paying film workers by time was of enormous significance: as *Fortune* put it, 'the chief expense in producing a motion picture is time' − expenditures for labor-power.

Somewhere between 70 and 80 per cent of direct costs were salaries and wages. The fewer 'unnecessary' people working in planning the film and the better the department could group daily- or weekly-paid technicians or players, the lower the costs.[7]

The allocation of costs seems to have affected the work practices during shooting. In 1916, Price, Waterhouse prepared an accounting procedure memorandum for film accountants. Optional methods of charging expenses might have been set up, but Price, Waterhouse (possibly following then-current practices) advised charging as much as possible to an individual film. Then, what could not be attributed on an individual basis became overhead – such as salaries for administrators and department heads and the studio's physical costs. Although Price, Waterhouse suggested several methods of distributing overhead, it preferred dividing it by the number of feet of exposed negative on the assumption that wasteful directors exposed more film. They also argued that rehearsals were cheap in comparison to many retakes because shooting involved many more laborers, more raw film, and higher consumption of electricity for lights. Such an accounting practice, or ones similar to it, discouraged multiple takes, improvisation, extensive re-arranging of the script on the set, and long takes. How much impact such accounting practices had upon the 'star' directors is questionable, but for those working around them and for those with less secure reputations, the pressure to control shooting was more intense.[8]

Accounting and efficiency practices influenced other aspects of filmmaking. Bookkeepers wrote the cost of all sets and costumes against the film for which they were made; as a result, any subsequent uses were free. This encouraged the re-use of sets and a return to the same genres. After Selig purchased an entire zoo in 1908, the company made a series of animal pictures. Paramount built a ship in 1927 which through its lifetime (until 1935) was used in *Special Delivery* (1927), *Fireman Save My Child* (1927), *Anybody's War* (1930), *Morocco* (1930), *Luxury Liner* (1933), *Four Frightened People* (1934), *Now and Forever* (1934), and others.[9]

The development of experts in efficient set construction was also an effect of economy measures. Studios, even with large stages, had limited physical space for the several films in production so the production department had to prepare carefully the most efficient use of the facilities. Sets could not be erected on those stages until just before use and afterwards had to be stored until any retakes had been shot. On set construction at Metro-Goldwyn-Mayer many years later, Cedric Gibbons wrote:[10]

> But let me emphasize one point – our object in set construction is *not* to fool the public, as so many people seem to think. As a matter of fact, it often costs us more to improvise a house than it would to build the real thing. Time is the essential factor. Time, and transportability. As a result, we have developed a corps of skilled technicians who, in the space of a few hours, can build a cottage and 'age' it so that it will appear to have stood for centuries. Or a ship, or a jungle, or whatever we may need.

By the mid-teens, sets were built in a factory area and then stored or moved to stages to save time and physical space and, in the long-run, costs.

To keep track of its operations and to provide data which would suggest the efficiency (or lack thereof) of any film and its laborers, the production department created elaborate routine reporting systems. Paperwork traced the cost of every stage of production. In 1918 one firm kept daily track of the number of production stills, scenes shot, total footage, net footage, number of scenes to complete the film, estimated days to completion, and the day's labor hours. On a large wall diagram-board (see fig 13.2), the production manager had a systematic description of where each director's film stood in its shooting schedule, how many players were working, and where the unit was shooting. Generally, the assistant director supplied the daily shooting reports to the production office. In such a planning system, different individuals assumed the responsibility for producing reports which kept track of the details necessary to guide the assembly of the film.[11]

Pre-shooting work

Script writing

We have already seen that the early divisions among writing tasks occurred when one person contributed stories and the cameraman or director reworked the material for shooting. The story writer may have been another member of the firm, a freelancer who was paid a nominal sum for the story, or a writer hired specifically to supply material. The companies followed the latter course more frequently once demand for new narratives intensified, around 1907. At that point, the firms began actively soliciting freelance material either through the purchase of copyrighted plays, novels, and stories (particularly after the *Ben-Hur* suit) or from unknowns who sent in stories. The firm delegated to editors and readers the selection of stories. By at least 1911, firms had a story reading/writing department with a head, readers, and writers.[12] Reliance on freelance submissions from unestablished writers decreased after studios began to draw regularly upon stories from adaptations and from employees' originals and after protection against plagiarism suits became important (there was little chance of discovering an outstanding scenario from an unknown). By the mid-1920s, agents were go-betweens for non-studio-generated plots.[13]

The emerging classical Hollywood style and the adoption of multiple-reel films in the early teens caused the new major separation in the writing process: the technical expert who specialized in translating a story into a continuity script. As the script became more important for planning and coordinating the work and as continuity conventions became more complex, this technician took over the preparation of the script. The scenario editor for Lubin said in 1913 that while formerly the editor supplied ideas to the director, 'now the director does not see the scenario, until it is handed to him for production, complete in every detail. . . . Four or five experts of our staff have read and discussed every phase of the script and every effort has been made to eliminate any flaws of structure.' Since the continuity writer also adapted all purchased copyright and freelance work, the material in its original form went through a standardizing process to meet the criteria of the quality film and format. The technician not only knew the continuity format and stylistic demands, but she or he also knew the studio's particular needs with respect to costume and set cost, standing sets, star and stock personalities, directorial and staff areas of skill,

and so on. Such a practice provided the studio with a standardized script designed to take the best advantage of its physical capacities and labor force. Thus, a similar blueprint confronted the workers time after time, making its use routine and fast. Such a standardizing process undoubtedly controlled innovation and contributed to the overall solidification of the classical Hollywood style.[14]

The splitting of writing expertise around 1913 – some workers excelling in creating stories, others in re-writing – produced experts in further subdivisions. Although atypically early, Vitagraph's scenario department in 1912 had another speciality area: 'In addition to the Scenario writers, title and sub-title draughtsmen are an adjunct.' In 1915 the call for such inter-title specialists increased, with one writer suggesting as a source 'the trained newspaperman or woman, one preferably skilled in the difficult art of writing head lines' (which suggests one function of the inter-titles). Thereafter, firms hired those specialists and others (such as gag-men for comedies).[15]

Two final developments in the subdivision and order of the writing process worth noting occurred in the 1920s. Although the Lubin firm used team-writing by mid-1913, it was customary by the early twenties for scripts to travel through several writers or groups of writers. (One writer in 1922 said Pathé once had a group of twelve writers on a story; the infamous teams at MGM had precedents.[16]) Seldom did one person do all the work all the way through. In addition, the studio added an intermediary step between the purchased original story and the continuity script: the 'treatment.' After the producer and staff selected a story for production, the treatment writer broke the story into sections and character plot, '[viewing] it with an eye to the special requirements and conditions of his own studio' and to the present market. This treatment would be in lengthy prose form. The principal decision-makers, including often the star for which it was intended, responded to it. Several treatments might be done before the project would receive a go-ahead to be put into a shooting script format by a continuity writer. The advantage of the treatment was several trial constructions of the film's blueprint without the extensive and expensive detail of the continuity script.[17]

Direction

With the subdivision of the labor process and the creation of the work position of the central producer, the director's range of work and technical management decisions decreased. The amount and type of control by a director depended on several factors: his interests and background, production needs of the firm, and the director's contractual power. The varied backgrounds allowed the studios to take advantage of any specializations these men provided – those with art backgrounds, for instance, might contribute to set design, as did William Cameron Menzies.[18] Those with more experimental tendencies (e.g., Maurice Tourneur) were sometimes given more leeway with the style (e.g., *The Bluebird*). After the diffusion of the central producer system, the major responsibilities of the director were his input into pre-shooting decisions, now a group system of decision-making, and his control of the staging of the action during shooting.

Research

The critics' and public's attention to details of accuracy (induced in part by the company's advertising) caused first the director and then the assistant director and often the set manager to spend time in research. By the mid-teens, this work resulted in firms employing a 'technical expert' to work on 'archaeological references.' Joseph Henabery recalled doing extensive research for D.W. Griffith and *Intolerance*, ending up with 15 feet of books on Babylon and Assyria. By the end of the decade, the expert had his or her own research department, and the staff would 'collect all available material and information that may be of value to motion picture production. These libraries have now become very extensive.' Clippings and files on all sorts of subjects and subscriptions to magazines filled out the reference materials for writers, costumers, and art directors.[19]

Art direction

The construction of sets involved several work functions which subdivided the director's work into two positions: the art director and the property manager, each with a staff. Following contemporary theatrical and vaudeville precedents, the early interior sets for films were backdrops painted by theatrical scenic painters. These artists included in their responsibilities using materials corrected for the properties of orthochromatic film stock. As David Sherrill Hulfish explained in 1911: 'The scenery used for setting the [film] stage differs from the dramatic stage by the absence of color. Plain black and white and neutral tints are most desirable, for color is objectionable in that it may be misleading in tone values when photographed.'[20]

By the early 1910s, theaters were using more three-dimensionality in their sets, film producers' became similarly interested in verisimilitude and depth, and production rates were increasing. As a result, the film companies started collecting permanent properties and building three-dimensional sets under the direction of a 'stage manager' or 'technical director.'[21] Using the script, the technical director and his assistants drew up scene and property plots, reducing the inefficiency and inaccuracies attendant upon unplanned construction. As early as 1913, these plots included pre-construction diagrams of the sets with camera set-ups precisely marked so that only the necessary portions of a set and props would be prepared. A 1914 discussion of the technical director mentioned that he needed to consider how a set would photograph with the camera at varying distances (an effect of closer framing and analytical editing), and Arthur Miller has recalled that in the mid-teens Anton Grot did drawings which considered the camera lens length. Set models started to be used by at least 1914: the director okayed their dramatic use while the technical director handled their artistic, photographic, and authenticity requirements. (See figs 13.3, 13.4, 13.5.) These technical directors were also responsible for preventing anachronisms in the sets, with which the research staff helped them out. The technical directors needed to understand aspects of the crafts of construction and cinematography, particularly the properties of the film stock and lenses; they obviously used that knowledge in their work.[22]

By the mid-teens, the studios started calling this position the 'art director.' The terminology may reflect the new source of some of these experts from painting and architecture and the current interest in 'new stagecraft,' the American version of recent European theatrical staging and lighting trends. These new art directors started taking over some of the cameraman's and director's decisions regarding lighting and composition. Will H. Bradley, 'art editor of the *Century Magazine*, the artist who has done so much for the poster in America' advised firms on 'correct lighting of interiors, artistic variations of chiaroscuro, and dramatic effect to be produced by psychological handling of color notes.' Besides Bradley and Grot, Wilfred Buckland, Robert Brunton, Hugo Ballin, Everett Shinn, William Cotton, Cedric Gibbons, and others began working for firms. Buckland, a former Belasco designer who worked for Famous Players-Lasky, followed the most recent theatrical lighting styles; Brunton,[23]* art director for Ince productions, had, according to a period description, 'a rich dramatic lighting' style; and Ballin provided sets to the Goldwyn Company containing a 'suggestion of Gordon Craig and Sam Hume.' The introduction after 1915 of these new art directors set up precedents of lighting for more than realistically motivated illumination and depth and of composing for more than visibility of action.[24]

By the late teens, sets had become complex constructions, with rooms in rows. One writer explained:[25]

This adds more realism and permits the artistic camera shots through vistas which could not be obtained if a single room were constructed at a time. . . . and when, in the further development of the plot, these rooms are shown more completely, we recall them and the memory serves as another means of knitting up the unity of impressions.

Architects were hired. Robert Haas was with Famous Players-Lasky by 1919, and Hans Dreier worked for its European branch from 1919 to 1923, when he came to Hollywood. Haas constructed sets which included ceilings visible in the film.[26] Such complications required cooperative planning among the craftspeople. One aid was even more extensive use of models. Jerome Lachenbruch described the process of set design for *Theodora* (1921):[27]

But in the case of this picture, a procedure that is sometimes employed in American productions was followed. It consisted in erecting miniatures of every set that was to be

constructed. For this alone, separate sets of blueprints had to be made. In a spectacle conceived on so magnificent a scale, the models were essential for the directorial staff to work out the pictorial grouping of thousands of players to define the various angles from which scenes [shots] were to be made, to test in miniature the effect of light at disparate heights, and finally to decide upon and record for future reference the exact action of the various players in the different scenes and sets.

The art director had influence over all aspects of the *mise-en-scène*'s design, but he had a large number of subordinate experts who carried out individual (detailed division) segments of the construction and dressing of the set. The choice of exterior locations had passed by 1913 from the director's concerns into the hands of the assistant director, or more often thereafter to 'location men.' By the mid-teens with the increasing organization and in-depth research practices within the industry, the companies collated photographic files of hundreds of locales. In the same period, the firms launched massive indexings of the props which they had started purchasing much earlier. By 1915, the work of supplying properties had subdivided to the property department head who also had staffs of experts to make what was not available for purchase or rent.[28]

Finally, composite photography became part of art direction. Although cinematographers developed most of the technology for composite work, the use of miniatures, glass shots, and mattes overlapped with areas of concern to the art director (see fig 13.6). Patents for the technologies and techniques predate the beginning of the industry, but standardization of precision registration around 1914 was particularly important in permitting certain special effects. This technology developed in the late teens and spread into general use in the 1920s. The firms employed these effects to create *mise-en-scène* − beautiful mountains instead of the tops of an adjacent set, multi-storied castles, and locales not available for mass transportation of hundreds of staff and players and tons of equipment. Experts in cinematography worked under the art director to create special effects. As a result, throughout the 1920s and in some cases through the 1930s and

1940s, the firms split special effects between the art and the cinematography departments rather than combining them into a separate unit or delegating all of the work to one department. As these techniques proliferated, individual staffs specialized in each process.[29] (The advantage to the split of the work is the spreading of technical knowledge across various sectors of the firm; the disadvantage is possible lack of communication and competitive rather than cooperative moves on the parts of the separate groups of workers.)

Costuming

From the earliest period of filming, the firms divided costumes into the modern and the historical. When modern dress was required, the players were supposed to furnish their own wardrobes, and reminiscences of the early period of casting often include hiring decisions based on the dress a woman wore to that studio that day. Special historical costumes, of course, were expensive, and firms renting such supplies to theater companies were glad to pick up the film business. After the narrative production increase in 1907, the individual firms began purchasing and making their own wardrobes as well as renting them, and out of this need came another theatrical carry-over, the position of the wardrobe mistress, common by the early teens. Besides preparing the costumes, she was responsible for considering the photographic effects of the textures and colors of her materials.[30]

With the advent of the employment of other experts around 1915, companies started adding fashion designers to costume the leading ladies; Ince announced his firm's hiring of Melville Ellis, 'designer and fashion expert of International reputation' that year. By 1922 at Famous Players-Lasky, the wardrobe director headed two sections of special costuming: character and women's fashions. From a wardrobe plot, the research department supplied photographs and descriptions of period clothes, and the character section reviewed its 50,000 costumes for appropriate ones and started construction of new designs. In women's fashions, a technical expert, the designer Ethel Chaffin, specialized in the gowns for the female leads. She supervised over one hundred women in five subdivided branches of costuming: dressmaking, stock materials, finished wardrobe, millinery, and fancy dress. Chaffin designed the

major pieces by draping and pinning and turned the actual construction over to assistants. In that way, she was able to create three thousand dresses in 1920. Speed and originality, she claimed, were the most important considerations in designing for films.[31]

Casting

When the director controlled all of his casting, he selected the leads from his stock company and the extras from anyone who appeared at the studio 'bull pens.' Gradually, around the early teens, the assistant director took over casting extras, and major players followed the theatrical practice of hiring agents. In late 1915, one firm announced its new plan for 'casting efficiency': it hired a theatrical agent to make a file of data on character types. The phrase 'type-casting' has literal implications within this mode of production. In order to set up such a system, the casting director, an expert who replaced the more casual approach which the firm had employed, needed some method to classify the potential players for his system. As Mary Pickford put it several years later, the casting director 'divided humanity in sections – young men, old men, comedians, tragedians'; the selected classification became somewhat permanent as it went down on a card with other statistics and into the casting director's indexed and cross-indexed files. With this procedure, the producer and director would choose the leads, and the casting director filled out the rest of the cast subject to their approval.[32]

In 1925, the industry as a whole, working from the advice of the trade association (the Motion Picture Producers and Distributors Association), tried to stop the exploitation of the extras. Multitudes of star-struck people had descended on Hollywood, most with little prospects of employment, and agents secured large percentages of these extras' fees in return for finding them one of the few openings. The firms formed the Central Casting Corporation to serve as a single hiring agency for all producers without the intervention of agents. Central Casting was also highly systematized. By 1930, 17,500 extras were registered.[33]

Make-up

As in theatrical traditions, film make-up was the responsibility of the individual player into the

1920s. 'How-to' books and company handouts explained the problems of the use of reds and whites with orthochromatic film stock and suggested how to avoid ending up with black eyelids and lips and halating complexions. Because of this, the cinematographer found himself checking out the various players' results and insisting on consistency (for continuity and verisimilitude) within an individual film. One standardizing aid was the support firm of Max Factor which had located in Los Angeles in 1908 and supplied make-up, wigs, and hair-pieces to stage and screen. By the mid-1920s, many studios had department heads and staffs of make-up artists to assist the players. First National created its department in 1924 with Perc Westmore in charge. Paramount placed Wally Westmore as head of its staff in 1926, and he remained there for forty-three years.[34]

Cinematography

Although the cameraman of the very early years may have made most of the management decisions, after the advent of the director system in 1907, his primary responsibilities were setting up lighting, placing boundary lines to signal the edges of the set area visible in the image, handling the camera, and providing special effects photography. After shooting, he turned his negatives over to the laboratories with instructions as to development.

As the style of the films employed more crosscutting and analytical editing and as their length increased in the early teens, there were greater problems in keeping records and order among pieces of film. In these years, the cameramen devised tactics to keep track of the individual shots. One report on the work process in 1913 said that the cameraman's assistant held up a scene number before each take was photographed; the purpose: 'in handling the film the developers know how to make their reports concerning any photographic deficiencies and the assemblers use the scene numbers as a guide.' Karl Brown, Billy Bitzer's assistant, supplies an example for this period in which he recorded for reference the place, lighting, special effects, camera stop number, and footage. By the 1920s, Hal Mohr said, 'we had charts all made out as to what [the laboratory workers] were supposed to do.' Thus, the cameraman's notes supplied

another paper record to coordinate with the continuity script, helping in the assembly of the film by various workers at different times and places.[35]

When longer films increased the cameraman's duties, his work became subdivided. By 1913, some cinematographers had assistants. By the early 1920s, three individuals handled camerawork with the subordinates as apprentices.[36]* The assistant's duties were to clean and repair equipment, to carry it to locations, and to assist the first cameraman in routine matters such as holding the slate, marking the playing area, and making the shooting notes. The second cameraman handled more responsible work and usually shot the second negative, which was an insurance negative and the one used for European prints. The first cameraman supervised the placement of lighting equipment, shot the primary negative, and advised the director in 'the composition or artistic arrangements of the photographic scene.'[37]

Owning twenty-six cameras, most valued between $3,000 and $4,000, Famous Players-Lasky in 1922 was apparently a bit atypical in that it supplied the cameramen with their cameras. Around 1915, cameramen began to purchase their own equipment because the studios' mechanical repair departments were bogged down with other work and could not fix company-owned cameras fast enough. The firms were also slow in purchasing accessories which the cinematographers wanted. Cameramen's personal ownership of the equipment probably lead to invention of accessories, although the general craft situation and an ideology of 'progress' also stimulated interest in technological development.[38] (Studios started owning the cameras again after sound technology increased their cost and studio synchronizing methods required uniformity in equipment.)

Shooting work

Assistant direction

Much of the preceding job descriptions has touched on the shooting segment of the work, but several other parts of the actual process of filming ought to be mentioned. If the assistant director played a key role in planning the work, he remained in the same essential supporting function during shooting. As liaison among the production department, the director, and the rest of the crew, the assistant director had the major responsibility of keeping everything running smoothly and efficiently. In a 1924 memo at Thomas Ince's studio, the assistant general production manager cautioned that the assistant director should have each set checked out the day before scheduled shooting. He should have present at that inspection the first cameraman, the head of the property department, the company [unit] property man, the chief electrician, and the company [unit] electrician as well as the director. Assistant directors also oversaw on the day of shooting the availability of the players, make-up, properties, and so forth. If a number of extras were in a scene, he directed their actions. (For big scenes, there might be several assistant directors.) For location shooting, he supervised the players' and crew's transportation, food, and lodging. Finally, he was supposed to keep costs down. Good assistant directors seldom became directors; they were too valuable to lose. Their normal promotion was to production supervision.[39]

Rehearsals

The number and type of rehearsals seem to have varied greatly throughout all periods, studios, and directors. When the director was making up the script as he went along, the players could not know in advance what the characterizations would be; rehearsals in those cases involved much improvisation and direction during shooting. After 1908, however, to get a story within the allotted footage of the one-reel film, the director had to make shots more concise, and rehearsals were used to time the action. Rehearsals also allowed the cameraman and electricians time to check the placement of lights. Probably earlier, but certainly by 1922, the studios had created another subdivision of work: stand-ins with the same coloring replaced the leads for the final checkups before shooting.[40]

Music during shooting

Once rehearsals were satisfactory and equipment was in place, the workers began shooting with directors at times coaching off-screen. The use of music during the shooting first occurred at least by 1907; a phonograph played during posing 'to add to the reality of the moving pictures.' In October 1915, the *Moving Picture World* recorded that George K. Spoor, an owner of Essanay, had a full orchestra play during an afternoon shooting of part of *The Raven* in order to raise the actors' work to the required emotional pitch. The paper noted: 'this is the first time [sic] in film history that music has been used in the production of photoplays.' As a publicity stunt, it worked. Several months later Equitable announced it had live music during all of its productions to enhance the acting, and the practice had become standard by 1918, some directors being satisfied with phonographs or a couple of musicians, others requiring orchestras. Here is an instance of the studio's willingness to spend money on an extra job function in the belief that it would enhance the performances and hence the film's quality.[41]

Order of shooting

The order of the taking of the shots was partially dictated by availability of locations and sets, but fairly early (by 1910) the procedure was to take the exteriors first, since interiors could be arranged to accommodate the idiosyncracies of the actual locations. This became more necessary when films relied upon frame cuts, direction-matching, cut-ins, matches-on-action, and sets staged so that exteriors were visible through windows. Other considerations also determined shooting order. The 'big set,' the most complicated construction, would be delayed until the end of the schedule to allow the art department the most time to complete it. Also the most dangerous scenes would be scheduled last, on the logic that if anything happened to the leading players it would not delay the film going to the distributor.[42 and 43]*

Multiple cameras

Another method of saving money was the occasional use of multiple cameras during shooting. Using two or more cameras occurred on and off from at least 1907. *The Show World* records Essanay filming with two 'as one film may not be a success, but if both turn out perfectly, there is always a chance to use them.' The extra footage, for instance, might be used in another film. So one usage of multiple cameras was to protect against needing retakes of a shot. When exports of American films increased after 1910, a second negative also served as the master for foreign prints. As the costs of spectacular scenes increased, multiple cameras helped in another way: the studios could stage a scene once but cover the action from different points and distances. A 1918 writer pointed out that more than twenty cameras might be used in a battle scene in which the set or locale would be destroyed during the take: 'the cameras are posted at advantageous positions, some on the ground level and some at an elevation, in order to get varying and unusual views.'[44] Cecil B. De Mille's shooting practice in the 1920s can be seen as an outgrowth of this procedure. And the practice as a whole is a result of keeping costs in hand while satisfying needs for spectacle, continuity, and differentiation of the product.

Continuity clerk

By the mid-teens, analytical editing and matching of action were common. Also by the late teens, effects lighting on the stars included backlighting and the beginnings of diffusion through lenses and gauzes in imitation of still photography and theatrical conventions of beauty. After an establishing shot was made, lighting and equipment had to be adjusted before the cut-in was taken. Consequently, the staff had to pay close attention to make sure details of action and *mise-en-scène* matched. Although continuity and verisimilitude had always been a responsibility of the director, of the cameraman, and of their staffs, the demand for accuracy increased the need for a paper record. By the mid- to late teens, a new sort of worker, a 'script assistant' or 'continuity clerk,' usually a woman, worked as an aide to the assistant director. Her duties were to take notes on continuity during shooting 'for future reference when carrying out the connecting scenes [shots].' She was also to check on all properties and costumes and notate every change a director made from the prepared script. These notes became part of the paper record sent to the film editors.[45]

Post-shooting work

Negative development and rushes

By the early teens, the cameraman no longer developed his negatives, and laboratory assistants were in charge of that under his direction. After

the cameraman exposed the film, he tagged it with his notes for developing the individual shots and sent it to either his studio lab or an independent lab for development. The lab prepared a print within twenty-four hours so that the staff could check the film for any 'minute flaws of detail, business or photography.' If there were multiple takes, the director or producer chose which ones he wanted.[46]

Editing

Before the system of analytical editing was formulated, assembling the film was a matter of joining the separate shots and adding permanent inter-titles, but as crosscutting, cut-ins, matches, dialogue inter-titles, etc., became standard, cutting became more time-consuming. By the early teens, cutters had taken over part of the director's work and assembled a rough cut following the continuity script, the camera assistant's slate numbers, and the directions from the review of prints. In later years, the cutters also used the continuity clerk's notes. Mohr recounts that when he joined Universal in late 1914, he and eight other cutters worked for fifty-four directors. Sometimes the director actually did the first cut but the written instructions usually relieved him of that routine task. Generally, however, he did a final cut. After the advent of the central producer system eliminated some of the director's responsibilities, the cutters often handled the final cut and titling even though the director and producer might still choose the scenes for the first cuts. By the late teens, the cutter had become the 'film editor,' a technical expert who refined the film from the rough cut to the final one. Working with the film editor during the drafting of the final version, an expert title writer polished the inter-titles.[47]

Previews and revisions

Besides censorship, the major reason for revisions of the film at this point was the firm's decision that the film did not meet its standards of a quality product. One way to determine whether it was adequate was to try it out − like opening a play out of town. Previews with actual audiences occurred at least as early as 1914, when Mutual studios in Los Angeles would check the reception of a film before doing the prints for distribution. Previews could trigger a whole series of revisions including rewrites and retakes. That, of course, became expensive. Sometime after 1925, Irving Thalberg made retakes a permanent part of the MGM procedure and budget, but that was an exception among the studios.[48]

Musical accompaniment

After the firm completed the film and while positive prints were made, musical accompaniment would be prepared. After 1909, Edison supplied cue sheets to pianists, and this became standard service for the exhibitors in the early 1910s. Pathé did an adaptation of the operatic music for its *Il Trovatore* in 1911, and musicians occasionally wrote original film music. Because of the length of features, this cost and effort was expended only for very special films.[49]

The film companies assigned work functions to particular job positions and created new positions for two chief reasons. First, the standards of continuity, verisimilitude, narrative clarity, and spectacle significantly affected Hollywood's production practices. Jobs such as continuity writer, art director, costumer, researcher, and continuity clerk were in part their result. Secondly, detailed division of labor facilitated mass production; in particular, 'scientific management' resulted in producers, planning departments, and craft experts in shooting the film, casting, executing special effects, and so forth. Assistants and speciality staffs increased. These positions, the work order, and the mode of production were in many instances the effect of the economic and ideological/signifying practices. In turn, the production practices often affected film form and technique. Most certainly, these practices provided the conditions for the existence of a group style. Moreover, production routines not only had to prove themselves efficient, they also had to enhance quality filmmaking. When both conditions were met, these routines became normative. Innovations could be effected but within the constraints of the overall standardized system.

Thus, what we think of as the Hollywood 'studio system' was in effect by the mid- to late teens. Although we shall see some important modifications later, the period dominated by the central producer (1914-31) contains the elements we have traditionally associated with the Hollywood mode of production. Part Five will show that the next management system, the 'producer-unit' system which begins in 1931, is a movement away from the strong central producer system into an era of management specialization. Before that change can be discussed, however, the development of the classical style of filmmaking must be considered in connection with this study of the organization of the mode of production. That is the work of the next part.

Part Three The formulation of the classical style, 1909-28

KRISTIN THOMPSON

We are the last who grew up with the movies. We saw Nazimova's films as they were made, not when they were revived, Academically; we sat in draughts and put up with fire, flicker, breaks, scented disinfectant – for what? For delight, magic, pleasure. Early Swedish and Sennetts and Italians were not early then. Rooms were naturally orange at night, and the country deep blue. It was part of the magic. Our companions were men who got rolled into doormats by fire engines. We heard of cinema first, and Chaplin came after. We are the last, as we were the first, to grow with it unprejudiced. We experienced something that will never be possible again. We gave to it and took from it, and we know that its secret is pleasure.[1]

Robert Herring, 1932

14 From primitive to classical

The cinema knows so well how to tell a story that perhaps there is an impression that it has always known how.[1]

André Gaudreault, 1980

In looking back to the silent cinema, it is all too easy to consider the period as remote, alien, and crude. The addition of sound, color, widescreen, and a panoply of recent developments seems to have hopelessly outdistanced the achievements of the early films. Yet it is remarkable that one must go back very far to find films which are so fundamentally different as to be incomprehensible today.

Historians have called these very early years of film production the 'primitive' period. This period is generally assumed to have begun with the cinema's commercial origins in 1894 and lasted until somewhere between 1906 and 1908. During most of the primitive period, films appealed to audiences primarily through simple comedy or melodrama, topical subjects, exotic scenery, trick effects, and the sheer novelty of photographed movement. Non-fiction films outnumbered narratives, at first, and the latter were usually imitations of popular theatrical forms of the day. According to the traditional account, the primitive style began to disappear as individual innovators like Edwin S. Porter and D.W. Griffith introduced devices such as crosscutting, the close-up, and so on. These devices are said to have influenced other filmmakers.[2*]

Most historians would agree that between the primitive period and the sophisticated studio production of the twenties, the US cinema moved from a narrative model derived largely from vaudeville into a filmmaking formula drawing upon aspects of the novel, the popular legitimate theater, and the visual arts, and combined with specifically cinematic devices. I do not propose here to challenge that general notion. Clearly there was a profound shift in both narrative and stylistic practices. But this shift did not come about because a few prominent filmmakers happened to decide to move their camera in or to break their scenes into more shots. When they did such things, these men and women were not creating isolated strokes of genius, but were responding to larger changes within a developing system. Not all of the many experiments that were tried in the early teens became part of Hollywood's paradigm. Only those solutions which held promise to serve a specific type of narrative structure caught on and became widely used. The predominance of narrative structure over the systems of time and space within the classical film can thus be seen as one result of early attempts to harness cinematic time and space to a storytelling function. Filmmakers quickly came to share certain assumptions about films, narratives, techniques, and audiences that guided them in their experiments.

I shall be suggesting that the formulation of the classical mode began quite early, in the period around 1909-11, and that by 1917, the system was complete in its basic narrative and stylistic premises. During the early and mid-teens, older devices lingered, but classical norms began to coalesce. The stylistic patterns which characterized the primitive period eventually disappeared. This was in part due to the fact that innovation was not simply a matter of a few daring filmmakers influencing others. It occurred within a set of institutions which were capable of controlling new ideas, fitting them into an existing model, and making them into normative principles. As Part Two has shown, trade journals, handbooks, and reviews disseminated and developed the norms of the classical model, while standardized studio organization was putting those norms into effect. Individual innovations were certainly important, but people like Griffith and Maurice Tourneur changed production practices and filmic techniques in limited ways, governed by the overall production system.

Nor was the shift from the primitive to the classical cinema a matter of either a growing sophistication or a discovery of a natural 'grammar' of the medium. The term 'primitive' is in many ways an unfortunate one, for it may imply that these films were crude attempts at what would later become classical filmmaking. While I use the word because of its widespread acceptance, I would prefer to think of primitive films more in the sense that one speaks of primitive art, either produced by native cultures (e.g., Eskimo ivory carving) or untrained individuals (e.g., Henri Rousseau). That is, such primitive art is a system apart, whose simplicity can be of a value equal to more formal aesthetic traditions. The classical cinema, then, was not a development directly out of the early primitive approach; the primitive cinema, as André Gaudreault puts it, cannot be considered 'the humus and the soil of which the sole virtue was to allow the germination of the other form.'[3] Rather, the classical cinema resulted from a major shift in assumptions about the relation of spectator to film and the relation of a film's form to its style.

As many historians have noted, the primitive cinema largely assumed that the spectator was equivalent to an audience member in a theater. Mise-en-scene often imitated theatrical settings, and actors behaved as if they were on an actual stage. The framing and staging of scenes in constructed sets placed the spectator at a distance from the space of the action, looking into it. Devices like crosscutting, montage sequences, and dissolves for elliding or compressing time were not in general use. The spectator witnessed either a continuous stretch of time over a whole film or discrete blocks of time in one-shot scenes with ellipses or overlaps between. Filmmakers provided few cues to guide the spectator through the action; there was little of the redundancy of narrative information which the classical cinema would habitually provide.

The classical cinema, on the other hand, assumes that the narration places a spectator within or on the edge of the narrative space. As we shall see, a variety of stylistic devices combined to extend that space out toward the plane of the camera, as well as to move the spectator's viewpoint periodically into the narrative space. This increasing depth of the playing area, in combination with greater three-dimensionality in the sets themselves, promoted that specific conception of verisimilitude which, as Chapter 9 has shown, was valued in the early classical period. While presenting to the spectator a more three-dimensional narrative space, however, the film now contained a set of cues to underscore the story action at all times. These two demands, a verisimilitude and narrative clarity, helped create the classical style of Hollywood filmmaking. Part One has already presented this system in its complete form. In this part, I shall be dealing with the early formulation of the classical system and its refinements in the late teens and twenties. This will not be a history of the 'first times' that given devices appear in the cinema. So many films from the silent period are lost or inaccessible that such a project would be doomed. But more importantly, an emphasis on first usages does not inform us about the wider impact of a device. To understand the classical cinema, we need to know when its techniques became normalized on a wide scale.

Even more importantly, we cannot look at devices in isolation from their typical functions. Techniques contribute to the creation of systems of causality, time, and space. A device already in use during the primitive period may continue to be used in the classical system, but may change its function.

In a study of standard practice, a concentration on filmmakers traditionally considered major – Griffith, Tourneur, Thomas H. Ince – would create a skewed impression of the norms. Rather, a variety of genres, filmmakers, and studios should contribute to create a broad picture. I have included films of the early teens from many studios – from the larger Patents Co. members, like Essanay, Vitagraph, and Edison, to the major independents, like Imp, Bison 101, and Thanhouser, to the smaller independents, like Crystal, Rex, Solax, Reliance, and Yankee. (Unfortunately some studios' outputs have virtually disappeared, so a complete sampling is impossible.)

A study that focused entirely on the most famous filmmakers and studios would run the risk of giving undue prominence to certain devices which might in fact have been limited or idiosyncratic. For example, most historians who study the early history of crosscutting devote their attention to the last-minute rescue situation, since they derive most of their examples from Griffith. Yet I shall be claiming that once crosscutting became standardized, it gained several other equally important functions. A cross-sectional survey of the type attempted here provides a tool for judging the actual importance of any given technique in the history of the American cinema.

An important question throughout will be the degree to which filmmakers and critics of the period were aware of newly formulated film techniques. We cannot always be sure that a device's appearance in a number of films implies that filmmakers were beginning to consider it a standard way of doing things. Fortunately, there exists a set of evidence paralleling the films themselves – contemporary discussions of filmmaking practice in how-to columns and books and in various theoretical and critical writings. These materials reveal that filmmakers and critics at the time recognized many of the changes in the continuity system, in acting style, in lighting practice, indeed in most of the areas we are exploring in this book.

With these sources – films and contemporary accounts – we should be able to survey the formulation of norms of narrative and stylistic structure in American filmmaking during the transitional years 1909 to 1917. The primitive and classical periods were not, of course, entirely different from each other nor unchanging within themselves. We may find at least two distinct phases within the primitive period itself: the earlier (1895-1902) includes primarily one-shot films, with documentaries more numerous than fiction films; after about 1902, multiple-shot films and the increasing use of staged narratives created a more complex approach to filmmaking. Then, from about 1909 to 1916, the transitionary phase toward the classical cinema occurred, with the classical paradigm in place by 1917. From that point on, silent cinema history became mainly a matter of adjustments, not basic changes.

The primitive film's relation to vaudeville

The early film's economic dependence on vaudeville, discussed in Chapter 10, helped determine the genres and formal norms of the primitive cinema. Exhibition circumstances, short length, and small-scale production facilities dictated the creation of films which modeled themselves largely on types of stage acts: the variety act, the fictional narrative, the scenic (views of interesting locales), the topical (presentations of current events), and the trick film.

These genres were recognized as such in the primitive period; they reflect the type of appeal the producers and exhibitors exploited in selling them – the trick film's technical novelty, the variety acts' presentation of famous vaudevillians to farflung audiences. In practice, however, many trick films and variety acts contained brief fictional narratives, so the categories overlap somewhat. For my purposes here, the most important groupings are general ones: documentary films versus fictional narratives.

Before 1903, most films shown on early vaudeville programs were documentaries. The early views were usually a single shot, taken from a static tripod or involving a pan or track from a moving vehicle. Brief, in black and white, and with little explanatory material, they seem of minimal interest today. The apparent crudity of these early documentaries has helped foster the myth that films were used to drive patrons out at the ends of vaudeville programs, or the notion that audience demand spurred the shift to narratives.

Before 1903, the typical film resembled a very simple vaudeville skit. The stage skit usually involved a couple of comics performing verbal and sight gags in a relatively static situation.[4] Early films are even simpler; while the vaudeville skit usually leads to a pay-off, the brief, single-shot film usually employs a more static narrative situation – a potential cause which never leads to an effect. For example, *The Old Maid in a Drawing Room* (1900, Edison) consists entirely of a medium shot of an elderly woman in evening dress seated and talking animatedly, facing a space off front; the film's entire interest arises from her comic appearance and gestures. There is no development. Some of these skit-like films are difficult to distinguish from motion-picture records of actual vaudeville comedy performances – a circumstance that reflects the indebtedness of the early narrative film to its stage mode.

Beginning about 1903, the film's single action became part of a brief series of causally linked events. This resulted in part from the increasing length of each film; there was also a greater complexity of production methods, which might mix interior and exterior shots within the same film. But greater lengths and heterogeneous material did not fundamentally change the narrative model derived from the skit. Films still depended upon an initial, often accidental event, rather than upon character motivation. In 1903 and 1904, the chase film, staged in a series of exterior locations, was becoming one of the most popular narrative genres.[5] Rather than confining itself to a simple, brief slapstick fight, the film might prolong its action by having one combatant flee, with the other chasing and passersby joining in. A relatively complicated film, like *The Life of an American Fireman* (Edwin S. Porter, 1903, Edison) or *The Runaway Match* (1903, AM&B) would incorporate a chase as part of a larger series of events. Through the period 1903 to 1908, simple narratives that follow one action – a chase, a rescue, a fight – in linear fashion dominate narrative filmmaking.

The second major vaudeville form from which film derived narrative principles was the playlet. When writers on this period assume that film imitated full-length nineteenth-century legitimate drama, they overlook the fact that there was this more accessible form closer at hand. Vaudeville initially adopted the playlet during a period of intense competition among entrepreneurs in New York in 1893-4. Wishing to book famous attractions to enhance drawing power, a few producers hired stars from the legitimate theater, who performed in condensed, twenty-minute versions of their original dramatic successes. This practice eventually brought such stars as Sarah Bernhardt and Ethel Barrymore to the vaudeville stage in the early teens.[6] Authors began writing original playlets, and the form developed into one specific to vaudeville. At the beginning, however, when film was most closely linked to vaudeville, the condensed plays were highly episodic series of highlights from existing works. They were in a sense the opposite of the

skit, since instead of prolonging the effects of one initial cause, the playlet packed a great deal of causal material into a short playing time.

When film producers began basing films upon lengthy literary works, they also tended to structure them as series of selected scenes from the originals. Porter's 1903 version of *Uncle Tom's Cabin* (Edison) no doubt imitated the popular stage productions of the novel, which had toured the country during the last decades of the nineteenth century.[7] But the condensation of the narrative into an episodic set of fourteen tableaux suggests as well the playlet form. A series of tableaux, often with explanatory phrases between, became a standard way of presenting a narrative in the later portion of the primitive period (e.g., *The Unwritten Law*, c. 1907, Lubin).

The playlets and the plays upon which they were based were frequently melodramas, and familiar melodramatic subject matter appears in primitive-period films. *The 100 to One Shot* deals with a man who wins on a long-shot bet at the track to save his fiancee and her father from eviction. Other popular motifs in primitive films were gypsies who steal a child and the father who disapproves of his son or daughter's choice of a marriage partner. Moreover, the episodic quality of the stage melodrama continues in films of the primitive period (and into the teens as well). Coincidence was permissible at virtually any point in the narrative, either to keep the story going or to provide a resolution at the end.

Neither the skit nor the playlet fosters the weave of causes from scene to scene which Part One has shown to be typical of the classical narrative. The primitive scene does not usually begin by closing off dangling causes or continue by creating new ones for scenes to come. Rather, the same cause lingers on, resulting in more and more effects (the skit), or each scene sets up a new set of premises to be worked out in one relatively self-contained stretch of action (the episodic playlet). As we shall see in the next chapter, this difference is a crucial one for distinguishing the classical from the primitive cinema.

Between 1906 and 1908, the sudden nickelodeon boom made film in many cases vaudeville's rival for audiences. The enormous success and quick spread of nickelodeons, combined with vaudeville's continued use of films, created a demand for more releases from the producers.

Robert C. Allen has shown that the producers responded, increasing their output from 10,000 feet weekly in November of 1906, to 28,000 feet by March, 1907; even this did not meet the demand.[8] As a result, filmmaking followed a trend which had begun about 1901-3: the production of larger proportions of narrative films in relation to documentaries.[9]* Initially comedies formed the greater part of the fiction output. Allen has persuasively shown that this increase was *not* in response to public demands – that in fact audiences regretted to some extent the replacement of scenics and topicals by narratives. Indeed, Allen found that sales in magic lantern slides showing exotic locales surged in 1908, at the point when producers went over decisively to narrative.[10] But with a steady demand established first by vaudeville theaters and later by nickelodeons as well, producers had to find some way of guaranteeing a regular flow of releases. This, as Chapter 10 has explained, resulted in a mass production of staged, narrative films.

The move to narrative was a key factor in encouraging a shift from primitive cinema to classical filmmaking. Certainly the early vaudeville structures held on for some years, partly because filmmakers had been trained under them, partly because films were still shown in vaudeville situations, and partly because the classical paradigm took several years to be formulated and to be widely accepted as a norm. But why was there a shift away from the approach to narrative prevalent in the primitive period?

The rise of the classical model

With the considerable elevation of public taste in the past two years and the still greater desire to do better things on the part of the film manufacturers, the 'trick' film, and the merely farcical, or horse play, pictures have taken a secondary place.[11]

Walter Prichard Eaton, 1909

One of the main causes in the shift from primitive to classical cinema involves a change in influences from the other arts, from an initial close imitation of vaudeville, to a greater dependence on short fiction, novels, and legitimate drama. But film narrative and style were not simply the sum of several inter-arts influences. However directly film may have imitated existing devices from theater or fiction, we must always ask how the device and its function changed when incorporated into works in the film medium.

Only in the first phase of the primitive cinema, when films were one shot long, were they nearly direct imitations of existing forms. Topicals and scenics were very similar to magic lantern slides and photographs. Records of vaudeville acts made little attempt to change the act for the screen. The abstracting functions which films performed – reducing their subjects to black and white, rendering them for the most part silently on a two-dimensional surface – were already familiar to audiences from other photographic media.

But with the steady demands by vaudeville and later by nickelodeons for more product came a tendency for the manufacturers to increase the length of the films, usually by adding shots. This greater length had two vital implications for the types of narratives used in the films.

On the one hand, greater length, whether in longer takes or in multiple shots, would allow more time for characterization and the development of psychological traits. The filmmaker could have simply added more characters and physical action to expand a skit-like situation, but this would tend to provide little change in the course of the film – the longer the film, the more apparent would be the static quality of the situation. Providing traits for the characters could motivate a changing situation; then it would be the characters, rather than the situation, which remained stable, unifying the string of events. A few simple traits could motivate a whole variety of circumstances, while at the same time providing a narrational thread to guide the spectator.

On the other hand, while characters could be a unifying force, cutting could be potentially *dis*unifying. Yet technological restrictions like limited camera-magazine capacities and production circumstances like the lack of a written script, might tend to discourage lengthy one-shot films. In fact, during the rise of the narrative film, from 1902 to 1908, the multiple-shot film gradually became the norm, although film lengths varied considerably during these years. At first, the association of shots with whole films was strong: 'Above all, the inventors of the cinema invented the shot, and this shot was at the time the alpha and omega of cinematographic expression.'[12] Indeed, sometimes producers would copyright every shot of a multiple-shot narrative as a separate film. In this way the title of each film/shot could serve as an explanatory inter-title, and the separate shots became self-contained tableaux. Producers also began to make series of scenic views of a single locale, each of which could be copyrighted separately; these could be exhibited individually or as a set.[13*] The initial reluctance to put several shots into a single film suggests a recognition of the potentially disruptive qualities of the cut. Unless the filmmaker finds cues for conveying the spatio-temporal relationship between shots, the effect of the cut is a perceptible break between bits of subject matter.

We have seen that the manufacturers realized how suitable fictional narrative films were for profitable mass production. Because of film's success, more footage was needed, and it proved more predictable to manufacture staged films than documentaries. In addition, all other things being equal, a longer narrative film was proportionately cheaper than a short one, since the same sets and personnel could be used to create a greater amount of footage.[14*] So the trend toward longer narratives continued throughout the silent period.

The spatio-temporal problems innate in the construction of the multiple-shot film helped guide the filmmakers' formulation of a classical narrative model. This is in one way a somewhat traditional view of film history — that the discovery and increasing use of cutting brought cinema from its initial dependence on theater into a more independent, 'cinematic' period. Yet historians have usually treated this change as an untroubled evolution — with editing freeing Porter, Griffith, and their followers to explore the 'grammar' of film. What I am suggesting here is that cutting was not entirely a liberation; it posed tremendous problems of how to maintain a clear narrative as the central interest of the film, while juxtaposing disparate times and spaces. The continuity rules that filmmakers devised were not natural outgrowths of cutting, but means of taming and unifying it. In a sense, what the psychological character was in the unification of

the longer narrative, the continuity rules were in the unification of time and space.

Filmmakers found themselves dealing with an increasingly disruptive set of devices as their films became longer and their narratives more complicated. When no standard way of conveying narrative information existed, experimentation was necessary. In the primitive period, films sometimes display anomalous devices. The famous repeated action in the last two shots of Porter's *Life of an American Fireman* (made in late 1902, Edison) has caused debate among historians, as to whether Porter's film indeed could have been released with such a problematic repetition of an entire scene. To argue that the repetition could not have been in the original assumes that the later norm of smooth story-telling was in existence by 1902 and that Porter must have known that overlapping time would disturb an audience. But in fact such repetitions of actions from different vantage points occur in other films of the period. These include *A Policeman's Love Affair* (1904, Lubin) — where the maid's greeting to the policeman is seen both from the street and from inside the house — and *The Tunnel Workers* (1906, AM&B) — where the foreman and the protagonist both go through a door and are seen repeating this action from the other side of the door.[15] The point here is that disruptive devices abound during the late primitive period and occasionally crop up in the early teens.[16*]

Time, space, and logic did not fit together unproblematically at this early point. The relationships among these systems were probably the same in the primitive period as in the classical — that is, narrative was the dominant consideration, with time and space subordinate to it. And many of the same techniques were in use during both periods — cut-ins, characters, intertitles, linear causality, and the like. The main changes that occurred in the shift from primitive to classical cinema took place *within* the individual systems of causality, time, and space.

The main vehicle for the change was a radically different conception of narration. During the primitive period, the narration usually remained omniscient, with actions placed in a block before the viewer — played out in long-shot view for the most part. (Even dreams, visions, and memories were seen in superimposition over only part of the frame, with the character still visible in the long shot, thus minimizing the subjective effect and keeping the narration omniscient.) As Gaudreault suggests, 'The narrator was not *conscious* of being a narrator.'[17] Inter-titles of neutral, non-self-conscious tone summarized action and introduced characters. But the narration seldom attempted to guide the spectator actively. The rare early cut-ins or camera movements which occurred stand out in this context as moments of more self-conscious narration aimed at shaping the onlooker's perception. (Later, when such moments became part of the norm, they would call considerably less attention to the process of narration, with continuity principles fore-grounding narrative flow and making cutting unobtrusive.) In short, classical narration tailored every detail to the spectator's attention; the primitive cinema's narration had done this only sporadically.

In the shift away from primitive cinema, filmmakers found ways to control the disruptive spatio-temporal effects of multiple shots and locales; they accomplished this by constructing a totalized model, making a unified narrative the top priority, and using guidelines within the model to control the spatial and temporal problems created by the film medium. With such a unified structure as the grounding for the entire film, cutting, ellipses, repetitions of events, could all come to serve a clear function. Such a film would not be difficult for a spectator to grasp.

Directly or indirectly, the cinema found models of unified narrative in other arts – the unities of drama, the single strong impression created by the classical short story, and the well-made play. But because the film medium had its own demands as well, not one influence came through unchanged, and classical film narrative was more than the sum total of the devices it borrowed.

Novel, short story, drama

The conditions for influence

As films grew longer, the status of the individual film on a program changed. Initially, eight or so short films might fill a twenty-minute slot in a vaudeville program of several hours. The overall emphasis was on variety, and the disparate films formed an act. As a consequence, no individual film was expected to stand by itself. But with the advent of the nickelodeon and the standardized 1,000-foot reel, a program would typically consist of only three or four films; each occupied a distinct place within the complete show, separated by song-slide presentations and possibly other live acts. Internal coherence became a more central issue. And when the feature film came to occupy virtually an entire evening's program (with overture and other entertainment often tailored to the film), it had to carry the burden of sustaining audience interest. Expanded length and the change in viewing circumstances undoubtedly played a large part in turning filmmakers away from a vaudeville model of narrative toward fiction and the drama.

In the early years, films had competed only with other vaudeville acts for a place on a program in an art form that had an established audience. But with the phenomenal growth of the film industry, its product began to vie with other entertainment commodities for customers. By the first half of the teens, films were competing with inexpensive popular fiction – short-story magazines and novels, *The Saturday Evening Post* and *Collier's*, for instance, offered 'one or two nights' enjoyment of the best serials and short stories for five cents.'[18] To lure those readers in at a similar price for a shorter period, film producers felt they had to raise the quality of their offerings. Thus, for the short film at least, the popular short story offered an existing model to be emulated.

The feature film, on the other hand, offered a more expensive, often lengthier evening's entertainment, one directly comparable to that offered by a play, and entrepreneurs showed early features in legitimate theaters with prices based upon live-drama admissions. The situation in the theater industry of the early teens gave film a competitive advantage and probably fostered the industry's move into features during that period. That advantage derived from the organization of the theatrical business around the turn of the century.

The legitimate theater in the early years of this century operated as a cluster of touring troupes, controlled by a small number of entrepreneurs centralized in New York. This centralized touring system had replaced the country's earlier theatrical organization, the individual local professional repertory company, around 1870. Theater historian Jack Poggi sums up the changes in the theater industry:[19]

> What happened to the American theater after 1870 was not very different from what happened to many other industries. First, a centralized production system replaced many local, isolated units. Second, there was a division of labor, as theater managing became separate from play producing. Third, there was a standardization of product, as each play was represented by only one company or by a number of duplicate companies. Fourth, there was a growth of control by big business.

The characteristics which Poggi lists have obvious parallels to the development of the film industry as described in Part Two. Film was able to compete successfully with legitimate drama because it provided a more efficient, more centralized system for staging a performance only once, recording it, and reproducing it for the mass audience with minimal transportation costs.[20*] Because of its success in competing with the drama, the film industry was able to standardize the multiple-reel feature, which in turn encouraged the move to a classical continuity system. But again, in order to compete with the drama for its audience, filmmakers realized the necessity of raising the quality of their offerings.

To a considerable extent, raising the quality of films to attract consumers of short fiction, novels, and plays required drawing directly or indirectly upon these other arts. Chapter 12 has shown that the film companies did this by adapting plays, stories, and novels. So for sources of subject matter, films turned definitively away from vaudeville skits. Producers also wanted to lure personnel, particularly established stars, away from the theater; adaptations of drama and literature, plus a general elevation of film's status among the arts, helped accomplish this.

But film drew upon these other arts in ways other than the direct appropriation of stories and personnel. The original scenarios used by the companies, whether done by their own staff writers or by freelancers, already felt the indirect impact of existing literary models. The film industry was fortunate in being able to tap a huge marketplace for popular fiction and drama. The writers working in this marketplace were often trained in popularized versions of traditional rules, and they could apply these rules to film scenarios as well.

The large freelance market for novels and short fiction had arisen only a few years before the invention of film. The development of a widespread native fiction had been discouraged by the lack of an international copyright law. Publishers tended to bring out editions of European novels and stories, which they could obtain without payment, rather than to pay American authors to write for them. Before 1891, when an international copyright law took effect, there had been only a very limited output of American short stories.[21] From about 1824 into the 1840s, literary annuals, ladies' magazines, and later gentlemen's magazines, fostered a brief flowering of the tale or sketch; these were generally considered hack work, although at their best such periodicals brought out the works of Hawthorne, Irving, and Poe. The 1850s were a fallow period for short fiction, but the tremendous commercial successes in America of Dickens's novels and of Stowe's *Uncle Tom's Cabin* (1852) marked the rise of the popular novel in America. With the founding during the 1860s of *The Atlantic Monthly* and *The Nation*, short fiction became increasingly respectable, and by the mid-1880s, the writing of short stories was becoming lucrative. The number of writers increased steadily.[22]

After the new international copyright law of 1891, popular fiction underwent a huge growth. Brander Matthews, a leading critic of the period, commented in 1898: 'This is perhaps the most striking fact in the history of the literature of the nineteenth century – this immense vogue of the novel and of the short story. Fiction fills our monthly magazines, and it is piled high on the counters of our bookstores.'[23] Novels were relatively easy to sell but took more time to write. Also, short stories were so popular at the time that a payment for a single story often was as great as the total royalties on a novel. For the vast number of part-time or casual writers, the short story proved attractive. By the late 1890s, there were so many weekly magazines and newspaper supplements that the writing of short stories could be considered an industry. And by 1900, syndicates existed to write, buy, and sell stories.[24]

There were also freelance playwrights, although this market was much smaller. A writer could not sell a play nearly so easily as a piece of fiction; the financial rewards, however, were potentially greater:[25]

Although there is far more pecuniary profit to the author from a successful play than from the average successful novel, and although in some countries, notably in France, the authorship of a play brings more instant personal recognition, playwriting demands a long and arduous period of apprenticeship. Even after years of familiarity with technical stagecraft, it is far more difficult to get a manuscript play accepted than it is to secure publication for a manuscript novel. Most authors choose, or are forced to follow, the easier path.

Authors could mail plays directly to managers or to stars, but many worked through agents. Chances of a sale were relatively slim. One 1915 playwriting manual described how an author could expect to wait while his or her manuscript languished for months on a manager's shelf.[26] Once a playwright succeeded in getting one play produced, however, she or he usually would be considered a professional, receiving reasonably high, regular royalties. There was also a small market for freelance writers of vaudeville playlets.[27] Again, the procedure involved royalties rather than outright sales.

The film industry entered the literary market in part by hiring established writers and in part by inviting submissions of synopses and scenarios. Staff writers and scenario editors came to the studios from a variety of backgrounds, but the most common previous occupations were journalism and popular-fiction writing. Journalists were presumably well-suited to the task because they had professional experience in writing and editing synoptic narratives. A trade journal noted in 1916: 'The best school for the would-be photoplay writer is the newspaper office. Many who were formerly newspaper men are now successful as writers for the silent drama. They know life, a good story, and the value of a gripping situation.'[28] Edward Azlant's examination of screenwriting before 1920 discusses several dozen prominent scenarists at the studios.[29] The largest number of this group came from journalism, followed by magazine-fiction writing, novel writing, and playwriting. These divisions are not

hard and fast, however. Many writers worked in several or all of these fields. Given the huge, lucrative freelance story market, few writers of any type failed to submit something to the magazines. Reporters, copy readers, and editors working for magazines and newspapers wrote short stories. (Stephen Crane, Edna Ferber, Willa Cather, James Cabell, Irwin Cobb, and Sinclair Lewis were among those who got their starts this way.)[30] Writers who worked at the studios or sent in their freelance efforts would usually have some experience with the popular fiction forms of the period.

Historians have dealt extensively with the impact of the drama and the novel on film form and style.[31] The concomitant influence of the short story, however, has been largely overlooked. An examination of the close relations between the freelance short story and scenario markets will demonstrate some of the conditions which encouraged narrative principles from all of these arts to enter the cinema.

In order to make narrative films on a regular, efficient basis, producers began to use the detailed division of labor described in Part Two. Narrative filmmaking necessitated a steady source of stories, a need which eventually resulted in the scenario staff. These workers performed specialized tasks: among other things, they wrote many of the original stories used and read the freelance synopses or scenario-scripts submitted to the studio. Chapter 12 has suggested that the heyday of the amateur scenarist was actually brief (from about 1907 to 1914), but these were important years in the transition from primitive to classical filmmaking. Vast changes took place in ideas about how a narrative film should be constructed. The backgrounds of both studio and freelance writers, as well as the normative advice they received, helped shape those ideas.

By 1910, the methods of obtaining stories for filmmaking purposes resembled those of the popular fiction magazines, which, as we have seen, had become popular in the 1890s. The prominent *Black Cat* magazine, for instance, started a trend toward using contests to encourage submissions of short stories. Motion-picture companies followed this strategy, and there were scenario contests conducted through the trade journals in the early teens.

Whether encouraged by prizes or by flat-fee

purchases, amateur and professional freelance writers flooded the studios with scenarios. Usual estimates in the trade journals and scenario guides suggest that only about one in a hundred scripts was actually accepted, and scenario editors frequently complained about the poor quality of the material they had to plow through. Very quickly, the studios' dependence on such submissions declined. By 1912, copyright problems and the expanding production of multiple-reel films made unsolicited stories less attractive; contract writers in scenario departments proved a more reliable, efficient source, and the most promising freelancers could be hired. Amateur scenarios were used almost exclusively for one- or two-reel films, the production of which declined as the feature became the standard basis for production in the mid-teens.

Little direct evidence indicates what proportion of the freelance material came from writers who had also tried their hand at short stories. Few films of this period credited their scenarists. But some indirect evidence suggests the importance of popular short fiction as a model for film narrative. For one thing, some of the books on how to write scenarios of the period came from authors who also provided advice on short-story writing.[32] In addition, a few major scenarists of the time have recalled their beginnings as short-story free-lancers. Frances Marion wrote fiction until requests for the screen rights to her stories led her to try doing scenarios; she eventually became a staff writer for several West Coast companies. Clifford Howard, who later became scenario editor for the Balboa and the American companies, wrote of having turned his outlines for short-story plots into scenarios when he heard how easy they were to sell. Others who had written short stories (usually in addition to work in other prose or dramatic forms) include: Roy L. McCardell, Lloyd Lonergan, Emmett Campbell Hall, Epes Winthrop Sargent, James Oliver Curwood, Eustace Hale Ball, Mary H. O'Connor, Beulah Marie Dix, and Clare Beranger.[33] There were undoubtedly others, but most freelancers remained anonymous, and their backgrounds are now untraceable. At least some scenarists, however, had learned their craft from magazine freelancing, rather than from the stage.

Most explicitly, trade journals recognized a parallel between the scenario and popular short-

story markets. These comparisons tend to come a little later in the period, during the middle and late teens, but they indicate an awareness that writers were often working for both markets. By about 1915 the industry began to realize that it was competing with the popular fiction magazines for good stories. *Motography* noted in early 1915: 'An able and recognized short story writer can command from five to ten cents a word for his manuscript. To such a writer an average short story of three thousand words brings a check for one hundred to three hundred dollars.' The article contrasted this with the average payment for a scenario, which ranged well below $100, and pointed out that 'at present the short story writer is only tempted to submit something made over from an oft-rejected story manuscript.' The author concluded: 'The film producers can afford to pay better prices than the magazines. Encourage the writer to try his ideas in scenario form first; he can make over his rejected scenarios into magazine articles as easily as he can do the opposite.'[34] A *Motion Picture News* editorial pointed out that fiction magazines attracted a large middle-class audience and educated it to appreciate good stories:[35]

They are sharp critics, these readers. They want pictures up to their established fiction standards.

It is regrettable, but it is a fact, that up to a few years ago, the large percentage of pictures released were of the same ordinary adventurous, or sentimental or funny character of the fiction in our popular publications of *thirty years* ago.

What is to be done then to get good stories? Simply this: Pay the price. . . .

Go directly to the best magazine writers and get their work by *paying at least what the magazine will pay.*

Throughout 1915 and into 1916, similar articles in the trade press called for the producers to raise their fees for scenarios, to attract something beyond the leavings of the fiction magazines.[36]

The possibility for influence from the short story, then, came in part from the contact with writers who sold stories in both the magazine and film markets. In addition, many of the writers who were employed as permanent staff members came from a similar background. Along with the novel and the drama, the short story provided classical models upon which the early film could draw.

Narrative principles

The length of a text has a great deal to do with how critics and writers perceive that a specific literary mode – a novel, a short story, a play – should be treated. The modern short story in a sense gained a distinct identity when Poe pointed out that its basic difference from the novel was that the short story could be read at a single sitting, and thus should convey a unified impression quite different from the principles of unity governing the longer form. Ever since, theorists have repeated the idea that the short story is not simply a story which is short.

In the same sense, the feature film was not simply an expanded one-reeler. The lengthier films – initially 1,000 feet, then two or three reels, then five – demanded new structural principles. In the other arts, full-blown sets of classical dicta on formal matters already existed. By drawing upon drama and literature for stories, the film industry also drew upon these dicta.

The short story, novel, and drama all had something to offer film. Like the short story and the drama, films (excepting serials) were consumed in a single stretch of time; hence filmmakers could use ideas of unity of impression, of a continuity of action rising to climax and falling, and so on. Yet films tended to move about in space more than most dramas or short stories; they dealt with more characters and lines of action in many cases, compressing a great deal of material into the brief span of two hours or less. Ideas of how to organize this material were available from theories of novel construction.

Cinema emerged in the middle of a reformulation of classical notions of unity in the literary arts. The very definition of the short story as Poe originated it (and as it has continued to the present day) was based upon unity. In the nineteenth century, the novel began to be considered a set of carefully interwoven lines of action. The drama, having passed through an emphasis on perfect structure in the nineteenth century, was now adjusting this notion to accommodate the character psychology of new 'realistic' trends.

These issues might well have remained concepts only for scholarly discussion, had it not been for the sudden rise in the 1880s and especially the 1890s of the huge literary market. With so many authors or potential authors trying to sell their works, there began a dissemination of simple guidelines for literary creation. We have seen already how in film, the freelance market of the teens gave rise to dozens of writing manuals. The same was true in other literary arts. The biggest boom in manual-publishing was for the short story, for here the market was largest. According to one literary historian, lesser critics seized upon the most important discussions of short fiction and quickly made them into a set of rules for the novice writer: 'These laws they proceeded to codify and promulgate. The first decade of the new century was the era of the short-story handbook.' The first appeared in 1898, and many others followed.[37] A number of other guides covered fiction in general, and a few concentrated on the novel; there were also manuals of playwriting. Such works reveal the popularization of classical aesthetic principles, many of which coincide with the traits of the developing classical paradigm in film.

The handbooks' discussions of drama and fiction invariably assume that 'Of course the prime structural necessity in narrative, as indeed in every method of discourse, is unity.'[38] Unity was most stringently demanded in the short story. The short story gained its modern definition in 1842, in Poe's famous review of Hawthorne's *Twice Told Tales*; in a passage universally quoted by aestheticians and manual-writers alike, Poe declared that the good short story, being designed to be read at one sitting, should be characterized by 'the unity of effect or impression.'[39] Although Poe's discussion had little impact in America at the time, it was revived in 1885 by Brander Matthews, a Columbia drama professor, whose writings on literature contributed greatly to popularizing Aristotelian canons of classical structure.[40] Thereafter writers, whether scholarly or popular, referred to the Poe/Matthews view as the ideal.

In order to achieve a unified short story, the general assumption went, the writer arranged every element of plot and character around the single strong impression which the story should create on its reader: 'The plot should revolve around a single, central, dominant incident, which in many cases will be the nucleus (in the mind of the author) from which the story originally developed.'[41] In 1904, another major critic, Clayton Hamilton, refined the Poe/ Matthews formula: 'The aim of a short-story is to produce a single narrative effect with the greatest economy of means that is consistent with the utmost emphasis.'[42] Everything in the narrative must function to build up toward the climax, which comes close to the end and creates the strong effect. This idea fed directly into the film scenario manuals; compare the following instructions, one from the Home Correspondence School's 1913 manual on short stories, the other from Phillips's scenario guide (1914):[43]

> Steps: (1) Determine at the outstart [sic] what tone you wish to strike, what effect you wish to produce. (2) Do not put into your story a single word, or action, or bit of description, or character, or *anything* that does not in some direct or indirect way help to produce the effect you desire. (3) Do not omit anything that may help to bring about the same result.

> The climax resolves itself into a definite purpose to guide the playwright; for he writes every scene with a view to its influence on the climax; if it has no influence on the climax, that is sufficient evidence that it is not necessary for his play purposes.

Virtually any manual on story writing offered a variant of this same advice. This was particularly applicable to the one- or two-reel films, and, as we shall see in the next chapter, short films tended to follow the short story's pattern of a steadily rising action leading to a climax late in the plot.

The short story was supposed to be unified in the extreme. Critics and theorists realized that the length of the novel tended to preclude its having such rigorous coherence; yet they still assumed that this trait was applicable and desirable in the longer form. 'Unlike the short-story, the novel aims to produce a series of effects − a cumulative combination of the elements of narrative − and acknowledges no restriction to economy of means.'[44] This does not mean, however, that the novel should be episodic, for unity implied threads running through the whole that connected every

part. Although the novelist might use more characters, more incidents, and more lines of action than the story-writer, all these still had to bear upon the entire plot. The novel should not fall into distinct episodes with separate climaxes, but should rise and fall with an overall ascent toward a final major climax. Again, no extraneous material was permitted, such as the stories interpolated into episodic novels (e.g., *Don Quixote*, *Humphrey Clinker*, *Pickwick Papers*).

These ideas about the novel were never as simply and distinctly codified as were the 'rules' for the short story, and hence their influence on film was perhaps less direct. But as scenarists adapted lengthy novels into feature films, they undoubtedly learned ways of sustaining multiple lines of action throughout an extended story. And indeed the episodic feature-length film is rare, outside the particular mode of the continuing serial. Films which deal with many characters and which cover lengthy time spans still manage to keep a core of causal lines which bind the elements together.

In the field of drama, practitioners and critics alike were still strongly under the influence of the 'well-made play' of the nineteenth century. The major French plays by Scribe, Sardou, Dumas *fils*, and others had been translated and were frequently performed in the United States around the turn of the century.[45] Dumas *fils* and especially the leading German proponent of the well-made play, Gustav Freytag, were to the drama of this period what Poe was to the short story; Freytag's *Technik des Dramas* was translated in 1894, but was quoted frequently before that by drama critics and theorists. Many of the most popular English-language playwrights of the day − Pinero, Shaw, Wilde − had been influenced by the well-made play, as had Ibsen. In the 1890s, books on dramatic structure typically reiterated Freytag's rigid, pyramidal schema (rising action, climax, falling action, catastrophe), which would guarantee a perfectly unified play.[46] This schema would produce a symmetrical play with the traditional five acts forming mirror-image parallels across the whole; *Othello* and *Macbeth* were considered excellent examples.

Critics of this period did not agree with the traditional French interpretation of the three 'Aristotelian' unities; the unities of time and space, in which the play's story was supposed to take place within twenty-four hours and in one locale, were dismissed. Instead, these writers focused on the unity of action:[47]

> This has been variously interpreted, but the most sensible view is, that all the incidents of the story must be made to cluster about a single central animating idea. One purpose must be seen to run throughout the whole series of incidents. If there are two series of incidents, they must be so woven together that, at the end of the story, it will be evident that one could not have taken place without the other. This constitutes the *unity of action*.

This passage suggests that unity in the drama was conceived in terms somewhat similar to Poe's 'unity of impression' for the short story. But here 'a single central animating *idea*' is the basis for the whole; as we shall see shortly, this 'central idea' became codified as the 'theme.'

After the turn of the century, the rigid structure derived from Freytag was dropped by critics, and there was a general reaction against the well-made play (and perhaps a tendency to underplay its continuing influence). The well-made play was derided as shallow, with empty structure overriding considerations of character psychology, realism, or social comment. One prominent expert on playwriting, William Archer, refused to use the standard term *dénouement* ('untying'): 'The play of intrigue being no longer the dominant dramatic form, the image of disentangling has lost some of its special fitness.' Archer also poked fun at Sardou for his overly complex exposition and situations.[48] Archer and his contemporaries abandoned the placement of the climax at the center of a play with a long falling action, or denouement, leading to a 'catastrophe.' Instead, for them the climax should come near the end, with all action rising generally in stages toward this moment – a model much closer to the literary structure assumed for the short story and novel of the period. Critics jettisoned the 'catastrophe' altogether. A 1915 playwriting manual gives the typical listing of parts of a play: exposition, development and complication of the intrigue rising toward the climax, the climax itself, and ending.[49] Critics of this period go directly back to Aristotle's requirement that every play's action

must have a beginning, a middle, and an end.[50]

Like the unified novel, the play should not be episodic. Archer commented on the play without unity: 'No part of it is necessarily involved in any other part. If the play were found too long or too short, an act might be cut or written in without necessitating any considerable readjustments in the other acts. The play is really a series of episodes.'[51] Here, as with the other literary forms, unity implies that all elements are necessary, and no necessary ones are missing; all the elements pertain to the main line(s) of action, rather than to separate incidents. Poe's 'unity of impression' is not, however, the basis for the play's coherence. Instead, critics considered the core of a play to be its 'theme': 'It appears reasonable that a play that is actually developed from a definite theme is most likely to possess both the unity and the simplicity, to say nothing of the freshness, which good drama requires.'[52] But this thematic center served the same unifying function as the single impression in short fiction. Everything in the play related to it, and hence could not be superfluous.

Theories of playwriting stressed one additional aspect of unity which was relevant to the cinema: thorough motivation and a resulting continuity of action. Plays, like films, occur in a steady temporal progression. The reader of a short story or novel can go back or can pause to ponder causes and effects, but the audience in a theater must understand the drama as it proceeds. Hence the importance of motivation. Archer quotes Dumas *fils*: ' "The art of the theatre is the art of preparations," ' and advises dramatists to[53]

> Place the requisite finger-posts on the road he would have us follow. . . . It is in nowise to the author's interest that we should say, 'Ah, if we had only known this, or foreseen that, in time, the effect of such-and-such a scene would have been entirely different!' We have no use for finger-posts that point backwards.

This passage invites comparison with the classical cinema's tendency to direct audience attention forward by frequent 'priming' of future events in the plot.

The careful preparation for events throughout the plot would help eliminate coincidence. Coincidence had been a staple of melodrama and the popular nineteenth-century theater in general; but with the growing emphasis on realism around the turn of the century, coincidence became passé. A 1915 playwriting manual stated:[54]

Time was when important coincidence was accepted in the theatre as a matter of course, or even of preference. To-day, however, it has been for the most part consigned to that limbo of antiquated devices and conventions which, for the present at least, has swallowed up the soliloquy, the 'apart,' and the 'aside,' along with eavesdropping behind portieres and letters fortuitously left lying about.

The elimination wherever possible of 'important coincidences' — especially coincidences to resolve plots — was desirable in the classical cinema as well.

Chapter 6 examined the scene-by-scene structure of the classical film, as causes are left dangling and picked up in alternation; this effect guarantees that the action never slackens between scenes. This, too, was noted as a desirable trait in drama; in 1912 Archer discussed how to maintain interest from act to act:[55]

The problem is, not to cut short the spectator's interest, or to leave it fluttering at a loose end, but to provide it either with a clearly-foreseen point in the next act towards which it can reach onwards, or with a definite enigma, the solution of which is impatiently awaited. In general terms, a bridge should be provided between one act and another, along which the spectator's mind cannot but travel with eager anticipation.

The 'clearly foreseen point' or the 'definite enigma' are comparable to the dangling cause; by setting these in place at the ends of acts, the playwright avoided the episodic structure inimical to a unified whole.

Although conceptions of unity differed somewhat for the short story, novel, and drama, they boiled down to a similar notion. The artwork was to be organized around a single central factor — an intended impression, a theme. No unrelated elements were admissible, and the elements that were present should be motivated. Such ideas were common currency by the time that studios began hiring professional writers from other

fields, buying the rights to literary works, and soliciting freelance scenarios from the public.

The same was true of the classical cinema's concept of character; it derived in part from a growing interest in the other arts during the same period in character psychology. Influenced by European Positivism in the second half of the nineteenth century, and especially by studies of human behavior, writers were increasingly interested in portraying realistic characters and their environments. Few were willing to go to the extremes of Zola's theory and approach their characters with a strictly scientific attitude, but critics and theorists were certainly aware of the French naturalist's work. In popularized form, they were willing to apply it. A concentration on character psychology could provide the motivational material necessary to a unified work. The two main issues concerning character revolved around character *development* and *psychology*.

In the short story, both were considered necessarily limited. The short story dealt with fewer characters than the novel or drama. To gain the maximum effect, one or two central characters were held to be ideal.[56] Since the story-writer had a limited time to create characters, they must be immediately striking and colorful, developing swiftly if at all, and 'that development must be hastened by striking circumstances.'[57] Such strictures could be of use to the film, particularly the one- or two-reeler, and even a feature film had far less time than a novel to develop character. In the classical cinema, our first impressions tend to be lasting ones, and the characters seldom have a complex set of traits.

In the novel, on the other hand, character development was considered paramount; it, rather than theme or impression, was often the major source of unity. Over the course of hundreds of pages, the author could slowly acquaint the reader with a whole set of central figures and could change their traits in a leisurely fashion. Character became the wellspring of the action, rather than an agent reacting to a series of incidents. Zola's naturalistic theory can be detected in Brander Matthews's 1898 summary:[58]

The best fiction of the nineteenth century is far less artificial and less arbitrary than the best fiction of the eighteenth century. Serious novelists now seek for the interest of their narratives not in the accidents that befall the hero, nor in the external perils from which he chances to escape, but rather in the man himself, in his character with its balance of good and evil, in his struggle against his conscience, in his reaction against his heredity and his environment.

The novels of George Eliot, and in particular *Middlemarch* (1872), were considered exemplars of the complex portrayal of developing characters.

Given an average feature length of five reels, the early classical film could hardly hope to create characters as complex as those of the Victorian novel. At most, an epic film could bring together large numbers of characters and events and suggest character development: Ben Cameron's change in *The Birth of a Nation* from a simple Southern gentleman to an avenging leader as a result of the war; Trina's gradual deterioration under the effects of her desire for money in *Greed*. On the whole, however, the quick, relatively simple characterizations of the classical film resemble more closely those of the period's drama.

The drama provided less time for character development than most novels would, and simplicity was necessary: 'Our people should be sufficiently rounded to appear human. Yet if they be developed with anything like the completeness of a George Eliot treatment, no time will be left for the fable. Therefore the need of economy. Character must be shown in swift and telling strokes.' A 'roundness' in the characters implied some complexity; characters with single traits were appropriate only to the broadest comedy or melodrama.[59] In general, then, the characters of a play frequently resembled those in a short story: established quickly with a few clear traits, changing minimally in the course of the action.

Dramatists and critics realized by the 1890s, however, that by covering only a brief span of time in a plot, the playwright could concentrate on character more closely and at the same time could promote unity: 'The greater emphasis . . . on the inner rather than the outer aspect of the dramatic situation may have something to do with the simplification of setting and compactness of treatment that marks the work of at least some groups of modern dramatists [e.g., Sudermann, Hauptmann, Ibsen].'[60] Ibsen was perhaps the most extreme instance of a severe compression of

time-span and locale for the sake of character revelation; to some critics, especially Archer, he was the ideal to which the playwright should aspire. (Here we find perhaps a greater lingering influence of the well-made play, modified by contemporary conceptions of realism, than some critics at the time would acknowledge.)

But again, the narrational means of the film did not encourage an imitation of such complex characterization methods as Ibsen's. Without spoken dialogue, detailed character revelation was difficult. Instead, the film stuck to simpler classical features of dramatic characterization:[61]

1 The characters must be suited to the story – the story to the characters.
2 The characters must be clearly distinguished from one another.
3 The characters must be self-consistent.
4 The characters must be so selected and arranged that each one may serve as a foil to another.

(The last dictum reflects the strong influence of Brunetière, whose views were universally quoted in the turn-of-the-century period. He had proclaimed that all dramatic conflict should result from a clash of wills.) All four of these statements could be used unchanged to describe characterization in the classical cinema. They indicate a complete balance between action and psychological delineation, with neither taking precedence.

Besides unity and characterization, several other elements familiar in popular contemporary fiction and drama reappear in the classical cinema's paradigm. In both fiction and the drama toward the end of the nineteenth century, an unobtrusive narration was increasingly considered desirable. Critics insisted upon a distinction between direct and indirect character presentation, preferring the latter:[62]

The modern writer no longer makes pages of statements about his characters, but he much more cleverly leads his reader to form his own opinions of them.

Characters in fiction may be made to reveal themselves in this more forcible and convincing, but less direct fashion, by telling what they say and what they do, by disclosing their thoughts and describing their acts and gestures.

What held for characterization was also true of other stylistic aspects of fiction: 'In the art of the story-teller, as in any other art, the less the mere form is flaunted in the eyes of the beholder the better.'[63] In the drama as well, stage effects would seem like mere tricks if not 'intimately related to the main theme of the play'; they should not 'distract attention to themselves.'[64] Unobtrusive technique tending toward the suppression of the narration began to be a trait of the early classical cinema; as we shall see, this principle guided changes in inter-titles, editing, and other devices.

In addition, beginning *in medias res* was a trait of both plays and short stories. The novel, with its more expansive period for development, could use this device or not. But for those arts consumed in Poe's 'single sitting' — the story, drama, and film — the quick opening allowed economy of means and created an immediate strong impression. A 1913 story manual suggests that Poe's tactic of beginning in the middle of the action's crisis was a strong one: 'In whatever part of the plot the story opens, the first and chief commandment for the short-story writer of today is to waste no time in beginning.'[65] In a play, the opening in the middle of events might provide a way of concentrating intensely on a complex psychological situation: 'The method of attacking the crisis in the middle or towards the end is really a device for relaxing, in some measure, the narrow bounds of theatrical representation, and enabling the playwright to deal with a larger segment of human experience.'[66] A film, too, by launching in at a point well into the story events, could engage the spectator's attention quickly, with the attendant benefits of concentrating and developing a few characters and events extensively.

In sum, models for structuring a film came, not from drama and fiction in general, but specifically from late nineteenth-century norms of those forms — norms which lingered on in popular stories, plays, and novels of this century. The cinema tended to avoid the more innovative, contemporary forms of drama and fiction. Strindberg, Ibsen, and Shaw, or Hardy, Conrad, and James figure very little in the formation of the classical cinema, either as narrative models or as direct sources for scenarios.

But while the film took principles of unity, of characterization, and of narration from the other literary arts, these principles were modified in actual usage by specific qualities of the medium. The film's classicism, while traditional, was unique.

For example, where prose fiction could provide a written narration to reveal internal states of the characters, the Hollywood film showed mostly gestures and facial expressions. Inter-titles might briefly characterize the figures, but the bulk of the action occurred in pantomime. As a result, the film created an objective, omniscient narration, moving occasionally toward the points-of-view of the characters; this type of narration is equivalent only to that portion of short-story narration which confines itself to descriptions of appearances.

Again, the expansion into features stimulated the creation of more leisurely scenes that linger over character traits. Some early features simply expanded the structure of the short film by adding more story material. *The Scarlet Road* (1916, Edison), for example, covers many years of an inventor's life as he strays with a nightclub singer, reforms, and finally makes good. Yet the individual scenes are nearly as brief and condensed as if the film were a one-reeler; the characters are still the stock figures of melodrama. (The protagonist's fiancée is characterized at the beginning with a brief scene of her hugging some tame rabbits, and we learn nothing more about her; we see her at intervals waiting patiently for her lover to return.) But some films display what Chapter 2 calls a 'balance between the fixed types of the melodrama and the dense complexity of the realist novel.' *The Wishing Ring* (Maurice Tourneur, 1914, World) and *The Eagle's Mate* (James Kirkwood, 1914, Famous Players) both linger over their characterizations. The first sequence of *The Wishing Ring* shows the comic details of the hero's drunken carousing with his fellow students — the neighbors waking up, the heroine appalled at the group's bad singing, a donkey braying along with the song, and finally the arrival of the local constabulary. A one-reeler would be likely to show the carousing in one shot, followed by a scene at the father's home as he receives the letter expelling the son from school. *The Wishing Ring* even finds time for tiny subplots among the villagers, helping to establish the quaint Victorian atmosphere that realistically motivates the central story line. These are no doubt rare among mid-teens films, but by 1917, many features were using stories with fewer, longer scenes and with fewer lengthy gaps of time between scenes.

Aspects of the mode of production helped mediate the effects the literary arts had upon unity and characterization in film plotting. The scenario script, and later the continuity script, with their accompanying scene plot, encouraged the use of multiple locations; the filmmaker could make several shots in one setting, then cut these in at intervals in the final film, at reasonable shooting costs. Hence throughout the teens, films contained increasing numbers of shots and moved about freely among locations. Since individual shots provided minimal chance for the various kinds of narration available to the fiction writer, one assumes that the filmmaker would want to provide variety by cutting away from the static take. Analytical editing and crosscutting could create an omnipresent narration, constantly guiding the spectator's attention to story events. In keeping with their compression of long time spans into a brief plot, one- and two-reelers tended to move around more in space than a unified short story might. Increasingly, a combination of circumstances − feature-length films, the star system, the ability of the script format to allow this stylistic complexity − encouraged more cutting within and between scenes. This in turn gave rise to the continuity editing system, explicitly formulated in the period 1909-17; we shall examine this system in Chapter 16.

With the rise of the feature, producers turned increasingly to staff writers experienced in adapting all sorts of material into film scripts. The scripts they turned out followed a standardized narrative form specific to cinema. One would be hard put to look at *The Eagle's Mate* (Kirkwood, 1914, Famous Players) next to *The Girl of the Golden West* (Cecil B. DeMille, 1915, Lasky) and tell from internal evidence which came from a novel and which from a play. The script format in itself would not guarantee such similarity, of course; it basically broke the existing work into shots. But the adaptation process would help iron out the differences in narratives taken from disparate sources in the other arts. Working from a synopsis rather than from the original play or book would tend to rearrange events and isolate them from their dramatic or fictional forms, while the devices of cutting and framing would create a specifically filmic mode of narration.

Ultimately, the film medium used the influence from the literary arts for its own purposes. In spite of a growing dependence on dialogue intertitles, films presented most of the action visually. This meant not only pantomime, but the transmission of information through objects, figure placement, lighting, and camera techniques. The classical system increasingly relied on editing, so that, by 1917, films often used separate shots for virtually every item of narrative information. This rapid juxtaposition of views differed significantly from either fiction or the drama; the film's narration could constantly shift in relation to the action, as in the novel, but the action could be visual, as in the drama. The resulting omniscient, omnipresent narration differed from all other art forms, for none could assemble disparate moving images. And as a result, the material that needed unifying was different for film than it was for other media. Based originally upon nineteenth-century conceptions of unity, the classical system remained consistent − answering on the one hand the need for efficient large-scale production and on the other the desire for a set of norms easily assimilable to a broad audience.

The formulation of the classical narrative

Cause and effect

During the primitive period (1894-1908), films tended to present narratives in such a way that they were minimally intelligible. Given a camera fixed for the most part at long-shot distance, actors simply performed with large gestures, holding up relevant objects briefly to give the spectator a better view. So long as an action was performed within the frame, its narrative function was apparently considered to be fulfilled.

Primitive framing and action did not always aid intelligibility, however. Sometimes a less important gesture at another part of the screen might cause the audience to miss the main action. *Tom, Tom, the Piper's Son* (1905, AM&B) contains an elaborate first shot full of moving people, in which the relevant action − the theft of the pig − is all but unnoticeable; this now-famous example is an extreme one, yet other films of the pre-1909 period show a tendency to present several actions at once. Even a brief, one-shot narrative like *The Dude and the Burglars* (1903, AM&B) keeps all its actors constantly gesturing, effectively dividing the small playing area into three centers of attention. In *The Pickpocket* (1903, AM&B), one shot in a chase structure places the fugitive in the background, with a minor character in the foreground looking on. By accident, the foreground woman blocks the central actions − the pickpocket knocking a policeman off his bicycle and the ensuing struggle (see fig 15.1). Then the woman turns front, obviously responding to the cameraman/director's warning that she is in the way, and she moves left to give us an unimpeded view (see fig 15.2). The fact that this shot was not redone for the finished film indicates the early assumption that as long as the events were on the screen, it was up to the audience to follow them. As late as 1909, Griffith uses a busy, illegible

bustle of action for the stockmarket shot in *A Corner in Wheat* (Biograph). Indeed, Griffith was later to refine this chaotic mise-en-scene into a characteristic framing with multiple points of interest, as in *The Musketeers of Pig Alley* (1912, Biograph). There, when one gangster pours a drug into the Little Lady's drink at lower center, our eye is also drawn to her at the right reading the postcard and to Snapper Joe's cigarette smoke puffing suddenly into the upper left. In the teens, Griffith was somewhat atypical in his tendency to avoid centering.

But with the general shift to the classical model, the status of narrative changes. Devices like editing, camera distance, inter-titles, and acting function more specifically to narrate causal information as clearly as possible. Cinematic technique, rather than remaining a novelty or means of recording, began to be considered a way to convey narrative through careful manipulation of audience attention. David Hulfish summarized this new conception in 1909:[1]

> To secure art in a motion picture, there must be an end to be attained, a thought to be given, a truth to be set forth, a story to be told, and the story must be told by a skillful and systematic arrangement or adaptation of the means at hand subject to the author's use.

By this point, a narrative is not something to be placed in front of an audience, but something to be 'given' or 'told.' A coherent narration must hold the film together − a narration usually not presented by an explicit narrator, but implicit in a specific, systematic combination of film devices.

In order to present a clear narrative, film-makers turned away from the primitive-period device of building a story around either an extended incident or an episodic series of tableaux. Chases did not disappear, but they occurred only in the context of a larger narrative, after careful preparation. One 1913 scenario guidebook offered this advice, derived from notions of unity in the novel, drama, and short story: 'Each scene [i.e., shot[2*]] should be associated with its purpose, which is to say that the outline of a play should comprehend: First, "cause" or beginning; secondly, development; third, crisis; fourth, climax or effect; fifth, denouement or sequence.'[3] This structure led away from both the extended incident (essentially a single drawn-out effect following an initial cause) and the episodic narrative. Now the ideal required a unified chain of causes and effects, varied by complicating circumstances (the development), concluding with a definite action which resolves the chain into a final effect (the climax) and which lingers to establish a new situation of stasis at the end.

Aside from slapstick comedies, many films in the early teens follow this pattern. *Her Mother's Fiancé* (1911, Yankee) is a relatively low-budget, unexceptional one-reeler, yet it is quite unified in its plot: 1) 'Cause,' the mother's fiancé, whom she has not seen in years, arrives to marry her; 2) 'development,' the mother's attractive daughter comes home from school; 3) 'crisis,' during a garden party the daughter and fiancé are in a rowboat caught in a storm and are marooned for the night; 4) 'climax,' they fall in love; and 5) 'denouement,' the mother forgives them both.

By the early teens, a compressed set of causes and effects of this type had replaced the primitive narrative structure almost completely. Eileen Bowser has concluded that comedies were the most popular fiction genre of the years 1900 to 1906, and that 'A very large number of them consisted of practical jokes.'[4] A how-to scenario column in a 1912 *Photoplay* dismissed the earlier form:[5]

The moving picture play has altogether outgrown themes of single individuals in a series of incidents that have no relation to one another except for the presence of the main character. For instance, the mischievous small boy in a series of pranks; the victim of sneezing powder in various mishaps, the near-sighted man, etc. They are all passé.

To some extent the advent of the feature film necessitated finding a means of constructing a lengthy narrative, one which could extend beyond such simple events. But the move toward causal unity was well under way already in the one-reel film. The feature film simply intensified the need which arose with the advent of the multiple-shot films in the early years of the century – to find a means of unifying an extensive series of disparate spatial and temporal elements in the plot in such a way that the spectator could grasp the story events.

The chain of separate events linked by causes and effects provided the answer. Again, this was recognized quite early; a 1912 scenario guidebook suggested that a scenario begin with a central idea and add 'a series of causes on the front end of it and a series of consequences on the other end.'[6] The chain of cause and effect would be so tightly constructed that no extraneous event could enter the film's plot. The basis of the American classical cinema's narrative aesthetic was compositional unity rather than realism. Reality might be full of random events and coincidences, but the filmmakers sought to motivate as much as possible causally. A contemporary review of Raoul Walsh's 1915 feature *The Regeneration* (Fox) was in general highly favourable about the acting and other aspects of the film; the reviewer was therefore inclined to forgive a fault he found: 'the fact that the ship is burned for no definite reason whatsoever. It was a series of wonderful scenes [shots], staged with the utmost realism, but it would have taken better effect if a cause had been given.'[7] For the reviewer, realism was not a matter of chance events; rather, it consisted of little 'touches,' bits of business or props added to scenes. But for the classical mode, even this realism must always be subordinate to a thorough-going compositional motivation.

Causality and motivation became especially important as fiction films became longer and more complex, with multiple lines of action. Most one- and two-reelers tended to follow the same characters fairly consistently with an omnipresent, objective narration. Crosscutting among several groups might occur, but often because of spatial separation, not because the characters were involved in separate lines of action. In *The Lonely Villa* (Griffith, 1909, Biograph), we never see the father engaging in any activities unconnected with his family after his departure — he simply goes away and then starts back on his rescue mission.

A few short films do introduce at least minimal second lines of action, however. In *The Loafer* (1911, Essanay), the drunkard protagonist has two aims. First, he vows revenge upon the leader of a masked mob that has beaten him up; secondly, after he has been given some plow-horses by a neighbor, he determines to reform. These lines come together when it is revealed that the leader of the mob was the same man who gave him the horses. *A Friendly Marriage* (1911, Vitagraph) involves a newly rich miner's daughter who enters into a marriage of convenience with an impoverished English nobleman. The two lines of action involve the husband's growing love for his wife and his secret attempts to earn a living by writing. At the end, it turns out that the wife also loves her husband and that her father's mine has failed, leaving them to live happily on the proceeds from the husband's successful novel. These two films and others like them stand out as having more complex narratives than the standard one-reelers of the day. Some of Griffith's most complicated Biograph shorts combine several story lines through crosscutting.

The dual line of action becomes common in the multiple-reelers. *The Cheat* (Cecil B. De Mille, 1915, Lasky) deals both with the husband's struggle to make a fortune and with the irresponsible wife's flirtation with the Japanese businessman. In *The Case of Becky* (Frank Reicher, 1915, Lasky), our concern lies both with the young doctor's attempt to rid a woman of a split personality and with the villain's efforts to exploit her condition in his hypnotism act.

Aside from encouraging the addition of lines of action, the multiple-reel film militated against a simple linear construction in another way. For a few years, exhibition practices bolstered this change. As Chapter 12 has shown, multiple-reelers were released one reel at a time, so that the parts would often be shown a week apart. Even after the studios began releasing all the reels as a unit in late 1911, theaters would typically show the second reel after a pause, and this custom continued into the mid-teens. Standard wisdom for scenarists at this point was to maintain an overall story, but to structure each reel with its own point of highest interest at the end, to maintain audience attention. Scenarios longer than one reel were considered more difficult, and advisors often warned beginners to avoid them. In 1913, experienced scenarist Capt. Leslie Peacocke described the difference: 'The plot of a two-reel must necessarily be stronger than that of a one-reel story and must carry a big "punch" to close the first part of the story and then work up stronger and stronger toward the climax.'[8] This practice held even into longer films. In general, this emphasis on structuring strong lines of continuing action into a series of climaxes would tend to make film narratives more complicated. With features comes a move away from the compressed 'single impression' narrative style of many one-reelers.

During the mid-teens, these multiple lines of action begin frequently to involve a romance plot. The young doctor in *The Case of Becky* (1915) falls in love with his patient, giving him the determination to cure her when others fail. One-reelers had usually included romantic relationships, but unless the love interest was the main action, it was simply assumed and given little attention. With little time for an epilogue, many short films resolved the entire plot in the final shot, with only a few seconds at the end reserved for the conventional embrace. But the greater length of multiple-reelers gave the romance more prominence. A separate shot or even sequence might be devoted to the final clinch (a device which became considered clichéd by the second half of the teens).

The classical narrative settled into a pattern of linear causality with multiple lines of intertwined actions. But there was at least one alternative narrative model which filmmakers could theoretically have adopted — a model based upon parallelism. A film may follow several lines of action which are not causally related, but which are similar in some significant way. American filmmakers of the silent period did occasionally experiment with parallelism. Porter's *The Kleptomaniac* (1905, Edison) and Griffith's *A Corner in Wheat* (1909, Biograph) and *One is Business, the Other Crime* (1912, Biograph) all use contrasting lines of action to create a conceptual point. The fact that all three of these films involve social criticism may suggest why parallelism proved such an unlikely option in the classical paradigm: it lends itself readily to ideological rather than personal subject matter. Griffith's *Intolerance* (1916) revived the parallel narrative, which proved too abstract for widespread use. The causal chain with an interweaving of lines of action won out easily over parallelism as the basis for the classical film.

The growing complexity of the plot reinforced the tendency toward a system of narration which could present information clearly. In general, films of the transitional period attempted to integrate narration into every aspect of the film – self-consciously at beginnings of films and scenes, unself-consciously within scenes. This was a departure from primitive-film practice.

Many primitive films did use expository titles at the beginnings of scenes to summarize what would happen in the upcoming action. But often other things happened as well, and the spectator was left to notice those unaided. Within the shot, framings and staging did not always single out the salient actions for the spectator. The exposition of primitive films often depends on presenting a situation which is apparent at a glance. The masked gunmen in *The Great Train Robbery* are obviously the robbers, the telegraph man's identity is equally evident, and so on. At the opposite extreme are films which are virtually unintelligible, because little narration of any sort aids our understanding. *The Unwritten Law* (c. 1907, Lubin) presents an enigmatic series of events without identifying characters or situations; an audience of the day could presumably grasp it only by being familiar with the Stanford White murder case upon which it is based. And there are mixed instances, where some events are obvious, yet the films leave certain information unclear. *The Policeman's Love Affair* (1904, Lubin) is a simple story of a policeman calling on a maid and being chased out by the lady of the house. The bulk of the action occurs in a long shot depicting the kitchen and an adjacent room where the lady sits. Yet only the edge of the wall between the two rooms is visible; we cannot see either side of it, and it appears as a stripe on the backdrop. As a result, the two rooms appear to be one, and the audience might be puzzled as to why the lady sits calmly reading as her maid gives food to the policeman and kisses him, apparently right under her eyes. Only when the lady opens the door between the two rooms does the wall become apparent. A slightly different framing would have made the space clear from the start, but we are left on our own to figure out the scene's layout.

The primitive film's presentation of narrative makes things both simple and difficult for the viewer. The stories are simple because causality occurs on the level of external action; we usually need not infer characters' motives in order to understand what it is happening. Summary titles sometimes help make things clear. The difficulties arise from the fact that framing, staging, and editing play only a minimal narrational role. These films are not saturated with narration the way the classical cinema is.

With the transition to classicism, narration gains a distinct structure. The classical film begins *in medias res*. This helps distinguish it from the primitive film. In the early films, there is virtually no difference between story events and the way they are presented in the plot. We seldom learn of any event we have not seen – characters do not recall events earlier than the film's opening scene. (Flashbacks generally repeat a shot seen earlier in the film.) By contrast, the classical film adds a limited dependence on events in the past, the ability to refer to the past verbally, and especially a sense of habitual actions. In the primitive film, we seem often to have stumbled on characters we know little about, and we witness their actions out of context. The classical film sets up characters by positing that they are certain types (they have lived in a certain environment, have done certain kinds of things habitually), then goes on to begin the action.

Character psychology, then, forms the basis of numerous changes that distinguish the classical from the primitive cinema. It serves both to structure the causal chain in a new fashion and to make the narration integral to that chain.

Traits, visions, and desires: the psychologically based character

Once you have created an appealing, heroic central character there will naturally spring up in your mind other characters with whom he or she comes into conflict. In that relationship lies the genesis of your plot.[9]

Frederick Palmer, 1921

In seeking models of characterization, the classical cinema turned away from vaudeville, with its stock figures, toward the short story, the novel, and the drama; in these media, characters had multiple traits from which actions could arise logically. In most genres, random incident became an unacceptable way of getting a plot moving or of resolving it. In 1911, *The Moving Picture World* declared that 'In farce-comedy alone can characterization be *subordinated* to incident and action,' adding that the most interesting stories were those which lead 'to some readjustment of the characters in action.'[10]

Director James Kirkwood wrote in 1916 about the desirability of basing narrative on character rather than situation:[11]

I believe that the most desirable sort of play today is modern and American, whether a swift-moving drama with strong, human characterization, or a comedy devoid of extravagance, its incidents growing out of the foibles of human nature rather than produced by one of the characters smiting another with what is commonly called a slapstick.

So, for example, a one-reel film, *The Girl at the Cupola* (1912, Selig) begins rather elaborately, setting up the fact that the heroine Jessie's fiancé is returning to her and that he is now known as 'the Business Doctor' for his skill at reorganizing failing businesses. Further, we discover that Jessie's father's steel mill has received a spate of cancelled orders. After the fiancé helps reorganize the business, we see the workers receive lower wages and decide to go on strike. Jessie sympathizes with the men and supports the strike; the bulk of the film depicts her and the men's conflict with the fiancé. Finally she succeeds in getting her father to restore fair wages. Although the characterization in this film is not elaborate, every action arises from the characters' traits and desires, and the ending involves a change of heart on the part of the father.

Yet, as this example shows, characters were not typically given traits beyond what was necessary to the drama. Again, the use of realistic motivation in the classical model is severely limited, serving the workings of the story. As Henry Albert Phillips wrote in 1914: 'Characters are subservient to climax. We have no use for any

manifestations of their character outside the needs of properly developing the big moment of the story. Character is the most effective means to our photoplay end.'[12] In the mid-teens, American filmmakers became adept at disguising dramatically necessary actions as realistic touches. An apparently casual or random gesture occurring in one scene will most likely turn out later to have been 'planting' an important bit of motivation for a later scene. In *The Wishing Ring* (Maurice Tourneur, 1914, World) the heroine's little dog appears in several comic scenes, seemingly peripheral to the plot; but later in the film it plays a key role by leading the search party to the heroine lying injured after she has fallen from a cliff. Less prestigious films also 'plant' material. *An Ill Wind* (1912, Universal, one reel) begins with a party held by some office workers; the hero Tom frightens the heroine with a toy mouse. Later a jealous co-worker arranges for Tom to be falsely accused of stealing a check from his employer. Tom spends three years in jail; upon his release he becomes a thief, breaking into the home of the heroine, who is now rich. She screams upon finding a man in her room, and police respond to the sound. But the heroine has learned of Tom's innocence in the check theft; she saves Tom by holding up the toy mouse and telling the police it was what caused her to scream. After the police depart, the brief epilogue shows Tom kneeling and thanking her for saving him. (In a later classical film, the fact that she had kept the mouse for three years would be used as a sign of her secret love for Tom; as it is, the film ends with no definite suggestion of renewed romance.) In these and other films, realism in character is primarily a means of reinforcing compositional motivation.

In the early transitional period, the move toward character psychology manifested itself mainly in the assigning of additional traits. The compressed action of the short films and early features did not permit the extensive use of repeated gestures and subjectivity. Instead, films continued to depend on stock characters, developed somewhat more fully than in the primitive period. Donald Crisp's *The Warning* (1914, Majestic) presents a character study, with the introductory inter-title describing the central figure as a 'wilful, indolent country girl.' The heroine is tempted by a salesman to go with him to the city, but a dream in which she sees herself abandoned provides 'the warning' she needs. At the end, she tells her mother she will not be wilful again. This use of the 'wilful' trait at beginning and end suggests that a film could occasionally be unified entirely by character. Even a film which would have been considered a minor effort in its day, a Lubin split-reel[13*] called *The Gambler's Charm* (G. Terwilliger, 1910) makes an effort to characterize the gambler briefly. At the beginning, the gambler Randall is attracted to a small child and gives it his lucky charm; later, in the saloon he shoots the child's father when the father tries to gamble with the charm as stakes. This film, only about seven minutes long, depends on the strongly contrasted traits of kindliness and vengefulness in Randall's character. With the rise of the feature, both acting and the repetition of characteristic gestures had more time to develop. An early scene in *Wild and Woolly* (John Emerson, 1917, Douglas Fairbanks Pictures Corp.) lingers over the comic business that establishes the hero's fanaticism for things Western.

But the growing dependence on character psychology went beyond external signs of traits. Films sometimes represented mental states visually. Dreams, visions, and memories became narrative staples around 1915. There had been isolated visual representations of mental events from almost the beginning of narrative film-making. The sleepwalking incident that ends with the heroine falling off a building in *The Somnambulist* (1903, AM&B) turns out to have been a dream; in the final shot, the heroine is back in bed and wakes up, gesturing in reaction to the nightmare. Porter used vignetted super-impositions for the vision scene in *The Life of an American Fireman* (1903, Edison) and separate shots for the dream in *The Dream of a Rarebit Fiend* (1906, Edison; in this film, superimpositions and whip pans suggest the mental condition of the drunken hero). Similarly, in *The Unwritten Law* (c. 1907, Lubin), the jailed protagonist has a dreamed flashback to earlier events, represented by a vignette superimposed on the cell's window (see fig 15.3). Visions and dreams continued to appear in occasional films throughout the primitive period and early teens: in *The Girl in the Armchair* (1912, Solax) a young man dreams of his gambling debts, and superimposed cards

whirl around his bed (see fig 15.4). But the compressed structure of the one- or two-reeler was perhaps an inhibiting factor in the use of subjective effects. They tend to appear either when the subjectivity is the basis for the whole film (*The Somnambulist, Dream of a Rarebit Field*) or when the narrative absolutely depends on showing the character's inner state. (In *The Girl at the Armchair*, the hero must undergo a considerable change of character as a result of his gambling experiences.)

Feature films permitted more leisurely characterization and hence more extensive use of subjective effects. Of the fourteen ES films examined from 1914, five contained dreams or visions, and three of these were features. By 1915, just over half of the ES films examined contained a vision, dream, or flashback. After this year – approximately the point at which features became the standard – short films tended more and more toward slapstick comedy; hence the visual representation of subjectivity crops up mainly in features. Some flashbacks do occur without subjective motivation, but most are prefaced by a character pausing to recall an earlier event.

Aside from subjectivity, a variety of other devices helped individualize the classical character. In the primitive period, few figures receive names, unless they represent historical personages or famous fictional characters. But the various central characters after 1909 do receive this additional touch. They do not, however, gain distinctive motifs, or 'tags,' until the mid-twenties: the tattoo in *A Woman of the World* (Malcolm St Clair, 1925, Famous Players-Lasky), which identifies the heroine as a sophisticated woman; or Harold Meadows's stammer in *Girl Shy* (Fred Newmeyer and Sam Taylor, 1924, Harold Lloyd Corporation); or Chico's repeated declarations in *Seventh Heaven* (Frank Borzage, 1927, Fox) that he is 'a very remarkable fellow.' Chapter 2 also discussed how the star system aids in distinguishing characters in the classical cinema. The parallel rise of that system and the classical cinema itself indicates the importance of stars for early characterization. In 1914 it was already unthinkable for Theda Bara to don Mary Pickford's golden curls or for 'Little Mary' to play a vamp. Stars were to a considerable degree the basis for the personae they played. In 1927, Jesse L. Lasky estimated that 'three-fourths of the material is picked to suit the personality of the star and one-fourth is picked for the material of the story itself and cast to suit that material.'[14] Even in the early teens, trade journals frequently advised freelance scenarists that studios were looking for stories for particular stars. These factors — subjectivity, proper names, 'tags,' and star personalities — all contributed to the increasing individualization of central characters.

But no matter how many traits they might possess, isolated characters were inadequate to initiate and sustain a unified, developing narrative line. Early in the transition toward the classical model, characters' goals began to be motivated by their traits. This was a considerable change from many early films, where characters simply react to situations that occur around them. (If a man's pocket is picked, he chases the thief.) No doubt some films of the primitive period present characters with goals, but these don't typically arise from a clear-cut trait of the character; it is given that a character-type wants something. In *The Widow and the Only Man* (1904, AM&B), we see that the man and the widow want to marry, but we get little sense of their backgrounds or motivations for their actions. The fact that he is really a poor clerk seeking her money is only revealed in the last shot, as the punch line of the comedy.

By the early teens, scenarists seem to have been aware of the goal-oriented protagonist, if not by that name; a 1913 guidebook advises writers:[15]

It should be remembered that 'want,' whether it be wanting the love of a woman, of a man, of power, of money or of food, is the steam of the dramatic engine. The fight to satisfy this 'want' is the movement of the engine through the play. The denouement is the satisfaction or deprivation of this desire which must be in the nature of dramatic and artistic justice.

Early goal-oriented protagonists tended to have rather simple, direct desires — marriage, paying off gambling debts, and so on. In *A Race With Time* (1913, Kalem) a railroad president and his son need to deliver a pouch of mail by a certain time in order to win a contract. Since they desire the contract, they proceed, hindered by the traps set for them by a rival line.

Goal orientation was common in early adaptations and historically based narratives. This suggests that the idea came from existing literary models, and Chapter 2 has shown that the late nineteenth-century dramatic theory of Brunetière had formulated goal orientation for characters. The protagonists of *Cinderella* (1911, Thanhouser), *Dr. Jekyll and Mr. Hyde* (1912, Thanhouser and 1913, Imp), *Damon and Pythias* (Otis Turner, 1914, Universal feature), and *The Coming of Columbus* (Colin Campbell, 1912, Selig feature) have obvious goals, all suggested by the source material.

Soon protagonists with strong desires were central to many films. The young doctor in *The Case of Becky* (Reicher, 1915, Lasky) falls in love with his patient, giving him the insight and daring to cure her split personality when others had failed. In *The Social Secretary* (John Emerson, script Anita Loos, 1916, Triangle-Fine Arts), the heroine sets out initially to get a secure job, then to prove that her employer's daughter's fiancé is a scoundrel. To some degree, certain star personalities helped to popularize the goal-oriented protagonist. Charles Ray, Douglas Fairbanks, and their imitators tended to play young men with clear-cut aspirations. In his comedies — especially those written by Anita Loos — Fairbanks typically played a character with an obsession of some sort. In *The Matrimaniac* (Paul Powell, 1916, Triangle-Fine Arts), he uses a variety of modern technological devices to reach his fiancée when her father spirits her away to avoid their marriage; in *Wild and Woolly* (Emerson, 1917, Douglas Fairbanks Pictures Corp.), he wants to be a cowboy. With a less comic tone, in film after film Ray played the same earnest country boy with dreams of higher things. The beginning of *The Hired Hand* (Victor Schertzinger, 1918, Ince) characterizes the hero Ezry quickly: he pauses while working in the field and gazes off into the distance (see fig 15.5). A title (fig 15.6) speaks of his 'vision' of 'bigger, finer things.' After the mid-teens, it becomes difficult to find a film without a protagonist striving for something.

Without obstacles, the goal could not sustain the film, and so classical narratives also set up conflicts. As one screenplay manual puts it:[16]

A story is the record of a struggle — a history of a conflict which has occurred or that might have occurred. Man's never-ending conflict with nature; the conflict of one man, as an individual animal, against another; the struggle of the individual against society as an institution; man's inner conflict of the 'good nature' against the 'bad nature' — of conscience against evil inclination — these and other general classifications embodying innumerable variations, contain the history of Life itself.

Yet character conflict was typically favored, since it gave priority to goal orientation. In *The Hired Hand*, for example, the hero's goal is to attend the state agricultural school; early in the film he finishes earning the $500 he needs for his freshman year. He also falls in love with the farm-owner's daughter. But her brother Walter, a wastrel bank employee, pressures Ezry into loaning him the money to replace a sum he has embezzled. This leads, as an inter-title puts it, to 'The broken bridge of dreams,' and Ezry goes back to working as a hired hand on the farm. Eventually, through his heroism, Ezry wins the daughter's hand, and at the end is well on the way to the career he had been striving for.

Character conflict was not a device created by the classical system. Primitive films, with their chases, comic romances, and robberies, had dealt in clashes of will. But as the transitional period went on, characters were increasingly individualized — through the names, traits, associations arising from their stars' personalities, and opposing goals. The greater complexity of character relationships that followed could sustain a multiple-reel film with a considerable variety of action.

Character and temporal relations

Each scene should be a step *forward* in the story, for there can be no such thing as going back.[17]

John Nelson, 1913

The advent of the feature film intensified the problem of temporal relations. Few films after 1908, aside from the simplest chase and trick narratives, would make plot time identical to story time, presenting an uninterrupted stretch of time across the whole. In proceeding from one high point in the causal chain to another, certain intervals would be eliminated, repeated, or re-ordered in the plot.

Similarly, temporal gaps between scenes needed distinct markers. This was relatively easy in the silent period, since inter-titles could specify the passage of time and set up the situation of the new scene. During the teens, time-covering inter-titles became something of a cliché, as we shall see. The narratives of early features often covered great spans of time; some compressed their action as much as a two-reeler would, rather than spreading it out and spending more time on individual scenes. As a result, the films added more story material, covering many years rather than days or weeks. Some features of the mid-teens would have gaps of years' duration at several points. But the increasing tendency was toward narratives covering briefer time-spans and containing lengthier scenes with more character development.

By attaching causality — and hence the spectator's attention to the flow of events — to the characters, the classical film gained a method for insuring a clear temporal progression. For example, character memory could motivate flashbacks. And by concentrating so thoroughly upon character actions, the film could make its narration less self-conscious as well. In contrast, unexplained ellipses or overlaps in time, such as the repeated rescue scene in *Life of an American Fireman* (see p. 162), would tend to call attention to the process of narration. In the primitive, and to some extent in the transitional period, situation was paramount; hence overlaps and gaps in the characters' movements were unimportant so long as the individual incidents fitted together into a comprehensible sequence. The spectator's continued expectation of a forward progression of action would lead him or her to overlook small discontinuities.

The classical cinema began to dictate that any deviations from chronological order be clearly marked as such. The early signal for a flashback was a superimposed vignette, as in *The Unwritten Law* example above (see fig 15.3). *After One Hundred Years* (1911, Selig) uses a superimposition over the entire frame for a flashback. All the 1912 ES films with flashbacks present the past events as separate shots. In both *The Cry of the Children* (Lois Weber, Thanhouser) and *The*

Deserter (Thomas H. Ince, Bison '101'), for example, single-shot flashbacks are bracketed by dissolves; in each, there is a character present who may be recalling the earlier scene – the subjective cues are not clear. *The High Cost of Living* (1912, Solax) frames its protracted flashback as the hero's courtroom testimony, marking its beginning and end with dialogue titles. (This film has dialogue inter-titles throughout the flashback, forming a sort of 'voiceover narration.')

After 1912, visions continue to be shown mostly as vignettes, but flashbacks and dreams are separate shots. Both fades and dissolves function interchangeably to introduce and end flashbacks; sometimes both will appear within the same film for this purpose. *The Regeneration* (Walsh, 1915, Fox), for example, has two flashbacks, a brief one set off by dissolves, a longer one by fades. In any case, however, flashbacks figure in the classical cinema as distinct interruptions of the chronological flow; motivation by character memory, as in *The Regeneration*, minimizes flashbacks' disruptive effects.

Chapter 4 has shown that deadlines are an important way of limiting and structuring the temporal span of a narrative, as well as of creating suspense; characters are almost invariably the source of deadlines. The deadline seems to have come into occasional use from the beginning of the transition to the classical mode. In *The Dynamiters* (a 1911 Imp split-reel), a drunken man joins an anarchist group and is given a time bomb to plant, set to go off at noon. When he sobers up, he races around trying to get rid of the bomb, finally leaving it in the anarchists' own hideout. Inter-titles punctuate the action, informing us that it is '20 minutes to 12,' '10 minutes to 12,' '5 minutes to 12,' and '12 o'clock.' A one-reel drama of the same year, *A Daughter of Dixie* (1911, Champion), handles a deadline situation somewhat more subtly. During the Civil War, a southern woman's Yankee boyfriend is caught by Confederates. The heroine holds the soldiers at bay with a rifle and promises her lover to delay them until four o'clock while he escapes. There follows an intercut scene, with shots of the fleeing soldier alternating with views of the heroine and soldiers watching a clock approaching four (see fig 15.7). The intercutting considerably compresses the passage of time, and

the unknown director suggests the omitted intervals by rearranging the group's positioning in the room at each return (see fig 15.8). Finally, as the clock reaches four, the Confederate soldiers point suddenly to it, and the heroine lets them leave (see fig 15.9). *Cinderella* (1911, Thanhouser) has a built-in deadline structure, carried through in this case with cutaways to a clock tower.

In the early teens, the occasional deadlines that appear are used to motivate an entire film. *A Race With Time* (1913, Kalem) sets up its deadline thoroughly, then works clocks into the setting of the scenes in a more casual way. A railroad owner receives a telegram: 'Test for mail contract to be held Dec. 17, 1912. Pouch must be in Stevenson at two o'clock or you forfeit in favor of Union Central.' When Union Central tries to sabotage the run by knocking out the engineer, the girlfriend of the owner's son leaps into the engine and takes it to Stevenson. Crosscutting builds suspense, as we see the officials and the son at Stevenson awaiting the train's arrival. The intercutting begins as follows:

1 Title: 'Stevenson'
2 LS: Group of men on platform, all with watches (fig 15.10).
3 MS: Man with stopwatch and pistol to signal end of race (fig 15.11).
4 LS: The moving train (fig 15.12).
5 MCU: Inside the cab, the heroine looking at the clock, which reads three minutes to two (fig 15.13).
6 MS: She stokes the fire.

And so on, alternating these elements, with the train clock later showing nearly two o'clock; a title announces 'On time,' just before the train pulls into the station.

By the time the principles of the classical cinema become fully established in the late teens, deadlines are an occasional local device within the longer structure of the feature. In *His Mother's Boy* (Schertzinger, 1917, Ince), the deadline is established only in the twelfth of thirteen scenes, when the villain, Banty, tells the hero, Matthew, to leave town by seven the next morning or face him in a shoot-out. Matthew has been characterized as a mama's boy, and he agonizes over whether to flee or get a gun. His fiancée, deploring his apparent cowardice, returns his engagement ring and the scene ends. The next, final scene irises in on a close-up of a clock, reading 6:44, and the scene continues in a boarding-house dining-room. Soon, the drunken Banty comes in, announcing that Matthew has ten minutes left. Matthew is finally driven to fight Banty, and after he wins, the heroine puts on his engagement ring; two lines – the cowardice problem and the romance – are resolved at once, and the film ends.

By the mid-twenties, the deadline was standard enough to be parodied. *Exit Smiling* (Sam Taylor, 1926, MGM) centers around a theater troupe performing a cliché-ridden melodrama in which the play's heroine must disguise herself as a vamp, seduce the villain, and keep him with her. As the play ends (in the second scene of the film) the heroine declares: 'Ten o'clock! My lover is saved!' Later on the film's heroine, Violet, imitates the play and uses the same trick to save the man she loves, with comic consequences, as her vamping turns into a tussle to prevent the villain from leaving before midnight. As the deadline passes, Violet poses dramatically, says, 'Twelve o'clock! My lover is saved!' and pulls a set of curtains in a doorway to imitate the stage finale. The gesture fails as the curtain rod falls on her head. This film not only makes fun of the deadline device, but acknowledges its origins in nineteenth-century popular theater.

Narration: the functions of inter-titles

The shift in the early teens toward a more psychologically based narrative also affected the types and uses of inter-titles. The two basic types of inter-titles were expository and dialogue. An expository title would either describe the upcoming action – a 'summary' title – or would simply establish the situation and allow the action within the images to present causes and effects. Moving away from the primitive period's considerable dependence upon summary titles, filmmakers gradually began to employ a higher proportion of establishing expository titles and dialogue titles. The dialogue title was one of the many devices which made narration less self-conscious and less overtly suppressive in the classical period; it helped characters take over more of the functions that expository inter-titles had performed.

The earliest films had no inter-titles. Their action was so simple that the main title could establish the basic idea clearly enough to sustain the entire film. Films with titles like *The Dude and the Burglars* (1903, AM&B), *Hold-up in a Country Grocery Store* (1904, Edison), and *A Policeman's Love Affair* (1904, Lubin) need no further explanation. But even at this point, some titles indicate the need for more expository matter. The officially copyrighted title of a Lubin 1905 chase comedy, *A Dog Lost, Strayed or Stolen $25.00 Reward Apply Mrs. Brown, 711 Park Ave.* must be one of the longest in American film history. In effect, it serves as a summary inter-title to set up the action of the first few shots, as we see the dog stolen, Mrs Brown placing a want ad, and the resulting crowds of people bringing dogs to her home. Other films of this period copyrighted each shot separately, and the titles that preceded each could serve as expository inter-titles.[18]* For example, *Parsifal* (Porter, 1904, Edison) has eight shots, with titles such as 'Interior of the Temple' and 'Return of Parsifal.'

But most films were copyrighted as a whole, and in these the summary inter-title eventually became standard. Kemp Niver, who has surveyed the entire collection of films preserved as paper prints, concludes that *Uncle Tom's Cabin* (Porter, 1903, Edison) is the earliest such film to have titles between shots.[19] In *Uncle Tom's Cabin* the title, 'Tom Refuses to flog Emal'ine,' is followed by a lengthy tableau shot of this action. By about 1910, the text of summary titles had expanded. In *Her Mother's Fiancé* (1911, Yankee), one title states: 'Home from School. The Widow's daughter comes home unexpectedly and surprises her mother.' By this point, however, these titles are not appearing between every shot, but often set up the action for a series of shots. Griffith's film *Fate's Turning* (1911, Biograph) has brief summaries ('Smitten by the waitress he neglects his fiancée'), but has only nine titles to thirty-four other shots. Summary titles of this sort are an extremely overt and redundant form of narration. They often present the spectator with an explicit hypothesis for upcoming action, rather than guiding him or her to form hypotheses on the basis of the actions themselves.

During the early transitional period, inter-titles came to have other functions than setting up action to come. Most importantly, they could cover temporal gaps between scenes, indicating a specific length for the lapse. In 1911 and early 1912, two scenario columns gave similar advice, using the current terms 'leader' and 'sub-title' to refer to the inter-title:

> Leader is also used to 'break' scenes where required. It may happen that two scenes are to be played in the same setting with an interval between. Without the leader the two scenes would follow with nothing to show the lapse of time. The action would appear continuous and the characters would either leave the stage to reappear immediately or another set of characters would fairly jump into the scene. A leader stating that it is 'the Next Day. The Quarrel is Renewed.' serves as a drop curtain to separate the scenes.[20]

> It may be employed to indicate the lapse of time, as 'Two Years Later.' It may be used to define the relationship between two characters, as 'The Jealous Husband.'
> But it is not the legitimate function of the sub-title to tell the whole story in anticipation of the characters' movements. Write no such leaders as 'Helen, detecting and understanding her lover's falseness, resolves to teach him a lesson by breaking their engagement.'[21]

The first passage recommends using the inter-title to avoid an elementary continuity error later to be known as the 'jump cut' (and indeed the author describes the problem using the word 'jump'). Jump cuts of the kind described occurred occasionally in primitive films, but they disappear once the transitional period begins about 1909. The second passage deplores lengthy summaries that give away action to be shown visually; in effect, the author advises against the use of overt narration, preferring to let the characters present information directly. Such advice was necessary; early teens films frequently use complicated titles of the type quoted.

But while expository titles came into narrative cinema quite early, dialogue titles were extremely rare in the primitive cinema. *The Ex-Convict* (Porter, 1904, Edison) uses one (without the quotation marks which would become standard as indicators of characters' speech). There are undoubtedly other such films. Dialogue titles do not appear consistently until around 1910, and from this point the functions previously performed only by summary expository titles become divided between expository and dialogue titles.

In a silent film, character dialogue can be cued by any of three factors: placement of the dialogue title, lip movements of the characters, and quotation marks in the title. While the early transitional years experimented with various alternatives, by 1915 usage had hardened into a redundant schema. Some early instances insert the dialogue titles where they are spoken (always returning to the same framing). In *The Unexpected Guest* (1909, Lubin), for instance, we see a woman in long shot pacing after reading a letter which reveals that her fiancé has fathered an illegitimate child. She does not move her lips and the title that follows lacks quotation marks ('I must know the truth'). Griffith's *Faithful* (1910, Biograph) also inserts a title at the moment of speech and lacks lip movements, but uses quotation marks. Other films from 1910 use quotation marks *and* lip movement, with the dialogue title placed at the point in the shot where it is spoken: *Brother Man* (Vitagraph) and *The Gambler's Charm* (Lubin).

By 1915, filmmakers would settle upon a standard approach to all three cues – placement, lip movement, and quotation marks. During the approximate period 1911-13, however, an alternative practice existed, in which the title, with quotation marks, could appear *before* the shot in which it was to be spoken; then, partway through the shot, a character would speak, with the lip movement and the narrative context cuing us that this is the moment when the line occurs. Here the dialogue title not only takes on the function of the summary expository title, but also occupies the same position, preceding the scene. Until 1913, both alternative placements occur about equally.[22*] Some films stick to one or the other placement throughout, while others use both.[23*]

This even mixture suggests that for a few transitional years, two different approaches were equally acceptable, but it does not necessarily imply that filmmakers were unaware of principles of title placement. Indeed, the delay in standardizing one placement arose from the fact that filmmakers saw different functional advantages in each approach. Various reviews and screenplay manuals debated function and placement of all titles, whether dialogue or expository.[24]* In a 1911 column, Epes Winthrop Sargent favored explanation given later in the scene; his reference here is to expository titles:[25]

> For one or two seconds following the return of the picture to the screen the mind of the spectator is still busy with the import of the leader, and any important action ocurring immediately following the leader is apt to be overlooked.
>
>   For this reason many directors hold the action slow for a moment following the leader, just as they refuse to let in a leader in the middle of a scene [shot]. . . . Sometimes the line is flashed before the scene opens, but this is objectionable in that it removes the element of suspense.

Another advisor on the writing of photoplays, A.R. Kennedy, gave other reasons for not breaking up a shot by titles; he wrote in 1912:[26]

> There is much to be said against throwing a leader into the middle of the scene [shot]. The spectator gets the effect of the actors' 'holding the pose' while he reads the leader. One often has a feeling of irritation at having a scene interrupted, and when the scene is resumed, it often takes an appreciable time to readjust one's mind. The continuity of the scene is broken and the illusion is spoiled.

Kennedy favored the use of titles mainly for time lapses. Specific discussions of where dialogue titles should go began at least as early as 1913, when a photoplay manual advises that 'whenever such leaders are employed, they should be made to *follow* the action and not to precede it.'[27]

In 1914, the dialogue title was increasingly placed at the point where the character spoke the line. The prevalence of one alternative may have had several causes. First, as some of the aforementioned scenario advisers imply, the anticipatory dialogue title would impair the suspense of a scene. Secondly, a cut from a speaking character to the written dialogue would make it easier to discern who was speaking and when the line occurred; this furthers the psychological individualization of characters. Thirdly, such a cut

would make the character's lip movement motivate the title, which would in turn create a less self-conscious narration. Fourthly, by placing the title at the moment when it was spoken, the film could preserve the temporal flow of the actions uninterrupted. Placement before the shot would present a story event (the line of dialogue) out of order (before its actual delivery within the shot), and this unmotivated rearrangement of chronology would prove unacceptable under the classical system. There were probably other reasons as well. The dialogue title is an interesting example of the classical cinema's having two possible devices which could become standard and weeding out the one which fits less well into its overall system of relations among causality, time, and space.

The eventual elimination of the dialogue title at the beginning of a scene follows a general movement toward suppressing excessive summarizing of action. 'The Reviewer' wrote in a 1912 *New York Dramatic Mirror*:[28]

> The insertion, therefore, of titles explaining something is about to be done and then following with a scene in which the characters do the action indicated, is not only ridiculous to the average spectator, but a procedure which spoils the dramatic sense and strength of the plot, since it ultimately destroys suspense and possibly the making of a dramatic climax.

Through the early teens, paralleling the rise of the dialogue title, the expository title tends to become less a summary of action. Instead, it introduces characters, gives an indication of the situation, and tells how much time has elapsed between scenes. The classical expository title does not preview action, but provides the concentrated, preliminary exposition described in Chapter 3. For example, *The Fatal Opal* (1914, Kalem two-reeler) sets up the initial situation with an expository title: 'Frank, Judge Morton's nephew, is in love with Alice Grey, an actress.' This laconic attempt to introduce as many facts as possible reflects the effort to begin the film's forward action *in medias res*. Titles in this film avoid summarizing, resembling instead chapter headings in fiction: 'The crowning insult' or 'An opportunity for revenge.' Even longer titles try to avoid giving away the events to follow: 'Not wishing to further antagonize his uncle, Frank says nothing of his marriage.' Here the title suggests Frank's thoughts and points out what is *not* done (something difficult to convey visually) in the following shot, in which Frank enters a room where his uncle is reading. From this, however, the film cuts directly to an escape scene at a nearby prison, avoiding altogether an expository title, since we can infer the situation from information given in earlier scenes. Finally, *The Fatal Opal* contains time-lapse titles like 'The following morning.' This sort of title had become a cliché by the mid-teens.

The title beginning 'Not wishing to further antagonize his uncle . . .' suggests the increasing use of expository titles to aid the presentation of psychological material, rather than simply to summarize action. In 1914 a scenario guide commented: 'Captions are not labels, but means of suggesting beyond the visible action and of furnishing deeper motives than those on the surface.'[29] Thus from about 1913 on, writings on film construction increasingly emphasized the reduction of the expository title to only those bits of information which could not be conveyed visually. Standard limits began to come into play. *Photoplay* critiqued a sample scenario in 1913: 'We have 53 words on the screen already, and 50 is about the limit for one reel.'[30]

Indeed, during the period from 1913 to 1916, there was a widespread belief that the film with no inter-titles was the ideal. Scriptwriters seemed to assume that every title in a film betrayed a weak point where its author had failed to convey the situation properly through images. In 1913, Famous Players' president Adolph Zukor was reported to be working toward eliminating titles from his company's films: ' "We are trying to let the story tell itself so far as possible," said he; "to do this we are introducing more scenes and connecting links." '[31] There were indeed some films that contained no titles, such as *Broncho Billy and the Greaser* (G.W. Anderson, 1913, Essanay).

But while a one-reel Western might be simple enough to follow unaided, filmmakers began to be convinced that the feature film necessitated at least occasional inter-titles. From 1916, when the feature film was standardized, the desire for title-less films yielded to an approach that emphasized cleverly written inter-titles. Anita Loos helped

popularize the idea that inter-titles could actively contribute to the film. Having written scenarios for Griffith shorts, she did only the inter-titles for *Intolerance* (1916). In that film, little jokes, elaborate descriptions, and asides to the audience make the narration more overt – as when the Boy is 'intolerated' away into prison or in the famous 'When women cease to attract men they often turn to reform as a second choice.' Loos went on to write many of the witty scripts and titles of Douglas Fairbanks's comedies. In such films, the inter-titles come to represent a narrating voice which goes beyond the neutral stating of facts. Loos utilized the possibility that certain genres – especially comedy – could motivate highly self-conscious narration. One transitional title between sequences in *Reaching for the Moon* (John Emerson, scripted by Emerson and Loos, 1917, Douglas Fairbanks Pictures Corp.) states simply 'But things are always darkest before the dawn.' This title adds no tangible information, but guides the viewer to expect both climax and resolution. Another Fairbanks film of the same year, *Wild and Woolly*, seems to come to an end as the hero gets on a train for the East, leaving the woman he loves standing tearfully on the platform. A title breaks in: 'But wait a minute, this will never do. We can't end a Western romance without a wedding. Yet – after they're married where shall they live? For Nell likes the East, And Jeff likes the West. So where are the twain to meet?' This leads into a brief epilogue where we see the couple leave an eastern-style house, stepping out into a western landscape. The specific appeal to genre – 'a Western romance' – combines with the film's comic tone to justify a playful narration that bares the device of the happy ending.

Loos-style inter-titles quickly became the fashion. They were, in a sense, the incorporation into the film of a narration, such as that in Dickens and Thackeray, which could flaunt its omniscience. *Hoodoo Ann* (Lloyd Ingraham, 1916, Triangle-Fine Arts) inserts this into the middle of one scene: 'A casual and mysterious stranger, whom we advise you to remember.' In *The Ghost of Rosie Taylor* (Edward Sloman, 1918, American), a title intervenes at one point to flash the action back to the point in time when 'The story, as it really happened, begins.' The tendency to use cleverly written titles is especially apparent in the comedy features of Buster Keaton and Harold Lloyd; there almost every expository title that begins a scene also makes a verbal joke of its own.

Still, the narrational intrusion through titles usually comes at codified moments – such as the openings of sequences, for a preliminary, concentrated exposition. Inter-titles making poetic generalizations often act as brief preludes in features of the late teens and the twenties. *Hoodoo Ann* prefaces its narrative with this statement: 'The greatest heart throbs of life are not always quickened into being by violence, sensation or thrills. Laughter, bitter tears and even tragedy frequent the humblest paths and create drama in the most obscure and peaceful corners of the earth.' The opening of a Mary Pickford feature, *Suds* (Jack Dillon, 1920, Mary Pickford Co.), sets up comedy with a plethora of inter-titles:

1 Title: Oh, this is no tale of gay romance,
          Of storm-swept shores, adventure-girt,
          Of bold, heroic circumstance,
          Of daring deeds, of luck, of chance,
          Of purple pain, of hectic hurt –
2 Title: No! no!
          NO! *NO!*
3 Title: No hero here with passion pants –
          This is *the tale* of a *shirt!*
4 MS.   Pixillation: Shirt in laundry wrap
          stands up and bows.
5 Title: What ho!
          Let's go!

This prologue in turn leads to two additional, more neutral inter-titles that establish the London locale of the action. Lois Weber begins her film *The Blot* (1921, Lois Weber Productions) more succinctly: 'Men are only boys grown tall.'

The Loos-style title, what we might term the 'literary' inter-title, became the norm for both comedies and dramas by the twenties (when it was commonly poked fun at as the 'rosy-fingered dawn' style of title writing). Although this style made the narration of the inter-titles more overt, it also provided an advantage that overrode that small problem. Apart from simply conveying information, such titles seemed to contribute something extra to the film; they were more than tacked-on labels. This appearance of double

functioning helped motivate inter-titles. Filmmakers no longer aimed at title-less films. When Charles Ray made one in 1921, *The Old Swimmin' Hole* (Joseph De Grasse, Charles Ray Productions), it was met with indifference by reviewers and public.

Another means of motivating expository titles was adopted in 1916. Rather than printing the white letters on plain black or bordered cards, filmmakers painted scenes over part or all of the background, thus creating the 'art title' card (see figs 3.2 and 15.6). Triangle was one of the earliest companies to use this device; in keeping with the central producer system's methodical breakdown of labor, the company had a department for painting the cards (fig 15.14; the same department supplied the paintings that hung on the walls of sets). A 1916 review of *The Aryan* (William S. Hart, 1916, Triangle) remarked that: 'The subtitles of Triangle productions have been worth attention for some time. At first they were pleasingly decorative; later they aided in interpreting the mood of the play. The text of the subtitles not only advanced the story, but when conversation was used, helped the characterization; and the skillful word pictures aided and completed the scene.'[32]

Art titles added considerable flexibility to the written texts. With a painting of a building or locale as if in 'long-shot' distance, the title could serve to establish the space of the scene to come. This might even mean that a set would not have to be built; the next shot could more directly to an interior. Victor Fleming's *When the Clouds Roll By* (1919, Douglas Fairbanks Pictures Corp.) shows few long shots of buildings or exteriors, but conveys a sense of various parts of New York City through art titles. One title shows the Washington Square arch, then cuts to a shot of Fairbanks walking along a path that could be in almost any park; similarly, a painting of a Greenwich Village street leads directly to interior shots of the heroine's studio apartment.

The art title could also contain a symbolic, sometimes non-diegetic object to convey an idea. Spiders, cupids, flowers, and all manner of clichéd imagery adorn the titles of silent films in the late teens and twenties. A 1916 commentator recognized the new function of the inter-title: 'It has grown even in its logical and consistent place, from a simple explanatory note, to a cleverly fitting link in the given chain of events, presented with a decorative background that conveys the force of the immediate situation in unmistakable symbols.'[33] The art card in effect made the inter-title into an extra shot, providing visual material as well as verbal. This additional material either supplemented or reinforced the information coming from the words and surrounding shots. Both art cards and 'literary' texts made inter-titles seem less disruptive to the narrative's flow. They also helped the narration go beyond the simple neutral summaries of the primitive period.

But during these same years (1914-17), film-makers realized the advantages of motivating inter-title texts as lines spoken by the characters. One advisor critiqued a sample scenario in 1916, concluding: 'Note the strength gained by inserting the subtitle in the action and having it a speech by one of the characters.'[34] In general, filmmakers worked to replace expository inter-titles with dialogue wherever possible. A Lubin serial of 1915, *Road o' Strife*, reportedly had only one expository title in its fifteen episodes – reading 'A Week Later.' Its director, Emmett Campbell Hill, described how he tried to blend in the dialogue titles to minimize any interruption of the action: 'Some dissolve in and out, others appear abruptly and slowly fade, still others merely flash on and instantly disappear, as a sharp, explosive "No!" seems to do. We have undertaken to visually approximate sound effects.'[35] The use of type size and other means to simulate sonic qualities was not uncommon, by the way; many silent films have small letters to suggest whispers and large ones for shouts. In *'Beau' Revel* (John Griffith Way, 1921, Thomas H. Ince), words with their letters out of line suggest a drunken man's speech. With or without such effects, dialogue titles were motivated as coming from a source within the scene, and hence were preferable to expository titles. Partly because of this, filmmakers seldom used art cards for dialogue titles.

Certainly by the late teens, dialogue titles outnumbered expository titles. Typically, expository titles come between scenes to set up new situations, but most titles within scenes tend to present dialogue. Fleming's *When the Clouds Roll By* (1919, Douglas Fairbanks Pictures Corp.) has seventeen scenes, four of which have no expository titles at all, and seven of which have

only one or two. In all, of the 216 inter-titles in the film (not counting credits and end titles), only thirty-three are expository. In James Cruze's *Hawthorne of the USA* (1919, Artcraft), every scene has at least one expository title, but 80 per cent of all the titles are dialogue.

In the mid-twenties, many films limit expository titles severely. Almost every film would use at least a couple at the beginning to introduce characters and situations. But frequently later scenes would contain one or no expository titles.[36]* By the middle and late twenties, the predominance of dialogue titles combines with the general handling of scenes to create films which were prepared for the introduction of sound. (Sound was far from a surprise to filmmakers and writers. Throughout the teens and twenties, the almost universal assumption was that sound, color, stereoscopy, and widescreen processes would eventually be adopted.) Dialogue titles also insured that most of the spectator's understanding of the narrative came directly from the characters themselves – from their words and gestures – rather than from an intervening narration's presentation.

A similar effect of placing verbal narration within the story space resulted from a related device – the insert. Inserts were not, strictly speaking, inter-titles; they were any written material in the space of the action which was shown in a separate shot – 'inserted' – within the main long view of the action. Letters, photographs, and newspaper headlines were commonly used for inserts. Inserts appeared occasionally in primitive-period films, but began to occur with greater frequency in the transitional period. Of the ES films from 1909 to 1916, 62 per cent have inserts. Many one-reelers begin with a person receiving a letter, which we then see in close-up in the second shot. Letters were a convenient way of beginning *in medias res*: 'Inserts should never be used in front of the first scene.'[37] After a short initial view of the main character and situation, the writing rapidly fills in past events and sets up causes for action to come.

Letters made versatile inserts, since they allowed the characters to give a variety of information about personal traits and travels, and to set up appointments. But newspapers proved useful as well, in conveying more general and public events. As Part One pointed out, the newspaper became a universal device in Hollywood, motivating written texts realistically and compositionally as coming from the world of the story. This advantage was realized by Sargent in 1911: 'A deal of information may be conveyed in a headline and the spectator seems to read the item over the character's shoulder rather than to have been interrupted by a leader.'[38] Numerous other scenario guides of the next few years recommended the use of headlines or short clippings for conveying information.[39] Other written texts could serve similar functions. In *Stella Dallas* (Henry King, 1926, Samuel Goldwyn), passages from a diary repeatedly appear in places where an expository inter-title might ordinarily be used. As with the dialogue inter-title, the insert seemed to come from within the story, helping make written narration less overt.

The 'American' style of acting

Few aspects of silent films seem so alien to the modern viewer as the performances of their actors. Yet all 'silent acting' was not the same. A more discriminating look reveals striking differences. Consider, for example, two films released almost exactly two years apart.

Figures 15.15 through 15.17 are frames from *The High Cost of Living* (October, 1912, Solax); the second example, figures 15.18 through 15.22, comes from *The Warning* (September, 1914, Majestic). The earlier film illustrates the pantomime style of silent acting. In this shot, the younger workers want to strike, and they invite the hero, Old Joel, out for a drink to talk over the situation. The man at the right gestures 'drinking' to him (see fig 15.15). Joel points to his own body, then to his grey hair (fig 15.16), as if to say, 'I'm too old for such things.' The other man then holds up a single finger and smiles persuasively ('Just one?'); then Joel also holds up a finger (fig 15.17), smiles, and agrees to go. No inter-title explains this bit of action.

The Warning is a one-reeler directed by Donald Crisp and starring Dorothy Gish. In a medium-long shot of a small apartment, the heroine receives a note from her lover telling her he has left her. In despair, she sits, and there follows a cut-in to a medium shot (fig 15.18). She sits staring numbly for a moment, then glances up at the gas lamp fixture at the upper left (fig 15.19). Her eyes widen as she realizes that she could commit suicide (fig 15.20). She reaches over and turns on the gas (fig 15.21), gets up, and exits right. Off-screen, she sits in another chair, with her face reflected in the mirror at the center rear (fig 15.22). Played in the long-shot framing of *The High Cost of Living*, Gish's performance would hardly be discernible.

The difference in acting styles and framing distance in these two films is considerable. Between approximately 1909 and 1913, acting styles in the American cinema underwent a distinct change: an exaggerated pantomime gave way to a system of emphasizing restrained gestures and facial expression. *The High Cost of Living* is typical of its period, yet by 1914, the year of *The Warning*, the telegraphic style usually occurs in combination with the facial style (except in slapstick comedies). This change was to a large degree responsible for the development of a broader range of camera distance, which in turn contributed to the development of continuity editing.

The codified pantomime style is readily apparent in films of the very early teens. Stock gestures that rely only minimally upon facial expression, and then only for reinforcement, are everywhere. Indeed, these films, which may seem to be somewhat confusing at first, become comprehensible once one watches for these gestures. In the three-reel *A Tale of Two Cities* (William Humphreys, 1911, Vitagraph), the second sequence introduces Dr Manette, who has been called in by the evil Marquis to examine a peasant woman whose lover has been killed. Manette comes into the room, kneels by the woman, then stands and makes several brief gestures: he points to the woman, places the tips of his fingers, with palms open, to his own forehead (see fig 15.23), moves his hands out about a foot in front of his head, flutters them, then lowers his hands in a helpless gesture while shaking his head. No dialogue title accompanies this, nor was there a summary title at the beginning of the scene. We rely entirely upon these gestures to interpret something like, 'Her reason is gone' (hand gestures) and 'There is nothing I can do' (shaking of head). One could catalogue many standard gestures in films before 1913. For example, when characters place an open hand palm down about three feet from the floor, that indicates 'child.' The child's growth can be shown by raising the hand to an appropriate point higher off the ground. In *Tangled Lives* (1911, Kalem), the hero, who had rescued the heroine years before in an Indian massacre, tells her he has fallen in love with her now that she has grown. There is again no inter-title, but he makes the 'child' gesture, raises his hand to about her height and then places it over his heart, while speaking emotionally to her. (Even here, the gestures are often smaller and more restrained than they would have been in a film five years earlier, and one must be on the lookout to catch them.)

During the transitional years of 1912 and 1913, the pantomime style was in the process of modifying into a more naturalistic approach to gestures. Still framed in long shot or *plan américain*, the actor used facial expression and non-conventionalized gestures, but with enough exaggeration that they would be visible. The increasing dependence on dialogue inter-titles aided in the formulation of this new acting style by taking over some of the informational functions of the codified gestures. The feature film would also promote it, by allowing, even encouraging, more time for character development. There may have been a small genre of character-sketch films, exemplified by *The Warning* and some of Griffith's early-teens work like *The Painted Lady* (1912, Biograph). By 1914, the new acting style had combined facial expression in closer shots with muted pantomime in the more distant framings. Technical improvements in lighting equipment, focusing devices, film stock, and make-up practice aided in the process by making it easier for the spectator to see details at a distance.

The change to closer framings and facial acting was apparently a two-step process. In the early teens, some critics noted a new style in Vitagraph productions; a French filmmaker, Victorin Jasset, described it in 1911:[40]

The Americans realized the interest that could be given to the play of the features in foreground shots and they served it, sacrificing the decor, the whole of the scene when it was necessary in order to present to the audience the figures of the characters who stay a bit more immobile.

Rapid acting horrified them, and the acting was calm, exaggeratedly calm.

James Morrison, an actor at Vitagraph, recalled the closer framings:[41]

We were the first to use the nine-foot line. When I started, they would frame the scene as in a theater, a long shot with everyone shown full length. We were the first ones to bring people up to within nine feet of the camera. The nine-foot line was a line of tape on the floor; if you came any closer, you'd go out of focus. The next innovation in the movies was when Griffith did the close-up. We thought of the nine-foot line, but we didn't think of the close-up.

The 'nine-foot line' would yield a framing with the actors cut off at the knees. This would hardly be enough to 'sacrifice the decor,' as Jasset claimed, but the effect on the figures was striking enough that the French termed this the 'American foreground' shot. The larger figures would make possible a more restrained pantomime − a first step toward the facial style of acting.

It has become a commonplace of film history to admit that D.W. Griffith did not invent the close-up, but to claim that he used it better than those who came before, thereby establishing it as a basic part of filmmaking practice. This may be the case, but the standardized close shot can be considered a by-product of a true Griffith innovation, the new acting style. With the advent of the multiple-reel film, better actors were drawn to the cinema because the firms could now afford to pay competitive salaries. Griffith drew together a repertory company of actors, in particular very young women, beginning with Pickford in 1909, and adding the Gish sisters, Dorothy Bernard, Blanche Sweet, and others. With them, he worked out a method of sustained performance centering on the face, the shot being held while a series of muted expressions come and go. Griffith himself described the process of 'learning' this method with his actors, in a 1914 interview:[42]

It is this learning step by step that brought about the 'close-up.' We were striving for real acting. When you saw only the small, full-length figures, it was necessary to have exaggerated acting, what might be called 'physical' acting, the waving of the hands and so on. The close-up enabled us to reach real acting, restraint, acting that is a duplicate of real life. But the close-up was not accepted at once.

Griffith's new method was not, of course, a duplicate of life. It was a stylized system, like the one before it; but it did involve restraint – the transmitting of feelings and thoughts through a series of facial suggestions.

The new approach to acting was widely recognized at the time and even labeled as specifically American. Exaggerated pantomime, although used in virtually all American primitive films, was considered to be of European origin. After all, European films, primarily French, Italian, and Danish, were numerous on American programs before World War I. As early as 1911, however, a reviewer found the influence beginning to run the other way; in discussing a Danish three-reeler, Great Northern's *The Temptations of a Great City*, a *Moving Picture World* reviewer commented on its lack of a 'foreign style of acting.' He compared the film's acting to 'the palmy days of the Biograph Company, when tense situations were worked up entirely with the eyes and slight movement.' The Europeans were, the review claimed, beginning to use the 'American style of acting.'[43] Many commentators of the 1911 to 1915 period speak of pantomime as the older style and of facial expression as more modern.

With the new acting style came closer framings. These were not actually close-ups; at this point, a distinction existed only between close and long shots. Any shot that cut off part of the human figure would be considered 'close.' Griffith's 'close-ups' were actually medium and medium-long shots. Films shot consistently using such framings, in addition to *The Warning* (1914), include *The Painted Lady* (1912) and *The Mothering Heart* (Griffith, 1913, Biograph).

Griffith's comments that the close shots were resisted at first are not without basis. There were a number of published attacks on framings which cut people off at the knees or waist. But such attacks did not, as historical myth would have it, accuse the shots of incomprehensibility. Instead, some contemporary critics felt that the closer framings violated traditional aesthetic principles. *The Moving Picture World* carried on a controversy over the subject. In 1911 the scenario columnist, Epes Winthrop Sargent, defended 'bust pictures' (as these close shots were sometimes called in the early teens): 'Many points may be cleared in a five-foot bust picture which would require twenty to thirty feet of leader to explain, and the bust picture always interests.'[44] But another writer of that same year attacked close shots, since the actors' figures 'assume unnecessarily large and, therefore, grotesque proportions.'[45]

Another participant in the *Moving Picture World* controversy was H.F. Hoffman, who wrote a diatribe against close shots in 1912. Here he specifically attributes these shots to the shift in acting styles and gives a description of the two styles which is worth quoting in full:[46]

Facial expression – that seems to be the dominating influence that brings about this inartistic result. The American producers, after they learned the rudiments of their craft, uncovered an entirely new school of pantomime. In the heyday of the business, when exhibitors were making fortunes out of small investments, the European picture had the call. Pantomime to the old world was an exact science. Every known gesture and expression had for years been labeled and catalogued as definitely as the rows of bottles in a chemist's shop. With the play-going public of America, the European school of pantomime at one time found favor over our crude home-made productions. Exhibitors clamored at the exchanges for foreign films. This was disheartening because it really did seem that the American product would never catch up. But at last the American producer found himself. He evolved a school of pantomime that swept away the antiquated formulas and proved to be such a revelation as to eclipse the Europeans themselves.

The difference between the two schools is broad and plain. The European school is based more upon bodily movements than upon the mobility of the face. The American school relies more upon the expression of the face and the suppression of bodily movement. It remained for the Americans to demonstrate that more dramatic emotion is the keynote of American pantomime.

Again, this shift is not a matter of a new and better style entirely replacing a crude style. During the teens, pantomime acting primarily in long shot shifted its function; with modifications, it became generically motivated in the work of silent comedians such as the Keystone company, Charles Chaplin, and Keaton.

The 'European' style was too telegraphic to remain the dominant acting method as films became longer and more psychologically based. Far from being cruder than the later style, 'European' pantomimic gestures briefly conveyed a good deal of information to the audience. One striking aspect of the early one-reelers is how much action they managed to pack into about sixteen minutes. This was in part due to those films' considerable dependence upon physical rather than psychological causality; causes were immediately obvious from the situation. The films also compressed the duration of the story events, either by using ellipses between most shots (with a one-shot-per-scene structure in many cases) or by presenting several actions simultaneously or in quick succession. But during the transitional period, filmmakers learned to sustain plots based upon fewer events, with less compression of story time, within or between scenes. At that point, a more leisurely acting style became desirable. If the camera could linger on the mobile face of a Lillian Gish or a Blanche Sweet, individual incidents, and especially psychological states, could now provide major causes and sustain whole segments of the film.

Unity and redundancy

The crystallization of these various temporal, causal, and character-oriented devices into a classical model of narrative in 1917 suggests the considerable impact that the feature film had on their development. Virtually all the traits I have discussed here appeared in short films during the transitional period. But one- and two-reelers usually built their narratives around a few key devices; a deadline, or incident, or character study could dominate the film. As features became the norm, however, individual devices were inte-

grated into the whole; they could serve a localized function, permitting other devices to come in as needed. A feature might contain elaborate character exposition at the beginning, with visions, *and* flashbacks, *and* a deadline, *and* a chase, and so on. This is not to suggest that features were simply strung-out one-reel narratives. Rather, the story's tight causal chain would create a more complex weave of events, motivating each new device in its place. While the chase in *Personal* (1904, AM&B) starts simply as the result of too many women answering an ad placed by a rich man,[47]* in *The Birth of a Nation* (1915), the ride of the Klan results from a lengthy and dense weave of events – the death of the little sister and the formation of the Klan, the southern family's proud defiance of the carpetbaggers, Stoneman's encouragement of Lynch's aspirations, and so on. Similarly, the flashback in the next-to-last scene of *Hoodoo Ann* (Lloyd Ingraham, 1916, Triangle-Fine Arts) brings to a climax two separate lines of action. The main line concerns Ann, who has been established in a series of scenes as a naive girl fond of play-acting. She fires a pistol while imitating a Western movie she has seen and thinks she has accidentally killed a man living next door. The subplot involves this man, a drunkard henpecked by his wife. He has been missing since Ann fired the shot, but he returns and describes how he ran away and hid from his wife – with his story shown as the flashback. This clears up the mystery, and the epilogue depicts Ann's wedding.

The feature film also permitted a greater amount of redundancy. A narrative might be easy to follow if the procedure for laying it out presented each event and trait clearly. But in its effort to help the spectator understand completely, the Hollywood cinema repeats information. The feature's length allowed time for developing parallelisms and motifs of behavior; it could linger over information and encouraged the shift to the new acting style.

By the 1920s, redundancy and thorough motivation were fully in place. *His People* (Sloman, 1925, Universal-Jewel) involves a Jewish couple and their two sons living in the ghetto of an American city. The father, David, favors Morris, who is a lawyer; but Morris has secretly concealed his ghetto origins from his rich Jewish boss, Judge Stein, and from his fiancée,

Stein's daughter, Ruth. David rejects his other son, Sammy, when the latter becomes a boxer, even though Sammy remains loyal to his family.

This narrative is motivated in a prologue when Sammy is seen as a boy, winning a street fight and bringing home groceries he buys with the money given to him by an onlooker. David, established as a peddler with a street stall, beats Sammy for fighting. Initial impressions formed in these scenes are crucial in determining the pattern subsequent events will take. After a ten-year interval, the film stresses the contrast between the two grown sons' actions by repeatedly juxtaposing their behavior: Morris courts Ruth, while Sammy has a romance with Mamie, the daughter of an Irish neighbor. (As with the choice of careers, Sammy transgresses family tradition by choosing a non-Jewish woman, yet he does not become a social-climber, as Morris does.) Morris asks for money to buy a dress suit, while Sammy fights for prize money to help his ailing father. The film also provides causal motivation for its effects. When Morris asks for money, David takes his own overcoat out to pawn; when David goes to his stall in the snow without his coat, he falls ill. This in turn leads Sammy to win the money so that his father can recuperate in a warmer climate. Ultimately Sammy's selflessness, in combination with the revelation of Morris's secret rejection of the family, leads David to realize the relative worth of his two sons and to reconcile with Sammy. The careful balance among elements and the thorough motivation evident in *His People* were common by the twenties.

The classical narrative, then, came to place more emphasis upon character, and to construct tightly organized causal chains. The 1917 cinema had not eliminated every disruption of time or causality throughout every film. But the basic principles had become dominant. In early 1918, actor and director Henry King summed up the changes he had observed in filmmaking:[48]

> There was a period when nearly every producer thought that action made a photoplay. Every scene and incident was full of restless movement. Then came the day of characterization, as opposed to and superceding the 'action' period, and this method has come to stay.
>
> Nearly all of the melodramas and westerns of two years ago raced through from two to four reels of film and there was little reserve force or character acting brought out. The hero was always distinctly heroic and good looking, the heroine was just that, and the supporting cast, as a rule, acted all over the shop, and if you will remember the general run of photoplays ran to periods, with the title 'several years later' showing up with tiresome frequency.
>
> In other words, we were satiated with swiftly moving action and did not really get acquainted with the characters of our stories. Nowadays the directors 'place' their characters so that an audience actually knows who and what they are and what sort of lives they lead, which makes what they do and how they do it understandable and real. You will also notice that many of the most entertaining stories cover comparatively short intervals of time.

Note that King even uses a specific term, to 'place,' in describing the more thorough establishment of character traits and background. All through the transitional and into the classical periods, the idea of a film's unity centered around the narrative − and, more specifically, character psychology.

16

The continuity system

If you have a diamond in the shape of a plot, give it the proper setting of continuity. Do not sink it in the tar of unmatched action.[1]

Epes Winthrop Sargent, 1915

The concept of continuity

We have seen how the move to longer multiple-shot films and later to multiple-reel films brought about a shift in narrative models. Filmmakers used the short story, drama, and novel as sources for new conceptions of causal and temporal unity. At the same time, they needed to find means of creating a unified spatial structure in which story events could take place. To a limited extent, these means could also come from the other arts: the film frame is analogous to the proscenium of a stage; the sudden leaps of time and space achieved by editing resemble the freedom of movement enjoyed by the novel's narrator.

But again, the filmic medium imposed its own unique demands. The filmmaker juxtaposes a series of disparate spaces, building from them an overall narrative space. That space is concrete, not the verbal construction of the novelist. Hence the filmmaker must be able to guide the spectator's understanding of spatial relations if the film's causal actions are to be clear. Editing, with its instantaneous changes of vantage point, presented a new aesthetic challenge, and filmmakers had to a considerable degree to thrash out their problems on their own. The resulting guidelines became the continuity system.

The formulation of the continuity editing system was not a direct development of devices from the primitive period. Classical films of the teens did not involve more complex, more correct usage of the same devices available to earlier filmmakers. Rather, fundamental changes in the systems of causality, time, and space brought about a profoundly new approach to filmmaking, and the functions of individual stylistic devices changed as well. Some techniques used infrequently in the primitive period – the cut-in, point-of-view and eyeline structures, dialogue inter-titles, and so on – became central means of constructing space and conveying narrative information in the teens. Key devices of the primitive cinema changed in their function. The lengthy tableau shots became establishing shots; expository titles which formerly anticipated action now merely established situations. The classical system is a change from the earlier one, not necessarily an improvement upon it.

With the growing emphasis on calculating how a film could be understood came new normative systems within the production sector. The growth of a trade press after 1907 (brought about by the nickelodeon boom and regularization of production) contributed to making these norms uniform across the industry. Almost from the beginning trade papers and instruction books emphasized a specific conception of what constitutes a good film. In one of the earlier scenario books, Herbert Case Hoagland, of Pathé Frères, gave this advice to writers:[2]

> *Let one scene* [shot] *lead into the next scene wherever possible.* Motion picture theater goers don't yearn for mental gymnastics and shouldn't be kept guessing as to who the characters are or why they are in the story at all. . . . Keep your scenes in a sequence easily followed by the onlooker.

Increasingly, the conception of quality in films came to be bound up with the term 'continuity.' 'Continuity' stood for the smoothly flowing narrative, with its technique constantly in the service of the causal chain, yet always effacing itself. Later, 'continuity' came specifically to refer to a set of guidelines for cutting shots together, but the original implications of the term lingered on. The 'continuity system' still connotes a set of goals and principles which underlie the entire classical filmmaking system.

One of the best descriptions of continuity was written before the term was being applied commonly to film. In 1910, a commentator in *The Nickelodeon* outlined what constituted great films:[3]

Their greatness has been established through the medium of a strong story, interpreted by artistic players and illuminated by splendid photography. Invariably the stories have been easily defined and followed and every gesture correctly interpreted. The director who knows his dramatic technique, that subtle, indiscernible thread or mesh, binding and blending scenes [shots] and parts into a harmonious whole is, perhaps, the greatest influence in making the story thoroughly convincing; thrilling us when we should be thrilled, making us laugh or cry at the appointed times, and leaving us, at the end of the film, in a beatific frame of mind, without a doubt to be cleared, without the jar of a false gesture.

The basic principles of Hollywood film practice are here already: the story as the basis of the film, the technique as an 'indiscernible thread,' the audience as controlled and comprehending, and complete closure as the end of all. Moreover, these ideas soon came to be accepted as a set of truisms. This remark might have appeared in virtually the same terms at any point in Hollywood's history since 1910.

This is not to say that the continuity system was conceived of by 1910. Most of its principles were set forth and tested in the years up to 1917. But given this set of goals for narrative film-making, each new technique or device could easily take its place within an overriding formal system.

The term 'continuity' itself soon came into common usage. Initially it occurred in the scenario columns and books. Filmmakers assumed that if a scenario were correctly constructed, shot by shot, they could simply follow it literally in

production, and their film would automatically have a continuously coherent narrative. So, until the late teens, references to 'continuity' are usually addressed to scenario writers and refer to a flow of story across changing shots. Compare these bits of advice:[4]

[From a 1912 *Photoplay* scenario column:] Continuity of events is a feature of the best pictures ever made. Avoid these 'twenty-year after' stories.

[A 1913 definition of 'continuity of action':] While unity of action is one of the fundamentals of a model dramatic action, this unity must be *visibly continuous* to render it distinctly and easily perceptible.

[A 1914 scenario book:] Unbroken continuity or perfect cohesion of story unity – of which every intelligent audience is ever conscious – that knows no such things as gaps, breaks or retrogressive movement.

[And a 1917 essay on the topic in *Photoplay*:] It is the placing of the many scenes that go to make up the photoplay in a logical sequence, so that the play may run perfectly smoothly, without breaks or jumps which otherwise would have to be covered by wordy and explanatory subtitles.

Some of these advisors were themselves also scenario editors for the production companies; their guidelines would help determine the kinds of material accepted for filming. In late 1913, Epes Winthrop Sargent's column in *The Moving Picture World* informed freelance writers that Phil Lang, at Kalem, wanted 'continuity' in the scripts submitted to him; these should have no 'jumps,' where the character in one shot appeared in the next one in a new locale.[5] By about 1915, trade journals like *Motography* began publishing 'how I did it' articles signed by filmmakers. In one of that year, William Desmond Taylor modestly characterized his direction of a serial, *The Diamond From the Sky*, saying that 'Its continuity is as near perfection as it is possible to obtain.'[6] In 1917, Ince described how films from his studios were always viewed many times, 'with the one idea of avoiding inconsistencies in continuity and technique.'[7]

'Continuity' quickly developed from a general notion of narrative unity to the more specific conception of a story told in visual terms and continuing unbroken, spatially and temporally, from shot to shot. This led to the word's being applied to the shooting script itself. As Chapter 12 has described, the continuity was a numbered list of shots used as a means of planning the entire production. Thus the shot became not a material unit but a narrative one (as evidenced by the almost universal use of the word 'scene' for a 'shot'). The implication here is that filmmakers took the narrative of a film to equal the sum total of all its shots. This procedure of decoupage precludes any notion of using segments of time and space for their own sake, of elevating them above the narrative at any point. A scenarist at Hoffman-Foursquare Pictures described good continuity scripting in 1917: 'No scene [shot] which does not advance the action can be allowed to have a place in the script. Every scene must be in its proper place.'[8] Most of the rules or guidelines that were gradually formulated during the teens had as their common purpose the subordination of devices to a dominant narrative. Not just shots, but everything, had to serve its narrative function. In 1914, Phillips wrote: 'We employ nothing – property, actor, scene [shots], spectacle, spoken word, insert, incident or device – in the perfect photoplay that has not a bearing on the climax of the play.'[9] In this chapter, we will see how editing rules were introduced during the teens and assimilated into the dominant filmmaking system.

Establishing shots

The long framing was the earliest device for creating and maintaining a clear narrative space. When other spatial devices were introduced – cut-ins, multiple spaces – the long shot ceased to present virtually all the action. Instead, it acquired a more specific function, that of establishing space. (The long shot can also have other functions, such as displaying spectacular mise-en-scene or suggesting a character's isolation in a vast space, but these usually occur in addition to the basic establishing function.) Multiple spaces involve cutting together shots that show entirely different locales, whether at a distance from each other or contiguous; analytical editing cuts to portions of a single space. In the classical system, the establishing shot is so important that these other devices usually are organized around it. A film can have multiple spaces without analytical editing, and vice-versa; but to maintain 'correct' continuity according to the classical system, both multiple-space cutting and analytical editing depend on establishing shots.

The earliest staged films of 1893 and several years thereafter were tiny scenes, single events hardly long enough to be narratives. Edison Kinetoscope films usually ran less than a minute; one 1893 Kinetoscope film shows a drunken man in medium-long shot, stumbling in a park; a policeman approaches and they struggle. In such films, there is automatic narrative continuity – one event entirely visible throughout.

With the increasing length of films, an extended narrative action might be played out, still within a single locale; historians have termed this one-shot scene the *tableau*. A one-shot film, *Street Car Chivalry* (1903, Edison), for example, shows a row of men sitting in a street car; they move to accommodate a pretty woman, then refuse to do the same for a homely woman until she tricks them. Here we have several events forming a brief narrative, but still played in long shot within a single space; without cuts, shifts in space and time do not occur, and hence continuity is not yet a factor.

But occasional films in the years 1897 to 1903 introduced multiple spaces. In most cases, such films string a series of tableaux together, with each scene acted out completely within the space of the image and without any movement of the action into a contiguous space. In some cases, each is preceded by an inter-title, as in the most famous example of this type, Porter's *Uncle Tom's Cabin* (Edwin S. Porter, 1903, Edison). There was no clear-cut progression from one technique to another during the primitive period. Single-shot films (*Street Car Chivalry*) and series of tableaux (*Uncle Tom's Cabin*) continued to exist side by side, lingering into the phase of films involving multiple spaces and cut-ins.[10]

Later, in the teens, when scenes were regularly cut up into multiple shots, the single long shot showing initial spatial relations became one portion of the scene, usually coming at the beginning. Its function then became specifically to establish a whole space which was then cut into segments or juxtaposed with long shots of other spaces. Early cut-ins to closer framings were rare and always came after longer views of the same space and before a return to the same long view – a re-establishing shot. There was thus little need for filmmakers to specify the placement and function of the establishing shot.

But in the mid-teens, close-ups were becoming standard: only a third of the ES films from 1912 had cut-ins, and only one had two of them; of the 1913 films, slightly over half had cut-ins (several with two or three, and a couple with cut-ins involving a distinct change of angle); by 1914, every ES film had at least one cut-in.

Now that filmmakers were regularly dealing with more than one shot per scene, they formulated guidelines specifying the placement of the establishing shot, cut-in, and re-establishing shot. Sargent commented in 1914 on the increasing use of close-ups: 'Lately we saw a subject in which a setting room was used. At various times three portions of this room were used for close-up pictures, instead of always using the full set.' Sargent approved the close view, but cautioned that 'it should be used sparingly, where the close-up is but a part of a scene, the opening and closing of which uses the full stage.'[11] This advice suggests that filmmakers in the early teens still thought of the long shot as the basis of the scene, with the cut-in an occasional, effective variant.

But in the second half of the teens, Hollywood's discourse sometimes assigned a more limited, specific function to the long view. Now it became a part of an overall scene consisting of many shots, and it served to establish spatial relationships. A 1918 trade-paper review of Lois Weber's *For Husbands Only* recommends 'a long shot placing the locations of the various situations during the time Miss Harris overhears the conversation between Cody and Miss Kirkwood.'[12] In the four years between Sargent's statement and this review, the conception of cutting had changed considerably. Earlier, a scene consisted of long shots, book-ending one or more close shots. After 1917, filmmakers would build scenes up from a variety of different angles, with the long shot often no more important than any other. Around 1920, Hollywood usage dubbed the long shot's function as that of 'establishing' characters'

relations in space.[13]*

By the mid-teens filmmakers had so normalized the establishing shot's function that they could systematically vary its placement within the scene. A film might begin its first scene on a close shot of a character's face, then later show an establishing view. Often an inter-title precedes the close shot, describing the character we are about to see for the first time. The first shot of *The Fatal Opal* (George Melford, 1914, Kalem) frames a man in medium shot, then cuts back to a long shot of him in a courtroom, revealing the man to be a judge. Some films insert a brief series of analytical close shots before establishing the whole space. In the opening of *The Case of Becky* (Frank Reicher, 1915, Lasky) we see the villainous hypnotist Balzano in medium close-up after a title introduces him; a cut to a *plan américain* shows him to be onstage doing his act. Only later in the scene does a long shot frame both the audience and the stage. Another 1915 film, *The Woman* (a one-reeler, production company unknown) starts with a shot/reverse-shot conversation between a couple, before a *plan américain* shows that they are at a party. We quickly learn the situation, while seeing the two characters' appearances. In all these cases, the function of beginning on a close shot is to show the appearance of the characters and create first impressions about them. An initial close view would also support the new acting style and would emphasize character as a source of narrative causality. None of these films, however, begins on a close shot in any scene after the opening, and all move to an establishing shot fairly soon.

In the later teens, filmmakers occasionally delayed the establishing shot for other purposes. A scene may mislead the spectator for comic effect, as in the second sequence of *Wild and Woolly* (John Emerson, 1917, The Douglas Fairbanks Corp.). The scene begins with a medium shot of Jeff seated in cowboy clothes by a teepee; a track back to long shot shows us that the 'campsite' is actually inside his bedroom. Here we get not only a clear view of a new character, but the delayed establishing view humorously undercuts our first impression. Another function of beginning on a close shot is to emphasize important details which reveal the narrative situation of the scene more clearly than a long shot would. In all these functions of the delayed long shot, compositional motivation justifies the use of the less predictable schema; the variation on the standard opening is not arbitrary.

Many films of the 1920s make subtle use of the delayed long shot. The opening of *Mantrap* (Victor Fleming, 1926, Famous Players-Lasky) provides an example of a quick revelation of narrative situation through detail. Without any introductory inter-title, the credits lead directly to a medium close-up of a woman's foot touching a man's, which he moves away (see fig 16.1); a tilt up shows the woman speaking to a point off right front (fig 16.2). The dialogue title that follows gives the situation: '— and he said I flirted. A clever lawyer like you should get me heaps of alimony!' After the title, we see a medium close-up of the woman, who raises a make-up case to cover her face (fig 16.3). The next shot shows her point-of-view of her own face in the mirror, which she then lowers to reveal the lawyer, with an annoyed expression on his face (fig 16.4); we later discover that his experience in handling divorces has led him to mistrust all women. Finally a tight long shot establishes them at his desk, with law books prominently visible to confirm that this is a lawyer's office (fig 16.5). The delayed establishing shot, while not the most probable schema, would remain a common alternative to the analytical breakdown of the scene.

Analytical editing

> An insert is filmed matter which is inserted in appropriate place in a scene, the film being cut for this purpose. This matter must appear and be known as an insert to the writer and manufacturer only; to the audience, it becomes the normal, logical, and only natural phenomena that could be presented under the circumstances.[14]
>
> Henry Albert Phillips, 1914

In primitive films, cut-ins occurred rarely and served a number of different functions. Most frequently, the move to a closer framing allowed the viewer to see facial expression more clearly,[15*] although the expression might be broad comic mugging rather than the later 'American'-style acting discussed in the previous chapter. Another common function for the closer

shot would be the revelation of a detail not sufficiently visible in the main tableau shot. But the cut-in could also simulate the point-of-view of a character within the scene, and occasionally it aided in the creation of a trick photographic effect.

Some of the closer shots to show facial expression were not, strictly speaking, cut-ins. Following the lead of *The Great Train Robbery*, quite a number of films of 1903-5 begin or end with medium shots of the characters; these may introduce the characters before the action proper begins, as in *The Widow and the Only Man* (1904, AM&B), where we see the two title characters in separate shots posing against a white background. *The Bold Bank Robbery* (1904, Lubin) begins similarly with a medium shot of the three smiling robbers in evening dress and ends with a cut-in within a prison scene; now the three are in convicts' stripes, frowning. Here the close shots structure the beginning and ending, providing a 'crime doesn't pay' moral for the whole. Some close shots for facial expression may constitute the entire action of a brief film, with no long shots to frame them, as in *The May Irwin — John C. Rice Kiss* (1896, Edison) and *The Old Maid in a Drawing Room* (1900, Edison). So the close shot for facial expression could either comprise a whole scene or come before a longer shot of the same action.

From its earliest occurrence until the early teens, the cut-in for detail comes between two long shots taken from the same camera set-up. Barry Salt has pointed out an early cut-in in *The Sick Kitten* (1903?), which he identifies as a re-release of *The Little Doctor*, a 1901 British film.[16] (Urban's 1903 catalogue in fact describes *The Sick Kitten* as an abridged version of *The Little Doctor*, offering both versions for sale. *The Little Doctor*, possibly originally entitled *The Little Doctor and the Sick Kitten*, was apparently made *c.* 1901. Only the shorter version is known to survive, but the Urban catalogue specifically mentions the cut to a closer view in *The Little Doctor*.) This brief film begins with a medium-long shot of two children preparing to administer a dose from a bottle marked 'Fisik' to a kitten sitting in the girl's lap (see fig 16.6). The cut-in to a medium close-up of the cat (fig 16.7) shows clearly the action of the cat lapping at the spoon's contents. Such small actions would have been indiscernible in the original framing. *The Sick Kitten* ends after a cut back to the medium-long-shot framing. A similar pattern occurs in *The Gay Shoe Clerk* (Porter, 1903, Edison), in which the central medium close-up emphasizes the detail of the customer raising her skirt to reveal her ankle; the cut-in thus explains to the audience why the clerk impulsively kisses her in the third shot, a re-establishing view of the store. In both these cases, the motivation for the cut-in is compositional, for without the closer view, we could not follow the action adequately.

Some early films motivate cut-ins as subjective shots. The subjective shot almost invariably is at least partly motivated realistically, since the camera lens is assumed to be imitating what a character's eye would see. In *Grandpa's Reading Glass* (1902, AM&B), a series of long shots shows some children examining objects with a magnifying glass. These shots alternate with close framings, masked as if from the children's point-of-view through the glass, of unmoving people or objects. In *The 100-to-One Shot* (1906, Vitagraph), there is a long shot of a grassy area in which horses are being walked before a race; the hero enters and finds a paper dropped by a rich bettor (see fig 16.8). A cut to a medium close-up, point-of-view shot shows his hands unfolding the paper (fig 16.9).

The earliest examples of point-of-view cut-ins occur in films which depend almost entirely upon the novelty effect of the close view. *Grandpa's Reading Glass* contains no other action and minimal causal progression; the whole thing consists of the children's series of examinations of objects and people. The cut-ins are motivated realistically (the children would see the objects from these points in space) and artistically (the close views are of interest in themselves), but not compositionally (they give us no new story information). But *The 100-to-One Shot* embeds its subjective shot within a larger narrative chain, motivating it compositionally by giving it causal functions; the paper in figure 16.9 contains a tip on a horse, which the hero reads and uses to win his bet. This compositionally motivated point-of-view cut-in later becomes the norm in the transitional period 1909-17.

Besides enlarging facial expression, providing details, and representing optical subjectivity, cut-ins during this period could construct a more

limited space within which special effects could be created. Two American Mutoscope and Biograph films which use extended and intricate pixillation shots are *The Tired Tailor's Dream* (1907) and *The Sculptor's Nightmare* (1908). In each, the basic space of the scene is established, then cut-ins eliminate the human figures in order to facilitate the lengthy stop-motion process of animating objects. Vitagraph's *Princess Nicotine* (J. Stuart Blackton, 1909) cuts in numerous times to tiny figures cavorting on a table. Here the special effects were mainly accomplished by building over-sized matches and cigarettes, with actresses playing the parts of the princess and her friend. When trick films declined after about 1909, so did the use of cut-ins for this purpose. But certain special effects would always depend on cutting to a new view of the scene's space.

Through most of the pre-1909 period, films seldom matched action or position between the long and close views. At the end of the first shot of *The Sick Kitten* (fig 16.6 is the last frame of this shot), the girl reaches for the bottle of medicine; at the beginning of the close shot (fig 16.7 is the first frame), her hand is already holding a spoon to the cat's mouth. There is no attempt to match on action or position, since the girl had not even begun to pour the medicine before the cut. A similar mismatch on her arm's position occurs at the cut back to the third and final shot. In the cut-in from *The 100-to-One Shot* (see figs 16.8 and 16.9), the close shot shows the hands and paper against a light, neutral background; given the surroundings visible in the long shot, the paper should be seen against grass. Here the mismatch is one of setting rather than position or action. *The Gay Shoe Clerk* does match the clerk's hand movement at one of the cuts. This may have been an accident, but at least the film successfully conveys a continuous event over the cuts by matching on position; *The Lost Child* (1904, AM&B) does the same thing on a cut-in to a pursued man holding up a guinea pig. The only other example of a match on action in the early years of the ES occurred in a much later film, *The Unexpected Guest* (1909, Lubin). In long shot, a man moves to a desk; then a cut to a medium close-up has an imprecise match on his hands cutting the PS away from a letter. There are undoubtedly other cut-ins with matches, but the usual use of a cut-in in the primitive period was to a static object or character. *The Unexpected Guest* is moving toward a conception of skilled matching which would become one sign of a well-executed classical film.

On the whole, however, before 1911 or so, cut-ins were not common for any purpose. Even when closer shots became more acceptable, most filmmakers initially sought to avoid cuts within a space. Frequently staging could render a cut-in unnecessary. If a filmmaker wanted to insure that facial expression was visible, the actors simply moved closer to the camera. In the first shot of *After One Hundred Years* (1911, Selig) a group of characters stand outside an inn; the innkeeper comes out to greet them (see fig 16.10). One man and the innkeeper come forward to talk, thereby identifying the film's central character (fig 16.11). This practice contrasts sharply with the more decentered framings of earlier years; compare the stock market shot from *A Corner in Wheat* (Griffith, 1909, AB) in which the bustling characters all claim equal attention. No framing or staging device guides the spectator's eyes to the most relevant actions in that shot. Similar framings with the characters stepping forward occur frequently in the early teens. In *Cinderella* (1911, Thanhouser), the Prince picks up the lost slipper in long shot, carries it forward, and extends it toward the camera, then goes back up the palace steps. *A Tale of Two Cities* (William Humphrey, 1911, Vitagraph) opens with a long shot of a party at the Marquis's home, with the Marquis in the depth of the shot (see fig 16.12). He comes into medium-long shot to give orders to a servant (fig 16.13). *At Old Fort Dearborn* (1912, Bison '101') contains a more elaborate example, with a long shot framing a soldier who comes out of a saloon and accosts an Indian woman (see fig 16.14). As an officer and the woman's father enter to stop him, the whole group moves forward (fig 16.15). After the Indians go out, the two men take one more step forward into *plan américain* as the officer berates the soldier (fig 16.16).

The practice of moving characters toward the camera has never entirely disappeared. But by the mid-teens the cut-in had become an equally important way of providing a closer view of the characters. At the same period, movement toward the camera was handled in a less obvious fashion, with a deeper setting extending the acting space forward. Movement toward the camera became

part of the realistically motivated staging of the scene, rather than a movement made solely to allow the spectator a better view. In *The Cheat* (Cecil B. DeMille, 1915, Lasky), for example, the husband and his friend stroll slowly and casually forward in the parlor after dinner. Here the movement is motivated by their desire to discuss their investment plans out of the earshot of guests in the depth of the room. There is no sense here, as there is in the earlier examples just described, of the actors crossing an empty foreground space simply to get closer to the camera. As with other devices, realistic and compositional motivation combine to make the mechanics of film style less noticeable.

In spite of attempts to use staging to avoid cut-ins, after 1910 filmmakers increased their dependence on closer shots. Sometimes the narrative situation necessitated a view of a detail which for some reason could not be brought forward to the camera. In the first scene of *After One Hundred Years*, as we have seen, the actors move into closer view. Later, in the last scene, the hero discovers a bullet-hole in the mantelpiece of his inn room (see fig 16.17). As he inspects it, there is a cut-in with a match on action (fig 16.18). *Shamus O'Brien* (Otis Turner, 1912, Imp) contains a *plan américain* in which the fugitive Shamus's family read a letter from him. Barely visible outside the slatted window is listening a treacherous neighbor who will turn Shamus in (see fig 16.19). There follows a close-up of the neighbor (fig 16.20), partly in order to catch his gleeful expression, but primarily to guarantee that we see this important bit of narrative information, which is partly hidden by the window in the long shot. In each case, the cut-in emphasizes a detail associated with a fixed portion of the set.

The *Shamus O'Brien* example shows how set construction could also necessitate a change of angle at the cut. But once the cut-in had come into general use, filmmakers did not always need such a pretext to vary the vantage point on the scene. *The Girl of the Cabaret* (1913, Thanhouser) establishes the hero, at foreground right, sitting at a table watching a cabaret violinist (fig 16.21). A cut-in catches his reaction, moving nearly 180° to the other side of the table from the long shot (fig 16.22). But most cut-ins still moved straight in to capture detail.

By the mid-teens, cut-ins routinely function not only to guarantee the visibility of narrative action, but to aid characterization as well. We saw in the previous chapter how the new facial acting style encouraged closer framings. This style may have been a major cause of the steadily increasing cutting tempo during the teens. Cecil B. DeMille, commenting in 1923 on the increase in the number of shots over the past ten years, attributed it to an increasing emphasis on character psychology:[17]

In the old days we would have 'shot' a struggle scene in a 'long shot,' showing, perhaps, two men fighting on the floor with a woman at one side. In the long shot we could get only a suggestion of the emotions being experienced. The physical action, yes, but the soul action, the reaction of the mentalities concerned, the surging of love, hate, fear, up from the heart and into the expressive muscles of the face, the light of the eyes, that, indeed, is something you can only get by a flash to a close-up or semi-close-up.

And it is these flashes, short but telling, that have caused some scenario writers to increase scene numbers.

A more regular use of crosscutting and contiguous spaces would also tend to increase the average number of shots per reel during this period. Along with the acting shift, the rise of the star system also encouraged the use of closer framings. Filmmakers moved in upon the famous faces in order to allow spectators to gaze upon their favourites. These closer shots were not the lingering glamor shots of the twenties and thirties, but they served somewhat the same function. Pickford's first appearance in her early feature *The Eagle's Mate* (James Kirkwood, 1914, Famous Players) epitomizes this usage. We see her first in a medium-long shot, emerging from the forest (see fig 16.23). Even though she is clearly recognizable from this view, a cut-in to a medium shot follows (fig 16.24). Here Mary plays with a bird on a branch – an action which helps to characterize her, but which also allows the camera to dwell on her. These actions could have been handled in one shot, but the division into two prolongs Pickford's entrance.

During the mid-teens, the cut-in quickly changed from an occasional necessity to a standard device in creating an omnipresent narration. For a few years, from about 1914 to 1917, practitioners seem to have conceived of cut-ins as a way simply to add variety and interest to a scene. Scenario guidebooks advised using cut-ins to speed up a scene, whether or not there was any specific reason to change framings. Consider the following statements:[18]

[1914] The close-view has no rival for breaking dangerously long scenes in a manner so natural and potential that oftentimes it makes a brilliant presentation of something that would in all probability have become tedious.

[1917] Main scenes must not be too long. If they threaten to be so, they must be broken up by close-ups or flash-backs [i.e., cutaways].

The cut-in thus contributed to the increasing tempo of editing in the teens. But after 1917, most writers advocated the use of close shots for specific narrative purposes – not just to liven up a scene's rhythm. A 1921 scenario manual echoed the earlier writers, saying: 'Occasionally the close-up is used to "break up" a sequence that would be too long and monotonous were the action therein contained shown in one lengthy and sustained long-shot'; however, the same writer specified that the usual uses of the close-up are 'to show a close, detailed view of that which is not sufficiently clear or which lacks emphasis in a more distant and general scene. In the case of a human face, it is occasionally necessary or desirous to show the details of expression, conveying an emotion.'[19] After 1914, no UnS or ES films lacked cut-ins, and about 1916, the cut-in with a match on a moving object was almost as frequent as the static match. Certainly by 1917, the advent of the classical period, filmmakers had formulated the analytical presentation of a scene through establishing, cutting in, and re-establishing.

Moreover, by 1917, the cut-ins could be taken from a variety of angles, as the films of Fairbanks, Ray, and Pickford show. A scene from a 1918 Ray film, *The Hired Hand* (Victor Schertzinger, Thomas Ince Corp.), begins with an establishing shot of mother, daughter, and servant in a kitchen (see fig 16.25). A medium shot of the mother follows; she looks off left and speaks (fig 16.26).

This leads to a reverse medium shot of the daughter looking right, listening (fig 16.27), and then to a re-establishing shot from a new angle, emphasizing the servant as she comes forward to speak with the mother (fig 16.28). Here the back wall provides a spatial anchor from shot to shot (note how the three lanterns on a shelf recur in each shot), but the filmmakers no longer conceive of the space as a flat, frontal tableau. Rather than simply cutting straight in, the filmmakers have created a new angle on the space for each shot. Guiding spectator attention through frequent shifts in vantage point, analytical editing became a familiar schema that aided easy comprehension of all classical films.

The introduction of the cut-in as a standard device and the resulting breakdown of a single scene into multiple shots bring up the question of screen direction (later to be called the 'axis of action' or '180° rule'). The maintenance of screen direction from shot to shot is one of the basic principles which American filmmakers would use to orient the spectator to the story action. There never was a period in the history of the US cinema when screen direction was random. Originally the tableau staging and framing precluded the need for any question of direction; space was presented whole. Furthermore, early cut-ins failed to disturb the clarity of this space. There was seldom any question of moving to the other side of the action. The standard painted sets had only a backdrop and perhaps two small segments of other walls at the sides. In order to keep the setting in the background of the closer shot, the camera had to stay on the same side of the characters. Since filmmakers usually did close-ups directly after the long shots, by simply carrying their cameras forward, problems seldom arose, even in exteriors done without sets.

Occasionally, in later films, there are closer shots, especially of characters, taken from the side of the action opposite to the vantage of the establishing shot. Such breaks in continuity are rare, and probably result from successive shots being done at different times from the long shot. (We have seen how shooting 'out of continuity' was necessary to maintain efficiency in the production process.) In *Girl Shy* (Fred Neumayer, 1924, Harold Lloyd Corp.), close-ups of Harold's typewriter after each fantasy scene, a close-up of the villain stroking the maid's hand, and a

medium shot of Harold pulling the lever to dump a workman from the back of a wagon, are all filmed from the opposite side to the establishing shot. Only one of these disjunctive cuts is compositionally motivated: since the villain conceals his gesture with his hat, we can see it only because the camera crosses over the axis of action. In the other two cases, we must assume either that the staff confused the direction when making the close shots or were willing to overlook a few irregularities. On the whole, however, violations of screen direction were so rare that contemporary writers did not refer to screen direction as a problematic aspect of cutting in, but only in relation to scenes of multiple contiguous spaces.

There can be little doubt that the concept of screen direction stems from the primitive period, when the spectator viewed the action from a distance, as if in a theater seat. In a play performed on a proscenium-arch stage, one does not suddenly see the action from the other side; stage right and left remain consistent. Later, as analytical editing became more common, the film spectator ceased to see the bulk of the action from a fixed point. The shifts created at the cuts by the narration do not imply that filmmakers conceived of the spectator as a disembodied spirit capable of moving anywhere within the space.

Analytical editing, Hollywood commentators tell us, follows the 'natural attention' of the spectator. First the onlooker surveys the scene (establishing shot); as the action continues, he or she focuses upon a detail (cut-in), or glances back and forth at the participants in a conversation (shot/reverse shot), or glances to the side when distracted by a sound or motion (cutaway). But while the attention may flit here and there, it never departs from the physical ties of the spectator to the degree that it crosses the line to view the opposite side of the action. Arbitrary as this conception of the spectator is, it has governed Hollywood practice from the earliest years.

By 1917, analytical editing was used consistently through whole films. And as early as 1915, Sargent offered a remarkable summary of the closer shot's use in a hypothetical scene:[20]

It is worth while noting the growing tendency to use the close-up. This was very intelligently handled in a recent Kalem when, to borrow an expression of a writer, 'they shot all over the darned room,' and got strongly effective results.

For an illustration let us say that the scene is laid in the Senate Chamber in Washington. Hawkins, a newcomer, is trying to force through a bill 'for the relief' of his sweetheart's father. Jorkins, one of the old Wheel horses and senior senator from the same state, seeks to defeat the bill because of his dislike for the girl's father. Hawkins is to make his big speech.

To show the matter adequately would require a tiresome stay in the same big set. One or the other of the leading players would be too far from the camera to show up well. In this case the large scene would show the floor of the chamber, but instead of holding the action there it would flash back and forth between the two men, to the girl and her father in the balcony, and perhaps to the press gallery where Hawkins' friend, a correspondent from the home paper, helps to swing the tide. All of the players would be seen in the occasional big set, but there would be a succession of close-up pictures of the principals, with an occasional return to the big scene. It would be perhaps a three-hundred-foot scene, yet divided up into perhaps twenty-five or thirty sections, avoiding monotony.

Sargent's description could almost apply to the filibuster scene of *Mr. Smith Goes to Washington* (Frank Capra, 1939, Columbia). His reference to 'the occasional big set' advocates the periodic return to a re-establishing shot, but no longer does Sargent consider the close-up as a brief interruption of the basic single long shot comprising the scene.

Analytical editing breaks a single locale into different views; cutting to create multiple spaces expands the narrative space outward. There are two basic patterns for editing multiple spaces together: joining contiguous spaces and cross-cutting (i.e., joining non-contiguous spaces). I shall examine the former first, since it was the first to develop into a standard way of constructing space.

Multiple spaces

Movement between spaces and screen direction

The film cutter must know continuity, have a slight knowledge of directions, and an eye keen and embracing.[21]

Frank Atkinson (cutter at Universal), 1924

When a film presents contiguous spaces in separate shots, it needs some method for showing the viewer that these spaces are indeed next to each other. There are different ways of providing cues: a character or object moving from one space to another might link them together; or a character looking offscreen in one direction might lead the viewer to surmise that the next shot shows the space that character sees.

Character movement was the most common cue for linking contiguous spaces in the early cinema; it appeared widely from about 1903. In *The Somnambulist* (1903, AM&B), we see the interior of a bedroom and three shots of various parts of a rooftop outside as a woman gets up and sleep-walks across the roof. There is a match on the action of her coming through the door that gives a strong cue for contiguous spaces; at the other cuts, she exits to and enters from offscreen. *A Search for Evidence* (1903, AM&B) presents several segments of a hotel corridor, shifting laterally two doors at a time, as a woman and man move through from right to left, peeking through each keyhole. *The Great Train Robbery* (Porter, 1903, Edison) contains a pair of shots in which the robbers move from their hold-up of the passengers by the side of the train to the engine, in which they make their escape.

The year 1903 also saw the release of some early chase films. The chase, with its characters moving from shot to shot, became one of the standard ways of using multiple spaces in subsequent years. *The Pickpocket* (1903, AM&B) begins with a long shot as a thief robs and beats a man. The thief runs out at the foreground. Other people run in to help the victim; then this group runs out at the foreground as well. There follow thirteen more shots of various spaces, with characters in different combinations running through, usually toward the front and from left to right (the main directional variation being that sometimes they exit to the right of the camera, sometimes to the left). The multiple spaces even include locales above and below each other as several policemen chase the pickpocket over high stacks of lumber.

The movement from shot to shot in such films is

usually fairly comprehensible, as long as the characters are recognizable. This is true whether or not they keep constant screen direction. In the case of *The Pickpocket*, screen direction is not always strictly maintained. But again, films tended from the start to keep the characters moving from space to space in a reasonably consistent direction. These chase films were probably the earliest to standardize a dependence on screen direction to link multiple contiguous spaces. As in *The Pickpocket*, all the characters in such films would exit entirely, and a cut would reveal a new space nearby, with the characters entering after the cut. In most outdoor chase shots, the characters moved diagonally from the rear to exit in the foreground, just to one side of the camera. Examples occur in the first film to popularize the chase genre in this country, *Personal* (1904, AM&B). Here a group of women pursue a man through each of the eleven shots; they exit variously left and right, but always move toward the front, passing close to the camera. Similar chases occur in the same company's *The Lone Highwayman* (1906), *Her First Adventure* (1908; see fig 16.29), and *Trying to Get Arrested* (Griffith, 1909).[22]* During the decade, movements through contiguous spaces appeared more frequently in non-chase situations as well.

As with analytical editing, the conception of screen direction between contiguous spaces probably derives in part from the fixed position of the spectator in proscenium theater. In the later decades of the nineteenth century, spectacular productions sometimes employed a series of perspective backdrops to change locales quickly; at times, characters might move across the stage repeatedly through several represented settings, suggesting a progress through contiguous spaces. For instance, Nicholas Vardac describes an 1887 production of *David Copperfield* which staged the famous shipwreck scene in which Steerforth dies. A series of three settings, all changed without the curtain being closed, moved the characters through space: beginning in 'The Ark Interior,' as the characters rush out to the rescue, moving to an area 'Near the Beach' as the rescue party runs across the stage, and finally to 'the Sea in a Storm' with the ship sinking and the characters rushing in to attempt the rescue. According to Vardac, the changes of backdrop were accom-

panied by 'sound effects, offstage noises, and the action itself running continuously.'[23] For Vardac, the three scenes resemble a series of film shots, with 'dissolves' between. But beyond this, one significant aspect of this staging is the fact that the actors run across the stage to the left, exit, run across toward the left again, and so on. Were they not to maintain this constant direction, it is not clear that the spatial relationships among the Ark, Beach, and Storm backdrops would be apparent. There is but a small step from such a series of contiguous spaces on the Victorian stage to the series of shots in a primitive chase film.

The early use of screen direction depended on the fact that there were few shots, and that the same framing seldom recurred elsewhere in the film. But filming numerous shots which would later have to fit together with other shots done in different locales, on different days, made screen direction harder to control. After 1909, with the introduction of the shooting script and its attendant scene plot, it became more convenient to shoot out of continuity. In 1911, Frank Woods commented upon inconsistent screen direction and its possible production causes:

> Attention has been called frequently in *Mirror* film reviews to apparent errors of direction or management as to exits and entrances in motion picture production. . . . A Player will be seen leaving a room or locality in a certain direction, and in the very next connecting scene, a sixteenth of a second later, he will enter in exactly the opposite direction. Now it may be argued quite logically that this need not necessarily be inartistic, because the spectator himself may be assumed to change his *point of view*, but (oh, that word!) the spectator will not look at it that way. Any one who has watched pictures knows how often his sense of reality has been shocked by this very thing. To him it is as if the player had turned abruptly around in a fraction of a second and was moving the other way.

Woods suggests that: 'It is probable that the trouble is due in some instances to the fact that interior scenes are made first and exteriors cannot always be made to accommodate themselves.'[24] Indeed, most changes in screen direction in films of the early teens seem to result from shooting in different locales, then trying to match up the results. Particularly problematic are movements between interior and exterior locales. There are also instances where the different interior sets were not planned to take entrances and exits into account, so that the character repeatedly changes direction between the two settings. Allan Dwan's *The Fear* (1912, American) shows an instance of a reversed screen direction which must have resulted from out-of-continuity shooting. Throughout the film, we see shots made on a rocky beach; in one such shot, a character exits toward the left front (see fig 16.30). In the next shot, he should approach from the right side of the frame, but he comes in left (fig 16.31). Since these two spaces are never seen in a single framing, we can assume that Dwan's unit probably filmed in two locations far separated from each other and that no one kept track of this particular movement. As a result, several movements and eyelines between these two spaces are regularly mismatched in the same way.

Despite such occasional inconsistencies of screen direction, both films and contemporary writings indicate that most filmmakers considered it an important factor. Of all the ES films for the period 1910 to 1915, inclusive, about two-thirds contained structures of multiple contiguous spaces through which characters moved. Of these, less than one-fifth contained any violations of screen direction. Charles G. Clarke, who became a cameraman in 1915, confirms that screen direction was a rule in force when he began to work. He describes the belief current at that time: 'If they exit left and enter left, they're bumping into themselves.'[25]

A 1912 Vitagraph one-reel film, *Alma's Champion*, exemplifies the standard adherence to constant screen direction. At the end of one shot the hero runs out front left (see fig 16.32), leaving the frame entirely. The cut reveals a nearby space, into which he runs from the right (fig 16.33). Note here the carefully balanced reverse angles, with the camera at the same basic mirror-image vantage in relation to the railroad tracks in each shot. In *The Warning* (Donald Crisp, 1914, Majestic), the heroine runs out left, again exiting entirely (see fig 16.34); in the next shot she runs in from the right (fig 16.35). This pattern is typical of the use of movements to cue contiguous spaces in the early teens.

In 1914, an occasional film avoided the complete exit and entrance by using frame cuts (that is, cutting with the character passing over the frameline itself). This sort of match is more difficult technically than simply cutting when no figures are visible onscreen. *The Eagle's Mate* has a cut as the Pickford character moves away from the sick man she has been tending. The cut comes exactly as she is halfway out of the frame (fig 16.36); in the next frame (fig 16.37), the new shot begins with her already halfway into the image. (As we shall see, these shots lead directly into a shot/reverse-shot conversation; this, combined with the sequence's initial establishing shot, constitutes a fairly complex construction of the scenic space.)

After 1915, quite a few films continued to violate screen direction in relation to movements, but often only once or twice in an entire feature film — no more than might occur in a film of the thirties or forties. One reason that violations of screen direction occurred at all is that there was no established method for avoiding them until the late teens, when the 'script girl' began to be a regularly assigned position. In the early teens, there seems to have been some attempt to solve the problem by specifying screen direction in the continuity script, extending its function as a blueprint guiding all aspects of production. Two 1913 screenplay advisers give the following instructions:[26]

Describe *where* each character *enters* or *exits* when necessary and *how* and *with whom*, i.e., tell where he enters or exits — whether from the house, garden, or door — tell how he enters or exits — whether arm-in-arm, frightened, walking, running, mounted, breathlessly, etc.

Describe when and where the characters are to enter the scene, giving the entrance, or the direction. If they are to be in the scene at the beginning of the film, state that they are 'discovered' and give their position.

In each case, the authors seem anxious to get the scenario writer to specify as much as possible about the characters, not only to maintain screen direction, but also to aid in matching on action.

This attempt to make screen direction part of the written plans apparently did not work, however. While some published specimen scenarios of this period mention directions of entrances, most fail to do so. And set designers went on making an occasional set that did not allow for the matching of exit and extrance from one locale to another. *The Italian* (Reginald Barker, 1915, New York Motion Picture Co.), for example, consistently mismatches movements from the outside of Gallia's house to the inside. Planning, then, did not always ensure proper screen direction.

In the mid-teens, the task of watching for directions of entrances and exits fell to someone on the set during shooting. A 1913 account suggests that it was perhaps partly the cinematographer's job; he 'must keep accurate account of every motion made during the run of the film. In this way he is also an assistant stage manager.'[27] When asked who was responsible for keeping track of the directions of the actors' movements in the mid-teens, Clarke also credited the cinematographer: 'I knew what the next shot would be and kept track of exits and entrances.'[28] Cameraman Hal Mohr confirms that at least some cinematographers watched for screen direction. Mohr had worked as an editor during the teens, but was behind the camera by 1921. Asked if his editing experience had helped him as a cameraman, Mohr replied:[29]

It helped me a lot. Script girls used to get kind of mad at me, because they'd never have a chance; I'd put pictures together, so I knew instinctively that the man had gotten off the horse and gone into the saloon on camera left, so he had to come in the next scene from camera right, or from center down. So I'd set up accordingly.

Clearly some cinematographers would be better at keeping track of continuity than others; all would have other duties that would preclude their devoting complete attention to screen direction.

As Chapter 13 has pointed out, directors and assistant directors also tried to watch for this. When the number of shots increased and screen direction became a normative rule, firms added a specific production role – the 'script girl,' or continuity clerk – to keep continuity notes during the shooting. Apparently the role of the script person emerged between 1917 and 1920.

By the late teens, not only did filmmakers watch for screen direction in shooting, but editors had developed tactics for correcting problems when they arose. Helen Starr's major 1918 *Photoplay* article on editing discusses screen direction:[30]

The matter of progression is most important. If an actor is seen in a dining-room set and if he goes out a door on the left of the set, it is obvious that when we next 'pick him up' in the parlor he must be seen entering the parlor at the right of the screen. But sometimes the cutter finds that the director has made a mistake in this regard. If so he can turn the film negative over.[31]*

Note Starr's assumption that the need for maintaining screen direction is 'obvious.' William Hornbeck, an editor who began as an assistant cutter at Keystone in 1917, discusses other ways of covering a problem; in describing how an editor would cut together two shots in which the screen direction was reversed, he recalled:[32]

You'd try to get a movement that would excuse it, a turn of the head or something – there were various tricks that you could try. You'd go to a closer shot or a longer shot. Oh, there's dozens of things you could devise. Make an insert even; if they were handling something, put an insert in.

In some cases, editors might even arrange to have shots redone – especially a close shot which would cost little to make and which could cover an error.

By the late teens, filmmakers counted on audiences' 'reading' screen direction in specific ways. Starr discussed how an editor could save money on a production; using a recent battle scene as an example, she quotes the editor's description of how the sequence was done:[33]

'There were only seventy real soldiers in that scene,' explained the cutter. 'We cut the picture so that it seemed as if thousands took part – first a long shot of the seventy fighting amid battle smoke on one side, then closer shots of a dozen or two soldiers running in from the right, another dozen running in from the left, another long shot of the seventy soldiers but now wearing the uniforms of the enemy and fighting on the opposite side, then back to a shot of the hero and his forces and so on throughout the picture.' It was just a matter of reverse camera shots and joining them together so carefully that any audience would be deceived.

In spite of Starr's casual conclusion, the passage (with its use of the term 'reverse camera shot' to mean basically what it means today) indicates an extensive grasp of the principles of continuity editing. The filmmakers understood and were putting into practice the effects of opposed screen direction and eyelines that the Soviet filmmaker Lev Kuleshov was to study in his famous experiments on editing conducted during the early 1920s. Screen direction, we may assume, had virtually reached the status of a rule by 1917.

The eyeline match

If character movement can cue contiguous spaces, so does character glance. Quite early, around 1902, filmmakers began using glances to create optical point-of-view (POV) shots, placing the camera in the spatial position of the character. Then, during the early transitional period, after about 1909, eyeline matches appear in films; in this device, the character glances to a point offscreen in one shot, and a cut reveals the seen space, but not from the spatial position of the character.

The POV shot can show either a portion of the space seen in the establishing shot, or it can show a contiguous space. Filmmakers who first employed the POV shot used it in both ways. In the early years, the POV shot was usually indicated not only by position but also by a mask. *Grandpa's Reading Glass* (1902, AM&B) uses a series of round masks to represent a magnifying glass; the POV shots show details of the larger space of the establishing shot. Similarly, the hero's view through binoculars in *The 100-to-One Shot* (1906, Vitagraph; see figs 16.38 and 16.39) shows a space already seen in the first shot. But in *A Search for Evidence* (1903, AM&B), POV shots done through a keyhole mask reveal a contiguous space, a series of hotel rooms behind closed doors.

In rare instances, an unmasked POV shot might be used in these early years. *The Runaway Match* (1903, AM&B) even contains a POV tracking shot. When the pursuing father's car breaks down, the camera continues tracking back from him along the road; he stands angrily gesticulating toward the camera as it moves to extreme-long shot. A reverse medium-long shot tracks forward following the car containing the eloping daughter and her fiancé, who wave and laugh directly into the camera; the preceding view of the father is revealed as their POV shot. *The Runaway Match* provides a good example of a device which was later to become a recognizable part of Hollywood's repertory of devices, but which at the time was more likely an isolated experiment.

The unmasked POV shot occurs more regularly from about 1911. Since most camera angles were at this point nearly horizontal, they were not particularly serviceable as POV cues. Nor had filmmakers developed a set of other cues for indicating that the camera occupied the character's place. The glance through a window provided virtually the only such cue, since the window frame within the image placed the character spatially. Thus *A Friendly Marriage* (1911, Vitagraph) contains a shot of the wife stopping by a church and looking off left front (see fig 16.40), followed by a view of her husband through the rectory window (fig 16.41). *A Tale of Two Cities* (1911, Vitagraph) also contains a window POV, with the bank clerk looking out a window in *plan américain*, followed by a *plan américain* of the mob outside. Lois Weber's *The Cry of the Children* (1912, Thanhouser) ends with a scene of the factory owner and his wife looking out a window, followed by an extreme-long shot of the factory. Other spatial cues soon began to appear. In Kirkwood's American Biograph drama, *The House of Discord* (1913), the heroine stands by the gate of an estate and watches her daughter ride past with a groom; there follows a POV shot of the pair going away down the road. Here the position of the road and the direction of movement of the couple on horseback tell us that the camera has been placed in the heroine's position in the second shot. In *Behind the Footlights* (1916, Vim Comedies), the hero looks out from behind the curtain of a vaudeville stage (see fig 16.42) and sees his girlfriend in the audience (fig 16.43). Here camera angle as well as the placement of orchestra members in the lower part of the frame signals POV. By 1917, most of the UnS and ES films use POV at least once, usually employing continuity cues of spatial relations from shot to shot to indicate POV, only occasionally including windows and binocular or keyhole masks.

By the late teens, the masked POV shot returned, but not with shapes suggesting binoculars or keyholes. Instead, masking became a conventional means of marking POV shots as such. In *Love and the Law* (Edgar Lewis, 1919, Edgar Lewis Productions), one scene contains a lengthy series of POV shots as the hero stands by a parked wagon, turns slowly around, and sees a series of shop signs; there are five shots of him looking in various directions, each followed by a masked shot of a sign (see figs 16.44 and 16.45). The sophistication of POV usage by the late teens is apparent in this series: each sign is at the precise angle and distance it would be in relation to the character's position, those on his side of the street being closer than ones across the street or further down the street. In accordance with Hollywood's growing use of redundancy, the spatial and masking cues supported each other in indicating POV. In later years, additional POV cues reinforced the principles formulated in the teens.

The eyeline match, where the second shot shows a space seen, but not from a character's spatial position, came into occasional use about 1910-11. In *The Gambler's Charm* (1910, Lubin), the gambler runs to the door of a saloon and fires his gun at a man running away outside, offscreen right (see fig 16.46). The cut leads to a shot of the man falling, with the gambler's stare offscreen giving us one important cue as to where this second space is (fig 16.47).

Of the 1912 ES films, one-fourth had eyeline matches. Only one violated screen direction: Dwan's *The Fear*, in the same situation described on page 205. At the end of the film's first shot, the father looks off front left (see fig 16.48) and sees his daughter by their house (fig 16.49). We assume at this point that in the second shot the father is offscreen right. As we discover later when the other character moves between the two spaces (see figs 16.30 and 16.31), the father really had been offscreen left. In contrast, *The Girl at the Cupola* (1912, Selig) maintains screen direction in a scene of a labor strike: the first shot shows the workers and the sympathetic boss's daughter

looking off front left (fig 16.50), with the cut revealing her fiancé, who is trying to keep the factory running with scab labor (fig 16.51). This second shot suggests that the group looking on is offscreen to the right, and indeed they are, as we discover when characters move between the two spaces.

Of the 1913 films examined, nearly half used eyeline matches, with only one across the line. By 1914, the majority of films have them, and by 1917, only an occasional film is without an eyeline match. *Weights and Measures* (1914, Victor) has a scene in which a man in a car is being followed by a woman in another car; he stops to get a drink at a well, with his car in the background facing left (see fig 16.52). The cut to the woman, who has stopped her car and is watching from a distance, matches correctly on the direction of her gaze. Being behind him, she should be off right in the first shot, and the direction of her gaze — off left — confirms this (fig 16.53). In *The Wishing Ring* (1914) the couple looks off right (fig 16.54), and the cut reveals that they see a gypsy camp (fig 16.55). They should be off left here, and indeed they are, as their subsequent entrance from that direction proves. These examples are typical of eyeline usage in the teens.

Shot/reverse shot

Scene 202 — Close-up of John's face, smiling at the wrongful accusation. He casts a glance toward the jury box.
Scene 203 — Fairly close-up of the members of the jury looking fixedly in the direction of John.[34]

Capt. Leslie T. Peacocke, 1917

If a single eyeline provides a strong spatial cue, then a second eyeline on the other side of the cut should create an even stronger spatial anchor for the spectator. This principle is commonly used to create the shot/reverse-shot (SRS) schema, one of the most prevalent figures in the classical Hollywood cinema's spatial system. The SRS also depends on screen direction.

As we have seen, the concept of the eyeline match existed by 1913-14. Cuts that change screen direction after a glance were distinctly in the minority. The same is true of the shot/reverse-shot pattern. (It is true that several early SRSs in the ES crossed the line, but these are from 1911 and 1912, when writers were just beginning to refer to screen direction.) No doubt one can find occasional violations throughout the teens. But this does not indicate the absence of a guideline – filmmakers in the thirties occasionally crossed the line on SRSs as well.

SRS was introduced near the beginning of the transitional period. Early instances of this technique show it already performing its classical function of presenting a conversation situation; balanced pairs of shots form the centerpiece of a scene that contains other contiguous cuts as well. Barry Salt has pointed out[35] an early example of SRS in Essanay's *The Loafer* (1911), a film which is generally remarkably advanced in its application of classical principles. The shots he describes come in the middle of a classically constructed sequence which opens with an establishing shot of the hero by a buggy (see fig 16.56). He has been a drunken loafer, was given a loan, and now is a respectable farmer. After the shot begins, the camera pans right to reframe a stranger approaching the hero to beg for money (fig 16.57). After the hero refuses him, the tramp goes out right (fig 16.58). A cut reveals a grassy stretch of ground, and the tramp comes in from the front left, turns, and begins to berate the hero (fig 16.59). In the next shot, we see the hero's reaction (fig 16.60); then he runs out right threateningly. Cut to a shot of the beggar (as fig 16.59), as he runs out right. There follows a long shot of the field, and both men dash in from the left. The scene continues with the hero running out left after the struggle. Next we see a shot of a farmhouse door, and the hero comes into frame from front right. This relatively extended sequence of nine shots (including a dialogue title and return to the same framing as fig 16.59) combines several movements to contiguous spaces maintaining screen direction, plus a SRS framed three-quarters on each figure, again obeying screen direction. An establishing shot and two reframings give further indication of careful planning along the lines of continuity principles.

SRS is rare in the early and mid-teens, typically used when characters are so far apart that an ordinary two-shot is not feasible. Here SRS serves to indicate that characters are close enough to see each other. *In Old Madrid* (Ince, 1911, Imp Co.) has a scene in which two groups converse across a river. The shots of both are *plan*

américain, and in each the characters face off left. (The movements through contiguous spaces in this film do obey screen direction, however.) In Solax's 1913 *A Comedy of Errors*, a wife waves to her husband as he departs for work (see figs 16.61 and 16.62).

SRS became more frequent around 1914, now occurring in some cases between people who are close to each other; a two-shot could easily have been used in these cases, but the director cut in for a pair of closer shots to catch reactions during conversations. *The Eagle's Mate* (Kirkwood, 1914, Famous Players) has a couple of SRS patterns. In one, a *plan américain* establishes the heroine taking care of an injured relative. A cut-in to medium-long shot shows her by the bed; she then moves to the foot of the bed in the frame cut illustrated in figures 16.36 and 16.37. Returning to a medium shot of the man, the film sets up a SRS between the two, with two shots of each (figs 16.63 and 16.64).

SRS was still minority practice in 1914, but many films use it more than once and in ways which are quite sophisticated in terms of the continuity system. *The Wishing Ring* has several instances of SRS, one in the comic first scene as two old men lean out different windows of the same building to talk to each other. Here the medium shot of the man in the higher window is taken from a low angle (fig 16.65), that of the man on the ground floor from a high angle (fig 16.66). Later SRSs involve the young couple in situations where they are not spatially separated, as the figures in this example are.

A remarkable scene from a 1914 film, *Detective Burton's Triumph* (a Reliance two-reeler) shows how subtle some filmmakers could be by this point in their application of eyeline directions in SRS. The scene occurs near the end of the film, when Burton and two other detectives go in disguise to a bar to spy upon the three robbers they have been trailing. An establishing shot (see fig 16.67) shows the robbers at the rear table, Burton alone at the center left, and his colleagues at the foreground table. In the medium shot that follows, Burton looks front, then glances off right at the crooks (fig 16.68). Next we see the two other detectives, one of whom glances off left, at Burton (fig 16.69). The cut returns us to the framing of Burton, who looks front at his friend and covertly signals to him (fig 16.70). In the next shot, the same framing as figure 16.69, the man at the right returns the signal. A shot of the robbers follows, with the one at the right glancing front and left at Burton, then drawing the center crook's attention to the signals; he, too, looks front and left (fig 16.71). There then follows an extended SRS series of fourteen additional medium shots with these framings, as the detectives glance at the robbers and at each other, exchanging signals, while the robbers look at both other tables and become more suspicious. Finally, after a total of nineteen medium reverse shots among the three tables, there is a return to the establishing shot, and a gun battle breaks out (fig 16.72). This sustained control of six eyeline directions is certainly not typical of its period; yet it is difficult to imagine the creation of such a scene if the basic principles of the eyeline match and SRS were not known by this point. Their widespread use would soon follow.

By 1915, SRS had become majority practice, and I found no film from 1916 and 1917 that lacked it. Films of 1915 that use the device range from the most prestigious features (*The Cheat* [Cecil B. DeMille, Lasky]) to extremely clumsy comedy shorts (*Cupid in a Hospital* [an L-KO Chaplin imitation]), indicating the widespread adoption of the SRS pattern. Not a single one of the SRS patterns in 1915 ES films violated screen direction.[36]* There are probably films from the late teens which avoid SRS, but certainly the pattern is almost universally accepted by this point. Figures 16.73 through 16.77 show other examples from the late teens, demonstrating how uniform this device had already become. Feature films were now using SRS throughout, and not only for distantly separated characters. These examples show characters who are within a few feet of each other and who have previously been seen together in establishing shots.

There is one striking difference between SRS in the teens and SRS as practiced in the 1930s. Sound films often place the camera behind the shoulder of one character when framing the other; shoulders provide one more spatial cue to orient the spectator. Occasional silent films do use shoulders or other portions of the body for such a function, although this remains minority practice until the sound period. Maurice Tourneur's *Victory* (1919, Tourneur) provides an early example (see figs 16.78 and 16.79), and *Mantrap*

(Fleming, 1926, Famous Players-Lasky) uses compositions very similar to those of sound films (figs 16.80 and 16.81). Such framings show up not infrequently during the twenties. Thus SRS became one of the most basic devices of the late teens and twenties classical cinema, appearing in most scenes. We may be surprised to find this particular device so common in a cinema in which characters' speech could not be heard, but passages built around dialogue (only partially conveyed through dialogue inter-titles) were an important basis of many silent films. By the late twenties, the handling of conversation situations was schematized in a way which would barely differ from that of sound films.

The classical cinema's dependence upon POV shots, eyeline matches, and SRS patterns reflects its general orientation toward character psychology. As Part One stressed, most classical narration arises from within the story itself, often by binding our knowledge to shifts in the characters' attention: we notice or concentrate on elements to which the characters' glances direct us. In the construction of contiguous spaces, POV, the eyeline match, and SRS do not work as isolated devices; rather, they operate together within the larger systems of logic, time, and space, guaranteeing that psychological motivation will govern even the mechanics of joining one shot to another. As a result, the system of logic remains dominant.

Crosscutting

Part One has defined 'crosscutting' as editing which moves between simultaneous events in widely separated locales. 'Parallel editing' differs in that the two events intercut are not simultaneous. Interestingly, crosscutting was seldom used before 1910. In *The Great Train Robbery*, Porter's narration returns from the robbers' flight to the situations at the telegraph office and dance hall, but he does not alternate shots in these locales. Similarly, in *The Kleptomaniac* (1905, Edison), Porter first shows the rich woman's actions and then the poor one's, in order to contrast the treatment of the two when they are arrested for stealing, but he does not alternate between them. In *A Corner in Wheat* (1909, AB), Griffith suggests cause and effect by cutting between the Wheat King and the poor people in the bakery.[37] Here the time scheme is unclear;

Griffith's editing device could be crosscutting or parallel editing. But as Chapter 15 discussed, the classical narrative seldom depended entirely upon parallel construction; *A Corner in Wheat* is one of the rare exceptions. On the whole, parallel editing, with its non-simultaneous lines of action, was also rare in American filmmaking from its earliest years.

The more conventional 'rescue' pattern of crosscutting, involving two persons or groups who eventually meet, occurs at least as early as 1906, in *The 100-to-One Shot* (Vitagraph). In this film, the hero goes out and wins money on a long shot to aid his fiancée and her father, who are about to be evicted. As they are being thrown out of their house by the landlord, the following brief series of shots creates suspense:

29 ELS: A street. A car in the distance drives
    straight forward and out right fore-
    ground.
30 LS: Interior of the house, as earlier,
    but with furniture gone. The landlord enters
    from the right, and, with the help of two
    officials, starts to lead the father out right.
31 ELS: A road. The car comes in from the
    background, drives forward, stops, and the
    hero gets out and runs out right.
32 As 32: The hero enters from the right
    (a violation of screen direction), tears up the
    landlord's paper, and pays him. The villains
    leave, and the film ends with rejoicing and an
    embrace.

Another example occurs in *Her First Adventure* (Wallace McCutcheon, 1908, AM&B), which is generally handled as a conventional chase until toward the end. Then a few shots alternate between pursued and pursuers. From 1909 on, Griffith begins to use the device occasionally and was probably responsible for popularizing it.

Crosscutting did not become widespread immediately, however. By 1912, slightly fewer than half the ES films used any crosscutting. Some of these include chases, as in *The Bandit of Tropico* (1912, Nestor) and *The Grit of the Girl Telegrapher* (1912, Kalem). Others simply use crosscutting to show two related events occurring in separate spaces. In *The Haunted Rocker* (1912, Vitagraph), there is one instance of crosscutting when the disapproving father goes to his club

while his daughter's lover visits her secretly at home. The following sequence occurs:

13 LS: The steps outside the house. The
    father goes out, then the lover goes to the
    door.
14 MLS: The parlor. The heroine sits in
    the rocking chair. Her lover enters and they
    embrace.
15 MLS: Interior of a men's club. The father
    comes in, has a drink, and leaves.
16 MLS, as 14: The heroine sits on her
    lover's lap in the rocker.
17 MLS: The front gate of the house. The
    father comes in, drunk.
18 New MLS: The rocker. The lovers stand
    hurriedly and hide behind a screen. The
    father enters, sees the moving chair, and is
    puzzled.

One noticeable trait of this sequence is the considerable compression of time made possible by the crosscutting. At each return to the previous action, a move forward in the narrative has occurred. The crosscutting represents simultaneous events, but also creates large ellipses which are less obvious because of the move away to another line of action. As crosscutting became more common, this ability to shorten plot duration remained one of its most important functions.

Contemporary writers recognized that crosscutting could condense narrative material, as well as create suspense. A 1914 scenario manual referred to the 'cutback' (as crosscutting was known at the time) as being 'employed to accelerate action and maintain suspense.'[38] In 1923 the *American Cinematographer* described how an editor could reduce an excess of footage to a finished film:[39]

By careful cutting and recutting the editor can
establish all the preliminary motivation
necessary and yet do it in a simple manner both
entertaining and retaining the full values. This
is usually handled by 'splitting sequences' or in
other words, handling two sequences at one
time, hitting the highlights or important parts
of each one yet telling it in the same amount of
film required to handle one of them if cut
individually.

Thus by elliding the relatively inessential moments of each story line, the omnipresent narration guides the spectator's attention through a string of the most salient actions.

In a sense, this compression through cross-cutting carried on the basic approach of the early teens, when short film lengths led to highly condensed presentations of action. At that point, summary titles, telegraphic pantomime gestures, and other devices had combined to pack a great deal of action into a short span. Now crosscutting could create a similar effect, but in a less obtrusive way.

With the feature film, such extreme condensation of action was not always necessary. Sometimes the opposite problem arose: how to sustain an action through a whole sequence. Some filmmakers found crosscutting to be the solution. Crosscutting permitted the action of a single sequence to be drawn out, where showing the actions in separate short scenes might make the film episodic. Cecil B. DeMille's feature *The Whispering Chorus* (1918, Artcraft) is an example. This seven-reeler has thirty sequences, eleven of which employ crosscutting between two lines of action which do not come together within any one sequence (as well as two others which juxtapose action in two locales without cutting between them). The story covers a long time span and involves a large number of separate locales and incidents. Without crosscutting, the film would consist of a string of brief scenes; with it, there is less sense of choppiness.

By 1914, most ES films used crosscutting, and after 1915, only a few films avoided it. Once crosscutting had been established, filmmakers continued to add more and more lines of action, the most famous instances being the multiple simultaneous rescues near the ends of *The Birth of a Nation* and *Intolerance*. Griffith, who was universally assumed at the time to have invented the cutback, was the prime experimenter in this. But apparently even he went too far; a review of his 1918 feature *The Great Love* (now lost) comments:[40]

> With the genius that Griffith alone commands, three almost separate stories have been carried through this picture. And in this point we think he went a trifle too far. In several places he is carrying as high as six different situations

along simultaneously by means of cutbacks.

Crosscutting became standardized as the interweaving of two or three lines of action – seldom more.

The crosscut scene had become a staple of the silent cinema by the late teens and twenties. More often than not, crosscutting provided a simple way of constructing an exciting story without the script writer's having to sustain a single line of action. It seems to have reached its most frequent usage for this purpose in the few years after 1915. By the twenties, script writers had gained more experience at creating situations which could sustain themselves for whole sequences. Crosscutting did not disappear, but became a more localized device, occurring mainly in scenes where the narration demanded the juxtaposition of multiple lines of action.

Parodies of continuity

Contemporary writings and stylistic usage in the sample films suggest that the continuity guidelines were known and widely accepted by 1917. But beyond this, there are a small number of films from the teens and twenties which parody various continuity guidelines and 'mistakes.' Artists are not likely to parody something which is not already established and familiar. Hence the existence of such films helps confirm the idea that the continuity system was in force at this early stage.

The earliest continuity-parody among the ES films is the extraordinary 1915 split-reel comedy, *Ye Gods! What a Cast!* Made by a very minor independent company, Luna, this film is an extended joke on the eyeline match. In the opening scene, the impoverished Hardluck Film Co. assigns the various roles in its new film to a woman and a man: she is to play the heroine, while he takes all six male roles. The man tries on all six costumes in this first scene, in order to establish the various characters' appearances in the audience's mind. The bulk of *Ye Gods! What a Cast!* consists of the resulting film, with the male actor, as six different characters, chasing himself, looking at himself, and conversing with himself in SRS. *Ye Gods! What a Cast!* contains 103 shots, all of which maintain screen direction. Here not only does the whole film depend on the eyeline match, but the humor in the situation would be incomprehensible unless we assume the audience could understand the play with eyelines.

Other films make fun of inconsistent mise-en-scene over the cut. In *Hoodoo Ann* (Lloyd Ingraham, 1916, Triangle-Fine Arts), Ann and her boyfriend attend a Western, *Mustang Charlie's Revenge*, at their local cinema. The film is a parody of old-fashioned, New-Jersey-made Westerns (its producer is 'The Hoboken Film Co.'), done in a deliberately crude style that contrasts sharply with the remainder of *Hoodoo Ann*. At one point, a title announces 'Father's Dear old tin pale' (a reference to the not infrequent misspellings of early-teens inter-titles), followed by a shot of the heroine inside a shack, going to the door while swinging the pail. A cut to the well outside follows, and the woman comes in carrying a wooden bucket, which she holds up prominently. Later, when she runs back into the shack, she has the tin pail again. This delightful film-within-a-film demonstrates Hollywood's awareness of its own changes in the space of a few years.

Other films made similar jokes. In 1918, *Photoplay* described *Nut Stuff*, another story about a filmmaking establishment, the 'Hardly Able Feature-Film Company'; this comedy short parodies 'the careless direction that permits a player to enter a room in one costume and leave it in another.' The film also contains exaggeratedly stock character types and canted framings which simulate bad cinematography.[41] Finally, a 1923 comedy short, *Uncensored Movies* (Hal Roach, 1923, Hal Roach) has Will Rogers imitate various movie stars of the day. As Tom Mix, he repeatedly tramples, rips, or dirties his elegant white hat, yet puts it on again in pristine condition after the cut.

There are undoubtedly other such parodies. Clearly filmmakers felt that at a simple level at least, audiences could notice and appreciate the humor of continuity errors.

The ready-made center of interest

The various continuity rules – establishing and re-establishing shots, cut-ins, screen direction, eyelines, SRS, crosscutting – served two overall purposes. On the one hand, they permitted the narrative to proceed in a clearly defined space. On the other hand, they created an omnipresent narration which shifted the audience's vantage point on the action frequently to follow those parts of the scene most salient to the plot.

Two statements from the twenties summarize these purposes succinctly and demonstrate that Hollywood practitioners understood their editing system as fully then as have practitioners ever since. A former editor for Ince wrote in 1922: 'The value of every scene and sequence must be carefully weighed and the man who attempts to do this must most surely be able to prepare and smooth the production for audience consumption.'[42] The second statement comes from a lecture given by actor Milton Sills in 1928; he begins by discussing how developing methods limited the length of shots:[43]

> This limitation proved desirable. It was found that by telling the story in flashes [contemporary term for very short shots], flitting from spot to spot in the fields of action, eliminating irrelevancies, isolating and emphasizing the significant moment, the film could do what the eye does naturally; namely, select and focus on the quintessential drama. The eye of the spectator did not have to seek the center of interest. It was there ready-made for its pleasure. . . . This practice spelt economy in attention, vividness of effect, and dramatic intensity. The close view, the medium shot, and the long shot could be intermingled by the skill of the director and the mechanics of the cutting room in such a way that the narrative was constantly moving from high light to high light.

Thus continuity editing constantly organizes the spectator's attention. In doing so, it acts in concert with other principles of the classical cinema – principles of depth and centering that guide the eye within shots.

17

Classical narrative space and the spectator's attention

The knot hole in the fence

In the shift from primitive to classical film practice, the spectator's implicit spatial relation to the action changed significantly. During the primitive period, the camera usually remained at a distance from the action, framing it in a way that suggested a stage seen by a spectator in a theater seat. Later films also have long shots, of course, that place at least some elements of the mise-en-scene far away from the camera. But primitive films combine this distant view with a relatively flat playing space which creates a gap immediately in front of the implicit viewer. Even when a crowd is supposedly milling about, jammed together, the figures typically do not stray into the foreground zone (see fig 17.1). In chases and other similar situations, the characters may move diagonally forward and exit close to the camera; but they appear in the foreground space only briefly at the end of the shot, usually after we have watched them move in from the extreme background. On the whole, the primitive cinema keeps the spectator looking across a void into an action in a separate space. A few exceptions, like cut-ins or track-ins, occur in rare situations where either essential narrative information or novelty dictates the closer view.

Classical film practice, on the other hand, removed the empty foreground between the spectator and the space of the narrative action. During the transition period (1909-16), several changes placed the spectator's vantage point directly on the edge of the playing area: the staging of the action in depth, changes in set design, considerable depth of field, and directional lighting. No longer was the action played out before the spectator in a shallow, removed area. Rather, the space extended outward. Like editing, cinematography, and other devices of the classical

system, the boundaries of narrative space became unnoticeable. Primitive-period mise-en-scene created a flat playing area within a box-like space, seldom suggesting space behind the set or to the sides. But classical staging and sets suggested space receding into the distance, and cut-ins foster a sense of additional space on the sides, by showing only portions of the whole area. Space now apparently stretched out indefinitely, appearing to include the viewer.

As we have seen, the primitive cinema's placement of the spectator at a distance did not always provide the best view for grasping important narrative information. But the omnipresent narration of the classical cinema situates the spectator at the optimum viewpoint in each shot. Staging, composition, and editing combine to move that viewpoint instantly as the action shifts. There arose the enduring Hollywood image of the spectator as an invisible onlooker present on the scene; filmmakers and theorists have invoked this idea to the present day in explaining the shot/reverse-shot pattern (an onlooker at a conversation turning the head back and forth), the cut-in, reframing (both of which follow the 'natural' attention of the onlooker), and virtually any other standard technique. This notion of the invisible spectator provides a neat reversal of the actual reason for the whole continuity system; while the classical cinema claims to follow the attention of the spectator, it actually guides that attention carefully by establishing expectations about what spatial configurations are likely to occur.

Although this idea came up only occasionally in the silent period, the basic idea of creating the spectator as an invisible onlooker at the ideal vantage point underlies the development of the classical system. One of the best formulations of this idea appeared in 1913; the author is describing the difference between the loose causality of comedy and the tighter structure of drama:[1]

> In the tragedy-form of the drama there is always a cause, a deed, and an effect. In the photo-drama, the film must create the impression among the audience that they are witnessing the three elements of the action, unknown to the characters of the play. They should be put in the position of being at the 'knot hole in the fence' at every stage in the play.

The 'knot hole in the fence' irresistibly brings to mind the concept of linear perspective; according to Renaissance perspective theory, the spectator could see the depth effect created by a painting's vanishing point by looking at it with one eye, from a single point in space. The space of the scene, both in the painting and in the classical film, is organized outward from the spectator's eye. But the knot-hole image specifies other aspects of the classical approach as well − the spectator looking directly into a space from its edge, unseen by anyone within that space. In the continuity system, however, the knot hole is not stationary, but moves to the ideal place for viewing. The displacement may be gradual in the case of camera movement, or instantaneous at a cut. The author's conception of the audience being 'put in the position' in relation to the narrative's causal events would be inconceivable in the primitive period, for it implies a fundamentally different approach to narration. The change helps define the basis of the classical cinema.

Staging in depth

Part of the impulse to place the action closer to the camera resulted from a desire to show the facial expressions of the actors. As we have already seen, filmmakers tended initially to have the actors move forward into *plan américain* or medium-long shot, avoiding cut-ins (see fig 16.10 through 16.16). This expanded the shallow playing area and utilized the empty space between set and camera. Increasingly, filmmakers avoided the awkwardness of such unmotivated movements; instead they placed the figures in several planes between the back of the set and a

spot closer to the camera. In 1911 *The Moving Picture World* claimed that 10 to 15 feet was the standard camera-subject distance, or 8 feet 'with those who amputate the lower limbs to show us facial expression.'[2] The main motive for moving the actors forward was probably to provide the spectator a better view of facial expression; incidentally, however, the practice of utilizing the foreground also brought the narrative space out toward the viewer. A 1912 review drew upon the 'invisible spectator' notion in defending the close shot; it is 'natural, as in life one does not see the entire form of a person with whom he is in close relation.'[3] Thus the close framing places the spectator on the edge of a deep playing space, looking primarily at the actor, but aware as well of a setting beyond.

But the 'American foreground,' as this closer framing came to be known, was not simply a matter of single figures moving forward. Several characters who might have stood side by side in a primitive staging would be likely, from the early teens on, to occupy several planes. *The Loafer* (1911, Essanay) opens with a shot of a drunkard arguing with his wife in a cabin (see fig 17.2). The set is a flat wall behind them, but the placement of the wife at the right foreground creates a conversation at a slight diagonal into depth away from the camera. The result does not display facial expression to the best advantage; in fact the actress playing the wife must turn a bit away from the camera to address the man. But it does eliminate to some degree the sense of an empty space in the foreground. Another, more striking example occurs in *A Friendly Marriage* (1911, Vitagraph). In one shot, a woman sits in the foreground as another woman brings a man into the scene (see fig 17.3). The two standing figures come forward and sit, forming a triangular grouping. At no point do we see the foreground woman's face; again, the motivation is realistic rather than compositional − to create a more three-dimensional playing space rather than to reveal expression. The grouping imitates how people would sit in a room, but the result impairs the scene's clarity. Later, analytical editing would permit the realistic motivation of groupings in space, combined with an optimum view of all narrative action.

Films of the early teens are full of examples of staging in depth; it would be hard to find a film done entirely in shallow tableaux. *The Bandit of Tropico* (1912, Nestor; fig 17.4) has a shot with the bandit waiting in the foreground and a stagecoach appearing suddenly in extreme depth through a gap in the trees; in *Weights and Measures* (1914, Victor; fig 17.5), the protagonist sits close to the camera at the left as the woman he awaits enters at the rear. By the late teens, staging in depth appears frequently; with deeper sets, the placement of the figures has come to appear casual (**Love and the Law*, 1919, Edgar Lewis; fig 17.6).

Staging in significant depth began at the period around 1910 when scenes still usually avoided analytical editing. But cut-ins added a sense of moving right into the space. The combination of multiple planes of action with multiple views from different distances was a powerful means of absorbing the viewer within the action. Mae Marsh's 1921 acting guide discusses the standardization of this approach by the late teens:[4]

> Most of the dramatic action is now played at three-quarters length; that is from the face to the knees. As we weave in and out of a scene, very often the entire body is shown . . . but the majority of the intermediate shots through which the dramatic action is conducted cut off the lower part of the body.

As this passage suggests, in the post-1917 classical period the establishing (and re-establishing) shot is the only point in the scene at which the viewer is at a distance from the totality of the narrative space. Once we have a view of the overall situation, analytical editing moves us inside, where the 'dramatic action' primarily occurs in a medium-distance view. The Hollywood cinema seldom used close-ups or extreme close-ups; but by the late teens and twenties, the medium close-up (showing shoulders and face) was common. Used for details, reactions, or intense emotions, the medium close-up often isolates the single figure from both the setting and from other figures. Depth, after all, implies that the spectator sees several objects in different planes. When only one item is dramatically relevant, a tight framing prevents our noticing the surrounding space, sometimes in combination with a mask at the edges of the frame to cut

down the prominence of the background (as in fig 17.7, from *A Temperamental Wife*). In the analytical editing system, the close shot becomes the extreme degree of the viewer's placement within the narrative space. Aware of the surroundings from the establishing shot, the viewer nevertheless sees the character filling most of the frame.

Thus each shot scale in the early classical period gained its own general functions not only for laying out narrative space, but also for drawing the spectator into and out of that space. This expansion from back to front tended to force a change in the shape of the set itself.

Settings and depth

Until about 1909, sets in narrative films resembled those of the legitimate theater and vaudeville. A painted backdrop stood perpendicular to the camera, with perhaps a few pieces of real furniture for use in the action. Figure 17.8 shows such a backdrop in use, with fireplace, doorframe, corner, window, sunbeam, and flowers all painted. Only the chair and table are three-dimensional. Such sets contrasted considerably with the depth of location shots, which would often be cut in beside them in the same film.

Since the characters remained at long-shot distance, in front of the backdrop, the resulting playing space was shallow, but wide, stretching the width of the frame. Let us assume that the *Moving Picture World* figures quoted earlier are accurate, and that the actors stayed about 10 to 15 feet away from the camera for a standard long view.[5] The backdrop in figure 17.8 is perhaps 14 feet wide. Thus in this case the actors have 14 feet in which to move back and forth, but only about 5 feet forward from the backdrop. A larger backdrop, placed further from the camera, would enlarge the playing space into depth. Such expansion, however, was limited: 'When a large stage setting is required the figures of the actors are made small upon the screen, which is objectionable.'[6] To understand why, one need only watch the 1904 *Parsifal* (Edison), where tiny figures move about, dwarfed by huge backdrops. Both this statement and *Parsifal* suggest that the actors would play directly in front of the backdrop, however far back from the camera it was situated.

The stage also used backdrops, although in combination with wings at the sides to mask the backstage area, to hide lighting instruments, and to suggest depth. (The film's frame served similar purposes and eliminated the need for wings.) In vaudeville, the depth at which the backdrop was placed defined the playing area, from a shallow space downstage for comic skits, to a deep, full stage for playlets and more elaborate acts.[7] Theaters had a stock set of backdrops for use in all situations. The box set had gradually become more prominent from the 1840s on, but as one theater historian put it in 1928, 'This present progressive century was well begun before all theatres had relinquished the old practice of representing closed rooms with open wings and borders.'[8] Large playhouses could afford to convert their setting practices, but smaller ones had little choice about retaining existing equipment. Vaudeville acts and touring legitimate troupes needed simple, portable scenery which could fit on any provincial theater's stage. Box sets finally replaced drops and wings on a widespread basis in the first decade of this century.

The cinema, with its initial close links to vaudeville, used its own version of the backdrop method. In addition to their conventional familiarity, flat drops offered economic advantages; they were cheaper than solid sets and took up less room on the small studio stages. Producers continued to use backdrops only as long as the film industry remained relatively small. Economic growth and stability followed in the wake of the nickelodeon boom and the formation of the MPPC. As soon as filmmakers were financially capable of introducing more elaborate, three-dimensional sets, they did so. The rising fortunes of the film industry are paralleled by the increasing importance of set design, until the heyday of the art director in the early twenties. The film industry's conversion to more three-dimensional sets also came at about the same time that the smaller theaters were converting to the use of box sets. Although not in the forefront in this change, neither did the film industry lag seriously behind the popular theatrical practice of the day.

By the time that the transition to the classical

cinema had begun, around 1909, there are signs that commentators were becoming discontented with painted sets. Compare these three remarks from the period:[9]

(1909) Is there any verisimilitude or truth in a picture of a woman weeping amidst the ruins of her home, when the canvas door evidently shakes and the flood of light which surrounds her obviously cannot come from the all-too-obviously *papier mâché* chandelier above her?

(1911) Artificial stage methods have been discarded by every successful company. Everywhere the tendency is toward truthful and compelling simulation of real life [i.e., building of actual sets and going on location].

(A 1911 review of *The Scarlet Letter* [Herbert Brenon, Imp]) The scene of the public street showing the stocks seemed rather flat and shallow. A street scene, above all others should convey the idea of depth or distance, which this scene did not. It is very obviously a painted drop upon which shadows fall, and it was also very easy to see the line of connection it made with the stage.

During the same years that these expressions of dissatisfaction appeared, filmmakers were beginning to alter set design in several important ways. Walls became more solid and now appeared at an angle to the camera. Three-dimensional trimmings were attached to the walls. Furniture was moved forward toward the camera. Moreover, whenever possible sets were built on location, so that real landscapes rather than painted flats frequently appeared outside windows in the early teens. All these devices give a greater sense of depth, and some also move the playing space out toward the camera. In conjunction with the placement of the actors in the foreground, this new approach to setting helped to place the spectator within or on the edge of the narrative space.

Even in using backdrops, filmmakers of the primitive period had sometimes attempted to create depth by the suggestion of a second wall. By placing a corner at the side of the frame and showing a bit of a wall extending forward, they avoided the completely flat drop effect. See figure 15.3 for an example. As should be clear from this shot, however, the second wall did not extend the playing space forward substantially.

One of the most famous early examples of a deep playing area is the banquet scene in *A Corner in Wheat* (D.W. Griffith, 1909, Biograph), where the long table juts directly forward; as a result, the group of well-wishers face the Wheat King at the right foreground, creating a dynamic composition. But other less startling examples occur in that same year. Lubin had abandoned the busy painted drops that characterized his earlier studio product. He put out several films in 1909 that faced the camera into a corner: *She Would Be an Actress* (the opening scene in the couple's dining room) and *An Unexpected Guest* (both the nurse's home and the young doctor's study). Another example is Griffith's *Faithful* (1910, Biograph), in which the hero's dining room has a centered corner, functional French windows, and several real pieces of furniture against the wall, as well as the dining table and chairs at the center (see fig 17.9). All three of these examples use painted flats rather than backdrops, to achieve a three-dimensional corner (as opposed to the painted corner in fig 17.8 above). The set in *She Would Be an Actress* contains a real china cupboard which is present purely for realistic effect; it never figures in the action. The *Faithful* set is substantial enough to hold a mirror. It is still possible to see the canvas rippling in the breeze in some films done in the open air during the teens, but this distraction soon disappears.[10]*

During the early teens, filmmakers began consistently placing furniture in the foreground, often extending out of sight at the lower frame-line. This practice has several advantages: It could motivate a character's move forward, and it could maintain the sense of deep space even when the characters remained at a distance. In one shot from *The Bells* (1913, Edison), the characters are not close to the camera, but the cluttered desk, the hat on the chair, and the table with its bowl, all convey a sense of the room extended forward (see fig 17.10). Note also that the back wall has several corners, placing the actors more firmly within a three-dimensional locale.

In addition to expanding the action forward from the back wall, there were attempts to suggest depth beyond that barrier. Real trees and vistas outside windows and doors were one solution, created by constructing the set outdoors, in front of the appropriate landscape. The multiple-room set was another solution. In the primitive period, the small size of stages would prevent the construction of a second room beyond the main one. But as larger permanent studios were built and outdoor filming became more feasible (due to the moves to warmer climates and the acquisition of studio lots), some filmmakers in the early to mid-teens began to place a large doorway at the rear of the set. Beyond, a substantial portion of another room would be visible.[11]* This enhanced the representation of spacious homes and made for a greater variety of staging possibilities. *The Girl in the Arm-Chair* (1912, Solax) contains a set with a parlor in the foreground and a hallway with staircase at the rear (fig 17.11). This set creates several distinct major playing spaces in depth, with the armchair at foreground right figuring in several key scenes, the safe at the left of the door doing likewise, and the hallway beyond providing dramatic entrances and exits (as in the frame shown). In fact, this set appears in many shots in the film; possibly its greater expense limited the total number of sets the film could use.

Expense was certainly a prime consideration in the early teens. Scenario guidebooks cautioned their readers that a narrative calling for too many sets could lead to a rejection slip. In 1913, one writer suggested that six was the usual limit, and another gave a formula: 'No one-reel picture should require more "sets" than would approximate one-third of the total number of scenes, feature and out-door pictures excepted.'[12] (One-reelers of this period contained perhaps fifty to sixty shots. Given that some of these were titles and exteriors, a figure of six sets is reasonable.)

By about 1913, it is likely that producers had reached the maximum expense for sets that could be supported by one-reel filmmaking. Longer films, however, made it possible to spend more lavishly on at least one set per film. Warning scenarists against narratives that demand expensive sets, one columnist used the cabaret set of *The Mothering Heart* (Griffith, 1913, Biograph) as an example; he explained that Biograph could afford such a set because it habitually sold a larger number of prints, and because 'it is a multiple-reel, so that the cost is partially distributed through two reels.'[13] The same principle would hold true for longer features. Fox reportedly built a six-room set for a Theda Bara feature in 1916. An estimate of that same year suggests that the cheapest sets would cost several hundred dollars, while 'a good restaurant or cabaret scene may cost from $2,000 to $5,000, depending on its elaborateness and size.' Chapter 9 has also noted that publicity played up the extravagant costs of the sets as 'production value.' Promoters claimed that the Babylon set in *Intolerance* cost $50,000 and that $35,000 was spent on one set in *Civilization* (1916, Ince).[14]

The growing expense of set-building went not simply into general enlargement but specifically into greater dimension in depth. Figure 17.12 from *The Eagle's Mate* (James Kirkwood, 1914, Famous Players), shows a typical teens 'box' set for a feature film. Such a set is like a rectangle with the invisible wall placed at one of the short sides. The principle is a functional one, since in a very large, wide set the side walls would not be visible within the frame, and the set would resemble a flat backdrop placed at a distance. The result is a deep playing area rather like an Italian Renaissance stage, but with solid walls replacing the layers of flat wings at the sides. As Chapter 13 points out, contemporary designers recognized that they were creating sets to suit the perspective limitations of the motion-picture lens. One of Hollywood's top art directors, Hugo Ballin, wrote in 1921: 'A lens represents one eye, it may be the right or the left. Therefore it is important in sets to get *depth*, not width. The depth of a motion picture is infinite, its width finite.'[15] Aside from the deep rectangular box set, there was the L-shaped set with two walls. The longer wall extended toward the foreground, and the camera filmed obliquely along it into the corner. This method also creates a sense of depth, while eliminating the need for building the third wall.

By itself, deep set design would not be enough to place the spectator within the playing space. But in combination with multiple planes of action and deep focus, the deep set contributed to the extension of that space forward toward the camera. Thus the set's depth perspective would be visible mainly in the establishing shot, while analytical editing would place the spectator's vantage point within the set. Set designers took the camera's placement into account; a 1922 commentator described the planning stages:[16]

Once the requirements of the sets have been established, the art director instructs members of his staff as to those requirements, the approximate size, the placing of such buildings as will be used, their use, the angle at which the camera will view the set and the distance at which it will be placed from the foreground in the long shots.

Planning promoted efficiency, preventing the crew from building more of the set than would appear within the frame. But it also helped create the optimum view. The camera would still stand outside the front boundary of the set in the establishing shots, but the front edge would extend just far enough to be outside the camera's field. (Such planning also encouraged standardization of lens lengths, so that the set designers could easily calculate the lens's exact field.) The spectator's vantage point is located on the scene's edge, poised to move into the space on the cut-in.

Studio set design in the mid- and late teens in a sense attempted to reconcile the split between painted backgrounds and location shooting that had existed during the primitive period. Primitive films often cut together shots done in shallow interior sets with those shot in the unlimited depth of real exteriors; for a classical film, such a disjunction would create a break in continuity. So classical design for the most part tried to suggest that settings had the depth of real locations and buildings.

The studios' ideal for authenticity and depth was location shooting itself. With no backdrop to cut off the spectator's view, the location shot could create a considerable sense of depth. In *Rory O'More* (Sidney Olcott, 1911, Kalem; filmed in Ireland) one framing places British soldiers in the foreground taking aim at the tiny figure of Rory, visible in the depth of the shot on the next ridge (see fig 17.13). In the location shot, there is less sense of looking across a neutral zone and into a delimited, rectangular space. Instead, the camera seems to be picking out one section of an expanse that goes on in every direction. The depth of most location shots helped place the spectator almost automatically at the edge of the narrative space.

But location shooting at great distances from the home studios proved excessively expensive. By the mid-teens, the elaborate construction of foreign locales was taking place habitually in the studios. *Scientific American* treated travel abroad as a thing of 'years ago'; it found that: 'To-day, in marked contrast, the producers find it easier to bring the foreign or distant spots to the studio, literally speaking. Accuracy enables them to convince the audience that the scenes are laid in the country called for by the story.' The advantages in studio shooting are that 'the producers have better laboratory facilities, understand the light better, can secure experienced players – and save time.'[17] Chapter 12 has described the increasing breakdown of the studios into specialized departments, including the art department. By using their own facilities, the producers could get better quality and more efficiency. With longer films, more actors, sets, and crews were involved in the shooting process; any savings of time saved commensurately large amounts of money in salaries. Add to this the traveling costs themselves, and the economies of all-studio-made shooting became considerable.[18]

From the mid-teens on, the switch from location shooting to large, deep studio sets was made possible by the acquisition of back lots and the erection of standing sets. Sets representing interiors were typically built either on indoor studio stages (especially in the eastern studios) or on outdoor stages (in the West and other sunny climes; see figure 17.14, Universal's stages *c.* 1915 in Universal City, near Los Angeles). But larger buildings would not fit on such platforms; filmmakers built them on plots of land adjacent to the studio buildings – the 'back lot.'[19]*

The introduction of the back lot, in combination with the growing prosperity of the larger companies, gave rise to some lavish settings. In the early teens, historical epics imitated the successful Italian features. The palace set in *The Coming of Columbus* (Colin Campbell, 1912, Selig three-reeler; fig 17.15) was considered by *Motography* to be the largest interior ever constructed for a film.[20] Later films contained sets that dwarfed this one. Figure 17.16, a production still from *The Queen of Sheba* (J. Gordon Edwards, 1921, Metro), shows the kind of spectacle which could be achieved on the studio back lot (note the echo of the *Cabiria* temple in the building at the right). Such large sets served all of Hollywood's aims, adding novelty through spectacle and placing the spectator on the edge of a playing space much deeper than that possible on

a theater stage.

It is worth noting that during the mid-teens, Hollywood set design decisively parted ways with theatrical practices of the period. At that point, the 'new stagecraft' of Gordon Craig, Max Reinhardt, Adolphe Appia, and other European producers and designers was having a major impact on American theater. The naturalistic design which had dominated for several decades under such people as David Belasco, gave way to a simplified, more stylized and atmospheric approach. Yet one could scarcely infer that this major change was going on by watching the films of the teens. Maurice Tourneur made an isolated pair of films using painted, stylized sets – *The Blue Bird* and *Prunella* (both 1918, Famous Players-Lasky) – but their dismal box-office showing ended his attempt to align Hollywood with the current theatrical scene. In general, Hollywood set design has developed its own methods, remaining true to its origins in the turn-of-the-century realist approach.

Chapter 13 has described the addition of staff members to design and supervise settings for film studios. First, during the approximate period 1907 to 1915, there was the stage manager, a role replaced by that of the art director. Art directors were expected on the one hand to create designs of great beauty or spectacle, and on the other to be expert enough to insure historical and geographic accuracy.

But as with other elements of the classical Hollywood film, beauty, spectacle, and historical accuracy were generally subordinate to narrative function. Harold Grieve, art director for the Marshall Neilan Studios, summed up this belief in 1926:[21]

> The day of sets for sets' sake is passed. For a successful picture, there must be coordination of a most intimate nature between sets and story, for the sets must help get over the feeling of the story. Mere realism or beauty alone is not sufficient. The sets must be built to harmonize with the intention of the director. They must always remain in the background, but they must fit the plot just as exactly as paper fits the wall of a room.

In order to coordinate set designs with the narrative, the art director had to be aware of other aspects of the planning. As even the California studios began increasingly to use artificially lit interior stages in the late teens, the art directors came to concern themselves with the total visual look of the shots. These art directors were coming from backgrounds in theater, in art, and in architecture; they would be accustomed to controlling or considering the effects of lighting. The art director would be likely to encourage his company to use studio interiors for greater flexibility of composition. The perpetual Hollywood comparison of setting and lighting design with painting (specifically, the Old Masters) came into being in the mid-teens. Increasingly, the art director collaborated with the director and cinematographer to plan the effects of lights and lenses. Famous Players-Lasky's art director, Wilfred Buckland, who had been trained as an engineer and architect, wrote in 1924:[22]

By approaching screen settings from the standpoint of the pictorial artists and not the architect leading art directors are revolutionizing the building of photoplay backgrounds.

Heretofore, the majority of art directors have been architects rather than artists. The setting has been made all-important and constructed with no thought of the action to take place within it. . . .

In building our settings around our characters, instead of first constructing our setting and then forcing the players into it, we are substituting for the old method an arrangement which aids and intensifies the movements of the actors — we concentrate the attention on the dramatic interest.

We also study our backgrounds, not only for pictorial composition, but for the relation of the tonal values to the figure. . . .

We are applying to our screen pictures the same laws and principles that the old masters applied to their paintings — laws which are as definite as those of physics and mechanics.

Our new school of screen artistry in settings considers also the lighting of our pictures, for on the camera's sensitized film we can paint with light and shade as an artist paints with pigment upon canvas.

This approach reached a high level of sophistication by the late silent period, with the work of William Cameron Menzies. Menzies made numerous sketches of shots, incorporating lighting, camera angle, and even lens length into the drawings (as in fig 17.17, from *The Beloved Rogue* [Alan Crosland, 1927, Feature Productions]).

By the late teens, as classical film practice had become standardized, deep sets containing multiple planes of playing area were the norm for American films. They aided in the general process of placing the spectator within the narrative space. The final touch in this process was the clear presentation of these planes using deep focus cinematography.

Deep focus cinematography

Through much of the silent period, filmmakers assumed that a considerable photographic depth of field was desirable for most shots. Critical attention to depth of field was evident as early as 1908:[23]

Motion-picture people will tell you — some of them — that you can't have foreground sharp with the distance. And they use lenses of a couple of inches in focal length! The trouble is they sometimes use lenses of too long focus with too large openings, and do not distinguish enough between a bright day and a cloudy one, a well-lighted spot and a dim one and consequently, do not diaphragm their lenses enough when, as it is frequently possible to do, in bright lights a prominent foreground is to be included.

The principles of achieving depth of field were certainly known from still photography. A fan's review of Essanay's 1910 *The Price of Fame* remarked in *The Nickelodeon*: 'Here the makers have secured a good depth to the picture without a loss of detail.'[24] Throughout the teens and twenties, the numerous guides to cinematography almost invariably assume that the greatest possible depth of field is the proper goal. They give clear instructions for achieving deep focus through the manipulation of f-stops, lens lengths, and lighting conditions.[25]

Many films from the teens suggest filmmakers were aware of such principles and could apply them. In most shots with multiple planes of action, the foreground character will be in medium shot, with the background kept in sharp focus. In 1913, Kalem's *A Race With Time* contains a shot (see fig 17.18) taken from behind a telegraph operator as his daughter appears in the distance and walks up to the window to give him his lunch. All planes are kept in focus throughout. There are several compositions in an early feature, *Damon and Pythias* (Otis Turner, 1914, Universal), that place characters near the lens, with other characters in planes beyond (fig 17.19). *The Case of Becky* (Frank Reicher, 1915, Lasky) shows how characters could be juxtaposed against rather busy backgrounds, which still remained in clear focus (fig 17.20). A similarly cluttered background appears behind the shot/reverse-shot passage in *Field of Honor* (Alan Holubar, 1917, Butterfly; figs 16.73 and 16.74). Such background objects, kept in sharp focus and brightly illuminated, tend to compete with the main figures for attention; a few years later, such background planes would be lit more dimly to minimize their distracting effects. A dance scene in *Love and the Law* (1919, Edgar Lewis) contains a shot with the camera moving close to one couple, while the band remains in clear focus beyond (fig 17.21).

As these examples show, the depth of field achieved in this period would not be of the type later associated with Gregg Toland, with the foreground character or object placed very close to the lens. But the characters could be in medium-shot framing, with the background kept sharply in focus. The avoidance of extreme depth of field may have resulted as much from aesthetic considerations as from technical ones. Most cut-ins still framed the actors in medium shot at this point; tight facial close-ups seldom appeared in films. In addition, some commentaries of the period suggest that the distortion caused by short focal-length lenses was considered disturbing and undesirable. A 1911 *Moving Picture World* article advised: 'Experienced photographers know that to get naturalness of effect in a picture a short focus lens should be avoided, otherwise you get distortion, that is unnecessary enlargement in parts of the pictures.'[26] Three years later a British cinematography guide suggested that foreground figures would seem grotesquely large in relation to the background:[27]

> The use of too short focus lenses and the consequent excessive nearness of the camera to the scene is the cause of those unpleasant pictures that we sometimes see, which are apt to suggest to the flippant-minded Gulliver among the Pygmies.

The suggestion here is that the distorting properties of the wide-angle lens – which enlarges foreground objects and diminishes those in distant planes – would make Toland-style deep focus distracting for audiences in the teens.

By the late silent period, however, exaggerated depth was appearing occasionally. The increased use of occasional tight close-ups, added to the greater variety of lens lengths in use, combined to make the large foreground object less incongruous, as figure 17.22, from *The Magician* (Rex Ingram, 1926, MGM) demonstrates. The villainous hypnotist looks down through an upper window, at the heroine in the courtyard below, visible in crisp focus. Depth functions narrationally here to suggest the hypnotist's mental control over the heroine. In general, an obvious separation of planes of action with deep focus was rare in the silent period, nor do whole films use the technique throughout. Yet the basic technology was clearly available, and filmmakers drew upon it occasionally for specific narrative purposes.

Aside from contemporary accounts and the films themselves, we know that the technology had to be available. Cinematographers began using glass shots in the early twenties; these involved placing a large glass sheet with a partial painting on it in a frame or clamp between the lens and the scene to be filmed. If properly aligned and lit, the painting blended in with the scene beyond.[28] But less attention has been given to the fact that glass shots implied a command of depth of field. A 1922 account describes how they depend upon the fact that:[29]

> with a 2-inch lens working at f-5.6, an average operating condition, the depth of field is so great that objects placed at close range and far away are all rendered sharply enough for practical purposes. The hyperfocal distance (based on a 100th inch circle of confusion) of a 2-inch lens at f-5.6 is 6 feet. In practice all objects from 5 feet

to infinity are rendered sufficiently sharp.

We must dismiss, then, any lingering notion that the silent period used only a crude, unintentional deep focus resulting from 'contrasty' ortho-chromatic film or from crude, slow lenses.[30*] If filmmakers did not place great stress upon deep focus, it was because such a basic assumption of their practice did not need reiteration: that one would seek as great a depth of field as shooting conditions permitted. In Chapter 21, we shall see that even after the growth of a soft style of filming, depth of field remained a concern.

Deep focus cinematography worked in combination with staging in multiple planes and with depth in set design. The spectator would not look across a space toward distant figures and setting. Instead, the larger foreground figures or setting elements would give an impression of nearness — the spectator would look past them into the deeper layers of the scene. Some shots would employ deep focus and multiple planes; other shots in the same sequence would not. The cut-in could seem to move the spectator's vantage point past the foreground elements, toward a portion of the space that had been clearly visible in a previous shot.

Together, staging, set design, and depth of field contributed to the extension of narrative space forward, with all its planes kept clearly visible. But without a change in lighting styles, the effect could be problematic. If a deep-focus composition keeps the background plane brightly lit, objects of minimal narrative significance may draw our eye away from the central action. We have already seen how in figures 16.77, 16.78, and 17.20, the busy walls at the rear attract an undue amount of attention. One additional technique, that of directional, selective lighting, was necessary in order to downplay the less significant areas of visible space within the frame.

Lighting for clarity and depth

During the teens, the adoption of arc equipment moved American film lighting practice away from a dominant use of diffused, overall illumination toward a concentration on 'effects' lighting. Effects were generally directional patches of light realistically motivated as having a specific source

within the story. During the primitive period, diffused lighting had been a part of the mise-en-scene which did not function narratively. It was the same whatever the narrative situation (excepting the occasional cases of fireplaces and windows). But with the classical drive to subsume every technique within the overall motivation of the narrative, there came an interest in varying lighting to suit the situation — to have the lighting issuing realistically from narrative space and varying with circumstances.

A 1918 article defined light effects:[31]

A sign of the increased artistry on the part of motion picture producers was the introduction, some years ago of 'light effects' in their interior scenes, a 'light effect' being broadly defined as that manner of lighting a scene which would produce in the resultant photographs the appearance, or effect, of the various objects or characters in the scene being lighted to an extent which would be expected under the natural conditions which the scene was intended to represent, and with the light on any given object coming from the direction which, likewise, would be noted under the natural conditions supposed to be duplicated in the scene.

Figures 17.23 and 17.24 show a light effect from *Shamus O'Brien* (1912, Imp). Shamus is hiding in a loft from his British pursuers. As he raises a trapdoor, a beam of light from below picks him out starkly. He raises the door further and, through a stop-motion effect, dim fill light falls on the wall behind. This is an early application of the principles described in the above definition.

With the technical improvement in arc lighting during the teens, light effects became easier to execute. In 1917, Kenneth MacGowan commented favorably upon the growing tendency toward effects lighting, citing an Ince production called *Chicken Casey*:[32]

Light becomes atmosphere instead of illumination. Coming naturally from some window, lamp, or doorway, it illumines the center of the picture and the people standing there, with a glow that in intensity, in volume, or in variety of sources has some quality expressive of the emotion of the scene.

Lighting still retained its invariable function of illuminating the scene enough for it to be photographed, of course. But as MacGowan suggests, 'natural' light sources and atmospheric enhancement of the narrative came to be important considerations as well.

As an illustration of the kind of lighting MacGowan is talking about, consider a four-shot segment from *The Clodhopper*, a 1917 Ince-produced feature (directed by Victor Schertzinger). In the first shot of the scene (see fig 17.25), we see the hero's shadow on the wall as he sits sewing late at night. An eyeline match shows his mother looking at the shadow; a stark light falls on her face, motivated by the candle she holds (fig 17.26). She looks around, and another eyeline match reveals the hero, also starkly lit, the lighting now motivated by the lantern at his elbow (fig 17.27). The fourth shot is an establishing shot of the whole, with more general lighting (fig 17.28). Here much of the effect of the mother discovering her son sitting up late to repair his old clothes is created by the use of light effects, which not only create the sense of lateness, but also help prolong the moment by motivating the mother's gradual discovery of her son's activities.

Light effects initially served a novelty function as well. Occasionally during the teens, advertisements in trade journals stressed special light effects in films, sometimes using illustrations from relevant scenes. Figure 17.29 shows an advertisement for an early 1912 Imp release, stressing the fireplace effect in the still as the main selling point of the film. In 1917, *Reel Life* ran an advertisement for the Signal Film Corp.'s production, *A Lass of the Lumberlands* (a Helen Holmes serial released through Mutual); the description in the advertisement mentions the film's 'unusual lighting effects' and says:

In Lighting effects, the new Mutual chapterplay, 'A Lass of the Lumberlands' is as unusual and superior to other serials as it is in plot, action, and enactment. Some of the wonderful night 'effects' are positively startling. It is almost uncanny to behold flashing headlights, brilliantly lighted Pullmans and tremendous bonfires, depicted on the screen with such reality.

This advertisement contains a still of three men in a car at night, picked out against the black background by a single low light source within the car.[33] Thus light effects fulfilled both stylistic and economic functions – verisimilitude, atmosphere, and product differentiation.

This tendency toward the motivation of light effects from within the diegetic space was not the only impulse behind the creation of a classical lighting style, however. Paralleling this tendency was a move away from diffusion toward modeling of figures and objects through selective lighting. These two tendencies go hand in hand, since selective lighting could draw upon naturalistic sources within the story space for its motivation. Yet the specific purpose of selective lighting was not so much an impression of naturalism as it was an aesthetically pleasing image and an illusion of greater depth.

Because filmmakers sought more and more selectivity in illumination, different lighting types gradually emerged. A 1915 writer indicates that a distinction between key and fill lights was common knowledge: 'It may be laid down as a safe rule in studio practice that there shall be, first, a primary source of light ... and in addition a secondary source, used to accentuate portions of the scene or action which it is desired to bring out in sharp relief.'[34] After 1910 the principles of back and side-lighting were employed to enhance the beauty of shots and to separate figure from background. In figure 17.30 from *The Loafer* (1911, Essanay), the camera has been placed in an exterior so as to keep the sun to the left and rear, behind the figures, outlining them partially with backlight. (See Appendix D, Diagram 2, for a contemporary illustration of how sidelighting could be done.)

Several types of lighting were in at least occasional use, then, before the mid-teens. But a great shift in American lighting practice started in 1915, with lighting effects and selective lighting becoming widespread in the various studios in succeeding years. There can be little doubt that the change is in large part due to the practices of the Cecil B. De Mille unit at the Lasky studio. In 1915, De Mille and his cinematographer, Alvin Wyckoff, used spotlights provided by art director Wilfred Buckland to produce low-key lighting effects in several productions: *The Warrens of Virginia* (released February), *Carmen*

(November), and, most noticeably, in *The Cheat* (December). Jesse L. Lasky used the lighting as a means of gaining publicity for his films; he wrote to *Motography* just before the release of *The Cheat*, saying: 'The picture should mark a new era in lighting as applied to screen productions.'[35]

Contemporary sources invariably credit this innovation to De Mille and his colleagues, and motivated low-key lighting arrangements soon came to be known as 'Lasky lighting.' One review of *The Cheat* commented on 'the development in the Lasky school of the purely photographic part. No school has attained greater achievements in this respect. We would have to admire the purely photographic part even if it were not subordinated to the plot. When it is thus subordinated the lighting effects may well be called a new dramatic force.'[36] This review articulates clearly the developing classical conception of lighting usage. Selective lighting adds a pleasing aesthetic quality to the image, but can be justified as having a source within the scenic space. Hence it enhances the narrative effect while providing a modicum of spectacle in its own right.

Figure 17.31 is from the famous opening scene of *The Cheat*; placed against an entirely dark background, the figure stands out in a single-source spotlight motivated as coming from a window offscreen right. Several major scenes, usually involving the Japanese businessman, use effects depending on directional spotlights. Other films from 1915 and 1916 copy Lasky lighting in a fairly direct way. In *His Phantom Sweetheart* (April 1915, Vitagraph), there is a shot with a figure illuminated starkly from the side by light coming from the next room (fig 17.32). *Dolly's Scoop* (Joseph De Grasse, 1916, Rex) has a scene with the heroine and her mother eating at a table lit by a single source, motivated as a hanging lamp; the rest of the room is in total darkness (fig 17.33).

Yet such extreme contrasts of light and dark, highly praised though they were at the time, did not become the standard way of creating a selective lighting set-up. The majority of films that used selective lighting after 1915 mixed key and fill, often adding a touch of backlight. De Mille's composition of one shot from *The Girl of the Golden West* (1915, Lasky) typifies the softer modeling of faces that became standard; the shot also shows a subdued lighting on the background

that renders it unobtrusively visible (fig 17.34). Other directors at Lasky used light effects less dramatically than De Mille had in *The Cheat*, demonstrating a combination of motivated sources and selective illumination (see fig 17.35).

Within a few years, other studios had adopted the two principles of motivated light sources and selective lighting, making these the basis of the classical approach to lighting. In 1917, studio head Edwin Thanhouser declared the changes in lighting practice over the past few years to be an innovation second in significance only to that of the feature film:

> A subdued shadow for an unimportant background, the accentuating of some individual face or expression or some particular action, the reflection of sunlight or moonlight through an open window, the definite sphere of radiation from an electric light, the soft glow of a fireplace, and hundreds of effects of light and shadow, all these have been perfected now, although but a few years ago, they were still in the category of crude experiments. By centering lights at different points, and subduing or omitting them altogether at others, the entire science of motion picture photography has been revolutionized.

By the end of the teens, films often extended and refined backlighting by using it to surround the entire figure — creating what was called 'rim' lighting. The accompanying frames from *The Four Horsemen of the Apocalypse* (Rex Ingram, 1921, Metro) and *A Cumberland Romance* (Charles Maigne, 1920, Realart Pictures Corp.) demonstrate how figures were carefully picked out against a subdued background by a set of lights pointing in from a variety of directions (figs 17.36 and 17.37). As Thanhouser concludes:[37]

> For the old style of diffusing light evenly over an entire scene has given place to the newer and better method, and it is now not uncommon to see a succession of Rembrandt-like pictures, the light effects of which rival, in that respect, some of the best conceptions of the Old Masters.

Filmmakers and writers were aware of the ability of selective lighting, and especially backlighting, to produce a greater impression of depth. By outlining figures in light, the filmmaker could make them stand out against a subdued background. This in turn was desirable because it kept the eye from wandering to the set and away from the main narrative action. In 1921, Frederick S. Mills, Lasky's electrical illuminating engineer, wrote:[38]

> By focusing a spotlight on the back of the heads of the principals, the image or images are caused to stand out from the background and the figures are more pronounced and thus better depth is obtained. If this were not done, the figures would go dead against the background, no matter how far out they stood in the perspective.

Later, in 1925, a presentation to the Society of Motion Picture Engineers demonstrated the effects of backlighting. The lecturers compared two stills from *Night Life of New York* (Allan Dwan, 1925, Famous Players-Lasky; see fig 17.38), showing three actors in medium shot against a dark background. In the first, backlighting is used:

> Note how the spotlight has been used to bring up each of the characters. These highlights on the heads of each of the two men separate them from the dark background at the same time revealing the position of Mr. Kelly's left arm. The dark coat of Miss Gish has been revealed in the same manner.

The second picture is the same composition, but with all the lighting coming from the front:[39]

> Here the dark heads of the men disappear into the background and there is no suggestion of the left arm position. Obviously spotlighting of this kind is necessary. . . . This effect and more especially that obtained from back lighting has been done in the last few years.

This careful modeling was especially important for glamor lighting. A set-up with a key light from the left, fill from the right, and a strong backlighting is evident in one medium close-up of Mary Miles Minter from *The Ghost of Rosy Taylor* (Edward Sloman, 1918, American; see fig 17.39). The use of backlighting on blonde hair was not

only spectacular but necessary — it was the only way filmmakers could get blonde hair to look light-colored on the yellow-insensitive ortho-chromatic stock.

Figure 17.40 shows how a close shot would combine a variety of lights, with arc floodlights at the sides, mercury-vapors and a reflector for fill light in front, and an arc spot at the rear to high-light the actress's blonde hair. The same basic types of lighting were used for long shots. The lighting set-up for *Mr. Billings Spends His Dime* (1923, Famous Players-Lasky; see fig 17.41) demonstrates the use of large floodlights in the foreground for overall illumination, with a considerable amount of sidelight coming from arc broadsides in stands. Note also the pairs of spotlights shining down from the tops of the set's walls at the rear. This combination tends to outline the figures in glowing light, as in figures 17.36 and 17.37.

The move away from diffused to selective light is apparent from lighting plots published in contemporary accounts. (The lighting plots and descriptions in Appendix D show shifts in approach through the period 1914 to 1925.) These various lighting set-ups represent the basic principles of arrangement; filmmakers could of course alter them according to circumstances. But the arrangement of lamps was the single greatest consumer of time during shooting; other personnel were paid for doing nothing while technicians changed the lights. So practice would tend toward standardized lay-outs for lighting. Usually only the larger budget films under imaginative directors, designers, and cinematographers, would display atypical effects.

As with other stylistic devices, lighting was ultimately judged by its contribution to the narrative. In spite of the many claims that Hollywood had an aesthetic of realism, film-makers would always sacrifice realism if this was necessary for a clearer understanding of the story. In 1924, cinematographer Norton F. Brodin summed up this distinction between realist and narrative functions:[40]

> People often ask if eventually the screen lighting will not be exactly like natural lighting — people in a room, for instance, being lighted through the one window of the room. It does not seem that this condition will ever arrive. What

the screen loses in voice it must make up in gesture and traveling as it must always, at a steady, fast rate, there must not be anything lost that will aid the plot and the development of it. Furthermore, it seems more important to photograph scenes advantageously from the angle of the subject, and the audience, too, rather than to be just correct in lighting. Every day we come closer to photographing scenes as they really are but never will we discard the art of photographing people and objects in the backgrounds for certain pleasing effects.

Brodin touches upon one recurring rationale for the classical narration – to show things 'advantageously' for the audience. In the primitive cinema, lighting helped the spectator to see; later, filmmakers began to consider light as it could function to help the spectator to understand more and more. By picking important figures out more brightly than their surroundings, selective lighting could emphasize them and could establish their position in the depth of the scene. Beauty and realism were additional functions, designed to make the viewer's understanding pleasurable and its technological sources in filmmaking unobtrusive.

Framing as a guide for the spectator

Depth placed the spectator on the edge of the narrative space and lighting helped pick out the salient objects in that space. But lighting was only reinforcing another strong cue for the spectator's attention – framing. Centering, the balanced composition, and the mobile frame to follow or reveal action could all work with or without selective lighting to guide the eye and to create expectations about the most important elements in a scene.

The principles of composition Chapter 5 has described as characteristic of the classical Hollywood cinema are in evidence from the early teens. Important characters and actions draw our eye because they occupy the center of the screen. The area about one-third of the way down from the top of the frame is a privileged one for faces; whether the framing is distant or close, the heads tend to line up there (see fig 17.42). A glance through the other illustrations in this section will

confirm that this practice was widespread early in the classical period.

When two figures are present, they usually balance one another, standing about equidistant from the center. (Again, fig 17.42 and other frames in this section demonstrate this.) In the primitive period, important actions sometimes took place at the extreme sides or corners of the frame. In *The Skyscrapers* (1905, AM&B), for example, the villain plants a stolen watch in the foreman's house for revenge; the foreman's daughter watches this from a hiding place and later is able to confront the villain in court and reveal his guilt. But in the planting scene, the daughter's hiding place is in the extreme upper left of the frame; even granting that original prints probably would have shown more than we see in modern ones, the framing still emphasizes the villain's gestures more than the daughter's, because he is at the center of the frame. The classical composition took care to guide the spectator's eye to the pertinent actions without effort.

One of the main impulses toward the mobile frame, or moving camera, came from the effort to maintain centering. By far the greatest number of films that used camera movement before the mid-twenties used it strictly to reframe rather than to track or pan with an extended movement. Jon Gartenberg has shown that occasional primitive films use panning or tracking.[41] Certainly the possibility of moving the camera was well-known almost from the beginning of cinema. But in the primitive period, the moving camera was associated more with scenics and topicals. These would often consist of shots in which the camera surveyed a location by panning in a circle or by moving while mounted on a vehicle. In such films, camera movement often created the main action or change by providing additional depth cues. Without camera movement, such films as Edison's series of views of Kicking Horse Canyon (1901) would show an unmoving landscape; they would offer little novelty value beyond that of a simple lantern slide of the same sight.

But the fiction film usually needed no such added motion. Figure movement provided the main interest, and in most cases staging could be done within the limits of the camera's range. Undoubtedly the static framing of most early narrative-film shots arose from the camera's imitation of a spectator in a theater seat. The flat back wall of the set did not extend much beyond the edges of the frame, and hence panning was often impossible – there was no new space to reveal. Certainly shots done out of doors use camera movements more frequently than those made in studio settings. (They occur, for example, in *The Great Train Robbery* [Porter, 1903, Edison], *A Bold Bank Robbery* [1904, Lubin], *The Skyscrapers* [1905, AM&B], and *Her First Adventure* [1908, AM&B].) Brief reframing pans became common in the teens; they occurred in about half the Extended Sample films from 1911, and they remained at about that frequency through the teens.

In spite of this common use of reframing, few films went on to employ lengthy pans or tracks. Some writers found panning distracting. One 1914 script guide commented:'Theoretically, the eye of the camera never moves, excepting in the disillusioning practice of some operators to follow the movement of energetic characters by "panoram-ing." '42 This opinion suggests that there was some resistance to camera movement, just as there had been to close framings. A moving camera would call attention to the frame itself, rather than the action within it. With the growing emphasis on centering the action, however, reframings were inevitable; if a figure moved partially out of the frame, there was no way to make the action visible but by re-centering. Commentators and practitioners soon realized that a small camera movement would be less distracting than a figure partially concealed by the frameline.

Reframing was not always a matter of casual adjustment to the vagaries of figure movement. Many reframings, especially from the mid-teens on, show strong evidence of planning. Figure 17.43 shows the situation at the beginning of a shot in *The Hired Hand* (Victor Schertzinger, 1918, Ince). The actors sit with their heads at the classical point, one-third of the way down from the top of the frame. Suddenly the camera tilts up, to a position where there seems to be too much space above the characters' heads (fig 17.44). In a classical film, this can imply only two things. Either the characters are about to stand up, or another character will enter the frame; whichever the case will be, the camera adjusts the balance of

the composition to anticipate the change. In this case, the characters stand up (fig 17.45). Such anticipatory reframings occur occasionally in the silent cinema; usually, however, the cinematographer tries to coordinate the reframing exactly with the figure movement, to make the camera shift less noticeable. In either case, the reframing soon became common enough not to be distracting to an audience accustomed to the device.

While the main use of camera movement was to center action, cinematographers made limited use of other functions for movement as well. Occasionally a film of the teens employs the mobile frame for a dramatic or comic revelation of new space. This coincides with the transitional period, in which films began to display more self-conscious narration; here the plot delays our knowledge of story events in order to increase their impact on us. In *At Old Fort Dearborn* (1912, Bison '101') a long shot shows a band of Indians on a hill (fig 17.46), then tilts down to show the results of a battle that has just taken place – a ruined wagon with dead driver and horses (fig 17.47). The second sequence of *Wild and Woolly* (John Emerson, 1917, Douglas Fairbanks Corp.) introduces the hero in medium shot, apparently seated at a campfire in front of a teepee; then the camera pulls back to reveal that the teepee is in fact in the hero's Manhattan apartment bedroom. Another common function for tracking or panning shots was to follow a vehicle's or figure's extended movement. Griffith helped popularize placing the camera on a platform attached to a car (as in *Intolerance*) or moving the camera back from racing horsemen (as with the galloping Klan members in *The Birth of a Nation*). Following a moving subject was undoubtedly the most common application of the tracking shot during the silent period.

Under the influence of the Italian epics that were popular in this country in the early to mid-teens, some directors and cinematographers tried using tracking and even crane shots for still other purposes. *Cabiria* (Giovanni Pastrone, 1914, Italy) especially caught filmmakers' attention, and the slow track independent of figure movement came to be known as the '*Cabiria* movement.' Several directors used such tracking shots. For *Intolerance*, Billy Bitzer recalled filming the Babylon set with the camera mounted on a pyramidal dolly 140 feet high, with an elevator to move the camera up and down; in addition, the dolly was on a set of six parallel railroad cars that moved it toward and away from the set.[43] Lois Weber directed an intricate tracking shot for a battle sequence in *The Dumb Girl of Portici* (1915, Weber). Figures 17.48 through 17.50 show how the camera tracks directly to the right along a row of pillars, past the action; then the camera moves diagonally backward and to the left, across the room and away from the pillars. In both these films, the camera moves independently of the action, displaying the epic proportions of the sets and the staging. Movement is an important depth cue, and a mobile framing guaranteed that huge sets like the *Intolerance* and *Dumb Girl of Portici* palaces did not appear as flat, painted surfaces. The studios would want to show off the large volumes of the decor they had paid for. At least one observer of the period noticed tracking shots as a trend:[44]

There is in vogue at some studios now a method of filming a large scene without losing detail that may be adopted generally. This consists in mounting the camera and tripod upon a rubber-wheeled platform, and moving camera and operator about the scene. Thus, first a corner may be photographed; then the camera moves and more of the scene enters the field of vision. Finally the lens may point only to the chief character in the scene.

In this there is the advantage of holding the connection between the different parts of the scene without interruption. At present, however, there is a sense of mechanics which to some may destroy the illusion of the picture.

There were no commercially made camera mounts for such movements, and each studio had to devise its own when the occasion arose. Nevertheless, most seemed to hit upon the same solution — an automobile frame and wheels with rubber tires to cushion the jolts occasioned by moving over rough ground. This apparatus served to make tracking shots, either following action or showing off a set. Several filmmakers have spoken of using such vehicles in the mid-teens,[45*] and by the end of the teens, the terms 'truck-up' and 'truck-back' were in use.[46]

Tracking, panning, and reframing movements remained in occasional use into the twenties.

They were relatively infrequent, however. Most films show such extensive planning that the mobile frame is not necessary. One carefully balanced and beautifully lit composition follows another. The cutting rate was typically so fast that each individual action had its own shot; there was little impulse to combine several actions by adjusting the framing within a shot. Ernst Lubitsch's films, such as *The Marriage Circle* and *Lady Windermere's Fan* (1924 and 1925, Warner Bros), offer good examples of how to avoid reframing. *The Marriage Circle* begins with a tilt up to reveal a character's reaction and contains a few later tracking shots that follow action, but the camera never reframes. One of the most skilfully photographed films of the early twenties, *The Four Horsemen of the Apocalypse* (Rex Ingram, cinematographer John F. Seitz, 1921, Metro), employs some impressive tracking shots during Valentino's tango scenes, but otherwise has only a couple of tiny reframing movements. On the whole, aside from tracking shots following chase scenes and the like, camera movement was a relatively minor part of Hollywood's stylistic repertory until late in the silent period.

The influence of German films in the mid-twenties — especially *Variety* (E.A. Dupont, 1925, Ufa) in 1926 — was considerable. Some cinematographers began to move their camera as freely as they could, once again devising many sorts of elevators, cranes, and elaborate dollies to imitate the German visual acrobatics. The new freedom of movement fitted well into Hollywood's existing practices. Mobile framing could function to display character perception through point-of-view shots, to substitute for editing in the creation of an omnipresent narration, to display the volume of large sets, or to aid in other specialized effects tailored to the needs of a given narrative situation. In *Hotel Imperial* (Maurice Stiller, 1926, MGM), Bert Glennon mounted his camera on an elevator which in turn hung from a set of overhead rails (fig 17.51). Charles Rosher claims to have learned the technique of the dolly suspended from tracks in the ceiling when he was observing the filming of *Faust* in Germany in 1926.[47] He and Karl Struss used it to spectacular effect in the famous camera movement through the swamp in *Sunrise* (F.W. Murnau, 1927, Fox). For *Seventh Heaven* (Frank Borzage, cinematographer Ernest Palmer, 1927, Fox) the camera was mounted on a large elevator to follow the characters vertically up several flights of stairs (fig 17.52). This sudden emphasis on mobile framing undoubtedly contributed to the sense many observers had during the early sound period that the camera was imprisoned in its soundproof booth. Actually, as Chapter 23 will show, early sound filming encouraged a return to reframing.

Continuity editing and the various devices discussed in this chapter – staging, set design, deep focus, lighting practices, and camera movement – combined to tailor space moment by moment to the demands of the narration. In the primitive period, space had been presented in a series of large blocks which kept the spectator at a distance, scanning the entire space to follow the action. By the late teens, films provided multiple cues to guide the eye and the understanding. In effect, omniscient narration began to manipulate the plot relations to a greater degree. The techniques of narration were unobtrusive because films thoroughly motivated their mise-en-scene and framing and matched their shots to create an uninterrupted flow. However strange or difficult silent films may appear to us today, we can still look at works from the late teens and twenties and find a standard classical presentation of causally relevant space and time.

18 The stability of the classical approach after 1917

Standard form is not an arbitrary Detail of a passing Mood, but a composite Assemblage of all that has proved effective in past Expression.[1]

Henry Albert Phillips, 1921

At the beginning of Part Three, I suggested that the classical cinema gained its full formulation in 1917. The initial coalescence of all the elements of classical filmmaking came at that particular time because a variety of practices in the industry had recently become dominant. New subdivisions in the work process created production roles like those of the art director, the master cutter, and the assistant cameraman, leading to a greater emphasis on specialization and defined procedures. Feature films forced more concentration upon a variety of techniques and permitted more money to be invested in each film. The supervisory segment of the studios fostered a division of labor and an attention to efficiency that would further support a systematic approach to filmmaking. Finally, a wide range of industry institutions were disseminating a normative description of the quality film.

I do not wish to imply that all films from 1917 on were complete or correct in their utilization of the classical system. Many drew upon it in a tentative or clumsy way; others could easily be mistaken for mid-twenties films. But few entirely fail to draw upon the system. And by the mid-twenties, classical filmmaking had reached a relative stability.

Undoubtedly a film of the mid-1920s is likely to look somewhat different from one of 1917. During the interval, filmmakers were assimilating the guidelines, which had reached the status of rules. Custom and practice made it easier to match on action smoothly, to light every interior scene with the same overall look, to motivate the movements of characters into various planes, and so on. Such practices were matters of skill; the use of classical guidelines could be more or less correct, but films of the late teens and of the twenties would appeal to the same basic principles. Films of the twenties frequently have a technical and stylistic perfection and an apparent ease missing from most teens films. To some extent this may be due to the fact that a new generation of directors and other filmmakers was already emerging. These people had made their first important films during the mid- to late teens, when the continuity system, effects lighting, and other central aspects of the classical style were being explicitly discussed as the way of doing things. Among directors, John Ford, Raoul Walsh, Edward Sloman, Victor Fleming, Clarence Brown, John Stahl, James Cruze, W.S. Van Dyke, Alan Crosland, Henry King, King Vidor, Rex Ingram, Frank Borzage, William C. deMille, Fred Niblo, and Malcolm St Clair were all expert in the classical system of the twenties, and all made their first major films during the period 1915 to 1920.

By the 1920s, directors, cinematographers, and other filmmakers had a range of models of the classical style to follow. As one 1928 commentator, referring to scenarists, suggested: 'What the trained writer of twelve years or more ago laboriously sweated over and figured out in continuity form, most young men who grew up with the movies (using the screen's evolutionary efforts for their main entertainment) know instinctively today.'[2] After 1917, a filmmaker's attempts to give his or her work a distinctive look would take place within well-defined limits. Filmmaking now was guided by a set of standards and norms often codified in print. A budding filmmaker could be taught the system and would be likely to receive basically the same advice from any experienced practitioner.

Learning standard style

There were no schools or classes held by the studios to teach newcomers how to make films, nor does there appear to have been any formal apprenticeship program at any studio. Certainly the system of assistants to directors, cinematographers, editors, art directors, and the like must have functioned as an informal apprenticeship program. Similarly, filmmakers usually had to work their way up, starting on less important films and moving on to the higher budget features. In 1920, Carl Laemmle described the system in force at Universal:

> Our directors and cameramen, and we hire only the most experienced, go through a new school when they join our organization. They have to work up from the one-reel pictures. Then they graduate to the serials and from there to the special attraction class. They are learning all the time. When they get in the special attraction class they have profited by their previous work. As a result, a Universal special attraction is not marred by a 'serial-ish tone.'

Finally, according to Laemmle, filmmakers would 'graduate' to making Universal-Jewels, the studio's highest line of films.[3]

A variety of practitioners have recalled their early experiences, and, given the absence of primary documentation from the period, these reminiscences are the best evidence we have as to how filmmakers learned their crafts. Young employees were sometimes willing to work long hours, learning skills not called for in their regular duties at the studio. Several have mentioned getting help from more experienced filmmakers who guided them along. Karl Brown worked as an assistant to Bitzer and Griffith, eventually going on to be a cinematographer and director on his own. Margaret Booth has recalled learning editing by watching director John M. Stahl: 'I used to stand by him while he cut, and he used to ask me to come in with him to see his dailies in the projection room. This way he taught me the dramatic values of cutting, he taught me about tempo – in fact he taught me how to edit.' On her own time, Booth practiced editing outtakes until Stahl promoted her to doing his first cut.[4] Dorothy Arzner, a script typist at Famous Players in 1919, got similar help from a cutter, Nan Heron, who eventually recommended her for promotion to script girl and editor. William Hornbeck tells a similar story about getting 'advice and tips' from F. Richard Jones at Keystone; Hornbeck has also recalled that when he began as a projectionist at Keystone, he 'kept watching and each runthrough I'd see what had been done to the film. I would learn from the others that were ahead of me.' The similarity of these stories suggests a pattern that may have been common – with young hopefuls either observing the procedures of more experienced filmmakers, or getting direct advice from them. The same sort of thing apparently happened with writers. When Clarence C. Badger joined the writing staff at Lubin about 1913, the head of that department taught him 'how to split up a story into scenes, in other words, how to write a shooting script.'[5] This method of learning technique would promote standardization of each specialized task. Such learning would be especially necessary in the areas most dependent upon technological knowledge, such as cinematography and laboratory work.

But aspiring filmmakers seem also to have learned the classical style quite simply by watching films. Compare these two remarkably similar accounts of learning style from a theater seat. The first, written long after the fact, is King Vidor's description of his attempts to learn how to direct, the night before he was due to shoot his first film, a freelance newsreel; this was about 1912. The second comes from a 1914 article in which a freelance scenarist told *Photoplay* readers how she had succeeded in selling forty scenarios and winning Vitagraph's scenario contest:[6]

> (Vidor) That evening I tried to increase my knowledge of motion-picture technique by going to the movies. I sat with a stop watch and notebook and tried to estimate the number of cuts or scenes in a thousand-foot reel, the length of individual scenes, the distance of the subject from the camera, and various other technical details.
>
> (Sterne) I went to the movies, pencil and paper in hand, determined to master the technique by study at close range. . . . Before long I had a rough idea of how many scenes constituted a comedy – how many a drama. I discovered

what style of pictures various companies required. Even now I find myself unconsciously counting inserts and scenes as a matter of habit.

The aspirants may have been more systematic than most, but their attention to precise and quantifiable factors accorded well with the studios' ideals.

Early scenario manuals sometimes urged writers to attend films to learn technique. A professional scenarist wrote in 1917:[7]

Every scenario writer should practice continuity writing persistently and should follow carefully the continuity of productions he sees upon the screen, and then he will readily pick the flaws in other writers' work and see where they themselves could better it if given the opportunity. Continuity writing is largely a matter of practice and keen observation.

Professionals within the industry were advising amateurs to do much the same thing they habitually did themselves. Various organizations encouraged filmmakers to gather and see each other's work. In the twenties, industry clubs and professional organizations often had projection rooms or special screenings. The studios themselves had access to prints, which they might show to their employees. Charles G. Clarke, who worked at Fox in the mid-twenties, recalls that the personnel regularly attended dinners which would be followed by screenings of films that studio officials wished them to be aware of. In 1922, the Chicago laboratory of the Rothacker company held a 'cutters' convention,' where a number of editors screened the films they were currently working on.[8]

Cinematographers saw each others' films frequently and influences passed freely among them. Arthur Miller recalled that 'cameramen were copycats; one copied the other, I copied someone, someone also copied me.' Clarke agrees that cinematographers could learn more about lighting, for example, from seeing other people's films than from experimentation. Asked about visually influential films of the period, he named *Four Horsemen of the Apocalypse*, *Broken Blossoms*, and *Way Down East*: 'The only way that you could know what was going on was to go to the movies and see.'[9] The speed with which any innovation became diffused across the industry tends to confirm these recollections.

Although the Hollywood production system favored a certain degree of innovation on the part of its employees, it generally rewarded their conformance to its established filmmaking approaches. As we have seen, an innovation had to be adaptable to the existing guidelines of narrative and stylistic construction before it could enter the system. Even a relative nonconformist would have to know the basic filmmaking paradigm in order to depart from it acceptably.

The contemporary recognition of standardization

All our directors are not great. There would be no fun for the picture audiences if they were. Fans would be deprived of that greatest of all pleasures, writing to the magazines to point out that Marie wore silk stockings going in the door and lace filigreed hose coming out of it.[10]

Peter Milne, 1922

Films and writings of the period demonstrate that certain devices and functions were consistent practice in Hollywood. But beyond this, there is written evidence that Hollywood considered itself standardized. Practitioners did not find the image of factory production detrimental; standardization was conceived as a positive force.

By the late teens and twenties, Hollywood writings were separating off the early years of filmmaking as a crude stage which had been surpassed. Although fond at all times of repeating the old saw that the movies were still in their 'infancy' (and hence capable of continual, rapid progress), people within the industry seem also to have believed that the art had reached a sort of plateau by the late teens. Writers referred especially to the older chase and trick films as typical of the crude material that would be unacceptable to modern audiences. Austin C. Lescarboura summed up this view in 1920:[11]

There is a vast difference between the photoplays of the present and those of a decade ago. But during the past two or three years progress along this line has been somewhat limited and not so obvious. The photoplay of to-day leaves little to be desired; motion-picture acting and story-telling technique and photography appear pretty nearly perfect.

In a sense Lescarboura's statement seems naive, for there were to be frequent changes in film-making devices in the years to come – most notably the introduction of soft-style cinemato-graphy and sound during the twenties. But he was also remarkably quick to pick up on the classical formula's transition into a period of relative equilibrium. The notions of rapid progress which writers had set forth in the mid-teens now took a back seat to a more tempered approach to change within a standardized system.

Even as early as the late teens, many writers and historians assumed that Griffith had single-handedly brought about the transition to the classical cinema. A 1917 account credited him with having 'wrought out the grammar of this new language in the world of art,' and with having 'established such well-defined rules of technique that nearly all the works in motion pictures can be traced in some manner to certain developments of his. The universal school of cutting, the closeup, the cutback . . .' This account also traces the formula used in comedy films to Mack Sennett, and concludes that 'the rules invented by these men are as inviolable as the rules of harmony, classified from the works of Mozart, Wagner and others.'[12] One could scarcely ask for a better summary of the Hollywood cinema as a 'classical' system.

There were numerous statements during the twenties, both praising and attacking Hollywood's standardization. Harold Lloyd recognized the balance of standardization and differentiation which characterized Hollywood when he described his films in 1926:[13]

If they are designed from slightly different angles, so that in a series of three pictures we can offer our whole bag of tricks and vary our appeal, then we have done what we aimed to do. And this will make for a certain standardization of comedies. Of course by this I do not mean that we create a rubber stamp or formula by which we make pictures. It is rather a standard of appeal from slightly different points, or a blending of average tastes.

This description seems overly modest in relation to Lloyd, whose silent features surely rank among the most polished and varied (and lucrative) works turned out by a single artist within the Hollywood system during the twenties. Yet the passage also suggests the power of that system to allow someone as inventive as Lloyd to turn out quality films quickly – films which would appeal predictably to a broad audience.

Hollywood practitioners and writers at least professed to believe that the system of norms was a response to the desires of audiences. Con-temporary accounts paint the viewer as quick to pick up on anachronisms or inconsistencies of mise-en-scene from shot to shot. The 'Why do they do it?' letters column of *Photoplay* encouraged readers to send in descriptions of errors they spotted. Invariably the letters referred to the handling of mise-en-scene (an 1887 model gun in a Civil War scene, an object switched from right to left hand at the cut). In 1916, *Photoplay* reported that fans also wrote in to the studios when they spotted errors:[14]

The same discriminating public which is responsible for the creation of art and technical directors is the *bete noir* of those officials, for technical flaws are quickly discovered by the 'outsiders' and some of the more enthusiastic fans do not hesitate about writing the producer to 'set him right.' Then the art director hears from the 'big boss.'

Although fault-finding on the part of the audience sometimes appears to be a headache for the studios, Chapter 9 has shown that Hollywood has a stake in promoting such an activity. By focusing spectator attention on nitpicking, the industry could enhance the publicity value of the art director's work; historical and geographical accuracy became a saleable aspect of the films.

The *Photoplay* column and other popular sources give no hint that ordinary moviegoers noticed violations of screen direction or other continuity rules. Yet practitioners still assumed that a spectator would sense flaws. Compare these two accounts of spectator to continuity.[15]

(1917) Ninety-nine picture fans in every hundred can instantly tell whether the continuity in a picture is good or bad. They will not stop to analyze it; that isn't necessary. They feel instinctively whether it is rhythmical or not; whether the scenes follow one another in proper sequence, and whether the correct values of each to the other are maintained.

(1918, speaking of a fan who has found a film's story hard to follow) But its faults were intangible. Had an English house been flashed on the screen as an old Southern homestead, or a girl shown playing tennis in an evening gown, then she could have explained the faults. The public are location and wardrobe wise by this time but they are not yet 'cutting wise.'

As a result of the idea that audiences were not consciously aware of cutting, the fan magazines tend to refer to it seldom; the second passage quoted above is a rare exception. Usually *Photoplay* and the other popular journals concentrated on art direction, costumes, special effects, and other techniques of mise-en-scene – hence perpetuating audience interest in them and not in editing. This bias, which has remained in force to the present, helps keep attention on spectacle while allowing editing to remain unobtrusive and unnoticed.

These opinions from the period leave little room for doubt that Hollywood was aware of its own standardization as it occurred. There are references to the various techniques as 'rules' and appeals to the norms of classical systems in other arts to justify those rules. Moreover, most practitioners saw the standard style as an aid to filmmaking rather than as a restriction. (Those for whom the norms *were* constraining – principally Erich von Stroheim, and to a lesser degree Rex Ingram, Maurice Tourneur, and Josef Von Sternberg – eventually left the American industry proper.)

From the late teens on, Hollywood's narrative and stylistic approaches would receive relatively small adjustments. One issue may serve as an indication of the degree of sophistication the classical filmmaking system had reached by the end of the teens. Beginning around 1920, a few contemporary writings discuss strategies for avoiding 'eye fatigue' for the viewer. So clear were the basic rules concerning spatial and temporal construction, that writers could turn their attention to such a minor problem. The solution was more continuity – of tonality and of composition. In 1920, Lescarboura summed up this solution; eye-strain, he wrote, was caused by:

sudden changes on the screen, either in the composition of successive scenes or in the degree of illumination. For instance, if in one scene the eyes have been drawn to a figure on the extreme left, and in the next the point of interest lies to the extreme right, the onlooker is immediately disconcerted and his eyes seek out the new point of interest only after suffering eyestrain and momentary confusion. Again, if one scene has been made in the open, in bright sunlight, and the next is uniformly dark, the quick change from a bright scene to a dark one and particularly vice versa is quite trying.

Already producers have given much attention to the matter of scene changes on the screen. The more advanced producers at this moment have more or less overcome all sudden changes in either light or points of interest. Where successive scenes do not match up sufficiently close to permit of going directly from one to the next, the various devices such as the 'fade-in' and 'fade-out,' the various vignettes, and so on are employed. In this manner the eyes are gradually removed from one scene and introduced to the next.

Lescarboura adds that tinting, toning, and art cards for titles all aid in achieving an even visual quality from shot to shot.[16]

A later observer in the Hollywood studios echoed these remarks in 1927, concluding:[17]

Pictorial rhythms must seem to sway from scene to scene, must pick up naturally from one to another, and must vary enough to avoid monotony.

Consider three consecutive scenes, A, B, and C. If at the close of A the interest is placed on the right, then scene B, although perhaps quite unconnected in subject matter with A, must begin with the interest concentrated almost at the point which the eye was watching at the close of A, or it must continue a movement suggested by A. Again, whatever the action may be that runs through B, scene C must pick up the interest at the local spot where B ceases.

So that the eye is danced about insensibly, but is never steeplechased.

This concern with graphic continuity carries forward concepts upon which the classical system was based. As with temporal and spatial relations, no breaks or shocks should jar the eye, lest attention be momentarily shifted from the narrative to the film's technical aspects. This notion is perhaps a minor one, but that is precisely the point; the major changes had taken place by the late teens. In the twenties, film-makers could work at perfecting an existing system.

A summary example: *Code of the Sea*

In the course of Part Three, we have seen that by the 1920s the stylistic devices of classical film-making were in use and that their range of functions was well-established. We have also seen to some degree that the systems of time and space were subordinate to that of causality. But in examining Hollywood's devices in a somewhat atomistic fashion, I have not yet shown that classical silent films drew thoroughly and exclusively upon these systematic relations. Only an analysis of a typical film can demonstrate that Hollywood had indeed created a stable, pervasive classical approach by the twenties.

Code of the Sea (Famous Players-Lasky) is in many ways a typical 'A' feature of 1924. Made by a relatively major but non-auteur director, Victor Fleming (who had already completed a dozen films since his switch from cinematographer to director), the film was a starring vehicle for Rod La Rocque.

Code of the Sea contains a unified cause-effect chain which reaches closure at the end, leaving no lines of action unresolved. An event in the past — the earliest event referred to in the film — provides the main cause. Bruce McDow's father, John, had been in charge of a lightship which warned vessels away from a rocky coast. During a storm, John had lost his nerve and sailed the lightship into shelter, thereby allowing an ocean liner to crash and its passengers to drown; John subsequently died, branded a coward. This all happens before the film's action begins. Bruce has grown up believing himself to have inherited his father's cowardice, and, as the film opens he loses his first job on the crew of a ship by being too scared to climb the mast. His girlfriend Jenny Hayden urges him to try again. Her father is the owner of a line of steamships, one of which had been in the fatal accident caused by John. Captain Hayden forbids Jenny to see Bruce, and favors another suitor, Stewart Radcliffe. This basic situation leads Jenny to help Bruce obtain a post aboard the same lightship his father had commanded. During a gale, Bruce proves his courage by saving the passengers aboard Captain Hayden's sinking yacht, including Jenny and Radcliffe. Bruce falls into the sea as the yacht goes under, but he is washed ashore unconscious the next morning, where Jenny finds him.

This story line is extremely simple; the film fills it out through variations on the elements of Bruce's despair and Jenny's urging him on. The characters provide the basis for most of the film's action. Each has a severely limited number of traits which we learn at his or her first appearance. An inter-title introduces Bruce by saying that this is his first sea voyage, and the shot that follows this title frames Bruce's apprehensive face. The captain orders him aloft, but he is too frightened to go and instead ends up peeling potatoes in the galley. Everything emphasizes Bruce's cowardice, and he behaves in a consistent fashion until he overcomes his fears. First impressions of the other characters are also valid and lasting. We initially see Jenny as she greets Bruce on the dock at his return. She obviously is in love with him, delighted at his return, and disappointed when he reveals his failure. Jenny will be the main causal impetus behind Bruce's character change. The inter-title that introduces Captain Hayden declares that he hates the name McDow, having lost his ship years before through John's cowardice. Within a few shots, Hayden forbids Jenny to see Bruce; later, after she fails to accept Radcliffe as a suitor, Hayden sends her on a yacht trip to forget Bruce. Radcliffe first appears taunting and bullying Bruce, and he continues to be a cad throughout. Except when some change of traits is clearly motivated, the characters remain true to our initial impressions of them.

Chapter 2 has mentioned that the star system reinforces the rapid construction of consistent characters and can prepare for 'plausible' character change. The only real star in the film is

Rod La Rocque, who had risen to fame during the years before the release of *Code of the Sea*. La Rocque was among the 'Latin lover' types who became prominent after Valentino's success in 1921 with *Four Horsemen of the Apocalypse*. Like Valentino, La Rocque had a general image of glamor, with a slightly foppish or flighty quality. He was more a sensitive than a he-man type, being quite capable of portraying weak or erring men who redeemed themselves eventually. Although he had played the villain in DeMille's *The Ten Commandments* the year before, La Rocque was, by mid-1924, a leading man. At the beginning of *Code of the Sea*, his star persona would lead the audience to believe in his doubts and fears, but to realize that Bruce McDow is probably not 'really' a coward. There is a strong hypothesis from the start that he only thinks he is, and this sets up later scenes where he overcomes his weakness.

This problem with cowardice sets up one main line of action; the second, following the frequent classical pattern, is a romance. The two lines initially are linked by the past connection between the two fathers. In the film's action, the romance with Jenny provides the incentive for Bruce to keep trying to overcome his fears. In the second scene, Jenny tells Bruce she knows of a way for him to 'conquer' himself. Later, she says his salvation will be to think of others. Although he has further doubts along the way, Bruce eventually does behave bravely, risking his life to save the passengers aboard the yacht.

Along the way to this goal, most of the causal agents are human. Jenny aids Bruce, Radcliffe and Hayden oppose him, and Bruce's own hidden strength pulls him through. The storm that provides him with his big chance is the only natural agent that intervenes, and it is there simply as a means of throwing Bruce into action. He, not the storm, determines the outcome.

The film's narrative is usually careful to provide motivation so that individual causes will not appear coincidental. The storm, although described as 'the worst gale within the memory of man,' could be expected in a geographical area that needs to keep a lightship on constant duty offshore. Bruce ends up working on the same lightship that had proved so disastrous for his father, but again a reason is supplied. The basic motivation is compositional; Bruce must reverse

his father's mistake, so Jenny provides the assignment letter. And her ability to do so is in turn motivated realistically; as the daughter of a rich ship owner, she knows the various maritime officials in the area, and she gets one of them to arrange for Bruce's assignment. Indeed, virtually the only cause not motivated in any way is the sudden placement of Bruce in command of the lightship after two months on the job. An inter-title abruptly informs the viewer that the captain has been transferred and that Bruce is now in charge. Classical unity would dictate some early mention of this transfer; this minor lapse is the only irregularity in the film's overall causal chain.

Not only is the narrative of *Code of the Sea* fairly simple and unified, but the film provides considerable redundant emphasis on the most basic causal factors. Bruce's cowardice is reiterated time and again. In the opening scene, he is apprehensive before given the order to go aloft; he is unable to obey and ends up in the galley peeling potatoes while the cook lectures him – 'Leap before you look.' In this scene the sailors taunt him, and in the second scene they come ashore and sing a song about the 'boogey-man' to him. (The inter-titles reinforce this point still further with 'shaky' lettering.) Everyone who meets Bruce subsequently mentions his cowardice in some way. Alone, he has visions of super-imposed 'Fears' which taunt him similarly with repeated references to his weakness (see fig 18.1).

Finally, several motifs function redundantly to reinforce this already obvious trait of Bruce's personality. Aside from the 'Fears' that appear in a couple of scenes, Bruce's timidity becomes associated with the potatoes he peels in the first scene. Later, seeing a bowl of potato peels in his mother's kitchen, Bruce becomes upset. But most consistently, the film uses Bruce's dog as a parallel for him. The dog meets Bruce on the pier in scene 2; an inter-title characterizes it as the only one who believes Bruce to be 'all that was good – and brave – and true.' Later in the scene, Radcliffe's fierce dog chases Bruce's dog, which turns tail and runs. Radcliffe then taunts Bruce as a 'cur' (stooping immediately after to pick a stray potato peel out of Bruce's cuff). Much later in the film, Hayden vows to take his daughter away from that 'mongrel,' Bruce. When Jenny assures Bruce she loves him, the dog apes Bruce's determination, barking to banish a superimposed phantom of Radcliffe's dog (paralleling Bruce's 'Fears'). So important does the dog parallel become that the epilogue continues after Bruce and Jenny's final embrace. In the film's final shots, Bruce's dog spots Radcliffe's dog and chases it off down the beach.

The narration presents the film's causality in a clear, straightforward fashion; the narration begins with credits over a live-action shot of waves on a rocky shore confirming the title. Early in the first scene, several expository inter-titles introduce characters and give information about them; the tone of these titles is neutral, creating a minimally self-conscious narration even at the opening. These expository titles are able to drop out of the scene quickly, since the film begins *in medias res*. We see Bruce behave in a cowardly fashion; then one of the sailors taunts him: 'Yer as yellow as yer father was!' Thus the major relevant past action — Bruce's father's cowardice — is introduced not by a self-conscious narrator, but by a character. Only later, at the end of the scene, does an expository title step in to inform us what the father's specific action had been (and this title is compositionally motivated by Bruce's glimpse of the lightship his father had commanded). Several subsequent scenes have no expository inter-titles, and the titles that do occur tend to come early in their respective scenes.

Code of the Sea contains extreme redundancy, but for the most part, repetition arises from the characters' actions rather than from restatements of information by the omniscient narration. A variety of devices repeatedly stresses Bruce's cowardice: the sailor's taunts, the cook's lecture in the first scene, Bruce's own ruminations and visions of his 'Fears,' Jenny's several exhortations to him to conquer himself, and especially the parallel scenes of his dog's timidity. Yet the expository titles barely mention this subject, functioning primarily to name characters and situations, or to indicate at one point that two months have passed. The narration remains essentially unself-conscious even at the film's end. The final shot is motivated as Radcliffe's point-of-view as he watches Bruce's dog chasing his along the beach into the distance. Hence the narration subordinates itself to the actions of the characters.

But even though the characters present much of the causal chain, the film's narration remains intermittently omniscient. Bruce carries much of the action and the audience's sympathy, yet we know things that he does not. The third scene takes place in the Haydens' home, concentrating upon Jenny's family and her father's wish for her to marry Radcliffe. Later, in the party scene, Bruce tries to save Jenny, whose dress has been accidentally set on fire. Just as he overcomes his fear and rushes to her aid, Radcliffe pushes him down. Bruce hits his head on a rock and doesn't remember that he had tried to help; instead he sees Radcliffe take credit for the rescue. In this segment the audience sees Radcliffe toss the careless match that causes the accident, even though Bruce and Jenny do not see this; and we know that Bruce did try to act bravely, while he thinks he held back. The extra knowledge the audience gains in this scene is important in motivating Bruce's eventual heroism in the storm scene. Even from the second scene onward, the audience senses that Jenny's faith in Bruce is justified (he is, after all, the star). Yet nothing in the film tells us overtly that Bruce is really brave; the omniscience of the narration is not apparent. Indeed, at times we seem very close to Bruce's subjective experiences. As with many Hollywood characters, he talks about his feelings frequently — with his mother and with Jenny — and we even see his mental images (fig 18.1). Thus the film keeps a balance between our sympathy with Bruce's worry that he will fail and our basic belief that he will succeed. In this way the film maintains suspense until the end, but also guarantees that the final triumph will not seem unmotivated.

Code of the Sea is unexceptional in its maintenance of clear temporal indicators. Most scenes are continuous, with fades between them to mark time lapses. The temporal relationship of each new scene to the preceding one is made clear early on. The first scene shows the ship approaching land, and the second takes place later the same day as Bruce comes ashore and meets Jenny. The third shows dinner at the Hayden household, with Radcliffe blaming Jenny's tardiness on her talk with Bruce; we can easily infer that only a little time has elapsed since scene 2.

Appointments mark off several intervals. Jenny invites a friend to a party to take place the next night; later she sets up a rendezvous for nine o'clock that same night. Although no durational limits are specified during the storm scene, there is the constant suggestion that the yacht will sink with Jenny aboard unless Bruce gets there in time. Crosscutting compresses time in two different scenes: Bruce's preparations for and walk to Jenny's party, intercut with the party's progress; and the extended rescue scene during the storm, which cuts among the yacht, Hayden's liner, the lightship, Bruce's launch, and the rescue party on the shore. In addition, faster editing rhythm during the storm scene marks this as the climactic stretch of the film's narrative.

The film's space remains true to Hollywood's continuity guidelines. *Code of the Sea* employs analytical editing in the conventional pattern, as in the shot/reverse shot from the opening scene (figs 18.2 and 18.3). Here the frontality of the classical cinema is apparent, as each character's body is turned toward the camera, with only the face angled toward the offscreen character. Both heads occupy the privileged spot, two-thirds of the way up the frame in the center. The same is true in figure 18.4, as Bruce talks to his mother. This shot shows a depth effect, with rim lighting picking out the figures against a darker background plane; three-point lighting models their faces. Overall there is little that departs from the various spatial rules of editing or framing; the few cuts that violate screen direction are decidedly exceptional.

Decoupage in *Code of the Sea* is similarly exemplary. In a period for which Chapter 6 claims the average number of shots was 750-900, the film has 871, with 133 inter-titles (15.2 per cent of the total – again matching the average of 15 per cent). Its number of sequences is relatively small – eleven, as opposed to the silent-period average of fifteen to sixteen. This disparity arises from the unusually lengthy rescue sequence.

But such correspondences to the norm are to be expected – *Code of the Sea* is one of the Unbiased Sample films from which these figures were derived. More importantly, the film's internal scene-by-scene organization already follows the pattern Chapter 6 has described as typical of the classical cinema as a whole. The film shows that by 1924, filmmakers were constructing scenes with brief initial expository passages, followed by developmental sections which close off an old dangling cause and set up at least one new cause

for a future scene. The important central party scene (number 7) begins with the party already in progress, echoing the *in-medias-res* opening of the whole film. An inter-title briefly states that it is 'party time'; then a long shot shows the living room of the Hayden house where the party is occurring. After only a few seconds of establishing material to set up the situation, time, and space, the action begins as Superintendent Beasley (the friend Jenny had invited earlier) enters to give Jenny a paper. This is the appointment for Bruce to a position aboard the lightship; at the end of scene 5, Beasley had promised Jenny he would obtain it. This closes off one previous cause. An intercut scene follows, setting up Bruce at home, preparing for the party. He reads a letter from Jenny arranging to meet him at nine o'clock; this prepares for the main action which will form the bulk of the scene. After he meets her, the development section of the scene occurs; Jenny gives him the letter, and the dress burns accidentally. The scene ends with two dangling causes. First, Hayden threatens to send Jenny on a yacht voyage; we will see this happen in scene 9. Secondly, Bruce sends the lightship-assignment letter back to Jenny, in despair over what he assumes is his own cowardice; this becomes the cause taken up in scene 8, as Jenny comes to Bruce's home and talks him into taking the job. Scene 8 in turn ends with the unanswered question of whether Bruce will succeed, and the two dangling causes come together in the climactic rescue sequence. Indeed, they represent the film's two lines of action – Bruce's cowardice and the romance.

No one film is the classical cinema, for no one film can explore every possibility the paradigm allows for. *Code of the Sea* is typical of classical usage in the mid-twenties, however, because it remains within the paradigm, using its principles in varied and flexible ways. While it adheres to classical guidelines almost entirely, we can find a couple of distinctive aspects about this film. Its climactic rescue-at-sea sequence is lengthy, taking up a larger portion of the whole than most Hollywood films would allot to a single scene. And the hero's repeated visions of his 'Fears' take symbolism further than might be typical – although they are by no means unique. Many films of the late teens and twenties show such inventiveness – often to a considerably greater degree than does *Code of the Sea*. But by this point, unlike in the early teens, inventiveness is a regularized part of the system – guided, limited, controlled. The classical cinema is now firmly in place.

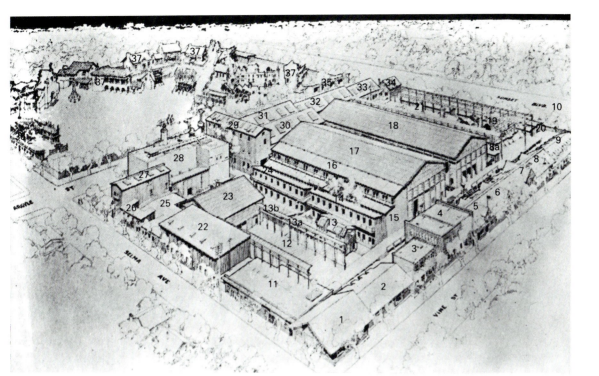

1	Property room	over dressing room used	of Stage No. 4
2	Outgoing property room	by Geraldine Farrar	21 Sail boat in tank
3	Star dressing room	13a Title department, and	22 Dark stage
	building	printing plant, and	23 Small glass stage
4	Wardrobe building	electrical department	24 Extra dressing rooms and
5	Engaging department	13b Projection room No. 2	hospital
6	Executive offices	14 Extra dressing room	25 Stock room
7	Cecil B. De Mille's office	15 Scene docks	26 Purchasing department.
8	Director's offices	16 Principal dressing rooms	Press photographer's
9	Scenario department	17 Stage No. 2	rooms
10	Mary Pickford's dressing	18 Stage No. 3	27 Old paint frame now
	room	18a Company dressing rooms,	upholstering and wall
11	Incoming property room	entire length of stage	papering department
12	Stage No. 1	19 Stage No. 4	28 Laboratory. Frame build-
13	Wilfred Buckland's office	20 Scene docks, entire length	ing under number now

removed and addition to
laboratory erected
29 Paint frame
30 Fitting room
31 Carpenter shops
32 Planing [sic] Mills
33 Property construction
department
34 Plaster shops and black-
smith shop
35 Garages
36 Douglas Fairbanks' offices
and dressing rooms
37 Exterior sets built for
productions

13.1 (above) The Lasky studio in 1918

13.2 (below) A firm's production chart, 1918

13.3 Art designers started set production with detailed sketches (1918)

THE MINIATURE CARDBOARD MODEL, ON A TABLE, FROM WHICH THE LARGE
SETS ARE TO BE MADE

The scene is from "Thais," and the street is one in Alexandria, Egypt.

13.4 Models of the sets might be prepared before construction began (1918)

THE BUILDINGS UNDER COURSE OF CONSTRUCTION FROM THE MODELS
JUST SHOWN

At the far end is the temple wherein Thais worships.

13.5 Sketches also supplied
information for scene painters (1918)

13.6 Miniatures (1918)

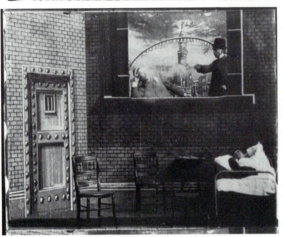

A vision that carries
him far beyond the
golden dust-haze into
the future. A future
of bigger, finer things.

15.1-15.2 (above) *The Pickpocket* (1903)
15.3 (centre left) *The Unwritten Law* (c. 1907)
15.4 (centre right) *The Girl in the Armchair* (1912)
15.5-15.6 (below) *The Hired Hand* (1918)

15.7-15.9 *A Daughter of Dixie* (1911)

15.10-15.13 *A Race With Time* (1913)

15.14 Art backgrounds for inter-titles being made in the Ince Art Department in the late teens

15.15-15.17 (opposite page and left) *The High Cost of Living* (1912)

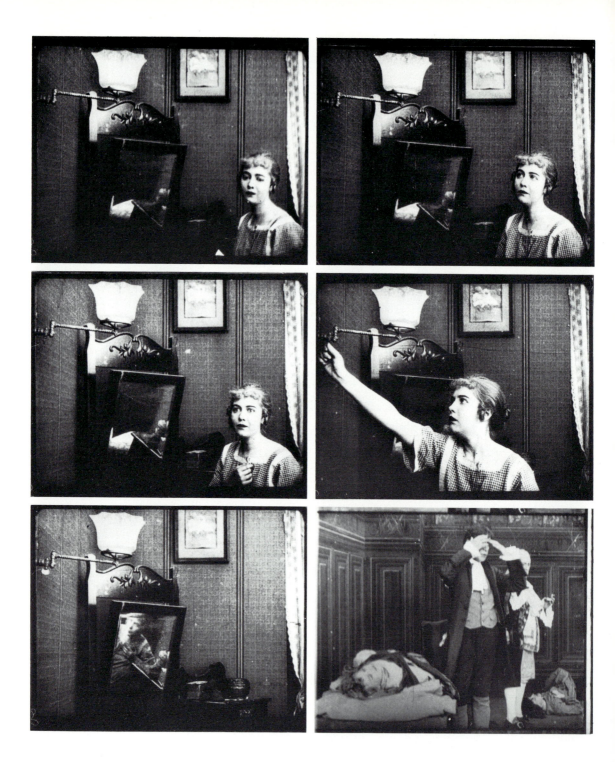

15.18-15.22 *The Warning* (1914)
15.23 (below right) *A Tale of Two Cities* (1911)

16.1-16.5 *Mantrap* (1926)

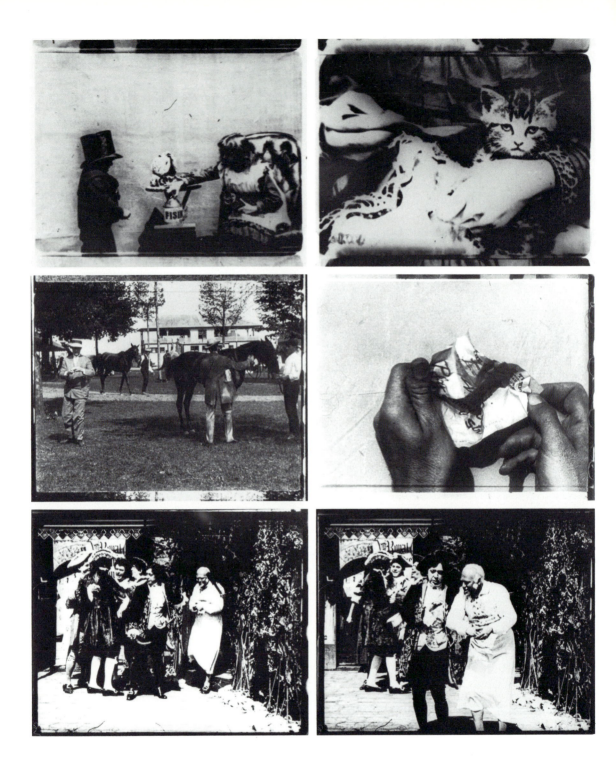

16.6-16.7 (above) *The Sick Kitten* (1903?)
16.8-16.9 (centre) *The 100-to-One Shot* (1906)
16.10-16.11 (below) *After One Hundred Years* (1911)

16.12-16.13 (above) *A Tale of Two Cities* (1911)
16.14-16.16 (centre and below) *At Old Fort Dearborn* (1912)

16.17-16.18 (above) *After One Hundred Years* (1911)
16.19-16.20 (centre) *Shamus O'Brien* (1912)
16.21-16.22 (below) *The Girl of the Cabaret* (1913)

16.23-16.24 (above) *The Eagle's Mate* (1914)
16.25-16.28 (centre and below) *The Hired Hand* (1918)

16.29 (above) *Her First Adventure* (1908)
16.30-16.31 (centre) *The Fear* (1912)
16.32-16.33 (below) *Alma's Champion* (1912)

16.34-16.35 (above) *The Warning* (1914)
16.36-16.37 (centre) *The Eagle's Mate* (1914)
16.38-16.39 (below) *The 100-to-One Shot* (1906)

16.40-16.41 (above) *A Friendly Marriage* (1911)
16.42-16.43 (centre) *Behind the Footlights* (1916)
16.44-16.45 (below) *Love and the Law* (1919)

16.46-16.47 (above) *The Gambler's Charm* (1910)
16.48-16.49 (centre) *The Fear* (1912)
16.50-16.51 (below) *The Girl at the Cupola* (1912)

16.52-16.53 (above) *Weights and Measures* (1914)
16.54-16.55 (below) *The Wishing Ring* (1914)

 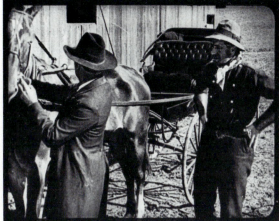

16.56-16.60 *The Loafer* (1911)

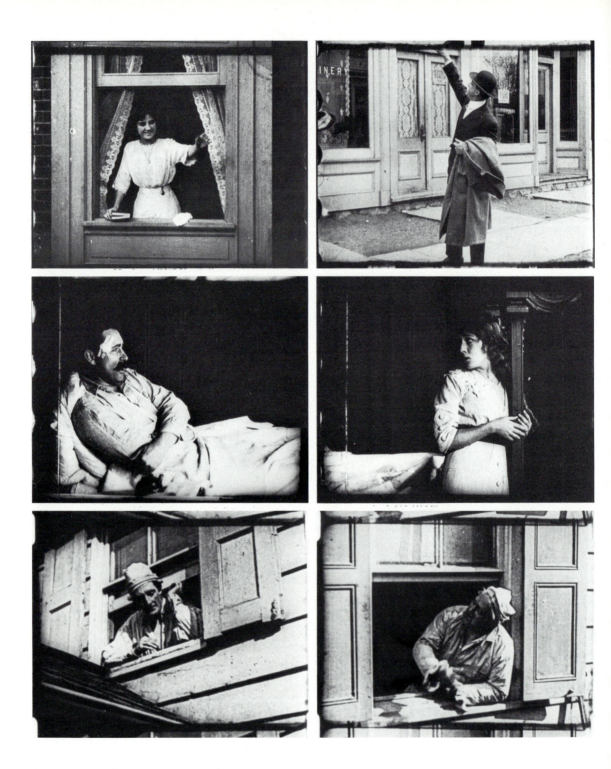

16.61-16.62 (above) *A Comedy of Errors* (1913)
16.63-16.64 (centre) *The Eagle's Mate* (1914)
16.65-16.66 (below) *The Wishing Ring* (1914)

16.67-16.72 *Detective Burton's Triumph* (1914)

16.73-16.74 (above) *Field of Honor* (1917)
16.75-16.77 (centre and below) *The Ghost of Rosie Taylor* (1918)

16.78-16.79 (above) *Victory* (1919)
16.80-16.81 (below) *Mantrap* (1926)

17.1 (above left) *The 100-to-One Shot* (1906)
17.2 (above right) *The Loafer* (1911)
17.3 (centre left) *A Friendly Marriage* (1911)
17.4 (centre right) *The Bandit of Tropico* (1912)
17.5 (below left) *Weights and Measures* (1914)
17.6 (below right) *Love and the Law* (1919)

17.7 (above left) *A Temperamental Wife* (David Kirkland, 1919, Constance Talmadge)

17.8 (above right) *The 100-to-One Shot* (1906)

17.9 (centre left) *Faithful* (1910)

17.10 (centre right) *The Bells* (1913)

17.11 (below left) *The Girl in the Armchair* (1912)

17.12 *The Eagle's Mate* (1914)

17.13 *Rory O'More* (1911)

17.15 *The Coming of Columbus* (1912)

17.16 Production still for *The Queen of Sheba* (1921)

17.14 A row of outdoor stages at Universal at about the time of the studio's opening in 1915

17.17 William Cameron Menzies's design for the astrologer's chamber in *The Beloved Rogue* (1927)

17.18 (above left) *A Race With Time* (1913)
17.19 (above right) *Damon and Pythias* (1914)
17.20 (centre left) *The Case of Becky* (1915)
17.21 (centre right) **Love and the Law* (1919)
17.22 (below) *The Magician* (1926)

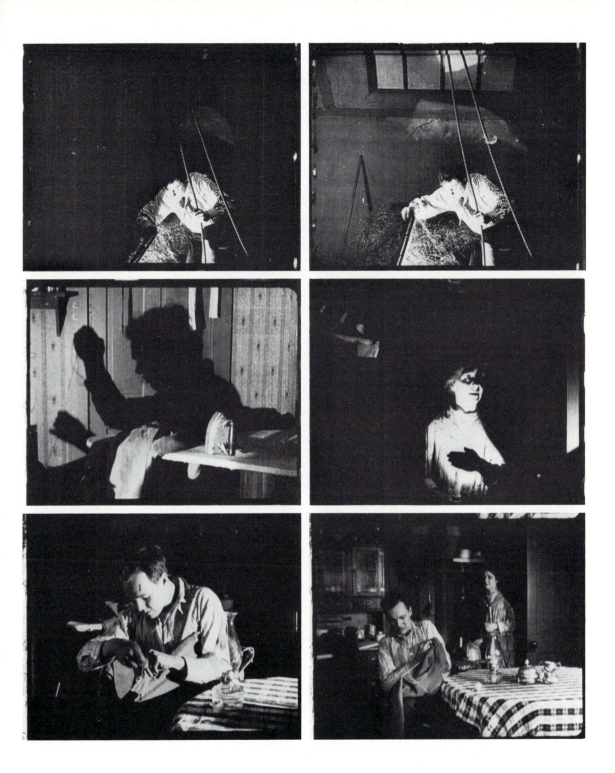

17.23-17.24 (above) *Shamus O'Brien* (1912)
17.25-17.28 (centre and below) *The Clodhopper* (1917)

MAN'S BEST FRIEND
Eclair Release, January 30

Old Silas Judson, stricken blind by fever and compelled, through poverty, to beg in the street, is cared for by a fatherless granddaughter who looks after their cheerless home while the old man goes into the street each day accompanied by his Pomeranian, a dog of unusual intelligence.

"Gyp" is subsequently stolen and falls into the hands of the daughter of a wealthy merchant. He is later sent to The Home for Friendless Animals when the merchant's daughter enquires about the purchase. On the way, "Gyp" escapes and his animal instinct carries him back to his blind master who has feebly started for home alone.

But, in crossing a busy street, the old man is struck by a passing car and seriously injured. The dog, realizing his master's condition, runs to the house and barks frantically at the door, whereupon the granddaughter follows him back to the scene of the accident.

In the meantime, the wealthy merchant, riding by in his auto, comes upon the old man and, entreated by his daughter, takes him to their home where he recovers sufficiently to be taken to his own little cottage after a short time.

The blind man's injury proved fatal, however, and they buried him in a corner of the public burying ground where little "Gyp" mourned his loss with the now friendless girl.

Fortunately the merchant's daughter learns of their pitiable condition and the two little waifs are given a good home, but "Gyp" and the little girl may be seen making regular visits to the grave of their dead friend where they place flowers and mourn in sacred silence.

WILLY PLAYS TRUANT
Eclair Release, February 1

Young Willy is a terrible boy. His nurse can hardly get him to dress. It is harder still to get him to school. Here, his exuberance causes discord in class. He fights with his classmates, turns over desks and benches and runs away, along the road, where he continues his mischievous actions. To escape them, Willy hides in a big laundry basket. The laundress, not knowing, carries it away and empties the contents into a tub in which she pours water. Willy finds the joke less amusing and gets out of the tub quickly, pulling an obstinate bed sheet behind him. He returns to his own home and hides under the table in shame.

But he left a trail behind which was discovered by his father who gives him a whipping. On the same reel,

EDUCATION OF THE BLIND
This picture initiates us into the life and education of the blind in all its details.

We show how they learn to read, write and count according to their

17.29 A 1912 *Moving Picture News* advertisement stressing light effects in the IMP release *The Power of Conscience*

17.30 (above left) *The Loafer* (1911)
17.31 (above right) *The Cheat* (1915)
17.32 (centre left) *His Phantom Sweetheart* (1915)

17.33 (centre right) *Dolly's Scoop* (1916)
17.34 (below left) *The Girl of the Golden West* (1915)
17.35 (below right) *Forbidden Paths* (Robert Thornby, 1917, Lasky)

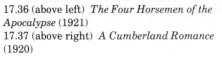

17.36 (above left) *The Four Horsemen of the Apocalypse* (1921)
17.37 (above right) *A Cumberland Romance* (1920)

FIG. 9.—Spotlighting is used in this set to separate the characters from the background and to accentuate the predominating features.

17.38 A comparison of the same composition from *Night Life of New York* (1925), with and without backlighting

FIG. 10.—The value and necessity of highlights are appreciated when this illustration is compared with Figure 9.

17.39 *The Ghost of Rosy Taylor* (1918)

17.40 Norma Talmadge in the United Studios, around 1923

506-2/10

17.41 Filming George Fawcett (center, with epaulettes) in *Mr. Billings Spends His Dime*, at Famous Players-Lasky (1923)

17.42 (above left) *Her Code of Honor* (John Stahl, 1919, Tribune-United)
17.43-17.45 (above right and centre) *The Hired Hand* (1918)
17.46-17.47 (below) *At Old Fort Dearborn* (1912)

17.48-17.50 *The Dumb Girl of Portici* (1915)

17.51 The camera elevator used for *Hotel Imperial* (1926)

17.52 A cutaway set and elevator permitted the camera to follow Chico and Diane during their ascent
to *Seventh Heaven* (1927)

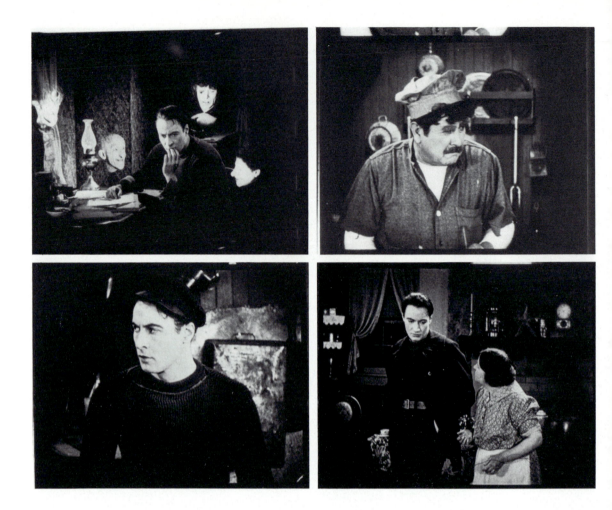

18.1 (above left) Four gruesome, superimposed faces represent Bruce's 'Fears' in *Code of the Sea* (1924)

18.2-18.3 (above right and below left) Bruce confronts the ship's cook in shot/reverse shot (*Code of the Sea*)

18.4 (below right) Classical guidelines of composition and editing in a shot from *Code of the Sea*

Opposite page

20.1 (above) A publicity photograph of the cutaway set from *The Hand of Peril* (1916)

20.2 (below) Allan Dwan's cinematographers at the American Film Co. in 1911: at left, R.D. Armstrong using a Moy camera, and Roy Overbaugh with a Williamson

20.3 (above left) The Pathé studio model, with its distinctive placement of the crank on the back of the camera body. The eyepiece for sighting through the lens between shots is to the left of the crank; its cover is open, but would be closed during filming to keep light off the film

20.4 (above right) A 1920 illustration of the Bell & Howell camera, showing its cranking-speed indicator, footage dial, and chart of shutter openings and f-stops

20.5 (above) Universal newsreel cameraman Norman Alley and his Akeley
20.6 (below) A Paramount Famous Lasky Western on location in the late twenties –
probably for *The Last Outlaw* (1927). First cameraman James Murray, at right with
his Bell & Howells, is backed up by another Bell & Howell with a long lens, as well
as by an Akeley. Gary Cooper sits by the script clerk, behind Murray

20.7 (above) Charles Rosher and Mary Pickford pose by the prototype Mitchell camera in 1920
20.8 (below) Sol Polito, right, and director Albert Roper, with a Mitchell camera, at the First National Studio

20.9 A Mitchell advertisement shows the back of the camera, with the body in filming position in the right view and in focusing position in the left view

20.10 The first Eyemo model, with handle attached for handheld shots

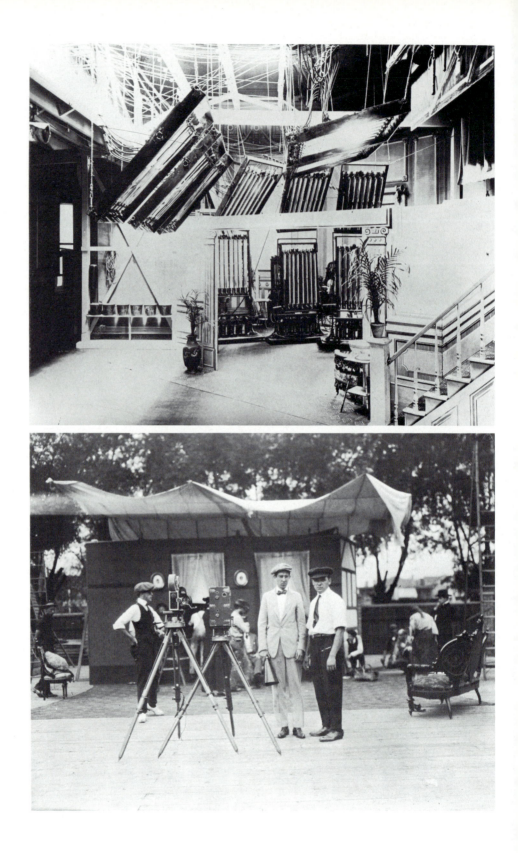

20.13 A corner of the main outdoor stage at Inceville

Opposite page
20.11 (above) The interior of the New York Biograph Studio in 1909. Banks of hanging and floor units
of mercury-vapor tubes provide the only illumination
20.12 (below) Diffusing cloth draped above an outdoor stage at Essanay in 1912; cameraman Jack Rose
is in dark pants and white shirt

20.14 Thomas Ince in the Triangle Studio at Culver City, 1916, showing off an array of Cooper-Hewitt
units. The glass studio roof and walls have been covered with cloth to facilitate artificial lighting. A
floor stand of mercury-vapors is in the center at each side, surrounded by a dozen wheeled goose-neck
units

20.15 (opposite below) Cameraman Ned Van Buren filming in the Edison studio with a Moy camera, with director John Collins seated on the bed railing talking to the actors. Diffusers hang below the glass roof, while hanging enclosed arcs and broadside arcs on floor stands provide additional light

20.16 (right) The sunlight arc and its accessories

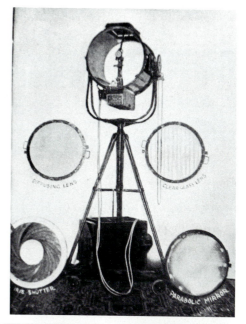

20.17 Transferring film from a rack to a drying drum at the Bloom Laboratory in Hollywood in 1918

21.1 (above) Cinematographer Joe La Shelle wears a blue glass around his neck, using it here to set up a shot of Colleen Moore. His camera is a Mitchell
Opposite page
21.2 (above left) A film editor at MGM, *c.* 1928, poses for a publicity shot. The small machine with the rounded top between the rewinds on his table is a Moviola Midget
21.3 (above right) The 1918 model Bell & Howell automatic splicer, with foot pedals to run the film through and clamps to apply pressure to the splice.
21.4 (below) Shooting a scene with Joan Crawford for *Duke Steps Out* (James Cruze, 1929, MGM). The Bell & Howell camera at center has a long lens and has been moved back to get a soft look, in combination with the diffusion disk overhead and diffusion screen behind the couple

21.5 Henrik Sartov's portrait of D.W. Griffith

Opposite page
21.9 (above) Henrik Sartov, at the camera, sets up a
shot of Lillian Gish for *La Bohème* (1926), while director
King Vidor and producer Irving Thalberg look on
21.10 (below) The camera crew for *Sparrows* (1926):
Charles Rosher stands at right (white shirt, dark tie)
with his Mitchell, with Karl Struss (in glasses) at center
behind his Bell & Howell, with gauze box attachment.
Hal Mohr (with glasses and mustache) is behind Struss,
and director William Beaudine sits in the lower center
(holding a megaphone)

21.6-21.7 *Way Down East* (1919)
21.8 *The Four Horsemen of the Apocalypse* (1921)

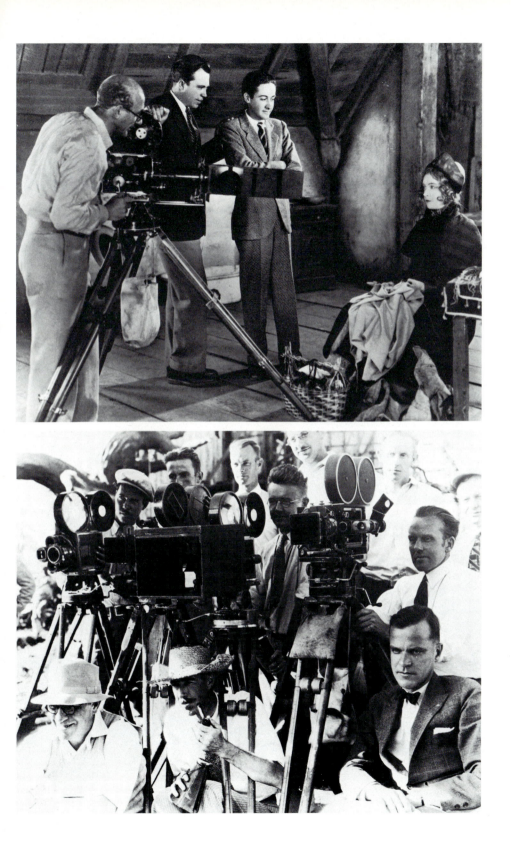

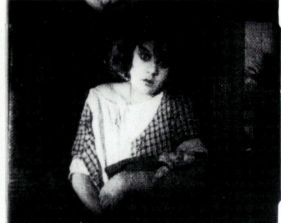

21.11-21.12 (above) *Foolish Wives* (1922)
21.13 (left) *Sparrows* (1926)

21.16 *Way Down East* (1919)

21.17 *Foolish Wives* (1922)

21.14 (above left) Clarence White's 1905 landscape
photograph, 'Morning'
21.15 (below) 'Mrs Eugene Meyer,' a portrait by Edward
Steichen
21.18 (right) A gum bichromate process was used to give
texture to a turn-of-the-century photograph – 'Cigarette
Girl – A Poster Design' – by Robert Demachy

22.1 Lighting Warners' *Singing Fool* (1928) with incandescent lamps. Al Jolson is on stage

23.1 (above) Several cameras and booths in Warners' Vitaphone Studios, Brooklyn (1926)
23.2 (below) A posed shot showing multiple cameras and a single microphone for *Gentlemen of the Press* (1929) in Paramount's Astoria, Long Island studio

23.3-23.10 (this page and opposite above) *The Lights of New York* (1928)

23.11-23.12 (centre) *Downstairs* (1932)

23.13-23.14 (below) *The Show* (1927). Cock Robin is on the left side of the room, Salome on the right. When he throws a record to the lower left, Salome turns to look sharply to our right. We are thus between the two, with the action occurring 'around' us. This volumetric space would become rare in early sound films

23.15-23.16 (above) Shot/reverse shot with multiple cameras: *Moby Dick* (1930)
23.18 (below) The 28-ton steel crane used to film *Broadway* (1929). The arm was over 30 feet long

23.17 Blimped cameras on various carriages for filming First National's *Sunny* (1930). Note the rolling tripod attached to the camera on the far right

24.1 A 1912 Reliance advertisement credits the author of the story

32 (Cont.1)

NAPOLEON:
(continuing)
...millions have been poured into the
Mexican conquest... millions for men and
more men -- ships munitions. I could
have conquered half of Europe at less
cost.

He stops, whirls on his heel to face them, and grinds
out the coal of his cigarette on the polished table.

NAPOLEON:
(continuing, to de Morny)
You and your banker friends got me
into this mess...

DE MORNY:
Your Majesty is unfair... The collection
of Mexico's debt was of secondary importance... Your Majesty intervened in
Mexico to block the spread of American
democracy.

NAPOLEON:
Democracy!... The rule of the cattle by
the cattle for the cattle... Abraham
Lincoln -- bah! Parliaments and plebi-
scites and proletarians -- A mob intox-
icated with ideas of equality -- cattle!
(he almost foams at the
mouth)
Well, am I to be destroyed by such filth...
Am I?

He looks from one minister to another, each of whom
evades his glare and turns questioning eyes on the remaining members of the Council... with no results.

NAPOLEON:
(continuing)
Well, what do you advise now! Shall we
evacuate Mexico... permit the humiliation
of French Imperialism by Benito Juarez -
an Indian bandit!... and be engulfed by
a revolution here at home?... Or shall
we wait for the Yankees to destroy us
on the Rio Grande?

DE MORNY:
If we evacuate Mexico now, we are certain to have trouble here at home. As
I see it, there is everything to lose
by an immediate wd thrawal.

(CONTINUED)

---

41 (Cont.)

CORPORAL:
Make your mark...
(pointing)
... here!

The peon marks and returns the board to the private.

CORPORAL:
What is your father's name?

PEON:
Doroteo Almengo.

The private writes and hands back the board again.

CORPORAL:
Mark here!

PEON:
But my father is dead, Senor.

CORPORAL:
Mark here! --

As the peon does.

DISSOLVE TO:

42. AN ASSEMBLY OF PEONS AND POORER-CLASS TOWNSFOLK
listening to a speaker who is standing on a bench in a
public plaza.

SPEAKER:
...You are being tricked, Companeros...
Do not write your names or make
your marks... The paper says we
want an emperor to come from Europe
and rule over us... We do not want
an emperor. We have a president,
Benito Juarez, who helped us poor
peons to get lands to farm... If
an emperor comes, he will take
them away. Then we shall starve
and be slaves again...

DISSOLVE TO:

A clatter of hoofs begins to SOUND OVER the scene. The
listeners turn, break and run in all directions, as
soldiers ride over them and close in on the speaker.

DISSOLVE TO:

25.1 Two pages from the final script for Warner Bros' *Juarez* (1939)

25.2 Scriptwriters for *Juarez* included John Huston, Aneas MacKenzie,
Wolfgang Reinhardt, and Abem Finkel

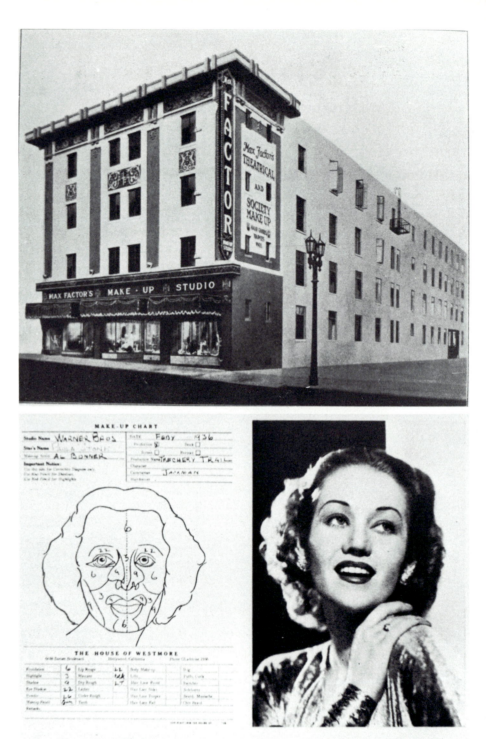

The drawing illustrates the way Paula Stone's corrective make-up is planned.
The photo shows how she looks in that make-up.

25.3 (above) Max Factor's new building (1929) for research in make-up
25.4 (below) A 1937 make-up chart at Warner Bros

25.5 An optical printer matted in the ceiling on this set
(1932)

25.6 In a November 1939 *American Cinematographer*
article, Byron Haskin described matte shot work at
Warner Bros. The bottom photograph showed the set as
built; the middle photograph was the negative with its
matte line; and the top photograph illustrated the
completed matte shot

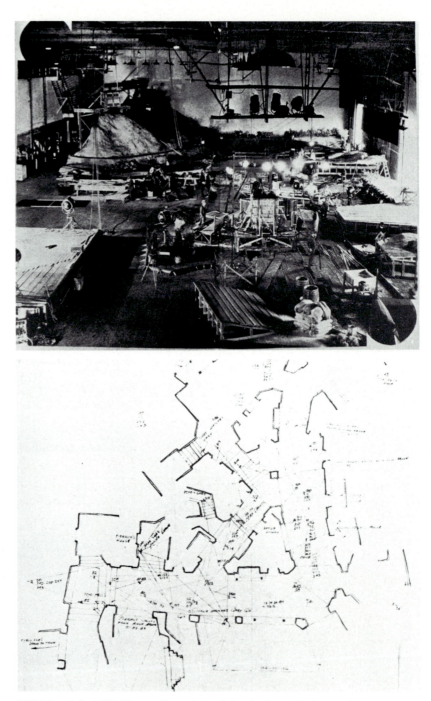

25.7 (above) In 1929, Warner Bros claimed that its Scientific Research Department worked in 'the largest building in the industry devoted exclusively to special process and miniature work.' The 150 × 300 foot stage included optical printers and enough room to shoot up to two dozen miniatures

25.8 (below) The floor plan of the Casbah set for *Algiers* (1938). After art director Alexander Toluboff designed the set, camera angles and movements for every scene were carefully planned

25.9 Several production stills from publicity about *Juarez*

25.10 Part of Warner Bros' 1939 staff of cinematographers with their ten new Studio Model Mitchells. Front row, left to right: E.B. McGreal; Charles Rosher; Ted McCord; Arthur Edeson; James Wong Howe; Sol Polito; Bun Haskin. Rear row, left to right: Sid Hickox; Warren Lynch; Arthur Todd; Lou O'Connell; Ernie Haller

27.1 (above left) *Casbah* (1948)
27.2 (above right) *The Kid Brother* (1927)
27.3 (centre left) Deep staging with fairly sharp focus in the rear planes: *Greed* (1924)
27.4 (centre right) Deep focus with a strong foreground and employing a wide-angle lens: *The Show* (1927)
27.5–27.6 (below) The hard-edged image in the late silent era: *So This Is Paris* (1926)

27.7-27.8 (above) The soft style in the late silent film: *Seventh Heaven* (1927)
27.9 (centre left) *Moby Dick* (1930)
27.10 (centre right) *A Midsummer Night's Dream* (1935)
27.11 (below left) *The Enchanted Cottage* (1945)
27.12 (below right) Wide-angle distortion in *Each Dawn I Die* (1939)

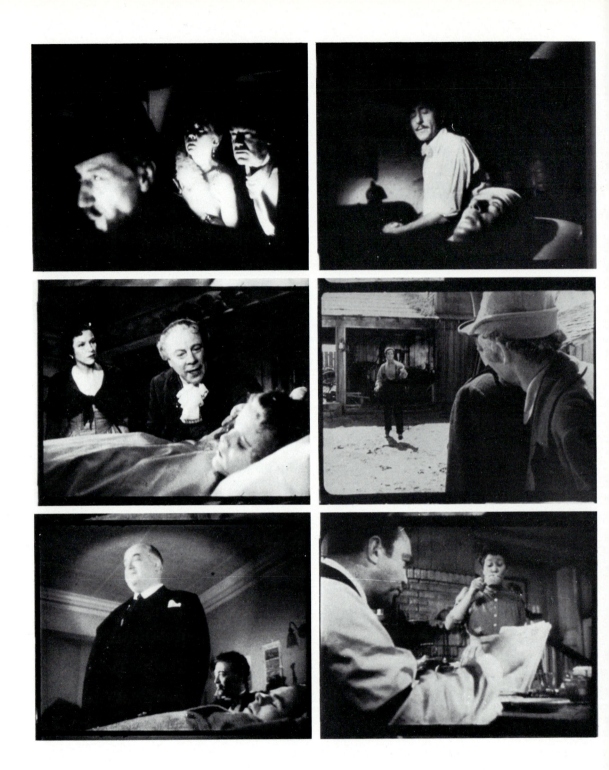

27.13 (above left) *Bulldog Drummond* (1929)
27.14 (above right) *A Farewell to Arms* (1932)
27.15 (centre left) *Anthony Adverse* (1936)

27.16 (centre right) *All That Money Can Buy* (1941)
27.17 (below left) *The Maltese Falcon* (1941)
27.18 (below right) *Our Town* (1940)

27.19 *Kings Row* (1941)

27.20 A drawing by William Cameron Menzies for *Alibi* (1929)

27.21 (above left) *Jezebel* (1938)
27.22 (above right) *Arrowsmith* (1931)
27.23-27.24 (below) Deep space shot/reverse shot in *Our Town* (1940)

27.25 (above) Gregg Toland (far left) and Howard Hawks (far right) using the Mitchell BNC to film *Ball of Fire* (1941)
27.26 (below left) Use of a wide-angle lens in *Dead End* (1937), shot by Toland for William Wyler
27.27 (below right) *These Three* (1936)

27.28 (above left) *These Three* (1936)
27.29 (above right) *Dead End* (1937)
27.30 (centre left) *The Long Voyage Home* (1940)

27.31 (centre right) *Dead End* (1937)
27.32 (below left) *Dead End* (1937)
27.33 (below right) *The Long Voyage Home* (1940)

27.34 (above left) *Citizen Kane* (1941)
27.35 (above right) *T-Men* (1948)
27.36 (centre left) *Gun Crazy* (1949)
27.37 (centre right) *The Maltese Falcon* (1941)
27.38–27.39 (below) *Kings Row* (1941)

27.40 (above left) *Ball of Fire* (1941)
27.41 (above right) *The Little Foxes* (1941)
27.42 (below left) **Manhandled* (1949)
27.43 (below right) *The Best Years of Our Lives* (1946)

27.44 (above) *The Best Years of Our Lives* (1946)
27.45-27.46 (below) *The Best Years of Our Lives* (1946)

28.1 (left) *At Sword's Point* (1952)
28.2 (right) *The Goldwyn Follies* (1938)

Rodgers and Hammerstein's "OKLAHOMA!", filmed in **TODD-AO**
Directed by Fred Zinnemann   Produced by Arthur Hornblow   Distributed by *Magna Theatre Corporation*
Printed in U.S.A.

29.1 Filming *Oklahoma!* (1955) with two Todd-A0 cameras. The size of the lens was due to its extreme angle of coverage. The film was also shot in CinemaScope; the Scope camera is center right

29.2 (above) *Carmen Jones* (1954)

29.3 (centre) A slightly off-center Scope composition, balanced by the glance: *Tip on a Dead Jockey* (1957)

29.4 (below) *Not Reconciled* (1964)

29.5-29.11 (this page and overleaf) *River of No Return* (1954)

29.9-29.11 (above) *River of No Return* (1954)
29.12 *Pierrot le fou* (1964)

Part Four Film style and technology to 1930

DAVID BORDWELL, JANET STAIGER,
and KRISTIN THOMPSON

19

Technology, style and mode of production

DAVID BORDWELL and JANET STAIGER

Technology is an important factor in American film history partly because it sells films. Since at least 1930, Hollywood has promoted mechanical marvels as assiduously as it has publicized stars, properties, and genres. Sound, color, widescreen, 3-D, stereophonic sound, 'Smell-o-vision,' and other novelties were marketing strategies as much as they were technical innovations. Today, a film like *Apocalypse Now* sells in part because of its Dolby sound, and *Star Wars*, *Superman*, *Tron*, *et al.* continue the cult of special effects. Indeed, special effects have exerted a perennial fascination for moviegoers, and popular magazines have never tired of showing how Hollywood wizardry could simulate bar-room brawls, snowstorms, sea battles, and earthquakes. The celebration of special effects is only a particular case of the tendency of Hollywood to promote technology as legerdemain. George Lucas's special effects firm is aptly named Industrial Light and Magic.

If we are to understand technology as a historical factor, we should not forget that it is as a benevolent but spectacular magic that it works to Hollywood's greatest advantage. Yet we cannot rest content with that image of technology. Within the film industry and allied spheres, there is nothing oneiric about technology; it is a concrete historical force. Trade journals, professional discussions, films, and the machines themselves furnish empirical evidence of a series of changes in design, engineering, and function. In dismissing hyperbole about magic, it is easy to swing toward fetishizing the physical materials and devices: lists of early sound or color systems, chronicles of the development of film stocks or lenses, 'histories' of Technicolor or Moviola or process projection. This too will not do. How can we explain technological change in Hollywood in relation to the classical style of filmmaking and the Hollywood mode of production? Answering

this question in concrete historical terms is the business of this part and Part Six of this book.

Technological change and the mode of production

It is precisely because of the economic value of 'industrial light and magic' that Hollywood instituted technological change as a business strategy. One inventor put it well: 'The persistent demands upon motion picture production for novel effects and broader methods of story-telling have necessarily instituted rapid and revolutionary developments in technique.'[1] In the Hollywood mode of production, we find that any technological change can be explained by one or more of three basic causes.

Production efficiency

The industry invested in some changes because of their economies. A new technology might cut costs by saving time or physical capital, or it might make the results of the work more predictable, or it might solve particular production problems. Composite photography, light meters, new aspects of camera design, viewing machines, faster film, machine processing, and varieties of lighting equipment performed such roles. 'In cinematography,' one 1927 writer explained, 'there is plenty of scope for the ingenious to exercise their talents. There seems to be, among the practisers of the craft, no end of the inventions or expedients, or the devising of new things to make the work easier or better.'[2] As Chapter 9 points out, the industry praised and rewarded innovations through trade acknowledgements, awards, and contracts. Such rewards in turn stimulated further innovation.

Product differentiation

The industry also effected technological changes because of the economic advantages of differentiating products. Chapter 9 has already shown that one of the most important goals of Hollywood's economic practices was distinguishing one firm's products from another. We are back to the fascination which technology holds for the spectator: the major innovations – synchronized sound, color, stereoscopy, widescreen, and stereophony – served to promote significant novelty in the product.

This product differentiation through technological change followed American industry's tradition of research and development. Before the 1900s, the solitary inventor was the chief source of scientific discovery. By the end of the nineteenth century, however, industry had begun to innovate technology in a much more systematic way. Major firms undertook large-scale research with the aim of product development or patent control. David F. Noble has shown that companies such as General Electric and Du Pont assimilated the private inventor into a corporate laboratory and channeled diffuse research efforts into specific programs.[3] Although the film industry wielded nothing like the vast research strength of the chemical or electrical industry, many technological innovations exploited by Hollywood were the result of careful strategies of product differentiation. Any firm will expend capital upon research and development if the firm believes that the technology will allow the firm to retain or expand its share of a market or move it into new markets. Douglas Gomery argues, for example, that Warner Bros's innovation of sound was the successful result of such a strategy.[4]

Adherence to standards of quality

In some instances, the film industry innovated technology because the industry's discourse marked certain innovations as desirable. This sounds circular, and it was. Hollywood's discourse, as revealed in advertising, trade papers, *et al.*, set forth standards of the quality film. Technological innovations which would help attain the goal became institutionalized research aims. An ideology of 'progress' (of a particular kind) led and controlled research. From the earliest period, certain technological innovations, such as sound and color, were assumed to be almost inevitable.

American cinema's technological research has been aimed at meeting a commitment to the standards canonized by the classical stylistic paradigm. Synchronized sound, color, widescreen, stereoscopy, and stereophony were justified as progress toward better storytelling, greater realism, and enhanced spectacle. Here is one writer on the value of true stereophonic sound:[5]

Pseudostereophonic methods can indeed be used if the producer is willing to sacrifice the lifelike perspective effects, the showmanship of offscreen dialogue, music or other sounds, and the improved fidelity particularly in sets described as 'boomy' – all of which are provided by true stereophonic methods.

When MGM introduced a widescreen process, 'Realife,' in 1930, one critic wrote: 'Ordinary "pan" shots permit the camera to cover the full arc only in shortened limited scenes. With "Realife" the camera covers all of the attackers in one sweep, and keeps them close enough so individual dramatic details may be seen.'[6] A cinematographer noted of Fox's 1930 'Grandeur,' a 70mm process:[7]

From the audience standpoint, *Grandeur* offers a series of spectacular surprises. In the first place, the new size and proportions of the screen are astounding. . . . Then, the wide proportion selected is almost exactly that of natural vision, and removes from the consciousness the dead black borderline which haunts the smaller screens. The absence of this borderline gives the large pictures a pseudostereoscopic effect which is very pleasing.

Hollywood's discourse praised these technologies for reinforcing classical standards, and the firms calculated that adherence to those standards would maintain or increase profits.

Even minor technological innovations which would not be noticeable to the audience – and thus could not be used in publicity – were sought by Hollywood. Filmmakers assumed that innovations like the automatic dissolving shutter (*c.* 1920) and refinements in sound recording techniques (through the 1930s and 1940s) cumulatively improved films, although audiences might not be able to pinpoint such improvements.

It is evident that these three causes for technological change can complement or collide with one another. Often, for instance, a change effected primarily for differentiating a product could be quite costly, particularly at the beginning. Obviously, the industry expected long-term advantages, but even small changes could be expensive. As Joseph Valentine remarked,[8]

> Cinematography is a good deal like a mathematical equation: change one factor, and you find it has become necessary to make corresponding changes in several others to keep the result correctly in balance. . . . [A change in the film stock means other changes] in order to keep the final result at the balance we call good cinematography.

Here the maintenance of stylistic norms becomes a controlling factor; product differentiation must not destroy stylistic standardization. The standards thus compel further research, which will solve problems and restabilize the system. No wonder that in 1938 a professional organization noted: 'It is frequently difficult to decide whether the development of the new tools is the cause or the result of the progress being made.'[9] In any instance, technological innovation may be introduced without full consideration of its impact on filmmaking; the mode of production responds by readjusting other factors in the equation. The rewards of cost efficiency, product differentiation, and creation of a quality film were often judged worth short-run imbalances.

Any such readjustment would have to consider a number of factors. Obviously, the style of the films would be affected, and we shall see in further chapters how the industry worked to reinstate classical schemata. In addition, existing technology would have to be retuned. A ripple effect modified adjacent technologies, as when Technicolor filming impelled Max Factor to recast its make-up formulas. Moreover, the mode of production had to accommodate the innovation. The most important strategy of accommodation was to insert new subdivisions into the work process. Adding a craft to the chain of assembly was consistent with the mode's system of serial manufacture. Furthermore, the new expert specialist continued the tradition of efficiency and delegation of work knowledge. Once the decision

to innovate and diffuse a technology was made, production firms had to determine how to introduce modifications most rapidly and smoothly, with the least disruption and cost. Two instances, one a failed innovation, the other a successful one, illustrate how institutions weighed the various factors introduced by new technology.

Three-dimensional films have been anticipated since the introduction of moving pictures. By 1909, experimenters had tried using anaglyphic (red/green) systems, alternating projectors, and double-printing negatives. MGM produced several 3-D shorts in the 1930s, and John A. Norling displayed a 3-D system at the 1940 World's Fair.[10] In February 1952, when film attendance was down and Hollywood sought ways to entice the consumer back into the theaters, Norling suggested 3-D: 'That the motion picture industry could use something to combat television's capture of more and more of the theatre audience is undeniable.'[11] By summer, a new company was shooting *Bwana Devil*. The film's sensational opening in Los Angeles seemed to presage a revolution, and in March of 1953, studios were eagerly engaged in extensive 3-D production. Yet in December 3-D was declared dead. Although stereoscopic pictures provided product differentiation, they failed. The technology could not assure a high-quality product at each screening, and another innovation, widescreen, seemed a more efficient way to provide the novelty the industry sought. 3-D did not become standard because its disadvantages outweighed its advantages.[12]

In contrast, the innovation of synchronized-sound films shows how the factors of novelty, economy, and adherence to norms might encourage the industry to make pervasive adjustments in its mode of production. When Warner Bros used sound-synched pictures to differentiate its product and seize a competitive advantage, the innovation initially cut down production efficiency, significantly increased costs, and threatened the standards of quality established during the previous decade. In this case, however, Warner Bros was willing to deal with the problems because it judged that the innovation would have a comparative advantage in the long run. Synch-sound pictures did provide product differentiation, they augured a significant increase in profits from rentals, and initial problems of sound quality were considered capable of being quickly resolved.

Moreover, Warner Bros and the rest of the industry would not have been able to introduce such a change in standard filmmaking techniques had not the system of serial manufacture been able to restabilize itself. Some short-term difficulties were swiftly resolved by established procedures. For instance, the studios now demanded story material laden with dialogue, but since the firms had for twenty years adapted Broadway plays, this posed no great obstacles. From the New York stage came writers, directors, and players experienced in handling dialogue. For a while, rehearsals played a larger part in the director's preparations, since companies hoped to avoid the expense of rewriting during shooting and sought to follow the theatrical procedures to which its new personnel were accustomed. This new production practice fell into disuse as the workers became accustomed to sound filming.[13] The problem of providing foreign-language versions was also quickly solved, with dubbing and sub-titling becoming standard by the end of 1931.[14]

In other respects, the mode of production adjusted to sound by sacrificing some flexibility in the filmmaking process. Improvised shooting declined because of sound's greater expense and its limited editing options. In the silent period, the film could be altered in the post-production phase by the insertion of inter-titles. Once a talkie was shot, however, script changes were more limited, unless the studio would pay the costs of rewriting and refilming. Likewise, cameramen lost control of cranking speed, and the machine development of negatives eliminated the possibility of adjusting the image quality during processing. Synchronized sound also required a longer editing phase, so that directors could not spend as much time supervising cutting.[15] If the value of a lost option was generally recognized, research might be directed to recover it, but in many instances, sound reduced choices and made production practices more uniform.

The major effect of synchronized-sound production was to create new subdivisions in the work process, the most usual way that the mode of production accommodated any large-scale technological change. Dialogue coaches and directors, speech experts, and dance directors are obvious examples of new roles. Studios added departments to select, compose, arrange, and orchestrate the film's musical accompaniment. These work processes were placed after editing, a position deplored by musicians but consistent with that allotted to musical accompaniment in the silent era.[16] Sound also removed the head of photography from his position as camera operator. With the rise of multiple-camera shooting in the early sound era, the first cinematographer became an executive supervising the team of 'operative cameramen.' By the 1930s, when multiple-camera shooting was abandoned, the director of photography remained a supervisor who did not handle the equipment during shooting.[17]

The most extensive addition to the structure of divided labor involved the employment of sound recording experts. The studios hired 75 to 80 per cent of their sound personnel from telegraphy, telephony, radio broadcasting, and electrical research laboratories.[18] In 1931, the RKO sound director, Carl Dreher, outlined a line-and-staff structure that assigned one group of workers to maintain the equipment and a second to use it (see fig. 19.1, p. 261). The maintenance engineer oversaw a staff that installed, tested, and repaired the sound-recording equipment. The recording supervisor, or chief mixer, supervised the recordists and assistant recordists during shooting.[19] Thus when Hollywood added a sound track to the silent picture, it added a labor process and divided the workers into a parallel hierarchy.

These new craft hierarchies seem to have been modeled upon existing ones. The music department paralleled the story and writing departments. Rights to music (like rights to stories) had to be purchased; famous composers (like celebrated writers) created original material to be reworked by others (arrangers and orchestrators, continuity scriptwriters). In addition, the sound staff was organized in a fashion parallel to that serving the cinematographer. The chief mixer paralleled the first cinematographer, while the mixer's recordists were the counterparts of the operative cameramen: just as the operative cameramen had responsibility for recording the image track as directed, so the sound recordists were charged with placing microphones and monitoring sound quality. Rerecording personnel collaborated with the chief mixer much as special-effects personnel worked with the cinematographer.[20]

The dissemination of sound filming stands as a typical case of how the Hollywood mode of production could accommodate technological change. With any such change, the industry could solve certain problems with established procedures, sacrifice some flexibility for the sake of the innovation, or create new divisions in the work order. By hiring experts, modeling new work structures upon old, and inserting new operations into an appropriate phase of the overall work sequence, Hollywood could insure that rapid and efficient production would continue according to quality standards. New technologies momentarily disrupted the labor process, but they were absorbed in ways which modified, not revolutionized, the mode of production.

Film technology and the classical style

If technological change can be attributed to such economic causes as production efficiency, product differentiation, and maintenance of a standard of quality, how can we grasp that change in relation to stylistic changes visible and audible in Hollywood films? In any sphere, historians typically address four aspects of change: direction, function, timing, and causation.

Changes in film style may be described in *directional* terms – away from this, toward something else. The most common explanation of stylistic change assumes an evolutionary pattern. André Bazin has proposed that the quest for a 'total cinema' of perfect realism gave film history a specific direction and made Hollywood style a step upon that path.[21] V.F. Perkins has argued that although technology moves toward such a total realism, the effect of this is to expand purely formal means. With the ever-increasing resources of cinema, the artist gains a greater range of choice: 'The more completely the cinema is able to duplicate "mere reality," the wider becomes the range of alternatives open to the filmmaker.'[22]

Such teleological accounts of style in history pose problems. Although a complete understanding of the Hollywood style cannot neglect the idea of progress, that idea cannot adequately explain the direction of stylistic change. Any such conception of progress ignores the ways in which technological change has often reduced stylistic options. The classical style has not changed in a cumulative or additive fashion, nor has technology always left room for a return to discarded practices. We have already seen, for instance, that synchronized sound forced certain workers to relinquish areas of control. It is not simply nostalgic to assert that the range of possibilities often became narrower: something was definitely lost when Hollywood abandoned the hand-cranked camera, rack-and-tank developing by inspection, and three-strip Technicolor. We cannot make a film today which looks like it was made in 1915, or 1925, or 1945 (even if, after a glance at today's grainy, muddy images, we wish we could).

Given the uneven movement of stylistic history, we may be more inclined to accept Jean-Louis Comolli's claim that style change has no inherent direction but is instead fundamentally 'nonlinear.' As an Althusserian Marxist, Comolli sees every technological innovation as torn by contradictions among economic pressures, ideological demands, and signifying practices. It is not just that photography fulfilled the bourgeois dream of capturing the world as a spectacle for a detached observer. Comolli asserts that photography also disrupted this ideology by *challenging* the eye as a source of knowledge. Similar contradictions are to be found in any historical relation of technology to film style.[23] Comolli's point is certainly sound: the direction of change in the classical Hollywood style has been not linear but dispersed, not a progress toward a goal but a series of disparate shifts. Yet even if the change is not lawlike, it is not capricious either. Hollywood's insistence upon standardization limited the shape which change could take. To describe this nonlinear but not random pattern, we need a nonteleological model of change.

Leonard Meyer has pointed out that several sorts of change exist in the history of the arts, and one sort which he identifies fits the case at hand. In *trended* change:[24]

Change takes place within a limiting set of preconditions, but the potential inherent in the established relationships may be realized in a number of different ways and the order of the realization may be variable [i.e., not specified by lawlike and invariant preconditions]. Change is successive and gradual, but not necessarily sequential; and its rate and extent are variable, depending more upon external circumstances than upon internal preconditions.

This conception is useful because it grants that stylistic change need not operate according to notions of revolution or rupture on the one hand or evolutionary unfolding on the other. We do not have to consider the coming of sound as a drastic break in the classical mode, nor need we accept Bazin's 'dialectical evolution of film language.' Once we admit that there is no lawlike pattern of development in Hollywood style, we can look for particular historical circumstances which govern the different ways that the classical paradigm has been realized and modified. This does not mean, however, that change is capricious. The category of trended change lets us see stylistic change as operating within a bounded set of possibilities, even if the causes or the timing of change derive from external spheres such as management decisions or technological innovations. Finally, Meyer's account lets us situate an individual's innovation within the stylistic preconditions that shape and limit it.[25]

This is to say that we can also consider the *functions* of stylistic change differently. For an evolutionary account, either utopian like Bazin's or more open-ended like Perkins's, any style change functions as one stride in a forward march. But Meyer's concept of trended change permits us to use Chapter 1's concept of functional equivalents to plot systematic shifts in stylistic devices. If, for example, a scene's space may be established by means of a long shot, a camera movement, an editing pattern, an introductory title, or voice-over narration, then we need to examine not only the change in devices but also their common function — the establishment of classical narrative space. From this standpoint, the history of Hollywood film style after 1917 is in large part a series of shifts in formal devices within the range of functions defined by the classical paradigm.

Those shifts can be analyzed for the ways in which they fulfill or extend the initial options. For instance, a camera movement – say a track back from a detail to a long shot – can establish the scene's locale while serving other canonized functions: creating a stronger cue for three-dimensional space, centering viewer attention, suspensefully delaying information, creating a

parallel to another tracking shot. Or consider the innovation of sound. In 1927, when sound was inserted into the already-constituted system of classical filmmaking, it was used in ways that supported the paradigm (e.g., voice for expressivity, sound effects for realism of locale). But sound also extended the paradigm: now vocal qualities could represent character psychology, now temporal continuity could be assured by diegetic speech or music. Even though the classical premises define a limited hierarchy of functions, new stylistic devices can realize those possibilities in domains that were previously not absorbed functionally. We are back at the issues discussed in Chapter 7, the ways in which controlled deviations from classical norms can reinforce the authority of those norms.[26]

Any consideration of stylistic change must also account for *timing* and *causation*, and these aspects force us to leave the purely stylistic realms of direction and function. Meyer's notion of trended change cannot rest content with a historical chronology that locks itself solely within the medium. Yuri Tynianov and Roman Jakobson have indicated the limits of an autonomous history of style, since immanent laws do not explain[27]

> the rate of change or the choice of a particular evolutionary path from among those which are in theory possible, since the immanent laws of literary (linguistic) evolution represent only an indeterminate equation whose solution may be any of a number (albeit limited) of possible solutions, but not necessarily a single one. The question of the specific evolutionary path chosen, or at least of the dominant, can be answered only by analyzing the correlation between the literary series and other historical series.

Thus the timing of stylistic change – why something happens when it does and not before or after – poses severe problems for a teleological account such as Bazin's. Bazin claims that the dream of total cinema predated the actual invention of the apparatus, but Comolli has retorted that all the important scientific preconditions for cinema existed fifty years before the first films. Again and again we find a lag between the technological preconditions of color or sound or widescreen and the actual utilization of them. Comolli claims that no autonomous logic of film style can explain this lag and that the best explanation is to be found in the socio-economic sphere. Technology does not get used until capitalism has a need for it at a certain juncture.[28] The history of Hollywood technology certainly bears this out; more often than not, economic factors of the three sorts already mentioned determine when certain devices became standardized. Hollywood studios became interested in incandescent lighting when tungsten units and panchromatic film stock made filming cheaper and more efficient in significant respects. Firms decided to switch over to sound motion pictures when Warners and Fox had proven financial benefits and an acceptable standard of quality. World War II constraints on set expenditures encouraged location shooting and the development of more portable equipment. Although widescreen cinema and stereophonic sound were technically feasible before World War II, they were not exploited until the studios faced a declining theater attendance in the postwar period. Comolli's emphasis upon the lag between technological possibility and extended use is helpful in explaining the timing of stylistic change.

Causation of stylistic change poses even more severe difficulties for an immanent account. The most common, and commonsensical, move has been to attribute stylistic and technical change to individual innovation. Two causal agents typically emerge: the inventor and the artist. Consider Perkins's account of the way camera movements were devised for F.W. Murnau's *The Last Laugh* (1924):[29]

When *The Last Laugh* was still in the script stage, Mayer went to the photographer Karl Freund to find out how far it was possible to film long sections of the film with a continuously mobile camera. When Freund satisfied him that it could be done, Mayer started writing afresh and constructed his screenplay to exploit the possibilities to the full.

The inventor/artist pairing generates a dialogic model of the causes of technological change. At any given starting point — the primitive cinema, the end of the 1920s — technology defines a horizon of possibilities. The filmmaker may either accept these constraints and work within them, or the filmmaker may innovate, for whatever reason (craving for novelty, the challenge of overcoming obstacles, etc.). When the artist demands an innovation, the technician responds. In his *Last Laugh* example, Perkins suggests that the technician works out the practical details of the artist's original insight. Horizon of possibilities, artistic innovation, technological implementation: these stages define the shuttling pattern that Perkins calls 'a constant two-way traffic between science and style, technology and technique.'[30]

What vitiates such arguments is the absolutism of the artist/inventor couplet. The model presupposes a small-scale task to be solved and an interpersonal scale of communication. Yet, as we have seen, technological change in the film industry has a broad impact, and research and invention are institutional to a very substantial degree. A vision of individuals talking to individuals does not explain the *systematic* effects of technology upon style. The artist/inventor pairing also does not explain why sometimes the technician innovates when no need is articulated by the artist. Eastman Kodak's development of ever-faster film stocks in the 1930s is one example. As one cameraman put it: 'We were like a bunch of sheep. When Eastman sent out a new batch — "This is going to do so and so." Well, all the cameramen wanted to try it and see it. And the directors had to have it ...'[31] The artist/inventor couplet, based on the filmmaker's posing a problem for the technician to solve, further ignores one crucial fact. Some solutions are more acceptable than others, and some are unacceptable altogether. The most elegant solution to a technical problem from an engineering standpoint may be rejected for reasons of 'showmanship' or production routines. At any historical moment, the mode of production and the classical paradigm permit only some solutions. And about what is permitted, the individual artist or inventor has very little to say.

Because the inventor/artist model fails to recognize broad causes of stylistic change, Comolli has argued for the necessity of recognizing economic and ideological factors. He has asserted that an autonomous history of film style and its mechanical/technical causes reduces to a chain of 'first times' and purely contingent links. Comolli calls for historical analysis which recognizes the importance of social ideology and the film industry as determining technological and stylistic change. This much is probably uncontroversial. Where Comolli breaks new ground is in insisting that both style and technology are causally determined by ideological processes.

It is often conceded, especially in French film theory, that monocular perspective in Renaissance painting is not only an artistic procedure but an ideologically determined mode of representation, embodying a bourgeois conception of the individual subject's relation to visible reality. It is less often conceded that the camera obscura or the photographic camera *as a machine* is inherently ideological. Comolli claims that no film technology is a neutral transmitter of the world 'out there'; the technology is produced in large part by a socially derived conception of that world and how we know it. For example, he finds the origin of cinema not in scientific inquiry but in nineteenth-century ideological pressures to represent 'life as it is' and in economic desires to exploit a new spectacle.[32]

Comolli's theory is far superior to the simpler account, but it remains sweepingly reductive. Cinema's construction of depth is reduced to 'Renaissance perspective' (itself a slogan for several perspective systems), deep focus is usually treated as only a matter of lens length, and most important, 'technology' and 'ideology' are flattened into abstract and ahistorical generalities. For Comolli, 'technology' includes not only the machines themselves but also many social processes that produce them: theories, scientific research, manufacture, and the labor of film production. These senses are never clearly distinguished. Similarly, Comolli makes the concept of 'ideology' do too much work; he assumes that 'bourgeois ideology' rests in place for three centuries, from Caravaggio to *Citizen Kane*. This objection echoes a point made by Raymond Williams:[33]

One thing that is evident in some of the best Marxist cultural analysis is that it is very much more at home in what one might call *epochal* questions than in what one has to call *historical* questions. That is to say, it is usually very much better at distinguishing the large features of different epochs of society, as commonly

between feudal and bourgeois, than at distinguishing between different phases of bourgeois society, and different moments within those phases: that true historical process which demands a much greater precision and delicacy of analysis than the always striking epochal analysis which is concerned with main lineaments and features.

Comolli's description of capitalist economy and bourgeois ideology is epochal in exactly Williams's sense. Our purpose here is to construct, without falling back into the atomistic dualism of artist and inventor, a more precisely historical account of Hollywood technology and style.

We can, for instance, immediately translate Comolli's concept of 'capitalist economics' into the more particular causes of technological change examined earlier − production economies, product differentiation, and adherence to standards of quality. Similarly, we can replace the broad concept of 'signifying practice' with the historical model of the classical film's style articulated in Parts One and Three of this book. And in looking for the agents of causal change, we must be sensitive to Sartre's criticism of 'lazy' Marxists who replace 'real, perfectly defined groups' by vague collectivities such as 'bourgeois ideology.'[34] In our argument, those concrete groups are the institutions which promoted and guided stylistic change by articulating the range of permissible solutions to technological problems.

In examining the ways that stylistic change in the period 1917-60 is tied to technological change, we will need to recognize the significant differences among the four aspects already noted. Business strategies can usually explain the causation and timing of stylistic change, while the direction and functions of the change must usually be constructed from the way that technology permitted novel devices to fill roles which the classical paradigm had already staked out. But where can we locate the historical agents of this process? In most cases, the agents are a set of specific institutions: manufacturing and supply firms and professional associations. These institutions transferred the industry's economic strategies and aesthetic precepts to the spheres of technological innovation and film form. In doing so, they fulfilled and elaborated the classical paradigm, spurring and guiding technological change. In short, specific firms and associations functioned as mediations − not in the sense that they temporally came between film production and film style, but in the sense that they shaped a particular relationship between the two.[35] By mediating between film style and economic imperatives, these institutions defined the range of practical possibilities open to Hollywood filmmaking.

Technology and Hollywood institutions

Only institutions could have systematized and guided technological research and development in an industry as complex as the American studio cinema. Technology's sources have always been tangled and diverse, its developments diffuse and interdependent. From the very beginning, cinema has relied upon discoveries and applications in other fields. Often, for instance, one finds sources of film technology in military research: zoom lenses were first developed for reconnaissance work, Cinerama came out of gunnery training exercises, and 3-D cameras used an interlock mechanism devised for missile tracking. Similarly, it has often happened that a technical development in one area of film offered possibilities for another area. The 1929-30 experiments with wide film came to little in themselves, but studio engineers seized upon the high-intensity projection lamps required by wide film and used them to improve the quality of rear-projection work.[36] While the imaginative insight belongs to individuals, institutions must select and promote certain leads as worth work.

In the earliest years of the American film industry, innovation tended to be sporadic, casual, and impelled by individual inquiry. But during the teens, economies of scale began to emerge and technological change became systematized. The industry's investment in technology required some mechanisms for producing, monitoring, and assimilating innovations. By 1920, the American film industry had come to depend heavily upon specific institutions for materials, tools, and processes.

What sort of institutions governed Hollywood's appropriation of technology? In other industries, the corporate research laboratory has been indispensable to technological innovation.

Although the major film studios claimed to have their own 'research departments,' most were small-scale design and machine shops.[37] No studio could afford the research facilities of a General Electric, a Union Carbide, or a Western Electric. More often, the burden of research fell to new, small, or marginal companies. In the film industry, small production firms were more likely to tackle research because it was a way to enter markets. Typically, after such small companies had financed initial research, a larger company would then invest in the technology. The most basic and significant research was performed by the manufacturers and suppliers of materials and equipment. In an important sense, Hollywood filmmaking only became a modern industry when it joined forces with corporate research.

The outstanding example of Hollywood's reliance upon a giant firm is Eastman Kodak. When in 1889 George Eastman supplied motion picture film for Edison's experiments, there began a dependence that has continued throughout the history of the American cinema. In the early years, Eastman's chief competitor, Lumière, produced a less dependable stock; by 1910, Eastman's negative dominated the world market. What kept the firm's quality so carefully controlled was its commitment to basic research. In the mid-1890s, Eastman began to institutionalize technical innovation by recruiting engineers and creating a testing department. In 1913, C.E.K. Mees, a London chemist and physicist whom Eastman had hired, founded the firm's research laboratory.[38] In his book, *The Industrial Organization of Scientific Research*, Mees explained that while some companies could be content with seeking minor refinements in their product, leading firms had to commit themselves to fundamental research with no obvious or immediate reward.[39] Hence the aim of the Eastman laboratory was nothing less than 'scientific understanding of photographic processes.'[40] The boldly theoretical research which Mees and his staff undertook yielded rich results for the motion picture industry. Expanded through the years, the Kodak laboratory introduced a panchromatic motion picture stock in 1913, reversal film in the 1920s, a range of amateur film stocks (including color), a series of ever-faster professional emulsions through the 1930s, 1940s, and 1950s, and a color negative film stock in 1950. The Eastman Research Laboratory also created much of the sensitometric theory that became indispensable for sound film processing after 1926.[41]

Other large enterprises applied some of their research facilities to supply technology to the film industry. Du Pont, Eastman's chief rival for the motion-picture raw-stock market, did not produce film until 1923, but as the principal producer of explosives since 1802, Du Pont already had a huge corporate research facility. Western Electric's subsidiary, Electrical Research Products Incorporated (ERPI), furnished much of the technological innovation for talking films. Western Electric was in turn the manufacturing subsidiary of American Telephone and Telegraph, whose corporate research program had been launched in 1910. Before World War II, AT&T's Bell Laboratory had a bigger budget for research than any university in America. Another major corporation, the National Carbon Company, supplied carbon rods and arc lamps for studio lighting and theater projection. As a subsidiary of Union Carbide, National Carbon drew upon the resources of a laboratory founded in 1921. Bausch and Lomb, which began as a firm making cheap spectacles, became prosperous because of its unprecedented mass-manufacture of lenses. Bausch and Lomb supplied lenses for Edison's Kinetoscope, introduced the standard Cinephor projection lenses and the Raytar and Baltar camera lenses, developed the optical systems used in film sound recording and reproduction, and supplied lenses for rear-projection and widescreen systems. Like its Rochester neighbor Eastman Kodak, Bausch and Lomb established its own research laboratory to maintain its supremacy in its field. A relative latecomer was the Radio Corporation of America, created in 1919 by General Electric, other firms, and the federal government. After a series of successes in radio manufacturing and broadcasting, RCA created its own Technical and Test Department in New York City. Although much research was done there (chiefly resulting in velocity microphones), it was not until 1934 that RCA embarked on massive corporate research, which was eventually to produce innovations in film sound recording.[42]

Smaller, more specialized, firms also served the film industry. None could afford to be as concerned with basic research as the giants were,

but all worked to varying degrees to innovate technology. Bell & Howell is the most notable instance. Donald J. Bell, a projectionist, met Albert Howell, a draftsman and mechanic for a projector-parts manufacturer. The two formed a firm in 1907. Bell deliberately sought to establish a standardized line of motion-picture machinery. Soon Bell & Howell had built the perforator that would become the industry norm. In a 1916 paper, Bell urged the industry to standardize the spacing, size, and shape of film perforations, and he devised a test gauge to measure deviations. The Bell & Howell metal camera, put on the market in 1909, eventually became the most popular 35mm camera of the silent era. The pilot-pin engineering that made the camera yield superior registration also made the Bell & Howell continuous printer a great success. Modified and improved through two decades, it was superseded in 1933 by the Bell & Howell automatic printer. Later innovations included magnetic sound striping, an additive color printer, and a 35mm reflex camera. Such engineering advances required an ample research department, and Bell & Howell's grew steadily. During World War II, the new Lincolnwood laboratories were busy twenty-four hours a day designing and building not only studio equipment but also gunsights, radar devices, gun cameras, portable projectors, and combat cameras.[43]

The Mitchell Camera Corporation lacked Bell's zeal for standardization, but it was also concerned with using company research to gain Hollywood business. The firm was born from the idea of a camera that would have the ability to rack the camera body sidewise quickly and bring the viewing glass into alignment with the taking lens; this would make framing and focusing easier and faster. In 1921, the company began to market the machine. George Mitchell had nothing like the research resources of Bell & Howell, but the coming of sound made the firm launch a new engineering effort. Bell & Howell was unable to quiet the slapping sound made by the pressure plate and the pilot-pin shuttle. The Mitchell firm redesigned its basic model — first as the NC (1932), then the BNC (1934) — and created the universally used studio camera of the decades before 1960.[44]

There were other specialized technical firms serving the studios, and to enter and stay in the market, many had to develop technology, on however modest a scale. Some, like Bell & Howell, worked within a traditional engineering framework. Peter Mole and Elmer Richardson, both trained as electrical engineers, wound up working for the Creco Lamp Company of Los Angeles. When they saw that the industry was switching to incandescent lighting for production, they noticed that no firm was providing such units. In 1927, the firm of Mole-Richardson was formed and quickly became the chief supplier of incandescent fixtures. The founders' engineering expertise enabled them to plan systematic research programs. They obtained the cooperation of GE, the National Carbon Company, and Corning Glass in designing and testing new lighting units, both incandescent and arc. Studios and firms began to come to them with problems to be solved and equipment to be built.[45] Mole boasted that each project required 'a combination of pure scientific research, practical photo-technical necessity, and production engineering.'[46] We shall encounter a similarly zealous engineering organization when we examine Technicolor's contribution to technological innovation.

Other firms lacked the engineer's gospel of scientific inquiry but understood the economic advantages of directed research. Max Factor, who had learned some chemistry as a doctor's assistant in Russia, opened a wig and make-up business in Los Angeles in 1908. Although he supplied make-up to the studios during the 1920s, his first major success was the standardizing of panchromatic make-up, which helped take the make-up process out of the player's hands and into the control of the studio. After 1928, to guarantee uniformity, Factor had to create careful testing and research procedures. By 1934, his factory had an assembly-line operation, a quality-control laboratory, and a research laboratory to develop new formulas. Every innovation in lighting or film stock sent studios to Factor, and the company devised make-up to suit faster emulsions, arc lamps, three-color Technicolor, and Eastman Color. In fact, the 1935 make-up developed for Technicolor became the pancake foundation make-up still used in cosmetics.[47]

The list of specialized service agencies is long. There is Moviola, which in the 1920s began furnishing Hollywood studios with precision previewing and editing machinery. There is Bardwell & McAlister, Mole-Richardson's chief competitor in supplying lighting equipment. There is Consolidated Film Industries, which innovated continuous machine processing. Rear-projection equipment, cutaway cars, even wind machines — for almost everything, from raw stock to camera cranes, the American film industry relied upon large and small manufacturers and suppliers.[48]

The service industries bore the brunt of technical innovation, but they had to keep abreast of the studios' needs. Certainly proximity helped. Most of the specialized firms began their operations in Los Angeles, and the larger firms established branches there. The first wave of settlement was over by the mid-twenties, when Technicolor had moved from Boston and the major raw-stock manufacturers (Eastman, Du Pont, Agfa) all had their Hollywood representatives. The second wave of settlement coincided with the coming of sound. At the end of the 1930s, RCA and Western Electric had offices in Los Angeles, as did the Chicago-based Bell & Howell.[49] 'Only in Hollywood,' wrote Mole in 1938, 'could designing and production engineers be in such close daily contact with the ultimate, practical users of their products.'[50] It was estimated in 1936 that, apart from the 16,000 people employed in the studios, another 14,000 worked for service firms.[51]

Still, to posit the process of technological innovation as a simple communication among neighbors is to ignore the difficulties within the artist/technician model: the fact that technical agencies could innovate on their own, the requisite that maker and user must share some conception of permissible innovation, and the need to explain large-scale technological change. The firms' research orientation insured the capacity to innovate. What the firms needed was guidance about the acceptable directions for innovation.

The film industry confronted engineers with a specific set of problems. For instance, the practices of Hollywood filmmaking did not entirely fit engineers' conceptions of efficiency. Peter Mole recalled that in the early days, he was surprised to discover that the correct solution from an engineer's point of view was not necessarily the most feasible one for film production. 'In order to give the cinematographer what he wanted we would be obliged to sacrifice engineering efficiency all the way along the line.'[52] Thus Hollywood's aesthetic specificity governed the range of permissible technical innovations. The researcher's work could not be abstractly instrumental; filmmaking presented 'artistic' problems absent from ordinary industrial research. In other words, the classical stylistic paradigm had to be made known, however implicitly, to the technical agencies. To communicate this paradigm, to foster standard solutions to problems, and to coordinate long-range research became tasks for Hollywood's professional societies and associations.

Like most oligopolies in American history, the film industry recognized the value of cooperation among firms. As early as the mid-teens, the industry possessed formal networks to disseminate standards of quality filmmaking, new technologies, and efficient production practices. Chapter 9 has traced the emergence of advertising that established grounds for competition, trade papers and handbooks that described and prescribed style and production procedures, and various trade, labor, and professional associations that permitted the exchange of information across companies. In 1922, the film companies officially demonstrated a commitment to industry-wide uniformity by reorganizing the trade association as the Motion Picture Producers and Distributors Association (MPPDA). Under the strong leadership of Will H. Hays, the MPPDA took steps to solidify the industry.[53] Besides controlling subject matter through self-censorship regulations, the MPPDA was credited with the 'encouragement of better business practice, such as standardized budgets, uniform cost accounting, uniform contracts, and the arbitration of disputes.'[54] Like the MPPDA, most industry groups included in their aims the sharing of information and a commitment to progress.

The same goals characterized the three most important agencies that guided technological innovation: the American Society of Cinematographers (founded 1918), the Society of Motion Picture Engineers (founded 1916), and the Academy of Motion Picture Arts and Sciences (founded 1927). The three agencies differed considerably in power, constituency, and purpose. The American Society of Cinematographers was a small fraternal association dedicated to creating a professional image for first cameramen at the Hollywood studios. The Society of Motion Picture Engineers, a larger group, drew its members from studio technical personnel and from the supply and manufacturing sector. The Academy of Motion Picture Arts and Sciences had by far the most authority in the industry, representing as it did the major studios, the producers, and many personnel. Although each group undertook a wide range of activities, it is their work in regulating technological change that is important here.

The American Society of Cinematographers

The American Society of Cinematographer (ASC) grew out of a few cameramen's clubs begun in 1913. Functioning chiefly as fraternal organizations, the clubs also encouraged the exchange of information and published their own journals.[55] In 1919, shortly after the clubs dissolved, the ASC was chartered, claiming as one of its objectives 'to advance the art and science of cinematography and to encourage, foster, and strive for pre-eminence, excellence, artistic perfection, and scientific knowledge in all matters pertaining to cinematography.'[56] In 1920, the ASC began publishing a monthly journal, *American Cinematographer*, which has continued to this day. The Society also held regular meetings, usually of an informal social nature. At some points, notably during a 1933 strike, the ASC became embroiled in labor disputes, but on the whole it never tried to represent cameramen in the workplace.[57] The group's chief purpose was to propose and maintain standards of professional work in cinematography.

It is evident that the ASC created a specific conception of the cameraman's role, one that combined aspects of 'artist' and 'technician.' The Society's motto, 'Loyalty, progress, and artistry,' embodies their ideals. Cinematographers took pride in finding ways to achieve novel effects or to make shooting more economical and efficient, and in Society meetings and in the pages of *American Cinematographer* the cinematographers shared their discoveries with their peers. Soon after the ASC was founded, it stated:[58]

When a cameraman encounters a difficult problem in his work which he cannot solve he can call on sixty-five fellow cameramen. The small producer with limited facilities for experimentation is benefited with this arrangement. It is equivalent to putting on his payroll the entire membership of the society, without the exhausting exercise of signing checks to cover their salaries.

Loyalty to professional standards and the pooling of information in the name of progress thus promoted standardization. As for the third goal of the motto, artistry, after 1910 the cinematographer saw his job as more than simply creating legible images. As the dominant spatial procedures (e.g., centering, balancing, depth) became more clearly defined, cinematographers turned their attention to the skilful achievement of classical goals. Beauty, spectacle, and technical virtuosity came to be recognized as signs of 'artistic' cinematography. Later we shall see how important this conception of technician-as-artist was to the development of the soft style in the 1920s and deep-focus cinematography in the 1930s and 1940s; for now, what is important is the ASC's role in guiding industry research.

While the ASC as a whole did not launch research programs, it did create committees to monitor current developments. In 1928, the ASC announced brief courses for its members in the technique of sound filming. The Wide Film Committee of 1930 sought to 'arrive at not only ideal proportions but those most readily realized in commercial practice.'[59] Two decades later, the ASC organized a committee to determine the most suitable type of cinematography for television production.[60] The pragmatically professional ASC needed to keep its members at a high level of proficiency when new technologies emerged.

That professionalism could not have been maintained, however, if the ASC had not, from the start, sought liaisons with the manufacturing firms. As one founder wrote, 'Our original purpose was to get cameramen to exchange ideas and thus encourage manufacturers to make better equipment, especially lighting equipment.'[61] *American Cinematographer* carried advertisements from film and equipment suppliers, and often articles would be devoted to innovations of interest to cinematographers. ASC meetings hosted manufacturers' representatives who demonstrated their latest equipment.[62] 'Our members,' wrote Charles G. Clarke, 'learn of these

innovations first.'[63] The firms also had representatives within the ASC. During the 1920s and 1930s, for instance, Emery Huse of Eastman was technical editor of *American Cinematographer*. In 1930, the ASC created the category of associate member, and researchers from Bausch and Lomb, Bell & Howell, Eastman, and other firms soon joined; many of the same men also served on the Society's research committee. On a few occasions, the ASC threw its weight entirely behind a technical improvement, as when in 1931 the Society officially recommended the new faster panchromatic films. In their turn, the firms sought testimonials from leading cinematographers, sending them equipment to try out.[64]

Almost no cinematographers had any formal research training, but their links to the technical agencies gave them the chance to invent and refine. Many ASC members held patents. Tony Gaudio was said to have patented the view-finder in use on the early Mitchell, with the cooperation of Mitchell and Bausch and Lomb engineers. In the 1940s, Karl Freund became affiliated with a firm manufacturing exposure meters and Linwood Dunn conceived a standardized optical printer built by the Acme Tool and Manufacturing Company. (This printer won an Academy Award of Merit in 1981.) In 1929, Jackson Rose conducted detailed color rendition tests of all currently available film stocks and was able to pinpoint the capacities of each; the results were quickly seized upon by Eastman and Du Pont as help in refining their products.[65] In such ways, the ASC constituted a valuable channel between the manufacturer and the film industry. The cinematographers were able to indicate directions for research to take, either by discussion in meetings or by active involvement in the process of innovation. Those directions were, to varying degrees, governed by the economic and stylistic determinations we have seen at work in Hollywood, and they were mediated by the specific professional ideology of the ASC itself. In subsequent chapters we shall examine in detail how this occurred.

The Society of Motion Picture Engineers

As David Noble has indicated, professional engineering societies and major corporations predicated industrial development upon uniformity.[66]

Without some uniformity in the types and dimensions of industrial products which went into the production of consumer goods, and standard specifications for the performance of equipment and machinery, the interchangeability of parts and the regularization of manufacturing processes upon which large-scale production depended were impossible. And without widely recognized standards of quality and readily available means of servicing products after sale, large-scale consumption was impossible. Standardization in industry was thus the *sine qua non* of corporate prosperity and, since the corporations were the locus of technological innovation, of scientific progress as well.

Since 1902, the United States Bureau of Standards was aggressively establishing standards of measurement, performance, and quality; in 1918, the American Engineering Standards Committee was created to coordinate the activities of all engineering societies. It is in this context that we must situate the formation of the Society of Motion Picture Engineers (SMPE). (In 1950, the Society changed its name to the Society of Motion Picture and Television Engineers [SMPTE]. We shall use its earlier name when describing its activities before that date.)

Engineering of various sorts – mechanical, optical, electrical, and chemical – had been necessary to the creation and maintenance of film technology since before 1895. Chapter 9 has detailed the formation of the SMPE in 1916. Although the SMPE charter members were generally not the university-trained men to be found in other engineering societies, the goal of standardization helped define their professional status. As C. Francis Jenkins pointed out at the SMPE's second meeting in 1916:[67]

Every new industry standardizes sooner or later, whether we will it or not. It is our duty, therefore, as engineers to wisely direct this standardization, to secure best standards of equipment, quality, performance, nomenclature, and, unconsciously, perhaps, a code of ethics. It is entirely a practical attainable ideal. But we should recognize our responsibility to fix standards with due regard for the interests of all concerned.

In 1930, the American Standards Association recognized the SMPE as the official representative of the film industry, and with American involvement in World War II, the SMPE was given federal support in determining and updating standards. Cooperating with the ASA and the American Engineering Standards Commission, the Society established standards and recommended practices for perforations, sprocket holes, dimensions, reels, lenses, splices, screen size and brightness, projection room layout, sensitometry, densitometry, and terminology.[68]

The SMPE's concern for standardization was frankly designed to support what Jenkins called 'the interests of all concerned' – that is, the growing service sector. In 1920, some SMPE members worked in the New York offices of film companies, but the power of the Society lay with the researchers from the major manufacturing firms: Bausch and Lomb, Corning Glass, Eastman, Union Carbide, Technicolor, General Electric, and Westinghouse. It was not until 1929, when the Society founded its Pacific Coast section, that the Society began to include more production personnel and workers in Los Angeles service firms. Modeling itself on older American engineering societies, the SMPE held conventions twice a year and established committees on procedures and standards. It published its proceedings, first as a set of *Transactions* (1916-29), then as *The Journal of the Society of Motion Picture [and Television] Engineers* or *JSMP[T]E* (1930-present). Based in the Engineering Societies Building in New York City, the *JSMPE* printed committee reports, technical papers, patents abstracts, and résumés of articles from other journals. The Society's conduct was governed by the conception of the engineer as both scientist and businessman. A 1925 SMPE policy statement explained:[69]

Modern business and especially manufacturing is founded on scientific research and sound engineering practice. Practically all engineering organizations are supported by, and have for their purpose, increased business for their members.

Experience has shown that in the long run the most business is developed for the majority of people by cooperation and the interchange of knowledge gained through research and practical application. To provide a medium for such exchange of data is one of the chief functions of an engineering organization.

Engineering *societies* differ from *commercial* organizations in that they do not let commercial considerations dominate their work, yet the results of their work are applied directly to business.

In adopting this goal of 'applied science,' the SMPE was accepting the engineer's role as defined by the profession in the late nineteenth century. The society's concern for standardization was thus part of a larger effort to help its member companies prosper.

Indeed, the entire history of the Society shows that it became a central forum for manufacturers. Its charter members included Donald Bell, two of the partners in Technicolor, and several electrical company engineers. During the 1920s, the presidents and governors were typically representatives of Edison, General Electric, Eastman, Technicolor, and other major firms. In the early 1930s, at about the same time that the ASC sought financial support from manufacturers, the SMPE created the category of sustaining member. By 1952, there were sixty-three such members, all principal service firms. SMPE conventions provided the occasion to display new equipment and processes and to discuss research findings. Often technical but seldom purely theoretical, the papers frequently announced innovations soon to be marketed. The conventions would often be held in manufacturers' home towns, yielding an opportunity for promotion. The Fall 1936 Convention in Rochester included a luncheon underwritten by Eastman, another by Bausch and Lomb, and a tour of each company's research facility.[70] In 1930, the Pacific Coast section met at the Mitchell plant to discuss wide film, since the principal wide-film camera was made by Mitchell; after a demonstration of the camera, the one hundred technicians attending were given a tour of the plant. Appropriately, at this 1930 meeting Emery Huse of Eastman pointed out that one of the most valuable functions of the SMPE was 'the contact it afforded between the industry and the many research organizations whose work so materially affected the progress of the motion picture industry.'[71]

The program and activities of the SMPE help us explain why there appears to be a progress or evolution in the history of film technology. The research in the service sector and the goals of the professional associations presupposed a fairly linear, accumulative development. In any industry, the policy of continuous innovation demands a constant revising of basic designs according to some conception of perfectability. A clear statement of this policy emerged from a 1934 speech by A.N. Goldsmith, then president of the SMPE. Goldsmith pointed out that engineering is a goal-oriented activity. Like his brethren in other industries, the motion picture engineer strives to perfect his product according to certain criteria: freedom of choice, portability, convenience, speed, simplicity, uniformity, and quality control.[72] Greater sensitivity of film stocks, more portable cameras, better lenses, increased recordable range of sound, the acceleration of laboratory rate and capacity – by Goldsmith's criteria, the history of Hollywood technology has constituted a progress comparable to that in other industries.

Given the engineer's gospel of perfectibility, the SMPE undertook to explain to its manufacturers the peculiar nature of motion picture engineering. Throughout the society's history, paper after paper attempts, as one put it, to 'reconcile the requirements of showmanship with the limitations of technical advances.'[73] The SMPE worked to communicate the Hollywood aesthetic to engineers, albeit seldom in 'aesthetic' terms. One of the most explicit statements comes, again, from Goldsmith. The motion picture engineer had as his task 'the presentation of a real or imagined happening to the audience in such approach to perfection that a satisfactory illusion of actual presence at the corresponding event is created.'[74] Here is a goal for the engineer to work toward. (A Bazinian teleology is packed into that phrase 'approach to perfection.') Goldsmith went on to claim that while the engineer strives for a total realism, the film artist (director, writer) alters the illusion of reality to achieve 'the most satisfactory audience response.'[75] To take another example: engineers had to learn to accommodate Hollywood's demand for unobtrusive technique. In 1930, John Otterson, President of ERPI, addressed the SMPE banquet:[76]

It is necessary for the artistic effect of motion

pictures that the process by which the result has been attained should be concealed. Due to this fact, I would say that the work of the engineer, as well as the motion picture industry of the future, lies in concealing the fact that an engineer has anything to do with motion pictures – to bring about such a natural effect that the public will not associate with it any mechanical or engineering process.

'Showmanship,' realism, invisibility: such canons guided the SMPE members toward understanding the acceptable and unacceptable choices in technical innovation, and these too became teleological. In another industry, the engineer's goal might be an unbreakable glass or a lighter alloy. In the film industry, the goals were not only increased efficiency, economy, and flexibility but also spectacle, concealment of artifice, and what Goldsmith called 'the production of an acceptable semblance of reality.'

To see Hollywood's technical institutions as aiming at a steady progress in film machinery is not to endorse the positions advanced by Bazin and Perkins. Both theorists perceived a teleological direction in technical change, but both erred as to the source and significance of the change. Bazin attributed the teleology to a universal urge of the human mind to duplicate reality, a 'mummy complex,' a myth of total cinema which in Bazin's view could 'in no way be explained on grounds of scientific, economic, or industrial evolution.' On the contrary: only the history of scientific and engineering research in the service of capitalism can explain both the cinema's progress and the very idea of progress itself. As for realism, which both Bazin and Perkins treated as the goal of technology's evolution, we can see from observations like Goldsmith's that this too was rationally adopted as an engineering aim – but wholly within the framework of *Hollywood's conception* of 'realism.' Otterson's remark about invisibility makes it clear that any absolute phenomenal realism is qualified by aesthetic criteria. 'The Cinema' is not 'evolving' toward a 'total realism.' Rather, institutions, such as the SMPE, chose in a specific historical context to modify an already-defined aesthetic system according to an ideology of progress.

The Academy of Motion Picture Arts and Sciences

The Academy of Motion Picture Arts and Sciences was chartered in 1927. It has had many fields of influence, the most publicized being its annual achievement awards, the least-known its role in the history of labor in Hollywood. In its 1937 revision of its purpose, the Academy declared itself to be a forum for all motion picture crafts, a clearing house for records of achievements, and a showcase for innovations. At first, the Academy possessed five branches (actors, directors, writers, producers, and technicians), with an initial membership of 350. It grew quickly, doubling its membership by 1932 and adding many branches in the next decade.[77]

Between 1927 and 1959, the Academy referred matters of technology to a specific body. Until 1932, this was the Producers-Technicians Committee, a revision of the MPPDA technical committee; as we shall see, the Academy committee was instrumental in guiding the industry's switchover to tungsten lighting, panchromatic film, and synchronized sound pictures. The Producers-Technicians Committee was renamed the Research Council, and, between 1932 and 1947, it operated with funds, labor, and equipment donated by the studios. In 1948, the council re-incorporated itself as a separate agency (once again funded by the MPPDA).[78] In its different incarnations, the Academy's research body represented the studios' recognition that large-scale development required collective action. In his book on the organization of scientific research, C.E.K. Mees pointed out that in many industries, the best research facility was a cooperative laboratory financed by a trade association. Such laboratories only succeeded, however, in industries in which little scientific work had been done and in which the basic technical processes were common knowledge.[79] In 1928, both such conditions existed in the film industry. Like their counterparts in other fields, the production companies rationally pooled their resources. In 1930, the Academy Technical Bureau claimed:[80]

Motion pictures may be called an art existing by grace of mechanics, but it is the art and not the mechanics of it that is sold to the public. Studios all need good cameras, for instance, but the only use of a camera is to photograph a scene. It is the value of the scene which will be in competition with the product of other studios. If every camera could be made twice as efficient, the competition would remain the same, but the industry as a whole would benefit and every studio in proportion.

The same logic was echoed in explaining the formation of the Motion Picture Research Council:[81]

By 1947 it was freely recognized that insofar as methods, processes, and equipment are concerned, there was no need for competition among the producers of motion pictures. Accordingly, it was practical to carry on the development of such equipment, processes, and methods in a common industry-sponsored technical organization.

Thus Hollywood recognized the collective rewards of organized research.

Through its research agency, the Academy did considerable work on standardization. When in 1930 it looked as if wide film would become a significant option, the Producers-Technicians Committee held meetings and gathered information toward the standardization of such formats. In the early years of sound, Academy committees proposed uniform theater projection equipment and studio recording processes. The Academy standardized script format, leaders, laboratory sensitometry, screen materials, and even the official shade of white to be filmed by panchromatic film (actually, pearl gray).[82] When 3-D films seemed promising, the Motion Picture Research Council held lectures for studio personnel, devised an instrument to help cinematographers reckon convergence, published a set of standards for exhibition, and developed a single-film 3-D projector.[83] Like the SMPE, the Academy created uniform procedures for reasons of efficiency and economy.

But, like the SMPE, the Academy realized that such standardization could not take place without close contacts with the service sector. Between 1928 and 1932, such contacts were somewhat ad hoc. With the creation of the Academy Research Council in 1932, the arrangement became more systematic. The council was composed of representatives from all five branches, a technical representative from each studio, and an advisory engineer from each major manufacturing company. At this point, the council's work was financed by the Association of Motion Picture Producers.[84] In 1933, however, the Academy was reorganized, and it declared a new aim: 'to cooperate and/or affiliate with any organization whose objective is the betterment of the motion picture industry as a whole, on such terms and conditions as may be mutually agreed upon.'[85] The new category of corporate member was created to enable manufacturers and suppliers to join the Academy. Corporate members could not participate in the work of the branches, but could be represented on the Research Council, and their fees would fund the council's activities. Later, in 1948, the Research Council was established as a separate corporation in order to be able to work closely with commercial firms:[86]

We are acting as a liaison between studios and suppliers. On one hand, suppliers are using the Council to distribute directly to those concerned in the studios information on new products. On the other hand, we are correlating studio needs and desires and presenting such information to the suppliers. This procedure saves time, standardizes methods and practices, and results in better and less expensive equipment.[87]

Thus the Academy's work as a coordinator of technical activity required the support of the service sector.

The support strengthened the already powerful suppliers. Academy meetings would host representatives of firms to demonstrate new equipment. More important, the Academy grew accustomed to turning to favored firms for help on projects. When the Research Bureau was studying the problem of projector distortion in 1932, it authorized its subcommittee to get technical assistance from Bausch and Lomb and Bell & Howell. In 1941, the Research Council committee on set noise needed information and so turned to the major electrical firms and the equipment manufacturers. Usually the Research Council would set out a problem, investigate alternative solutions, and communicate the industry's preference to the suppliers.[88] For example, in 1938, the Academy began to standardize a production process jealously guarded by most studios: rear projection. The committee included not only studio technicians but also engineers from Bausch and Lomb, Technicolor, Mole-Richardson, Mitchell, the National Carbon Company, and other firms. In February of 1939, the results were published and sent to all equipment companies. Seven months later, the committee chairman reported that Mole-Richardson had designed a new lamp housing, Mitchell was completing a new projection head, and Bell & Howell had taken orders for seventy-six new lenses – all to Academy specifications. Again, in 1947, the council's Basic Sound Committee held meetings of studio technicians and manufacturers to discuss magnetic recording. The manufacturers demonstrated their products, and the studios supplied specifications about frequency range, volume, speed, and other features.[89] After the Motion Picture Research Council had conceived a new piece of equipment, 'Normally we would provide manufacturing firms with performance specifications or a complete design, and they would manufacture and sell directly to the industry.'[90] This was what happened when the Research Council collected data and drew up plans for a standardized camera crane. Since no companies were willing to make the crane for the open market, the council licensed the design exclusively to Houston Fearless, collated studio orders, and placed an initial order for twenty-five.[91] In such ways, the Academy got a desirable level of technical quality, but also sustained the principal manufacturers.

Relations among the technical agencies

The ASC, the SMPE, and the Academy functioned to standardize technology and to link the production sector with the service industries. Occasionally there was friction. Sometimes the SMPE's zeal for standardization was blocked by the producers' recalcitrance. For instance, the SMPE noted peevishly in 1937 that although it had officially adopted a new uniform perforation several years before, the industry simply refused to change. Similarly, during the 1930 fad for wide film, the SMPE spent months researching the problem but by then the industry had decided against the innovation, leaving the Society with an ASA-approved set of standards for an obsolete format. Sometimes distributors and exhibitors became embroiled in standardization battles as

well, as in the disputes over a standard reel length during the 1930s. Even apparently straightforward problems, such as standardizing screen dimensions, aperture ratios, and sound-track dimensions, occupied the Academy, the ASC, the SMPE, the exhibitors, and the projectionists' union for many years.[92]

On the whole, however, the ASC, the Academy, and the SMPE were able to work closely and cooperatively. Their mutual concern for uniformity, for monitoring technological developments, and for linking the film industry to its service companies made possible the smooth assimilation of large-scale technological change. At the same time, the three professional associations could assure that the fundamental premises of the classical paradigm of narrative construction and film style would, however tacitly, shape research and innovation.

To trace this process, we must look not only to the historical agents – the manufacturers and suppliers and the regulating institutions – but also to their discourses. What these institutions said is as important as what they did. The agencies' discourse often acknowledges the ways in which a given innovation can save money, differentiate the product, or further the progress toward a standard of quality. Moreover, in the very language of these institutions we find admonitions about the range and nature of *permissible* innovations. It is in fact one job of the regulating agencies to reiterate what counts as an acceptable technological change. At this point, the abstract duality between 'artist' and 'inventor' looks particularly thin. Conferences, papers, and meetings address issues that involve both engineering and film style. Through the discourses and practices of these institutions, the principles of the classical model were continually reformulated, redirected, and translated into problem/solution terms. Finally, we shall have to scrutinize the films themselves for their stylistic operations. As traces or deposits of technological change, the films yield evidence for the fundamental continuity of the classical paradigm. The idea of functional equivalence, the capacity of various techniques to play similar roles, enables us to analyze the ways in which changing stylistic devices extend and reaffirm the premises of Hollywood filmmaking. The next four chapters will show how, from the beginning of the classical period through the coming of sound, Hollywood's institutions innovated technology, how they explained their innovations, and how the classical paradigm was affected.

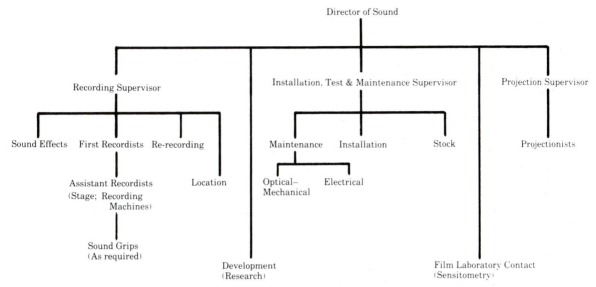

Fig. A—Organization of sound department using portable equipment; film recording only

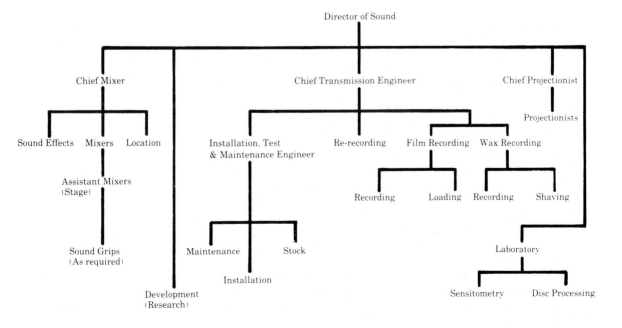

Fig. B—Organization of sound department using centralized installation; film and disc recording

19.1 The organization of sound personnel at RKO, 1931

20 Initial standardization of the basic technology

KRISTIN THOMPSON

'The Hollywood pioneers' – a phrase so familiar we need not ask to whom it refers. It evokes a notion of the early American film industry's growth: small groups of daring individuals striking out on their own toward the West, especially California, working under crude conditions (barns for studios, bathtubs for developing tanks), and finally carving out a new industry with their own resources. Even some of the names of these groups – Champion, Yankee, Bison '101', Broncho, American 'Flying A' – conjure up images of American history and the Old West. Historians have drawn upon the pioneer metaphor until it seems to constitute an adequate characterization of the whole period.[1]*

There is nothing wrong with the metaphor itself; early film companies did send units into desolate territory to make films, and they did use a good deal of their own initiative to solve immediate problems. But we cannot stop with that view, appealingly romantic though it be (transforming the early filmmakers into the cowboys of their own stories). It gives only a one-sided picture of the filmmaking institutions that were developing. Far from being completely on their own in a wilderness, the early film companies tended to locate in or near cities, and they had links to major manufacturing firms from the start. The number of those links increased steadily as the industry expanded. As we have seen, Eastman Kodak, the National Carbon Company, and Bausch and Lomb researched and provided supplies initially, and a support sector grew up around filmmaking.

The large, existing companies in this support sector supplied those technological devices which could be adapted from existing products: lighting instruments, lenses, film stock, make-up, and the like. Such devices also promised a continuing market. As long as films kept being made and

studios were expanded or refurbished, all these products would be in continual demand.

But machines to handle the filmstrip itself – cameras, processing equipment, and projectors – were specialized items. They could not be simply modified from machines that already existed, and although this equipment was vital, the market was limited. Firms and cameramen seldom replaced their instruments, and once the industry had leveled off its expansion, the demand for new cameras would not be great enough to interest a major corporation. So film-handling equipment was supplied by a group of smaller, specialized firms.

The support firms' relation to the industry was relatively casual before the mid-teens, for there was no regularized means of communication between the two groups. As we shall see, the decisions of individuals had more effect at this point than they later would. This was a pre-institutional period, when various apparati competed in a market which had not yet become systematized. The previous chapter discussed the formation of a set of institutions to guide technological change, beginning with the Society of Motion Picture Engineers in 1916. Systematic innovation benefited the support sector as well as the film industry. By the twenties, the film companies were spending more on expanding their studio facilities and less on technology, since they were by that point adequately equipped. Increased communication of needs helped prevent wasted effort by the support firms in supplying this reduced demand.

But even in these pre-institutional years, standardization of equipment tended to occur, due to conditions in the film equipment market. Either type of support company – the large, existing corporation or the specialized firm – would foster the adoption of similar equipment across the industry. The corporation could dominate the field by size and by utilizing its research facilities to create the best product. In a limited market, competition would tend to eliminate all but a few of the smaller, specialized firms, whose product would also then dominate the field.

By the end of the teens, for example, there were only a few brands of cameras or lighting instruments available. It was simply not economical or efficient to have a machine for each specialized trick the filmmakers could think up; but within the given range of possibilities offered by the standard machines, there was plenty of room for different styles and for experimentation.

Technological change in the pre-1920 period was already governed by the three considerations outlined in the previous chapter: production efficiency, product differentiation, and standards of quality. A couple of examples from the mid-teens may show how filmmakers worked to balance these factors in determining whether change would take place.

Throughout the teens, studios sought a combination of techniques that would make location shooting at night practical. At the time most night scenes were simply shot during the day and then tinted blue, with possibly an inter-title to indicate the time of day. In 1915, both portable floodlights and generators were available for night shooting, but these were still too expensive for general use. Those rare films which did go on location at night gained a considerable novelty value. Universal/Imp's *The House of Fear*, made in 1915, was promoted in the trade and fan press as an early use of this lighting equipment.[2*] Quality and novelty resulted, but not efficiency. Few films in the mid- and late teens used this equipment. But by 1919, with the introduction of high-powered arcs (recently invented as search-lights for military use) and better portable generators, the system became cheap enough to be feasible. From that year on, it was much more common to find 'night for night' scenes in Hollywood films done outside the studio. We can examine the standardization of this new lighting device using the four aspects of technological change Chapter 19 has described. The direction of change here follows the Hollywood paradigm, in that night shooting permits a clearer indication of the temporal relations in a film. In function, it would replace or supplement the blue tinting or inter-titles, and it would create a less self-conscious narration than would either of those devices. The timing of the change results from the conjunction at a certain point of new lighting and generating equipment. Both economic imperatives and the stylistic paradigm contribute to the causation for the change: the companies were in the process throughout the mid- and late teens of equipping their studios with artificial illumination, as filmmakers employed more effects lighting. All these factors favored the eventual adoption of exterior night lighting.

But some innovations of the teens fell by the wayside; already Hollywood's criteria for technical change were in place and left no room for them. For example, in 1916, Maurice Tourneur's film *The Hand of Peril* (World) contained a cutaway set in which nine rooms were visible at the same time, stacked in three stories (see fig 20.1). This again was heavily promoted, with pictures and stories in the trade press. The set's function in relation to the paradigm was clear; it showed several separate actions simultaneously in a single long shot. *The Motion Picture News* hailed it as an alternative to crosscutting.[3] The timing of this innovation was logical enough. During the mid-teens, the art director was a new production role, and features were allowing more money to be spent on larger and more spectacular sets. Tourneur in particular had recently gained success and had a growing reputation as an experimenter. The use of the set was presumably caused by a desire for novelty. But a cutaway set remained a highly unlikely stylistic alternative, for it did not follow the direction of trended change dictated by the Hollywood paradigm, which was at that time nearing its stable form. Such a set would make redundancy difficult to achieve, by presenting simultaneous events; it would discourage centering within the frame; and it would certainly call attention to the process of narration. In addition, a large set of this type would be more expensive to build than a group of individual rooms (due to the need for a larger stage and for the upper stories to have solid floors and ceilings to support the actors). Finally, an effective stylistic alternative was already in use: smaller sets and crosscutting. Isolated experiments like this set may be found in many films throughout

Hollywood's history. Yet the paradigm quickly became so all-encompassing, so complete, that it filtered out those devices that were not useful to it.

This chapter will examine the initial standardization of basic technology in the film industry. Why were certain cameras, lighting instruments, or processing systems adopted? And what did they offer the filmmaker as a range of possibilities? The answers to these questions should allow us to see how technology contributed to the early development of the stylistic paradigm. In answering them we will spend considerable time on teens and even pre-teens equipment, rather than concentrating on the classical period itself. This early equipment set the pattern for the rest of Hollywood's history and also demonstrates the range of equipment available during the process of standardization.

Standardizing cameras

My fondest hope for the industry – Standardization.[4]

Donald J. Bell, 1930

Hollywood would adopt camera technology on the basis of a set of criteria. Two areas of these criteria have to do with the *quality* of the exposed film:

The capability to create a clear, steady image
  (Good lenses, a steady registration system, and no light leaks)
Controllability
  (Gauges to indicate the speed of cranking and the footage remaining, adequate sighting while filming, and smooth mobility of the camera body)

Two additional groups of criteria deal with *efficiency* in the filming process:

Durability
  (Sturdiness, freedom from frequent replacement and repair)
Ease of handling
  (Portability, fast focusing and framing systems, fast adjustment and changing of attachments, easy loading of film stock)

And one additional desirable quality of the camera promotes *novelty* in the finished product:

Versatility
  (Special effects options, reverse-motion capability, single-frame crank, a variety of lenses, mattes, etc.)

(As we shall see, this set of criteria applies *in toto* or in part to some other types of film technology as well, including lighting instruments.) In general, the camera contributes less to the novelty of a film than other equipment might; its techniques tend to create quality and efficiency.

In the absence of other restraints – relatively high cost, patents control, lack of supply – the camera that best meets these various needs would be standardized across the industry. But as we shall see, there was no point in silent film history when all the ideal conditions existed simultaneously. Differences in costs of cameras or the failure of any one camera to perform all the necessary operations led to a small range of cameras remaining standard in Hollywood.

The early process of standardization fell into two general periods. Initially, the Motion Picture Patents Company's (MPPC) control of the industry through patents limited the availability of the most desirable types of cameras. This period lasted until the crucial Latham-loop court decision of 1912, after which followed a period of a comparatively free market. In the second period, several new cameras gradually came into widespread use, and the cameras of the first period fell into disuse.

Before 1912, there were several types of motion-picture cameras in use. Major Woodville Latham had patented a loop device in 1895, and the MPPC controlled the patent. Until 1912, all cameras used by non-licensed production companies either infringed the patent or used alternative principles for moving the film along its path. In this case, legal and economic conditions in the production situation limited technological development; for the independents, efficiency, quality, and novelty remained goals, but they were superceded by the necessity to remain in business with a legal or apparently legal camera mechanism. The Patents Company members' belief that they legally monopolized the industry apparently led to a relative lack of technological innovation. (Lack of innovation is not an inevitable result of patent control, since the period of control is limited; in the years 1914 to 1919, the patents would be running out for the MPPC. A reasonable strategy would have been to continue research and innovation. Yet there is evidence that Edison at least made little effort to improve the camera design, as we shall see.)

The primary non-infringing camera was the Biograph model, used at the American Mutoscope and Biograph Company from 1896. It had been designed specifically to circumvent Edison's patent and hence was atypical of silent film cameras in general. Its large size set the Biograph camera apart, but its main unique feature was the fact that it used an unperforated film stock over two inches wide. The camera's intermittent mechanism was a pair of rollers like those of a wringer washer, with the operator adjusting the amount of film pulled down for each exposure. While filming, the camera would punch two holes into the film's edges as the frame was being exposed – one on either side – producing a very steady image.[5]* The Biograph camera had the ability to provide a clear image because of its size, but it was relatively difficult to handle, and thus inefficient. In 1899, the company built a more compact camera of the common box type, using standard 35mm film, but the interior mechanism was still overly complex, and when American Biograph joined the Patents Company in 1908, they turned to a more orthodox system.[6]

As Chapter 19 pointed out, the American film industry became modern to the degree that it allied itself with corporate research. Yet during the years of Patents Company control, the member firms could not form such alliances; they had to get their cameras as best they could. Since Edison never sold cameras, even to Patents Company members, they were forced to buy cameras or to make their own; all but Kalem and Essanay chose the latter course. W. Wallace Clendenin gives a good summary of these: Selig's box-type camera made by Andrew Schustek; Lubin's copy of the French Pathé studio model; Vitagraph's unique camera that shot two rolls of negative in the same camera simultaneously.[7] It was also legal for the Patents Company members to buy foreign-made cameras, as long as they continued to pay in their license fees. We shall examine these foreign cameras shortly, since they were also popular with the independents.

Because the independent companies were operating on the fringe of legality, they also failed to create any alliances with large corporations to guarantee a supply of reliable equipment. Instead, they tried several different strategies to get hold of any camera minimally capable of producing an image; if they were lucky, they got one which could do a little better than that.

Some independents tried to remain within the law by obtaining a 'non-infringing' camera. Gimmicks abounded and inventors had a brief field day; the trade papers before 1912 are full of advertisements for new, supposedly non-infringing cameras (as well as for lawyers specializing in patents suits). The principal type of camera that did not employ a Latham loop substituted the 'beater' movement. Clendenin describes it thus: 'A beater camera had only one loop, this being above the gate. From the bottom of the gate the film ran directly to the lower sprocket in a straight line. After each exposure this stretch of film was struck by a rotating arm which would displace the film approximately one frame at the aperture.' According to Clendenin, this gave an extremely unsteady picture, necessitating the use of a pilot pin and making for a very loud-running camera. Such cameras, then, did not meet the requirements of quality and controllability for the production of a clear image. Arthur Miller recalled that John Arnold had a Bianchi camera at the Yankee Film Company about 1911; it produced a picture that 'jumped all over the screen.' Cameramen for non-Patents Company firms sometimes used a French Gaumont camera, which also employed a beater movement.[8] In contrast to the Biograph camera, the beater cameras were relatively portable, but their image quality would have precluded their use under less restrictive circumstances.

Because the beater cameras were so unacceptable, many if not most of the independents used loop cameras, either domestic or foreign. In many cases these were the same cameras being used by the small, non-patent-holding members of the MPPC. For companies willing to operate illegally, the advantages for quality and efficiency were obvious. Cameras employing the Latham loop could combine convenient size with relatively steady registration; thus they provided ease of handling and a quality image.

During the Patents Company's reign, from 1908 to 1912, foreign cameras became increasingly popular. Perhaps the lack of improvement in the original American-designed cameras led producers to adopt the more sophisticated French and English models. Several major brands were English: the Moyer (popularly known as the Moy), used at Kalem and later at Edison, World, Universal, and a few at Keystone; the Prestwich Model 5, which was used on most of the Keystone comedies; and the Williamson. (See fig 20.2 for a comparison of the Moy and Williamson cameras.) The French Debrie Parvo and the Eclair were used by many American companies.[9] But the most popular camera which emerged from the pre-1913 period was the French-made Pathé Professional camera (see fig 20.3, a 1912 Pathé). This camera had outside magazines holding 400 feet of film, with the crank on the back. The Pathé Professional combined many of the features desirable for a studio camera: the dial above the crank is the footage indicator, and it had a focusing scale, film punch, diaphragm setting indicator, and magnifier for focusing directly through the lens onto the film before shooting. It was portable, weighing twenty-two pounds.[10] As we shall see, it remained the standard camera for some years.

There were a number of other imported cameras which found occasional use in the American studios. With few exceptions, they had basically the same technology as far as facilitating shooting went. Cameramen focused them through the lens before shooting, either through focusing tubes in the camera body or through magnifying glasses on the side which focussed on an enlarged image from the film in the gate, reflected by a mirror into the viewer. Most cameras ran in reverse for making dissolves, had footage counters, and had shutters with openings that could only be changed while the camera was not running (making in-camera fades difficult); their tripods had pan and tilt cranks; they usually took rolls of films of 200 feet or 400 feet.

The pre-1913 period, then, had a degree of standardization, but constraints outside considerations of efficiency, product differentiation, and quality limited the possible technical changes. The independents were hardly in a position to foster technical change through cooperation with manufacturing firms; they were more concerned with holding onto the best cameras they could obtain. Numerous historical accounts describe how the independents sometimes disguised the outsides of their cameras or sought to hide from Patents Company detectives during this period. The Patents Company's detectives sought not so much to intimidate crews of independent companies, but to look inside the cameras to see if they used the loop device; without proof of such usage, the Patents Company's officials could not take legal action.[11] And the Patents Company firms, although in a better position to promote the growth of specialized camera manufacturers with research facilities, appear not to have done so. Possibly the problems of industrial expansion and of organizing distribution methods were higher priorities. At any rate, patent control delayed the move toward a modern industrial approach to the creation of standard cameras.

But in 1912 a legal decision eliminated the problem. The court decided that an earlier French patent invalidated the Latham claim.[12] The loop device became open to anyone's use. From this point, the dependence on European cameras declined, and the major American silent cameras, Bell & Howell and later Mitchell, began to take over the industry. Standardization could proceed without restraints issuing from outside the production sitration.

As older cameras began to wear out, they were gradually replaced by newer American models. A few European makes retained their popularity for some time, however; this was primarily due to the fact that many cameramen owned their own cameras or had become loyal to the brand they habitually used. Among the European makes, the Pathé studio camera retained its popularity the longest. In 1917 the *Cinema News* described the reasons:[13]

Cameramen as a rule prefer the Pathé Professional camera because of its mechanical simplicity, its expert workmanship and its steadiness on the screen. Other cameras may possess these same qualifications, but have failed as yet to attain the popularity of the Pathé.

The writer also notes that Pathés were not as readily available since the war cut down their production in France. As in the case of the earlier patents control, a factor outside actual production considerations interfered to affect the choice of camera; possibly the inability to obtain Pathés hastened the move over to Bell & Howells.

The Pathé's lingering popularity after the introduction of the Bell & Howell in the period 1909-12 may also be due to relative cost. Cameramen would be unlikely to change equipment once they had an outfit, especially when they could simply modify their camera's attachments as new technology developed. And the Pathé was consistently a cheaper camera than the Bell & Howell.[14]* The Pathé camera remained a significant force in American film production into the twenties.

The Bell & Howell Company (founded January 1, 1907 by Donald J. Bell and Albert Howell) was the first notable American company to sell cameras to the industry; as such it marked a new step for the film industry toward modern business practices. Indeed, the initial impulse for the formation of the company was an arrangement between Bell & Howell and George Spoor, for whom Bell had worked as a projectionist; Bell & Howell was to supply Spoor with projectors. When Spoor formed Essanay, his need for projectors disappeared, and the Bell & Howell Company's market dried up. The partners' next project was not in the film line at all; they built 'an automatic machine, a very efficient one, producing three thousand strawberry boxes per hour,' but the cost was not covered by the contract terms; they turned back to cinema equipment.[15] So the Bell & Howell Company, in spite of its modest beginnings, was a true supply firm, undertaking research and invention and fitting into the growing support sector of the industry. Its next uniform products would be not strawberry boxes but perforators and cameras.

The Bell & Howell Company provides a good example of technological innovation in the pre-institutional era, when individual decisions counted for a good deal. Rather than responding to a call from the film industry, Bell independently conceived of a goal of standardization for the industry. He recalled: 'My years of experience as an operator [i.e., projectionist] and designer of projectors established in my mind the paramount necessity of producing a standard perforator, this to be our first development toward

affecting standardization of all motion picture producing machinery.' His partner was a machinist and draftsman, capable of designing equipment to meet this goal. After the perforator, Howell went on to design the Bell & Howell Standard camera, a box-type camera somewhat like the Moy and Williamson. Apparently only two of these 1907 cameras were made, going to the Kalem and Essanay companies.[16]

But Howell soon came up with a new model, the all-metal Bell & Howell Professional Model (known as the 2709; see fig 20.4). A complete camera outfit at the time cost about $1,000, far higher than any other camera on the market. So in spite of the Bell & Howell's technical superiority, there was a long delay before it made headway in the studios.

The main advantages of the camera were its steady registration, its focusing system, and its all-metal construction with ball-bearing shafts. The fine registration resulted from a unique system for moving and holding the film at the aperture. Rather than simply having a claw to pull the film down in a straight line as most cameras did, the Bell & Howell had a pressure plate which released when the film moved, allowing it to pass with minimal friction. As a result, the film moved back to the claws, which pulled it down and forward onto a pair of pilot pins at the aperture plate. The pressure plate then clamped the film down for exposure.[17] The resulting combination of pressure plate and registration pins gave the best registration of any motion picture camera. So, better than any other silent camera, the Bell & Howell satisfied one criterion of quality, the creation of a steady image.

The Bell & Howell also innovated a rackover focusing device which was easier to use and more efficient in its consumption of shooting time. Most cameras necessitated sighting through the body by means of a tube or mirror viewer; the cinematographer saw a tiny inverted image on a ground glass plate or on the actual film in the shooting aperture. A 1927 cinematography handbook described the Bell & Howell focusing system:[18]

The direct focusing device does not make use of the actual aperture, but of a corresponding one on the opposite side of the turret. Thus the camera is set at the left side of the tripod and the lens focussed upon the screen provided. When this is done the lens is locked. Then the camera is pushed to the right of the tripod, the lens turret swung through 180 degrees, which brings the lens from focussing position to taking position, yet due to moving the camera, the lens is still in its former position. This allows focussing without disturbing the film, and allows a solid pressure plate to be used.

Aside from being less clumsy and unsure, this system saved time and film. No frames were lightstruck while focusing, as occurred in other cameras. Hence the cameraman did not have to perform the additional task of cranking the lightstruck portion out of the aperture. He saw through the lens exactly what area the film would register during shooting without having to use a magnifying tube; so centering and other procedures of framing became easier. The Bell & Howell focusing system added a greater degree of control, as well as ease of handling; hence it fostered quality and efficiency.

The Bell & Howell's metal body, with its ball bearings at all shafts, was also advantageous. The exterior magazines were more light-tight than those of the wooden Pathé, which sometimes warped and had to be wrapped to prevent light leaking onto the film. Also, the crank revolved with little effort. As Kevin Brownlow points out, 'After a good turn, you could release the handle and it would revolve a turn or so on its own.'[19] The minimization of friction would make a steady cranking rate easier to obtain, since in trying to overcome drag, the operator's hand would sometimes go slower on the upswing and faster on the downswing. A uniform cranking speed would contribute to image quality.

In spite of its obvious superiority, the 1909 all-metal Bell & Howell took a relatively long time to make any impact on American production. Essanay again bought the first one, but sales were minimal. Indeed, 1912 seems to have been the first year that Bell & Howell sold any appreciable number of cameras, leading some recent historians to date the invention of the camera in that year.[20]* After 1912, sales increased slowly. By 1915, *The Static Club Bulletin* reported that 'Bell & Howells are getting common as Kodaks.'[21] Soon Ince bought them for his Santa Monica

studio, and American followed suit. Harry Perry recalled that Lasky bought its first Bell & Howells in 1919: 'Two of them were around the studio for a year before anyone would touch them. We preferred the old Pathés'; but by 1927, 'The Lasky Studios had no Mitchell cameras. We relied upon Bell & Howells and Akeleys.'[22] According to Clendenin, '1920 saw the studios almost 100% Bell & Howell equipped; in that year the company sold 142 cameras.'[23]

Perry referred to the Akeley camera, now largely forgotten or regarded as an exclusively news-oriented camera. During the twenties, however, the Akeley (see fig 20.5) became a common specialty camera in commercial studio production as well. It added a degree of controllability which no other camera of the period had; with its extremely long lenses and gyroscopic tripod head, it served specifically for filming scenes of rapid action that required telephoto panning. It was actually invented for filming wild animals in the bush; a naturalist, Carl E. Akeley, brought it out in 1917. There was a slight delay in introducing the camera into the industry, due to the heavy demand for Akeleys by the Signal Corps during World War I.[24]

The Akeley was significantly different from other cameras, both European and American. Its tripod head was gyroscopic, allowing it to be panned without a crank, and ensuring that the Akeley could be set up quickly on uneven ground and still deliver a level image. It could pan with relative smoothness using lenses as long as six inches and had a floating viewing tube which could be moved freely to a comfortable angle no matter what position the camera occupied.[25] The cinematographer could sight through the lens while shooting, a rare feature in silent cameras.

By 1927 there were Akeley specialists working in most of the major studios. Figure 20.6 shows a location unit using an Akeley in addition to the standard Bell & Howell cameras. The American Society of Cinematographers held meetings of its Akeley specialists and declared in *American Cinematographer*: 'The Akeley camera has entered the professional production field and is there *to stay*. The truly splendid Akeley achievements which have lately graced our biggest and best productions have sanctioned the use of the Akeley "shots" as an important factor in the story-telling qualities of the motion picture.' In 1926, Charles G. Clarke confirmed that the camera 'has become so widely used that nowadays scenarios specify "Akeley shot." '[26] Although it played a limited part in the overall process of shooting a narrative film, the Akeley's special functions led to its widespread use in the studios by the mid-twenties.

The impact of Akeley usage becomes apparent in films of the second half of the twenties especially. Tom Mix's film *The Great K. and A. Train Robbery* (Lewis Seiler, 1926, Fox) contains an elaborate stunt during which Mix hangs high in the air on a rope suspended from a cliff top down to Tony's saddle. Many of the closer shots of Mix, plus his slide down the rope, utilize Akeleys to get telephoto and pan effects. *Ben-Hur* (Fred Niblo, 1926, MGM), *Wings* (William Wellman, 1927, Paramount), and *Hell's Angels* (Howard Hughes, 1930, Caddo Co.) are among the more famous films to employ Akeleys. Indeed, many of the spectacular aerial scenes that became popular in the late twenties and early thirties were made possible by this camera. More standard films of the period also contain occasional Akeley shots (often for fight scenes, chases, and races); these are usually quite distinctive and easily recognizable. But the special advantages of the Akeley also limited it to occasional usage. Its smaller 200-foot magazines made it less versatile, and its image was less steady than that of either the Bell & Howell or the Mitchell.

In 1920 the Mitchell camera prototype was turned over to Charles Rosher for use in filming *The Love Light* (Frances Marion, 1921, Mary Pickford Productions).[27] Figure 20.7 shows Rosher and Mary Pickford with the new camera, which Rosher used throughout the silent period. By 1921, the Mitchell company was selling cameras, trying to break into the market that Bell & Howell had recently taken over.

Within a few years, Mitchells became popular, but they did not have enough advantages over the Bell & Howell to make great inroads until the introduction of sound. At that point the Bell & Howell's pressure plate's noise made it difficult to use, and the quieter Mitchell gained the advantage at the expense of a slight loss of registration quality. The Mitchell camera resembled the Bell & Howell physically, but differed in that it was built in two parts rather than one. The camera body of a Mitchell rested within an L-shaped base below and in front. The Mitchell's advantages over the Bell & Howell were primarily two: a faster focusing system and built-in matte holders. The Mitchell had a four-lens turret similar to the Bell & Howell's, but it did not need to be turned during the focusing process. A small handle (to which Sol Polito is pointing in fig 20.8) moved the Mitchell to the side along tracks on the base, with the lenses remaining in place, attached to the front of the base (fig 20.9). This brought the viewfinder on the left of the camera to a position behind the taking lens, and the cameraman focused. Bringing the camera to the left put the aperture behind the taking lens, and the camera was ready to shoot. The viewfinder then became a parallax viewer which could be used during shooting if desired. This very quick process improved upon the Bell & Howell system, as the Bell & Howell had improved upon earlier cameras. Clarke says that the Bell & Howell's rackover device — initially so efficient compared to other cameras' focusing methods — had become 'a slow, cumbersome way of working,' in relation to the rising costs of studio production.[28] The front of the Mitchell base created great ease of handling, since it contained an iris, four-way mattes, matte disc, turret plate, and turret; the iris could be adjusted to any point of the aperture, to allow the easy use of irises anywhere in the frame.[29] The Bell & Howell required a matte attachment, which had to be disengaged from the camera body during the rackover process, then re-engaged. But the Mitchell never equalled the registration system of the Bell & Howell; hence neither camera established a clear superiority over the other during the twenties.

The Mitchell company promoted its camera energetically. Many back and inside covers of *American Cinematographer* have advertisements which either illustrate details of the technical advantages (as in fig 20.9) or reproduce letters from prominent directors and cameramen praising the camera. In 1922, Mitchell appointed representatives in New York and San Francisco, and by 1923 had to go to a 72-hour week to deal with a backlog of orders. At this time, there were approximately thirty Mitchells in use in the Hollywood studios.[30] Mitchells and Bell & Howells remained the two standard studio cameras through the late silent period.

One other camera that came into occasional use in the late silent period deserves brief mention. After the success of Bell & Howell's 16mm Filmo camera, introduced in 1923, the firm brought out a 35mm version, the Eyemo, in 1925. The Eyemo (fig 20.10) was designed as a newsreel camera; at seven pounds, it was far lighter than the standard studio cameras, which generally weighed over twenty pounds. A wrist strap and screw-on handle facilitated handheld shots, while without the handle, the camera could attach to a regular tripod. It held 100 feet of film and ran 35 feet on one wind of its spring motor. Although used primarily for documentary work (and by many filmmakers as a home-movie camera), it also proved helpful in feature production. For aerial photography, its motor allowed it to be strapped on, say, the wing of an airplane and run from the plane's seat. With the German influence of the mid-twenties, cinematographers increasingly were interested in photographing from odd angles, and the Eyemo was easy to tuck into small, awkward places. For dangerous stunts, the Eyemo helped keep the cinematographer safe; Daniel Clark reportedly used one to shoot over the edges of cliffs and in similar situations for Tom Mix films at Fox. Like the Akeley, the Eyemo served only as a specialized camera around the studios; it was not particularly efficient (requiring frequent reloading) or versatile (having a limited range of lenses and special-effects capabilities) for regular use. But it performed one type of function very well, and the Eyemo remained in use for decades into the sound period.[31]

Major advances in camera technology quickly tended to become uniform throughout the industry. For example, before about 1919, most cameras did not have automatic dissolving shutters. That is, the shutter opening could not be closed during filming to produce fades and dissolves. Fades were created through the stopping down of the diaphragm, but since the diaphragm did not close completely, a small dot at the center would fail to go dark. In films of the teens, it is possible to see these partial fades, or occasionally to see the center of the fade go suddenly dark as the cameraman puts his hand over the lens to complete the fade. But in the late teens, the Akeley and a few other cameras introduced the automatic dissolving shutter, which could be closed down while the camera was running, permitting complete fades. By 1919, several cameras came equipped with the device. The Badgley shutter was available to add to the Pathé and other cameras.[32] The Mitchell camera had an automatic dissolving shutter from the beginning. The introduction of this particular device took only a few years, and it resulted in noticeably superior dissolves and fades in films of the twenties. Possibly the improved quality of fades and dissolves helped bring about the decline in the use of the iris after the teens.

Standardizing lighting instruments

Many of the same criteria which guided Hollywood in its choice of camera technology also determined what kinds of lighting instruments the studios would use. The two sets of criteria to promote quality are the same:

The capability to create a clear, steady image
    (Lack of flicker, brightness, correct degree of diffusion, actinicity)
Controllability
    (Steady light, dimmer control while shooting)

Criteria of efficiency fall into three categories; since lamps consumed electric current in widely different ways and in large quantities, comparisons among the various types of lighting were necessary:

Durability
Ease of handling
    (Automatic functioning with remote control, portability, easy changing of bulbs or carbons)
Efficiency
    (A high proportion of lumens vs. heat produced per watt of current)

Lighting instruments could also provide novelty through certain properties:

Versatility
    (Directionality, flexible positioning, capacity for a variety of effects)

No one type of light excelled in all these categories. The most efficient type – mercury-vapor tubes – was also the least directional, and hence was almost useless for effects, or motivated, illumination. But arc lamps, which gave a strongly directional light, were difficult to handle. The lamp that best solved the handling problem – the incandescent – was both inefficient and low in actinicity. And while the least expensive source was sunlight, it was also the least controllable. Consequently, film studios of the classical period typically used a combination of types of light, or found ways to compensate for the problems created by the one type chosen. Across the industry there was a standardization of several types of lighting instruments.

As we saw in Chapter 17, the overall movement of the transitional period was from an almost complete dependence on overall, diffused illumination to a style employing directional effects lighting. This followed the general trended change of Hollywood style, in that it gave each film's light a set of realistically motivated sources within the narrative space (e.g., sun, candles, lamps). For this reason, the desirable traits in a lighting instrument differ in type from those of a camera. The camera records the scene, but is not itself a part of the narrative. But the light forms part of the mise-en-scene, and the instrument producing that light should ideally enhance the light's representational qualities. For instance, filmmakers often want light produced by a studio lamp to imitate moonlight shining through a window, or a match held in cupped hands, or a candle on a table. A successful imitation demands that the lamp be directional, so that the spectator can see where the beam of light is supposedly coming from. It should be flexible in its positioning – easy to place behind that window, in the actor's hands, or in some concealed spot near the candle's flame. It should also be capable of a series of effects – from the strong glare of sunlight to the dimmest flicker of a tiny flame. In practice, again, most lamps cannot do all these things, and so a range of instruments came into conventional use.

Of course, once the studio has outfitted itself with the most durable lamps it can find, its management will not be eager to invest in new equipment. Any innovation had to offer a distinct advantage in one of the sets of criteria to induce the studios to change.

Mercury-vapor lamps and diffused sunlight

During the first decade of filmmaking, most films were shot in daylight. American Mutoscope and Biograph built a stage on the roof of a New York building to catch the sun; Lubin did the same in Philadelphia. Edison's Black Maria, the first film studio, was enclosed, but had a roof with a panel which could be raised to admit the sun. Both the Black Maria and the American Mutoscope and Biograph stages rotated to catch the sunlight evenly throughout the day. In such usage, the stages faced south, causing the light to come directly into the set from behind the camera and above.

But sunlight was relatively uncontrollable. Even with a revolving stage, the hours when shooting was practical were limited. From the earliest years to the late teens, there was a gradual move toward artificial light, which could be turned on and adjusted at will.

The first type of artificial light which came into general usage was the Cooper-Hewitt mercury-vapor lamp. This type of lighting was invented in 1901, by Peter Cooper-Hewitt, and was marketed for commercial and industrial use by the Cooper-Hewitt Electric Company, a subsidiary concern of Westinghouse.[33] Allan Dwan, who worked for the Cooper-Hewitt company at that time, has described the advantages of these lamps for commercial situations: 'We made up the tubes and put them in the Chicago Post Office for sorting mail; they're very fine on the eyes, and the mail-sorters could work many hours more a day without eyestrain.'[34] The mercury-vapor's gentleness on the eyes resulted from its color spectrum, which was concentrated in the blue-green portion; it lacked the red end of the spectrum, which is more conducive to eyestrain. This same fact made this lamp's light ideal for making motion pictures in the pre-panchromatic period, since blue and green lights were extremely actinic for orthochromatic film. (Actinicity refers to the proportion of the light which actually registers as an image on the film stock. For orthochromatic film, a light containing mainly red and yellow wavelengths would be low in actinicity, no matter how bright it might appear to the eye; blue or green light, even though less bright, would be more actinic for this type of film.)

The first 'dark' studio (the term used in the

teens for a studio lit entirely by artificial lights) appears to have been the Biograph studio at 11 East 14th Street in New York, into which the company moved in 1903 (fig 20.11); the building had a roof stage, but also a room inside the building lit by Cooper-Hewitts. Other companies followed suit; Lubin, for example, built a studio with Cooper-Hewitts in Philadelphia in 1907.[35] Mercury-vapors were efficient in their use of electrical current, highly actinic, more controllable than sunlight, and they produced a clear image. Their lack of directionality was not yet a limitation, since effects lighting was still in only occasional use. So great were their advantages that they remained a basic type of artificial light well after the widespread introduction of arc lamps.

Mercury-vapor lamps did not imitate the daylight of the open-air stages. Sunlight, unless diffused, provides a hard, bright light in parallel rays. See, for example, figure 17.8, which shows a scene shot with undiffused sunlight; the result is a harsh frontal light that creates strong shadows. Mercury-vapor lamps, which were long tubes similar in appearance and working to neon lights, provided a softer illumination which was automatically diffused by the larger area covered by the source.

Evidence is sketchy, but it was apparently only after the introduction of mercury-vapor lamps that filmmakers began to diffuse sunlight by hanging muslin in large sheets over their stages.[36]* Diffusers provided only limited control of sunlight, but they cut down on contrast and thus created a clearer image, with details in shadows more visible than they would be in direct sunlight. Numerous production stills from the early teens show diffusion cloth over sets (see fig 20.12). Diffusion became quite systematized, however. In 1913, *Motography* reported that Universal's head carpenter at its west coast studio had worked out a new system of pulleys and rollers to control the diffusers on its outdoor stages. Up to twenty diffusers could be placed over a set of 40 square feet, thereby eliminating all shadows.[37] Figure 20.13 shows an arrangement of diffusers over an open stage at Inceville. These panels of diffusers apparently also had a mechanism for sliding back and forth, as the gaps at the upper right show.

Around 1906, glass studios began replacing the open-air rooftop stages, especially in the East, where rain and other inclement weather posed frequent problems. Edison and Biograph both set up permanent glass studios that year to replace their roof-top and backyard methods. Vitagraph built a glass studio that same year, and Selig did the same in 1907. But even in such studios diffusion became important. Again by the early teens, contemporary sources describe special diffusing glass which was used in the construction of these studios. In 1912, the American Film Co. built its new Chicago studio using diffusion glass, which was 'expected to add considerably to the photographic results.'[38] The best glass for diffusion purposes was not simply pebbled or translucent glass; it involved rows of tiny prismatic ridges which broke up the light that entered. The resulting small spectra would not be noticeable, as they would diffuse back into white light. The advantage, however, was that prism glass did not cut down the amount of light passing through, while other types of textured translucent glass did. The 1906 Vitagraph studio, for example, used this type of glass, as did the 1912 American studio. Glass studios remained standard across the industry through most of the silent period, although in the late teens and early twenties, firms increasingly depended on 'dark' studios, lit entirely by artificial light. By the early teens, then, the standard approach to lighting an interior set, whether actually shot indoors or outdoors, was to throw a diffused, even light over the whole; shadows and glaring highlights were undesirable.

Peter Mole has described the standard types of mercury-vapor units: the 'broadside' unit, ranging from six to eight tubes, on wheeled stands (these are the ones most frequently seen in production stills); 'gooseneck' units, which started with a broadside unit and added a second unit above, angled downward; and low front-lighting units, usually of four tubes, for special underlighting effects.[39] Overhead banks were similar to the broadsides, but hung on wires, tilted slightly up to face the rear of the set. These would be relatively fixed, but the portability of the wheeled floor units would be an advantage in dealing with rows of the 6-foot tubes (see fig 20.14). These units were built especially for motion-picture work; they were not simply the hanging types Dwan described installing in the Chicago post office.

Mercury-vapor lamps were ideally suited for orthochromatic film, and they had other advantages which led to their continued use after the introduction of other lighting sources. In 1922, Alfred Hitchins, the Director of Ansco Research Laboratory, conducted spectrographic tests to compare the most common types of artificial lighting available for motion pictures – mercury-vapors, arcs, and incandescents – and found the mercury-vapor lamps best all-round. He concluded that the Cooper-Hewitts were desirable because they yielded the best actinicity, provided automatic diffusion, gave little glare even when used in great numbers, gave off little heat, and consumed less electricity, with no cost for replacing carbons.[40] In other words, the mercury-vapor was highly efficient: it gave off more light in proportion to heat per watt than any other available light source. Even in recent years, the high-pressure mercury-vapor quartz lamp is one of the most efficient lamps and is in wide use in filmmaking and in street-lighting. These advantages made the Cooper-Hewitt a staple of filmmaking throughout most of the silent period. Only the increasingly widespread use of panchromatic film in the mid-twenties rendered their use less advantageous, due to their lower actinicity with this stock.

Mercury-vapor lamps were so common in the studios that by 1918 motion pictures were the fourth industry in the United States in their use, following automobile manufacturers (e.g., Buick, Ford), munitions manufacturers (e.g., Remington, Winchester), and machine-tool builders (e.g., Erie Forge). Virtually every motion picture studio had Cooper-Hewitts.[41]

The main disadvantage of the Cooper-Hewitts was their inability to provide directional light. They could not cast sharp shadows or pools of limited light; they could not model a figure. Their diffused light was an even wash over the entire set. In effect, this light did not come from within the narrative; it did not vary to suit the situation. While it did not distract from the story, it did not add anything either. As the classical system developed, the concept of making style contribute to the narrative became dominant. Filmmakers needed a type of light which could be manipulated in a variety of ways, according to the narrative demands of a scene.

Thus, in spite of their superior efficiency, the mercury-vapor lamps began to give way to other units which could provide hard, directional illumination for effects lighting. Hollywood developed its three-point lighting system, described in Chapter 5. By the late teens and twenties, filmmakers were mixing smaller numbers of mercury-vapors with other types of lamps. The tube units often functioned to provide fill light, while arcs and, later, incandescents took over the task of creating highlights and modeling figures and setting. The more expensive arcs offered less efficiency and controllability, but they did permit a lighting style capable of serving narrative because their directional beams could be realistically motivated as coming from a source within the scene. Quality and novelty induced studios to invest in new lighting instruments.

Arc lamps

Histories of early film lighting have suggested that the film studios adopted arc lighting wholesale from contemporary stage instruments. Yet some lamps used in filmmaking derived from technology used in public illumination, primarily street lighting. Certain devices came from the theater or from photo-engraving, while in the late teens, modern wartime searchlights quickly made their way to Hollywood. More generally, looking at the early cinema in a limited perspective and seeing it as slavishly imitating the theater perpetuates the view that early films were clumsy products of a technically limited and backward industry, aping a more advanced, established art. Instead, the motion picture industry and the theater both take their place in the larger development of arc and incandescent lighting.

The carbon arc competed with the gas light for public utility usage during the late 1800s and was not generally employed until after widespread distribution of electricity made it feasible in the 1880s. By 1910, the carbon arc had surpassed gas and oil as the most common source of street lighting.[42]

Carbon arcs were first used in theatrical practice on a limited basis by the Paris Opera, which employed them in 1846 as floodlights; in 1860 it used the first electric arc spotlight. But arcs created a number of problems; they hissed, could not be dimmed from the dimmer board as gas could, and produced a harsh white light. Each individual instrument had to have its own separate stagehand in constant attendance, due to fire regulations. Because of these disadvantages, arc lighting only supplemented gaslight and served for special effects and spotlighting. So in the theater arc lights competed with gaslight and limelight (introduced around 1857 and capable of serving as the illumination in a spotlight). But theaters also began installing incandescent lamps directly after their introduction in 1879. By 1900, incandescent lighting was almost universally used.[43] The gradual improvement of incandescent filaments culminated in 1913 with the marketing of drawn-tungsten fibres in an inert gas environment. These gradually replaced arcs in theatrical spotlighting.

So the simple introduction of carbon arc lighting fixtures in film studios is hardly enough to warrant the assumption that studio practice derived from stage practice. Nor did filmmakers adopt the standard theater procedure of using arcs for follow spots, although they did borrow the other common usage of arcs, for special effects like sunbeams and fireplaces. Barry Salt has found a number of early films which use arc lamps in isolated scenes for effects of this sort: Edwin S. Porter's *The Seven Ages* (1905, Edison), D.W. Griffith's *Edgar Allan Poe* (1909, AB), *Oliver Twist* (1909, Vitagraph), and others.[44] In most such cases, arc lamps supplement the standard diffuse light in order to suggest a specific source of strong illumination. In the early teens, such usage became slightly more frequent.

But the more widespread early use of arcs was as floodlights; these provided diffused light, and commonly were used in combination with mercury-vapors. The arc flood's chief advantage over the mercury-vapor would have been its concentration of brightness into a small area; its bluish-white light was comparable in actinicity to the Cooper-Hewitt's. The diffused arc lamp derived in some cases from street lighting. As early as 1897, the American Mutoscope and Biograph Company used 400 modified street arcs to illuminate Madison Square Garden when its cameramen filmed the Jeffries-Sharkey fight. Apparently Biograph also experimented with this technique for its indoor New York studio; one lighting historian says the company installed thirty-six Bogue arcs in their 14th Street facilities, before replacing them with Cooper-Hewitts.[45]

1908 seems to have been the year that arcs came into occasional but regular use in the studios. The Kliegl company, which had made its first arcs for stage use in 1896, came out with a motion picture unit in 1908. Although this was the most prominent, it was by no means the only brand of arc lamp used in motion picture work in the silent period.

A common early type of studio lamp was the enclosed arc, derived from street lighting. These lamps typically hung in rows above the sets, supplemented by banks of mercury-vapors on stands, or by open arc broadside floodlights on stands. Figure 20.15 shows a stage at the Edison studio, with enclosed arcs overhead; their hoods have been placed at an angle to direct light down into the set from the top front. This illustration also shows a couple of Kliegl arc 'broadsides,' used for floodlighting. Peter Mole described the introduction of broadsides about 1912: 'According to cinematographers active at the time, the Wohl was one of the first, if not actually the first of these units used. It, like most of its successors for a decade or more, was an adaptation of units previously made for photoengraving.'[46] Here we find yet another field from which the film studios adapted their lighting equipment.

Aside from open broadsides, of the type shown in figure 20.15, during the early teens, studios were adopting a relatively recent innovation in lighting, the white flame arc. Flame arcs were innovated in 1898; they consisted of chemical salts mixed in with the carbon to control the spectrum of the light produced. These, too, were soon enclosed, and the result was an intense light that needed infrequent maintenance, since the carbons burned less quickly. Motion picture studios used these, since they were highly actinic with orthochromatic stock. The *American Cinematographer* stated that American Biograph replaced its 'low-intensity enclosed "street-lighting" arcs with white flame carbon-arcs that provided the cinematographer with a controllable light source having twice the power and penetration capability of anything he had worked with before.' By 1919, Vitagraph's Brooklyn studio was equipped with 225 units, using an average of twenty per set.[47]

The primary function of this arc equipment in the early teens was to provide additional overall illumination; beyond this, the directional control of arc lights made them suitable for creating occasional effects. Mole describes the use of hard light from arc floods in the period from roughly 1913 to 1915; these arcs were 'generally used in conjunction with the softer vapor tubes. Before the introduction of arc spot-lighting equipment, they were the only sources of strongly directional "hard" light available.'[48] So limited light effects were possible, but the more spectacular low-key arrangements made famous by *The Cheat* and other mid-teens films depended on the introduction of spotlights. These apparently reached the studios about 1914, through the Lasky company.

In 1914, Lasky hired Wilfred Buckland, David Belasco's supervising artist in charge of production, as its art director. In New York, Buckland had been assisted by the Kliegl brothers, who had been Belasco's theater electricians. The brothers had developed an arc spotlight they called the 'Klieg light.' According to Buckland's later recollections, he obtained two Klieg spotlights for the Lasky company. (Again, film production was not lagging far behind theatrical practice; one of Belasco's most famous and spectacular uses of these spots had been in his 1910 production, *The Return of Peter Grimm*.) Arthur Miller recalled working with George Fitzmaurice of the Astra Film Co. in late 1915 or early 1916: 'Eighty amp spotlights had appeared on the scene and their use brought about a noticeable increase in light effect photography. Flat lighting gave way to modeling with highlight and shadow.' The changes Miller describes affected much of the industry's lighting practice, as we have seen. Perhaps as a direct result of the Lasky use of spotlights, small or 'baby' spotlights appeared about this time, for simulating small light sources like candle flames.[49] Here we have another case of individual decision in the pre-institutional era leading to the introduction of new equipment. Buckland obtained lighting units because he was accustomed to using them, and the success of the resulting films apparently led to a widespread adoption of such lighting.

The only major development in arc lighting after the mid-teens came about as a result of the war. This was the high-power arc searchlight created for various uses on the battleground, including spotting airplanes. This unit became available to the film industry in early 1918.[50] The

president of the Sun-light Arc Company described the value of this arc to filmmakers: 'Perfect in effect as natural sun; there as long as you desire. What's more beautiful than depth, perfect definition; this is art.'[51] The 'sun-arc' was the first lighting unit in history which was actually as bright as sunlight.

Studios began using these arcs almost immediately. By the time these lamps became available, the institutions for influencing technological change were coming into existence. The *Transactions of the Society of Motion Picture Engineers* discussed the new units thoroughly, as did the *American Cinematographer* several years later; these journals promoted sunlight arcs by explaining their numerous advantages. They were controllable, making intense light possible at night. They were relatively flexible, due to four attachments (see fig 20.16): 'a parabolic mirror, an iris shutter, a frosted glass door, and a clear glass door.' By setting the lamp at full flood position, the filmmakers could get a 130° sweep of 100,000 candlepower (with the glass door in use to prevent the common irritation known as 'Klieg-eyes,' caused by the ultra-violet rays in the light burning the eye). Four lamps could light an exterior set at night. The iris shutter could close the light down to a spot, without the necessity of a focusing lens. To achieve a softer, diffused light of 60,000 candles, the cinematographer added the diffusing glass. Finally, the parabolic mirror could intensify the light to a 1,600,000 candlepower spot.[52] So the sun arc was versatile, providing both directional and diffused light. High-power arc searchlights helped to solve a problem which had plagued filmmakers for years – how to shoot on location at night economically. They also could be used to light large sets in dark studios.

By 1918, the significant types of arc lighting were available to motion picture producers. They presented a flexible range of equipment which could be used in various combinations for effects and selective lighting. From this point, changes involved the technology less than the standardization of approaches to applying the equipment. Lighting innovations came mainly in the application of incandescent illumination to motion picture production.

Editing and laboratory technology

On casual inspection, the equipment employed in

editing and developing a film in the teens was very simple in comparison with the cameras and lighting instruments then in use. The Bell & Howell 1909 Professional Model was a sophisticated instrument; by the late teens, filmmakers were combining mercury-vapors and arcs for complex effects. But the film these technologies produced then went to a laboratory where it was dipped in an open wooden tank to be developed — a process called rack-and-tank developing. The cutter then snipped the shots with a pair of scissors and clamped the ends between finger and thumb. While camera and lighting equipment constituted a fairly complex technology, the realm of editing and processing employed mere tools. As with handcranking on the camera, these non-mechanical, labor-intensive methods lingered on after automated devices became available in the early twenties. While these laboratory and editing methods were simple, some of them allowed a degree of direct supervision and control which was later lost.

Automation during the twenties was mainly a matter of efficiency, although in a few instances it added quality as well; some machines, like automatic splicers, could actually improve the look of the finished product. But machine developing minimized novelty and, some cinematographers might have argued, quality. Automated processing diminished the variation which individual filmmakers could introduce into their work by personal supervision. Essentially, hand laboratory work was somewhat comparable to serial manufacturing, with handmade products; automated developing introduced a standardization more akin to what Marx called machine industry.

Editing

There were a variety of circumstances under which pieces of film would be cut and spliced together. The actual decisions as to what shots would be used in the final film were made by the head editor, or master cutter, who usually made a positive workprint, assisted by cutters. Here technical efficiency was not important; the main time expended was in judging tempo, in matching action, and so on. The splices need not be of perfect quality, since the workprint was never shown to the public. Once the workprint was complete, the editor or cutter spliced the negative

to match it. Here the technical quality of the splices was crucial; they had to be made so that the splice line would not be visible on the screen; extra time taken to make them correctly would be acceptable, since the process was only necessary once per film.

But in the silent period, positive prints were also joined by splices. This was partly because the developing racks could only hold sections of two hundred feet or less, and partly because shots to be tinted or toned the same color were all temporarily fastened together, then after the coloring bath detached and spliced into their proper places in the print. The job of assembling positive release prints fell to 'joiners.' They had to make quality splices which would run through projectors many times with minimal breakage. Efficiency was also a primary concern, since joiners had to work on multiple prints of the same film, and they did not need to take time to make decisions. Finally, projectionists would splice, or 'patch,' the film when it broke. This aspect of cutting also demanded both efficiency and quality, since the showing would be delayed until the splice was made, and the print still had to go through as many additional projections as possible.

Editors, cutters, joiners, and projectionists would at various times perform the same basic task of splicing. But because their aims differed, they did not always have the same equipment available to assist them.

During the teens and into the twenties, splicing equipment was simple indeed. Most cutters and joiners had no guide to align the two pieces of film or clamp to apply pressure to the splice while it dried; they sat at a table with a pair of rewinds, a light box over which the film passed, a pair of scissors, and a bottle of cement with brush. Finding the correct spot, the worker would snip the shots apart, scrape the portion to be spliced, brush on the cement, and press the spice with his or her fingers.[53*] The handmade splice gave the editor no extra degree of control; the important decision here was where to cut. Thereafter the main considerations were quality and efficiency in making the negative and positive prints.

A simple clamp with tracks for lining up the film ends could help make a straight splice that would go through a printer or projector. The Edison Film Mender was apparently the first hand splicer, but it could be used only in theaters, being built onto the Edison Universal Kinetoscope projector after at least 1908. It did not cut or scrape the film, however, but was only a sprockethole guide and clamp. This may reflect an attempt by the newly formed MPPC to protect its prints from inexperienced projectionists; after all, the companies were now renting their prints rather than selling them. The MPPC also claimed in advertising that it was improving its members' service, especially to second- and third-run houses. The Edison Film Mender was perhaps one step in that direction. During the teens and twenties, some projectionists reportedly used a similar device called a 'splicing block' or 'patch press,' to line up the perforations and apply pressure while the film cement dried.[54] But many theater owners were reluctant to invest in even an inexpensive splicer when their projectionists' fingers could serve the same purpose. Throughout the silent period, observers reported that most film mending in theaters was done entirely by hand.

In 1919, *Photoplay* described splicing in theaters as involving no guides whatsoever, and 'The same process is used in the factories [i.e., studios] for joining the sections of new film.' Bebe Daniels has recalled learning to edit from Dorothy Arzner in the mid-twenties, using the hand-splicing method in making workprints and negatives. So the main method for splicing the film at the studios changed little throughout the silent period. By the late twenties, some editing rooms had added a small, clamp-type splicer, 'secured permanently to the table between the rewinds.'[55]

By the early twenties, technicians were beginning to see the incongruity of lavishing thousands of dollars upon the shooting phase, only to put the pieces together in such an unsophisticated fashion. The problem was not so significant in the studios, where the negative was carefully edited and under the direct supervision of expert personnel. But release prints frequently came back to company exchanges in bad shape, and considerable footage was being lost through repeated and careless splicing. In 1919, Paramount even hired an expert to find out why so much damage was being done to release prints. Concluding that sloppy splices at the exchanges were the main factor, he proposed a further

division of labor, with a supervisor put in charge of inspection and joining at each exchange office. Standardization was also increased: 'We adopted a standard scraping tool, which was nothing more than a flat piece of flexible steel, ground to a scraping edge, and not to a cutting edge.'[56] There was also a running battle between the distribution exchanges and the projectionists over the types of splices to be used. Projectionists would take out the narrow splices used by the exchanges and replace them with wide ones; the exchanges then replaced these new splices, and so on, until the print lost so much footage that it had to be discarded. It was not until 1926 that the SMPE cooperated with Eastman Kodak to make formal recommendations for standard splice widths.[57]*

The late standardization of splicing procedures probably resulted from the fact that pre-twenties editing was at least minimally acceptable; it served its purpose. But another tool of the editor's trade – the workprint – came into standard use earlier. In the early teens, filmmakers sometimes made editing decisions while cutting the negative itself. Cameraman Charles Rosher recalled working at the Nestor studio, which opened in late 1911 in Hollywood:[58]

> Although we had a developing room, we had no printing machinery. The picture was cut directly from the negative, and we thought nothing of running original negative through the projector. Scratches and abrasions were mere details. When the negative was cut, the completed reel was sent to New York or Chicago for printing.

Allan Dwan has described his experiences heading a unit in California for the American Film company in similar terms. These descriptions refer to small, independent companies, and in each case the director's unit is working at a distance from the company's laboratory. But American's scenario editor recalled that even when that company set up a major studio in Santa Barbara in 1915, there was no laboratory on the premises, cutting was still done on the negative, and the positive prints were made at the home office in Chicago. Within a year, however, the Santa Barbara studio got a printer and began to make workprints. It is quite possible that the major companies that made films entirely at their home studios in the East used workprints earlier than this. The earliest published reference to workprints I have found occurs in 1911; David Hulfish calls them 'proofs':[59]

> Thus there is produced a final proof picture of the complete film as it is to be released to the public. The final proof is projected before the producer and critics and if approved it is turned over to the photographer [i.e., head of the laboratory] as 'copy.' The photographer cuts his negative into lengths, both motion scenes and titles, splicing them together to reproduce a complete continuous negative of the approved 'copy.'

We may assume that workprints were probably standardized across the industry during the first half of the teens.

The tendency to cut the negative directly in the early teens could have resulted from several factors. With scenarios that laid out all the shots in a numbered list, the cutter's job was relatively simple; there were perhaps only a few dozen shots to put in correct order. There were almost never retakes, so the editing process did not involve choices between different shots of the same action. The lack of significant numbers of cut-ins similarly meant that matching and choices among different views of the same action were usually unnecessary. But editing became more complicated as the teens progressed. Greater numbers of shots were involved, retakes became more common, and the breakdown of the scene analytically required that several decisions be made to insure a smooth continuity. The cutter needed a clear view of the action and might also have to handle the film more often. Rosher claimed that 'scratches and abrasions were mere details' in 1911, but repeated viewing and handling for more complex editing would also increase print wear. In addition, the greater emphasis on quality control as the studio mode of production developed would dictate that something like a workprint be devised. Not only would a preliminary positive cut of the film save negative wear and permit the cutters to see better what they were doing, but it would allow studio supervisors to make sure the film was progressing along its planned lines. The longer production time of the multiple-reel film also encouraged

closer monitoring of the project at each step. The entire expense of a production was calculated around the negative as a finished object and was often figured as so much per foot of negative (see fig 12.17). This precious object needed to be preserved; reshooting later would be expensive. As one cinematography guide put it in 1927, 'The negative is *never* projected. To project the negative is to risk scratching it in the projector mechanism.'[60] Workprints were a means of quality control.

The standardization of editing procedures like splice widths and workprints had little obvious impact on the look of the films. Certainly the cutting rate increased steadily throughout the teens and into the early twenties, with the average shots per reel perhaps doubling between 1911 and 1921. The use of workprints would make cutting so many shots together easier but would not be a necessity. Faster cutting may have encouraged the use of workprints, or vice versa. Workprints would make for smoother continuity cutting, with matches on action being easier to achieve. Editing technology in general must have influenced film style in a minor but pervasive way, permitting existing stylistic devices to be better executed.

Laboratory technology

When the exposed film came from the camera, it would be spooled off its core and wound around a rectangular wooden frame, or 'rack,' with small pegs at intervals to keep the film from slipping. The laboratory technicians then lowered the rack into a series of wooden tanks containing the various developing solutions. (Robert Paul reportedly invented the rack-and-tank system in England in 1895, making birch frames that would hold 40-foot lengths of film.[61]) Once the negative was developed the rack was placed on a support that allowed it to pivot as the film wound onto large framework drums, to be turned until dry. (In figure 20.17, the technicians have a rack on such a pivot, in a horizontal position, and are winding the film off onto a drum.)

The rack-and-tank method permitted filmmakers to introduce considerable variation into the image at the developing stage. Thus, rather than having to gauge their image entirely to suit fixed developing methods, as they would often have to do in the sound period, cinematographers had more leeway in giving instructions for custom handling. Some of the information the laboratory received was in the form of a paper record. One 1913 account said that an exposed can of film would be 'numbered and tagged with a record of the lighting, temperature, and humidity at the time of taking, and sent to the dark rooms.'[62] Another method of conveying information to the laboratory was the film punch, a standard part of most studio cameras, which could be pressed to make a hole in the film or to notch its edge. The punch was necessary because in developing, the 400-foot or 1,000-foot roll emerging from the camera magazine would have to be cut into 200-foot lengths — the most a single rack would hold. To prevent the technician from cutting in the middle of a shot, the punch would be used between shots to mark safe cutting points. Cinematographers could also use multiple punch holes to create a code indicating other things. The cinematographer might do a few preliminary turns of the crank at the beginning of a shot, punch several times, then shoot the action: 'The leader of the film ahead of the marker holes may by cut off and developed to learn whether the exposure is correctly timed, and whether regular or special developer shall be used in the development.'[63] Film could be inspected during the developing process under a red light, since orthochromatic film stock was insensitive to red.

Perhaps the most common manipulation of the negative in developing during the teens was the attempt to correct for under- or overexposure. If the light in the shooting situation was too dim, the cinematographer would sometimes go ahead and shoot, underexposing with the assumption that the laboratory could make up for the problem. According to Karl Struss, 'If the cameraman made a mistake in overexposing, why they'd pull it, you see. They wouldn't get the right degree of contrast in there.'[64] A pulled film would have less than normal contrast. Similarly, for underexposure, the laboratory would push the film in developing, creating more contrast.

Laboratory pushing and pulling of negatives to correct exposure continued through much of the silent period. Some cinematographers apparently believed that such chemical manipulation literally altered the original exposure time of the frames, producing a good negative by adding or taking away light. Indeed, this belief may have

been one major reason why many opposed mechanized developing.

But the concept of a good negative was itself relative, depending on the function of the shot in the film. A cinematographer who knew how to expose an image correctly might still use hand developing to manipulate it. Special treatment of the film was employed, not simply for covering errors, but for creative purposes as well. Rack-and-tank developing was important to the soft style of cinematography, as we shall see in the next chapter. Various major cinematographers have recalled working closely with the laboratory in order to achieve special effects in photography. Hal Mohr spoke of his work in the twenties:[65]

> Even up to the time I was doing *The Jazz Singer* [1927], I'd get there a half-hour ahead of time and go to the laboratory. At that time we made tests of every setup, and the negative developer had all my test strips lying on a lightbox. I'd go through with the lab man, and they'd all be developed to a certain time. There were many cases where you deliberately overexposed a scene for a certain effect, or you deliberately underexposed a scene. When you'd overexpose, the purpose was they'd short-develop it, to get a soft, flat effect; where you'd underexpose, the purpose would be that they'd force the development, to build up contrast.

Often cinematographers went to the laboratories on their own time (as Mohr's statement suggests), for their official duties may not always have included consultation with laboratory technicians. Later, as we shall see, machine processing effectively eliminated the possibility of collaboration between laboratory and cinematographer, except in extraordinary cases.

Through the teens, the rack-and-tank system changed little, but cinematographers' attitudes did change, and as a result they began exploring the possibilities of control over the developing stage. The basic demand of studio filmmaking upon a film's photography was that it be 'clear' — that it show the mise-en-scene adequately for spectator understanding. But during the mid-teens, as we have seen, cinematographers, in collaboration with art directors, began to go beyond mere clarity, striving to achieve beauty as well. While camera and lighting technologies offered the most obvious means for assembling striking compositions, some cinematographers also discovered laboratory manipulation. Thus the greater variety of photographic styles that became apparent in the late teens and twenties can be attributed in part to an increased understanding of laboratory technology. This change goes hand in hand with the growing importance of the art director and the standardization of selective lighting during these same years. Photographic beauty became a staple of Hollywood's quality product.

21 Major technological changes of the 1920s

KRISTIN THOMPSON

Dramatically motion pictures will scarcely rise to higher heights than now attained. The finer shades of feeling and temperament are now conveyed to the screen in sincerity equal to the best in the older form of art. . . . The most marked changes that years succeeding the publication of this volume will bring about will be in further mechanical development.[1]

Homer Croy, 1918

By 1920, with the industry-wide adoption of Bell & Howell cameras and with the introduction of the sun-arc, the main phase of technological standardization was ending. Similarly, the style paradigm had been formulated and had reached a certain stability.

Before 1920, technological change could be rapid because many innovations offered major advantages by reducing inefficiency or by fostering progress in quality or novelty. But in the late silent period, the introduction of technology slowed. Some of the important changes had only a minor effect on the look of the films. Panchromatic film stock, which had been available for years, finally became more advantageous than orthochromatic. Panchro was more efficient, but the visible difference in the finished film was minimal. Similarly, the automation of developing and editing was largely an efficiency move; quality received a slight boost, but the novelty value was nil. Perhaps the main stylistic change during the twenties was the soft style of cinematography, and this in part depended upon the manipulation or modification of existing techniques. Now the changes were refinements – the replacement of one adequate device with a more advantageous one – rather than introductions of basic technology.

The change from orthochromatic to panchromatic stock

Audiences today looking at films from the silent period usually see contrasty 16mm or even 8mm prints, with stark, chalky whites and deep blacks. Perhaps such prints, as much as any other factor, have led to the myth of the crude early cinema. Historians and fans alike have perpetuated the notion that orthochromatic film, used in the majority of films until the mid-twenties, was a slow, contrasty, insensitive stock.

Yet the contrastiness of most modern prints arises from the conditions under which the film has been preserved. Often films survive only in a positive release print rather than a negative. The striking of a duplicate negative, or the repeated duping of positive prints over the years adds considerable contrast. If one sees a well-preserved positive print taken directly from an original orthochromatic negative, the range of grays most likely will be impressive (see, for example, figs 5.5, 5.15, and 5.16, taken from an original nitrate positive). Given an equal state of preservation, it is usually impossible to tell a film shot on orthochromatic from one shot on panchromatic.

But historians have assumed ortho was an inferior stock; several suggest that as soon as panchromatic stock became available, filmmakers switched over to it.[2]* Yet panchromatic stock was available in this country from 1913 on, failing to become the basic negative in use across the industry until about 1927. Why did cinematographers cling to ortho so long? In fact there were several reasons why panchro remained an unattractive alternative for years after its introduction. Only after improvements were made in panchro did cinematographers turn to it, and then they did so rapidly.

Orthochromatic film's main limitation was its

insensitivity to the yellow and red areas of the spectrum. Panchromatic, as its name implies, is sensitive to the entire visible spectrum. If all other properties of the two types of stock were equal, panchro would be more desirable, because it renders all colors in a more accurate relation to each other, even in black and white. Not only would panchro enhance the quality of the image, but it would be more efficient, requiring less time on the set to arrange compensatory filters, make-up, and the like. But the other properties were not equal until 1925.

In spite of its insensitivity to the red ranges, ortho was adequate to its purpose of rendering black and white images; filmmakers could avoid reds and yellows or use filters to alter image tonality. The impulse toward the invention of a panchromatic motion picture stock came in the limited area of experimentation with color cinematography. Charles Urban needed such a stock for his British Kinemacolor system. Kinemacolor used alternate frames photographed and then projected through red and green filters. But ortho stock would not register effectively through the red filter. In late 1909, Kinemacolor held a demonstration screening in New York, and a company soon formed to exploit the process in the United States. Although production by the Kinemacolor Company of American began in 1910, its films did not reach theaters until early 1913; the Patents Co. had attempted to keep color films out by threatening to cut off supplies of films to any theater that showed Kinemacolor. Kinemacolor of America reached an agreement with the Patents Co. in August of 1913.[3] In September of that same year, Eastman Kodak marketed its first panchromatic stock.[4] According to the founder of Eastman's research laboratory, Eastman was considering marketing the film for use in relation to Léon Gaumont's additive color process (a color system similar to Kinemacolor, except that it used three colored filters instead of two).[5] Whether Eastman was responding to Kinemacolor needs, or to Gaumont, or both, there is little doubt that it brought out its panchro stock in 1913 in response to the needs of experimenters in color filmmaking.

The simple fact that panchro was now available did not create a rush to abandon ortho. Panchro had three great disadvantages at this time, any one of which would probably have precluded its extensive use for black-and-white cinematography. Not only was panchro far more expensive and significantly slower than ortho, it was also physically unstable. The negative had to be used within weeks of its manufacture, or it would deteriorate.[6] For the next ten years Eastman would supply panchro 'in small quantities as experimental material.'[7] For Kinemacolor and the other companies working to create a satisfactory color process, a supply of panchro would be essential.[8] This same stock was supplied to studio cinematographers in the late teens and early twenties for limited usage on a trial basis. But for virtually all commercial film production, panchromatic film stock became largely a dead issue for the remainder of the teens. Presumably the failure of Kinemacolor in 1914, plus the fact that cinematographers had not adopted the new stock, combined to discourage Eastman from attempting to expand the market.

Cinematographers went on using ortho. Only three complaints about the stock appeared consistently in technical journals: clouds did not show up, since blue skies photographed as flat white (this also made good day-for-night effects difficult, even with filters); blonde hair photographed too dark; and light blue eyes photographed nearly white. But cinematographers could compensate to solve such problems. Throughout the silent period, cameramen reported using orange filters to get cloud effects. As we have already seen, back-lighting helped solve the 'blonde' problem; it could render the hair not only light in color, but also beautifully glowing. The solution to one problem posed by ortho actually ended by enhancing glamor photography.

The failure of light blue eyes to register created a similar problem for attractive close-ups of actors, especially women. James Wong Howe recalled that his first fame as a cinematographer came when he worked out a solution for Mary Miles Minter in 1922. She had pale blue eyes, and Howe managed to make them photograph dark by placing a screen of black velvet so that it would reflect into the lens from her eyes.[9] Some cinematographers used yellow filters for their close shots of such actors.

Other more general problems could be solved by controlling the colors in the objects photographed. Since red photographed as black, attempts were made to avoid deep reds. A careless make-up job could cause the actors' lips to appear black. Max Factor manufactured make-up to compensate for this problem. Even the contrast created by stark whites could be controlled through color manipulation:[10]

> Under the modern studio vapor lights, white photographs glaringly and is unpleasant on the screen, offering, for one thing, too much contrast to other surrounding objects which are darker and therefore have a different photographic light value. For that reason, garments and objects usually white in everyday life are usually pink and often yellow when being used for movie studio purposes.

But this does not mean that ortho was highly contrasty in relation to panchro. Even in the sound period when panchro was in universal use, objects to be filmed were seldom stark white. As with ortho, lights shining on a white shirt-front could set up a strong glare on panchro stock. So color compensation was not a problem that disappeared with the abandonment of ortho stock.

In using ortho, the cinematographer had to be able to judge what relative tones of gray the various colors in the mise-en-scene would translate into the film stock. (A red and a blue object might appear equally dark to the eye, but on the film the blue object would appear very light grey, the red one nearly black.) But here again the cinematographers worked out a method that minimized the problematic properties of ortho stock. By the mid-teens, they had realized that it was possible to view the scene through a blue filter to gauge its final look on the film. Since ortho registered primarily in the blue range, the filter simulated the tonalities that would result photographically (see fig 21.1). Outdoors, directors and cinematographers alike often wore blue-lensed glasses.

By the early twenties, cinematographers had managed to adjust to most of the problems inherent in ortho stock. In addition, as we have seen, ortho offered a tremendous advantage in the developing process; it could be inspected under a ruby-red light without fogging the negative. For all these reasons, then, the slow adoption of panchromatic stock is understandable.

Nevertheless, an improved panchro would be useful, offering a fuller sensitivity without compensating measures. In 1919 and into the early twenties, references to panchro began to crop up again in technical journals. The stock was still slower than ortho, so its main use was for out-door shots, where there was plenty of white light. Panchro gave sky shots which were superior to those achievable with ortho and filters. Cinematography experts reported that the 'up-to-date photographer ... goes in for beautiful cloud effects and color values, using color screens, vignetting devices, and panchromatic films.'[11] By 1921, the American Cinematographer was giving this advice to cameramen going on location: 'Don't forget for location long [tripod] legs, small tripod, panchromatic film and filters.'[12] But panchro was too slow for most studio use. Arcs and mercury-vapor lamps, ideal for blue-sensitive stock, were less efficient for panchro, which instead worked well with the yellower incandescent light. The studios still lit large sets with arcs and vapors, and would only use 'inkies' for close framings, where less light was needed. So from the late teens to the mid-twenties, panchro was used mainly for location shooting or studio portrait close-ups.

Experimentation soon allowed cinematographers and lab workers to increase the speed of the slow panchro stock. In 1922, the SMPE's Committee on Progress reported a new method giving 100 per cent greater speed. The improvement made it possible 'to photograph interiors by artificial light or exteriors on cloudy days' with panchro.[13] The following year, the Committee on Films and Emulsions found that studios were increasing the speed of panchro by immersing it in a mild ammonia bath.[14]

The increased speed of panchro in the early twenties made its use practical for entire films. The Headless Horseman (Edward Venturini, 1922, Sleepy Hollow Corp.) is generally held to be the first feature to have used panchro throughout. This film provides evidence that studios could get panchro if they wanted it, even during the 'experimental' period; panchro became a regular Eastman Kodak product only in 1923. In a 1926 interview, Henry King recalled shooting Romola (1925, Inspiration Pictures) in 1923-4, using panchro entirely. He remarked especially on its speed: 'We were surprised at the little light needed, for while it was generally supposed that panchromatic was slower than common stock, it proved a great deal faster.'[15] This is somewhat implausible, but the stock King used could well have been about equal in speed with ortho.

The real breakthrough in the dissemination of panchromatic did not come until 1925, when Eastman lowered its price to a level commensurate with ortho and began actively to promote the stock. Apparently the manufacturers and studio officials were in no hurry to put panchro into wide use prior to that year. In 1927 John Grierson described this resistance: 'The Eastman people who are responsible were themselves terribly slow in promoting the film in the world of cinema. Again, the use of panchromatic in interior work would involve changes in the system of lighting, and some experiment with softer lights and proper filters.'[16] As Chapter 19 suggested, innovations in one area of technology can affect other areas, ultimately requiring a considerable investment beyond the cost of the initial innovation. In the case of panchromatic, the studios might be willing to undertake the changes because the incandescent lamps used with panchro would be cheaper to run than arcs. Yet the studios would be likely to approach the conversion cautiously. Grierson was also right about the need for experimentation; in 1928 the film production companies and support industries cooperated on a series of Mazda tests of incandescent lights and panchromatic stock. The next chapter will describe these.

In an introduction to Grierson's article, the American Cinematographer's editor suggested that the burden of proving panchro's worth had been left to the cinematographers, some of whom sought its introduction:

> This demand has little by little spurred the manufacturer of film to invest great sums in perfecting this and subsidiary products. It has forced the manufacturer of lighting apparatus to adapt it to the new film. It has encouraged the laboratories to perfect the handling of this material so as to make its use safe and commercially practical.

Aside from resistance by laboratories, lighting manufacturers, and Eastman, the editor saw reluctance on the part of the producers:[17]

It was up to the cinematographer to become the natural link between these interests and the adoption of this revolutionary measure. It was up to him to foster and make known the advantages that he *knew* to exist, but which he had to *sell* to all parties interested in the making of motion pictures.

We must take these claims with a grain of salt, since the American Cinematographer had an interest in creating an image of its members as innovators. Still, it seems likely that the years 1919 to 1925 would be used as a period of limited experimentation with panchro in various circumstances. Cinematographers would hope to distinguish themselves by their achievements during this period. The success reported by filmmakers like King with *Romola* or cinematographer Ned Van Buren on *The Headless Horseman* would encourage the industry to proceed with the wide introduction of panchro, in spite of the attendant costs.

But whatever the cause, Eastman began to promote panchro. In 1925 it issued a pamphlet describing the stock: 'It is of great advantage in close-ups; the flesh tones are much more accurately rendered and the whole appearance is more natural when panchromatic film is used. It is also valuable for outdoor sets, the general tones of the landscape being better rendered, and clouds being photographed as they appear in a blue sky.' The stock could be used under arc light with a filter, but its speed increased when used under tungsten lamps, since the incandescent light was more actinic for panchro. Eastman claimed that their panchro negative was about equal in speed to ortho when used under arcs or in sunlight. It could also be hypersensitized.[18]

By 1925, Eastman had eliminated the two physical inferiorities of panchro. It was now more stable. Robert Flaherty's use of it in the south seas for *Moana* in 1925 proved that panchro would not deteriorate in heat. And the speed was now acceptable. By lowering the price, Eastman removed the last restraint. During 1926 Hollywood moved rapidly to use panchro. Bert Glennon praised it after using it for *Hotel Imperial* (Maurice Stiller, 1926, Famous Players-Lasky). The cast of *Old Ironsides* (James Cruze, cinematographer Alfred Gilks, 1926, Famous Players-Lasky) reportedly were able to work without make-up, due to panchro's superior rendition of flesh tones. George Barnes used panchro for *The Winning of Barbara Worth* (Henry King, 1926, Samuel Goldwyn), and the list goes on.[19]

On 31 January 1927, a meeting was held in Hollywood which signaled a recognition of the standardized use of panchro stock. The ASC and Eastman Kodak sponsored an evening of lectures and experimental film clips; two hundred guests listened to talks on graininess, duplicate negatives,[20*] and filters.[21]

Many productions continued to mix film stocks, however, employing panchro primarily for exteriors. Karl Struss recalled having used this approach on *Sunrise*. For cinematographers who wanted some special photographic quality that required inspection of the negative during development, the use of panchro would be confining, because the red inspection light used for ortho would fog the panchro. But on the whole the conversion was widespread by 1928: 'Officials report that a year ago the studios were using approximately 85 per cent. orthochromatic (ordinary) and 15 per cent. panchromatic, but today the percentages are almost exactly reversed.'[22] The introduction of faster 'Type II' panchro stock in 1928 put ortho at an additional disadvantage, and within a few years it was a thing of the past for regular studio use.[23*]

In the light of all this, we must abandon the traditional view of orthochromatic as an inferior, contrasty, slow stock. As Van Buren, one of the first cinematographers to work extensively with panchro, pointed out in 1930: 'The earlier [i.e., pre-1928] type panchromatic films gave more contrasty results pictorially than the regular negative. Furthermore, the cameraman was confronted with the idea that to use panchromatic negative properly it was necessary to use light filters.'[24] (The filters were for use in the studios with arcs and vapor lamps.) The 1928 'Type II' softer stock was the first panchro which was *less* contrasty than ortho. The dominant film stock of the silent period, orthochromatic, was excellent for use in both the hard-edged and the soft styles. It permitted a thorough control impossible with automatic developing and completely dark developing rooms. The discontinuation of ortho was logical, but so was its lengthy tenure as the basis of silent production.

Automatic editing and developing devices

Soon after the establishment of the studio system and its division of labor during the teens, there was a move to automate some key parts of the post-shooting stages. Machines were introduced to develop the film, to allow the editor to view it, and to splice it. Efficiency and quality control were the impulses behind this new technology.

Automated editing devices did not affect the degree of control filmmakers had over the editing stage. Such devices were labor-saving equipment. Typically, cutters looked at the images by holding the strip of film over a light box, perhaps employing a magnifying glass. Most cutters could 'read' the image to follow movement as they pulled the shots through their fingers against the light. Yet what they were looking at was a strip of still photographs, and judgments of tempo and matches on action were necessarily rough.

Some editors devised viewing machines for themselves. By removing the head from an old projector, the editor could contrive a machine that could run and stop the film. The editor would then be able to watch the shots in movement.[25] But most editors did not bother, preferring to trust their own sense of the film's tempo as it ran through their fingers. They could check their work by running it on a regular projector. Silent-period editor Margaret Booth has described how she worked in the twenties: 'As we cut the picture, we would continually screen it. We would make the necessary adjustments, and then screen it again. Cut it and run it, cut it and run it. And gradually we would make our rhythm, our pattern, for the picture.'[26] Editor William Hornbeck claims that this practice was already going on in 1916-17, when he worked at Keystone as a projectionist for such sessions.[27] But it was more efficient to enable the editor to run individual segments without summoning a projectionist for a screening each time the film needed checking.

The first editing viewer to be manufactured was the Moviola, which has remained a major brand name in the industry. After several trial machines, inventor Iwan Serrurier marketed the Moviola Midget in 1924 (see fig 21.2). Mounted between the rewinds by the editor's light box, the Midget ran the film through at a constant rate; the operator controlled it with a foot pedal. By the late silent period, virtually all studios had installed the Midget, and it remained the industry standard until sound necessitated the introduction of a new model.[28]* Moviolas promoted quality by making continuity and tempo easier to judge, and they made the editing process more efficient.

As part of the general move toward automated assembly of the film, automatic splicing machines came into use in the industry. As with the question of standard splice sizes, this device applied mainly to the companies' joining rooms rather than to their editing departments. Whole prints had to be assembled from the short strips of positive film coming out of the laboratories. (Even in the days of automatic developing machines, tinted or toned prints had to have a splice at every color change.) Workers, mostly women, sat making splices in a preordained order. Since they were making no decisions, they needed no time to consider options; automation would increase efficiency.

In 1918, Bell & Howell introduced an automatic splicer (fig 21.3), but it was designed only to splice negatives. That is, it made a strong .03-inch ($\frac{1}{32}''$) splice exactly on the frameline, so that the splice did not extend into the frame itself and hence was not visible on the screen. This made for a quality negative, but did not aid greatly in speeding up the editing process, since most editing time was consumed in the assembling and repairing work at the joining rooms and exchanges. So laboratories requested that Bell & Howell modify its machine to make it usable for positive film. As we have seen, positive film was typically spliced with a .156-inch ($\frac{5}{32}''$), or full-hole, splice; the adjustment was mainly a matter of making the machine do splices of various widths.

This adjustment was done by early 1922, when one author described the machine's advantages: it permitted an experienced worker to do four or five times as many splices as by hand; its pilot pins provided accurate registration of the two strips of film; the machine scraped the film, cut the ends, eliminated excess film cement; and its heating unit dried the splice quickly.[29] By the mid-twenties, this machine was in widespread use in studios and exchanges; as in its use with negatives, it added quality by making splices that would be less noticeable on the screen. Since a splice line on the screen calls attention to the cut,

invisible splices helped the continuity system of editing.

Automatic developing was also more efficient than the rack-and-tank system it replaced; but unlike editing, the new developing machines did sometimes place restrictions on filmmakers' choices. Automatic developing machines began to gain wide attention in the industry about 1921, when over half a dozen models were available in the United States. One of these models could handle as much as 4,000 feet of film an hour in 40 square feet of laboratory area and could be run by one operator; it replaced equipment which would take up 1,500 square feet and require several employees to run. Since the strips of film were longer, a finished positive reel could contain two splices rather than the previous average of about forty.[30]

These machines caught on within the next few years, but were almost exclusively limited to the processing of positive release prints. As originally manufactured, they would not handle negatives, and there was no great pressure from within the film industry for machine processing of negatives. On the one hand cinematographers preferred the control offered by the rack-and-tank method; on the other, there was some fear that irreplaceable negatives could be damaged by equipment breakdown. By 1925, one manufacturer was able to report: 'The machine development of positive film calls for no special remarks for it is rapidly becoming the accepted practice and most of the big laboratories are equipped with developing machines of one form or another.' He went on to urge the use of machines for negatives as well, pointing out that the same machine could easily be modified to run at the slower speed that negatives required.[31]

But apparently this suggestion went largely unheeded during the silent period. Finally the adoption of sound in the late twenties necessitated machine developing for negatives; most importantly, the chemicals and timing had to be absolutely standardized in order to preserve the fidelity of the sound track. So the conversion was not wholly one of choice, but one forced upon many filmmakers by a change in another area of technology. Quality control of sound took precedence over that of the image, for sound was the major novelty upon which film popularity was based at the time. Cinematographer John Seitz, who was noted for his close collaboration with the laboratory during the silent period, has recalled the alteration of approaches:[32]

> Motion-picture photography of the silent era was an optical and chemical business. The addition of sound changed it to more of an electrical business. The talking picture made it necessary to standardize film developing, thereby taking away much of the individuality of the cinematographer.

In the sound period, cinematographers could still introduce variations into their work, but mainly during the shooting phase; most stylistic touches had to be made in lighting and cinematography. In the 1930s, many studio laboratories standardized the films' photographic qualities. At Warner Bros, the laboratory head Fred Gage tried to get a characteristic studio look, but would push or pull film for varying degrees of contrast. Mike Leshing of 20th Century-Fox's laboratory and Daniel Clark of the Camera Department tried for complete standardization of exposure and development throughout the studio. Similarly, John Nickolaus tried to create an MGM style; according to Clarke, Nickolaus instructed him not to use diffusion filters when shooting, since the laboratory would give all films the correct degree of softness during the developing stage.[33] Thus the increasing technical sophistication of Hollywood did not always imply a straightforward 'progress.' Some cinematographers lost a great deal more than simply the ability to move their cameras freely when sound arrived. In particular, automatic processing put restrictions on a new stylistic impulse which had arisen during the twenties, the soft style of cinematography.

The soft style of cinematography

During the late teens and especially the 1920s, many Hollywood filmmakers experimented with and gradually adopted a soft style of cinematography. By 'the soft style,' I do not simply mean shallow focus. This was one way of softening an image, but cinematographers also drew upon a range of other devices: low-contrast developing, gauzes, filters, soft-edged vignettes, smoke — anything that could reduce contrast and create

diffusion. As we have seen in Chapter 17, for most of the silent period the main cinematographic style emphasized sharp focus and depth of field: a 'hard-edged' look. The soft style was to prove an enduring alternative to this approach.

Recent accounts tend to credit Billy Bitzer and Henrik Sartov's work in *Broken Blossoms* (D.W. Griffith, 1919, D.W. Griffith Corp.) for the innovation of soft photography, especially in their close shots of Lillian Gish.[34] There is no doubt that *Broken Blossoms* was very influential, in spite of the fact that it uses fewer soft-style shots than many of the films that followed it. But its gauzy shots of the Chinese harbor and of Lucy sleeping in the moonlight in the Yellow Man's room apparently struck other cinematographers of the period as a radical break with customary practice.

Yet there are indications that softness had been considered a desirable visual quality for some years before 1919. Soft filming began with close shots of actors, in an attempt to imitate still photography. A 1914 cinematography manual describes quite specifically how to achieve this effect:[35]

> For portrait pictures in a regular studio with a background it will be well to use a side light, and use as large an opening in the lens as possible, and the highest shutter speed with which you can get a properly timed negative. In this manner you can get a softer and more pronounced relief between the object and the background. The negative should be somewhat thinner than a landscape negative or an outdoor exposure and somewhat softer, and should be developed and printed for softness instead of contrast. By giving less time in the printing or using a warmer developer this softness may be obtained.

This author treats the use of soft lighting and shallow focus as a matter of separating the salient characters from the less important background. A 1917 source adds the idea that soft cinematography enhances the beauty of the composition:[36]

> Beautiful scenes, involving artistic close-ups that hold the interest to the actors, soft and clear effects, pleasing angles which give the best expression and expressiveness to the

whole, or any part thereof, are always noticed and appreciated by an audience, regardless of the enthralling interest of the drama.

So a second early justification for using the soft style was beauty – not simply feminine beauty, but beauty of the whole composition. These two functions would continue through the twenties as the basic justification of the soft style.

The first passage above suggests that during the early teens, experiments with the soft style depended upon manipulations the cinematographer could perform using existing technology: placing the lights, opening the aperture, or altering the developing process. In the mid-teens, however, filmmakers began to create specific tools for this purpose. In 1916, for example, Triangle-Fine Arts director Paul Powell was reportedly using a diffusing lens for 'highly poetic scenes' in *The Marriage of Molly O.*[37] There is considerable evidence that Karl Struss's Pictorial Lens, originally created for his delicately hazy still photographs of the early decades of the century, made its way into filmmaking in the same year, probably on this production.[38*] But it was not until the early twenties that soft-focus lenses became widely available for motion-picture cameras.

During the later teens, cinematographers experimented with other ways of softening their images, placing gauze or filters over their lenses. In 1917 one author commented on the use of diffusing filters over the lens: 'Screens of various materials which do not cut off all the light rays, are being used by cameramen.' These little screens were made from wire screening or translucent portrait film, exposed and developed to the desired degree of opacity; the cameraman would then punch a hole in the center, to create a haziness around the edge of the frame[39] (see figs 16.79 and 16.80). Sources do not discuss the reasons for this usage, aside from the idea of beauty. But one purpose was probably to isolate the figures from the background, concentrating the spectator's attention on the face.

Accessories to create soft effects were commercially available; with these, a cinematographer could get his regular, sharp-focus anastigmat lens to simulate a soft-focus lens. In 1922, Karl Brown described how an anastigmat lens

may be made to give acceptable soft images by means of various attachments, such as diffusion disks, etc. A diffusion disk, such as the Eastman Diffusion Disk, is a piece of optical glass, flat on one surface, and having the other surface broken up with slight waves or bands, the intensity and frequency of the bands determining the amount of diffusion.

Other such screens were available, and Brown pointed out that a great variety of meshes of chiffon and gauze were used for the same purposes, with the advantage that the center could be cut or burned out, again to create soft-edged vignettes.[40]

With the increasingly widespread use of soft shots in the early twenties, it became more efficient to have special lenses as a standard tool of the cinematographer, so that he would not need to spend time improvising an effect. During this period, a variety of brands of soft lenses became available to the cinematographer. Brown's series, 'Modern lenses,' in *American Cinematographer*, gave an excellent account of both the optics of soft lenses and the specifications of the various makes – the Wollensak Verito, the Kalostat, and the Dallmeyer. Brown described the workings of these lenses:[41]

Most soft focus lenses depend upon spherical aberration, chromatic aberration, or a combination of the two in various degrees. The usual soft focus image shows a more or less firm main image overlapped and underlaid with a less intense out-of-focus secondary image, the spread and intensity of which can be varied with the diaphragm.

Spherical aberration depends upon the fact that the marginal rays passing through the lens element focus in a different plane than the central rays; most lenses add elements to correct for this. A soft-focus lens deliberately leaves this aberration at least partially uncorrected. The Struss Pictorial Lens, for example, consisted of a single lens element. In chromatic aberration, the light is broken into its component colors in passing through the lens, and the various colors focus on different planes. Brown pointed out that chromatic aberration is harder to judge in focusing, since the differences are not visible to the eye when the many tiny spectra overlap to create white light.[42] Hence most soft-focus lenses correct chromatic aberration to some extent.

Brown also discussed something which is easy to overlook in dealing with the twenties soft-focus style; he explained how these lenses 'show a great increase in depth of field over an anastigmat of the same aperture and focal length, and this varies with the formula. Some soft lenses show an increase of several hundred per cent. greater acceptable depth of field over a similar ana-stigmat.'[43] Thus in discussing the history of depth of field usage, we should not directly compare the aperture settings of the ultraspeed and soft-focus lenses of the twenties with the regular lenses in use at the time. Such comparisons will most likely be inaccurate.

Instead, there were different approaches to soft filming in the twenties. One involved actual shallow focus, filming a scene with a long lens from a distance, thereby throwing the background out of focus. This might be supplemented by gauzed lights, gauzed lens, and so on. But there was also a trend toward soft style maintaining depth of field. As Brown's description of soft-focus lenses suggests, such lenses could provide spherical aberration, but maintain depth of field, so that the foreground would be as fuzzy as other planes. The selective application of gauze, not only to the lens and lamps, but also to the *mise-en-scène* elements, could also create a diffusion effect in selected planes, without affecting focus.

The tendency toward selective focus was not a strong one during the teens, as we saw in examining cinematography and depth of field. Most cinematographers would strive to achieve as great a depth of field as possible under the given conditions. Standard lens lengths in this period were 2 and 3 inches; a 3-inch lens gave a slightly fuzzy background, but barely enough to be noticeable in the typical *plan américain*. Lenses as long as 4-inches were available from an early date.[44]*

In the twenties cinematographers were employing a greater variety of lenses – not only faster and softer, but also longer. Clarke recalled that Billy Bitzer did the close-ups for *Way Down East* (1920, D.W. Griffith Corp.) with a 6-inch lens to make the backgrounds go out of focus. Bitzer experimented with and bought new lenses frequently, according to Clarke. By 1927, McKay's *Handbook of Motion Picture Photography* listed standard lenses as 35mm (1⅜″), 2-inch (50mm), 3-inch (75mm), 4-inch (100mm), and 6-inch (150mm); he described the shallow focus tendencies familiar to us from thirties Hollywood:[45]

In photographing distant scenes, use the small stop for universal sharpness, but for objects in the middle distance and foreground, open the lens to f8 or larger. This will soften the distance and provide atmospheric depth.

In filming people, focus sharply upon them and let the background go fuzzy. This will prevent extraneous objects in the background from spoiling the effect of the picture. This process for using out of focus planes for securing pictorial effects is known as differential focussing.

So visual softness could be obtained by long lenses as well as by soft lenses and specific accessories (see fig 21.4). Given this range of tools, certain cinematographers between 1919 and 1929 experimented with different ways of achieving the hazy, luminous effects characteristic of the soft style.

One of the earliest impulses toward a soft style came from the continuing imitation of portrait photography (fig. 21.5). Some films would use the regular hard-edged style for most of their shots, but close shots would suddenly go fuzzy. In 1920, Billy Bitzer and Henrik Sartov worked together on close shots of Lillian Gish for *Way Down East*. Bitzer had begun his career using the hard-edged style, but was interested in experimenting with lenses. Sartov was a portrait photographer originally and he and Bitzer tried for this soft look in their close-ups of the heroine. Several shot/reverse-shot situations demonstrate clearly how soft the treatment of Gish is (fig 21.6), in comparison with the photography of the villain, for example (fig 21.7).

Another film shot in 1920 was *The Four Horsemen of the Apocalypse*, which had a considerable impact on other filmmakers of the period. Its cinematographer, John F. Seitz, used lenses, gauze, developing tricks, and other devices to soften his images. One famous scene involved a hazy effect in the background of a cafe setting (fig 21.8). Here everything remains in sharp focus, but the background planes drop off noticeably in their degree of contrast. Seitz may have used smoke to help achieve this effect. The use of low contrast creates a series of beautiful compositions; the scene was frequently singled out for praise in contemporary reviews. Seitz also used gauze, lighting, and low-contrast developing for glamor effect, as in the first meeting of the hero and heroine. In figure 17.36, the hero is lit from top and sides, with the background thrown slightly out of focus. This is a far cry from the evenly lit, deep focus shots of several years earlier (see figs 16.73 and 16.74).

In *Four Horsemen* the glamor shots of the actors are only part of a larger pattern, where softness and low contrast in the cinematography create pictorial beauty in many other types of images as well. It inspired other cinematographers to experiment increasingly with soft-style techniques. Some of the most spectacular effects they achieved involved the use of gauze, and a number of the great soft-style films of the late silent era owe their visual quality as much to gauze as to optical qualities of lenses. Rosher, Struss, and Sartov were leaders in this area. In figure 21.9, Sartov sets up a close shot of Lillian Gish for *La Bohème* (1926, MGM). Sartov's gauze box is visible on the front of the camera; its length offers a variety of options for placing gauzes and filters at different positions. Figure 21.10 shows the camera crew of one of the major soft-style films, *Sparrows* (William Beaudine, 1926, Pickford Corp.). The large black box on the front of Struss's Bell & Howell is his own matte box. (Cinematographers typically built a number of their camera accessories themselves.) According to Struss, he would fasten gauze and other materials inside this box with thumbtacks.[46]

Within a short period, cinematographers placed gauze scrims within the mise-en-scene, sometimes actually visible to the camera and the audience. In their 1922 film *Foolish Wives*, Erich von Stroheim and cinematographer Ben Reynolds used gauze for several important shots. Here the function is not beauty. These shots always mark the villain's point-of-view of certain characters. In one shot, Count Karamzin, filmed in the hard-edged style, looks offscreen (fig 21.11); his POV of the counterfeiter's daughter is filmed through a gauze, with the texture of the filter visible, in focus between the lens and the actress (fig 21.12).

Rosher made famous the use of large sheets of gauze behind the figures to give the background a washed-out, overexposed look without sacrificing depth of field. A contemporary review praised the effect in his 1923 film *Rosita*, saying it contained 'an almost perfect perspective of the third dimension, or stereoscopic effect, showing the figures in bold relief in the foreground, at the same time keeping the background sharply in focus yet obtaining the long-sought for effect of showing distances on a flat surface.'[47] This effect probably reached its culmination in the Mary Pickford film *Sparrows*, in 1926. There one can see the foregrounds of the scenes done around the swamp farm clearly, while the background beyond the surrounding clumps of trees suddenly goes relatively dim; the reviewer's description of the distance appearing to be on a flat surface is apt – yet every detail remains in focus (fig 21.13).

This remarkable film brought together the talents of Rosher, Struss, and Hal Mohr. Struss has recalled the use of gauze in this film in an interview: 'We put enormous gauzes in the trees, thirty by sixty feet; and we had three in a line. They all had to be backlit, and we used special reflectors. Miss Pickford was always shot through gauzes, but this was something else again.'[48] Mohr has added information about the soft look of *Sparrows*. Rosher dealt with Consolidated Film Laboratories to achieve a special look through the developing process. As Mohr described it:[49]

We'd go into a situation where you'd be shooting, let us say, into a terrific backlight, a lot of reflected light coming in, and so on. It would call for, in those days, a f-8 stop – well, we'd photograph it at 4, or 4.5, and that's several stops overexposed. Then Aller [at Consolidated] would skin-develop it; as soon as the image would show through, it was stopped. . . . That's how we got this soft, ethereal look. Of course, we used a lot of fog machines, also.

The result was a film that used the soft style consistently throughout the sequences, without losing image definition.

This extremely soft, luminous style, suffusing virtually every image of a film, was not widespread. Certainly there are many films, possibly the majority, in the mid-1920s, that retain the sharp-focus, hard-edged lighting style. Yet a soft shot here and there for glamor effects was a likely paradigmatic alternative. And a consistent soft style had become one way of shooting prestigious films, as with *Sparrows* and *The Four Horsemen of the Apocalypse*. Rosher was Pickford's regular cinematographer and was in constant demand among the biggest female (and occasionally male) stars in Hollywood for his ability to create glamorous close-ups.

What factors brought about the soft style? Clearly soft-style cinematography did not promote efficiency. When workers are hanging giant gauzes, calculating special exposure and developing methods, or buying extra lenses, shooting time and expenses go up. But on high-budget films especially, considerations of product differentiation and quality would outweigh limited inefficiency. The soft style first crops up primarily in films made by powerful independent companies (especially those releasing through United Artists) or auteur directors. The main impetus for experimentation in this field came from the cinematographers themselves, and from their directors and actors, in a quest for what they viewed as quality images. Cinematographers often created their own lenses, camera attachments, and processes. On *Four Horsemen*, Seitz provided the laboratory with special chemical formulas to be used in custom developing the separate shots. (Metro had gone back to the director-unit system for this very high-budget film, and thus Ingram and Seitz had an unusually high degree of control.) We have seen how Struss's own Pictorial Lens made its way into the industry. Rosher said he developed the Rosher Kino Portrait Lens in the mid-1920s. Such cinematographers and directors employed the soft style initially; then stars began to demand it as they realized how it enhanced their looks. Alice Terry and Rudolph Valentino became stars overnight as a result of *Four Horsemen*, and the soft glamor close shots of them may have contributed a good deal to their appeal. Rosher used his Kino Portrait lens to photograph close-ups of Pickford and John Barrymore. He has recalled amusingly his use of the soft style to make Barrymore look younger in *The Tempest* (Sam Taylor, 1928, Joseph M. Schenck Productions, released United Artists).[50] Close shots of the Barrymore character are hazy; a medium close-up of him looking off at the heroine and her friends bathing in a river surrounds him with tiny glints of light sparkling on willow leaves, creating a cloud of fuzziness. These shots, as well as views of Richard Barthelmess in *Way Down East* and the treatment of a few other male stars in the twenties indicate that women were not the only subjects of the soft-style treatment. Women usually got heavier gauzing, but certain men were associated with glamor as well. Some stars could control the assignment of a cinematographer. If Lillian Gish or Pickford wanted someone like Rosher, experienced in glamor photography, he was most likely the person she would have.[51]* The Hollywood cinema uses the human figure as its center of interest, and a technique that could enhance that figure might well be worth the additional expense in production.

Aside from the added quality attained through glamor, it was the case that a good many of the most successful films of the decade used soft-style filming. Seitz was reportedly the highest-paid cinematographer of the twenties and the only one whose name was used in advertising.[52] Hollywood institutions also helped to make the soft style the 'quality' style of the day by rewarding practitioners. The first Academy Awards for cinematography were given to Rosher and Struss in 1927, for their collaborative work on *Sunrise*. Other soft-style films figured prominently in the awards, including *Seventh Heaven*, *Street Angel*, and *The Tempest*. By the years 1926-8, the soft style had reached its peak in the silent period.

Why would cinematographers and other filmmakers create the soft style to begin with? The strongest influences came from a style prevalent in still photography at the time, the Pictorialist school active in America from about the turn of the century into the twenties. Pictorialism was practiced primarily by the Photo-Secessionist group started in 1902 by Alfred Stieglitz, and it influenced many prominent photographers of the period. The international Pictorialist movement began earlier, in the late 1800s, as an attempt to promote photography as an art; proponents manipulated the image, either in the taking or developing stage, to stylize it and to emphasize its similarity to the graphic arts.

There were some direct connections between cinematography and Pictorialist still photography. Some of the earliest soft-focus cinematography lenses were simply adapted versions of lenses in use on still cameras. The Struss Pictorial

Lens is one example. Struss was himself a still photographer in the Pictorialist tradition before going into film, as was Henrik Sartov. Also, a number of cinematographers were professional or amateur still photographers. (Issues of *American Cinematographer* and *International Photographer* frequently reproduced stills taken by cinematographers, often in a hazy Pictorialist style.) By the mid-teens, when Pictorialism begins to appear in films, it had become the prevailing fashion in photography; and by the late twenties, it was the standard academic style against which many still photographers were reacting. There was little danger of following avant-garde trends by taking Pictorialism into the film industry.

Beaumont Newhall has described the work of American Pictorialist photographers like Clarence H. White and Edward Steichen as being 'characterized by soft focus, deep shadows relieved with brilliant highlights and strong, linear compositions.'[53] Figures 21.14 and 21.15 show the Pictorialist style in landscape and portrait work; both of these could be useful to filmmakers. Compare them with figures 21.16 and 21.17. The frame from *Way Down East* could almost pass for a Pictorialist still photograph. In *Foolish Wives*, the mesh filter in the view of the monk makes the surface resemble that of a painting; it comes very close to a similar effect used by the Pictorialists (fig 21.18). For stills, a cloth-like texture is created by special printing with the gum bichromate method.[54]

These examples of Pictorialist still photography reflect the influence of French Impressionist painting in their indistinct, fuzzy renditions. Impressionism was itself an academic style by the mid-teens. This was the period during which filmmakers were eager to prove that cinema, too, was an art. So Hollywood was in about the same position in the late teens that the Pictorialist photographers had been in twenty years before; cinematographers hoped that by imitating earlier, established styles in the other arts, they could achieve the same public status themselves.

In many cases, cinematographers succeeded: soft-style photography was singled out for praise in reviews, and the public flocked to see the beautifully hazy images of their favorite stars. And in the hands of experts like Rosher and Struss, Pictorialism enhanced the cinematography of their films. Yet the influence of Pictorialism brought its own problems, as several contemporary accounts suggest. Brown comments on the abuses of soft focus:

> The worst error into which the cameramen have in the past fallen is excessive diffusion, and failure to control 'runaround' and halo. Perhaps too close attention to the work of prominent pictorialists has caused this. . . . An acceptable amount of halo on sun-lit foliage is delightful in a still picture, but an identical picture in motion on the screen would be impossible, due to the twinkling of the appearing and disappearing haloes as the foliage moves. A slight runaround does not matter in a still portrait, but on the screen it appears and vanishes as the subject moves and changes high lights.

Brown also points out a problem which has plagued Hollywood cinematographers ever since, in their search for complete continuity: 'The pictorialist does not have to show his pictures in immediate contrast to sharp scenes; the cameraman must.'[55] Another commentator brought up similar objections in 1926:[56]

> From the pictorialist photographers the motion picture makers have borrowed one implement of especial value − and danger. This is the soft focus lens. . . . It is easily misused. With it very lovely and delicate portrait photography, for example, is possible, but such portraits appear strangely out of place when sandwiched in between scenes in sharp-definition photography.

The soft style, then, presented particular problems for the continuity system. Frequent changes in degree of contrast or fuzziness from shot to shot would call attention to editing and other stylistic devices. This is noticeable in films from the first half of the twenties especially; in *Four Horsemen*, the degree of softness changes frequently. Yet apparently the enhanced beauty of composition and the glamor of the figures was considered worth the sacrifice of a small degree of continuity. Later, as we shall see, machine developing in the sound period lessened the difference among shots, minimizing the continuity problem − if at the expense of a great deal of the variety of the early soft style.

The support sector of the film industry co-operated in the introduction of soft-style technology. Members of the ASC would test new lenses and make recommendations for changes. In 1922, Brown's series on 'Modern lenses' included a report on a soft lens for still cameras, the Graf Variable, which was about to appear on the market for motion-picture cameras as well. Brown had tested the first one made and reported favorably on it to *American Cinematographer* readers. He ends his series by urging other cameramen to help American companies to test their lenses and thereby to surpass German lens makers. At least some laboratories were willing to give the kind of individualized service demanded for complicated soft effects. Tom Storey, who had collaborated with Seitz at Metro's laboratory on the developing of *Four Horsemen*, opened his own laboratory in 1922; Storey was called 'a believer in individuality in photography and plans to work directly with cameramen whose film he handles, giving personal service and attention to every detail.'[57] Such cooperation would foster the dissemination of the soft style, since laboratory personnel could learn the techniques from the experimenters, then suggest them to other cinematographers seeking advice.

Since sound negatives had to be developed by machine to ensure absolute uniformity of contrast in the track, cinematographers could no longer order custom hand-developing after the silent period. Instead, some studios decided to standardize a soft, slightly diffused look to their films. The result was a relatively uniform, low-contrast, slightly fuzzy gray look. Heavily gauzed close-ups would still stand out as fuzzier than the long shots, but the difference was not nearly so noticeable as it had been in the early twenties.

Sound took the soft style partially out of the cinematographers' control and made it a matter of studio policy. In effect, the soft style became more pervasive, but less varied. It was also cheaper. Rather than spending costly time on the set arranging gauzes or in the laboratory concocting special developing formulas, studios demanded a narrower set of options. Adjustments of the lens would throw a background out of focus; standard filters and developing baths could give all shots a similarly gray look; the softer panchromatic film stocks introduced in the late twenties and early thirties also promoted low contrast. The inefficiency of the twenties soft-style filming was eliminated, but at the expense of novelty, and, arguably, of some quality. The soft style has remained with us to the present to some degree, but the twenties probably represented the height of cinematographers' control of this technique.

22 The Mazda tests of 1928

DAVID BORDWELL

I confidently believe, however, that in the course of a few years the present system of motion picture lighting will be replaced by a system of illumination by incandescent lamps.[1]

Frederick S. Mills, 1921

In early 1928, Hollywood technicians were mobilized for a common effort of unprecedented scope. On a set donated by Warner Bros, open every weekday and some evenings, forty cinematographers exposed 800 hours of film. The purpose was to test panchromatic film and incandescent lighting under studio conditions. Today, this massive enterprise is almost wholly forgotten. Historians do not mention it; the films are apparently lost; many participants have only faint recollections. Yet the Mazda tests, as they were called at the time, are of capital importance in the history of Hollywood technology. The tests established service firms as the chief sources of systematic, industry-wide technical innovation and made the Academy the coordinator of large-scale technological change. At the same time, the 1928 tests forged the links among the Academy, the Society of Motion Picture Engineers, and the service sector that made for efficient technical progress.

The film industry's conversion to sound did not directly trigger the studios' interest in incandescent lighting on the set. At first, cutting production costs supplied a more compelling motive. The 1926-7 film season had shown a marked falloff in earnings, and studios were eager to cut expenses.[2] Incandescent, or tungsten, lighting (also called 'Mazda' lighting because of the GE trademark) seemed to many producers one step toward lower costs. Although arc and mercury-vapor lamps were the chief types of studio lighting during the early 1920s, some cinematographers used incandescent lighting occasionally, and many cameramen expected incandescent light eventually to become the industry standard. In 1927, with a growing use of panchromatic film and a greater demand for production economy, several studios began to use incandescents. Tungsten lighting was thought to be more efficient than arc lighting for several reasons: incandescents used less current, required less maintenance, were simpler to change, and were more portable. In late 1927, nine studios went on record as believing that using incandescents had cut lighting costs in half, and some companies estimated that as much as two hours of production time per day could be saved by the 'inkies.'[3]

At this point, however, incandescent lighting was crude and unsystematized. Most studios were building their own fixtures or converting arc units, while a few studios were buying units from the new firm of Mole-Richardson. There was no standard and many production problems remained to be solved. In November 1927, at a meeting of the Academy Technicians' Branch, two members predicted that incandescent illumination would soon be universally adopted. (It is likely that the knowledge that Warners had experimented with Mazdas for its talkies made the issue even more pressing.) The problem was that very few cinematographers knew how to use tungsten lighting. As a result, the Technicians' Branch proposed a series of tests, to be coordinated by the branch and the American Society of Cinematographers.[4]

Such tests constituted an ideal project for the newly formed Academy, but it also offered the SMPE an opportunity it had been awaiting. Since its founding, the SMPE had few members on the West Coast; nearly all the service firms were in New York, Rochester, Boston, and Chicago. At its spring 1927 convention, the SMPE discussed the need to form strong bonds with Hollywood. K.C.D. Hickman's paper, 'Hollywood and the Motion Picture Engineers,' insisted that the manufacturing and research sector had to connect with its customers:[5]

> We have firstly to disseminate continually and all the time general scientific knowledge, together with that practical instruction so prized by the field worker; and secondly, we have to get the other man to describe his business so that we may anticipate his needs of tomorrow. This is not a kindness nor even a duty. It is a commercial act as necessary as advertisement to a soap manufacturer.

The solution, Hickman claimed, was to bring Hollywood technicians into the SMPE, even though they were not scientists in any strict sense. Hickman's point was reinforced by a warning from Eastman Kodak's John I. Crabtree. He pointed out that there was just beginning in Hollywood a new professional society, the Academy, and there 'the engineer is only in a minority; in other words, the society would include actors, scenario writers, and so on, and engineers. Once that society is established, I don't know where the Society of Motion Picture Engineers will fit.'[6] The result was that the SMPE scheduled its April 1928 convention for Los Angeles.

The timing was superb. After the Academy's Mazda tests had been planned, J.A. Ball of Technicolor suggested to the Technicians' Branch that the lighting demonstrations be held just before the SMPE's April convention, since that would make it easier to attract experts from the major manufacturers.[7] As it happened, the results of the tests were announced immediately after the SMPE convention.

Since most studios were already convinced of incandescent lighting's cost efficiency, it is plain that most participants were not interested in comparing arc light to incandescent. (Nor did the tests address the usefulness of mercury-vapor lamps, since the latter favored the green band of the spectrum and were thus unsuited to panchromatic film.) Some emphasis, of course, fell upon production economy, and a few tests measured one system against another with respect to labor and production time. But most

tests assumed the feasability of Mazdas and went on to explore their range and determine their weaknesses. What the producers wanted was practice in using incandescents, information on how one could use them most efficiently, and a means of notifying suppliers what to supply. It was important, then, that manufacturers participate in the tests. The Technicians' Branch invited all suppliers of incandescent equipment and panchromatic film to send representatives and new equipment. General Electric contributed thousands of dollars worth of lamps, and Mole-Richardson sent their entire line of products. Du Pont, Eastman, and Agfa supplied free film and processing. Max Factor donated a make-up artist and make-up materials. Eventually, over a dozen service firms participated in the tests.[8] For the first time, the manufacturers had a chance to display their wares for systematic comparison.

The tests were conducted between 18 January and early March of 1928. All members of the ASC and of the Academy were invited to use the facilities. Aside from the daily tests on Warner Bros' set, twelve major public demonstrations were held. The ASC edited the 72,000 feet of film into eight reels and screened them on 17 April at the Hollywood Chamber of Commerce. Since the SMPE convention had ended only three days before, many members extended their stay to see the film and to participate in the discussions that followed.[9]

The Academy proposed no official recommendations at the close of the Mazda tests, but it was hardly necessary, since the adoption of incandescent lighting had been felt as almost inevitable.[10] The ASC made its own position clear:[11]

> It was decided from the results obtained in the tests that the tungsten incandescent lamp is superior to all other types of light source now in use in the following respects: convenience; economy of power and operating labor; ready controllability; freedom from smoke and dirt; superior color of light permitting correct tone reproduction of colored objects when used with panchromatic color sensitive motion picture film.

Moreover, thanks to the tests, engineers and manufacturers now knew more exactly what problems Hollywood had with Mazdas and panchromatic. Early in 1928, the Academy had already assembled and disseminated a dossier of studio attitudes toward Mazda lighting, including criticisms (that the light was too diffuse, too weak, too hot). These dossiers were made available to the manufacturers. At the close of the tests, the results were published as *Academy Report's No. 1: Incandescent Illumination*, and the document was sent to the research departments of the firms, as a guide to innovation and development.[12] This was the manufacturers' chance to do what Hickman had suggested: to get the other man to describe his business.

The Mazda tests were a turning point in the history of Hollywood technology. For one thing, they established incandescent light and panchromatic film as the industry's norm for three decades. It is often thought that sound filming directly caused the adoption of panchromatic and tungsten lighting, but we can now see that the case was more complex. It was while the Mazda tests were under way that *The Jazz Singer* was recognized as a box-office success and that the major studios signed with ERPI for sound rights (May 1928). When the Academy published the official test reports in July 1928, the first all-talking feature, *The Lights of New York*, was released.[13] Thus investigation into panchromatic film and incandescent lighting paralleled and reinforced Hollywood's decision to adopt sound. As Charles G. Clarke puts it: 'When sound came, we were ready.'[14] (See fig. 22.1.)

Stylistically, the tests reflected certain classical principles developed before the 1920s. The Warner Bros set, for instance, was a baronial hall with fireplace, easy chairs, table, piano, and raftered ceiling – a typical upper-class interior for a silent film. Test exposures were made to the established formulas of camera distance and angle. Records of the test films reveal incipient narrative situations, as when a young man and woman in evening clothes greet one another in a room, or when the couple, sitting in a darkened library, are interrupted by the woman's father.[15] Most important, the decision to match incandescent lighting with panchromatic film favored the dominance of a somewhat diffused photographic style. The previous chapter has shown that the heavily diffused soft style was one option in the 1920s; Mazda lamps helped any film obtain

a moderately soft look akin to that of the prestigious late silent films. As one cinematographer put it in the Academy report: 'In order to obtain soft photography with Arc lights it is necessary to diffuse. The Mazda lamp, on the other hand, has a softness to it that does not need the amount of diffusion, if any, required by the hard light.'[16]

The 1928 tests constituted a turning point in still other ways. In the short run, service firms that adapted to the prevalence of incandescent lighting prospered. During the tests, Max Factor created a make-up for panchromatic film that became the industry standard. Mole-Richardson, virtually the only company manufacturing incandescent equipment, flourished.[17] In the long run, the Mazda tests established the Academy as the coordinator and clearing house for technical innovation. The SMPE, for its part, obtained its link to Hollywood. At its April convention, held under the Academy's auspices, the Society hosted many papers from Hollywood industry workers – scriptwriters, directors, laboratory technicians, and theater managers. More importantly, the workers were exhorted to join the SMPE under premises that considerably stretched its conception of the professional engineer: 'Every man contributing a real part in the motion picture industry qualifies as an engineer.'[18]

Most significantly, the Mazda tests, coming on the heels of the Vitaphone shorts, *Don Juan*, and *The Jazz Singer*, mark Hollywood's recognition that it needed to support technical research in a directed, explicit way. The Academy gave the SMPE a banquet at the close of its convention, and the engineers took the opportunity to lecture their hosts on the necessity for industrial research and development. A representative from General Electric pointed out that in modern companies, scientific research was considered an investment. C.E.K. Mees, founder of Eastman's research laboratory, said that now, thanks to the SMPE, the producers could cooperate closely with the manufacturers.[19]

Before the Mazda tests, technological innovation was fairly haphazard and uncoordinated, relying on individual firms such as Cooper-Hewitt, Eastman, and Bell & Howell, or on institutional imperatives such as the creative role constructed for the cinematographer. After the tests, Hollywood had a network for the organized articulation of technical questions and the systematic search for answers. On 20 April 1928, at the very close of the Mazda tests, the Academy announced its intention to create a technical bureau which would use 'all research laboratories for the immediate benefit that we ourselves can gain.'[20] The bureau would contract with firms to solve particular problems, standardize materials with the cooperation of the Federal Department of Standards, and eventually create its own research laboratory. On 8 August 1928, the Academy Technical Bureau was established.[21] The bureau's head was J.A. Ball − a principal engineer at Technicolor, an active member of the SMPE, a founding member of the Academy, and the man who had proposed synchronizing the Mazda tests with the SMPE convention.

23

The introduction of sound

DAVID BORDWELL

The talking pictures of the future will follow the general line of treatment heretofore developed by the silent drama. They will be motion pictures in which the characters will talk by audible speech instead of printed subtitles. The talking scenes will require different handling, but the general construction of the story will be much the same.[1]

> Frank Woods, Secretary of the Academy of Motion Picture Arts and Sciences, 1928

Attempts to synchronize sound and image were part of Edison's research program, and several firms introduced technologies through the early 1920s. Invariably, synchronization and amplification systems proved inadequate, and exhibitors failed to adopt the equipment. As Douglas Gomery has shown, the decisions by Warner Bros and Fox to introduce sound in the mid-1920s eventually forced the major firms to compete. Warners and Fox, both minor firms, saw the technology as a method of product differentiation and a means of appealing to smaller exhibitors unable to afford a live stage program of the sort offered in the first-run theaters. Drawing upon Western Electric's corporate research program and control of patents, Warner Bros formed Vitaphone in 1926 and embarked on a strategy of step-by-step introduction of sound films. Fox brought out its Movietone News later that year. The success of these endeavors was apparent. In early 1927, MGM, First National, Paramount, Universal, and Producers Distributing Corporation requested the Motion Picture Producers and Distributors Association, the industry's trade association, to investigate the competing sound systems. In May 1928, the major firms signed with Western Electric's subsidiary ERPI and the industry faced a wholesale conversion of its equipment and production procedures.[2]

With the shift to a new technology came adjustments in film style. This chapter first examines how the technology was standardized through the efforts of Hollywood's institutions. Once we understand this process we can consider the logic of image/sound relations that adjusted sound to classical norms. Finally, the chapter considers how certain stylistic devices, such as editing schemata and camera movement, changed with the introduction of sound.

Technical agencies and the standardization of sound

The 1928 Mazda tests may be regarded as a trial run for the technological standardization required by sound. Indeed, in 1929, the Academy claimed that research into sound was modeled upon research into incandescent illumination. The situation was simply more intensified. Sound firmly initiated a pattern of industry-wide expansion and cooperation. In the silent era, most technological matters had been left to the cameraman, the laboratory, the studio machine shop, and a few key manufacturers. With sound film production, however, studios had to acquire expensive and sophisticated equipment. In the silent days, the cinematographer had often supplied his own camera; now a studio required a department and a staff to maintain its cameras. Editing changed from a scissors, glue, and rewinds operation to one requiring more elaborate equipment (gang sprockets, machines to number sound frames, the sound Moviola). More importantly, film companies began to rely more heavily on trained engineers, draftsmen, and machinists. In the silent era, such men had worked primarily for manufacturers; now a studio might well employ a staff of these experts.[3]

Furthermore, producers became dependent upon manufacturers and professional associations to an unprecedented degree.

To solve some small-scale problems, producers could call on their own 'research' departments. Most studios had machine shops for solving day-to-day practical problems, but the introduction of sound created larger research facilities in some studios. At Paramount, for instance, Farciot Edouart took the lead in studying and improving various rear-projection systems. At MGM, John Arnold and Douglas Shearer, heads of camera and sound departments respectively, created a tradition of in-house research. In these studios, when a researcher arrived at a design, the studio shop would built a prototype. If that showed promise, a manufacturer would be requested to produce the equipment for the studio's use or for wider marketing. Articles in the professional journals and demonstrations at SMPE, ASC, and Academy meetings could serve to publicize the device. For example, in 1929, Shearer assigned his staff to build a flexible microphone boom. The MGM shop built a prototype, then asked Mole-Richardson to produce several. By the next year, the Mole-Richardson Boom was enthusiastically promoted and came into use in the major studios.[4]

Such demands on outside firms caused a great expansion in the technical service sector between 1928 and 1930. Kodak established the Eastman Service Building on Santa Monica Boulevard in 1929; the facility was equipped with a lounge, a reference library, a test laboratory, and a private theater, all at the disposal of cinematographers. Later in the same year, Du Pont furnished its Hollywood building with a 'baby set' that would enable cinematographers to make tests. Mole-Richardson, prospering with the general adoption of incandescent lighting, moved to expanded quarters in 1928, built an addition a year later, and by June of 1930 employed fifty-seven engineers, technicians, and clerical personnel. In 1929, the Mitchell Camera Company opened a new, bigger factory. By the end of 1930, Eastman had completed an up-to-date film processing plant in Hollywood. Outside Los Angeles, manufacturers were no less responsive. In 1929, Bell Telephone built a New York research laboratory devoted entirely to solving problems of sound film.[5] At the same time, in Chicago, Bell & Howell completed its large Rockwell Engineering

Laboratory, declaring that the four hundred engineers in this facility would devote themselves to innovations and standardization in motion pictures and that the laboratory was at the disposal of the industry: 'Assignments on any phase of new picture developments are invited.'[6]

The growth of manufacturers still did not empower them to solve the film industry's problems of development and standardization. It was the Academy that took over the function of coordinating the service companies and the professional organizations with the production sector. Representing the studios, the Academy defined the industry's needs and goals. As early as September of 1928, the Academy's *Bulletin* claimed that 'The Academy with its five creative branches is obviously the only central clearing house for this essential process of self-education on sound synchronization.'[7] Between May and October of 1928, the branch units held thirteen major meetings on problems of sound film. At a higher level, the Academy went beyond simply sharing information. It took the initiative in articulating and solving technical problems by creating the Producers-Technicians Committee out of Ball's Academy Technical Bureau. Chaired by Irving Thalberg of MGM, this crucial committee consisted of producers drawn from the major studios and of representatives of such organizations as Technicolor, ERPI, RCA, and the SMPE. From 1929 to 1931, the committee conducted a series of recording courses which established a common set of sound procedures along what Frank Woods called 'non-competitive lines.' By May of 1930, 900 studio employees had finished the course.[8] The Producers-Technicians Committee took another step toward uniformity by isolating the three most pressing problems of the transitional period – silencing the arc lamp, silencing the camera, and constructing soundproof set material. A series of subcommittees, always including engineers from ERPI or RCA, adopted an inquiry method modeled on that of the Mazda tests: surveys of studio practice, tests under controlled conditions, consultations with firms, and publication of results. The Academy disseminated the Committee's recommendations to the production companies, the professional associations, and the manufacturers.[9]

Once the Academy had defined critical production or exhibition problems, it could work with the manufacturers and the professional groups to solve them. Consider the problem of silencing the arc lamp. Although incandescent lighting had been proven superior for panchromatic film, the early Mazda bulbs lacked both the carrying power and the sharp shadows yielded by arcs; many cinematographers preferred the arcs' photographic quality. In great numbers, Mazdas were also very hot. Moreover, if the studios abandoned the arc, they would be throwing money away. A representative of the National Carbon Company pointed out that in 1928 the studios owned between two and three million dollars' worth of arc lamp equipment, and it would be a severe loss to discard it all. Yet arc lamps gave off a high-pitched whistle that microphones picked up. In spring of 1930, the Producers-Technicians Committee investigated how various studios silenced arc equipment. The committee found that Fox's chief engineer had devised a choke coil to filter the commutator ripple of the arcs. The committee concluded that the choke coil was the best solution.[10] Other studios did not hasten to return to arc lighting (chiefly because Eastman Kodak quickly introduced its Type II panchromatic film, balanced specifically for incandescent light), but research by the National Carbon Company continued in the 1930s, and the results were disseminated through the technical journals. This work proved essential when Technicolor demanded quiet arc lamps in the middle 1930s.

Aided by the SMPE's engineering efforts, the Academy established links to key manufacturers during the transition to sound. The Academy tacitly strengthened major suppliers by inviting representatives of Western Electric, Movietone, and other firms to conduct demonstrations at branch meetings. The Academy's power over equipment standardization is well-illustrated by the work done on camera silencing devices. Given the demands of the classical style, camera noise became a vexing problem: just as the viewer should not glimpse the camera's reflection in a mirror, he or she should not hear the camera's whir. Once the problem of silencing the camera was defined, the Producers-Technicians Committee narrowed the range of acceptable solutions. The subcommittee, consisting of the vice-president of ERPI and an engineer from RCA, surveyed the various booths, bungalows, and

blimps used in the studios to muffle camera noise. Manufacturers cooperated: Mitchell furnished data on camera maintenance and ERPI donated access to its laboratory. In 1930, the committee proposed an ideal, standardized blimp, which a Pathé engineer promptly built; the design won an Academy Award. At the same time, Mole-Richardson used the academy's recommended specifications to design tripods which would support the new blimp. But the blimps were still too heavy to be efficient on the set. After surveying sixty cinematographers, the Producers-Technicians Committee learned that most wanted the camera body and mechanisms to be silenced, and so the committee resolved to consult with the manufacturers.[11] When the Research Council superseded the committee, it took camera silencing as a major goal and decided to help in several ways:[12]

> To coordinate the ideas of individual experimenters, assist the manufacturers and provide facilities in the studios for further development work if necessary. To draw up specifications for the guidance of manufacturers. . . . To supervise tests of any new cameras and associated equipment.

With this support, Bell & Howell, Mitchell, and the Fox studios worked throughout the 1930s to create silent-running cameras.[13]

Throughout the decade, the academy continued to monitor sound innovations. The presence of RCA and ERPI representatives on the Producers-Technicians Committee was essential, for these were the outside firms best equipped to undertake far-reaching innovations in sound recording and reproduction. It is important to recall that such firms and not the film industry created sound-on-film in the first place; as Gomery has shown, it was Western Electric who approached Warner Bros and the private research laboratory of Case-Sponable who approached Fox. The most basic equipment – microphones, recorders, speakers, and synchronous motors – had all been developed outside the film industry, in radio, phonography, and telephony. Once the studios and the professional organizations had laid out the direction of inquiry, the gigantic research capabilities of ERPI and RCA were turned to the solving of particular problems. Between 1932 and 1935, the two firms created directional microphones, increased the frequency range of film recording, reduced ground noise (resulting from the particle size of the recording medium − optical film − and from residual noise from amplification systems) and extended the volume range with 'push-pull' sound tracks. Such developments impelled the Academy Research Council to sponsor an updated series of sound-recording courses for studio workers in 1936. The basic course was conducted by an ERPI engineer, and over two hundred technicians attended. A year later, under the aegis of the Academy, the major studios adopted a uniform recording characteristic to insure comparable reproduction. The later part of the decade saw even more important improvements: RCA's ultraviolet recording system (1936) which increased frequency response, its 'high-range' process for greater volume range (1937), the achievement of multiple-channel recording (1938), and the adoption of fine-grain film for better variable-density recording (1939). While the Academy neither financed nor innovated such improvement, in its role as a clearing house it made the industry's needs known and helped spread and organize a uniform usage of the innovations. Once a certain standardization in recording was accomplished, the Academy turned its attention to standardizing reproduction through a series of recommendations concerning theater sound.[14]

Style: the image-sound analogy

What was stabilized by all these efforts? What purposes governed the adjustments, modifications, and revisions of technology? Sound cinema was not a radical alternative to silent filmmaking; sound as sound, as a material and as a set of technical procedures, was inserted into the already-constituted system of the classical Hollywood style. This meant that sound technique was on the whole brought into conformity with silent filmmaking norms. Throughout the practices and discourses of the technical agencies from 1927 to 1932, one finds a highly coherent set of analogies between image and sound, between the visual and the auditory construction of narrative space and time. In these analogies, the recording of speech is modeled upon the way

cinematography records visible material, and the treatment of music and sound effects is modeled upon the editing and laboratory work applied to the visual track.

In the technical discourse of Hollywood during the 1930s, the link between sound recording and cinematography rests upon a biological analogy. Combined, camera and microphone resemble a limited but lifelike human body. 'The technic of acoustic control,' claimed the most influential article on sound recording, 'is based on letting the camera be the eye and the microphone the ear of an imaginary person viewing the scene.'[15] From this analogy there extend many parallels. Just as cinematography is monocular, sound recording must work with only one 'ear.' Technical adjustments must compensate for this: the cinematographer must work to create an impression of visual depth and the sound recordist must create 'sound perspective.'[16] To the cinematographer's control of space through lighting and composition corresponds the recordist's control of volume and reverberation:[17]

> The resulting flatness or 'depth' in recorded sound is comparable to the lack of perspective in a photographed picture. . . . These handicaps can be overcome to a certain degree by careful attention to the acoustic conditions existing within the set in sound recording, and by skilful lighting of the actors and their backgrounds in photography.

Sets must be designed not only to provide convincing visual depth but also to evoke auditory space. Just as manipulation of focus and framing eliminates unwanted background detail, techniques for reducing ground noise create a 'foreground' vocal space: 'Because of the background of silence, the player's voice is more lifelike than ever.'[18] One sound engineer compared sound recording to lighting by defining 'high key' sound (for comedies), 'low key' sound (for drama) and 'contrasted' sound (for melodrama).[19] And while the cinematographer had his filters and diffusion lenses to govern the transmission of visual information, by 1931 the recordist had his wind gags, microphone baffles, and electric filters to compensate for boomy sets or to distort speech deliberately (as for telephone conversations).[20]

Furthermore, the vocal track must be as mobile as the visual track. For every cut from point to point there must be an auditory shift as well. 'I can give you a closeup of a sound, just as I can give you a closeup of a person.'[21] In the late 1920s, there was a considerable controversy about whether it was more 'natural' for a close-up's volume to be louder than the volume for a long shot, but by the early 1930s, it was evident that volume should be in rough proportion to shot scale. This would maintain what William deMille called 'the proper illusion of distance.'[22] It is not only cutting that raises this issue. How is the single ear of the imaginary observer to accompany its single eye during camera movement? The earliest microphones were stationary because they had their own amplifiers attached, and the slightest noise of movement would be picked up. To follow sound it was necessary to rig several mikes and fade one up and one down as the actor moved. Technicians worked to create mobile mikes, and in 1930, Mole-Richardson manufactured its microphone boom. Later in the decade MGM and Mole-Richardson equipped the boom with a telescoping arm and rebuilt it of aluminium. While the French director Jean Epstein was calling for a drastic disparity of microphone and camera positions, for an independent path for the microphone and a formal play with sound distance, the Hollywood aesthetic stressed a harmony of the moving camera and the moving microphone. The mike boom was analogous to the camera dolly or crane.[23] Like a camera carriage, the boom made it possible to record continuous movement: 'The microphone-boom operator on the set must "follow" as skilfully as any Operative Cinematographer or Akeley-camera specialist.'[24] And, like a camera carriage, the boom could shift recording positions quickly and save production time.

In Hollywood's conception of the monocular, monaural 'invisible observer,' sound was considered to consist essentially of the human voice. Until the late 1930s, the post-dubbing of voices gave poor fidelity, so most dialogue was recorded direct.[25] More importantly, in sound cinema the voice became as central to the sound track as the human figure was to the image track. Like bodily build and facial expression, the voice individuates, it characterizes, it marks traits for narrative development, it gives access to

psychological-causal factors. Of course cinematic speech need not function in these ways, as we can tell from the disembodied, anonymous voices that crisscross films like Jean-Luc Godard's *Le gai savoir*, Marguerite Duras's *India Song* (1975), or Dziga Vertov's *Enthusiasm* (1931). But in Hollywood, dialogue constitutes the chief vehicle of narrative action and must be personalized no less than body, face, and space.

The centrality of speech became a guideline for innovations in sound recording. Directional microphones cut down reverberation from sets and reduced noise from the camera, allowing the dialogue to stand out more intelligibly. Increasing the fidelity of recording through extended volume and frequency range heightened the dramatic possibilities of vocal timbre, pitch, and loudness. Ultraviolet recording sought to eliminate the 'fuzzy high notes' and sibilants: 'Women's voices will be especially benefited.'[26] The primary energy was thus invested in staging the visual spectacle – the human figures in surroundings – and coordinating that with a staging of the characters' voices. Body and voice, the *person*: that is what one records, on image and on sound, for use in narrative.

In particular, many of the 1930s sound improvements aimed at a clearer articulation of the voice in relation to music. This was important not only in the musical film but also in dramas, since in the late 1930s the 'symphonic' score was becoming prominent. RCA's 'high-range' process created at least a 6-decibel difference between voice and music. Multiple-channel recording developed from a similar need to guarantee the primacy of the voice. Throughout most of the 1930s, musical numbers were recorded on two tracks – singing on one, accompaniment on the other – which would be balanced at the dubbing stage. For *One Hundred Men and a Girl* (1937), RCA engineers made it possible to record the orchestra on seven tracks and the singer on one, all to be mixed later.[27] Such innovations were governed by the assumption that music must support the expressive human voice, the sonic equivalent of the face.

Since the voice is compared to the visual field that the camera records, sound effects and music become important at later stages of production. What editing and optical effects are to shooting, sound editing and dubbing become to sound recording. Editing and laboratory effects work over the visual track, selecting and assembling shots, tightening transitions, blending scenes by dissolves or wipes, creating montage sequences. Similarly, sound editing and dubbing rework the auditory track. The victory of Movietone's optical sound system over Warner's disk system was at least partly due to the fact that putting optical sound on film enabled it to be cut as freely as the visual track. In 1930, Moviola produced the first of many sound models, and by the same year various sound takes were being cut together to assemble the best tracks. The 'bloop' or sound splice allowed unwanted sounds to be painted out of the track as easily as an unwanted frame could be snipped. Edge numbering, already provided by the film manufacturer on the raw stock, was introduced for the sound track as well, thus permitting perfect synchronization. By 1932, the average film was said to be about 50 per cent re-recorded, and in the same year another editor reported that all sound effects were put in the film after the picture track had been cut. Re-recording sound effects was also compared to process photography: the sound 'background' of a restaurant crowd or a traffic-filled street was like the back-projection added to give realism and to save money. The analogies generated corresponding terminology regarding auditory 'fades' and 'dissolves.'[28]

The clearest example of the assimilation of sound to classical norms has always been music. The chief difference between silent and sound film composing was quantitative, in that less music was needed for the dialogue film. This limited the formal inventiveness of the composer. The music could enter only in short passages, bits and pieces to tie together a montage sequence, connect scenes, or underscore an action or line of dialogue. Hence the chief formal device of film composing continued to be the leitmotif, the tag that identified characters or situations. 'Every character should have a theme,' Max Steiner declared. 'Music aids audiences in keeping characters straight in their minds.'[29] Erich Wolfgang Korngold boasted that *Anthony Adverse* (1936) had a theme for 'each major character, mood, or idea.'[30] As we have seen in Chapter 3, this practice was already a Hollywood convention in the silent era. Other parts of the film would call for specially composed passages, all pleonastic:

fanfares or songs for the opening credits, crescendos for suspense, marches for military scenes, and so on. Although it became more fragmentary, film music in the sound era still functioned as a factor in narrational continuity. Coming at the last phase of production, music became the glue that joins scenes, the polish that brightens a point, or what Bernard Herrmann called 'a kind of binding veneer that holds a film together.'[31]

The technical agencies, then, sought to map onto the sound cinema the classical norms governing the visual track – norms going back into the silent cinema. Yet the image/sound analogy was only a partial one. To some degree, sound actually changed the visual style of Hollywood films.

Let us take a particular pair of examples: Ernst Lubitsch's *The Marriage Circle* (Warners, 1924) and his remake, *One Hour With You* (Paramount, 1932). Granting important differences of narrative, several of the scenes are enough alike to point up the range of stylistic alternatives. One scene in both films shows an errant husband being seduced by his wife's best friend. At the same time, his unsuspecting wife and his best friend roam through the garden looking for them. The fundamental similarities are apparent: psychological causality, parallel situations, motivic construction (a pesky scarf in one version, a tie in the second), spatial coherence (the garden as a consistent locale, obedience to the 180° rule), and temporal unity (simultaneous action rendered through crosscutting). One can even argue that the expository inter-titles in *The Marriage Circle* find their functional equivalent in the spoken and sung address to the audience in *One Hour With You*. Still, several small-scale differences are instructive.

For one thing, of course, the performances in the sound version are less mobile; in using voices to signal the characters' feelings, the later film plays down facial expression and bodily movement. Moreover, although both scenes run almost exactly the same length, the silent version has several more shots (forty-one as opposed to twenty-five; only three of the forty-one are titles). This means that the silent version's shots run about seven seconds each, while the sound version's average shot length is almost eleven seconds. Conversely, *One Hour With You* makes more use of camera movement. There are many reframings, while *The Marriage Circle* has none. There is also much more panning and tracking in the sound version, especially independently of figure movement. Finally, the later film's photography has a softer, lower-contrast quality; *The Marriage Circle* defines figures, planes, and volumes with comparative crispness.

These parallel sequences are emblematic of the relation of Hollywood's silent style to its sound style: differences of stylistic devices (voice, shot length, cutting rhythm, camera mobility) but fundamental similarity of the systems (coherence of causality, space, and time). The transition from silence to sound was a matter of finding functional equivalents: new techniques appeared, but they served constant formal purposes. One technique might wholly replace a prior one; with the introduction of sound, dialogue inter-titles left the classical paradigm. Or a device might simply become the preferred paradigmatic alternative, as when reframing replaced quick cutting as a means of keeping moving figures centered. More complexly, vocal expressivity might reinforce facial and bodily expressivity or it might become the chief transmitter of story information, making visual cues secondary. Some stylistic devices of the early sound cinema, such as over-the-shoulder shot/reverse-shot cutting and a moderately soft photographic style, were already present in the late silent period (see Chapter 21). And we have already seen how the classical paradigm's principles continued to dominate sound cinema, through the work of the technical organizations in promulgating the image/sound analogy. What needs explaining is how new stylistic devices came to supplant or supplement old ones. The films of the transitional years 1928-31 show how fresh devices became functional within the canonized systems and how they occasionally managed to extend those systems in new directions.

1928-31: multiple-camera shooting

There are some significant misconceptions about early talkies. Consider this typical description: 'The camera stood still while the players mouthed their lines. Cuts were rare.'[32] Or this, of *Lights of New York* (1928): 'The story stood still to record

scenes of seemingly endless dialogue. The director cut sparingly, if at all.'[33] But such descriptions are inaccurate. For one thing, cutting is plentiful in these early talkies, with many shots per scene (an average of thirty in *Lights of New York*). Furthermore, the camera itself is not at all still. It may track in or out, and it frequently pans to follow character movement and reframes to center characters, indeed much more so than in the silent cinema.

It is true that with the coming of sound, cutting did decrease somewhat. Between 1917 and 1927, the average shot ran between five and six seconds; between 1928 and 1934, the length was closer to eleven seconds. It is obvious that the shot lengthened to accommodate the speaking of lines. (Lest this be taken as 'natural,' we should remember that the continuity of speech need not be respected in the way that Hollywood does. In Marcel Hanoun's *L'Authentique Procès de Carl-Emmanuel Jung* (1966), one medium-length sentence is fractured into eight separate shots.) But in neither period can the average shot lengths be explained by technical constraints. In the silent era, arc lamps began to flicker after a few minutes and rack-and-tank developing set a limit of 200 feet on any one shot, yet there is no technological reason why every shot was not one to two minutes long. When sound was introduced, incandescent lamps could be operated longer than arcs, camera reels became standardized at 1,000 feet, and machine processing could accommodate 1,000-foot lengths of film.[34] Yet the shots in the transitional films of 1928-31 are still comparatively short. In an era when every shot could have run ten minutes, the paradigmatic range of shot lengths almost never exceeded twenty seconds; most commonly, a film's average shot length would lie between eight and fourteen seconds. Even the most talky and self-conscious example, the infamous *Lights of New York* (1928), has an average shot length of only nine seconds. What is remarkable about the transitional films is not how long the takes are but how relatively short they are; although the technology permitted a shot to be drastically prolonged, Hollywood remained a cinema of cutting.

It is evident that the classical model continued to dominate filmmakers' stylistic decisions. Part Three has shown that by 1920, Hollywood had bound cinematic storytelling closely to cutting.

There was an insistence upon many shots, both to analyze a scene's action and to intercut one scene with others. In Chapter 6, we found that the post-1917 silent film would contain between 500 and 800 shots per hour. There were economic and stylistic rationales for this heavily edited decoupage: a conception of the realistic quality film militated against the long take (which was more susceptible to error); editing permitted personnel to adjust the product in final stages of production; continuity cutting was seen as the chief narrational means for manipulating space and time. Given the centrality of editing within the classical paradigm, the coming of sound represented a threat. For both economic and stylistic reasons, the option of editing had to be preserved. The task became that of inserting sound into the already existing model of filmmaking. The immediate result was the standardization of multiple-camera filming.

Multiple-camera shooting, which was the dominant studio practice from 1929 to 1931, shows how hard American filmmakers worked to maintain the classical model of film style (see figs 23.1 and 23.2). For, after all, why not simply film with only one camera? Why set up the action to be filmed by two to nine cameras simultaneously? The difficulties were formidable. Microphones had to be concealed, scenes had to be lit for several angles, and most film shot was wasted. What made all this trouble worthwhile was the option of cutting, especially cutting to a variety of angles. Silent filmmaking had developed the power of the narration to penetrate the dramatic space, to analyze it from many angles. The psychological development of the drama depended upon fluid shifts from long shots to angle and reverse-angle positions, to inserts, and to close-ups. Wesley Miller pointed out in 1931 that the silent film's ability 'to cut from place to place, to recognize no limits of time or space, had made it possible to play upon the imagination of the audience to the point where they were almost in the scenes depicted before them on the screen.'[35] This fluidity had to be restored.

Multiple-camera shooting was not a new idea. In silent films, scenes of spectacle (such as the chariot race in *Ben-Hur*) or scenes with un-repeatable actions (stunts, fires, crashes, explosions) would be filmed by several cameras from different angles. It was not, however, until

the Vitaphone shorts that multiple-camera filming proved a necessity. Because the sound was recorded on disks, the action could not be interrupted for a change of camera position, and post-synchronization was not yet developed. To avoid the 'unfilmic' stasis of a single six-minute take, Vitaphone filmmakers shot with batteries of cameras.[36] In *The Light Cavalry Overture* (c. 1927), for example, the orchestra performance is filmed by three cameras. Even the Vitaphone shorts with individual soloists use at least two cameras, yielding a full-figure framing and a *plan américain*.

It is thus no surprise that the earliest talkies have a repetitive, even routine, method of cutting up the narrative space. A sequence from *Lights of New York* (1928) offers a prototype. Establishing shot: a 35mm lens films the action from more or less straight on as the thugs wait in the Hawk's office (fig 23.3). During the conversation, we cut to medium-long shots from a camera filming from straight on or from a side angle (figs 23.4 through 23.10). The enlargement of scale in these shots comes from the use of long focal-length lenses, not from a physically closer camera location. The variety of camera positions (six cameras at two general angles on the action) makes an effort to recapture the spatial omnipresence characteristic of silent film narration.

This scene shows how multiple-camera shooting struck a compromise between the technical necessity of sound and the filmmaking style of the silent era. At bottom, the sequence is perfectly classical: cutting analyzes the space; the semi-circular arrangement of the booths guarantees obedience to the 180° rule; matches on action are facilitated. But there is also a loss. In the *Lights* sequence, the framing is seldom closer than medium shot. There are no high or low angles. Most importantly, now that shifts of shot scale are effected through drastic changes in lens lengths, perspective jumps from shot to shot. For example, cutting from figure 23.3 to figure 23.4 yields a move from a fairly short focal-length lens to a very long one (probably 150-200mm). The sudden flattening of space produced by the longer lenses (figs 23.7 and 23.9) is quite disconcerting. Yet if the cut-in is less drastic, we can wind up with odd lateral cuts, resulting from two cameras placed side by side and using lenses of the same focal length (see figs 23.11 and 23.12, from *Down-

stairs, 1932). Thus multiple-camera shooting does not completely recover the sense of penetrating the scene's space that changing camera positions and more moderate lens lengths supplied in the silent cinema. One need only compare the shots from *The Show* (1927, figs 23.13 through 23.14) to see how a late silent film deploys a greater frontality of figures and variety of angles, and a volumetric shot/reverse-shot space that enables the audience, as Miller put it, to feel that 'they are almost in the scenes depicted before them on the screen.'

The years 1929-31 saw consistent attempts to overcome the monotony of a sequence such as the *Lights of New York* example. Scenes in *On With the Show!* (1929), *Glorifying the American Girl* (1929), and *Applause* (1929) use more high and low angles than does *Lights*. Other films place the camera booths at more oblique angles to a conversation, so that a dialogue scene will contain over-the-shoulder shots. A film like *Moby Dick* exemplifies how by 1930 the director could put the multiple cameras at extreme high and low angles and create a variety of shot/reverse-shot patterns. The scene of Ahab's brother and his wife (figs 23.15 and 23.16) is a good instance of how strongly the developed multiple-camera style resembled that of later sound films. Hollywood made no attempt to explore systematically the possibilities of multiple-camera filming for spatial disorientation and discontinuity cutting; not until Akira Kurosawa's films (e.g., *Record of a Living Being* [1955], *High and Low* [1963]) does an alternative aesthetic of multiple-camera filming emerge. Hollywood was content to try to recover the conventional patterns of the silent film.

Multiple-camera shooting presented Hollywood's technical agencies with two tasks. First, to insure continued production, multiple-camera filming had to be made as efficient as possible. *JSMPE*, *American Cinematographer*, and other journals disseminated information on how to stage and shoot in this fashion.[37] Secondly, filmmakers were aware that multiple-camera shooting was only a short-term compromise. The task was to return to the practices of silent production as much as possible: the action broken into bits, to be staged and shot in controllable segments; a single camera which could be shifted easily to make one shot after another; the ability to control timing and meaning during the editing stage.

Engineers and researchers thus turned to several problems. The camera had to be liberated from its soundproof booth, which meant designing blimps and casings for the camera body. As we have seen, the Academy Research Council spurred manufacturers to design quieter cameras and camera containers. The camera also had to rest on a different kind of support. Wooden tripods transmitted camera noise to the legs and floor, creating vibrations picked up by microphones. Moreover, the blimp had increased the weight of the camera considerably. In the silent era, the cinematographer could quickly shift his camera and tripod from spot to spot. But once out of the booth, the sound camera could no longer be supported by a tripod and could not be moved so easily. So from 1930 onward, Bell & Howell, Mole-Richardson, Fearless, and other firms introduced a series of rolling camera carriages (see fig 23.17). Dollies, perambulators, 'rotambulators,' and small cranes enabled the crew to set up one shot after another with an ease akin to that of silent film production.[38] By 1933, shooting a sound film came to mean shooting a silent film with sound.

By the end of 1931, the efforts of the technical agencies had succeeded, and the period of multiple-camera filming ended. As a transitional form, it preserved the classical decoupage until a new technology could be brought into conformity with the style and the work habits of the silent era. But multiple-camera filming also *extended* the range of the classical style.

Talking pictures created a concrete and inflexible tempo for the Hollywood film. Duration in a silent picture, even one accompanied by music, has a more abstract quality: crosscutting, inter-titles, ellipses, and even the varying rates of shooting and projection create a malleable, plastic duration. What one writer called 'the actual time-elapsed speed' of the talkie was more fixed, rooted in the pace of recorded speech.[39] In 1929, the discrepancy between silent tempo and sound was highly visible; Harold Franklin hoped that 'The abrupt change of tempo when the dialogue stops and the action resumes will somehow be blended into a smooth-running continuity.'[40] The operative term is, of course, continuity. Given that sentences and speeches must be tied to a coherent diegetic world, how can one preserve an even flow of sound and image? The transitional period found several solutions: shorter and more plentiful scenes, the montage sequence, and what one observer called 'an almost constantly moving camera.'[41]

Considering their reputations for visual blandness, the 1928-31 talkies have a surprising amount of camera movement. Tracking shots follow characters, travel down aisles or corridors, or begin on a detail and glide back to a full view. There seems to have been a fad for starting a film with a striking camera movement before settling down to a pithier shooting style (see, for instance, *Sunny Side Up* [1929] and *Street Scene* [1931]). Such camera movements did not spring suddenly into existence; as Chapters 7 and 17 indicate, the German cinema's mobile camerawork influenced Hollywood during the late silent era. Even reframings — the dominant type of camera movement in the sound era — may be seen in many late silent films, such as *For Heaven's Sake* (1926) and *The Michigan Kid* (1928). As with multiple-camera shooting, what was one free choice during the late silent era came to be judged necessary and normal in the early sound period. In this context, the celebrated camera movements in *Applause* (Rouben Mamoulian, 1929) and *Hallelujah!* (King Vidor, 1929) seem not individual innovations but extensions of common practice.

Moreover, we have seen that certain camera movements — lateral pans to follow characters and to reframe compositions — were part and parcel of multiple-camera shooting. The long lenses scanned the space, just as telephoto TV cameras pan back and forth across sports events today. Even after multiple-camera shooting became rare, the lateral pan or track to follow action continued as a dominant stylistic device. A character enters a room and walks to a desk. In a 1925 film, there would be an extreme-long shot of the room as the character enters, then a long shot of the character walking, and then a medium-long shot of the character halting by the desk. But in a 1933 film, the camera would frame the door in a medium-long shot and pan or track as the character walks to the desk. Evidently the practice of scanning the scene from a booth suggested ways that lateral camera movement could solve the problem of continuity and tempo that speech had created.

Once clear signals had been sent from the production end, technical agencies strove to realize the possibilities of camera mobility. The camera carriages of the sound era were created not only to convey the bulky camera between set-ups but also to make moving shots. For instance, the 1930 Mole-Richardson perambulator sought 'to eliminate the difficulties encountered in the ceaseless changing from stationary to travel shots or vice-versa.'[42] Bell & Howell's 1932 'rotambulator' was equipped with a rotating oiled base that made for smooth panning. The 1933 Fearless Camera Dolly was a lighter machine, using hydraulics to achieve smooth elevation. Sometimes units were built solely in order to execute complex moving shots: the Universal crane used for *Broadway* (1929; see fig 23.18), William Cameron Menzies's 'perambulator-elevator' (1930), the Fox camera carriage (1933). The Academy sponsored demonstrations of new dollies and booms. Technical journals announced the newest designs; professional conventions included displays of equipment. Sometimes a studio staff would design a carriage that would then be built in quantity by an outside firm. In 1930 Mole-Richardson modified a rolling tripod developed at MGM, and six years later Fox and Fearless cooperated on a dolly.[43] In sum, Hollywood's technical corps responded to the demand for increased camera mobility.

Although some cinematographers criticized the excesses of early 1930s camera mobility, there was no doubt that camera movement had become a significant instance of virtuosity, a source of spectacle in its own right. One writer pointed out that in *All Quiet on the Western Front*, the use of a crane turned an ordinary scene into:[44]

> an impressive and extraordinary example of the camera-man's art. . . . Such photography, interspersed throughout the more commonplace scenes, does much to determine the success or failure of any motion picture. The problem of keeping the plot moving along and at the same time impressing the beauty and color of the setting upon the spectator is solved in many cases by the camera crane.

As a continuity factor, camera movement appealed to the cinematographer's pride in invisible craftsmanship; as a fleeting display of prowess, camera movement testified to his expertise.

The vogue for flashy camera movements in the early 1930s is thus part of a larger process that includes the re-introduction of reframing. All these camera movements helped the classical style recover control of spatial and, particularly, temporal smoothness. Panning and tracking lent a greater sense of depth to the shot; in this way, the mobile camera compensated somewhat for the flatness produced by the telephoto lenses in multiple-camera filming.[45] Joseph Dubray of Bell & Howell pointed out that although Hollywood learned of camera movement in the silent era, 'The new technic proved invaluable as a means of sustaining the tempo of an action which the spoken word has a tendency to slacken.'[46] By the middle 1930s, writers were praising dolly shots because they aided 'the continuity and smoothness of action of the motion picture story.'[47] We have, then, a good example of different techniques being recognized as functionally equivalent. As we saw in comparing *The Marriage Circle* with *One Hour With You*, the omnipresent point-of-view which cutting had provided during the silent era was replaced to some extent by a ubiquity yielded by camera movement. None the less, the fundamental functions which both techniques fulfilled − narrative continuity, clear definition of space, covert narrational presence, control of rhythm − remained constant.

As a transitional form, multiple-camera shooting also affected production procedures of the 1930s. As Chapter 19 mentioned, multiple-camera shooting created a new production role: the number of camera operators increased, and the 'first cinematographer' became the supervisor. Another consequence was the 'master scene' technique. In the silent period, it was con-ventional to film each action in a separate shot without substantial overlaps of action between shots. Multiple-camera shooting, however, accustomed cinematographers and directors to having one complete record of the action in long shot. Edward DuPar recalled that for the Vitaphone shorts, he operated the 'close-up' camera and often had to change lenses. Every time he did, 'a few frames of the picture would be lost, but as the long shot camera was going all the time, we could always cut back and keep everything in sync.'[48] For later features, the long-shot camera provided an uninterrupted reference point − the so-called master scene or master shot. Although multiple-camera shooting was abandoned, the 'master shot' concept held on. After 1932, it became standard practice to film the entire scene once straight through in long shot. Then key actions would be repeated and shot from closer positions. This procedure obviously allows control in editing: one always has coverage for every action, always has a shot to go back to. (A few directors, such as John Ford, denied producers and editors that coverage by refusing to shoot master shots.[49]) Such calculated overshooting produced a very standardized set of choices at the editing stage.[50]

The differences between silent and sound visual style, then, can be seen as issuing in large part from attempts during the transitional years 1928-31 to retain the power of editing in the classical style. Slightly longer takes, with more camera movement, emerged as functional equivalents for controlling spatial, temporal, and narrative continuity. Technical agencies worked to make these equivalents viable and efficient. It is during this period that basic premises of the classical style were transmitted into the sound cinema.

Part Five The Hollywood mode of production, 1930-60

JANET STAIGER

24

The labor-force, financing and the mode of production

Chapter 19 examined the relationship between production practices and technological change, probably the most significant of the factors in the means of production for this industry. This chapter will look at two other aspects of the mode of production, the labor-force and the ownership and financing of the films. We need to consider the interconnections between these factors and production practices. These interconnections while present from the very start of the American film industry have usually been considered most complex after the vertical integration of the major studios, the conversion to sound, and the unionization of the labor-force. What traditional historians have tended to ignore is that labor-force activities and financing *reinforced* rather than contradicted or changed the production system as it had been constructed. In the case of the labor-force, we will find that union jurisdictional disputes and fights for individual worker recognition reinforced and solidified the subdivision of the work and practices of differentiation.

Ownership involved economic agents which contributed capital to permit the firm to operate. Some historians have argued that the film industry changed when its financing methods shifted from capitalism to advanced capitalism. While it is apparent that advanced capitalism affected the industrial structure, the implications for the mode of production are not so clear.

The labor-force and the mode of production

Like the labor-force in any US industry, film workers wanted a greater share of the earnings through increased wages and salaries and more favorable working conditions. And just as in any other industry, the owners sought to avoid this,

fearing loss of their profits. In the film industry, the labor-force was composed of both management and non-management workers, each presenting different bargaining problems – also the case in most industries. On the one hand, the industry perceived some skilled laborers and 'talent' as contributing desired knowledge, craftsmanship, and special abilities. (Stars, for instance, were seen as having a monopoly on a particular personality.) On the other hand, for work positions in which there was a ready supply of willing and able replacements, the companies had a bargaining advantage. Thus, the differentials between workers' bargaining powers were large, and, as a result, the earliest labor coalitions for collective action to improve wages and conditions arose in the less skilled work areas. The more skilled and desired workers organized into guilds and only later into unions.[1]*

Since the earliest labor difficulties in the teens, a pattern of union and management conflict has occurred. The firms used strike-breakers, and the organizing unions competed among themselves, slowing down the workers' gains. Murray Ross's extensive history of the unionizing of the industry through 1941 traces a classic pattern: workers strike, top management makes countermoves (in the interests of the owners), and the State intervenes either to promote or retard union goals. (The State's interest in harmonious industrial relations during political and economic crises – wars and the depression – contributed to compromises and eventual recognition of the unions by the firms.)[2]

Yet one of the effects of union activities and State intervention was the reinforcement and solidification of the division of labor. In many instances, unions battled less against the owners and more against competing unions for jurisdiction of work functions. These struggles resulted in very distinctly drawn job boundaries. Between 1918 and 1921 three major strikes produced compromises on wages, but the firms retained an open shop. During these and future strikes, members of rival organizing groups not only crossed picket lines, but offered their member-workers at lower rates than the striking group. To solve this internecine warfare the feuding unions drew strict jurisdictional boundaries. In 1925 and 1926, the International Brotherhood of Electrical Workers (IBEW) and the United Brotherhood of Carpenters and Joiners achieved control over general construction, and the International Alliance of Theatrical Stage Employees (IATSE) acquired jurisdiction for the actual processes of shooting films – constructing property and scenery, handling lighting, and creating miniatures. With the internal dispute settled (and IATSE's control of theater projectionists), the film companies collectively recognized five unions in the Studio Basic Agreement of 1926. This union victory set the precedent for future collective contracts.

In subsequent years, squabbles broke out again and again among organizing unions, often when new technology introduced new work functions. B.B. Kahane, vice president of Columbia, rationalized this in 1948 during another strike: 'The issue simply is this: Who does what work, and who pays dues to whom. That is an issue solely between the unions. It is not an issue between the unions and us.' An instance of the necessity to redefine lines (often done amicably despite the management's representation to the contrary) was the introduction of liquid rubber to replace textile padding of actors' bodies. 'In Hollywood, as elsewhere, jurisdiction is frequently determined by the materials used or fabricated.' This particular dispute was avoided when the Motion Picture Costumers were alloted control of body padding and the Make-Up Artists took responsibility for all rubber aids. Such earth-shaking disputes were solved by the segregation of work functions to very specific job positions which, in turn, were allocated to particular unions. When the state and federal governments intervened, particularly after 1932, they also tended to codify whatever work arrangement on which all disputing parties would compromise. As a result, unionizing practices did not contest the production system; they reinforced and furthered

the solidification of the subdivision of the work.[3]

As important as prior accounts of unionization are, they do not stress an important area of labor activities – the fight by *individual* craft workers for recognition and bargaining power. Proper recognition could lead to greater personal power in contract agreements (beyond the minimums established in any union contracts). As pointed out in Chapter 9, the industrial discourse encouraged the individual craft worker to strive to attain the standards of the quality film and to innovate in acceptable ways. The worker seeks public acknowledgment of his or her contribution to the film not merely because of pride, but also because the worker's future bargaining status is at stake. If a worker could gain recognition for either achieving the standard of excellence or innovating successfully, then his or her bargaining power would increase. Two major means of achieving public recognition were credits and awards, and, as a result, these became very important to the worker.

The credit system was an early practice. Apparently at least by 1897 Edison added a title to its films which carried the firm's name and a copyright statement. The practice there was following US legal constructions to retain property rights. (Company titles and trademark decorations became more elaborate, particularly when illegal duplication of prints threatened profits.) In 1911, the industry credited Edison with the innovation of listing the members of the cast on a brief introductory title card. Since Edison advertised its hiring of stage players, this is not a surprising move (and its carry-over from theater programs is evident). Once the firms were exploiting the players' names, the major reason to hold back on this credit practice was the 1,000-foot limit of the one-reel film (and the viewers' patience). In early 1912 Edison added the story writer's name (but not the continuity techni-cian's). The industry argued that this practice encouraged submissions from famous writers and decreased possibilities of plagiarism. Other firms quickly followed suit (see fig 24.1).[4]

Advertising in the US film industry exploited very few labor areas, in part because its product standards emphasized the narrative. For the average consumer, the important labor areas were the stars, writers, and directors – the most obvious creators of that narrative. These workers could use public recognition to boost their 'exchange-value' to the firm, the same way that the firm used that public recognition as an exchange-value to entice the spectator to its products. However, the function of screen credits for most of the other workers was slightly different: the recognition sought was less public than intra-industrial. Credits tied the name of a worker to a film and became a means of achieving status in the industry. As an instance of how important this was to the workers, we can note the elaborate criteria which the writers' guild set up to determine credits for its members. Once it had become common for several individuals to write a film script, overloading the credits with names did not acknowledge the dominant contributors or provide much recognition for anyone. As a result, the 1932 Academy writers' agreement and its 1934 revision tried to provide a solution. All writers on a script would review the cutting continuity and final film and among themselves unanimously decide on one or two names for the credits. (If they failed to make a unanimous decision, credits were left to the studio's discretion.) As the Academy explained:[5]

> The object of reducing the number of writing credits on the screen is to give the screen playwright a better chance for recognition in the industry and by the public. The names of the authors are big assets to books and plays. For many years the names of directors have been built into assets in selling motion pictures. Writers' names can be made equally valuable, but never as long as from three to seven names are used on the screen. . . .
>
> However, the writer has had to rely largely on his screen credits in securing work at other studios.

To acknowledge all the workers, the Academy published a monthly bulletin listing the writers on a film and distributed it to relevant managers in the various firms.

Also symptomatic of this fight for recognition was the Academy's activities to publicize workers' efforts with its annual awards. Achievement awards for the 'best' picture, the 'best' cinematography, special achievement in scientific or technical contributions, and so on not only set up a state-of-the-art standard, but also reinforced the

workers' attempts to achieve recognition in their work categories. In a production system in which a laborer's worth depended on the creation of exchange-value, credits and awards became very important. As such the craftsman-laborer sought to achieve what the industry rewarded, and, consequently, the worker achieved what the industry established as its needs: the quality film with acceptable innovations.

The activities of the labor-force, then, reinforced production practices. As unions compromised over their areas of control, they defined strict divisional lines between work functions and positions. This was necessary to insure workers' job security and to improve salaries and working conditions, and the union job definitions also confirmed the separation of conception from execution in film production. As a result, Hollywood's labor union activities intensified the structure. In addition, the fight for craftsmen-worker recognition perpetuated the practices of standardization and differentiation. Workers used the advertising function of tying a name to a film in hopes of future gain from recognition on the basis of the quality of that film. The work of the Academy and subsequent craft organizations participated in the standardization of the industry, including improving the product within defined parameters.

Advanced capitalism, the mode and the product

Two types of financing and ownership have occurred in the film industry: capitalism and advanced capitalism (also called finance or monopoly capitalism). Advanced capitalism implies the concentration and centralization of capital. It is characterized by a massive vertical and horizontal integration for economy of scale, a shift from identifiable owners to joint-stock firms, and a multinational range in marketing control. The standard analysis is that advanced capitalism in the general economy of the United States began to surge forth around the turn of the century and that it definitely characterized the economy after World War I. Film histories accept this characterization as applicable to the film industry, the shift being dated between 1919 and 1935. (The beginning of advanced capitalism in the film industry is Paramount's movement into total integration with its theater purchases in 1919. I date the end of the shift as 1935 because after 1929 several of the major firms went into receiverships and bankruptcy; as the firms emerged from court control the identifiable ownerships were dissolved into joint-stock ownerships.) Although there is no doubt that advanced capitalism affected the industry's structure and conduct, I am interested in a different question: how does the financing of film production and the shift to advanced capitalism affect the mode of production and the films?

How did financing affect the product? Outside financing of films started when production costs increased. With the multiple-reel film and the star system, the firms expended a much higher outlay per film. Simultaneously, the retention of ownership of the negative by the producer and the extended-run system delayed the return on liabilities for up to a year. While waiting for this return, the studios needed outside capital to finance new productions. By 1917 the companies used three major external financing techniques. The studio might persuade a distribution firm to finance part of the negative costs. In this method, distributors could deposit advance money from exhibitors in banks as collateral for loans to the producers. Thus the distributors acted as finance arrangers (in many respects, as they do today). Or a studio might receive direct financing from loans by private individuals (sometimes loan sharks) or banks and investment firms. Or a studio might issue public stock underwritten by investment firms – a method which spread ownership and helped move the firms into advanced capitalism.[6]

Whatever the method, the grounds for acquiring these external funds were always the difference between being or not being able to make films. In early 1919, Paramount requested a loan of $10,000,000 from Kuhn, Loeb and Company to purchase theaters. As investment bankers, Kuhn, Loeb and Company had been financing public utility and industrial companies, so before deciding about the loan request, it asked an affiliate to investigate Paramount and the industry. While the entire report demonstrated Paramount's dominance in the industry and its sound financial status, the basis for Kuhn, Loeb's positive response was in large part due to the perceived quality of the firm's product.[7] The

method the investigator used to make that judgment is symptomatic of the system of standards this book has been describing:[8]

> In judging the quality of the company's product, the investigating corporation mentioned three main factors, dramatic material, stars, and directors. A large reservoir of dramatic material had been established through arrangements by the corporation with authors and theatrical producers. A comparison of the stars' ages, salaries, and probable future screen life with those of other leading producers showed the corporation to be in the lead. An equally imposing corps of directors was employed.

Choosing these three factors provided an additional economic support for an ideological/signifying practice. With financing, and on that basis potential market strength, determined by the quality of the product, story, stars, and directors were further reinforced as factors necessary to and dominant in product design. The financiers explicitly supported and maintained Hollywood's existent film standards.

In the 1920s, as outside financing increased, film finance firms organized for the sole purpose of extending capital for negative production. These firms and the established banks and investment houses continued to require these quality standards (plus good distribution) as the basis for the use of their capital and banking facilities. A typical early film investment company was the Cinema Finance Corporation formed about 1921 by a group of Los Angeles bankers, Harry Chandler (publisher of the Los Angeles *Times*), Thomas Ince, and several other producers. The company, its secretary explained, furnished financing on three criteria: 'First, a producer's demonstrated ability, both business and artistic, and his absolute integrity. Secondly, a suitable story and cast, and thirdly, a satisfactory releasing arrangement with reputable distributing company.' As for the large established sources of capital, the Bank of Italy and the Bank of America in California, for example, were involved in loaning funds to film firms from about 1912 on. Attilio H. Giannini, vice president of the Bank of Italy, explained that he required a financial statement, a star lead, a solid story, and a known director. Producing firms with contracts to release through distributors that owned their own theaters had a 'distinct advantage' over those that did not, and larger firms developed a line of credit. Beyond that, Giannini said, he would stay out of managing the firm and the product. By 1927 he recognized a flourishing competition to loan money to film companies. Thus, financing by outside capital reinforced not only the industry's adherence to efficient, contemporary business practices but also its product practices of the dominance of the story and the use of stars. Furthermore, in judging a firm, the investors considered the director as a key manager. They looked at his ability to bring in a project on time and to make that film within the norm.[9]

Besides understanding how financing affected the films, we can reformulate some implications of advanced capitalism for the mode. In their analyses of the film industry and financing, earlier film historians have responded to that theory of advanced capitalism most influentially formulated by Rudolf Hilferding's *Das Finanz-kapital* (1910). Hilferding argued a theory of growth. The industrial revolution and business competition at the end of the nineteenth century stimulated the concentration and centralization of capital while an increase in size was useful for economical production and as a barrier to entry. Size became a competitive advantage. Vertical and horizontal integration spread risks and insured stability in long-term production, while formerly competitive firms found collusion more profitable than cut-throat competition. Challenging neo-classical economics, the Marxist Hilferding believed that the concept of competition did not work as a tool for analyzing business strategies once advanced capitalism developed. Prices, for instance, were no longer determined by supply and demand; because of the oligopolistic and monopolistic structures of collusion, firms could *set* prices to reap profits larger than under 'pure competition' markets.[10]

Many scholars (including Ernest Mandel) have expanded Hilferding's analysis. With the growth of external financing and joint-stock corporations, collusion could be direct. Financiers could place representatives on boards of directors and control the industry and the economy through inter-locking directorships. Of particular concern were the 'spheres of influence' of Rockefeller and Morgan.[11]

The problem for film historians was to apply this theory to the film industry and then to production practices. In an early analysis, F.D. Klingender and Stuart Legg listed the growing involvement of financiers in the film industry and went on to argue that the introduction of sound equipment (controlled by the electrical and telephone companies) gave the Morgan and Rockefeller spheres of influence virtual control over the major film companies. This was accomplished indirectly through their control of sound equipment and patents and directly through the number of their key executives on the boards of directors. Klingender and Legg do not theorize any change in production practices, but they do imply an effect on the product. Writing in the middle of the 1930s depression, they claim: 'Whether the movies will regain their former financial success ultimately depends on whether the Morgans and Rockefellers will find it in their interest in the unceasing change of American life to provide the masses with the type of pictures that alone will induce them to flock to their cinemas.'[12] Robert Sklar perceived the absurdity of this analysis: there is 'every indication that Wall Street's interest coincided with that of Hollywood's old hands – to make as much money as possible.' (As a matter of fact, as we have seen, the grounds for financing film production by investment houses explicitly supported the accepted standards of the quality film as well as profit maximization.) Sklar then writes that it is not so important 'who owns the movie companies but who manages them.'[13] Indeed, Klingender and Legg ignore the significance of management hierarchies which place certain types of decisions in various work positions.

In fact, more recent analyses of advanced capitalism suggest revisions in our approach to its effects. According to John Kenneth Galbraith and to Paul M. Sweezy, the first analysis of advanced capitalism was inadequate in part because of its own logic and material history. Galbraith points out that financial spheres such as Rockefeller's and Morgan's realms of interest still provide competition. In the film industry, the historical evidence is that investment groups competed for control of the companies and that ERPI and RCA (the major sound technology firms) both vied for the industry's business.[14]

Sweezy argues against the Hilferding/Mandel

analysis on other grounds: once an industry is oligopolistic, companies shift to internal sources of funds, and banks and investment firms move into a secondary position. After an initial use of finance capital for the transitional move to advanced capitalism, the power of collusion and price setting and the distance between stockholders and managers permit the use of retained earnings and issues of stock shares as sources of funds for growth. So although external capital may be important for a while, the advantages of autonomy from factors external to the firm promote rapid movement away from it. Sweezy's formulation contributes two elements to a revised theory of advanced capitalism. First, he reminds us that the State insures property relations; for instance, the federal and state governments are willing to compromise with workers' demands to promote industrial tranquility (which we noted in the discussion on the film labor-force). Secondly, Sweezy argues that the theory needs to reanalyze the significance of the conception of ownership to the means of production. In the classical Marxist economics of the Hilferding/Mandel analysis, what is significant is who owns the means of production, with the presumption that ownership equals control. That equation, however, is complicated by the joint-stock company. After all, stockholders in advanced capitalism do not direct the capital of the company; managers representing these owners do.[15]

Sweezy, joined by Paul A. Baran in *Monopoly Capital* (1966), suggests a new paradigm, one of the analysis of 'control' of the firm, to replace the 'sphere of influence' theory. The 'control' theory shifts interest from ownership to management – a move to cope with the shift from the owner-run firm in capitalism to the manager-run firm in advanced capitalism. This model creates a necessity to theorize managerial goals as distinct from owner goals.[16] Management's goals may not produce direct profit maximization for the owners; instead, managerial actions may include retention of profits for corporate and personal use.[17] (This theorization provides the background for what Mae D. Huettig and others noticed about the top film management: before payment of dividends, they voted themselves large salaries and bonuses which in several cases caused stockholder suits.[18])

The effects of the structural shift to manager-run firms are several, but two become important for Hollywood's mode of production. The first effect is the managers' concern for the general growth of the firm rather than high dividends. To control long-term planning and stability, the firm must expand, thus insuring steady supplies of raw materials, provisions for capital, and minimization of risks.[19]* In the film industry, growth led not only to the fully integrated firms of the 1920s through the 1940s, but also to the conglomerates of the post-1960s. With growth comes the second effect – diversification and then decentralization. Economists have linked decentralized management structures to complications produced by diversified business functions. As a result, management functions continued increasingly to split between strategic and tactical ones. As Richard Edwards points out, a complex management structure controls the work (and the workers) through an 'institutionalization of hierarchical power.' Furthermore, effective decision-making resides in diverse and multiple levels of the bureaucracy. Thus, not only top- but middle-management may be central to business decisions. Galbraith argues, in addition, that in a highly technological industry this separation may be further enhanced. It becomes difficult to question the judgment of specialists and experts: a 'distinction [must be made] between ratification of a group's decision based on information and actual decision-making.'[20]

This revised theory of advanced capitalism indicates new methods for analyzing the film industry. Furthermore, when we study its implications to Hollywood's mode of production, we find that advanced capitalism confirmed the practices. The work structure and procedures remained as before, and middle-level management retained its prerogatives over the routines of filmmaking. When earnings were inadequate, boards of directors did not rearrange (or question) the work order but replaced the top manager, the head of production. As Bing Crosby observed about the line dividing the front office from the rest of the studio: 'Back of that line everyone has been at Paramount for thirty-four years or more; in front of it they change every six months.'[21] Middle-management, Galbraith's effective decision-makers, continued to operate as before, as did the entire system of structural control.

Pertinent, then, to a study of Hollywood's mode of production is an analysis of who managed the firms – an analysis which considers the stylistic paradigms and economic practices operating as received norms for these managers. What advanced capitalism did do to the mode of production was to intensify the existent mode by reasserting the production hierarchies of management. This reinforced the control of the management structure, particularly the power wielded by the tactical experts whose knowledge of the technology and work process placed product design in their control. Thus, the impact of advanced capitalism confirmed the production practices, maintaining them as the established order. The standard became even more the standard.

Independent production

In discussions of the move to advanced capitalism, one way to argue that the shift affected the mode of production and films in the United States is to show that it shut off the small competitor. In the American film industry, this usually translates into eliminating commercial independent production. Showing that advanced capitalism and financing reinforced the dominant mode of production and group style does not consider their possible effects on optional, subordinate modes and products. So it is important to analyze not only the dominant system but also alternatives in the industrial structure and market, the most important alternative being independent production. We need to consider independent production in the same terms we have been using in considering the dominant system: the relations in its work process, its means of production, the financing of its films, its conception of quality films, and its system of consumption.

What is an independent producer? Used loosely, the term applies to David O. Selznick, Samuel Goldwyn, and Charles Chaplin in United Artists as well as to Monogram, Maya Deren, and Pare Lorentz. Temporarily, I will use the term as it was generally used in Hollywood. An independent production firm was a small company with no corporate relationship to a distribution firm. An independent producer might have a contract with a distributor or participate in a distribution alliance, but it neither owned nor was owned by a distributing company. The term also implied a

small firm: independents produced only a few films per year. Thus, they did not commit themselves to a full-year supply of product to exhibitors.

Independent production in this sense began to appear during the diffusion of multiple-reel films around 1911-14. While several economic conditions led to its existence, three stand out. A single producer-distributor of multiple-reelers had difficulty gearing up production to the level necessary to supply all the films an exhibitor could use during a year (104 for a twice-weekly change). The attempt to reach full supply carried over from the 'service' period of the one-reelers, but it was also necessary for a conversion to a full feature-film exhibition system.[22] In addition, significant at this time was the growth in salaries, share-returns, and box-office power to certain individual workers. Stars and other talents were able to finance their own production companies by accumulating the necessary capital or by attracting investors. One more factor promoting independent production was the strength of optional distribution alliances and states'-rights exchanges which expected to deal with a multitude of sources for their product. First National and other such distribution groups not only bought films from these independents, but they offered to finance productions.

According to one estimate, independents made one-third of the features produced between 1916 and 1918. Price, Waterhouse explained several techniques an independent used to secure distribution: contracting with a larger producer or distributor to manufacture a number of films on order (e.g., the producers at United Artists); producing a film and then selling it; or making a film which the production company then promoted and road-showed itself.[23]

In the early 1920s, there were plenty of outlets for independent films; for the 1925-6 season, states'-rights distributors handled 248 of the 696 releases; First National and United Artists, an additional 60; with an undetermined number within other national distributors' output. As the last section pointed out, financing was available from several sources, with judgments being made on the bases of a producer's demonstrated ability, a suitable story and cast, and satisfactory distribution.[24]

Independent firms often did not own the entire

means of production. One writer in 1922 observed that most producers did not 'own, or even have entire studios for the filming of their pictures.' Understandably, a company producing only a few films a year could not maintain the costs of a physical facility and the large staff necessary by then to make a standard quality feature film. Instead, these firms turned to such facilities as United Studios which could supply not only space and equipment but support personnel as well, organized in the standard departments. In addition to these rental studios, some of the larger companies (such as Universal) also rented space and labor support to independents.[25]

The advanced-capitalism movement of the mid- and late 1920s changed the situation somewhat. As the soon-to-be-majors consolidated and organized their control of first-run exhibition, the independent production company found its access to the top-profit theaters cut off unless it had distribution contracts with the majors or United Artists – although only a very few (e.g., Goldwyn) had the status of sufficiently high-cost production to be in this position. Without the possibility of first-run distribution, financing from outside capital sources became difficult. Another difficulty during this period was the industry's conversion to sound. Since the majors contracted for huge amounts of equipment, sufficient quantities for the independent studios were not available until mid-1929. The depression, of course, added to the problem of securing financing.[26]

By 1931, however, double-feature programming and its need to supply the demand of the second- and subsequent-run houses for 208 films a year (two films for twice-weekly changes) gave independent firms a resurgence. As the *Motion Picture Herald* reported:[27]

Practically all important independent theatres have now equipped with sound; a more substantial response and favorable reaction has been felt from independents' bankers, while the condition of state right exchanges, after a hectic two-year period, now are [sic] beginning to assume a more healthy aspect.

The paper reported the entrance of a number of new companies as well as the reactivation of others. Twenty-two independents planned 192 features, 247 shorts, and 8 serials for the 1931-2 season.

This optimism continued, and within a year the independents formed a protective association, in part to bargain collectively with the labor unions. In 1936, Sidney Kent, then president of Twentieth Century-Fox, estimated that there were, besides the seven majors, twenty-five to thirty active producing firms which each made between three and ten films a year. The 'healthiest,' such as Selznick and Goldwyn, released through United Artists. Some such as Republic, Monogram, and Producers Releasing Corporation eventually integrated into national distribution; others used states'-rights exchanges. Banks and firms such as Consolidated Film Industries (a major independent laboratory) acted as suppliers of capital. Independents continued to rent space and service from studios, with their rental costs balancing the overhead costs of the major companies.[28]

Much independent production, then, was within the mainstream of the American film industry. In most cases, independents followed the director-unit, central producer, or producer-unit system of management (e.g., Chaplin, Monogram, Selznick). Nor was the overall mode of a detailed division of labor ever in question; (the independents hired union workers too). This is of major importance in any analysis of the Hollywood mode versus 'independent production.' Moreover, the type of financing was not at issue (although getting it may have been). Some firms were privately owned; others used finance companies, banks, and public stock issues – all just like the majors. Access to the standard technology was not a problem (except for one brief period). Raw film stock, cameras, lighting equipment, and processing by the same firms that supplied the majors were available to the independents. Usually the standard for the design of the product was not an issue either. Finally, at least into the mid-1920s, access to first-run exhibition was about the same if the firm's production expenditures were comparable to the major companies.

With advanced capitalism, some narrowing of possibilities for independents did occur. Firms with higher costs-per-film, firms with 'talents' and quality design, could still get national distribution in first-run theaters. For other independents, if they adhered to the standard design but were without major first-run exhibition outlets, their returns were limited, and, consequently, their best chance to compete was with the majors' B-product. Here the catch-22 situation operated. They could not get better financing without good distribution, but to get distribution required evidence of a secure financial program and the ingredients for a quality product.

Without a doubt, the majors did cut off first-run exhibition, thus good distribution, and thus prospects of financing. Independents, however, potentially had access to subsequent-run theaters. Moreover, a large number of unaffiliated exhibitors tried during the 1930s and 1940s to compete with the powerful affiliated majors. Had an independent's films been successful in trial cases, it would be reasonable for those interested in profit maximization to support them.

Furthermore, some writers have argued a contradiction within the capitalists' aims which might have encouraged interest in unusual independent projects. The question is to what extent would major firms support films which might advocate (even tacitly) political or social actions that might, on the long-term, harm the capitalist system (e.g., positive representations of communism, criticisms of dominant political policies). Terry Lovell points out that some firms might seek short-term profits despite any longer-range disadvantageous effects. Thus, the capitalist might undermine his or her own goal of profit maximization. As a result, independent projects, despite perhaps rather problematic content, might be financed if they seemed to augur box office success.[29]

Thus, while the majors monopolized first-run exhibition and consequently the higher-priced product, a conduct generally regarded as unfair competition, some independents competed with them, independents had outlets in subsequent-run commercial exhibition, and independents with potentially profitable projects might secure financing. Commercial independent production in the terms we have been analyzing the dominant studio mode of production seems to have organized itself in similar fashion. Its relations in its work processes were that of a hierarchy with divided labor; its means of production were identical; financing came from the same sorts of investors on the same grounds, with some people owning the firm and other workers being employed. Independent production's conception of quality films generally was within the classical paradigm; and its systems of consumption were commercial theatrical exhibition. If, however, we widen our consideration of filmmakers to the likes of Maya Deren or Pare Lorentz, we do face alternatives to Hollywood. Here do arise variations from the commercial mode, and we will consider the issue of alternative modes of film practice in Chapter 31.

As we have seen in previous chapters, the production practices and product design constructed by the American film industry did not change after 1930. The actions of the labor-force strengthened both the subdivision of labor and the economic practices of standardization and differentiation. Likewise, once film firms turned to external sources of capital, those sources accepted the industry's assessment of what constituted a profitable product. With the shift to advanced capitalism, the manager-run company reaffirmed the control of the management structure and hierarchy. Finally, commercial independent production moved with the mainstream of the system.

25

The producer-unit system: management by specialization after 1931

The 'producer-unit' system of production (1931-55)

Good pictures are created, not manufactured.[1]

Motion Picture Herald, 1931

Efficiency experts trained in other industries are usually baffled when they try to fit the making of a movie to their standard rules. The fact is, a movie is essentially a hand-craft operation, a one-of-a-kind custom job – but it must be made on a factory basis, with production-line economics, if we're to hold the price down within reach of most of the people. The job is to do this without losing the picture's individuality.[2]

Dore Schary, Metro-Goldwyn-Mayer producer, 1950

In 1931 the film industry moved away from the central producer management system to a management organization in which a group of men supervised six to eight films per year, usually each producer concentrating on a particular type of film. Like other changes in the mode, this introduced greater specialization, in this case in the upper-management levels.

In fact, over the period of the central producer system, specialization in the producer function was already occurring. Dominating the detailed division of labor from 1914 through the 1920s, the central producer system had provided a single controlling manager over the production of a firm's films. W.C. Harcus described the 1930 typical studio organization for SMPE members: a general manager supervised the production of fifty or so films per year. Under him were the executive manager (in charge of financial and legal affairs and routine studio functions), the production manager (in charge of pre-shooting and post-

shooting work), the studio manager (in charge of various support departments), and a set of supervisors to help plan the films. The prototypical example of the central producer at this time was Irving Thalberg at MGM. Thalberg had gradually organized a set of subordinates, associate supervisors, the number of which by the early 1930s had grown to ten men. Each of these men had an area of specialization: sophisticated stories, animal stories, genre films and 'curios,' Marie Dressler films, sex 'fables,' and sad stories. With a project in mind, Thalberg and the selected associate would assign a writer, a director, and the leads. The associate then took over following the rewrites until a script was ready for Thalberg's revisions. The associate supervisor's decisions about cost estimates, sets, costumes, the rest of the staff, and so on were not final until approved by Thalberg. Despite this subdivision of supervision, a strong central producer was still in charge.[3]

Howard Lewis explains that around 1926 when theater attendance declined some firms believed that the films had become 'stereotyped' and attributed the problem to the fact that one individual had charge of producing thirty to fifty films a year. A proposed solution was a system in which a number of producers would supply product and the firm would merely finance the negatives. Lewis writes that the firm considering this was diverted from the change by the sound and merger movements.[4]

In 1931 when attendance dropped off again, Lewis recounts that another company was said to be considering the change, including a profit-sharing program. The reason for the proposal was the belief that central control by producers and directors 'had a tendency to minimize originality and the transfusion of new ideas.' The use of a profit-sharing incentive would eliminate pressures of creation by time, and the firm would act almost as an independent facility. It would contract individually with talent for a number of films and would allow the filmmakers to work on its premises with no further interference. Eventually, the company rejected its first plan, but late in 1931 the firm did go to another plan. Lewis notes that one of the first firms to make the move was Columbia in October 1931. In November Fox and Paramount also instituted new management systems.

The trade papers reported part of these activities while they were in progress, helping rapidly spread the concept of 'unit production.' In June 1931, the *Motion Picture Herald* wrote that 'a movement is under way . . . to band together a number of the industry's prominent directors for the purpose of carrying out . a plan of unit production. . . . The group would function . . . along the lines of the now defunct Associated Producers. . . .'[5] Subsequent articles attributed the idea to David Selznick. Selznick and Lewis Milestone had in mind an independent production system in which a number of producers would each make one film at a time. Selznick promoted the plan on two grounds − 'cost and quality' − grounds dear to Hollywood. He argued:[6]

Through unit production there is a saving in overhead of between 30 and 40 per cent. The only good reason for factory production in any line of business is to lower cost. Now, the minute you remove the reason for factory production it is no longer useful.

Under the factory system of production you rob the director of his individualism, and this being a creative industry that is harmful to the quality of the product made.

In editorials and columns, the *Motion Picture Herald* praised the plan, with Terry Ramsaye proclaiming that the idea 'tends toward a restoration of some part of the individualism which seems to be an essential factor in creative effort.' The Selznick-Milestone firm was not to test this procedure; Selznick, instead, signed as production head for RKO Radio Pictures within two months.[7]

Meanwhile, other events were affecting the industry; most notably, the depression had started to force economy moves in the studios. One survival tactic was a type of collusion: an across-firm truce limited the budgets for the top films to $200,000, and the companies agreed to halt bidding wars for stars. Another tactic was cutting out expensive or non-productive workers. Three directing teams replaced John Ford at Fox, saving 50 per cent of his salary with the potential of three times the output. MGM fired writers in its story department, and Fox eliminated its reading department. Salaries were cut.[8]

In late October 1931, Columbia announced its installation of 'the unit system of production':[9]

The associate producers are Sam Briskin, Jack Bachman, Ralph Block, and J.K. McGuiness. Harry Cohn, vice president in charge of production, will confer with each producer on details for each film.

The individual producers will follow their films through to completion, and submit them to Cohn for final consultation. The new system is expected to allow greater freedom of action, singleness of purpose, and consequent better results in production.

When, in the next two weeks, Selznick took over RKO Pictures and RKO Pathe, 'that company officially adopted the unit system of production championed by Selznick.' Next came Fox. Winfield Sheehan and Sol Wurtzel would be producers with four associate producers. 'Sheehan estimates that economies in effect at the Fox studios will save about $1,000,000 annually. He believes a saving of about $20,000 on each picture will result under the unit system, totaling $1,000,000 on the 50 features scheduled.' Paramount followed in late November. That firm had been extensively considering 'radical recommendations for elimination of waste.' As constituted, B.P. Schulberg headed seven associate producers.[10]

Although the institution of unit production in the studios had a different format than Selznick initially envisioned, his reasons for proposing it do seem to be the motivations of the films. A central producer could not keep as close a tab on day-to-day operations and costs as could a producer supervising one or two films at a time. In terms of quality, the image of individualism in creativity seems compatible with then-current ideologies. Both of these factors (abetted by industry discourse) resulted in a rather rapid changeover in management organization.

Lewis calls this unit system 'decentralization of production,' possibly following a current business term.[11] Yet the elimination of a central producer who made or approved most of the routine decisions and the creation of a set of fairly autonomous producers cannot be equated with 'decentralization' since the studios retained centralized physical facilities and labor. In other words, no multi-divisional production operation was set up. (The scale of production did not justify such an action.) The producer-unit system may have imitated approved business standards (or responded to discourses about creativity and the independent artist), but the end result is not fairly termed decentralization.

In a sense, the producer-unit system was a revision of the director-unit system but with the producer in charge and a central staff which planned the work process. The producer-unit system also followed the industry's earlier tendency toward type-casting and specialization, since these studio producers were identified with certain categories – which might be as illogically divided as *Fortune*'s 1932 list of MGM's associate producers.

Studios now had one more management structure as an option, and they could employ it when they found it advantageous. A later section of this chapter will survey the structures utilized by the major studios during the 1930s and 1940s. The central producer had gradually gathered a corps of associates; given their experience in filmmaking, the disappearance of the central producer eliminated a higher authority but did little to change their routine activities. This change to a new system fitted into the dominant production practices, as a brief review of the modifications in those practices will show.

Further subdivisions of the work in the 1930s and 1940s

During the 1930s and 1940s, various changes in the work procedures occurred, including the addition of some small steps and the creation of a new department and several management positions. As Chapter 19 noted, when the production system faced new technologies, its solution was adding specialists and new steps in the chain of assembly. The same process is at work here; several of these changes are, in fact, attributable to new technologies, but several are also due to general expansion of the system.

The increased work activities in several departments resulted in further specializations and several new steps in the work order. The most significant of these were in story acquisition, script writing, research, casting, pre-shooting production, cinematography, make-up, and marketing research.

The procedures of finding suitable story material intensified. Studios embarked upon complete coverage of worldwide publishing. East and west coast editorial departments hired up to fifty employees; scouts talked to agents and famous writers, sometimes gaining access to a manuscript or galleys before publication. The reading staff would prepare ten- to seventy-five-page synopses which the editorial staff analyzed and assessed in a one-page summary. Extensive files with cross-checking by 'plot structure, the dramatic possibilities, and the characteristic comic or tragic elements of the story' covered almost everything published. If a studio purchased a 'property,' the other studios kept track of it in case they decided to buy it later. In the early- or mid-1930s, story conferences started, with verbal discussions of the possibilities of the stories before treatments were made.[12]

With dialogue, a new element entered the continuity script, and this disrupted its established format. In addition, the post-sound shooting practice of the master-shot affected the work situation. Each studio adapted the old script format differently. When the Academy initiated its Research Council in 1932, one of the tasks with which the academy charged it was the standardization of script format. The academy summarized its problem and added the directive:[13]

As a result [of the change to talking films] the placement, order, numbering, and display of the various parts [of the continuity script] – dialogue, action, set descriptions, camera instructions, etc. vary widely among the studios and are constantly subject to change. This unnecessarily complicates the work of those who handle the scripts during production.

. . . .

Proposed: To conduct such surveys as may be

necessary to establish the basis for the various present practices. To correlate this information and secure general agreement on a recommended form of script that will be most legible, graphic, and convenient in practical use by actors, directors, writers, executives and the various production departments.

The form that eventually became standard (the master-scene) was a combination of theatrical and pre-sound film scripts, a variant of the continuity synopsis used in the 1920s (see figs 25.1, 25.2).

The research department added tasks. It aided the legal department in avoiding accidental use of real street names, phone numbers, and people's names (which might lead to lawsuits). The studios also added a separate research library for music. That library searched for copyright sources, catalogued music purchased by the firm, and determined authentic versions of older works.[14]

Casting activities remained similar to those before 1931 although the loans of players were common and agents started functioning to some extent as producers. In a loan situation the renting studio paid the player's salary plus an additional 75 per cent to the studio to compensate for the player's unavailability there. Warners loaned Perc Westmore, its head make-up artist, to RKO for *The Hunchback of Notre Dame* for a fee of $10,000. The deals could involve capital exchange rather than outright cash. Jimmy Stewart has said: 'Your studio could trade you around like ball players. I was traded once to Universal for the use of their back lot for three weeks.'[15]

Agents, particularly the firms of Myron Selznick and the William Morris Agency, functioned not only as go-betweens in setting up contracts but also as personal representatives, managing a client's total career. By the late 1930s, with clients working throughout the entertainment fields, some agencies occasionally 'block-booked' their talent. They also 'packaged' shows by providing a complete set of entertainers for a producer (often in radio). These activities started moving the agency from functioning as a support firm into producing activities as well.[16]

An additional step in pre-shooting production was script timing. H.G. Tasker described that work for the Society of Motion Picture Engineers:[17]

A group of now experienced script analysts study the proposed story to determine the playing time of each scene of the production and, from the total, determine how long the picture would run. It is at once shortened to proper release length before filming, thus avoiding the common and expensive procedure of throwing away several reels of completed negative in order to boil the picture down to acceptable length.

What had been common procedure in the one-reel period (to estimate and reduce the narrative to fit release-length restrictions) and in the 1920s (to cut costs wherever possible through careful planning) became in the 1930s, as Tasker put it, 'a neat bit of engineering.'

The introduction of Technicolor added a camera assistant who was expert in the process. The Technicolor Corporation insisted on this, wanting to insure quality color production (but also preventing access to its patented technology). The new Technicolor assistant concentrated on the camera's operation, did daily tests, kept the daily log, and handled the slate and the 'lily,' a color chart for lab control. He also acted as the liaison with the Technicolor laboratories.[18]

The standardization of make-up in the Academy sound tests (see fig 25.3) not only simplified directions to the players but more importantly insured continuity throughout the entire film. By the early 1930s, the studio make-up department had taken over the major players' responsibility for selecting and applying make-up although extras continued to do their own. For a major player, the studio would do an extensive initial make-up session in cooperation with the cinematographer. Once everyone agreed on the facial design of powders, paints, and plastics, a chart – another paper record – would outline the areas and make-up codes for reference and continuity between the days of shooting (see fig 25.4).[19]

Marketing research, likewise, became more complicated. While MGM routinely previewed and then extensively reshot and re-edited, other studios, for more expensive productions, took care to predetermine the effect of a general release. For Paramount's *Night at the Opera*, half a dozen scenarists composed a version which was pre-tested in small towns for six months, after which the story was rewritten on the basis of the audiences' reactions.[20]

In the early 1940s, the studios started using more formal methods of market research. By 1946, eleven studios tested their rough-cut films with George Gallup's Audience Research, Inc. (ARI). By 1949, the *Motion Picture Herald* reported that independent production companies that had pre-tested their title, script, and cast with ARI met much more favorable loan-request responses from bankers. Leo A. Handel who ran his own audience research company, the Motion Picture Research Bureau, believed that with firms finally renting on a film-by-film basis (see Chapter 26), a pre-estimate of a response was more useful: the firms could better determine what rental fee to charge exhibitors. These two reasons for the institutionalization of marketing research was probably joined by a third. With declining audiences after World War II, knowledge about who was going to films became more important.[21]

Technology produced a new department: during the 1930s, as special process work and composite photography increased in complexity and precision (see figs 25.5, 25.6) the work of such experts became recognized as an important subdivision of the labor process. Although work units with the art and cinematography departments specialized in this during the 1920s, some firms now organized separate, unified departments. Interestingly enough, Warner Bros' unit in 1929 had the title 'Special Research Department' and resulted from the merger of the special process departments at Warners and First National when the former bought the latter (fig 25.7). The head, Fred Jackman, had ten subordinates, each had his own speciality. In September 1932 RKO reorganized all of its effects workers into a single department; its head Vernon Walker consulted with the art and photography directors. The company justified the move as increasing economy and efficiency and allowing concentrated effort on 'the highly specialized work.' MGM retained part of its special effects with the art department until 1936 when it separated that section into an individual unit; that department prepared miniatures, process work, and full-sized composites while another department handled matte paintings and optical effects. In addition, several support companies offered special process work.[22]

Apart from small added steps and the creation

of the special effects department, the principal change during the period was the addition of management positions. The production department added a unit head for each film. The new unit manager split the responsibilities for coordinating the film with the assistant director. Generally, the unit manager handled pre-shooting organization and budget control while the assistant director worked as the aid to the director.[23]

Similarly, the art department subdivided the work with a supervising art director assigning a unit art director. This unit art director did the layouts, sketches, and planning and checked back with the supervisor for approval of the work. Part of this trend was due to the increased complexity of the art work. Hans Dreier, art director at Paramount in 1937, pointed out that with color and sound, the staff had to consider special camera filters, set paints, and wall construction for resonance. The studio had to follow insurance requirements and state building laws, particularly for parts of the sets which the players used. As a result, it was customary for sketches and set models to consider lighting, camera placement, and lenses, and the staff would calculate lighting, camera, and microphone movements (fig 25.8). If the film was made in color, a Technicolor advisor supervised the coordination of all the colors of sets, costumes, and props.

Finally, sometime in the mid-1930s, the 'production designer' position appeared for a few films. The production designer − the prototype was William Cameron Menzies − assimilated several work areas: he did art direction but also sketched camera set-ups and might even direct the film. Menzies's control over the look of a film was probably a result of his successes in designing and the introduction of German films and talking pictures in the late 1920s. (For more on Menzies, see Chapter 27.)[24]

This brief summary cannot detail the work of all the 276 professions and trades which, as of the 1940s, contributed to a motion picture.[25] Later modifications were, in effect, extensions of the earlier practices. Only minor changes occurred, and this supports the conclusion that the effects of advanced capitalism were not felt at the middle-management or specialist's level in this technological industry. The firms accommodated increased work and changes in technology by adding specialists and more record-keeping to guide the making and assembling of the quality film. This is not imply that there were no variations within production practices; in fact, each studio organized itself a bit differently from the others.

The studios and their systems of production: 1930s and 1940s

A look at the seven major producing studios will reveal what management systems were in effect. Three implications of these systems deserve special note.

First, whether a central producer or a producer-unit system controlled the work decisions, all of the department organizations followed the standard structures and work practices. Despite the apparent differences among studios' management structures, production practices were overwhelmingly uniform across the industry. Description after description of the department heads, their staffs, and work activities are similar, partly because of the industrial discourse's emphasis upon efficient practices and partly because of the unionization, which reinforced a uniform subdivision and work procedure. Such a general conformity helps explain the stylistic similarities between films made by many different workers in a number of studios.

Secondly, given the standardization of the product, we need to understand smaller deviations, particularly when they contribute to an innovation which becomes standard. Here we are interested in controlled stylistic change. Industrial discourse encouraged innovations, but these have to be seen in the context of the particular work situations. Production practices are part of the conditions for the existence of stylistic practices. Thus, any assignment of creative responsibility for a film must consider what decisions were allocated to what positions and note deviations among studios. It is at the point of management structures that variations in allocation of effective-decision-making occur. Beyond that, the standard procedures take hold. Furthermore, there were small variations in major decision-making not only among studios but within them. Upper-level management seems

to have paid much greater personal attention to the more expensive productions. Certainly the preparations for these extended through more than one production season, compared to the rapid pre-shooting plans of the lower-cost A-product, which might see art direction start only a month or less in advance of shooting. B-product was hardly supervised at all by the first-string managers; most studios considered it the training ground for younger staff.

Thirdly, quality films – as defined by the box office – did not come so much from variation within the management systems but from overall investment in the top laborers, materials, and technology, which is probably why there is variance among studios. Now whether or not we would agree that box office success is a worthwhile criterion for the excellence of a film, it was the case that that was a primary factor for Hollywood (although Hollywood executives continually bemoaned the fact that films considered more prestigious and high-class often failed at the box office). Mae Huettig noted in 1941 that 'it is a fixed belief in Hollywood and throughout the motion picture industry that the quality of firms is generally commensurate with cost.' The ranking of the firms with respect to box-office successes was: United Artists, MGM, Twentieth Century-Fox, Warner Bros, Paramount, RKO, Universal, and Columbia.[26]

Certainly this information will not support much hypothesizing, but it does agree with the general consensus on how well these companies met the industry's standards in quality film-making. Furthermore, the top three firms also ranked in the same order for highest expenditures-per-film. What is of interest to us is that box office success did not come only to studios that allowed one individual much control but also to those which used collective decision-making procedures and much mass production. The three leaders all employed different management systems: United Artists used director-units and producer-units; Twentieth Century-Fox, a central producer; and MGM, a producer-unit. This consideration is important for any discussion of one system versus another. In the following survey, as far as possible, the studios are ranked in descending order of management control.

Twentieth Century-Fox

In 1930 Fox had a central producer system in which the central producer Winfield Sheehan seems to have left many decisions in the directors' realm. Sheehan participated in script and casting selection, knew the financial and production situations for each film, and checked the dailies. The company's production department head Sol Wurtzel assumed Sheehan's responsibilities in his absence, and each production had a unit manager. The director generally decided takes and supervised the final cut, which was checked by Sheehan, Wurtzel, the writer, and others.[27]

In November 1931, Fox shifted to a producer-unit system plan with two producers and four associates. Under this system, by 1933 Sheehan handled about twelve films a year, Wurtzel did the cheaper product, and Jesse L. Lasky, the rest. In 1935 Twentieth Century and Fox merged, bringing in Darryl F. Zanuck and initiating a modified central producer arrangement. Wurtzel was left in charge of a little less than half the product, had his own set of writers, directors, and associate producers, and reported to Zanuck every week. Zanuck supervised the upper half of the output with greater and lesser degrees of dominance. Zanuck made the story purchase choices, controlled story conference decisions, chose the leads, and took the casting director's advice on minor players. But while his control was overt in pre-shooting, he generally left his directors alone on the set. According to his assistant, some directors had freedom to shoot as they saw fit while others were required to follow the script or consult with the producer. Zanuck stepped back in during post-shooting production. While watching rushes, he gave instructions to the editor, dictated comments to the director, and chose takes and their arrangements. John Ford apparently was one of the very few directors usually exempted from this control. Zanuck did retakes for photography as well as acting. Zanuck became an independent producer releasing through Twentieth Century-Fox in 1956; until then, the work process he managed followed a strict central control.[28]

Warner Bros

Warner Bros employed a producer-unit system with relatively rigorous attention to cost-efficiency production. Until 1933 Zanuck was the major

production executive, but when he left, Hal B. Wallis became associate executive in charge of production under Jack Warner, studio head. In 1937, Wallis was using six associate producers, including Bryan Foy (who handled all of the B product). The other producers had specialities: for example, Lou Edelman made 'service' pictures and 'headliners' (films from events reported in the press), while Henry Blanke handled the more prestigious biography films including *The Adventures of Robin Hood, Juarez, The Story of Louis Pasteur*, and *The Life of Emile Zola*. Wallis devoted more of his attention to the company's specials, initiated many of the scripts, and approved all of them.[29]

The studio expected directors to follow the scripts, which in many cases they had little hand in writing. During the early 1930s, the exceptions to this included Jack Warner's son-in-law, Mervyn LeRoy, who after early box office successes did what he wanted with his own budget, had some players under personal contract, and shared in profits. The other exceptions were directors of the highest budget films: consider, for instance, the making of *Juarez* between 1937 and 1939 (fig 25.9). After Jack Warner and Wallis had chosen a Paul Muni biography picture, Blanke and director William Dieterle picked a head writer and three others. The research department started assembling background material; later the vice consul of Mexico acted as a technical advisor; and Wallis, Blanke, Muni, and Dieterle took a six-week tour of Mexico, following the events in Juarez' history. Art director Anton Grot and his assistant did 3,643 set sketches and models, and draughtsmen prepared 7,360 scale blueprints. A wardrobe head organized most of the costumes while the studio's 'style creator' Orry-Kelly designed eighteen gowns for the female lead.[30]

For the programmers and B-films, writers, directors, and other personnel had set working hours and a per-day expected piece-rate production. Retakes after shooting was over were most unusual. Under the supervision of Jack Warner and Wallis, directors participated in cutting unless shooting took them away. Studio composers received the film after the final cut. Warners also invested heavily in capital assets, such as its special process and sound equipment (fig 25.10). In the late 1930s, Warners started some special unit productions with producer-directors such as Anatole Litvak, William Wyler, and Howard Hawks, and in the early 1940s began distributing independent productions.[31]

Metro-Goldwyn-Mayer

MGM's Irving Thalberg functioned as a central producer until his illness in 1932. At that point, Louis B. Mayer hired son-in-law David Selznick to produce a set of films with his own unit. While Thalberg was in Europe, Mayer shifted the studio structure, turning Thalberg's staff into associate producers. Selznick, Thalberg on his return, Hunt Stromberg, Walter Wanger, Joseph L. Mankiewicz, and others (with Harry Rapf doing the B product) filled out a staff line answerable only to Mayer. While Mayer has been accused of deliberately diluting Thalberg's power – and that was the change's effect – it must also be noted that the new structure followed the general pattern developing in the industry. (That may have made it easier for Mayer to justify the change.) After 1933, Thalberg averaged six films a year for MGM until his death.[32]

After Mayer returned from New York City from the yearly production meetings, he would have a large staff meeting. Then the associate producers were on their own. They assigned unit staff members under each department head to each film, and as far as possible tried to keep work units together film after film. MGM, like Twentieth Century-Fox, Warner Bros, and other studios, had a tendency, however, to avoid consulting cinematographers during pre-shooting work. The company also almost always limited their directors to the shooting phase, with films following one after another. If MGM demanded retakes, as it often did, and if the initial director was in another production, other directors might do the re-shooting.

In 1948, Mayer adopted a modified central producer system with Dore Schary in charge of production. During Schary's tenure there until 1956, he managed the MGM product of thirty to thirty-five films per year with a set of fairly independent associate producers. The making of *An American in Paris* (Vincente Minnelli, 1950) during Schary's control has been documented in a series of interviews with the cast and technical staff. Its production history repeats the Hollywood pattern with the exception of the ballet sequence, which was planned and shot after the completion of the 'book' (the narrative) and the rest of the numbers.[33]

Universal

Universal also had a producer-unit system by the mid-1930s. During the 1930-6 period the company focused on the subsequent-run exhibition market and the B half of the double feature. When Universal's ownership changed hands in 1936, the policy shifted toward A production. Universal added independent arrangements to its operations in the late 1930s.[34]

In 1937, to acquaint SMPE members with current Hollywood filmmaking procedures, Universal hosted a conference tour, describing the making of a typical film in their studio. The producer Robert Presnell discussed problems of budgeting a lower-cost A film: since he could not afford higher-salaried actors, he often used new personalities. He had to plan in advance for a specific number of shooting days to meet the budget, so he would instruct script writers to limit the number of sets for the story. Since Deanna Durbin was Universal's rising new star, the SMPE group watched her pre-record 'Sunbeams' for *One Hundred Men and a Girl* (1937). The supervising art director, John Harkrider, described sketches, blueprints, models, set dressing, and costuming and emphasized Universal's innovative use of pastel-colored paints on the set: 'The colors impart the correct atmosphere from the aesthetic, logical, and psychological standpoints.' Through specialization and integration of the work, Universal's staff of experts created their motion pictures.

In 1946, when Universal merged with International, a new production manager, James Pratt, took over the department, instituting lengthy two-day meetings in which every production worker on a film came in and discussed the project. The intent of the meetings was to foresee every problem before shooting started. As Pratt recalled:[35]

It takes the whole team, it's a collaborative art that requires the efforts of all, every son of a gun from the doorman to the front office guy, you know. And I tried my best to actuate that, to create a respect, a mutual regard between the so-called creative group and the so-called backlot group.

Like the other studios, Universal worked to integrate its disparate craftspeople into an efficient, organized labor-force.

Paramount

Throughout the 1930-50 period, Paramount had a looser organization than other studios. The studio used a director-unit system with a central producer system of planning and departmental centralization. From 1928 through 1931, under Lasky and B.P. Schulberg, a set of associate producers 'advised' the directors who had a greater amount of decision-making and co-ordinating powers than in other studios. In fact, the associate producer and a unit manager were often assigned to a production after the director was chosen. The director, his assistant, and the editor assembled the final cut.[36]

In November 1931, Paramount moved to a producer-unit system with seven associate producers. In 1935, the organization had run through a series of production executives, including a 1935 team of Ernst Lubitsch and Henry Herzbrun. Lubitsch supervised a few films, leaving the other productions on their own. When the board of directors changed that year, the new president put William Le Baron in charge. Joseph Kennedy's 1936 investigation of Paramount revealed cost overruns, random shooting schedules, and inefficient use of players and stars, and, again, the company replaced the top production management – this time with Adolph Zukor as studio head. Zukor, like Mayer and Jack Warner, acted as the liaison with New York management and as major purchaser of talent, but remained a broad decision-maker. Zukor supported Le Baron as production head and George Bagnall as studio manager, which helped secure conformance to schedules and budgets. Half the total output was assigned to B-product and a single producer with his associates, and the management left him on his own. For the other half, about twenty-six films for 1937, two systems operated under Le Baron. One system was a variant of the director-unit system, giving the director-producer charge of his production: once he had a story and cast idea, he cleared it with Le Baron and received a budget. The other system was a producer-unit one in which a producer acted in a supervisory manner over a director. For all of these, Paramount maintained a staff in sixty departments. Paramount also followed an earlier policy of releasing films produced by independents, such as the early 1930s films by writers Ben Hecht and Charles MacArthur. Despite subsequent changes in studio top-management, most of the middle-line executives remained constant throughout the period.[37]

RKO Radio Pictures

RKO had one of the most changing histories of top-management control, but employees at the technical level remained fairly stable. During the early 1930s, RKO's policy was the high-cost film, with independent producers supplying a number of additional films. There was also a program of B-product. When a new investment group bought minority control, RKO shifted to a double system: as at Paramount, part of the top management staff were producer-directors; the other part, a group of producers. As RKO president from 1938 to 1942, George Schaefer eliminated independent production with his director-unit and producer-unit systems and generally allowed the units their own control after initial decisions and approval. RKO followed standard practices with centralized departments, unit managers, and unit art directors. It had one of the best special effects departments in Hollywood and many of the remarkable shots in *Citizen Kane* (Orson Welles, 1941) were due to its work. In 1942, Charles Koerner took over as production head, and RKO returned to a policy of renting space in the studio to independents. In the mid-1940s under Schary, the firm made higher- and moderate-budget films and released the work of independents. When Howard Hughes took over the company, production schedules disintegrated and independent releases became dominant.[38]

Columbia

The last of the seven, Columbia, was the first to move to a producer-unit plan in which it concentrated on lower-budget films until the firm had several box office successes in 1934. One of the most careful planners of production schedules, the studio throughout the period invited short-term independent production deals with successful directors, the best known of which was Frank Capra.[39]

This review indicates the variance among the

studios in their allocation of top-management decisions regarding the films. However, when cinematographer Lucien Ballard responded to an interviewer's question as to whether there were differences among the studios, he said, 'No; when you're a professional, you know what you're doing, and it shouldn't make a difference whether it's at Paramount or Fox or Warners. But after [Josef von] Sternberg left [Columbia], I was under contract to Columbia, and, you know, the biggest pictures there were eighteen-day pictures!'[40] On the one hand, while cost allocations made a difference in production time and production value, it is more difficult to find cases in which the management structure made any specific difference in standard work practices.

On the other hand, some management structures may have inhibited alternative shooting techniques. Arthur Miller recounts an instance at Twentieth Century-Fox in which director Edmund Goulding tried to shoot each scene for *The Razor's Edge* in a single take. Studio head Zanuck apparently stopped this, however, because 'Zanuck wanted medium shots and plenty of close-ups to play with when the time came to edit a picture.' Since Zanuck took strong control of the post-shooting work, the practice of the long take would work against his ability to rearrange and rework the film.[41] This may also have been the situation at Warners. Director Vincent Sherman recalled:[42]

Having seen many of John Ford's pictures, I can imagine that he does a lot of cutting with the camera. We couldn't do that at Warner Brothers. If we started doing that at Warners, we would have been in trouble right away. We knew that we had to cover a scene from many angles so there would be a choice, so that Wallis and Warner would have a choice of what they wanted. Now, sometimes we wanted to have a choice ourselves on these things.

Here, desire by management for control of the film's look and sound seems to have hindered any stylistic options. (But recall, too, that Sherman accepts the most probable alternatives within the classical paradigm.)

It might not be just top management who worked to sustain the classical style. MGM editor Adrienne Fazan reported that Editorial Supervisor Margaret Booth expected her to go to close-ups, although Vincente Minnelli might intentionally not have provided them: 'Minnelli sometimes fell in love with certain sequences, and he didn't want them to be broken up or shortened. So he shot that way [no close-ups and long takes with camera movement] on purpose so that it could not be changed in the editing room.' But studios satisfied their desire for close-ups by blowing up frames during editing – so even if a director tried to out smart the studio by avoiding close-ups, technology provided a solution.[43]

As Booth had an impact on editing procedures, MGM production manager Walter Strohm may have controlled experimentation with large camera movements. In recalling the studio's filming practices, Strohm said that he believed the use of a camera boom had to be watched: Many directors 'became very awkward and mechanical, and you became conscious of a boom and not of the action. . . . You just couldn't have a boom put on a shooting schedule without my approval, and I didn't give it often.' For Minnelli, however, Strohm readily granted his permission because he believed that Minnelli knew how to make acceptable camera movements.[44]

It should be clear that Hollywood's criteria of the quality film usually guided individual decisions, no matter what position or which worker had the power to make them. Together, groups of craftspeople worked on a film project, collaborating on the commodity. Furthermore, Hollywood's mode of production, despite its modifications and minor variations through the 1930s and 1940s, continued to specialize the work tasks and to function with standardized production practices. Many workers felt positive about the collective work process. As Schary remarked later about the period:[45]

One of the lost things you can look back on in that era and say was good was the system of patronage that enabled us to keep together a group of highly talented people and let them function rather freely and profitably.

Serial manufacture of a standardized product resulted in a collaborative work situation in which craftspeople jointly mass produced a great number of remarkable (and, admittedly, not so remarkable) films.

26 The package-unit system: unit management after 1955

The 'package-unit' system of production

When historians speak of the structure of the industry after World War II, they describe it as a period of the ending of mass production of films and the diffusion of independent production. As noted in Chapter 24, commercial independent filmmaking occurred as a minority strategy in the United States through the 1930s, with mass production by the major studios as the dominant approach to filmmaking. An independent film company was a firm which was not owned by nor owned a distribution organization. Rather, the company had several distribution options: it could make a film on contract with a distributor, it could make one and then sell it, or it could make one and then distribute it through road-showing. An independent's output was also small, usually no more than ten films per year. After the war when the production sector made fewer films, and those chiefly through independents, it adopted a new method of organizing the labor: the 'package-unit' system of production.

Recall that the definition of commercial independent production is not based on its organization of the mode of production; in fact, an independent firm could use any of the systems. Firms such as David O. Selznick or Samuel Goldwyn which produced a larger number of films might use a producer-unit system; some such as Charles Chaplin with a very small output might opt for the director system, modified with some pre-shooting planning. Thus, rather than confuse the industrial structure and the mode of production, we must remember that the production system we are about to study is a distinct concept from the industrial structure.

What, then, was the 'package-unit' system of production and how was it a change from the prior system? The signal concept is that of package.

Rather than an individual company containing the source of the labor and materials, the entire industry became the pool for these. A producer organized a film project: he or she secured financing and combined the necessary laborers (whose roles had previously been defined by the standardized production structure and subdivision of work categories) and the means of production (the narrative 'property,' the equipment, and the physical sites of production).

The major differences between this system of production and the prior one, the producer-unit system, were the transitory nature of the combination and the disappearance of the self-contained studio. With the old producer-unit system, a producer had a commitment to make six to eight films per year with a fairly identifiable staff. The package-unit system, however, was a short-term film-by-film arrangement. Of course, often many subordinate members of the labor hierarchy worked time and again with the same people because of skills and work habits; workers' employment was, none the less, based on a film not a firm. With the disappearance of the self-contained studio, the means of production was also a short-term combination. Instead of a filming unit owning its entire means of production for use in film after film, the unit leased or purchased the pieces for a particular project from an array of support firms. Costumes, cameras, special effects technology, lighting and recording equipment were specialities of various support companies, available for component packaging.

There continued, however, a number of characteristics from prior systems, making the package-unit system still an instance of detailed division of labor. Because of the success of the former methods of filmmaking and because the labor pool for the industry was still unionized (to protect the lower- and middle-echelon workers), the labor structure was one of a subdivision of work and a management hierarchy. Technological expertise, in part a result of the specialized support firm, also reinforced this. With such a system, craft specialization continued to increase, and detailed knowledge of each work process belonged to only some of the workers. Still acting as standardizing mechanisms, the professional associations continued to function as the means of easing the introduction of new equipment and securing the interchangeability of the parts and their technicians.

This system of production was intricately tied to the postwar industrial shift: instead of the mass production of many films by a few manufacturing firms, now there was the specialized production of a few films by many independents. The majors acted as financiers and distributors. As independent production gained predominance, the industry also constructed the package-unit system, causing the close connection between the industrial structure and the mode.

The move to a reduced output supplied primarily by independents occurred in two phases. During the first half of the 1940s, incentives for the shift included the elimination by a 1940 consent decree of blind selling and block booking, certain effects of World War II, and an apparent tax advantage. After the war, the movement intensified because of income losses, divorcement of exhibition from production and distribution, and new distribution strategies. By the mid-1950s, limited output, independent production, and the package-unit system typified Hollywood.

The early 1940s

Commercial independent production had always been part of the industrial structure in the United States. Even in the 1930s, a period dominated by the major integrated firms, independents found methods to finance and distribute their products. United Artists and even some of the majors worked with the better independents.[1]

When the producer-unit system was introduced in the 1930s (see Chapter 25), its proponents argued that it would improve the quality of the films. The reasoning followed ideological lines regarding ideas of innovation and authorship: allow certain workers to specialize on selected projects and better films would result. Despite this, however, the distribution and exhibition

system held the industry in check. Its regular release schedule did not encourage the companies to move very far away from mass production.

An incentive to do so developed out of a 1940 consent decree in the federal government's antitrust suit against the affiliated majors (those firms with full integration into exhibition). In an attempt to settle the complaints against their trade practices of blind selling and block booking all their product, the majors agreed to trade shows and blocks of no-more-than-five films.[2] This change encouraged the companies to load up each film with as much talent and spectacle as possible so that all the blocks-of-five would attract exhibitors. Furthermore, concentrating on fewer and higher-priced films fell in line with monopolistic practices. The affiliated majors could indirectly collude, reducing the total number of A and Super-A products, most desired by the exhibitor, and still achieve similar profit returns. Even when the consent decree lapsed in 1943, the firms did not return to their former practices.[3]

Another incentive to move away from mass production was a result of World War II. With more disposable income, people turned to movie-going, and attendance figures climbed, eventually to their all-time peak in 1946. As part of this, the top-budget films commanded longer runs. Again, certain conditions favored reduction of output and concentration on more expensive films. Even the companies formerly specializing in 'B' pictures began shifting their policies by adding special A-budget films.[4]

Into the gap between current and former product-supply levels stepped the independents. By 1943, the trade papers noted a surprising increase in available capital for film projects, and, at the same time, talents such as James Cagney, Hal Wallis, and Joseph Hazen started setting up independent deals with their former employers. By the end of the war, a virtual wave of independent companies had formed while majors now offered 'decentralised' control and 'semi-independent status' to many other desired employees. The independents were encouraged to leave studio employment not only because almost every film was now making money, but because the US wartime tax laws favored forgoing salaries and setting up private companies instead. In fact, for a while, single-picture firms seemed the most profitable method although the Bureau of Internal

Revenue halted that practice.[5]

By the end of World War II, the effects of the 1940 consent decree, wartime film attendance trends, and tax laws promoted a move away from mass production and toward independent production. By the end of 1946, every major firm except MGM had some independent projects as part of their regular production schedule.

Later incentives to continue the trend

With the war over we might wonder why the industry did not return to its earlier structure. Postwar conditions, however, reinforced the independent trend as fewer and selectively produced films seemed the best way to make profits.

More typical consumption patterns returned, with a significant reduction in film-going by the public. Although A-products continued to do well, the average film found itself in difficulty. Furthermore, foreign countries, particularly Britain, set up restrictions on exporting film revenues. This hindered the ability of US companies to use that foreign income to offset domestic losses.[6]

With both problems harming profit-making, the studios responded in a familiar pattern: they reduced short-term costs and fixed liabilities. The number of employed film workers declined. In addition, the companies turned to location shooting outside Los Angeles and the United States. This both reduced some costs and, in the case of non-US productions, might unfreeze blocked foreign revenues.[7]

By 1950, additional factors led to continued domestic income losses: population shifts, changing recreational habits, regional unemployment, and particularly competition with television. By 1953, film firms were investigating 3-D and widescreen technologies as means to differentiate their products from television (see Chapter 29).[8]

As income losses continued, the advantage of independent deals was clear. One-time packages reduced fixed costs and allowed more studio flexibility. Furthermore, in 1948, the courts ordered the majors to separate their exhibition holdings from the production-distribution sectors of the firms. This eased any self-generated need to return to mass production. Instead, a firm could concentrate on making fewer, specialized projects

and financing or buying the more desirable independent films.

Finally, another incentive to move away from mass production was the industry's new distribution strategies. Recognizing changing consumption patterns and targeting parts of the population as its most likely and desired audiences, the industry concentrated even more on a highly differentiated film. Moreover, ignoring marginal theaters, the film companies moved toward aiming films primarily at first-run audiences only.[9]

As the majors increasingly financed independent films, the new independent production companies turned to the already-available army of support firms for their technology, studio space, and technical experts. Furthermore, the unions functioned as a labor pool, supplying skilled workers to the independents as well as the growing television industry. By 1956, even MGM was making outside deals. With the industrial shift to independent production, the package-unit system of filmmaking replaced the older studio-system.[10]

The package-unit system in operation

Although still an instance of divided labor with a structural hierarchy, the package-unit system differed from former systems in its industry-wide pooling of labor and materials, the disappearance of the self-contained studio, and the transitory combination of labor-force and means of production. As we have noted, these were all effects of the industrial shift away from mass production and toward film-by-film financing and planning. Several other differences deserve some attention.

The package-unit system further intensified the need to differentiate the product on the basis of its innovations, its story, its stars, and its director. With the major firms supplying financing and other benefits that were not visible to the consumer, the use of a studio brand name became only another (if slightly larger) line on the poster. Instead, the names of individuals and the unique package were marketed, particularly to certain audiences. When *Gidget*, starring James Darren and Sandra Dee, was released in 1959, advertising and promotion aimed the film at the teen market, with a personal endorsement from Dick

Clark, 'idol and trend-setter extraordinary of young America.'[11] The goal of aiming a film at a heterogeneous audience was no longer standard.

The advertising stress on certain workers also increased distinctive laborers' bargaining power. In a package-unit system, the worker returned to the labor-supply after each project, ready to negotiate his or her next deal. When Vincente Minnelli chose Joseph Ruttenberg as director of photography for *Gigi* (1956, MGM), *American Cinematographer* explained:[12]

Minnelli, who has a passion for moving camera shots, acquired both an expert craftsman and a recognized exponent of the 'fluid' camera. During his long and successful career at MGM, Joseph Ruttenberg has achieved photography with a boom-mounted camera that has won high praise from his contemporaries and contributed largely to the photographic achievements that have netted him three Academy Awards. . . .

Ruttenberg's labors in *Gigi* won him a fourth Oscar.

With the package-unit system, the assembling of the project's components was usually done by the major studios and individual producers, but talent agencies also commonly did this producer function. The William Morris Agency had packaged complete programs for the radio since the late 1930s, and Music Corporation of America (MCA), Famous Artists, and others joined the field. As talent started crossing into more media, such as television, these agencies facilitated the package-unit system. Experts and specialists in casting, they helped pull together writers, actors, directors, stories, and producers: the major part of a deal. By 1959, MCA was so powerful that it bought control of Universal Studios, the physical plant of Universal Pictures. Besides that holding, its subsidiaries included its Hollywood talent agency (MCA Artists, Ltd), a distributor of television films (MCA-TV), a packager of live television shows (Management Corporation of America), and one of the biggest producers of television films (Revue Productions). Examples of MCA's packages included the 1958 films *The Young Lions* (MCA represented stars Marlon Brando, Montgomery Clift, and Dean Martin) and *The Big Country* (MCA represented the director

William Wyler and stars Gregory Peck, Charlton Heston, Carroll Baker, and Charles Bickford.)[13]

Although not directly a result of the package-unit system, another change affected the production of films: location shooting abroad often resulted in variations from the standard division of labor. Not only was foreign labor sometimes cheaper but many of the postwar trade agreements with foreign countries encouraged the use of their crews as a means of unfreezing earnings. The diffusion of independent production also spread the sources of funding, with companies seeking the best financial arrangement regardless of country. Even if a US firm distributed a film, the legal ownership of the product might be partly or wholly non-American. Once again, economic concerns affected the mode of production. Producing films outside the United States – the famous 'runaway' productions as well as investment in foreign filmmaking – made utilization of other production practices an important factor. Such productions commonly employed local laborers at the middle and lower levels, causing the foreign country's domestic work structures to alter the normal US processes in some cases. In 1953, forty-eight films had some foreign location shooting, with Hollywood either partially or fully financing the project. Reasons for such a large number included 'the need for authentic background and locale,' tax advantages, foreign policies, foreign private financing, 'split hemisphere' deals, lower production costs, and the importance of the foreign box office. N. Peter Rathvon was already advocating the 'international picture' in which the production was 'conceived and filmed to serve the screen demands of two countries.'[14]

The effect of such joint productions on the division of labor was to alter the number of people on crews, to redefine labor responsibilities, and to change the general work conditions. For foreign-based films, crews were usually a mixture of nationalities. In shooting *Gigi* in Paris, Ruttenberg discovered that the French crew did not 'rough in' a set. In Hollywood, the head electrician (the 'gaffer') anticipated a set-up and 'roughed in' the basic lighting arrangements (easy with the standardized lighting patterns). With that done, the cinematographer directed the minor refinements. In France, however, Ruttenberg found that the head cinematographer directed every lighting placement. For *The Nun's Story* (1959), director of photography Franz Planer supervised an Italian camera operator. Burnett Guffey's principal crew in Okinawa for *Hell to Eternity* (1960) was American, but his two other teams of cameramen were Japanese. (He used an interpreter.) Robert Aldrich had an American cameraman but indicated that he had to cope with a chiefly British staff and German crew for the Berlin-based shooting of *Ten Seconds to Hell* (1959); for *The Angry Hills* (1959), British and Greek crews shot part of the locations in Greece and England.[15] We can mark slight individual variations within the mode of production once foreign-based shooting became so important in the 1950s and afterwards. These variations, however, were only on location; in Hollywood, practices did not change.

Finally, the package-unit system also slightly changed the division of labor and the work hierarchy. This was a result of paying some workers by profit-shares rather than time. Profit-sharing could, of course, have been provided for all the workers, but generally it was arranged only for certain personnel — those in the middle- and upper-management levels. The probable reason for this is that the lower-echelon workers, in keeping with the wage differentials, would receive percentages which might very well be lower than their secure union wage schedule. Only the most powerful workers — major stars, directors, sometimes writers — could demand a large enough piece of the picture to make profit-sharing attractive.

The effect of profit-sharing was to encourage more cooperative pre-shooting planning with less strict division of certain labor functions. With a regular mass-production schedule and a fixed output, the employer had had to encourage speed in production. Concentrating the specialists, and only those workers, in their areas of expertise produced a faster rate of output since they could quickly repeat time and again the same job. Such a system also discouraged other workers from participating in planning since this would take them away from their routine tasks and would divert earnings to pay their time in planning. When the industry abandoned a regular-release schedule, the deadline effect was reduced. Furthermore, with profit-sharing, concern for loss of money due to time spent on the job was gone. If a worker paid by profits wanted to spend his or her time functioning in several capacities and contributing to planning, the pressure to meet a deadline was off. Also it was up to him or her to determine how valuable his or her time was. When workers paid by time were involved, then the deadline effect returned, particularly in shooting schedules.

During the 1940s, Hollywood personnel perceived the new flexibility in planning as a remarkable contrast to the prior system. Cinematographer Lee Garmes, for instance, contributed to much of the pre-shooting plans for *Spectre of the Rose* (1956) and had complete charge of camera distances, angles, and lighting. In 1947, the Screen Writers Guild arranged with Zanuck and Schary to let writers watch shooting activities so they could learn that part of the production practices. (Schary records that in the economy moves around 1950, MGM started letting middle-level workers do two or three tasks to reduce costs — so this cannot be completely seen as altruistic or due to the industrial transformation.[16]) Although much more common after 1960, by the late 1940s, individuals combined positions: writer-director Billy Wilder for *Sunset Boulevard* (1950), producer-director Stanley Kramer for *The Defiant Ones* (1958), star-director-producer John Wayne for *The Alamo* (1960).[17]

Although some labor processes were less strictly divided, such changes existed only in certain parts of the middle- and upper-management levels of the work structure: producing, writing, directing, and acting. Directors or stars who had previously moved from shooting one film immediately to the next now took over a business function, spending a larger part of their time negotiating each new film deal. The older system was as much in force as ever for the other departments and lower-level workers. This had to do in part with the complexity of the technologies and in part with the union contracts which specified minimal conditions of work for those employees. The unions bargained with those who hired their workers. When independent production started increasing in the mid-1940s, the new independent producers united into their own trade associations and collectively bargained with the unions. In 1946 besides the Association of Motion Picture Producers, which was the bargaining group for ten major studios, two other associations existed: the Society of Independent Motion Picture Producers, which represented twenty-five independents, and the Independent Motion Picture Producers Association, which included thirty-two smaller independents, Monogram, and Producers Releasing Corporation. Even though the unions might consider special difficulties which the independents faced, scales and minimal work conditions were bargained. Thus, as Chapter 24 suggested, the unions – while protecting their member-workers – also contributed to the continuance of the detailed division of labor mode.[18]

The Hollywood mode of production: an evaluation

You had a feeling on [the MGM] lot that they made the best pictures in the world, which they did. A great feeling![19]

Ed Woehler, Unit Production Manager,
Metro-Goldwyn-Mayer

What occurred in the Hollywood mode of production was the result of its conditions of existence: the economic and ideological/signifying practices which individual firms and institutions took as their initial models. Furthermore, the industry changed these models to suit its particular medium and situations, and, through its own internal organization, the industry generated its own structure. As John Ellis writes, 'the history of cinema cannot be read off from its conditions of existence,' which is why this extended look at the formations and effects that resulted in the particular mode of production has been necessary.

The Hollywood mode of production changed continually. Conceptions of efficiency and quality developed the subdivisions of the execution of the work. Economy moves helped cause the subdivision of the jobs of assistant directors, unit managers, production department workers. Narrative coherence and clarity supported the movement of star personalities to the foreground and their directors toward the top of the management pyramid. Verisimilitude provided a need for researchers, art directors, specialized construction crews, and composite photography experts. Continuity techniques encouraged the use of continuity writers, continuity clerks, expert editors, and make-up artists. Spectacle and emotional effects led to specialists in technological *tours de force* and novelties.

Subdivisions of the work occurred initially as a method to increase film output and to insure the movies' predictable quality and appearance. Subsequently, the divisions of labor occurred as they did for several reasons, primarily because of examples in related work areas (the stage mode of production and concurrent US business practices), because of conceptions of work necessary to achieve a particular look and sound in the film, and because of technological change and unionization. Workers used the script first as a rough outline of the story and then as a blueprint that precalculated costs, prechecked narrative continuity and coherence, and provided on paper a permanent memory that guided the assembly of a film made in many phases and places by various craftspeople. Technological change was encouraged and accommodated. Labor activities and advanced capitalism tended to reinforce a divided labor system with a structural and hierarchical management.

Each management system in one or a few areas differed from the prior one, changed out of it. But in many ways each new system retained much of its predecessor's organization. In a rather surprising way, the dominant systems participated in a cycle effect. From a period in which deadlines were less important (the cameraman system), the systems moved through periods in which mass production very much enforced deadlines (the director, the director-unit, the central producer, and the producer-unit systems), to the last period (the package-unit system) in which release dates did not have the force of earlier years. Throughout these changes, directors of capital assigned control of production to a rather powerful worker: the cameraman, then the director, then the producer, and finally, often, the star. The cycle, however, never returned to the origin. Gone were the conditions of the existence for inventor-cameraman-owner W.K.L. Dickson's trip in 1900 to film the Boer War. Gone were the conditions for D.W. Griffith's one-reel Biographs and Thomas Ince's scientifically managed factory. Even later visions of returning to the golden era of mass production in the studio were altered by more contemporary ideologies of specialized, individually controlled films. Francis Ford Coppola wanted the studio he purchased in 1979 to be an 'all inclusive gathering of talent utilizing the best features of the powerful and productive studios of the 30s and 40s.'[20] But he also explained:[21]

> The movies I really want to make can only be made after we get the studio in L.A. to be an all-electronic studio, so that it's all stages and guys building things; a totally electronic medium. You put some guys in there for a week and they come out with a film with gigantic sets, just like that. You can make it and cut electronically. I'm trying to make a film factory that works incredibly well and then I'll get it turning out these class B pictures, take a really wonderful story like *The Black Stallion*, a really wonderful story that everyone can understand, and give it a really arty class treatment. Just make movies like that, a lot of them. Then, when I've got this whole big factory going, then I want to take it over and just make *one* film.

If the Hollywood mode of production has provoked praise in some quarters, in others, it has been an example not of the good but the bad, and, occasionally, the ugly. Many workers found it alienating, depressing, stifling. Cinematographers continually complained about the stupidity of the producers in not bringing them in on the planning phases of a film, and writers described the destruction of the Great American screenplay. The plot of *A Star Is Born* had a basis in the lives of the actors and actresses who were often manipulated by publicity and the vicissitudes of the box office. Hollywood was also criticized for the aesthetic quality of its films. Dudley Nichols wrote: 'It is too much the modern factory-system – each man working on a different machine and never in an integrated creation. It tends to destroy that individuality of style which is the mark of any superior work of art.' V.F. Perkins believed that the corporate boss of the package-unit studio must 'encourage indecision and cowardice' – with presumed effects on the films.[22]

Undoubtedly, Hollywood deserves criticism for parts of its mode of production. However, that criticism has to be carefully applied. It is unfair to represent its production practices as uniformly dehumanizing and merely formulaic. For one thing, the tension between standardization and differentiation allowed two worthwhile goals for workers: first, a standard of making a quality film; second, the encouragement to innovate, to redefine that standard. Such a dual system created a flexibility and a tolerance within, admittedly, ideological and economic boundaries.

Nor is it fair to think of production in this industry as monolithic. The mode had various degrees of rigidity in the work order, within the hierarchical structure, and in regard to deadlines. In Hollywood filmmaking at the craftsman's level of work, manufacturing never reached the degree of dehumanization that it has in other industries. Making a film was not working on a Ford moving assembly-line. Even at mass production's peak in the central producer and producer-unit systems, middle-management as craftsmen had much control over their sections of work and their work conditions. Within an instance of serial manufacture, these craftsmen were organized into a collective group, with varying degrees of exchange of ideas for every film the company turned out.

In fact, I would argue, the auteurist tendency to attempt to attribute particular stylistic innovations to a single worker (producer, director, writer) may have reinforced the hierarchical system. Certainly the movement from the early 1930s has been increasingly in the direction of assuming that one individual ought to control almost all aspects of the filming so that that individual's personal vision can be created. The introduction of the producer-unit system in 1931 and package-unit filmmaking in the 1940s followed this ideological attitude toward authorship without consideration of its effect on the rest of the mode of production.

What was valuable in the Hollywood mode of production was its combination of the expertise of multiple crafts. Groups of specialists, although in divided labor, made films which just seem difficult to conceive having been created by workers in other work arrangements. Not that that should be the criterion by which to judge a mode of production if the effects of the work situation or the signifying practices are abhorrent. But much is commendable in joint-work projects in which the skills of individuals are combined to make something perhaps otherwise not possible.

Others have noticed this about the Hollywood

work mode. Many workers felt a great sense of pride in the craftsmanship which went into the films. George Gibson, head of scenic art at MGM, believed that the studio system allowed a special type of creative association:[23]

Creativity demands a continuing relationship with people, the people who work for you and you, in turn, work for someone else. It's the only way that I think any kind of creative effort can be accomplished. We weren't aping anybody. We were doing a job that was a very demanding and highly disciplined type of job. We couldn't do it any other way. Everything had to go into it that we knew how best to put into it.

.... All I know is that the [MGM scenic art] building represented the best that there was in the field of scenic art, both as a place to work and to the personnel who were working in it. It was the best there was, best there's ever been.

Cinematographer Hal Rossen also thought this:[24]

[Leonard Maltin]: Many people have criticized the studio system, saying that it hampered creativity. Did you feel this way as a cameraman?

Rossen: I am a product of the studio system, star system, and I thought it was a very good way to make pictures. I'm sure it hampered some, but when I think of the great help it gave so many many more than it hampered, I think it helped a great deal more than it hampered.

.... I was so happy with my work, I wanted to see it on the screen. I had the best time in the world, and for that I was paid.

If Coppola's remarks quoted earlier about his hopes for a factory gathering of the best talent exhibit a nostalgia for the studio era, it is in part because of the value of the mass production approach. The package-unit system, although still a collective work arrangement, lost long-term stability while it gained some degree of creative power for a few top managers. In achieving the freedom to seek out, negotiate, and plan every project, the package-unit director or star tied up more of her or his time in business dealing than in filmmaking. On the other hand, if the entire mode as an instance of serial manufacture did allow collectivity, it also divided labor and set up hierarchies; not all laborers had equal opportunities to contribute to the conception and execution of the work. This has been the case from the director system through the package-unit system.

All of this should remind us that any system or mode of production has contradictions. But we might also remember that if we want to appreciate the work of artists/craftsmen/laborers in the creation of an object, we might consider contemplating the precision, expertise, and skill the various lower-echelon workers, the technical experts, and the other managers gave to the films as they contributed their share of knowledge, creativity, and labor-power to what was known as the Hollywood film.

Part Six Film style and technology, 1930-60

DAVID BORDWELL

By 1931, Hollywood had a model of how the mode of production could initiate and assimilate a new technology. During the next two decades, the producer-unit system provided a stable basis for technological innovation. These are very active years for the Academy Research Council, the Society of Motion Picture Engineers, the American Society of Cinematographers, and manufacturers' research departments. It is within this solid framework that we must locate the trended stylistic changes in deep-focus cinematography and Technicolor filmmaking. The last principal innovations, widescreen and stereophony, coincided with the rise of package-unit production and represented the last major studio-sponsored technical initiatives. The causation and timing of each technological change can, in the last analysis, be attributed to such economic pressures as product differentiation and the promotion of quality standards. The changes created some production inefficiencies and extra expenses, but in each case the Hollywood mode of production absorbed the innovation and restabilized itself. The classical style promptly assigned the new techniques to already-canonized functions; reciprocally, some of the new devices extended and enriched the classical paradigm.

27

Deep-focus cinematography

Deep-focus cinematography has held a great interest for film aestheticians, and the reasons are not obscure. It is a technological development which can be clearly correlated with stylistic consequences: the evidence seems to be baldly there on the screen. Just as importantly, deep focus seems to invite a stress upon innovation as such – André Bazin called it 'a dialectical step forward in the evolution of film language' – and upon the individual innovators (Orson Welles, William Wyler, Gregg Toland, *et al.*). The argument being made in this book tries to frame the central problems somewhat differently.

First, what are we trying to explain? 'Deep focus' itself requires some definition: the 'deep focus' of Lumière is not that of Renoir, and that of Renoir is not that of Welles. Nor will a simple opposition of depth and flatness in image composition take us very far. Most simply, we are asking why at specific periods the classical paradigm favored certain renditions of depth over others. Why is a shot like figure 27.1, with its fairly close foreground plane and sharply focused rear plane, so rare in 1937 and yet quite ordinary a decade later? To answer such a question, we must not simply link technological devices to the image; we must examine how such 'deep focus' functioned within the classical paradigm. The issue of innovation should in its turn be treated in an institutional context. This is not to say that individual filmmakers do not count, but the nature of their contributions will be largely defined by the ways that the mode of production encouraged and appropriated individuals' innovations. In certain ways, deep focus extended the range of the classical paradigm. To investigate deep-focus cinematography, we will need to look at the historical role played by specific technical agencies, especially the American Society of Cinematographers.

In discussing how films may represent depth, we must keep several distinctions in mind. Spatial depth is not simply one 'thing'; it is a quality we attribute to widely different sorts of images. One distinction that must be maintained is that between mise-en-scene and cinematography. You can represent spatial depth through composition, setting, and light and shadow; and you can represent depth through choice of lens, amount of light, aperture, film stock, and optical process work. For example, Jean Renoir's films of the 1930s often produce depth by composing significant action on two planes or by using doors and windows to frame distant action; yet usually only one of these planes will be in sharp focus. Similarly, one can have every plane of a shot in sharp focus, as in Carl Theodor Dreyer's *La Passion de Jeanne d'Arc* (1928), and yet because of the ambiguous composition and the blank decor relatively little depth is demarcated. The distinction between deep-space mise-en-scene and deep-focus cinematography lets us isolate various ways that the classical Hollywood style has represented space.

A second distinction is no less important: that between device and function. It is one thing to say that *Citizen Kane* (1941), or any film, contains shots of unprecedented spatial depth; it is another thing to claim that that device functions in a new way. The innovations, sources, and first times exhumed by film historians often become less startling if placed in their functional context, within a film or within a tradition.

The soft style in the sound period

During the 1920s, the classical representation of a shot's depth obeyed a few simple principles. Typically, the principal actors performed on one

341

or two planes only, and the surroundings (wall, road, horizon) constituted general background planes. There would usually be one plane of interest, the figure in the foreground (e.g., a close-up or medium shot of the hero) or, less often, a figure in the middle ground (e.g., the hero framed by a tree or doorway in the foreground). Great depth is more common in long shots than in closer framings. In *The Kid Brother* (1927), Harold waves goodbye to his girlfriend in the distance (fig 27.2), but the foreground plane is still at a considerable distance from us. Medium shots could also use marked depth, as in figures 27.3 and 27.4, but such compositions are rare in American silent films. On the whole, deep-space staging in the shot obeys a fixed rule: the greater the shot scale (that is, the closer it comes to being a long shot), the greater the potential depth; the less the shot scale, the shallower the space.

What of deep-focus cinematography? Again, Chapter 21 has shown that in the 1920s, the American cinema contained two distinct impulses, one toward sharp-focus filming, another toward a softer and more diffused look. Not until the second half of the 1920s did a certain photographic softness become generally accepted. By April 1928 Joseph Dubray could write: 'It is acknowledged by cinematographers in general that the need of absolutely sharp definition is a thing of the past. The dramatic quality of present day cinematography demands a certain softness of contours throughout the whole image.'[1] Several factors contributed to the soft look: soft-focus lenses, filters, diffusion of the light sources, different developing procedures, and the increased use of Mazda lamps. The style owed a good deal to much older trends in still photography, whereby pictures were considered 'artistic' and painterly if they had a blurry softness about them. Whether the image was crisp or diffused, however, the arrangement of the players in the shot did not fundamentally differ. Compare two sets of shots (figs 27.5 through 27.8) from *So This Is Paris* (Lubitsch, 1926) and *Seventh Heaven* (Borzage, 1927). The cinematographic styles are significantly different (determined by differences in studio, genre, and filmmaker) but the depth of each shot's playing space is comparable: medium close-ups of a figure and a background, long shots with greater depth.

The introduction of sound modified the soft style. In certain respects, the image remained soft in focus and definition, and Patrick Ogle has pointed out how certain factors favored that quality (the supremacy of the Mazda lamp, the use of low-contrast developing solutions, the cinematographers' insistence on shooting at maximum aperture).[2] Certainly the practice of multiple-camera shooting also had an effect. The need to light the set for several camera positions created a flat illumination, while the extremely long lenses used for multiple-camera filming tended to weaken definition. Yet the softness of the early sound films is not the softness of *Sunrise* (1927), *Seventh Heaven*, or *The Tempest* (1928). In the outstanding films of the silent soft style, the blurring of edges and textures was often accompanied by dark blacks and sparkling highlights; the image shimmered. In the early sound films, the image can be said to be soft only insofar as it is grayer, with lower contrast.

The difference was due to several factors. Machine-developing tended to standardize a middle-range degree of contrast in processing all shots. Moreover, early incandescent illumination simply could not produce crisp definition. In 1928, Karl Struss and Charles Rosher, two chief practitioners of the soft style, complained that with Mazdas the colors blended too much: arcs could pick out wrinkles in fabrics, but Mazdas could not distinguish two black-clothed figures when they came into contact. Proponents of incandescents found this a desirable 'softness,' while antagonists called it 'blurred, foggy composition.'[3] Theater projectionists protested that they could not focus these images; the National Carbon Company even advertised new projector carbons for 'the modern soft, low key or fuzzy film.'[4] Furthermore, the fact that most 1928-31 shots were filmed through a pane of glass (because the camera was in a booth or blimp) gave early talkie photography a lack of definition that one observer called 'mushy.'[5] (See fig 27.9.) Finally, the soft films not only diffused the light sources but also applied very heavy diffusion filters to the lens. (The filters were ranked from 1 to 4, the heaviest.) Sometimes the cinematographer would also set up taut sheets of mesh or other material between various planes of the shot. (See fig 21.11 through 21.13.) After the coming of sound, cinematographers avoided such heavy diffusion. Scrims were not generally used between planes, and much lighter diffusion filters (scaled from $\frac{1}{2}$ to beyond $\frac{1}{32}$) became the norm.[6] The result was a smooth and slight overall blurring that sought to be both unnoticeable and constant from shot to shot. After the early 1930s, the sparkling, heavily diffused soft style was used only to convey a fantasy atmosphere (see figs 27.10 and 27.11).

Once a modified 'soft' style became the norm for the sound era, the service firms responded. The earliest panchromatic film had been relatively slow and contrasty, but in 1928 Eastman marketed a lower-contrast, more sensitive stock. In 1931, the firm introduced Super Sensitive Panchromatic, the first stock created specifically for Mazda light, low contrast, and 'softer highlight rendering.'[7] Proponents claimed that the film itself produced the softness that would otherwise have to be created by lighting and filters. Eastman quickly improved the Super Sensitive stock by adding an anti-halation backing that gave a brighter image with more shadow detail. Within two years, both Du Pont and Agfa had introduced similar emulsions. While other service agencies quickly adapted to the film stock – Bausch and Lomb introduced its Raytar lenses designed for fast film, and Max Factor devised appropriate make-up – cinematographers pondered exactly how to use the new panchromatic.[8]

Producers expected that the sensitive emulsions, being at least twice as fast as the old ones, would lead to a lowering of lighting levels and consequently a decrease in costs. At first, this did not happen. A 1931 Academy survey discovered that most studios using fast film did not consume less amperage.[9] Cinematographers were using the same number of lighting units and were not stopping down the lens because 'sharp photography is not artistic photography.'[10] But when the ASC officially recommended the new fast films to its members, it pointed out that 'with the present lightings and smaller lens openings, improved definition can be obtained without sacrifice of those qualities of softness which have always been the artistic aim of cinematographers.'[11] After 1931, most cinematographers chose to keep the lens at full aperture, cut down the light levels, and save money on the set.

Cinematography in the 1930s thus became a give-and-take between the technical agencies and the cinematographers. The agencies were committed to 'progress': faster and finer-grained films, faster lenses, more portable and powerful light sources. Throughout the decade, suppliers introduced a series of faster emulsions, culminating in 1938 with Agfa Supreme, Du Pont Superior II, and Eastman Plus X and Super XX. Mole-Richardson perfected an incandescent spotlight with Fresnel focusing lenses in 1935, and at the same period created a new series of lightweight and automatic-feed arc lamps. Most cinematographers in turn chose to keep a soft style. The faster films and more powerful lights were used to reduce set lighting levels, sometimes by as much as seventy per cent. The arc lamp had never been completely abandoned when sound arrived, but after 1935 it was not uncommon for cameramen to mix incandescents with the improved Mole-Richardson arcs, again in the name of control, economy, and efficiency.[12] The faster films also reduced the need for modeling light. As one cinematographer put it:[13]

The film itself [Plus X] now does half the work of separating the different planes of your picture. People stand out more clearly from their backgrounds. Even separating the planes in close shots – the little matter of keeping a coat-lapel from blending into the background of a garment – of giving an illusion of depth to faces and figures – is easier with the new film.

The speed of the new films allowed some cinematographers to rely more on spotlighting. Because dolly shots often made floor lighting cumbersome, most lights were hung above the set; but the light was often so distant from the action that only powerful spotlights could work effectively. Mole-Richardson cooperated and designed a variety of spots with controllable beam-spreads and a dimmer that regulated the intensity of light at any point.[14] In short, most cinematographers sought to maintain a balance between technological novelty and the 'artistic' demand for soft images. Yet some cinematographers experimented with ways to produce harder, more sharply defined shots. What explains this penchant for innovation?

As an organization, the ASC replicated, in its own particular terms, the tension between standardization and differentiation at work in the production sector generally. On the one hand, the ASC asked the cinematographer to be a crafts-man, cleanly obeying the rules. At the same time, he was expected to originate techniques. 'Bert Glennon introducing new method of interior photography'; 'Reverse studio lighting methods to put big night spots on the screen'; 'A new viewpoint on the lighting of motion pictures' – such titles, from *American Cinematographer* and *JSMPE*, indicate the degree to which novelty had become institutionalized. Every article told the same story. The cinematographer encounters a particular problem on a production. He devises a mechanism or procedure to solve the problem in a way that might prove useful on other productions. The article concludes that the solution could improved quality, differentiate the product, or cut expenses. For example, when Hal Mohr devised a ball-and-socket lens mount to keep several planes in focus, the *American Cinematographer* featured an article in which he explained that such shots made the scene more dramatic and easier to shoot. The article concluded that 'the device can be of inestimable value in the Cinematographer's efforts to reconcile the dramatic purpose of Cinematography with the mechanical limitations of the camera.'[15] Similarly, Bert Glennon was praised as 'a man whose progressiveness and sincerity has kept the photographic competition moving.'[16] Not only the cameraman's employer but his professional association encouraged him to innovate.

While some cinematographers sought to intro-duce new lighting techniques, camera supports, or filters, others experimented with the rendering of depth. Some cinematographers used lenses wider than the 50mm norm to increase depth of field. James Wong Howe (*Transatlantic* and *Viva Villa!*, 1933) and Hal Mohr (*Tess of the Storm Country*, 1932) are the most famous instances, but many early sound films (e.g., *Applause, *Young Sinners) use a short focal-length lens occasionally. Mohr used his ball-and-socket mount for *Green Pastures* (1936) and *Bullets or Ballots* (1936). Bert Glennon employed a 25mm lens for *Stagecoach* (1939). In *Each Dawn I Die* (1939), Arthur Edeson made fairly close shots with a wide-angle lens (see fig 27.12). Tony Gaudio's 'precision lighting' was an attempt to increase depth by creating strong key light with less fill. Coated lenses, which increased light transmission and enabled

cameramen to stop down the aperture, began to be used in the late 1930s in films like *Tobacco Road* (1940), which Arthur Miller shot with remarkably little backlighting.[17]

Such developments in deep-focus cinemato-graphy encouraged some directors to stage more ambitiously in depth. Deep-space compositions crop up occasionally throughout the early sound era (see figs 27.13 through 27.15 for instances). Such shots are chiefly remarkable for placing the foreground plane in medium shot, even if it is not in focus. But on the whole, the 1930s cinema adhered to the staging practices of the 1920s. Not until 1940 and 1941 do films systematically place foregrounds quite close to the camera and in sharp focus. This prototypical 'deep-focus' look is usually associated with *Citizen Kane*, but this film, available for industry viewing in April 1941, appeared in the midst of a string of similar efforts.

There is, for example, *The Stranger on the Third Floor* (available to the trade in September 1940), in which Boris Ingster and his cinemato-grapher Nicholas Musuraca played and filmed courtroom scenes in considerable depth. There is William Dieterle's *All That Money Can Buy* (July 1941), shot by Joseph August, with its striking backlighting, wide-angle shots, and emphatically close foregrounds (fig 27.16). There is *Meet John Doe* (March 1941), in which George Barnes used wide-angle lenses and rapid rack-focusing to create great depth. There is also *The Maltese Falcon* (September 1941), whose looming ceilings, foreshortened views, and striking depth of field make Arthur Edeson's cinematography strongly akin to Toland's work (fig 27.17). There are, in particular, two films designed by William Cameron Menzies, *Our Town* (May 1940) and *Kings Row* (December 1941), both directed by Sam Wood. Many shots in *Our Town* are staged in remarkable depth, with looming foreground objects and great depth of focus (fig 27.18). *Kings Row* is no less claustrophobic, with huge fore-grounds and a dense organization of actors and decor (fig 27.19). One of the most important exponents of deep space and deep focus, Menzies sketched each shot in advance and even specified the lens to be used.[18] Unlike Toland, who was to argue for the realism of deep space, Menzies excelled in using depth to create contorted, fantastic perspective. His set designs for *The Tempest* (1928), *Bulldog Drummond* (1929), and other films had a calculated Germanic look which exploited unusual angles for deep-space compositions (fig 27.20; compare figs 1.1 and 17.17). Whether or not Menzies influenced Toland (who assisted George Barnes on *Bulldog Drummond*), his work anticipates the grotesquely monumental depth of *Citizen Kane*.

These innovations are not all that drastic. Within the context of the classical style, such depth devices were quickly assigned familiar functions. For instance, staging in depth often enhanced centering, as when the foreground figures are silhouetted or out of focus and our attention is drawn to the lighted middle ground (see fig 27.21). At other moments, a deep-focus composition will function as an establishing shot, especially in a cramped setting (for example, fig 27.22). Or the spatial depth will constitute a variant on the familiar shot/reverse-shot (figs 27.23 and 27.24). Sometimes the depth is motivated generically, as in the skewed sets of a horror film like *The Bat Whispers* (1931). Stylized or 'realistic,' before *Citizen Kane*, staging and shooting in depth went generally unnoticed because the devices fitted comfortably into roles allotted by the classical style.

Gregg Toland and deep focus

The innovations of Gregg Toland should be seen not only in the context of the development of 1930s technology but also in the context of the ASC as a professional organization. Patrick Ogle has examined the ways in which Toland synthesized various innovations of the decade — wide-angle lenses, fast film, arc lighting for black and white, coated lenses, the new silenced Mitchell camera (figs 27.25 and 27.26). But Ogle assigns the cause of this to Toland's artistic desire to experiment.[19] What Ogle's purely technical account misses is the way the concept of artistic experimentation was defined by the institutions within which Toland worked. Certainly as an independent producer, Samuel Goldwyn gave Toland a strong incentive to differentiate the studio's product. The most pertinent stimulus, however, was supplied by Toland's professional organization.

The ASC articulated a contradictory task for the cameraman. He was, firstly, to be an artist.

The ASC encouraged its members to think of themselves as creative people, comparable to the screenwriter or director. Implicitly, then, each cinematographer's work was to have something distinctive about it. We have already seen the stress laid on individual innovations and virtuosity. But at the same time, the ethos of the craft held that the cinematographer's work must go unnoticed by the layman. The ideal, remarked John Arnold, president of the ASC, 'is to so perfectly suit the cinematography to the story that the former is imperceptible, and the latter is subtly heightened.'[20] Arthur Miller claimed that the viewer should forget that he or she has seen cinematography in watching a film.[21] To avoid distracting from the story, the cinematographer's style would have to adapt itself to each film. The *American Cinematographer* praised one cameraman because 'The casual observer viewing these two films would hardly suspect they were photographed by the same man.'[22] The model is unobtrusive artistry, innovation that does not challenge reigning norms. Gregg Toland's problematic position in the early 1940s arose from the conflicting demands of individual artistry and self-effacing professionalism.

For a few years, Toland was the most famous cinematographer in Hollywood, and indeed the world. He began very young: an assistant cameraman at age sixteen, George Barnes's assistant at twenty-two, and at twenty-seven the youngest first cameraman in Hollywood. During his work with Goldwyn, Toland was entrusted with many of the studio's most important projects, such as Eddie Cantor and Anna Sten vehicles. Toland was admitted to the ASC in 1934, when he was barely thirty. For the next six years, no cinematographer received more public attention. In the pages of *American Cinematographer*, Toland explained how he used the new Mitchell camera, shot low-key, planned every set-up, used arc lighting for black and white, and devised new photographic gadgets. He shot a string of prestigious films (*Les Miserables* [1935], *These Three* [1936], *Dead End* [1937], *Kidnapped* [1938], and *Goldwyn Follies* [1938]). After winning the Academy Award for black-and-white cinematography for *Wuthering Heights* (1939), he clinched his fame with *The Grapes of Wrath*, *The Westerner*, and *The Long Voyage Home* (all 1940). With the reputation of being a fast, efficient worker and a meticulous attender to details of laboratory work, Gregg Toland at the age of thirty-six was the most powerful cameraman in Hollywood. He had an unprecedented long-range contract with Goldwyn, which was said to include a provision that he must be allowed to direct a film.[23] (At his death, he was also one of the few stockholders in Goldwyn Productions.) No wonder, then, that the *American Cinematographer* noted that most cinematographers believed that 'Toland's acknowledged brilliance has placed him in the most nearly ideal position any Director of Photography has enjoyed since the halcyon days when D.W. Griffith and Billy Bitzer were between them creating the basic technique of the screen.'[24]

Like many of his peers during the 1930s, Toland occasionally experimented with technical devices to give greater depth: arc lamps, faster film, lens coating, and wide-angle lenses. Many of Toland's shots display qualities common in other cinematographers' work. Sometimes the shot will have considerable spatial depth in the composition, but the foreground will be decoratively darkened or unfocused (fig 27.27). Sometimes a short-focal-length lens at an unusual angle will yield a shot/reverse-shot pattern (fig 27.28). Almost always, however, the 1920s principle holds: long shots have greater depth of field than closer shots. Even as late as *Wuthering Heights*, when a shot's foreground may be in medium close-up, one plane or another is out of focus. When Cathy is at the table, for instance, she is in focus in the middle ground and Hindley's shoulder and the servant's hand are out of focus in the foreground. Nevertheless, Toland's work of the late 1930s deserves closer consideration. First, several of the films he worked on make a systematic use of depth of space and of focus that was generally rare at the time; and secondly, in some images we can find what would become Toland's individual use of deep focus.

Wuthering Heights (March 1939), shot for William Wyler at Goldwyn, employs certain aspects of the setting as motifs, and these aspects usually have to do with depth. In general, there is Wuthering Heights itself, a low, mazelike set with raked floors and low ceilings similar to those in *Stagecoach* (released February 1939). More specifically, depth is used as a motif to contrast eras within the story. When as youngsters Cathy and Heathcliff peer into the Grange, the camera

tracks past them to the window to reveal the ball inside. The penetration into the room expresses Cathy's fascination with the glittering life there. Years later, with Cathy now Lockley's wife and mistress of the Grange, Heathcliff the gentleman calls on them. As the three leave the room, the camera suddenly tracks back, through the same window. The contrast of periods and the sense of change issue from the parallel camera movements into and out of depth.

Dead End (1937) is in many respects even more remarkable. The confinement to a single set and a loose unity of duration (one day) mark the film as fairly theatrical. Within these conventions, however, Toland and Wyler create a constant interplay in depth. The various lines of action are interwoven within deep space: Wyler will shift our attention from a foreground action to a new action in the background. This practice poses no great problem for depth of focus, since typically the foreground is still in long shot. But in one virtuosic framing, two hoodlums in a restaurant plan to kidnap the rich man's son (fig 27.29). The men are in focus in profiled close-up; outside the window, a woman wheels a baby carriage across the street. The woman is too far away to be in focus, and her child is not the target of the scheme, but the fact that she occupies frame center and is the only moving figure in the shot gives her a symbolic salience. Here is the sort of staging in extreme depth, with a significant element in foreground close-up and a thematically important element in a distant plane, that will become familiar in *Citizen Kane*.

The Long Voyage Home (October 1940) was praised by *American Cinematographer* for Toland's memorable shots, and it is possible that it exercised considerable influence on deep-focus films of 1941. As in *Dead End*, there is little backlighting, but the sensitivity of the film stock picks out various planes. Again, the action is staged in depth, especially along the ship's deck. Since the background plane is often only a few feet beyond an extremely close foreground plane, both planes can be in sharp focus (fig 27.30).

Toland's late 1930s career is of interest chiefly because in the three films mentioned, a fairly rigorous use of depth becomes central to the overall construction of space. Moreover, while many shots resemble other cinematographers' explorations of deep-focus imagery at the period, certain images in *Dead End* and *The Long Voyage Home* bear the mark of Toland's distinctive treatment of deep space and deep focus. The characteristic Toland shot is lit low-key, with little fill or backlighting. There are several significant planes of depth, all in focus. There is an exaggeratedly enlarged foreground plane – usually a face. Most importantly, heads crowd into the frame, competing for attention by position (centered, uncentered), size, movement, glance, and aspect (profile, frontal).

An excellent example of the Toland trademark occurs in figure 27.31, when the Bogart character terrorizes the young boy. There are not only several planes (from the beanie in extreme lower foreground to the wall in the distance) but several distinct areas of action in the shot. A comparable zigzag of our attention operates in figure 27.32. In the scene of the group song from *The Long Voyage Home* (fig 27.33), the foreground element is not so exaggerated, but the frontality is even more marked. Furthermore, the typical Toland composition crams all the dramatically significant elements into the frame. This has the effect of making the shot notably static: all the figures are visible from only one vantage point; any camera or figure movement would impede our sightlines. Toland's densely organized compositions do not, as Bazin argued, make our perception existentially free; instead, dialogue, gesture, and figure aspect direct our attention. We must also remember that such packed shots are legible because they are carefully imbedded in an orthodox context of clear establishing shots, analytical cutting, and close-ups. Such compositions' use of deep space and deep focus will become dominant in Toland's 1941 work.

If Toland was striving, within his professional context, to distinguish his own contribution, what do we make of *Citizen Kane* (released April 1941)? The film's stylistic features – the diagonal perspectives (with ceilings), the splitting of action into two or more distinct planes, the use of an enlarged foreground plane (close-up or even extreme close-up), the low-key lighting, and the persistent frontality – all had been seen, in fragmentary fashion, in Toland's previous work. But *Kane* enabled Toland to consolidate a unified 'look' as his trademark.

In this film, deep focus is elevated to a coherent style on the basis of two principles. The first is the dramatic expanse of the sets. The *Inquirer* offices, the auditoriums and opera stages, Xanadu, even the Kane family cabin and the El Rancho nightclub, are all conceived as enormous spaces, both high and deep. Here Toland's deep focus functions in traditional ways: even on these vast sets, the angles still operate within patterns of shot/reverse shot (e.g., Kane and Susan shouting across the cavernous hall in Xanadu) or of establishing shots (e.g., Gettys watching Kane's rally from a balcony). A second, more innovative principle made *Kane*'s deep focus flagrant: the use of unusually long takes. Toland claimed that in the interest of 'simplification,' Welles decided to avoid cuts.[25]

> We pre-planned our angles and compositions so that action which would ordinarily be shown in direct cuts would be shown in a single, longer scene – often one in which important action might take place simultaneously in widely-separated points in extreme foreground and background. . . . Welles' technique of visual simplification might combine what would conventionally be made as two separate shots – a close-up and an insert – in a single, non-dollying shot.

The important phrase here is 'non-dollying.' In *Kane*, the static, cramped quality of Toland's particular brand of depth is given full sway by the use of the almost unmoving long take. The most famous deep-focus shots in the film – Susan's music lesson, the scene of Kane signing away his newspapers (fig 27.34), Kane's firing of Leland, Susan's attempted suicide, and most of the shot in Mrs Kane's boarding house – all are notably rigid and posed, relying greatly upon frontality and narrowly circumscribed figure movement. These shots call attention to themselves not only because they are so deep but also because they are so prolonged and fixed.

Citizen Kane was, then, an opportunity for Toland to make flamboyant deep focus identified with his own work. Welles had come to Hollywood with no professional film experience, and (according to Welles) Toland had sought out the *Kane* assignment. After the filming was completed, Toland was at pains to claim several innovations. For greater realism, he explained, many sets were designed with ceilings, which required him to light from the floor. Since the sets were also deep, he relied on the carrying power of arc lamps. Furthermore, since Welles and Toland had decided to stage action in depth, Toland sought great depth of focus by using Super XX film, increasing the lighting levels, and using optically coated wide-angle lenses.[26] As a result, Toland claimed to be able to stop down his lens 'to apertures infinitely smaller than anything that has been used for conventional interior cinematography in many years.'[27] In an era when f-2.3 and f-2.8 were the common apertures, Toland boasted that he shot all *Kane's* interiors at f-8 or smaller apertures.[28]* The result shifted the traditional limits of deep space. In yielding a depth of field that extended from about eighteen inches to infinity, Toland's 'pan-focus' made it possible to have a sharp foreground plane in medium shot or even close-up and still keep very distant background planes in focus.

In justifying pan-focus for *Citizen Kane*, Toland walked the cinematographer's narrow line between artistic innovation and modest craftsmanship. Welles allowed originality full play, Toland claimed. But experimentation was controlled by certain demands. Static long takes in the name of 'simplification' could be justified as a more efficient production procedure, allowing dialogue scenes to be shot more quickly. There was a stylistic demand as well, which Toland labeled 'realism.' Realism of space, because the eye sees in depth: 'For all practical purposes it is a perfect universal-focus lens.' Realism of time, because cuts call the audience's attention to 'the mechanics of picture-making.' In all, realism in the name of continuity and concealed artifice: 'Both Welles and I . . . felt that if it was possible, the picture should be brought to the screen in such a way that the audience would feel it was looking at reality, rather than merely a movie.'[29] The terms of the rationale are familiar, but 'the most style-conscious cameraman of his time,' as Toland was later called, did not quite get away with it.[30] The visual style of *Citizen Kane* was sensed as so unusual that the Toland 'look' became famous but also came under considerable criticism within the industry.

Citizen Kane's distinctive cinematography made Toland the only Hollywood cameraman whose name was known to the general public. In 1941, Toland signed five major articles about his shooting technique, one of which appeared in *Popular Photography* and another in *Theatre Arts*. In June, *Life* ran an extensive feature about *Kane*: nominally about Welles, the article devoted most space to explaining 'pan-focus' using illustrations especially prepared by Toland. Toland's name was kept in the limelight by the release of two more films in 1941, *The Little Foxes* (August) and *Ball of Fire* (December). By the end of the year, amateur enthusiasts were learning how to apply pan-focus to their home movies and Goldwyn was reported to be offering Toland the most lucrative and prestigious contract any cinematographer had received.[31]

Toland's professional peers had a more mixed response to his work. True, he had publicized the cinematographer as a creative artist. None the less, many cinematographers felt that Toland's work swerved too far from the orthodox style.[32] *Kane* was criticized for distorted perspectives and excessive shadows. Charles G. Clarke pointed out in *American Cinematographer* that although the soft style had been abused, Toland had gone too far to the other extreme. For one thing, *Kane's* small apertures gained depth at the price of 'that illusion of roundness which – fully as important as depth of definition – is a necessity in conveying the illusion of three-dimensional reality in our two-dimensional pictures.'[33] Clarke went on to claim that exaggerated depth of field sacrificed selectivity, the ability to control audience attention by focusing on only the most important character. Toland was often criticized on these grounds. The *American Cinematographer's* review of *How Green Was My Valley* (December 1941) hits Toland in almost every sentence:[34]

[Arthur] Miller makes eloquent use of the modern increased-depth technique. But he does it without lapsing into the brittle artificiality which has so often accompanied the use of this technique. His scenes have depth – often to a surprising degree – but they also have qualities of 'good photography' which are all too often lost in attaining unusual depth of field. His scenes have depth, yes; but they also have a lifelike roundness, a soft plasticity of image, and a pleasing gradational range which have all too often been sacrificed in pursuit of depth.

Commentary in *American Cinematographer* about *The Little Foxes* was even more critical, complaining that simultaneous action in foreground and background created confused, scattered compositions: 'The eye hardly knows where to look.'[35]

Such responses to Toland's work were not simply jealousy. They were signals that Toland had developed too eccentric a style. His artistry was no longer unobtrusive. The reaction against Toland's lack of volumes and selectivity was caused by his refusal to use edge-lighting, his rigid placement of figures, his relatively undiffused close shots of women, his cramped compositions, and especially the lengthy takes that prolonged the viewer's awareness of depth.

One other factor, not mentioned at the time of *Kane*'s release, seems an important cause of the film's 'brittle artificiality.' So strong was the mystique surrounding Toland that his 'pan-focus' lens work was given credit for shots that were not made as he had claimed. During the late 1930s, the RKO Special Effects Unit, under Vernon Walker, had become famous for its realistic matte and optical printer work.[36] In 1941, no writers acknowledged that many of *Citizen Kane*'s deep-focus effects had been created by Walker's unit. Several of the Xanadu shots, ceilings included, were mattes. The shot of Kane firing Jed Leland was done in back-projection. In 1943, Linwood Dunn, supervisor of RKO's optical printer work, claimed: 'The picture was about 50% optically duped, some reels consisting of 80% to 90% of optically-printed footage. Many normal-looking scenes were optical composites of units photographed separately...'.[37] (Again, William Cameron Menzies had anticipated this practice, using back-projection and mattework for depth effects in *Our Town*.) Even shots not optically treated were not necessarily strict 'pan-focus.' Dunn points out that Susan's suicide scene, for example, was a multiple exposure, the foreground planes of the shot being exposed separately and the focus being changed for each plane.[38] At the time, Toland did not admit that many deep-focus shots were not done in the camera. Indeed, many of the illustrations accompanying his 1941 articles and interviews are captioned as examples of pan-focus when they are actually optically printed images. In his later films, Toland had no recourse to such optical work, which explains why

their depth of field is not so extreme. *Kane*'s use of special effects gave it a cartoonish look which was not greatly imitated. That Arthur Miller, not Toland, won the Academy Award for black-and-white cinematography in 1941 and that *Citizen Kane* looks not quite like any later Hollywood film suggest that Toland's extreme style had to be modified to fit classical norms.

Deep-focus cinematography in the 1940s and 1950s

If *Kane* was more controversial than copied, where lies Toland's significance? Even while criticizing Toland, Clarke claimed that deep focus gave the cinematographer a new tool, 'a better way of meeting the requirements of any story-situation. Let us hope that if the pendulum of cinematographic style swings back again toward increased softness, we will not forget this technique.'[39] Toland set a new standard for technical prowess: after him, a skilled cinematographer had to know how to use coated lenses, fast film, floor-level lights, and great depth of field. Moreover, although extreme deep focus had been attempted before, the publicity attending Toland made deep focus an active issue for the first time. Cinematographers were forced to face exactly how deep focus would be used, as Clarke put it, in particular story situations.

One of those situations was defined, following Toland, as 'realism.' In Chapter 7, we saw that in the 1940s a realist aesthetic somewhat modified classical practice. This was conceived as partly an 'objective' verisimilitude, especially of setting and lighting. Filming on location was initially encouraged by wartime economy measures in production, and it was facilitated by the fact that military demand had resulted in the production of more portable and versatile equipment.[40]*

Once the war ended, manufacturers created equipment and film stocks that helped location filming. 35mm camera design was least changed. A very few filmmakers did use Eyemos, Arriflexes, or Eclair Camerettes, but lightweight cameras were rarely used in Hollywood before the 1960s. Sometimes a cinematographer might use a combat camera, such as the Cunningham, for 'realistic action scenes.' More development took place in other fields. Several companies began to supply powerful portable photoflood units. After William Daniels used photofloods extensively on *Naked City* (1948), filmmakers began to take these lamps to location because they could run off house current. Photoflood lighting was also feasible because of increased film speed.[41] In 1947, Paramount and Du Pont began to use latensification to raise film speed quite considerably. (Latensification is a process which converts underexposed film to acceptable printing quality by re-exposing the film to a weak light.) By 1950 latensification was standard practice in several studios.[42]

> It is now possible to shoot location scenes in office buildings, narrow halls, alleys, etc., using only a few photofloods for illumination and, by giving the negative the latensification treatment, insure an acceptable print.
> Moreover, it is possible to achieve print quality in such footage that makes it no problem at all to edit it with scenes shot with normal studio lighting.

Soon after, in 1954, Eastman dramatically increased black-and-white film speed by introducing Tri-X (ASA 250 daylight, 200 tungsten). At the end of the decade, Eastman produced a sharper black-and-white stock and a color film suited for location shooting.[43]

Location shooting, taken in conjunction with low-key ('mood') lighting, helped define one distinct postwar cinematographic practice. Chapter 7 shows that this practice did not fundamentally violate classical principles of causal and generic motivation. Now we can see that this conception of 'realism' also owed something to a standardization of deep-focus shooting. Certain traits became common to many 'realistic' films of the 1940s and 1950s. First, there was the increased use of short focal-length lenses. The wide-angle lenses necessary for achieving deep focus were handy for cinematographers working in close quarters on location: by exaggerating distances, the short focal-length lens made actual locations, such as small rooms, seem more spacious. Moreover, in some shooting situations, full and sharply-focused shots of several figures would be impossible without a lens which could expand the angle of view.

The 35mm and 30mm lenses became more common. Frank Planer, in describing his work on *Criss Cross* (1948), remarked: 'To give the picture added realism through photography, we filmed every scene with the 30mm lens to carry a wire-sharp depth of focus throughout the frame.'[44] Whereas the 50mm lens was considered standard until the war, by 1950 the 35mm had become the norm; by 1959, cinematographers were said to have almost completely discarded the 50mm lens.[45] Another innovation of the late 1940s, the Garutso modified lens, was designed to increase depth of field without increasing the amount of light. With the Garutso, even location filming could use fairly wide apertures and still get good depth of field.[46] Thus many films of the period retained great depth of playing space and depth of focus on location. Several films shot on location used deep-focus extensively (*Act of Violence* [1948], *Lady from Shanghai* [1948], *Johnny Belinda* [1948], *A Double Life* [1948], *Asphalt Jungle* [1950], and *Viva Zapata!* [1952]).

Furthermore, just as Toland had used the faster Eastman stocks with more light, so some cinematographers took advantage of faster films and latensification to increase depth of field. Tri-X, initially designed for television filming, could be used on location to achieve depth of field, as in *Blackboard Jungle* and *Black Tuesday* (both 1955). Similarly, latensification was praised for enabling the cinematographer to stop down for greater depth. Joe MacDonald reported that latensification enabled him to film some shots for *Viva Zapata!* (1952) at an aperture of f-22. Comparable results had already been obtained in *Sunset Boulevard* and *Asphalt Jungle* (both 1950).[47]

In some ways, then, Clarke's prophecy was fulfilled. Deep focus gave the cinematographer 'a better way of meeting the requirements of any story-situation.' Deep focus became one paradigmatic alternative (see figs 27.35 and 27.36). Yet it was not a drastically new one. Cinematographers continued to use diffusion filters and three-point lighting, and they sought innovations like the Garutso lens (which yielded a great depth of field without the hard, contrasty effects of stopping down the lens). Just as Hollywood had quickly lauded, then revised, the extreme low-key 'Lasky lighting' in *The Cheat* (1915), so cinematographers toned down Toland's idiosyncratic style. Even in non-location films, deep focus and deep space were assimilated to existing norms of genre and decoupage. A horror film like *Hangover Square* (1945) could use bizarre low angles and depth to signify a threatening atmosphere. Other films absorbed deep focus into normal shooting and cutting patterns. If the shot was not a static long take (as in *Kane*), an occasional deep-focus composition could effectively establish or reestablish a locale (fig 27.37). If the deep shot was not exaggeratedly frontal, it could create a crisp over-the-shoulder reverse angle (figs 27.38 and 27.39). Toland himself used his particular brand of deep focus in such conventional ways for the comedy *Ball of Fire* (December 1941), which − although not entirely free of the rigid poses of *Kane* − does avoid the long take and fits the deep shots into orthodox shot/reverse-shot combinations or into grotesque comic juxtapositions (fig 27.40).

While many filmmakers of the 1940s inserted the deep-focus composition into a classical decoupage, some directors explored another possibility. For Wyler, as Bazin pointed out, the shot in depth constituted an equivalent of a normally edited breakdown of the scene. Action and reaction, cause and effect, are now shown within the same shot. But frontality, evenly spaced figures, and glances all function to guide the spectator's perception of the image. The pragmatic Wyler justified his practice as wholly traditional, creating 'smooth continuity, an almost effortless flow of the scene.'[48] Thus in *The Little Foxes*, when Zan glimpses her boyfriend eating with another woman, Wyler refrains from cutting in to him; but since Zan turns her back to us, our attention is driven to the background (fig 27.41). Other filmmakers followed the same principle, although with more open compositions; in figure 27.42, from *Manhandled* (1949), the detective notices the water cooler in the nearest plane, and his glance cues us to look at it. In both examples, the single shot does duty for a series of eyeline-matched close-ups. Thus filmmakers either inserted deep-focus shots into a traditional sequence or implanted the classical editing principles within the deep-focus shots themselves. Either way, the classical paradigm remained in place. Hollywood deep-focus cinematography created only what Leonard Meyer calls trended change.

Toland's own career after 1942 is a measure of the assimilation of deep focus to classical norms. After returning from the Navy, he shot *The Best Years of Our Lives* (1946) for Wyler and Goldwyn. The film has several deep-focus shots, but now Toland almost never jams many faces into the frame and never makes the foreground plane close and frontal. Compare figure 27.43, of Fred and Peggy in the drugstore and the manager in the distance, with the famous shot in Mrs Kane's boarding house; or compare the intimate space of the parlor in figure 27.44 with the depth of the stairwell in figure 5.25, from *The Little Foxes*. Toland's postwar compositions are relatively spacious and open, with more recourse to reframing, and none are allowed to take on the rigidity of *Kane*'s long-take tableaux. The most famous example of the new flexibility in Toland's compositions is the scene in Butch's tavern, when Al looks from Homer playing the piano in the foreground to the phone booth in the distance, where Fred is calling Peggy (fig 27.45). In *Kane*, our attention would be drawn to the booth by decor, lighting, and sharply-angled perspective. Here, Wyler cuts in closer (fig 27.46). The scene is analyzed for us.

Toland's professional practices changed as well. Wyler recalled that in the postwar films Toland had recourse to a sliding diffusion screen 'to keep the sharp focus of realism, without being harsh or unflattering to the women he photographed.'[49] In interviews, Toland justified his quest for deep focus as always subservient to the film's story. But he did continue his experiments. Toland was associated with his trademark − wire-sharp depth in cinematography − until his death in 1948 and thereafter. For *Roseanna McCoy* (1949), he was said to have perfected an 'ultimate focus' lens that could stop down to f-64. He was reported to carry in his wallet a strip of film bearing a shot with a focal depth of three inches to infinity; in the foreground was a face.[50]

Toland, then, did not overthrow the classical style. The film that posed the most problems, *Citizen Kane*, was not typical, partly because of its reliance upon optical work, partly because of its lighting, compositions, and long takes. None the less, Toland's innovations not only made his reputation; they also influenced his peers. After 1942, in good part through the activities of the ASC, Hollywood cinematography adopted a less picturesque deep-focus style better suited to the demands of classical narrative and decoupage. Long takes would be used, but not in conjunction with static deep-focus compositions. The ability to execute a shot in depth became one more mark of the expert cinematographer, but the wary professional chose not to call attention to deep focus by making it a personal trademark.

28 Technicolor

One source of spectacle in early silent films was color – tinting, toning, and handcoloring. For years many firms worked persistently to secure a predictable and reasonably priced photographic color that would conform to Hollywood's stylistic standards. In 1929, over twenty companies claimed basic color patents, but a single firm won control of the field.[1] Technicolor's supremacy resulted from several factors. The firm carefully developed, revised, and publicized its process. The company was generally sensitive to the business and engineering requirements of Hollywood film production. Moreover, Technicolor Corporation worked effectively with the professional associations, especially the SMPE (in which Technicolor staff members were prominent). The success of Technicolor during the 1930s and 1940s can be measured both by its increased volume of business and its several Academy Awards.

Technicolor is an instance of a service firm initiating research within a specialized area. In such situations, major production firms tended to let smaller firms initiate a new technology, withholding investment until severe problems had been ironed out. This explains why Technicolor lived precariously for such a long time – sixteen years without making a profit. It took that long to harness a significant novelty to Hollywood's standards of cost efficiency and quality.

The company was founded in 1916 by Herbert Kalmus, Daniel Comstock, and W. Burton Wescott as an outgrowth of their industrial-engineering consulting firm. The earliest Technicolor process, an additive method, aroused little interest. (An additive color process blends light of primary colors on the screen surface, rather than using pigments or dyes in the film strip itself. Technicolor's earliest method superimposed red-and-green-filtered images on the screen.) In the 1920s, a two-strip Technicolor process was used almost exclusively in sequences in black-and-white movies. Technicolor's first boom came during the years 1929-31. The firm had devised a new two-strip subtractive process and its celebrated imbibition printing method.[2]* Warner Bros, having innovated talking pictures, used the improved Technicolor for *On With the Show!* (1929), and other studios followed suit. But within three years, the decline in release-print quality and the cost of the process made firms halt Technicolor filming. In 1932, Joseph A. Ball created a three-strip method that offered much better color rendition. (For this method, Ball added a three-color beamsplitter and a third strip of film, so that each matrix – red, blue, green – had its own separation negative.) Tested on Walt Disney cartoons (beginning with *Flowers and Trees* [1932]), a live-action short (*La Cucaracha* [1934]), and then on a feature (*Becky Sharp* [1935]), Technicolor attracted attention again. The success of *Trail of the Lonesome Pine* (1935), *A Star Is Born* (1937), *Adventures of Tom Sawyer* (1938), and *Gone With the Wind* (1939) confirmed Technicolor's new powers. Soon the firm could not keep up with the producers' demands. Presided over by Herbert Kalmus, Technicolor virtually monopolized Hollywood color filming until the early 1950s.[3]

To win Hollywood's support, Technicolor employed a time-tested business tactic, that of supplying research prototypes. Every new Technicolor process was demonstrated in a sample film financed by the company itself or by a sympathetic backer. Kalmus and his colleagues produced *The Gulf Between* (1917) to display the additive process, *Toll of the Sea* (1922) to exhibit the initial two-color procedure, and *The Flag* (1927) and *The Viking* (1928) to publicize the revised two-color process. By the time Technicolor was ready to showcase the three-strip process in a feature film, Merriam C. Cooper and John Hay Whitney formed an independent firm, Pioneer Films, to make *La Cucaracha* and *Becky Sharp*.[4] Again and again Kalmus's company had to assume responsibility for proving that its color method could meet the industry's standard of quality.

The issue of production economies also dogged Technicolor. Even after the three-strip method was proven viable, the studios did not rush to convert. One principal reason was that Technicolor was hard to adjust to demands of cost and labor-time. In 1936, Technicolor could increase a picture's budget by $100,000 to $300,000, an enormous amount during the Depression. A Technicolor film consumed more production time, required more electrical power, and could not draw upon the studio library of stock footage. Many producers doubted that Technicolor's novelty compensated for the expense. As *American Cinematographer* put it, if the color was unnatural, the audience noticed it (and that was bad); if the color was good, the audience forgot about it (thus it was not worth the cost).[5]

Technicolor was sensitive to demands for cost effectiveness because its founders were experienced engineers. Both Kalmus and Comstock were graduates of the Massachusetts Institute of Technology and had taught there; they employed three MIT physics students to work on the process; even the firm's name paid tribute to 'Tech.' As industrial consultants, Kalmus, Comstock, and Wescott had gained a sound reputation for research. And as engineers, Technicolor's directors decided on a 'progressive step development' strategy for nurturing their color process little by little, with a three-color process as the ultimate goal. It was Ball, one of Comstock's students and a prominent member of the SMPE and the Academy, who designed the three-color camera and guided Technicolor research through the 1930s.[6] It was generally acknowledged that Comstock, Leonard Troland, and Ball were the inventors while Kalmus was the promoter: 'Businessmen regard Dr. Kalmus as a scientist and scientists regard him as a businessman.'[7] But even Kalmus continued to experiment in solving engineering problems in his spare time.

Throughout the years, Technicolor followed many industrial-engineering principles to maximize efficiency. The company started a research laboratory. It retained a staff to design and build special printers and processing machinery. Laboratory chief Gerald Rackett pointed to his operation as a model of successful engineering. Although the cameras were built by Mitchell, they were designed and repaired in the optical and machine shops of Technicolor. The plant was a paragon of industrial organization. Management carefully divided the labor, limited knowledge to specialties, and discouraged transfers across departments. Entering sensitive areas required security passes. Only the firm's executives had a total view of research development and patented processes.[8]

After the 1935 color boom, Technicolor controlled its quality by placing restrictions on production practices. Because the 1929-31 color vogue had resulted in untrained cinematographers using the process, the firm wanted to supervise production to a great degree. Filming procedures became standardized. To make a Technicolor film, a producer had to rent the cameras, hire a Technicolor cameraman (eventually to be called a 'camera optical engineer'), use Technicolor make-up, and have the film processed and printed by Technicolor. The producer would also have to accept a 'color consultant' who would advise what color schemes to use on sets, costumes, and make-up. Every day the camera magazines were inspected in the Technicolor laboratory, checked out by the cinematographer, and returned at the end of the day. Only trained crews could operate the camera, and the production's cinematographer had to work closely with the Technicolor cameraman. The firm also adjusted itself to studio differences, supplying motors for various studios' electrical and sound requirements.[9]

Before 1950, few of Technicolor's research innovations spilled over beyond the improvement of its own color process. In the mid-1930s, the firm devised a remote-control focusing device that was occasionally used on black-and-white films. Technicolor also spurred the development of bright process-projection equipment. The most significant innovation of all occurred in 1935. Since the three-color process was balanced for daylight, arc lighting most closely approximated the film's needs. But most studios' arc equipment dated back to the 1920s. Technicolor commissioned Mole-Richardson to design silent, efficient arc units that would yield a uniform, flat distribution of light. Two years later, Mole-Richardson introduced a new line of side arcs, overhead 'scoops,' and spotlights. These lamps soon became common in both color and black-and-white filming.[10]

As a service company, Technicolor maintained almost complete control of its product; as a color process, it had to conform to classical norms. Hollywood's use of Technicolor was almost entirely motivated by genre. It was to the firm's advantage to stress that color was simply an increase in realism applicable to any film, but the argument did not convince.[11] On the whole, Technicolor was identified with the musical comedy, the historical epic, the adventure story, and the fantasy — in short, the genres of stylization and spectacle. During the 1920s, Technicolor sequences were inserted into *The Merry Widow* (1925), *Beau Geste* (1926), *Ben-Hur* (1926), *The Ten Commandments* (1923), and others; in *The Big Parade* (1925) and *The Wedding March* (1928), the process was used for scenes of pageantry. *The Black Pirate* (1926), one of the first two-strip Technicolor features, made extensive use of color for spectacle. The 1929-31 Technicolor boom was identified with the rise of the musical. (*Desert Song*, *Glorifying the American Girl*, *Golddiggers of Broadway*, *Rio Rita*, *Show of Shows*, *King of Jazz*, and *Whoopee* are the best-known.) Contemporary accounts emphasize that two-color (red-green) Technicolor was best suited for 'musical revues' because they appeal by virtue of costume and artificial settings: 'Color pictures [scripts] which depend for their effect upon outdoor sets will be of comparatively little value to studios using a color process which cannot obtain good blues in sea and sky.'[12]

Even after Ball devised the more 'realistic' three-strip color method, color films remained codified by genre. There were musicals (*The Dancing Pirate* [1935], *Vogues of 1938* [1937], *Goldwyn Follies* [1938], *Down Argentine Way* [1940], *The Gang's All Here* [1943]). There were historical spectacles and adventure tales in exotic locales (*Adventures of Robin Hood* [1938], *Drums Along the Mohawk* [1939], *Northwest Mounted Police* [1940], *Western Union* [1941], *The Black Swan* [1942], *For Whom the Bell Tolls* [1943]). A Western (e.g., *Jesse James* [1939]), a comedy (e.g., *Nothing Sacred* [1937]), or a romance set in an exotic locale (e.g., *The Garden of Allah* [1936]) also had an occasional chance of being filmed in color. *The Women* (1940) justified color by its lengthy interpolated fashion show, while *An American Romance* (1944) uses color to reinforce its 'epic' account of an immigrant making good. It is probable that two films of 1939 played a central role in defining color's generic range: *Gone With the Wind*, a historical spectacle, was credited with having proven that color could add to a film's box-office appeal, and *The Wizard of Oz* used Technicolor only for the central Oz fantasy, not for a rendering of Dorothy's everyday life in Kansas. Like certain kinds of music or lighting, the presence of color was governed by genre conventions.[13]

Other conventions of the classical paradigm limited Technicolor's use. While Technicolor could play up the spectacular and the artificial, the industry cautioned that color must not distract from the story. It was widely felt that two-strip Technicolor musicals had been weak films bolstered by the novelties of color and sound; this diagnosis was confirmed by the lukewarm response given to *Becky Sharp* (1935). 'Never use color for the sake of color alone,' warned a Selznick art director in 1937. 'It is only something which is added to the story, and the story should not be made for the sake of it.'[14]

Technicolor was aware of Hollywood's demands. From the outset, the firm had understood that in order to succeed commercially color would have to favor principal narrative elements. Around 1920, a producer explained the problem to Comstock:[15]

> The human being is the center of the drama, not flowers, gardens, and dresses. The face is the center of the human being. And the eyes are the center of the face. If a process is not sharp enough to show clearly the whites of a person's eyes at a reasonable distance, it isn't any good no matter what it is.

The plausible rendering of complexion and expression became the chief goal of Technicolor's research. One critic pointed out problems of definition in the 1916-23 efforts: 'When the figures retreat to any distance, it is difficult to distinguish their expression.'[16] Complaints about *Becky Sharp*'s 'overripe' and 'scarletina' skin tones made Technicolor ask Max Factor to devise pancake make-up. Throughout the 1930s, Technicolor calmed cinematographers' fears that color would aggravate facial blemishes.[17] The firm was at pains to compromise between developing a 'lifelike' rendition of the visible spectrum and developing a treatment of the human face that would accord with classical requisites of beauty and narrative centrality.

To fit Technicolor's recording capacities smoothly to Hollywood's needs, the firm created the role of color consultant. Natalie Kalmus, Herbert's wife, had been the first model for Technicolor filming. She and Kalmus were divorced in 1921 (although they continued to live in the same house for another twenty-five years), and one condition of the divorce made Natalie the color supervisor on most Technicolor productions. A former art student, she insisted that sets and costumes be in cool colors, the better to set off the tones of the characters' faces. She is sometimes credited with Technicolor's reluctance to film bright or saturated colors, the assumption being that pastels were less harsh and distracting. The same worry that Technicolor would look artificial governed the ban on symbolically colored lighting, a constraint not completely overcome until *South Pacific* (1958).[18]

Natalie Kalmus also promoted the idea that Technicolor could yield not a flat and candy-box image, but actually a more rounded and deep one. With the proper color separation of foreground and background, she wrote, 'it is possible to make it appear as though the actors were actually standing there in person, thus creating the illusion of a third dimension.'[19] On the whole, cinematographers accepted this dictum. They shot Technicolor with softer and flatter light, using less backlight and letting the color difference separate the planes. A frame like figure 28.1 shows how color areas could distinguish planes without need for edge lighting. As late as 1957, the SMPTE was still advocating low-contrast lighting for color (no more than a 3:1 key-fill ratio). Most cinematographers used the same arrangement of lighting units for color and black and white; only the intensity and number of the sources differed.[20] The effect was far from transgressive, as can be seen from almost any shot in a 1930s or 1940s Technicolor film. High-key Technicolor shooting yielded an image that conformed to the norms of softness, low contrast, and diffusion characteristic of 1930s cinematography (see fig 28.2). The rarer low-key Technicolor shot still possesses a softness, especially in shadow areas, consistent with Hollywood norms. Classical ideals of volume, separation of planes, and dim backgrounds were amply satisfied by Technicolor cinematography.

Just as sound filming practices strove to recover the standardized procedures of the silent era, so Technicolor filming attempted to become as much as possible like monochrome filming. Color brought with it three changes: a very slow film stock, the need for arc lighting, and the awkward three-strip camera. Many cinematographers accepted certain inevitable demands, such as the necessity of gauging light by exposure meters. But knowing that light levels were a problem, Technicolor constantly tried to increase its film speed. The company's efforts resulted in a faster, fine-grained stock first used on *Gone With the Wind* (1939). Combined with Mole-Richardson's portable arc units, this film stock put color cinematography somewhat closer to monochrome methods. Nonetheless, by 1948, a cinematographer could still point out that for low-key filming, color required ten lighting units for every two used in black and white, and that changes in light intensity affected not only exposure but color gradations, often for the worse.[21]

From an engineering standpoint, Technicolor filming could not become fully consonant with mainstream production practice as long as it utilized a three-strip method. The bulky cameras were hard to maneuver, complicated to thread, difficult to maintain. It is clear that Herbert Kalmus set as a goal a monopack film that could be used in any camera. In 1939, he announced that in a year Technicolor would employ a single camera negative. Monopack was used for sequences in some films (*Dive Bomber* [1941], *Captains of the Clouds* [1942], *Forest Rangers* [1942], *Lassie Come Home* [1943]) and for one entire film (*Thunderhead – Son of Flicka* [1944]), but the process was declared unsatisfactory. It was even slower than ordinary Technicolor stock, it rendered interior sets poorly, and the processing often gave contrasty results. Researchers were uncertain as to whether a single-strip negative film could ever yield consistently good release prints in large quantity. World War II delayed research on the process, but Kalmus was also hesitant, probably recalling the difficulties he had faced after rushing into an untried process in 1929. Expecting monopack to come eventually, Technicolor built no more three-strip cameras.[22] (This decision caused further problems, since Technicolor could not satisfy the postwar demand for color.) When a color negative film arrived, however, Technicolor was not its originator.

Initially, Technicolor and Eastman Kodak had agreed not to compete for monopack color film. Through the research work of Comstock and Troland, Technicolor held crucial patents on monopack. A cross-licensing agreement allowed Eastman to use the process for Kodachrome, its amateur-gauge process. From 1937 to 1939, Technicolor and Eastman jointly researched a feasible 35mm color negative. The result was the monopack Technicolor process that saw limited use in the 1940s. In 1947, a government antitrust suit charged Eastman and Technicolor with monopolistic practices. Among other claims, the suit alleged that Technicolor had colluded with Eastman to restrict the development of monopack. Eastman soon signed a consent decree whereby it would license all its patents on the open market, with no priority given to Technicolor. In early 1950, Technicolor signed a consent decree that terminated its relations with Eastman. At least as important as the government suit was the fact that in 1945 the original Troland patents had expired. By the time that Technicolor had submitted to the suit, Eastman had already announced its own color negative process.[23]

It took about four years for Eastman Color to dethrone Technicolor: the three-strip camera was last used on *Foxfire* (1954). What gave Eastman Color the edge was that it could be used in any camera and processed and printed by generally conventional means. Within two years, most studios began to use Eastman Color to a degree, some claiming it as the basis of their 'own' system (e.g., Warnercolor, Columbia's Super Cinecolor). In 1953, Eastman introduced an improved, faster negative stock and corresponding print and internegative stocks. At about the same time, studios discovered that Technicolor dye-imbibition printing did not yield enough resolution for the new widescreen processes. Thus Eastman Color was used to film *The Robe, How to Marry a Millionaire, Beneath the Twelve-Mile Reef* (all 1953), and other early anamorphic films. As of November 1955, most widescreen productions were shooting Eastman Color negative.[24]

Technicolor adjusted as best it could. Its lab processed a great deal of Eastman negative and often made release prints by its color-separation method. It eventually adapted its imbibition method to widescreen needs; Technicolor designed printers that could make films in any format. Moreover, until the 1960s, Technicolor was the only Hollywood laboratory with the capacity to process and print 65mm and 70mm gauges. The firm also introduced electronic print timing and a (short-lived) anamorphic process of its own, Technirama. None the less, Technicolor's use in motion pictures declined. In 1947, 90 per cent of 35mm color was Technicolor; ten years later, the firm met only half the industry's color needs. After 1953, Technicolor operated as primarily a laboratory and a research firm (working for television, NASA, and the military).[25]

Technicolor's future was settled when Eastman entered the 35mm color market. A specialized firm concentrating on short-term and small-scale problems could not compete effectively with the basic-research program of Eastman Kodak. Eastman held thousands of patents, supported an immense laboratory, and invested millions in color research every year. (Eastman Color monopack grew directly out of the firm's development of color couplers for still photography.) Most likely, Technicolor had long realized how precarious its control was and, expecting Eastman to devise monopack eventually, created the licensing agreements to give itself the first chance at the process. But color negative came too late, and three-color Technicolor gave way to a method which promised greater cost efficiency and compatibility with other innovations (e.g., widescreen). During its two decades of hegemony, Technicolor demonstrated that an engineering firm could flourish by shaping technological innovation to the economic and stylistic needs of its customers.

29

Widescreen processes and stereophonic sound

The early 1950s saw the most pervasive technological innovations in Hollywood since the late 1920s. A series of processes changed the size of the screen, the shape of the image, the dimensions of the films, and the recording and reproducing of sound. There were triple-camera and -projector systems like Cinerama (introduced in 1952) and CineMiracle (1957). Of the single-camera and -projector processes, VistaVision (1954) consisted of shooting (and, initially, showing) the film on its horizontal axis to give a wider and less grainy image. There were several anamorphic processes, which in shooting or printing squeezed onto the film a wide field of view to be unsqueezed in projection: the most famous of these processes was CinemaScope (1953). There were also the wide-film systems, such as Todd-AO (1955), which was shot on 65mm and projected at 70mm (see fig 29.1). It was possible to combine processes, such as in the anamorphic wide-film systems (CinemaScope 55 [1955], Ultra-Panavision [1956]). Nearly all of these widescreen systems included stereophonic reproduction.

Jean-Louis Comolli's conception of the lag between technical possibility and ideological need is clearly pertinent to these postwar innovations. In almost every respect, widescreen cinema was technically feasible at least two decades before its acceptance. In 1929, for example, Ralph Fear proposed putting a wide image on film by a method similar to that of VistaVision. In fact, the VistaVision cameras used in the 1950s were originally designed in the late 1920s for the Fox Natural Color system, a two-color additive process. Henri Chrétien's anamorphic system was known in the early 1930s, long before it was purchased and renamed CinemaScope. 'Widescope,' a two-lens system comparable to Cinerama, was demonstrated to the SMPE as early as 1922; three-lens Cinerama had its source

in the spherical film projection at the 1934 World's Fair. Wide film gauges became of particular interest in 1929 and 1930. There was the Spoor Natural Vision (63mm), the Paramount process (56mm), Fox Grandeur (70mm), and MGM's Realife (wide film reduced to 35mm for projection). The Grandeur process had the greatest success, with the Mitchell Company furnishing precision cameras and the International Projector Corporation manufacturing Super-Simplex 70mm projection equipment. For a time, it appeared that widescreen would become common. The SMPE, ASC, and Academy held several forums on standardization (at one of which Sergei Eisenstein pleaded for a square image format). Although there were difficulties with focus and illumination, by December of 1930, the SMPE was confident enough to report that the engineering problems could be solved if the producers would only agree on a single process. That too seemed to be settled, since in July 1930 several major studios announced plans to shoot on 65mm, enlarge the sound track area, and project the film in 70mm (the Todd-AO and Ultra-Panavision procedure of later years). But the major production firms apparently decided that in a Depression economy, the novelty would not repay the investment, so extensive work on wide-film processes came to a halt.[1]

Stereophonic sound was also anticipated during the 1930s. Many of the wide-gauge processes sought to expand the soundtrack area for greater fidelity. For the first Fox Grandeur film, *Happy Days* (1930), the 70mm film yielded a wider sound track which was said to give 'a more perfect reproduction of the human voice.'[2] A 1932 paper defending Chrétien's anamorphic process suggested that the Hypergonar could put two tracks on the film and thus create 'the acoustical equivalent of the stereoscopic effect.'[3] Bell

Telephone was experimenting continually with stereophonic recording and reproduction, holding technical demonstrations in 1934 and 1938. At the SMPE convention in the fall of 1937, ERPI demonstrated stereophonic recording on film. ('The illusion of position is very strong.'[4]) Two years later, another exhibition proved that auditory perspective could be controlled at the dubbing phase as well. With the help of RCA, Warner Bros had a brief fling with 'Vitasound,' a two-channel reproduction system, used on *Four Wives* (1939) and *Santa Fe Trail* (1940). The most famous experiment in stereophonic sound was Walt Disney's *Fantasia* (1940), which utilized RCA's 'Panoramic' process. Many producers expected that stereophonic sound would soon come – the spring 1941 SMPE convention hosted five papers on the subject – but America's entry into World War II curtailed systematic nonmilitary work.[5]

Economic factors can help explain the timing of the reintroduction of widescreen and stereophonic systems. As Chapter 26 points out, between 1950 and 1952, film production companies were feeling severe losses in earnings, partly due to the competition of television. Most producers believed that some novelty was needed to recapture the audience. In late 1952, both Cinerama and 'Natural Vision' 3-D[6]* attracted public attention, and in November film firms' earnings started to rise steadily.[7] Although 3-D survived only a little over a year and Cinerama remained an exceptional roadshow process, the film industry committed many resources to devising other alternatives to television.

Research organizations such as the SMPTE or the Academy Motion Picture Research Council did not initiate widescreen processes; most were innovated by small, independent firms (e.g., Fred Waller's Cinerama, Robert Gottshalk's Panavision). Problems with the systems soon arose, though. For instance, all of the processes required a greatly enlarged theater screen – this was indeed one of their points of novelty. But there was a limit to how much the projected image could be magnified without losing certain standards of quality, such as brightness and definition. More powerful projector lamps could be used, but graininess remained a major difficulty. Thus engineers had to increase the area exposed on the original negative. Nearly all of the major

systems reduced grain by filling more negative area: VistaVision by exposing the film strip horizontally; CinemaScope by making the perforations smaller and enlarging the aperture; Todd-AO and other systems by using wider film. To effect such changes, the small manufacturers and the studios required the cooperation of major manufacturers and of the mediating agencies. Specific solutions were needed for such problems as the perspective distortion in early anamorphic lenses and the peripheral flicker visible in some widescreen systems.[8]

Once the production sector decided upon the widescreen strategy, the service companies became important sources of research and improvement. Mitchell initially supplied the cameras for VistaVision, Todd-AO, and Panavision. Phillips of Holland designed 70mm projectors. Eastman Kodak responded to the new production demands by computing the best negative areas for minimum grain and maximum information. Cinematographers sought to improve definition and depth in widescreen productions by stopping down their lenses. The smaller apertures, combined with the bigger widescreen sets and the longer focal lengths of widescreen lenses, all demanded much more light than had been customary in the late 1940s. While lamp makers such as General Electric designed high-wattage studio lamps, Eastman introduced two faster emulsions which permitted the lowering of light levels.[9]

Widescreen processes established one new supply firm as solidly as sound had established Mole-Richardson. Panavision began as a company developing and building anamorphic projector lenses. MGM asked the firm to develop a widescreen system free of distortion that would be compatible with Cinerama, anamorphic, and wide-gauge processes. The result, 'Ultra-Panavision,' was a 65mm/70mm process that created a negative from which a print in any format could be extracted. Relying upon Technicolor's laboratory expertise, Panavision could yield prints in ratios of 1.33:1, 1.85:1, 2:1, 2.25:1, 2.55:1, and 3:1. This made all systems compatible, and the results, first seen in *Ben-Hur* (1960), won Panavision an Academy Technical Award.[10]

CinemaScope was the most-utilized widescreen process of the period. In early 1953, after some years of work on widescreen and stereophonic processes, Twentieth Century-Fox announced purchase of the rights to Henri Chrétien's Hypergonar anamorphic process. Fox did little to dispell the belief that CinemaScope was a combination of Cinerama and 3-D: its advertisements exaggerated the curvature of the screen and proclaimed, 'You see it without glasses!' (Although the 'Scope ratio was initially planned to be 2.66:1, the addition of magnetic sound tracks meant that it had to be reduced to 2.55:1. Optical sound further reduced the picture area to 2.35:1.) CinemaScope quickly emerged as the compromise widescreen system. It offered a significantly different product, but required the fewest changes in exhibition procedures: only new lenses, a new screen, and some minor retooling in projection machinery. The problems with loss of projection light were solved by an aluminized lenticular screen and new lamphouses. Bausch and Lomb designed anamorphic camera and projection lenses which improved definition and reduced distortion. Exhibitors quickly converted: by 1957, four out of five American theaters could show a film in CinemaScope. Similarly, the number of 'Scope releases rose steadily between 1953 and 1958, with many films shot in other processes (Technirama, MGM 65, Todd-AO) winding up with 35mm prints in the anamorphic format. (Of the major studios, only Paramount obstinately resisted the process.) The SMPTE proposed CinemaScope standards, which were approved by the American Standards Association in 1956.[11] In short, CinemaScope succeeded at least partly because it was sufficiently novel, it was improved with the help of the service companies, and it was easiest to accommodate to standardized production and exhibition practices.

Stereophonic sound was initially planned as an integral part of CinemaScope. Some industry technicians had criticized *Fantasia* because stereo was not very dramatic as an accompaniment to an image of normal size and shape.[12] In 1948, after several experiments, Twentieth Century-Fox's director of research pointed out that 'increased effectiveness of stereophonic sound is obtained if used with a picture of greater aspect ratio than presently used.'[13] The growing use of magnetic recording after the war made stereophonic sound technically and economically feasible. The two major processes of 1952, Cinerama and Natural Vision 3-D, both used stereo. With the help of Western Electric and ERPI, Fox engineers perfected a three-channel stereo system. Unlike most widescreen processes, which reproduced stereophonically from a monaural studio recording, CinemaScope productions were also recorded in stereo. Three microphones, spread across a sound boom, yielded the sound to be played through the three theater speakers. A fourth track carried added sound effects. Simplex, Kinevox, MagnaSync, and Westrex all supplied the four-channel sound head necessary for projecting 'Scope magnetic sound, and the SMPTE accepted the modifications in perforation shape that made room for the magnetic tracks.[14]

Despite all this cooperation, stereophonic sound posed problems. It was, as we shall see, difficult to cut with regard to the image. The magnetic tracks decayed with use and picked up stray noise. Exhibitors were reluctant to install new sound heads and speakers. By 1956, only about one-fourth of the CinemaScope installations in the United States and Canada had magnetic playback facilities. Because of the expense of making both optical and magnetic release prints, Fox in 1957 turned to a combined 'MagOptical' print format that made the CinemaScope ratio officially 2.35:1.[15] Stereo sound remained confined chiefly to roadshow theaters.

Many critics believed that widescreen filming decisively changed Hollywood film style. André Bazin, though critical of the distorted optics of CinemaScope and Cinerama, saw these innovations as a progressive step away from a montage-based cinema.[16] 'The wide screen can only hasten what we like in the most modern tendencies in the cinema: the reduction of all artifice external to the content of the image itself, of all expressionism of time or space.'[17] The revisionist Bazinians of *Cahiers du cinéma* and *Movie* quickly seized upon the widescreen processes as proof of the mystique of mise-en-scene. With CinemaScope, François Truffaut exulted, film had moved closer to total realism.[18] Charles Barr's influential essay, 'CinemaScope: before and after,' argued that the wide screen could delineate the narrative situation more subtly through a greater 'gradation of emphasis.' CinemaScope also encouraged an active and alert state of mind in the spectator: 'We have to make a positive act of interpreting, of "reading" the shot.' Now editing could not abstract a detail from its context; even a close-up, Barr argued, becomes a part of its 'natural' situation.[19] In mainstream usage, however, widescreen cinema belied these assertions. Hollywood's widescreen filmmaking was but another instance of trended change, a new set of stylistic devices brought into line with the classical schemata.

Like Technicolor, widescreen was initially motivated generically. The expanded format was believed well-suited for spectacle: the travelogue (*This Is Cinerama* [1952], *Cinerama Holiday* [1955]), the historical pageant (*The Robe* [1953], *Knights of the Round Table* [1953]), the adventure film (*Beneath the Twelve-Mile Reef* [1953], *King of the Khyber Rifles* [1954]), the musical (*Carmen Jones* [1954], *Seven Brides for Seven Brothers* [1954], *Oklahoma* [1955]), and the Western (*Broken Lance* [1954], *Sitting Bull* [1954]). (Bazin: 'Like a fish in the biggest aquarium, the cowboy is most at ease on the wide screen.'[20]) Rather than enhancing realism, the monumental screen size and shape tended toward stylization and the enhancement of spectacle.

But, like color and sound, widescreen posed potential problems for the classical style. Cinematographers and directors had difficulty in guiding the audience's attention to the significant elements in the frame. Spatial orientation was also disturbed. Before Panavision, the widescreen processes had to use longer lenses, which produced shallower depth of field. If, to get greater depth of field, the cinematographer used a lens of shorter focal length, distortion increased drastically. Actors looking off at the same object seemed to be looking in slightly different directions; horizon lines could warp; a panning shot could produce a giddying heave of perspective.[21] In addition, editing was felt to jolt the audience. 'Rapid cutting,' claimed Kenneth MacGowan, 'is disturbing on the wide screen.'[22] Other problems were peculiar to certain systems — especially Cinerama and Todd-AO — and remained unsolved.[23]* It is evident, however, that the crucial difficulties of widescreen were resolved within the terms of the classical paradigm.

We might expect that some deep-focus procedures would have been quickly applied to widescreen cinema. But the shallow depth of field of most widescreen lenses precluded anything like the looming sharp foregrounds of Toland's work for Welles or Wyler. Depth in the widescreen

format obeyed the principle established in the teens: the further the foreground plane from the camera, the greater the potential depth of field. Most of the celebrated uses of deep-focus in CinemaScope, for instance, place the foreground plane no closer than medium shot. And almost never does widescreen filming yield greater use of depth than the modified deep-focus style of the 1940s.[24] (Indeed, for some years, interior scenes in widescreen films tended to be somewhat shallower in focus than was the case in the previous decade.) The widescreen process did, however, affect the length of the take and shot composition.

It is generally assumed that widescreen filming triggered a move to lengthier shots. If *Cahiers du cinéma* writers hailed CinemaScope for its ability to make editing less important, no less 'Bazinian' was Hollywood's own attitude. Henry Koster, director of *The Robe*, asserted that a cut in to a close-up was now unnecessary, since virtually every detail in the shot was magnified. Charles G. Clarke suggested that cutting should be avoided in CinemaScope because each change of shot demanded more viewer adjustment than did cutting in regular format. Todd-AO cameramen were told to stay well back from the players and to avoid close-ups.[25] We might then expect that the average shot length jumps dramatically for widescreen films. Although the average shot duration did lengthen somewhat when widescreen processes were introduced, the classical system fairly quickly restabilized itself.

Certainly early (1953-5) CinemaScope films lean to longer takes. The typical range is between 180 and 350 shots per hour for 'Scope films, as opposed to 300-520 shots per hour for non-Scope ones. In practice, the ASL of early widescreen films is four to seven seconds longer than the eleven-second non-widescreen norm. But the range of paradigmatic options soon broadened. After 1955, a CinemaScope film might contain between 200 and 600 shots per hour, with the 300-400 shot range being most common. This range falls within the common Academy-ratio norm (200-500 shots per hour). Thus a later widescreen film's ASL might be anywhere between six and eighteen seconds. By 1959 it was possible to cut a CinemaScope film as rapidly as a 1930s Warners' film: both *Journey to the Center of the Earth* (1959) and *Wild River* (1960) have an ASL of slightly over six seconds. As in early sound decoupage, what is remarkable is not how long most widescreen takes are but how comparatively short they are.

The formal effects of the somewhat longer widescreen take were slight. Very few Hollywood directors exploited the wide screen for unusually lengthy takes, and those tended to be directors like George Cukor and Otto Preminger who had made the long take an integral part of their decoupage before widescreen processes arrived. Moreover, the single-take scene remained as rare in Hollywood as it had ever been. While there are relatively fewer shots per scene in the widescreen films of the 1950s, the number is still high: about nineteen shots per scene in the UnS. In other filmmaking traditions, the long takes of Kenji Mizoguchi, Miklós Jancsó, Jean-Marie Straub and Danièle Huillet, and Jean-Luc Godard create a film of large durational chunks, of segments impossible to frame within an orthodox decoupage; the long take becomes a major structural factor. But in Hollywood filmmaking, the innovation of widescreen had no such radical effect. *The Letter* (1940), *Citizen Kane* (1941), and other films were predecessors of this 'crossbred' decoupage: the long take was permitted only as a privileged rhetorical device controlled by classical cutting patterns. The single-take scene was, in other words, a secondary paradigmatic alternative to the classically edited scene, and widescreen shots almost always functioned in a pattern of establishment, analysis, shot/reverse shot, and the like. (See figs 5.42 and 5.43.)

Examining Welles's use of wide-angle lenses, Bazin coined the term 'lateral depth of field' to describe 'the exceptional openness of this angle of vision.'[26] Depicting George and Fanny in the kitchen in *The Magnificent Ambersons* (1942), or depicting the Amberson ball, Welles created multiple centers of interest, not necessarily in great depth, but spread across the screen. Such lateral compositions became more prominent with widescreen ratios. Clarke pointed out that a horizontal composition was more comfortable for the viewer; Elia Kazan called it more relaxed, 'more like a stage – more "across." '[27] Doubled and triangular compositions looked less cramped than in the regular format; it was easy to string several heads and shoulders across the frame. (See fig 29.2.) The director then had to guide our attention to a single figure at any given moment,

chiefly through lighting, camera position, sound, and frontal positioning. In framing a single figure in medium shot, the dominant widescreen practice is to avoid exact centering; the actor is positioned slightly off-center, leaving space for his or her gaze or for pertinent background material (fig 29.3).[28] Using the lateral stretch this way, the Hollywood filmmaker confirms our sense of the unity of profilmic space: the glance and the setting charge the empty area with narrative meaning. An alternative practice would refuse to let the character's gaze impregnate the empty space, as in figure 29.4, from Straub/Huillet's *Not Reconciled* (1964).

Both the long take and lateral staging practices, as devices, operated within the spatial system of classical decoupage. Several Hollywood artists admitted as much. Working on her second CinemaScope film, Fox editor Barbara Webb used 'one-foot cuts' in a fight scene and concluded that the task was exactly like cutting a film in the ordinary format.[29] Although the shots might be lengthier, Leon Shamroy pointed out, 'this won't be apparent to most audiences because any well-edited film looks like one long uninterrupted strip of film anyway.'[30] This was also apparent to Bazinian devotees of the wide screen. Truffaut was delighted that CinemaScope would not overturn the classical style: 'The close-ups of Victor Mature in *The Robe* are completely convincing; the faces are as diffused as those in *Notorious*; a long scene with Lauren Bacall reassures us of the persistence of the *plan américain*...'[31] Charles Bitsch found *A Star Is Born* (1954) virtually the Hegelian synthesis of all previous cinema:[32]

> Notice: fast cutting, ten-minute takes, the most skillful camera movements, the most daring match-cuts, the most difficult framings – everything is there. We have finally the material proof that in CinemaScope everything is possible. With *A Star Is Born*, CinemaScope is born.

Since cinematographers worried about directing attention, filmmakers struggled to retain the stability of continuity editing. We do not find in Hollywood widescreen filming the disjunctive cutting of Akira Kurosawa's Tohoscope *High and Low* (1963), in which cuts take us across the 180° line but keep the shot scale constant, so that from shot to shot we must search for cues to reorient ourselves to the space.

Even Hollywood's auteurist uses of the widescreen do not deviate significantly. In the critical literature, probably the most-praised widescreen shot is that from *River of No Return* (1954). Harry has lifted Kay off the raft and her valise of clothes has fallen into the river (fig 29.7). V.F. Perkins writes:[33]

> Kay's gradual loss of the physical tokens of her way of life has great symbolic significance. But Preminger is not over-impressed. The bundle simply floats away offscreen while Harry brings Kay ashore. It would be wrong to describe this as understatement. The symbolism is in the event, not in the visual pattern, so the director presents the action clearly and leaves interpretation to the viewer.

As the scene continues, Kay and Harry join Matt and Mark on the shore. After Kay and the boy have gone off to the cabin, Harry and Matt slowly follow and talk. As the camera tracks and pans right with them, we glimpse far in the background Kay's valise still floating down river (fig 29.11). Barr praises the 'natural' integration of such details as characteristic of the virtues of the wide screen. 'The spectator is "free" to notice the bundle, and when he does so, free to interpret it as significant.'[34]

If we situate the shots in their context, however, we see that they rely almost completely upon classical principles. When Kay loses her bundle, the camera reframes sharply to the right as she looks at it (fig 29.8); there is also a chord on the musical track; the glance, the music, and the camera call our attention to the valise. Our subsequent view of the bundle being carried away in the background is not 'free'; on the contrary, it is heavily motivated. First, the bundle is kept in frame for a long time (figs 29.9 and 29.10). When Matt and Harry pass (fig 29.11), the bundle is more or less centered. Furthermore, Preminger has 'primed' this orientation a few shots earlier, when Matt ran to the edge of the river (fig 29.5). Our orientation in figure 29.11 is thus a repetition of an earlier one. As we saw in Chapter 5 (figs 5.50 through 5.53) the classical film commonly establishes space in a neutral way a few shots

before we are to notice a particular aspect of it; we absorb the new (narratively significant) information against a background of familiarity. In *River of No Return*, Preminger primes his shots again and again. (For example, when Kay first comes onstage to sing, she passes a roulette wheel; in the next shot, when Matt strolls through the saloon to look at Kay, the roulette wheel jumps to our notice because it is moving and because, for the first time, we can hear its soft ticking spin.) Finally, one can argue that noticing the bundle when it moves down river in the background is not vital to our comprehension of the film. Perkins is surely right about the symbolic significance of Kay's gradual loss of her things, but the point is reiterated visually and verbally throughout the film. After the raft scene, when Kay is cleaning her shoes, she tells Mark: 'They're all I've got left.' Later she loses her guitar as well. The last shot of the film, a close-up of her discarded shoes, signals her abandonment of her old life. So the narrative point of the raft scene – that she loses her valise – is one that no spectator, 'free' or not, can fail to grasp. One can admire the devices which Preminger employs in the scene while still recognizing that the scene's spatial system remains strictly within the classical range of choices.

In 1954, Jacques Rivette looked forward to a new art brought by CinemaScope:[35]

> The director will learn to sometimes assert the entire surface of the screen, to activate it by his zest, to play a diverse and tight game there – instead of staking out the poles of the drama, to create zones of silence, surfaces of repose, or provocative gaps, knowing ruptures; quickly tiring of chandeliers and vases introduced at the sides of the image to balance medium-shots, he will discover the beauty of empty spots, of open and free spaces through which the wind glides; he will unburden the image, no longer fearing holes or imbalances, and will multiply compositional violations the better to obey the truths of cinema.

Such a passage evokes the compositional fractures of Kurosawa's, Godard's, Nagisa Oshima's, and Jancsó's widescreen films (see fig 29.12), but it does not describe Hollywood's normal practice. Novel devices were absorbed into orthodox systems, which in turn remained within the classical paradigm. With a little adjustment and with some help from the supply companies and the professional associations, widescreen filmmaking offered only trended changes in the classical style.

Part Seven Historical implications of the classical Hollywood cinema

DAVID BORDWELL and
JANET STAIGER

30

Since 1960: the persistence of a mode of film practice

The previous chapters have shown the complex and shifting relations between style and mode of production in Hollywood filmmaking. There is no question that economic factors have strongly affected the development of the classical style. The steady demands for more footage in the first two decades of the industry contributed to the development of the multiple-shot film and later to features. At the same time, narrative filmmaking proved the most efficient, controllable approach and soon came to dominate the companies' output. In subsequent years, technological change was often the result of economic imperatives, and the particular moment of an innovation's adoption can be traced to a specific attempt to improve efficiency or differentiate the product.

In the last analysis, however, stylistic factors can explain the most specific and interesting aspects of Hollywood filmmaking. The particular nature of the classical norms depended upon models of storytelling drawn from literature, theater, music, and the visual arts. After 1917, the principle of using narrative logic to control systems of space and time became central. Maintaining narrative dominance and its particular systems (e.g., psychological motivation, continuity editing) was a central cause for the emergence of successive production systems. Once the director-unit method was succeeded by the central-producer system around 1914, a rigid mass-production framework was in place, to be elaborated and perpetuated in the producer-unit system of the 1930s and 1940s. Even when mass-production declined with the package-unit system of the middle 1950s, a detailed division of labor and a hierarchical work order remained. The classical style was critical in reinforcing both economic practices (e.g., cost efficiency) and ideological/signifying practices (e.g., the standard of the quality film). Within the mode of produc-

tion, the tensions of standardization and differentiation, the increase in specialization, and the tendency of Hollywood's institutions to focus energy and capital toward a controlled uniformity all crucially depended upon the norms of the classical style.

Similarly, while technological change had to be economically beneficial in the long run, the directions and functions of such change were strongly contained by stylistic premises. Classical norms dictated how cameras, lighting, laboratory equipment, sound recording, deep-focus cinematography, color, and widescreen could be introduced and used. By 1920, specific institutions – manufacturers and suppliers, professional organizations – had generated activities and discourses that were able to assimilate technological change to Hollywood's parameters.

Self-professed pragmatists are fond of asserting that Hollywood makes movies to make money, not to make art. This is supposed to bring the interlocutor down with a thump, to quell a preoccupation with 'aesthetics' by a hardheaded call to business practices. Yet in a capitalist society there is no opposition of business and art: most artists make art to make money. And one could make movies more cheaply if one did not recognize conventions of narrative construction, spectacle, verisimilitude, continuity, and so on. Between 1917 and 1960, these conventions constituted Hollywood's very definition of a movie itself, so our pragmatist's claim must be revised: Hollywood makes *classical* movies to make money. Historically, the classical style played a major, if not the central, role in the American film industry and its mode of production.

By confining our history of this cinema to the four decades after 1917, we may have seemed to assume Stendhal's definition of classicism as a style which gives the greatest possible pleasure to an audience's ancestors.[1] But plainly the principles of classical filmmaking still hold sway. It is now pertinent to consider to what extent the Hollywood mode of production and the classical style have changed in the last two decades. Again, we shall find that in most cases the desire to maintain and vary the classical style has played the determining part in Hollywood's film practice.

Capital and Elective Affinities

Sergei Eisenstein has slipped into a difficult and absurd situation. He has suddenly found himself proclaimed a world-class director, a genius, he has been heaped with political and artistic decorations. . . .

. . . . It comes as no surprise therefore that Eisenstein has announced his intention to film Marx's Capital – no lesser theme would do.[2]

Osip Brik, 1928

Since 1960, there have been several modifications in the US film industry, but most of them have had only minor effects on the mode of production. While new trade practices, such as four-walling, saturation booking, platforming, extensive market analyses, revising advertising campaigns in the middle of release, year-round bidding, and recutting and redistributing a film, have emerged in recent years, none of these affects the mode of production in any significant way.[3] For example, recutting and re-releasing a film is an extension of earlier years' practice of using previews and retakes before release. Similarly, the demographic analyses produced by market research take to new levels of precision the audience research of the 1940s.

One might argue that conglomerate ownership of film production has affected the mode, but this does not seem to be the case. This change in the structure of the industry can actually be seen in part as fostered by one symptom of the package-unit system – the blockbuster film. After the 1940s, when the industry concentrated on fewer, specialized projects, it developed an interest in the film which did spectacularly at the box office. Such a highly profitable film permits a company to use the film's excessive earnings for growth purposes, particularly for diversifying into areas which might provide a stable growth income to

counterbalance the more speculative film-finance operations. Although some film firms became parts of conglomerates through mergers with larger corporations not in the entertainment field (Paramount became part of Gulf & Western in 1966, for instance), other film companies created their own conglomerate organizations through diversification. Earnings from blockbusters contributed to various acquisitions, often in the leisure field: hotels and recreation areas, publishing firms, video equipment and cable television, record companies, pinball- and electronic-game machine manufacturers. Twentieth Century-Fox invested part of its Star Wars (1977) profits in a Coca-Cola bottling company; Jaws (1975) permitted Universal to do the same. As Time noticed: 'The acquisition will move the movie business toward controlling not only what the audience sees but what they buy in the lobby.'[4] Such a conglomerate structure might be different from the earlier industrial structure, but as Alfred D. Chandler, Jr, points out, conglomerate ownership leads to decentralized management control.[5] Each branch ends up with the power to make tactical decisions for its own area. Thus, just as the shift to advanced capitalism during the 1920s and 1930s did not significantly change the mode of film production, so the current major firms act primarily as financiers and distributors, allowing individual package units to operate on their own once a deal is set.

On the whole, recent years have witnessed only a continuation of the package-unit system.[6] What is currently called 'clout' is the power of the worker's perceived value to determine his or her share of the next project. Gone are long-term option contracts which controlled profit-share increases. Some top talent, the 'superstars,' even determine whether or not a project is financed – something which seldom happened during the earlier periods. One writer-producer described the comparative status of these top talents: 'If Robert Redford and Sydney Pollack want to shoot "Telephone Pole," they can go to any studio for financing. Or if Barbra Streisand wants to film herself atop the Wailing Wall shouting, "Look, Ma! Top of the World!" who would say no?'[7] Exhibitors book by stars, and stars who are popular find financing. So do directors. Vincent Canby in reviewing Martin Scorsese's New York,

New York (1977) wrote that the French would explain the film by 'the *Politique des Comptables*. Here: the accountant theory. Put another way, it's "you're as good as your last picture, Sam," meaning that the amount of freedom and clout that a director has at any moment depends pretty much on the grosses of his most recent film.' For Canby, this explains 'why directors of very profitable films so often follow up with films that are in some fashion self-indulgent and out-of-control.'[8]

Only workers in producing, writing, directing, and acting have this noticeable power and flexibility in their division of labor. The package-unit system remains in effect in the rest of the structure. Talent agencies, such as International Creative Management, have continued as producers, putting together packages; in 1977, five of the major film firms employed top managers who were formerly agents.[9] Technology and unions still keep the labor crafts specialized. For example, Robert Faulkner has detailed the standard employment process of Hollywood recording musicians. As a holdover from the self-contained studio period, many of the freelancers have a commitment to work for a studio if contacted ninety-six hours in advance, and composers and conductors can specify whom they want hired. A contractor assembles the orchestra. Union contract agreements prearrange wage scales and working conditions.[10] Thus, as Chapter 24 suggests, the unions, while protecting their members, have also contributed to the continuation of detailed division of labor.

Production processes have changed only in very minor ways. By the late 1950s, on occasion, shooting procedures resembled television multiple-camera practices. One camera would continuously cover the action while one or two other ones filmed the action sporadically and then quickly moved to set up for new shots. Saving shooting time was the primary reason for adopting this technique. On the other hand, for more extravagant affairs, shooting times have lengthened. As Michael Cimino explained during production of *Heaven's Gate* (1980):[11]

At one time . . . when certain parts of films were unsatisfactory, people could go back and reshoot. It was rather standard practice. If one needed an extra scene, one went back and did it; or if one didn't like the score, one rescored the film. It was possible because everyone was under contract. We no longer have that kind of option. Most of what we shoot is on location, often under difficult circumstances, and there is no going back. There is no reconstructing sets, there is no getting the actors back together. And we certainly don't want to be sitting in a cutting room a year after shooting is completed and wishing, if I had only gotten this or that. By then it's too late.

Despite such a narrowing of production options, the package-unit system still utilizes detailed division of labor. Conceiving the work remains the prerogative of the upper- and middle- management, and the subdivision of work continues. The script is still the blueprint, and most films are planned carefully with experts attending to craft details. The standard of the quality film remains dominant. Cimino's project, for instance, revelled in details of authenticity: 'Every article of clothing, every structure, every sign . . . is based on a photograph of the period.'[12] Producer Joann Carelli claimed: 'The special thing about *Heaven's Gate* is that nobody has reproduced these times as they actually were. When this Western comes to the screen, it will be the first time you have seen a moving documentation of that era.'[13] Yet Cimino adjusted the historical facts to make a story. As reporter Rex McGee comments:[14]

The facts of the Johnson County War are somewhat at odds with the version in *Heaven's Gate*, a point which doesn't disturb Cimino in the slightest. 'It was not my intention to write a history book,' Cimino said. 'I'm telling a story that interests me and hopefully will interest other people. One uses history in a very free way. After all, you're not trying to rewrite it or reinvent it. You're using it as context. The specific facts of that incident recounted in a literal way would be of no interest.'

Osip Brik's observation about Eisenstein may seem less out of place now that we recognize that the package-unit system of production gives some creative personnel a power to choose projects and working conditions. In the Hollywood mode of production, however, conceiving a film of Marx's

Capital is an improbable alternative. Spectacle, technological *tours de force*, and human emotions – above all, love – are more likely pretexts than political economy. And so we are left with Francis Ford Coppola, the current prototype of the independent and visionary director, who wants to make *Elective Affinities*, based on Goethe's novel. Coppola has explained how he would treat the proposed quartet of films. Although the whole project would be 'a big movie,' the films would also be 'very, very intimate epics.' *Elective Affinities* would deal with love: 'male-female love; sexual love; romantic love; spiritual love.' Coppola's film incorporates rocket ships, 'the birth of the universe,' politics, and 'the first moving hologram.' He also contemplates a step toward vertical integration: entering the exhibition field:[15]

L.A. Weekly: But you're going to show this film in your own theatre, aren't you?

Coppola: Right. And do you know where the theatre will be? In the Rocky Mountains. We're going to build this incredible theatre there – 2,000 seats on the top of the Rockies. You go in there and it's just glass so you can see the view. Then, at a certain point, the glass gets dark and you're in a totally dark room and then – ultimately – you get a color hologram.

L.A. Weekly: Is this your design concept?

Coppola: No, but underneath it, underneath it, there is a hotel. A hotel in the Rockies. You go there for the weekend to see *Elective Affinities*. It's a weekend event. You go, you get a great room and at night on your television set, anytime, whenever the hell, you can see any part of the film over and over again. If you want to see a scene that you didn't understand or you don't know what you felt about it or you missed it . . .

L.A. Weekly: It seems like a new film form.

Coppola: It is. It's a new kind of mental theme park.

The China Syndrome *and* Tout va Bien

Hollywood? Yes, but this cultural phenomenon is much stronger than any other and it cannot disappear. It can't; the proof is that it continues stronger than ever.[16]

Jean-Luc Godard

Just as the Hollywood mode of production continues, the classical style remains the dominant model for feature filmmaking. Any number of well-known films of the last two decades offer examples, but consider as one instance *The China Syndrome* (1979). The project exemplifies the package-unit system: the scriptwriter (Michael Gray) induced the producer and star (Michael Douglas) to assemble the project, a process aided by the 'matchmaking' of Columbia Pictures.[17] Stylistically, the film not only demonstrates the endurance of the classical paradigm, but it shows how that paradigm's formal operations shape the film's presentation of controversial political issues.

The story action of *The China Syndrome* adheres completely to the canons of classical construction. After an initial cause (a nearly disastrous breakdown in a nuclear plant), individual characters endowed with goals struggle against obstacles. Television reporter Kimberly Wells wants to cover hard news, her cameraman Richard Adams seeks to do investigative journalism, and Jack Goodell the nuclear plantworker wants to make the plant safe. These characters run into opposition: the television station executives want to pacify Kimberly and dismiss Richard, while the nuclear plant owners work to silence Jack. In addition, the star system sustains these character roles. Michael Douglas, as Richard, continues playing the impetuous young idealist established in his television series, *The Streets of San Francisco*. In the role of Kimberly, Jane Fonda reenacts the middle-class woman's discovery of 'liberation' which underpins her later films (*A Doll's House* [1973], *Julia* [1977], *Coming Home* [1978], *Nine to Five* [1981]) and which is tied to the myth of her personal life.[18] Jack Lemmon trades on one aspect of his star persona: the organization man gifted with conscience (*Mr. Roberts* [1955], *The Apartment* [1960], *Save the Tiger* [1973]). (Of course, the character's name, Jack Goodell, echoes the star's name, while the reference to the character's Navy career recalls Lemmon as Ensign Pulver in *Mr. Roberts*, which starred Jane Fonda's father.) The opposing forces are played by actors stereotyped as heavies, either suave bureaucrats or thugs. Finally, generic conventions operate to shape the story action. The film is a detective story (what caused the accident?), with Jack, Kimberly, and Richard following up clues. The film is also a gangster film, with the cigar-smoking corporate managers playing the role of the mob: thugs intimidate Jack, kill the sound man Hector, and in a car chase pursue Jack to the plant. In such ways, the film renders its ostensibly progressive subject by the most traditional means.

The China Syndrome tames its central political issue by means of the standard device of the double plot. Here the pretext action is the nuclear accident at Ventana, while the real action is Kimberly's quest to win her reportorial spurs. The film makes the personal goal take precedence over the social issue by situating its protagonists in an ambivalent position with respect to the problem of nuclear safety. (The credits, a montage sequence showing Kimberly and Richard driving to Ventana, is accompanied by a song, 'Somewhere in Between.') Kimberly and Richard want to reveal the cover-up, but they do not take a position on nuclear power per se. Jack Goodell is just as compromised. He explains that 'the system works,' and nothing in the film confutes this: the mechanical design of the plant is sound. What Jack's sleuthing discovers is shoddy workmanship and cost-cutting in plant construction. Jack is central to the narrative's reshaping of the political issue, since he redefines the problem as one of faulty execution and individual greed, not of the economic system that puts nuclear power into corporate hands. While the double plot makes the nuclear issue a means to Kimberly's goal, Jack's investigation shifts the political problem to one of technical causes and a subcontractor's dishonesty. The film's narrative action identifies its protagonists as 'somewhere in between' the anti-nuclear demonstrators (seen testifying at a public hearing) and the nuclear industry.[19]

The evasive double plot also yields classical closure. Jack has barricaded himself in the plant control room and insists on telling the truth over television. Plant authorities distract him by triggering another turbine trip, and the police rush in and shoot him. But this trip convinces Jack's assistant (as the first accident had convinced Jack) that the cover-up must be revealed. So coming outside to the reporters, Ted

Spindler takes up Jack's mantle and promises to tell all. Although Jack dies, his goal – full disclosure – is achieved. Moreover, Kimberly's poised and resourceful coverage convinces her station bosses that she can handle 'serious' material. In her commentary, Kimberly says of the Ventana scandal: 'Let's hope it doesn't end here,' but in fact the film has used up the nuclear-power pretext action. In the last shot, two television monitors serve as emblems for the film's two lines of action. On one, the coverage of the accident is replaced by a commercial for microwave ovens. On the other monitor, we see Kimberly and Richard joyfully embracing – the canonic last shot of the classical Hollywood film, the man and woman celebrating the achievement of their personal goals. The public problem is not theirs to solve.

Narration in *The China Syndrome* also conforms to classical principles. The action stretches over five days, each clearly demarcated. There are appointments and deadlines, both explicit ('I want that film on my desk before he gets back') and implicit (the rush to stop the first turbine trip, Hector's race to get Jack's evidence to the hearing, the last-minute rescue situation in the control room). The film follows plotlines through crosscutting, especially in the last third. Shifts of locale are motivated narratively; scenes completely obey rules of spatial coherence. (The sequences in the plant control room constitute excellent examples of the classical definition of space through eyelines and reverse angles.) The anatomy of each segment follows the standard pattern of establishment, new information, and 'hooking' to the next.

We can see the classical presuppositions of *The China Syndrome*'s narration most clearly in the film's contrast between cinema and television. As we have seen, classical narration aims to create the impression that it proceeds directly from the story action (thanks to multiple motivation and other factors). Television is a perfect foil for this process. In *The China Syndrome*, television is limited, contained, and manipulated. The TV image passes through many hands (the studio console, the power supply at Ventana); at any point, the image can be interrupted or halted. At the limit, there is straightforward censorship. Television mediates reality; it disjoins and fragments. Film, on the other hand, is immediate.

When Richard, Hector, and Kimberly visit the plant, Richard surreptitiously films the turbine trip. Shooting from the hip, he can casually record all the relevant information about the accident: by scrutinizing Richard's film, scientists can tell what really happened. Cinema makes the event completely readable simply by recording it.

It would be easy to say that in these ways cinema is celebrated as realistic and transparent, but here, as usual in the classical cinema, realistic motivation is at the service of compositional motivation: verisimilitude depends on coherence. So, for instance, Richard's documentary footage ends with a shot of Jack, desperately relieved that the plant pulled through. Certainly this image suggests that cinema can not only record the event, but also reveal the human truth of the event. That revelation, however, also gains its truth status from its confirmation of our view of Jack: we saw the same concerned expression on his face during the accident, and it reappears at later moments of crisis. Television is not simply distanced and artificial, it is fragmentary (e.g., the schizophrenic shots of the control room monitors). Cinema reasserts continuity of meaning: Richard's film, document of a fiction, corroborates the unity of the fiction.

Operating within classical premises, *The China Syndrome* cannot question the homogeneity of film technique without questioning its own style. Godard's work offers an instructive alternative here. In *Numéro Deux* (1975), the fragmentary nature of television imagery furnishes a tool of analysis. Similarly, *Tout va bien* (1972) resembles the story of *The China Syndrome* in several ways, but Godard makes the inquiry into cinema central to his political purpose, thus refusing unified narrative, motivated technique, and continuity devices. *The China Syndrome* shows that the classical paradigm continues to flourish, partly by absorbing current topics of interest and partly by perpetuating seventy-year-old assumptions about what a film is and does.

Blow-up and The Conversation

Hollywood no longer exists in the same way, but it re-exists in another way.[20]

Jean-Luc Godard

The China Syndrome represents the way that most American commercial cinema has continued the classical tradition. But some would argue that during the late 1960s and 1970s more venturesome filmmakers took fresh directions. Scorsese, Coppola, Robert Altman, Paul Schrader, Woody Allen, and others are often cited as contemporary directors who have created a 'New Hollywood' or a 'Hollywood Renaissance.'

It has been claimed that several of these directors have created a 'youth revolution': Cimino directed his first Hollywood film at the age of thirty-one, Scorsese at thirty, Coppola at twenty-eight, Brian DePalma and Steven Spielberg at twenty-seven. Yet the Hollywood director has customarily started young. Allan Dwan, Raoul Walsh, Frank Borzage, Henry King, Charles Chaplin, John Ford, King Vidor, W.S. Van Dyke, William Wellman, Frank Capra, Mervyn LeRoy, George Stevens, Garson Kanin, Orson Welles, Budd Boetticher, Robert Wise, Stanley Donen, Richard Fleischer, Stanley Kubrick, John Frankenheimer, Robert Mulligan, and Roger Corman all began directing before they were thirty. William K. Howard started when he was only twenty-one, William Wyler when he was twenty-three. It is rarer to find a Hollywood director who started 'late' – say, after forty.

Nor have the New Hollywood directors significantly changed the mode of film production. Michael Pye and Lynda Myles argue that film-school training gave younger directors a unified vision of their craft, since as students they had to learn writing, editing, sound, and camerawork.[21] But this knowledge is itself a sparse sampling of all the crafts that contribute to a top-budget professional motion picture. (The 'versatility' of the film-school graduates has enabled publicity mechanisms to promote the New Hollywood films as creations of a single artistic vision.) Nor can the film-school training be considered innocent, since many university film departments have taken upon themselves the task of transmitting dominant standards to students eager to enter the industry. Moreover, as we have seen, the New Hollywood maintains the division of labor established decades earlier. Even if one person plays the roles of screenwriter, director, and producer, these remain supervisory functions not different from those enjoyed by independent producer-directors like Alfred Hitchcock, Howard

Hawks, John Ford, and others during the 1940s and 1950s.

The New Hollywood has also been defined by its technological feats: sophisticated special effects, new camera supports (Panaflex, Steadicam, the Louma crane), television viewfinding, time-coded synchronization, computer-assisted storyboarding, and expanded multitrack sound recording.[22] Parts Four and Six, however, have shown that Hollywood has always used technological innovation to promote films. Recent developments are no exception to this trend. Coppola and George Lucas have proven themselves especially alert to promoting technical 'breakthroughs.' Expectably, recent innovations have been justified in utterly orthodox ways — in the name of economy, realism, unobtrusiveness, spectacle, and narrative supremacy. Here is Altman on the value of multi-track sound: 'Suddenly leaving that track there live . . . we were able to put their lines in, and it just gave that sense of reality to the thing that otherwise it wouldn't have had.'[23] His sound recordist adds that Altman demands a track which will 'color, highlight, and augment his story.'[24] Steadicam's manufacturer claims that it duplicates normal vision; cameramen praise the device for saving money and time; Haskell Wexler points out that it allows for spectacular camera movements.[25] The f-0.7 lens in *Barry Lyndon* (1975) is explained as a way 'to preserve the natural patina and feeling of these old castles at night as they actually were.'[26] When journalistic panegyrics publicize such technological innovations, the New Hollywood becomes a manifestation of what Ernest Mandel has called the specific form of bourgeois ideology under late capitalism: 'belief in the omnipotence of technology.'[27]

The strongest argument for a New Hollywood rests upon the claim that the directors' works constitute a non-classical approach to narrative and technique. The case was anticipated in 1971 by Peter Lloyd, who claimed to find a disintegration in the Hollywood style after 1961. Lloyd argued that narrative structure had splintered, genre conventions had dissolved, linearity had been replaced by ambiguity, and the individual protagonist could no longer be seen as heroic.[28] In the mid-1970s, Thomas Elsaesser suggested that the New Hollywood of *Thieves Like Us* (1974), *Sugarland Express* (1974), *Easy Rider*

(1969), and *American Graffiti* (1973) revealed unmotivated protagonists, picaresque journey structures, and a self-consciousness that slipped into pastiche, parody, or 'the pathos of failure.'[29] While Lloyd's and Elsaesser's observations are apt, these new films do not constitute a sharply distinct style, but can better be explained by that process of stylistic assimilation we have seen at work throughout Hollywood's history. As the 'old' Hollywood had incorporated and refunctionalized devices from German Expressionism and Soviet montage (see Chapters 7 and 17), the 'New' Hollywood has selectively borrowed from the international art cinema.

The category of the art cinema includes the internationally distributed films identified with such directors as Federico Fellini, Ingmar Bergman, François Truffaut, Luchino Visconti, and Bernardo Bertolucci.[30] Just as in the classical Hollywood cinema, formal principles cohere to create a distinct group style and a unified set of viewing strategies.

Formally, the art cinema employs a looser, more tenuous linkage of events than we find in the classical film. In *L'Avventura* (1960), for example, Anna is lost and never found; in *A bout de souffle* (1959), the reasons for Patricia's betrayal of Michel remain unknown. The art cinema motivates this slackening by two principles: realism and authorial expressivity.

The art film defines itself as realistic. It will show us actual locations, 'realistic' eroticism, and genuine problems (e.g., contemporary 'alienation,' 'lack of communication'). Most important, the art cinema depicts psychologically ambivalent or confused characters. Whereas characters in the Hollywood film have clear-cut traits and objectives, the characters of the art cinema lack precise desires and goals. Characters may act for inconsistent reasons (Marcello in *La Dolce Vita* [1960]) or may question themselves about their goals (Borg in *Wild Strawberries* [1957]). Choices become vague or nonexistent. Hence a certain drifting, episodic quality to the art film's narrative.

What takes up the forward causal momentum is an exploration of the nature and sources of psychological states. The art cinema is concerned less with action than reaction; it is a cinema of psychological effects in search of their causes. The dissection of feeling is often represented explicitly as therapy and cure (e.g., *Persona* [1966]), but even when it is not, the forward flow of causation is braked and characters pause to seek the aetiology of their feelings. The protagonist becomes a supersensitive individual, and in the course of the search he or she may come to the edge of psychological breakdown.

A conception of realism also affects the film's spatial and temporal construction. The options range from a documentary factuality (e.g., *Il posto* [1961]) to intense psychological subjectivity (e.g., *Hiroshima mon amour* [1959]). Thus room is left for two viewing strategies. Violations of classical conceptions of time and space are justified as the intrusion of an unpredictable daily reality or as the subjective reality of complex characters. Manipulations of story order remain anchored to character subjectivity, as in *8 1/2* (1963). In similar ways, the representation of space will be motivated as documentary realism (e.g., location shooting, available light), as character revelation (a pan cross an apartment), or in extreme cases as purely mental imagery.

At the same time, the art cinema foregrounds the author as a structure in the film's system. Sometimes the author is represented as a biographical individual, and the film solicits confessional readings (e.g., Fellini's and Truffaut's films). More often, the author is identified with an overt narration. The author comes forward chiefly as patterned violations of the classical norm. Deviations from the classical canon – an unusual angle, a stressed bit of cutting, a prohibited camera movement, an unmotivated shift in lighting or setting, indeed any failure to motivate cinematic space and time by cause-effect logic – can be read as 'authorial commentary.' Or the art film may foreground the narrational act by posing enigmas. In the classical film, the puzzles are born of *story*: what is in her past? what will he do now? In the art film, the puzzle is one of *narration*: who is telling this story? how is this story being told? why tell the story this way? A telltale sign of such narrational presence is the flashforward – the narration's anticipation of a future story action. The flashforward is unthinkable in the classical narrative cinema, which seeks to retard the ending and to motivate a step-by-step narration. But art films like *Love Affair; or, the Case of the Missing Switchboard Operator* (1967) and *Stavisky* (1974) force us to notice how the narrator

teases us with knowledge that no character can have.

Realism and authorial expressivity, then, will be the means whereby the art film unifies itself. Yet verisimilitude, objective or subjective, can be incompatible with an intrusive author. The art cinema solves the problem by means of ambiguity. The art film is nonclassical in that it emphasizes unplugged gaps and unresolved issues. But these very deviations get placed, resituated as realism (in life, things happen this way) or authorial commentary (the ambiguity is symbolic). Thus the art film solicits a particular viewing procedure. Whenever confronted with a problem in causation, temporality, or space, we first seek realistic motivation. (Is a character's mental state causing the uncertainty? Is life just leaving loose ends?) If we are thwarted, we seek narrational reasons. (What is being 'said' here? What significance justifies the violation of the norm?) Ideally, the film hesitates, suggesting all at once character subjectivity, life's untidiness, and author's vision. Uncertainties persist, but are understood as such, as *obvious* uncertainties. Whereas the classical film solicits a univocal reading, the slogan of the art cinema might be, 'When in doubt, read for maximum ambiguity.'

This excursion into the art cinema has been necessary to show how the New Hollywood has absorbed several conventions of the mode. But such absorption has not been simple copying; art-film principles have been merged with certain conventions of the classical style. The process is easiest to see at the level of technique. Recent American film has bent art-film devices to causally or generically motivated functions: the jump-cut used for violence or comedy, the sound bridge for continuity or shock effect, the elimination of the dissolve as a transition, and the freeze-frame used to signify finality. (Compare the narrative irresolution of the freeze-frame in *Les 400 coups* [1959] with its powerful closure in *Butch Cassidy and the Sundance Kid* [1969].) Editor Ralph Rosenblum cites *Hiroshima mon amour* and *A bout de souffle* (both 1959) as having influenced the brief and abrupt flashbacks in *The Pawnbroker* (1965).[31] Certain technical tics of the art cinema have proven easy to assimilate.

There are more pervasive indications that an 'art cinema' has emerged in Hollywood. Like the European art film, the 'new Hollywood' film is sharply aware of its relation to the 'old Holly-wood': DePalma's rehashes of Hitchcock, Lucas's use of Warners' war films and Universal serials as prototypes for *Star Wars*, remakes of serials (*Superman* [1979] and *Flash Gordon* [1981]) and cartoons (*Popeye* [1980]), Bogdanovich's attempts to revive the screwball comedy and the musical. Scorsese explains that he studied 1940s musicals before shooting *New York, New York* (1977). The song 'Hurray for Hollywood' in *The Long Goodbye* (1973) functions partly to stress the differences between this detective film and its predecessors.

In keeping with the definition of a non-Hollywood Hollywood, American films are imitating the look of European art films: Bresson is copied in *Taxi Driver* (1976) and *American Gigolo* (1980), Truffaut and Fellini in Paul Mazursky's work, Bergman in *Interiors* (1978), Godard in Alan Pakula's *Klute* (1971). More interestingly, the new directors sometimes flaunt the act of narration, as in the parallel-time structure of *Godfather II* (1974), the opening credits of *Nashville* (1975), or the gratuitous tracking shot in *Taxi Driver* that leaves the protagonist behind. In *McCabe and Mrs. Miller* (1971), the Leonard Cohen songs serve as a symbolic commentary on the action; at the end of *Blue Collar* (1978), an earlier line from the film is repeated nondiegetically over a freeze-frame. Altman's *Three Women* (1977) is a veritable orgy of art-film narration, creating dream/reality confusion and symbolic transmutations deriva-tive of *Persona*. So strong has the cult of the director become that Scorsese and Mazursky can play roles in their films and Coppola can in *Apocalypse Now* (1979) portray, naturally, a filmmaker. Pascal Kané points out that in many recent Hollywood films the active role of the traditional hero has been transferred to the director-as-creator; the film's unity can be recovered, as in the art cinema, at the level of authorial 'statement.'[32]

Yet two factors keep the New Hollywood from becoming only a pastiche of the continental art cinema. First, there is the almost complete conservatism of style. No recent American director has produced an idiosyncratic style comparable to even Truffaut's or Bergman's, let alone to that of Antonioni or Bresson. The classical premises of time and space remain powerfully in force, with only minor instrumental changes (e.g., multiple cameras to capture reverse angles, zooms doing duty for tracking shots). Altman, probably the most interesting stylist to emerge in the New Hollywood, none the less uses techniques in ways which conform to the dominant paradigm. Secondly, even the most ambitious directors cannot escape genres. New Hollywood cinema consists of gangster and outlaw films, thrillers, Westerns, musicals, science-fiction films, comedies, and an occasional melodrama. *Apocalypse Now* is primarily and almost entirely a war movie. *Blue Collar*, a film of putative social significance, includes fight scenes reminiscent of prison films like *Brute Force* (1947), a caper intrigue, and even a car chase. Classical film style and codified genres swallow up art-film borrow-ings, taming the (already limited) disruptiveness of the art cinema. We can watch this process clearly at work in a famous film by the most prestigious director of his generation.

Francis Ford Coppola's *The Conversation* (1974) is, fundamentally, a detective story. Harry Caul, an expert in audio surveillance, is hired to record a conversation between a young man and woman. As he assembles his documentation, he begins to suspect that the couple is in danger from his mysterious employer, the director of a company. The film thus follows classical detective patterns: Harry must uncover and interpret clues to reveal the truth. Some of the clues are highly conven-tional. The director's sinister assistant warns Harry not to get involved with the tapes because they are dangerous and 'someone may get hurt.' Later, Harry is able to decipher more and more of the conversation and to pick out the date of a hotel rendezvous. At first Harry refuses to turn over the tapes, but they are stolen by a spy sent by the director. Convinced that the director in-tends to kill the couple, Harry visits the hotel at the time mentioned in the conversation. There he overhears and glimpses a murder. The twist in the plot comes when he learns that it is the company director who has been killed by the daughter and the young man with the help of the director's assistant. Harry has misinterpreted the clues. The film ends with him immured at home, unable to report the crime because he is himself being bugged.

The genre conventions – investigation, threat, and evasion maneuvers – provide most of the film's causal impetus. Narrationally the film operates from a classical base as well. The opening, which reveals Harry's crew recording the conversation, immediately establishes the principal characters and the paramount issues of the film: what did the couple say, and what does it mean? During the recording, interference distorts the speech; as the film proceeds, Harry's re-recording clarifies more and more. We move toward enlightenment. The consistency of narrative space is assured not only by composition and cutting but also by sound perspective; a line is unclear only when it is necessary to be (momentarily) unclear. Narrative time is homogeneous, achieved through a short durational span (a few days) and a tight mesh of appointments (going to a surveillance convention, meeting other wiretappers, meeting the company director) leading to the crucial deadline, the mysterious Sunday rendezvous at the Jack Tar Hotel. Scenes are linked by dialogue hooks, as when Coppola cuts from the taped conversation ('Three o'clock – room 773') to Harry at the hotel lobby asking for room 773; the next scene begins with a close-up of the door of room 773. There are even two montage sequences, functioning to compress story time.

Except for the elements which must remain enigmatic for the sake of the mystery, characters and situations are redundant and consistent. At first it is unclear why the call girl Meredith should be attracted to Harry, but later he and we discover that she has been an agent for the director and has stolen the incriminating tape. As the protagonist, Harry states his initial goal explicitly in the first scene: 'I don't care what they're talking about. All I want is a nice fat recording.' His plastic raincoat, his neutral business suit, his halting manner, his habit of backing away from other characters – all define Harry as anonymous, solitary, and fearful of human contact. Before he knocks on his girl-friend's door, Harry dodges behind the staircase to see if anyone is watching. After he is inside her apartment, Amy asks why she once saw him hiding on the stairs; her question confirms our inferences about his behavior. Later, Harry's Catholicism is redundantly stressed. The last shot, which shows Harry alone in his apartment, is thus a logical culmination of his movement toward isolation.

Into this classical context, *The Conversation* imports strategies and devices taken from the art cinema. If the investigation is the pretext action, the second plotline presents an uncertain protagonist in a psychological crisis. Harry is alienated, psychically drifting. As he says in the second scene, 'I don't have anything personal. Nothing of value.' His professional goal, achieving the perfect recording, is mitigated by a sense of guilt. Years before, his bugging inadvertently caused a family's death. Now Harry cannot decide whether to intervene in the situation he has discovered. He goes to confession, and he dreams of warning the director's daughter. In the same dream, he reveals facts from his childhood and fantasizes the murder that might come to pass. The paralytic, drifting protagonist of the art film fits badly into the detective role: where Sam Spade would have tried to prevent the murder in room 773, Harry can only listen, then crumple up on the bed in an agony of indecision. Finally, Harry cannot solve the mystery in time – a good example of how the failed protagonist of the art cinema can stand not far from the failed hero of the film noir. (Compare other recent private-eye films such as *Chinatown* [1974] and *Night Moves* [1975].)

The film gives us access to the protagonist's state of mind through his behavior, speech, dreams, and, chiefly, through Harry's dissection of the tape. Here Coppola exploits an ingenious narrational device. When Harry plays the tape, the film shows us images of the crucial conversation, so we see the characters speaking the lines we hear. (These are not always the shots that we saw in the opening scene.) We are inclined to read these images as flashbacks, cued by the recording: that is, the sound is 'objective,' but the images are Harry's recollections. It is during these replays that we hear the young man say, 'He'd kill us if he could.' These lead us to share Harry's suspicions of the company director. But at the film's end, when Harry discovers his error, another flashback shows us the young man saying, '*He'd* kill *us* if he could.' Not only the image but the sound has been subjective; we have shared Harry's mental state to a greater degree than we have realized. (Coppola's duplicity extends to playing Harry's subjective version of the tape not only when Harry is alone but in a more 'objective' scene, when the director and his assistant are present; we are thus led still further to assume, wrongly, that the tape is as we hear it.) As Walter Murch, the sound editor for the film, puts it: 'The tape becomes his obsession, so it gets replayed at various points in the film, for various reasons, in different spaces and in different realities. Sometimes it's totally in his head – you're listening to the tape, but the way *he* imagines it.'[33]

There is more than character subjectivity at work, though, for *The Conversation* also uses authorial intervention to increase ambiguity. Many shots, especially in Harry's apartment, hold on empty spaces, connoting not only the vacant quality of his life but also marking the presence of a commenting narration. Other shots, such as one of a mirror at the convention, have obvious symbolic functions. Coppola also creates ambiguity by refusing to assign certain images either to the character or to the narration. During Harry's dream, an image of the murder yet to come can be read as Harry's premonition or as the narration's flashforward. The same calculated uncertainty is engendered when Harry examines the murder room and blood begins overflowing the toilet bowl. Is the image objective (i.e., the blood from the crime emerging after the cleanup) or subjective (Harry's imagination)? Near the end of the film, Harry learns of the director's death (supposedly in a car crash) and goes to the firm. There the daughter, the young man, and the director's assistant are fending off reporters. Coppola alternates shots of the characters in the present, shots taken from earlier sequences, and shots showing the murder of the father in the hotel room. These interspersed images can be read in several ways: as fragmentary flashbacks (daughter, boyfriend, assistant, and Harry each recalling certain events), as Harry's swift inferences about what must have happened, or as

the narration's intervention to explain the story to us. The soundtrack produces similar problems, with distorted music (recalling the murder scene) underscoring fragments of the original conversation.

The Conversation exemplifies how the New Hollywood has absorbed narrational strategies of the art cinema while controlling them within a coherent genre framework. Although the film's narration switches from objectivity to character subjectivity to authorial commentary, a puzzle and solution remain firmly at the center of the story. Thanks to genre conventions, the film finally reveals that the young couple committed the murder, presumably to take control of the corporation. It is true that this conclusion is not spelled out to the degree that it would be in a classical film, but nothing in the action contradicts this reading and a great deal (the thwarting of Harry's investigation, the bugging of his apartment) supports it. Even the misleading presentation of the crucial conversation is partly motivated by the duplicitous narration characteristic of the detective film. (Recall a similar device in *The Maltese Falcon*, discussed in Chapter 3.) Contrast Antonioni's *Blow-up* (1966), a film with which *The Conversation* is often compared. In that film, the detective puzzle cannot be solved. The protagonist has only the vaguest suspicions; we have no access to the murder plot, to motives, or to any evidence but the photograph. Antonioni glancingly cites the detective-puzzle situation, whereas Coppola expands it in order to anchor the film within generic expectations. The New Hollywood can explore ambiguous narrational possibilities but those explorations remain within classical boundaries.

31 Alternative modes of film practice

The longevity of the classical cinema accounts partly for its influence. We often forget that Hollywood cinema has affected nearly every sphere of Western cultural life, from building design to conceptions of physical beauty. Certainly the classical style has influenced other narrative media – modern literature, advertising, comic strips, and photography. Even if we confine our survey to the sphere of filmmaking, we cannot ignore the extent to which the classical film has become a model for the entire world.

By the end of the 1920s, the classical style dominated the world's screens. The pattern of events was similar almost everywhere. World War I would force a country to cut back its film production, but theaters would still need motion pictures. American films, imported in huge numbers, became stupendously popular. In Italy audiences quickly succumbed to the appeal of Chaplin, Pickford, and Fairbanks, and domestic producers recovered only by erecting trade barriers. In postwar France, for every French film in circulation there were four American ones; what was widely called *la crise du scénario* came down to an inability to duplicate the vigor of the Hollywood narrative.[1] A German critic ruefully recalled his compatriots' dismay that 'America, with all her faults, could nevertheless do one thing and she could do it well – and that the Germans realized. She could produce popular films – films that were stupid, inane, and often immoral, but for all that, films that did fill the theatres.'[2] British critics complained that their country's films had succumbed to slavish copying of Hollywood. When the Danish director Urban Gad wrote a book on filmmaking he championed both American principles of style and the Hollywood division of labor.[3] The emergence of classical narrative form and style after 1917 provided a stable and powerful *exemplum* for European cinema.

Hollywood did not limit its colonizing to Europe. In Japan, as early as 1919 American films were the most popular foreign ones, and after the 1923 Kanto earthquake severely damaged Japanese studios, Hollywood established its economic domination of the import trade.[4] One Japanese film historian wrote that with the coming of American films, 'Japanese producers were taught for the first time what a true motion picture must be like, and the new conception was fully illustrated by the American example.'[5] Well into the 1930s, Japanese cameramen and directors studied American films, sometimes even counting and timing shots.[6] In India, the same sort of assimilation occurred. As elsewhere, Hollywood was able to offer its films at lower rentals than domestic producers could, and by 1927, most of the films seen in India were American.[7] And there is little need to elaborate upon the classical cinema's influence upon the young film industry of Soviet Russia. Lev Kuleshov's defense of 'Americanitis' and V.I. Pudovkin's admiration for the use of 'plastic material' in *Tol'able David* are well-known. Eisenstein wrote admiringly of Ford and Griffith and recalled his discovery of smooth continuity editing:[8]

> I myself remember what exertions it cost me, at the start of my career in cinema, to learn to see on the screen a scene, let us say, in which Douglas Fairbanks puts out a cigarette – to see it not as a single action but professionally, i.e., in all three of its montage segments: 1) mid-shot – takes cigarette out of mouth; 2) close-up – hand extinguishes cigarette on ashtray; 3) knees-up shot – having dropped the cigarette-butt, Douglas walks away from table!

Two effects of Hollywood's international dominance stand out. First, it spurred Europeans to imitation. French Westerns, pseudo-DeMille sex comedies, and *King Kong Made in Japan* (1933) offer only the most striking symptoms of a much deeper commitment to the classical mode. It is evident that the 'ordinary film' of France, Germany, and even Japan and Russia constructed causality, time, and space in ways characteristic of the normal Hollywood film.[9] The accessibility of Hollywood cinema to audiences of different cultures made it a transnational standard. This trend has, of course, continued to the present.

There is, however, a second effect of Hollywood's international prominence: the need within various countries to distinguish domestic films from the American product. The growth of 'national film styles' after 1919 can best be seen as an attempt to compete economically with the classical style.[10] The German cinema drew upon native art movements (e.g., Expressionism) and literary traditions to create a distinctly Teutonic quality. French Impressionist cinema also sought to constitute an alternative to the American style. The Japanese cinema drew upon its indigenous culture as a way to draw audiences away from the American import. (In various ways, all these attempts created contradictions within each nation's film practice.) When the nationalism strategy did not work, there were a few attempts to create international film syndicates that might compete with Hollywood. Nationalist strategies continue to the present; the most recent examples are the Australian cinema and the anti-colonialist cinema of Third World countries.

The classical style extends its influence to other filmmaking domains as well. It has changed the history of animation; Walt Disney built his career upon transposing the narrative and stylistic principles of classical cinema into animated film. (Recall *Pinocchio* [1940], with its depth compositions, complex crane shots, and goal-oriented protagonist.) Hollywood has also standardized a style for documentary filmmaking. Industrial and government films, educational shorts, and training films, although often non-narrative in structure, call upon the devices and systems of Hollywood filmmaking. World War II combat films, for example, attempted to duplicate Hollywood techniques and production values. Contemporary television has continued this

influence: shot/reverse shot, eyeline matching, and edge lighting are obvious borrowings.[11] The multiple-camera shooting of early talkies foreshadowed the dominant shooting procedures in studio television. Even the amateur cinema has been cut to the classical pattern. From the early 1920s, when 16mm filming became available, Eastman Kodak has urged amateurs to follow the dominant practice. Script your film in advance, make sure the camera is level, balance your compositions, use backlighting and lots of close-ups.[12] Industry journals like *American Cinematographer* gave tips on how the home moviemaker could accomplish Hollywood effects. In sum, it is not too much to say that our conception of any film (or television show), fictional or not, rests chiefly upon assumptions derived from the classical Hollywood cinema.

The most dispiriting evidence of the identification of the cinema as a whole with the classical film style comes from the writings of film theorists, who should know better. There is ample excuse for Hugo Münsterberg to believe that every film must have unified action and consistent characters; he was writing in 1916, when classical filmmaking was emerging.[13] There is less reason for psychologists writing sixty years later to call mismatched editing 'bad' cutting and justify the term by appeal to manuals of Hollywood practice.[14] And there is no excuse for a linguist to assert in 1980 that viewers find a scene without cuts 'unacceptable' in the sense that speakers of a language find ungrammatical utterances unacceptable as sentences; or that cuts which cross the axis of action are not 'filmic' (i.e., 'structurally correct and therefore well-formed').[15] One consequence of defining historical modes of film practice is thus to caution against taking The Cinema as an unproblematic identity; too many theories have blindly repeated as axioms the protocols of one (excessively obvious) cinema.

The historical hegemony of Hollywood makes acute and urgent the need to study film styles and modes of production that differ from Hollywood's. But a great deal more needs to be done in order to specify the salient differences involved. Theorists usually discuss alternatives to the classical cinema in general and largely negative terms. If the classical style is 'invisible,' we will then praise films that show the camera. To the pleasure of the classical style, critics have counterposed a cinema of 'unpleasure' or frustration or boredom; to a representation of depth, a cinema of flatness or 'materiality.' Working with such mighty opposites, it becomes easy to claim that the favored filmmaker (Godard, Vertov, Stan Brakhage, whoever) 'subverts' or 'deconstructs' the dominant style. One task of this book has been to show that such polarities lack nuance and precision. Moreover, one cannot simply oppose narrative or pleasure; one must at the same time show how films can construct systematic alternatives.

Recently, theorists have begun to propose a subtler range of modes of film practice. In an essay on *Vent d'est* (1969), Peter Wollen has drawn up a columnar set of oppositions between Godard's 'counter-cinema' and Hollywood filmmaking. Colin MacCabe has suggested a threefold typology: the classic realist text, the progressive realist text, and the avant-garde text. Paul Willemen constructs a four-part scheme based on whether the film prevents, allows, encourages, or requires an 'active reading.' Using a different four-part taxonomy, Noël Burch and Jorge Dana distinguish among classical films, films with a 'stylistic' (e.g., *Citizen Kane*), films which intermittently escape ideological determination, and films which play upon dominant codes in order to question them. The prototype of such typologies remains that of Jean Narboni and Jean-Louis Comolli, which lists seven ways in which a film can relate to the dominant ideology.[16]

In the light of these attempts (none of which has been elaborated further), it may seem mandarin to propose still another typology; but this book does suggest a systematic approach to the problem. We might start with the functions that some alternative film styles have assigned to particular devices. Plainly, many filmmakers have graded and discriminated formal factors which the classical style lumps together. Just as Impressionist painters dissolved line in order to sharpen a sense of color differences, so have some films promoted a single formal device to a level where we become sensitive to its more minute variations. Because in the classical paradigm the camera can rest at any height, we seldom notice particular differences. But when Yasujiro Ozu decides on a single camera height as the very basis of his scenography, the most minute

inflections of position register with great force. In the classical style, the close-up gains its importance from its rarity; in certain Soviet films or in Dreyer's *La Passion de Jeanne d'Arc* (1928), the close-up becomes the norm and the decoupage must adjust to the consequent fragmentation of the scene. In the Hollywood style, lengthy camera movements alternate with fixed and shorter shots; when, however, Jancsó refuses to contain the mobile take within a clearly segmented scene, every camera movement leaps to our notice. Imagine the orthodox 180° conversation scene; now imagine the scene shot, as in Straub and Huillet's *History Lessons* (1973), from a series of symmetrically disposed high-angle positions moving in a near half-circle around the characters.[17] What one critic wrote of Mizoguchi applies to other filmmakers as well: they emit 'a note so pure that the slightest variation becomes expressive.'[18]

It is not enough, however, to see oppositional styles as the promotion of a formal device: this is only a point of departure for recognizing alternative stylistic *systems*. Ozu's camera height, Jancsó's use of camera movement, Eisenstein's use of the close-up only make sense as forces within a definite and dynamic interaction of story and narration. Consider Mizoguchi's use of shot space in three of his 1936-40 films (*Naniwa Elegy*, *Sisters of Gion*, and *Story of the Last Chrysanthemums*). The films might all be loosely called melodramas, and the takes are very long (average shot lengths of 23 seconds, 33 seconds, and 59 seconds respectively). So far, this hardly distinguishes Mizoguchi's work from that of the American John Stahl, whose 1930s melodramas also use long takes (19 seconds average for *Back Street* [1932], 35 seconds for *Magnificent Obsession* [1935]). But Mizoguchi's work challenges the classical style in a way Stahl's does not: Mizoguchi systematically withholds our access to the character's psychological behavior, especially facial expression. The long take becomes only one instrument of this strategy. Mizoguchi typically stages the scene's action in long shot, using chiaroscuro lighting or aspects of the set to block our vision of the characters. Stahl's long takes, on the other hand, are clearly-lit medium shots of the characters in profile or three-quarters view; thus the shot is wholly at the service of the actor. Mizoguchi demotes the actor's body and face to a parity with other elements in the shot (lighting, architecture, props). In the classical tradition, frontality of body position dominates, but Mizoguchi will play extensive scenes with all characters, or the most important ones, turned away from the camera. The shape and rhythm of the spectator's activity is changed when the 'establishing' shot does not give way to nearer and clearer vantage points, to a pattern of shot/reverse shots, to reaction shots, or to the final close-up that reveals the heart of the action before we are whisked to the next scene. Mizoguchi's scenography promotes values not present in the classical film: separating the voice from the body and using the former as the chief carrier of emotion; saturating shot duration with recollection and anticipation of gestures; exploring environment; and creating an ambiguity of character psychology as well as of spatial depth. What enables these values to emerge, however, is the rigorously systematic quality of Mizoguchi's alternative narration, the way camerawork, lighting, acting, setting, and causality function together.[19]

By using the three levels of generality suggested in Chapter 1, it would be possible to sort out alternative styles. We could characterize any alternative by its specific devices, by its systems, and by the principles of relations among systems. For instance, Eisenstein's *Strike* (1925), *Potemkin* (1925), and *October* (1928) constitute an opposition to Hollywood style at all three levels: an alternative set of techniques (e.g., overlapping and macaronic editing); different systems of narrative causality (the mass protagonist motivated by class interests), of time (the dialectical laws of history), and of space (place treated as a locus of class conflict); and a specific relation among these systems (narrative can be interrupted and qualified by a rhetorical narration). Or Michael Snow's *Wavelength* (1968) can be considered to foreground certain non-classical devices (the jerky zoom, the colored superimpositions) and to change the hierarchy of systems in the film's overall form. Here space and time are not vehicles for story causality, and narrative elements (character, action, suspense) enter only intermittently, with a spatio-temporal progression (the zoom) providing the dominant shape of the film. As with the Hollywood cinema, we must not fetishize devices, since any device

can be appropriated by any style: television commercials borrow from Eisenstein, and Antonioni's *The Passenger* (1975) borrows from *Wavelength*. The systemic level is the crucial contextual link between particular elements and the most fundamental formal principles.

We could also use the theoretical account of narration offered in Chapters 2-7 to distinguish alternative modes of filmmaking. Those chapters have drawn upon examples from non-classical traditions to suggest specific ways in which narration could create new patterns of self-consciousness, knowledge, and communicativeness and to show how the viewer's gap-spotting and gap-filling activity could be guided along different directions. Mizoguchi's scenography would be a pertinent example: the refusal of frontality, legible lighting, and analytical editing is effectively a self-conscious refusal of the omnipresence and communicativeness of classical narration.

It would be tempting to mount an exhaustive typology of all possible alternatives to the classical Hollywood style — a paradigm of paradigms, so to speak. Is there a middle course between simply calling hundreds of films non-classical (each in its own way) and mechanically deducing possible variants? Apart from the dominant and long-lived Hollywood style, only a few other general modes of film practice have existed. Three significant ones would be the 'art cinema,' the avant-garde cinema, and the 'modernist' cinema. We have already sketched out the art cinema as a group style. What we are calling the avant-garde consists centrally of a rejection of narrative causality. Examples would be *La région centrale* (1971), *Zorns Lemma* (1970), *Scorpio Rising* (1964), *Mothlight* (1963), *Ballet Mécanique* (1924), and *Man With a Movie Camera* (1928). More positively, the avant-garde typically takes as its task the creation of film form out of the spatial and temporal possibilities of the medium. The 'modernist' cinema could be described as one in which spatial and temporal systems come forward and share with narrative the role of structuring the film. That is, narration is no longer the most important aspect of plot; other structures can compete for our attention. Hence these films often pose problems of how to unify themselves: a dynamic of unity and fragmentation is set up within the text. The modernist category is very roomy – we could include most works of Ozu, Dreyer, Jacques Tati, Mizoguchi, Jacques Rivette, Robert Bresson, Eisenstein, Godard, Oshima, Straub/Huillet, Marguerite Duras, Yvonne Rainer, *et al.* One would need to make many more distinctions, both historical and theoretical, to sort out various ways in which certain films could be called 'modernist.'

There is a danger that someone might freeze these tendencies into rigid categories, sort or judge films along these lines, even write articles advocating that Wim Wenders's *The Wrong Move* (1975) is a modernist film rather than art film. Although this typology is couched in an objectivist language, it is best thought of as a set of roughly distinct viewing hypotheses. Every film offers some leeway: you can read *Dog Star Man* (1965) as an art film (myth and autobiography become important here), and auteur criticism usually consists of reading certain classical films as if they were art films. Yet the leeway is not infinite. (Try to read *Dog Star Man* as a classical narrative film.) While alternative viewing hypotheses can activate new aspects of a film, the object is not phantasmic; it solicits some readings and pretty definitely forecloses others. The critic should be able to specify what viewing activities the film asks for and where his or her analysis diverges from them, cuts into the film at a bias. (Surrealist critics have been exemplary in their explicit recognition of when their readings 'irrationally enlarge' the operations of a film by Sternberg or Stuart Heisler.[20]) One useful way to keep our sense of alternative styles at once flexible and precise is to use the concept of mode of production to situate the styles historically.

Some alternative modes of production can be identified with characteristics of entire national film industries. The Soviet system of filmmaking after 1930 is an instance of the overt insertion of State ideological direction in the filmmaking process. Assuming the role of directors of capital, the Communist Party assigned its members as top managers of the production studios. Picked because of his administrative successes, the head of the studio might have no knowledge of filmmaking. Although he was the top administrator, the actual power lay with the secretary that the Party also assigned to the studio. Under the administrative head were two divisions: an 'artistic-creative' council of directors, cameramen, producers, and writers, which formulated the scripts and supervised and approved their production; and a 'technical' division, which supplied materials and technicians. As in other Soviet factories, production groups made open, competitive pledges to cut costs and to film efficiently, although world-famous directors such as Eisenstein and Alexander Dovzhenko exceeded budgets, particularly when handling a State-commissioned project. In the United States, a firm made a film to make profits. In the USSR, the studios expected some projects' earnings to support the industry, but ideological correctness was more important than box-office success. Such earnings did not come easy; there was a problem of slow output. In 1935-36, a committee studied other production systems and suggested re-organization along 'American lines.' They set up a division of labor and a production head as in the Hollywood mode, but the Party and committees remained the top decision-makers in the studios.[21]

If the alternative practices of the Soviets produced a slow output, the Japanese film industry of the 1950s involved fast mass-production. The typical film had a short production time, normally using only one take and a lot of editing in the camera. Music might be written during the shooting without the composer even seeing rushes of the film. The Japanese mode also included another labor position – the lighting supervisor, who controlled the placement of lamps. Following other Japanese industries, the film firms were unionized but on an industrial basis, so jurisdictional disputes such as those in the United States did not occur. Rather than starting anywhere in the structure, workers hoping to advance to directing expected to move slowly up the hierarchy.[22]

Because of the world-wide imitation of Hollywood's successful mode of production, however, oppositional practices have generally not been launched on an industry-wide basis. Most alternatives have sprung from the choice of individual filmmakers or filmmaking groups. One major area of variation involves the status of the script. In examining the effects wrought by *cinéma direct*, Comolli has shown that there has emerged a tendency to challenge the sovereignty of the script in the fiction film. Some filmmakers have written scripts and then not used them; Tati claims to film and cut *par coeur*, while Straub and Huillet on some films prepared a detailed script but then did not use it during shooting. Janscó typically uses no conventional script, only a few notes, and he decides on the figure behavior and camera movement only after pacing around the location. Some filmmakers habitually write the script on short order for each day's shooting. Wenders claims to have written *Kings of the Road* (1976) each night before shooting in order to take advantage of changing situations; during the filming of *Zabriskie Point* (1970), Antonioni did not permit his staff to discuss the constantly changing script because 'political events go by too fast for the cinema to keep up.'[23]

Other filmmakers have challenged the script more radically. Dziga Vertov's conception of montage, extended to include the acts of observation and shooting, forced the filmmaker to surrender the usual distinctions between script and filming: for Vertov, scripting occurred throughout the production process. Godard claimed to have a 'dialectical' notion of film-making: adapt the scenario against its source, shoot against the scenario, edit against the footage, and mix sound against the images. One can employ group methods of scripting as well. The makers of *The Battle of Chile* (1973-76) shot footage for two weeks with no plan, then met to determine production roles and the film's final argument. For *My Night at Maud's* (1969), director Eric Rohmer and the cast and crew worked and lived together. Although most of the script was prepared before filming, each night everyone met to discuss and revise the dialogue.[24]

Alternative methods of shooting have often sought to promote 'realism' in the finished product or to generate greater cooperation during production. One tactic, employed by Dreyer and Straub/Huillet, is to shoot in continuity, that is, in the order in which the sequences will appear in the finished film. This practice is often defended as a means to enhance actors' performances. By building his films out of abnormally long takes, Mizoguchi compelled his cast and crew to work together with a sustained attention that differed considerably from the quick and routine totting up of shots demanded in Hollywood. A comparable process was at work in the production of Laura Mulvey and Peter Wollen's *Riddles of the Sphinx* (1977), in which the entire crew had to figure out

ways to remain unseen during the several 360° pan shots. Such *esprit de corps* prevailed in Rohmer's production of *My Night at Maud's* and *Claire's Knee* (1970). The production team was small (no assistants or intermediaries), and all workers shared profits. Rohmer acted as prop man, while the producer also did the electrical work. Shooting in continuity, the group took advantage of the natural change of seasons and filmed at the time of day, place, and season specified by the script.[25] 'A scene which occurs in the script at four in the morning will be shot then because Rohmer believes that the actor will have a particular type of tension in his face befitting the hour.'[26]

Post-production phases of alternative modes of film practice often stress the contribution sound can bring to the film. While a few Hollywood filmmakers preferred to have the music prepared before shooting was finished,[27] the traditional practice, as we have seen, was to add music and sound effects after editing. For *Pierrot le fou* (1965), however, Antoine Duhamel wrote an untimed score from which Godard then used bits and pieces at various points, sometimes cutting the image to fit. As for dialogue, filmmakers such as Tati and Fellini often dispense with it during shooting and then insert it during the editing phase. Other filmmakers prefer to use only direct sound and refuse to tamper with it in the post-filming process. Alexander Kluge believes such direct sound creates 'authenticity,' while Straub and Huillet claim that it provides an 'obstacle' for the actors that makes their performances more 'concrete.'[28] In such ways, oppositional modes of filmmaking can suggest sonic possibilities which the smoothly embellished Hollywood soundtracks cannot.

It would be naive to think that alternative styles necessarily lead to alternative production procedures, still less to fundamental shifts in the mode of production. Yet just as we must define the classical mode partly by its standardization of production and division of labor, so a historically specific description of alternative modes must construct the ideological, technological, and economic bases that support them. In general, most oppositional cinemas have handed over a great many production decisions to the director — hence the commonplace notion of 'personal' filmmaking in Europe or in the avant-garde. But even if the director has played a privileged role, she or he cannot be seen as simply the prime mover of the film. For example, an analysis of the modernist cinema's or the art cinema's mode of production would have to trace the ideological notion of the *film d'art*, the national styles that grew up in opposition to Hollywood after World War I, the importance of the director's taking over the role of the scriptwriter, the functions of the independent and small-scale producer, the creation of an international audience of college-educated viewers, the scope of international coproduction after World War II, and the link of cinema to modernism in other arts (e.g., the post-Jamesian novel for the art cinema; Meyerhold, Brecht, or *le nouveau roman* for various modernist filmmakers). The postwar American avant-garde can be seen to depend extensively upon 16mm technology, an ideology of personal expression cultivated in poetry and painting, a new audience in colleges and art galleries, the growth of private and government arts foundations, and a recasting of commercial division of labor (the film studio becoming more like a painter's studio).

It is in the context of militant filmmaking that the most radical alternatives to the dominant mode of production have been tried out. Here the directors's role has not been so privileged. An early instance was *Kühle Wampe* (1931), whose makers (scenarists, director, composer, producer, and lawyer) constituted themselves as an 'author' in a legal sense. In explaining their aims, the participants pointed to a link between their collective identity and their leftist political position. 'We came more and more to treat organization [of production tasks] as an essential component of artistic work. This was only possible because the work as a whole was political work.'[29] In the late 1960s, many militant filmmaking collectives became active, and several claimed that sharing political goals within a non-hierarchical mode of production affected the look and sound of the films. A famous manifesto by the Brazilians Octavio Getino and Fernando Solanas called for a guerilla cinema that, among other things, changed the division of labor: 'Each member of the group should be familiar, at least in a general way, with the equipment being used: he must be prepared to replace another in any phase of the production. The myth of irreplaceable technicians must be exploded.' The result was a 'third

cinema,' experimental and technically imperfect by Hollywood standards, and aiming at 'unfinished, unordered, violent works.'[30] Most famous of all militant collectives is probably the Dziga Vertov Group, composed of Godard, Jean-Pierre Gorin, and perhaps some other members. The Group celebrated the death of the film author and claimed that on Group productions all workers were paid equally and every shot was discussed politically. Shot on 16mm with limited sound facilities, the Dziga Vertov Group films deliberately 'started from zero,' working from initially simple images and sounds and testing them against one another for political functions. Godard commented on why he used a group method: 'It's an attempt to smash the usual dictatorship of the director. To try to have other people be in the movie on a little more equal basis than just as technicians or slaves. To try to make no hierarchy.'[31] One cannot reduce alternative styles to their productive contexts, but radical cinema, especially of a modernist sort, has insistently demanded a revolutionizing of the means and relations of production in ways that have affected film style.

Radical cinema has also been militant in addressing issues of consumption. Films are not conceived of as commodities for exchange and generation of profits but as ideological instruments for social action. Brecht reportedly wanted a sequence in *Hangmen Also Die* (1943) to be extractable for audience discussion of types of social behavior. Cine Liberacíon, an Argentinian film collective, argued directly against Hollywood where 'man is viewed as a consumer of ideology, not as the creator of ideology.'[32] With screenings and discussions of their films, the group provides an arena for political discussion.

Finally, in constructing alternatives to Hollywood, we must recognize that the historical centrality of that mode creates a constant and complex interchange with other modes. No absolute, pure alternative to Hollywood exists. Godard's use of Hollywood conventions (even in his post-1968 work), Rainer Werner Fassbinder's borrowings from melodramas and gangster films, Rivette's revision of Lang and Jancsó's of Ford – all attest to filmmakers' impulse to use classicism as a reference point. Straub speaks of *Fort Apache* (1948) as Brechtian and of *Othon* (1971) as Hitchcockian, while Brakhage remarks: 'My childhood, like that of Gregory [Markopoulos] and Kenneth [Anger], was saturated by Hollywood movies. Most of us still go to them quite gratefully and enjoy them in the same milieus that we did as children. So we are all the time borrowing possibilities from the Hollywood movie.'[33] You can trace a Hollywood technical process such as back projection from its classical use to its cubistic possibilities in films like *The Chronicle of Anna Magdalena Bach* (1968). Likewise, Hollywood's mode of production continues to exert a power that can be opposed only by a knowledge of its past and its functions. The historical and aesthetic importance of the classical Hollywood cinema lies in the fact that to go beyond it we must go through it.

Envoi

From the speeches at the Society of Motion Picture Engineers banquet, Hotel Pennsylvania, New York, 22 October 1930

MR HAYS: The next presentation is Mr Paul Gulick, publicity director of Universal.

MR GULICK: Personally, I am very glad to meet face to face the gentlemen who caused the revolution in the motion picture business. You don't look revolutionary to me; you are able spokesmen and leaders; you have talked rationally and seem to formulate plans which will be helpful.

My business is that of press agent, and it is my business to make people like the pictures and pay at the box-office that Mr Thompson told you about. I have never had any ability to become an engineer. The only accomplishment I have attained is to get my name mentioned on the program tonight so that I can tell my wife where I have been.

MR HAYS: The next, my friends, is a very great artist and most distinguished international representative of this great business, Mr Sergei Eisenstein, the director who is here from Russia.

MR EISENSTEIN: Mr President, Ladies, and Gentlemen: I don't like to make speeches. Please don't mind if my speech is bad; my feelings are not – I am smiling.

You know, everybody asks the employees if they like the boss, 'Hollywood.' The joke of that boss is that it will not smile. When you visit Hollywood you are shown the marvelous installations and the results of research, and at the end you are always invited to look at the pictures. The differences between the technical and artistic accomplishments are tremendous. I don't want to say that the pictures are not good, but behind the screen production, from the artistic point of view you feel the lack of research such as is behind every engineering achievement. When I arrived in Hollywood I wanted to know: 'Is there a university or high school of motion pictures?' And I received the answer: 'No, there is not; the business developed so quickly – but we can have everybody outstanding on Broadway for our business; we can have the best singers and artists so we don't need a university.' Now, I think that is not the way to insure a really great development in art, and when we see such remarkable results on the technical side, it is because there is a scientific basis for them. I will say that you have some scientific organizations which work on this subject, such as Harvard and Yale. I had the honor of speaking in both places and saw what use is made of research there, but it is almost nothing. They are occupied with the theater drama, and I think that these universities, isolated as they are from the real motion picture business, can never provide the producers with the knowledge they must have. The only institution which approaches what I have in mind is the Academy of Motion Picture Arts and Sciences. I want to say in leaving, that the greatest thing to be accomplished for the future of the motion picture business is the foundation of a high school or university for research on the artistic side.

MR HAYS: The next and last: A recent graduate of the University of Southern California, who has come to New York on a visit, who is incidentally the star in a very great new picture which I have thought enough of to see twice in the projection room, whose shooting is as straight as his love is charming – Mr John Wayne.

MR WAYNE: I want you all to know that I consider it a very great honor to be presented here to people who are creating and aiding in the adjustment of our industry. This occasion recalls to mind the words of my partner in the picture, *The Big Trail*. One day we were watching the movements of the wagons, horses, and cattle in the picture and he said, 'We actors are like that; we are driven and shoved, we don't know where.' It is you people who are giving us something to work with, and I hope everything is going to be 'ok' with sound.

Appendix A   The unbiased sample

To discover the norms of ordinary filmmaking in American studio features of the period 1915-60, we took a sample. (See Chapter 1.) Our initial source was a list of 29,998 feature titles released in the United States since 1915; this list is to be found in *The 1961 Film Daily Yearbook of Motion Pictures*, edited by Chester B. Bahn (New York: Film Daily, 1961), pp. 281-395. After eliminating all films obviously not from an American studio, we used a random-number table to select 841 titles. We located one hundred of these films in the collections of 16mm distributors, of private collectors, and of four research archives: the Motion Picture Division of the Library of Congress; the Museum of Modern Art Film Library; the Wisconsin Center for Film and Theater Research, University of Wisconsin-Madison; and the Film Archive of the University of California at Los Angeles.

This was not, strictly speaking, a random sample. Every film made in American studios did not have an equal chance to be viewed, since not every film has survived. None the less, our selection procedures represent the closest a researcher can come to random sampling when dealing with historical artifacts. The point remains that our choices were not biased by personal preferences or conceptions of influential or masterful films.

The viewing procedures were uniform. Two collaborators viewed each film simultaneously on a horizontal viewing table. One of us enumerated shots, scenes, and reframings, and tabulated reel lengths and credits. The other viewer notated the film shot by shot, indicating shot scale and angle, figure movement and expression, costume, camera movements, setting, lighting, optical devices, narrative motifs, music, effects, and significant

Table: 1: The Unbiased Sample by periods and studios

	1916	1917-28	1929-39	1940-49	1950-59	1960	Totals
Paramount		8	4	4	1		(17)
Metro-Goldwyn-Mayer		5	4	4	1		(14)
Universal		4		1	1		(6)
Columbia			3	2	4		(9)
Warner Bros			13	4			(17)
RKO			1	1	2		(4)
Twentieth Century-Fox			1	4	2	1	(8)
Goldwyn			1				(1)
Monogram				1			(1)
United Artists				1			(1)
Edison	2	3					(5)
Triangle		1					(1)
Sennett		1					(1)
Other		8	3	3	1		(15)
	2	30	30	25	12	1	(100)

dialogue. Notes on each film ran between twenty and sixty pages. In some cases, the films were reviewed to check for errors.

Certain omissions in the sample were unavoidable. Because comparatively few silent films have survived, those located were likely to be 'quality' products considered worth preserving. Similarly, the output of some 'B' studios was difficult to sample because most such films have not been preserved. The high concentration of Warner Bros films during the period 1929-39 resulted from the fact that the studio's output for these years is completely preserved at three archives; no other studio's output of these years is so accessible to scholars. (It may also be relevant that between 1930 and 1937, Warner Bros typically released more features than did any other studio.) Despite these qualifications, the resulting sample films break into a broad representation of studios and periods, as Table 1 shows. On this table, silent cinema is represented by the first two columns, sound by the next four, and totals by the last.

For reference purposes, a list of all Unbiased Sample films follows. Credits were taken from the films themselves. Dates are those given in the *Film Daily Yearbook*. For 1920s releases, additional information on some titles was supplied by *The American Film Institute Catalogue of Motion Pictures Produced in the United States: Feature Films, 1921-1930* (New York: Bowker, 1971).

Unbiased Sample Films

ADVENTURE ISLAND. 1947. Production: Pine-Thomas. Distributor: Paramount. Direction: Peter Stewart. Cinematography: Jack Greenhalgh. Script: Maxwell Shane. Source: story, R.L. Stevenson and Lloyd Osborne. Art direction: F. Paul Sylos. Editing: Howard Smith. Music: Darrell Calker. Cast: Rory Calhoun, Rhonda Fleming, Paul Kelly.

THE ADVENTUROUS BLONDE (Torchy Blane series). 1937. Production: First National. Distributor: Warner Bros. Direction: Frank McDonald. Cinematography: Arthur Todd. Script: Robertson White and David Diamond. Art direction: Max Parker. Editing: Frank Magee. Cast: Glenda Farrell, Barton MacLane, Anne Nagel.

AFFAIR IN HAVANA. Production: Dudley Pictures International Corporation of Cuba. Distributor: Allied Artists. Direction: Laslo Benedek. Cinematography: Alan Stensvold. Script: Burton Lane and Maurice Zimor. Source: original story, Janet Green. Art direction: Gabriel Scognamillo. Editing: Stefan Arnsten. Music: Ernest Gold. Cast: John Cassavetes, Raymond Burr, Sara Shane.

AN AMERICAN ROMANCE. 1944. Production/distribution: MGM. Direction: King Vidor. Cinematography: Harold Rosson. Script: Herbert Dalmas and William Ludwig. Source: story by Vidor. Art direction: Cedric Gibbons and Urie McCleary. Editing: Conrad A. Nervig. Music: Louis Gruenberg. Cast: Brian Donlevy, Ann Richards, Walter Abel.

APPLAUSE. 1929. Production/distributor: Paramount. Direction: Rouben Mamoulian. Cinematography: George Folsey. Script: Garrett Fort. Source: story, Beth Brown. Editing: John Bessler. Cast: Helen Morgan, Joan Peers, Fuller Mellish Jr.

APPOINTMENT FOR LOVE. 1941. Production/distributor: Universal. Direction: William A. Seiter. Cinematography: Joseph Valentine. Script: Bruce Manning and Felix Jackson. Source: story, Ladislaus Bus-Fekete. Art direction: Jack Otterson. Editing: Ted Kent. Music: Frank Skinner. Cast: Charles Boyer, Margaret Sullavan, Rita Johnson.

THE ARKANSAS TRAVELER. 1938. Production/distributor: Paramount. Direction: Alfred Santell. Cinematography: Leo Tover. Script: Viola Brothers Shore, George Sessions Perry. Source: story, Jack Cunningham. Art direction: Hans Dreier, Earl Hedrick. Editing: Paul Weatherwax. Music: Boris Morris. Cast: Bob Burns, Fay Bainter, John Beal.

AT SWORD'S POINT. 1952. Production/distributor: RKO. Direction: Lewis Allen. Cinematography: Ray Rennahan. Script: Walter Ferris, Joseph Hoffman. Source: story, Aubrey Wisberg, Jack Pollexfen. Art direction: Albert S. D'Agostino, Jack Okey. Editing: Samuel E. Beetley, Robert Golden. Music: Roy Webb. Cast: Maureen O'Hara, Cornel Wilde, Robert Douglas.

BALALAIKA. 1939. Production: MGM. Distributor: Loew's. Direction: Reinhold Schunzel. Cinematography: Joseph Ruttenberg, Karl

Freund. Script: Leon Gordon, Charles Bennett, Jacques Deval. Source: play, Eric Maschwitz, George Posford, Bernard Grun. Art direction: Cedric Gibbons, Eddie Imazu. Editing: George Boemler. Music: Herbert Stothart. Cast: Nelson Eddy, Ilona Massey, Charlie Ruggles.

BEGGARS OF LIFE. 1928. Production: Paramount Famous Lasky. Distributor: Paramount. Direction: William A. Wellman. Cinematography: Henry Gerrard. Script: Benjamin Glazer. Source: story, Jim Tully. Editing: Alyson Shaffer. Cast: Wallace Beery, Richard Arlen, Louise Brooks.

BLACK HAND. 1949. Production/distributor: MGM. Direction: Richard Thorpe. Cinematography: Paul C. Vogel. Script: Luther Davis. Source: story, Leo Townsend. Art direction: Cedric Gibbons, Gabriel Scognamillo. Music: Alberto Columbo. Cast: Gene Kelly, J. Carrol Nalsh, Teresa Celli.

THE CADDY. 1953. Production: York Pictures. Distributor: Paramount. Direction: Norman Taurog. Cinematography: Daniel L. Fapp. Script: Edmund Hartmann, Danny Arnold. Source: story, Arnold. Art direction: Hal Pereira, Franz Bachelin. Editing: Warren Low. Music: Joseph J. Lilley. Cast: Dean Martin, Jerry Lewis, Donna Reed.

THE CANTERVILLE GHOST. 1944. Production/distributor: MGM. Direction: Jules Dassin. Cinematography: Robert Planck. Script: Edith Harvey Blum. Source: story, Oscar Wilde. Art direction: Cedric Gibbons, Edward Carfagno. Editing: Chester W. Schaeffer. Cast: Charles Laughton, Robert Young, Margaret O'Brien.

CASBAH. 1948. Production: Marston. Distributor: Universal International. Direction: John Berry. Cinematography: Irving Glassberg. Script: Ladislaus Bush-Fekete, Arnold Manoff. Source: novel, Detective Ashelbe. Art direction: Bernard Herzbrun. Editing: Edward Curtiss. Music: Harold Arlen. Cast: Yvonne DeCarlo, Tony Martin, Peter Lorre.

THE CASE OF THE LUCKY LEGS (Perry Mason series). 1935. Production: First National. Distributor: Warner Bros. Direction: Archie L. Mayo. Cinematography: Tony Gaudio. Script: Brown Holmes, Ben Machson, Jerry Chodorov. Editing: James Gibbon. Cast: Warren William, Genevieve Tobin, Patricia Ellis.

CODE OF THE SEA. 1924. Production: Famous Players-Lasky. Distributor: Paramount. Direction: Victor Fleming. Cinematography: Edgar Shoenbaum. Script: Bertram Millhauser. Source: story, Byron Morgan. Cast: Rod La Rocque, Jacqueline Logan, George Fawcett.

CORPORAL KATE. 1926. Production: DeMille Pictures Corp. Distributor: Producers Distribution Corp. Direction: Paul Sloane. Cinematography: Jacob Badaracco. Script: Albert Shelby LeVino. Source: story, Zelda Sears, Marian Orth. Cast: Vera Renolds, Julia Faye, Kenneth Thomson.

THE COURAGE OF THE COMMONPLACE. 1917. Production: Edison. Direction: Ben Turbett. Source: Mary Raymond Shipman Andrews. Cast: Leslie Austin, Mildred Havens, Stanley Wheatcroft.

CRIME DOCTOR'S MAN HUNT (Crime Doctor series). 1946. Production/distributor: Columbia. Direction: William Castle. Cinematography: Philip Tannura. Script: Leigh Brackett. Source: radio series, Max Marcin; story, Eric Taylor. Art direction: George Montgomery. Editing: Dwight Caldwell. Music: Mischa Bakaleinikoff. Cast: Warner Baxter, Ellen Drew, William Frawley.

DANCE CHARLIE DANCE. 1937. Production: First National. Distributor: Warner Bros. Direction: Frank McDonald. Cinematography: Warren Lynch. Script: Crane Wilbur, William Jacobs. Source: play, George S. Kaufman. Art direction: Carl Jules Weyl. Editing: Frank Magee. Music: M.K. Jerome, Jack Scholl. Cast: Stuart Erwin, Jean Muir, Allen Jenkins.

DEEP VALLEY. 1947. Production: Warner Bros–First National. Distributor: Warner Bros. Direction: Jean Negulesco. Cinematography: Ted McCord. Script: Salka Viertel, Stephen Morehouse Avery. Source: novel, Dan Totheroh. Art direction: Max Parker, Frank Durlauf. Editing: Owen Marks. Music: Max Steiner. Cast: Ida Lupino, Dane Clark, Wayne Morris.

THE DEVIL BAT. 1940. Production: Jack Gallagher. Distributor: Producers Releasing Corp. Direction: Jean Yarborough. Cinematography: Arthur Martinelli. Script: John Thomas Neville. Source: story, George Bricker. Art direction: Paul Palmentola. Editing: Holbrook N. Todd. Music: David Chudnow. Cast: Bela Lugosi, Suzanne Kaaren, Dave O'Brien.

DOWNSTAIRS. 1932. Production/distributor:

MGM. Direction: Monta Bell. Cinematography: Harold Rosson. Script: Lenore Coffee, Melville Baker. Source: story, John Gilbert. Art direction: Cedric Gibbons. Editing: Conrad A. Nervig. Cast: John Gilbert, Paul Lukas, Virginia Bruce.

EASY TO LOOK AT. 1945. Production/distributor: Universal. Direction: Ford Beebe. Cinematography: Jerome Ash. Script: Henry Blankfort. Source: story, Blankfort. Art direction: John B. Goodman, Robert Clatworthy. Editing: Saul A. Goodkind. Music: Charles Newman, Arthur Altman. Cast: Gloria Jean, Kirby Grant, George Dolenz.

FIRE DOWN BELOW. 1957. Production: Warwick Films. Distributor: Columbia. Direction: Robert Parrish. Cinematography: Desmond Dickinson. Script: Irwin Shaw. Source: novel, Max Catto. Art direction: John Box. Editing: Jack Slade. Music: Arthur Benjamin, Kenneth V. Jones, Douglas Gamley. Cast: Rita Hayworth, Robert Mitchum, Jack Lemmon.

FROM HERE TO ETERNITY. 1953. Production/distributor: Columbia. Direction: Fred Zinneman. Cinematography: Burnett Guffey. Script: Daniel Taradash. Source: novel, James Jones. Art direction: Cary O'Dell. Editing: William Lyon. Music: Morris Stoloff. Cast: Burt Lancaster, Montgomery Clift, Deborah Kerr.

GIDGET. 1959. Production/distributor: Columbia. Direction: Paul Wendkos. Cinematography: Burnett Guffey. Script: Gabrielle Upton. Source: novel, Frederick Kohner. Art direction: Ross Bellah. Editing: William Algon. Music: Morris Stoloff. Cast: Sandra Dee, James Darren, Cliff Robertson.

GOING HIGHBROW. 1935. Production/distributor: Warner Bros. Direction: Robert Florey. Cinematography: William Rees. Script: Edward Kaufman, Sy Bartlett. Source: story, Ralph Spence. Art direction: Esdras Hartley. Editing: Harold McLernen. Music: Louis Alter, John Scholl. Cast: Guy Kibbee, Zasu Pitts, Edward Everett Horton.

THE HASTY HEART. 1949. Production/distributor: Warner Bros. Direction: Vincent Sherman. Cinematography: Wilkie Cooper. Script: Ronald MacDougall. Source: play, John Patrick. Art direction: Terence Verity. Editing: E.B. Jarvis. Music: Jack Beaver. Cast: Ronald Reagan, Patricia Neal, Richard Todd.

HIGH TIME. 1960. Production: Bing Crosby Productions. Distributor: Twentieth Century-Fox. Direction: Blake Edwards. Cinematography: Ellsworth Fredericks. Script: Tom Waldman, Frank Waldman. Source: story, Garson Kanin. Editing: Robert Simpson. Music: Henry Mancini. Cast: Bing Crosby, Fabian, Tuesday Weld.

HIS DOUBLE LIFE. 1933. Production: Eastern Service Studio. Distributor: Atlantic Pictures. Direction: Arthur Hopkins. Cinematography: Arthur Edeson. Script: Arthur Hopkins, Clara Beranger. Source: novel and play, Arnold Bennett. Art direction: Joe Schulze, Walter Keller. Editing: Arthur Ellis. Music: Karl Stark, James Hanley. Cast: Roland Young, Lillian Gish, Montague Love.

HOUSEWIFE. 1934. Production/distributor: Warner Bros. Direction: Alfred E. Green. Cinematography: William Rees. Script: Manuel Seff, Lillie Hayward. Source: story, Robert Lord, Hayward. Art direction: Robert M. Haas. Editing: James Gibbon. Music: Mort Dixon, Allie Wrubel. Cast: George Brent, Bette Davis, Ann Dvorak.

IMPACT. 1948. Production: Cardinal Pictures. Distributor: United Artists. Direction: Arthur Lubin. Cinematography: Ernest Laszlo. Script: Dorothy Reid, Jay Dratler. Source: story, Dratler. Art direction: Rudi Feld. Editing: Arthur H. Nadel. Music: Michel Michelet. Cast: Brian Donlevy, Ella Raines, Charles Coburn.

INDIANAPOLIS SPEEDWAY. 1939. Production/distributor: Warner Bros. Direction: Lloyd Bacon. Cinematography: Sid Hickox. Script: Sig Herzig, Wally Klein. Source: story, Howard Hawks. Art direction: Esdras Hartley. Editing: William Holmes. Music: Adolph Deutsch. Cast: Ann Sheridan, Pat O'Brien, John Payne.

THE INNOCENCE OF RUTH. 1916. Production: The Edison Studios. Distributor: Kleine-Edison. Direction: John H. Collins. Cast: Edward Earle, T. Tamamoto, Viola Dana.

INTERLUDE. 1957. Production: Ross Hunter. Distributor: Universal. Direction: Douglas Sirk. Cinematography: William Daniels. Script: Daniel Fuches, Franklin Coen, Inez Cook, Dwight Taylor. Source: novel, James Cain. Art direction: Alexander Golitzen, Robert E. Smith. Editing: Russell E. Schoengarth. Music: Frank Skinner. Cast: June Allyson, Rossano Brazzi,

Marianne Cook.

THE KING AND THE CHORUS GIRL. 1937. Production/distributor: Warner Bros. Direction: Mervyn LeRoy. Cinematography: Tony Gaudio. Script: Norman Krasna, Groucho Marx. Source: story. Art direction: Robert M. Haas. Editing: Thomas Richards. Music: Werner R. Heymann. Cast: Fernand Gravet, Joan Blondell, Edward Everett Horton.

KING OF THE RODEO. 1928. Production: Universal-Jewel. Distributor: Universal. Direction: Henry MacRae. Cinematography: Harry Neumann. Script: George Morgan. Source: story, B.M. Bower. Art direction: David Garber. Editing: Gilmore Walker. Cast: Hoot Gibson, Kathryn Crawford.

KING OF THE ZOMBIES. 1941. Production/distributor: Monogram. Direction: Jean Yarbrough. Cinematography: Mark Stengler. Script: Edmund Kelso. Art direction: Charles Clague. Editing: Richard Currier. Music: Edward Kay. Cast: Dick Purcell, Joan Woodbury, Manton Moreland.

LADY AND GENT. 1932. Production/distributor: Paramount. Direction: Stephen Roberts. Cinematography: Harry Fischbeck. Script: Grover Jones, William Slavens McNutt. Cast: George Bancroft, Wynne Gibson, Charles Starrett.

THE LATE GEORGE APLEY. 1947. Production/distributor: Twentieth Century-Fox. Direction: Joseph L. Mankiewicz. Cinematography: Joseph La Shelle. Script: Philip Dunne. Source: play, John P. Marquand, George S. Kaufman; novel, Marquand. Art direction: James Basevi, J. Russell Spencer. Music: Alfred Newman. Cast: Ronald Colman, Vanessa Brown, Richard Hayden.

LORNA DOONE. 1921. Production: Thomas H. Ince Corp. Distributor: Associated First National Pictures. Direction: Maurice Tourneur. Cinematography: Henry Sharp. Script: Katherine Speer Reed, Cecil G. Mumford, Wyndham Gittens. Source: novel, Richard Doddridge Blackmore. Art direction: Milton Menasco. Cast: Madge Bellamy, May Giracci, John Bowers.

THE LOST EXPRESS. 1926. Production: Anchor Film Distributors. Distributor: Rayart Pictures Corp. Direction: J.P. McGowan. Cast: Helen Holmes, Henry Barrows, Eddie Barry.

A LOST LADY. 1933. Production/distributor: First National. Direction: Alfred E. Green. Cinematography: Sid Hickox. Script: Gene Markey, Kathryn Scola. Source: story, Willa Cather. Art direction: Jack Okey. Editing: Owen Marks. Cast: Barbara Stanwyck, Frank Morgan, Ricardo Cortez.

LOVE AND THE LAW. 1919. Production: Edgar Lewis. Direction: Lewis [?]. Source: story, William Hamilton Osborne. Cast: Glen White, Tom Williams, Arthur Bauer.

THE MAD MARTINDALES. 1942. Production/distributor: Twentieth Century-Fox. Direction: Alfred Werker. Cinematography: Lucien Andriot. Script: Francis Edwards Faragoh. Source: play, Wesley Tower. Art direction: Richard Day, Lewis Creber. Editing: Nick De Maggio. Music: Emil Newman. Cast: Jane Withers, Marjorie Weaver, Alan Mowbray, Jimmy Lydon.

THE MAN WHO LAUGHS. 1928. Production/distributor: Universal. Direction: Paul Leni. Cinematography: Gilbert Warrenton. Script: J. Grubb Alexander. Source: novel, Victor Hugo. Art direction: Charles D. Hall, Joseph Wright, Thomas O'Neil. Editing: Maurice Pivar, Edward Cahn. Cast: Conrad Veidt, Mary Philbin, Olga Baclanova.

MANHANDLED. 1949. Production/distributor: Paramount. Direction: Lewis R. Foster. Cinematography: Ernest Laszlo. Script: Foster, Whitman Chambers. Source: story, L.S. Goldsmith. Art direction: Lewis H. Creber. Editing: Howard Smith. Music: Darrell Calker. Cast: Dorothy Lamour, Sterling Hayden, Dan Duryea.

MERRY-GO-ROUND. 1923. Production/distributor: Universal. Direction: Rupert Julian, Erich von Stroheim. Cinematography: Charles Kaufman, William Daniels. Art direction: E.E. Sheeley. Editing: James McKay. Cast: Norman Kerry, Dorothy Wallace, Anton Vaverka.

MERRY WIVES OF RENO. 1934. Production/distributor: Warner Bros. Direction: H. Bruce Humberstone. Cinematography: Ernest Haller. Script: Robert Lord. Source: story, Lord, Joe Traub. Art direction: Jack Okey. Editing: Thomas Pratt. Music: Leo Forbstein. Cast: Guy Kibbee, Glenda Farrell, Donald Woods.

THE MICHIGAN KID. 1928. Production: Universal-Jewel. Distributor: Universal.

Direction: Irvin Willatt. Cinematography: Charles Stumar. Script: Peter Milne. Source: story, Rex Beach. Editing: Harry Marker. Cast: Conrad Nagel, Renée Adorée, Lloyd Whitlock.

MICKEY. 1918. Production: Mack Sennett. Distributor: Film Booking Office. Direction: Richard Jones. Cast: Mabel Normand, George Nichols, Wheeler Oakman.

THE MIRACLE WOMAN. 1931. Production/distributor: Columbia. Direction: Frank R. Capra. Cinematography: Joseph Walker. Script: Jo Swerling. Source: play, John Meehen, Robert Riskin. Editing: Maurice Wright. Cast: Barbara Stanwyck, David Manners, Sam Hardy.

MISS LULU BETT. 1921. Production: Famous Players-Lasky. Distributor: Paramount. Direction: William C. deMille. Cinematography: L. Guy Wilky. Script: Clara Beranger. Source: novel and play, Zona Gale. Cast: Theodore Roberts, Lois Wilson, Milton Sills.

MR. SKEFFINGTON. 1944. Production/distributor: Warner Bros. Direction: Vincent Sherman. Cinematography: Ernest Haller. Script: Julius J. and Philip G. Epstein. Source: story, 'Elizabeth.' Art direction: Robert Haas. Editing: Ralph Dawson. Music: Franz Waxman. Cast: Bette Davis, Claude Rains, Walter Abel.

MONSIEUR BEAUCAIRE. 1948. Production/distributor: Paramount. Direction: George Marshall. Cinematography: Lionel Linden. Script: Melvin Frank, Norman Panama. Source: novel, Booth Tarkington. Art direction: Hans Dreier, Earl Hedrick. Editing: Arthur Schmidt. Cast: Bob Hope, Joan Caulfield, Patric Knowles.

MY FAVORITE BRUNETTE. 1947. Production/distributor: Paramount. Direction: Elliott Nugent. Cinematography: Lionel Linden. Script: Edmund Belion, Jack Rose. Art direction: Hans Dreier, Earl Hedrick. Music: Robert Emmett Dolan. Cast: Bob Hope, Dorothy Lamour, Peter Lorre.

THE NARROW TRAIL. 1917. Production: Thomas H. Ince. Direction: William S. Hart. Cinematography: Joe August. Script: Harvey S. Thew. Source: story, Hart. Cast: William S. Hart, Sylvia Bremer, Milton Ross.

THE NIGHT HOLDS TERROR. 1955. Production/distributor: Columbia. Direction: Andrew Stone. Cinematography: Fred Jackman, Jr. Script: Stone. Editing: Virginia Stone. Cast: Jack Kelly, Hildy Parks, John Cassavetes.

NO LEAVE, NO LOVE. 1946. Production: MGM. Distributor: Loew's. Direction: Charles Martin. Cinematography: Harold Rosson, Robert Surtees. Script: Martin, Leslie Kardos. Source: original. Art direction: Cedric Gibbons, Preston Ames. Editing: Conrad A. Nervig. Music: Georgie Stoll. Cast: Van Johnson, Keenan Wynn, Pat Kirkwood.

ON DANGEROUS GROUND. 1917. Production: William A. Brady. Distributor: World. Direction: Robert Thornby. Cinematography: Lucien Andriot. Source: novel, Burton E. Stevenson. Cast: Gail Kane, Carlyle Blackwell, William Baily.

ONE FRIGHTENED NIGHT. 1935. Production: Nat Levine. Distributor: Mascot. Direction: Christy Cabanne. Cinematography: Ernest Miller, William Nobles. Script: Wellyn Totman. Source: story, Stuart Palmer. Editing: Joseph H. Lewis, Ray Curtiss. Cast: Charley Grapewin, Mary Carlisle, Arthur Hohl.

ONE TOUCH OF NATURE. 1917. Production: Edison. Direction: Edward H. Griffith. Source: story, Peter B. Kyne. Cast: John Drew Bennett, Viola Cain, George Henry.

PARACHUTE JUMPER. 1933. Production: Warner Bros–Vitaphone. Distributor: Warner Bros. Direction: Alfred E. Green. Cinematography: James Van Trees. Script: John Francis Larkin. Source: story, Rian James. Art direction: Jack Okey. Editing: Ray Curtiss. Cast: Doug Fairbanks, Jr., Bette Davis, Frank McHugh.

PAROLE FIXER. 1939. Production/distributor: Paramount. Direction: Robert Florey. Cinematography: George Barnes. Script: William R. Lipman, Horace McCoy. Source: book, J. Edgar Hoover. Art direction: Hans Dreier, John Goodman. Editing: Harvey Johnston. Cast: William Henry, Virginia Dale, Robert Paige.

PARTNERS IN CRIME. 1928. Production: Paramount Famous Lasky. Direction: Frank Strayer. Cinematography: William Marshall. Script: Grover Jones, Gilbert Pratt. Source: story, Jones, Pratt. Editing: B.F. Zeidman. Cast: Wallace Beery, Raymond Hatton, Mary Brian.

PENTHOUSE. 1933. Production: Cosmopolitan. Distributor: MGM. Direction: W.S. Van Dyke. Cinematography: Lucien Andriot, Harold Rosson. Script: Frances Goodrich, Albert

Hacker. Source: story, Arthur Somers Roche. Art direction: Alexander Toluboff. Editing: Robert J. Kern. Music: Dr. William Axt. Cast: Warner Baxter, Myrna Loy, Charles Butterworth.

PLAY GIRL. 1941. Production/distributor: RKO. Direction: Frank Woodruff. Cinematography: Nick Musuraca. Script: Jerry Cady. Source: story, Cady. Art direction: Van Nest Polglase, Albert D'Agostino. Editing: Harry Marker. Music: Paul Sawtell. Cast: Kay Francis, James Ellison, Mildred Coles.

PRINCE OF PLAYERS. 1954. Production: Philip Dunne. Distributor: Twentieth Century-Fox. Direction: Philip Dunne. Cinematography: Charles G. Clarke. Script: Moss Hart. Source: book, Eleanor Ruggles. Art direction: Lyle Wheeler, Mark Lee Kirk. Editing: Dorothy Spencer. Music: Bernard Herrmann. Cast: Richard Burton, Maggie McNamara, John Derek.

RIVER OF NO RETURN. 1954. Production: Stanley Rubin. Distributor: Twentieth Century-Fox. Direction: Otto Preminger. Cinematography: Joseph LaShelle. Script: Frank Fenton. Source: story, Louis Lantz. Art direction: Lyle Wheeler, Addison Hehr. Editing: Louis Loeffler. Music: Cyril J. Mockridge. Cast: Robert Mitchum, Marilyn Monroe, Rory Calhoun.

ROARING TIMBER. 1937. Production/distributor: Columbia. Direction: Phil Rosen. Cinematography: James S. Brown, Jr. Script: Paul Franklin, Robert James Cosgriff. Source: story, Cosgriff. Art direction: Dwight Caldwell. Cast: Jack Holt, Grace Bradley, Ruth Donnelly.

THE ROYAL PAUPER. 1917. Production: Edison. Distributor: K.E.S.E. Direction: Ben Turbett. Script: Henry Albert Phillips. Cast: Francine Larrimore, Helen Strickland, William Wadsworth.

SARATOGA. 1937. Production/distributor: MGM. Direction: Jack Conway. Cinematography: Roy June. Script: Anita Loos, Robert Hopkins. Source: story, Loos. Art direction: Cedric Gibbons. Editing: Elmo Veron. Music: Edward Ward. Cast: Clark Gable, Jean Harlow, Lionel Barrymore.

THE SCARLET ROAD. 1916. Production: George Kleine Photodrama. Distributor: Kleine-Edison Feature. Cast: Malcolm Duncan, Della Connor, Ira Shepard.

SH! THE OCTOPUS. 1937. Production/distributor: Warner Bros. Direction: William McGann. Cinematography: Arthur Todd. Script: George Bricker. Source: two plays, Ralph Spence; Ralph Murphy, Donald Gallagher. Art direction: Max Parker. Editing: Clarence Kolster. Cast: Hugh Herbert, Allen Jenkins, Marcia Ralston.

SHALL WE DANCE. 1937. Production/distributor: RKO. Direction: Mark Sandrich. Cinematography: David Abel. Script: Allan Scott, Ernest Pagano. Source: story, Lee Loeb, Harold Buchman. Art direction: Van Nest Polglase, Carroll Clark. Editing: William Hamilton. Music: George Gershwin. Cast: Fred Astaire, Ginger Rogers, Edward Everett Horton.

THE SHOCK PUNCH. 1925. Production: Famous Players-Lasky. Distributor: Paramount. Direction: Paul Sloane. Cinematography: William Miller. Script: Luther Reed. Source: story, John Monk Saunders. Art direction: Ernest Fegte. Editing: William Le Baron. Cast: Richard Dix, Frances Howard, Theodore Babcock.

THE SHOW. 1927. Production/distributor: MGM. Direction: Tod Browning. Cinematography: John Arnold. Script: Waldemar Young. Source: novel, Charles Tenny Jackson. Art direction: Cedric Gibbons, Richard Day. Editing: Errol Taggart. Cast: John Gilbert, Renée Adorée, Lionel Barrymore.

SHOW PEOPLE. 1928. Production/distributor: MGM. Direction: King Vidor. Cinematography: John Arnold. Script: Agnes Christine Johnston, Laurence Stallings. Art direction: Cedric Gibbons. Editing: Hugh Wynn. Cast: Marion Davies, William Haines, Dell Henderson.

THE SIN OF HAROLD DIDDLEBOCK. 1946. Production: California Pictures Corp. Direction: Preston Sturges. Cinematography: Robert Pittack. Script: Sturges. Source: story, Sturges. Art direction: Robert Usher. Editing: Thomas Neff. Music: Werner R. Heyman. Cast: Harold Lloyd, Jimmy Conlin, Raymond Walburn.

THE SPEED SPOOK. 1924. Production: East Coast Films. Distributor: C.C. Burr. Direction: Charles Hines. Cinematography: Charles E. Gilson, Johnny Geisel. Script: Raymond S. Harris. Source: story, William Wallace Cook. Cast: Johnny Hines, Edmund Breese, Faire Binney.

SPEEDY. 1928. Production: Harold Lloyd Corp. Distributor: Paramount. Direction: Ted Wilde.

Cinematography: Walter Lundin. Script: John Grey, Lex Neal, Howard Rogers, Jay Howe. Cast: Harold Lloyd, Ann Christy, Bert Woodruff.

STEAMBOAT BILL, JR. 1928. Production: Buster Keaton Productions. Distributor: United Artists. Direction: Charles F. Reisner. Cinematography: Dev Jennings, Bert Haines. Script: Carl Harbaugh. Technical direction: Fred Gabourie. Editing: Sherman Kell. Cast: Buster Keaton, Ernest Torrence, Marion Bryon.

SUNDAY DINNER FOR A SOLDIER. 1944. Production/distributor: Twentieth Century-Fox. Direction: Lloyd Bacon. Cinematography: Joe MacDonald. Script: Wanda Tuchock, Melvin Levy. Source: story, Martha Cheavens. Art direction: Lyle Wheeler, Russell Spencer. Editing: J. Watson Webb. Music: Alfred Newman. Cast: Anne Baxter, John Hodiak, Charles Winninger.

SWEEPSTAKES WINNER. 1939. Production: First National. Distributor: Warner Bros. Direction: William McGann. Cinematography: Arthur Edeson. Script: John Krafft, Albert DeMond. Art direction: Stanley Fleischer. Editing: Frank Magee. Cast: Marie Wilson, Johnnie Davis, Allen Jenkins.

THE THREE MUST-GET-THERES. 1922. Production: Max Linder Productions. Distributor: Allied Producers and Distributors. Direction: Max Linder. Cinematography: Harry Vallejo, Max Dupont. Script: Linder. Source: novel, Alexandre Dumas. Cast: Linder, Frank Cooke, Caroline Rankin.

THE TIGER'S COAT. 1920. Production: The Dial Film Company. Distributor: W.W. Hodkinson Corp. through Pathé Exchange, Inc. Direction: Roy Clements. Cinematography: R.E. Irish. Script: Jack Cunningham. Source: book, Elizabeth De Jeans. Art direction: E.P. Hunziker. Cast: W. Butts, Myles McCarthy, F. Weed.

UNCERTAIN GLORY. 1944. Production/distributor: Warner Bros. Direction: Raoul Walsh. Cinematography: Sid Hickox. Script: Laszlo Vadney, Max Brand. Source: story, Joe May, Vadney. Art direction: Robert Haas. Editing: George Amy. Music: Adolph Deutsch. Cast: Erroll Flynn, Paul Lukas, Lucille Watson.

VICTORY. 1919. Production: Maurice Tourneur. Distributor: Paramount/Artcraft. Direction:

Maurice Tourneur. Cinematography: René Guissart. Script: Stephen Fox. Source: novel, Joseph Conrad. Art direction: Floyd Mueller. Cast: Jack Holt, Seena Owen, Wallace Beery.

WE GO FAST. 1941. Production/distributor: Twentieth Century-Fox. Direction: William McGann. Cinematography: Harry Jackson. Script: Thomas Lennon, Adrian Scott. Source: story, Doug Welch. Art direction: Richard Day, Lewis Creber. Editing: Fred Allen. Music: Emil Newman. Cast: Lyn Bari, Alan Curtis, Sheila Ryan.

THE WHIP HAND. 1951. Production/distributor: RKO. Direction: William Cameron Menzies. Cinematography: Nicolas Musuraca. Script: George Bricker, Frank L. Moss. Source: story, Roy Hamilton. Art direction: Albert S. D'Agostino, Carroll Clark. Editing: Robert Golden. Music: Paul Sawtell. Cast: Carla Ralenda, Elliott Reid, Edgar Barrier.

WHITE SHADOWS IN THE SOUTH SEAS. 1928. Production: Cosmopolitan. Distributor: MGM. Direction: W.S. Van Dyke. Cinematography: Clyde de Vinna, George Nogle, Bob Roberts. Script: Jack Cunningham. Source: book, Frederick O'Brien. Editing: Ben Lewis. Cast: Monte Blue, Raquel Torres, Robert Anderson.

WHITE ZOMBIE. 1932. Production: Victor Halperin. Distributor: United Artists. Direction: Victor Halperin. Cinematography: Arthur Martinelli. Script: Garnett Weston. Source: story, Weston. Editing: Howard McLernon. Cast: Bela Lugosi, Madge Bellamy, Joseph Cawthorn.

THE WHOLE TOWN IS TALKING. 1935. Production/distributor: Columbia. Direction: John Ford. Cinematography: Joseph August. Script: Jo Swerling, Robert Riskin. Source: story, W.R. Burnett. Editing: Viola Laurence. Cast: Edward G. Robinson, Jean Arthur, Arthur Hohl.

WINE OF YOUTH. 1924. Production/distributor: MGM. Direction: King Vidor. Cinematography: John J. Mescall. Script: Carey Wilson. Source: play, Rachel Crothers. Art direction: Charles Cadwallader. Editing: Hugh Wynn. Cast: Eleanor Boardman, William Haines, Ben Lyon.

WINGS OF THE NAVY. 1939. Production: Cosmopolitan. Distributor: Warner Bros. Direction: Lloyd Bacon. Cinematography: Arthur Edeson. Script: Michael Fessier. Source: original. Art direction: Esdras Hartley. Editing:

George Amy. Cast: George Brent, Olivia de Havilland, John Payne.

A WOMAN OF THE WORLD. 1925. Production: Famous Players-Lasky. Distributor: Paramount. Direction: Malcolm St Clair. Cinematography: Bert Glennon. Script: Pierre Collings. Source: novel, Carl Van Vechten. Cast: Pola Negri, Charles Emmett Mack, Holmes Herbert.

WUTHERING HEIGHTS. 1939. Production: Goldwyn. Distributor: United Artists. Direction: William Wyler. Cinematography: Gregg Toland. Script: Charles MacArthur, Ben Hecht. Source: novel, Emily Brontë. Art direction: James Basevi. Music: Alfred Newman. Cast: Merle Oberon, Laurence Olivier, David Niven.

YOU FOR ME. 1952. Production/distributor: MGM. Direction: Don Weis. Cinematography: Paul C. Vogel. Script: William Roberts. Source: story, Roberts. Art direction: Cedric Gibbons, Eddie Imazu. Editing: Newell P. Kimlin. Cast: Peter Lawford, Jane Greer, Gig Young.

YOUNG SINNERS. 1931. Production/distributor: Twentieth Century-Fox. Direction: John Blystone. Cinematography: John Seitz. Script: William Conselman. Source: play, Elmer Harris. Art direction: Gordon Wiles. Music: James F. Hanley. Cast: Hardie Albright, Thomas Meighan, Dorothy Jordon.

Appendix B   A brief synopsis of the structure of the United States film industry, 1896–1960

1896-1909

Between 1896 and 1909, the industry moved from a structure of pure competition in production, distribution, and exhibition to a structure of an apparent monopoly in production with efforts to monopolize distribution and exhibition. Thomas Edison filed a patent application on a moving picture camera and film in 1891. That patent application was granted in 1897. Wasting no time, Edison filed patent infringement suits against other manufacturers of moving picture cameras and projectors. At that point, Vitagraph, Selig Polyscope, Lubin, American Mutoscope and Biograph, and others were already engaged in activities of manufacturing and distributing film equipment and short film subjects. Between 1897 and 1907, Edison and other patent holders sued one another, seeking to establish and enforce their patent privileges. In 1907, the highest courts finally validated one of Edison's camera patents. As a result, almost every camera generally used was in the position of infringing that patent, and competitors recognized Edison's legal strength. In early 1908, Edison licensed the use of his patented inventions to Lubin, Selig Polyscope, Vitagraph, two new manufacturers of films (Kalem and Essanay), and two film importers (Georges Méliès and Pathé Frères). This group was the Film Service Association. The major remaining film manufacturer, Biograph, purchased the Latham loop patent in February 1908. The Latham loop was necessary in projectors and useful in cameras. With that patent and several others, Biograph licensed several importers, including Kleine Optical Company, and filed suits against infringers of its patents.

By mid-1908, the situation boiled down to two equipment and film manufacturing combinations and three major sets of patent − Edison's which were important for the camera and film; Biograph's, essential for projection and useful in the camera; and Armat's (a small firm), useful for projection. With the patent situation essentially a stalemate, the companies not merely cross-licensed one another (a feasible and legal solution), but they formed a patent pool which had the effect of a virtual monopoly in the production of equipment and films. The Motion Picture Patents Company was incorporated in fall 1908 and began formal operation in January 1909. Licensees of the Patents Company had the right to manufacture film commodities providing they paid a fee. Selected distributors of films were also offered licenses to deal in these products as were selected exhibitors.

1909-1912

Difficulties arose immediately, however. Many distributors and exhibitors resented having to pay fees. By January 1909, a trade organization formed to fight the Patents Company. Members of the association collectively sought supplies of films from European importers (who had been largely cut out of the US market as a result of Patent Company's policies). Members also formed new domestic film production companies including the New York Motion Picture Company, the Independent Motion Picture Company (Imp), Rex, Thanhouser, Powers, Nestor, American Flying A, and so on. These unlicensed manufacturers became known as the independents.

Another difficulty for the Patents Company in its attempt to monopolize the industry was that the licensed distributors were not always as diligent in securing license fees from exhibitors nor as efficiently organized as they could be: profits were not all that the Patents Company believed they might be. Between early 1909 and spring 1910, the number of licensed exchanges dwindled from over one hundred to sixty-nine. In April 1910, the various licensed manufacturers formed the General Film Company. General Film was to engage in the efficient distribution of licensed films and equipment and to collect fees and rentals from the exhibitors. General Film proceeded to purchase the formerly licensed distribution exchanges. By fall 1911, it had acquired fifty-eight exchanges and had cancelled the licenses of ten others, with one distributor left: the Greater New York Film Rental Company owned by William Fox. Fox refused to sell his exchange or to accept the cancellation of his license, and he filed suit against General Film. Although Fox eventually lost the case, the situation of the obvious monopolistic activities of the Patents Company members interested the federal government. The government filed charges in 1912 against General Film and the Patents Company members under antitrust legislation.

Although the independent film manufacturers initially relied on their trade association, once the Patents members formed General Film, the independents also organized a distribution alliance. In May 1910, the Motion Picture Distributing and Sales Co. was organized to distribute product for the independents, but it did not attempt to purchase exchanges. Thus, by mid-1910, the industry was characterized by an oligopoly at the distribution level: two alliances of manufacturers effectively split the film business in the United States. Both alliances moved into multinational distribution at this time as well.

This state of affairs was short-lived. Despite the strength of the distribution alliances, barriers to entry were low enough to attract new firms. In addition, the independents realigned several times as members sought a greater share of the market. In spring 1912, Majestic Film Company left the Sales Company. Its owner and others set up Mutual Film to purchase exchanges and the Film Supply Company of America to distribute the product of many of the independents. The remaining firms announced the formation of Universal Film Manufacturing Company. During that year, alliances shifted several times; by the end of 1912, Mutual, Film Supply, and Universal were all separate independent distribution alliances competing against General Film, which controlled about 60 per cent of the business.

1912-18

Between 1911 and 1916, the multiple-reel film was diffused and became the dominant product in the exhibition market. Generally, outside the mainstream exhibition system at first, such films were often distributed for roadshows (first-class theaters were hired for limited runs) or sold to states'-rights exchanges (these exchanges bought the rights to exhibit the film in a specified geographical area). Multiple-reel films released within the regular distribution system were problems. Since all the companies' films were usually sold at a uniform price per foot – regardless of negative cost – the more pretentious multiple-reelers, often with expensive stars, were at a distinct disadvantage in recouping costs. Time for return on costs was thus longer, too. Finally, longer runs for the feature films disrupted the distributors' systems since the normal format was a daily exchange of product.

Although both licensed and independent manufacturers went into multiple-reel production, many new firms formed for that sole purpose. These firms needed a national system to facilitate their distribution. Although attempted earlier, one of the first contenders to provide a regularized, national release of feature films was Warners' Features Company in late 1913. In spring 1914, several other multiple-reel manufacturers, Famous Players, Jesse L. Lasky Feature Film Company, and Bosworth (producing Pallas and Morasco films) allied with a new distribution firm, Paramount. The firm's purpose was to release multiple-reelers on a regular basis. World Film reorganized, offering another feature-film supply source. By July 1914, three major one-reel distribution alliances – General Film, Universal, and Mutual – and four major feature distribution alliances – Warners', Paramount, World, and Film Box Office (Fox's feature film company) dominated the industry.

While new distribution alliances formed, those of the Patents Company reorganized. Although fighting the charges of antitrust violations and filing new patent suits against competitors, General Film companies also constructed new distribution alliances to release their feature product. In April 1915, Vitagraph, Lubin, Selig, and Essanay incorporated V-L-S-E to distribute feature product made by those firms; Kleine and Edison formed Kleine-Edison Feature Film Service later that year. In fall 1915, the US district court decided against the Patents Company in regard to the antitrust suit. An appeal was denied, and in 1918 a decree forbidding a patent pool went into effect. A major patent suit also was decided against the Patents Company in January 1916, with the decision affirmed on appeal. Vitagraph purchased the interests of the other V-L-S-E members, and in May 1916 formed Greater Vitagraph, a feature film producer and distributor. Selig and Essanay signed with Kleine-Edison, forming KESE to distribute feature product while General Film continued to release their one-reelers.

The independent alliance also reorganized once again. Mutual changed when part of its manufacturers left to form Triangle in summer 1915. Although Triangle eventually failed, it was an initial attempt at vertical integration: production and distribution was combined in one firm, and the company leased showcase theaters which provided an entry into the exhibition sector of the film industry.

Famous Players combined with the Lasky Corporation and organized Famous Players-Lasky as a holding company in summer 1916. In the fall, Morosco and Pallas merged into it, and Artcraft was formed to distribute special feature product. In December, Famous Players-Lasky acquired the assets of Paramount. This firm reorganized a year later (December 1917), merging in many of its subsidiaries. Thus, by 1917, feature film companies were merging and vertically integrating their production and distribution sectors. One-reel distribution alliances declined in market power as the industry shifted to the multiple-reel film.

1918-48

The period of 1918-48 witnessed full integration and many mergers of film companies. In addition, ownership shifted from private hands to public stock ownership. From a multitude of production firms and exhibitors and a set of distribution alliances developed five fully integrated, powerful film companies. Three other firms were large enough to merit inclusion in the industrial oligopoly.

In fall 1916, Vitagraph, Famous Players-Lasky, and Triangle, among others, were integrated into at least two levels of the industry and provided national distribution of the most important feature films. Exhibitors, contesting prices asked by the distributors for the product, formed First National Exhibitors' Circuit in spring 1917. As a franchise and buying agent for twenty-four of the largest exhibitors with major first-run theaters, First National offered to purchase independently-produced films. In fact, it threatened Paramount's (and the others') access to some of the better first-run theaters. Although considering other options, in 1919, Famous Players-Lasky financed a stock issue of ten million dollars, using the proceeds to purchase a string of theaters. As such, it became a fully integrated firm with producing, distributing, and exhibiting operations within the same company. In the next several years, First National and Paramount vied for control of theaters.

In the early 1920s, theater acquisition slowed down, but company purchases and mergers of firms picked up in the second half of the decade. Warners Bros purchased control of Vitagraph (1925), Stanley Theater chain (1928), and First National (1928). Paramount bought controlling interest in the Publix Theater chain (1926). Loew's, a New York City theater chain, acquired Metro Pictures Corporation (1920) and merged with Goldwyn Pictures and Louis B. Mayer Pictures (1924). Fox Film Corporation and a subsidiary purchased West Coast Theaters (1925) and the Roxy Circuit and Poli chain (1927-8). Fox even worked in 1929 toward acquisition of controlling interest in Loew's, only to have the US government and events of the depression halt that. RKO formed in 1928 out of Film Booking Company (a distributor and then producer) and the Keith-Albee and Orpheum Theater circuits. In 1931, RKO purchased the studio and exchanges of Pathé. Universal purchased some second-run houses in 1929, and Columbia organized a national distribution system. By 1930, six fully integrated firms, one producer-distributor, and United Artists (a distributor for independent product, formed in 1919) lead the industry, with an oligopolistic control of the major product and of first- and many second-run theaters. Unaffiliated exhibitors might be organized into circuits and into a vocal trade association, but the major companies controlled the structure and conduct of the industry. Small independent producing companies supplied films, but their market strength was minor compared to the leading firms.

When the depression hit the industry, the film companies found themselves in a precarious situation. Attendance (and box office receipts) declined. Film producers cut costs, and exhibitors tried double-features and give-aways to lure the consumer back into the theaters. Companies with short-term notes from recent acquisitions and from the costs of the conversion to sound equipment could not meet their scheduled payments. Fox was in trouble by the end of 1929, and the firm had to reorganize (which it did by 1933). In 1935, Fox merged with a small independent, forming Twentieth Century-Fox. Paramount went into receivership in 1933, then bankruptcy. Under a protective committee, it had reorganized by 1936. Loew's was controlled by Fox when Fox went into receivership; under court action, Loew's stock was put into a trust, and eventually the stock was sold to the public. RKO went into bankruptcy in 1934. After a reorganization, the courts approved the new company format in 1939. Warners, Columbia, and United Artists managed to avoid bankruptcy despite serious problems. When the depression

affected it, Universal sold most of its theaters. In 1933 it went into receivership until new owners reorganized the firm in 1936. In 1946, Universal participated in the firm's first merger since the company's formation in 1912: it acquired the independent production company International Pictures.

1948-60

Subject to federal investigation of its structure and conduct since 1912, the film industry was eventually required to divorce its production-distribution sectors from its exhibition holdings (for more details, see Chapter 26). Although some firms were slow to capitulate, eventually they did. Paramount divorced its theater sector in 1949; RKO, 1950; MGM and Twentieth Century-Fox, 1952; and Warners, 1953. Although there were still oligopolies in each sector (production-distribution and exhibition), the major firms were no longer fully integrated. Independent production companies became more dominant, for a number of reasons, and most turned to the major firms' release networks as the means to achieve national and international distribution. Although independent production characterized the production sector, financing came primarily from the major producer-distributors which still controlled the industry.

Appendix C   Principal structures of the US film industry, 1894–1930

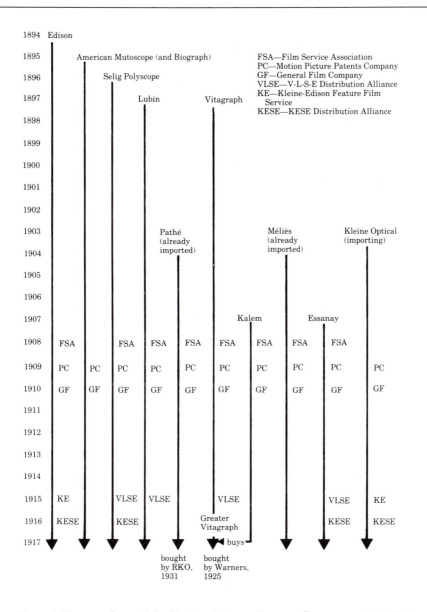

Chart 1 The members of the Motion Picture Patents Company, 1894-1917

FSA—Film Service Association
PC—Motion Picture Patents Company
GF—General Film Company
VLSE—V-L-S-E Distribution Alliance
KE—Kleine-Edison Feature Film Service
KESE—KESE Distribution Alliance

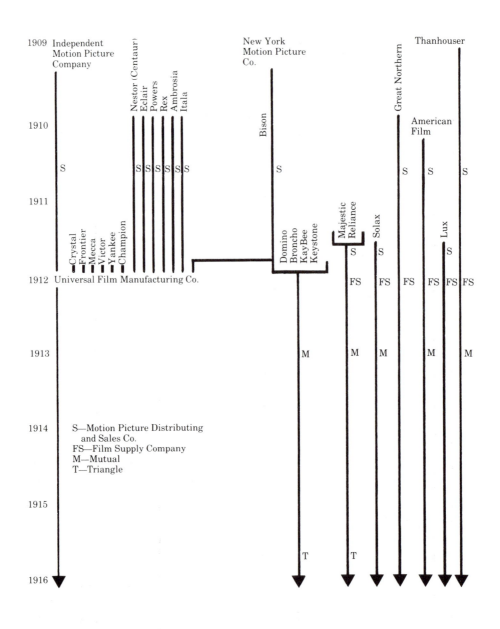

Chart 2 The independents, 1909-16

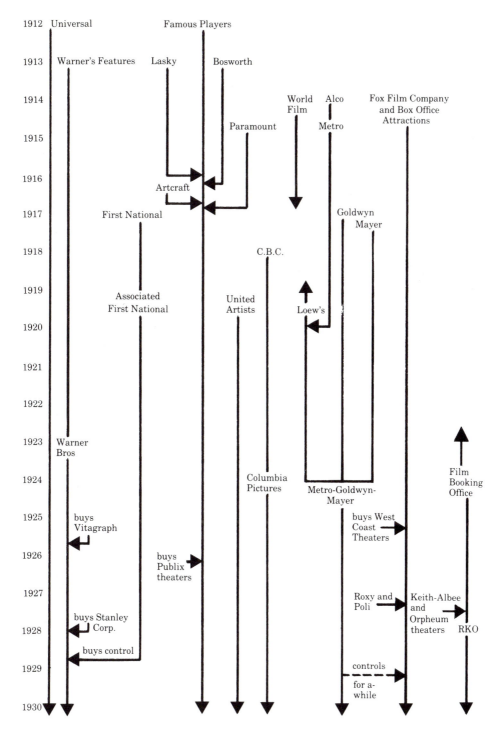

Chart 3 The formation of the major studios, 1912-30

Appendix D Lighting plots and descriptions

Note: These plots have been redrawn following the originals. In each case the camera's field is represented by dotted lines.

Diagram 1 This plot, published in 1914, was done by H.M. Lomas, a British lighting expert who nevertheless used many examples from American films in his discussion. In diagram 1a, the entire set is lit by floodlights – overhead arcs and 'guillotine' floorstand units at the sides. Each guillotine unit would have either four diffused arcs or a row of twenty-four mercury-vapor tubes.

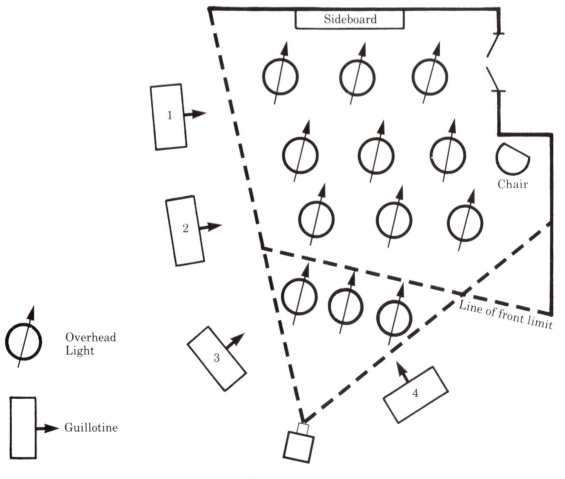

Diagram 1a

Lomas assumes here that the light is motivated as coming from a window offscreen left, so there are more floor units on that side than on the right. As the side view (diagram 1b) shows, the overhead arcs are hung lower toward the front of the set, and they are closer together (as shown in the overhead view); this makes the light on the foreground figures more intense than that on background figures and objects.

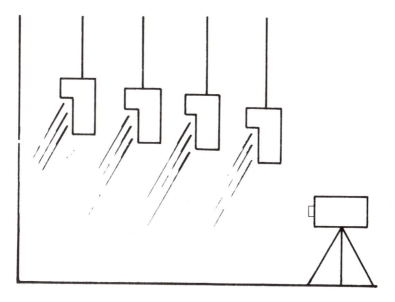

Diagram 1b

Diagram 2 Also done in 1914 by Lomas, this plot shows how to achieve a strong side light on a moving figure. The actor moves from position 1, 10 feet away from the light source, and stops at 2, 20 feet away. With a strong enough light, the side light on the figure will not diminish appreciably. (Note the early use of an 'L-shaped' set. There would usually be other lights in use in addition to the two pairs of arcs.)[1]

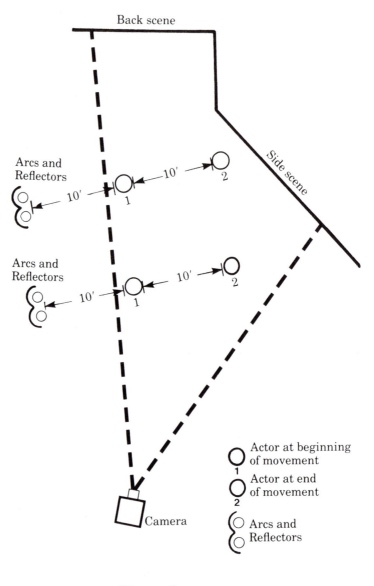

Diagram 2

Diagram 3 Diagrams 3 through 7 are from L.G. Harkness Smith's 1915 survey of different types of lighting possibilities, mostly for box sets. Smith's plots provide a large amount of overall diffused fill light and include a key light for accentuation, placed in each case offscreen right. Diagram 3 represents a small, 10' x 12' set, with sixteen arc floods (represented by dots) hanging in rows 12 feet above the set (A through D) and a twin-arc broadside 5 feet in front of the set, angled toward the foreground figures to provide highlights (E). The overhead lights are placed 'sufficiently far forward to project the light backward and downward at an angle of 45 deg. upon the scene.'[2]

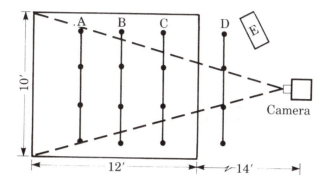

Diagram 3

Diagram 4 A larger box set, 20' x 20', with three rows of overhead arcs (A through C), again 12 feet above the floor. A larger key light is provided by two diffused quadruple-arc floor-stands (D and E) at the side.

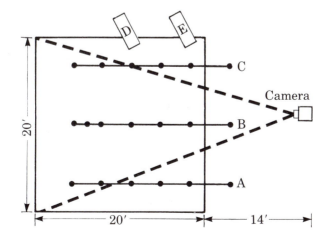

Diagram 4

Diagram 5 A still larger set, 25' x 25', with seven rows of overhead arcs (A through G). Two diffused twin-arc stands (H and K) provide highlights from the sides. (Compare diagrams 3 through 5 with figure 20.15.)

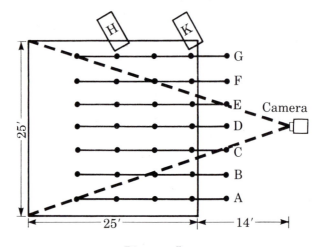

Diagram 5

Diagram 6 Smith considers the combination of mercury-vapors and arcs more satisfactory than either type used alone, and this plot shows such a combination. Here one bank of ten mercury-vapor tubes (A) hangs at a 45° angle to the set, 10 feet above the floor. Three floor units (B through E) contain eight tubes each. Floor units of quadruple diffused arcs (F and G) again provide highlights.

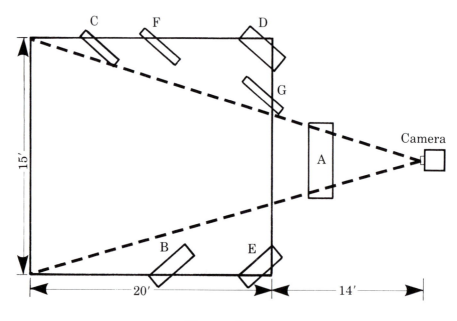

Diagram 6

Diagram 7 Here the set is L-shaped and smaller, 10' x 15', to demonstrate a standard way of doing fireplace scenes, the most common light effect of the pre-1915 period. For this set-up, the lighting consists entirely of twin-arc portable floods. One lamp unit (A) is situated behind the fireplace (E), shining an undiffused light onto the actor (D).

One bank of four diffused twin-arc lamps hangs above the set (C), and a diffused twin-arc floor unit is angled in from offscreen right (B). The relatively small amount of fill light will allow the harsh, undiffused arc to cast a distinct glow to simulate firelight.[3]

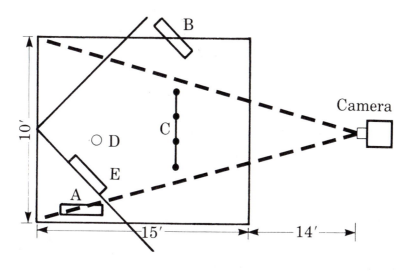

Diagram 7

Diagrams 8a and 8b These diagrams were published in 1915 in *The Illuminating Engineer*; they show the typical scheme for lighting a large stage in an American glass studio using Cooper-Hewitt lamps. The purpose here is to supplement daylight with artificial diffused light in order to prolong the hours during which it was possible to do filming. The keystone-shaped area represents the playing space. Rectangular shapes show the racks of tubular lamps hung at a 30° angle,

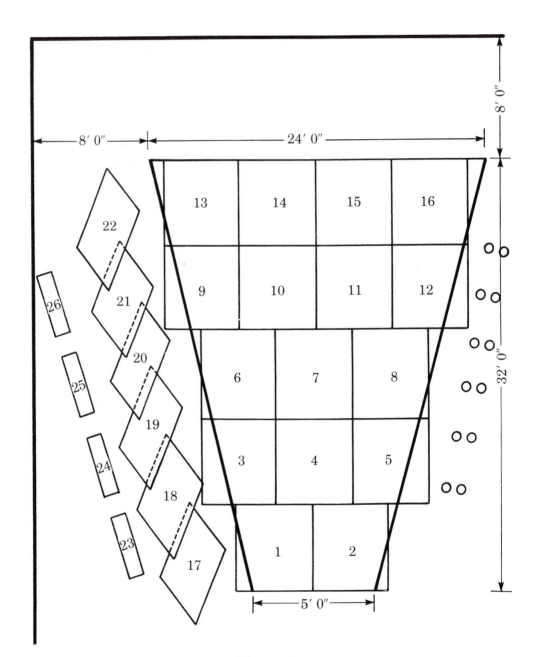

Diagram 8a

directly over the stage; parallelograms represent additional units placed high and at a 45° angle to the side of the stage; the long narrow rectangles signify floor units; and the small circles show the position of smaller quartz mercury lamps (an improved unit introduced in 1913 and designed especially for film work). The total number of tubes in such an arrangement might typically be 208, with 136 overhead (about 8 per unit), 32 in the units at a 45° angle (5-6 tubes each), and 48 in

the floor stands (with 12 tubes each). Note that the angled and floor units are all placed to one side to provide a sort of crude key light, giving some modelling to the figures.

Diagram 8b is a side view of the set. As with the overhead arcs in Diagram 1b, these lamps are placed higher toward the back of the stage: the overhead units closest to the camera are about 8 feet above the front line, while the rear units are 18 feet off the floor.[4]

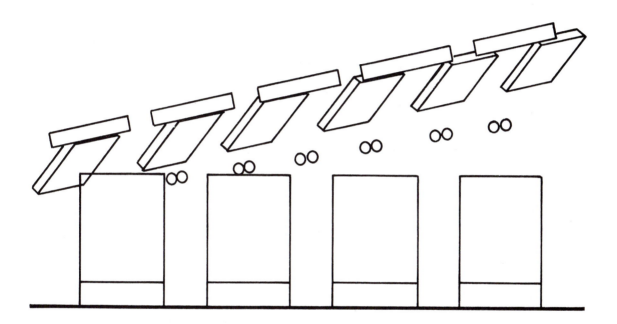

Diagram 8b

Diagram 9 In a major 1919 address to the Society of Motion Picture Engineers, William Roy Mott discussed the use of white flame arcs for lighting an L-shaped set. By now, the conception of lighting had changed drastically: in this case many of the light rays are sent into the set from the side, and even from slightly behind the figures. The plot does not show the overhead lights which would be used in such a scene (arc floods or mercury-vapors, as in earlier diagrams), but does indicate optional lamps placed outside the doors, to be directed onto the set as from a motivated source. According to Mott, there should be 50 per cent more light coming from the sides than from the top, and the L-shaped arrangement is better for achieving this than the box set. The large white-flame arc floor units at the sides direct light into the set slightly away from the camera, but the reflectors placed beside them direct a portion of the light toward the front of the set:[5]

This gives a good reflection on surfaces sidewise to the light because the light is **reflected so** obliquely that a large amount is carried to the camera from side surfaces, and this arrangement gives the much desired line and Rembrandt effects, or as better known to the motion picture artist as molding and modelling effects.

Mott is describing rim light here. With such floods of oblique light, the figures could move about the set without ever losing their bright outlines.[6]

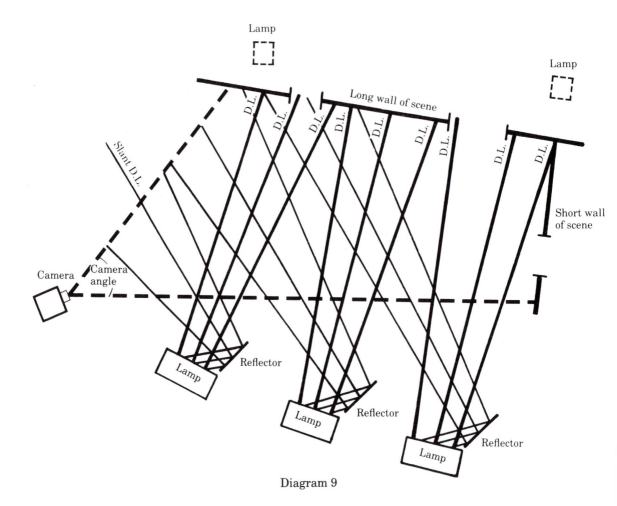

Diagram 9

Diagram 10 Diagrams 10 through 12 are from a 1925 lecture before the SMPE, in which Wiard B. Ihnen and D.W. Atwater gave suggestions for avoiding flat, frontal lighting in a simple box set 12 feet wide. Light such a set with broadside arcs from the front and sides, they said, and 'the result is a flat picture with no detail, distance, or separation between actors and background. Each arc would cast a separate shadow on the opposite wall.'[7] Their first alternative, Diagram 10, simply adds a couple of overhead spotlights on the top of the set walls; these help eliminate the shadows and add a bit of modelling on the figures.

Diagram 11 Another simple solution involves moving the actors from the corner out into the middle of the set and moving the camera closer in. This leaves room for a pair of spotlights to be placed on either side of the actors; sidelight will also help model the figures.

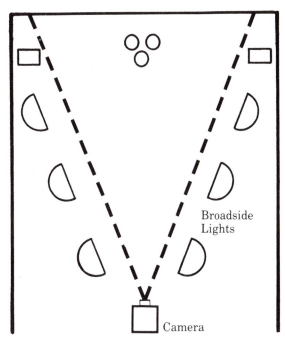

Broadside Lights

Camera

Diagram 11

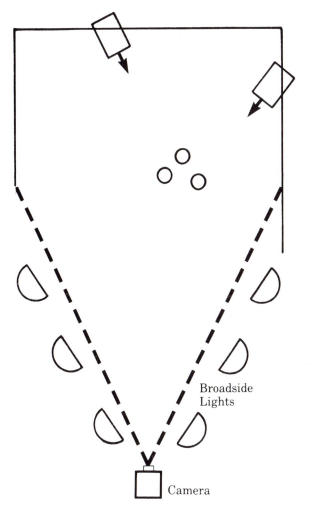

Broadside Lights

Camera

Diagram 10

Diagram 12 This plot illustrates a more complex, but more common solution to the problem. By adding openings in the set walls (doors, windows), the filmmakers could motivate the placement of spotlights outside the set, aiming in at the actors in the corner. This last approach involves considerable planning in the design of the set to accommodate the lighting instruments. By having specialized knowledge of both lighting and set design, the art director could provide a practical arrangement combining the two effectively.[8]

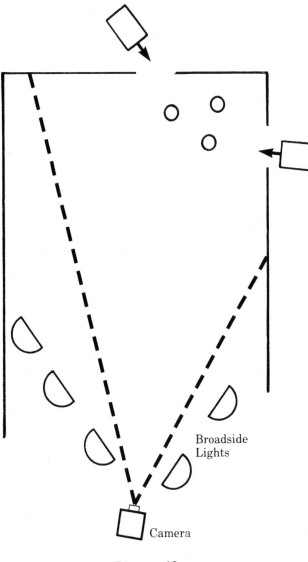

Broadside
Lights

Camera

Diagram 12

Notes

In notes and bibliographic entries, frequently cited items are abbreviated as follows:

AC American Cinematographer
AMPAS Academy of Motion Pictures Arts and Sciences
EK Edison Kinetogram
IP International Photographer
IPro International Projectionist
JSMPE Journal of the Society of Motion Picture Engineers
JSMPTE Journal of the Society of Motion Picture and Television Engineers
MPH Motion Picture Herald
MPN Moving Picture News/Motion Picture News
MPW Moving Picture World/Motion Picture World
NKL The Nickelodeon
NYDM New York Dramatic Mirror
PTD The Photodramatist
TSMPE Transactions of the Society of Motion Picture Engineers

Asterisked note numbers indicate substantive notes containing additional discussion.

Preface

1 Quoted in Anthony Slide, *'Film Fan Monthly* Interviews Ruth Waterbury,' in Leonard Maltin (ed.), *Hollywood: The Movie Factory* (New York: Popular Library, 1976), p. 239; T.W. Adorno, *Minima Moralia*, tr. E.F.N. Jephcott (London: New Left Books, 1974), p. 201; Will H. Hays, 'Introduction,' Cora W. Taylor, *Masters and Masterpieces of the Screen* (New York: Collier, 1927), p. 6; quoted in Leo Rosten, *Hollywood: The Movie Colony, The Movie Makers* (New York: Harcourt, Brace, 1941), p. 368; John Ford in a 1964 BBC television interview.
2 George Kubler, *The Shape of Time* (New Haven: Yale Unversity Press, 1962), p. 6.
3 See David Bordwell, 'Textual analysis, etc.,' *Enclitic*, nos 10-11 (1982): 125-36.

4 Among the most important of the revisionist film historians are J. Douglas Gomery, Robert C. Allen, Vincent Porter, and Tom Gunning.
5 Raymond Williams, 'Base and superstructure in Marxist cultural theory,' in his *Problems in Materialism and Culture* (London: New Left Books, 1980), pp. 47-8.
6 On this point, see Terry Eagleton, *Criticism and Ideology* (London: New Left Books, 1976), pp. 45-8.

Part One

1 E.H. Gombrich, *Norm and Form: Studies in the Art of the Renaissance* (London: Phaidon, 1971), p. 98.

Chapter 1 An excessively obvious cinema

1 Leading accounts of group style in art history are James S. Ackerman and Rhys Carpenter, *Art and Archaeology* (Englewood Cliffs, New Jersey: Prentice-Hall, 1963), pp. 164-86; E.H. Gombrich, 'Style,' in *International Encyclopedia of the Social Sciences*, ed. David Sills (New York: Macmillan, 1968), vol. 5, pp. 352-61; Meyer Schapiro, 'Style,' in *A Modern Book of Aesthetics*, ed. Melvin Rader, 4th ed. (New York: Holt, Rinehart, & Winston, 1973), pp. 270-80. See also Berel Lang (ed.), *The Concept of Style* (University of Pennsylvania Press, 1979).
2 A. Haut-Pré, 'Les moving pictures américaines,' *Ciné-Revue*, no. 32 (11 September 1925): 10; Marcel Zahar and Daniel Burret, 'Une visite à Jean Renoir,' *Cinéa-Ciné pour tous*, no. 59 (15 April 1926): 15.
3 André Bazin, *What Is Cinema?*, tr. Hugh Gray (Berkeley: University of California Press, 1967), p. 29.
4 André Bazin, 'La Politique des auteurs,' in *The New Wave*, ed. Peter Graham (New York: Doubleday, 1968), pp. 143, 154.
5 'Sept hommes à débattre,' *Cahiers du cinéma*, no. 150-51 (December 1963-January 1964): 20.
6 *Ibid.*

7   *Ibid.*, p. 16.

8   See Jan Mukařovský, 'The aesthetic norm,' in *Structure, Sign, and Function*, ed. and tr. John Burbank and Peter Steiner (New Haven: Yale University Press, 1977), pp.49-54.

9   *Ibid.*, p. 54.

10 See Tzvetan Todorov, *Poétique* (Paris: Seuil, 1968), pp. 67-77; David Bordwell and Kristin Thompson, *Film Art: An Introduction* (Reading, Mass.: Addison-Wesley, 1979); David Bordwell, *The Films of Carl-Theodor Dreyer* (Berkeley: University of California Press, 1981), pp. 1-8.

11 See, for example, Martin Walsh, 'Brecht and Straub-Huillet: The frontiers of language,' *Afterimage*, no. 7 (Summer 1978): 13-19.

12 Noël Burch, *To the Distant Observer* (Berkeley University of California Press, 1979), p. 19.

13 R.L. Gregory, *The Intelligent Eye* (New York: McGraw-Hill, 1970) and R.L. Gregory and E.H. Gombrich, (eds.), *Illusion in Nature and Art* (London: Duckworth, 1973), pp. 54-95, 193-243.

14 Meir Sternberg, *Expositional Modes and Temporal Ordering in Fiction* (Baltimore: Johns Hopkins University Press, 1978), pp. 50-3.

15 E.H. Gombrich, *Art and Illusion* (Princeton: Princeton University Press, 1969), pp. 93-178.

16 *Ibid.*, p. 60.

17 Beth Day, *This Was Hollywood* (London: Sidgwick & Jackson, 1960), pp. 13-18. See also Richard Griffith, *Anatomy of a Motion Picture* (New York: St Martin's Press, 1959), pp. 5-14, 91-111.

18 Roman Jakobson, 'Entretien sur le cinéma,' in *Cinéma: Théorie, Lectures*, ed. Dominique Noguez (Paris: Klincksieck, 1973), p. 65.

19 Edgar Allan Poe, 'The purloined letter,' *The Complete Tales and Poems of Edgar Allan Poe* (New York: Modern Library, 1938), p. 222.

Chapter 2 Story causality and motivation

1   Roman Jakobson, 'The dominant,' in *Readings in Russian Poetics*, ed. Ladislav Matejka and Krystyna Pomorska (Cambridge, Mass.: The MIT Press, 1971), p. 82.

2   See Boris Tomashevsky, 'Thematics,' in Lee T. Lemon and Marion J. Reis (eds), *Russian Formalist Criticism: Four Essays* (Lincoln: University of Nebraska Press, 1965), pp. 66-8; Tzvetan Todorov, 'Some approaches to Russian Formalism,' *20th Century Studies*, 7/8 (December 1972): 6-19.

3   Francis Taylor Patterson, *Cinema Craftsmanship* (New York: Harcourt, Brace & Howe, 1920), p. 5.

4   André Bazin, *What Is Cinema?*, tr. Hugh Gray (Berkeley: University of California Press, 1967), p. 134.

5   Pierre Sorlin, *The Film in History* (Oxford: Blackwell, 1980), pp. 93-4.

6   David Grimsted, *Melodrama Unveiled* (Chicago: University of Chicago Press, 1968), pp. 183-95.

7   Ian Watt, *The Rise of the Novel* (Berkeley: University of California Press, 1974), pp. 13-32.

8   Quoted in Peter Milne, *Motion Picture Directing* (New York: Falk Publishing Co., 1922), p. 116.

9   Howard T. Lewis, *The Motion Picture Industry* (New York: Van Nostrand, 1933), pp. 7-10.

10 Max Ophuls, 'Hollywood, petite île . . . ,' *Cahiers du cinéma*, no. 54 (Noël 1955), pp. 5-7.

11 Quoted in Eric Sherman, *Directing the Film: Film Directors on their Art* (Boston: Little, Brown, 1976), p. 50.

12 Richard Dyer, *Stars* (London: British Film Institute, 1979), pp. 110-50.

13 On this point, see '*Morocco* de Joseph von Sternberg,' *Cahiers du cinéma*, no. 225 (November-December 1979): 9-13. For an excellent analysis of a star's persona, see Wade Jennings, 'Nova: Garland in *A Star is Born*,' *Quarterly Review of Film Studies*, 4, no. 3 (Summer 1979): 321-37.

14 Frederick Palmer, *Technique of the Photoplay* (Hollywood: Palmer Institute of Authorship, 1924), pp. 67-8.

15 Bazin, *What Is Cinema?*, p. 62.

16 Ferdinand Brunetière, 'The law of the drama,' in *European Theories of the Drama*, ed. Barrett H. Clark (New York: Crown, 1961), p. 407.

17 Walter S. Bloem, *The Soul of the Moving Picture* (New York: E.P. Dutton, 1924), p. 132.

18 Quoted in Peter Bogdanovich, *Allan Dwan: The Last Pioneer* (Berkeley: University of California Press, 1971), p. 26.

19 Patterson, *Craftsmanship*, p. 117.

20* These prescriptions have hardly changed. A 1980 essay on screenwriting tells us that the story must center upon consistent changes in a relationship from start to finish ('Change. Obstacles surmounted or not surmounted.') and that each event must grow out of the preceding one ('Event A generates Event B. A and B combine to make C. Get it?'). See David Freeman, 'The great American screenplay competition,' *Esquire*, 93, no. 6 (June 1980): 28.

21 Tom Terris, *Writing the Sound and Dialogue Photoplay* (Hollywood: Palmer Institute of Authorship, 1930), p. 11.

22 John Emerson and Anita Loos, *How to Write Photoplays*, (Philadelphia: George W. Jacobs & Co., 1920), p. 11.

23 Barrett C. Kiesling, *Talking Pictures* (Richmond, Virginia, Johnson Publishing Co., 1937), p. 2.

24 Lewis Herman, *A Practical Manual of Screen Playwriting for Theater and Television Films* (New York: New American Library, 1974), p. 88.

25   Bertolt Brecht, *Ecrits sur le theatre I* (Paris: L'Arche, 1972), p. 275.

26   See Stephen Heath, 'Lessons from Brecht,' *Screen*, 15, no. 2 (Summer 1974): 122.

27   Tomashevsky, 'Thematics,' pp. 77-87.

28   Jonathan Culler, *Structuralist Poetics* (London: Routledge & Kegan Paul, 1975), pp. 140-60.

29   Gérard Genette, *Figure II* (Paris: Seuil, 1969), pp. 72-6.

30   Howard T. Dimick, *Modern Photoplay Writing* (Franklin, Ohio: James Knapp Reeve, 1922), pp. 233-4.

31   Frances Marion, 'Scenario writing,' in *Behind the Screen: How Films Are Made*, ed. Stephen Watts (New York: Dodge, 1938), p. 33.

32   Quoted in Sherman, *Directing the Film*, p. 28.

33   Alvin Wyckoff, 'Motion picture lighting,' *Annals of the American Academy of Political and Social Science*, 128, no. 217 (November 1926): 64; John Arnold, 'Shooting the movies,' in *We Make the Movies*, ed. Nancy Naumburg (New York: Norton, 1937), p. 160.

34   Frederick Foster, 'High key vs. low key,' *AC*, 38, no. 8 (August 1957): 506.

35   Marc Vernet, 'Freud: effets spéciaux; mise en scène: USA,' *Communications*, 23 (1975): 223-34.

36   *Ibid.*, p. 229.

37   See Tomashevsky, 'Thematics,' pp. 84-7.

38   Kiesling, *Talking Pictures*, p. 115.

39   Parker Tyler, *The Hollywood Hallucination* (New York: Simon & Schuster, 1970), p. 12.

40   See, for example, Ezra Goodman, 'A director who realizes the importance of cinematographers,' *AC*, 26, no. 7 (July 1945): 243; Herb A. Lightman, ' "The Killers": teamwork on film production,' *AC*, 27, no. 12 (December 1946): 458; Lightman, 'Exponent of the moving camera,' *AC*, 29, no. 11 (November 1948): 376.

41* The Russian Formalist concept of baring the device is a marked improvement upon the currently fashionable idea of 'reflexivity'; according to the Formalists, even the most 'realistic' art works find ways to point to their own artificiality, since all art works aim (in different ways) to heighten the viewer's perception of art's specific materials and methods. On 'laying bare the device,' see Victor Shklovsky, 'Sterne's *Tristram Shandy*: Stylistic Commentary,' in Lemon and Reis, *Russian Formalist Criticism*, pp. 25-57. Kristin Thompson has shown that Hollywood films may make baring of the device central to their structure; see 'The duplicitous text: an analysis of *Stage Fright*,' *Film Reader*, 2 (January 1977): 52-64; 'Closure within a dream: point-of-view in *Laura*,' *Film Reader*, 3 (February 1978): 90-105.

Chapter 3 Classical narration

1   John Cromwell, 'The voice behind the megaphone,' in *We Make the Movies*, ed. Nancy Naumburg (New York: Norton, 1937), p. 60.

2   André Bazin, *What Is Cinema?*, tr. Hugh Gray (Berkeley: University of California Press, 1967), p. 32.

3   Arthur Edwin Krows, *The Talkies*, (New York: Henry Holt & Co., 1930), pp. 168-9.

4   Noël Burch, *Theory of Film Practice*, tr. Helen R. Lane (New York: Praeger, 1973), pp. 110-13. See also Burch, 'De "Mabuse" à "M",' in *Cinéma: Théorie, Lectures*, ed. Noguez, pp. 228-9.

5   Meir Sternberg, *Expositional Modes and Temporal Ordering in Fiction* (Baltimore: Johns Hopkins University Press, 1978), pp. 56-7.

6   The term 'narrator' has uncomfortably human overtones and is easily confused with the author of the narrative text. These problems have been cogently examined in Edward Branigan's *Point of View in the Cinema: A Theory of Narration and Subjectivity in Classical Film* (New York: Mouton, 1984).

7   Sternberg, *Expositional Modes*, pp. 236-305.

8   Ronald Levaco and Fred Glass, 'Quia ego nominor Leo,' in *Le cinéma américain*, ed. Raymond Bellour (Paris: Flammarion, 1980), pp. 21-2.

9   Thierry Kuntzel, 'Le travail du film 2,' *Communications*, no. 23 (1975): 142, 188.

10   John Emerson and Anita Loos, *How to Write Photoplays* (Philadelphia: George W. Jacobs & Co., 1920), p. 29.

11   *Ibid.*, pp. 36, 66. See also Frederick Palmer, *Photoplay Writing* (Los Angeles: Palmer Photoplay Corporation, 1921), p. 29.

12   Francis Patterson, *Scenario and Screen* (New York: Harcourt, Brace, 1928), p. 69.

13   Krows, *The Talkies*, p. 109.

14   A. Haut-Pré, 'Les moving pictures américaines,' *Ciné-Revue*, no. 32 (11 September 1925), pp. 8-9.

15   Sternberg, *Expositional Modes*, pp. 39-58.

16   Emerson and Loos, *Photoplays*, p. 94.

17   *Ibid.*, p. 95.

18   See Pierre Sorlin, *The Film in History* (Oxford: Blackwell, 1980), pp. 53-64.

19   See Herb Lightman, 'The magic of montage,' *AC*, 30, no. 10 (October 1949): 361; Don Livingston, *Film and the Director* (New York: Macmillan, 1953), pp. 56-7.

20   Jean-Paul Sartre, 'Quand Hollywood veut faire penser,' *L'écran français*, no. 5 (3 August 1945): 3.

21   A. Lindsley Lane, 'The camera's omniscient eye,' *AC*, 16, no. 3 (March 1935): 95.

22   Quoted in Thomas Elsaesser, 'Why Hollywood,' *Monogram*, no. 1 (April 1971): 8.

23 Lane, 'The camera's omniscient eye,' p. 95. See also Frederick Y. Smith, 'The cutting and editing of motion pictures,' in *The Technique of Motion Picture Production*, ed. Society of Motion Picture Engineers (New York: Interscience, 1944), pp. 130-9.

24 On 'impossible' camera angles, see Stephen Heath, 'Narrative space,' *Screen*, 17, no. 3 (Autumn 1976): 95-7.

25 See Editors of *Cahiers du cinéma*, 'John Ford's *Young Mr. Lincoln*,' *Screen*, 13, no. 3 (Autumn 1972): 34

26 On repetition in the classical film, see Ben Brewster, 'Notes on the text, "John Ford's *Young Mr. Lincoln*," ' by the editors of *Cahiers du cinéma*,' *Screen*, 14, no. 3 (Autumn 1973): 29-43; Raymond Bellour, 'Le blocage symbolique,' *Communications*, no. 23 (1975): 347; Bellour, 'Ciné-repetitions,' *Screen*, 20, no. 2 (Summer 1979): 65-72.

27 Eugene Vale, *The Technique of Screenplay Writing* (New York: Grosset & Dunlap, 1972), p. 37; Frances Marion, *How to Write and Sell Film Stories* (New York: Covici, Friede, 1937), p. 144.

28 Quoted in Eric Sherman, *Directing the Film: Film Directors on their Art* (Boston: Little, Brown, 1976), p. 125.

29 'Casey Robinson on "Dark Victory," ' *Australian Journal of Screen Theory*, no. 4 (1978): 6.

30 'Igor Stravinsky on film music as told to Ingolf Dahl,' *Cinema* [Hollywood], 1, no. 1 (June 1947): 7.

31 Clarence E. Sinn, 'Music for the picture,' *MPW*, 8, no. 1 (7 January 1911): 27.

32 Leonid Sabaneev, *Music for the Films*, tr. S.W. Pring (London: Pitman, 1935), pp. 20-1,29.

33 Hanns Eisler, *Composing for the Films* (London: Dobson, 1947), pp. 10, 61; Bertolt Brecht, *Ecrits sur le théâtre I* (Paris: L'Arche, 1972), pp. 468-9.

34 James L. Smith, *Melodrama* (London: Methuen, 1973), pp. 1-5, 31; Nicholas Vardac, *Stage to Screen* (Cambridge, Mass.: Harvard University Press, 1949), pp. 81, 118, 159.

35 Theodor Adorno, *In Search of Wagner*, tr. Rodney Livingstone (London: New Left Books, 1981), pp. 43-6.

36 Sinn, 'Music for the picture,' p. 76. See also Sinn's columns in *MPW*, 8, no. 3 (21 January 1911): 135, and *MPW*, 8, no. 8 (25 February 1911): 409; and W. Stephen Bush, 'Giving musical expression to the drama,' *MPW*, 9, no. 5 (12 August 1911): 354-5.

37 G.P. Von Harleman and Clarke Irvine, 'News of Los Angeles and vicinity,' *MPW* 29, no. 4 (22 July 1916): 620.

38 Roy Prendergast, *Film Music: A Neglected Art* (New York: Norton, 1977), pp. 10, 39; Mark Evans, *Soundtrack: The Music of the Movies* (New York: Da Capo, 1979), p. 22. See also Claudia Gorbman, 'The Drama's Melos,' *Velvet Light Trap*, no. 19 (1982): 35-9.

39 Evans, *Soundtrack*, p. 27.

40 Hugo Riesenfeld, 'Music and motion pictures,' *Annals of the American Academy of Political and Social Science*, 128, no. 217 (November 1926): 60.

41 Brecht, *Ecrits I*, p. 468.

42 Quoted in Roy Pickard, *The Hollywood Studios* (London: Muller, 1978), p. 140.

43 See Adorno, *In Search of Wagner*, p. 76; Bertolt Brecht, *Journal de travail* (Paris: L'Arche, 1976), p. 270.

44 Parker Tyler, *The Hollywood Hallucination* (New York: Simon & Schuster, 1970), p. 155.

45 Quoted in Lawrence Morton, 'An interview with George Antheil,' *Film Music Notes*, 10, no. 1 (September-October 1950): 5.

46 'Constantin Bakaleinikoff,' *Film Music Notes*, 2, no. 2 (November 1942): n.p.

47 Robert Nelson, 'Film music: color or line?,' *Hollywood Quarterly*, 2, no. 1 (October 1946): 59-62. See also Leonard Rosenmann, 'Notes on the score to *East of Eden*,' *Film Music*, 14, no. 5 (May-June 1955): 3-12.

48 Miklós Rózsa, 'Lust for Life,' *Film and TV Music*, 16, no. 1 (Fall 1956): 3-6.

49 Nelson, 'Film music: Color or line?' p. 59.

50 Aaron Copland, 'Second thoughts on Hollywood,' *Modern Music*, 16, no. 3 (March-April 1940): 141-7.

51 Thierry Kuntzel pointed this out in a colloquium on film analysis at the University of Wisconsin-Milwaukee Center for Twentieth Century Studies, Fall 1975.

52 Marion, *Film Stories*, pp. 85-6.

53 Emerson and Loos, *Photoplays*, pp. 104-5.

54 Raymond Bellour, 'To analyze, to segment,' *Quarterly Review of Film Studies*, 1, no. 3 (August 1976): 331.

55 Mortimer J. Adler, *Art and Prudence* (New York: Longmans Green, 1937), p. 533; Cedric Gibbons, 'The set as an actor,' *AC*, 12, no. 10 (February 1932): 30; see also Charles G. Clarke, *Professional Cinematography* (Hollywood: American Society of Cinematographers, 1964), p. 84.

56 See, for example, Christian Metz, *Film Language* tr. Michael Taylor (New York: Oxford, 1974), p. 195; Stephen Heath, 'Film performance,' *Ciné-Tracts*, 1, no. 2 (Summer 1977): 8-9, 16; Stephen Heath, 'On screen in frame,' *Quarterly Review of Film Studies*, 1, no. 3 (August 1976): 261.

57 See Sternberg,. *Expositional Modes*, p. 71.

58 *Ibid.*, pp. 93-6.

59 Howard T. Dimick, *Modern Photoplay Writing* (Franklin, Ohio: James Knapp Reeve, 1922), pp. 155-60.

60 Richard Mealand, 'Hollywoodunit,' in *The Art of the Mystery Story*, ed. Howard Haycraft (New York:

Grosset & Dunlap, 1947), p. 300.
61 Sternberg, *Expositional Modes*, p. 94.
62 *Ibid.*, pp. 243-6.
63 *Ibid.*
64 Roland Barthes, *S/Z*, tr. Richard Miller (New York: Hill & Wang, 1974), pp. 75-7, 84-8.
65 Sternberg, *Expositional Modes*, pp. 51, 240-1.
66 Henry Albert Phillips, *The Photodrama* (Larchmont, New York: Stanhope-Dodge, 1914), p. 64.
67 Vale, *The Technique of Screenplay Writing* (New York: Grosset & Dunlap, 1972), p. 81.

Chapter 4 Time in the classical film

1 Jean Epstein, 'Art d'événément,' *Ecrits sur le cinéma*, vol. 1 (Paris: Lherminier, 1974), pp. 181-2.
2 Eugene Vale, *The Technique of Screenplay Writing* (New York: Grosset & Dunlap, 1972), p. 64.
3 *Ibid.*
4 E.H. Gombrich, 'Moment and movement in art,' *Journal of the Warburg and Courtauld Institutes*, 27 (1964): 299.
5 Kuntzel, 'Le travail du film, 2,' *Communications*, no. 23 (1975): 152.
6 Emerson and Loos, *How to Write Photoplays* (Philadelphia: George W. Jacobs & Co., 1920), p. 48.
7 Thomas Elsaesser, 'Narrative cinema and audience-oriented aesthetics,' unpublished seminar paper (London: British Film Institute/SEFT seminar, n.d.).
8 See 'Exit dissolves?,' *Cinemeditor*, 6, no. 3 (September 1956): 2.
9 Ed Gibbons, 'Montage marches in,' *IP*, 9, no. 9 (October 1937): 28.
10 See Emerson and Loos, *How to Write Photoplays*, p. 82; I.J. Wilkinson and W.H. Hamilton, 'Motion picture editing,' *JSMPE*, 36, no. 1 (January 1941): 103-4. For a discussion of issues around the match-on-action, see Jean-François Tarnowski, 'De quelques problèmes de mise-en-scène,' *Positif*, no. 158 (April 1974): 46-60; 'Courriers des lecteurs,' *Positif*, no. 173 (September 1975): 77-8; Jean-François Tarnowski, 'De quelques points de théorie du cinéma,' *Positif*, no. 188 (December 1976): 47-55.
11 Sidney Cole, 'The film editor,' in *Working for the Films*, ed. Oswald Blakeston (London: Focal Press, 1947), pp. 156-7.
12 See Barry Salt, 'Film style and technology in the Thirties,' *Film Quarterly*, 30, no. 1 (Fall 1976): 20.
13 Maury Hughes, 'Laps 'n Wipes,' *IP*, 12, no. 5 (June 1940): 9.
14 Tamar Lane, *The New Technique of Screenwriting* (New York: Whittlesey House, 1936), pp. 72-3.
15 Arthur Erwin Krows, *The Talkies* (New York: Holt, 1930), p. 130.

16 Gombrich, 'Moment and Movement,' p. 302.
17 For example, in Karel Reisz and Gavin Millar, *The Technique of Film Editing* (New York: Hastings House, 1968), pp. 323-36; Lewis Herman, A. *Practical Manual of Screen Playwriting for Theater and Television Films* (New York: New American Library, 1974), pp. 107-8.
18 On the use of silence for rhythm, see David Bordwell, *The Films of Carl-Theodor Dreyer* Berkeley: University of California Press, 1981), pp. 148-53; on the Navajo films, see Sol Worth and John Adair, *Through Navajo Eyes* (Bloomington: Indiana University Press, 1972), pp. 142-207.
19 Vale, *The Technique of Screenplay Writing*, p. 53.
20 See, for example, 'The language of music,' *What's Happening in Hollywood*, no. 17 (13 January 1945): 2-3; Herb A. Lightman, 'Staging musical routines for the camera,' *AC* 28, no. 1 (January 1947): 9.
21 Emerson and Loos, *How to Write Photoplays*, p. 81.
22 Julian C. Hochberg, *Perception*, 2nd ed. (Englewood Cliffs, N.J.: Prentice-Hall, 1978), p. 209.
23 Robert Parrish, *Growing Up in Hollywood* (New York: Harcourt Brace Jovanovich, 1976), p. 183.
24 Christian Metz, *Film Language* tr. Michael Taylor (New York: Oxford University Press, 1974), pp. 128-9.
25 A. Nicholas Vardac, *Stage to Screen: Theatrical Method from Gawick to Griffith* (Cambridge, Mass.: Haward University Press, 1949), pp. 27, 47, 65.
26 Sergei Eisenstein, *Film Form*, tr. Jay Leyda (New York: Meridian, 1957), pp. 195-255.
27 Emerson and Loos, *How to Write Photoplays*, pp. 32-3.
28 See, for example, Krows, *The Talkies*, pp. 130-1.

Chapter 5 Space in the classical film

1 Ranald MacDougall, 'Sound – and fury,' *The Screen Writer*, 1 (September 1945): 1.
2 Don Livingston, *Film and the Director* (New York: Macmillan, 1953), p. 30. On 'bad' cuts, see Julian Hochberg and Virginia Brooks, 'The perception of motion pictures,' in *Handbook of Perception*, vol. 10: 'Perceptual ecology,' ed. Edward C. Carterette and Martin P. Friedman (New York: Academic Press, 1978), p. 283.
3 Arthur Hardy and R.W. Conant, 'Perspective considerations in taking and projecting motion pictures,' *TSMPE*, 12, no. 33 (1928): 117. See also Alfred Guzzetti, 'Narrative and the film image,' *New Literary History*, 6, no. 2 (Winter 1975): 384.
4 Cecil B. DeMille, 'The public is always right,' in *Hollywood Directors 1914-1940*, ed. Richard Koszarski (New York: Oxford University Press, 1976), p. 168.

5   Robert Surtees, 'Color is different,' *AC*, 29, no. 1 (January 1948): 11; Jean Douchet, 'Rencontre avec Leon Shamroy,' *Cahiers du cinéma*, no. 147 (September 1963): 34; Cecil B. DeMille, 'Motion picture directing,' *TSMPE*, 12, no. 34 (1928): 295-309; Charles Higham, *Hollywood Cameramen* (London: Thames & Hudson, 1970), pp. 35-6, 38.

6   Quoted in Eric Sherman, *Directing the Film: Film Directors on their Art* (Boston: Little, Brown, 1976), p. 106.

7   See, for example, Lewis W. Physioc, 'Pictorial composition,' *AC*, 9, no. 2 (May 1928): 20-1.

8   See Samuel Y. Edgerton, Jr., *The Renaissance Rediscovery of Linear Perspective* (New York: Harper & Row, 1976), p. 26.

9   In conversation with the author.

10   See 'Unique photographic assignment,' *IP*, 22, no. 7 (July 1950): 5-6.

11   Welford Beaton, 'Grouping characters to make them face camera,' *The Film Spectator*, 5, no. 7 (26 May 1928): 6.

12   Quoted in Andrew Sarris (ed.), *Interviews With Film Directors* (New York: Avon, 1967), pp. 106-7.

13   James Mitchell Leisen, 'Some problems of the art director,' *TSMPE*, 12, no. 33 (1928): 76.

14   Victor Milner, 'Painting with light,' *Cinematographic Annual*, vol. 1, ed. Hal Hall (Hollywood: American Society of Cinematographers, 1930; rep. New York: Arno Press, 1972), p. 93.

15   Don Livingston, *Film and the Director* (New York: Macmillan, 1953), p. 70.

16   See Bazin, *What Is Cinema?*, p. 33, and Claude Bailblé, 'Programming the look,' *Screen Education*, nos 32/33 (Autumn/Winter 1979/80): 127-8.

17   For a discussion of Ozu's use of shallow focus, see Kristin Thompson and David Bordwell, 'Space and Narrative in the Films of Ozu,' *Screen*, 17, no. 2 (Summer 1976): 46-7.

18   Milner, 'Painting with light,' p. 94; Max Factor, 'Standardization of motion picture make-up,' *JSMPE*, 28, no. 1 (January 1937): 61.

19   Carlyle Ellis, 'Art and the motion picture,' *Annals of the American Academy of Political and Social Science*, 128, no. 217 (November 1926): 55.

20   Morton Eustis, 'Designing for the movies,' *Theatre Arts*, 21 (October 1937): 786-92; Barrett C. Kiesling, *Talking Pictures: How They Are made, How to Appreciate Them* (Richmond, Virginia: Johnson, 1937), pp. 96-7; A.B. Laing, 'Designing motion picture sets,' *Architectural Record*, 74 (July 1933): 63; Hal Herman, 'Motion picture art direction,' *AC*, 28, no. 11 (November 1947): 397; Herman Blumenthal, 'Cardboard counterpart of the motion picture setting,' *Production Design*, 2, no. 1 (January 1952): 2-21; Hans Dreier, 'Designing the sets,' in *We Make the Movies*, ed. Nancy Naumburg

(New York: W.W. Norton, 1937), p. 86.

21   Quoted in Peter Bogdanovich, *Allan Dwan* (New York: Praeger, 1971), p. 86.

22   See Edgerton, *Renaissance Rediscovery of Linear Perspective*.

23   Hans Dreier, 'Motion picture sets,' *JSMPE*, 17, no. 5 (November 1931): 789-91; Kiesling, *Talking Pictures*, p. 97; Ray Hoadley, *How to Make a Motion Picture* (New York: Crowell, 1939), p. 25. Sometimes miniatures and forced perspectives were used to make sets appear larger than they were. See Dreier, 'Designing the sets,' in *We Make the Movies*, ed. Naumburg, p. 84, and, as a case study, Herb Lightman, 'Shooting "Oklahoma!" in Todd-A0,' *AC*, 36, no. 4 (April 1955): 244.

24   Pierre Francastel, *Peinture et société* (Paris: Gallimard, 1950), pp. 59-65.

25   Leon S. Becker, 'Technology in the art of producing motion pictures,' in *The Technique of Motion Picture Production*, ed. SMPE (New York: Interscience, 1944), pp. 5-6.

26   On sound perspective, see Hardy and Conant, 'Perspective,' pp. 117-18; E.A. Wolcott, 'Recent improvements in equipment and technic in the production of motion pictures,' *JSMPE*, 23, no. 3 (October 1934): 211-12; Carl Dreher, 'Recording, re-recording and editing of sound,' *JSMPE*, 16, no. 6 (June 1931): 757; J.P. Maxfield, 'Acoustic control of recording for talking motion pictures,' *JSMPE*, 14, no. 1 (January 1930): 85-7; Ralph H. Townsend and A.P. Hill, 'Sound stages,' in *Recording Sound for Motion Pictures*, ed. Lester Cowan (New York: McGraw-Hill, 1931), pp. 242-3; H.B. Santee, 'Western Electric sound projection systems for use in motion picture theatres, Part II,' *TSMPE*, 12, no. 35 (1928): 683; Earl I. Sponable, 'Some technical aspects of the Movietone,' *TSMPE*, 11, no. 31 (1927): 473. On stereophonic sound, see J.E. Ney, 'Stereophonic,' *IP*, 9, no. 7 (August 1937): 5; Lorin D. Grignon, 'Experiment in stereophonic sound,' *JSMPTE*, 61, no. 3 (September 1953): 366-8; Loren Ryder, 'Expanded sound and picture at Paramount,' *International Sound Technician*, 1 (August 1953): 41.

27   Alan Williams, 'Is sound recording like a language?' *Yale French Studies*, no. 60 (1980): 58. See also Colin MacCabe *et al.*, *Godard: Images, Sounds, Politics* (Bloomington: Indiana University Press, 1980), p. 112.

28   Herman, *Practical Manual of Screen Playwriting*, p. 101.

29   Fred Balshofer and Arthur C. Miller, *One Reel a Week* (Berkeley: University of California Press, 1967), p. 193; John Arnold, 'Shooting the movie,' in *We Make the Movies*, ed. Naumberg, p. 166; John Arnold, 'Cinematography – professional,' in *The*

Complete Photographer, vol. 2, ed. W.D. Morgan (New York: National Education Alliance, 1943), p. 764; John Boyle, 'Black and white cinematography,' in *Technique of Motion Picture Production*, ed. SMPE, pp. 14-15.

30 For examples of this position see Heath, 'Narrative space,' pp. 73-90, and Guy Fihman, 'D'où viennent les images claires?' in *Cinéma: Théorie, lectures*, ed. Noguez, pp. 200-2.

31 See Julian Hochberg, 'The psychophysics of pictorial perception,' *Audio-Visual Communications Review*, 10 (1962): 39-40.

32 B. Schlanger, 'A method of enlarging the visual field of the motion picture,' *JSMPE*, 30, no. 5 (May 1938): 504.

33 E.H. Gombrich, 'The "What" and the "How": perspective representation and the phenomenal world,' in *Logic and Art*, ed. Richard Rudner and Israel Scheffler (Indiana: Bobbs-Merrill, 1972), p. 143.

34 On Hollywood's eye-level camera, see Krows, *The Talkies*, pp.158-9, and Herman, *Practical Manual of Screen Playwriting*, p. 119.

35 E.H. Gombrich, *Art and Illusion*, (Princeton: Princeton University Press, 1969) p. 179.

36 See Pascal Bonitzer, ' "Réalité" de la dénotation,' *Cahiers du cinéma* no. 229 (May 1971): 39-41.

37 Jan and Cora Gordon, *Star-Dust in Hollywood* (London: Harrap, 1930), pp. 105-6.

38 Bazin, *What Is Cinema?*, pp. 31-2.

39 Quoted in Sherman, *Directing the Film*, p. 105. For the most scholastic spelling out of the continuity rules, see Daniel Arijohn, *Grammar of the Film Language* (New York: Hastings House, 1976).

40 MacCabe *et al.*, *Godard*, p. 68.

41 See Jean Mitry, *Esthétique et psychologie du cinéma*, vol. 2 (Paris: Editions Universitaires, 1967), pp. 72-7.

42 Edward Branigan, 'Formal permutations of the point-of-view shot,' *Screen*, 16, no. 3 (Autumn 1975): 57-8.

43 King Vidor, *On Film Making* (New York: McKay, 1972), p. 137.

44 On Dreyer, see Bordwell, *Films of Dreyer*, pp. 120-4; on Bresson, see Jean-Pierre Oudart, 'Cinema and suture,' *Screen*, 18, no. 4 (Winter 1977-8): 35-47.

45 Martha Robinson, *Continuity Girl* (London: Hale, 1937), p. 47.

46 See Hochberg and Brooks, 'Perception of motion pictures,' pp. 282-6.

47 Julian C. Hochberg, *Perception*, 2nd ed. (Englewood Cliffs, N.J.: Prentice-Hall, 1978) p. 208.

48* Readers familiar with contemporary film theory will have noticed that my account of the shot/reverse-shot pattern both overlaps with and diverges from Jean-Pierre Oudart's analysis of the 'suture.' Like Oudart, I have emphasized that an implicit, offscreen space opens and closes a gap and thus implies a process of narration; like Oudart (and unlike most commentators upon Oudart), I have treated the 'Absent One' entailed by the image as the narration, not another character in the fiction. The most significant difference is this: Oudart implies that the 'suturing' effect of editing is best explained as an activity of the viewer's unconscious. The process I have described works in the preconscious, as Noël Carroll has pointed out, and we can bring its operations to light in a straightforward fashion. See Oudart, 'Cinema and suture,' pp. 35-47; Stephen Heath, 'Notes on suture,' *Screen*, 18, no. 4 (Winter 1977/78): 66-76; Jean-Pierre Oudart, 'L'effet de réel,' *Cahiers du cinéma*, no. 228 (March-April 1971): 19-26; Noël Carroll, 'Toward a theory of film editing,' *Millennium Film Journal*, no. 3 (1978): 93-5.

49 Gombrich, *Art and Illusion*, p. 222.

50 E.H. Gombrich, 'Standards of truth: the arrested image and the moving eye,' *Critical Inquiry*, 7, no. 2 (Winter 1980): 248-9.

Chapter 6 Shot and scene

1 André Bazin, 'La technique de *Citizen Kane*,' *Temps modernes*, 2, no. 17 (1947): 945.

2 Theodor W. Adorno, 'Scientific experiences of a European scholar in America,' in *The Intellectual Migration: Europe and America, 1930-1960*, ed. Donald Fleming and Bernard Bailyn (Cambridge, Mass.: Harvard University Press, 1969), p. 366.

3 Vladimir Nilsen, *The Cinema as a Graphic Art*, tr. Stephen Garry (New York: Hill & Wang, 1959), p. 185.

4 Barry Salt, 'Statistical style analysis of motion pictures,' *Film Quarterly*, 28, no. 2 (Winter 1974-5): 13-22. Note (p. 14) that Salt's figures are not derived from an unbiased sample and were not obtained by watching each film in its entirety.

5 See L.E. Clark, 'Sound stage equipment and practice,' *AC*, 11, no. 6 (October 1930): 23; James R. Cameron, *Sound Motion Pictures: Recording and Reproducing* (Woodmont, Conn.: Cameron Publishing Co., 1934), p. 93; 'Questions and answers,' *IP*, 9, no. 1 (February 1937): 23; Kiesling, *Talking Pictures*, pp. 180, 231; 'Cinematographers show how to achieve production economies,' *AC*, 21, no. 8 (August 1941): 360-2.

6 See Raymond Bellour, 'To analyze, to segment,' *Quarterly Review of Film Studies*, 1, no. 3 (August 1976): 336-45.

7 'Sept hommes à débattre,' *Cahiers du cinéma*, nos 150-1 (December 1963-January 1964): 16.

8   Metz, *Film Language*, pp. 131-3.

9   Walter B. Pitkin and William M. Marston, *The Art of Sound Pictures* (New York: Appleton, 1930), p. 98.

10 Kuntzel, 'Le travail du film, 2,' p. 153.

11 Raymond Williams, 'A lecture on realism,' *Screen*, 18, no. 1 (Spring 1977): 66.

12 Cited in O. Eyquem, 'Otto Ludwig Preminger,' in *Dictionnaire du cinéma*, ed. Raymond Bellour and Jean-Jacques Brochier (Paris: Editions Universitaires, 1966), p. 568.

13 See Cromwell, 'The voice behind the megaphone,' in *We Make the Movies*, ed., Naumburg, p. 60.

14 A good discussion is in Livingston, *Film and the Director*, pp. 41-4.

15 I. James Wilkinson and W.H. Hamilton, 'Motion picture editing,' *JSMPE*, 36, no. 1 (January 1941): 102.

16 Quoted in Sherman, *Directing the Film*, p. 99.

17 Barthes, *S/Z*, p. 160.

Chapter 7 The bounds of difference

1   Stephen Heath, 'Narrative space,' *Screen*, 17, no. 3 (Autumn, 1976): 71.

2   Diane Waldman, 'Horror and domesticity: the modern Gothic romance film of the 1940s' (Madison, Wisconsin: unpublished PhD dissertation, 1981), pp. 164-93.

3   Tyler, *Hallucination*, pp. 15-19; Parker Tyler, *Magic and Myth of the Movies* (New York: Simon and Schuster, 1970), p. 248; Richard Dyer, *Stars* (London, British Film Institute, 1979), pp. 146-9.

4   Tyler, *Hallucination*, p. 161.

5   David Grimsted, *Melodrama Unveiled* (Chicago: University of Chicago Press, 1968), pp. 234-40.

6   Alan Williams, 'The musical film and recorded popular music' (unpublished essay), p. 11.

7   Frank Krutnik, '*The Shanghai Gesture*: the exotic and the melodrama,' *Wide Angle*, 4, no. 2 (1980): 36-42; Griselda Pollock, 'Report on the Weekend School,' *Screen*, 18, no. 2 (Summer 1977): 105-13; Geoffrey Nowell-Smith, 'Minnelli and melodrama,' *Screen*, 18, no. 2 (Summer 1977): 113–18. The source of most contemporary analyses of melodrama is Thomas Elsaesser's essay, 'Tales of sound and fury,' *Monogram*, no. 4 (1972): 2-15.

8   Elsaesser, 'Tales of sound and fury,' p. 12.

9   Daniel Gerould, 'Russian Formalist theories of melodrama,' *Journal of American Culture*, no. 1 (1978): 158.

10 Laura Mulvey, 'Notes on Sirk and melodrama,' *Movie*, no. 25 (Winter 1977/78): 53-7.

11 S.J. Perelman, *The Best of S.J. Perelman*, with a critical introduction by Sidney Namlerep (New York: Modern Library, 1947), pp. 51-2.

12 Quoted in Roy Prendergast, *Film Music: A Neglected Art* (New York: Norton, 1977), pp. 45-6.

13 *Ibid.*, pp. 80-4, 119-20.

14 Leonard Rosenmann, 'Notes on the score to *East of Eden*,' *Film Music*, 14, no. 5 (May-June 1955): 11.

15 Louis and Bebe Barron, '*Forbidden Planet*,' *Film Music*, 15, no. 5 (Summer 1956): 18.

16 Carlyle Ellis, 'Art and the motion picture,' *Annals of the American Academy of Politica and Social Science*, 1928, 128, no. 217 (November 1926): 56.

17 Interview with Charles G. Clarke, conducted by David Bordwell and Kristin Thompson, 12 June and 3 July 1980 in Hollywood, California.

18 Ira B. Hoke, 'Akeley has wide range of adaptability,' *AC*, 9, no. 9 (December 1928): 30.

19 Linwood G. Dunn, 'Explaining "Montage," ' *AC*, 23, no. 8 (August 1942): 359. See also Rudolf Messel, *This Film Business* (London: Ernest Bess, 1928), pp. 261-3.

20 See M.L. Tandon, 'Montage,' *IP*, 6, no. 10 (November 1934): 2-3; Paul E. Bowles, 'The relation between continuity and cutting,' *IP*, 6, no. 9 (October 1934): 10-11, and *IP*, 6, no. 12 (January 1935): 10-11, 28-9; Ed Gibbons, 'Montage marches in,' *IP*, 9, no. 9 (October 1937): 25-9; Vernon L. Walker, 'Rhythmic optical effects for musical pictures,' *AC*, 17, no. 12 (December 1936): 504, 514; Karl Freund, 'Just what is "Montage"?' *AC*, 15, no. 5 (September 1934): 204, 210.

21 Slavko Vorkapich, 'The psychological basis of effective cinematography,' in 'Transitions and time lapses,' *AMPAS Academy Technicians' Branch Technical Digest*, no. 10 (28 September 1934): 8.

22 *Ibid.*, p. 9.

23 See also Lewis Jacobs, 'Montage for motion pictures,' *The Complete Photographer*, vol. 7, ed. Willard D. Morgan (New York: Education Alliance, 1943): 2609-19; Herb A. Lightman, 'The magic of montage,' *AC*, 30, no. 10 (October 1949): 382; and Vladimir Petric, 'Soviet revolutionary film in America (1926-1935)' (PhD dissertation, New York University, 1973), pp. 404-9.

24 Raymond Borde and Etienne Chaumeton, *Panorama du film noir américain* (Paris: Editions d'aujourd'hui, 1976); Alain Silver and Elizabeth Ward, *Film Noir: An Encyclopedic Reference to the American Style* (Woodstock, New York: The Overlook Press, 1979); Raymond Durgnat, 'The family tree of film noir,' *Cinema* [Britain], no. 6/7 (August 1970): 49.

25 E.H. Gombrich, *Norm and Form: Studies in the Art of the Renaissance* (London: Phaidon, 1966), p. 88.

26 Jean-Pierre Chartier, 'Les américains aussi font des films "noirs," ' *Revue du cinéma*, no. 2 (November 1946): 67-70. See also Borde and

Chaumeton, *Panorama*, p. 155.

27 Borde and Chaumeton, *Panorama*, pp. 1-2.

28 Silver and Ward, *Film Noir*, p. 323.

29 See E. Ann Kaplan, 'Introduction,' *Women in Film Noir* (London: British Film Institute, 1978), p. 4; Christine Gledhill, '*Klute*,' in *Women in Film Noir*, ed. Kaplan, pp. 14-19.

30 Borde and Chaumeton, *Panorama*, pp. 185-6.

31 Paul Schrader, 'Notes on film noir,' *Film Comment*, 8, no. 1 (Spring 1972): 11-13.

32 Janey Place and L.S. Peterson, 'Some visual motifs of film noir,' *Film Comment*, 10, no. 1 (January 1974): 31.

33 See Boileau-Narcejac, *Le roman policier* (Paris: Payot, 1964), p. 154.

34 *Ibid.*, pp. 123-6; Borde and Chaumeton, *Panorama*, pp. 17-29; Raymond Chandler, 'The simple art of murder,' in *The Art of the Mystery Story*, ed. Howard Haycraft (New York: Grosset & Dunlap, 1947), pp. 222-37.

35 Julian Symons, *Mortal Consequences* (New York: Harper & Row, 1972), pp. 133-8, 178-89.

36 See Howard Haycraft, 'The whodunit in World War II and after,' in *Mystery Story*, ed. Haycraft, pp. 536-42.

37 James Wong Howe, 'Visual suggestion can enhance "rationed" sets,' *AC*, 23, no. 5 (June 1942): 236-7; Harry B. Warner, 'Waste more deadly than sabotage,' *IP*, 14, no. 2 (March 1942): 25; 'Cinematographers show how to achieve production economies,' *AC*, 21, no. 8 (August 1941): 360-2; Ezra Goodman, 'A cinematographer speaks,' *AC*, 26, no. 4 (April 1945): 120-1; Robert Joseph, 'Filming a motion picture in one set,' *AC*, 25, no. 10 (October 1944): 336; Joseph Valentine, 'Using an actual town instead of movie sets,' *AC*, 23, no. 10 (October 1942): 440-1; Ezra Goodman, 'Post-War motion picture,' *AC*, 26, no. 5 (May 1945): 160; James Wong Howe, 'The documentary film and Hollywood techniques,' in *Proceedings of the Conference Held in 1943 Under the Sponsorship of the Hollywood Writers' Mobilization and the University of California* (Berkeley: University of California Press, 1944), pp. 94-6; James Wong Howe, 'Documentary technique in Hollywood,' *AC*, 25, no. 1 (January 1944): 10, 32. See also Paul Kerr, 'Out of what past? Notes on the B film noir,' *Screen Education*, no. 32/33 (Autumn 1979-80): 45-65.

38 Leon Shamroy, 'Future of cinematography,' *AC*, 28, no. 10 (October 1947): 358. See also Herb Lightman, '13 rue Madeleine,' *AC*, 28, no. 3 (March 1947): 89; Herb A. Lightman, 'Mood in the motion picture,' *AC*, 28, no. 2 (February 1947): 48-9, 69.

39 Cited in John Baxter, 'Something more than night,' *The Film Journal*, 2, no. 4 (1975): 9.

40 See John Berger, *The Success and Failure of Picasso* (London: Penguin, 1966). For an attempt to see authorship in the cinema as a constructed 'biographical legend,' see David Bordwell, *The Films of Carl-Theodor Dreyer* (Berkeley: University of California Press, 1981), pp. 9-24.

41 Leonard B. Meyer, 'Toward a theory of style,' in *The Concept of Style*, ed. Berel Lang (University of Pennsylvania Press, 1979), p. 27.

42 See Noël Burch, *Theory of Film Practice*, tr. Helen R. Lane (New York: Praeger, 1973), p. xviii.

43 V.F. Perkins, *Film as Film* (New York: Penguin, 1972), p. 130.

44 Peter Wollen, *Signs and Meanings in the Cinema*, 2nd ed. (Bloomington: Indiana University Press, 1972), p. 77.

45 *Ibid.*, p. 170.

46 Meir Sternberg, *Expositional Modes and Temporal Ordering in Fiction*, (Baltimore: Johns Hopkins University Press, 1978), pp. 98-158.

47 Pascal Kané, '*Sylvia Scarlett*: Hollywood cinema reread,' *Sub-stance*, no. 9 (1974): 37-40; Jean-Pierre Oudart, 'Un discours en défault,' *Cahiers du cinéma*, no. 232 (October 1971): 5-6.

48 See, for example, Kané, '*Sylvia Scarlett*,' pp. 37-8; Oudart, 'Un discours,' pp. 6-7; and Claudine Eizykman, *La jouissance-cinéma* (Paris: 10/18, 1975), pp. 10-21.

49 Quoted in Martin Jay, *The Dialectical Imagination* (Boston: Little, Brown, 1973), p. 214.

50 Quoted in Christian Braad Thomsen, 'Five interviews with Fassbinder,' in *Fassbinder*, ed. Tony Rayns, 2nd ed. (London: British Film Institute, 1980), p. 82.

51 See David Bordwell, 'Happily ever after, part two,' *The Velvet Light Trap*, no. 19 (1982): 2-7.

52 Karl Marx and Frederick Engels, *The German Ideology*, ed. C.J. Arthur (New York: International Publishers, 1977), pp. 108-9.

53 See Lewis Herman, *A Practical Manual of Screen Playwriting for Theater and Television Films* (New York: New American Library, 1974), p. 126; Martha Robinson, *Continuity Girl* (London: Hale, 1937), p. 26; Bowles, 'The relationship between continuity and cutting,' p. 10; and Jack Russell, 'What is an insert?' *IP*, 11, no. 12 (January 1940): 9, 44.

54 Gibbons, 'Montage marches in,' p. 29.

55 Nick Grinde, 'Pictures for peanuts: a study from Hollywood,' *Penguin Film Review*, no. 1 (1946): 14.

56 See Anne Bauchens, 'How we use these devices to increase production value,' in 'Transitions and time lapses,' *AMPAS Technical Digest*: 6-8; Gordon Jennings, 'Special effects and montage for *Cleopatra*,' *AC*, 15, no. 8 (December 1934): 350-4; 'Montage,' *IP*, 12, no. 12 (January 1941): 3, 13; Robert Parrish, *Growing Up in Hollywood* (New York: Harcourt Brace Jovanovich, 1976), pp. 163-6.

Chapter 8 The Hollywood mode of production: its conditions of existence

1 Jean-Louis Comolli, 'Technique et idéologie,' *Cahiers du cinéma*, nos 229, 230, 231, 233, 234-5, and 241 (May 1971-September-October 1972).

2 John Ellis, 'The institution of cinema,' *Edinburgh '77 Magazine*, no. 2 (1977), 56-66; Geoffrey Nowell-Smith, 'On the writing of the history of the cinema: some problems,' *Edinburgh '77 Magazine*, no. 2 (1977), 8-12. Also see: John Hill, 'Ideology, economy and the British cinema,' in *Ideology and Cultural Production*, ed. Michèle Barrett, Philip Corrigan, Annette Kuhn, and Janet Wolff (New York: St Martin's Press, 1979), pp. 112-34; Michèle Barrett, Philip Corrigan, Annette Kuhn, and Janet Wolff, 'Representation and cultural production,' in *Ideology and Cultural Production*, pp. 9-24.

3 Karl Marx and Frederick Engels, *Selected Works* (New York: International Publishers, 1968), p. 182. Also see *The German Ideology* and *Capital* in particular. More recent theorists include Louis Althusser, 'Ideology and the ideological state apparatuses (notes towards an investigation),' in *Lenin and Philosophy and other Essays*, trans. Ben Brewster (New York: Monthly Review Press, 1971), pp. 127-86; Terry Eagleton, *Criticism & Ideology: A Study in Marxist Literary Theory* (London: Verso Edition, 1978); Barry Hindness and Paul Q. Hirst, *Pre-Capitalist Modes of Production* (London: Routledge & Kegan Paul, 1975); Antony Cutler, Barry Hindess, Paul Hirst, and Athar Hussain, *Marx's Capital and Capitalism Today* (London: Routledge & Kegan Paul, 1977 and 1978). Outside the scope of my question (although an important problem) is the determination of classes and the methods by which certain classes appropriate surplus value. On these problems, see Hindess and Hirst, *Pre-Capitalist Modes of Production*, and Talal Asad and Harold Wolpe, 'Concepts of modes of production,' *Economy and Society*, 5, no. 4 (November 1976), 470-506.

4 Peter F. Drucker, 'Work and tools,' in *Technology, Management & Society* (New York: Harper & Row, Publishers, 1970), pp. 43-54.

5 Historical background for this section comes from: John Chamberlain, *The Enterprising Americans: A Business History of the United States*, rev. ed. (New York: Harper & Row Publishers, 1974); Alex Groner, *The American Heritage History of American Business & Industry* (New York: American Heritage Publishing Co., Inc., 1972); David F. Noble, *America by Design: Science, Technology, and the Rise of Corporate Capitalism* (New York: Alfred A. Knopf, 1977); Harry N. Scheiber, Harold G. Vatter, and Harold Underwood Faulkner, *American Economic History*, 9th ed., rev. (New York: Harper & Row, Publishers, Inc., 1976); Monte Calvert, *The Mechanical Engineer in America, 1830-1910* (Baltimore: Johns Hopkins University Press, 1967); John Perry, *The Story of Standards* (New York: Funk & Wagnalls Company, 1955).

6 Henry Ford cited in Scheiber, *et al., American Economic History*, p. 225.

7 Perry, *The Story of Standards*, p. 126.

8 Frank L. Eidmann, *Economic Control of Engineering and Manufacturing* (New York: McGraw-Hill Book Company, Inc., 1931), p. 204.

9 John D. Rockefeller cited in Chamberlain, *Enterprising Americans*, p. 150.

10 Eidmann, *Economic Control*, p. 261.

11 This section relies heavily on Harry Braverman, *Labor and Monopoly Capital: The Degradation of Work in the Twentieth Century* (New York: Monthly Review Press, 1974). On social division of labor, see pp. 70-5.

12 *Ibid.*, pp. 63-4.

13 Also see: Karl Marx, *Capital*, vol. 1, ed. Frederick Engels, 1887, trans. Samuel Moore and Edward Aveling (New York: International Publishers, 1967), pp. 350-6.

14 Marx, *Capital*, 1, chs 13, 14, and 15, particularly pp. 336-86.

15* *The McGraw-Hill Dictionary of Modern Economics* defines these. '*Vertical Integration*: the operation of a single firm at more than one stage of production. The most comprehensive type of vertical production would include productive stages from the processing of the raw material to the completion and distribution of the finished product.' '*Diversification*: the participation by a single firm in the production or sale of widely divergent kinds of goods and services.' '*Horizontal Integration*: the situation existing in a firm whose products or services are competitive with each other. The term also applies to the expansion of a firm into the production of new products that are competitive with older ones.' *The McGraw-Hill Dictionary of Modern Economics: A Handbook of Terms and Organizations*, 2nd ed. (New York: McGraw-Hill Book Company, 1973), pp. 263, 174-5, and 275.

16 Marx, *Capital*, 1, p. 420. Marx also deals with the consequent segregation of jobs by genders; see Marx, *Capital*, 1, pp. 459-503.

17 Cutler, *et al., Marx's Capital and Capitalism Today*, vol. 2, p. 190, and vol. 1, pp. 304-10. An earlier discussion of the manager is in James Burnham, *The Managerial Revolution* (Bloomington, Indiana: Indiana University Press, 1941).

18 Alfred D. Chandler, Jr, *Strategy and Structure: Chapters in the History of the American Industrial Enterprise* (Cambridge, Massachusetts: The M.I.T.

Press, 1962), pp. 11-12. On the problem of the class of the professional manager, see Pat Walker, ed. *Between Labor and Capital* (Boston: South End Press, 1979); Nicos Poulantzas, 'The problems of the capitalist state,' in *Ideology in Social Science: Readings in Critical Social Theory*, ed. Robin Blackburn (New York: Pantheon Books, 1972), pp. 238-62; Erik Olin Wright, *Class, Crisis and the State* (n.p.: NLB, 1978), pp. 30-110.

Chapter 9 Standardization and differentiation: the reinforcement and dispersion of Hollywood's practices

1 William C. de Mille, *Hollywood Saga* (New York: E.P. Dutton & Co., Inc., 1939), p. 123.

2 John Perry, *The Story of Standards* (New York: Funk & Wagnalls Co., 1955), p. 125.

3 Ralph K. Davidson, Vernon L. Smith, and Jay W. Wiley, *Economics: An Analytical Approach*, rev. ed. (Homewood, Illinois: Richard D. Irwin, Inc., 1962), pp. 28-9.

4 Harry Braverman, *Labor and Monopoly Capital: The Degradation of Work in the Twentieth Century* (New York: Monthly Review Press, 1974), p. 266.

5 Information for this section is from: John Chamberlain, *The Enterprising Americans: A Business History of the United States*, rev. ed (New York: Harper & Row Publishers, 1974); Alex Groner, *The American Heritage History of American Business & Industry* (New York: American Heritage Publishing Co., 1972); Harry N. Scheiber, Harold G. Vatter, and Harold Underwood Faulkner, *American Economic History* 9th ed., rev. (New York: Harper & Row, 1976).

6 Motion Picture Patents Co., 'Memorandum for the Motion Picture Patents Company and the General Film Company concerning the investigation of their business by the Department of Justice,' submitted by M.B. Phillipp and Francis T. Homer, 18 May 1912, TS (New York: Museum of Modern Art), p. 42.

7 *Edison Films*, Supplements 168, 185, and 200 (Orange, New Jersey: Edison Manufacturing Company, February 1903, October 1903, January 1904), pp. 2-3, 5, and 5-7, respectively, rpt. in *Spellbound in Darkness: A History of the Silent Film*, ed. George C. Pratt, rev. ed. (Greenwich, Connecticut: New York Graphic Society Ltd., 1973), pp. 29-30, 34, and 34-6.

8 ' "The Iced Bullet" a novel and thrilling detective story,' *The Triangle*, 3, no. 11 (6 January 1917), 5; L.F. Cook, 'Of interest to the trade,' *NKL*, 3, no. 1 (January 1910), 21.

9 'The Motion Picture Story Magazine,' *MPW*, 8, no. 5 (4 February 1911), 228.

10 'Film stories in Sunday papers,' *NYDM*, 67, no. 1725 (10 January 1912), 30; Harold MacGrath, *The Adventures of Kathlyn*, Kathlyn Williams De Luxe Edition (Indianapolis: The Bobbs- Merrill Company, 1914).

11 'Cleveland,' *MPW*, 8, no. 20 (20 May 1911), 1126.

12 Howard Thompson Lewis, *Cases on the Motion Picture Industry* (New York: McGraw-Hill Book Company, Inc., 1930), p. 63.

13 R.R. Nehls, 'The efficiency plan of film salesmanship,' *MPW*, 14, no. 3 (19 October 1912), 237; David Sherrill Hulfish, *Cyclopedia of Motion-Picture Work* (Chicago: American School of Correspondence, 1911), I, pp. 276-82. 'Spectator,' ' "Spectator's" comments,' *NYDM*, 65, no. 1692 (4 January 1911), 28.

14 Cited in Benjamin B. Hampton, *History of the American Film Industry from its Beginnings to 1931* (1931; rpt, New York: Dover Publications, 1970), p. 37.

15 'Doings in Los Angeles,' *MPW*, 12, no. 11 (15 June 1912), 1014; 'Comments on the films,' *MPW*, 8, no. 2 (14 January 1911), 88.

16 Sybil Rosenfeld, *A Short History of Scene Design in Great Britain* (Totowa, New Jersey: Rowman & Littlefield, 1973), pp. 76-8; Oscar G. Brockett, *The Theatre: An Introduction* (New York: Holt, Rinehart & Winston, 1964), pp. 246-55.

17 Ad, *MPW*, 11, no. 7 (17 February 1912), between 570 and 571; Samuel Goldwyn cited in James P. Cunningham, 'Asides and interludes,' *MPHerald*, 142, no. 3 (18 January 1941), 35. Russell Merritt astutely points out how the historian may be trapped by the fascination of these profilmic details used to establish an exchange-value; see his 'On first looking into Griffith's Babylon: a reading of a publicity still,' *Wide Angle*, 3, no. 1 (1979), 12-21.

18 Glenn Loney, 'Heyday of the dramatized novel [1900-1906],' *Educational Theatre Journal*, 9, no. 3 (October 1957), 194-200; 'Noted dramatists to write moving picture plays,' *MPW*, 2, no. 13 (28 March 1908), 263; 'Motion picture play writing as an art,' *EK*, 1, no. 3 (1 September 1909), 12. Also see the *Kinetograms* for 15 December 1909 and 1 January 1910.

19 Alfred L. Bernheim, *The Business of the Theatre: An Economic History of the American Theatre, 1750-1932* (New York: Benjamin Blom, Inc., 1932), p. 27; 'The Edison Stock Company,' *EK*, 1, no. 4 (15 September 1909), 13; 'Our Stock Company,' *EK*, 1, no. 5 (1 October 1909), 13-4; Anthony Slide, 'The evolution of the film star,' *Films in Review*, 25 (December 1974), 591-4; 'Marion Leonard Shanghaid,' *MPNews*, 5, no. 1 (6 January 1912); ad, *MPNews*, 5, no. 4 (27 January 1912), 35.

20   Anthony Slide, *Aspects of American Film History Before 1920* (Metuchen, New Jersey: The Scarecrow Press, Inc., 1978), p. 1.

21   'Gem tells when!' *MPNews*, 4, no. 52 (30 December 1911), 24-6; C.B. Clapp, 'Florence Lawrence famous picture star,' *NYDM*, 68, no. 1754 (31 July 1912), 13.

22   'The Essanay Company out West,' *The Denver Post*, rpt. in *Spellbound in Darkness*, ed. Pratt, pp. 127-30; 'From tyranny to liberty,' *EK*, 3, no. 2 (15 August 1910), 11.

23   'Spectator,' ' "Spectator's" Comments,' *NYDM*, 66, no. 1721 (13 December 1911), 28; 'Will present play productions,' *MPW*, 11, no. 2 (13 January 1912), 109-10; 'The independent situation,' *MPW*, 12, no. 11 (15 June 1912), 1016.

24   'Motion picture nomenclature,' *AC*, 3, no. 2 (1 May 1922), 25.

25   Magnus W. Alexander, *The Economic Evolution of the United States: Its Background and Significance* (New York: National Industrial Conference Board, Inc., 1929), pp. 36-8; Groner, *American Heritage History*, pp. 92, 262. Information about the theatrical trade association, the National Association of Producing Managers, which organized in the early 1900s to effect stronger copyright protection is in Arthur Edwin Krows, *Play Production in America* (New York: Henry Holt and Company, 1916), pp. 276-7.

26   'The independent movement,' *NKL*, 1, no. 1 (February 1909), 39-40; William Horsley, 'From pigs to pictures,' (part 1), *IP*, 6, no. 2 (March 1934), 3; Ralph Cassady, Jr, 'Monopoly in motion picture production and distribution: 1908-1915,' *Southern California Law Review*, 32, no. 4 (Summer 1959), 363, 371-2; Laurence F. Cook, 'Convention of the independent alliance,' *NKL*, 2, no. 4 (October 1909), 105-10; 'Motion Picture Distributing and Sales Co.,' *MPNews*, 4, no. 15 (15 April 1911), 25-6.

27   'The Motion Picture Exhibitors' League of America,' *MPW*, 13, no. 7 (17 August 1912), 621; 'Motion Picture Exhibitors' Association of Greater New York goes on record in favor of a national convention of exhibitors,' *MPW*, 8, no. 14 (8 April 1911), 753; Edward Hobday, 'Importance of trade organizations,' *MPW*, 9, no. 6 (19 August 1911) 444; M.A. Neff, 'Big meeting of Ohio exhibitors,' *MPW*, 8, no. 18 (6 May 1911), 1007; 'Local organization necessary to a national convention' and 'Exhibitors' league meeting,' *MPW*, 8, no. 20 (20 May 1911), 1114-15, 1122; 'National organization,' *MPW*, 9, no. 5 (12 August 1911), 365; 'Exhibitors form national league: report of organization meeting,' *MPW*, 9, no. 6 (19 August 1911), 440-3; 'The goat man,' 'On the outside looking in,' *Motography*, 6, no. 5 (November 1911), 237-8.

28   'The first international exposition,' *MPW*, 17, no. 3 (19 July 1913), 324-7; also see 'Manufacturers organize,' *MPW*, 21, no. 11 (12 September 1914), 1488.

29   Howard T. Lewis, *The Motion Picture Industry* (New York: D. Van Nostrand Company, Inc., 1933), p. 267*n*; 'Renters organize for protection,' *MPW*, 20, no. 9 (30 May 1914), 1242; 'Exchanges correct abuses legally,' *MPW*, 30, no. 4 (28 October 1916), 526-7.

30   'A commendable step,' *Moving Picture Publicity*, 2, no. 5 (July 1914), 18; 'Standards of practice for ad-filmers,' *Moving Picture Publicity*, 2, no. 5 (July 1914), 22-3; 'Ad. film folks meet to discuss organization,' *MPW*, 29, no. 9 (24 August 1914), 1221; 'M.P. advertising men organize,' *MPW*, 29, no. 7 (12 August 1916), 1089; 'Motion publicity men organize,' *MPW*, 29, no. 8 (19 August 1916), 256.

31   'Independents propose organization,' *MPW*, 21, no. 11 (12 September 1914), 1521.

32   'Our man about town,' 'Observations,' *MPW*, 21, no. 13 (26 September 1914), 1764; W. Stephen Bush, 'The Motion Picture Board of Trade of America,' *MPW*, 25, no. 13 (26 September 1915), 2156; Bernard M. Corbett, 'Cash in advance vs. open account,' *MPW*, 27, no. 1 (1 January 1916), 67; 'Decision in Vitagraph-Metro case,' *MPW*, 27, no. 13 (25 March 1916), 2015; 'Film men discuss organization,' *MPW*, 28, no. 13 (24 June 1916), 2210; 'Film men form temporary organization,' *MPW*, 29, no. 4 (22 July 1916), 612-13; 'The great get-together meeting,' *MPW*, 29, no. 7 (12 August 1916), 1074.

33   G.P. Von Harleman and Clarke Irvine, 'News of Los Angeles and vicinity,' *MPW*, 27, no. 3 (15 January 1916), 408-9.

34   Frederick James Smith, 'The evolution of the motion picture, VIII: from the standpoint of the film censor,' *NYDM*, 70, no. 1807 (6 August 1913), 25, 33; Martin Field, 'A short history of film censorship,' *The Screen Writer*, 3, no. 2 (July 1947), 9-11; Lewis, *Motion Picture Industry*, pp. 366-91; 'Motion Picture Exhibitors' Association of Greater New York goes on record in favor of a national convention of exhibitors,' *MPW*, 8, no. 14 (8 April 1911), 753; 'Report of the National Board of Censorship,' *MPW*, 8, no. 19 (13 May 1911), 1066-7; 'National Board changes its name,' *MPW*, 28, no. 3 (15 April 1916), 446; R.V.S., 'Scenario construction,' *MPW*, 8, no. 6 (11 February 1911), 294; Epes Winthrop Sargent, 'The scenario writer,' *MPW*, 11, no. 4 (27 January 1912), 294.

35   Charles R. Metzger, 'Pressure groups and the motion picture industry,' in *The Motion Picture Industry*, ed. Gordon S. Watkins (Philadelphia: American Academy of Political and Social Science, 1947), pp. 110-15; 'Among the exhibitors,' *MPW*, 8,

no. 13 (1 April 1911), 705; Richard V. Spencer, 'Los Angeles Notes,' *MPW*, 8, no. 11 (18 March 1911), 586; Epes Winthrop Sargent, *The Technique of the Photoplay*, 2nd ed. (New York: The Moving Picture World, 1913), p. 116.

36 F.H. Richardson, 'Projection department,' *MPW*, 12, no. 10 (8 June 1912); George Blaisdell, 'Nicholas Power urges standardization,' *MPW*, 21, no. 2 (11 July 1914), 222-3; Frank M. Byam, 'Standardization,' *MPW*, 21, no. 5 (1 August 1914), 690; Frank M. Byam, 'Standardization and the motion picture camera,' *MPW*, 21, no. 7 (15 August 1914), 946.

37 'Plans of Bureau of Standards,' *MPW*, 28, no. 10 (3 June 1916), 1673; 'Society of Motion Picture Engineers,' *MPW*, 29, no. 7 (12 August 1916), 1086; Society of Motion Picture Engineers, *The Society of Motion Picture Engineers* (New York: Society of Motion Picture Engineers, 1930), pp. iii-iv; Kemp R. Niver, 'Motion-picture film widths,' *JSMPTE*, 77 (August 1968), 814; 'Society of Motion Picture Engineers,' *MPW*, 30, no. 4 (28 October 1916), 533; Loyd A. Jones, 'A historical summary of standardization in the Society of Motion Picture Engineers,' *JSMPE*, 21, no. 4 (October 1933), 280-93.

38 Groner, *American Heritage History*, pp. 70, 217-18; Scheiber, *et al.*, *American Economic History*, pp. 167-70, 251-6, 311-12.

39 'An operators' league, and why?' *MPW*, 1, no. 1 (9 March 1907), 21; Phil Whitman, 'Western correspondent,' *MPNews*, 5, no. 3 (20 January 1912), 35; F.H. Richardson, 'Trouble department,' *MPW*, 8, no. 4 (28 January 1911), 187-8; 'Moving Picture Workers' Local No. 422,' *MPW*, 8, no. 11 (18 March 1911), 591; 'Enthusiastic meeting of New York operators,' *MPW*, 8, no. 13 (1 April 1911), 700; 'Moving Picture Machine Operators, Local 186, I.A.T.S.E. (Springfield, Mass.) wage schedule of 1910 and 1911,' and 'Scale of wages of Local 35, New York City,' *MPW*, 8, no. 19 (13 May 1911), 1079.

40 'The Screen Club is a fact,' *MPW*, 13, no. 12 (21 September 1912), 1163; 'Doings at Los Angeles,' *MPW*, 14, no. 12 (21 December 1912), 1175; P.M. Powell, 'Doings at Los Angeles,' *MPW*, 15, no. 2 (11 January 1913), 142; 'Spectator,' ' "Spectator's" comments,' *NYDM*, 67, no. 1735 (20 March 1912), 25; William Lord Wright, 'For those who worry o'er plots and plays,' *MPNews*, 5, no. 14 (6 April 1912), 21; 'The photoplay dinner,' *MPW*, 13, no. 12 (21 December 1912), 1169; William Lord Wright, *Photoplay Writing*, (New York: Falk Publishing Co., Inc., 1922), pp. 217-18; 'Woods heads Authors' League,' *NYDM*, 70, no. 1840 (25 March 1914), 31.

41 Epes Winthrop Sargent, 'The photoplaywright,' *MPW*, 19, no. 13 (28 March 1914).

42 'The League Protective Bureau,' *The Script*, 1, no. 6

(October 1914), 6.

43 'The editor,' 'Motion picture cameramen's organizations in America,' *IP*, 7, no. 9 (October 1935), 3; Static Club Constitution (October 1915) (Los Angeles: American Cinematographers), p. 51.

44 Fred F. Balshofer and Arthur C. Miller, *One Reel a Week* (Berkeley: University of California Press, 1967), p. 146.

45 'Static Club,' *MPW*, 25, no. 2 (10 July 1915), 272. Also see Minutes of Static Club, particularly 11 May 1915 (Los Angeles: American Cinematographers).

46 'Static Club,' *MPW*, 25, no. 2 (10 July 1915), 272-3; Lewis W. Physioc, 'The history of the Cinema Camera Club,' *Cinema News*, 1, no. 5 (15 February 1917), 5-6; 'The editor,' 'Motion picture cameramen's organizations in America,' *IP*, 7, no. 9 (October 1935), 3; George Blaisdell, 'Arnold again head of A.S.C.,' *AC*, 20, no. 5 (May 1939), 198; Balshofer and Miller, *One Reel a Week*, p. 123.

47 Murray Ross, *Stars and Strikes: Unionization of Hollywood* (New York: Columbia University Press, 1941).

48 John Francis Barry and Epes W. Sargent, *Building Theatre Patronage: Management and Merchandising* (New York: Chalmers Publishing Company, 1927), p. iii; Epes Winthrop Sargent, 'Technique of the photoplay,' *MPW*, 9, no. 2 (22 July 1911), 108-9; Sargent, *The Technique of the Photoplay*; 'The art of writing scenarios,' *MPW*, 8, no. 8 (25 February 1911), 419.

49 Archer McMackin, 'How moving picture plays are written,' *NKL*, 2, no. 6 (December 1909), 171-3.

50 'Letters and questions,' *NYDM*, 68, no. 1753 (24 July 1912), 25-6.

51 'Reviews of licensed films,' *NYDM*, 62, no. 1618 (25 December 1909); 15; S.M. Spedon, *How and Where Moving Pictures Are made by The Vitagraph Company of America* (New York: Vitagraph Company of America, [1912]), [p. 13]; James Slevin, *On Picture-Play Writing: A Hand-Book of Workmanship* (Cedar Grove, New Jersey: Farmer Smith Incorporated, 1912), p. 86; Louis Reeves Harrison, *Screencraft* (New York: Chalmers Publishing Co., 1916), pp. 115-18; 'Heard in studio and exchange,' *Reel Life*, 3, no. 24 (28 February 1914), 8; 'The practical side of pictures,' *Reel Life*, 4, no. 3 (4 April 1914), 25.

52 Clarence E. Sinn, 'Music for the pictures,' *MPW*, 8, no. 3 (21 January 1911), 135.

53 F.H. Richardson, 'The advancement of projection,' *MPW*, 21, no. 2 (11 July 1914), 218-19; Epes Winthrop Sargent, 'Advertising for exhibitors,' *MPW*, 9, no. 11 (23 September 1911), 876-7; Epes Winthrop Sargent, *Picture Theatre Advertising* (New York: The Moving Picture World Chalmers

Publishing Company, 1915); Clyde Martin, 'Working the sound effects,' *MPW*, 10, no. 4 (28 October 1911), 283; Mark Evans, *Soundtrack: The Music of the Movies* (New York: Hopkinson & Blake, 1975), p. 8; Carl Louis Gregory, 'Motion picture photography,' *MPW*, 25, no. 2 (10 July 1915), 283-4.

54 Raymond Williams, 'Base and superstructure in Marxist cultural theory,' *New Left Review*, 82 (November-December 1973), 8-9.

55 Epes Winthrop Sargent, 'Photoplay criticism,' *The Writer's Monthly*, 29, no. 5 (May 1927), 391-2. Also see Frances Taylor Patterson, *Scenario and Screen* (New York: Harcourt, Brace & Company, 1928), p. 82.

56 Rouben Mamoulian, 'Common sense and camera angles,' *AC*, 12, no 10 (February 1932), 26.

57 Harry C. Carr, 'What next – ?,' *Photoplay*, 11 (March 1917), 62.

58 Hugo Ballin, 'The scenic background,' *The Mentor*, 9, no. 6 (1 July 1921), 22.

59 Cedric Gibbons, 'The art director,' in *Behind the Screen: How Films Are Made*, ed. Stephen Watts (New York: Dodge Publishing Company, 1938), p. 41.

60 George Cukor, 'The director,' in *Behind the Screen*, ed. Watts, pp. 21-2.

61 Lee Garmes, 'Photography,' in *Behind the Screen*, ed. Watts, p. 107.

62 *Ibid.*, p. 108.

63 Frederick Foster, 'High key vs. low key,' *AC*, 38, no. 8 (August 1957), 506.

64 Hunt Stromberg, 'The producer,' in *Behind the Screen*, ed. Watts, p. 8.

65 Gregg Toland, 'I broke the rules in *Citizen Kane*,' *Popular Photography*, 8, no. 6 (June 1941), 55, 90-1.

66 Vincent Sherman in *Directing the Film: Film Directors on their Art*, ed. Eric Sherman (Boston: Little, Brown & Company, 1976), p. 293.

67 Stanley Cortez in Charles Higham, *Hollywood Cameramen: Sources of Light* (London: Thames & Hudson, 1970), p. 98.

68 Joe Henry, 'Techniques of Hollywood cinematographers,' *AC*, 38, no. 1 (January 1957), 34.

69 John Davis, 'When will they ever learn? A tale of mad geniuses, scientists, artists, and a director (also mad),' *The Velvet Light Trap*, no. 15 (Fall 1975), 13.

70 Tim Onosko, '53: The new era: A brief history of the three-dimensional film,' *The Velvet Light Trap*, no. 11 (1974), 13; 'No women in John Ford's Fox Picture,' *The Ohio Showman*, 5, no. 19 (14 December 1929), 28.

71 George Stevens in William R. Weaver, 'Seek new ways, says Stevens,' *MPHerald*, 168, no. 2 (12 July 1947), 33.

Chapter 10 The director system: management in the first years

1 Alfred L. Bernheim, *The Business of the Theatre: An Economic History of the American Theatre, 1750-1932* (New York: Benjamin Blom, 1932), pp. 37-40; John L. Fell, *Film and the Narrative Tradition* (Norman: University of Oklahoma Press, 1974), p. 8; 'A combination scheme,' *NYDM*, 35, no. 895 (22 February 1896), 17; Frank Luther Mott, *A History of American Magazines* (New York: D. Appleton & Co., 1957), pp. 1-44; Russel Blaine Nye, *The Unembarrassed Muse: The Popular Arts in America* (New York: The Dial Press, 1970).

2 Robert C. Allen, *Vaudeville and Film 1895-1915: A Study in Media Interaction* (New York: Arno Press, 1980), pp. 23-92; A.R. Fulton, 'The machine,' rpt. in *The American Film Industry*, ed. Tino Balio (Madison: University of Wisconsin Press, 1976), pp. 27-31; 'Edison's Vitascope,' *NYDM*, 35, no. 905 (2 May 1896), 19, rpt. in *Spellbound in Darkness: A History of the Silent Film*, ed. George C. Pratt, rev. ed. (Greenwich, Connecticut: New York Graphic Society, 1973), p. 16 (both accounts of the Vitascope presentation give details of the coloring of the films); Robert C. Allen, 'Contra the Chaser Theory,' *Wide Angle*, 3, no. 1 (1979), 4; Brett Page, *Writing for Vaudeville* (Springfield, Mass.: The Home Correspondence School, 1915), pp. 7-10.

3 Allen, *Vaudeville and Film*, pp. 112-13; 'The evolution of exhibition,' *MPW*, 29, no. 3 (15 July 1916), 367-425.

4 'The art of moving photography,' *Scientific American*, 76, no. 16 (17 April 1897), 249-50.

5 'The evolution of exhibition,' *MPW*, 29, no. 3 (15 July 1916), 367-425; Allen, 'Contra the Chaser Theory,' 4-11; George Pratt, 'No magic, no mystery, no sleight of hand,' *Image*, 8 (December 1959), 192-211, rpt. in *The American Film Industry*, ed. Balio, p. 54; Raymond Fielding, 'Hale's Tours: ultra-realism in the pre-1910 motion pictures,' *Cinema Journal*, 10, no. 1 (Fall 1970), 34-47. The Pratt source is an excellent recovery of the types of films shown in one city during the first years of commercial cinema.

6 Frederick James Smith, 'The evolution of the motion picture, I: from the standpoint of the film producer,' *NYDM*, 69, no. 1792 (23 April 1913), 26, 30; Terry Ramsaye, 'The motion picture,' *The Annals* (of the American Academy of Political and Social Science), 128 (November 1926), 7-9; Earl Theisen, 'Part of the story of lighting,' *IP*, 6, no. 3 (April 1934), 10; Pratt, 'No magic, no mystery,' p. 55.

7 Garth S. Jowett, 'The first motion picture

audiences,' *Journal of Popular Film*, 3 (Winter 1974), 39-54.

8 William F. Hellmuth, Jr, 'The motion picture industry,' in *The Structure of American Industry*, ed. Walter Adams, rev. ed. (New York: The Macmillan Company, 1954), p. 362; 'The evolution of exhibition,' *MPW*, 29, no. 3 (15 July 1916), 367-425; Benjamin B. Hampton, *History of the American Film Industry from its Beginnings to 1931* (1931; rpt, New York: Dover Publications, 1970), pp. 44-5; Robert C. Allen, 'Film history: the narrow discourse,' in *Film: Historical-Theoretical Speculations, The 1977 Film Studies Annual*, (Part Two), ed. Ben Lawton and Janet Staiger (Pleasantville, New York: Redgrave Publishing Co., 1977), p. 14; 'Growth of the film business,' *Billboard*, 18, no. 37 (15 September 1906), 16, rpt in *Spellbound in Darkness*, ed. Pratt, pp. 42-3; Robert C. Allen, 'Motion picture exhibition in Manhattan, 1906-1912: beyond the nickelodeon,' *Cinema Journal*, 18, no. 2 (Spring 1979), 11; Lucy Frances Pierce, 'The nickelodeon,' *NKL*, 1, no. 1 (January 1909), 10; 'Copyright laws vs. moving pictures and the cameraphone,' *MPW*, 2, no. 14 (4 April 1908), 290.

9 Hugo Münsterberg, *The Film: A Psychological Study: The Silent Photoplay in 1916* (1916; rpt, New York: Dover Publications, 1970), pp. 9-10.

10 Harry C. Carr, 'What next – ?' *Photoplay*, 11, no. 4 (March 1917), 60.

11 Allen, 'Film history,' pp. 13-15.

12 W.K.L. Dickson, *The Biograph in Battle: Its Story in the South African War Related with Personal Experiences* (London: T. Fisher Unwin, 1901), p. 157.

13 Besides Dickson, descriptions of this system are in: G.W. Bitzer, *Billy Bitzer: His Story* (New York: Farrar, Straus & Giroux, 1973), pp. 7-69; Albert E. Smith, *Two Reels and a Crank* (Garden City, New York: Doubleday & Co., 1952), pp. 1-159; Fred F. Balshofer and Arthur C. Miller, *One Reel a Week* (Berkeley: University of California Press, 1967); Charles Musser, 'The early cinema of Edwin Porter,' *Cinema Journal*, 19, no. 1 (Fall 1979), 1-38; Kemp R. Niver, *The First Twenty Years: A Segment of Film History* (Los Angeles: Artisan Press, 1968); Paul C. Spehr, 'Filmmaking at the American Mutoscope and Biograph Company,' *The Quarterly Journal of the Library of Congress*, 37, no. 3-4 (Summer-Fall 1980), 413-21.

14 Leonard Maltin, *The Art of the Cinematographer: A Survey and Interviews with Five Masters*, rev. ed. (New York: Dover Publications, 1978), p. 77.

15 'How the cinematographer works, and some of his difficulties,' *MPW*, 1, no. 11 (18 May 1907), 165.

16 Bitzer, *Billy Bitzer*, pp. 7-69; Smith, *Two Reels*, pp. 1-159; Balshofer and Miller, *One Reel a Week*;

'Manufacture of moving pictures is a science,' *The Show World* (6 July 1907), 17; W.W. Winters, 'Moving pictures in the making,' *NKL*, 1, no. 1 (January 1909), 25-6.

17 Oscar Brockett, *The Theatre: An Introduction* (New York: Holt, Rinehart & Winston, 1964), p. 279.

18 Besides Brockett, pp. 279-84, see Helen Krich Chinoy, 'The emergence of the director,' in *Directors on Directing*, ed. Toby Cole and Helen Krich Chinoy, rev. ed. (Indianapolis: Bobbs-Merrill Co., 1963), pp. 1-77; Marvin Felheim, *The Theater of Augustin Daly: An Account of the Late Nineteenth Century American Stage* (Cambridge, Mass.: Harvard University Press, 1956), p. 17; Oral Sumner Coad and Edwin Mims, Jr, *The American Stage* New Haven, Connecticut: Yale University Press, 1929), pp. 234-62. For an excellent description of the US theatrical mode of production a few years later (1916), see Arthur Edwin Krows, *Play Production in America* (New York: Henry Holt & Co., 1916), pp. 239-341.

19 'Manufacture of moving pictures is a science,' *The Show World* (6 July 1907); 17; Kalton C. Lahue, *Motion Picture Pioneer: The Selig Polyscope Company* (Cranbury, New Jersey: A.S. Barnes & Co., 1973), p. 14; *The 1933 Motion Picture Almanac* (New York: Quigley Publishing Co., 1933).

20 'How the cinematographer works, and some of his difficulties,' *MPW*, 1, no. 11 (18 May 1907), 165-6; 'How the cinematographer works and some of his difficulties,' *MPW*, 1, no. 14 (8 June 1907), 212-13; 'How the cinematographer works and some of his difficulties,' *MPW*, 1, no. 15 (15 June 1907), 230; 'How the cinematographer works,' *MPW*, 1, no. 19 (13 July 1907), 298, 300; 'How the cinematographer works,' *MPW*, 1, no. 34 (27 October 1907), 536-7; 'How the cinematographer works,' *MPW*, 1, no. 41 (14 December 1907), 660-3; 'How moving pictures are made,' *MPW*, 2, no. 20 (16 May 1908), 434-5.

21 Edward W. Townsend, 'Picture plays,' *Outlook*, 93 (27 November 1909), 704.

22 'How the cinematographer works,' *MPW*, 1, no. 41 (14 December 1907), 660-3; 'How moving pictures are made,' *MPW*, 2, no. 20 (16 May 1908), 434-5.

23* Peter F. Drucker in his study of the interconnections among a task, its tools, and a work organization notes that the introduction of certain tools may make a traditional organization of work untenable. Others see technologies as a method of reinforcing class divisions. Pat Walker argues that divisions of labor created through the introduction of new technology 1) can deprive a worker of the understanding of a production process, making it seem that mental labor is more valuable than manual; 2) can physically separate the workers; and 3) can fragment jobs into 'an arbitrary hierarchy of skill levels.' Generally, this seems to have been the case in the US film industry. See Peter F. Drucker, 'Work and tools,' in *Technology, Management & Society* (New York: Harper & Row, 1970), pp. 43-54; Pat Walker, ed., *Between Labor and Capital* (Boston: South End Press, 1979), p. xvi.

24 'Gregory is Fleming's aide,' *Reel Life*, 3, no. 21 (7 February 1914), 2; 'Studio and exchange notes,' *Reel Life*, 3, no. 5 (18 October 1913), 3.

25 Epes Winthrop Sargent, 'The photoplaywright,' *MPW*, 14, no. 11 (14 December 1912), 1075. On the division of labor also see: David Sherrill Hulfish, *Cyclopedia of Motion-Picture Work* (Chicago: American School of Correspondence, 1911), vol. 2, pp. 75-6.

26 Epes Winthrop Sargent, *The Technique of the Photoplay*, 2nd ed. (New York: The Moving Picture World, 1913), p. 8.

27 Gene Gauntier, 'Blazing the trail,' *Woman's Home Companion*, 55, no. 11 (November 1928), p. 181; Edward W. Townsend, 'Picture plays,' *Outlook*, 93 (27 November 1909), 706.

28 W.W. Winters, 'Moving pictures in the making,' *NKL*, 1, no. 1 (January 1909), 25-6.

29 'Spectator,' ' "Spectator's" comments,' *NYDM*, 66, no. 1718 (22 November 1911), 24; 'Spectator,' ' "Spectator's" comments,' *NYDM*, 68, no. 1757 (21 August 1912), 24.

Chapter 11 The director-unit system: management of multiple-unit companies after 1909

1 Eugene Dengler, 'Wonders of the Diamond-S Plant,' *Motography*, 6, no. 1 (July 1911), 7-19, rpt. in Kalton C. Lahue, *Motion Picture Pioneer: The Selig Polyscope Company* (Cranbury, New Jersey: A.S. Barnes & Co., 1973), p. 83.

2 'Advice to Hollywood,' *MPHerald*, 167, no. 8 (24 May 1947), 61.

3 'New schedule of Edison releases,' *EK*, 3, no. 7 (1 November 1910), 2; J. Berg Esenwein and Arthur Leeds, *Writing the Photoplay* (Springfield, Mass.: The Home Correspondence School, 1913), pp. 16-17; David Sherrill Hulfish, *Cyclopedia of Motion-Picture Work* (Chicago: American School of Correspondence, 1911), vol. 2, pp. 113-15.

4* At this point several women directors such as Lois Weber, Jeanne Macpherson, Alice Guy-Blaché, and Gene Gauntier had made films, but just as now, they were in the vast minority. George C. Pratt, *Spellbound in Darkness: A History of the Silent Film*, rev. ed. (Greenwich, Connecticut: New York Graphic Society, 1973), p. 83; Lahue, *Motion Picture Pioneer*, p. 13.

5 Anthony Slide, *Early American Cinema* (New York:

A.S. Barnes & Co., 1970), p. 53; Lahue, *Motion Picture Pioneer*, p. 13; Richard Dale Batman, 'The founding of the Hollywood motion picture industry,' *Journal of the West*, 10 (October 1971), 611.

6 'The Imp Company invades Cuba,' *MPW*, 8, no. 3 (21 January 1911), 146.

7 Ad, *MPNews*, 4, no. 6 (11 February 1911), 26; 'Our roving commissioner,' 'A chat with Mr. David Horsley,' *MPNews*, 5, no. 5 (3 February 1912), 19.

8 Slide, *Early American Cinema*, pp. 47-56; Batman, 'Founding,' 611; 'A dozen Lubin favorites,' *NYDM*, 67, no. 1728 (31 January 1912), 55; 'American plans in the West,' *MPW*, 8, no. 1 (7 January 1911), 31; Margaret I. MacDonald, 'Trip to New Rochelle to the Thanhouser Plant,' *MPNews*, 5, no. 3 (20 January 1912), 28-30; 'Roving commissioner,' 'A visit to the offices of the Powers Motion Picture Company', *MPNews*, 5, no. 12 (23 March 1912), 34.

9 Richard V. Spencer, 'Los Angeles as a producing center,' *MPW*, 8, no. 14 (8 April 1911), 768; 'Los Angeles the Mecca,' *NYDM*, 65, no. 1679 (22 February 1911), 29-30; Batman, 'Founding,' 611-22; the Los Angeles number of *MPW*, 25, no. 2 (10 July 1915); Robert Florey, *Filmland* (Paris: Editions de cinémagazine, 1923), pp. 31-42; W. Wallace Clendenin, 'Hollywood studios of the early years,' *IP*, 6, no. 1 (February 1934), 12-13; Clifford M. Zierer, 'Hollywood – world center of motion picture production,' in *The Motion Picture Industry*, ed. Gordon S. Watkins (Philadelphia: American Academy of Political and Social Science, 1947), pp. 12-17; Albert Marple, 'Making pictures in California,' *The Motion Picture Supplement*, 2, no. 2 (April 1916), 37-9, 73; Richard Alan Nelson, 'Movie mecca of the South: Jacksonville, Florida, as an early rival to Hollywood,' *Journal of Popular Film and Television*, 8, no. 3 (Fall 1980), 38-51.

10 'Four Vitagraph reels,' *MPW*, 8, no. 26 (1 July 1911), 1506; 'A glimpse behind the scenes,' *MPW*, 9, no. 5 (12 August 1911), 380; P.M. Powell, 'Doings in Los Angeles,' *MPW*, 15, no. 2 (11 January 1913), 142; 'Griffith surrounds himself with screen notables,' *Reel Life*, 3, no. 10 (22 November 1913), 1; 'Where the movies are made,' *Reel Life*, 6, no. 9 (15 May 1915), 22; Richard V. Spencer, 'Los Angeles notes,' *MPW*, 8, no. 13 (1 April 1911), 704; Fred F. Balshofer and Arthur C. Miller, *One Reel a Week* (Berkeley: University of California Press, 1967), p. 77; 'Great activity at Keystone Studios in Edendale, Los Angeles, California,' *Reel Life*, 3, no. 7 (1 November 1913), 3; 'Heard in studio and exchange,' *Reel Life*, 4, no. 4 (11 April 1914), 14; 'Three companies added to Keystone Organization,' *The Triangle*, 1, no. 21 (11 March 1916), 3; ' "More Keystones," says Sennett,' *MPW*, 27, no. 12 (18 March 1916), 1831.

11 Balshofer and Miller, *One Reel a Week*, p. 67; 'Amicus,' 'Artistic directions of the photoplay,' *MPW*, 10, no. 5 (4 November 1911), 369-70; 'Separate producers for drama and comedy,' *MPW*, 8, no. 14 (8 April 1911), 755-6; Louis Reeves Harrison, 'The reject manuscript,' *MPW*, 8, no. 13 (1 April 1911), 695.

12 H.O. Stechhan, 'Efficiency in studio management,' *Motography*, 14, no. 8 (21 August 1915), 353.

13 On the changing physical arrangement of factories in the United States for a comparison to the film industry, see Daniel Nelson, *Managers and Workers: Origins of the New Factory System in the United States 1880-1920* (Madison: The University of Wisconsin Press, 1975), pp. 11-33.

14 'The new Solax plant: A modern structure representing the last word in moving picture plant architecture,' *MPNews*, 6, no. 12 (21 September 1912), 10-11.

15 H.Z. Levine, 'Exchange Assets,' *MPW*, 17, no. 7 (16 August 1913), 734.

16 'Improved facilities at Triangle-Fine Arts,' *The Triangle*, 2, no. 8 (16 December 1916), 3; 'Motion picture colony under one roof,' *Scientific American*, 120, no. 25 (21 June 1919), 651; also see on the 1919 Fox studio, 'The Fox film building,' *Architecture and Building*, 52, no. 5 (May 1920), 53-4. 'New Horsley Plant completed,' *Reel Life*, 6, no. 10 (31 July 1915), 21; Marple, 'Making pictures in California,' 37-9, 73.

17 'S. Lubin's latest,' *NYDM*, 66, no. 1718 (22 November 1911), 25; 'Doin' things at Lubin's,' *MPW*, 10, no. 7 (18 November 1911), 545; Nelson, *Managers and Workers*, pp. 101-21.

18 'Los Angeles letter,' *MPW*, 25, no. 8 (21 August 1915), 1301.

19 S.M. Spedon, *How and Where Moving Pictures are made by The Vitagraph Company of America* (Brooklyn, New York: Vitagraph Company of America, [1912]), [p. 13]; 'Artisans of the motion picture film,' *Scientific American*, 115, no. 10 (2 September 1916), 210-11, 224-5; 'Los Angeles letter,' *MPW*, 25, no. 8 (21 August 1915), 1301; Carl Louis Gregory, 'Motion picture photography,' *MPW*, 25, no. 4 (24 July 1915), 654; 'New Inceville Studios represent millions,' *The Triangle*, 2, no. 6 (27 May 1916), 6; 'Thomas H. Ince in New York with big plans for the future,' *The Triangle*, 2, no. 5 (20 May 1916), 1; 'Ince talks of Culver City,' *MPW*, 28, no. 10 (3 June 1916), 1697; Frederick S. Mills, 'Film lighting as a fine art,' *Scientific American*, 124, no. 8 (19 February 1921), 148.

20 Spedon, *How and Where*, p. 13; Balshofer and Miller, *One Reel a Week*, p. 143.

21 Homer Croy, *How Motion Pictures Are Made* (New York: Harper & Bros, 1918), pp. 134, 200; H.H. Van Loan, 'How I Did It,' (Los Angeles: The Whittingham Press, 1922), pp. 148-54; 'Artisans of the motion picture films,' *Scientific American*, 115, no. 10 (2 September 1916), 225; James Hood MacFarland, 'Architectural problems in motion picture production,' *American Architect*, 118, no. 2326 (21 July 1920), 68-9; Jerome Lachenbruch, 'The photoplay architect,' *American Architecture*, 120, no. 2377 (28 September 1921), 221; Edward Carrick, 'Moving picture sets: a medium for the architect,' *Architectural Record*, 67, no. 5 (May 1930), 441.

22 'The ambiguous picture – some causes,' *MPW*, 8, no. 1 (7 January 1911), 4.

23 Clara F. Beranger, 'The photoplay – a new kind of drama,' *Harper's Weekly*, 56, no. 2907 (7 September 1912), 13; Eustace Hale Ball, *The Art of the Photoplay* (New York: Veritas Publishing Co., 1913), pp. 28, 38-9, 52-3; Ernest A. Dench, *Making the Movies* (New York: Macmillan, 1915), pp. 2-3; C.G. Winkopp, *How to Write a Photoplay* (New York: C.G. Winkopp, 1915), p. 9; Esenwein and Leeds, *Writing the Photoplay*, p. 200; Frances Agnew, *Motion Picture Acting* (New York: Reliance Newspaper Syndicate, 1913), p. 79; John B. Rathbun, 'Motion picture making and exhibiting,' *Motography*, 9, no. 11 (31 May 1913), 405-8. On inter-titles and crosscutting see: Epes Winthrop Sargent, 'Technique of the photoplay,' *MPW*, 9, no. 5 (12 August 1911), 363-4; Esenwein and Leeds, *Writing the Photoplay*, p. 180; Everett McNeil, 'Outline of how to write a photoplay,' *MPW*, 9, no. 1 (15 July 1911), 27; Epes Winthrop Sargent, *The Technique of the Photoplay*, 2nd ed. (New York: The Moving Picture World, 1913), p. 49; reviews from 1909 excerpted and reprinted in *Spellbound in Darkness*, ed. Pratt, pp. 59-60; Epes Winthrop Sargent, 'The technique of the photoplay,' *MPW*, 9, no. 7 (26 August 1911), 525; Epes Winthrop Sargent, 'The photoplaywright,' *MPW*, 18, no. 12 (20 December 1913), 1405.

24 Archer McMackin, 'How moving picture plays are written,' *NKL*, 2, no. 6 (December 1909), 172-3; Edward W. Townsend, 'Picture plays,' *Outlook*, 93 (27 November 1909), 704-6.

Chapter 12 The central producer system: centralized management after 1914

1 Douglas Gomery, 'The economics of U.S. film exhibition and practice,' *Ciné-Tracts*, no. 12 (Winter 1981), 36-40.

2 'Keith's Union Square – Vaudeville,' *NYDM* 33, no. 858 (8 June 1895), 10.

3 Joseph Medill Patterson, 'The nickelodeons: the poor man's elementary course in the drama,' *The*

Saturday Evening Post, 180, no. 21 (23 November 1907), 10-11, 38, rpt in *Spellbound in Darkness: A History of the Silent Film*, ed. George C. Pratt, rev. ed. (Greenwich, Conn.: New York Graphic Society, 1973), pp. 46, 48-52; Russell Merritt, 'Nickelodeon theaters 1905-1914: building an audience for the movies,' in *The American Film Industry*, ed. Tino Balio (Madison: University of Wisconsin Press, 1976), pp. 59-79; Douglas Gomery, Lectures, Seminar in Social and Economic Problems in American Film History (University of Wisconsin-Madison, Fall 1977); Robert C. Allen, 'Motion picture exhibition in Manhattan, 1906-1912: beyond the nickelodeon,' *Cinema Journal*, 18, no. 2 (Spring 1979), 2-15.

4   Allen, 'Motion picture exhibition,' 12; Patterson, 'The nickelodeons,' p. 48.

5   'Construction/decorations,' *MPW*, 8, no. 2 (14 January 1911), 82. Also see: 'A matter of evolution,' *NYDM*, 65, no. 1672 (4 January 1911), 3.

6   Robert Grau, 'The theatre of cinematography,' *MPW*, 8, no. 17 (29 April 1911), 936; 'Achievements of "Nineteen-Eleven,"' *MPW*, 11, no. 2 (13 January 1912), 106-7; 'Observations by our man about town,' *MPW*, 9, no. 6 (19 August 1911), 453.

7   Ad, *MPW*, 8, no. 4 (28 January 1911), 203; David Sherrill Hulfish, *Cyclopedia of Motion-Picture Work* (Chicago: American School of Correspondence, 1911), vol. 2, p. 171; Epes Winthrop Sargent, 'Buying a theater,' *MPW*, 11, no. 12 (23 March 1912), 1047; C.B. Crain, Jr, 'Choosing the location,' *MPW*, 21, no. 8 (22 August 1914), 1088-9; Richard V. Spencer, 'The "Liberty Theater," Los Angeles,' *MPW*, 8, no. 13 (1 April 1911), 701; 'Proper illumination of moving picture and other theaters,' *MPW*, 8, no. 4 (28 January 1911), 184; Frederick A. Taylor, *Moving Pictures: How They Are Made and Worked*, new ed. (Philadelphia: J.B. Lippincott Co., 1914), pp. 139-40; Clarence E. Sinn, 'Music for the picture,' *MPW*, 8, no. 8 (25 February 1911), 409; Harry Alan Potamkin, 'Music and the movies,' *Musical Quarterly*, 15, no. 2 (April 1929), 281-96; 'The voice with the picture,' *MPW*, 8, no. 13 (1 April 1911), 706; 'A screen suggestion,' *MPW*, 8, no. 14 (8 April 1911), 754; 'Checking room in moving picture houses,' *MPW*, 8, no. 23 (10 June 1911), 1312; 'Theater chair signalling,' *MPW*, 24, no. 13 (26 June 1915), 2104.

8   'About moving picture films,' *Complete Illustrated Catalog of Moving Picture Films, Stereopticons, Slides, Films* (Chicago: Kleine Optical Co., October 1904), pp. 30-1, rpt in *Spellbound in Darkness*, ed. Pratt, pp. 36-7.

9   W. Stephen Bush, 'Feature programs,' *MPW*, 14, no. 6 (9 November 1912), 529. Also see 'The Kinetogram,' *EK*, 3, no. 3 (1 September 1910), 2.

10   Exhibitors still had advertising problems, particularly the daily change. Samples of contemporary analyses are throughout the trade papers but see: L.F. Cook, 'Advertising the picture theater,' *NKL*, 3, no. 9 (1 May 1910), 331-2; John M. Bradlet, 'The open market,' *MPW*, 8, no. 7 (10 February 1911), 349-51; 'How he got them coming,' *MPW*, 8, no. 5 (4 February 1911), 252; 'The will o' the wisp,' *MPW*, 8, no. 23 (10 June 1911), 1294; Epes Winthrop Sargent, 'Advertising for exhibitors,' *MPW*, 9, no. 11 (23 September 1911), 876. These are symptomatic as well of how the discourse of the industry diffused particular economic and ideological/signifying practices.

11   Kevin Brownlow, *The Parade's Gone By* (New York: Alfred A. Knopf, 1968), p. 386. Brownlow gives background information on the theatrical presentation.

12   Ralph Cassady, Jr, 'Monopoly in motion picture production and distribution: 1908-1915,' *Southern California Law Review*, 32, no. 4 (Summer 1959), 375-6; Georges Sadoul, *Histoire de l'art du cinéma: Des origines a nos jours*, 3rd ed. (Paris: Flammarion, 1949), pp. 71-3; 'Noted dramatists to write moving picture plays,' *MPW*, 2, no. 13 (28 March 1908), 263; 'Motion picture play writing as an art,' *EK*, 1, no. 3 (1 September 1909), 12.

13   Pratt, *Spellbound in Darkness*, p. 86; 'Spectator,' '"Spectator's" comments,' *NYDM*, 65, no. 1676 (1 February 1911), 29; 'Higher ideals,' *MPW*, 8, no. 24 (17 June 1911), 1355.

14   'Facts and comments,' *MPW*, 9, no. 6 (19 August 1911), 436.

15   'Reviews of notable films,' and W. Stephen Bush, 'Standard fiction in films,' *MPW*, 9, no. 12 (30 September 1911), 954-6, 950-3; W. Stephen Bush, 'Do longer films make better show?' *MPW*, 10, no. 4 (28 October 1911), 275; 'Another step forward,' *MPW*, 9, no. 2 (22 July 1911), 102; 'Mabel Taliaferro on new years,' *NYDM*, 66, no. 1721 (13 December 1911), 29; 'Mildred Holland in pictures,' *MPW*, 10, no. 11 (16 December 1911), 881.

16   W. Stephen Bush, 'Do longer films make better show?' *MPW*, 10, no. 4 (28 October 1911), 275.

17   Brownlow, *The Parade's Gone By*, p. 386; Jeanne Allen, 'Copyright protection in theatre, vaudeville and early cinema,' *Screen,* 21, no. 2 (Summer 1980), 79-91.

18   K.S. Hover, 'The *Ben Hur* copyright case,' *NKL*, 2, no. 3 (September 1909), 82.

19   Gene Gauntier, 'Blazing the trail,' *Woman's Home Companion*, 55, no. 10 (October 1928), 186; K.S. Hover, 'The "Ben Hur" copyright case,' *NKL*, 2, no. 3 (September 1909), 81-2; 'Ben-Hur case finally decided,' *NYDM*, 66, no. 1718 (22 November 1911), 26; Epes W. Sargent, 'The Ben Hur Case,' *MPW*, 10,

no. 10 (9 December 1911), 793. This decision was reaffirmed in *Famous Players* v. *Selig Polyscope* (1913); see 'Famous Players film company wins legal battle,' *MPNews*, 7, no. 3 (18 January 1913), 17.

20 Epes W. Sargent, 'The Ben Hur case,' *MPW*, 10, no. 10 (9 December 1911), 793; William Lord Wright, 'William Lord Wright's page,' *MPNews*, 5, no. 2 (13 January 1912), 32.

21 Richard V. Spencer, 'Los Angeles notes,' *MPW*, 8, no. 11 (18 March 1911), 587; 'For those who worry o'er plots & plays,' *MPNews*, 6, no. 3 (20 July 1912), 20-1; 'Eclair Co. gets exclusive rights to O. Henry stories,' *MPNews*, 7, no. 4 (25 January 1913), 15; 'Lubin gets Klein plays,' *MPW*, 15, no. 6 (8 February 1913), 552; 'Adolph Zukor, the benefactor of posterity,' *MPNews* 7, no. 4 (25 January 1913), 14-15; 'Lasky gets Belasco plays,' *MPW*, 10, no. 10 (6 June 1914);'W. Stephen Bush, 'Belasco on motion pictures,' *MPW*, 20, no. 11 (13 June 1914), 1513.

22 William Lord Wright, 'For photoplay authors real and near,' *NYDM*, 75, no. 1934 (15 January 1916), 35; 'Woods buys *The Cheat*,' *Variety*, 42, no. 8 (21 April 1916), 3; Alfred A. Cohn, 'The author gets his,' *Photoplay*, 13 (February 1918), 79-80, 122.

23 William Lord Wright, 'For photoplay authors, real and near,' *NYDM*, 74, no. 1910 (28 July 1915), 30; Walter Prichard Eaton, 'The latest menace of the movies,' *The North American Review*, 212 (July 1920), 80-7.

24 'Spectator,' ' "Spectator's" comments,' *NYDM*, 65, no. 1676 (1 February 1911), 29; 'Three reel pictures a success,' *MPW*, 8, no. 12 (25 March 1911), 639; '*Romeo and Juliet* in two reels,' *MPW*, 9, no. 5 (12 August 1911), 380; 'Three reel subjects in one day,' *NYDM*, 66, no. 1708 (13 September 1911), 22; 'Spectator,' ' "Spectator's" comments,' *NYDM*, 66, no. 1709 (20 September 1911) 26; 'Bison-101 feature pictures,' *MPW*, 11, no. 4 (27 January 1912), 298; W. Stephen Bush, 'The feature of the single reel,' *MPW*, 16, no. 3 (19 April 1913), 256; 'Facts and comments,' *MPW*, 17, no. 5 (2 August 1913), 511; 'Facts and comments,' *MPW*, 19, no. 1 (3 January 1914), 22; W. Stephen Bush, 'Feature programs,' *MPW*, 14, no. 6 (9 November 1912), 529; John M. Bradlet, 'Exhibitors' meeting at Columbus, Ohio – national league proposed,' *MPW*, 8, no. 20 (20 May 1911), 1124.

25 Ad, '*Dante's Inferno*,' *MPW* 8, no. 27 (8 July 1911), 1594-5; 'Spectator,' ' "Spectator's" comments,' *NYDM*, 66, no. 1703 (9 August 1911), 20.

26 'A great triumph,' *MPW*, 9, no. 7 (26 August 1911), 530.

27 Epes Winthrop Sargent, 'The feature and the price,' *MPW*, 13, no. 5 (3 August 1912), 431; '*Enoch Arden*' and 'Lectures for superior plays,' *MPW*, 8, no. 24 (17 June 1911), 1358-9; '*The Battle Hymn of the Republic* – Vitagraph,' *MPW*, 8, no. 26 (1 July 1911), 1497; James S. McQuade '*The Coming of Columbus*,' *MPW*, (September 1912), rpt. in Kalton C. Lahue, *Motion Picture Pioneer: The Selig Polyscope Company* (Cranbury, New Jersey: A.S. Barnes & Co., 1973), pp. 124-7; James S. McQuade, 'The Belasco of motion picture presentations,' *MPW*, 10, no. 10 (9 December 1911), 796-8; James S. McQuade, 'A de luxe presentation of *Cinderella*,' *MPW*, 11, no. 4 (24 January 1912), 288.

28 'Will present big productions,' *MPW*, 11, no. 2 (13 January 1912), 109-10; 'Spectator,' ' "Spectator's" comments,' *NYDM*, 67, no. 1739 (17 April 1912), 24-5.

29 'Roving commissioner,' 'Great Northern Special Feature Film Co.,' *MPNews*, 5, no. 1 (6 January 1912), 13. Also see: J. Berg Esenwein and Arthur Leeds, *Writing the Photoplay* (Springfield, Mass.: The Home Correspondence School, 1913), p. 145; William Lord Wright, 'For those who worry o'er plots and plays,' *MPNews*, 8, nos. 12 and 13 (20 September 1913 and 27 September 1913), 16 and 22.

30 'Picture and stage realism,' *MPW*, 15, no. 5 (1 February 1913), 477.

31 Robert Grau, 'Is the two-dollar-a-seat picture theater in sight?' *MPW*, 9, no. 12 (30 September 1911), 959; 'The listener chatters,' *Reel Life*, 4, no. 3 (4 April 1914), 6; C.W. Carrison, 'Fortunes in the movies', *Photoplay*, 6, no. 5 (October 1914), 169; 'The listener chatters,' *Reel Life*, 4, no. 4 (11 April 1914), 6.

32 '*Birth of a Nation* closes New York run,' *MPW*, 27, no. 2 (8 January 1916), 250; 'Griffith engages theater,' *MPW*, 23, no. 8 (20 February 1915); Richard Dale Batman, 'The founding of the Hollywood motion picture industry,' *Journal of the West*, 10 (October 1971), 623; William Lord Wright, 'For photoplay authors, real and near,' *NYDM*, 74, no. 1908 (14 July 1915), 30; 'Long runs more general,' *MPW*, 26, no. 1 (2 October 1915), 114; 'Production values of certain film dramas,' *The Triangle*, 1, no. 1 (30 October 1915), 4.

33 Don D. Lescohier, 'Working conditions,' in *History of Labor in the United States*, ed. John R. Commons (1935; rpt, New York: Augustus M. Kelley, 1966), vol. 3, pp. 303-15. I am following Lescohier but also see Harry Braverman, *Labor and Monopoly Capital: The Degradation of Work in the Twentieth Century* (New York: Monthly Review Press, 1974), pp. 85-137; David F. Noble, *America by Design: Science, Technology, and the Rise of Corporate Capitalism* (New York: Alfred A. Knopf, 1977), pp. 82-3; Daniel Nelson, *Managers and Workers: Origins of the New Factory System in the United*

States 1880-1920 (Madison: University of Wisconsin Press, 1975), pp. 48-78. Richard Edwards has written an excellent account of the types of control over the worker, moving from simple control to technical and bureaucratic control. See his *Contested Terrain: The Transformation of the Workplace in the Twentieth Century* (New York: Basic Books, 1979).

34   Thomas Nixon Carver, 'The economic foundations: the condition of large-scale production,' in *Scientific Foundations of Business Administration*, ed. Henry Clayton Metcalf (New York: Williams & Wilkins Co., 1926), p. 73.

35   'Putting the move in the movies,' *Saturday Evening Post*, 188, no. 46 (13 May 1916), 14-15, 96-8, 100-1.

36* The term 'unit' has continued, however, to describe the production personnel assigned to any particular project. Thus, although in subsequent years the industry spoke of units, they were either temporary, one-film groupings or a holdover from the multiple-unit production system. In the 1940s, when the majors started moving into financing and supplying rental space for independent projects (see chapter 26), those groups were also called units.

37   'Universal issues a strong program,' *MPNews*, 5, no. 23 (8 June 1912), 20; 'H.O. Davis talks system,' *MPW*, 28, no. 7 (13 May 1916), 1142.

38   W.E. Wing, 'Tom Ince, of Inceville,' *NYDM*, 70, no. 1827 (24 December 1913), 34.

39   Janet Staiger, 'Dividing labor for production control: Thomas Ince and the rise of the studio system,' *Cinema Journal*, 18, no. 2 (Spring 1979), 16-25.

40   E.W.S., 'Changes in Lubinville,' *MPW*, 16, no. 8 (24 May 1913), 790; 'For those who worry o'er plots and plays,' *MPNews*, 7, no. 25 (21 June 1913), 16.

41   'Studio efficiency,' *MPW*, 17, no. 6 (9 August 1913), 624.

42   'Studio management,' *MPW*, 26, no. 6 (30A October 1915), 982; 'The higher efficiency,' *Cinema News*, 1, no. 1 (15 December 1916), 6; 'Here's efficiency for you,' *Motography*, 19, no. 15 (13 April 1918), 707.

43   'Jesse L. Lasky announces plans,' *NYDM*, 77, no. 2003 (12 May 1917), 22.

44   William S. Hart, *My Life East and West* (Boston: Houghton Mifflin, 1929), p. 211. Kevin Brownlow lists some of the famous teams in the silent period in *The Parade's Gone By*, p. 71.

45   Aitken Brothers Papers, 1909-39, Boxes 1-9: Scripts and Scenarios, TS and MS (Madison, Wisconsin: Wisconsin State Historical Society and Wisconsin Center for Film and Theater Research).

46   Peter Milne, *Motion Picture Directing* (New York: Falk, 1922), p. 136.

47   Brownlow, *The Parade's Gone By*, pp. 85-93, 282; on the theatrical work procedure of that period see: Arthur Edwin Krows, *Play Production in America*

(New York: Henry Holt & Co., 1916). Charles Chaplin also employed this scripting method until *The Great Dictator*; see Timothy J. Lyons, ed., 'Roland H. Totheroh interviewed: Chaplin films,' *Film Culture*, nos. 53-54-55 (Spring 1972), 238-46.

48   Milne, *Motion Picture Directing*, p. 76.

49   Besides Brownlow and Milne, see Karl Brown, *Adventures with D.W. Griffith*, ed. Kevin Brownlow (New York: Farrar, Straus & Giroux, 1973); C. Blythe Sherwood, 'The art director is accredited: the vision that makes *Dream Street* come true,' *Arts and Decoration*, 15 (May 1921), 36-7.

50   Milne, *Motion Picture Directing*, pp. 42-3, 52; Cecil B. DeMille, 'Building a photoplay,' in *The Story of the Films*, ed. Joseph P. Kennedy (Chicago: A.W. Shaw Co., 1927), pp. 123-50; Frances Taylor Patterson, *Scenario and Screen* (New York: Harcourt, Brace & Co., 1928), pp. 91-4; Bert Glennon, 'Cinematography and the talkies,' *AC*, 10, no. 11 (February 1930), 7, 45.

51   'Playing the end game,' *Time*, 30 July 1979, p. 84.

52   'Chaplin seeks to enjoin *Carmen*,' *MPW*, 28, no. 6 (6 May 1916), 949; 'Essanay vs. Chaplin,' *MPW*, 28, no. 10 (3 June 1916), 1704; 'No injunction for Chaplin,' *MPW*, 28, no. 11 (10 June 1916), 1897; 'Chaplin loses *Carmen* suit,' *MPW*, 29, no. 2 (8 July 1916), 236. On employer-employee law for the period, see: Louis D. Frohlich and Charles Schwartz, *The Law of Motion Pictures Including the Law of the Theater* (New York: Baker, Voorhis, & Co., 1918), pp. 26-7, 109, 169, 205-6.

53   Charles Higham, *Warner Brothers* (New York: Charles Scribner's Sons, 1975), p. 23.

54   Jon Tuska, *The Detective in Hollywood* (Garden City, New York: Doubleday & Co., 1978), pp. 296-7.

Chapter 13 The division and order of production: the subdivision of the work from the first years through the 1920s

1   'A Bird's-eye view of the Lasky studio at Hollywood, California,' *Photoplay*, 13, no. 6 (May 1918), 30-1; 'From forest to film,' *Photoplay*, 13, no. 5 (April 1918), 94.

2   Leonard Maltin, *The Art of the Cinematographer: A Survey and Interviews with Five Masters*, rev. ed. (New York: Dover Publications, 1978), p. 107.

3   For background on US advertising history, see Alex Groner, *The American Heritage History of American Business & Industry* (New York: American Heritage Publishing Co., 1972), pp. 255, 262.

4   'Giving the public what it wants,' *Motography*, 15, no. 3 (15 January 1916), 113-14; William W. Hodkinson, 'Stage stars must prove their worth,'

Motography, 15, no. 5 (29 January 1916), 235-6; 'New department installed,' *Motography*, 18, no. 2 (14 July 1917), 98; Jesse L. Lasky, 'Production problems,' in *The Story of the Films*, ed. Joseph P. Kennedy (Chicago: A.W. Shaw Co., 1927), p. 118; Howard T. Lewis, *The Motion Picture Industry* (New York: D. Van Nostrand Co., Inc., 1933), pp. 37-44, 87-9; Howard Thompson Lewis, *Cases on the Motion Picture Industry* (Harvard Business Reports, vol. 8) (New York: McGraw-Hill Book Co., 1930), pp. 132-7.

5   Cecil B. DeMille, 'Building a photoplay,' in *The Story of the Films*, ed. Kennedy, pp. 134-5; Lewis, *the Motion Picture Industry*, pp. 37-40.

6   Epes Winthrop Sargent, 'The photoplaywright,' *MPW*, 15, no. 1 (4 January 1913), 44; Frederick James Smith, 'The evolution of the motion picture, V: from the standpoint of the player,' *NYDM*, 69, no. 1800 (18 June 1913), 24-5; Eustace Hale Ball, *The Art of the Photoplay* (New York: Veritas Publishing Co., 1913), p. 26; William Lord Wright, *Photoplay Writing* (New York: Falk Publishing Co., 1922), pp. 171-3; George Landy, 'The mysterious assistant director,' *PTD*, 4, no. 6 (November 1922), 17-18, 42.

7   'Twentieth Century-Fox,' *Fortune*, 12 (December 1935), 85.

8   Price, Waterhouse & Co., *Memorandum on Moving Picture Accounts* (New York: Price, Waterhouse & Co., 1916), pp. 11-18.

9   Price, Waterhouse & Co., *Memorandum*, pp. 11-18; Anthony Slide, *Early American Cinema* (New York: A.S. Barnes & Co., 1970), p. 23; Frederick A. Talbot, *Moving Pictures: How They Are Made and Worked*, new ed. (Philadelphia: J.B. Lippincott Co., 1914), pp. 172-4; Kalton C. Lahue, *Motion Picture Pioneer: The Selig Polyscope Company* (Cranbury, New Jersey: A.S. Barnes & Co., 1973), pp. 128-9; Wright, *Photoplay Writing*, pp. 105-8; Walter B. Pitkin and William M. Marston, *The Art of Sound Pictures* (New York: D. Appleton & Co., 1930), pp. 274-9; Earl Theisen, 'Hollywood notebook,' *IP*, 7, no. 1 (February 1935), 10.

10   Cedric Gibbons, 'The art director,' in *Behind the Screen: How Films Are Made* (New York: Dodge Publishing Co., 1938), p. 47.

11   Homer Croy, *How Motion Pictures Are Made* (New York: Harper & Bros, 1918), pp. 148-50.

12   Epes Winthrop Sargent, 'The photoplaywright,' *MPW*, 14, no. 11 (14 December 1912), 1075; 'Studio gossip,' *NYDM*, 66, no. 1708 (13 September 1911), 23; 'A lady scenario editor,' *NYDM*, 67, no. 1726 (17 January 1912), 29; 'With the western producers,' *MPW*, 9 (19 August 1911), 449.

13   Epes Winthrop Sargent, 'The earmark on the film,' *MPW*, 9, no. 7 (26 August 1911), 521; Joseph Medill

Patterson, 'The nickelodeon, the poor man's elementary course in the drama,' *The Saturday Evening Post*, 180, no. 21 (23 November 1907), 10-11, 38, rpt. in *Spellbound in Darkness: A History of the Silent Film*, ed. George C. Pratt, rev. ed. (Greenwich, Conn.: New York Graphic Society, 1973), pp. 46, 48-52; Archer McMackin, 'How moving picture plays are written,' *NKL*, 2, no. 6 (December 1909), 171-3; 'Motion picture play writing as an art,' *EK*, 1, no. 3 (1 September 1909), 12; 'Giving credit where credit is due,' *MPW*, 6, no. 10 (12 March 1910), 370; R.V.S., 'Scenario construction,' *MPW*, 8, no. 6 (11 February 1911), 294; Eugene Dengler, 'Wonders of the Diamond-S Plant,' *Motography*, 6, no. 1 (July 1911), 7-19; Epes Winthrop Sargent, 'The photoplaywright,' *MPW*, 13, no. 11 (14 September 1912), 1073; Lawrence S. McCloskey, 'The professional writer and the photoplay,' *MPW*, 14, no. 4 (26 October 1912), 341; Epes Winthrop Sargent, 'The photoplaywright,' *MPW*, 14, no. 9 (30 November 1912), 874; Epes Winthrop Sargent, 'The photoplaywright,' *MPW*, 14, no. 10 (7 December 1912), 973. Even in the 'high' period of purchasing manuscripts from unknowns (1908-14), the usual acceptance rate was generally given as 1 per cent of submissions; see, for instance, Frederick James Smith, 'The evolution of the motion picture, IV: from the standpoint of the scenario editor,' *NYDM*, 69, no. 1798 (4 June 1913), 25, 32. On selling a script in the mid-1920s, see Laurence D'Orsay, 'Can I sell my scenario?' *The Writer's Monthly*, 28, no. 4 (October 1926), 301.

14   Frederick James Smith, 'The evolution of the motion picture, IV: from the standpoint of the scenario editor,' *NYDM*, 69, no. 1798 (4 June 1913), 25; 'The technical difficulties of scenario writing,' *Reel Life*, 3, no. 9 (15 November 1913), 3; 'Noted authors to write for Mutual,' *MPW*, 19, no. 1 (3 January 1914), 29; 'The listener chatters,' *Reel Life*, 4, no. 5 (18 April 1914), 6; Epes Winthrop Sargent, 'The photoplaywright,' *MPW*, 23, no. 4 (23 January 1915), 510.

15   S.M. Spedon, *How and Where Moving Pictures are made by The Vitagraph Company of America* (Brooklyn, New York: Vitagraph Company of America [1912]), [p. 20]; William E. Wing quoted in William Lord Wright, 'For photoplay authors, real and near,' *NYDM*, 74, no. 1908 (14 July 1915), 30.

16   Wright, *Photoplay Writing*, p. 219.

17   Clifford Howard, 'Author and talkies,' *Close Up*, 5, no. 3 (September 1929), 222-3; Wright, *Photoplay Writing*, p. 219; Clifford Howard, 'A Hollywood close-up,' *Close Up*, 2, no. 1 (January 1928), 12-22.

18   Backgrounds are in: *The 1933 Motion Picture Almanac* (New York: Quigley Publishing Co., 1933); 'The Personal Side of the Pictures,' *Reel Life*,

5, no. 12 (5 December 1914), 18.

19 Arthur Edwin Krows, 'Once more – consider the status of motion pictures,' *The Triangle*, 3, no. 3 (4 November 1916), 15; Joseph Henabery quoted in Kevin Brownlow, *The Parade's Gone By* (New York: Alfred A. Knopf, 1968), pp. 50-6; Lee Royal *The Romance of Motion Picture Production* (Los Angeles: Royal Publishing Co., 1920), p. 32; Melvin Riddle, 'From pen to silversheet,' *PTD*, 3, no. 8 (January 1922), 35-7; G. Harrison Wiley, 'Solving Your Photoplay Puzzles,' *PTD* 4, no. 9 (February 1923), 21-4.

20 Lewis S. Physioc, 'The scenic artist (the cameraman's new ally),' *IP*, 8, no. 2 (March 1936), 3, 22-3; David Sherrill Hulfish, *Cyclopedia of Motion-Picture Work* (Chicago: American School of Correspondence, 1911), vol. 2, p. 28.

21 'Freelance,' 'Seen on the curtain,' *MPW*, 8, no. 20 (20 May 1911), 1120-1. Specific background on contemporary theatrical sets is in Brander Matthews, *A Book about the Theater* (New York: Charles Scribner's Sons, 1916), pp. 127-40; Brooks McNamara, 'Scene design: 1876-1965: Ibsen, Chekhov, Strindberg,' *Drama Review*, 13, no. 2 (Winter 1968), 77-91; Elizabeth R. Hunt, 'Acting scenery,' *The Drama*, no. 8 (November 1912), 153-62; and histories of the theater in general.

22 Lucy Frances Pierce, 'The nickelodeon,' *NKL*, 1, no. 1 (January 1909), 7-10; Mabel Condon, 'What happens to the scenario,' *Motography*, 9, no. 5 (1 March 1913), 149, 151; Epes Winthrop Sargent, *The Technique of the Photoplay*, 2nd ed. (New York: Moving Picture World, 1913), p. 21; 'The technical director,' *Reel Life*, 4, no. 6 (25 April 1914), 26; Fred F. Balshofer and Arthur C. Miller, *One Reel A Week* (Berkeley: University of California Press, 1967), p. 130; 'Scene building for our Mutual girl,' *Reel Life*, 5, no. 1 (19 September 1914), 23.

23* Before coming to screen work, Brunton had been the technical director and property master for the Boston Opera Company and had designed for A.L. Erlanger, Alfred A. Aarons, and Florenz Ziegfeld. He did the scenery and stage effects for the 1914, 1915, and 1916 Follies. See *The 1933 Motion Picture Almanac*.

24 On 'new stagecraft' and lighting conventions which started in the US in 1911, see William Leigh Sowers, 'The progress of the new stagecraft in America,' *The Drama*, no. 28 (November 1917), 570-89; Arthur Pollock, 'Illumination and the drama,' *The Drama*, no. 13 (February 1914), 93-109; Francis Lamont Pierce, 'Youth, Art, and Mr. Belasco,' *The Drama*, no. 26 (May 1917), 176-91; Arthur Edwin Krows, *Play Production in America* (New York: Henry Holt & Co., 1916), p. 157; Oral Sumner Coad and Edwin Mims, Jr, *The American Stage* (New Haven, Conn.: Yale University Press, 1929), p. 337. 'Artisans of the motion picture films,' *Scientific American*, 115, no. 10 (2 September 1916), 224; Arthur Edwin Krows, 'Once more – consider the status of motion pictures,' *The Triangle*, 3, no. 3 (4 November 1916), 15; Edwin Jay Herts, 'The importance to the film of interior details,' *MPW*, 26, no. 5 (30 October 1915), 781; Alfred A. Cohn, 'The art director,' *Photoplay*, 10, no. 3 (August 1916), 43-6, 177; Kenneth MacGowan, 'As the movies mend,' *The Seven Arts*, 2 (September 1917), 665-7; *The 1933 Motion Picture Almanac*; J.C. Jessner, 'In and out of Los Angeles studios,' *MPNews*, 11, no. 24 (19 June 1915), 48. Also see: John Emerson and Anita Loos, *How to Write Photoplays* (1920; rpt, Philadelphia: George W. Jacobs & Co., 1923), p. 87; Austin Celestin Lescarboura, *Behind the Motion Picture Screen*, 2nd ed. (New York: Scientific American Publishing Co., 1921), pp. 116-20; G. Harrison Wiley, 'The dream factory,' *PTD*, 3, no. 4 (September 1921), 21-4; Melvin M. Riddle, 'From pen to silversheet,' *PTD*, 3, no. 8 (January 1922), 35-7; Jack Grant, 'Hollywood's art director,' *AC*, 22, no. 5 (May 1941), 219.

25 James Hood MacFarland, 'Architectural problems in motion picture production,' *American Architect*, 118, no. 2326 (21 July 1920), 67-8.

26 *Ibid.*, 65-6; 'The architecture of motion picture settings,' *American Architect*, 118, no. 2324 (7 July 1920), 1-5; *The 1933 Motion Picture Almanac*.

27 Jerome Lachenbruch, 'The photoplay architect,' *American Architect*, 120, no. 2377 (28 September 1921), 220.

28 Ball, *The Art of the Photoplay*, pp. 20-2; Croy, *How Motion Pictures Are Made*, pp. 120-1; Lescarboura, *Behind the Motion Picture Screen*, p. 32; Melvin M. Riddle, 'From pen to silversheet,' *PTD*, 3, no. 11 (April 1922), 25-6; Melvin M. Riddle, 'From pen to silversheet,' *PTD*, 4, no. 3 (August 1922), 9-10.

29 H.H. Van Loan, *'How I Did It,'* (Los Angeles: Whittingham Press, 1922), pp. 149-53; Clifford Howard, 'A Hollywood close-up,' *Close Up*, 2, no. 1 (January 1928), 21; Tim Onosko, 'Made in Hollywood, USA: a conversation with A. Arnold Gillespie,' *The Velvet Light Trap*, no. 18 (Spring 1978), 46-50.

30 Frances Agnew, *Motion Picture Acting* (New York: Reliance Newspaper Syndicate, 1913), p. 76; Sargent, *The Technique of the Photoplay*, p. 21; 'Making wardrobes for the movies,' *Reel Life*, 4, no. 2 (28 March 1914), iii.

31 'Los Angeles letter,' *MPW*, 25, no. 8 (21 August 1915), 1301; Slide, *Early American Cinema*, p. 70; Melvin M. Riddle, 'From pen to silversheet,' *PTD*, 3, no. 9 (February 1922), 29-30; Melvin M. Riddle, 'From pen to silversheet,' *PTD*, 3, no. 10 (March

1922), 31-2.

32 Joseph Henabery in Brownlow, *The Parade's Gone By*, p. 44; Agnew, *Motion Picture Acting*, pp. 49-51; Croy, *How Motion Pictures Are Made*, pp. 114-15; 'Casting efficiency,' *MPW*, 26, no. 11 (11 December 1915), 1985; Mary Pickford in *Cinema: A Practical Course in Cinema Acting* (London: Standard Art Book Co., [1919]), p. 29; Royal, *The Romance of Motion Picture Production*, pp. 30-4; Lescarboura, *Behind the Motion Picture Screen*, p. 32; Wright, *Photoplay Writing*, pp. 170-3; Melvin M. Riddle, 'From pen to silversheet,' *PTD*, 3, no. 12 (May 1922), 25-6; Edgar J. Kelly and Muro, *Acting for Pictures: How Its* [sic] *Done and How To Do It* (New Orleans: Coste & Frichter Publishing Co., 1916), p. 14; Inez and Helen Klumph, *Screen Acting: Its Requirements and Rewards* (New York: Falk Publishing Co., 1922), p. 165.

33 Murray Ross, *Stars and Strikes: Unionization of Hollywood* (New York: Columbia University Press, 1941), pp. 64-88; 'Academy discourages would-be celebrities,' *The Ohio Showman*, 8, no. 3 (24 February 1931), 1.

34 Melvin M. Riddle, 'From pen to silversheet,' *PTD*, 4, no. 1 (June 1922), 25-6; James Barker, 'Make-up for fast film,' *AC*, 12, no. 7 (November 1931), 11; Earl Theisen, 'The Max Factor make-up factory,' *IP*, 6, no. 6 (July 1934), 9. On make-up standards during the orthochromatic period, see: Agnew, *Motion Picture Acting*, pp. 77-8; William Lord Wright, 'William Lord Wright's page,' *MPNews*, 7, no. 2 (11 January 1913), 14; Frederick James Smith, 'The evolution of the motion picture, VII: from the standpoint of the photoplaywright,' *NYDM*, 70, no. 1805 (23 July 1913), 31; Catherine Carr, ed., *The Art of Photoplay Writing* (New York: Hannis Jordon Co., 1914), p. 46; Frank Westmore and Murial Davidson, *The Westmores of Hollywood* (New York: Berkeley Publishing Corporation, 1976), pp. 35, 402, 60-3.

35 Ball, *The Art of the Photoplay*, p. 22; John H. Rathbun, 'Motion picture making and exhibiting,' *Motography*, 9, no. 8 (19 April 1913), 275-8; 'The new Solax Plant,' *MPNews*, 6, no. 12 (21 September 1912), 10-11; Epes Winthrop Sargent, 'The photoplaywright,' *MPW*, 17, no. 8 (23 August 1913), 837; Karl Brown, *Adventures with D.W. Griffith*, ed. Kevin Brownlow (New York: Farrar, Straus & Giroux, 1973), p. 16; Maltin, *The Art of the Cinematographer*, p. 82.

36* Cinematographers have been much more traditional than their colleagues in the training of their craftspeople. Many started at the 'bottom,' working in the laboratories and moving up to assistants and finally head cameramen. Coming from a family of still photographers, Tony Gaudio first worked in Vitagraph's laboratory and in 1911 took charge of all the cameramen at IMP in Los Angeles. Besides Brown, Sidney Hickox, Jackson Rose, Gregg Toland, and many others also progressed through a semi-formal apprenticeship. The early formation in 1914 of cinematographers' clubs also indicates the same concern for craft tradition and training. See *The 1933 Motion Picture Almanac*.

37 Brown, *Adventures with D.W. Griffith*, pp. 14-18; Melvin M. Riddle, 'From pen to silversheet,' *PTD*, 4, no. 5 (October 1922), 9-10. Also see: Carl Louis Gregory, *Motion Picture Photography*, ed. Herbert C. McKay, 2nd ed. (New York: Falk Publishing Co., 1927), p. 25; William Luhr and Peter Lehman, ' "Would you mind just trying it?': an interview with special effects artist Linwood Dunn, ASC,' *Wide Angle*, 1, no. 1 (rev. ed.) (1979), 78-9.

38 Carl Louis Gregory, 'Motion picture photography,' *MPW*, 25, no. 8 (21 August 1915), 1315; H. Lyman Broening, 'The cinematographer's investment,' *AC*, 4, no. 7 (October 1923), 4; Gregory, *Motion Picture Photography*, p. 92.

39 'Special order no. 20,' 26 November 1924, Thomas Ince Papers (New York: Museum of Modern Art); George Landy, 'The mysterious assistant director,' *PTD*, 4, no. 6 (November 1922), 17-18, 42; C.H. Mitchell, *Assistant Director's Compendium* (Hollywood: Jesse L. Lasky Feature Play Company, April 1916).

40 Agnew, *Motion Picture Acting*, p. 79; John B. Rathbun, 'Motion picture making and exhibiting,' *Motography*, 9, no. 11 (31 May 1913), 407; J. Berg Esenwein and Arthur Leeds, *Writing the Photoplay* (Springfield, Mass.: Home Correspondence School, 1913), p. 200; Klumph and Klumph, *Screen Acting*, p. 175.

41 'How the cinematographer works,' *MPW*, 1, no. 19 (13 July 1907), 298, 300; Peter Milne, *Motion Picture Directing* (New York: Falk Publishing Co., 1922), pp. 162-3; 'Spoor adds orchestra,' *MPW*, 26, no. 5 (30 October 1915), 805; 'Music for Equitable players,' *MPW*, 27, no. 4 (22 January 1916), 605; Croy, *How Motion Pictures Are Made*, p. 130.

42 James E. McQuade, 'Making "Selig" Pictures,' *The Film Index*, 4, no. 47 (20 November 1909), 4-6, rpt in Lahue, *Motion Picture Pioneer*, p. 58; 'Spectator,' ' "Spectator's" comments,' *NYDM*, 65, no. 1681 (8 March 1911), 29; Croy, *How Motion Pictures Are Made*, pp. 110, 120.

43* Stars had been insured for the production period from at least mid-1914. Thomas Ince's studio bought a $25,000 policy on George Beban when 'Beban nearly lost his life under a street car, after falling from an automobile.' In October 1915 the New York Motion Picture Co. took out a policy on Ince's life for $250,000 which they announced 'marks a new epoch in the taking of precautionary measures against financial loss.' The beneficiary was the company. By 1925, 'freak insurance policies' also had publicity value. *Photoplay* listed some: Louise Fazenda had her $100,000 policy that her braids would not be hurt or cut; Cecille Evans was 'the first girl to have her legs insured' – for $100,000; Ramon Novarro was insured for $3,000,000 to protect the investment in *Ben Hur*; and Ben Turpin would collect $100,000 if his eyes went straight. 'In and out of Los Angeles studios,' *MPNews*, 10, no. 19 (14 November 1914), 35-7; 'Los Angeles film brevities,' *MPW*, 26, no. 4 (23 October 1915), 604; Croy, *How Motion Pictures Are Made*, p. 120; 'Some freak insurance policies,' *Photoplay*, 28, no. 6 (November 1925), 40-1.

44 'Manufacture of moving pictures is a science,' *The Show World* (6 July 1907), 17; Lescarboura, *Behind the Motion Picture Screen*, p. 28; Hulfish, *Cyclopedia of Motion-Picture Work*, vol. 2, pp. 106, 138 (Hulfish says that multiple cameras with different makes were also used to confuse Patents Company's detectives); Croy, *How Motion Pictures Are Made*, p. 126.

45 Alice Eyton, ' "Unknown" women of the films,' *The Story World and Photodramatist*, 4, no. 10 (April 1923), 38; L.C. MacBean, *Kinematograph Studio Technique* (London: Sir Isaac Pitman & Sons, 1922), p. 15; 'Long shot, medium shot and close-up,' *Photoplay*, 21, no. 3 (February 1922), 30; Klumph and Klumph, *Screen Acting*, p. 49; Frances Taylor Patterson, *Scenario and Screen* (New York: Harcourt Brace & Co., 1928), p. 94; Virgil E. Miller, *Splinters from Hollywood Tripods* (New York: Exposition, 1964), between pp. 62-3; Helen Starr, 'Putting it together,' *Photoplay*, 14, no. 2 (July 1918), 52-4; 'Following the magic camera on locations east and west,' *Photoplay*, 21, no. 5 (April 1922), 29.

46 Eugene Dengler, 'Wonders of the "Diamond-S" Plant,' *Motography*, 6, no. 1 (July 1911), 15; 'A glimpse behind the scene,' *MPW*, 9, no. 5 (12 August 1911), 380.

47 Ball, *The Art of the Photoplay*, pp. 26-8; Epes Winthrop Sargent, 'The photoplaywright,' *MPW*, 15, no. 1 (4 January 1913), 44; Epes Winthrop Sargent, 'The photoplaywright,' *MPW*, 17, no. 8 (23 August 1913), 837; 'The cutting of a moving picture,' *Reel Life*, 3, no. 26 (14 March 1914), vi; Maltin, *The Art of the Cinematographer*, p. 78; 'Ince's big picture completed,' *MPW*, 27, no. 10 (11 March 1916), 1638; Starr, 'Putting it together,' 52-3; Jack G. Leo, 'Greater scenario department,' *MPW*, 33, no. 3 (21 July 1917), 382; Royal, *Romance of Motion Picture Production*, p. 42; Emerson and Loos, *How To Write Photoplays*, pp. 38-9; Frances

Taylor Patterson, *Cinema Craftsmanship: A Book for Photoplaywrights* (New York: Harcourt Brace & Co., 1921), pp. 92-4; Wright, *Photoplay Writing*, pp. 73-4; Bradley King, 'More studio secrets,' *PTD*, 3, no. 12 (May 1922), 5-6; Melvin M. Riddle, 'From pen to silversheet,' *PTD*, 4, no. 7 (December 1922), 9-10.

48 Harry E. Aitken, 'Out of quantity – quality,' *MPW*, 21, no. 2 (11 July 1914), 211; 'Metro-Goldwyn-Mayer,' *Fortune*, 6 (December 1932), 51-8+, rpt in *The American Film Industry*, ed. Tino Balio (Madison, Wisconsin: University of Wisconsin Press, 1976), p. 258; also see for a case of extensive revisions after previews: Robert E. Sherwood, 'The phantom jinx,' *Photoplay Magazine*, 29, no. 2 (January 1926), 113, rpt in *Spellbound in Darkness*, ed. Pratt, pp. 394-6.

49 'Incidental music for Edison pictures,' *EK*, 1, no. 4 (15 September 1909), 12-13; Clarence E. Sinn, 'Music for the picture,' *MPW*, 8, no. 24 (17 June 1911), 1370; Clarence E. Sinn, 'Music for the picture,' *MPW*, 9, no. 2 (22 July 1911), 116; Max Winkler, 'The origin of film music,' *Films in Review*, 2, no. 10 (December 1951), 34-42; Carl Van Vechten, *Music and Bad Manners* (New York: A.A. Knopf, 1916), p. 53.

Part Three The formulation of the classical style, 1909-28

1 Robert Herring, 'Enthusiasm?,' *Close Up*, 9, no. 1 (March 1932): 23-4.

Chapter 14 From primitive to classical

1 André Gaudreault, 'Temporalité et narrative: le cinéma des premiers temps (1895-1908),' *Etudes littéraires*, 13, no. 1 (April 1980): 109.

2* William K. Everson includes a chapter on 'The birth of film grammar' in *American Silent Film* (New York: Oxford University Press, 1978), pp. 30-53; Kevin Brownlow has one on 'The experimenters' in *The Parade's Gone By* (New York: Alfred A. Knopf, 1968), pp. 21-8. Both of these authors maintain that Griffith was the prime mover in the introduction of cinematic techniques. Other authors dispute this view, but mainly with the purpose of calling attention to other, less famous directors. Barry Salt suggests Reginald Barker as 'the missing link' in the development of analytical editing in 'The early development of film form,' *Film Form*, 1, no.1 (Spring 1976): 102. There has been a move recently to bring forward other names from the oblivion into which most of the early teens' cinema has fallen, as in Richard Koszarski's anthology *The Rivals of D.W. Griffith* (Minneapolis: Walker Art Center, 1976). This re-assignment of credit, however, does little to alter the traditional view of the classical cinema as a teleological growth toward a natural film grammar waiting to be discovered.

3 Gaudreault, 'Temporalité et narrative,' p. 111.

4 For sample scripts of skits and other vaudeville forms, see Brett Page's *Writing for Vaudeville* (Springfield, Mass.: Home Correspondence School, 1915).

5 Eileen Bowser, 'The Brighton project: an introduction,' *Quarterly Review of Film Studies*, 4, no. 4 (Fall 1979): 523.

6 Robert C. Allen, *Vaudeville and Film 1895-1915: A Study in Media Interaction* (PhD dissertation, University of Iowa, 1977; rep. New York: Arno Press, 1980), p. 43; Douglas Gilbert, *American Vaudeville* (New York: Whittlesley House, 1940), p. 6.

7 Nicholas Vardac hardly leaves room for doubt that the film owes a great deal to the play, with his stills from a stage production juxtaposed to frames of the film. See figures 61 through 64 in his *Stage to Screen* (Cambridge, Mass.: Harvard University Press, 1949).

8 Allen, *Vaudeville and Film 1895-1915*, pp. 214-25.

9* The percentage of narratives in the total US output increased rapidly after 1902. In 1904, documentaries were barely holding their own; figures for copyrighted films of 1904 show these proportions of genres: documentaries, 42 per cent, comedies, 45 per cent, dramas, 8 per cent, and trick films 5 per cent. From 1906, the new institution of the nickelodeon increased the pressure on producers, leading to a decisive domination of the field by fiction films a few years later. In 1907, drama was up to 17 per cent of the total, with comedy at 50 per cent, and in 1908, drama increased to 66 per cent, with comedy trailing at 30 per cent. These figures are based upon copyrighted films only. (See *ibid.*, pp. 181, 212.)

Current work being done by Charles Musser seems to confirm the claim that fiction films became the dominant product of the industry before the nickelodeon era began in 1906. He has found evidence to suggest that in 1904 at least some fiction films sold in greater numbers of prints than did scenics and topicals from the same producer. See Charles Musser, 'The nickelodeon era begins: establishing the foundations for Hollywood's mode of representation,' *Framework*, nos. 22/23 (Autumn 1983): 11. Musser's extensive work in progress on the primitive period is tentatively entitled *The Emergence of Cinema in America: Edwin Porter*

and the Edison Manufacturing Company.

10 Allen, *Vaudeville and Film 1895-1915*, pp. 214-15.

11 Walter Prichard Eaton, 'Canned drama,' *American Magazine*, 68, no. 5 (September 1909): 494.

12 Gaudreault, 'Temporalité et narrative,' p. 113.

13* For examples of such narrative films, see Kemp Niver's description of the multiply copyrighted shots for *The Ex-Convict* (1904, Edison), *Rip* (1902, AM&B), and others, in *Motion Pictures from the Library of Congress Paper Print Collection 1894-1912* (Berkeley: University of California Press, 1967), pp. 182, 212, 164, 142-3. Documentaries handled in a similar way include the twenty views of the *Westinghouse Works* and *Westinghouse Air Brake Company* (1904, AM&B), which add up to a lengthy series, and the four different films of Kicking Horse Canyon, Canada (1901, Edison). In his forthcoming work on the primitive cinema, *The Emergence of Cinema in America*, Charles Musser deals with the production and exhibition of films made as series of separately released shots.

14* Film lengths increased slowly for several reasons. Producers had to build up a sufficient base to support more expensive films (and hence potentially to generate greater profits). Also, it appears that many exhibitors resisted longer films, believing that a greater variety of short films would draw more viewers. See *Complete Illustrated Catalog of Moving Picture Machines, Stereopticons, Slides, Films* (Chicago: Kleine Optical Co., 1905); rep. in George Pratt (ed.), *Spellbound in Darkness*, rev. ed. (Greenwich, Conn.: New York Graphic Society, 1973), p. 41.

15 Gaudreault finds additional examples from the primitive period in his 'Temporalité et narrative,' pp. 119-20.

16* For example, *Kid Canfield, Notorious Gambler* (1912, Champion) contains a scene in which Canfield goes into a side room of his gambling den and straps on what an inter-title identifies as a 'sleeve machine,' a mechanism for cheating at cards. Two non-diegetic shots follow, close shots illustrating the workings of the machine. The next shot returns us to the main room of the gambling den, with Canfield already back at the table and engaged in a game. The non-diegetic insert was a rare device for American filmmakers, but here audience understanding of the sleeve machine's workings is vital to the narrative, and the filmmakers settled upon a novel method of conveying information. I take this scene to be somewhat comparable to the earlier films' repeated actions – a solution to a problem, but one which did not prove widely acceptable within the guidelines of the Hollywood system.

17 Gaudreault, 'Temporalité et narrative,' p. 116. Emphasis in original.

18 'The Weakness of the strong,' *MPN*, 11, no. 1 (9 January 1915): 29.

19 Jack Poggi, *Theater in America: The Impact of Economic Forces 1870-1967* (New York: Cornell University Press, 1968), p. 26.

20* The touring theater company, the touring vaudeville act, and the film can all be seen as ways of distributing a theatrical entertainment to a far-flung mass audience. Poggi attributes the rise of the touring theater company in part to the expanding railroad system of the 1860s, which for the first time enabled groups to haul people and sets around the country efficiently. The invention of cinema created a similar change; like the railroads, the cinema made wide distribution of a standard product possible. Film did not begin to compete with theater immediately because, as we have seen, producers could not organize an entire production, distribution, and exhibition system all at once; they depended initially upon vaudeville, which began to decline in the teens as a result of film's competition. By this point, early film entrepreneurs – e.g., Marcus Loew, William Fox, Adolph Zukor – were building distribution and exhibition circuits which would eventually lead to the industry's vertical integration. These men were able to build up the industry because they took advantage of problems in the touring system of theater. Poggi sees the rise of features around 1912 as coinciding with 'the very time when production costs in the legitimate theater were becoming burdensome.' Between 1913 and 1928, the transportation costs alone rose 80 per cent for theatrical troupes. See *ibid.*, pp. 6, 78, 36.

21 C. Alphonso Smith, *The American Short Story* (Boston: Ginn & Co., 1912), p. 39; Fred Lewis Pattee, *The Development of the American Short Story* (New York: Harper & Bros, 1923), pp. 81, 130.

22 Pattee, *The Development of the American Short Story*, pp. 31, 70-5, 145, 150, 167, 191, 310.

23 Brander Matthews, 'The study of fiction,' [1898], in his *The Historical Novel and Other Essays* (New York: Charles Scribner's Sons, 1901), p. 81; for further discussion of the increasingly lucrative field of professional writing in the 1890s, see also Matthews, 'Literature as a profession,' pp. 203-4 in this same volume.

24 Bliss Perry, *A Study of Prose Fiction* (Boston/New York: Houghton, Mifflin & Co., 1902), p. 330; Pattee, *The Development of the American Short Story*, p. 337.

25 Perry, *A Study of Prose Fiction*, p. 65.

26 Charlton Andrews, *The Technique of Play Writing* (Springfield, Mass.: Home Correspondence School, 1915), p. 230.

27 At least one book-length guide appeared to dispense advice on writing playlets and other vaudeville forms: Page's *Writing for Vaudeville*.

28 Gilson Willets [Selig staff writer], 'Photoplay writing not an easy art,' *Motography*, 16, no. 14 (30 September 1916): 763.

29 Edward Azlant, 'The theory, history, and practice of screenwriting, 1897-1920' (PhD dissertation, University of Wisconsin, 1980).

30 Pattee, *The Development of the American Short Story*, p. 337.

31 Vardac's *Stage to Screen* remains the major study of nineteenth-century theater and early film. Concentration on film and the nineteenth-century novel has come more recently, stemming primarily from Colin MacCabe's 'Realism and the cinema: notes on some Brechtian theses,' *Screen*, 15, no. 2 (Summer 1974): 7-27. In *Film and the Narrative Tradition* (Norman: University of Oklahoma Press, 1974), John L. Fell relates early film to a variety of nineteenth-century narrative arts.

32 Besides his manuals on *The Photodrama* (Larchmont, New York: Stanhope-Dodge Publishing Co., 1914) and *The Feature Photoplay* (Springfield, Mass.: The Home Correspondence School, 1921), Henry Albert Phillips also authored *The Plot of the Short Story* and *Art in Short Story Narration* (both advertised in *The Photodrama* as publications of the Stanhope-Dodge Publishing Co.). J. Berg Esenwein was editor of the Home Correspondence School's 'Writer's Library.' In addition to co-authoring *Writing the Photoplay* (with Arthur Leeds [Springfield, Mass., 1913]), he contributed many works on short fiction to the series.

33 'Film stories change rapidly,' *Motography*, 18, no. 16 (20 December 1917): 813; Clifford Howard, 'The cinema in retrospect,' *Close Up*, 3, no. 5 (November 1928): 18; Azlant, *The Theory, History, and Practice of Screenwriting*.

34 'The need for more originality,' *Motography*, 13, no. 5 (30 January 1915): 167.

35 William A. Johnston, 'About stories,' *MPN*, 11, no. 21 (29 May 1915): 35. Emphases in original.

36 See also, 'The story writers' opportunity,' *Motography*, 14, no. 20 (13 November 1915): 1025; 'The weakness of the strong,' *MPN*, 11, no. 1 (9 January, 1915): 29, 48.

37 Pattee, *The Development of the American Short Story*, p. 364.

38 Clayton Hamilton, *A Manual of the Art of Fiction* (Garden City, New York: Doubleday, Page, & Co., 1918), p. 61.

39 Pattee, *The Development of the American Short Story*, p. 135; Pattee reprints Poe's review in full, pp. 134-7.

40 Brander Matthews, 'The philosophy of the short-story,' [1885], rep. in his *Pen and Ink* (New York: Charles Scribner's Sons, 1902), pp. 75-106.

41 J. Berg Esenwein and Mary Daroven Chambers, *The Art of Story-Writing* (Springfield, Mass.: Home Correspondence School, 1913), p. 107.

42 Quoted in Hamilton, *A Manual of the Art of Fiction*, p. 177.

43 Esenwein and Chambers, *The Art of Story-Writing*, p. 106; Phillips, *The Photodrama*, p. 134.

44 Hamilton, *A Manual of the Art of Fiction*, p. 186.

45 For a survey of the well-made play, see Stephen S. Stanton, 'Introduction,' *Camille and Other Plays* (New York: Hill & Wang, A Mermaid Dramabook, 1957), pp. vii-xxxix.

46 For examples, see Elizabeth Woodbridge, *The Drama: Its Laws and Its Techniques* (Boston/Chicago: Allyn & Bacon, 1898), p. 77; Alfred Hennequin, *The Art of Play Writing* (Boston/New York: Houghton, Mifflin & Co., 1897), p. 98; W.T. Price, *The Technique of the Drama* (New York: Brentano's, 1892), pp. 76-109. For the original formulation, see Gustav Freytag, *Freytag's Technique of the Drama*, trans. Elias J. MacEwan, 2nd ed. (Chicago: S.C. Griggs & Co., 1896), pp. 114-40.

47 Hennequin, *The Art of Play Writing*, p. 89. For similar discussions, see Price, *The Technique of the Drama*, p. 64, and Woodbridge, *The Drama*, p. 20.

48 William Archer, *Play-Making: A Manual of Craftsmanship* (Boston: Small, Maynard & Co., 1912), pp. 331, 214-15.

49 Andrews, *The Technique of Play Writing*, pp. 75-106.

50 See, for examples, Archer, *Play-Making*, p. 85; Andrews, *The Technique of Play Writing*, p. xi.

51 Archer, *Play-Making*, p. 191.

52 Andrews, *The Technique of Play Writing*, pp. 122-3.

53 Archer, *Play-Making*, pp. 201, 207.

54 Andrews, *The Technique of Play Writing*, pp. 122-3.

55 Archer, *Play-Making*, p. 177.

56 Esenwein and Chambers, *The Art of Story-Writing*, p. 108.

57 Perry, *A Study of Prose Fiction*, p. 309.

58 Matthews, 'The Study of Fiction,' p. 105.

59 Andrews, *The Technique of Play Writing*, p. 32.

60 Woodbridge, *The Drama*, p. 15.

61 Hennequin, *The Art of Play Writing*, p. 86.

62 Esenwein and Chambers, *The Art of Story-Writing*, p. 180.

63 Matthews, 'The study of fiction,' p. 94.

64 Brander Matthews, 'The art of the stage-manager,' in his *Inquiries and Opinions* (New York: Charles Scribner's Sons, 1907), pp. 301-2.

65 Esenwein and Chambers, *The Art of Story-Writing*, p. 166.

66 Archer, *Play-Making*, p. 113.

Chapter 15 The formulation of the classical narrative

1   David S. Hulfish, *The Motion Picture, Its Making and Its Theater* (Chicago: Electricity Magazine Corporation, 1909), p. 55.

2* Throughout the silent period, the prevalent term for what we would today call the 'shot,' was 'scene.' This arose from the fact that most scenes were only one shot long in early films. Even when scenes began to be broken up regularly into several shots, 'scene' kept its initial meaning. Surprisingly, there seems to have been no word during this period to designate the extended dramatic unit we term a 'scene' or 'sequence.' Scenarios labelled shots 'Scene 1' and so on, with perhaps a gap between shot descriptions to indicate a major change of action.

3   John Nelson, *The Photo-play* (Los Angeles: Photoplay Publishing Co., 1913), p. 167.

4   Eileen Bowser, 'The Brighton Project: an introduction,' *Quarterly Review of Film Studies*, 4, no. 4 (Fall 1979): p. 520.

5   'How to write a scenario,' *Photoplay*, 2, no. 2 (March 1912): 71.

6   Herbert Case Hoagland, *How to Write a Photoplay* (New York: Magazine Maker Publishing Co., 1912), p. 6.

7   Peter Milne, 'The Regeneration,' *MPN*, 12, no. 13 (2 October 1915): 83.

8   Quoted in William Lord Wright, 'For those who worry o'er plots and plays,' *MPN*, 8, no. 13 (27 September 1913): 22.

9   Frederick Palmer, *Palmer Plan Handbook*, rev. ed. (Los Angeles: Palmer Institute of Authorship, 1921), p. 27.

10 Louis Reeves Harrison, 'Characterization,' *MPW*, 8, no. 17 (29 April 1911): 937. Emphasis in original.

11 James Kirkwood, 'Motion picture stories scarce,' *Motography*, 16, no. 2 (8 July 1916): 80.

12 Henry Albert Phillips, *The Photodrama* (Larchmont, New York: Stanhope-Dodge Publishing Co., 1914), pp. 75-6.

13* A 'split-reel' is a short (500 feet) film, spliced together with and rented with another split-reel to make up a standard, 1,000-foot length. These were usually minor films – often comedies, animated films, or newsreels. The fact that classical devices appear in split-reels is one of the best indications that the new guidelines were being standardized throughout the industry – not just in the most expensive, outstanding films.

14 Jesse L. Lasky, 'Production problems,' in Joseph P. Kennedy, ed., *The Story of the Films* (Chicago: A.W. Shaw Co., 1927), p. 121.

15 Eustace Hale Ball, *The Art of the Photoplay*, 2nd ed. (New York: G.W. Dillingham Co., 1913), p. 50.

16   Palmer, *Palmer Plan Handbook*, p. 38.

17   Nelson, *The Photo-play*, p. 167.

18*   The contemporary term was not 'inter-title.' During the early teens, writers called inserted titles 'leaders' or 'sub-titles' (the latter because the credits were the main titles). By the mid-teens, 'leader' had largely been dropped in favor of 'sub-title,' which persisted through the silent period.

19   Kemp Niver, *The First Twenty Years* (Los Angeles: Artisan Press, 1968), pp. 34, 80, 91, 98, 101.

20   Epes Winthrop Sargent, 'Technique of the photoplay,' *MPW*, 9, no. 5 (12 August 1911): 363.

21   Robert Saunders Dowst, 'Technicalities of scenario writing,' *Motography*, 7, no. 1 (January 1912): 16.

22*   The four dialogue titles in *A Tale of Two Cities* (1911, Vitagraph) all come where spoken, and the same is true of the single dialogue title in *A Daughter of Dixie* (1911, Champion). On the other hand, the following films use one to four dialogue titles, all placed before the shot where spoken: *The Dynamiters* (1911, Imp), *A Friendly Marriage* (1911, Vitagraph), *In Old Madrid* (Thomas H. Ince, 1911, Imp), and *The Loafer* (1911, Essanay).

23*   In *The Bells* (1913, Edison), two of the three titles are placed where spoken; in *A Comedy of Errors* (1912, Solax), the titles divide two and two in placement; in *The House of Discord* (James Kirkwood, 1912, Biograph), five of the six dialogue titles precede the shots in which the lines occur.

24*   Barry Salt has suggested that the placement of dialogue titles at the point in the scene where they are spoken was minority practice around 1911 to 1913, adding, 'It is doubtful that the principle had yet been realized.' (See Barry Salt, 'The early development of film form,' *Film Form*, 1, no. 1 [Spring 1976]: 99.) Yet, as we have seen, both placements were in equal use, and contemporary accounts demonstrate that commentators were aware of the difference.

Salt's claims tend to perpetuate the notion that the early teens was a relatively crude period, with filmmakers groping toward the discovery of a preordained film grammar. In general, Salt's admirable attempts to outline the usage of various techniques in the early American cinema are limited by a neglect of evidence from written sources. Although one can learn much from the films – as Salt does – certain aspects of contemporary awareness of style can emerge only from documents.

25   Sargent, 'Technique of the Photoplay,' p. 363.

26   Quoted in William Lord Wright, 'For those who worry o'er plots and plays,' *MPN*, 6, no. 26 (28 December 1912): 12.

27   Nelson, *The Photo-play*, p. 181. Emphasis in original.

28   'The Reviewer,' 'Views of the Reviewer,' *NYDM*, 68, no. 1752 (17 July 1912): 27.

29   Phillips, *The Photodrama*, p. 53.

30   Marc Edmund Jones, 'Why my photoplays do not sell,' *Photoplay*, 4, no. 3 (August 1913): 8.

31   George Blaisdell, 'Adolf Zukor talks of Famous Players,' *MPW*, 15, no. 2 (11 January 1913): 136.

32   Genevieve Harris, 'The Aryan,' *Motography*, 15, no. 14 (1 April 1916): 766.

33   Arthur Edwin Krows, 'Once more – consider the status of motion pictures,' *The Triangle*, 3, no. 3 (4 November 1916): 13.

34   Robert Emmett Welsh, *A-B-C of Motion Pictures* (New York: Harper & Bros., 1916), p. 100.

35   'Unique captions in *Road o' Strife*,' *Motography*, 13, no. 13 (27 March 1915): 470.

36*   William C. deMille's *The Bedroom Window* (1924, Famous Players-Lasky) has one or two expository titles in nine of its eleven sequences, none in the other two. It uses an average of ten dialogue titles per sequence. *Peter Pan* (Herbert Brenon, 1924, Famous Players-Lasky) goes further, with only seven expository titles spread over its nine scenes (with none in five scenes), yet 277 dialogue titles. Relatively small numbers of expository titles are used in such films as: *Are Parents People?* (Malcolm St Clair, 1925, Famous Players-Lasky), *The Goose Woman* (Clarence Brown, 1925, Universal-Jewel), *Lady Windermere's Fan* (Ernst Lubitsch, 1925, Warner Bros), *Ella Cinders* (Alfred E. Green, 1926, John McCormick Productions), *La Boheme* (King Vidor, 1926, MGM), *Exit Smiling* (Sam Taylor, 1926, MGM), *A Gentleman of Paris* (Henry d'Abbadie D'Arrast, 1927, Paramount Famous Lasky), and *Hula* (Victor Fleming, 1927, Paramount Famous Lasky). These are mostly fairly prestigious films by major directors, but the practice filtered down to some of the more standard films as well, as is evident in *Footloose Widows*, a Louise Fazenda comedy (Roy del Ruth, 1926, Warner Bros), which has only nine expository intertitles among a total of 184.

37   Nelson, *The Photo-play*, p. 177.

38   Epes Winthrop Sargent, 'Technique of the photoplay,' *MPW*, 9, no. 5 (12 August 1911): 364.

39   See, for examples, William Lord Wright, 'For those who worry o'er plots and plays,' *MPN*, 6, no. 16 (19 October 1912): 16; Nelson, *The Photo-play*, p. 178; and Phillips, *The Photodrama*, p. 56.

40   Victorin Jasset, 'Le cinéma contemporain,' *Ciné journal* (October-November 1911), quoted in Jean Mitry, *Histoire du cinéma* Vol. 1 (Paris: Editions universitaires, 1967), p. 413.

41   Quoted in Kevin Brownlow, *The Parade's Gone By* (New York: Alfred A. Knopf, 1968), p. 16.

42   Robert E. Welsh, 'David W. Griffith speaks,' *NYDM*, 71, no. 1830 (14 January 1914): 49, 54, rep. in Pratt, *Spellbound in Darkness*, pp. 110-11.
43   'Temptations of a great city,' *MPW*, 8, no. 24 (17 June 1911): 1367.
44   Epes Winthrop Sargent, 'Technique of the photoplay,' *MPW*, 9, no. 4 (4 August 1911): 281.
45   'Too near the camera,' *MPW*, 8, no. 12 (25 March 1911): 633.
46   H.F. Hoffman, 'Cutting off the feet,' *MPW*, 12, no. 1 (6 April 1912): 53.
47* Even this can only be inferred from the film's title and opening, although Eileen Bowser suggests there may have been an insert of the ad itself at the beginning, missing from existing prints. Bowser, 'The Brighton project: an introduction,' p. 523.
48   Henry King, 'Too much action,' *Cinema News* (March 1918): 9.

Chapter 16 The continuity system

1   Epes Winthrop Sargent, 'The photoplaywright,' *MPW*, 23, no. 7 (13 February 1915): 977.
2   Herbert Case Hoagland, *How to Write a Photoplay* (New York: Magazine Maker Publishing Co., 1912), p. 12. Emphasis in original.
3   H. Kent Webster, 'Little stories of great films,' *The Nickelodeon*, 3, no. 1 (1 January 1910): 13.
4   'How to write a scenario,' *Photoplay*, 2, no. 2 (March 1912): 71; John Nelson, *The Photo-play* (Los Angeles: Photoplay Publishing Co., 1913), p. 78; Henry Albert Phillips, *The Photodrama* (Larchmont, New York: Stanhope-Dodge Publishing Co., 1914), p. 52; Capt Leslie T. Peacocke, 'Logical continuity,' *Photoplay*, 11, no. 5 (April 1917): 111.
5   Epes Winthrop Sargent, 'The photoplaywright,' *MPW*, 18, no. 12 (20 December 1913): 1405.
6   S.S. Hutchinson, 'From the master producer's standpoint,' *Motography*, 14, no. 1 (3 July 1915): 5.
7   Thomas H. Ince, 'Ince makes war on inconsistency,' *Motography*, 19, no. 8 (23 February 1918): 361.
8   Pierre V.R. Key, 'Continuity is important factor,' *Motography*, 18, no. 20 (17 November 1917): 1034.
9   Phillips, *The Photodrama*, p. 49.
10   For discussions of this non-linear pattern, see Noël Burch, 'Porter, or ambivalence,' *Screen*, 19, no. 4 (Winter 1978/79): 91-105, and Charles Musser, 'The early cinema of Edwin S. Porter,' *Cinema Journal*, 19, no. 1 (Fall 1979): 1-38.
11   Epes Winthrop Sargent, 'The photoplaywright,' *MPW*, 20, no. 1 (4 April 1914): 56.
12   'Hellfire and brimstone,' *Camera!*, 1, no. 19 (18 August 1918): 7.
13* Throughout the teens, the term 'long shot' was the principal one used to designate the overall view of the set. Mae Marsh's 1920 *Screen Acting* guide defines the long view's function: 'The long shot is usually taken to establish the atmosphere and setting of a scene.' A 1922 guidebook glossary defined 'establish' as: 'To make known the relationship of a character to other characters or to his environment, or to make known his identity and type.' This is essentially the meaning the term has had ever since. This usage appears in reviews as well; one writer criticized *The Perfect Sap* in 1926: 'There is one entire sequence played entirely in close-ups. It is an interior scene, played in a room, but the room is not established. There are four characters in it, but at no time is their relation to one another shown. It is just a succession of faces.' These uses of the term 'establishing' confirm that filmmakers and critics were aware of this specific function of the long shot, but such awareness preceded the term itself. See Mae Marsh, *Screen Acting* (New York: Frederick A. Stokes Co., 1921), p. 91; *Opportunities in the Motion Picture Industry* (Los Angeles: Photoplay Research Society, 1922), p. 110; Welford Beaton, 'This one killed by poor direction,' *The Film Spectator*, 3, no. 4 (16 April 1927): 9.
14   Phillips, *The Photodrama*, p. 54.
15* Eileen Bowser claims that the display of facial expression 'remains the most common use of close views for the whole period 1900-1906.' ('The Brighton project: an introduction,' *Quarterly Review of Film Studies*, 4, no. 4 (Fall 1979): 518.)
16   Barry Salt, 'Film form 1900-06,' *Sight and Sound*, 47, no. 3 (Summer 1978): 150.
17   Cecil B. De Mille, 'What psychology has done to pictures,' in Ruth Wing, ed., *The Blue Book of the Screen* (Hollywood: The Blue Book of the Screen, Inc., 1923), p. 380.
18   Phillips, *The Photodrama*, p. 60; Peacocke, 'Logical continuity,' p. 112.
19   Frederick Palmer, *Palmer Plan Handbook*, rev. ed. (Los Angeles: Palmer Institute of Authorship, 1921), pp. 101, 100.
20   Epes Winthrop Sargent, 'The photoplaywright,' *MPW*, 23, no. 4 (23 January 1915): 510.
21   Frank Atkinson, 'Pause before you become a film cutter,' in Laurence A. Hughes (ed.), *The Truth about the Movies by the Stars* (Hollywood: Hollywood Publishers, 1924), p. 343.
22* Historians have argued persuasively that the chase film originated in England with such films as *Fire!* and *Stop Thief* (both J.H. Williamson, 1901 and 1900) – see particularly Barry Salt, 'Film form 1900-06,' p. 149. Certainly the popular import, *Rescued by Rover* (Cecil Hepworth, 1905) keeps

perfect screen direction, with the dog moving always out from the rear to exit foreground left as it goes to the gypsy's lair. Rover then goes in exactly the opposite direction as he returns home.

23   Nicholas A. Vardac, *Stage to Screen* (Cambridge, Mass.: Harvard University Press, 1949), p. 32.

24   'Spectator' [Frank Woods], 'Spectator's Comments,' *NYDM*, 65, no. 1681 (8 March 1911): 29. Emphasis in original.

25   Interview with Charles G. Clarke, conducted by David Bordwell and Kristin Thompson, 12 June and 3 July 1980, in Hollywood, California.

26   Nelson, *The Photo-play*, p. 219, emphasis in original; John B. Rathbun, 'Motion picture making and exhibiting,' *Motography*, 9, no. 13 (28 June 1913): 472.

27   John H. Rathbun, 'Motion picture making and exhibiting,' *Motography*, 9, no. 8 (19 April 1913): 278.

28   Interview with Charles G. Clarke.

29   Quoted in Leonard Maltin, *The Art of the Cinematographer* (New York: Dover Publications, 1978), pp. 79-80.

30   Helen Starr, 'Putting it together,' *Photoplay*, 14, no. 2 (July 1918): 54.

31*   William Hornbeck has confirmed that Starr was right in claiming that editors sometimes turned the negative over to correct for errors:

> Yes. You would have to be careful about hair-combs and be sure that there wasn't a design on one arm that wasn't on the other. You had to be very careful. But often, if there was no identification to show that everything was lefthanded instead of righthanded, that was done a lot.

Interview with William Hornbeck, conducted by David Bordwell and Kristin Thompson, 9 July 1980, Ventura, California.

32   *Ibid.*

33   Starr, 'Putting it together,' pp. 53-4.

34   Peacocke, 'Logical continuity,' p. 112.

35   Barry Salt, 'The early development of film form,' *Film Form*, 1, no. 1 (Spring 1976): 98.

36*   Noël Burch has claimed that the SRS lagged behind other guidelines within the continuity system of editing. At one point he states that 'the system thus constituted as a visual entity had become fully operational in the United States before the end of World War I,' with the exception of the 'full head-on reverse-angle' (his term for what I have been calling the shot/reverse shot); see Noël Burch, 'Film's institutional mode of representation and the Soviet response,' *October*, no. 11 (Winter 1979): 83. Elsewhere he specifies further how he considers the

development of the SRS to have proceeded: 'from alternating views of characters facing one another in profile shots, to head-on views of them facing each other "through" the camera spectator.' More importantly, Burch claims that the reason the SRS eyelines did not obey screen-direction guidelines was that such guidelines did not yet exist. The move into the story space involving analytical editing and the SRS pattern was, he says, fraught 'with moments of contradiction, one of the most significant, perhaps, being the period (around 1915) when the possibility of face-to-face opposing shots had begun to appear, but not yet the concept of the eyeline match.' Burch cites no examples from the period. See Noël Burch, *Correction Please, Or How We Got Into Pictures* (Arts Council of Great Britain, n.d.), p. 8.

Doubtless there are many SRSs from the teens that mismatch eyeline direction, but most do not. As we have seen, the directional eyeline match existed as minority practice from at least 1910, and certainly by 1915, SRSs would usually obey the 180° rule. If Burch were correct in his claim that the principle of the eyeline match was not known by 1915, the scene from *Detective Burton's Triumph* described in the text would have been impossible. I have found no films from the silent period in which SRS patterns consistently involve characters looking into the camera; there may be some such films, but head-on SRS would certainly be exceptional. In general Burch's claims about this period are hampered by a lack of evidence, both from the films and from contemporary sources. For an analysis of his historical work on American film, see David Bordwell's and my 'Linearity, materialism, and the study of the early American cinema,' *Wide Angle*, 5, no. 3 (1983): 4-15.

37   According to the recently discovered shot order of the original negative; see Eileen Bowser, 'Addendum to "The reconstitution of *A Corner in Wheat*,"' *Cinema Journal*, 19, no. 1 (Fall 1979): 101-2.

38   Phillips, *The Photodrama*, p. 140.

39   Leroy Stone, 'The importance of film editing,' *AC*, 3, no. 12 (March 1923): 4.

40   'Hellfire and brimstone,' *Camera!*, 1, no. 20 (18 August 1918): 7.

41   'A film satire,' *Photoplay*, 14, no. 1 (June 1918): 61.

42   Del Andrews, 'The film editor: his training and qualifications,' in *Opportunities in the Motion Picture Industry* (Los Angeles: Photoplay Research Society, 1922), p. 77.

43   Milton Sills, 'The actor's part,' in Joseph P. Kennedy, *The Story of the Films* (Chicago: A.W. Shaw Co., 1927), pp. 184-5.

Chapter 17 Classical narrative space and the spectator's attention

1   John B. Rathbun, 'Motion picture making and exhibition,' *Motography*, 9, no. 13 (28 June 1913): 471.

2   Untitled, *MPW*, 8, no. 15 (15 April 1911): 815. Recall that this journal published several articles opposing framings that showed anything less than full figures.

3   'The Reviewer,' 'Views of the Reviewer,' *NYDM*, 68, no. 1761 (18 September 1912): 24.

4   Mae Marsh, *Screen Acting* (New York: Frederick A. Stokes Co., 1921), p. 92.

5   Frederick A. Talbot confirms that 'A photográph at a distance of twelve feet presented people of normal height.' See his *Moving Pictures: How They Are Made and Worked*, new ed. (London: William Heinemann, 1914), p. 201.

6   David S. Hulfish, *The Motion Picture: Its Making and Its Theater* (Chicago: Electricity Magazine Corporation, 1909), p. 36.

7   For descriptions and a diagram of a vaudeville stage's areas, see Brett Page, *Writing For Vaudeville* (Springfield, Mass.: Home Correspondence School, 1915), pp. 27-31.

8   Arthur Edwin Krows, *Equipment for Stage Production* (New York: D. Appleton & Co., 1928), p. 31.

9   C.H. Claudy, 'Pictorial possibilities in moving-pictures,' *Photo-era*, 22, no. 4 (April 1909): 173; 'Spectator' [Frank Woods], 'Spectator's comments,' *NYDM*, 66, no. 1723 (27 December 1911): 28; 'The Scarlet Letter (Imp),' *MPW*, 8, no. 16 (22 April 1911): 881-2.

10* The practice of shooting into a corner rather than perpendicularly toward a backdrop may have moved cinema away from vaudeville, but comparable things were going on in the popular theater of the period. In 1916, Arthur Edwin Krows wrote of the 'now-familiar "V-shape" – that is, the walls of the room being slanted backward to meet each other, so as apparently to show just a corner of the interior.' See Arthur Edwin Krows, *Play Production in America* (New York: Henry Holt & Co., 1916), p. 174. This did not mean that film and theater devices were identical in effect, however, since the theater spectator could never have a sense of the side walls extending out to surround him or her. But by cutting in and placing the camera close to a section of the playing space, the filmmaker could create that sense.

11* Again, attempts to suggest space beyond the walls of the set parallel similar tendencies in the theater. Stage settings used backing flats to suggest adjacent rooms and exteriors beyond doors and windows; the cyclorama for representing sky and other atmospheric effects was becoming common usage. Several contemporary critics and historians made much of the production of Clyde Fitch's *The City* (1909) for its use of space beyond the back wall. A door in the main room opened onto a hallway and staircase; when one central character exited through this door, his subsequent collapse and death were conveyed entirely through sound and glimpses of neighbors hurrying past in the hall. See Clayton Hamilton, *Studies in Stagecraft* (New York: Henry Holt & Co., 1914), pp. 20-1; Krows, *Play Production in America*, p. 174.

12   Marc Edmund Jones, 'Why my scenarios do not sell,' *Photoplay*, 4, no. 3 (August 1913): 91; John Nelson, *The Photo-play* (Los Angeles: Photoplay Publishing Co., 1913), p. 79.

13   Marc Edmund Jones, 'The photoplay forum,' *Photoplay*, 4, no. 4 (September 1913): 108.

14   'Six-room "set,"' *Motography*, 16, no. 14 (30 September 1916): 752; 'Artisans of the motion picture films,' *Scientific American*, 115, no. 10 (2 September 1916): 225.

15   Hugo Ballin, 'The scenic background,' *The Mentor*, 9, no. 4 (1 July 1921): 22. Emphasis in original.

16   Max Parker. 'The art director – his duties and qualifications,' *Opportunities in the Motion Picture Industry* (Los Angeles: Photoplay Research Society, 1922), p. 58.

17   'Artisans of the motion picture films,' p. 225.

18   For an interesting account of one disastrous attempt to shoot on location – the 1926 *Ben Hur* production – see Kevin Brownlow, *The Parade's Gone By* (New York: Alfred A. Knopf, 1968), Ch. 36.

19* The size and hence the great depth of some of these sets were economically feasible in part because some of them could be used more than once. These were the standing sets, kept on the back lot for use over a stretch of time. For example, the Ford Theater set from *The Birth of a Nation* also appears in *The Regeneration* (Raoul Walsh, 1915, Fox); similarly, the same kitchen set shows up in at least two Charles Ray films, *His Mother's Boy* and *The Hired Hand* (both Victor Schertzinger, 1917 and 1918, Ince; this set is visible in fig 16-25 through 16-28). In the late twenties, Paramount had a standing set representing half of a full-sized ocean liner; this set figures in such Paramount films as *The Docks of New York* (Joseph Von Sternberg, 1928, Paramount), but could be rented out to other studios. It also served as a storehouse. See Chapter 13 for a discussion of the advantages of standing sets for studio economy.

But most sets were built for one film only. According to Thomas Brierley, the Christie Film Company's technical director:

Sets are seldom used over and over. Practical studio managers and technical men have found that it is in the long run more economical to 'strike' a set after it is finished and build the new one all over again, than to dismantle and go to the trouble and expense of storing.

A great number of standing sets would be uneconomical because it is financially advantageous to a company to keep as much of its physical plant continually busy as possible. A set which occupied space but was used only at wide intervals would waste money. Hence standing sets were only of the type likely to be used frequently, such as restaurants, theaters, and western streets. See Jan and Cora Gordon, *Star-Dust in Hollywood* (London: George G. Harrap and Co., 1930), p. 92. This page has a sketch of the ship set. Thomas Brierley, 'The construction of settings,' in Laurence A. Hughes (ed.), *The Truth about the Movies by the Stars* (Hollywood: Hollywood Publishers, 1924), p. 321.

20 'A big set required,' *Motography*, 10, no. 4 (23 August 1913): 140.

21 Harold Grieve, 'Background stuff,' *The Motion Picture Director*, 3, no. 3 (November-December 1926): 28.

22 Wilfred Buckland, 'The art director,' in Hughes (ed.), *The Truth about the Movies by the Stars*, p. 320.

23 C.H. Claudy, 'The degradation of the motion-picture,' *Photo-era*, 21, no. 4 (October 1908): 163-4.

24 'Some recent films reviewed: criticism by the fans,' *The Nickelodeon*, 3, no. 4 (15 February 1910): 96.

25 Frederick Talbot, *Practical Cinematography and Its Applications* (Philadelphia: Lippincott, 1913), p. 47; *How to Take and Make Moving Pictures* (Denver: Ford's [An equipment-manufacturing firm]), p. 25.

26 'Too near the camera,' *MPW*, 8, no. 12 (25 March 1911): 633.

27 H.M. Lomas, *Picture Play Photography* (London: Ganes, 1914), p. 26.

28 For excellent illustrations of glass shots, see Brownlow, *The Parade's Gone By*, p. 218, and William K. Everson, *American Silent Film* (New York: Oxford University Press, 1978), pp. 246-7.

29 Dr Alfred B. Hitchins, 'A method of using miniatures or models for the introduction of extra detail in motion pictures,' *TSMPE*, no. 15 (9-12 October 1922): 41.

30* Patrick Ogle's article, 'Technological and aesthetic influences upon the development of deep focus cinematography in the United States,' *Screen Reader* (London: SEFT, 1977), pp. 81-108, is an important examination of the subject in relation to the silent period, but it has perpetuated this notion about early deep focus. Ogle's data on the silent period are sketchy, and he draws incorrect conclusions several times from his facts. Ignoring the pre-1915 period altogether, he implies that cinematography from *The Birth of a Nation* to the soft-focus period (which Ogle dates as beginning in the late twenties) may have had a tendency to use more depth of field because of the contrastiness of orthochromatic film stock in comparison with panchromatic. He notes the introduction of panchromatic stock in 1913, but dismisses it as having not 'proved popular' (p. 85). He assumes that the simple fact of the invention of panchromatic stock meant cinematographers immediately had a choice of using it, but preferred ortho for its familiarity and contrastiness. Yet, as we shall see in greater detail in Chapter 21, early panchro was hardly the desirable alternative to ortho that it later became. It was far slower, more expensive, and highly unstable physically; during the silent period, deep focus was indeed easier to achieve with ortho, more because of ortho's speed than its supposed contrastiness.

31 'On light effects,' reprinted from *MPW* in *Cinema News*, 2, no. 11/12 (November-December 1918): 12.

32 Kenneth MacGowan, 'On the screen,' *The New Republic*, 12, no. 150 (15 September 1917): 188.

33 Advertisement, *Reel Life* (6 January 1917): 11.

34 L.G. Harkness Smith, 'Electric lighting for motion-picture studios,' *Electrical World*, 65, no. 17 (24 April 1915): 1040.

35 'Lasky praises *The Cheat*,' *Motography*, 14, no. 24 (11 December 1915): 1223.

36 W. Stephen Bush, 'Analyzing a winner,' *MPW*, 17, no. 3 (15 January 1916): 432.

37 Edwin Thanhouser, 'The great development in lighting,' *Cinema News*, 1, no. 5 (15 February 1917): 12.

38 Frederick S. Mills, 'Film lighting as a fine art,' *Scientific American*, 124, no. 8 (19 February 1921): 148.

39 Wiard B. Ihnen and D.W. Atwater, 'The artistic utilization of light in the photography of motion pictures,' *TSMPE*, no. 21 (18-21 May 1925): 30.

40 Norbert F. Brodin, 'Something about the cameraman,' in Hughes (ed.), *The Truth about the Movies by the Stars*, pp. 327-8.

41 Jon Gartenberg, 'Camera movements in Edison and Biograph films, 1900-1906,' *Cinema Journal*, 19, no. 2 (Spring 1980): 1-16.

42 Henry Albert Phillips, *The Photodrama* (New York: Stanhope-Dodge Publishing Co., 1914), p. 104.

43 Billy Bitzer, '*Intolerance*: the sun play of the ages,' *IP*, 7, no. 9 (October 1934): 24.

44 Will M. Ritchey, 'Tricks of the trade,' *Motography*, 16, no. 10 (2 September 1916): 542.

45* These include producer Fred Balshofer in making

The Second in Command (1915, Quality Pictures) and Allan Dwan for *David Harum* (1915, Famous Players). Hal Mohr claims to have used a platform on tracks in 1914 for a film called *The Daughter of the Gods* (not the Herbert Brenon film *A Daughter of the Gods*, done in 1916). By 1918, one historian discussed the moving platform with inflated tires as a common device for filming large sets. See Fred J. Balshofer and Arthur Miller, *One Reel a Week* (Berkeley/Los Angeles: University of California Press, 1967), p. 118; Peter Bogdanovich, *Allan Dwan: The Last Pioneer* (New York: Praeger, 1971), p. 34; Leonard Maltin, *The Art of the Cinematographer* (New York: Dover Publications, 1978), p. 78; Homer Croy, *How Motion Pictures Are Made* (New York: Harper & Bros, 1918), pp. 130-2.

46 Frederick Palmer, *Palmer Plan Handbook*, rev. ed. (Los Angeles: Palmer Institute of Authorship, 1921), p. 162.

47 Brownlow, *The Parade's Gone By*, p. 232.

Chapter 18 The stability of the classical approach after 1917

1 Henry Albert Phillips, *The Feature Photoplay* (Springfield, Mass.: Home Correspondence School, 1921), p. 11.

2 Madeleine Matzen, 'The high price continuity writer,' *The Film Spectator*, 5, no. 9 (23 June 1928): 26. Note that Matzen refers precisely to the pre-1917 period here.

3 'Laemmle explains "diploma system" for his directors and cameramen,' *MPW*, 43, no. 7 (14 February 1920): 1104.

4 Karl Brown, *Adventures With D.W. Griffith* (New York: Farrar, Straus & Giroux, 1973); Kevin Brownlow, *The Parade's Gone By* (New York: Alfred A. Knopf, 1968), p. 202.

5 Brownlow, *The Parade's Gone By*, pp. 286 and 308; Interview with William Hornbeck, conducted by David Bordwell and Kristin Thompson, 9 July 1980, Ventura, California; Clarence C. Badger, 'Reminiscences of the early days of movie comedies,' in Marshall Deutelbaum (ed.), *'Image' on the Art and Evolution of the Film* (New York: Dover Publications, 1979), p. 96.

6 King Vidor, *A Tree is a Tree* (New York: Harcourt, Brace & Co., 1953), p. 28; Elaine Sterne, 'Writing for the movies as a profession,' *Photoplay*, 6, no. 5 (October 1914): 156.

7 Capt. Leslie T. Peacocke, 'Logical continuity,' *Photoplay*, 11, no. 5 (April 1917: 114.

8 Interview with Charles G. Clarke, conducted by David Bordwell and Kristin Thompson, 12 June and 3 July 1980, in Hollywood, California; Untitled, *AC*, 3, no. 3 (1 June 1922): 12.

9 Quoted in Leonard Malton, *The Art of the Cinematographer* (New York: Dover Publications, 1978), p. 64; interview with Charles G. Clarke.

10 Peter Milne, *Motion Picture Directing* (New York: Falk Publishing Co., 1922), p. 21.

11 Austin C. Lescarboura, *Behind the Motion-Picture Screen* (London: Hutchinson & Co., 1920), p. 406.

12 Lewis W. Physioc, 'Twenty-five years of motion pictures,' *Cinema News*, 1, no. 16 (1 November 1917): 12, 16.

13 Harold Lloyd, 'The hardships of fun making,' *Ladies Home Journal* (May 1926), rep. in Richard Koszarski (ed.), *Hollywood Directors 1914-1940* (New York: Oxford University Press, 1976), p. 132.

14 Alfred A. Cohn, 'The art director,' *Photoplay*, 10, no. 3 (August 1916): 46.

15 Pierre V.R. Key [scenario writer and ad and sales manager, Hoffman-Foursquare Pictures], 'Continuity is important factor,' *Motography*, 18, no. 20 (17 November 1917): 1033; Helen Starr, 'Putting it together,' *Photoplay*, 14, no. 2 (July 1918): 52.

16 Lescarboura, *Behind the Motion-Picture Screen*, pp. 408, 410.

17 Jan and Cora Gordon, *Star-Dust in Hollywood* (London: Harrap & Co., 1931), pp. 105-6. This book was not written by Hollywood practitioners, but by a British couple, one an artist, the other a writer, who gained entry to the Paramount studio through their friendship with a writer employed there. They had access to the departments, and, being new to filmmaking, they evidently described all its stages as explained to them by the studio staff. The result is an unusually explicit presentation of classical production methods (as this quotation indicates).

Chapter 19 Technology, style, and mode of production

1 Otto Durholz, 'Durholz describes his novel lens,' *IP*, 6, no. 3 (April 1932): 10.

2 E.G. Lutz, *The Motion-Picture Cameraman* (New York: Charles Scribner's Sons, 1927; rep. New York: Arno, 1972), p. 125.

3 David F. Noble, *America By Design* (New York: Knopf, 1977), pp. 5-6. See also J.D. Bernal, *Science and Industry in the Nineteenth Century* (Bloomington: Indiana University Press, 1970), pp. 153-60, and Thomas C. Cochrane and William Miller, *The Age of Enterprise* (New York: Harper & Bros, 1961), p. 306.

4 J. Douglas Gomery, 'The coming of the talkies: invention, innovation, and diffusion,' in *The American Film Industry*, ed. Tino Balio (Madison: University of Wisconsin Press, 1976), pp. 193-211.

5 Lorin D. Grignon, 'Experiment in stereophonic sound,' *JSMPE*, 61, no. 3 (September 1953): 375.

6 ' "Realife" in *Billy the Kid* new departure in pictures,' *The Ohio Showman*, 7, no. 7 (23 September 1930): 10.

7 William Stull, 'Seventy millimetres,' *AC*, 10, no. 11 (February 1930): 43.

8 Joseph Valentine, 'Make-up and set painting aid new film,' *AC*, 20, no. 2 (February 1939): 54.

9 'Report of the studio lighting committee,' *JSMPE*, 30, no. 3 (March 1938): 295.

10 David S. Hulfish, 'Some questions answered,' *The Nickelodeon*, 1, no. 6 (June 1909): 156; David S. Hulfish, *The Motion Picture: Its Making and Its Theater* (Chicago: Electricity Magazine Corporation, 1909), pp. 118-22; Tim Onosko, '1953: the new era: a brief history of the three-dimensional film,' *The Velvet Light Trap*, no. 11 (1974): 12-16; 'Germans make gains,' *AC*, 18, no. 9 (September 1937): 377; V. Solyev, 'Soviets working in new stereoscopic pictures,' *AC*, 18, no. 12 (December 1937): 502, 504-5, 524.

11 J.A. Norling, 'Stereoscopic motion pictures,' *AC*, 33, no. 2 (February 1952): 66, 78-80. See also Arthur Gavin, 'All Hollywood studios shooting 3-D films,' *AC*, 34, no. 3 (March 1953): 108-10, 134-6; Charles G. Clarke, 'Practical filming techniques for three-dimensional and wide-screen motion pictures,' *AC*, 34, no. 3 (March 1953): 107, 128-9, 138.

12 'Is 3-D dead?' *AC*, 34, no. 12 (December 1953): 585-6, 608-12.

13 Marguerite G. Ortman, *Fiction and the Screen* (Boston: Marshall Jones Co., 1935), p. 82; 'Directors of stage in exodus to coast,' *The Ohio Showman*, 3, no. 16 (24 November 1928): 3; Murray Ross, *Stars and Strikes: Unionization of Hollywood* (New York: Columbia University Press, 1941), p. 30.

14 C.J. North and N.D. Golden, 'Meeting sound film competition,' *JSMPE*, 15, no. 6 (December 1931): 757-8.

15 'Two directors,' *The Ohio Showman*, 4, no. 18 (15 June 1929): 5; Howard T. Lewis, *The Motion Picture Industry* (New York: D. Van Nostrand Co., 1933), p. 45; MPPDA, 'The motion picture industry,' in *The Development of American Industries*, ed. John George Glover and William Bouck Cornell (New York: Prentice-Hall, 1932), p. 754; Margaret Booth, 'The cutter,' in *Behind the Screen: How Films Are Made*, ed. Stephen Watts (New York: Dodge Publishing Co., 1938), p. 149.

16 Verna Arvey, 'Present day musical films and how they are made possible,' *Etude*, 49 (January 1931): 16-17; Max Winkler, 'The origin of film music,' *Films in Review*, 2, no. 10 (December 1951): 42.

17 Walter Blanchard, 'Aces of the camera XXIX: Sol Polito, A.S.C.,' *AC*, 24, no. 6 (June 1943): 212; Bert Glennon, 'Cinematography and the talkies,' *AC*, 10, no. 11 (February 1930): 7, 45; Charles Higham, *Hollywood Cameramen* (Bloomington: Indiana University Press, 1970), p. 40; 'How lighting units are developed today,' *AC*, 18, no. 5 (May 1937): 189.

18 Carl Dreher, 'Sound personnel and organization,' in *Recording Sound for Motion Pictures*, ed. Lester Cowan (New York: McGraw-Hill, 1931), p. 340.

19 *Ibid.*, pp. 340-54.

20 *Ibid.*

21 André Bazin, *What Is Cinema?*, tr. and ed. Hugh Gray (Berkeley: University of California Press, 1967), pp. 17-40.

22 V.F. Perkins, *Film as Film* (New York: Penguin, 1972), p. 56.

23 J.-L. Comolli, 'Technique et idéologie,' *Cahiers du cinéma*, no. 229 (May 1971): 4-5. See also Dugald Williamson, 'Technique and ideology,' *Australian Journal of Screen Theory*, nos 5-6 (1978): 67-81.

24 Leonard Meyer, *Music, the Arts, and Ideas* (Chicago: University of Chicago Press, 1967), p. 99.

25 *Ibid.*, p. 128.

26 On the importance of functional concepts in the history of art, see Yuri Tynianov, 'On literary evolution,' *Russian Poetics in Translation*, no. 4 (1977): 32.

27 Yuri Tynianov and Roman Jakobson, 'Problems of research in literature and language,' *Russian Poetics in Translation*, no. 4 (1977): 50.

28 Comolli, 'Technique et idéologie,' pp. 12-15.

29 Perkins, *Film as Film*, p. 49.

30 *Ibid.*, p. 48.

31 Norman O. Dawn, 'Innovations in cinematography,' *The American Film Institute/Louis B. Mayer Oral History Collection* (Glen Rock, New Jersey: Microfilming Corporation of America, 1977), p. 187.

32 Comolli, 'Technique et idéologie,' pp. 4-15.

33 Raymond Williams, *Problems in Materialism and Culture* (London: New Left Books, 1980), p. 38.

34 Jean-Paul Sartre, *Search for a Method*, tr. Hazel E. Barnes (New York: Vintage, 1963), p. 45.

35 See Erik Olin Wright, *Class, Crisis, and the State* (London: New Left Books, 1978), p. 23.

36 Farciot Edouart, 'The Paramount transparency process projection equipment,' in *Technique of Motion Picture Production*, ed. SMPE (New York: Interscience, 1944), pp. 104-9.

37 See H.G. Stechnan, 'Efficiency in studio management,' *Motography*, 14, no. 8 (21 August 1915): 353; 'Motion picture colony under one roof,' *Scientific American*, 120, no. 25 (21 June 1919): 651; 'The Fox film building,' *Architecture and Building*, 52, no. 5 (May 1920): 53-4; James G. Stewart, 'The evolution of cinematic sound: a personal report,' in *Sound and the Cinema: The Coming of Sound to American Film*, ed. Evan William Cameron (Pleasantville,

New York: Redgrave, 1980), p. 42; William Stull, 'Twentieth Century-Fox holds preview for its big camera,' *AC*, 21, no. 9 (September 1940): 396-8; Arthur Edeson, 'Utility features new light crane,' *AC*, 15, no. 1 (May 1934): 10. The most active studio-based research departments were at MGM, where John Arnold and Douglas Shearer won fame for their technical innovations. See 'Industry news,' *AC*, 37, no. 9 (September 1956): 514; 'Color, recording gains cited in SMPE progress report,' *IPro*, 11, no. 1 (July 1936): 14, 22-6; 'First pix with all sound aids,' *IP*, 9, no. 3 (April 1937): 14.

38   Reese V. Jenkins, *Images and Enterprise: Technology and the American Photographic Industry, 1839 to 1925* (Baltimore: Johns Hopkins University Press, 1975), pp. 147, 179-80, 277-9, 302-11. See also C.E.K. Mees, *From Dry Plates to Ektachrome* (New York: Ziff-Davis, 1961), pp. 43-58.

39   C.E.K. Mees, *The Organization of Industrial Scientific Research* (New York: McGraw-Hill, 1920), pp. 2-10.

40   Quoted in Jenkins, *Images*, p. 310.

41   See George A. Blair, 'The development of the motion picture raw film industry,' *Annals of the American Academy of Political and Social Science*, 128, no. 217 (November 1926): 50-1; Emery Huse, 'Sensitometry,' *Cinematographic Annual*, 1 (1930), p. 115; Gordon Chambers and Ian D. Wratten, 'The Eastman Type IIb Sensitometer as a control instrument in the processing of motion picture film,' *JSMPE*, 21, no. 3 (September 1933): 218-23.

42   On Du Pont, see Noble, *America by Design*, pp. 115-17; George R. Rocher, 'Motion picture film,' *AC*, 8, no. 9 (December 1927): 4. On Western Electric, see Noble, *America by Design*, pp. 114-15. On National Carbon Company, see 'National Carbon's new labs,' *IPro*, 31, no. 12 (December 1956): 21. On Bausch and Lomb, see Earl Theisen, 'Science steps into optics,' *IP*, 8, no. 7 (August 1936): 10, 26-7; W.B. Rayton, 'New lenses for projecting motion pictures,' *JSMPE*, 35, no. 1 (July 1940): 89-97; 'Bausch and Lomb new Cinephor f:2 lens series,' *IPro*, 15, no. 5 (May 1940): 24. On RCA, see Robert C. Bitting, 'Creating an Industry,' *JSMPE*, 74, no. 11 (November 1965): 1015-17.

43   Donald Bell, 'A letter from Donald Bell,' *IP*, 2, no. 1 (February 1930): 18-20; Donald Bell, 'Motion picture film perforation,' *TSMPE*, no. 2 (1916): 8-10; Earl Theisen, 'The story of Bell and Howell,' *IP*, 5, no. 9 (October 1933): 6-7, 24-5; '40 Years for Bell and Howell,' *AC*, 28, no. 12 (December 1947): 434-5; Joseph A. Dubray, 'The evolution of motion picture film processing apparatus,' *Cinematographic Annual*, 2 (1931), pp. 271-90; A.S. Howell, B.E. Stechbart, and R.F. Mitchell, 'The Bell and Howell fully automatic sound picture production printer,'

JSMPE, 19, no. 4 (October 1932): 305-28; 'Automatic sound and picture printers,' *IP*, 8, no. 12 (January 1936): 25; Bell & Howell Engineering Department, 'Magnetic striping techniques and characteristics,' *International Sound Technician*, 1, no. 11 (January 1954): 16-17.

44   'With the pioneers,' *IP*, 1, no. 6 (July 1929): 28; Sol Polito, 'BNC Mitchell silent camera,' *IP*, 11, no. 4 (May 1934): 7; 'Silencing the Bell & Howell camera for sound work,' *AC*, 9, no. 12 (March 1929): 13-16; A.S. Howell and J.A. Dubray, 'The motion picture camera in sound pictures,' *TSMPE*, 13, no. 37 (1929): 135-49; Edward T. Estabrook, 'New camera marvel unveiled,' *IP*, 5, no. 2 (March 1933): 8; 'Silencing the camera,' *AC*, 9, no. 19 (January 1929): 6; 'New type Mitchell camera,' *IP*, 9, no. 1 (February 1938): 9; Earl Theisen, 'The evolution of the motion picture camera,' *IP*, 5, no. 6 (June 1933): 42; Edmund M. Digiulio, E.E. Manderfield, and George A. Mitchell, 'An historical survey of the professional motion picture camera,' *JSMPTE*, 76, no. 7 (July 1967): 666.

45   'Two men of Tek-Nik-Towne,' *IP*, 2, no. 5 (June 1930): 88; Keva Marcus, '20 years of starlighting,' *IP*, 19, no. 12 (December 1947): 5; 'Pan and sound put inkies on top,' *IP*, 10, no. 3 (April 1938): 43; Mary Eunice McCarthy, *Hands of Hollywood* (Hollywood: Photoplay Research Bureau, 1929), pp. 60-1; Peter Mole, 'Will there always be a need for carbon arcs?' *AC*, 31, no. 2 (February 1951): 72; Peter Mole, 'Twice the light and twice the carrying power,' *AC*, 32, no. 3 (March 1951): 93, 111.

46   'Studio contacts aid lamp design,' *IP*, 10, no. 7 (August 1938): 15.

47   Earl Theisen, 'The Max Factor make-up factory,' *IP*, 6, no. 6 (July 1934): 8-9; Max Factor, 'Movie make-up,' *AC*, 9, no. 1 (April 1928): 8; undated press release, Max Factor Company, pp. 1-2; Max Factor, 'Standardization of motion picture make-up,' *JSMPE*, 38, no. 1 (January 1937): 60; Vern Murdock, 'Make-up: now an exact art,' *IP*, 10, no. 3 (April 1938): 48-9; Max Factor, 'Make-up, the cameraman's ally,' *Cinematography*, 1, no. 5 (August 1930): 6, 25; Max Factor, 'Coordinating makeup with film,' *AC*, 16, no. 7 (July 1935): 286, 297; Max Factor, 'Make-up for the new Technicolor process,' *AC*, 17, no. 8 (August 1936): 331, 334; Nancy Smith, 'The new Max Factor Technicolor make-up,' *IP*, 8, no. 5 (June 1936): 10; Fred Basten, *Glorious Technicolor* (New York: A.S. Barnes, 1980), p. 71; Eva Gardiner, 'Trends in film make-up,' *IP*, 28, no. 5 (May 1956): 18-19; Walter Ramsey, 'Make-up magic for today's color films,' *AC*, 36, no. 9 (September 1955): 526-9.

48   Genevieve Hauge, 'The evolution of the Moviola,' unpublished manuscript at Margaret Herrick

Library, AMPAS (c. 1938); 'Moviola expansion plans,' *AC*, 27, no. 1 (January 1946): 18; interview with Sidney P. Solow, conducted by David Bordwell, Hollywood, California, on 1 July 1980; 'Pan and sound,' p. 48; Louis Hockman, 'Come-apart cars let camera in,' *Popular Science*, 155, no. 4 (October 1949): 153-6; Earl Theisen, 'In the motion picture prop and research department,' *IP*, 6, no. 7 (August 1934): 5.

49 Jenkins, *Images*, pp. 287-91; Basten, *Glorious Technicolor*, pp. 32, 47, 90-1; 'Bell & Howell builds for tomorrow,' *AC*, 12, no. 5 (September 1931): 1; 'Sure advance coming in sound,' *AC*, 20, no. 4 (April 1939): 163; 'Hollywood's service army,' *IP*, 10, no. 2 (March 1938): 11-13.

50 'Studio contacts,' p. 16.

51 R.D. Sangster, 'Hollywood – Ye Old Tek-Nik Towne,' *IP*, 8, no. 9 (October 1936): 10.

52 Mole, 'Will there always . . . ,' p. 72.

53 Raymond Moley, *The Hays Office* (Indianapolis: Bobbs-Merrill, 1945); Will H. Hays, *The Memoirs of Will H. Hays* (Garden City: Doubleday, 1955).

54 Halsey, Stuart, and Company, 'The motion picture industry,' in *The American Film Industry*, ed. Tino Balio (Madison: University of Wisconsin Press, 1976), p. 175.

55 H. Lyman Broening, 'Beginning of the ASC,' *AC*, 9, no. 1 (April 1928): 28, 35; Fred W. Jackman, 'Birthday of the ASC,' *AC*, 23, no. 1 (January 1942): 5.

56 Quoted in 'Six decades of "Loyalty, progress, art,"' *AC*, 60, no. 6 (June 1979): 596.

57 Charles G. Clarke, *History of the American Society of Cinematographers* (Hollywood: ASC, 1977), pp. 5-6. See also Murray Ross, *Stars and Strikes* (New York: Columbia University Press, 1941), pp. 145-6.

58 ' "Loyalty, progress and art" is slogan of West Coast club of cinematographers,' *MPW*, 44, no. 13 (26 June 1920): 1777.

59 'ASC School,' *AMPAS Bulletin*, no. 14 (18 September 1928): 7; letter from John F. Seitz to John Arnold (16 October 1930), on file at the American Society of Cinematographers.

60 Victor Milner, 'ASC inaugurates research on photography for television,' *AC* 30, no. 3 (March 1949): 86, 100-2.

61 Lewis W. Physioc. quoted in 'Six decades,' p. 576.

62 Ralph B. Farnham, 'Mercury cadmium lamps for studio set lights,' *AC*, 30, no. 2 (February 1949): 47, 58-60; letter from Fred Jackman to Charles Rosher (29 October 1950), on file at the American Society of Cinematographers; 'Hollywood Bulletin Board,' *AC*, 34, no. 4 (April 1953): 150.

63 Clarke, *History of the ASC*, p. 10.

64 'Society of American Cinematographers,' *AC*, 14, no. 3 (July 1933): 85; 'ASC recommends fast film,'

AC, 12, no. 3 (July 1931): 19; Jack McCoskey, 'The new Bell & Howell camera,' *IP*, 16, no. 1 (February 1944): 13-14; 'Lighting equipment received for ASC experimental library,' *AC*, 7, no. 5 (August 1926): 6.

65 Walter Blanchard, 'Aces of the camera XV: "Tony" Gaudio,' *AC*, 23, no. 3 (March 1942): 112, 137; Alex Evelove, 'Long record and more honor for Tony Gaudio in his screen work,' *AC*, 19, no. 6 (June 1938): 230-1; Lars Moen, 'New "Spectra" meter,' *IP* 20, no. 12 (December 1948): 7-8, 17; Linwood Dunn, 'The new Acme-Dunn optical printer,' *AC*, 25, no. 1 (January 1944): 11, 29; W.G.C. Bosco, 'Aces of the camera: Jackson J. Rose,' *AC*, 25, no. 7 (July 1944): 228, 248, 250; Fred W. Jackman, 'Birthday of the ASC,' *AC* 23, no. 1 (January 1942): 5; Jackson Rose, 'Color rendition,' *IP*, 2, no. 5 (June 1930): 9-16, 28; Fred W. Jackman, 'Patents and the cinematographer,' *AC*, 14, no. 9 (January 1934): 358, 380; Herb A. Lightman, 'Changing trends in cinematography,' *AC*, 30, no. 1 (January 1949): 11.

66 Noble, *America By Design*, p. 70.

67 C. Francis Jenkins, 'Chairman's address,' *TSMPE*, no. 2 (1916): 3.

68 E.A. Williford, 'Twenty-four years of service in the cause of better projection,' *JSMPE*, 36, no. 3 (March 1941): 295; J.W. McNair, 'Do standards inhibit progress?' *JSMPTE*, 66, no. 9 (September 1957): 525; 'The SMPE – its aims and accomplishments,' *Projection Engineering*, 2, no. 12 (December 1930): 18.

69 'The Society of Motion Picture Engineers: its aims and accomplishments,' *JSMPE: Index, July 1916-May 1926* (New York: SMPE, 1926), p. 5.

70 J.L. Crabtree, 'The Society of Motion Picture Engineers and its relation to production during the past year,' *International Review of Educational Cinematography*, 3, no. 1 (January 1931): 35; 'Sustaining members,' *JSMPTE*, 58, no. 5 (May 1952), part 2: 71-2; 'Fall 1936 Convention,' *JSMPE*, 27, no. 5 (October 1936): 473.

71 G.F. Rackett, 'Pacific Coast Section, SMPE, Minutes of Meeting February 27, 1930,' *JSMPE*, 14, no. 4 (April 1930): 465.

72 A.N. Goldsmith, 'Problems in motion picture engineering,' *JSMPE*, 23, no. 6 (December 1934): 350-4.

73 W.W. Lozier, 'Foreword: screen brightness symposium,' *JSMPE*, 61, no. 2 (August 1943): 213-4.

74 Goldsmith, 'Problems,' p. 350.

75 *Ibid.*

76 'Banquet speeches,' *JSMPE*, 14, no. 2 (February 1931): 223-38.

77 Pierre Normon Sands, *A Historical Study of the Academy of Motion Picture Arts and Sciences (1927-*

1947) (New York: Arno Press, 1973), pp. 29, 37-8, 82-4; *Statement of Policy for the Reorganized Academy* (Hollywood: AMPAS, 1937), pp. 2-3; 'Academy of Motion Picture Arts and Sciences shows growth,' *Projection Engineering*, 4, no. 3 (March 1932): 20. On the academy and labor, see Ross, *Stars and Strikes,* pp. 27-57; Dudley Nichols, 'Report to the Screen Writers' Guild,' *Authors' League of America Bulletin*, no. 22 (November 1938): 11; Herbert Kline, 'The Academy's Last Supper,' *New Theatre*, 3, no. 4 (April 1936): 32-3; Frank Woods, 'The Academy of Motion Picture Arts and Sciences,' *TSMPE*, 12, no. 33 (1928): 27-8; Nancy Lynn Schwartz, *The Hollywood Writers' Wars* (New York: Knopf, 1982), pp. 8-12.

78 Sands, *Historical Study*, pp. 197-8; 'The Motion Picture Producers Association research laboratory,' *AC*, 9, no. 2 (May 1928): 34; 'Technical bureau transformed,' *AMPAS Bulletin*, no. 28 (29 January 1930): 1; 'The Hollywood scene,' *Motion Picture Herald*, 167, no. 6 (10 May 1947): 28; William Koenig, 'The organization and activities of the Research Council of the Academy of Motion Picture Arts and Sciences,' *JSMPE*, 29, no. 5 (November 1937): 484-5; W.F. Kelley, 'Motion Picture Research Council,' *JSMPE* 51, no. 4 (October 1948): 418-19.

79 Mees, *Organization*, p. 49.

80 Quoted in Sands, *Historical Study*, p. 87.

81 W.F. Kelley and W.V. Wolfe, 'Technical activities of the Motion Picture Research Council,' *JSMPTE*, 56, no. 2 (February 1951): 178.

82 Fred Westerberg, 'The Academy's Symposium,' *IP*, 2, no. 9 (October 1930): 14-15; 'The Academy of Motion Picture Arts and Sciences,' *Projection Engineering*, 5, no. 2 (February 1933): 10-11; John K. Hilliard, 'The theatre standardization activities of the Research Council of the Academy of Motion Picture Arts and Sciences,' *JSMPE*, 35, no. 4 (October 1940): 388-96.

83 Motion Picture Research Council, '3-D projection requisites,' *IPro*, 28, no. 3 (March 1953): 12-13; Motion Picture Research Council, 'Addendum: 3-D projection,' *IPro*, 28, no. 4 (May 1953): 14-15; 'Hollywood bulletin board,' *AC*, 34, no. 5 (May 1953): 202; Gavin, 'All Hollywood studios,' p. 135; Armin J. Hill, 'The Motion Picture Research Council 3-D calculator, *AC*, 34, no. 8 (August 1953): 373, 398.

84 Sands, *Historical Study*, pp. 87-8; 'Research in Hollywood,' *Projection Engineering*, 4, no. 11 (November 1932): 9.

85 'Draft of new by-laws,' *AMPAS Bulletin*, no. 14 (22 June 1933): 1.

86 Richard Shale, *Academy Awards* (New York: Ungar, 1978), p. 15.

87 Kelley, 'Research Council,' p. 423.

88 'Research Council,' *AMPAS Bulletin*, no. 42 (8 February 1932): 7; Darryl F. Zanuck, 'First meeting of Research Council,' *AMPAS Technical Bulletin*, supplement no. 12 (20 August 1932): 3-4; *AMPAS Technical Bulletin*, supplement no. 19 (17 December 1932): 7; AMPAS Research Council, 'Report on the arc lamp noise tests,' *JSMPE*, 36, no. 5 (May 1941): 559-71.

89 'Wanger pic important for process work,' *IP*, 19, no. 12 (January 1939): 16-18; Academy Research Council, *Recommendations on Process Projection Equipment* (Hollywood: AMPAS, 1939); Farciot Edouart, 'The work of the Process Projection Equipment Committee of the Research Council, Academy of Motion Picture Arts and Sciences,' *JSMPE* 33, no. 3 (September 1939): 253; 'Magnetic recording symposium by Academy,' *IPro*, 22, no. 3 (March 1947): 9, 28-9.

90 Kelly, 'Research Council,' p. 422.

91 Andre Crot, 'Research Council small camera crane,' *JSMPE*, 52, no. 3 (March 1949): 273, 279; Frank E. Lyon, 'The Research Council camera crane,' *AC*, 30, no. 7 (July 1949): 242; Kelly, 'Research Council,' p. 422.

92 'Report of the Color Committee,' *JSMPE*, 29, no. 1 (July 1937): 54-6; 'Report of the Standards and Nomenclature Committee,' *JSMPE*, 17, no. 3 (September 1931): 431-3; 'Report of the Standards Committee,' *JSMPE*, 31, no. 6 (December 1938): 619-22.

Chapter 20 Initial standardization of the basic technology

1* We find it in titles of books – Katton Lahue's *Motion Picture Pioneer: The Selig Polyscope Company* (New York: A.S. Barnes & Co., 1973) and *Hollywood: The Pioneers* by Kevin Brownlow and John Kobal (New York: Alfred A. Knopf, 1979) – and in chapter headings – 'The pioneering age of the film,' in *'Image' on the Art and Evolution of the Film*, ed. Marshall Deutelbaum (New York: Dover Publications, 1979) and 'The lawless film frontier,' in *A Million and One Nights* by Terry Ramsaye (New York: Simon & Schuster, 1926) – as well as in innumerable passages of prose.

2* *The House of Fear* used the recently introduced Panchroma Twin Arc Light, a 19-pound lamp designed to fold up into a suitcase, which ran on AC or DC current. See 'New lamp for night pictures,' *Photoplay*, 7, no. 4 (March 1915): 160; Ernest Dench, *Making the Movies* (New York: Macmillan, 1915), p. 116; Hanford C. Judson, 'In search of *The House of Fear*,' *MPW*, 22, no. 19 (5 December 1914): 1388-9.

3 'Action in 9 rooms shown at once in film by director Tourneur of World-Equitable,' *MPN*, 13, no. 13 (1 April 1916): 1903; see also Victor Freeburg's *The Art of Photoplay Making* (New York: Macmillan, 1918), p. 43.

4 Donald J. Bell, 'A letter from Donald Bell,' *IP*, 2, no. 1 (February 1930): 19.

5* As W. Wallace Clendenin describes this perforation, 'These holes were always exactly placed in relation to the aperture, no matter what the spacing of the frames might be.' The Biograph printers used 'feeler' pilot pins which would slide along the edges of the moving negative until the perforations passed, at which point the pins slipped in and stopped the negative and pre-perforated positive (sandwiched together in the aperture) while the frame was printed. This perforation in the camera produced the steady image. See W. Wallace Clendenin, 'Cameras of yesteryear,' Pt 2, *IP*, 21, no. 2 (February 1949): 14.

6 Billy Bitzer, *Billy Bitzer, His Story* (New York: Farrar, Straus & Giroux, 1973), pp. 20-1.

7 Clendenin, 'Cameras of yesteryear,' Pt 2, pp. 12-13.

8 Clendenin, 'Cameras of yesteryear,' Pt 2, p. 13; Fred J. Balshofer and Arthur C. Miller, *One Reel a Week* (Berkeley: University of California Press, 1967), p. 52; Clendenin, 'Cameras of yesteryear,' Pt 2, p. 13; quoted in Leonard Maltin, *The Art of the Cinematographer* (New York: Dover Publications, 1978), pp. 74-5.

9 Charles G. Clarke, *Early Film Making in Los Angeles* (Los Angeles: Dawson's Bookshop, 1976), p. 17; Clendenin, 'Cameras of yesteryear,' Pt 2, p. 12; W. Wallace Clendenin, 'Cameras of yesteryear,' Pt 1, *IP*, 21, no. 1 (January 1949): 20-1. On Debrie cameras, see 'Milestone movie cameras,' *AC*, 50, no. 1 (January 1969): 79; and 'New features announced on latest models of Debrie cameras,' *AC*, 7, no. 2 (May 1925): 23.

10 Clendenin, 'Cameras of yesteryear,' Pt 1, pp. 18, 20.

11 Balshofer and Miller's *One Reel a Week* provides one of the best extended descriptions of this period.

12 'Loop litigation ends,' *Motography*, 8, no. 5 (31 August 1912): 186; for excellent summaries of the ruling in MPPC vs Independent Motion Picture Company of America (IMP) in the latter's favor, and of the final decision later the same year upholding that ruling, see 'Important patent decision,' *MPW*, 11, no. 7 (17 February 1912): 560, and 'Latham loop patent adjudicated,' *MPW*, 13, no. 8 (24 August 1912): 747.

13 'Questions and answers,' *Cinema News*, 1, no. 8 (1 April 1917): 7.

14* A Bell & Howell outfit, including a tripod, one lens, one magazine, and a carrying case, cost about $1,000 in the early teens. In 1922, the Motion Picture Apparatus Co. advertised a Pathé outfit, with a tripod, lens, and six magazines, for $850. See Bell, 'A letter from Donald Bell,' p. 20; advertisement, The Motion Picture Apparatus Co., *AC*, 3, no. 6 (September 1922): 17.

15 Bell, 'A letter from Donald Bell,' p. 19.

16 *Ibid.*

17 Clendenin, 'Cameras of yesteryear,' Pt 3, *IP*, 21, no. 3 (March 1949): 18.

18 Herbert C. McKay, *Handbook of Motion Picture Photography* (New York: Falk Publishing Co., 1927), pp. 65-6. For a demonstration of this focusing process in action, see the final sequence of Von Sternberg's *The Last Command* (1927, Paramount).

19 Kevin Brownlow, *The Parade's Gone By* (New York: Alfred A. Knopf, 1968), p. 213. This may even be an underestimate; several times in King Vidor's *Show People* (1928, MGM) cameramen release their cranks, which go on turning for some time with no visible slowdown.

20* Aside from the higher price of the camera, patent infringement may have affected Bell & Howell sales. The fact that the loop patent was invalidated in 1912 may have increased the company's business. Bell remarked in passing that the Patents Company 'made a claim against us for infringement, asked many thousands of dollars from us, and gladly took one thousand, which was paid to avoid further annoyance.' See Bell, 'A letter from Donald Bell,' p. 20.

21 Clendenin, 'Cameras of yesteryear,' Pt 3, p. 17; Untitled, *The Static Club Bulletin*, 1, no. 6 (16 November 1915): 3-4.

22 Harry F. Perry, with Oscar G. Estes, Jr., '40 years behind a motion picture camera, (unpublished typescript on file at the American Film Institute's Louis B. Mayer Library, Los Angeles; dated March, 1960), pp. 13, 92.

23 Clendenin, 'Cameras of yesteryear,' Pt 3, p. 18.

24 Carl Louis Gregory, 'Motion picture photography,' *MPW*, 32, no. 5 (3 May 1917): 792; Roe Fleet, 'Aces of the camera: Wilfred M. Clines,' *AC*, 28, no. 4 (April 1947): 123.

25 Ira B. Hoke, 'An erect image-finder for the Akeley,' *AC*, 9, no. 3 (June 1928): 36.

26 'The Akeley specialists,' *AC*, 8, no. 7 (October 1927): 7; Charles G. Clarke, 'Amateur camera makes intimate shots possible,' *AC*, 7, no. 2 (May 1926): 19.

27 'Milestone movie cameras,' p. 116.

28 Interview with Charles G. Clarke, conducted by David Bordwell and Kristin Thompson, 12 June and 3 July 1980, in Hollywood, California.

29 'A camera out of the West,' *AC*, 2, no. 18 (1 October 1921): 13.

30 'Mitchell appoints agents in North and East,' *AC*, 3,

no. 5 (August 1922): 7; 'Mitchell increases production program; to build new plant,' *AC*, 4, no. 3 (June 1923): 22.

31 J.H. McNabb [President, Bell & Howell], 'A new camera for screen news cinematographers,' *TSMPE*, no. 23 (5-8 October 1925): 79-81; advertisement, Bell & Howell, *AC*, 7, no. 2 (May 1926): 14-15; H. Mario Raimondo Souto, *The Technique of the Motion Picture Camera* (New York: Hastings House, 1977), pp. 128-9; Victor Milner, 'A.S.C. member answers amateurs,' *AC*, 7, no. 1 (April 1926): 5.

32 Carl L. Gregory and G.J. Badgley, 'Attachments to professional cinematograph cameras,' *TSMPE*, no. 8 (14-16 April 1919): 80, 82.

33 George C. Keech, 'Mercury lamps for moving pictures,' *The Nickelodeon*, 3, no. 9 (May 1910): 233.

34 Peter Bogdanovich, *Allan Dwan: The Last Pioneer* (New York: Praeger, 1971), p. 15.

35 Peter Mole, 'The evolution of arc broadside lighting equipment,' *JSMPE*, 32, no. 4 (April 1939): 399; Balshofer and Miller, *One Reel à Week*, p. 6.

36* Fred Balshofer refers in his memoirs to using muslin to diffuse sunlight on sets at the Crescent Film Co. in 1908. In his book *Early Filmmaking in Los Angeles*, Charles G. Clarke also dates the use of muslin over sets representing interiors as being about 1908. This date may be approximate, but certainly the diffusion of sunlight had become a standard practice by the early teens. See Balshofer and Miller, *One Reel a Week*, p. 20; Clarke, *Early Filmmaking in Los Angeles*, p. 22.

37 'New diffusion system,' *Motography*, 9, no. 12 (14 June 1913): 436.

38 Motion Picture Producers and Distributors of America, Inc., 'The motion picture industry,' in John George Glover and William Bouck Cornell (eds), *The Development of American Industries* (New York: Prentice-Hall, 1932), p. 746; Anthony Slide, *The Big V: A History of the Vitagraph Company* (Metuchen, New Jersey: Scarecrow Press, 1976), p. 14; Kalton C. Lahue (ed.), *Motion Picture Pioneer: The Selig Polyscope Company* (Cranbury, New Jersey: New York: A.S. Barnes & Co., 1973), p. 43; 'American secures remarkable lens,' *Motography*, 7, no. 4 (April 1912): 180.

39 Mole, 'The evolution of arc broadside lighting equipment,' p. 399.

40 Dr Alfred B. Hitchins, 'Artificial lighting of motion picture studios,' *AC*, 3, no. 6 (September 1922): 22.

41 'Cooper-Hewitt lights,' *Cinema News*, 2, no. 11 (October 1918): 19.

42 Sarah Pressey Noreen, *Public Street Illumination in Washington, D.C.* (Washington: G.W. Washington Studies, n.d.), p. 23; Eddy S. Feldman, *The Art of Street Lighting in Los Angeles* (Los Angeles:

Dawson's Book Shop, 1972), p. 17; Paul W. Keatin, *Lamps for a Brighter America* (New York: McGraw-Hill, 1954), p. 7.

43 Theodore Fuchs, *Stage Lighting* (Boston: Little, Brown & Co., 1929), pp. 45, 47; Gösta M. Bergman, *Lighting in the Theater* (Stockholm: Almquist & Wiksell International, 1977), pp. 273-88.

44 Barry Salt, 'A letter to the editor,' *Screen*, 17, no. 1 (Spring 1976): 120.

45 Earl Theisen, 'Part of the story of lighting,' *IP*, 4, no. 3 (April 1934): 10.

46 Mole, 'The evolution of arc broadside lighting equipment,' p. 399.

47 'The A-B flaming arc,' *The Nickelodeon*, 2, no. 4 (October 1910): 128-9; 'The evolution of motion picture lighting,' *AC*, 50, no. 1 (January 1969): 95; William Roy Mott, 'White light for motion picture photography,' *TSMPE*, no. 8 (14-16 April 1919): 34.

48 Mole, 'The evolution of arc broadside lighting equipment,' p. 400.

49 Jack Grant, 'Hollywood's first art director,' *AC*, 22, no. 4 (May 1941): 238; Balshofer and Miller, *One Reel a Week*, pp. 126-7; 'Apfel has a patent,' *MPW*, 21, no. 13 (26 September 1914): 1760.

50 Advertisement, *Cinema News*, 2, no. 3 (February 1918): back cover.

51 J. Justice Harmer, 'Artificial sunlight,' *Cinema News*, 2, no. 2 (January 1918): 9.

52 P.R. Basset [of the Electrical Illuminating Engineers Society], 'Flexibility and uses of light,' *AC*, 4, no. 3 (June 1922): 12, 23-4.

53* An excellent close view of this process in action appears in the publicity documentary, *A Tour of the Thomas H. Ince Studio* (c. 1923, Ince). This film in general gives a good account of the various departments and shows a few candid (not staged) views of units filming on interior stages.

54 Maxwell Harper Hite, *Lessons in How to Become a Successful Moving Picture Operator* (Harrisburg, 1908), pp. 71-7; David Sherrill Hulfish, *Motion-Picture Work* (Chicago: American Technical Society, 1915; rep. New York: Arno, 1970), p. 79; Earl J. Denison, 'My troubles, your troubles and our troubles and how we can get around them without trouble,' *The American Projectionist*, 4, no. 7 (July 1926): 4.

55 'What happens when the film breaks,' *Photoplay*, 16, no. 5 (5 October 1919): 60; Brownlow, *The Parade's Gone By*, p. 283; McKay, *Handbook of Motion Picture Photography*, p. 165.

56 Earl J. Denison, 'Sprockets and splices,' *TSMPE*, no. 17 (1-4 October 1923): 180.

57* The projectionists generally believed that a wide splice was necessary for strength and holding power. A 1914 projectionist-advice column suggested: 'The best place to cut the film for splicing is below the first perforation below the printing line [i.e., frame line], say about halfway between that perforation and the one below.' Such a splice would be about $^3/_{16}$ of an inch wide, with an entire sprocket hole of one strip of film lined up over one from the other strip. (This would be termed a 'full-hole' splice in the twenties.) Some projectionists even made two-hole overlaps (with the splice line visible in the center of the frame!), but this column cautions against this, pointing out that the one-hole splice would go 'through the sprocket wheels with less commotion.' See The Operator, 'The practical side of pictures,' *Reel Life*, 4, no. 17 (11 July 1914): 20.

By the twenties, formal tests began to be made, and these revealed that even a one-hole overlap caused too wide a splice. In going through the sprocket gears, a wide, thick splice was less flexible, would pull more, and hence would cause a break more easily. In 1922, the SMPE heard evidence that a beveled splice only $^1/_{32}$-inch (.03") wide was sufficient for negatives, but that one $^5/_{64}$-inch (.078") wide was necessary for positives. The Society also got the results of Eastman's tests of splice strength in 1926, which found that unspliced film's tensile strength was 14.2 kilograms, while that of a .078-inch ($^5/_{64}$") splice was 10.5 KG, and of a larger .156-inch ($^5/_{32}$", or full-hole) splice was actually smaller, at 10.4 KG. But since projectionists could not be persuaded to give up the full-hole splice, in 1926 the Society finally gave its recommendations on standard splice widths as follows: .03-inch ($^1/_{32}$") for negatives, .156-inch ($^5/_{32}$") for positive prints. See J.H. McNabb, 'Film splicing,' *TSMPE*, no. 14 (1-4 May 1922) 43; S.E. Sheppard and S.S. Sweet, 'Note on the strength of splices,' *TSMPE*, no. 25 (3-6 May 1926): 145; 'Report of Standards and Nomenclature Committee,' *TSMPE*, no. 27 (4-7 October 1926): 20.

58 Brownlow, *The Parade's Gone By*, p. 31.
59 Bogdonovich, *Allan Dwan: The Last Pioneer*, p. 24; Clifford Howard, 'The cinema in retrospect,' *Close Up*, 3, no. 6 (December 1928): 38; David Sherrill Hulfish, *Cyclopedia of Motion-Picture Work* (Chicago: American School of Correspondence, 1911): vol. 2, p. 111.
60 McKay, *Handbook of Motion Picture Photography*, p. 170.
61 J.I. Crabtree, 'The motion-picture laboratory,' *JSMPTE*, 64, no. 1 (January 1955): 14.
62 'Motion pictures in the making,' *NYDM*, 70, no. 1806 (30 July 1913): 25-6.
63 Hulfish, *Motion-Picture Work* (1915), Pt. 2, p. 140.
64 John Harvith, 'Karl Struss remembers,' in Susan and John Harvith (eds), *Karl Struss: Man with a Camera* (Bloomfield Hills, Michigan: Cranbrook

Academy of Art/Museum, 1976), p. 11.
65 Quoted in Maltin, *The Art of the Cinematographer*, p. 80.

Chapter 21 Major technological changes of the 1920s

1   Homer Croy, *How Motion Pictures Are Made* (New York: Harper & Bros., 1918), pp. 354-5.
2* The assumption that panchro was innately superior to ortho has given rise to some inaccurate accounts of panchro's introduction. Jean Mitry dates the introduction of panchro as 1918, thereby suggesting that its adoption progressed smoothly into the twenties (*Histoire du cinéma*, vol. 3 [Paris: Editions universitaires, 1973], p. 490). Eric Rhode ignores the existence of panchro before the twenties and credits its entire introduction to Robert Flaherty's *Moana*, as late as 1926 (*A History of the Cinema From Its Origins to 1970* [New York: Hill & Wang, 1976], pp. 248-9.). Charles Harpole assumes that because panchro was an experimental stock for Eastman in 1913, it was not available to film-makers until 1923, when it became a regular product; as we shall see, however, filmmakers could get panchro if they cared to order it from 1913 on (*Gradients of Depth in the Cinema Image* [New York: Arno Press, 1978], p. 56). We have seen that Patrick Ogle correctly dates the introduction of panchro in 1913, but he concludes simply that it 'had not proved popular,' without giving reasons ('Technological and aesthetic influences upon the development of deep focus cinematography in the United States,' *Screen Reader*, [London: Society for Education in Film and Television, 1977], p. 85).
3   S.D. Levings, 'Urban-Smith Kinemacolor demonstration,' *The Nickelodeon*, 3, no. 1 (1 January 1910): 7; for accounts of Kinemacolor of America, see D.B. Thomas, *The First Colour Motion Pictures* (London: Her Majesty's Stationery Office, 1969), p. 30, and Gorham Kindem, 'The demise of Kinemacolor: technological, legal, economic, and aesthetic problems in early color cinema history,' *Cinema Journal*, 20, no. 2 (Spring 1981): 9-12.
4   Earl Theisen, 'The history of nitrocellulose as a film base,' *JSMPE*, 20, no. 3 (March 1933): 261; Earl Theisen, 'Tracing the history of silver grain,' *IP*, 4, no. 10 (November 1932): 24; J.I. Crabtree, 'The motion-picture laboratory,' *JSMPTE*, 64, no. 1 (January 1955): 19.
5   C.E. Kenneth Mees, 'History of professional black-and-white motion-picture film,' *JSMPTE*, 63 (October 1954), rep. Raymond Fielding (ed.), *A Technological History of Motion Pictures and Tele-*

vision (Berkeley: University of California Press, 1967), p. 125.

6 Frederick A. Talbot, *Moving Pictures: How They Are Made and Worked*, new ed. (London: William Heinemann, 1914), pp. 292-4.

7 Mees, 'History of professional black-and-white motion-picture film,' p. 125; see also Emery Huse and Gordon A. Chamber, 'Three new Eastman negative emulsions: Background X, Plus X, and Super XX,' *AC*, 19, no. 12 (December 1938): 487.

8 See Roderick T. Ryan, *A History of Motion Picture Color Technology* (London/New York: Focal Press, 1977), pp. 26-35, for a discussion of Kinemacolor and four other American companies of this period.

9 Charles Higham, *Hollywood Cameramen* (London: Thames & Hudson, 1970), p. 78.

10 Jonas Howard, 'There are no "motion" pictures!' *Photoplay*, 16, no. 5 (October 1919): 60.

11 Carl L. Gregory and G.S. Badgley, 'Attachments to professional cinematographic cameras,' *TSMPE*, no. 8 (14-16 April 1919): 84-5.

12 'The log of a great picture,' *AC*, 2, no. 20 (1 November 1921): 10.

13 'Report of the Committee on Progress,' *TSMPE*, no. 14 (1-4 May 1922): 175.

14 'Report of the Committee on Films and Emulsions,' *TSMPE*, no. 16 (7-10 May 1923): 260.

15 'Director advocates panchromatic stock,' *AC*, 7, no. 7 (October 1926): 6.

16 John Grierson, 'Putting richness into the photoplay,' *AC*, 8, no. 7 (October 1927): 22.

17 Editor's note introducing Grierson, 'Putting richness into the photoplay,' p. 4. Emphases in original.

18 *Eastman Panchromatic Negative Film For Motion Pictures* (Rochester, New York: Eastman Kodak, 1925), pp. 5, 7-8.

19 Renee Van Dyke, 'Paragraphs pertaining to plays and players,' *Cinema Art*, 5, no. 8 (October 1926): 54; Daniel B. Clark [President of ASC], 'A cinematographic forecast for 1927,' *AC*, 7, no. 10 (January 1927): 10, 21-2.

20* Up to 1927, the additional negative for export prints had been shot by a second camera on the set. Duplication in the lab rendered an excessively contrasty negative. But that year Eastman introduced its Duplicating Film, containing a yellow dye; used in combination with filters, this stock held down contrast to an acceptable level and made it unnecessary to shoot two negatives. See J.I. Crabtree, 'The motion-picture laboratory,' *JSMPTE*, 64, no. 1 (January 1955): 21-2.

21 'Record lectures held on new film subjects,' *AC*, 7, no. 11 (February 1927): 6, 21.

22 Scott Eyman, 'An interview with Karl Struss,' *The Journal of Popular Film*, 4, no. 4 (1975): 314; Herbert C. McKay, 'Panchromatic versus ordinary

film,' *Photo-Era*, 61, no. 1 (July 1928): 58.

23* Ortho continued to be manufactured until July of 1942. After 1936, Eastman apparently ceased manufacturing it as a regular studio negative, for it had clearly been replaced by the faster panchro stocks. It lingered on as a stock for certain special purposes, however: it still would be used in negative for the blue strip in bi- or tri-pack color systems, and was occasionally used for such purposes as positive back projection prints (where its extremely fine grain would be advantageous). But improvements in various panchro stocks eventually eliminated even these minor uses. See Mees, 'History of professional black-and-white motion-picture film,' p. 125; Emery Huse, 'The characteristics of Eastman motion picture negative films,' *AC*, 17, no. 5 (March 1936): 192; *Motion Picture Laboratory Practice and Characteristics of Eastman Motion Picture Films* (Rochester, New York: Eastman Kodak Co., 1936), pp. 42-4; Jackson J. Rose, *American Cinematographer Hand Book and Reference Guide* (Hollywood: ASC, 1942), pp. 31-2.

24 Ned Van Buren, 'Light filters and their use in cinematography,' *Cinematographic Annual*, 1 (1930): 127.

25 Earl Theisen, 'The story of the Moviola,' *IP*, 7, no. 19 (November 1935): 4.

26 Kevin Brownlow, *The Parade's Gone By* (New York: Alfred A. Knopf, 1968), p. 304.

27 Interview with William Hornbeck, conducted by David Bordwell and Kristin Thompson, 9 July 1980, Ventura, California.

28* In 1919, Serrurier registered the name 'Moviola' as a trademark. His intention was to create a machine for home projection of 35mm films. As a result, the first model was a self-contained cabinet with a small screen extending toward the front. This back-projection system resembled an upright cabinet Victrola – the machine from which Serrurier derived the name. He apparently sold only three of these machines during the period 1923-4. The machine was certainly a failure as far as its intended purpose went, but in September 1924 an editor at the Douglas Fairbanks Studio told Serrurier he was interested in the Moviola's mechanism; Serrurier then discarded the bulky cabinet and screen, attaching the modified mechanism to a board. In this form, the Fairbanks company purchased it; sales to Universal and Pickford followed. With this success, Serrurier devised a model which could be manufactured on a regular basis, the Midget. The Mitchell Camera Co. made twelve, of which the first went to MGM in November 1924. Sales were brisk enough to necessitate a second manufacturer, machineshop operator W.S. Austin, to participate with Mitchell. See Mark Serrurier,

'The origins of the Moviola,' *JSMPTE*, 75, no. 7 (July 1966): 702, 707; Theisen, 'The story of the Moviola,' p. 4.

29   J.H. McNabb, 'Film splicing,' *TSMPE*, no. 14 (1-4 May 1922): 41-2.

30   *Ibid.*, p. 21; Harry A. Mount, 'Developing motion picture film with automatic machinery,' *Scientific American*, 125, no. 11 (10 September 1921): 181.

31   Alfred B. Hitchins [Technical Director, Duplex Motion Picture Industries, Inc.], 'Machine development of negative and positive motion picture film,' *TSMPE*, no. 22 (18-21 May 1925): 52.

32   Brownlow, *The Parade's Gone By*, p. 212.

33   Interview with Stanley Cortez, conducted by David Bordwell and Kristin Thompson, 3 July 1980, in Hollywood, California; interview with Charles G. Clarke, conducted by Bordwell and Thompson, 12 June and 3 July 1980, in Hollywood, California.

34   'Fifty years – or more – of evolving camera technique,' *AC*, 50, no. 1 (January 1969): 53; Fred J. Balshofer and Arthur C. Miller, *One Reel a Week* (Berkeley: University of California Press, 1967), p. 140; Arthur C. Miller, 'Setting the record straight,' *IP*, 32, no. 5 (May 1960): 108.

35   *How To Take and Make Moving Pictures* (Denver: Ford's [an equipment manufacturer], 1914), p. 24.

36   Henry Clay Foster, 'Cinematography and the public,' *Cinema News*, 1, no. 15 (1 October 1917): 1.

37   Arthur Edwin Krows, 'Once more – consider the status of motion pictures,' *The Triangle*, 3, no. 3 (4 November 1916): 13.

38* *The Marriage of Molly O* was supervised by Griffith at Triangle-Fine Arts. An account in 1926 stated that Powell 'had the lens made (to fit motion picture camera requirements) and experimented with it before using it (legitimately and effectively) to tell an inserted fairy story in an Irish photoplay released by Triangle' – presumably *The Marriage of Molly O*. In a much later account, John Harvith states in *Karl Struss: Man With a Camera* that the Struss Pictorial Lens was the 'first soft-focus lens used in motion pictures'; Harvith quotes a 1922 *American Cinematographer* article which claimed that a three-inch version of the lens had been built for John Leezer in 1916. Leezer was a cameraman at the Triangle-Fine Arts studio under Griffith. Finally, Struss recently explained that he had licensed a company in Brooklyn to make his Pictorial lens, and that they made a few in shorter lengths for motion picture work. See Carlyle Ellis, 'Art and the motion picture,' *Annals of the American Academy of Political and Social Science*, 128 (November 1926): 56; John Harvith, 'Karl Struss: man with a camera,' in Susan and John Harvith (eds.), *Karl Struss: Man With a Camera* (Bloomfield Hills, Michigan: Cranbrook Academy of Art/Museum, 1976), pp. 1-2; interview with Karl Struss, conducted by David Bordwell and Kristin Thompson, 10 July 1980, in Hollywood, California.

39   Austin C. Lescarboura, ' "Shooting" the photoplay,' *Scientific American*, 117, no. 11 (15 September 1917): 199.

40   Karl Brown, 'Modern lenses,' Pt 2, *AC*, 3, no. 3 (1 June 1922): 12.

41   *Ibid.*, p. 4.

42   Karl Brown, 'Modern lenses,' Pt 3, *AC*, 3, no. 4 (1 July 1922): 4.

43   *Ibid.*

44* In 1909, David Hulfish mentioned standard lenses as 2 to 4 inches; in 1913, John H. Rathbun repeated this, saying that 'the usual focal length' was 3 inches. *American Cinematographer* surveyed the studios in 1922 and found typical lens lengths as 32 mm (approximately $1^1/_4$ "), 40mm ($1^1/_2$"), 50mm (2"), and 75mm (3"). See David S. Hulfish, *The Motion Picture, Its Making and Its Theater* (Chicago: Electricity Magazine Corporation, 1909), p. 18; John H. Rathbun, 'Motion picture making and exhibiting,' *Motography*, 9, no. 8 (19 April 1913): 277; Glenn Robert Kershner, 'Lens angles of the cinema camera,' *AC*, 3, no. 8 (November 1922): 14-15.

45   Interview with Charles G. Clarke; Herbert C. McKay, *Handbook of Motion Picture Photography* (New York: Falk Publishing Co., 1927), pp. 60, 123.

46   Interview with Karl Struss.

47   Quoted in Brownlow, *The Parade's Gone By*, p. 230.

48   Higham, *Hollywood Cameramen*, pp. 124-5.

49   Leonard Maltin, *The Art of the Cinematographer* (New York: Dover Publications, 1978), p. 81.

50   Brownlow, *The Parade's Gone By*, p. 234.

51* Gish was Ufa's first choice to play Gretchen in the 1926 German film of *Faust*, but according to the film's designer, Robert Herlth, she would only take the role on the condition that Rosher would film her. Since Herlth and his collaborator Walter Rohrig insisted on a different cinematographer, the entire plan to use Gish fell through. See Lotte Eisner, *Murnau* (Berkeley: University of California Press, 1973), p. 69.

52   Erique J. Rebel *et al.*, 'Great cameramen,' *Focus on Film*, no. 13 (1973): 67.

53   Beaumont Newhall, *The History of Photography*, rev. ed. (New York: Museum of Modern Art, 1964), p. 104.

54   For additional examples of the gum bichromate method, see Newhall, *The History of Photography*, p. 103, and Helmut and Alison Gernheim, *A Concise History of Photography* (New York: Grosset & Dunlap, 1965), pp. 173-8.

55   Brown, 'Modern lenses,' Pt 2, p. 12.

56   Ellis, 'Art and the motion picture,' pp. 55-6.

57 Karl Brown, 'Modern lenses,' Pt 5, *AC* 3, no. 5 (August 1922): 5, 20; Advertisement, William Horsley's Film Laboratories, *AC*, 3, no. 1 (1 April 1922): 12; 'Among the laboratories,' *AC* 3, no. 1 (1 April 1922): 13.

Chapter 22 The Mazda tests of 1928

1 Frederick S. Mills, 'Film lighting as a fine art,' *Scientific American*, 124, no. 8 (19 February 1921): 158.

2 Benjamin B. Hampton, *History of the American Film Industry, From Its Beginnings to 1931* (New York: Dover, 1970), pp. 369-74; Jan and Cora Gordon, *Star-Dust in Hollywood* (London: Harrap, 1930), pp. 269-74; J. Douglas Gomery, The coming of sound to the American cinema: a history of the transformation of an industry' (Unpublished PhD dissertation (University of Wisconsin: Madison, 1975), pp. 219-22.

3 Daniel B. Clark, 'A cinematographic forecast for 1927,' *AC*, 7, no. 10 (January 1927): 10; Peter Mole, 'The use of globe lamps,' *AC*, 8, no. 8 (November 1927): 18; R.E. Farnham, 'Motion picture lighting with incandescent lamps,' *Cinematographic Annual*, 1 (1930), p. 253; 'A new era in lighting,' *AC*, 8, no. 5 (August 1927): 22; Peter Mole, 'The tungsten lamp situation in the studio,' *TSMPE*, 11, no. 3 (September 1927): 582-4; Academy of Motion Picture Arts and Sciences, *Academy Reports No. 1: Transactions, Enquiries, Demonstrations, Tests, Etc., on the Subject of Incandescent Illumination as Applied to Motion Picture Production* (Hollywood, California: AMPAS, 1928), pp. 10-14.

4 AMPAS, *Academy Reports No. 1*, pp. 5-6; 'Technicians hold important meeting,' *AMPAS Bulletin*, no. 5 (25 November 1927): n.p.

5 K.C.D. Hickman, 'Hollywood and the Motion Picture Engineers,' *TSMPE*, 11, no. 29 (April 1927): 36.

6 *Ibid.*, p. 29.

7 AMPAS, *Academy Reports No. 1*, p. 7.

8 'First of incandescent meetings held; shots made by John Arnold,' *Exhibitors Herald and Moving Picture World*, 90, no. 4 (28 January 1928): 31; 'A Mazda marathon,' *AC*, 8, no. 11 (February 1928): 24; 'Mazda lighting,' *AMPAS Academy Bulletin*, no. 7 (1 February 1928): 1; AMPAS, *Academy Reports no. 1*, pp. 5, 10-11, 23-7; Max Factor, 'The art of motion picture make-up,' *Cinematographic Annual*, 1 (1930), pp. 157-71.

9 Earl Theisen, 'Part of the story of lighting,' *IP*, 6, no. 3 (April 1934): 12; AMPAS, *Academy Reports No. 1*, pp. 5-9, 18-21; 'Mazda lighting,' *AMPAS Academy Bulletin*, no. 8 (1 March 1928): 1-2; 'Mazda

enquiries close,' *AMPAS Academy Bulletin*, no. 10 (3 May 1928): 3.

10 For technical results of the tests, see Research Committee of the American Society of Cinematographers, 'Incandescent tungsten lighting in cinematography,' *TSMPE*, 12, no. 34 (1928): 453-63.

11 'Report on experiments on Mazda lighting sponsored by the Academy of Motion Picture Arts and Sciences and prepared by the Research Committee of the American Society of Cinematographers,' *AC*, 9, no. 2 (May 1928): 8.

12 'The Mazda tests,' *AC*, 9, no. 1 (April 1928): 30-2; 'Academy Secretary's Annual Report,' *AMPAS Bulletin*, no. 16 (22 November 1928): 10-13; R.E. Farnham, 'Incandescent lighting improving,' *AC*, 10, no. 1 (April 1929): 31-2; 'Technicians investigate arcs,' *AC*, 10, no. 12 (March 1930): 221.

13 See 'Plan and sound put inkies on top,' *IP*, 10, no. 3 (April 1938): 45.

14 Interview with Charles G. Clarke, conducted by David Bordwell and Kristin Thompson, 12 June and 3 July 1980, in Hollywood, California.

15 The set is illustrated in *AC*, 8, no. 12 (March 1928): 19. The footage is described in detail in AMPAS, *Academy Reports No. 1*, pp. 18-21.

16 Quoted in AMPAS, *Academy Reports No. 1*, p. 16.

17 Max Factor, 'Panchromatic make-up,' *AC*, 9, no. 2 (May 1928): 22; E.W. Beggs, 'Motion picture studio lighting,' *Motion Picture Projection*, 2, no. 5 (February 1929): 7, 30.

18 W.B. Cook, 'Presidential address,' *TSMPE*, 12, no. 33 (1928): 15.

19 'Speeches presented at the banquet given by the Academy of Motion Picture Arts and Sciences in honor of the Society of Motion Picture Engineers,' *TSMPE*, 12, no. 33 (1928): 19-24.

20 AMPAS, *Academy Reports No. 1*, p. 63.

21 'Technical bureau started,' *AMPAS Academy Bulletin*, no. 13 (11 August 1928): 5.

Chapter 23 The introduction of sound

1 Frank Woods, 'The sound motion picture situation in Hollywood,' *TSMPE*, 12, no. 35 (1928): 629.

2 Edward W. Kellogg, 'History of sound motion pictures,' in *A Technological History of Motion Pictures and Television*, ed. Raymond Fielding (Berkeley: University of California Press, 1967), pp. 174-220; J. Douglas Gomery, 'The coming of the talkies: invention, innovation, and diffusion,' in *The American Film Industry*, ed. Tino Balio (Madison: University of Wisconsin Press, 1976), pp. 193-211.

3 'Survey of sound problems,' *AMPAS Bulletin*, no. 23 (9 July 1929): 4-5; 'What sound has done,' *Variety* (13 March 1929): 1; Hatto Tappenback,

'Practical exposure meters under present photographic conditions,' *Cinematographic Annual*, 2 (1931), pp. 233-6; Virgil E. Miller, 'Camera-department organization and maintenance,' *AC*, 13, no. 6 (October 1932): 6-7, 40-1; 'The magic of the cutting room,' *IP*, 1, no. 7 (August 1929): 20. See also Rick Altman, 'Introduction,' *Yale French Studies*, no. 60 (1980): 5-11.

4   L.A. Hawkins, 'Research in industry,' *AC*, 9, no. 2 (May 1928): 35-8; 'Banquet speeches,' *JSMPE*, 17, no. 3 (September 1931): 423-4; 'Biggest stage on earth devoted to special process work,' *AC*, 10, no. 1 (April 1929): 20-1, 35; 'Columbia moves ahead,' *IP*, 8, no. 4 (May 1936): 31; Gordon A. Chambers, 'Process photography,' *Cinematographic Annual*, 2 (1931), pp. 223-7; Elmer C. Richardson, 'A microphone boom,' *JSMPE*, 15, no. 1 (July 1930): 41-5. See also Chapter 19, note 37.

5   'Brulator-Eastman technical service lab,' *AC*, 9, no. 12 (March 1929): 7; 'Eastman research lab opened in Hollywood,' *AC*, 10, no. 2 (May 1929): 23; Eastman Kodak, *An Eastman Service* (Rochester: Eastman Kodak, n.d.); 'Smith and Aller provide experimental stage for cameramen,' *AC*, 10, no. 6 (September 1929): 21, 43; 'The Dupont baby set,' *IP*, 1, no. 8 (September 1929): 6; 'Mole-Richardson expand,' *AC*, 9, no. 6 (September 1928): 32; 'Two men of Tek-Nik Towne,' *IP*, 2, no. 5 (June 1930): 88, 120; 'The Mitchell's new home,' *AC* 9, no. 11 (February 1929): 34; 'Eastman's processing plant most completely equipped,' *IP*, no. 9 (October 1930): 37; 'Progress in the motion picture industry,' *JSMPE*, 14, no. 2 (February 1930): 233.

6   Advertisement for Bell & Howell *IP* 1, no. 8 (September 1929): 13. See also 'Bell & Howell expand,' *IP*, 1, no. 8 (September 1929): 16; 'New engineering laboratory for Bell & Howell completed,' *AC*, 10, no. 6 (September 1929): 45.

7   'What is the Academy doing?' *AMPAS Bulletin*, no. 14 (18 September 1928): 1-2.

8   'Academy Secretary's Annual Report,' *AMPAS Bulletin*, no. 16 (22 November 1928): 10-13; 'Writers in Hollywood give varied views on "talkers,"' *Variety* (9 May 1928): 9; 'Directors and talkers,' *Variety* (16 May 1928): 9, 42; Harold B. Franklin, *Sound Motion Pictures* (Garden City: Doubleday, Doran, 1929), pp. 223-4; 'Sound development programs,' *AMPAS Bulletin*, no. 24 (15 August 1929): 1; Irving Thalberg, 'Technical activities of the Academy of Motion Picture Arts and Sciences,' *JSMPE*, 15, no. 1 (July 1930): 5; 'Producers-technicians meeting,' *AMPAS Bulletin*, no. 32 (7 June 1930): 4; Pierre Norman Sands, *A Historical Study of the Academy of Motion Picture Arts and Sciences (1927-1947)* (New York: Arno Press, 1973), pp. 133-5; 'Academy sound school a success,' *AMPAS Bulletin*, no. 26 (30 October 1929): 2-3; Frank Woods, 'The Academy of Motion Picture Arts and Sciences and its service as a forum for the industry,' *JSMPE*, 14, no. 4 (April 1930): 437-40.

9   Sands, *Historical Study*, pp. 187-93; AMPAS Producers-Technicians Committee, *Acoustic Analysis of Set Materials* (Hollywood: AMPAS, 1930); 'Practical problems basis for technical programs,' *AMPAS Bulletin*, (21 September 1931): 9, 12; 'Technical committees active,' *AMPAS Bulletin* no. 29 (27 February 1930): 5.

10   'Sound men and cinematographers discuss their mutual problems,' *AC*, 10, no. 5 (August 1929): 8; Pat Dowling, 'Bringing the art back,' *AC*, 10, no. 8 (November 1929): 21; C.W. Handley, 'Color carbons,' *AC*, 8, no. 11 (February 1928): 22; 'A tribute to the engineer,' *IP*, 2, no. 4 (May 1930): 48; 'Technicians investigate arcs,' *AC*, 10, no. 12 (March 1930): 22; 'How arcs are silenced,' *Cinematography*, 1, no. 4 (July 1930): 12, 25-6; 'Silence with arc lamps,' *IP*, 1, no. 12 (January 1930): 8-10, and 2, no. 1 (February 1930): 44; AMPAS, *Methods of Silencing Arcs* (Hollywood: AMPAS, 1930); E.W. Beggs, 'Motion picture studio lighting,' *Motion Picture Projection*, 2, no. 5 (February 1929): 96.

11   AMPAS, *Camera Silencing Devices* (Hollywood: AMPAS, 1930), pp. 1-30; 'Quarterly technical meeting,' *AMPAS Bulletin*, no. 30 (18 April 1930): 4; Gordon S. Mitchell, 'Camera noise silencing blimps,' *Projection Engineering*, 3, no. 3 (March 1931): 12-14; L.E. Clark, 'Some considerations in the design of sound-proof camera housings,' *JSMPE*, 15, no. 2 (August 1930): 165-70; 'Camera silencing devices,' *Cinematography*, 1, no. 4 (July 1930): 10-11; 'Analysis of camera silencing devices,' *Projection Engineering*, 2, no. 3 (March 1930): 13; 'Development of silent camera given suport,' *AMPAS Bulletin* (14 May 1931): 14; 'Camera silencing,' *Projection Engineering*, 3, no. 5 (May 1931): 13.

12   'Synopsis of technical reports and action authorized by the Research Council,' *AMPAS Technical Bulletin*, supplement no. 12 (20 August 1932): 7.

13   William Koenig, 'The organization and activities of the Research Council of the Academy of Motion Picture Arts and Sciences,' *JSMPE*, 29, no. 5 (November 1937): 485-6.

14   E.C. Wente, 'Contributions of telephone research to sound pictures,' *JSMPE*, 27, no. 2 (August 1936): 189-93; J. Douglas Gomery, 'The coming of sound to the American cinema: A history of the transformation of an industry' (Unpublished PhD dissertation, University of Wisconsin-Madison, 1975), pp. 118-34, 175-8; Patrick Ogle, 'The development of sound systems: the commercial era,' *Film Reader*, 2 (1977): 199-212; 'The ribbon microphone,' *Projection*

Engineering, 4, no. 7 (July 1932): 18-19; Cecil B. Fowler, 'A new recording system,' *Motion Picture Projection*, 6, no. 1 (November 1932): 22-4; F.L. Hopper, 'Wide-range recording,' *JSMPE*, 22, no. 4 (April 1934): 253-9; H.G. Tasker, 'Slide-rule sketches of Hollywood,' *JSMPE*, 28, no. 2 (February 1937): 158; J.K. Hilliard, 'Push-pull recording,' *JSMPE*, 30, no. 2 (February 1938): 156, 161; William Stull, 'Ultra-violet recording with "black light," ' *AC*, 17, no. 8 (August 1936): 329, 335-6; 'The influence of sound accompaniment on the dramatic value of pictures,' *IPro*, 15, no. 4 (April 1940): 20-1; 'Push-pull ultra-violet recording,' *IPro*, 15, no. 2 (February 1940): 23-4; 'One Hundred Men and a Girl,' *Cinema Progress*, no. 2 (August 1937): 24; 'Progress in the motion picture industry,' *JSMPE*, 24, no. 5 (May 1940): 455-84; 'Report on the adaptation of fine-grain films to variable-density sound technics,' *JSMPE*, 34, no. 1 (January 1940): 3-11; Koenig, 'Organization and activities,' pp. 485-7; Jack Duerst, 'An outline of the work of the Academy Research Council SubCommittee on Acoustical Characteristics,' *JSMPE*, 36, no. 3 (March 1941): 282-3; John K. Hilliard, 'Notes on the procedure for handling high volume release prints,' *JSMPE*, 30, no. 2 (February 1938): 209-14; 'Academy recommendations on theatre sound reproducing equipment,' *IPro*, 13, no. 7 (July 1938): 14-15, 29-30; 'Sound track standards revised,' *IPro*, 15, no. 7 (July 1940): 17, 28; Douglas Shearer, 'The voice of the screen,' *The Lion's Roar*, 3, no. 4 (July 1944): n.p.

15   J.P. Maxfield, 'Technic of recording control for sound pictures,' *Cinematographic Annual*, 1 (1930), p. 412.

16   Charles Felstead, 'Monitoring sound motion pictures,' *Projection Engineering*, 2, no. 12 (December 1930): 10-11, 14; 'Technicians' branch meeting,' *AMPAS Bulletin*, no. 21 (12 May 1929): 2; Carl Dreher, 'Recording, re-recording, and editing of sound,' *JSMPE*, 16, no. 6 (June 1931): 756-7; Wesley C. Miller, 'The illusion of reality in sound pictures,' in *Recording Sound for Motion Pictures*, ed. Lester Cowan (New York: McGraw-Hill, 1931), p. 214. See also Mary Ann Doane, 'Ideology and the practice of sound editing and mixing,' in *The Cinematic Apparatus*, ed. Stephen Heath and Teresa De Lauretis (New York: St Martins, 1980), pp. 47-56.

17   Charles Felstead, 'Motion picture sound recording,' *IP*, 6, no. 2 (March 1934): 24.

18   Alexander Walker, *The Shattered Silents: How the Talkies Came to Stay* (New York: William Morrow & Co., 1979), p. 194. See also John L. Cass, 'The illusion of sound and picture,' *JSMPE*, 14, no. 3 (March 1930): 323-6; and Dreher, 'Recording, re-recording,' p. 758.

19   Harold Lewis, 'Getting good sound is an art,' *AC*, 15, no. 2 (June 1934): 65, 73-4.

20   L.E. Clark, 'Accessory and special equipment,' in *Recording Sound*, ed. Cowan, pp. 123-44.

21   Benjamin Glazer, 'The photoplay with sound and voice,' in *Introduction to the Photoplay*, ed. John Tibbetts (Shawnee Mission, Kansas: National Film Society, 1977), p. 95.

22   William deMille, 'Talkie technic,' *AC* 9, no. 12 (December 1929): 17. See also Mordaunt Hall, 'The reaction of the public to motion pictures with sound,' *TSMPE*, 12, no. 35 (1928): 613; 'Open forum,' *TSMPE*, 12, no. 36 (1928): 1129; Wesley C. Miller, 'Sound pictures the successful production of illusion,' *AC*, 10, no. 9 (December 1929): 5, 20-1; L.E. Clark, 'Accessory and special equipment,' p. 127.

23   George Groves, 'Motion picture sound recording,' *American Film Institute/Louis B. Mayer Oral History Collection* (Glen Rock, New Jersey: Microfilming Corporation of America, 1977), pp. 19-21, 50-60; James G. Stewart, 'The evolution of cinematic sound: a personal report,' in *Sound and the Cinema: The Coming of Sound to American Film*, ed. Evan William Cameron (Pleasantville, New York: Redgrave, 1980), p. 44; L.E. Clark, 'Sound stage equipment and practice,' *AC* 11, no. 6 (October 1930): 22; 'New lighting, electrical and set units developed during 1930,' *AC*, 11, no. 9 (January 1931): 24-5; Charles Felstead, 'Monitoring sound motion pictures,' *Projection Engineering*, 3, no. 1 (January 1931): 15; Earl Theisen, 'Hollywood offstage,' *IP*, 8, no. 10 (October 1936): 14; 'Micks and mikes,' *IP*, 1, no. 12 (January 1930): 30; 'Light boom,' *IP*, 9, no. 6 (July 1937): 20-1; L.D. Grignon, 'Light-weight stage pick-up equipment,' *JSMPE*, 29, no. 2 (August 1937): 191-6; Jean Epstein, quoted in *Realism in the Cinema*, ed. Christopher Williams (London: Routledge & Kegan Paul, 1980), pp. 193-7.

24   Harold Lewis, 'Getting good sound is an art,' *AC*, 15, no. 2 (June 1934): 65, 73-4.

25   Kenneth Lambert, 'Sound re-recording: its effects upon reproduction,' *IPro*, 4, no. 1 (November 1932): 16, 28-9.

26   'Sounder sounds,' *Business Week* (29 February 1936): 27. See also James R. Cameron, *Sound Motion Pictures: Recording and Reproducing* (Woodmont, Conn.: Cameron Publishing Co., n.d.), p. 116.

27   H.G. Tasker, 'Multiple-channel recording,' *JSMPE*, 31, no. 4 (October 1938): 381-5.

28   Maurice Pivar, 'Sound film editing,' *AC*, 13, no. 1 (May 1932): 11-12; H.W. Anderson, 'Re-recording, or dubbing film for sound pictures,' *Projection Engineering*, 2, no. 12 (December 1930): 12; Kenneth Lambert, 'Sound re-recording,' *AMPAS*

Technical Bulletin, supplement no. 9 (20 July 1932): 11; H.J. McCord, 'The sound film editor,' *AC*, 12, no. 12 (April 1932): 41; Dreher, 'Recording, re-recording,' p. 759; Maurice Pivar, 'Sound film editing,' *American Photography*, 27, no. 9 (September 1933): 560-1; 'New Moviola,' *IP*, 5, no. 4 (May 1933): 18; F.D. Williams, 'Methods of bloop-ing,' *JSMPE*, 30, no. 1 (January 1938): 105-6; 'Glossary of technical terms used in the motion picture industry,' *TSMPE*, 13, no. 37 (1929): 49; M.W. Palmer, 'Film-numbering device for cameras and recorders,' *JSMPE*, 14, no. 3 (March 1930): 327-31; Earl Theisen, 'The story of the Moviola,' *IP*, 7, no. 10 (November 1935): 4.

29 Quoted in Roy Prendergast, *Film Music: A Neglec-ted Art* (New York: Norton, 1977), p. 42.

30 Quoted in Mark Evans, *Soundtrack: The Music of the Movies* (New York: Da Capo, 1979), p. 26.

31 Bernard Herrmann, 'Reminiscence and reflection,' in *Sound and the Cinema*, ed. Cameron, p. 120.

32 Gerald Mast, *A Short History of the Movies* (Indianapolis: Bobbs-Merrill, 1976), p. 222.

33 *Ibid.*, p. 224.

34 Elmer C. Richardson, 'Progress in studio illumin-ation during 1929,' *AC*, 10, no. 9 (December 1929): 41; Leigh M. Griffith, 'The technical status of the film laboratory,' *TSMPE*, 12, no. 33 (1928): 173-94; C. Roy Hunter, 'A negative developing machine,' *TSMPE*, 12, no. 33 (1928): 195-8; Arthur Reeves, 'How to simply develop sound film,' *IP*, 4, no. 4 (May 1932): 14.

35 Wesley Miller, 'Illusion of reality', in *Recording Sound*, ed. Cowan, p. 210. See also Fitzhugh Green, *The Film Finds Its Tongue* (New York: Putnam's, 1929), pp. 66-7.

36 See Green, *Tongue*, pp. 166-7, 220-40; Armand Falnieres, 'Enter – the silent director,' *Cinema Art*, 6, no. 2 (April 1927): 26-7; 'Fresh details on "Vitaphone" filming,' *AC*, 7, no. 11 (February 1927): 11, 15; Fred J. Balshofer and Arthur C. Miller, *One Reel a Week* (Berkeley: University of California Press, 1967), p. 174.

37 See Lewis W. Physioc. 'Technique of the talkies,' *AC*, 9, no. 5 (August 1928): 24-5; J.P. Maxfield, 'Technic of recording control for sound pictures,' *Cinematographic Annual*, 1 (1930), p. 417; Karl Struss, 'Photographing with multiple cameras,' *TSMPE*, 13, no. 38 (1929): 477-8; Victor Milner, 'Painting with light,' *Cinematographic Annual*, 1, (1930), p. 92; J. Garrick Eisensberg, 'Mechanics of the talking movies,' *Projection Engineering*, 1, no. 3 (November 1929): 22-4; Charles Felstead, 'Monitor-ing sound motion pictures,' *Projection Engineering*, 3, no. 1 (January 1931): 15; James R. Cameron and Joseph A. Dubray, *Cinematography and Talkies* (Woodmont, Conn.: Cameron Publishing Company,

1930), p. 186; 'Progress Committee Report,' *JSMPE*, 19, no. 2 (August 1932): 123. See also Edward Bernds, 'The birth of the talkies,' *American Film*, 6, no. 10 (September 1981): 34-6, 65.

38 'What they use in Hollywood,' *Cinematographic Annual*, 1 (1930), pp. 549, 575; 'Analysis of camera silencing devices,' *Projection Engineering*, 2, no. 3 (March 1930): 13-14; Elmer C. Richardson, 'Tilt heads and rolling tripods for camera blimps,' *JSMPE*, 15, no. 1 (July 1930): 46-52.

39 A. Lindsley Lane, 'Cinematographer plays leading part in group of creative minds,' *AC*, 16, no. 2 (February 1935): 58. See also Walter B. Pitkin and William M. Marston, *The Art of Sound Pictures* (New York: Appleton, 1930), pp. 121-6.

40 Franklin, *Sound Motion Pictures*, p. 230.

41 Tamar Lane, *The New Technique of Screenwriting* (New York: Whittlesey, 1936), p. 37.

42 'A new Mole-Richardson production,' *IP*, 2, no. 4 (May 1930): 6; 'Mole-Richardson construct peram-bulator to eliminate shifting on travel shots,' *IP*, 2, no. 11 (December 1930): 45.

43 'Report of the Progress Committee,' *JSMPE* 20, no. 6 (June 1933): 468; Lewis W. Physioc. 'Unterrified inventors show work,' *IP*, 4, no. 5 (June 1932): 4; John F. Seitz, 'New camera-carriage saves time,' *AC*, 14, no. 1 (May 1933): 8, 35; J. Henry Kline, 'Kamera kiddie kars,' *IP*, 5, no. 5 (May 1933): 44-5; Frank Graves, 'The Universal camera crane,' *TSMPE*, no. 38 (1929): 303-7; 'Devises "rotary shot,"' *IP*, 2, no. 10 (November 1930): 45; 'Progress in the motion picture industry,' *JSMPE*, 27, no. 1 (July 1936): 11-12.

44 Gordon S. Mitchell, 'The camera crane used in making intricate shots,' *Projection Engineering*, 3, no. 2 (February 1931): 14.

45 J.A. Ball, 'Scientific foundations,' in *Introduction to the Photoplay*, ed. Tibbetts, p. 10.

46 Joseph Dubray, 'The rotambulator – a new motion picture camera stand,' *JSMPE*, 22, no. 3 (March 1934): 201.

47 A. Lindsley Lane, 'Rhythmic flow – mental and visual,' *AC*, 16, no. 4 (April 1935): 138.

48 Roe Fleet, 'Aces of the camera: Ed B. DuPar, ASC,' *AC*, 27, no. 12 (December 1946): 456.

49 See Balshofer and Miller, *One Reel*, pp. 184-98; Michael Killanin, 'Poet in an iron mask,' *Films and Filming*, 4, no. 5 (February 1958): 9.

50 A. Lindsley Lane, 'Cinematographer plays,' p. 49; Mary Eunice McCarthy, *Hands of Hollywood* (Hollywood: Photoplay Research Bureau, 1929), p. 31; Karl Struss, 'The camera battery,' *IP*, 1, no. 6 (July 1929): 17; Barrett C. Kiesling, *Talking Pictures* (Richmond, Virginia: Johnson, 1937), p. 181; Anne Bauchens, 'Cutting the film,' in *We Make the Movies*, ed. Nancy Naumberg (New York:

Norton, 1937), p. 213; Carl Dreher, 'Stage technique in the talkies,' *AC*, 10, no. 9 (December 1929): 16; Eric Sherman, *Directing the Film: Film Directors on Their Art* (Boston: Little Brown & Co. 1976), pp. 104-5, 120; Nick Grinde, 'Pictures for peanuts,' *Penguin Film Review*, no. 1 (1946): 48-9; Don Livingston, *Film and the Director* (New York: Macmillan, 1953), pp. 44-5. 'Covering' footage is still a mainstay of Hollywood production; see Ralph Rosenblum, *When the Shooting Stops . . The Cutting Begins* (New York: Penguin, 1980), pp. 135-6.

Chapter 24 The labor-force, financing and the mode of production

1* Bargaining power is reflected in terms of salaries and contractual rights. It is difficult to find comparable statistics on this from reliable sources. William S. Hart claimed that in the mid-teens his average cowboy actor earned $5 plus board per week, his leading actress received $40 per week, as star and director he made $125 per week, while some other 'new stars' were making $1,800 to $3,500 per week just for acting. In the first part of the 1920s, two other listings also indicate a wide range of pay schedules. See William S. Hart, *My Life East and West* (Boston: Houghton Mifflin Co., 1929), p. 214; Robert Florey, *Filmland* (Paris: Editions de cinémagazine, 1923), pp. 45-6; Laurence A. Hughes, ed., *The Truth About the Movies by the Stars* (Hollywood: Hollywood Publishers, 1924), p. 293. On actors' salaries in 1933, see Murray Ross, *Stars and Strikes: Unionization of Hollywood* (New York: Columbia University Press, 1941), p. 108.

2 Ross, *Stars and Strikes*; early evidence of labor action is in: Richard V. Spencer, 'Los Angeles notes,' *MPW*, 8, no. 12 (25 March 1911), 644; F.H. Richardson, 'Projection department,' *MPW*, 9, no. 4 (5 August 1911), 286; F.H. Richardson, 'Projection department,' *MPW*, 15, no. 2 (11 January 1913), 155-6; 'Trade board holds regular meeting,' *MPW*, 28, no. 4 (22 April 1916), 601; 'Studio extras would organize,' *MPW*, 29, no. 10 (9 September 1916), 1673; G.P. Von Harleman and Clarke Irvine, 'News of Los Angeles and vicinity,' *MPW*, 29, no. 10 (9 September 1916), 1677.

3 On jurisdictional disputes in the 1930s and 1940s, besides Ross, see: Robert Joseph, 'Re: unions in Hollywood,' *Films*, 1, no. 3 (Summer 1940), 34-50; 'More trouble in paradise,' *Fortune*, 34, no. 5 (November 1946), 154-9, 215+; Murray Ross, 'Labor relations in Hollywood,' in *The Motion Picture Industry*, ed. Gordon S. Watkins (Philadelphia: American Academy of Political and Social Science, 1947), pp. 58-64; Anthony A.P. Dawson, 'Holly-wood's labor troubles,' *Industrial and Labor Relations Review*, 1, no. 4 (July 1948), 638-47; US Education and Labor Committee, House, 'Jurisdictional disputes in motion-picture industry,' hearings before special subcommittee, 80th Cong., 1st and 2nd sess. (Washington, DC: Government Printing Office, 1948), vols 1, 2, and 3.

4 Earl Theisen, 'The evolution of the motion picture story,' *IP*, 8, no. 4 (May 1936), 12; 'Our new titles,' *EK*, 3, no. 4 (1 September 1910), 2; Earl Theisen, 'The story of slides & titles,' *IP*, 5, no. 11 (December 1933), 4-6; 'Aida (Edison),' *MPW*, 8, no. 20 (20 May 1911), 1140 (specific reference as 'notable' is given to the cast list on the titles); J. Berg Esenwein and Arthur Leeds, *Writing the Photoplay* (Springfield, Mass.: Home Correspondence School, 1913), pp. 90-3; Epes Winthrop Sargent, 'The scenario writer,' *MPW*, 10, no. 13 (28 December 1911), 1062; William Lord Wright, 'William Lord Wright's page,' *MPNews*, 5, no. 2 (13 January 1912), 32; 'Credit for scenarios,' *EK*, 6, no. 1 (1 February 1912), 15; William Lord Wright, 'For those who worry o'er plots and plays,' *MPNews*, 5, no. 9 (2 March 1912), 22; 'Spectator,' ' "Spectator's" comments,' *NYDM*, 67, no. 1735 (20 March 1912), 25; 'Reliance to publish authors' names,' *NYDM*, 67, no. 1735 (20 March 1912), 25.

5 'Revised administrative procedure for credits to screen authors,' *Academy of Motion Picture Arts & Sciences Bulletin*, 1934, no. 8 (9 August 1934), p. 21. Later descriptions of this are in Maurice Rapf, 'Credit arbitration isn't simple,' *The Screen Writer*, 1, no. 2 (July 1945), 31-6; Hortense Powdermaker, *Hollywood: The Dream Factory* (New York: Little Brown & Co., 1950), pp. 154-5.

6 Price, Waterhouse & Co., *Memorandum on Moving Picture Accounts* (New York: Price, Waterhouse & Co., 1916), p. 26; Paul H. Davis, 'Financing the movies,' *Photoplay*, 11, no. 3 (February 1917), 66.

7 US Interstate Commerce Committee, Senate, 'Compulsory block-booking and blind selling in motion-picture industry,' hearings before subcommittee, 74th Cong., 2nd sess., on S. 3012, February 27, 28, 1936 (Washington, DC: Government Printing Office, 1938), p. 15; Howard Thompson Lewis, *Cases on the Motion Picture Industry* (Harvard Business Reports, vol. 8) (New York: McGraw-Hill, 1930), pp. 68-79.

8 Lewis, *Cases*, p. 71.

9 Maurice Barber, 'Requirements of financing,' *AC*, 3, no. 1 (1 April 1922), 20-1; Benjamin B. Hampton, *History of the American Film Industry from its Beginnings to 1931* (1931; rpt, New York: Dover Publications, 1970), p. 380; Lewis, *Cases*, pp. 46-51; Attilio H. Giannini, 'Financial aspects,' in *The Story of the Films*, ed. Joseph P. Kennedy (Chicago:

A.W. Shaw Co., 1927), pp. 77-97; Motion Picture Producers and Distributors Association, 'The motion picture industry,' in *The Development of American Industries*, ed. John George Glover and William Bouck Cornell (New York: Prentice-Hall, 1932), p. 758; Halsey, Stuart & Co., 'The motion picture industry as a basis for bond financing,' in *The American Film Industry*, ed. Tino Balio (Madison: University of Wisconsin Press, 1976), pp. 172, 190.

10 Ernest Mandel, *Marxist Economic Theory*, trans. Brian Pearce (New York: Monthly Review Press, 1968), vol. 2, pp. 393-440; Paul M. Sweezy, *The Theory of Capitalist Development* (New York: Modern Reader Paperbacks, 1942), pp. 239-328; Paul A. Baran and Paul M. Sweezy, *Monopoly Capital: An Essay on the American Economic and Social Order* (New York: Modern Reader Paperbacks, 1966).

11 Mandel, *Marxist Economic Theory*, vol. 2, pp. 413-33.

12 F.D. Klingender and Stuart Legg, *Money Behind the Screen* (London: Lawrence & Wishart, 1937), pp. 68-79.

13 Robert Sklar, *Movie-Made America: A Cultural History of American Movies* (New York: Vintage Books, 1976), pp. 156-65.

14 John Kenneth Galbraith, *The New Industrial State*, 2nd ed. (New York: New American Library, 1971), p. 92. See in particular Fox and Paramount: 'The case of William Fox,' *Fortune*, 1 (May 1930), 48-9+; 'Formation of trusteeship announced by Wm. Fox,' *The Ohio Showman*, 5, no. 19 (14 December 1929), 25; '*Body and Soul* is (here) put together,' *Fortune*, 4 (August 1931), 26-34+; Daniel Bertrand, W. Duane Evans, and E.L. Blanchard, 'Investigation of concentration of economic power: study made for the temporary national economic committee,' monograph no. 43, 'Motion picture industry – pattern of control' (Washington, DC: Government Printing Office, 1941), p. 60; 'Theatres and motion pictures,' *Standard Trade and Securities*, 75, no. 22 (20 February 1935), TH-52-54; Howard T. Lewis, *The Motion Picture Industry* (New York: D. Van Nostrand Co., 1933), pp. 361-3; 'Paramount,' *Fortune*, 15 (March 1937), 87-96+; US Securities and Exchange Commission, 'Report on study and investigation of work, activities, personnel and functions of protective and reorganization committees, pursuant to sec. 211 of securities exchange act of 1934' (Washington, DC: Government Printing Office, 1936-8), vol. 1, pp. 6-64; and vol. 2, pp. 78-121, 196-200; William T. Raymond, 'SEC probes Paramount reorganization,' *Barron's*, 15, no. 15 (24 June 1935), 24; Douglas Gomery, 'The coming of the talkies: invention, innovation, and diffusion,' in *The

American Film Industry*, ed. Balio, p. 207.

15 Sweezy, *The Theory of Capitalist Development*, pp. 267, 242-4; also see Galbraith, *The New Industrial State*, p. 101; Paul Hirst, *On Law and Ideology* (Atlantic Highlands, New Jersey: Humanities Press, 1979), pp. 96-152.

16 Baran and Sweezy, *Monopoly Capital*, pp. 15-16; James Early in Baran and Sweezy, pp. 25-8.

17 Richard Caves, *American Industry: Structure, Conduct, Performance*, 4th ed. (Englewood Cliffs, New Jersey: Prentice-Hall, 1977), p. 4; Rubin Marris, 'A model of the "managerial" enterprise,' *Quarterly Journal of Economics*, 77, no. 2 (May 1963), p. 188; Oliver E. Williamson, 'Managerial discretion and business behavior,' *American Economic Review*, 53, no. 5 (December 1963), p. 1049.

18 Mae D. Huettig, *Economic Control of the Motion Picture Industry: A Study in Industrial Organization* (Philadelphia: University of Pennsylvania Press, 1944), pp. 100-1.

19* In a case study of management at A & P, the managers measured the success of the firm not by profit on sales but by return on investments. In fact, they became concerned over 'excessive profits' which indicated that retained earnings were not being rechanneled into growth. See M.A. Adelman, *A & P: A Study in Price-Cost Behavior and Public Policy* (Cambridge, Mass.: Harvard University Press, 1959), pp. 30, 36; Galbraith, *The New Industrial State*, p. 88.

20 Alfred D. Chandler, Jr, *Strategy and Structure: Chapters in the History of the American Industrial Enterprise* (Cambridge, Mass.: M.I.T. Press, 1962), p. 11; Richard Edwards, *Contested Terrain: The Transformation of the Workplace in the Twentieth Century* (New York: Basic Books, 1979), p. 21; Galbraith, *The New Industrial State*, pp. 92-7.

21 'Paramount: Oscar for profits,' *Fortune*, 35, no. 6 (June 1947), 218.

22 Price, Waterhouse & Co., *Memorandum*, p. 9.

23 *Ibid.*, pp. 24-5.

24 Hampton, *History*, pp. 187, 320; William Marston Seabury, *The Public and the Motion Picture Industry* (New York: Macmillan, 1926), pp. 280-1, 286; Maurice Barber, 'Requirements of financing,' *AC*, 3, no. 1 (1 April 1922), 20-1.

25 George Landy, 'The "independent" film studio,' *PTD*, 4, no. 4 (September 1922), 7-8, 42; Hampton, *History*, p. 205; Lee Royal, *The Romance of Motion Picture Production* (Los Angeles: Royal Publishing Co., 1920), pp. 66-7.

26 Hampton, *History*, pp. 318-19; Geoffrey Shurlock, ' "Versions," ' *AC*, 11, no. 9 (January 1931), 22; Gomery, 'The coming of the talkies,' p. 208; David O. Selznick, *Memo from David O. Selznick*, ed. Rudy Behlmer (1972; rpt, New York: Avon Books, 1973),

p. 72; Pat Dowling, 'Independents burst into sound,' *AC*, 10, no. 7 (October 1929), 7, 40.

27 '100 features from independents in new season as market opens,' *MPHerald*, 103, no. 5 (2 May 1931), 12.

28 'Independents to do 192 features,' *MPHerald*, 103, no. 8 (23 May 1931), 24; 'Curtailment by larger studios prompts independents to expand,' *MPHerald*, 106, no. 2 (9 January 1932), 9; 'Independent producers unite to capitalize on wider market,' *MPHerald*, 106, no. 4 (23 January 1932), 21; US Interstate and Foreign Commerce Committee, 'Motion-picture films,' hearing before subcommittee, 74th Cong., 2nd sess., March 9-26, 1936 (Washington, DC: Government Printing Office, 1936), p. 242; Charles Flynn and Todd McCarthy, 'The economic imperative: why was the B movie necessary?' *Kings of the Bs* (New York: E.P. Dutton, 1975); 'Theatres and motion pictures,' TH-51; Tim Onosko, 'Monogram: its rise and fall in the forties,' *The Velvet Light Trap*, no. 5 (Summer 1972), 5-9; Merrill Lynch, Pierce, Fenner & Beane, *Radio, Television, Motion Pictures* (New York: Merrill Lynch, Pierce, Fenner & Beane, 1950), pp. 21, 24.

29 Edward Buscombe, 'Bread and circuses: economics and the cinema,' Conference on Cinema Histories, Cinema Practices, Asilomar, California, 25-29 May 1981, p. 4.

Chapter 25 The producer-unit system: management by specialization after 1931

1   Florabel Muir, 'Hollywood considers the unit,' *MPHerald*, 104, no. 7 (15 August 1931), 12.

2   Dore Schary and Charles Palmer, *Case History of a Movie* (New York: Random House, 1950), p. 56.

3   W.C. Harcus, 'Making a motion picture,' *JSMPE*, 17, no. 5 (November 1931), 802-4; 'Metro-Goldwyn-Mayer,' *Fortune*, 6 (December 1932), rpt in *The American Film Industry*, ed. Tino Balio (Madison: University of Wisconsin Press, 1976), p. 260; David Gordon, 'Mayer, Thalberg, and MGM,' *Sight and Sound*, 45 (Summer 1976), 187.

4   Howard T. Lewis, *The Motion Picture Industry* (New York: D. Van Nostrand Co. 1933), pp. 98-106.

5   'New associated director group for unit production is proposed,' *MPHerald*, 103, no. 13 (27 June 1931), 29.

6   'Industry to test unit producing to shave cost, improve quality,' *MPHerald*, 104, no. 5 (1 August 1931), 9.

7   *Ibid.*, 9, 23; Florabel Muir, 'Hollywood considers the unit,' *MPHerald*, 104, no. 7 (15 August 1931), 12, 35.

8   '$200,000 Top Film Cost,' *Variety* 104, no. 4 (6

October 1931), 3; 'Producers agree to bar unfair bidding in star contract raids,' *MPHerald*, 106, no. 3 (26 January 1932), 19; '3 directing teams replace John Ford at Fox – drawing but half his salary,' *Variety*, 104, no. 8 (3 November 1931), 2; 'Thalberg orders story department cut at M-G-M,' *Variety*, 104, no. 8 (3 November 1931), 3; 'Fox cuts off readers dept.,' *Variety*, 104, no. 7 (27 October 1931), 4; 'Fox salary slash from 5% to 25% covering all depts. and executives,' *Variety*, 104, no. 7 (27 October 1931), 4; 'Fox budget now $225,000 per picture, first studio near discussed figure,' *Variety*, 104, no. 7 (27 October 1931), 5.

9   'Columbia adopts unit production,' *MPHerald*, 105, no. 5 (31 October 1931), 17; also see: 'Unit production for Col. includes new personnel,' *Variety*, 104, no. 7 (27 October 1931), 5.

10 'Radio and Pathe sales forces consolidate under Lee Marcus,' *MPHerald*, 105, no. 6 (7 November 1931), 9, 30; 'Holding brands,' *Variety*, 104, no. 9 (10 November 1931), 4; 'Fox starts unit production plan; Sheehan at head,' *MPHerald*, 105, no. 7 (14 November 1931), 26; 'Fox Studio heads stay, says Tinker,' *MPHerald*, 105, no. 11 (12 December 1931), 17; 'Cohen's economy plan at Par for Zukor's OK,' *Variety*, 104, no. 9 (10 November 1931), 5; 'Cohen favors unit system for Par,' *Variety*, 104, no. 10 (17 November 1931), 2; 'Schulberg proposal changed by Zukor,' *Variety*, 104, no. 11 (24 November 1931), 5; 'Paramount names seven associates for unit system,' *MPHerald*, 105, no. 9 (28 November 1931), 13.

11 Alfred D. Chandler, Jr, *Strategy and Structure: Chapters in the History of the American Industrial Enterprises* (Cambridge, Mass.: M.I.T. Press, 1962), pp. 320-3.

12 On story and writing practices, see: William James Fadiman, 'Selling books to movies,' *The Publishers' Weekly*, 126, no. 12 (22 September 1934), 1085-7; William J. Fadiman, 'The sources of movies,' in *The Motion Picture Industry*, ed. Gordon S. Watkins (Philadelphia: American Academy of Political and Social Science, 1947), pp. 37-40; Lewis, *The Motion Picture Industry*, pp. 30-3; Samuel Marx, 'Looking for a story,' in *We Make the Movies*, ed. Nancy Naumberg (New York: W.W. Norton & Co., 1937), pp. 16-31; Frances Marion, *How to Write and Sell Film Stories* (New York: Covici-Friede Publishers, 1937), pp. 14-16; Marguerite G. Ortman, *Fiction and the Screen* (Boston: Marshall Jones Company, 1935); pp. 77-8; Barrett C. Kiesling, *Talking Pictures: How They are Made, How to Appreciate Them* (Richmond, Virginia: Johnson Publishing Co., 1937), pp. 39-53; 'Paramount: Oscar for profits,' *Fortune*, 35, no. 6 (June 1947), 216-18; Motion Picture Producers Association, *1956 Annual Report*

on the Motion Picture Producers Association (New York: Motion Picture Producers Association, 1956), p. 15; Sidney Howard, 'The story gets a treatment,' in *We Make the Movies*, ed. Naumberg, pp. 32-52; Ray Hoadley, *How They Make a Motion Picture* (New York: Thomas Y. Crowell, 1939), pp. 14-15; Martin Field, 'Type-casting screen-writers,' *Penguin Film Review*, no. 6 (April 1948), 29-31; William J. Fadiman, 'The type-writer jungle,' *Films and Filming*, 7, no. 3 (December 1960), 8.

13   *Academy of Motion Picture Arts & Sciences, Technical Bulletin*, Supplement no. 19 (23 December 1932).

14   On research and legal departments, see: Kiesling, *Talking Pictures*, pp. 81-91; 'Research in motion pictures,' *IP*, 13, no. 12 (January 1942), 16; Fred Stanley, 'Film tune sleuths,' *The New York Times*, rpt in *Film Music Notes*, 8, no. 3 (January-February 1949), 17-18; Schary and Palmer, *Case History*, pp. 30-2.

15   On casting, see: Kiesling, *Talking Pictures*, pp. 127-47; Phil Friedman, 'The players are cast,' in *We Make the Movies*, ed. Naumberg, pp. 106-16; Jimmy Stewart in Kodak ad, *American Film*, 5, no. 5 (March 1980), 9; Earl Theisen, 'Eyes toward Hollwood,' *IP*, 7, no. 8 (September 1935), 22-3; Hoadley, *How They Make a Motion Picture*, p. 37; Frank Westmore and Murial Davidson, *The Westmores of Hollywood* (New York: Berkeley Publishing Corp., 1976).

16   On agencies, see: 'The Morris Agency: put their names in lights,' *Fortune*, 18 (September 1938), 67+.

17   On script timing, see: H.G. Tasker, 'Current developments in production methods in Hollywood,' *JSMPE*, 24, no. 1 (January 1935), 4-5. *An American in Paris* (1951, MGM) was also timed, resulting in the loss of several pre-planned numbers; see, Donald Knox, *The Magic Factory: How MGM Made An American in Paris* (New York: Praeger Publishers, 1973).

18   On cinematography, see: AC and *IP* throughout; John Arnold, 'Shooting the movies,' in *We Make the Movies*, ed. Naumberg, pp. 143-72; Virgil E. Miller, 'Camera-department organization and maintenance,' *AC*, 13, no. 6 (October 1932), 6-7, 40-1; 'Close-Ups,' *IP*, 11, no. 5 (June 1939), 12-13; C.W. Handley, 'The advanced technic of Technicolor lighting,' *JSMPE*, 29, no. 2 (August 1937), 174-5; William H. Daniels, 'Camera script clerk experiment by Daniels at MGM real success,' *AC*, 19, no. 3 (March 1938), 102-6; 'Just what is so mysterious about color,' *AC*, 17, no. 10 (October 1936), 414, 424-6; Jimmie Stone, 'The assistant cameraman's job,' *IP*, 11, no. 11 (December 1939), 12-13, 22-3; 'Lighting-sets,' *IP*, 9, no. 5 (June 1937), 31-2; John

Alton, *Painting with Light* (New York: Macmillan, 1949), pp. 1-3; Nathan Levinson, 'Recording and re-recording,' in *We Make the Movies*, ed. Naumberg, pp. 173-98; James R. Cameron, *Sound Motion Pictures Recording and Reproducing: With Chapters on Motion Picture Studio and Film Laboratory Practices*, 8th ed. (Coral Gables, Florida: Cameron Publishing Co., 1959), pp. 314-51.

19   On make-up, see: Max Factor, 'The Art of motion picture make-up,' in *Cinematographic Annual 1930*, vol. 1, ed. Hal Hall (Hollywood, California: American Society of Cinematographers, 1930), pp. 157-71; Kiesling, *Talking Pictures*, pp. 148-54; James Barker, 'Make-up for fast film,' *AC*, 12, no. 7 (November 1931), 11, 24; Max Factor, 'Standardization of motion picture make-up,' *JSMPE*, 28, no. 1 (January 1937), 52-62; Perc Westmore, 'Cooperation bulks big in work of make-up,' *AC*, 18, no. 12 (December 1937), 496-7.

20   Marion, *How to Write and Sell Film Stories*, pp. 59-60.

21   William R. Weaver, 'Studios use audience research to learn what pleases customers,' *MPHerald*, 164, no. 3 (20 July 1946), 37; William R. Weaver, 'Audience research has Hollywood renaissance,' *MPHerald*, 175, no. 6 (7 May 1949), 29; Leo A, Handel, *Hollywood Looks at Its Audience* (Urbana: University of Illinois Press, 1950), pp. 4-7.

22   On special effects, see: 'Biggest stage on earth devoted entirely to special process work,' *AC*, 10, no. 1 (April 1929), 20-1, 35; Hans Dreier, 'Motion picture sets,' *JSMPE*, 17, no. 5 (November 1931), 789-91; Fred W. Jackman, 'The special-effects cinematographer,' *AC*, 13, no. 6 (October 1932), 12-13, 42-4; 'Close-ups,' *IP*, 11, no. 8 (September 1939), 21-2; William Luhr and Peter Lehman, ' "Would you mind just trying it": an interview with special effects artist Linwood Dunn, ASC,' *Wide Angle*, 1, no. 1 (rev. ed.) (1979), 80; Don Jahraus, 'Making miniatures,' *AC*, 12, no. 7 (November 1931), 9-10, 41; 'R-K-O trick departments consolidated,' *AC*, 13, no. 6 (October 1932), 45; 'Rear projection big advance,' *IP*, 9, no. 3 (April 1938), 30-3; 'Winter made to order,' *IP*, 8, no. 2 (March 1936), 23; R. Seawright and W.V. Draper, 'Photographic effects in the feature production of *Topper*,' *JSMPE*, 32 (January 1939), 60+.

23   On production departments, unit managers, and assistant directors, see: W.C. Harcus, 'Making a motion picture,' *JSMPE*, 17, no. 5 (November 1931), 805; Clem Beauchamp, 'The production takes shape,' in *We Make the Movies*, ed. Naumberg, pp. 64-79; Kiesling, *Talking Pictures*, pp. 93-5, 159-63; [Paul R. Harmer], 'Estimating the cost of a motion picture production – the work sheet,' *IP*, 8, no. 9 (October 1934), 12-13; Robert Presnell, 'Preparing a

story for production,' *JSMPE*, 29, no. 4 (October 1937), 350-5; Robert Edward Lee, 'On the spot,' in *We Make the Movies*, ed. Naumberg, pp. 90-105; Cameron, *Sound Motion Pictures*, pp. 308-9; Carlisle Jones, 'Why and what is an assistant director,' *IP*, 6, no. 4 (May 1934), 20; John Van Pelt, 'The assistant director,' *IP*, 8, no. 12 (January 1937), 26-7; Leslie Wood, *The Romance of the Movies* (London: William Heinemann, Ltd., 1937), pp. 311-14.

24   On art direction, see: Hans Dreier, 'Motion picture sets,' *JSMPE*, 17, no. 5 (November 1931), 789-91; Ralph Flint, 'Cedric Gibbons,' *Creative Art*, 11 (October 1932), 116-19; James Wong Howe, 'Visual suggestion can enhance "rationed" sets,' *AC*, 23, no. 6 (June 1942), 246-7; Hans Dreier, 'Designing the sets,' in *We Make the Movies*, ed. Naumberg, pp. 80-9; Cedric Gibbons, 'The art director,' in *Behind the Screen: How Films Are Made*, ed. Stephen Watts (New York: Dodge Publishing Co., 1938), pp. 41-50; Hoadley, *How They Make a Motion Picture*, pp. 18-20; Kiesling, *Talking Pictures*, pp. 92-111; Hal Herman, 'Motion picture art direction,' *AC*, 28, no. 11 (November 1947), 396-7, 416-17; Gordon Wiles, 'Imagination in set design,' *AC*, 13, no. 3 (July 1932), 8-9, 31; Gordon Wiles, 'Small sets,' *AC*, 13, no. 5 (September 1932), 11-12, 28; Donald Deschner, 'Edward Carfagno: MGM art director,' *The Velvet Light Trap*, no. 18 (Spring 1978), 30-4; Donald Deschner, 'Anton Grot: Warners art director 1927-1948,' *The Velvet Light Trap*, no. 15 (Fall 1975), 18-22; John Harkrider, 'Set design from script to stage,' *JSMPE*, 29, no. 4 (October 1937), 358-60; Earl Theisen, 'In the motion picture prop and research department,' *IP*, 6, no. 7 (August 1934), 4-5, 23; Lewis W. Physioc, 'The scenic artist,' *IP*, 8, no. 2 (March 1936), 3, 22-3; Lansing C. Holden, 'Designing for color,' in *We Make the Movies*, ed. Naumberg, pp. 239-52; Natalie M. Kalmus, 'Color consciousness,' *JSMPE*, 25, no. 2 (August 1935), 139-47.

On William Cameron Menzies, see: Ezra Goodman, 'Production designing,' *AC*, 26, no. 3 (March 1945), 82-3, 100; 'The layout for *Bulldog Drummond*,' *Creative Arts*, 5 (October 1929), 729-34.

25   For descriptions of work practices in other areas during this period, see the following:

On producers: Hunt Stromberg, 'The producer,' in *Behind the Screen*, ed. Watts, pp. 1-12; Jesse L. Lasky, 'The producer makes a plan,' in *We Make the Movies*, ed. Naumberg, pp. 1-15; Kiesling, *Talking Pictures*, pp. 48-54; David O. Selznick, 'The functions of the producer and the making of feature films,' excerpts from a lecture, 1 November 1937, rpt in David O. Selznick, *Memo from David O.*

Selznick, ed. Rudy Behlmer (1972; rpt, New York: Avon Books, 1973), pp. 545-5.

On the special problems of low-budget productions: Robert Presnell, 'Preparing a story for production,' *JSMPE*, 29, no. 4 (October 1937), 350-5; Nick Grinde, 'Pictures for peanuts,' *The Penguin Film Review*, no. 1 (August 1946), rpt in *Hollywood Directors 1941-1976*, ed. Richard Koszarski (New York: Oxford University Press, 1977), pp. 56-67.

On costuming: Kiesling, *Talking Pictures*, pp. 112-18; Hoadley, *How They Make a Motion Picture*, pp. 40-2; Adrian, 'Clothes,' in *Behind the Screen*, ed. Watts, pp. 53-7.

On pre-scoring: Bernard Brown, 'Prescoring for song sequences,' *JSMPE*, 29, no. 4 (October 1937), 356-67; Herb A. Lightman, 'Staging musical routines for the camera,' *AC*, 28, no. 1 (January 1947), 8-9, 32.

On shooting practices: 'How lighting units are developed today,' *AC*, 18, no. 5 (May 1937), 189; Robert Edward Lee, 'On the spot,' in *We Make the Movies*, ed. Naumberg, p. 100; John W. Boyle, 'Black and white cinematography,' *JSMPE*, 39, no. 8 (August 1942), 83-92; H.G. Tasker, 'Slide-rule sketches of Hollywood,' *JSMPE*, 28, no. 2 (February 1937), 159-60 (on synching methods at various studios).

On direction: John Cromwell, 'The voice behind the megaphone,' in *We Make the Movies*, ed. Naumberg, pp. 53-63; Clem Beauchamp, 'The production takes shape,' in *We Make the Movies*, ed. Naumberg, pp. 70-1; Cameron, *Sound Motion Pictures*, pp. 78-83.

On laboratory work: 'Theatres and motion pictures,' *Standard Trade and Securities*, 75, no. 22 (20 February 1935), TH-51; 'The laboratory,' *IP*, 5, no. 5 (June 1933), 14; James R. Wilkinson, 'Motion picture laboratory practices,' *JSMPE*, 39, no. 9 (September 1942), 166-85.

On editing: Cameron, *Sound Motion Pictures*, pp. 78-83; James Wilkinson and E.W. Reis, 'Editing and assembling the sound picture,' in *Recording Sound for Motion Pictures*, ed. Lester Cowan (New York: McGraw-Hill, 1931), pp. 196-209; W.C. Harcus, 'Finishing a motion picture,' *JSMPE*, 19, no. 6 (December 1932), 553-60; Frederick Y. Smith, 'The cutting and editing of motion pictures,' *JSMPE*, 39, no. 10 (November 1942), 284-93; Maurice Pivar, 'Sound film editing,' *AC*, 13, no. 1 (May 1932), 11-12, 46; 'The laboratory,' *IP*, 5, no. 5 (June 1933), 14; Kiesling, *Talking Pictures*, pp. 216-26; Maurice Pivar, 'Film editing,' *JSMPE*, 19, no. 4 (October 1937), 363-72; Anne Bauchens, 'Cutting the film,' in *We Make the Movies*, ed. Naumberg, pp. 199-215; Susan Dalton and John Davis, 'John Cromwell,' *The Velvet Light Trap*, no. 10 (Fall

1973), 23-5; Allan Balter, 'After the last shot is made,' *AC*, 36, no. 7 (July 1955), 398-9, 431-3; Ralph Dawson, 'How *Anthony Adverse* was cut,' *AC*, 17, no. 8 (August 1936), 345, 356.

On music composition, recording, and rerecording: Cameron, *Sound Motion Pictures*, pp. 352-411; George Antheil, 'On the Hollywood front,' *Modern Music*, 14, no. 1 (November-December 1936), 46-7; George Antheil, 'Breaking into the movies,' *Modern Music*, 14, no. 2 (January-February 1937), 82-6; Charles Previn, 'Setting music to pictures,' *JSMPE*, 29, no. 4 (October 1937), 372-3; Edwin Wetzel, 'Assembling a final sound-track,' *JSMPE*, 29, no. 4 (October 1937), 374-5; Kiesling, *Talking Pictures*, p. 210; Bernard B. Brown, 'Prescoring and scoring,' *JSMPE*, 39, no. 9 (October 1942), 228-31; L.T. Goldsmith, 'Re-recording sound motion pictures,' *JSMPE*, 39, no. 10 (November 1942), 277-83; Adolph Deutsch, 'Three strangers,' Pts 1 and 2, *Film Music Notes*, 5, nos, 7 and 8 (March and April 1946), 16-19, 19-22; 'Information on film music in the United States,' *Film Music Notes*, 8, no. 4 (March-April 1949), 12-14; C. Sharpless Hickman, 'Movies and music,' *Film Music*, 13, no. 1 (September-October 1953), 21-2; Hans W. Heinsheimer, *Menagerie in F Sharp* (Garden City, New York: Doubleday & Co., 1947), pp. 236-56; Selznick, *Memo*, p. 157; Mark Evans, *Soundtrack: The Music of the Movies* (New York: Hopkinson & Blake, 1975), p. 144; Roy M. Prendergast, *Film Music: A Neglected Art* (New York: W.W. Norton & Co., 1977).

On previews and audience testing: Deutsch, 'Three strangers,' Pt 2; pp. 21-2; Bernard D. Cirlin and Jack N. Peterman, 'Pre-testing a motion picture: a case history,' *Journal of Social Issues*, 3, no. 3 (Summer 1947), 39-41.

On publicity materials: George Blaisdell, 'How moving pictures are moved by stills,' *AC*, 20, no. 10 (October 1939), 438-40; Howard Dietz, 'Public relations,' in *Behind the Screen*, ed. Watts, pp. 158-65.

26 Mae D. Huettig, *Economic Control of the Motion Picture Industry: A Study in Industrial Organization* (Philadelphia: University of Pennsylvania Press, 1944), pp. 88-92.

27 'Body and Soul (here) put together,' *Fortune*, 4 (August 1931), 26-34+.

28 Lewis, *The Motion Picture Industry*, pp. 98-106; 'Twentieth Century-Fox,' *Fortune*, 12 (December 1935), 85-93+; Gordon Wiles, 'Imagination in set design,' *AC*, 13, no. 3 (July 1932), 8-9, 31; Gordon Wiles, 'Small sets,' *AC*, 13, no. 5 (September 1932), 11-12, 28; US Interstate Commerce Committee, Senate, 'Anti "block booking" and "blind selling" in the leasing of motion picture films,' hearings on S.

280, 76th Cong., 1st sess., April 3-17, 1939 (Washington, DC: Government Printing Office, 1939), pp. 322-32; US Interstate and Foreign Commerce Committee, House, 'Motion-picture films (compulsory blockbooking and blind selling),' hearings on S. 280, 76th Cong., 3rd sess., May 13-June 4, 1940 (Washington, DC: Government Printing Office, 1940), p. 451; Fred J. Balshofer and Arthur C. Miller, *One Reel A Week* (Berkeley: University of California Press, 1967), pp. 189, 192; Walter Blanchard, 'Aces of the camera XVI: Arthur Miller, A.S.C.,' *AC*, 23, no. 4 (April 1942), 183; Charles Higham, *Hollywood Cameramen: Sources of Light* (London: Thames & Hudson, 1970), pp. 134-5, 150-2; Dan Ford, *Pappy: The Life of John Ford* (Englewood Cliffs, New Jersey: Prentice-Hall, 1979), pp. 92-109; 'Research in motion pictures,' *IP*, 13, no. 12 (January 1942), 16; Allan Balter, 'After the last shot is made,' *AC*, 36, no. 7 (July 1955), 398-9, 431-3; 'Name Adler to Zanuck post,' *MPHerald*, 202, no. 6 (11 February 1956), 18.

29 'Warner – F.N. production is combined; Zanuck in charge,' *MPHerald*, 103, no. 8 (23 May 1931), 32.

30 '*Juarez* declared really great picture,' *AC*, 20, no. 4 (April 1939), 167-70; 'Warner Brothers,' *Fortune*, 16, no. 6 (December 1937), 110-13, 206-20.

31 Deschner, 'Anton Grot,' 18-22; 'Moving mountain at Warner Brothers,' *IP*, 13, no. 4 (May 1941), 26-7; Perc Westmore, 'Cooperation bulks big in work of make-up,' *AC*, 18, no. 12 (December 1937), 496-7; Nathan Levinson, 'Recording and re-recording,' in *We Make the Movies*, ed. Naumberg, pp. 173-98; Selznick, 'The functions of the producer,' p. 545; Tom Flinn, 'William Dieterle: the plutarch of Hollywood,' *The Velvet Light Trap*, no. 15 (Fall 1975), 23-8; 'Biggest stage on earth devoted entirely to special process work,' *AC*, 10, no. 1 (April 1929), 20-1, 35; William Stull, 'Fred Gage creates great lab at Warners' Burbank studio,' *AC*, 19, no. 3 (March 1938), 96, 105-6; G.M. Best and F.R. Gage, 'A modern studio laboratory,' *JSMPE*, 35, no. 3 (September 1940), 294-314; Ralph Dawson, 'How *Anthony Adverse* was cut,' *AC*, 17, no. 8 (August 1936), 345-6; Adolph Deutsch, 'Three strangers,' Pts. 1 and 2, 16-19, 19-22; Vincent Sherman in *Directing the Film: Film Directors on their Art* (Boston: Little Brown & Co., 1976), pp. 112, 246; 'Outside producers for Warners; 11 "Names" in new studio jobs,' *MPHerald*, 138, no. 6 (10 February 1940), 60; Rudy Behlmer, 'Introduction: from legend to film,' *The Adventures of Robin Hood* (Madison: University of Wisconsin Press, 1979), pp. 11-41.

32 'Metro-Goldwyn-Mayer,' *Fortune*, pp. 256-70; W. Dixon Powell, 'MGM: The studio at its zenith,' *The Velvet Light Trap*, no. 18 (Spring 1978), 1-7; Samuel Marx, *Mayer and Thalberg: The Make-Believe*

Saints (New York: Random House, 1975); Howard Sharpe, 'The private life of a talking picture,' *Photoplay*, 49, no. 2 (February 1936), 32-3, 101-3 (the first of six articles by Sharpe on how films were made at MGM; the last is in *Photoplay*, 50, no. 1 [July 1936]); Marion, *How to Write and Sell Film Stories*; Marx, 'Looking for a story,' pp. 16-31; *Behind the Screen*, ed. Watts (devoted entirely to short pieces by key MGM personnel); Arnold, 'Shooting the movies,' in *We Make the Movies*, ed. Naumberg, pp. 156-60; Gordon, 'Mayer, Thalberg, and MGM,' 187; William H. Daniels, 'Camera script clerk experiment by Daniels at MGM real success,' *AC*, 19, no. 3 (March 1938), 102, 106; 'Loew's, Inc.,' *Fortune*, 20 (August 1939), 25-30+, rpt in *The American Film Industry*, ed. Balio, pp. 278-94; Dennis Giles, 'The ghost of Thalberg: MGM 1946-1951,' *The Velvet Light Trap*, no. 18 (Spring 1978), 8-14; US Judiciary Committee, Senate, 'Motion pictures and juvenile delinquency,' interim report from subcommittee pursuant to S. Res. 1973, 84th Cong., 2nd sess. (Washington, DC: Government Printing Office, 1956), pp. 52-3; Schary and Palmer, *Case History*.

33 Knox, *The Magic Factory*, pp. 117, 120.

34 'How motion pictures are made,' *JSMPE*, 29, no. 4 (October 1937), 350-75; Maurice Pivar, 'Sound film editing,' *AC*, 13, no. 1 (May 1932), 11-12, 46; 'Deanna Durbin,' *Fortune*, 20 (October 1936), 66+; Joseph Valentine, 'Make-up and set painting aid new film,' *AC*, 20, no. 2 (February 1939), 54-7, 82-5; Jack Otterson, 'Simplifying of set design brings production value,' *AC*, 20, no. 8 (August 1939), 357-8; 'Why *100 Men and a Girl* makes a hit on screen,' *AC*, 18, no. 11 (November 1937), 453, 458-60.

35 Lutz Bacher, interview with James Pratt, 2 September 1978.

36 Jesse L. Lasky, 'Production problems,' in *The Story of the Films*, ed. Joseph P. Kennedy (Chicago: A.W. Shaw Co., 1927), pp. 99-102.

37 '2,000 move Bagdad to Broadway,' *MPHerald*, 104, no. 6 (8 August 1931), 86-7, 92; 'From the script to the screen,' *MPHerald*, 104, no. 6 (8 August 1931), 90, 99; Lewis, *The Motion Picture Industry*, pp. 30-47, 98-106; 'Paramount,' *Fortune*, 15 (March 1937), 87-96+; Ortman, *Fiction and the Screen*, pp. 86-8; 'Warner Brothers,' *Fortune*, 216; Bauchens, 'Cutting the film,' pp. 199-215; Dreier, 'Designing the sets,' pp. 80-9; 'Close-ups: Guy Bennett, operative cameraman,' *IP*, 11, no. 3 (April 1939), 5-6; C. Sharpless Hickman, 'Movies and music,' *Film Music*, 13, no. 1 (September-October 1953), 21-2; 'Paramount: Oscar for profits,' *Fortune*, 218-21.

38 Dannis Peary, 'Mark Robson remembers RKO, Welles, and Val Lewton,' *The Velvet Light Trap*, no. 10 (Fall 1973), 32-7; Russ Merritt, 'R.K.O. Radio: the little studio that couldn't,' *Marquee Theatre* (Madison, Wisconsin: WHA-TV Channel 21, n.d.), pp. 7-25; Ellen Spiegel, 'Fred & Ginger meet Van Nest Polglase,' *The Velvet Light Trap*, no. 10 (Fall 1973), 17-22; John Davis, 'A studio chronology,' *The Velvet Light Trap*, no. 10 (Fall 1973), 6-12; Beauchamp, 'The production takes shape,' pp. 64-79; Friedman, 'The players are cast,' pp. 106-16; 'Koerner gets new 7-year RKO contract,' *MPHerald*, 151, no. 5 (1 May 1943), 45; 'RKO has 18 films completed now, Schary reports,' *MPHerald*, 167, no. 6 (10 May 1947), 19; 'RKO: it's only money,' *Fortune*, 47 (May 1953), 122-7+; Luhr and Lehman, ' "Would you mind just trying it," ' 80.

39 Lewis, *The Motion Picture Industry*, pp. 98-106; Edward Buscombe, 'Notes on Columbia Picture Corporation 1926-1941,' *Screen*, 16, no. 3 (Autumn 1975), 65-82.

40 Leonard Maltin, *The Art of the Cinematographer: A Survey and Interviews with Five Masters*, rev. ed. (New York: Dover Publications, 1978), p. 108.

41 Balshofer and Miller, *One Reel A Week*, pp. 189, 192; Higham, *Hollywood Cameramen*, pp. 150-2.

42 Vincent Sherman in *Directing the Film*, ed. Sherman, p. 112.

43 Knox, *The Magic Factory*, pp. 172-3.

44 *Ibid.*, p. 109.

45 *Ibid.*, p. 39.

Chapter 26 The package unit system: unit management after 1955

1 For an expanded version of the economic and ideological factors in this shift, see Janet Staiger, 'Individualism versus collectivism,' *Screen*, 24, no. 4-5 (July-October 1983), 68-79.

2 Good summaries of the events surrounding *United States* v. *Paramount, et al.*, are in Ernest Borneman, 'United States versus Hollywood: the case study of an antitrust suit,' *Sight and Sound*, 19 (February and March 1951), 418-20+, 448-50+, rpt in *The American Film Industry*, ed. Tino Balio (Madison: University of Wisconsin Press, 1976), pp. 332-45; Raymond Moley, *The Hays Office* (Indianapolis: Bobbs-Merrill Co., 1945), pp. 206-12; US Select Committee on Small Business, Senate, 'Motion-picture distribution trade practices, 1956,' report, 27 July 1956 (Washington, DC: Government Printing Office, 1956), pp. 5-6; Michael Conant, *Antitrust in the Motion Picture Industry: Economic and Legal Analysis* (Berkeley: University of California Press, 1960). For a summary and excerpts of the 1940

consent decree, see Daniel Bertrand, W. Duane Evans, and E.L. Blanchard, 'Investigation of concentration of economic power study made for the Temporary National Economic Committee,' monograph no. 43, 'Motion picture industry – pattern of control,' 76th Cong., 3rd sess. (Washington, DC: Government Printing Office, 1941), pp. 73-85.

3   'Hollywood places greater value on stars in blocks-of-5 selling,' *MPHerald*, 142, no. 9 (1 March 1941), 12; 'Mandatory block-of-five sales end for 5 majors,' *MPHerald*, 148, no. 10 (5 September 1942), 17; 'Majors to sell in blocks with decree big "if," ' *MPHerald*, 151, no. 11 (12 June 1943), 17-18.

4   'Hollywood in uniform', *Fortune*, 25 (April 1942), 92-5+; 'Playdates on top films increase 30 per cent,' *MPHerald*, 151, no. 12 (19 June 1943), 14; 'Through the editor's finder,' *AC*, 24, no. 6 (June 1943), 213; 'Monogram to offer 40 for 1943-44,' *MPHerald*, 151, no. 12 (19 June 1943), 40.

5   'War booming market for independent product,' *MPHerald*, 153, no. 7 (13 November 1943), 14; 'Cagney, U.A. in five-year pact,' *MPHerald*, 152, no. 12 (18 September 1943), 44; 'Wallis sets five year Paramount production deal,' *MPHerald*, 155, no. 9 (27 May 1944), 36; Ernest Borneman, 'Rebellion in Hollywood: a study in motion picture finance,' *Harper's*, 193 (October 1946), 337-43; Frederic Marlowe, 'The rise of the independents in Hollywood,' *Penguin Film Review*, no. 3 (August 1947), 72; 'Review of the film news,' *AC*, 26, no. 10 (October 1945), 33; Frank Capra, 'Breaking Hollywood's "pattern of sameness," ' *The New York Times*, 5 May 1946, rpt in *Hollywood Directors*, ed. Koszarski, pp. 83-9; 'Paramount: Oscar for profits,' *Fortune*, 35, no. 6 (June 1947), 90-5, 208-21; 'Talent planning to fight capital gains tax ruling,' *MPHerald*, 164, no. 5 (3 August 1946), 73. On financing methods during this period through the early 1960s, see, as a start, besides Borneman, Donald M. Nelson, 'The independent producer,' in *The Motion Picture Industry*, ed. Gordon S. Watkins (Philadelphia: American Academy of Political and Social Science, 1947), pp. 49-75; 'Movies: end of an era?' *Fortune*, 39 (April 1949), pp. 99-102+; Terry Sanders, 'The financing of independent feature films,' *The Quarterly of Film, Radio, and Television*, 9, no. 4 (1955), 380-9; Freeman Lincoln, 'The comeback of the movies,' *Fortune*, 51, no. 2 (February 1955), 127-31, 155-8; 'The derring-doers of movie business,' *Fortune*, 57 (May 1958), 137-41+; William Fadiman, 'Cowboys and Indies,' *Films and Filming*, 10, no. 6 (March 1964), 51-2.

6   'Industry must readjust price and cost: Cowdin,' *MPHerald*, 168, no. 3 (19 July 1947), 13; 'Pressures force issues down on stock market,' *MPHerald*, 169, no. 13 (27 December 1947), 13.

7   'Editorial,' *The Screen Writer*, 4, no. 3 (September 1948), 4; Anthony A.P. Dawson, 'Hollywood's labour troubles,' *Industrial and Labor Relations Review*, 1, no. 4 (July 1948), 642; William R. Weaver, 'Studio employment – a 12-year study,' *MPHerald*, 174, no. 6 (5 February 1949), 15; 'Employment at studios hit 13-year low in 1949,' *MPHerald*, 178, no. 8 (25 February 1950), 35; Norman Keane, *'Jigsaw* filmed without sound or sets,' *AC*, 29, no. 12 (December 1948), 412, 427-8; William R. Weaver, 'Studios hold gains with six pictures starting,' *MPHerald*, 170, no. 6 (7 February 1948); 25; Fred Hift, 'Those big city scenes are really shot on the spot,' *MPHerald*, 177, no. 13 (24 December 1949), 25; 'Hollywood is traveling abroad for production,' *MPHerald*, 170, no. 3 (17 January 1948), 13; 'Seek to melt frozen funds,' *MPHerald*, 174, no. 13 (26 March 1949), 36; 'British pact signed and U.S. ready to deliver,' *MPHerald*, 170, no. 12 (20 March 1948), 13; William R. Weaver, 'Impact of British-U.S. deal on production is worrying Hollywood,' *MPHerald*, 171, no. 7 (15 May 1948), 27; 'Report 20th-Fox will make 12 top films in Europe,' *MPHerald*, 172, no. 10 (4 September 1948), 12; '20th-Fox to offer 32 in month-by-month schedule,' *MPHerald*, 172, no. 12 (18 September 1948), 17; 'Shoot more films abroad,' *MPHerald*, 176, no. 4 (23 July 1949), 16.

8   'Video hurts, survey says,' *MPHerald*, 178, no. 6 (11 February 1950), 22; US Select Committee on Small Business, 'Motion-picture distribution trade practices, 1956,' report, 27 July 1956 (Washington, DC: Government Printing Office, 1956), pp. 22-31. For overall studies of the 1946-52 period, see: William F. Hellmuth, Jr, 'The motion picture industry,' in *The Structure of American Industry*, ed. Walter Adams, rev. ed. (New York: Macmillan, 1954), p. 379; Merrill Lynch, Pierce, Fenner & Beane, *Radio, Television, Motion Pictures* (New York: Merrill Lynch, Pierce, Fenner & Beane, 1950), pp. 2-5; US Select Committee on Small Business, Senate, 'Problems of independent motion picture exhibitors, 1953,' report, 83rd Cong., 1st sess. (Washington, DC: Government Printing Office, 1953), p. 3; Chris Hugo, 'The economic background,' *Movie*, 27/28 (Winter 1980/Spring 1981), 43-9.

9   'Six majors plan 7 films sold at advanced prices,' *MPHerald*, 168, no. 9 (30 August 1947), 23; 'Importers seek theatre outlets,' *MPHerald*, 166, no. 6 (8 February 1947), 50.

10   'New special effects company formed,' *AC*, 28, no. 2 (February 1947), 66; 'Motion picture center: Hollywood's newest studio,' *AC*, 28, no. 9 (September 1947), 314-15; Fred Hift, 'Coast talent poised over television pond,' *MPHerald*, 174, no. 9 (26 February 1949), 19. See *AC* through the 1950s but particu-

larly: Victor Milner, 'A.S.C. inaugurates research on photography for television,' *AC*, 30, no. 3 (March 1949), 86, 100-2; John De Mos, 'The cinematographer's place in television,' *AC*, 30, no. 3 (March 1949), 87, 102, 104-5; Walter Strenge, 'In the best professional manner,' *AC*, 32, no. 5 (May 1951), 186, 200-1; Leigh Allen, 'Television film production,' *AC*, 33, no. 2 (February 1952), 69; Frederick Foster, 'The big switch is to TV!' *AC*, 36, no. 1 (January 1955), 26-7, 38-40; Arthur Miller, 'Hollywood's cameramen at work,' *AC*, 38, no. 9 (September 1957), 580-1. Estimates for 1955 were that ten times the work for television compared to theatrical exhibition was being done in Hollywood; Morris Gelman, 'The Hollywood story,' *Television Magazine*, 20 (September 1963). Lincoln, 'Comeback of the movies,' p. 130; 'Outlook for 1956,' *MPHerald*, 202, no. 1 (7 January 1956), 8; films listed as in production for January through March 1950, 1955, and 1959, *Motion Picture Herald*; 'Top grossing pictures of 1956,' *MPHerald*, 206, no. 1 (5 January 1957), 12-13; 'Name Adler to Zanuck post,' *MPHerald*, 202, no. 6 (11 February 1956), 18; Vincent Canby, 'Hollywood pushes into TV production arena,' *MPHerald*, 198, no. 4 (22 January 1955), 13; Jay Remer, 'Hollywood eyes TV as new production source,' *MPHerald*, 202, no. 2 (14 January 1956), 12; William R. Weaver, 'Hecht-Hill-Lancaster plan nine features,' *MPHerald*, 206, no. 1 (5 January 1957), 20.

11 'Gimmicks for a *Gidget*,' *MPHerald*, 214, no. 4 (31 January 1959), 38.

12 Arthur E. Gavin, 'Location-shooting in Paris for *Gigi*,' *AC*, 39, no. 7 (July 1958), 424-5.

13 Richard Dyer MacCann, 'The independent producer: independence with a vengeance,' *Film Quarterly*, 15 (Summer 1962), 14-21; Robert H. Stanley, *The Celluloid Empire: A History of the American Movie Industry* (New York: Hastings House, 1978), pp. 251-2; Vincent Canby, 'How big is big MCA?' *MPHerald*, 214, no. 7 (21 February 1959), 23-6.

14 '1953 film year,' *1954 Film Daily Yearbook* (New York: Film Daily, 1954), 48; William R. Weaver, 'Hollywood scene,' *MPHerald*, 198, no. 2 (8 January 1955), 28.

15 Arthur E. Gavin, 'Location-shooting in Paris for *Gigi*,' *AC*, 39, no. 7 (July 1958), 424-5; Herb A. Lightman, 'Shooting black and white in color,' *AC*, 40, no. 8 (August 1959), 486-7, 499-500; George J. Mitchell, 'Multiple cameras cut shooting time of *Hell To Eternity*,' *AC*, 41, no. 7 (July 1960), 412-14, 434, 436-8; Robert Aldrich, 'Learning from my mistakes,' *Films and Filming* (June 1960), rpt in *Hollywood Directors*, ed. Koszarski, pp. 298-304.

16 Dore Schary and Charles Palmer, *Case History of a Movie* (New York: Random House, 1950), p. 68; this is also Martin Field's explanation in 'Hollywood report on a "Trend,"' *Penguin Film Review*, no. 9 (1949), 100-2.

17 Herb A. Lightman, 'The camera and production value,' *AC*, 27, no. 9 (September 1946), 312-14, 339; George Seaton, 'One track mind on a two way ticket,' *The Screen Writer* (September 1947), rpt in *Hollywood Directors*, ed. Koszarski, p. 133.

18 'More trouble in paradise,' *Fortune*, 34, no. 5 (November 1946), 155-6; Nelson, 'The independent producer,' p. 49.

19 Donald Knox, *The Magic Factory: How MGM Made 'An American in Paris'* (New York: Praeger Publishers, 1973), pp. 205-6.

20 David Linck, 'Zoetrope takes cue from studios of '30s and '40s,' *Box Office*, 116, no. 18 (5 May 1980), 1.

21 Francesca Riviere, 'Rebirth next: an exclusive interview with Francis Ford Coppola,' *L.A. Weekly*, 28 November 1979, p. 40.

22 Dudley Nichols, 'The writer and the film,' (1959), rpt in *Film: A Montage of Theories*, ed. Richard Dyer MacCann (New York: E.P. Dutton & Co., 1966), p. 74; V.F. Perkins, *Film as Film: Understanding and Judging Movies* (Harmondsworth: Penguin Books, 1972), p. 166.

23 Knox, *The Magic Factory*, pp. 205-6.

24 Leonard Maltin, *The Art of the Cinematographer: A Survey and Interviews with Five Masters*, rev. ed. (New York: Dover Publications, 1978), pp. 97-8, 103.

Chapter 27 Deep-focus cinematography

1 Joseph Dubray, 'Large aperture lenses in cinematography,' *TSMPE*, 12 no. 33 (1928): 206.

2 Patrick Ogle, 'Technological and aesthetic influences upon the development of deep focus cinematography in the United States,' *Screen Reader*, 1, ed. John Ellis (London: British Film Institute, 1977), pp. 87-8. See also Peter Mole, 'Will there always be a need for carbon arcs?' *AC*, 31, no. 2 (February 1951): 72-3; Charles W. Handley, 'History of motion picture studio lighting,' *A Technological History of Motion Pictures and Television*, ed. Raymond Fielding (Berkeley: University of California Press, 1967), p. 122.

3 Michael Leshing, 'Time and temperature control,' *IP*, 16, no. 4 (May 1944): 22; Mary Eunice McCarthy, *Hands of Hollywood* (Hollywood: Photoplay Research Bureau, 1929), p. 60; 'Projection faults denounced,' *AMPAS Bulletin*, no. 13 (11 August 1928): 4; Frank Woods, 'The sound motion picture situation in Hollywood,' *TSMPE*, 12, no. 35

(1928): 626; Carl F. Gregory, 'Limitations of modern lenses,' *Cinematography*, 1, no. 2 (May 1930): 9, 29; James Wong Howe, 'Lighting,' *Cinematographic Annual*, 2 (1931): 50-1; J.J. Finn, 'The indictment against "soft lighting,"' *IPro*, 1, no. 3 (December 1931): 20.

4   'Bring them back for more,' *Motion Picture Projection*, 2, no. 9 (June 1929): 5.

5   William Stull, 'Solving the "ice-box" problem,' *AC*, 10, no. 6 (September 1929): 7. See also Lewis W. Physioc, 'Exposure control serious problem,' *IP*, 2, no. 4 (May 1931): 6-8; Lewis W. Physioc, 'Problems of the cameraman,' *JSMPE*, 17, no. 3 (September 1931): 408-9.

6   George H. Scheibe, 'Filters for special effects,' *AC*, 14, no. 12 (April 1934): 486; Lewis W. Physioc, 'Physioc writes of camera problems,' *IP*, 3, no. 8 (September 1931): 5-6; John Arnold, 'Shooting the movies,' in *We Make the Movies*, ed. Nancy Naumburg (New York: Norton, 1937), p. 154; Lewis W. Physioc, 'More about lighting,' *IP*, 8, no. 7 (August 1936): 5; George Scheibe, 'Soft focus,' *IP*, 11, no. 3 (April 1939): 6; Charles B. Lang, Jr, 'The purpose and practice of diffusion,' *AC*, 14, no. 5 (September 1933): 171, 193-4; John Arnold, 'Cinematography – professional,' *The Complete Photographer*, vol. 2, ed. Willard D. Morgan (New York: National Education Alliance, 1943), p. 765. Cf. Vladimir Nilsen, *The Cinema as a Graphic Art*, tr. Stephen Garry (New York: Hill & Wang, 1959), pp. 151, 177.

7   Emery Huse and Gordon A. Chambers, 'Eastman Supersensitive Panchromatic Type Two motion picture film,' *Cinematographic Annual*, 2 (1931), p. 107.

8   Oliver Marsh, 'Super-sensitive film in production,' *AC*, 12, no. 1 (May 1931): 11; Hal Hall, 'Improvements in motion picture film,' *Cinematographic Annual*, 2 (1931): 93-102; Charles G. Clarke, 'Fast improvements of fast film,' *AC*, 12, no. 3 (July 1931): 10, 40; V.B. Sease, 'Du Pont's new panchromatic film,' *AC*, 13, no. 5 (September 1932): 17, 25; P. Arnold, 'A motion picture negative of wider usefulness,' *JSMPE*, 23, no. 3 (September 1934): 160-6; 'Symposium of new motion picture apparatus,' *JSMPE*, 17, no. 3 (September 1931): 387; James Barker, 'Make-up for fast film,' *AC*, 12, no. 7 (November 1931): 11, 24.

9   Clyde DeVinna, 'New angles on fast film,' *AC*, 12, no. 2 (June 1931): 19, 22; Fred Westerberg, 'New negative to improve quality,' *IP*, 2, no. 4 (May 1931): 29.

10 'Quality photography: a measure of superior craftsmanship,' *IPro*, 2, no. 3 (May 1932): 12. See also, 'Report of the Studio Lighting Committee,' *JSMPE*, 17, no. 4 (October 1931): 645-55.

11 'ASC recommends fast films,' *AC*, 12, no. 3 (July 1931): 19.

12 For summary accounts of 1930s innovations, see Emery Huse and Gordon A. Chambers, 'New Eastman emulsions,' *IP*, 10, no. 11 (December 1938): 23-7; 'Pan and sound put inkies on top,' *IP*, 10, no. 3 (April 1938): 43-8; Joseph Valentine, 'Make-up and set painting aid new film,' *AC*, 20, no. 2 (February 1939): 54-6, 85; 'Lighting the new fast films,' *AC*, 18, no. 12 (December 1937): 494; 'Report of the Studio Lighting Committee,' *JSMPE*, 33, no. 1 (July 1939): 97-100.

13 L.W. O'Donnell, quoted in 'Lighting the new fast films,' pp. 69-70.

14 'Report of the Studio Lighting Committee,' *JSMPE*, 30, no. 3 (March 1938): 294-8; G. Gaudio, 'A new viewpoint on the lighting of motion pictures,' *JSMPE*, 29, no. 2 (August 1937): 157-68.

15 Hal Mohr, 'A lens mount for universal focus effects,' *AC*, 17, no. 9 (September 1936): 371.

16 John Castle, 'Bert Glennon introducing new method of interior photography,' *AC*, 20, no. 2 (February 1939): 82.

17 James Wong Howe, 'Upsetting traditions with *Viva Villa!*' *AC*, 15, no. 2 (June 1934): 64, 71-2; 'Riddle me this,' *AC*, 13, no. 6 (October 1932): 16; Castle, 'Bert Glennon,' p. 83; Gaudio, 'New viewpoint,' pp. 157-68; 'Lighting *Tobacco Road*,' *IP*, 13, no. 1 (February 1941): 3, 7.

18 James Wong Howe, in *Hollywood Cameramen*, ed. Charles Higham (London: Thames & Hudson, 1970), p. 88. See also, 'The layout for *Bulldog Drummond*,' *Creative Art* (October 1929): 729-34, and William Cameron Menzies, 'Pictorial beauty in the photoplay,' in *Introduction to the Photoplay*, ed. John C. Tibbetts (Shawnee Mission, Kansas: National Film Society, 1977), p. 166.

19 Ogle, 'Technological and aesthetic influences,' pp. 92-3.

20 John Arnold, 'Art in cinematography,' *AC*, 12, no. 12 (April 1932): 25.

21 Quoted in Leonard Maltin, *Behind the Camera: The Cinematographer's Art* (New York: New American Library, 1971), p. 69.

22 Herb A. Lightman, 'Documentary style,' *AC*, 30, no. 5 (May 1949): 176.

23 Harry Burdick, 'Intense preparation underlies Toland's achievements,' *AC*, 16, no. 6 (June 1935): 240, 247; Gregg Toland, 'Using arcs for lighting monochrome,' *AC*, 22, no. 12 (December 1941): 559; 'Adjustment for dolly head,' *AC*, 16, no. 6 (June 1935): 246; Gregg Toland, 'Practical gadgets expedite camera work,' *AC*, 20, no. 5 (May 1939): 215-8; 'Toland with Twentieth's *Kidnapped* awarded camera honors for July,' *AC*, 19, no. 7 (July 1938): 274; 'Toland's *Dead End* selected in caucus one of

three best,' *AC*, 19, no. 4 (April 1938): 141-2; 'Ace cinematographer Gregg Toland passes,' *Los Angeles Times* (29 September 1948): n.p.

24   Walter Blanchard, 'Aces of the camera XIII: Gregg Toland, ' *AC*, 23, no. 1 (January 1942): 15.

25   Gregg Toland, 'Realism for *Citizen Kane*,' *AC*, 22, no. 2 (February 1941): 54, 80.

26   *Ibid.*, Gregg Toland, 'I broke the rules in *Citizen Kane*,' *Popular Photography*, 8, no. 6 (June 1941): 55; 90-1.

27   Toland, 'Realism,' 55.

28* There persists among American cinematographers the belief that Toland also used the 'Waterhouse stop' method to achieve small apertures. Joseph Walker explained:

With the advent of sound we all had difficulty matching the exposure with different lenses, especially very short focus lenses at small apertures. Some of the diaphragms were so sloppy there could be a half-stop difference at f:11, depending on whether you stopped the lens down to f:11 or opened it up to f:11. My own solution was to own four complete sets of lenses and try to match the calibrations.

Gregg Toland used very short focus lenses on *Citizen Kane* and used them at small apertures. His solution, and a very practical one, was to use the 'Waterhouse Stop' system, whereby a small piece of metal with an accurately drilled hole in it is inserted in a slot in the lens barrel, in place of the conventional diaphragm. A different metal strip for every stop is needed but this way the f-stop would match on all lenses that were prepared in this way.

I think these lenses were shown at a meeting at the ASC.

(Letter from Joe Walker to Charles G. Clarke, 23 May 1972. In ASC files.) In his articles, Toland makes no mention of using the Waterhouse stop method, but it is possible that he did.

29   Toland, 'Realism,' pp. 54-5.

30   Joseph V. Mascelli, 'What's happened to photographic style?' *IP*, 30, no. 1 (January 1958): 6.

31   Gregg Toland, 'The motion picture cameraman,' *Theatre Arts*, 25, no. 9 (September 1941): 647-54; 'Orson Welles: once a child prodigy, he has never quite grown up,' *Life*, 10, no. 21 (26 May 1941): 108-16; John Mescall, 'Pan-focus for your home movies,' *AC*, 22, no. 12 (December 1941): 576, 593; Blanchard, 'Aces', 15, 36. See also Hal McAlpin, 'Let's shoot 'em sharp,' *IP*, 15, no. 12 (January 1943): 7-9.

32   Mescall, 'Pan-focus,' p. 576; 'Through the editor's

finder,' *AC*, 22, no. 9 (September 1941): 424; ' "Increased range" system promises to revolutionize photography,' *IPro*, 16, no. 6 (June 1941): 12; 'Report of the Studio Lighting Committee,' *JSMPE*, 38, no. 3 (March 1942): 282.

33   Charles G. Clarke, 'How desirable is extreme focal depth?' *AC*, 23, no. 1 (January 1942): 14.

34   'Photography of the month,' *AC*, 23, no. 2 (February 1942): 66.

35   'Photography of the month: *The Little Foxes*,' *AC*, 22, no. 9 (September 1941): 425.

36   Linwood Dunn, 'Optical printer Handy Andy,' *IP*, 10, no. 5 (June 1938): 14-16; 'Special effects at RKO,' *IP*, 12, no. 11 (December 1940): 4; 'First rear projection specifications,' *IP*, 11, no. 2 (March 1939): 22.

37   Quoted in Walter Blanchard, 'Unseen camera aces II: Linwood Dunn, ASC,' *AC*, 24, no. 7 (July 1943): 268.

38   Interview with Linwood Dunn, conducted by Kristin Thompson and David Bordwell, July 1980, Hollywood, California. See also Donald Chase, *Filmmaking: The Collaborative Art* (Boston: Little, Brown, 1975), pp. 293-7; Peter Bogdanovich, 'The Kane mutiny,' *Esquire*, 77, no. 4 (October 1972): 100-1.

39   Clarke, 'How desirable,' p. 36.

40* Mitchell, for instance, developed a lightweight, single-system 35mm camera for combat photography, while Art Reeves designed a field camera that used reflex viewing. RCA paralleled the advances in photography with portable sound-recording equipment. Military demand also elevated 16mm to the status of a semi-professional gauge. Hollywood studios had used 16mm occasionally for wardrobe, location, and acting tests before the war, but after 1942, the usage increased, partly because 16mm stock was not rationed as strictly as 35mm. James Wong Howe enthusiastically predicted that 16mm would soon become the production standard because it was cheaper and the equipment was more flexible. See E.J. Tiffany, 'Mitchell 35mm single system sound camera,' *AC*, 24, no. 9 (September 1943): 330-43; Art Reeves, 'The Art Reeves reflex motion picture camera,' *JSMPE*, 44, no. 6 (June 1945): 436-42; Ainslie R. Davis, 'New light weight recording equipment serves in the war effort,' *JSMPE*, 42, no. 6 (June 1944): 327-48; William Stull, '16mm gains in studio use,' *AC*, 13, no. 10 (October 1942): 442; Ezra Goodman, 'Post-war motion pictures,' *AC*, 26, no. 5 (May 1945): 160.

41   Ralph Lawton, '*Champion*,' *AC*, 30, no. 6 (June 1949): 196, 218; Frederick Foster, 'Economy lighting with photofloods,' *AC*, 31, no. 1 (January 1950): 10-11, 20.

42   Phil Tannura, 'The practical use of latensification,' *AC*, 31, no. 2 (February 1951): 54, 68-70. See also Leigh Allen, 'New speed for films,' *AC*, 30, no. 12 (December 1949): 440, 456.

43   Emery Huse, 'Tri-X – new Eastman high-speed negative motion picture film,' *AC*, 35, no. 7 (July 1954): 335, 364; Emery Huse, 'Eastman Plus-X panchromatic negative film (type B),' *AC*, 37, no. 9 (September 1956): 542, 546; Frederick Foster, 'A faster color negative,' *AC*, 40, no. 6 (June 1959): 364-5, 368, 370.

44   Jack Taylor, 'Dynamic Realism,' *IP*, 20, no. 9 (September 1948): 6-7.

45   Charles L. Anderson, 'Filming with perspective control,' *AC*, 31, no. 10 (September 1950): 313; 'Choosing and using lenses,' *AC*, 40, no. 5 (May 1959): 296.

46   R.M. Newbold, 'The Garuzo lens in motion picture photography,' *AC*, 31, no. 7 (September 1949): 320; Leigh Allen, 'Deep focus and longer takes,' *AC*, 31, no. 7 (July 1950): 234-5, 257; Hal Mohr, 'Why I used the Garutso lens in filming *The Four Poster*,' *AC*, 33, no. 11 (November 1952): 482, 500-1.

47   Stanley Cortez, 'Tri-X in feature film production,' *AC*, 35, no. 1 (January 1955): 33, 44-5; Herb Lightman, 'The filming of *Viva Zapata!*' *AC*, 33, no. 4 (April 1952): 155; Herb Lightman, 'Old master, new tricks,' *AC*, 31, no. 9 (September 1950): 318; Herb Lightman, 'Realism with a master's touch,' *AC*, 31, no. 8 (August 1950): 286-8.

48   William Wyler, 'No magic wand,' *Screen Writer*, 2, no. 9 (February 1947): 10.

49   'A letter from William Wyler,' *Sequence*, no. 8 (Summer 1949): 68.

50   Lester Koenig, 'Gregg Toland, film-maker,' *Screen Writer*, 3, no. 7 (December 1947): 30-1; 'Gregg Toland, one of top lensers, dies at 44,' *Daily Variety* (29 September 1948): 6; 'Letter From Wyler,' pp. 68-9.

Chapter 28 Technicolor

1   For a history of color systems, see Roderick T. Ryan, *A History of Motion Picture Color Technology* (New York: Focal Press, 1977). See also Howard T. Lewis, *The Motion Picture Industry* (New York: Van Nostrand, 1933), p. 138.

2*   In the two-color subtractive method, a beam-splitter prism exposed two frames at once, one through a red filter and one through a green filter. A print was made from each set of images and the two prints were cemented together, yielding a relief image on each side of the film. One side was then dyed red, the other blue-green. Imbibition processing improved the method by dyeing each negative's relief-image print (its 'matrix') and immediately stamping it onto another film; the process resembled half-tone lithography.

3   F.J. Taylor, 'Mr. Technicolor,' *Saturday Evening Post*, 222 (22 October 1949): 131-3; 'Technicolor,' *Fortune*, 13 (June 1936): 40, 46, 54; Joseph Mascelli, 'The million dollar bubble,' *IP*, 23, no. 10 (October 1951): 6, 8-10; William Stull, 'Technicolor bringing new charm to screen,' *AC*, 18, no. 6 (June 1937): 237; Fred Basten, *Glorious Technicolor* (New York: A.S. Barnes, 1980), pp. 23-197; 'Abstracts,' *JSMPE*, 14 no. 1 (January 1930): 139-40; 'Progress in the motion picture industry,' *JSMPE*, 14, no. 2 (February 1930): 245; 'Technicolor orders 18 new cameras,' *Hollywood Filmograph*, 10, no. 16 (3 May 1930): 26; 'Technicolor expansion program in operation,' *Technicolor News and Views*, 1, no. 1 (April 1929): 1-2; 'Increase in popularity of Technicolor productions graphically shown by 35-millimeter positive print footage output, 1932-1947,' *Technicolor News and Views*, 10, no. 2 (August 1948): 2; 'Technicolor gaining,' *AC*, 25, no. 5 (May 1944): 178; J.A. Ball, 'The Technicolor process of 3-color cinematography,' *IPro*, 8, no. 6 (June 1935): 12; Howard C. Brown, 'Will color revolutionize photography?' *AC*, 17, no. 7 (July 1936): 284-5.

4   See Basten, *Glorious Technicolor*, pp. 29-58; 'Color film increase,' *Business Week* (22 May 1937): 47.

5   Jimmie Stone, 'The assistant cameraman,' *IP*, 11, no. 11 (December 1939): 23; 'Why all this hubbub regarding color?' *AC*, 17, no. 8 (August 1936): 327, 334-5; '*Ziegfeld Girl*,' *AC*, 22, no. 4 (May 1941): 223.

6   'Eliminating guesswork in cinematography,' *Scientific American*, 115 (9 December 1916): 532, 535-6; Taylor, 'Mr. Technicolor,' p. 131; Basten, *Glorious Technicolor*, pp. 20-3, 29, 81, 199; 'What? Color in the movies again?' *Fortune*, 10, no. 4 (October 1934): 93-4, 161.

7   'What? Color in the movies again?' p. 166.

8   Stull, 'New charm,' p. 236; 'A cinema world wonder,' *IP*, 2, no. 5 (June 1930): 84-6; Robert L. Greene, 'The camera optical engineer,' *IP*, 22, no. 5 (May 1950): 8-9; Basten, *Glorious Technicolor*, pp. 84-93.

9   'Technicolor system,' *IP*, 10, no. 1 (February 1938): 9-10; Ira B. Hoke, 'Grooming camera battery for 1931,' *IP*, 2, no. 11 (December 1930): 15, 40; Stone, 'Assistant cameraman,' p. 13; Basten, *Glorious Technicolor*, pp. 66-7.

10   William Stull, 'Following focus by remote control,' *AC*, 17, no. 2 (February 1936): 53, 60; William Stull, 'Process shots aided by triple projector,' *AC*, 20, no. 8 (August 1939): 363-6, 376; Farciot Edouart, 'The evolution of transparency process photography,' *AC*, 24, no. 10 (October 1943): 380, 382; Elmer C.

Richardson, 'Production use tested the "Ultra H.I. Arc,"' *IP*, 8, no. 3 (April 1936): 26-7; Peter Mole, 'Twice the light and twice the sunlight for color cinematography,' *AC*, 16, no. 8 (August 1935): 332-3; R.E. Farnham, 'Lighting requirements of the three-color Technicolor process,' *AC*, 17, no. 7 (July 1936): 282-3, 292; E.C. Richardson, 'Recent developments in high-intensity arc spotlamps for motion picture production,' *JSMPE*, 28, no. 2 (February 1938): 206-12; W. Howard Greene, 'Low-key lighting may be as easy in color as it is in monochrome,' *AC*, 19, no. 4 (April 1938): 146, 151; 'Pan and sound put inkies on top,' *IP*, 10, no. 3 (April 1938): 47; Ray Rennehan, 'Rennehan talks Technicolor,' *IP*, 9, no. 8 (September 1937): 24.

11 See, for example, Lyle Wheeler, 'Art direction for color by Technicolor,' *Technicolor News and Views*, 11, no. 2 (June 1949): 2-3.

12 Walter B. Pitkin and William M. Marston, *The Art of Sound Pictures* (New York: Appleton, 1930), p. 261.

13 For a good discussion of how color can be seen as lacking realistic motivation, see Ed Buscombe, 'Sound and color,' *Jump Cut*, no. 17 (1978): 23-5.

14 Lansing C. Holden, 'Color: the new language of the screen,' *Cinema Arts*, 1, no. 2 (July 1937): 64. See also Philip E. Rosen, 'Believe color will not aid dramatic cinematography,' *AC*, 4, no. 5 (August 1923): 4.

15 Quoted in Basten, *Glorious Technicolor*, p. 30.

16 *Ibid.*, p. 27.

17 *Ibid.*, p. 57; D.K. Allison, 'Common sense of color,' *IP*, 9, no. 8 (September 1937): 7-9.

18 Taylor, 'Mr. Technicolor,' p. 27; Basten, *Glorious Technicolor*, pp. 54, 70; Lansing C. Holden, 'Designing for color,' in *We Make the Movies*, ed. Nancy Naumburg (New York: Norton, 1937), p. 240; Natalie Kalmus, 'Color consciousness,' *IPro*, 8, no. 6 (June 1935): 17; Arthur E. Gavin, '*South Pacific* – New concept in color photography,' *AC*, 39, no. 5 (May 1958): 294-6, 318-19.

19 Natalie Kalmus, 'Colour,' in *Behind the Screen: How Films Are Made*, ed. Stephen Watts (New York: Dodge, 1938), p. 122.

20 'Rennehan talks Technicolor,' p. 25; Peter Mole, 'Lighting equipment for natural-color photography,' *IP*, 8, no. 5 (June 1936): 17; John Arnold, 'Cinematography – professional,' in *The Complete Photographer* vol. 2, ed. Willard D. Morgan (New York: National Education Alliance, 1943), p. 767; James Wong Howe, 'Reaction on making his first color production,' *AC*, 18, no. 10 (October 1937): 409-11; SMPTE, *Elements of Color in Professional Motion Pictures* (New York: SMPTE, 1957), pp. 44, 70; E.C. Richardson, 'Recent developments in motion picture set lighting,' *JSMPE*, 29, no. 2 (August 1937): 183.

21 Ray Rennehan, 'Natural-color cinematography today,' *AC*, 16, no. 7 (July 1935): 288, 294; 'Faster color film cuts light a half,' *AC*, 20, no. 8 (August 1939): 355-6; C.W. Handley, 'Advanced technic of Technicolor lighting,' *IP*, 9, no. 5 (June 1937): 10; William Stull, 'New charm,' p. 236; W. Howard Green, 'Creating light-effects in Technicolor,' *IP*, 8, no. 12 (January 1937): 10-11, 25; Winton Hoch, 'The Technicolor cameraman,' *IPro*, 21, no. 10 (October 1946): 20-2, 34; Robert Surtees, 'Color is different,' *AC*, 28, no. 1 (January 1948): 10-11, 31; Joe Valentine, 'Lighting for Technicolor as compared with black and white photography,' *IP*, 20, no. 1 (January 1948): 7-10.

22 Basten, *Glorious Technicolor*, pp. 137-46; 'Technicolor to employ standard camera negative in year, Dr. Kalmus predicts,' *Technicolor News and Views*, 1, no. 8 (November 1939): 1-2; 'Company's feature volume largest in history,' *Technicolor News and Views*, 3, no. 2 (April 1941): 1-2; Winton Hoch, 'Technicolor cinematography,' in *The Technique of Motion Picture Production*, ed. SMPE (New York: Interscience, 1944): 20-2, 34; Taylor, 'Mr. Technicolor,' pp. 133-4; 'Technical news,' *JSMPE*, 43, no. 1 (July 1944): 68; Charles G. Clarke, 'Practical utilization of monopack film,' *IP*, 18, no. 1 (February 1946): 11-12, 29; 'Technicolor establishes new records in a troubled year,' *Technicolor News and Views*, 4, no. 2 (April 1942): 1, 3; 'The Technicolor monopack process,' *Technicolor News and Views*, 7, no. 3 (September 1945): 1-2; Herbert T. Kalmus, 'Technicolor's post war plans,' *Technicolor News and Views*, 5, no. 4 (December 1943): 1, 4; Herbert T. Kalmus, 'Future of Technicolor,' *IP*, 16, no. 4 (May 1944): 29; Charles G. Clarke, 'We filmed *Kangaroo* entirely in Australia,' *AC*, 33, no. 6 (July 1952): 292-3, 315-7; William J. Kenney, 'Monopack as medium for three-color process,' *IP*, 16, no. 12 (January 1945): 12.

23 The most detailed examination of Technicolor's relation to Eastman Kodak is George E. Frost and S. Chesterfield Oppenheim, 'A study of the professional color motion picture antitrust decrees and their effects,' *The Patent, Trademark and Copyright Journal of Research and Education*, 4, no. 1 (Spring 1960): 1-39, and 4, no. 2 (Summer 1960): 108-49. See also Basten, *Glorious Technicolor*, p. 146; 'Technicolor,' *Fortune*, p. 54; Howard C. Brown, 'Movies in color,' *IP*, 8, no. 6 (July 1936): 26; Ed Gibbons, 'Color,' *IP*, 9, no. 6 (July 1937): 5-7; 'Technicolor system,' *IP*, 10, no. 1 (February 1938): 10; Ed Gibbons, 'Color progress dominates 1939 technical horizon,' *IP*, 10, no. 12 (January 1939): 9-10; 'Technicolor answers anti-trust action,' *Technicolor News and Views*, 10, no. 1 (January 1948): 1; 'Color film suit settled in US consent decree,' *Los Angeles*

Times (25 November 1948): sec. 2, p. 2; 'Eastman gets color patents,' *Hollywood Reporter* (10 July 1951): 1, 4; 'Government case against Technicolor terminated,' *Technicolor News and Views*, 12, no. 1 (March 1950): 1-2.

24 'Color in the motion picture,' pp. 164, 166; 'Six companies now testing Eastman Color,' *Hollywood Citizen-News* (10 November 1949): 19; Earl Theisen, 'Notes on the history of color in motion pictures,' *IP*, 8, no. 5 (June 1936): 8-9, 24; Don Hooper, 'Negative-positive color,' *IP*, 9, no. 8 (September 1937): 27-9; W.T. Hanson, 'Color negative and color positive film for motion picture use,' *JSMPTE*, 58, no. 8 (March 1952): 223-5; W.T. Hanson and W.I. Kisner, 'Improved color films for color motion-picture production,' *JSMPTE*, 61, no. 6 (December 1953): 670-2; Basten, *Glorious Technicolor*, pp. 149, 160; Frederick Foster, 'Eastman negative-positive color films for motion pictures,' *AC*, 34, no. 7 (July 1953): 322-33, 348; Robert A. Mitchell, 'Color and its reproduction on film,' *IPro*, 31, no. 2 (February 1956): 17; James Morris, '1954 seen as biggest year for color,' *IPro*, 29, no. 1 (January 1954): 7-8; Robert A. Mitchell, 'To which IP replies,' *IPro*, 30, no. 8 (August 1955): 16; '1945 to 1955: ten years of progress in projection technology,' *IPro*, 30, no. 12 (December 1955): 24, 38; 'Summary of current widescreen systems of photography,' *AC*, 36, no. 11 (November 1955): 676; 'CinemaScope,' *International Sound Technician*, 1, no. 2 (April 1953): 2; Robert A. Mitchell, 'Anatomy of CinemaScope,' *IPro*, 29, no. 6 (June 1954): 10; 'Warner Brothers debuts "Warnercolor" ' *AC*, 33, no. 3 (March 1952): 122; Edwin A. DuPar, 'Warner-Color – newest of color film processes,' *AC*, 33, no. 9 (September 1952): 384-5. See also R.M. Wiener, 'Color film often doomed at birth – in the lab,' *Box Office* (5 May 1980): 1, 5, 30.

25 Jackson J. Rose, *American Cinematographer Handbook and Reference Guide*, ninth ed. (Hollywood: American Cinematographer, 1956), p. 59; 'Closeups,' *AC*, 35, no. 3 (March 1954): 122; Herbert T. Kalmus, 'President's message,' *Technicolor News and Views*, 15, no. 2 (November 1953): 2; Lloyd Thompson, 'Progress Committee Report for 1959,' *JSMPTE*, 69, no. 5 (May 1960): 302; 'Technicolor improves color printing process,' *IPro*, 30, no. 5 (May 1956): 14; Lowell A. Bodger, 'Ultra-wide screen systems,' *AC*, 43, no. 7 (July 1962): 441; Basten, *Glorious Technicolor*, pp. 156-9, 197; Bob Allen, 'Wide screen production picking up,' *IP*, 33, no. 11 (November 1961): 222.

Chapter 29 Widescreen processes and stereophonic sound

1 Ralph G. Fear, 'Wide image on standard film,' *AC*, 10, no. 5 (August 1929): 17, 44; John R. Bishop and Loren L. Ryder, 'Paramount's "Lazy-8" double-frame camera,' *AC*, 34, no. 12 (December 1953): 606; John D. Elms, 'Demonstration and description of the Widescope camera,' *TSMPE*, no. 15 (1922): 124-9; Fred Waller, 'Cinerama goes to war,' in *New Screen Techniques*, ed. Martin Quigley (New York: Quigley, 1953), pp. 119-20; William Stull, 'Seventy millimeters,' *AC*, 10, no. 11 (February 1930): 9, 42-3; Edmund M. DiGiulion, E. C. Manderfield, and George A. Mitchell, 'An historical survey of the professional motion picture camera,' *JSMPTE*, 76, no. 7 (July 1967): 668; Paul Allen, 'Wide film development,' *Cinematographic Annual*, 1 (1930), pp. 186-7; H.H. Dunn, 'New giant movies,' *Popular Mechanics*, 53, no. 5 (May 1930): 709; Fred Westerberg, 'Is 35mm passing?' *IP*, 1, no. 9 (October 1929): 28-34; George A. Mitchell, '70mm film versus other sizes,' *IP*, 2, no. 3 (April 1930): 3, 7; 'Progress in the motion picture industry,' *JSMPE*, 15 no. 6 (December 1930): 759, 763; James R. Cameron, 'The new wide film arrives,' *Projection Engineering*, 1, no. 2 (October 1929): 26, 38.

2 'Grandeur film makes debut at Fox Carthay Circle Theatre,' *Hollywood Filmograph*, 10, no. 7 (1 March 1930): 9.

3 Henri Dain, 'Memorandum on widening the field of camera lenses,' *JSMPE*, 19, no. 6 (December 1932): 527.

4 J.P. Maxfield, 'Demonstration of sterophonic recording with motion pictures,' *JSMPE*, 30, no. 2 (February 1938): 132. See also 'Reproducing orchestral music in auditory perspective,' *IPro*, 5, no. 3 (May 1933): 14-16; Harvey Fletcher, 'Transmission and reproduction of speech and music in auditory perspective,' *JSMPE*, 22 no. 5 (May 1934): 314-29; and Franklin L. Hunt, 'Sound pictures in auditory perspective,' *JSMPE*, 31, no. 4 (October 1938): 351-7.

5 W.H. Offenhauser and J.J. Israel, 'Some production aspects of binaural recording for sound motion pictures,' *JSMPE*, 32, no. 2 (February 1939): 139-55; 'Warners' "Vitasound" praised at showing,' *AC*, 21, no. 12 (December 1940): 547; 'RCA's "Panoramic" sound system ready soon,' *IPro*, 16, no. 1 (January 1941): 30; *JSMPE*, 37, no. 4 (October 1941): 331-405; 'Report of the Committee on Sound,' *JSMPE*, 41, no. 4 (October 1943): 292-6. See also 'Movies soon to have three dimensions in both sight and sound,' *Architectural Record*, 83, no. 1 (January 1938): 38.

6* Anaglyphic (red/green) stereoscopic processes have

been used sporadically since early in the century, but most stereoscopic cinema of the 1950s employed Edwin Land's Polaroid process, first patented in 1928. The 'Natural Vision' Corporation applied polarization to cinema with *Bwana Devil* (1952), an independent production acquired by United Artists. Some studios, such as Warners and Columbia, obtained licenses to use 'Natural Vision,' while other studios built their own systems.

7   'New dimensions perk up Hollywood,' *Business Week* (14 March 1953): 122-3; Robert A. Mitchell, 'Visibility factors in projection,' *IPro*, 28, no. 5 (May 1953): 10.

8   G.H. Cook, 'Modern cine camera lenses,' *JSMPTE*, 65, no. 3 (March 1956): 155; Walter R. Greene, 'New CinemaScope "55,"' *IP*, 28, no. 3 (March 1956): 5; Ron Ross, 'Cameraman's comments,' *IP*, 27, no. 4 (April 1955): 7.

9   'Filming *The Ten Commandments*,' *IP*, 28, no. 10 (October 1956): 6; Herb A. Lightman, 'Why MGM chose "Camera 65,"' *AC*, 41, no. 3 (March 1960): 192; Lloyd Thompson, 'Progress Committee Report for 1956,' *JSMPTE*, 66, no. 5 (May 1957): 242; Arthur Rowan, 'Todd-AO – newest wide-screen system,' *AC*, 35, no. 10 (October 1954): 526; George Howard, 'Design improvements in high-wattage filament lamps respond to studio needs,' *AC*, 39, no. 4 (April 1958): 228; 'Industry news,' *AC*, 36, no. 5 (May 1955): 254; Lowell A. Bodger, 'Ultra-wide screen systems,' *AC*, 43, no. 7 (July 1962): 426; Petro Vlahos, 'Motion-Picture Studio Lighting and Process Photography Committee Report,' *JSMPTE*, 64, no. 8 (August 1955): 447; '3-D and wide screen news roundup,' *AC*, 34, no. 7 (July 1953): 308; N.H. Groet, T.J. Murray, and C.E. Osborne, 'Two high-speed color films and a reversal print film for motion picture use,' *JSMPTE* 69, no. 11 (November 1960): 815-16; Merle L. Dundon and Daan M. Zwick, 'A high-speed color negative film,' *JSMPTE*, 68, no. 11 (November 1959): 735-6; Norwood L. Simmons, 'The new Eastman color negative and color print films,' *AC*, 43, no. 6 (June 1962): 362-3, 385.

10 DiGuilio *et al.*, 'Historical survey,' p. 669; Lightman, 'Why MGM . . . ,' pp. 163, 192; Darrin Scot, 'Panavision's progress,' *AC*, 41, no. 5 (May 1960): 302-4; Bob Allen, 'Wide screen production picking up,' *IP*, 33, no. 11 (November 1961): 215; J. Victor, 'From any angle,' *IP*, 28, no. 5 (May 1956): 6; 'New products,' *JSMPTE*, 66, no. 12 (December 1957): 800; Lloyd Thompson, 'Progress Committee Report for 1958,' *JSMPTE*, 68, no. 5 (May 1959): 278; Lloyd Thompson, 'Progress Committee Report for 1959,' *JSMPTE*, 69, no. 5 (May 1960): 311; Scott Henderson, 'The Panavision story,' *AC*, 58, no. 4 (April 1977): 414-33.

11 Loren L. Ryder, 'Modernization desires of a major studio,' *JSMPE*, 47, no. 3 (September 1946): 226; '50-mm film tests seen as industry effort to neutralize competitive threat,' *IPro*, 21, no. 14 (April 1946): 8; Bob Mintz, 'The big changeover,' *AC*, 34, no. 10 (October 1953): 481, 497-9; Charles R. Daily, 'Progress Committee Report,' *JSMPTE*, 64, no. 5 (May 1955): 226; Robert A. Mitchell, ' "Matching" aperture and lenses,' *IPro*, 30, no. 5 (May 1955): 7-11, 33-4; Charles R. Daily, 'Progress Committee Report,' *JSMPTE*, 62, no. 5 (May 1954): 227; Derik J. Southall, 'Twentieth Century-Fox presents a CinemaScope picture,' *Focus on Film*, no. 31 (November 1978): 8-26, 47; Lloyd Thompson, 'Progress Committee Report for 1958,' *JSMPTE*, 68, no. 5 (May 1959): 290; Lloyd Thompson, 'Progress Committee Report for 1957,' *JSMPTE*, 67, no. 5 (May 1958): 242.

12 'C-Scope leads new methods,' *The 1954 Film Daily Year Book of Motion Pictures*, ed. Jack Alicoate (New York: Film Daily, 1954), p. 59; Martin Quigley, 'Introduction,' in Quigley, *New Screen Techniques*, pp. 10-11.

13 Loren Grignon, 'Experiment in stereophonic sound,' *JSMPE*, 52, no. 3 (March 1949): 280-91.

14 '1945 to 1955: ten years of progression in projection technology,' *IPro*, 30, no. 12 (December 1955): 39; Loren D. Grignon, 'Experiment in stereophonic sound,' *JSMPTE*, 61, no. 3 (September 1953): 365; Dolph Thomas, 'Problems in stereophonic sound,' *International Sound Technician*, 1, no. 3 (May 1953): 21; Ralph Lawton, ' "Penthouse" 4-track sound reproducers,' *AC*, 34, no. 10 (March 1954): 502-3; Lloyd Thompson, 'Progress Committee Report for 1956,' *JSMPTE*, 66, no. 5 (May 1957): 242.

15 'Editor's comment,' *IPro*, 30, no. 7 (July 1955): 16; '20th-Fox adopts small-sprocket Magoptical,' *IPro*, 32, no. 3 (March 1957): 21.

16 Bazin's comments can be found in 'Fin du montage,' *Cahiers du cinéma*, no. 31 (January 1954): 43; 'Un peu tard . . . ,' *Cahiers du cinéma*, no. 48 (June 1955): 45-7; 'Massacre en cinémascope,' *Arts*, no. 525 (20-26 July 1955): 1, 5.

17 André Bazin, 'Le cinémascope sauvera-t'il le cinéma?' *Esprit*, 12, no. 10-11 (October-November 1953): 683.

18 François Truffaut, 'En avoir plein la vue,' *Cahiers du cinéma*, no. 25 (July 1953): 22-3.

19 Charles Barr, 'CinemaScope: before and after,' *Film Quarterly*, 16, no. 4 (Summer 1963): 11, 18.

20 André Bazin, 'Beauté d'un Western,' *Cahiers du cinéma*, no. 55 (January 1956): 35.

21 Herb A. Lightman, 'Shooting *Oklahoma!* in Todd-AO,' *AC*, 36, no. 4 (April 1955): 210; Charles G. Clarke, 'And now 55mm,' *AC*, 36, no. 12 (December

1955): 707; Walter R. Greene, 'New CinemaScope, "55," ' *IP*, 28, no. 3 (March 1956): 6; Gayne Rescher, 'Wide angle problems in wide screen cinematography,' *AC*, 37, no. 5 (May 1956): 300, 310, 322-3; Arthur Gavin, 'CinemaScope: what it is, how it works,' *IPro*, 28, no. 4 (April 1953): 10.

22 Kenneth MacGowan, 'The wide screen of yesterday and tomorrow,' *Quarterly of Film, Radio, and Television*, 11, no. 3 (Spring 1957): 238.

23* Cinerama set up many obstacles for the cinematographer. The 'blend lines' between the three panels were visible, so the camera crew had to find vertical objects or shadows to conceal the breaks. If an actor were not placed wholly within one panel, the blend lines would bisect the body. The camera could not be panned or tilted because, again, of the distortions caused by the blend lines. And the three cameras required three separate lighting set-ups, since the diaphragms of all three cameras were interlocked to keep exposure constant. Todd-AO was no less cumbersome. Since movement perpendicular to the lens tended to blur, action had to be staged along diagonals. Because Todd-AO had no optical printers, fades and dissolves had to be done in lighting. The Todd-AO lenses also yielded a very shallow depth of field. Both Cinerama and Todd-AO, after some initial success in the 1950s, became moribund because their novelty value did not compensate for their expense and lack of flexibility in production. See William Daniels, 'Cinerama goes dramatic,' *AC*, 43, no. 1 (January 1962): 50-3; Joseph Brun, 'The Cinerama technique,' *AC*, 35, no. 6 (June 1954): 291, 301-2; Lightman, 'Shooting *Oklahoma!*,' pp. 243-4; Aaron Nadell, 'Cinerama – a step in the right direction,' *IPro*, 27, no. 10 (October 1952): 11; Herb A. Lightman, 'Filming the first Cinerama feature,' *AC*, 43, no. 9 (September 1962): 537, 560-1.

24 Ron Ross and Vic Heutschy, 'Cameraman's comments,' *IP*, 25, no. 11 (November 1953): 10; Charles G. Clarke, 'CinemaScope photographic techniques,' *AC*, 36, no.6 (June 1955): 11-12.

25 See the several essays grouped as 'Le Cinéma-Scope,' *Cahiers du cinéma*, no. 31 (January 1954): 36-48. See also Henry Koster, 'Directing in Cinema-Scope,' in Quigley, *New Screen Techniques*, pp. 171-3; Clarke, 'CinemaScope photographic techniques,' p. 12; Robert Wise, 'How my editorial background helps me as a director,' *American Cinema Editors: First Decade Anniversary Book*, ed. Frederick Y. Smith (Hollywood: ACE, 1961), pp. 25-9.

26 André Bazin, *Orson Welles*, tr. Jonathan Rosenbaum (New York: Harper & Row, 1978), pp. 67-74.

27 Clarke, 'CinemaScope photographic techniques,' pp. 11-12; quoted in *Kazan on Kazan*, ed. Michel Ciment (New York: Viking, 1974), pp. 122-3.

28 See Gavin, 'CinemaScope: what it is,' p. 10.

29 Barbara McLean Webb, 'Pioneering in Cinema-Scope,' *Cinemeditor*, 3, no. 4 (December 1953): 3.

30 Leon Shamroy, 'Filming *The Robe*,' in Quigley, *New Screen Techniques*, p. 180.

31 Truffaut, 'En avoir plein la vue,' p. 23.

32 Charles Bitsch, 'Naissance du CinémaScope,' *Cahiers du cinéma*, no. 48 (June 1955): 41-2.

33 V.F. Perkins, 'River of No Return,' *Movie*, no. 2 (September 1962): 18.

34 Barr, 'CinemaScope – before and after,' p. 11.

35 Jacques Rivette, 'L'âge des metteurs en scène,' *Cahiers du cinéma*, no. 31 (January 1954): 48.

Chapter 30 Since 1960: the persistence of a mode of film practice

1   René Wellek, 'The term and concept of classicism in literary history,' in *Discriminations* (New Haven: Yale University Press, 1970), p. 68.

2   Osip Brik, 'The Lef arena,' *Screen Reader*, ed. John Ellis (London: SEFT, 1977), p. 316.

3   A relentlessly snappy account of recent developments may be found in James Monaco, *American Film Now* (New York: New American Library, 1979), pp. 1-137. Less zoot-suited prose dominates Thomas Guback, 'Theatrical film,' in *Who Owns the Media?*, ed. Benjamin H. Companie (New York: Harmony, 1979), pp. 179-241.

4   'Jaws tries to swallow Coke?' *Time* (24 October 1977): 76.

5   Alfred D. Chandler, Jr, *Strategy and Structure: Chapters in the History of the American Industrial Enterprise* (Cambridge, Mass.: MIT Press, 1962).

6   For a description of the current system of production, see David Lees and Stan Berkowitz, *The Movie Business* (New York: Vintage Books, 1981).

7   Steve Shagan quoted in Andrew Laskos, 'The greatest movies never made,' *American Film*, 4, no. 10 (September 1979): 50.

8   Vincent Canby, 'Let's call it "the accountant's theory" of filmmaking,' *New York Times* (10 July 1977): sec. 2, p. 11.

9   Richard Dyer MacCann, 'The independent producer: independence with a vengeance,' *Film Quarterly*, 15, no. 3 (Summer 1962): 14-21; Robert H. Stanley, *The Celluloid Empire* (New York: Hastings House, 1978), pp. 251-2; Robert Lindsay, 'The new tycoons of Hollywood,' *New York Times Magazine* (7 August 1977): 20; Karen Stabiner, 'Playing hardball with a hot agent,' *American Film*, 6, no. 9 (July-August 1981): 40-5, 67.

10 Robert R. Faulkner, *Hollywood Studio Musicians: Their Work and Careers in the Recording Industry* (Chicago: Aldine, Atherton, 1971), pp. 46-50.

11   Arthur E. Gavin, '*Hear Me Good* shot in straight continuity,' *AC*, 38, no. 9 (September 1957): 572-3, 602-3; 'Industry news,' *AC*, 40, no. 81 (August 1959): 454; Rex McGee, 'Michael Cimino's way west,' *American Film*, 6, no. 1 (October 1980): 78.

12   McGee, 'Way west,' pp. 36-7.

13   *Ibid.*

14   *Ibid.*

15   Francesca Riviere, 'Rebirth next: an exclusive interview with Francis Ford Coppola,' *L.A. Weekly* (28 November 1979): 40.

16   Jean-Luc Godard, *Introduction à une véritable histoire du cinéma* (Paris: Albatros, 1980), p. 100.

17   Ben Fong-Torres, '*The China Syndrome*,' *Rolling Stone*, no. 288 (5 April 1979): 50-5; Aaron Latham, 'Hollywood vs. Harrisburg,' *Esquire*, 91, no. 10 (22 May 1979): 77-86.

18   On Jane Fonda's star persona, see Richard Dyer, *Stars* (London: British Film Institute, 1979), pp. 72-98.

19   For the makers' attitudes toward the characters' ambivalence, see Fong-Torres, '*China Syndrome*,' p. 55.

20   Godard, *Introduction*, p. 100.

21   Michael Pye and Lynda Myles, *The Movie Brats: How the Film Generation Took Over Hollywood* (New York: Holt, Rinehart & Winston, 1979), p. 58.

22   D.W. Samuelson, 'A survey of current film production techniques,' *AC*, 58, no. 9 (September 1977): 918-19, 922-3; D.W. Samuelson, 'Introducing the Louma crane,' *AC*, 60, no. 12 (December 1979): 1226-7, 1260-1, 1274.

23   Interview with Robert Altman, Paris Film Festival 1976, transcribed by Geoffrey Miller.

24   Quoted in Lear Levin, 'Robert Altman's innovative sound techniques,' *AC*, 61, no. 4 (April 1980): 368, 384.

25   Ed DiGiulio, 'Steadicam-35 – a revolutionary new concept in camera stabilization,' *AC*, 57, no. 7 (July 1976): 786-7; 'The first feature use of Steadicam-35 on *Bound for Glory*,' *AC*, 57, no. 7 (July 1976): 778.

26   Ed Digiulion, 'Two special lenses for *Barry Lyndon*,' *AC*, 57, no. 3 (March 1976): 318.

27   Ernest Mandel, *Late Capitalism*, tr. Joris De Bres (London: New Left Brooks, 1975), p. 501. For a good instance of evangelistic enthusiasm for technological innovation, see Charles Schreger, 'The second coming of sound,' *Film Comment*, 14, no. 5 (September-October 1978): 34-7.

28   Peter Lloyd, 'An outlook,' *Monogram*, no. 1 (April 1971): 11-13.

29   Thomas Elsaesser, 'The pathos of failure,' *Monogram*, no. 6 (1975): 13-19.

30   See Robin Wood, *Personal Visions* (London: Gordon Fraser, 1976), pp. 20-9; David Bordwell, 'The art cinema as a mode of film practice,' *Film Criticism*, 4, no. 1 (Fall 1979): 56-64; Steve Neale, 'Art cinema as institution,' *Screen*, 22, no. 1 (1981): 11-39.

31   Ralph Rosenblum, *When the Shooting Stops . . . The Cutting Begins* (New York: Penguin, 1980), pp. 142-9.

32   Pascal Kané, '*Sylvia Scarlett*: Hollywood cinema reread,' *Sub-stance*, no. 9 (1974): 35.

33   Quoted in Jordan Fox, 'Walter Murch – making beaches out of grains of sand,' *Cinefex*, no. 3 (December 1980): 51.

Chapter 31 Alternative modes of film practice

1   Carlo Lizzani, *Storia del cinema italiano 1895-1961* (Firenze: Parenti, 1961), p. 42; René Jeanne and Charles Ford, *Histoire encyclopédique du cinéma*, vol. 1 (Paris: Laffont, 1947), pp. 121-2; Charles Pathé, 'Le crise du cinéma,' *Le film*, no. 102 (25 February 1918): 8; Charles Pathé, 'Etude sur l'évolution de l'industrie cinématographique française,' *Le film*, no. 120 (1 July 1918): 12. For a discussion of the influence of the American cinema upon French culture at this period, see David Bordwell, *French Impressionist Cinema: Film Culture, Film Theory, and Film Style* (New York: Arno Press, 1980), pp. 34-5; for an analysis of European responses to this domination, see Janet Staiger and Douglas Gomery, 'The history of world cinema: models for economic analysis,' *Film Reader*, 4 (1979): 35-44.

2   Rudolf Messel, *This Film Business* (London: Ernest Benn, 1928), p. 259.

3   Hugh Castle, 'The battle of Wardour Street,' *Close Up*, 4, no. 3 (March 1929): 10-11; Urban Gad, *Filmen: Dens Midler og Maal* (Copenhagen: Gyldendal, 1919).

4   'The movies most popular in Japan,' *Japan Advertiser* (10 March 1919): 2.

5   Akira Iwasaki, 'An outline history of Japanese cinema,' in *Cinema Yearbook of Japan 1936-37*, ed. Tadashi Iizima (Tokyo: Sanseido, 1937), p. 3.

6   Harry A. Mimura, 'Professionals and amateurs of Japan,' *IP*, 5, no. 9 (October 1933): 14.

7   Erik Barnouw and S. Krishnaswamy, *Indian Film*, 2nd ed. (New York: Oxford University Press, 1980), pp. 41-2, 66.

8   Sergei M. Eisenstein, *Montage*, tr. Michael Glenny (forthcoming).

9   See, for example, Michèle Lagny, Marie-Claire Ropars, and Pierre Sorlin, 'Analyse d'un ensemble filmique extensible: Les films français des années 30,' in *Théorie du film*, ed. Jacques Aumont and J.-L. Leutrat (Paris: Albatros, 1980), pp. 132-64.

10   Kristin Thompson, work in progress upon the

European avant-garde of the 1920s.

11 Television's use of continuity techniques is discussed in David Antin, 'Video: distinctive features of the medium,' in *Esthetics Contemporary*, ed. Richard Kostelanetz (Buffalo: Prometheus, 1978), pp. 393-4.

12 For the application of the Hollywood style to amateur moviemaking, see *Your First 50 Pictures* (Rochester: Eastman Kodak, 1930), pp. 3-4; *Making the Most of Your Cine-Kodak* (Rochester: Eastman Kodak, 1925), pp. 4-16; A.L. Gaskill and D.A. Englander, *Pictorial Continuity* (New York: Duell, Sloan and Pearce, 1947); and Emil C. Brodbeck, *Handbook of Basic Motion Picture Techniques* (New York: McGraw-Hill, 1950).

13 Hugo Münsterberg, *The Film: A Psychological Study* (Reprint, New York: Dover, 1970), pp. 80-2.

14 Julian Hochberg and Virginia Brooks, 'The perception of motion pictures,' in *Handbook of Perception*, vol. 10: 'Perceptual ecology,' ed. Edward C. Carterette and Morton P. Friedman (New York: Academic press, 1978), pp. 282-4.

15 John M. Carroll, *Toward a Structural Psychology of Cinema* (The Hague: Mouton, 1980), pp. 54-80.

16 Peter Wollen, 'Counter-cinema: *Vent d'est,*' *Afterimage*, no. 4 (Autumn 1972): 6-16; Colin MacCabe, 'Realism and the cinema,' *Screen*, 15, no. 2 (Summer 1974): 7-27; Paul Willemen, 'Notes toward the construction of readings of Tourneur,' in *Jacques Tourneur*, ed. Claire Johnston and Paul Willemen (Edinburgh: Edinburgh Film Festival, 1975), pp. 18-19; Noël Burch and Jorge Dana, 'Propositions,' *Afterimage*, no. 5 (Spring 1974): 46-8; Jean Narboni and Jean-Louis Comolli, 'Cinema/ideology/criticism,' in *Screen Reader*, ed. John Ellis (London: SEFT, 1977), pp. 5-8.

17 See Martin Walsh, 'The frontiers of language: Straub/Huillet's *History Lessons*,' *Afterimage*, no. 7 (Summer 1978): 21-3.

18 Quoted in Michel Mesnil, *Kenji Mizoguchi* (Paris: Seghers, 1965), p. 151.

19 A more extensive account of Mizoguchi's style is offered in David Bordwell, 'Mizoguchi and the evolution of film language,' in *Language and Cinema*, ed. Stephen Heath and Patricia Mellencamp (Los Angeles: American Film Institute, 1983), pp. 107-15.

20 For examples of Surrealist criticism of Hollywood cinema, see *The Shadow and Its Shadow*, ed. Paul Hammond (London: British Film Institute, 1978).

21 Paul Babisky and John Rimberg, *The Soviet Film Industry* (New York: Praeger, 1955), pp. 29-87.

22 Joseph L. Anderson and Donald Richie, *The Japanese Film: Art and Industry* (New York: Grove, 1959), pp. 332-50.

23 André Bazin and François Truffaut, 'Entretien avec Jacques Tati,' *Cahiers du cinéma*, no. 83 (May 1958): 11; Richard Roud, *Jean-Marie Straub* (New York: The Viking Press, 1972), p. 62; Jan Dawson, *Wim Wenders* (Toronto: Festival of Festivals, 1976), p. 13; Jack Hamilton, 'Antonioni's America,' *Look*, (18 November 1969): 40.

24 Dziga Vertov, quoted in *Film Makers on Film Making*, ed. Harry M. Geduld (Bloomington: Indiana University Press, 1969), pp. 103-4; 'The Vertov Papers,' tr. Marco Carynyk, *Film Comment*, 8, no. 1 (Spring 1972): 48; Zuzana M. Pick, 'A special section on Chilean cinema,' *Ciné-Tracts*, no. 9 (Winter 1980): 38-49; Melton S. Davis, 'Boy talks with girl, boy argues with girl, boy says . . . ,' *New York Times Magazine* (21 November 1971): 88ff.

25 Yoda Yoshikata, 'Souvenirs sur Mizoguchi,' *Mizoguchi* (*Cahiers du cinéma* hors série, 1978): 13ff; Davis, 'Boy talks . . . ,' pp. 88ff.

26 Davis, 'Boy talks . . . ,' p. 88.

27 Mark Evans, *Soundtrack: The Music of the Movies* (New York: Hopkinson & Blake, 1975), p. 144; David O. Selznick, *Memo From David O. Selznick*, ed. Rudy Behlmer (New York: Avon Books, 1973), p. 157.

28 Francis Porcile, *Présence de la musique à l'écran* (Paris: Cerf, 1969), p. 197; 'Entretien avec Jean-Marie Straub et Danièle Huillet,' *Cahiers du cinéma*, no. 223 (August 1970): 53; Roud, *Jean-Marie Straub*, pp. 9, 62, 118.

29 Bertolt Brecht, *et al.*, 'Collective presentation (1932),' *Screen*, 15, no. 2 (Summer 1974): 43.

30 Octavio Getino and Fernando Solanas, 'Towards a third cinema,' *Afterimage*, no. 3 (Summer 1971): 28-9.

31 Michael Goodwin *et al.*, 'The Dziga Vertov film group in America,' *Take One*, 2, no. 10 (March-April 1971): 10. See also Michael Goodwin and Greil Marcus, *Double Feature: Movies and Politics* (New York: Outerbridge & Lazard, 1972), p. 19. And compare Marcel Martin, 'Le groupe "Dziga-Vertov,"' *Cinéma 70*, no. 151 (December 1970): 86-7.

32 Getino and Solanas, 'Towards a third cinema,' 32.

33 Quoted in Eric Sherman, *Directing the Film* (Boston: Little, Brown, 1976), p. 294.

Appendix D Lighting plots and descriptions

1 Diagrams 1 and 2 from H.M. Lomas, *Picture Play Photography* (London: Ganes, 1914), pp. 82-3.

2 L.G. Harkness Smith, 'Electric lighting for motion-picture studios,' *Electrical World*, 65, no. 17 (24 April 1915): 1040.

3 Diagrams 3 through 7 from Smith, 'Electric lighting for motion-picture studios,' pp. 1040-2.

4 William A.D. Evans, 'The artificial lighting of moving picture studios,' *The Illuminating Engineer*, 8 (June 1915): 286-7.
5 William Roy Mott, 'White light for motion picture photography,' *TSMPE*, no. 8 (14-16 April 1919): 32.
6 *Ibid*.

7 Wiard B. Ihnen and D.W. Atwater, 'The artistic utilization of light in the photography of motion pictures,' *TSMPE*, no. 21 (18-21 May 1925): 26.
8 Diagrams 10 through 12 from Ihnen and Atwater, 'The artistic utilization of light in the photography of motion pictures,' p. 27.

Select bibliography

Journals

Academy of Motion Picture Arts and Sciences Bulletin (and *Supplements*), 1929-35
American Cinematographer (AC), 1921-80
American Projectionist, 1923-31
Camera!, 1918
Cinema: The Magazine of the Photoplay, 1930
Cinema Arts, 1937
Cinema News, 1916-19
Cinema Progress: The Film and Life, 1936-9
Cinematography, 1930-1
Cinemeditor, 1952-63
The Drama, 1911-18
The Eclair Bulletin, 1912-13
The Edison Kinetogram (EK), 1909-16
Exhibitors Herald and Moving Picture World, 1928
Film Music Notes, 1946-57
The Film Spectator, 1926-9
Image, 1952-6
International Photographer, 1931-62
International Projectionist, 1931-60
International Sound Technician, 1953-4
Journal of the Society of Motion Picture [and Television] Engineers (JSMP[T]E), 1930-80 (Previously titled *Transactions of the Society of Motion Picture Engineers*)
Motion Picture, 1924
Motion Picture [Producers and Distributors] Association of America Annual Reports, 1931/32-1956
The Motion Picture Director, 1925-7
Motion Picture Herald (MPHerald), 1931-2, 1940-50, 1955-7, 1959
Motion Picture News (MPNews), 1908-16
Motion Picture Projectionist, 1927-33
Motography, 1911-18 (Previously titled *The Nickelodeon*)
Moving Picture World (MPW), 1907-16
New York Dramatic Mirror (NYDM), 1911-17
The Nickelodeon (NKL), 1909-11 (See *Motography* for continuation)
The Ohio Showman, 1928-33
Perspective: Quarterly Review of Progress: Photography,

Cinematography, Sound and Image Recording, 1959-66
The Photodramatist (PTD), 1921-3
Photoplay, 1912-35
Production Design, 1951-3
Projection Engineering, 1929-33
Reel Life, 1913-17
The Screen Writer, 1945-8
The Script, 1914
The Silver Sheet, 1921-3
Sound Waves, 1928-9
The Static Club Bulletin, 1916
Technicolor News and Views, 1939-55
Transactions of the Society of Motion Picture Engineers (TSMPE), 1916-29 (See *Journal of the Society of Motion Picture [and Television] Engineers* for continuation)
The Triangle, 1915-17
V-L-S-E Pals, 1915-16
Writer's Monthly, 1925-39

General background, theory, and method

Andrew, Charlton, *The Technique of Play Writing*, Springfield, Mass.: Home Correspondence School, 1915.

Archer, William, *Play-Making: A Manual of Craftsmanship*, Boston: Small, Maynard & Co., 1912.

Bailblé, Claude, 'Programming the look: a new approach to teaching film technique,' *Screen Education*, nos 32/33 (Autumn/Winter 1979/80), pp. 99-131.

Bailblé, Claude, 'Le son. Programmation de l'écoute,' *Cahiers du cinéma*, no. 292 (September 1978), pp. 53-9; no. 293 (October 1978), pp. 5-12; no. 297 (February 1979), pp. 44-54; no. 299 (April 1979), pp. 18-27.

Baran, Paul A. and Paul M. Sweezy, *Monopoly Capital: An Essay on the American Economic and Social Order*, 1966, reprint, New York: Modern Reader Paperbacks, 1968.

Baudry, Pierre, 'Les aventures de l'Idée (sur 'Intolerance'), 1,' *Cahiers du cinéma*, no. 240 (July-August 1972), pp. 51-8; part 2, *Cahiers du cinéma*, no. 241 (September-October 1972), pp. 31-45.

Bazin, André, *What Is Cinema?* tr. and ed. Hugh Gray, vol. 1, 1967, vol. 2. Berkeley: University of California Press, 1971.

Bernal, J.D. *Science and Industry in the Nineteenth Century*, Bloomington: Indiana University Press, 1971.

Bernheim, Alfred L. *The Business of the Theatre: An Economic History of the American Theatre, 1750-1932*, New York: Benjamin Blom, 1932.

Braverman, Harry, *Labor and Monopoly Capital: The Degradation of Work in the Twentieth Century*, New York: Monthly Review Press, 1974.

Burch, Noël, *Theory of Film Practice*, tr. Helen R. Lane, New York: Praeger, 1973.

Burch, Noël and Jorge Dana, 'Propositions,' *Afterimage*, no. 5 (Spring 1974), pp. 40-67.

Burnham, James, *The Managerial Revolution*, Bloomington: Indiana University Press, 1941.

Buscombe, Edward, 'Bread and circuses: economics and the cinema,' paper, Asilomar, California: Conference on Cinema Histories, Cinema Practices, 25-29 May 1981.

Carroll, Noël, 'Toward a theory of film editing,' *Millennium Film Journal*, no. 3 (Winter/Spring 1979), pp. 79-99.

Caves, Richard, *American Industry: Structure, Conduct, Performance*, 4th ed., Englewood Cliffs, New Jersey: Prentice-Hall, 1977.

Chamberlain, John, *The Enterprising Americans: A Business History of the United States*, rev. ed., New York: Harper & Row, 1974.

Chandler, Alfred D., Jr, *Strategy and Structure: Chapters in the History of the American Industrial Enterprise*, Cambridge, Mass.: MIT Press, 1962.

Chinoy, Helen Krich, 'The emergence of the director,' in *Directors on Directing*, ed. Toby Cole and Helen Krich Chinoy, rev. ed. Indianapolis: Bobbs-Merrill Company, 1963, pp. 1-77.

Comolli, Jean-Louis. 'Technique et idéologie,' *Cahiers du cinéma*, no. 229 (May 1971), pp. 4-15, 16-21; no. 230 (July 1971), pp. 51-7; no. 231 (August-September 1971), pp. 42-9; no. 233 (November 1971), pp. 39-45; nos 234-5 (December 1971, January/February 1972), pp. 94-100; no. 241 (September/October 1972), pp. 20-4.

Cutler, Antony, Barry Hindess, Paul Hirst, and Athar Hussain, *Marx's Capital and Capitalism Today*, 2 vols, London: Routledge & Kegan Paul, 1977, 1978.

Davies, Gill, 'Teaching about narrative,' *Screen Education*, no. 29 (Winter 1978/79), pp. 56-76.

'Dossier on Melodrama,' *Screen*, 18, no. 2 (Summer 1977), pp. 105-19.

Downer, Alan S., 'Players and the painted stage: nineteenth century acting,' *Publications of the Modern Language Association of America*, 61, no. 2 (June 1946), pp. 522-76.

Drucker, Peter F., *Technology, Management and Society*, New York: Harper & Row, 1970.

Eagleton, Terry, *Criticism and Ideology: A Study in Marxist Literary Theory*, London: Verso Edition, 1978.

Easthope, Antony, 'Notes on genre,' *Screen Education*, nos 32/33 (Autumn/Winter 1979/80), pp. 39-44.

Eizykman, Claudine, *La jouissance-cinéma*, Paris: Union Générale d'Editions, 1975.

Elsaesser, Thomas, 'Why Hollywood,' *Monogram*, no. 1 (April 1971), pp. 4-10.

Elsaesser, Thomas, 'Tales of sound and fury,' *Monogram*, no. 4 (1972), pp. 2-15.

Elsaesser, Thomas, 'Narrative cinema and audience-oriented aesthetics,' London: BFI/SEFT seminar paper, n.d.

Esenwein, J. Berg and Mary Davoren Chambers, *The Art of Story-Writing*, Springfield, Mass.: Home Correspondence School, 1913.

Felheim, Marvin, *The Theater of Augustin Daly: An Account of the Late Nineteenth Century American Stage*, Cambridge, Mass.: Harvard University Press, 1956.

Fihman, Guy, 'D'où viennent les images claires?' in *Cinéma: théorie, lectures*, ed. Dominique Noguez, Paris: Klincksieck, 1973, pp. 193-206.

Galbraith, John Kenneth, *The New Industrial State*, 2nd ed., New York: New American Library, 1971.

Gilbert, Douglas, *American Vaudeville*, New York: Whittlesley House, 1940.

Greenleaf, William (ed.), *American Economic Development since 1860*, New York: Harper & Row, 1968.

Groner, Alex, *The American Heritage History of American Business & Industry*, New York: American Heritage Publishing Co., 1972.

Gutman, Herbert G., *Work, Culture and Society in Industrializing America*, 1976, reprint, New York: Random House, 1977.

Guzzetti, Alfred. 'Narrative and the film image,' *New Literary History*, 6, no. 2 (Winter 1975), pp. 379-92.

Hamilton, Clayton, *A Manual of the Art of Fiction*, Garden City, New York: Doubleday, Page & Co., 1918.

Heath, Stephen, 'On screen in frame,' *Quarterly Review of Film Studies*, 1, no. 3 (August 1976), pp. 251-65.

Heath, Stephen, 'Narrative space,' *Screen*, 17, no. 3 (Autumn 1976), pp. 68-112.

Heath, Stephen, 'Notes on suture,' *Screen*, 18, no. 4 (Winter 1977/78), pp. 48-76.

Hennequin, Alfred, *The Art of Playwriting*, Boston: Houghton, Mifflin Co., 1897.

Hindess, Barry and Paul Q. Hirst, *Pre-Capitalist Modes of Production*, London: Routledge & Kegan Paul, 1975.

Hochberg, Julian and Virginia Brooks, 'The perception of motion pictures,' in *Handbook of Perception*, vol.

10, 'Perceptual ecology,' eds Edward C. Carterette and Morton P. Friedman, New York: Academic Press, 1978, pp. 259-304.

Hofstadter, Richard, *The Age of Reform*, New York: Vintage Books, 1955.

Horkheimer, Max, 'Art and mass culture,' in *Critical Theory*, New York: Seabury Press, 1972, pp. 273-90.

Hoxie, Robert Franklin, *Scientific Management and Labor*, 1918, reprint, New York: Augustus M. Kelley, 1966.

Hudson, Ray M. 'Organized effort in simplification,' *The Annals of the American Academy of Political and Social Science*, no. 87 (May 1928), pp. 1-8.

Jenkins, Reese V., *Images and Enterprise: Technology and the American Photographic Industry, 1839 to 1925*, Baltimore: Johns Hopkins University Press, 1975.

Krows, Arthur Edwin, *Play Production in America*, New York: Henry Holt & Co., 1916.

Kubler, George, *The Shape of Time: Remarks on the History of Things*, New Haven: Yale University Press, 1962.

Kuntzel, Thierry, 'Le travail du film, 2,' *Communications*, no. 23 (1975), pp. 136-89.

Lebel, Jean-Patrick, *Cinéma et idéologie*, Paris: Editions sociales, 1971.

Leblanc, Gérard, 'Welles, Bazin et la RKO,' *Cinéthique*, no. 6 (January-February 1970), pp. 27-32.

Lescohier, Don D., 'Working conditions,' in *History of Labor in the United States*, ed. John R. Commons, vol. 3, 1935, reprint, New York: Augustus M. Kelley, 1966, pp. 303-15.

MacCabe, Colin, 'Realism and the cinema: notes on some Brechtian theses,' *Screen*, 15, no. 2 (Summer 1974), pp. 7-27.

MacCabe, Colin, 'Theory and film: principles of realism and pleasure;' *Screen*, 17, no. 3 (Autumn 1976), pp. 7-27.

Mandel, Ernest, *Late Capitalism*, tr. Joris De Bres, London: New Left Books, 1975.

Mandel, Ernest, *Marxist Economic Theory*, tr. Brian Pearce, vol. 2, 1968, reprint, New York: Monthly Review Press, 1970.

Marx, Karl, *Capital: A Critical Analysis of Capitalist Production*, vol. 1, ed. Frederick Engels, New York: International Publishers, 1967.

Matthews, Brander, *A Book About the Theater*, New York: Charles Scribner's Sons, 1916.

Matthews, Brander *The Historical Novel and Other Essays*, New York: Charles Scribner's Sons, 1901.

Matthews, Brander, *Pen and Ink*, 3rd ed., New York: Charles Scribner's Sons, 1902.

Mees, C.E. Kenneth, *The Organization of Industrial Scientific Research*, New York: McGraw-Hill, 1920.

Metz, Christian, 'History/discourse: note on two voyeurisms,' *Edinburgh '76 Magazine*, no. 1, pp. 21-5.

Nelson, Daniel, *Managers and Workers: Origins of the New Factory System in the United States 1880-1920*. Madison: University of Wisconsin Press, 1975.

Noble, David F., *America by Design: Science, Technology, and the Rise of Corporate Capitalism*, New York: Alfred A. Knopf, 1977.

Nowell-Smith, Geoffrey, 'Facts about films and facts of films,' *Quarterly Review of Film Studies*, 1, no. 3 (August 1976), pp. 272-5.

Nowell-Smith, Geoffrey, 'Minnelli and melodrama,' *Screen*, 18, no. 2 (Summer 1977), pp. 113-18.

Nye, Russel Blaine, *The Unembarrassed Muse: The Popular Arts in America*, New York: Dial Press, 1970.

Oudart, Jean-Pierre, 'Cinema and suture,' *Screen*, 18, no. 4 (Winter 1977/78), pp. 35-47.

Oudart, Jean-Pierre, 'Un discours en défault,' *Cahiers du cinéma*, no. 232 (October 1971), pp. 4-12.

Page, Brett, *Writing for Vaudeville*, Springfield, Mass.: Home Correspondence School, 1915.

Pattee, Fred Lewis, *The Development of the American Short Story: An Historical Survey*, New York: Harper & Bros, 1923.

Perrier, Jean-Louis, 'L'oeil tranché,' *Cinéthique*, nos 7-8 (n.d.), pp. 20-4.

Perry, Bliss, *A Study of Prose Fiction*, Boston: Houghton, Mifflin & Co., 1902.

Perry, John, *The Story of Standards*, New York: Funk & Wagnalls Co., 1955.

Poggi, Jack, *Theater in America: The Impact of Economic Forces 1870-1967*, Ithaca, New York: Cornell University Press, 1968.

Price, W.T., *The Technique of the Drama*, New York: Brentano's, 1897.

Pryluck, Calvin, 'The aesthetic relevance of the organization of film production,' *Cinema Journal*, 15, no. 2 (Spring 1976), pp. 1-6.

Scheiber, Harry N., Harold G. Vatter, and Harold Underwood Faulkner, *American Economic History*, 9th ed., rev. New York: Harper & Row, 1976.

Smith, C. Alphonso *The American Short Story*, Boston: Ginn & Co., 1912.

Smith, James L., *Melodrama*, London: Methuen, 1973.

Sternberg, Meir, *Expositional Modes and Temporal Ordering in Fiction*, Baltimore: Johns Hopkins University Press, 1978.

Suleiman, Susan Rubin, 'Redundancy and the "readable" text,' *Poetics Today*, 1, no. 3 (Spring 1980), pp. 119-41.

Sweezy, Paul M., *The Theory of Capitalist Development*, 1942, reprint, New York: Modern Reader Paperbacks, 1968.

Terfloth, John H., 'The pre-Meiningen rise of the director in Germany and Austria,' *Theatre Quarterly*, 6, no. 21 (1976), pp. 65-86.

Todorov, Tzvetan, 'Some approaches to Russian Formalism,' *Twentieth Century Studies* 7/8 (December 1972), pp. 6-19.

Tomashevsky, Boris, 'Literary genres,' *Russian Poetics in Translation*, no. 5 (1978), pp. 52-93.

Tyler, Parker, *The Hollywood Hallucination*, New York: Simon & Schuster, 1970.

Tyler, Parker, *Magic and Myth of the Movies*, New York: Simon & Schuster, 1970.

Tynyanov, Yury, 'Plot and story-line in the cinema,' *Russian Poetics in Translation*, no. 5 (1978), pp. 20-1.

Walker, Pat (ed.), *Between Labor and Capital*, Boston: South End Press, 1979.

Watt, Ian, *The Rise of the Novel: Studies in Defoe, Richardson, and Fielding.* Berkeley: University of California Press, 1974.

Willeman, Paul, 'Notes toward the construction of readings of Tourneur,' in *Jacques Tourneur*, eds Clair Johnston and Paul Willeman. Edinburgh: Edinburgh Film Festival, 1975, pp. 16-35.

Williams, Alan, 'Is sound recording like a language?' *Yale French Studies*, no. 60 (1980), pp. 51-66.

Williams, Raymond, 'Base and superstructure in Marxist cultural theory,' *New Left Review*, no. 82 (November-December 1973), pp. 3-16.

Woodbridge, Elizabeth, *The Drama: Its Laws and Its Techniques*, Boston: Allyn & Bacon, 1898.

Film books and articles

AMPAS, *Academy Reports No. 1: Transactions, Enquiries, Demonstrations, Tests, Etc., on the Subject of Incandescent Illumination as Applied to Motion Picture Production*, Hollywood: AMPAS, July 1928.

Academy Technical Digest: Fundamentals of Sound Recording and Reproduction for Motion Pictures, Hollywood: AMPAS, 1930.

AMPAS Research Council, *Motion Picture Sound Engineering Lectures*, New York: Van Nostrand, 1938.

Agnew, Frances, *Motion Picture Acting*, New York: Reliance Newspapers Syndicate, 1913.

Allen, Robert C., 'Contra the chaser theory,' *Wide Angle*, 3, no. 1 (1979), pp. 4-11.

Allen, Robert C., 'Film history: the narrow discourse,' in *Film: Historical-Theoretical Speculations: The 1977 Film Studies Annual (Part Two)*, eds Ben Lawton and Janet Staiger, Pleasantville, New York: Redgrave Publishing Co., 1977, pp. 9-17.

Allen, Robert C., 'Motion picture exhibition in Manhattan: 1906-1912: beyond the nickelodeon,' *Cinema Journal*, 18, no. 2 (Spring 1979), pp. 2-15.

Allen, Robert C., *Vaudeville and Film 1895-1915: A Study in Media Interaction*, New York: Arno Press, 1980.

Alton, John, *Painting With Light*, New York: Macmillan, 1949.

The American Film Institute/Louis B. Mayer Oral History Collection, Glen Rock, New Jersey: Microfilming Corporation of America, 1977.

The Annals of the American Academy of Political and Social Science, 128 (November 1926), special number: 'The motion picture in its economic and social aspects,' ed. Clyde L. King and Frank A. Tichenor.

'The architecture of motion picture settings,' *American Architect*, 118, no. 2324 (7 July 1920), pp. 1-5.

'Artisans of the motion picture films,' *Scientific American*, 115, no. 10 (2 September 1916), pp. 210-11, 224-5.

Arvey, Verna, 'Present day musical films and how they are made possible,' *Etude*, 49 (January 1931), pp. 16-17, 61, 72.

Balio, Tino (ed.), *The American Film Industry*, Madison: University of Wisconsin Press, 1976.

Ball, Eustace Hale, *The Art of the Photoplay*, New York: Veritas Publishing Co., 1913, 2nd ed. New York: G.W. Dillingham Co., 1913.

Balshofer, Fred F. and Arthur C. Miller, *One Reel a Week*, Berkeley: University of California Press, 1967.

Barry, John Francis and Epes W. Sargent, *Building Theatre Patronage: Management and Merchandising*, New York: Chalmers Publishing Co., 1927.

Basten, Fred E., *Glorious Technicolor: The Movies' Rainbow*, New York: A.S. Barnes, 1980.

Batman, Richard Dale, 'The founding of the Hollywood motion picture industry,' *Journal of the West*, 10 (October 1971), pp. 609-23.

Becker, Leon S., 'Technology in the art of producing motion pictures,' in *The Technique of Motion Picture Production*, ed. SMPE, New York: Interscience, 1944, pp. 1-10.

Bell, Donald J., 'A letter from Donald Bell,' *IP*, 2, no. 2 (February 1930), pp. 18-21.

Bellour, Raymond (ed.), *Le cinéma américain*, 2 vols, Paris: Flammarion, 1980.

Beranger, Clara F. 'The photoplay – a new kind of drama,' *Harper's Weekly*, 56, no. 2907 (7 September 1912), p. 13.

Bertrand, Daniel, Review Division, National Recovery Administration, *Evidence Study, no. 25: Motion Picture Industry*, November 1935, Washington DC: Government Printing Office, 1935.

Bertrand, Daniel, W. Duane Evans, and E.L. Blanchard, 'Investigation of concentration of economic power,' study made for Temporary National Economic Committee, 76th Congress, 3rd Session, pursuant to Public Resolution 113 (75th Cong.): *Monograph no. 43, Motion Picture Industry – Pattern of Control*, Washington, DC: Government Printing Office, 1941.

Bertsch, Marguerite, *How to Write for Moving Pictures: A Manual of Instruction and Information*, New York:

George H. Doran Co., 1917.

Bitzer, G.W., *Billy Bitzer: His Story*, New York: Farrar, Straus & Giroux, 1973.

'Body and Soul is (here) put together,' *Fortune*, 4 (August 1931), pp. 26-34.

Bogdanovich, Peter, *Allan Dwan: The Last Pioneer*, New York: Praeger, 1971.

Borde, R. and E. Chaumeton, *Panorama du film noir américain*, 1953, reprint, Paris: Editions d'aujourd'hui, 1976.

Bowser, Eileen, 'The Brighton Project: an introduction,' *Quarterly Review of Film Studies*, 4, no. 4 (Fall 1979), pp. 509-38.

Branigan, Edward, 'Color and cinema: problems in the writing of history,' *Film Reader*, 4 (1979), pp. 16-34.

Brewster, W.E., 'Tungsten lamps for studio work,' *Motography*, 17, no. 4 (27 January 1917), pp. 201-4.

Brown, Karl, *Adventures With D.W. Griffith*, ed. Kevin Brownlow, New York: Farrar, Straus, & Giroux, 1973.

Brown, Karl, 'Modern lenses,' *American Cinematographer*, 3, no. 2 (1 May 1922), pp. 4-10; 3, no. 3 (1 June 1922), pp. 4-5, 12; 3, no. 4 (1 July 1922), pp. 4-5; 3, no. 4 (August 1922), pp. 4, 20; 3, no. 6 (September 1922), pp. 5, 20.

Brownlow, Kevin, *The Parade's Gone By*, New York: Alfred A. Knopf, 1968.

Buscombe, Edward, 'Notes on Columbia Picture Corporation 1926-1941,' *Screen*, 16, no. 3 (Autumn 1975), pp. 65-82.

Cahiers de la Cinématheque, no. 29 (Summer 1976), special number on Hollywood.

Cahiers du cinéma, no. 54 (Christmas 1955), special number, 'Situation du Cinéma Américain.'

Cahiers du cinéma, nos 150-151 (December 1963-January 1964), special number on American cinema.

Cahiers du cinéma editors, 'John Ford's *Young Mr. Lincoln*,' *Screen*, 13, no. 3 (Autumn 1972), pp. 5-44.

Cameron, Evan William (ed.), *Sound and the Cinema: The Coming of Sound to American Film*, Pleasantville, New York: Redgrave, 1980.

Carr, Catherine (ed.), *The Art of Photoplay Writing*, New York: Hannis Jordon Co., 1914.

Cassady, Ralph, Jr, 'Monopoly in motion picture production and distribution: 1908-1915,' *Southern California Law Review*, 32, no. 4 (Summer 1959), pp. 325-90.

Chase, Donald (for The American Film Institute), *Filmmaking: The Collaborative Art*, Boston: Little, Brown & Co., 1975.

'Cinerama – the broad picture,' *Fortune*, 47, no. 1 (January 1953), pp. 92-3, 144-50.

Cirlin, Bernard D. and Jack N. Peterman, 'Pre-testing a motion picture: a case history,' *Journal of Social Issues*, 3, no. 3 (Summer 1947), pp. 39-41.

Clarke, Charles G., 'CinemaScope photographic techniques,' *AC*, 36, no. 6 (June 1955), pp. 336-7, 362-4.

Clendenin, W. Wallace, 'Cameras of yesteryear,' *IP*, 21, no. 1 (January 1949), pp. 16-21; 21, no. 2 (February 1949), pp. 12-14; 21, no. 3 (March 1949), pp. 16-18.

Conant, Michael, *Antitrust in the Motion Picture Industry: Economic and Legal Analysis*, Berkeley: University of California Press, 1960.

Cornwell-Clyne, Adrian, *Colour Cinematography*, London: Chapman & Hall, 1951.

Cornwell-Clyne, Adrian, *3-D Kinematography and New Screen Techniques*, London: Hutchinson's Scientific and Technical Publications, 1954.

Cowan, Lester (ed.), *Recording Sound for Motion Pictures*, New York: McGraw-Hill, 1931.

Crabtree, J.I., 'The motion-picture laboratory,' *JSMPTE*, 64, no. 1 (January 1955), pp. 13-34.

Croy, Homer, *How Motion Pictures Are Made*, New York: Harper & Bros, 1918.

Davis, John, 'A studio chronology,' *The Velvet Light Trap*, no. 10 (Fall 1973), pp. 6-12.

Dawson, Anthony A.P., 'Hollywood's labour troubles,' *Industrial and Labor Relations Review*, 1, no. 4 (July 1948), pp. 638-47.

Dench, Ernest A., *Advertising by Motion Pictures*, Cincinnati: Standard Publishing Co., 1916.

Dench, Ernest A., *Making the Movies*, New York: Macmillan, 1915.

Deschner, Donald, 'Anton Grot: Warner art director 1927-1948,' *The Velvet Light Trap*, no. 15 (Fall 1975), pp. 18-22.

Deschner, Donald, 'Edward Carfagno: MGM art director,' *The Velvet Light Trap*, no. 18 (Spring 1978), pp. 30-9.

Deutelbaum, Marshall (ed.), *'Image' on the Art and Evolution of the Film*, New York: Dover Publications, 1979.

Dewhurst, H., *Introduction to 3-D*, New York: Macmillan, 1954.

Dickson, W.K.L., *The Biograph in Battle: Its Story in the South African War Related with Personal Experiences*, London: T. Fisher Unwin, 1901.

Di Giulio, Edmund M., E.C. Manderfield, and George A. Mitchell, 'An historical survey of the professional motion picture camera,' *JSMPTE*, 76, no. 7 (July 1967), pp. 665-70.

Dimick, Howard T., *Modern Photoplay Writing: Its Craftsmanship*, Franklin, Ohio: James Knapp Reeve, 1922.

Dreher, Carl, 'Recording, re-recording, and editing of sound,' *JSMPE*, 16, no. 6 (June 1931), pp. 756-65.

Dreher, Carl, 'Sound personnel and organization,' *Cinematographic Annual*, 1 (1930), pp. 335-46.

Dreher, Carl, 'Stage technique in the talkies,' *AC*, 10, no. 9 (December 1929), pp. 2-3, 16, 46.

Dyer, Richard, *Stars*, London: British Film Institute, 1979.

Edmondson, William R., 'Evolution of the "mike" boom,' *International Sound Technician*, 1, no. 9 (November 1953), pp. 3-7.

Edouart, Farciot, 'Economic advantages of process photography,' *AMPAS Technical Bulletin*, supplement no. 9 (20 July 1932), pp. 1-10.

Eisler, Hanns [and Theodor Adorno], *Composing for the Films*, London: Dennis Dobson, 1947.

Emerson, John and Anita Loos, *How to Write Photoplays*, 1920; reprint, Philadelphia: George W. Jacobs & Co., 1923.

Esenwein, J. Berg and Arthur Leeds, *Writing the Photoplay*, Springfield, Mass.: Home Correspondence School, 1913.

Eustis, Morton, 'Designing for the movies: Gibbons of MGM,' *Theatre Arts*, 21 (October 1937), pp. 783-98.

Evans, Mark, *Soundtrack: The Music of the Movies*, New York: Hopkinson & Blake, 1975.

Factor, Max, 'Standardization of motion picture make-up,' *JSMPE*, 28, no. 1 (January 1937), pp. 52-62.

Fadiman, William J., 'Books into movies,' *Publishers' Weekly*, 126, no. 10 (8 September 1934), pp. 753-5.

Fadiman, William, 'Cowboys and Indies,' *Films and Filming*, 10, no. 6 (March 1964), pp. 51-2.

Fadiman, William J., 'The typewriter jungle,' *Films and Filming*, 7, no. 3 (December 1960), pp. 8, 36, 42.

Famous Players-Lasky Corporation, *The Story of the Famous Players-Lasky Corporation*, New York: Famous Players-Lasky Corporation, 1919.

Farnham, R.E., 'Incandescent lighting improves,' *AC*, 10, no. 1 (April 1929), pp. 31-3.

Faulkner, Robert R., *Hollywood Studio Musicians: Their Work and Careers in the Recording Industry*, Chicago: Aldine, Atherton, 1971.

Fell, John L., *Film and the Narrative Tradition*, Norman: University of Oklahoma Press, 1974.

Feuer, Jane, 'Hollywood musicals: mass art as folk art,' *Jump Cut*, no. 23 (October 1980), pp. 23-5.

Field, Martin, 'Type-casting screen-writers,' *Penguin Film Review*, no. 6 (April 1948), pp. 29-32.

Fielding, Raymond, 'Hale's Tours: ultrarealism in the pre-1910 motion picture,' *Cinema Journal*, 10, no. 1 (Fall 1970), pp. 34-47.

Fielding, Raymond, *The Technique of Special Effects Cinematography*, 3rd ed., New York: Hastings House, 1974.

Fielding, Raymond (ed.), *A Technological History of Motion Pictures and Television*, Berkeley: University of California Press, 1967.

Florey, Robert, *Filmland*, Paris: Editions de Ciné-magazine, 1923.

Forrest, David, 'Music and the movies,' *International Sound Technician*, 1, no. 3 (May 1953), pp. 4-6, 19, 24.

'The Fox film building,' *Architecture & Building*, 52, no. 5 (May 1920), pp. 53-4.

Franklin, Harold B., *Sound Motion Pictures from the Laboratory to their Presentation*, Garden City, New York: Doubleday, Doran & Co., 1930.

Freeburg, Victor Oscar, *The Art of Photoplay Making*, New York: Macmillan, 1918.

Freeburg, Victor Oscar, *Pictorial Beauty on the Screen*, 1923, reprint, New York: Arno Press, 1970.

Frohlich, Louis D. and Charles Schwartz, *The Law of Motion Pictures including the Law of the Theatre*, New York: Baker, Voorhis, & Co., 1918.

Gale, Arthur L., *How to Write a Movie*, New York: Brick Row Book Shop, 1936.

Gartenberg, Jon, 'Camera movement in Edison and Biograph films, 1900-1906,' *Cinema Journal*, 19, no. 2 (Spring 1980), pp. 1-16.

Gaudio, G., 'A new viewpoint on the lighting of motion pictures,' *JSMPE*, 29, no. 2 (August 1937), pp. 157-68.

Gaudreault, André, 'Temporalité et narrativité: le cinéma des premiers temps (1895-1908),' *Etudes littéraires*, 13, no. 1 (April 1980), pp. 107-37.

Gauntier, Gene, 'Blazing the trail,' *Woman's Home Companion*, 55, no. 10 (October 1928) through 56, no. 3 (March 1929).

Gavin, Arthur, 'All Hollywood studios shooting 3-D films,' *AC*, 34, no. 3 (March 1953), pp. 108-10, 134-6.

Geduld, Harry M., *The Birth of the Talkies: From Edison to Jolson*, Bloomington: Indiana University Press, 1975.

Gomery, J. Douglas, 'The coming of sound to the American cinema: a history of the transformation of an industry,' unpublished PhD. thesis, University of Wisconsin-Madison, 1975.

Gomery, Douglas, 'The economics of US film exhibition policy and practice,' *Ciné-Tracts*, no. 12 (Winter 1981), pp. 36-40.

Gomery, Douglas, 'Towards an economic history of the cinema: the coming of sound to Hollywood,' in *The Cinematic Apparatus*, ed. Teresa de Lauretis and Stephen Heath, New York: St Martin's Press, 1980, pp. 38-46.

Gordon, Jan and Cora, *Star-Dust in Hollywood*, London: George C. Harrap & Co., 1931.

Green, Fitzhugh, *The Film Finds Its Tongue*, New York: Putnam's, 1929.

Gregory, Carl Louis, 'The early history of wide films,' *JSMPE*, 14, no. 1 (January 1930), pp. 27-31.

Gregory Carl Louis, *Motion Picture Photography*, New York: Falk Publishing Co., 1920.

Gregory, Carl Louis, *Motion Picture Photography*, ed. Herbert C. McKay, 2nd ed., New York: Falk Publishing Co., 1927.

Griffith, Linda Arvidson, *When the Movies Were Young*, 1925, reprint, New York: Dover Publications, 1969.

Griffith, Richard, *Samuel Goldwyn: The Producer and His Films*, New York: Museum of Modern Art, 1956.

Grignon, Lorin D., 'Experiment in stereophonic sound,' *JSMPTE*, 61, no. 3 (September 1953), pp. 364-79.

Groves, George, 'Playback records in motion picture production,' *International Sound Technician*, 1, no. 4 (June 1953), pp. 2-5, 28.

Guback, Thomas, 'Theatrical film,' in *Who Owns the Media?*, ed. Benjamin H. Compaine, New York: Harmony Books, 1979, pp. 179-241.

Hall, Ben M., *The Best Remaining Seats: The Story of the Golden Age of the Movie Palace*, New York: Bramhall House, 1961.

Hall, Hal (ed.), *Cinematographic Annual*, 2 vols, Hollywood: American Society of Cinematographers, 1930-1.

Hampton, Benjamin B., *History of the American Film Industry from its Beginnings to 1931*, 1931, reprint, New York: Dover Publications, 1970.

Handel, Leo A., *Hollywood Looks at Its Audience*, Urbana: University of Illinois Press, 1950.

Hankins, M.A., 'History of motion-picture set lighting equipment,' *JSMPTE*, 76, no. 7 (July 1967), pp. 671-4.

Happé, L. Bernard, *Basic Motion Picture Technology*, 2nd ed., New York: Hastings House, 1975.

Harpole, Charles H., 'Ideological and technological determinism in deep-space cinema images,' *Film Quarterly*, 33, no. 3 (Spring 1980), pp. 11-22.

Harrison, Louis Reeves, *Screencraft*, New York: Chalmers Publishing Co., 1916.

Harvith, Susan and John, *Karl Struss: Man with a Camera*, Bloomfield Hills, Michigan: Cranbrook Academy of Art/Museum, 1976.

Hart, William S., *My Life East and West*, Boston: Houghton Mifflin, 1929.

Hays, Will H., *The Memoirs of Will H. Hays*, Garden City, New York: Doubleday & Co., 1955.

Hays, Will H., *See and Hear*, New York: Motion Picture Producers and Distributors of America, 1929.

Hellmuth, William F., Jr, 'The motion picture industry,' in *The Structure of American Industry*, ed. Walter Adams, rev. ed., New York: Macmillan, 1954, pp. 360-402.

Henderson, Scott, 'The Panavision story,' *AC*, 58, no. 4 (April 1977), pp. 414-15, 422-3, 432-3.

Herman, Lewis, *A Practical Manual of Screen Playwriting for Theater and Television Films*, New York: New American Library, 1974.

Higham, Charles, *Hollywood Cameramen: Sources of Light*, London: Thames & Hudson, 1970.

Hitchins, Dr Alfred B., 'Artificial lighting of motion picture studios,' *AC*, 3, no. 6 (September 1922), pp. 14, 21-2.

Hoagland, Herbert Case, *How to Write a Photoplay*, New York: Magazine Maker Publishing Co., 1912.

Hoffman, H.G., 'Cutting off the feet,' *MPW*, 12, no. 1 (6 April 1912), p. 53.

How to Take and Make Moving Pictures, Denver: Ford's, 1914.

Howard, Clifford, 'Author and talkies,' *Close Up*, 5, no. 3 (September 1929), pp. 218-25.

Howard, Clifford, 'The cinema in retrospect,' *Close Up*, 3, no. 5 (November 1928), pp. 16-25; 3, no. 6 (December 1928), pp. 31-41.

Howard, Clifford, 'A Hollywood close-up,' *Close Up*, 2, no. 1 (January 1928), pp. 12-22.

Howard, Clifford, 'The menace around the corner,' *Close Up*, 6, no. 1 (January 1930), pp. 59-66.

Howard, Clifford, 'Writers and pictures,' *Close Up*, 3, no. 3 (September 1928), pp. 33-8.

Huettig, Mae D., *Economic Control of the Motion Picture Industry: A Study in Industrial Organization*, Philadelphia: University of Pennsylvania Press, 1944.

Hughes, Laurence A. (ed.), *The Truth about the Movies by the Stars*, Hollywood: Hollywood Publishers, 1924.

Hughes, Rupert, 'Early days in the movies,' *Saturday Evening Post*, 207, no. 40 (6 April 1935), pp. 18-9; 207, no. 41 (13 April 1935), pp. 30-1.

Hugo, Chris, 'The economic background,' *Movie*, nos 27/28 (Winter 1980/Spring 1981), pp. 43-9.

Hulfish, David Sherrill, *Cyclopedia of Motion-Picture Work*, 2 vols, Chicago: American School of Correspondence, 1911.

Hulfish, David S., *The Motion Picture: Its Making and Its Theater*, Chicago: Electricity Magazine Corporation, 1909.

Hulfish, David Sherill, *Motion-Picture Work*, 1915, reprint, New York: Arno, 1970.

Huse, Emery, 'The characteristics of Eastman motion picture negative films,' *AC*, 17, no. 5 (May 1936), pp. 190-2, 202-3.

Ihnen, Wiard B. and D.W. Atwater, 'The artistic utilization of light in the photography of motion pictures,' *TSMPE*, no. 21 (18-21 May 1925), pp. 21-37.

International Photographer, 10, no. 3 (April 1938), tenth anniversary number.

Irving, James, *The Irving System*, Auburn, New York: Authors' Press, 1919.

'Is 3-D dead? A survey by the editors,' *AC*, 34, no. 12 (December 1953), pp. 585-6, 608-12.

Jamey, Frank T., 'Push-pull recording and reproduction: the what, why, and how,' *IPro*, 13, no. 9 (September 1938), pp. 20-2.

Jensen, Paul, 'The coming of sound,' in *The Sound Film: An Introduction*, ed. Arthur Lennig, Troy, New York: Walter Snyder, 1969, pp. 77-110.

Joseph, Robert, 'Re: unions in Hollywood,' *Films*, 1, no. 3 (Summer 1940), pp. 34-50.

Jowett, Garth S., 'The first motion picture audiences,' *Journal of Popular Film*, 3 (Winter 1974), pp. 39-54.

Kalmus, H.T., 'Technicolor adventures in cinemaland,' *JSMPE*, 31, no. 6 (December 1938), pp. 564-85.

Kané, Pascal, 'Sylvia Scarlett: Hollywood cinema re-read,' Sub-stance, no. 9 (1974), pp. 34-43.

Kaplan, E. Ann (ed.), Women in Film Noir, London; British Film Institute, 1978.

Kellogg, Edward W., 'History of sound motion pictures,' 1955, reprint, in A Technological History of Motion Pictures and Television, ed. Raymond Fielding, Berkeley: University of California Press, 1967, pp. 174-220.

Kelly, Edgar J. and Muro, Acting for Pictures: How Its [sic] Done and How to Do It, New Orleans: Coste & Frichter Publishing Co., 1916.

Kennedy, Joseph P. (ed.), The Story of the Films, Chicago: A.W. Shaw Co., 1927.

Kerr, Paul, 'Out of what past? Notes on the B film noir,' Screen Education, nos 32/33 (Autumn 1979/80), pp. 45-65.

Kiesling, Barrett C., Talking Pictures: How They Are Made, How To Appreciate Them, Richmond, Virginia: Johnson Publishing Co., 1937.

Kindem, Gorham A., 'Hollywood's conversion to color: the technological, economic, and aesthetic factors,' Journal of the University Film Association, 31, no. 2 (Spring 1979), pp. 29-36.

Kingslake, Rudolf, 'The development of the zoom lens,' JSMPTE, 69, no. 8 (August 1960), pp. 534-44.

Kinsila, Edward Bernard, Modern Theatre Construction, New York: Chalmers Publishing Co., 1917.

Klein, Adrian Bernard, Colour Cinematography, Boston: American Photographic Publishing Co., 1936.

Klingender, F.D. and Stuart Legg, Money Behind the Screen, London: Lawrence & Wishart, 1937.

Klumph, Inez and Helen, Screen Acting: Its Requirements and Rewards, New York: Falk Publishing Co., 1922.

Knox, Donald, The Magic Factory: How MGM Made 'An American in Paris', New York: Praeger Publishers, 1973.

Koszarski, Richard (ed.), Hollywood Directors 1914-1940, New York: Oxford University Press, 1976.

Koszarski, Richard (ed.), Hollywood Directors 1941-1976, New York: Oxford University Press, 1977.

Koszarski, Richard (ed.), The Rivals of D.W. Griffith: Alternate Auteurs 1913-1918, Minneapolis: Walker Art Center, 1976.

Koszarski, Richard, '60 filmographies: the men with the movie cameras,' Film Comment, 8, no. 2 (Summer 1972), pp. 27-57.

Krows, Arthur Edwin, 'Once more – consider the status of motion pictures,' The Triangle, 3, no. 3 (4 November 1916), pp. 13, 15.

Krows, Arthur Edwin, The Talkies, New York: Henry Holt & Co., 1930.

Lachenbruch, Jerome, 'The photoplay architect,' American Architect, 120, no. 2377 (28 September 1921), pp. 219-23.

Lahue, Kalton C., Dreams for Sale: The Rise and Fall of the Triangle Film Corporation, Cranbury, New Jersey: A.S. Barnes & Co., 1971.

Lahue, Kalton C., Motion Picture Pioneer: The Selig Polyscope Company, Cranbury, New Jersey: A.S. Barnes & Co., 1973.

Lane, Tamar, The New Technique of Screen Writing: A Practical Guide to the Writing and Marketing of Photoplays, New York: McGraw-Hill, 1936.

Lauritzen, Einar and Gunnar Lundquist, American Film-Index 1908-1915, Stockholm, Sweden: Film-Index, 1976.

Lees, David and Stan Berkowitz, The Movie Business, New York: Vintage Books, 1981.

Lescarboura, Austin Celestin, Behind the Motion-Picture Screen, 2nd ed., New York: Scientific American Publishing Co., 1921.

Lescarboura, Austin C., ' "Shooting" the photoplay,' Scientific American, 117, no. 11 (15 September 1917), pp. 192-3, 199-200.

Levinson, Nathan, 'Sound in motion pictures,' JSMPE, 38, no. 5 (May 1942), pp. 468-82.

Lewis, Howard Thompson, Cases on the Motion Picture Industry, New York: McGraw-Hill, 1930.

Lewis, Howard T., The Motion Picture Industry, New York: D. Van Nostrand Co., 1933.

Lightman, Herb A., 'Why MGM chose "Camera 65," ' AC, 41, no. 3 (March 1960), pp. 162-3, 192.

Lindsay, Vachel, The Art of the Moving Picture, rev. ed., 1922, reprint, New York: Liveright Publishing Corp. 1970.

Livingston, Don, Film and the Director, New York: Macmillan, 1953.

Lomas, H.M., Picture Play Photography, London: Ganes, 1914.

Loos, Anita, Kiss Hollywood Good-by, New York: Ballantine, 1975.

Lowrey, Carolyn, The First One Hundred Noted Men and Women of the Screen, New York: Moffat, Yard & Co., 1920.

Luhr, William and Peter Lehman, ' "Would you mind just trying it": an interview with special effects artist Linwood Dunn, ASC,' Wide Angle, 1, no. 1 (rev. and expanded, 1979), pp. 78-83.

Lutz, E.G., The Motion-Picture Cameraman, 1927, reprint, New York: Arno Press, 1972.

Lytton, Grace, Scenario Writing Today, Boston: Houghton Mifflin Co., 1921.

MacCann, Richard Dyer, Hollywood in Transition, Boston: Houghton Mifflin Co., 1962.

MacCann, Richard Dyer, 'The independent producer: independence with a vengeance,' Film Quarterly, 15 (Summer 1962), pp. 14-21.

MacFarland, James Hood, 'Architectural problems in motion picture production,' American Architect, 118, no. 2326 (21 July 1920), pp. 65-70.

Macgowan, Kenneth, 'Cross-roads of screen and stage,' *The Seven Arts*, 1 (April 1917), pp. 649-54.

Macgowan, Kenneth, 'The wide screen of yesterday and tomorrow,' *Quarterly of Film, Radio, and Television*, 11, no. 3 (Spring 1957), pp. 217-41.

Madison, Wisconsin, Wisconsin State Historical Society and the Wisconsin Center for Film and Theater Research, Aitken Brothers Papers, 1909-39.

Maltin, Leonard, *The Art of the Cinematographer: A Survey and Interviews with Five Masters*, rev. ed., New York: Dover Publications, 1978.

Maltin, Leonard (ed.), *Hollywood: The Movie Factory*, New York: Popular Library, 1976.

Mamoulian, Rouben, 'Common sense and camera angles,' *AC*, 12, no. 10 (February 1932), pp. 8-9, 26.

'Manufacture of moving pictures is a science,' *The Show World* (6 July 1907), p. 17.

Manvell, Roger, and John Huntley, *The Technique of Film Music*, London: Focal Press, 1957.

Marion, Frances, *How to Write and Sell Film Stories*, New York: Covici Friede, 1937.

Marlowe, Frederic, 'The rise of the independents in Hollywood,' *Penguin Film Review*, no. 3 (August 1947), pp. 72-5.

Marsh, Mae, *Screen Acting*, New York: Frederick A. Stokes Co., 1921.

Matthews, Glenn E., 'Historic aspects of the SMPTE,' *JSMPTE*, 75 (1966), pp. 856-67.

Maxfield, J.P., 'Acoustic control of recording for talking motion pictures,' *JSMPE*, 14, no. 1 (January 1930), pp. 85-95.

McCarthy, Todd and Charles Flynn, *Kings of the Bs: Working Within the Hollywood System*, New York: E.P. Dutton, 1975.

McCarty, Clifford, 'Filmusic for silents,' *Films in Review*, 8, no. 3 (March 1957), pp. 117-18, 123.

McCarty, Clifford, 'Filmusic librarian,' *Films in Review*, 3, no. 5 (June-July 1957), pp. 292-3.

McKay, Herbert C., *The Handbook of Motion Picture Photography*, New York: Falk Publishing Co., 1927.

Mees, C.E. Kenneth, 'History of professional black-and-white motion-picture film,' 1954, reprint, in *A Technological History of Motion Pictures and Television*, ed. Raymond Fielding, Berkeley: University of California Press, 1967, pp. 125-8.

Meloy, Arthur S., *Theatres and Motion Picture Houses*, New York: Architects' Supply & Publishing Co., 1916.

The Mentor, 9, no. 6 (1 July 1921), special number on motion pictures.

Merrill Lynch, Pierce, Fenner & Beane, *Radio, Television, Motion Pictures*, New York: Merrill Lynch, Pierce, Fenner & Beane, 1950.

Merritt, Russ, 'R.K.O. Radio: the little studio that couldn't,' in *Marquee Theatre*, ed. Hayward Allen, Madison, Wisconsin: WHA-TV, Channel 21, University of Wisconsin-Extension Television Center, n.d., pp. 7-25.

'Milestone movie cameras,' *AC*, 50, no. 1 (January 1969), pp. 78-9, 116.

Miller, Don, *'B' Movies*, New York: Curtis Books, 1973.

Mills, Frederick S., 'Film lighting as a fine art,' *Scientific American*, 124, no. 8 (19 February 1921), pp. 148, 157-8.

Milne, Peter, *Motion Picture Directing: The Facts and Theories of the Newest Art*, New York: Falk Publishing Co., 1922.

Mitchell, C.H. (ed.), *Assistant Director's Compendium*, Hollywood: Jesse L. Lasky Feature Play Co., April 1916.

Mitchell, George, 'Sidney Olcott,' *Films in Review*, 5, no. 4 (April 1954), pp. 175-81.

Mitchell, George, 'Thomas H. Ince,' *Films in Review*, 11, no. 10 (October 1960), pp. 464-84.

Mitry, Jean, *Histoire du cinéma: art et industrie*, vols I-III, Paris: Editions universitaires, 1967-73; vols IV-V, Paris: Delarge, 1980.

Mole, Peter, 'The evolution of arc broadside lighting equipment,' *JSMPE*, 32, no. 4 (April 1939), pp. 398-411.

Mole, Peter, 'Twice the light and twice the carrying power,' *AC*, 32, no. 3 (March 1951), pp. 93, 111, 113, 115.

Mole, Peter, 'Will there always be a need for carbon arcs?' *AC*, 31, no. 2 (February 1951), pp. 50-1, 72-3.

Moley, Raymond, *The Hays Office*, Indianapolis: Bobbs-Merrill Co., 1945.

'More trouble in paradise,' *Fortune*, 34, no. 5 (November 1946), pp. 154-9ff.

'The Morris Agency: put their names in lights,' *Fortune*, 18, no. 3 (September 1938), p. 67ff.

'Motion picture colony under one roof,' *Scientific American*, 210, no. 25 (21 June 1919), p. 651.

Motion Picture Laboratory Practice and Characteristics of Eastman Motion Picture Films, Rochester, New York: Eastman Kodak Co., 1936.

Motion Picture Producers and Distributors of America, 'The motion picture industry,' in *The Development of American Industries*, ed. John Georges Glover and William Bouck Cornell, New York: Prentice-Hall, 1932, pp. 745-61.

Mott, William Roy, 'White light for motion picture photography,' *TSMPE*, no. 8 (14-16 April 1919), pp. 7-41.

'Movie missionary,' *Fortune*, 32, no. 4 (October 1945), p. 149ff.

'Movies: end of an era?' *Fortune*, 39, no. 4 (April 1949), pp. 99-102ff.

Munden, Kenneth W. (ed.), *The American Film Institute Catalog of Motion Pictures Produced in the United States: Feature Films 1921-1930*, New York: Bowker, 1971.

Mulvey, Laura, 'Notes on Sirk and melodrama,' *Movie*, no. 25 (Winter 1977/78), pp. 53-7.

Münsterberg, Hugo, *The Film: A Psychological Study*, 1916, reprint, New York: Dover Publications, 1970.

Musser, Charles, 'The early cinema of Edwin Porter,' *Cinema Journal*, 19, no. 1 (Fall 1979), pp. 1-38.

Naumburg, Nancy (ed.), *We Make the Movies*, New York: W.W. Norton & Co., 1937.

Nelson, John, *The Photo-play*, Los Angeles: Photoplay Publishing Co., 1913.

Nelson, Richard Alan, 'Movie mecca of the South: Jacksonville, Florida, as an early rival to Hollywood,' *Journal of Popular Film and Television*, 8, no. 3 (Fall 1980), pp. 38-51.

Nelson, Robert U., 'Film music: color or line?' *Hollywood Quarterly*, 2, no. 1 (October 1946), pp. 57-65.

Nisbett, Alex, *The Technique of the Sound Studio*, New York: Hastings House, 1962.

Niver, Kemp R., *The First Twenty Years: A Segment of Film History*, Los Angeles: Artisan Press, 1968.

Niver, Kemp R., *Motion Pictures From the Library of Congress Paper Print Collection 1894-1912*, Berkeley: University of California Press, 1967.

North, Joseph H., *The Early Development of the Motion Picture, 1887-1909*, New York: Arno Press, 1973.

Ogle, Patrick, 'The development of sound systems: the commercial era,' *Film Reader*, 2 (1977), pp. 199-212.

Ogle, Patrick, 'Technological and aesthetic influences upon the development of deep focus cinematography in the United States,' *Screen Reader 1*, ed. John Ellis, London: SEFT, 1977, pp. 81-108.

Onosko, Tim, 'Monogram: its rise and fall in the forties,' *The Velvet Light Trap*, no. 5 (Summer 1972), pp. 5-9.

Onosko, Tim, 'RKO Radio: an overview,' *The Velvet Light Trap*, no. 10 (Fall 1973), pp. 2-4.

Ortman, Marguerite G., *Fiction and the Screen*, Boston: Marshall Jones Co., 1935.

Palmer, Frederick, *Palmer Plan Handbook*, rev. ed., Los Angeles: Palmer Institute of Authorship, 1921.

Palmer, Frederick, *Photoplay Plot Encyclopedia: An Analysis of the Use in Photoplays of the Thirty-Six Dramatic Situations and Their Subdivisions*, 2nd ed., rev., Los Angeles: Palmer Photoplay Corp., 1922.

'Paramount,' *Fortune*, 15, no. 3 (March 1937), pp. 87-96ff.

'Paramount: Oscar for profits,' *Fortune*, 35, no. 6 (June 1947), pp. 90-5, 208-21.

Parsons, Louella O., *How to Write for the 'Movies,'* rev. ed., Chicago: A.C. McClurg & Co., 1917.

Patterson, Frances Taylor, *Cinema Craftsmanship*, New York: Harcourt, Brace, & Howe, 1920.

Patterson, Frances Taylor, *Scenario and Screen*, New York: Harcourt, Brace, & Co., 1928.

Peacocke, Capt Leslie T., 'Logical continuity,' *Photoplay*, 11, no. 5 (April 1917), pp. 111-14.

Perkins, Frank C., 'Photographing the New York subway,' *Scientific American*, 93, no. 1 (1 July 1905), p. 12.

Phillips, Henry Albert, *The Photodrama*, Larchmont, New York: Stanhope-Dodge Publishing Co., 1914.

Photoplay Research Society, *Opportunities in the Motion Picture Industry*, Los Angeles: Photoplay Research Society, 1922.

Pitkin, Walter B. and William M. Marston, *The Art of Sound Pictures*, New York: D. Appleton & Co., 1930.

Platt, Agnes, *Practical Hints on Acting for the Cinema*, New York: E.P. Dutton & Co., 1923.

'Pour une histoire du mélodrame au cinéma,' *Les Cahiers de la Cinémathèque*, no. 28 (1979).

Powdermaker, Hortense, *Hollywood: The Dream Factory*, New York: Little, Brown & Co., 1950.

Powell, Ardon Van Buren, *The Photoplay Synopsis*, Springfield, Mass.: Home Correspondence School, 1919.

Powell, W. Dixon, 'MGM: the studio at its zenith,' *The Velvet Light Trap*, no. 18 (Spring 1978), pp. 1-7.

Pratt, George C., *Spellbound in Darkness: A History of the Silent Film*, rev. ed., Greenwich, Conn.: New York Graphic Society, 1973.

Price, Waterhouse, & Co., *Memorandum on Moving Picture Accounts*, New York: Price, Waterhouse, & Co., 1916.

'Putting the move in the movies,' *Saturday Evening Post*, 188, no. 46 (13 May 1916), pp. 14-15, 96-8, 100-1.

Pye, Michael and Lynda Myles, *The Movie Brats: How the Film Generation Took Over Hollywood*, New York: Holt, Rinehart & Winston, 1979.

Quigley, Martin, Jr (ed.), *New Screen Techniques*, New York: Quigley, 1953.

Reisz, Karel and Gavin Millar, *The Technique of Film Editing*, New York: Hastings House, 1968.

Rescher, Gayne, 'Wide angle problems in wide screen cinematography,' *AC*, 37, no. 4 (May 1956), pp. 300-1, 322-3.

'La revolution du parlant,' *Cahiers de la Cinémathèque*, nos 13-14-15 (1974).

'RKO: it's only money,' *Fortune*, 47, no. 5 (May 1953), pp. 122-7ff.

Ross, Murray, *Stars and Strikes: Unionization of Hollywood*, New York: Columbia University Press, 1941.

Rosten, Leo C., *Hollywood: The Movie Colony, The Movie Makers*, New York: Harcourt, Brace, & Co., 1941.

Rowan, Arthur, 'Todd-AO – newest wide-screen system,' *AC*, 35, no. 10 (October 1954), pp. 494-6, 526.

Ryan, Roderick T., *A History of Motion Picture Color Technology*, New York: Focal Press, 1977.

Ryder, Loren, 'Expanded sound and picture at Paramount,' *International Sound Technician*, 1, no. 6 (August 1953), pp. 3-9.

Salt, Barry, 'The early development of film form,' *Film Form*, 1, no. 1 (Spring 1976), pp. 91-106.

Sands, Pierre Norman, *A Historical Study of the Academy of Motion Picture Arts and Sciences (1927-1947)*, New York: Arno Press, 1973.

Sargent, Epes Winthrop, *Picture Theatre Advertising*, New York: Moving Picture World Chalmers Publishing Co., 1915.

Sargent, Epes Winthrop, *The Technique of the Photoplay*, 2nd ed., New York: Moving Picture World, 1913.

Schary, Dore and Charles Palmer, *Case History of a Movie*, New York: Random House, 1950.

Schechter, Harold and David Everitt, *Film Tricks: Special Effects in the Movies*, New York: Harlin Quist, 1980.

Scot, Darrin, 'Panavision's progress,' *AC*, 41, no. 5 (May 1960), pp. 302, 304, 320-2, 324.

Seabury, William Marston, *The Public and the Motion Picture Industry*, New York: Macmillan, 1926.

Selznick, David O., *Memo From: David O. Selznick*, ed. Rudy Behlmer, New York: Avon Books, 1973.

Serrurier, Mark, 'The origins of the Moviola,' *JSMPTE*, 75, no. 7 (July 1966), pp. 701-3.

Sexton, Randolph Williams and B.F. Betts (eds), *American Theatres of Today*, 2 vols, New York: Architectural Book Publishing Co., 1927.

Shale, Richard (ed.), *Academy Awards*, New York: Ungar, 1978.

Sherman, Eric, *Directing the Film: Film Directors on Their Art*, Boston: Little, Brown & Co, 1976.

Sherwood, C. Blythe, 'The art director is accredited: the vision that makes "Dream Street" come true,' *Arts and Decoration*, 15 (May 1921), pp. 36-7.

Silver, Alain and Elizabeth Ward, *Film Noir: An Encyclopedia Reference to the American Style*, Woodstock, New York: Overlook Press, 1979.

Sklar, Robert, *Movie-Made America: A Cultural History of American Movies*, New York: Random House, 1975.

Slevin, James, *On Picture-Play Writing: A Hand-book of Workmanship*, Cedar Grove, New Jersey: Farmer Smith Incorporated, 1912.

Slide, Anthony, *Aspects of American Film History Before 1920*, Metuchen, New Jersey: Scarecrow Press, 1978.

Slide, Anthony, *Early American Cinema*, New York: A.S. Barnes & Co., 1970.

Slide, Anthony, 'The evolution of the film star,' *Films in Review*, 25 (December 1974), pp. 591-4.

Smith, Albert E., *Two Reels and a Crank*, Garden City, New York: Doubleday & Co., 1952.

Smith, Frederick James, 'The evolution of the motion picture,' *NYDM*, 69, no. 1792 (23 April 1913) through 70, no. 1817 (15 October 1913).

Smith, L.G. Harkness, 'Electric lighting for motion-picture studios,' *Electrical World*, 65, no. 17 (24 April 1915), pp. 1040-2.

SMPE (ed), *The Technique of Motion Picture Production*, New York: Interscience Publishers, 1944.

SMPTE, *Elements of Color in Professional Motion Pictures*, New York: SMPTE, 1957.

Souto, H. Mario Raimondo, *The Technique of the Motion Picture Camera*, 3rd rev. and enlarged ed., New York: Hastings House, 1977.

Spedon, S.M., *How and Where Moving Pictures are Made by the Vitagraph Company of America*, Brooklyn, New York: Vitagraph Company of America [1912].

Sponable, E.I., 'Historical development of sound films,' *JSMPE*, 48, no. 4 (April 1947), pp. 275-303.

Staiger, Janet, 'Dividing labor for production control: Thomas Ince and the rise of the studio system,' *Cinema Journal*, 18, no. 2 (Spring 1979), pp. 16-25.

Stanley, Robert H., *The Celluloid Empire: A History of the American Movie Industry*, New York: Hastings House, 1978.

Starr, Helen, 'Putting it together,' *Photoplay*, 14, no. 2 (July 1918), pp. 52-4.

Stull, William, 'Development of mobile camera-carriages and cranes,' *AC*, 14, no. 1 (May 1933), pp. 12-13, 36-7.

Stull, William, 'Summing up modern studio lighting equipment,' *AC*, 16, no. 10 (October 1935), pp. 424-5, 435-6.

Stull, William, 'Technicolor bringing new charm to screen,' *AC*, 18, no. 6 (June 1937), pp. 234-7, 242.

'Summary of current wide-screen systems of photography,' *AC*, 36, no. 11 (November 1955), pp. 654-6, 674-6.

Talbot, Frederick A., *Moving Pictures: How They Are Made and Worked*, new ed., London: William Heinemann, 1914.

Terriss, Tom, *Writing the Sound and Dialogue Photoplay*, Hollywood: Palmer Institute of Authorship, 1930.

Theisen, Earl, 'Evolution of the motion picture camera,' *IP*, 5, no. 6 (June 1933), pp. 6-9, 42.

Theisen, Earl, 'The history of nitrocellulose as a film base,' *JSMPE*, 20, no. 3 (March 1933), pp. 259-62.

Theisen, Earl, 'Part of the story of lighting,' *IP*, 6, no. 3 (April 1934), pp. 10-12, 26.

Tibbetts, John C. (ed.), *Introduction to the Photoplay*, 1929, reprint, Shawnee Mission, Kansas: National Film Society, 1977.

Toland, Gregg, 'Composition in motion pictures,' *The Complete Photographer*, no. 16 (1942), pp. 996-1004.

Townsend, Edward W., 'Picture plays,' *Outlook*, 93 (27 November 1909), pp. 703-10.

Transitions and Time Lapses: Fades, Wipes and Dissolves, Their Use and Value to the Production. AMPAS Academy Technical Branch Technical Digest, no. 10 (28 September 1934).

'Twentieth Century-Fox,' *Fortune*, 12, no. 6 (December

1935), pp. 85-93ff.

US Education and Labor Committee, House, *Jurisdictional disputes in motion-picture industry, hearings before special subcommittee*, 80th Cong., 1st and 2nd sess., pursuant to H. Res. 111, Washington, DC: Government Printing Office, 1948.

US Small Business, Select Committee on, Senate, *Motion-picture distribution trade practices, 1956, report on problems of independent motion-picture exhibition*, 27 July 1956, Washington, DC: Government Printing Office, 1956.

Vale, Eugene, *The Technique of Screenplay Writing*, New York: Grosset & Dunlap, 1972.

Van Loan, H.H., *'How I Did It,'* Los Angeles: Whittingham Press, 1922.

Vardac, A. Nicholas, *Stage to Screen: Theatrical Method from Garrick to Griffith*, Cambridge, Mass.: Harvard University Press, 1949.

Vernet, Marc, 'Freud: Effets spéciaux: Mise en scène: USA,' *Communications*, no. 23 (1975), pp. 223-34.

'Vingt ans après,' *Cahiers du cinéma*, no. 172 (November 1965), pp. 28-30.

Walker, Alexander, *The Shattered Silents: How the Talkies Came to Stay*, New York: William Morrow & Co., 1979.

'Warner Brothers,' *Fortune*, 16, no. 6 (December 1937),

pp. 110-13, 206-20.

Watts, Stephen (ed.), *Behind the Screen: How Films Are Made*, New York: Dodge Publishing Co., 1938.

Welsh, Robert Emmett, *A-B-C of Motion Pictures*, New York: Harper and Bros [c. 1916].

Westmore, Frank and Murial Davidson, *The Westmores of Hollywood*, New York: Berkeley Publishing Corp., 1976.

'What? Color in the movies again?' *Fortune*, 10, no. 4 (October 1934), pp. 92-7.

Wheeler, Leslie J., *Principles of Cinematography: A Handbook of Motion Picture Technology*, 4th ed. Hastings-on-Hudson: Morgan & Morgan, 1969.

Winkopp, C.G., *How to Write a Photoplay*, New York: C.G. Winkopp, 1915.

Wollen, Peter, 'Counter cinema: Vent d'Est,' *Afterimage*, no. 4 (Autumn 1972), pp. 6-16.

Wright, William Lord, *Photoplay Writing*, New York: Falk Publishing Co., 1922.

Wysotsky, Michael Z., *Wide-Screen Cinema and Stereophonic Sound*, tr. A.E.C. York, New York: Hastings House, 1971.

Young, Freddie and Paul Petzold, *The Work of the Motion Picture Cameraman*, New York: Hastings House, 1972.

Photograph credits

In the following listing, the numerals in the form 1.1 etc. are figure numbers. Any stills not credited are from the authors' private collections. All frame enlargements, script pages, and advertisements were printed by Kristin Thompson.

Academy of Motion Picture Arts and Sciences: 17.14, 17.17, 17.52, 27.20

Allied Artists: 5.23 (© 1957)

American Cinematographer: 20.6, 20.7, 20.9 (1 December 1921, back cover), 20.12, 20.13, 20.15, 25.3 (February 1929, p. 30), 25.4 (December 1937, p. 497), 25.5 (October 1932, p. 12), 25.6 (November 1939, p. 495), 25.7 (April 1929, pp. 20-1), 25.8 (August 1938, p. 313), 25-9 (April 1939), p. 168, 25.10 (January 1939, pp. 24-5

Bison 101 Archive: 13.1, 17.40, 17.41, 20.2, 20.3, 20.5, 20.8, 20.11, 20.14, 20.17, 21.1, 21.4, 21.9, 22.1, 23.1, 23.2, 23.17, 27.25

Columbia: 3.1 (© 1955)

Eagle-Lion: 7.1, 27.35 (© 1947)

Twentieth-Century Fox: 5.5 (© 1944), 5.8 (© 1954), 5.42 and 5.43 (© 1957), 27.7 and 27.8 (© 1927), 29.2 (© 1954), 29.5 and 29.11 (© 1954)

Goldwyn: 1.1 (© 1929), 5.6 (© 1946), 5.25 (© 1941), 27.13 (© 1929), 27.22 (© 1931), 27.26 (© 1937), 27.27 and 27.28 (© 1936), 27.29 (© 1937), 27.31 and 27.32 (© 1937), 27.40 (© 1941), 27.41 (© 1941), 27.43 and 27.46 (© 1946), 28.2 (© 1938)

MGM: 1.2 (© 1927), 3.17 and 3.20 (© 1944), 5.3 (© 1921), 5.26 (© 1921), 5.28 (© 1924), 5.33 (© 1921), 7.2 (© 1933), 17.22 (© 1926), 17.36 (© 1921), 21.8 (© 1921), 23.11 and 23.12 (© 1932), 23.13 and 23.14 (© 1927), 27.3 (© 1924), 27.4 (© 1927), 29.3 (© 1957)

Moving Picture News: 9.1 (18 November 1911, p. 9), 9.2 (27 September 1913, p. 3), 9.4 (27 September 1913, pp. 4-5), 9.5 (1911), 9.6 (6 May 1911, p. 4), 9.7 (12 August 1911, p. 23), 9.8 (23 September 1911, back cover), 9.9 (7 January 1911, p. 4), 9.10 (28 October 1911, n.p.), 9.11 (5 October 1912, p. 27), 17.29 (20 January 1920, p. 46), 24.1 (23 November 1912, p. 39)

Moving Picture World: 9.3 (4 March 1911, p. 485), 9.12 (10 July 1915, p. 268), 9.13 (10 July 1915, p. 272), 9.14 (21 October 1911, p. 200), 11.1 (11 February 1911, p. 290), 11.2 (8 June 1912, p. 907), 11.5 (18 May 1912, p. 621), 11.6 (10 July 1915, p. 235), 11.7 (10 July 1915, p. 239), 12-1 (27 May 1911, p. 1181), 12.2 (22 April 1911, p. 887), 12.3 (1 April 1911, p. 701), 12.4 (2 October 1915, p. 134), 12.5 (6 November 1915, p. 1185), 12.6 (8 July 1911, pp. 1594-4), 12.7 (24 June 1911, p. 1430), 20.16 (28 February 1920, p. 1435), 21.3 (26 October 1918, p. 526)

Museum of Modern Art: 1.3, 17.51, 23.18, 29.1

New Yorker: 5.44 and 5.45 (© 1964), 29.4 (© 1964)

Paramount: 3.2 (© 1924), 3.5 to 3.7 (© 1928), 3.14 to 3.16 (© 1953), 5.1 (© 1953), 5.4 (© 1924), 5.7 (© 1932), 5.15 and 5.16 (© 1924), 5.27 (© 1949), 5.34 (© 1925), 5.35 (© 1949), 18.1 to 18.4 (© 1924), 27.2 (© 1927), 27.14 (© 1932), 27.42 (© 1949)

The Photodramatist: 11.9 (December 1922, p. 11)

Scientific American: 11.3 (21 June 1919, p. 651)

Transactions of the Society of Motion Picture Engineers: 17.38 (No. 21, May 1925, p. 31. Copyright © 1925 by the Society of Motion Picture Engineers, New York, New York)

Universal: 2.1 to 2.5 (© 1948), 27.1 (© 1948)

United Artists: 5.22 (© 1921), 27.36 (© 1949)

Walter Wanger: 27.30 (© 1940), 27.33 (© 1940)

Wisconsin Center for Film and Theater Research: 2.6, 3.3, 3.8 to 3.13, 3.22 to 3.25, 3.26 to 3.28, 4.1 and 4.2, 4.3 to 4.5, 5.9 to 5.10, 5.11 to 5.14, 5.18 and 5.19, 5.21, 5.24, 5.29, 5.30, 5.31, 5.36, 5.40 and 5.41, 5.46 and 5.47, 5.48 and 5.49, 5.50 to 5.53, 6.7 to 6.9, 6.10 to 6.40, 12.8 to 12.19

(Aitken Bros. papers), 20.2, 21.2, 23.3 to 23.10, 23.15 and 23.16, 25.1 and 25.2 (Warner Bros. scripts), 27.5 and 27.6, 27.9, 27.10, 27.11, 27.12, 27.15, 27.16, 27.17, 27.19, 27.21, 27.34, 27.37, 27.38 and 27.39, 28.1

Misc. books and articles: 11.4 (Lescarboura, 1919, p. 399), 11.8 (Lee Royal *The Romance of Motion Picture Production*, LA: 1920, p. 67), 13.2 and 13.6 (Croy, pp. 149, 69, 111, 77, 205), 20.1 (Richard Kosarski, 'Maurice Tourneur', *Film Comment* [March 1973], p. 29), 20.4 (Lescarboura, p. 81), 20.10 (Gregory, *Motion Picture Photography*, 2nd ed., p. 437), 21.5 (Brown, *Adventures with D. W. Griffith*), 21.14 and 21.15 (William Innes Homer, *Alfred Steiglitz and the American Avant-Garde* [Boston: New York Graphic Society, 1977], pp. 25, 56), 21.18 (Beaumont Newhall, *The History of Photography* [New York: Museum of Modern Art, 1964], p. 103)

Index